r_t	Expected rate of return (or cost of capital) in period t. We omit the subscript where the expected return is identical in each period. Sometimes we use a *second* subscript to define the date at which the investment is made. Thus, $_{t-1}r_t$ is the (spot) rate of return on an investment made at $t - 1$ and paying off at time t.
$\tilde{r}_t$	Uncertain actual rate of return in period t
r_D	Rate of return on firm's debt
r_E	Expected rate of return on firm's equity
r_f	Risk-free interest rate
r_m	Expected rate of return on the market portfolio
$r_\$$	Dollar rate of interest
r^*	Adjusted cost of capital
$s_{\text{SFr}/\$}$	Spot rate of exchange between Swiss francs and dollars
t	Time
T_c	Rate of corporate income tax
T_p	Rate of personal income tax
V	Market value of firm: $V = D + E$
β	Beta: A measure of market risk
δ	Delta: hedge ratio
λ	Lambda: Market price of risk $= \dfrac{r_m - r_f}{\sigma_m^2}$
ρ_{12}	Rho: Correlation coefficient between investments 1 and 2
σ	Sigma: Standard deviation
σ_{12}	Sigma: Covariance of investment 1 with investment 2
σ^2	Sigma squared: Variance
Σ	Capital sigma: "The sum of"

PRINCIPLES OF CORPORATE FINANCE

McGRAW-HILL SERIES IN FINANCE

Consulting Editor: *Charles A. D'Ambrosio, University of Washington*

Principles of Corporate Finance

THIRD EDITION

Richard A. Brealey □ **Stewart C. Myers**

Midland Bank Professor of Corporate Finance
London Business School

Gordon Y Billard Professor of Finance
Sloan School of Management
Massachusetts Institute of Technology

McGRAW-HILL BOOK COMPANY

New York   St. Louis   San Francisco   Auckland   Bogotá   Caracas   Colorado Springs
Hamburg   Lisbon   London   Madrid   Mexico   Milan   Montreal   New Delhi   Oklahoma City
Panama   Paris   San Juan   São Paulo   Singapore   Sydney   Tokyo   Toronto

PRINCIPLES OF CORPORATE FINANCE

1 2 3 4 5 6 7 8 9 0   D O C   D O C   8 9 3 2 1 0 9 8

ISBN 0–07–007386–4

This book was set in Meridien by Waldman Graphics, Inc.
The editors were Scott D. Stratford and Larry Goldberg;
the designer was Joan Greenfield; the production supervisor was Salvador Gonzales.
The cover photograph was provided by Elaine Caine.
Drawings were done by Fine Line Illustrations, Inc.
R. R. Donnelley & Sons Company was printer and binder.

Library of Congress Cataloging-in-Publication Data

Brealey, Richard A.
  Principles of corporate finance.

  Includes bibliographies and index.
    1. Corporations—Finance.   I. Myers, Stewart C.
II. Title.
HG4026.B667   1988   658.1′5   87-35287
ISBN 0-07-007386-4

About the Authors

RICHARD A. BREALEY

London Business School. Currently Deputy Principal, Midland Bank Professor of Corporate Finance and member of the Governing Body. Past President of European Finance Association and Director of the American Finance Association. Current research interests include portfolio theory and international finance. Member of editorial board of *Midland Corporate Finance Journal*. Other books include *Introduction to Risk and Return from Common Stocks*, and *Modern Developments in Investment Management* (ed., with J. H. Lorie). Formerly with Sun Life Assurance Company of Canada and Keystone Custodian Funds of Boston.

STEWART C. MYERS

Gordon Y Billard Professor of Finance at the Massachusetts Institute of Technology's Sloan School of Management. Research Associate of the National Bureau of Economic Research and past President and Director of the American Finance Association. His research is primarily concerned with the valuation of real and financial assets, corporate financial policy, and financial aspects of government regulation of business. Member of the editorial board of the *Journal of Financial Economics* and the *Midland Corporate Finance Journal*. Coauthor of *Optimal Financing Decisions* (with A. A. Robichek) and editor of *Modern Developments in Financial Management*.

To Our Parents

Contents

PART THREE   PRACTICAL PROBLEMS IN CAPITAL BUDGETING

PART FOUR   FINANCING DECISIONS AND MARKET EFFICIENCY

Preface

THIS BOOK DESCRIBES the theory and practice of corporate finance. We hardly need explain why financial managers should master the practical aspect of their job, but a word on the role of theory may be helpful.

Managers learn from experience how to cope with routine problems. But the best managers are also able to respond rationally to change. To do this you need more than time-honored rules of thumb; you must understand *why* companies and financial managers behave the way they do. In other words, you need a *theory* of corporate finance.

Does that sound intimidating? It shouldn't. Good theory helps you understand what is going on in the world around you. It helps you ask the right questions when times change and new problems must be analyzed. It also tells you what things you do *not* need to worry about.

Throughout the book we show how to use financial theory to solve practical problems, and also to illuminate the facts and institutional material that students of corporate finance must absorb.

Of course the theory presented in this book is not perfect and complete—no theory is. There are some famous controversies in which financial economists cannot agree on what firms ought to do. We have not glossed over these controversies. We set out the main arguments for each side and tell you where we stand.

There are also a few cases where theory indicates that the practical rules of thumb employed by today's managers are leading to poor decisions. Where financial managers appear to be making mistakes, we say so, while admitting that there may be hidden reasons for their actions. In brief, we have tried to be fair but to pull no punches.

Once understood, good theory is common sense. Therefore we have tried to present it at a commonsense level. We have avoided abstract proofs and heavy mathematics. However, parts of the book may require a significant intellectual effort for those unused to economic reasoning. We have marked the most difficult sections with asterisks, and suggest that you skim these sections on the first reading.

A WORD ABOUT LEARNING AIDS

There are no ironclad prerequisites for reading this book except algebra and the English language. An elementary knowledge of accounting, statistics, and microeconomics is helpful, however. The study guide for this book (Charles A. D'Ambrosio and Stewart D. Hodges, *Study Guide to Accompany Principles of Corporate Finance, McGraw-Hill, New York, 1988*) includes chapter summaries, additional illustrations, problems, and other useful material. McGraw-Hill Book Company also will make available a very useful microcomputer software package that uses Lotus 1-2-3 templates and menu-driven programs to help apply the concepts in the book to problem-solving.

Each chapter of this book closes with a summary, an annotated list of suggestions for further reading, a quick and easy quiz, and several more challenging questions and problems. Answers to the quiz questions may be found at the end of the book, along with present value tables and a glossary.

We should mention two matters of style now to prevent confusion later. First, you will notice that the most important financial terms are set in **boldface** type the first time they appear. Second, most algebraic symbols representing dollar values are set in capital letters. Other symbols are lower-case letters. Thus the symbol for a dividend payment is DIV; the symbol for a percentage of rate of return is r. We hope this will make our algebra easier to follow.

CHANGES IN THE THIRD EDITION

Readers of the second edition of this book may be interested to know what's different about the third, apart from polishing. First, we have added a chapter on hedging. This sets out general principles and introduces some of the principal derivative instruments such as financial futures and swaps. When the first edition of this book appeared in 1981 some of these instruments were novelties. Now they trade in huge volumes, and are part of any financial manager's tool kit. We have also included a second chapter on options, which allows us to say more about how they should be valued and to work through a number of applications.

Updating was needed for all but the most basic material. For example, the 1986 Tax Reform Act necessitated major changes to the chapters on capital budgeting, dividend policy, and capital structure.

Finally there are changes in emphasis. For example, the growth of contested takeovers has led us to discuss the techniques of modern merger warfare at greater length. We have also looked at leveraged buy-outs and other forms of corporate restructuring. Of course there are occasions of *reduced* emphasis. Thus, we have devoted less space to antitrust law because fewer mergers have attracted antitrust challenges.

We think the third edition is a greater improvement of the second than the second was of the first.

ACKNOWLEDGMENTS

We have a long list of people to thank for their helpful criticism of earlier editions or drafts of this edition: George Aragon, Boston College; Zvi Bodie, Boston University; Ian Cooper, London Business School; Benoit Deschamps, Georgia State University; Jerome L. Duncan, Jr., Memphis State University; Frank Fabozzi, Lehigh University; Manak C. Gupta, Temple University; Dana Johnson, Virginia Polytechnic Institute and State University; Costas Kaplanis, Salomon Brothers; Evi Kaplanis, London Business School; William Kistler, Long Island University; Arnold Langsen, California State University, Hayward; William A. McCullough, University of Florida; Surendra Mansinghka, San Francisco State University; Saman Majd, Salomon Brothers; Patrick Regan, BEA Associates; Scott Richard, Carnegie Mellon University; Richard Ruback, Massachusetts Institute of Technology; Lemma W. Senbet, University of Wisconsin; Richard Shepro, Mayer, Brown & Platt; Bernard Shinkel, Wayne State University; Gordon Sick, University of Alberta; Lakshme Shyam Sunder, Dartmouth College; John Thatcher, Clarkson University; and Michael Whinihan, The Ohio State University. We extend special thanks to Charles D'Ambrosio, the editor of the McGraw-Hill series in finance. We also thank Deborah Hannon and Diana Brealey, who typed our manuscript.

This list is almost surely incomplete. We know how much we owe to our colleagues at the London Business School and MIT's Sloan School of Management. In many cases, the ideas that appear in this book are as much theirs as ours. Finally, we record the thanks due our wives, Diana and Maureen, who by now must be thoroughly sick of this book.

Richard A. Brealey
Stewart C. Myers

PART ONE

VALUE

Why Finance Matters

This book is about financial decisions by corporations. We should start by saying what these decisions are and why they are important.

To carry on business a modern company needs an almost endless variety of **real assets**. Many of them are tangible assets, such as machinery, factories, and offices; others are intangible, such as technical expertise, trademarks, and patents. All of them unfortunately need to be paid for. To obtain the necessary money the company sells pieces of paper called **financial assets**, or securities. These pieces of paper have value because they are claims on the firm's real assets. Financial assets include not only shares of stock but also bonds, bank loans, lease obligations, and so on.

The financial manager faces two basic problems. First, how much should the firm invest, and what specific assets should the firm invest in? Second, how should the cash required for investment be raised? The answer to the first question is the firm's **investment**, or **capital budgeting, decision**. The answer to the second is its **financing decision**. The financial manager attempts to find the specific answers which make the firm's shareholders as well off as possible.

Success is usually judged by value: Shareholders are made better off by any decision which increases the value of their stake in the firm. Thus, you might say that a good investment decision is one that results in purchase of a real asset that is worth more than it costs—an asset that makes a net contribution to value. The secret of success in financial management is to increase value. That is a simple statement, but not a very helpful one. It is like advising an investor in the stock market to "buy low, sell high." The problem is how to do it.

1-1 WHY FINANCE IS CHALLENGING AND INTERESTING

There may be a few activities in which one can read a textbook and then "do it," but financial management is not one of them. That is why finance is worth studying. Who wants to work in a field where there is no room for experience, creativity, judgment, and a pinch of luck? Although this book cannot supply any of these items, it does present the concepts and information on which good financial decisions are based.

There are many reasons that the financial manager's job is challenging and interesting. Here are four important ones.

The Importance of Capital Markets

The first reason is that the financial manager must act as an intermediary, standing between the firm's operations and **capital markets**, where the firm's securities are traded. The financial manager's role is shown in Figure 1-1, which traces the flow of cash from investors to the firm and back to investors again. The flow starts when securities are issued to raise cash (arrow 1 in the figure). The cash is used

3

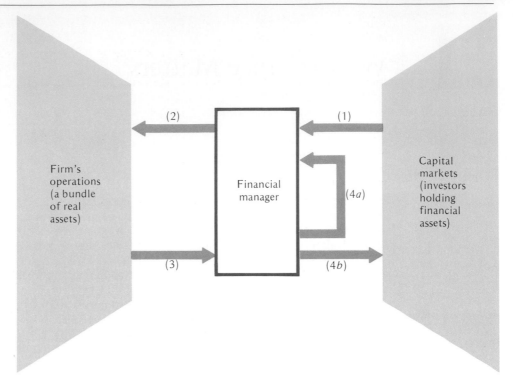

FIGURE 1-1

Flow of cash between capital markets and the firm's operations. Key: (1) Cash raised by selling financial assets to investors; (2) cash invested in the firm's operations and used to purchase real assets; (3) cash generated by the firm's operations; (4a) cash reinvested; (4b) cash returned to investors. (*Source:* From *Modern Developments in Financial Management,* S. C. Myers, ed. Copyright © 1976 by Praeger Publishers, Inc., New York. Reprinted by permission of Holt, Rinehart and Winston.)

to purchase real assets used in the firm's operations (arrow 2). (You can think of the firm's operations as a bundle of real assets.) Later, if the firm does well, the real assets generate cash inflows which more than repay the initial investment (arrow 3). Finally, the cash is either reinvested (arrow 4a) or returned to the investors who purchased the original security issue (arrow 4b). Of course the choice between arrows 4a and 4b is not a completely free one. For example, if a bank loans the firm money at stage 1, the bank has to be repaid this money plus interest at stage 4b.

Figure 1-1 shows that the financial manager has to deal with capital markets as well as the firm's operations. Therefore, the financial manager must understand how capital markets work.

The financing decision always reflects some theory about capital markets. For example, suppose a firm chooses to finance a major expansion program by issuing bonds. The financial manager must have considered the terms of the issue and concluded that it was fairly priced. That required a theory of how bonds are priced. The financial manager must also have asked whether the firm's stockholders would be made better or worse off by the extra debt standing between them and the firm's real assets. That required a theory of how corporate borrowing affects the well-being of stockholders.

The investment decision cannot be separated from capital markets either. A firm which acts in its stockholders' interest should accept those investments which increase the value of their stake in the firm. But that requires a theory of how common stocks are valued.

Understanding Value

Understanding how capital markets work amounts to understanding how financial assets are valued. This is a subject on which there has been remarkable progress over the past 10 to 20 years. New theories have been developed to explain the prices of bonds and stocks. And, when put to the test, these theories have worked well. We therefore devote a large part of this book to explaining these ideas and their implications.

Time and Uncertainty

The financial manager cannot avoid coping with time and uncertainty. Firms often have the opportunity to invest in assets which cannot pay their way in the short run and which expose the firm and its stockholders to considerable risk. The investment, if undertaken, may have to be financed by debt which cannot be fully repaid for many years. The firm cannot walk away from such choices—someone has to decide whether the opportunity is worth more than it costs and whether the additional debt burden can be safely borne.

Understanding People

The financial manager needs the opinions and cooperation of many people. For instance, many new investment ideas come from plant managers. The financial manager wants these ideas to be presented fairly; therefore, the proposers should have no personal incentives to be either overconfident or overcautious. Take another example. In some firms the plant manager needs permission from the head office to buy a company car but not to lease it, and the line of least resistance may be to lease the car. In other firms the plant manager needs permission from the head office to buy or lease, and the line of least resistance may be to travel everywhere by cab. The financial manager has to be aware of these effects and has to devise procedures that will avoid as far as possible any conflicts of interest.

These are not the only reasons that financial management is interesting and challenging. We think that as you read this book you will find many others.

1-2 WHO IS THE FINANCIAL MANAGER?

In this book we will use the term *financial manager* to refer to anyone responsible for a significant corporate investment or financing decision. But except in the smallest firms, no *single* person is responsible for all the decisions discussed in this book. Responsibility is dispersed throughout the firm. Top management is of course continuously involved in financial decisions. But the engineer who designs a new production facility is also involved: The design determines the kind of real asset the firm will hold. The advertising manager may also make important investment decisions in the course of his or her work. A major advertising campaign is really an investment in an intangible asset. If potential customers are aware of your product and convinced they should buy it, you have an asset that will pay off in future sales and earnings.

Nevertheless, there are managers who specialize in finance. The **treasurer** is

TABLE 1-1
Some typical responsibilities of the treasurer and controller

Treasurer	Controller
Banking relationships	Accounting
Cash management	Preparation of financial statements
Obtaining financing	Internal auditing
Credit management	Payroll
Dividend disbursement	Custody of records
Insurance	Preparing budgets
Pensions management	Taxes

Note: This table is not an exhaustive list of tasks treasurers and controllers may undertake.

usually the person most directly responsible for obtaining financing, managing the firm's cash account and its relationships with banks and other financial institutions, and making sure the firm meets its obligations to the investors holding its securities. Typical responsibilities of the treasurer are listed in the left-hand column of Table 1-1.

For small firms, the treasurer is likely to be the only financial executive. However, larger corporations usually also have a **controller**. The right-hand column of Table 1-1 lists the typical controller's responsibilities. Notice that there is a conceptual difference between the two jobs. The treasurer's function is primarily custodial—he or she obtains and manages the company's capital. By contrast, the controller's function is primarily one of inspecting to see that the money is used efficiently. The controller manages budgeting, accounting, and auditing.

The largest firms usually appoint a financial vice-president, who acts as the chief financial officer, overseeing both the treasurer's and the controller's work. In addition, the financial vice-president is deeply involved in financial policymaking and corporate planning. Often he or she will have general managerial responsibilities beyond strictly financial issues.

Major capital investment projects are so closely tied to plans for product development, production, and marketing that managers from these areas are inevitably drawn into planning and analyzing the projects. If the firm has staff members specializing in corporate planning, they are naturally involved in capital budgeting too. Usually the treasurer, controller, or financial vice-president is responsible for organizing and supervising the capital budgeting process.

Because of the importance of many financial issues, ultimate decisions often rest by law or by custom with the board of directors.[1] For example, only the board has the legal power to declare a dividend or to sanction a public issue of securities. Boards usually delegate decision-making authority for small- or medium-sized investment outlays, but the authority to approve large investments is almost never delegated.

---

[1] Often the firm's chief financial officer is also a member of its board of directors.

1-3   TOPICS COVERED IN THIS BOOK

This book covers investment decisions first, then financing decisions, and finally a series of topics in which investment and financing decisions interact and cannot be made separately.

In Parts One, Two, and Three we look at three different aspects of the investment decision. The first is the problem of how to value assets, the second is the link between risk and value, and the third is the management of the investment process. Our discussion of these topics occupies Chapters 2 to 12.

Eleven chapters devoted to the simple problem of "finding real assets that are worth more than they cost" may seem excessive, but that problem is not so simple in practice. Also, a conceptual base must be laid. So far, we have only asserted that increasing value is the appropriate financial objective for the firm. That assertion will have to be proved. We will also require a theory of how long-lived, risky assets are valued, and that requirement will lead us to basic questions about capital markets. For example:

- How are corporate bonds and stocks valued in capital markets?
- What risks are borne by investors in corporate securities? How can these risks be measured?
- What compensation do investors demand for bearing risk?
- What rate of return can investors in common stocks reasonably expect to receive?

Intelligent capital budgeting and financing decisions require answers to these and other questions about how capital markets work.

Financing decisions occupy Parts Four through Seven. We begin in Chapter 13 with another basic question about capital markets: "Do security prices reflect the fair value of the underlying assets?" The reason that this question is so important is that the financial manager must know whether securities can be issued at a fair price. Exactly how and when securities should be issued are the subjects of the remaining chapters in Part Four.

Parts Five, Six, and Seven continue the analysis of the financing decision, covering dividend policy, debt policy, risk management, and the alternative forms of debt. Literally dozens of different financing instruments are described and analyzed, including debentures, convertibles, leases, eurobonds, financial futures, and many other exotic beasts. We will also describe what happens when firms find themselves in financial distress because of poor operating performance, excessive borrowing, or both. Futhermore, we will show how financing considerations sometimes affect capital budgeting decisions.

Part Eight covers financial planning. Decisions about investment, dividend policy, debt policy, and other financial issues cannot be reached independently. They have to add up to a sensible overall financial plan for the firm, one which increases the value of the shareholders' investment yet still retains enough flexibility for the firm to avoid financial distress and to pursue unexpected new opportunities.

Part Nine is devoted to decisions about the firm's short-term assets and liabilities. There are separate chapters on three topics: channels for short-term borrowing or investment, management of liquid assets (cash and marketable securities), and management of accounts receivable (money lent by the firm to its customers).

Part Ten covers three important problems which require decisions about both investment and financing. We first look at mergers and acquisitions. Then we consider international financial management. All the financial problems of doing business at home are present overseas, but the international financial manager faces the additional complication of dealing in more than one currency.

The final chapter in Part Ten describes how pension plans are created and financed by corporations. Pension plan management is not a traditional subject in corporate finance texts, but we think it should be. Pensions represent an enormous liability for corporations in the United States.

Part Eleven is our conclusion. It also discusses some of the things that we *don't* know about finance. If you can be the first to solve any of these puzzles, you will be justifiably famous.

1-4   SUMMARY

In Chapter 2 we will begin with the most basic concepts of asset valuation. However, let us first sum up the principal points made in this introductory chapter.

The overall task of financial management can be broken down into (1) the investment, or capital budgeting, decision and (2) the financing decision. In other words, the firm has to decide (1) how much to invest and what assets to invest in and (2) how to raise the necessary cash. The objective is to increase the value of the shareholders' stake in the firm.

The financial manager's job is a challenging and interesting one. He or she acts as an intermediary between the firm and the capital markets. Good financial managers understand how capital markets work and how long-lived, risky assets are valued. They also work to devise procedures and incentives that encourage others in the firm to act sensibly when financial problems arise.

In small companies there is often only one financial executive. However, the larger corporation usually has both a treasurer and a controller. The treasurer's job is to obtain and manage the company's financing. By contrast, the controller's job is one of inspecting to see that the money is used correctly. In large firms there may also be a financial vice-president who acts as the firm's chief financial officer.

Of course all managers, not just finance specialists, face financial problems. In this book we will use the term *financial manager* to refer to any person confronted with a corporate financing or investment decision.

QUIZ

1. Read the following passage: "Companies usually buy _(a)_ assets. These include both tangible assets such as _(b)_ and intangible assets such as _(c)_ . In order to pay for these assets, they sell _(d)_ assets such as _(e)_ . The decision regarding which assets to buy is usually termed the _(f)_ or _(g)_ decision. The decision regarding how to raise the money is usually termed the _(h)_ decision." Now fit each of the following terms into the most appropriate space: *financing, real, bonds, investment, executive airplanes, financial, capital budgeting, brand names.*
2. Which of the following statements more accurately describes the treasurer rather than the controller?
   (*a*) Likely to be the only financial executive in small firms
   (*b*) Monitors capital expenditures to make sure that they are not misappropriated
   (*c*) Responsible for investing the firm's spare cash
   (*d*) Responsible for arranging any issue of common stock
   (*e*) Responsible for the company's tax affairs
3. Which of the following are real assets, and which are financial?
   (*a*) A share of stock

(*b*) A personal IOU
(*c*) A trademark
(*d*) A truck
(*e*) Undeveloped land
(*f*) The balance in the firm's checking account
(*g*) An experienced and hardworking sales force
(*h*) A corporate bond

2

Present Value and the Opportunity Cost of Capital

Companies invest in a variety of real assets. These include tangible assets such as plant and machinery and intangible assets such as management contracts and patents. The object of the investment, or capital budgeting, decision is to find real assets which are worth more than they cost. In this chapter we will show what this objective means in a country with extensive and well-functioning capital markets. At the same time we will take the first, most basic steps toward understanding how assets are valued. It turns out that if there is a good market for an asset, its value is exactly the same as the market price.

There are a few cases in which it is not that difficult to estimate asset values. In real estate, for example, you can hire a professional appraiser to do it for you. Suppose you own an apartment building. The odds are that your appraiser's estimate of its value will be within a few percent of what the building would actually sell for.[1] After all, there is continuous activity in the real estate market, and the appraiser's stock-in-trade is knowledge of the prices at which similar properties have recently changed hands.

Thus the problem of valuing real estate is simplified by the existence of an active market in which all kinds of properties are bought and sold. For many purposes no formal theory of value is needed. We can take the market's word for it.

But we have to go deeper than that. First, it is important to know how asset values are reached in an active market. Even if you can take the appraiser's word for it, it is important to understand *why* that apartment building is worth, say, $250,000 and not a higher or lower figure. Second, the market for most corporate assets is pretty thin. Look in the classified advertisements in *The Wall Street Journal*: it is not often that you see a blast furnace for sale.

Companies are always searching for assets that are worth more to them than to others. That apartment house is worth more to you if you can manage it better than others. But in that case, looking at the price of similar buildings will not tell you what your apartment house is worth under your management. You need to know how asset prices are determined. In other words, you need a theory of value.

We start to build that theory in this chapter. We will stick to the simplest problems and examples in order to make basic ideas clear. Readers with a taste for more complication will find plenty to satisfy them in later chapters.

---

[1] Needless to say, there are some kinds of properties that appraisers find really difficult to value—for example, nobody knows the potential selling price of the Taj Mahal or the Parthenon or Windsor Castle. If you own such a place, we congratulate you.

2-1   INTRODUCTION TO PRESENT VALUE

Later in this chapter we will prove why the concept of present value is useful. However, that concept will go down more easily if you first acquire an intuitive understanding of it.

Suppose your apartment house burns down, leaving you with a vacant lot worth $50,000 and a check for $200,000 from the fire insurance company. You consider rebuilding, but your real estate adviser suggests putting up an office building instead. The construction cost would be $300,000, and there would also be the cost of the land, which might otherwise be sold for $50,000. On the other hand, your adviser foresees a shortage of office space and predicts that a year from now the new building would fetch $400,000 if you sold it. Thus you would be investing $350,000 now in the expectation of realizing $400,000 a year hence. You should go ahead if the **present value** of the expected $400,000 payoff is greater than the investment of $350,000. Therefore, you need to ask yourself, "What is the value today of $400,000 1 year from now, and is that present value greater than $350,000?"

Calculating Present Value

The present value of $400,000 1 year from now must be less than $400,000. After all, *a dollar today is worth more than a dollar tomorrow*, because the dollar today can be invested to start earning interest immediately. This is the first basic principle of finance.

Thus, the present value of a delayed payoff may be found by multiplying the payoff by a **discount factor** which is less than 1. (If the discount factor were more than 1, a dollar today would be worth *less* than a dollar tomorrow.) If C_1 denotes the expected payoff at time period 1 (1 year hence), then

$$\text{Present value (PV)} = \text{discount factor} \times C_1$$

This discount factor is expressed as the reciprocal of 1 plus a *rate of return:*

$$\text{Discount factor} = \frac{1}{1 + r}$$

The rate of return r is the reward that investors demand for accepting delayed payment.

Let us consider the real estate investment, assuming for the moment that the $400,000 payoff is a sure thing. The office building is not the only way to obtain $400,000 a year from now. You could invest in United States government securities maturing in a year. Suppose these securities yield 7 percent interest. How much would you have to invest in them in order to receive $400,000 at the end of the year? That's easy: you would have to invest $400,000/1.07, which is $373,832. Therefore, at an interest rate of 7 percent, the present value of $400,000 1 year from now is $373,832.

Let's assume that, as soon as you've committed the land and begun construction on the building, you decide to sell your project. How much could you sell it for? That's another easy question. Since the property produces $400,000, investors would be willing to pay $373,832 for it. That's what it would cost them to get a $400,000 payoff from investing in government securities. Of course you could always sell your property for less, but why sell for less than the market will bear? The $373,832 present value is the only feasible price that satisfies both buyer and seller. Therefore, the present value of the property is also its market price.

To calculate present value, we discount expected future payoffs by the rate of return offered by comparable investment alternatives. This rate of return is often referred to as the **discount rate, hurdle rate**, or **opportunity cost of capital**. It is called the *opportunity cost* because it is the return forgone by investing in the project rather than investing in securities. In our example the opportunity cost was 7 percent. Present value was obtained by dividing $400,000 by 1.07:

$$PV = \text{discount factor} \times C_1 = \frac{1}{1 + r} \times C_1 = \frac{400,000}{1.07} = \$373,832$$

Net Present Value

The building is worth $373,832, but this does not mean that you are $373,832 better off. You committed $350,000, and therefore your **net present value** is $23,832. Net present value **(NPV)** is found by subtracting the required investment:

$$NPV = PV - \text{required investment} = 373,832 \quad 350,000 = \$23,832$$

In other words, your office development is worth more than it costs—it makes a *net* contribution to value. The formula for calculating NPV can be written as

$$NPV = C_0 + \frac{C_1}{1 + r}$$

remembering that C_0, the cash flow at time period 0 (that is, today) will usually be a negative number. In other words, C_0 is an investment and therefore a cash *outflow*. In our example, $C_0 = -\$350,000$.

A Comment on Risk and Present Value

We made one unrealistic assumption in our discussion of the office development: Your real estate adviser cannot be *certain* about future values of office buildings. The $400,000 figure represents the best *forecast*, but it is not a sure thing.

Therefore, our conclusion about how much investors would pay for the building is wrong. Since they could achieve $400,000 with certainty by buying $373,832 worth of United States government securities, they would not buy your building for that amount. You would have to cut your asking price to attract investors' interest.

Here we can invoke a second basic financial principle: *A safe dollar is worth more than a risky one.* Most investors avoid risk when they can do so without sacrificing return. However, the concepts of present value and the opportunity cost of capital still make sense for risky investments. It is still proper to discount the payoff by the rate of return offered by a comparable investment. But we have to think of *expected* payoffs and the *expected* rates of return on other investments.

Not all investments are equally risky. The office development is riskier than a government security but is probably less risky than drilling a wildcat oil well. Suppose you believe the project is as risky as investment in the stock market and that you forecast a 12 percent rate of return for stock market investments. Then 12 percent becomes the appropriate opportunity cost of capital. That is what you are giving up by not investing in comparable securities. You can now recompute NPV:

$$PV = \frac{400,000}{1.12} = \$357,143$$

$$NPV = PV - 350,000 = \$7143$$

If other investors agree with your forecast of a $400,000 payoff and with your assessment of a 12 percent opportunity cost of capital, then your property ought to be worth $357,143 once construction is under way. If you tried to sell it for more than that, there would be no takers, because the property would then offer an expected rate of return lower than the 12 percent available in the stock market. The office building still makes a net contribution to value, but it is much smaller than our earlier calculations indicated.

In Chapter 1 we said that the financial manager must be concerned with time and uncertainty and their effects on value. This is clearly so in our example. The $400,000 payoff would be worth exactly that if it could be realized instantaneously. If the office building is as risk-free as government securities, the 1-year delay reduces value to $373,832. If the office building is as risky as investment in the stock market, then uncertainty reduces value by a further $16,689 to $357,143.

Unfortunately, adjusting asset values for time and uncertainty is often more complicated than our example suggests. Therefore, we will take the two effects separately. For the most part, we will dodge the problem of risk in Chapters 2 through 6, either treating all payoffs as if they were known with certainty or talking about expected cash flows and expected rates of return without worrying how risk is defined or measured. Then in Chapter 7 we will turn to the problem of understanding how capital markets cope with risk.

Present Values and Rates of Return

We have decided that construction of the office building is a smart thing to do, since it is worth more than it costs—it has a positive net present value. To calculate how much it is worth, we worked out how much one would have to pay to achieve the same income by investing directly in securities. The project's present value is equal to its future income discounted at the rate of return offered by these securities.

We can reexpress our criterion by saying that our property venture is worth undertaking because the return exceeds the cost of capital. The return on the capital invested is simply the profit as a proportion of the initial outlay:

$$\text{Return} = \frac{\text{profit}}{\text{investment}} = \frac{400,000 - 350,000}{350,000} = 14\%$$

The cost of capital invested is once again just the return forgone by *not* investing in securities. In our present case, if the office building is about as risky as investing in the stock market, the return forgone is 12 percent. Since the 14 percent return on the office building exceeds the 12 percent cost, we should start digging the foundations of the building.

Here then we have two equivalent decision rules for capital investment.[2]

1. *Net present value rule*. Accept investments that have positive net present values.
2. *Rate-of-return rule*. Accept investments that offer rates of return in excess of their opportunity costs of capital.[3]

---

[2] You might check for yourself that these are equivalent rules. In other words, if the return 50,000/350,000 is greater than r, then the net present value $-350,000 + [400,000/(1 + r)]$ *must* be greater than 0.

[3] The two rules can conflict when there are cash flows in more than two periods. We address this problem in Chapter 5.

FIGURE 2-1
Notice how borrowing and lending enlarge the individual's choice. By borrowing against future cash flow *F*, an individual can consume an extra *BD* today; by lending current cash flow *B*, the individual can consume an extra *FH* tomorrow.

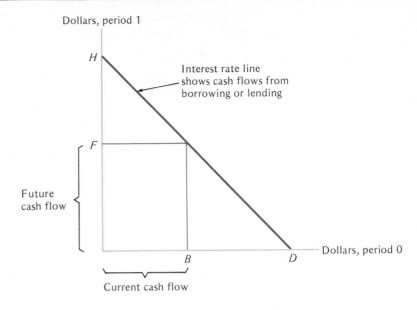

*2-2   FOUNDATIONS OF THE NET PRESENT VALUE RULE[4]

So far our discussion of net present value has been rather casual. Increasing NPV *sounds* like a sensible objective for a company, but it is more than just a rule of thumb. We need to understand why the NPV rule makes sense and why we look to the bond and stock markets to find the opportunity cost of capital.

Figure 2-1 illustrates the problem of choosing between spending today and spending in the future. Assume that you have a cash inflow of *B* today and *F* in a year's time. Unless you have some way of storing or anticipating income, you will be compelled to consume it as it arrives. This could be inconvenient or worse. If the bulk of your cash flow is received next year, the result could be hunger now and gluttony later. This is where the capital market comes in. It allows the transfer of wealth across time, so that you can eat moderately both this year and next.

The capital market is simply a market where people trade between dollars today and dollars in the future. The downward-sloping line in Figure 2-1 represents the rate of exchange in the capital market between today's dollars and next year's dollars; its slope is $1 + r$, where r denotes the 1-year rate of interest. By lending all your present cash flow, you could increase your *future* consumption by $(1 + r)B$ or *FH*. Alternatively, by borrowing against your future cash flow, you could increase your *present* consumption by $F/(1 + r)$ or *BD*.

Let us put some numbers into our example. Suppose that your prospects are as follows:

- Cash on hand: $B = \$20,000$
- Cash to be received 1 year from now: $F = \$25,000$

If you do not want to consume anything today, you can invest \$20,000 in the capital market at, say, 7 percent. The rate of exchange between dollars next year and dollars today is 1.07: This is the slope of the line in Figure 2-1. If you invest \$20,000 at 7 percent, you will obtain $\$20,000 \times 1.07 = \$21,400$. Of course, you

---

[4] Sections marked with an asterisk contain more difficult material and may be skipped on a first reading.

also have \$25,000 coming in a year from now, so you will end up with \$46,400. This is point H in Figure 2-1.

What if you want to cash in the \$25,000 future payment and spend everything today on some ephemeral frolic? You can do so by borrowing in the capital market. The present value formula tells us how much investors would give you today in return for the promise of \$25,000 next year:

$$PV = \frac{C_1}{1 + r} = \frac{25,000}{1.07} = \$23,364$$

This is the distance BD. The total present value of the current and future cash flows (point D in the figure) is found by adding this year's flow.

$$C_0 + \frac{C_1}{1 + r} = 20,000 + \frac{25,000}{1.07} = \$43,364$$

This is the formula that we used before to calculate net present value (except that in this case C_0 is positive).

What if you cash in but then change your mind and want to consume next year? Can you get back to point H? Of course—just invest the net present value at 7 percent.

$$\text{Future value} = 43,364 \times 1.07 = \$46,400$$

As a matter of fact, you can end up anywhere on the straight line connecting D and H depending on how much of the \$43,364 current wealth you choose to invest. Figure 2-1 is actually a graphical representation of the link between present and future value.

*How the Capital Market Helps to Smooth Consumption Patterns

Few of us save all our current cash flow or borrow fully against our future cash flow. We try to achieve a balance between present and future consumption. But there is no reason to expect that the best balance for one person is best for another.

Suppose, for example, that you have a prodigal disposition and favor present over future consumption. Your preferred pattern might be indicated by Figure 2-2: You choose to borrow BC against future cash flow and consume C today. Next year you are obliged to repay EF and, therefore, can consume only E. By contrast, if you have a more miserly streak, you might prefer the policy shown in Figure 2-3: You consume A today and lend the balance AB. In a year's time you receive a repayment of FG and are therefore able to indulge in consumption of G.[5]

Both the miser and the prodigal *can* choose to spend cash only as it is received, but in these examples both prefer to do otherwise. By opening up borrowing and lending opportunities, the capital market removes the obligation to match consumption and cash flow.

[5] The exact balance between present and future consumption that each individual will choose depends on personal taste. Readers who are familiar with economic theory will recognize that the choice can be represented by superimposing an indifference map for each individual. The preferred combination is the point of tangency between the interest-rate line and the individual's indifference curve. In other words, each individual will borrow or lend until 1 plus the interest rate equals the marginal rate of time preference (i.e., the slope of the indifference curve).

FIGURE 2-2
The prodigal chooses to borrow
BC against tomorrow's cash
flow, in order to consume *C* today and *E* tomorrow.

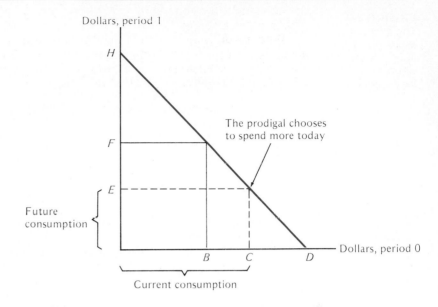

***Now We
Introduce
Productive
Opportunities**

In practice individuals are not limited to investing in capital market securities: They may also acquire plant, machinery, and other real assets. Thus, in addition to plotting the returns from buying securities, we can also plot an investment-opportunities line which shows the returns from buying real assets. The return on the "best" project may well be substantially higher than returns in the capital market, so that the investment-opportunities line may be initially very steep. But, unless the individual is a bottomless pit of inspiration, the line will become progessively flatter. This is illustrated in Figure 2-4, where the first $10,000 of in-

FIGURE 2-3
The miser chooses to lend *AB*,
in order to consume *A* today
and *G* tomorrow.

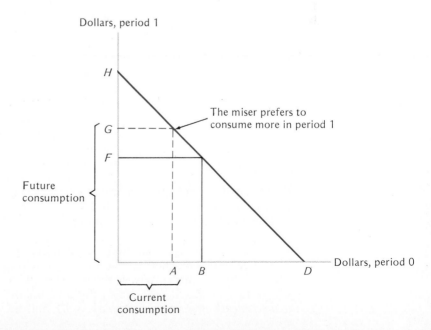

FIGURE 2-4
The effect of investment in real
assets on cash flows in periods 0
and 1. Notice the diminishing
returns on additional units of
investment.

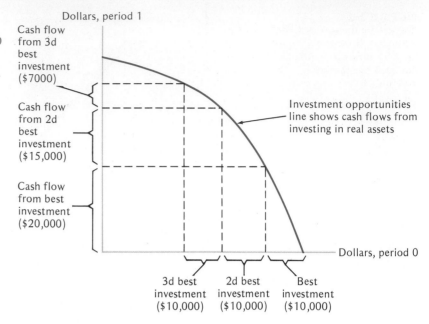

vestment produces a subsequent cash flow of $20,000, whereas the next $10,000
offers a cash flow of only $15,000. In the jargon of economics, there is a declining
marginal return on capital.

We can now return to our hypothetical example and inquire how your welfare
would be affected by the possibility of investing in real assets. The solution is
illustrated in Figure 2-5. To keep our diagram simple, we shall assume that you
have maximum initial resources of *D*. Part of this may come from borrowing
against future cash flow; but we do not have to worry about that, because, as we
have seen, the amount *D* can always be deployed into future income. If you choose
to invest any part of this sum in the capital market, you can attain any point along
the line *DH*.

Now let us introduce investment in *real assets* by supposing that you retain *J*
of your initial resources and invest the balance *JD* in plant and machinery. We
can see from the curved investment-opportunities line that such an investment
would produce a future cash flow of *G*. This is all very well, but maybe you do
not want to consume *J* today and *G* tomorrow. Fortunately you can use the capital
market to adjust your spending pattern as you choose. By investing the whole of
J in the capital market, you can increase *future* income by *GM*. Alternatively, by
borrowing against your entire future earnings of *G*, you can increase *present* income
by *JK*. In other words, by *both* investing *JD* in *real assets* and borrowing or lending
in the capital market, you can obtain any point along the line *KM*. Regardless of
whether you are a prodigal or a miser, you have more to spend either today or
next year than if you invest *only* in the capital market (i.e., choose a point along
the line *DH*). You also have more to spend either today or next year than if you
invest *only* in real assets (i.e., choose a point along the curve *DL*).

Let us look more closely at the investment in *real assets*. The maximum sum
that could be realized today from the investment's future case flow is *JK*. *This is
the investment's present value*. Its cost is *JD*, and the difference between its present

FIGURE 2-5
Both the prodigal and the miser have initial wealth of *D*. They are better off if they invest *JD* in real assets and then borrow or lend in the capital market. If they could invest *only* in the capital market, they would be obliged to choose a point along *DH;* if they could invest *only* in real assets, they would be obliged to choose a point along *DL*.

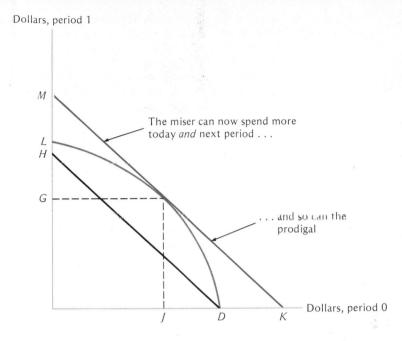

value and its cost is *DK. This is its net present value.* Net present value is the addition to your resources from investing in *real assets.*

Investing the amount *JD* is a smart move—it makes you better off. In fact it is the smartest possible move. We can see why if we look at Figure 2-6. If you invest *JD* in real assets, the net present value is *DK*. If you invest, say, *ND* in real assets, the net present value declines to *DP*. In fact investing either more or less than *JD* in real assets *must* reduce net present value.

Notice also that by investing *JD*, you have invested up to the point at which the investment-opportunities line just touches and has the same slope as the

FIGURE 2-6
If the prodigal or the miser invests *ND* in real assets, the NPV of the investment would be only *DP*. The investor would have less to spend both today and tomorrow.

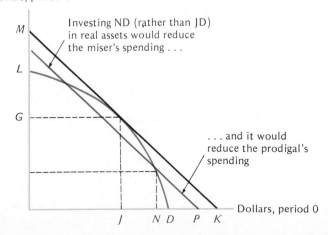

interest-rate line. Now the slope of the investment-opportunities line represents the return on the marginal investment, so that *JD* is the point at which the return on the marginal investment is exactly equal to the rate of interest. In other words, you will maximize your wealth if you invest in *real* assets until the marginal return on investment falls to the rate of interest. Having done that, you will borrow or lend in the capital market until you have achieved the desired balance between consumption today and consumption tomorrow.

We now have a logical basis for the two equivalent rules that we proposed so casually at the end of Section 2-1. We can restate the rules as follows:

1. *Net present value rule.* Invest so as to maximize the net present value of the investment. This is the difference between the discounted, or present, value of the future income and the amount of the initial investment.
2. *Rate-of-return rule.* Invest up to the point at which the marginal return on the investment is equal to the rate of return on equivalent investments in the capital market. This is the point of tangency between the interest-rate line and the investment-opportunities line.

*A Crucial Assumption

In our examples, the miser and the prodigal placed an identical value on the firm's investment. They agreed because they faced identical borrowing and lending opportunities. Whenever firms discount cash flows at capital market rates, they are implicitly making some assumptions about their shareholders' opportunities to borrow and lend. Strictly speaking, they are assuming:

1. That there are no barriers preventing access to the capital market and that no participant is sufficiently dominant as to have a significant effect on price
2. That access to the capital market is costless and that there are no "frictions" preventing the free trading of securities
3. That relevant information about the price and quality of each security is widely and freely available
4. That there are no distorting taxes

In sum, they are assuming a perfectly competitive capital market. Clearly this is at best an approximation, but it may not be too bad a one. There are nearly 50 million stockholders in the United States. Even a giant institution like the Morgan Guaranty Trust Company controls no more than 2 or 3 percent of publicly traded stocks. Second, the costs of trading in securities are generally small both in absolute terms and relative to the costs of trading in real assets such as office buildings and blast furnaces. Finally, though there obviously are cases in which investors have possessed privileged information, the mighty power of avarice and the Securities and Exchange Commission ensure that potentially profitable information seldom remains for long the property of one individual.[6]

Even though our conditions are not fully satisfied, there is considerable evidence that security prices behave almost as if they were. This evidence is presented and discussed in Chapter 13.

---

[6] Avarice helps because any other individual who can obtain this information can use it to make trading profits.

FIGURE 2-7
Here there are separate borrowing and lending rates. The steep line represents the interest rate for a borrower; the flatter line represents the rate for a lender. In this case the prodigal and the miser prefer different levels of capital investment.

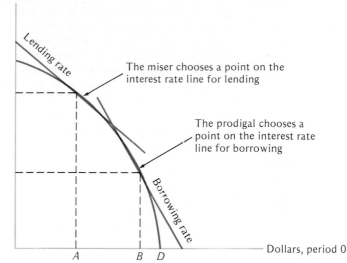

Dollars, period 1

Lending rate

The miser chooses a point on the interest rate line for lending

The prodigal chooses a point on the interest rate line for borrowing

Borrowing rate

Dollars, period 0

A $\qquad$ *B* *D*

*Imperfect Capital Markets

Suppose that we did not have such a well-functioning capital market. How would this damage our net present value rule?

As an example, Figure 2-7 shows what happens if the borrowing rate is substantially higher than the lending rate. This means that when you want to turn period 0 dollars into period 1 dollars (i.e., lend), you move *up* a relatively flat line; when you want to turn period 1 dollars into period 0 dollars (i.e., borrow), you move *down* a relatively steep line. You can see that would-be borrowers (who must move down the steep line) prefer the company to invest only *BD*. In contrast, would-be lenders (who must move *up* the relatively flat line) prefer the company to invest *AD*. In this case the two groups of shareholders want the manager to use different discount rates. The manager has no simple way to reconcile their differing objectives.

No one believes that the competitive market assumption is fully satisfied. Later in this book we will discuss several cases in which differences in taxation, transaction costs, and other imperfections must be taken into account in financial decision making. However, we will also discuss research which indicates that, in general, capital markets function fairly well. That is one good reason for relying on net present value as a corporate objective. Another good reason is that net present value makes common sense; we will see that it gives obviously silly answers less frequently than its major competitors. But for now, having glimpsed the problems of imperfect markets, we shall, like an economist in a shipwreck, simply *assume* our life jacket and swim safely to shore.

2-3   A FUNDAMENTAL RESULT

The present value rule really dates back to the work of the great American economist Irving Fisher, in 1930.[7] What was so exciting about Fisher's analysis was his discovery that the capital investment criterion has nothing to do with the individual's preferences for current versus future consumption. The prodigal and the miser are unanimous in the amount that they want to invest in real assets. Because they have the same investment criterion, they can cooperate in the same enterprise and can safely delegate the operation of that enterprise to a professional manager. Managers do not need to know anything about the personal tastes of their shareholders and should not consult their own tastes. Their task is to maximize net present value. If they succeed, they can rest assured that they have acted in the best interests of their shareholders.

Our justification of the net present value rule has been restricted to two periods and to certain cash flows. However, the rule also makes sense for cases in which the cash flows extend beyond the next period. The argument goes like this:

1. A financial manager should act in the interest of the firm's stockholders.
2. Each stockholder wants three things:
    (*a*) To be as rich as possible, that is, to maximize current wealth
    (*b*) To transform that wealth into whatever time pattern of consumption he or she most desires
    (*c*) To choose the risk characteristics of that consumption plan
3. But stockholders do not need the financial manager's help to reach the best time pattern of consumption. They can do that on their own, providing they have free access to competitive capital markets. They can also choose the risk characteristics of their consumption plan by investing in more or less risky securities.
4. How then can the financial manager help the firm's stockholders? By increasing the market value of each stockholder's stake in the firm. The way to do that is to seize all investment opportunities that have a positive net present value.

This gives us the fundamental condition for the successful operation of a capitalist economy. Separation of ownership and management is a practical necessity for large organizations. Many corporations have hundreds of thousands of shareholders, no two with the same tastes, wealth, or personal opportunities. There is no way for all the firm's owners to be actively involved in management: It would be like running New York City through a series of town meetings for all its citizens. Therefore, authority has to be delegated. The remarkable thing is that managers of firms can all be given one simple instruction: Maximize net present value.

Other Corporate Goals

Do real managers really follow this simple instruction? Some idealists say that managers should not be obliged to act in the selfish interests of their stockholders. Some realists argue that, regardless of what managers ought to do, they in fact look after themselves.

Let us respond to the idealists first. We do not know how energetically managers seek to maximize net present value, but we are reminded of a survey of businesspeople that inquired whether they attempted to maximize profits. They indignantly rejected the notion, protesting that they were responsible, God-fearing,

---

[7] I. Fisher, *The Theory of Interest*, Augustus M. Kelley, Publishers, New York, 1965 (Reprinted from the 1930 edition). Our graphical illustration closely follows the exposition in E. F. Fama and M. H. Miller, *The Theory of Finance*, Holt, Rinehart and Winston, New York 1972.

and so on: Their responsibilities went far beyond the narrow profit objective. But when the question was reformulated and they were asked whether they could increase profits by raising or lowering their selling price, they replied that neither policy would do so.[8] In a rather similar vein, we suspect that many managers do not have an explicit objective of maximizing net present value and yet can think of no action that would do other than to reduce it.

Suppose, however, that we do believe that management should have these wider responsibilities. Management still must be able to analyze a decision from the shareholders' point of view if it is to strike a proper balance between their interests and those of consumers, employees, and society at large. The net present value calculation tells them how much a particular decison helps or hinders stockholders.

Now, how about the realists who say that managers look after their own interests rather than those of their shareholders? We agree that managers do look to their own interests. But shareholders would not hand over their capital if they believed that their managers would dissipate it in luxury and leisure. What is it that prevents such dissipation—or at least keeps it down to acceptable proportions?

First, compensation packages can be designed to align managers' and stockholders' interests. For example, top managers are usually given options to buy stock in the business; the options pay off only if the business does well. Second, managers who are successful in increasing shareholder wealth will find that they can move on to better jobs and higher salaries. Managers who ignore shareholder wealth may find their companies taken over by some other firm more concerned with profitability. After the takeover, they may also find themselves out on the street.

No compensation plan can ensure that managers always try to increase shareholders' wealth, but good managers know that it is in their long-run interest to demonstrate that the shareholders' pockets are close to the managers' hearts.

2-4 SUMMARY

In this chapter we have introduced the concept of present value as a way of valuing assets. Calculating present value is easy. Just discount future cash flow by an appropriate rate, usually called the *opportunity cost of capital*, or *hurdle rate*.

$$\text{Present value (PV)} = \frac{C_1}{1 + r}$$

Net present value is present value plus any immediate cash flow.

$$\text{Net present value (NPV)} = C_0 + \frac{C_1}{1 + r}$$

Remember that C_0 is negative if the immediate cash flow is an investment, that is, if it is a cash outflow.

The discount rate is determined by rates of return prevailing in capital markets. If the future cash flow is absolutely safe, then the discount rate is the interest rate on safe securities such as United States government debt. If the size of the future cash flow is uncertain, then the expected cash flow should be discounted at the expected rate of return offered by equivalent-risk securities. We will talk more about this in Chapter 7.

---

[8] Cited in G. J. Stigler, *The Theory of Price*, 3d ed., The Macmillan Company, New York, 1966.

Cash flows are discounted for two simple reasons: first, because a dollar today is worth more than a dollar tomorrow, and second, because a risky dollar is worth less than a safe one. Formulas for PV and NPV are numerical expressions of these ideas. We look to rates of return prevailing in capital markets to determine how much to discount for time and for risk. By calculating the present value of an asset, we are in effect estimating how much people will pay for it if they have the alternative of investing in the capital markets.

The concept of net present value allows efficient separation of ownership and management of the corporation. A manager who invests only in assets with positive net present values serves the best interests of each one of the firm's owners—regardless of differences in their wealth and tastes. This is made possible by the existence of the capital market, which allows each shareholder to construct a personal investment plan that is custom-tailored to his or her own needs. For example, there is no need for the firm to arrange its investment policy to obtain a sequence of cash flows that matches shareholders' preferred time patterns of consumption. The shareholders can shift funds forward or back over time perfectly well on their own, provided they have free access to competitive capital markets. In fact, their plan for consumption over time is constrained by only two things: their personal wealth (or lack of it) and the interest rate at which they can borrow and lend. The financial manager cannot affect the interest rate but can increase stockholders' wealth. The way to do so is to invest in assets having positive net present values.

FURTHER READING

The pioneering works on the net present value rule are:

I. Fisher: *The Theory of Interest*, Augustus M. Kelley, Publishers, New York, 1965. Reprinted from the 1930 edition.

J. Hirschleifer: "On the Theory of Optimal Investment Decision," *Journal of Political Economy*, **66**:329–352 (August 1958).

For a more rigorous textbook treatment of the subject, we suggest:

E. F. Fama and M. H. Miller: *The Theory of Finance*, Holt, Rinehart and Winston, New York, 1972.

If you would like to dig deeper into the question of how managers may be motivated to maximize shareholder wealth, we suggest:

M. C. Jensen and W. H. Meckling: "Theory of the Firm: Managerial Behavior, Agency Costs, and Ownership Structure," *Journal of Financial Economics*, **3**:305–360 (October 1976).

E. F. Fama: "Agency Problems and the Theory of the Firm," *Journal of Political Economy*, **88**:288–307 (April 1980).

QUIZ

1. C_0 is the initial cash flow on an investment, and C_1 is the cash flow at the end of 1 year. The symbol r is the discount rate.
   (*a*) Is C_0 usually positive or negative?
   (*b*) What is the formula for the present value of the investment?
   (*c*) What is the formula for the net present value?
   (*d*) The symbol r is often termed the *opportunity cost of capital*. Why?
   (*e*) If the investment is risk-free, what is the appropriate measure of r?

2. If the present value of $150 paid at the end of 1 year is $130, what is the 1-year discount factor? What is the discount rate?

3. Calculate the 1-year discount factor DF_1 for discount rates of (a) 10 percent, (b) 20 percent, and (c) 30 percent.

4. A merchant pays $100,000 for a load of grain and is certain that it can be resold at the end of 1 year for $132,000.
   (a) What is the return on this investment?
   (b) If this return is *lower* than the rate of interest, does the investment have a positive or a negative net present value?
   (c) If the rate of interest is 10 percent, what is the present value of the investment?
   (d) What is the net present value?

5. What is the net present value rule? What is the rate-of-return rule? Do the two rules give the same answer?

*6. In Figure 2-8, the sloping line represents the opportunities for investment in the capital market and the solid curved line represents the opportunities for investment in plant and machinery. The company's only asset at present is $2.6 million in cash.
   (a) What is the interest rate?
   (b) How much should the company invest in plant?
   (c) How much will this investment be worth next year?
   (d) What is the average rate of return on the investment in plant?
   (e) What is the marginal rate of return?
   (f) What is the present value of this investment?
   (g) What is the net present value of this investment?
   (h) What is the total present value of the company?
   (i) How much will the individual consume today?
   (j) How much will he or she consume tomorrow?

7. We can imagine the financial manager doing several things on behalf of the firm's stockholders. For example, the manager might:
   (a) Make shareholders as wealthy as possible by investing in real assets with positive net present values.

FIGURE 2-8
See Quiz, question 6.

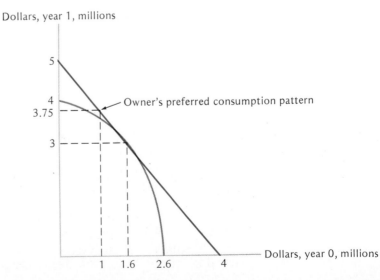

(b) Modify the firm's investment plan to help shareholders achieve a particular time pattern of consumption.

(c) Choose high- or low-risk assets to match shareholders' risk preferences.

(d) Help balance shareholders' checkbooks.

But in well-functioning capital markets, shareholders will vote for *only one* of these goals. Which one? Why?

QUESTIONS AND PROBLEMS

1. In Section 2-1, we analyzed the possible construction of an office building on a plot of land appraised at $50,000. We concluded that this investment had a positive NPV of $7,143.

   Suppose E. Coli Associates, the genetic engineers, offer to purchase the land for $60,000, $30,000 paid immediately and $30,000 after 1 year. United States government securities maturing in 1 year yield 7 percent.

   (a) Assume E. Coli is sure to pay the second $30,000 installment. Should you take their offer or start on the office building? Explain.

   (b) Suppose you are *not* sure E. Coli will pay. You observe that other investors demand a 10 percent return on their loans to E. Coli. Assume that the other investors have correctly assessed the risks that E. Coli will not be able to pay. Should you accept E. Coli's offer?

2. Write down the formulas for an investment's net present value and rate of return. Prove that NPV is positive *only* if the rate of return exceeds the opportunity cost of capital.

3. What is the net present value of a *firm's* investment in a U.S. Treasury security yielding 15 percent and maturing in 1 year? *Hint:* What is the opportunity cost of capital? Ignore taxes.

4. Calculate the NPV and rate of return for each of the following investments. The opportunity cost of capital is 20 percent for all four investments.

Investment	Initial Cash Flow, C_0	Cash Flow in Year 1, C_1
1	− 10,000	+ 20,000
2	− 5,000	+ 12,000
3	− 5,000	+ 5,500
4	− 2,000	+ 5,000

   (a) Which investment is most valuable?

   (b) Suppose each investment would require use of the same parcel of land. Therefore you can take only one. Which one? *Hint:* What is the firm's objective? To earn a high rate of return? Or to increase firm value?

*5. Redraw Figure 2-5 to scale to represent the following situation:

   (a) A firm starts out with $10 million in cash.

   (b) The rate of interest r is 10 percent.

   (c) To maximize NPV the firm invests today $6 million in real assets ($C_0 = -6$ million). This leaves $4 million which can be paid out to the shareholders.

   (d) The NPV of the investment is $2 million.

   When you have finished, answer the following questions:

   (e) How much cash is the firm going to receive in year 1 from its investment?

   (f) What is the marginal return from the firm's investment?

(*g*) What is the present value of the shareholders' investment after the firm has announced its investment plan?

(*h*) Suppose shareholders want to spend $6 million today. How can they do this?

(*i*) How much will they then have to spend next year? Show this on your drawing.

*6. Resketch Figure 2-5 to show how the firm's investment plan should be affected by a decline in the interest rate. Mark the NPV of the revised investment plan. Show whether the miser or the prodigal would be better off.

*7. Look again at Figure 2-5. Suppose the firm decides to invest *more* than *JD* in real assets. Redraw the interest-rate line to show the NPV of the revised investment plan. Show that both the miser *and* the prodigal are worse off.

*8. The interest-rate line in our diagrams always has a slope greater than 1. Why?

9. "The discount rate is the rate at which the company will be able to reinvest its cash flows." Is that right? Discuss.

10. Respond to the following comment: "It's all very well telling companies to maximize net present value, but 'net present value' is just an abstract notion. What I tell my managers is that profits are what matters and it's profits that we're going to maximize."

11. Respond to the following comment: "It's no good just telling me to maximize my stock price. I can easily take a short view and maximize today's price. What I would prefer is to keep it on a gently rising trend."

12. Here's a harder question. It is sometimes argued that the net present value criterion is appropriate for corporations but not for governments. First, governments must consider the time preferences of the community as a whole rather than those of a few wealthy investors. Second, governments must have a longer horizon than individuals, for governments are the guardians of future generations. What do you think?

13. Give examples of potential conflicts of interest between managers and shareholders. Why do managers generally work hard to make the firm successful?

3 How to Calculate Present Values

In Chapter 2 we learned how to work out the value of an asset that produces cash exactly 1 year from now. But we did not explain how to value assets that produce cash 2 years from now or in several future years. That is the first thing that we must do in this chapter. We will then have a look at some short-cut methods for calculating present values and at some specialized present value formulas.

By then you will deserve some payoff for the mental investment you have made in learning about present values. In Chapter 4 we will try out the concept on common stocks, and after that we will tackle the firm's capital investment decisions at a practical level of detail.

3-1 VALUING LONG-LIVED ASSETS

Do you remember how to calculate the present value PV of an asset that produces a cash flow (C_1) 1 year from now?

$$PV = DF_1 \times C_1 = \frac{C_1}{1 + r_1}$$

The discount factor for year 1 cash flows is DF_1, and r_1 is the opportunity cost of investing your money for 1 year. Suppose you will receive a certain cash inflow of $100 next year ($C_1 = 100$) and the rate of interest on 1-year United States Treasury bills is 7 percent ($r_1 = .07$). Then present value equals

$$PV = \frac{C_1}{1 + r_1} = \frac{100}{1.07} = \$93.46$$

The present value of a cash flow 2 years hence can be written in a similar way as

$$PV = DF_2 \times C_2 = \frac{C_2}{(1 + r_2)^2}$$

C_2 is the year 2 cash flow, DF_2 is the discount factor for year 2 cash flows, and r_2 is the annual rate of interest on money invested for 2 years. Continuing with our example, suppose you get another cash flow of $100 in year 2 ($C_2 = 100$). The rate of interest on 2-year Treasury notes is 7.7 percent per year ($r_2 = .077$); this means that a dollar invested in 2-year notes will grow to $1.077^2 = \$1.16$ by the end of 2 years. The present value of your year 2 cash flow equals

$$PV = \frac{C_2}{(1 + r_2)^2} = \frac{100}{(1.077)^2} = \$86.21$$

Valuing Cash Flows in Several Periods

One of the nice things about present values is that they are all expressed in current dollars—so that you can add them up. In other words, the present value of cash flow $A + B$ is equal to the present value of cash flow A plus the present value of cash flow B. This happy result has important implications for investments that produce cash flows in several periods.

We calculated above the value of an asset that produces a cash flow of C_1 in year 1, and we calculated the value of another asset that produces a cash flow of C_2 in year 2. Following our additivity rule, we can write down the value of an asset that produces cash flows in *each* year. It is simply

$$PV = \frac{C_1}{1 + r_1} + \frac{C_2}{(1 + r_2)^2}$$

We can obviously continue in this way and find the present value of an extended stream of cash flows:

$$PV = \frac{C_1}{1 + r_1} + \frac{C_2}{(1 + r_2)^2} + \frac{C_3}{(1 + r_3)^3} + \cdots$$

This is called the **discounted cash flow** (or **DCF**) formula. A shorthand way to write it is

$$PV = \sum \frac{C_t}{(1 + r_t)^t}$$

where Σ refers to the sum of the series. To find the *net* present value we add the (usually negative) initial cash flow, just as in the period 1 case:

$$NPV = C_0 + PV = C_0 + \sum \frac{C_t}{(1 + r_t)^t}$$

*Why the Discount Factor Declines as Futurity Increases— And a Digression on Money Machines

If a dollar tomorrow is worth less than a dollar today, one might suspect that a dollar the day after tomorrow should be worth even less. In other words, the discount factor DF_2 should be less than the discount factor DF_1. But is this *necessarily* so, when there is a different interest rate r_t for each period?

Suppose r_1 is 20 percent and r_2 7 percent. Then

$$DF_1 = \frac{1}{1.20} = .83$$

$$DF_2 = \frac{1}{(1.07)^2} = .87$$

Apparently the dollar received the day after tomorrow is *not* necessarily worth less than the dollar received tomorrow.

But there is something wrong with this example. Anyone who could borrow and lend at these interest rates could become a millionaire overnight. Let us see how such a "money machine" would work. Suppose the first person to spot the opportunity is Hermione Kraft. Ms. Kraft first lends $1000 for 1 year at 20 percent. That is an attractive enough return, but she notices that there is a way to earn an *immediate* profit on her investment and be ready to play the game again. She reasons as follows. Next year she will have $1200 which can be reinvested for a further year. Although she does not know what interest rates will be at that time, she does know that she can always put the money in a checking account and be sure of having $1200 at the end of year 2. Her next step, therefore, is to go to her bank and borrow the present value of this $1200. At 7 percent interest this present value is

$$PV = \frac{1200}{(1.07)^2} = \$1048$$

Thus Ms. Kraft invests $1000, borrows back $1048, and walks away with a profit of $48. If that does not sound like very much, remember that the game can be played again immediately, this time with $1048. In fact it would take Ms. Kraft only 147 plays to become a millionaire (before taxes).[1]

Of course this story is completely fanciful. Such an opportunity would not last long in capital markets like ours. Any bank that would allow you to lend for 1 year at 20 percent and borrow for 2 years at 7 percent would soon be wiped out by a rush of small investors hoping to become millionaires and a rush of millionaires hoping to become billionaires. There are, however, two lessons to our story. The first is that a dollar tomorrow *cannot* be worth less than a dollar the day after tomorrow. In other words, the value of a dollar received at the end of 1 year (DF_1) must be greater than the value of a dollar received at the end of 2 years (DF_2). There must be some extra gain[2] from lending for 2 periods rather than 1: $(1 + r_2)^2$ must be greater than $1 + r_1$.

Our second lesson is a more general one and can be summed up by the precept "There is no such thing as a money machine."[3] In well-functioning capital markets, any potential money machine will be eliminated almost instantaneously by investors who try to take advantage of it. Therefore, beware of self-styled experts who offer you chance to participate in a "sure thing."

Later in the book we will invoke the *absence* of money machines to prove several useful properties about security prices. That is, we will make statements like "The prices of securities X and Y must be in the following relationship—otherwise there would be a money machine and capital markets would not be in equilibrium."

How Present Value Tables Help the Lazy

In principle there can be a different interest rate for each future period. This relationship between the interest rate and the maturity of the cash flow is called the **term structure of interest rates**. We are going to look at term structure in Chapter 23, but for now we will finesse the issue by assuming that the term structure is "flat"—in other words, the interest rate is the same regardless of the date of the cash flow. This means that we can replace the series of interest rates $r_1, r_2, \ldots, r_t,$ etc., with a single rate r and that we can write the present value formula as

$$PV = \frac{C_1}{1 + r} + \frac{C_2}{(1 + r)^2} + \cdots$$

So far all our examples can be worked out fairly easily by hand. Real problems are often much more complicated and require the use of an electronic calculator

---

[1] That is, $1000 \times (1.04813)^{147} = \$1,002,000$.

[2] The extra return for lending 2 years rather than 1 is often referred to as a *forward rate of return*. Our rule says that the forward rate cannot be negative.

[3] The technical term for money machine is **arbitrage**. There are no opportunities for arbitrage in well-functioning capital markets.

that is specifically programmed for present value calculations or the use of present value tables. Here is a somewhat complex example which illustrates how such tables are used.

You have some bad news about your office building venture (the one described at the start of Chapter 2): the contractor says that construction will take 2 years instead of 1 and requests payment on the following schedule:

1. A $100,000 down payment now. (Note that the land, worth $50,000, must also be committed now.)
2. A $100,000 progress payment after 1 year.
3. A final payment of $100,000 when the building is ready for occupancy at the end of the second year.

Your real estate adviser maintains that despite the delay the building will be worth $400,000 when completed.

All this yields a new set of cash-flow forecasts:

Period	$t = 0$	$t = 1$	$t = 2$
Land	− 50,000		
Construction	− 100,000	− 100,000	− 100,000
Payoff			+ 400,000
Total	$C_0 = -150,000$	$C_1 = -100,000$	$C_2 = +300,000$

If the interest rate is 7 percent, then NPV is

$$\text{NPV} = C_0 + \frac{C_1}{1 + r} + \frac{C_2}{(1 + r)^2}$$

$$= -150,000 - \frac{100,000}{1.07} + \frac{300,000}{(1.07)^2}$$

Table 3-1 shows how to set up the calculations and how to get NPV. The discount factors can be found in Appendix Table 1 at the end of the book. Look at the first two entries in the column headed *7 percent*. The top one is .935 and the second is .873. Thus you do not have to compute $1/1.07$ or $1/(1.07)^2$—you can pull the figures from the present value table. (Notice that the other entries in the *7 percent* column give discount factors out to 30 years and the other columns cover a range of discount rates from 1 to 30 percent.)

Fortunately the news about your office venture is not all bad. The contractor is willing to accept a delayed payment; this means that the present value of the

TABLE 3-1
Present value worksheet

Period	Discount Factor		Cash Flow	.	Present Value
0		1.0	− 150,000		− 150,000
1	$\frac{1}{1.07} =$	.935	− 100,000		− 93,500
2	$\frac{1}{(1.07)^2} =$	.873	+ 300,000		+ 261,900
				Total = NPV =	$18,400

contractor's fee is less than before. This partly offsets the delay in the payoff. As Table 3-1 shows, the net present value is $18,400—not a substantial decrease from the $23,800 calculated in Chapter 2. Since the net present value is positive, you should still go ahead.

3-2 LOOKING FOR SHORTCUTS—PERPETUITIES AND ANNUITIES

Sometimes there are shortcuts that make it very easy to calculate the present value of an asset that pays off in different periods. Let us look at some examples.

Among the securities that have been issued by the British government are so-called **perpetuities**. These are bonds that the government is under no obligation to repay but that offer a fixed income for each year to perpetuity. The rate of return on a perpetuity is equal to the promised annual payment divided by the present value:[4]

$$\text{Return} = \frac{\text{cash flow}}{\text{present value}}$$

$$r = \frac{C}{\text{PV}}$$

We can obviously twist this around and find the present value of a perpetuity given the discount rate r and the cash payment C. For example, suppose that some worthy person wishes to endow a chair in finance at a business school. If the rate of interest is 10 percent and if the aim is to provide $100,000 a year in perpetuity, the amount that must be set aside today is

$$\text{Present value of perpetuity} = \frac{C}{r} = \frac{100,000}{.10} = \$1,000,000$$

How to Value Growing Perpetuities

Suppose now that our benefactor suddenly recollects that no allowance has been made for growth in salaries, which will probably average about 4 percent a year. Therefore, instead of providing $100,000 a year in perpetuity, the benefactor must

---

[4] You can check this by writing down the present value formula

$$\text{PV} = \frac{C}{1 + r} + \frac{C}{(1 + r)^2} + \frac{C}{(1 + r)^3} + \cdots$$

Now let $C/(1 + r) = a$ and $1/(1 + r) = x$. Then we have

$$\text{PV} = a(1 + x + x^2 + \cdots) \tag{1}$$

Multiplying both sides by x, we have

$$\text{PV}x = a(x + x^2 + \cdots) \tag{2}$$

Subtracting (2) from (1) gives us

$$\text{PV}(1 - x) = a$$

Therefore, substituting for a and x,

$$\text{PV}\left(1 - \frac{1}{1 + r}\right) = \frac{C}{1 + r}$$

Multiplying both sides by $(1 + r)$ and rearranging gives

$$r = \frac{C}{\text{PV}}$$

provide $100,000 in year 1, 1.04 × $100,000 in year 2, and so on. If we call the growth rate in salaries g, we can write down the present value of this stream of cash flows as follows:

$$PV = \frac{C_1}{1 + r} + \frac{C_2}{(1 + r)^2} + \frac{C_3}{(1 + r)^3} + \cdots$$

$$= \frac{C_1}{1 + r} + \frac{C_1(1 + g)}{(1 + r)^2} + \frac{C_1(1 + g)^2}{(1 + r)^3} + \cdots$$

Fortunately, there is a simple formula for the sum of this geometric series.[5] If we assume that r is greater than g, our clumsy-looking calculation simplifies to

$$\text{Present value of growing perpetuity} = \frac{C_1}{r - g}$$

Therefore, if our benefactor wants to provide perpetually an annual sum that keeps pace with the growth rate in salaries, the amount that must be set aside today is

$$PV = \frac{C_1}{r - g} = \frac{100,000}{.10 - .04} = \$1,666,667$$

How to Value Annuities

An **annuity** is an asset that pays a fixed sum each year for a specified number of years. The equal-payment house mortgage or installment credit agreement are common examples of annuities.

Figure 3-1 illustrates a simple trick for valuing annuities. The first row represents a *perpetuity* that produces a cash flow of C in each year *beginning in year 1*. It has a present value of

$$PV = \frac{C}{r}$$

The second row represents a second *perpetuity* that produces a cash flow of C in each year *beginning in year $t + 1$*. It *will* have a present value of C/r in year t and it therefore has a present value today of

$$PV = \frac{C}{r(1 + r)^t}$$

Both perpetuities provide a cash flow from year $t + 1$ onward. The only difference between the two perpetuities is that the first one *also* provides a cash flow in each of the years 1 through t. In other words, the difference between the two perpetuities is an annuity of C for t years. The present value of this annuity is, therefore, the difference between the values of the two perpetuities:

$$\text{Present value of annuity} = C\left[\frac{1}{r} - \frac{1}{r(1 + r)^t}\right]$$

---

[5] We need to calculate the sum of an infinite geometric series $PV = a(1 + x + x^2 + \cdots)$ where $a = C_1/(1 + r)$ and $x = (1 + g)/(1 + r)$. In footnote 4 we showed that the sum of such a series is $a/(1 - x)$. Substituting for a and x in this formula we find that

$$PV = \frac{C_1}{r - g}$$

FIGURE 3-1
An annuity that
makes payments
in each of years 1
to *t* is equal to
the difference be-
tween two perpe-
tuities.

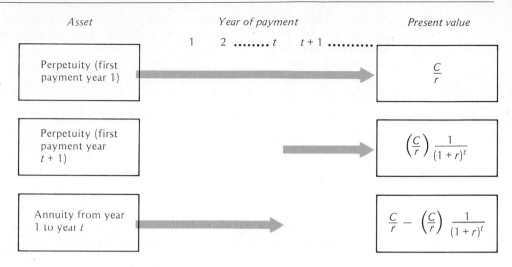

The expression in brackets is the *annuity factor*, which is the present value at discount rate *r* of an annuity of $1 paid at the end of each of *t* periods.[6]

Suppose, for example, that our benefactor begins to vacillate and wonders what it would cost to endow the chair by providing $100,000 a year for only 20 years. The answer calculated from our formula is

$$PV = 100,000 \left[\frac{1}{.10} - \frac{1}{.10(1.10)^{20}} \right] = 100,000 \times 8.514 = \$851,400$$

Alternatively, we can simply look up the answer in the annuity table in the Appendix at the end of the book (Appendix Table 3). This table gives the present value of a dollar to be received in each of *t* periods. In our example *t* = 20 and the interest rate *r* = .10, and therefore we look at the twentieth number from the top in the *10 percent* column. It is 8.514. Multiply 8.514 by $100,000, and we have our answer, $851,400.

You should always be on the lookout for ways in which you can use these formulas to make life easier. For example, we sometimes need to calculate how

---

[6] Again we can work this out from first principles. We need to calculate the sum of the finite geometric series

$$PV = a(1 + x + x^2 + \cdots + x^{t-1}) \tag{1}$$

where $a = C/(1 + r)$ and $x = 1/(1 + r)$. Multiplying both sides by x, we have

$$PVx = a(x + x^2 + \cdots + x^t) \tag{2}$$

Subtracting (2) from (1) gives us

$$PV(1 - x) = a(1 - x^t)$$

Therefore, substituting for a and x,

$$PV \left(1 - \frac{1}{1 + r} \right) = C \left[\frac{1}{1 + r} - \frac{1}{(1 + r)^{t+1}} \right]$$

Multiplying both sides by $(1 + r)$ and rearranging gives

$$PV = C \left[\frac{1}{r} - \frac{1}{r(1 + r)^t} \right]$$

much a series of annual payments earning a fixed annual interest would amass to by the end of t periods. In this case it is easiest to calculate the *present* value and then multiply it by $(1 + r)^t$ to find the future value.[7] Thus suppose our benefactor wished to know how much wealth \$100,000 would produce if it were invested each year instead of being given to those no-good academics. The answer would be

$$\text{Future value} = \text{PV} \times 1.10^{20} = \$851,400 \times 6.727 = \$5.73 \text{ million}$$

How did we know that 1.10^{20} was 6.727? Easy—we just looked it up in Appendix Table 2 at the end of the book: "Future Value of \$1 at the End of t Periods."

3-3 COMPOUND INTEREST AND PRESENT VALUES

There is an important distinction between **compound interest** and **simple interest**. When money is invested at compound interest, each interest payment is reinvested to earn more interest in subsequent periods. In contrast, the opportunity to earn interest on interest is not provided by an investment that pays only simple interest.

Table 3-2 compares the growth of \$100 invested at compound versus simple interest. Notice that in the simple interest case, *the interest is paid only on the initial investment of \$100.* Your wealth therefore increases by just \$10 a year. In the compound interest case, you earn 10 percent on your initial investment in the first year, which gives you a balance at the end of the year of $100 \times 1.10 = \$110$. Then in the second year you earn 10 percent on this \$110, which gives you a balance at the end of the second year of $100 \times 1.10^2 = \$121$.

Table 3-2 shows that the difference between simple and compound interest is nil for a 1-period investment, trivial for a 2-period investment, but overwhelming for an investment of 20 years or more. A sum of \$100 invested during the American Revolution and earning compound interest of 10 percent a year would now be worth \$49 billion. Don't you wish your ancestors had shown rather more foresight?

The two top lines in Figure 3-2 compare the results of investing \$100 at 10 percent simple interest and at 10 percent compound interest. It looks as if the rate of growth is constant under simple interest and accelerates under compound interest. However, this is an optical illusion. We know that under compound interest our wealth grows at a *constant* rate of 10 percent. Figure 3-3 is in fact a more useful presentation. Here the numbers are plotted on a semilogarithmic scale and the constant compound growth rates show up as straight lines.

Problems in finance generally involve compound interest rather than simple interest, and therefore financial people always assume that you are talking about compound interest unless you specify otherwise. Discounting is a process of compound interest. Some people find it intuitively helpful to replace the question "What is the present value of \$100 to be received 10 years from now, if the opportunity cost of capital is 10 percent?" with the question "How much would

---

[7] For example, suppose you receive a cash flow of C in year 6. If you invest this cash flow at an interest rate of r, you will have by year 10 an investment worth $C(1 + r)^4$. You can get the same answer by calculating the *present value* of the cash flow $\text{PV} = C/(1 + r)^6$ and then working out how much you would have by year 10 if you invested this sum today.

$$\text{Future value} = \text{PV}(1 + r)^{10} = \frac{C}{(1 + r)^6}(1 + r)^{10} = C(1 + r)^4$$

TABLE 3-2
Value of $100 invested at 10 percent simple and compound interest

| | SIMPLE INTEREST | | | COMPOUND INTEREST | | | |
Year	Starting Balance	+ Interest =	Ending Balance	Starting Balance	+	Interest	=	Ending Balance
1	100	+ 10 =	110	100	+	10	=	110
2	110	+ 10 =	120	110	+	11	=	121
3	120	+ 10 =	130	121	+	12.1	=	133.1
4	130	+ 10 =	140	133.1	+	13.3	=	146.4
10	190	+ 10 =	200	236	+	24	=	259
20	290	+ 10 =	300	612	+	61	=	673
50	590	+ 10 =	600	10,672	+	1,067	=	11,739
100	1,090	+ 10 =	1,100	1,252,783	+	125,278	−	1,378,061
200	2,090	+ 10 =	2,100	17,264,116,020	+	1,726,411,602	=	18,990,527,622
210	2,190	+ 10 =	2,200	44,778,670,810	+	4,477,867,081	=	49,256,537,891

I have to invest now in order to receive $100 after 10 years, given an interest rate of 10 percent?" The answer to the first question is

$$PV = \frac{100}{(1.10)^{10}} = \$38.55$$

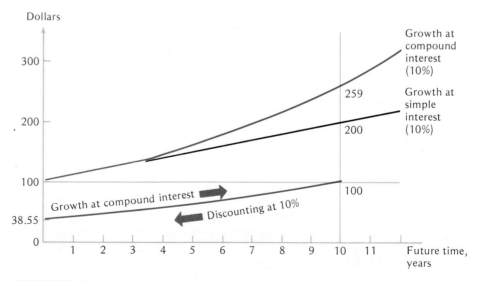

FIGURE 3-2
Compound interest versus simple interest. The top two ascending lines show the growth of $100 invested at simple and compound interest. The longer the funds are invested, the greater the advantage with compound interest. The bottom line shows that $38.55 must be invested now to obtain $100 after 10 periods. Conversely, the present value of $100 to be received after 10 years is $38.55.

FIGURE 3-3
The same story as Figure 3-2, except that the vertical scale is logarithmic. A constant compound rate of growth means a straight ascending line. This graph makes clear that the growth rate of funds invested at simple interest actually *declines* as time passes.

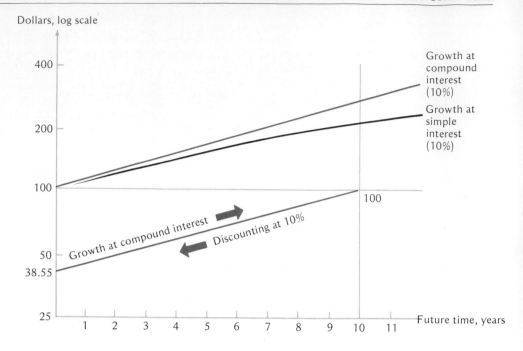

And the answer to the second question is

$$\text{Investment} \times (1.10)^{10} = 100$$

$$\text{Investment} = \frac{100}{(1.10)^{10}} = \$38.55$$

The bottom lines in Figures 3-2 and 3-3 show the growth path of an initial investment of \$38.55 to its terminal value of \$100. One can think of discounting as traveling *back* along the bottom line, from future value to present value.

---

*A Note on Compounding Intervals

So far we have implicitly assumed that each cash flow occurs at the end of the year. This is sometimes the case. For example, in France and Germany most corporations pay interest on their bonds annually. However, in the United States and Britain most pay interest semiannually. In these countries, the investor will be able to earn an additional 6 months' interest on the first payment, so that an investment of \$100 in a bond that paid interest of 10 percent per annum compounded semiannually would amount to \$105 after the first 6 months, and by the end of the year it would amount to $1.05^2 \times 100 = \$110.25$. In other words, 10 percent compounded semiannually is equivalent to 10.25 percent compounded annually. More generally, an investment of \$1 at a rate of r per annum compounded m times a year amounts by the end of the year to $\$[1 + (r/m)]^m$, and the equivalent annually compounded rate of interest is $[1 + (r/m)]^m - 1$.

The attractions to the investor of more frequent payments did not escape the attention of the savings and loan companies. Their rate of interest on deposits was traditionally stated as an annually compounded rate. The government stipulated a maximum annual rate of interest that could be paid but made no mention of the compounding interval. When interest ceilings became effective, savings and loan companies changed progressively to semiannual and then to monthly compounding. Thus the equivalent annually compounded rate of interest increased first to $[1 + (r/2)]^2 - 1$ and then to $[1 + (r/12)]^{12} - 1$.

Eventually one company quoted a **continuously compounded rate**, so that payments were assumed to be spread evenly and continuously throughout the year. In terms of our formula, this is equivalent to letting m approach infinity.[8] This might seem like a lot of calculations for our savings and loan companies. Fortunately, however, someone remembered high school algebra and pointed out that as m approaches infinity $[1 + (r/m)]^m$ approaches $(2.718)^r$. The figure 2.718—or e, as it is called—is simply the base for natural logarithms.

The sum $\$1$ invested at a continuously compounded rate of r will, therefore, grow to $e^r = (2.718)^r$ by the end of the first year. By the end of t years it will grow to $e^{rt} = (2.718)^{rt}$. Appendix Table 4 at the end of the book is a table of values of e^{rt}. Let us practice using it.

Example 1: Suppose you invest $\$1$ at a continuously compounded rate of 10 percent $(r = .10)$ for 1 year $(t = 1)$. The end-year value is simply $e^{.10}$, which you can see from the second row of Appendix Table 4 is $\$1.105$. In other words, investing at 10 percent a year *continuously* compounded is exactly the same as investing at 10.5 percent a year *annually* compounded.

Example 2: Now suppose you invest $\$1$ at a continuously compounded rate of 11 percent $(r = .11)$ for 1 year $(t = 1)$. The end-year value is now $e^{.11}$, which you can see from the second row of Appendix Table 4 is $\$1.116$. In other words, investing at 11 percent a year *continuously* compounded is exactly the same as investing at 11.6 percent a year *annually* compounded.

Example 3: Finally, suppose you invest $\$1$ at a continuously compounded rate of 11 percent $(r = .11)$ for 2 years $(t = 2)$. The final value of the investment is $e^{rt} = e^{.22}$. You can see from the third row of Appendix Table 4 that $e^{.22}$ is $\$1.246$.

There is a particular value to continuous compounding in capital budgeting, where it may often be more reasonable to assume that a cash flow is spread evenly over the year than that it occurs at the year's end. It is very easy to adapt our previous formulas to handle this. For example, suppose that we wish to compute the present value of a perpetuity of C dollars a year. We already know that if the

---

[8] When we talk about *continuous* payments, we are pretending that money can be dispensed in a continuous stream like water out of a faucet. One can never quite do this. For example, instead of paying out $\$10,000$ every year, our benefactor could pay out $\$100$ every $8\frac{3}{4}$ hours or $\$1$ every $5\frac{1}{4}$ minutes or 1 cent every $3\frac{1}{6}$ seconds but could not pay it out *continuously*. Financial managers *pretend* that payments are continuous rather than hourly, daily, or weekly because (1) it simplifies the calculations, and (2) it gives a *very* close approximation to the NPV of frequent payments.

payment is made at the end of the year, we divide the payment by the *annually* compounded rate of r:

$$PV = \frac{C}{r}$$

If the same total payment is made in an even stream throughout the year, we use the same formula but substitute the *continuously* compounded rate.

For any other continuous payments, we can always use our formula for valuing annuities. For instance, suppose that our philanthropist has thought more seriously and decided to found a home for elderly donkeys, which will cost $100,000 a year, starting immediately, and spread evenly over 20 years. Previously, we used the annually compounded rate of 10 percent; now we must use the continuously compounded rate of $r = 9.53$ percent ($e^{.0953} = 1.10$). To cover such an expenditure, then, our philanthropist needs to set aside the following sum:[9]

$$PV = C \left(\frac{1}{r} - \frac{1}{r} \times \frac{1}{e^{rt}} \right)$$

$$= 100,000 \left(\frac{1}{.0953} - \frac{1}{.0953} \times \frac{1}{6.727} \right) = 100,000 \times 8.932 = \$893,200$$

Alternatively, we could have short-cut these calculations by using Appendix Table 5. This shows that, if the annually compounded return is 10 percent, then $1 a year spread over 20 years is worth $8.932.

If you look back at our earlier discusssion of annuities, you will notice that the present value of $100,000 paid at the *end* of each of the 20 years was $851,406. Therefore, it costs the philanthropist $41,800—or 5 percent—more to provide a continuous payment stream.

Often in finance we need only a ballpark estimate of present value. An error of 5 percent in a present value calculation may be perfectly acceptable. In such cases it doesn't usually matter whether we assume that cash flows occur at the end of the year or in a continuous stream. At other times precision matters, and we do need to worry about the exact frequency of the cash flows.

3-4 SUMMARY

The difficult thing in any present value exercise is to set up the problem correctly. Once you have done that, you must be able to do the calculations, but they are

---

[9] To understand this formula it may help to remember that an annuity is simply the difference between a perpetuity received today and a perpetuity received in year t. A continuous stream of C dollars a year in perpetuity is worth C/r where r is the continuously compounded rate. Our annuity, then, is worth

$$PV = \frac{C}{r} - \text{present value of } \frac{C}{r} \text{ received in year } t$$

Since r is the continuously compounded rate, C/r received in year t is worth $(C/r) \times (1/e^{rt})$ today. Our annuity formula is therefore

$$PV = \frac{C}{r} - \frac{C}{r} \times \frac{1}{e^{rt}}$$

sometimes written as

$$\frac{C}{r} (1 - e^{-rt})$$

not difficult. Now that you have worked through this chapter, all you should need is a little practice.

The basic present value formula for an asset that pays off in several periods is the following obvious extension of our 1-period formula:

$$PV = \frac{C_1}{1 + r_1} + \frac{C_2}{(1 + r_2)^2} + \cdots$$

You can always work out any present value using this formula, but when the interest rates are the same for each maturity, there may be some shortcuts that can reduce the tedium. We looked at three such cases. First, there was the case of an asset that pays C dollars a year in perpetuity. Its present value is simply

$$PV = \frac{C}{r}$$

Second, there was the case of an asset whose payments increase at a steady rate g in perpetuity. Its present value is

$$PV = \frac{C}{r - g}$$

Third, there was the case of an annuity that pays C dollars a year for t years. To find its present value we take the difference between the values of two perpetuities:

$$PV = C\left[\frac{1}{r} - \frac{1}{r(1 + r)^t}\right]$$

Our next step was to show that discounting is a process of compound interest. It is the amount that we would have to invest now at compound interest r in order to produce the cash flows C_1, C_2, etc. When someone offers to lend us a dollar at an annual rate of r, we should always check how frequently the interest is to be compounded. If the compounding interval is annual, we will have to repay $(1 + r)^t$ dollars; on the other hand, if the compounding is continuous, we will have to repay 2.718^{rt} (or, as it is usually expressed, e^{rt}) dollars. Very often in capital budgeting we are willing to assume that the cash flows occur at the end of each year, and therefore we discount them at an annually compounded rate of interest. Sometimes, however, it may be fairer to assume that they are spread evenly over the year; in this case we must make use of continuous compounding.

Present value tables will help us to perform many of these calculations. You have been introduced now to tables that show:

1. Present value of $1 received at the end of year t
2. Future value of $1 by the end of year t
3. Present value of $1 received at the end of each year until year t
4. Future value of $1 invested at a continuously compounded rate of interest
5. Present value of $1 received continuously for t years when the annually compounded interest rate is r

Finally, we introduced in this chapter two very important ideas which we will come across several times again. The first is that you can add present values: if your formula for the present value of $A + B$ is not the same as your formula for the present value of A plus the present value of B, you have made a mistake. The second is the notion that there is no such thing as a money machine: if you think you have found one, go back and check your calculations.

FURTHER READING

The material in this chapter should cover all you need to know about the mathematics of discounting; but if you wish to dig deeper, there are a number of books on the subject. Try, for example:

> R. Cissell, H. Cissell, and D. C. Flaspohler: *The Mathematics of Finance*, 6th ed., Houghton Mifflin Company, Boston, 1982.

QUIZ

1. At an interest rate of 12 percent, the 6-year discount factor is .507. How many dollars is $.507 worth in 6 years if invested at 12 percent?
2. If the present value of $139 is $125, what is the discount factor?
3. If the 8-year discount factor is .285, what is the present value of $596 received in 8 years?
4. If the cost of capital is 9 percent, what is the present value of $374 paid in year 9?
5. A project produces the following cash flows:

Year	Flow
1	432
2	137
3	797

   If the cost of capital is 15 percent, what is the project's present value?
6. If you invest $100 at an interest rate of 15 percent, how much will you have at the end of 8 years?
7. An investment of $232 will produce $312.18 in 2 years. What is the annual interest rate?
8. An investment costs $1548 and pays $138 in perpetuity. If the interest rate is 9 percent, what is the net present value?
9. It costs $2590 to insulate your home. Next year's fuel saving will be $220. If the interest rate is 12 percent, what percentage growth rate in fuel prices is needed to justify insulation? Assume fuel prices will grow in perpetuity at the rate g.
10. A common stock will pay a cash dividend of $4 next year. After that, the dividends are expected to increase indefinitely at 4 percent per year. If the discount rate is 14 percent, what is the present value of the steam of dividend payments?
11. If you invest $502 at the end of each of the next 9 years at an interest rate of 13 percent, how much will you have at the end?
12. Harold Filbert is 30 years of age and his salary next year will be $20,000. Harold forecasts that his salary will increase at a steady rate of 5 percent per annum until his retirement at age 60.
    (a) If the discount rate is 8 percent, what is the present value of these future salary payments?
    (b) If Harold saves 5 percent of his salary each year and invests these savings at an interest rate of 8 percent, how much will he have saved by age 60?
    (c) If Harold plans to spend these savings in even amounts over the subsequent 20 years, how much can he spend each year?
13. A factory costs $400,000. You reckon that it will produce an inflow after operating costs of $100,000 in year 1, $200,000 in year 2, and $300,000 in

year 3. The opportunity cost of capital is 12 percent. Draw up a worksheet like that shown in Table 3-1 and use tables to calculate the net present value.

14. Do not use tables for these questions. The interest rate is 10 percent.
    (*a*) What is the present value of an asset that pays $1 a year in perpetuity?
    (*b*) The value of an asset that appreciates at 10 percent per annum approximately doubles in 7 years. What is the approximate present value of an asset that pays $1 a year in perpetuity beginning in year 8?
    (*c*) What is the approximate present value of an asset that pays $1 a year for each of the next 7 years?
    (*d*) A piece of land produces an income that grows by 5 percent per annum. If the first year's flow is $10,000, what is the value of the land?

15. Use the tables at the end of the book for each of the following calculations:
    (*a*) The cost of a new automobile is $10,000. If the interest rate is 5 percent, how much would you have to set aside now to provide this sum in 5 years?
    (*b*) You have to pay $12,000 a year in school fees at the end of each of the next 6 years. If the interest rate is 8 percent, how much do you need to set aside today to cover these bills?
    (*c*) You have invested $60,476 at 8 percent. After paying the above school fees, how much would remain at the end of the 6 years?
    *(*d*) You have borrowed $1000 and in return have agreed to pay back $1762 in 5 years. What is the *annually* compounded rate of interest on the loan? What is the *continuously* compounded rate of interest?

QUESTIONS AND PROBLEMS

✓ 1. Use the *discount factors* shown in Appendix Table 1 at the end of the book to calculate the present value of $100 received in:
    (*a*) Year 10 (at a discount rate of 1 percent).
    (*b*) Year 10 (at a discount rate of 13 percent).
    (*c*) Year 15 (at a discount rate of 25 percent).
    (*d*) Each of years 1 through 3 (at a discount rate of 12 percent).

✓ 2. Use the *annuity factors* shown in Appendix Table 3 to calculate the present value of $100 in each of:
    (*a*) Years 1 through 20 (at a discount rate of 23 percent).
    (*b*) Years 1 through 5 (at a discount rate of 3 percent).
    (*c*) Years 3 through 12 (at a discount rate of 9 percent).

3. (*a*) If the 1-year discount factor is .88, what is the 1-year interest rate?
    (*b*) If the 2-year interest rate is 10.5 percent, what is the 2-year discount factor?
    (*c*) Given these 1- and 2-year discount factors, calculate the 2-year annuity factor.
    (*d*) If the present value of $10 a year for 3 years is $24.49, what is the 3-year annuity factor?
    (*e*) From your answers to (*c*) and (*d*), calculate the 3-year discount factor.

✓ 4. A factory costs $800,000. You reckon that it will produce an inflow after operating costs of $170,000 a year for 10 years. If the opportunity cost of capital is 14 percent, what is the net present value of the factory? What will the factory be worth at the end of 5 years?

✓ 5. Halcyon Lines is considering the purchase of a new bulk carrier for $8 million. The forecast revenues are $5 million a year and operating costs are $4 million. A major refit costing $2 million will be required after both the fifth and tenth years. After 15 years, the ship is expected to be sold for scrap at $1.5 million. If the discount rate is 8 percent, what is the ship's NPV?

6. As winner of a breakfast cereal competition, you can choose one of the following prizes:
   (a) $100,000 now
   (b) $180,000 at the end of 5 years
   (c) $11,400 a year forever
   (d) $19,000 for each of 10 years
   (e) $6500 next year and increasing thereafter by 5% a year forever
   If the interest rate is 12 percent, which is the most valuable prize?

7. Refer back to the story of Ms. Kraft in Section 3-1.
   (a) If the 1-year interest rate were 25 percent, how many plays would Ms. Kraft require to become a millionaire? (*Hint:* You may find it easier to use a calculator and a little trial and error.)
   (b) What does the story of Ms. Kraft imply about the relationship between the 1-year discount factor, DF_1, and the 2-year discount factor, DF_2?

8. Siegfried Basset is 65 years of age and has a life expectancy of 12 years. He wishes to invest $20,000 in an annuity that will make a level payment at the end of each year until his death. If the interest rate is 8 percent, what income can Mr. Basset expect to receive each year?

9. James and Helen Turnip are saving to buy a boat at the end of 5 years. If the boat costs $20,000 and they can earn 10 percent a year on their savings, how much do they need to put aside at the end of years 1 through 5?

10. Kangaroo Autos is offering free credit on a new $10,000 car. You pay $1000 down and then $300 a month for the next 30 months. Turtle Motors next door does not offer free credit but will give you $1000 off the list price. If the rate of interest is 10 percent a year, which company is offering the better deal?

11. Recalculate the net present value of the office building venture in Section 3-1 at interest rates of 5, 10, and 15 percent. Plot the points on a graph with NPV on the vertical axis and the discount rates on the horizontal axis. At what discount rate (approximately) would the project have zero NPV? Check your answer.

12. (a) How much will an investment of $100 be worth at the end of 10 years if invested at 15 percent a year simple interest?
    (b) How much will it be worth if invested at 15 percent a year compound interest?
    (c) How long will it take your investment to double its value at 15 percent compound interest?

13. You own an oil pipeline which will generate a $2 million cash return over the coming year. The pipeline's operating costs are negligible and it is expected to last for a very long time. Unfortunately, the volume of oil shipped is declining, and cash flows are expected to decline by 4 percent per year. The discount rate is 10 percent.
    (a) What is the present value of the pipeline's cash flows if its cash flows are assumed to last forever?
    (b) What is the present value of the cash flows if the pipeline is scrapped after 20 years?
    [*Hint* for part (b): Start with your answer to part (a), then subtract the present value of a declining perpetuity starting in year 21. Note that the forecasted cash flow for year 21 will be much less than the cash flow for year 1.]

*14. If the interest rate is 7 percent, what is the value of the following three investments?
  (*a*) An investment that offers you $100 a year in perpetuity with the payment at the *end* of each year
  (*b*) A similar investment with the payment at the *beginning* of each year
  (*c*) A similar investment with the payment spread evenly over each year

*15. Refer back to Section 3-2. If the rate of interest is 8 percent rather than 10 percent, how much would our benefactor need to set aside to provide each of the following?
  (*a*) $100,000 at the end of each year in perpetuity
  (*b*) A perpetuity that pays $100,000 at the end of the first year and that grows at 4 percent a year
  (*c*) $100,000 at the end of each year for 20 years
  (*d*) $100,000 a year spread evenly over 20 years

*16. For an investment of $1000 today, the Tiburon Finance Company is offering to pay you $1600 at the end of 8 years. What is the annually compounded rate of interest? What is the continuously compounded rate of interest?

*17. How much will you have at the end of 20 years if you invest $100 today at 15 percent *annually* compounded? How much will you have if you invest at 15 percent *continuously* compounded?

  18. You have just read an advertisement reading, "Pay us $100 a year for 10 years and we will pay you $100 a year thereafter in perpetuity." If this is a fair deal, what is the rate of interest?

4 Present Value of Bonds and Stocks

We should warn you that being a financial expert has its occupational hazards. One is being cornered at cocktail parties by people who are eager to explain their system for making creamy profits by investing in stocks and bonds. Fortunately, these bores go into temporary hibernation whenever the market goes down.

We may exaggerate the perils of the trade. The point is that there is no easy way to ensure superior investment performance. Later in the book we will show that changes in security prices are fundamentally unpredictable and that this result is a natural consequence of well-functioning capital markets. Therefore, in this chapter, when we propose to use the concept of present value to price common stocks and bonds, we are not promising you a key to investment success; we simply believe that the idea can help you to understand why some investments are priced higher than others.

We begin with a brief review of how bonds are valued. It is brief because we shall be considering some of the refinements of bond valuation in Chapter 23. After our discussion of bonds, we will look at the valuation of common stocks. We will explain the real difference between growth stocks and income stocks and the significance of earnings per share and price-earnings multiples. Finally, in the appendix to this chapter, we discuss some of the special problems managers and investors encounter when they calculate the present values of entire businesses.

A word of caution before we proceed. Everybody knows that common stocks are risky and that some are more risky than others. Therefore, investors will not commit funds to stocks unless the expected rates of return are commensurate with the risks. The present value formulas we have discussed so far can take account of the effects of risk on value, but we have not yet told you exactly *how* to do so. Recognize, therefore, that risk comes into the following discussion in a loose and intuitive way. A more careful treatment of risk starts in Chapter 7.

4-1 A QUICK LOOK AT HOW BONDS ARE VALUED

When you own a bond, you receive a fixed set of cash payoffs. Each year until the bond matures, you get an interest payment and then at maturity you also get back the face value of the bond.

Suppose that in July 1986 you invest in a 13¾ percent 1991 U.S. Treasury bond. The bond has a coupon rate of 13¾ percent and a face value of $1000. This means that each year until 1991 you receive an interest payment of .1375 × 1000 = $137.50. The bond matures in July 1991: At that time, the Treasury pays you the final $137.50 interest, plus the $1000 face value.[1] The cash flows from owning

---

[1] The face value of the bond is known as the *principal*. Therefore, when the bond matures, the government pays you principal and interest.

the bond are therefore as follows:

CASH FLOWS (DOLLARS)				
1987	1988	1989	1990	1991
137.5	137.5	137.5	137.5	1,137.5

What is the 1986 market value of this stream of cash flows? To determine that, we need to look at the return provided by similar securities. Medium-term U.S. Treasury securities in mid-1986 offered a return of about 7.6 percent. That is what investors were giving up when they bought the 13¾ percent Treasury bonds. Therefore, to value the 13¾ percent bonds we need to discount the prospective stream of cash flows at 7.6 percent.

$$PV = \sum_{t=1}^{5} \frac{C_t}{(1 + r)^t}$$

$$= \frac{137.5}{1 + r} + \frac{137.5}{(1 + r)^2} + \frac{137.5}{(1 + r)^3} + \frac{137.5}{(1 + r)^4} + \frac{1137.5}{(1 + r)^5}$$

$$= \frac{137.5}{1.076} + \frac{137.5}{(1.076)^2} + \frac{137.5}{(1.076)^3} + \frac{137.5}{(1.076)^4} + \frac{1137.5}{(1.076)^5}$$

$$= \$1248.16$$

Bond prices are usually expressed as a percentage of face value. Thus, we can say that our 13¾ percent Treasury bond is worth $1248.16, or 124.82 percent.

We could have phrased our question the other way around and asked, "If the price of the bond is $1248.16, what return do investors expect?" In that case, we would need to find the value of r that solves the following equation:

$$1248.16 = \frac{137.5}{1 + r} + \frac{137.5}{(1 + r)^2} + \frac{137.5}{(1 + r)^3} + \frac{137.5}{(1 + r)^4} + \frac{1137.5}{(1 + r)^5}$$

The rate r is often called the bond's **yield to maturity** or **internal rate of return**. In our case r is 7.6 percent. If you discount the cash flows at 7.6 percent, you arrive at the bond's price of $1248.16. As we shall see in Chapter 5, the only *general* procedure for calculating r is by trial and error. But specially programmed electronic calculators can be used to calculate r, or you can use a book of bond tables that show values of r for different coupon levels and different maturities.

In calculating the value of 13¾ percent Treasury bonds, we made two approximations. First, we assumed that interest payments occur annually. In practice, most U.S. Treasury bonds make coupon payments *semiannually*. Therefore, instead of receiving 137.50 every year, an investor who held 13¾ percent bonds would receive $68.75 every *half* year. Second, we treated the 7.6 percent yield as an annually compounded rate. Bond yields are usually quoted as semiannually compounded rates.

You may have noticed that the formula that we used for calculating the present value of 13¾ percent Treasury bonds was slightly different from the general present value formula that we developed in Section 3-1. In the latter case, we allowed for the fact that r_1, the rate of return offered by the capital market on 1-year investments, may be different from r_2, the rate of return offered on 2-year investments. Later in Chapter 3 we finessed this problem by assuming that r_1 is the same as r_2.

In this chapter we again assume that investors use the same rate to discount cash flows occurring in different years. That does not matter as long as short-term rates are approximately the same as long-term rates. But often when we value bonds we must discount each cash flow at a different rate. There will be more about that in Chapter 23.

4-2 HOW COMMON STOCKS ARE VALUED

Today's Price

The cash payoff to owners of common stocks comes in two forms: (1) cash dividends and (2) capital gains or losses. Usually investors expect to get some of each. Suppose that the current price of a share is P_0, that the expected price at the end of a year is P_1, and that the expected dividend per share is DIV_1. The rate of return that investors expect from this share over the next year is defined as the expected dividend per share DIV_1 plus the expected price appreciation per share $P_1 - P_0$, all divided by the price at the start of the year P_0:

$$\text{Expected return} = r = \frac{DIV_1 + P_1 - P_0}{P_0}$$

This return that is expected by investors is often called the **market capitalization rate**.

Let us now see how our formula works. Suppose Fledgling Electronics stock is selling for $100 a share ($P_0 = 100$). Investors expect a $5 cash dividend over the next year ($DIV_1 = 5$). They also expect the stock to sell for $110 a year hence ($P_1 = 110$). Then the expected return to the stockholders is 15 percent:

$$r = \frac{5 + 110 - 100}{100} = .15, \text{ or } 15\%$$

Correspondingly, if you are given investors' forecasts of dividend and price and the expected return offered by other equally risky stocks, you can predict today's price:

$$\text{Price} = P_0 = \frac{DIV_1 + P_1}{1 + r}$$

For Fledgling Electronics $DIV_1 = 5$ and $P_1 = 110$. If r, the expected return on securities in the same "risk class" as Fledgling, is 15 percent, then today's price should be $100:

$$P_0 = \frac{5 + 110}{1.15} = \$100$$

How do we know that $100 is the right price? Because no other price could survive in competitive capital markets. What if P_0 were above $100? Then Fledgling stock would offer an expected rate of return that was *lower* than other securities of equivalent risk. Investors would shift their capital to the other securities and in the process would force down the price of Fledgling stock. If P_0 were less than $100, the process would reverse. Fledgling's stock would offer a *higher* rate of return than comparable securities. In that case, investors would rush to buy, forcing the price up to $100.

The general conclusion is that at each point in time *all securities in an equivalent risk class are priced to offer the same expected return*. This is a condition for equilibrium in well-functioning capital markets. It is also common sense.

We have managed to explain today's stock price P_0 in terms of the dividend DIV_1 and the expected price next year P_1. Future stock prices are not easy things to forecast directly. But think about what determines next year's price. If our price formula holds now, it ought to hold then as well:

$$P_1 = \frac{DIV_2 + P_2}{1 + r}$$

That is, a year from now investors will be looking out at dividends in year 2 and price at the end of year 2. Thus we can forecast P_1 by forecasting DIV_2 and P_2 and we can express P_0 in terms of DIV_1, DIV_2, and P_2:

$$P_0 = \frac{1}{1 + r}(DIV_1 + P_1) = \frac{1}{1 + r}\left(DIV_1 + \frac{DIV_2 + P_2}{1 + r}\right) = \frac{DIV_1}{1 + r} + \frac{DIV_2 + P_2}{(1 + r)^2}$$

Take Fledgling Electronics. A plausible explanation why investors expect its stock price to rise by the end of the first year is that they expect higher dividends and still more capital gains in the second. For example, suppose that they are looking today for dividends of $5.50 in year 2 and a subsequent price of $121. That would imply a price at the end of year 1 of

$$P_1 = \frac{5.50 + 121}{1.15} = \$110$$

Today's price can then be computed either from our original formula

$$P_0 = \frac{DIV_1 + P_1}{1 + r} = \frac{5.00 + 110}{1.15} = \$100$$

or from our expanded formula

$$P_0 = \frac{DIV_1}{1 + r} + \frac{DIV_2 + P_2}{(1 + r)^2} = \frac{5.00}{1.15} + \frac{5.50 + 121}{(1.15)^2} = \$100$$

We have succeeded in relating today's price to the forecasted dividends for 2 years (DIV_1 and DIV_2) plus the forecasted price at the end of the *second* year (P_2). You will probably not be surprised to learn that we could go on to replace P_2 by $(DIV_3 + P_3)/(1 + r)$ and relate today's price to the forecasted dividends for 3 years (DIV_1, DIV_2, and DIV_3) plus the forecasted price at the end of the *third* year (P_3). In fact we can look as far out into the future as we like, removing P's as we go. Let us call this final period H. This gives us a general stock price formula

$$P_0 = \frac{DIV_1}{1 + r} + \frac{DIV_2}{(1 + r)^2} + \cdots + \frac{DIV_H + P_H}{(1 + r)^H}$$

$$= \sum_{t=1}^{H} \frac{DIV_t}{(1 + r)^t} + \frac{P_H}{(1 + r)^H}$$

The expression $\sum_{t=1}^{H}$ simply means the sum of the discounted dividends from year 1 to year H.

Table 4-1 continues the Fledgling Electronics example for various time horizons, assuming that the dividends are expected to increase at a steady 10 percent compound rate. The expected price P_t increases at the same rate each year. Each line in the table represents an application of our general formula for a different value of H. Figure 4-1 provides a graphical representation of the table. Each column shows the present value of the dividends up to the time horizon and the present

TABLE 4-1
Applying the stock valuation formula to Fledgling Electronics

| Horizon Period (H) | EXPECTED FUTURE VALUES | | PRESENT VALUES | | |
	Dividend (DIV_t)	Price (P_t)	Cumulative Dividends	Future Price	Total
0	—	100	—	100.00	100
1	5.00	110	4.35	95.65	100
2	5.50	121	8.51	91.49	100
3	6.05	133.10	12.48	87.52	100
4	6.66	146.41	16.29	83.71	100
10	11.79	259.37	35.89	64.11	100
20	30.58	672.75	58.89	41.11	100
50	533.59	11,739.09	89.17	10.83	100
100	62,639.15	1,378,061.23	98.83	1.17	100

Assumptions:
1. Dividends increase at 10 percent per year, compounded.
2. Capitalization rate is 15 percent.

value of the price at the horizon. As the horizon recedes, the dividend stream accounts for an increasing proportion of present value, but the *total* present value of dividends plus terminal price always equals $100.

How far out could we look? In principle the horizon period H could be infinitely distant. Common stocks do not expire of old age. Barring such corporate hazards as bankruptcy or acquisition, they are immortal. As H approaches infinity, the present value of the terminal price ought to approach zero, as it does in the final column of Figure 4-1. We can, therefore, forget about the terminal price entirely and express today's price as the present value of a perpetual stream of cash dividends. This is usually written as

$$P_0 = \sum_{t=1}^{\infty} \frac{DIV_t}{(1 + r)^t}$$

FIGURE 4-1
As your horizon recedes, the present value of the future price (shaded area) declines but the present value of the stream of dividends (unshaded area) increases. The *total* present value (future price and dividends) remains the same.

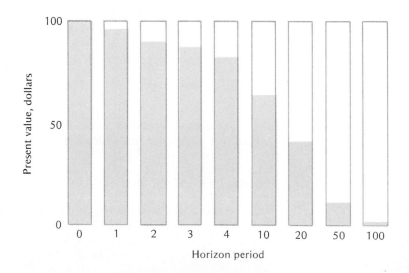

where the sign ∞ is used to indicate infinity. This discounted cash flow (DCF) formula for the present value of a stock is just the same as it is for the present value of any other asset. We just discount the cash flows—in this case the dividend stream—by the return that can be earned in the capital market on securities of comparable risk. Some find the DCF formula implausible because it seems to ignore capital gains. But we know that the formula was *derived* from the assumption that price in any period is determined by expected dividends *and* capital gains over the next period.

Remembering our rule about adding present values, we might be tempted to conclude that the *total* value of a company's common stock must be equal to the discounted stream of *all* future dividends paid by the company. But we need to be a little careful here. We must only include the dividends that will be paid on *existing* stock. The company may at some future date decide to sell more stock and this will be entitled to its share of the subsequent dividend stream. The total value of a company's existing common stock is, therefore, equal to the discounted value of that *portion* of the total dividend stream which will be paid to the stock outstanding today. It sounds obvious but it is surprising how often people forget.

4-3 A SIMPLE WAY TO ESTIMATE THE CAPITALIZATION RATE

In Chapter 3 we encountered some simplified versions of the basic present value formula. Let us see whether they offer any insights into stock values. Suppose, for example, that we forecast a constant growth rate for a company's dividends. This does not preclude year-to-year deviations from the trend: it means only that *expected* dividends grow at a constant rate. Such an investment would be just another example of the growing perpetuity that we helped our fickle philanthropist to evaluate in the last chapter. To find its present value we must divide the annual cash payment by the difference between the discount rate and the growth rate:

$$P_0 = \frac{\text{DIV}_1}{r - g}$$

Remember that we can use this formula only when g, the anticipated growth rate, is less than r, the discount rate. As g approaches r, the stock price becomes infinite. Obviously r must be greater than g if growth really is perpetual.

Our growing perpetuity formula explains P_0 in terms of next year's expected dividend DIV_1, the projected growth trend g, and the expected rate of return on other securities of comparable risk r. Alternatively, the formula can be used to obtain an estimate of r from DIV_1, P_0, and g:

$$r = \frac{\text{DIV}_1}{P_0} + g$$

The market capitalization rate equals the **dividend yield** (DIV_1/P_0) plus the expected rate of growth in dividends (g).

These two formulas are much easier to work with than the general statement that "price equals the present value of expected future dividends."[2] For instance, imagine that you are analyzing Sears, Roebuck and Company early in 1986 when

---

[2] These formulas were first developed in 1938 by Williams and were rediscovered by Gordon and Shapiro. See J. B. Williams, *The Theory of Investment Value*, Harvard University Press, Cambridge, Mass., 1938; and M. J. Gordon and E. Shapiro, "Capital Equipment Analysis: The Required Rate of Profit," *Management Science*, **3**:102–110 (October 1956).

its stock is selling for about $45 a share. Dividend payments for 1986 are expected to be $1.76 a share. Now we can calculate the first half of our formula:

$$\frac{\text{Dividend}}{\text{yield}} = \frac{\text{DIV}_1}{P_0} = \frac{1.76}{45} = .039$$

The hard part is to estimate g. One line of reasoning starts with Sears's **payout ratio**, the ratio of dividends to earnings per share (EPS). This has generally been around 45 percent. In other words, each year Sears plows back into the business about 55 percent of earnings per share:

$$\frac{\text{Plowback}}{\text{ratio}} = 1 - \frac{\text{payout}}{\text{ratio}} = 1 - \frac{\text{DIV}_1}{\text{EPS}_1} = 1 - .45 = .55$$

Also, Sears's ratio of earnings per share to book equity per share is about 13 percent. This is its **return on equity**, or **ROE**:

$$\frac{\text{Return on}}{\text{equity}} = \text{ROE} = \frac{\text{EPS}_1}{\substack{\text{book equity} \\ \text{per share}}} = .13$$

Sears has always been a stable company, and it may not be too unreasonable to assume that these relationships will continue to hold. Suppose we forecast that Sears will earn 13 percent of book equity and reinvest 55 percent of that. Then book equity will increase by $.55 \times .13 = .072$. Since we assumed that the return on equity and the payout ratio are constant, earnings and dividends per share will also increase by 7.2 percent:

$$\frac{\text{Dividend growth}}{\text{rate}} = g = \frac{\text{plowback}}{\text{ratio}} \times \text{ROE} = .55 \times .13 = .072$$

Now you have your estimate of the market capitalization rate (i.e., the rate of return that investors use to discount Sears's future dividends):

$$r = \frac{\text{DIV}_1}{P_0} + g = .039 + .072 = .111, \text{ or about } 11\%$$

Using the DCF Model to Set Electricity Prices

Although our estimate of the market capitalization rate for Sears stock seems reasonable enough, there are obvious dangers in analyzing any single firm's stock with such simple rules of thumb as the constant-growth DCF formula. First, the underlying assumption of regular future growth is at best an approximation. Second, even if it is an acceptable approximation, errors inevitably creep into the estimate of g. Remember, however, that r is not the personal property of Sears: in well-functioning markets investors must capitalize the dividends of *all* securities in Sears's risk class at exactly the same rate. This means that we may do better to take a large sample of securities of equivalent risk, estimate r for each, and use the average of our estimates. Here is a practical example.

One task of the U.S. Federal Energy Regulatory Commission (FERC) is to set prices for interstate sales of electric power. These are almost always wholesale transactions. That is, an electric utility with surplus generating capacity will sell power to a utility in a neighboring state. The buyer may have a shortage of capacity or it may not be able to produce electricity as cheaply as the seller.

The sale price is supposed to cover all costs of producing and transporting the electricity, including interest and tax payments, *and* to provide a reasonable profit for the seller. What is "reasonable"? It is the profit that provides a fair rate of return to the seller on its equity investment in generating equipment, transmission lines, and so on. What is a "fair" rate of return? It is usually interpreted as r, the market capitalization rate for the selling firm's common stock. That is, the expected rate of return on investments made by electric utilities ought to be the same rate offered by securities having risks equivalent to the utility's common stock.[3]

Thus, FERC's problem of determining fair profits boils down to estimating r for the common stock of the electric utilities it regulates. This is done case by case, as each utility appears before FERC to justify its prices for interstate sales. The case-by-case analyses typically rely on DCF formulas.

FERC also calculates quarterly a "generic" or "benchmark" estimate of r for the electric utility industry. In July 1986, for example, the benchmark was

$$r = \frac{DIV_1}{P_0} + g$$

$$= .0764 + .0454 = .1218, \text{ or about } 12\%[4]$$

Some Warnings about Constant-Growth Formulas

These simple constant-growth DCF formulas are extremely useful rules of thumb, but they are no more than that. Naive trust in the formulas has led many financial analysts to silly conclusions.

First, remember the difficulty of estimating r by analysis of one stock only. Try to use a large sample of equivalent-risk securities. Even that may not work, but at least it gives the analyst a fighting chance, because the inevitable errors in estimating r for a single security tend to balance out across a broad sample.

Second, resist the temptation to apply the formula to firms having high current rates of growth. Such growth can rarely be sustained indefinitely, but the constant-growth DCF formula assumes it can. This erroneous assumption leads to an overestimate of r.

Consider Growth-Tech, Inc., a firm with $DIV_1 = \$.50$ and $P_0 = \$50$. That firm has plowed back 80 percent of earnings and has had a return on equity (ROE) of 25 percent. This means that *in the past*

Dividend growth rate = plowback ratio × ROE = .80 × .25 = .20

The temptation is to assume that the future long-term growth rate (g) also equals .20. This would imply

$$r = \frac{.50}{50.00} + .20 = .21$$

---

[3] This is the accepted interpretation of the U.S. Supreme Court's directive in 1944 that ". . . the returns to the equity owner [of a regulated business] should be commensurate with returns on investments in other enterprises having corresponding risks." *Federal Power Commission v. Hope Natural Gas Company*, 302 U.S. 591 at 603.

[4] We say "about 12 percent" because it's pointless to pretend that expected returns can be estimated to four decimal places. Utilities and regulators find themselves arguing about these decimal places, however. If a utility has a $1 billion equity investment, that .18 percent amounts to .0018 × (1,000,000,000) = $1,800,000, or $1.8 million *per year*.

The 12.18 percent estimate of r was published by FERC in "Notice of Benchmark Rate of Return on Common Equity for Public Utilities," July 16, 1986. The estimate was based on dividend yields and forecasted dividend growth rates for a sample of 99 electric utility common stocks.

But this is silly. No firm can continue growing at 20 percent per year forever, except possibly under extreme inflationary conditions. Eventually, profitability will fall and the firm will respond by investing less.

In real life the return on investment will decline *gradually* over time, but for simplicity let's assume it suddenly drops to 16 percent at year 3 and the firm responds by plowing back only 50 percent of earnings. Then g drops to $.50(.16) = .08$.

Table 4-2 shows what's going on. Growth-Tech starts year 1 with assets of $10.00. It earns $2.50, pays out 50 cents as dividends, and plows back $2. Thus it starts year 2 with $10 + 2 = \$12$. After another year at the same ROE and payout, it starts year 3 with equity of $14.40. However ROE drops to .16 and the firm earns only $2.30. Dividends go up to $1.15, because the payout ratio increases, but the firm has only $1.15 to plow back. Therefore subsequent growth in earnings and dividends drops to 8 percent.

Now we can use our general DCF formula to find the capitalization rate r:

$$P_0 = \frac{DIV_1}{1 + r} + \frac{DIV_2}{(1 + r)^2} + \frac{DIV_3 + P_3}{(1 + r)^3}$$

Investors in year 3 will view Growth-Tech as offering 8 percent per year dividend growth. We will apply the constant-growth formula:

$$P_3 = \frac{DIV_4}{r - .08}$$

$$P_0 = \frac{DIV_1}{1 + r} + \frac{DIV_2}{(1 + r)^2} + \frac{DIV_3}{(1 + r)^3} + \frac{1}{(1 + r)^3}\frac{DIV_4}{r - .08}$$

$$= \frac{.50}{1 + r} + \frac{.60}{(1 + r)^2} + \frac{1.15}{(1 + r)^3} + \frac{1}{(1 + r)^3}\frac{1.24}{r - .08}$$

We have to use trial and error to find the value of r that makes P_0 equal $50. It turns out that the r implicit in these more realistic forecasts is approximately .099, quite a difference from our "constant-growth" estimate of .21.

A final warning. Do not use the simple constant-growth formula to test whether the market is correct in its assessment of a stock's value. If your estimate of the

TABLE 4-2
Forecasted earnings and dividends for Growth-Tech. Note the changes in year 3: ROE and earnings drop, but payout ratio increases, causing a big jump in dividends. However subsequent growth in earnings and dividends falls to 8 percent per year. Note that the increase in equity equals the earnings not paid out as dividends.

Year	1	2	3	4
Book equity	10.00	12.00	14.40	15.55
Earnings per share, EPS	2.50	3.00	2.30	2.49
Return on equity, ROE	.25	.25	.16	.16
Payout ratio	.20	.20	.50	.50
Dividends per share, DIV	.50	.60	1.15	1.24
Growth rate of dividends	—	.20	.92	.08

value is different from that of the market, it is probably because you have used poor dividend forecasts. Remember what we said at the beginning of this chapter about simple ways of making money on the stock market. There aren't any.

4-4 THE LINK BETWEEN STOCK PRICE AND EARNINGS PER SHARE

Investors often use the terms *growth stocks* and *income stocks*. They seem to buy growth stocks primarily for the expectation of capital gains, and they are interested in the future growth of earnings rather than in next year's dividends. On the other hand, they buy income stocks primarily for the cash dividends. Let us see whether these distinctions make sense.

Imagine first the case of a company that does not grow at all. It does not plow back any earnings and simply produces a constant stream of dividends. Its stock would be rather like the perpetual bond described in the last chapter. Remember that the return on a perpetuity is equal to the yearly cash flow divided by the present value. The expected return on our share would thus be equal to the yearly dividend divided by the share price (i.e., the dividend yield). Since all the earnings are paid out as dividends, the expected return is also equal to the earnings per share divided by the share price (i.e., the earnings-price ratio). For example, if the dividend is $10 a share and the stock price is $100, we have

$$\text{Expected return} = \text{dividend yield} = \text{earnings-price ratio}$$

$$= \frac{\text{DIV}_1}{P_0} \qquad = \frac{\text{EPS}_1}{P_0}$$

$$= \frac{10.00}{100} \qquad = .10$$

The price equals

$$P_0 = \frac{\text{DIV}_1}{r} = \frac{\text{EPS}_1}{r} = \frac{10.00}{.10} = \$100$$

The expected return for growing firms can also equal the earnings-price ratio. The key is whether earnings are reinvested to provide a return greater or less than the market capitalization rate. For example, suppose our monotonous company suddenly hears of an opportunity to invest $10 a share next year. This would mean no dividend at $t = 1$. However, the company expects that in each subsequent year the project would earn $1 per share, so that the dividend could be increased to $11 a share.

Let us assume that this investment opportunity has about the same risk as the existing business. Then we can discount its cash flow at the 10 percent rate to find its net present value at year 1:

$$\text{Net present value per share at year 1} = -10 + \frac{1}{.10} = 0$$

Thus the investment opportunity will make no contribution to the company's value. Its prospective return is equal to the opportunity cost of capital.

What effect will the decision to undertake the project have on the company's share price? Clearly none. The reduction in value caused by the nil dividend in year 1 is exactly offset by the increase in value caused by the extra dividends in

TABLE 4-3
Effect on stock price of investing an additional $10 in year 1 at different rates of return. Notice that the earnings-price ratio overestimates r when the project has negative NPV and underestimates it when the project has positive NPV.

Project Rate of Return	Incremental Cash Flow, C	Project NPV in Year 1[a]	Project's Impact on Share Price in Year 0[b]	Share Price in Year 0, P_0	$\dfrac{EPS_1}{P_0}$	r
.05	$ .50	$-$ $ 5.00	$-$ $ 4.55	$ 95.45	.105	.10
.10	1.00	0	0	100.00	.10	.10
.15	1.50	$+$ 5.00	$+$ 4.55	104.55	.096	.10
.20	2.00	$+$ 10.00	$+$ 9.09	109.09	.092	.10
.25	2.50	$+$ 15.00	$+$ 13.64	113.64	.088	.10

[a] Project costs $10.00 ($EPS_1$). NPV $= -10 + C/r$, where $r = .10$.
[b] NPV is calculated at year 1. To find the impact on P_0, discount for 1 year at $r = .10$.

later years. Therefore, once again the market capitalization rate equals the earnings-price ratio:

$$r = \frac{EPS_1}{P_0} = \frac{10}{100} = .10$$

Table 4-3 repeats our example for different assumptions about the cash flow generated by the new project. Note that the earnings-price ratio, measured in terms of EPS_1, next year's expected earnings, equals the market capitalization rate (r) *only* when the new project's NPV $= 0$. This is an extremely important point—managers frequently make poor financial decisions because they confuse earnings-price ratios with the market capitalization rate.

In general, we can think of stock price as the capitalized value of average earnings under a no-growth policy, plus PVGO, the **present value of growth opportunities**:

$$P_0 = \frac{EPS_1}{r} + PVGO$$

The earnings-price ratio, therefore, equals

$$\frac{EPS_1}{P_0} = r \left(1 - \frac{PVGO}{P_0} \right)$$

It will underestimate r if PVGO is positive and overestimate it if PVGO is negative. (The latter case is less likely, since firms are rarely *forced* to take projects with negative net present values.)

*Calculating the Present Value of Growth Opportunities for Fledgling Electronics

Although in our last example both dividends and earnings were expected to grow, this growth made no net contribution to the share price. The stock was in this sense an "income stock." Now let us compare this case with that well-known "growth stock," Fledgling Electronics. You may remember that Fledgling's market capitalization rate, r, is 15 percent. The company is expected to pay a dividend of $5 in the first year, and thereafter the dividend is predicted to increase indefinitely by 10 percent a year. We can, therefore, use the simplified constant-growth formula to work out Fledgling's price:

$$P_0 = \frac{\text{DIV}_1}{r - g} = \frac{5}{.15 - .10} = \$100$$

Suppose that Fledgling has earnings per share of $8.33. Its payout ratio is then

$$\text{Payout ratio} = \frac{\text{DIV}_1}{\text{EPS}_1} = \frac{5.00}{8.33} = .6$$

In other words, the company is plowing back $1 - .6$, or 40 percent of earnings. Suppose also that Fledgling's ratio of earnings to book equity is ROE = .25. This explains the growth rate of 10 percent:

$$\text{Growth rate} = g = \text{plowback ratio} \times \text{ROE} = .4 \times .25 = .10$$

The capitalized value of Fledgling's earnings per share if it had a no-growth policy would be

$$\frac{\text{EPS}_1}{r} = \frac{8.33}{.15} = \$55.56$$

But we know that the value of Fledgling stock is $100. The difference of $44.44 must be the amount that investors are paying for growth opportunities. Let's see if we can explain that figure.

Each year Fledgling plows back 40 percent of its earnings into new assets. In the first year Fledgling invests $3.33 at a permanent 25 percent return on equity. Thus the cash generated by this investment is $.25 \times 3.33 = \$.83$ per year starting at $t = 2$. The net present value of the investment as of $t = 1$ is

$$\text{NPV}_1 = -3.33 + \frac{.83}{.15} = \$2.22$$

Everything is the same in year 2 except that Fledgling will invest $3.67, 10 percent more than in year 1 (remember $g = .10$). Therefore at $t = 2$ an investment is made with a net present value of

$$\text{NPV}_2 = -3.33 \times 1.10 + \frac{.83 \times 1.10}{.15} = \$2.44$$

Thus the payoff to the owners of Fledgling Electronics stock can be represented as the sum of (1) a level stream of earnings, which could be paid out as cash dividends if the firm did not grow, and (2) a set of tickets, one for each future year, representing the opportunity to make investments having positive NPVs. We know that the first component of the value of the share is

$$\text{Present value of level stream of earnings} = \frac{\text{EPS}_1}{r} = \frac{8.33}{.15} = \$55.56$$

The first ticket is worth $2.22 in $t = 1$, the second is worth $2.22 \times 1.10 = \$2.44$ in $t = 2$, the third is worth $2.44 \times 1.10 = \$2.69$ in $t = 3$. These are the forecasted cash values of the tickets. We know how to value a stream of future cash values that grows at 10 percent per year: use the simplified DCF formula, replacing the forecasted dividends with forecasted ticket values:

$$\text{Present value of growth opportunities} = \text{PVGO} = \frac{\text{NPV}_1}{r - g} = \frac{2.22}{.15 - .10}$$

$$= \$44.44$$

Now everything checks:

$$\text{Share price} = \text{present value of level stream of earnings}$$
$$+ \text{ present value of growth opportunities}$$

$$= \frac{\text{EPS}_1}{r} + \text{PVGO}$$

$$= \$55.56 + \$44.44$$

$$= \$100$$

Why is Fledgling Electronics a growth stock? Not because it is expanding at 10 percent per year. It is a growth stock because the net present value of its future investments accounts for a significant fraction (about 44 percent) of the stock's price.

Stock prices today reflect investors' expectations of future operating *and investment* performance. Growth stocks sell at high price-earnings ratios because investors are willing to pay now for expected superior returns on investments that have not yet been made.[5]

A General Expression Linking Dividends and Growth Opportunities

Zeus made a habit of appearing in unusual disguises to unsuspecting maidens. The general DCF formula for valuing stocks is rather like that: it keeps cropping up in different forms. Here is another useful version of the formula.

Cash not retained and reinvested in the business is often known as **free cash flow**:

$$\text{Free cash flow} = \text{revenue} - \text{costs} - \text{investment}$$

But cash that is not reinvested in the business is paid out as dividends. So dividends per share are the same as free cash flow per share, and the general DCF formula can be written in terms of per share revenues, costs, and investment:

$$P_0 = \sum_{t=1}^{\infty} \frac{(\text{Free cash flow per share})_t}{(1 + r)^t}$$

Notice that it is *not* correct to say that a share's value is equal to the discounted stream of its future earnings per share. That would recognize the *rewards* of investment (in the form of increased revenues) but not the *sacrifice* (in the form of investment). The correct formulation states that share value is equal to the discounted stream of free cash flow per share.

To summarize, we can think of a stock's value as representing either (1) the present value of the stream of expected future dividends, or (2) the present value of free cash flow, or (3) the present value of average future earnings under a no-growth policy plus the present value of growth opportunities.

Some companies have such extensive growth opportunities that they prefer to pay no dividends for long periods of time. Up to the time when this chapter was written, Digital Equipment Corporation (DEC) had never paid dividends, because any cash paid out to investors would have meant either slower growth or raising capital by some other means. Investors were evidently happy with management's

---

[5] Michael Eisner, the chairman of Walt Disney Productions, made the point this way: "In school you had to take the test and then be graded. Now we're getting graded, and we haven't taken the test." This was in late 1985, when Disney stock was selling at nearly 20 times earnings. See Kathleen K. Wiegner, "The Tinker Bell Principle," *Forbes*, December 2, 1985, p. 102.

decision to reinvest the earnings. How else can we explain DEC's $11 billion market value in 1986?

Investors are willing to forgo cash dividends today in exchange for higher earnings and the expectation of high dividends sometime in the future. Thus DEC's common stock is not really a counterexample to the statement that stock price equals the present value of expected future dividends. DEC's dividends may continue to be zero for many years, but they are likely to be positive sooner or later. Eventually growth must slow down, releasing funds that can be paid to the stockholders. It is that prospect which makes DEC shares valuable today.

The inevitable deceleration of rapid growth is illustrated by the history of IBM, the most famous growth stock of the period after World War II. IBM has paid dividends since the 1930s, but most IBM stockholders bought the stock for growth, not dividends. Throughout the 1950s and 1960s the dividend yield (dividend per share as a percent of stock price) was very low—usually between 1 and 2 percent. Sales, earnings, and dividends grew at compound annual rates of roughly 20 percent.

That kind of growth cannot continue forever. By the mid-1970s IBM lacked investment opportunities attractive enough to justify continued growth at that rate. Yet its existing businesses remained healthy and profitable. Consequently, the firm accumulated cash at an embarrassing rate. It had $6.1 *billion* in cash and marketable securities at the end of 1976 and $5.4 billion at year-end 1977. It was therefore not surprising to find IBM paying more and more generous dividends: in 1978 it paid $2.88 per share on earnings per share of $5.32, a 54 percent payout ratio. Also, IBM spent about $1.4 billion in 1977 and 1978 to repurchase its own shares. That is, IBM distributed cash to its shareholders by buying shares from them. As Chapter 16 explains, this is essentially equivalent to paying a cash dividend.

What Do Price-Earnings Ratios Mean?

The **price-earnings ratio** is part of the everyday vocabulary of investors in the stock market. People casually refer to DEC stock as "selling at a high P/E." You can look up P/Es in stock quotations given in the newspaper. (However, the newspaper gives the ratio of current price to the most recent earnings. Investors are more concerned with price relative to *future* earnings.) Unfortunately, some financial analysts are confused about what price-earnings ratios really signify and often use the ratios in odd ways.

Should the financial manager celebrate if the firm's stock sells at a high P/E? The answer is usually yes. The high P/E shows that investors think that the firm has good growth opportunities (high PVGO), that its earnings are relatively safe and deserve a low capitalization rate (low *r*), or both. However, firms can have high price-earnings ratios not because price is high but because earnings are low. A firm which earns *nothing* (EPS = 0) in a particular period will have an *infinite* P/E as long as its shares retain any value at all.

Are relative P/Es helpful in evaluating stocks? Sometimes. Suppose you own stock in a family corporation whose shares are not actively traded. What are those shares worth? A decent estimate is possible if you can find a traded firm that has the same profitability, risks, and growth opportunities as those of your firm. Multiply your firm's earnings per share by the P/E of the counterpart firm.

Does a high P/E indicate a low market capitalization rate? No. There is *no* reliable association between a stock's price-earnings ratio and the capitalization rate *r*. The ratio of EPS to P_0 measures *r* only if PVGO = 0, and only if EPS is the average future earnings the firm could generate under a no-growth policy.

What Do Earnings Mean?

Another reason P/Es are hard to interpret is the difficulty of interpreting and comparing earnings per share, the denominator of the price-earnings ratio. What do earnings per share mean? They mean different things for different firms. For some firms they mean more than for others.

The problem is that the earnings that firms report are book, or accounting, figures, and as such reflect a series of more or less arbitrary choices of accounting methods. Almost any firm's reported earnings can be changed substantially by adopting different accounting procedures. A switch in the depreciation method used for reporting purposes directly affects EPS, for example. Yet it has *no* effect on cash flow, since depreciation is a noncash charge. (The depreciation method used for tax purposes *does* affect cash flow.) Other accounting choices which affect reported earnings are the valuation of inventory, the procedures by which the accounts of two merging firms are combined, the choice between expensing or capitalizing research and development, and the way the tax liabilities of the firm are reported. The list could go on and on.

We shall discuss the biases in accounting income and profitability measures in Chapter 12, after we have used present value concepts to develop measures of true, economic income. For the moment, we just want you to remember that accounting earnings are slippery animals.

4-5 SUMMARY

In this chapter we have used our new-found knowledge of present values to examine the market price of bonds and common stocks. In each case the value of the security is just like that of any other asset: it is equal to the stream of cash payments discounted at the rate of return that investors expect to receive on comparable securities.

The cash payments on a bond consist of the regular interest payments together with the final payment of the bond's face value. The rate of interest which makes the discounted value of these cash flows equal to the bond's market price is known as the bond's *yield to maturity* or *internal rate of return*.

Common stocks do not have a fixed maturity; their cash payments consist of an indefinite stream of dividends. Therefore, the present value of a common stock is

$$PV = \sum_{t=1}^{\infty} \frac{DIV_t}{(1 + r)^t}$$

However, we did not *derive* our DCF formula just by substituting DIV_t for C_t. We did not *assume* that the investors purchase common stocks solely for dividends. In fact, we began with the assumption that investors have relatively short horizons and invest for both dividends and capital gains. Our fundamental valuation formula is, therefore,

$$P_0 = \frac{DIV_1 + P_1}{1 + r}$$

This is a condition of market equilibrium: if it did not hold, the share would be overpriced or underpriced, and investors would rush to sell or buy it. The flood of sellers or buyers would force the price to adjust so that the fundamental valuation formula holds.

This formula will hold in each future period as well as the present. That allowed us to express next year's forecasted price in terms of the subsequent stream of dividends DIV_1, DIV_2, ...

We also made use of the formula for a growing perpetuity presented in Chapter 3. If dividends are expected to grow forever at a constant rate of g, then

$$P_0 = \frac{\text{DIV}_1}{r - g}$$

We showed how it is often helpful to twist this formula around and use it to estimate the capitalization rate r, given P_0 and estimates of DIV_1 and g.

Finally we transformed the general DCF formula into a statement about earnings and growth opportunities:

$$P_0 = \frac{\text{EPS}_1}{r} + \text{PVGO}$$

The ratio EPS_1/r is the capitalized value of the earnings per share that the firm would generate under a no-growth policy. PVGO is the net present value of the investments that the firm will make in order to grow. A "growth" stock is one for which PVGO is large relative to the capitalized value of EPS. Most growth stocks are stocks of rapidly expanding firms, but expansion alone does not create a high PVGO. What matters is the profitability of the new investments.

One thing we did *not* discuss is how an entire business is valued. (We looked only at present value *per share* of common stock.) Applying our present value formulas to a firm or line of business is easy in principle, but messy in application. Take a look at the appendix to this chapter: you may find the messy parts interesting.

In earlier chapters you should have acquired—we hope painlessly—a knowledge of the basic principles of valuing assets and a facility with the mechanics of discounting. Now you know something of how common stocks are valued and market capitalization rates estimated. In Chapter 5 we can begin to apply all this knowledge in a more specific analysis of capital-budgeting decisions.

APPENDIX: VALUING A BUSINESS BY DISCOUNTED CASH FLOW

Investors routinely buy and sell shares of common stock. Companies frequently buy and sell entire businesses—as, for example, when General Motors purchased Hughes Aircraft for $5 billion in 1985, or when Union Carbide sold its battery division to Ralston Purina for $1.4 billion in 1986.

Do the discounted cash flow formulas we presented in this chapter work for entire businesses as well as shares of common stock? Sure: it doesn't matter whether you forecast dividends per share or the total free cash flow of a business. Value today always equals future cash flow discounted at the opportunity cost of capital.

Of course things are never as easy in practice as they seem in principle. We have included this appendix to show some of the practical challenges that managers who value businesses often run into. This appendix walks you through the mechanics of valuing businesses. It also shows how smart application of some basic financial concepts can make discounted cash flow less mechanical and more trustworthy.

Forecasting Free Cash Flow for a Business

Rumor has it that Establishment Industries is interested in buying your company's concatenator manufacturing operation. Your company is willing to sell if it can get the full value of this rapidly growing business. The problem is to figure out what its true present value is.

TABLE 4-4
Forecasts of free cash flow, in millions of dollars, for the Concatenator Manufacturing Division. Rapid expansion in years 1–6 means that free cash flow is negative, because required additional investment outstrips earnings. Free cash flow turns positive when growth slows down after year 6.

Year	1	2	3	4	5	6	7	8	9	10
Asset value	10.00	12.00	14.40	17.28	20.74	23.43	26.47	28.05	29.73	31.51
Earnings	1.20	1.44	1.73	2.07	2.49	2.81	3.18	3.36	3.57	3.78
Investment	2.00	2.40	2.88	3.46	2.69	3.04	1.59	1.68	1.78	1.89
Free cash flow	−.80	−.96	−1.15	−1.39	−.20	−.23	1.59	1.68	1.79	1.89
Earnings growth from previous period (percent)	20	20	20	20	20	13	13	6	6	6

Notes:
1. Starting asset value is $10 million. Assets required for the business grow at 20 percent per year to year 4, at 13 percent in years 5 and 6, and at 6 percent afterward.
2. Profitability is constant at 12 percent.
3. Free cash flow equals earnings minus net investment. Net investment equals total capital expenditures less depreciation. Note that earnings are also calculated net of depreciation.

Table 4-4 gives a forecast of free cash flow. The table is similar to Table 4-2, which forecasted earnings and dividends per share for Growth-Tech, based on assumptions about Growth-Tech's assets per share, return on equity, and the growth of its business. For the concatenator business, we also have assumptions about assets, profitability—in this case, after-tax operating earnings relative to assets—and growth. Growth starts out at a rapid 20 percent per year, then falls in two steps to a moderate 6 percent rate for the long run. The growth rate determines the net additional investment required to expand assets, and the profitability rate determines the earnings thrown off by the business.[6]

It turns out that free cash flow, the bottom line in Table 4-4, is negative in years 1 through 6. The concatenator business is paying a negative dividend to the parent company; it is absorbing more cash than it is throwing off.

Is that a bad sign? Not really: the business is not running a cash deficit because it is unprofitable, but only because it is growing so fast. Rapid growth is good news, not bad, so long as the business is earning more than the opportunity cost of capital. Your company, or Establishment Industries, will be happy to invest an extra $800,000 in the concatenator business next year, so long as the business offers a superior rate of return.

Valuation Format

The value of a business is usually computed as the discounted value of free cash flows out to a **valuation horizon** (H), plus the forecasted value of the business at the horizon, also discounted back to present value. That is,

---

[6] Table 4-4 shows *net* investment, which is total investment less depreciation. We are assuming that investment for replacement of existing assets is covered by depreciation, and that net investment is devoted to growth.

We could have reported gross investment in Table 4-4. However, that would have required adding depreciation back to earnings to get operating cash flow. The bottom line, free cash flow, would be the same.

$$PV = \underbrace{\frac{FCF_1}{1 + r} + \frac{FCF_2}{(1 + r)^2} + \cdots + \frac{FCF_H}{(1 + r)^H}}_{PV(\text{free cash flow})} + \underbrace{\frac{PV_H}{(1 + r)^H}}_{PV(\text{horizon value})}$$

Of course, the concatenator business will continue after the horizon, but it's not practical to forecast free cash flow year by year to infinity. PV_H stands in for free cash flow in periods $H + 1$, $H + 2$, etc.

Valuation horizons are often chosen arbitrarily. Sometimes the boss tells everybody to use 10 years because that's a round number. We will try year 6, because growth of the concatenator business seems to settle down to a long-run trend in year 7.

Estimating Horizon Value

There are several common formulas or rules of thumb for estimating horizon value. First, let us try the constant-growth formula. This requires free cash flow for year 7, which we have from Table 4-4, a long-run growth rate, which appears to be 6 percent, and a discount rate, which some high-priced consultant has told us is 10 percent. Therefore,

$$PV(\text{horizon value}) = \frac{1}{(1.1)^6}\left[\frac{1.59}{.10 - .06}\right] = 22.4$$

The present value of the near-term free cash flows is:

$$PV(\text{cash flows}) = -\frac{.80}{1.1} - \frac{.96}{(1.1)^2} - \frac{1.15}{(1.1)^3} - \frac{1.39}{(1.1)^4}$$

$$- \frac{.20}{(1.1)^5} - \frac{.23}{(1.1)^6}$$

$$= -3.6$$

and therefore, the present value of the business is:

$$PV(\text{business}) = PV(\text{free cash flow}) + PV(\text{horizon value})$$

$$= -3.6 \qquad\qquad + 22.4$$

$$= \$18.8 \text{ million}$$

Now, are we done? Well, the mechanics of this calculation are perfect. But doesn't it make you just a little nervous to find that 119 percent of the value of the business rests on the horizon value? Moreover, a little checking shows that the horizon value can change dramatically in response to apparently minor changes in assumptions. For example, if the long-run growth rate is 8, rather than 6 percent, the value of the business increases from \$18.8 to \$26.3 million.[7]

In other words, it's easy for a discounted cash flow business valuation to be mechanically perfect and practically wrong. Smart financial managers try to check their results by calculating horizon value in several different ways.

[7] If long-run growth is 8 rather than 6 percent, an extra 2 percent of period 7 assets will have to be plowed back into the concatenator business. This reduces free cash flow by \$.53 to \$1.06 million. So,

$$PV(\text{horizon value}) = \frac{1}{(1.1)^6}\left(\frac{1.06}{.10 - .08}\right) = \$29.9$$

$$PV(\text{business}) = -3.6 + 29.9 = \$26.3 \text{ million}$$

Suppose you can observe stock prices for mature manufacturing companies whose scale, risk, and growth prospects today roughly match those projected for the concatenator business in year 6. Suppose further that these companies tend to sell at price-earnings ratios of about 11. Then you could reasonably guess that the price-earnings ratio of a mature concatenator operation will likewise be 11. That implies:

$$PV(\text{horizon value}) = \frac{1}{(1.1)^6}(11 \times 3.18) = 19.7$$

$$PV(\text{business}) = -3.6 + 19.7 = \$16.1 \text{ million}$$

Suppose also that the market-book ratios of the sample of mature manufacturing companies tend to cluster around 1.4. (The market-book ratio is just the ratio of stock price to book value per share.) If the concatenator business's market-book ratio is 1.4 in year 6:

$$PV(\text{horizon value}) = \frac{1}{(1.1)^6}(1.4 \times 23.43) = 18.5$$

$$PV(\text{business}) = -3.6 + 18.5 = \$14.9 \text{ million}$$

It's easy to poke holes in these last two calculations. Book value, for example, often is a poor measure of the true value of a company's assets. It can fall far behind actual asset values when there is rapid inflation, and it often entirely misses important intangible assets, such as your patents for concatenator design. Earnings may also be biased by inflation and a long list of arbitrary accounting choices. Finally, you never know when you have found a sample of truly similar companies.

But remember, the purpose of discounted cash flow is to estimate market value—to estimate what investors would pay for a stock or business. When you can *observe* what they actually pay for similar companies, that's valuable evidence. Try to figure out a way to use it. One way to use it is through valuation rules of thumb, based on price-earnings or market-book ratios. A rule of thumb, artfully employed, sometimes beats a complex discounted cash flow calculation hands down.

A Further Reality Check

Here is another approach to valuing a business. It is based on what you have learned about price-earnings ratios and the present value of growth opportunities.

Suppose the valuation horizon is set not by looking for the first year of stable growth, but by asking when the industry is likely to settle into competitive equilibrium. You might go to the operating manager most familiar with the concatenator business and ask:

Sooner or later you and your competitors will be on an equal footing when it comes to major new investments. You may still be earning a superior return on your core business, but you will find that introductions of new products or attempts to expand sales of existing products trigger intense resistance from competitors who are just about as smart and efficient as you are. Give a realistic assessment of when that time will come.

"That time" is the horizon after which PVGO, the net present value of subsequent growth opportunities, is zero. After all, PVGO is positive only when investments can be expected to earn more than the cost of capital. When your competition catches up, that happy prospect disappears.[8]

We know that present value in any period equals the capitalized value of next period's earnings, plus PVGO:

$$PV_t = \frac{earnings_{t+1}}{r} + PVGO$$

But what if PVGO = 0? At the horizon period H, then:

$$PV_H = \frac{earnings_{H+1}}{r}$$

In other words, when the competition catches up, the price-earnings ratio equals $1/r$, because PVGO disappears.

Suppose competition is expected to catch up by period 8. We can recalculate the value of the concatenator business as follows.

$$PV(\text{horizon value}) = \frac{1}{(1 + r)^8} \left(\frac{\text{earnings in period 9}}{r} \right)$$

$$= \frac{1}{(1.1)^8} \left(\frac{3.57}{.10} \right)$$

$$= \$16.7 \text{ million}$$

$$PV(\text{business}) = -3.6 + 16.7 = \$13.1 \text{ million}$$

Conclusion

We now have four estimates of what Establishment Industries ought to pay for the concatenator business. The estimates reflect four different methods of estimating horizon value. There is no "best" method, although in many cases we put most weight on the last method, which sets the horizon date at the point when management expects PVGO to disappear. The last method forces managers to remember that sooner or later competition catches up.

Our calculated values for the concatenator business range from $13.1 to $18.8 million, a difference of almost $6 million. The width of the range may be disquieting, but it is not unusual. Discounted cash flow formulas only estimate market value, and the estimates change as forecasts and assumptions change. Managers cannot know market value until an actual transaction takes place.

FURTHER READING

There are a number of discussions of the valuation of common stocks in investment texts. We suggest:

W. F. Sharpe: *Investments*, 3d ed., Prentice-Hall, Inc., Englewood Cliffs, N.J., 1985.

J. H. Lorie, P. Dodd and M. Hamilton Kimpton: *The Stock Market: Theories and Evidence*, 2d ed., Richard D. Irwin, Inc., Homewood, Ill., 1985.

R. A. Brealey: *An Introduction to Risk and Return from Common Stocks*, 2d ed., The MIT Press, Cambridge, Mass., 1983.

J. B. Williams's original work remains very readable. See particularly Chapter V of:

J. B. Williams: *The Theory of Investment Value*, Harvard University Press, Cambridge, Mass., 1938.

---

[8] We cover this point in more detail in Chapter 11.

The following articles provide important developments of Williams's early work. We suggest, however, that you leave the third article until you have read Chapter 16:

> D. Durand: "Growth Stocks and the Petersburg Paradox," *Journal of Finance*, **12**:348–363 (September 1957).
>
> M. J. Gordon and E. Shapiro: "Capital Equipment Analysis: The Required Rate of Profit," *Management Science*, **3**:102–110 (October 1956).
>
> M. H. Miller and F. Modigliani: "Dividend Policy, Growth and the Valuation of Shares," *Journal of Business*, **34**:411–433 (October 1961).

There have also been many applications of the present value model. Two good examples are:

> R. C. Higgins: "Growth, Dividend Policy and Capital Costs in the Electric Utility Industry," *Journal of Finance*, **29**:1189–1201 (September 1974).
>
> B. G. Malkiel: "Equity Yields, Growth and the Structure of Share Prices," *American Economic Review*, **53**:467–494 (December 1963).

QUIZ

1. Calculate the present value of each of the following bonds, assuming a yield to maturity of 8 percent:

YTM = 8%

Bond	Annual Coupon, %	Maturity
A	6	1
B	6	2
C	6	4
D	10	2
E	10	4

2. Recalculate the present value of the bonds in question 1 assuming the yield to maturity changes to 10 percent. Does a rise in the return that investors require have a larger effect on the price of long-term bonds or short-term bonds?

3. Company X is expected to pay an end-of-year dividend of $10 a share. After the dividend its stock is expected to sell at $110. If the market capitalization rate is 10 percent, what is the current stock price?

4. Company Y does not plow back any earnings and is expected to produce a level dividend stream of $5 a share. If the current stock price is $40, what is the market capitalization rate?

Why not constant growth formula?

5. Company Z's dividends per share are expected to grow indefinitely by 5 percent a year. If next year's dividend is $10 and the market capitalization rate is 8 percent, what is the current stock price?

6. If company Z (see question 5) were to distribute all its earnings, it could maintain a level dividend stream of $15 a share. How much, therefore, is the market actually paying per share for growth opportunities?

7. Which of the following statements are correct?

(*a*) The value of a share equals the discounted stream of future earnings per share. *(ignores cost of investments)*

(*b*) The value of a share equals the present value of earnings per share assuming the firm does not grow, plus the net present value of future growth opportunities.

(*c*) The value of a share equals the discounted stream of future dividends per share.

8. Under what conditions does r, a stock's market capitalization rate, equal its earnings-price ratio, EPS_1/P_0?

When pvgo = 0

QUESTIONS AND PROBLEMS

1. What would happen to the value of 13¾ percent Treasury bonds, 1991 (see Section 4-1), if the market rate of interest (*a*) fell to 6 percent and (*b*) rose to 9 percent? (Assume annual coupon payments.)

2. Calculate the value in 1986 of the following U.S. Treasury bonds, assuming that the rate of interest is 7.5 percent compounded semiannually.
   (*a*) 14½ percent, 1989
   (*b*) 8¾ percent, 1994
   (*c*) 13¾ percent, 2006
   (In your calculations recognize that coupon payments occur semiannually.)

3. Rework Table 4-1 under the assumption that the dividend on Fledgling Electronics is $10 next year and that it is expected to grow by 5 percent a year. The capitalization rate is 15 percent.

4. (*a*) Look in *The Wall Street Journal*. Can you find the dividend yield on the Dow Jones Industrial Average?
   (*b*) Assume that the expected return on common stocks is 8 percent higher than on short-term Treasury bills. Use the constant-growth model to estimate the expected dividend growth for the Dow Jones average.
   (*c*) Estimate the change in the Dow Jones average if investors reduce their forecast of the dividend growth by 2 percent.

5. Look in a recent issue of *The Wall Street Journal* at "NYSE-Composite Transactions."
   (*a*) What is the latest price of IBM stock?
   (*b*) What is the annual dividend payment and the dividend yield on IBM stock?
   (*c*) What would the yield be if IBM changed its yearly dividend to $8?
   (*d*) What is the P/E ratio on IBM stock?
   (*e*) Use the P/E ratio to calculate IBM's earnings per share.
   (*f*) Is IBM's P/E higher or lower than that of Exxon?
   (*g*) What are the possible reasons for the difference in P/E?

6. Look up Georgia Pacific's current stock price and yearly dividend payment. Assume that the payment is expected to grow at a constant rate g.
   (*a*) What expected rate of return is indicated by (i) $g = .02$, (ii) $g = .05$, or (iii) $g = .10$?
   (*b*) Make an estimate of g from the company's plowback rate and return on equity. What expected rate of return is indicated by your estimate?

7. You believe that next year the Dong Lumination Company will pay a dividend of $2 on its common stock. Thereafter you expect dividends to grow at a rate of 4 percent a year in perpetuity. If you require a return of 12 percent on your investment, how much should you be prepared to pay for the stock?

*8. Rework the analysis of the present value of the growth opportunities for Fledgling Electronics, assuming (i) that the dividend is $10 next year, (ii) that it is expected to grow by 5 percent a year, and (iii) that it plows back a constant 20 percent of earnings.
   (*a*) What is next year's expected earnings per share (EPS_1)?
   (*b*) What is the return on book equity (ROE)?
   (*c*) What is PVGO?

√**9.** Explain carefully why different stocks may have different P/Es. Show how the price-earnings ratio is related to growth, dividend payout, and the required return.

10. Suppose that there is a general increase in the rates of return that investors require. Show what effect this would have on the prices of short-term bonds (e.g., 1-year bonds), long-term bonds (e.g., perpetuities), income stocks, and growth stocks.

11. Each of the following formulas for determining shareholders' required rate of return can be right or wrong depending on the circumstances:

(a) $r = \dfrac{DIV_1}{P_0} + g$

(b) $r = \dfrac{EPS_1}{P_0}$

For each formula construct a *simple* numerical example showing that the formula can give wrong answers and explain why the error occurs. Then construct another simple numerical example for which the formula gives the right answer.

√**12.** Phoenix Motor Corporation has pulled off a miraculous recovery. Four years ago, it was near bankruptcy. Now its charismatic leader, a corporate folk hero, may run for president.

Phoenix has just announced a $1 per share dividend, the first since the crisis hit. Analysts expect an increase to a "normal" $3 as the company completes its recovery over the next 3 years. After that, dividend growth is expected to settle down to a moderate long-term growth rate of 6 percent.

Phoenix stock is selling at $50 per share. What is the expected long-run rate of return from buying the stock at this price? Assume dividends of $1, $2, and $3 for years 1, 2, 3. A little trial and error will be necessary to find r.

*__13.__ Look again at the financial forecasts for Growth-Tech given in Table 4-2. This time assume you *know* that the opportunity cost of capital is $r = .12$ (discard the .099 figure calculated in the text). Assume you do *not* know Growth-Tech's stock value. Otherwise follow the assumptions given in the text.

(a) Calculate the value of Growth-Tech stock.

(b) What part of that value reflects the discounted value of P_3, the price forecasted for year 3?

(c) What part of P_3 reflects the present value of growth opportunities (PVGO) after year 3?

(d) Suppose that competition will catch up with Growth-Tech by year 4, so that it can only earn its cost of capital on any investments made in year 4 or subsequently? What is Growth-Tech stock worth now under this assumption? (Make additional assumptions if necessary.)

14. Consider a firm with existing assets that generate an EPS of $5. If the firm does not invest except to maintain existing assets, EPS is expected to remain constant at $5 a year. However, starting next year the firm has the chance to invest $3 per share a year in developing a newly discovered geothermal steam source for electricity generation. Each investment is expected to generate a permanent 20 percent return. However, the source will be fully developed by the fifth year. What will be the stock price and earnings-price ratio assuming investors require a 12 percent rate of return? Show that the earnings-price ratio is .20 if the required rate of return is 20 percent.

15. Compost Science, Inc. (CSI), is in the business of converting Boston's sewage sludge into fertilizer. The business is not in itself very profitable. However, to induce CSI to remain in business, the Metropolitan District Commission (MDC) has agreed to pay whatever amount is necessary to yield CSI a 10 percent book return on equity. At the end of the year CSI is expected to pay a $4 dividend. It has been reinvesting 40 percent of earnings and growing at 4 percent a year.

(a) Suppose CSI continues on this growth trend. What is the expected long-run rate of return from purchasing the stock at $100? What part of the $100 price is attributable to the present value of growth opportunities?

(b) Now the MDC announces a plan for CSI to treat Cambridge sewage. CSI's plant will, therefore, be expanded gradually over 5 years. This means that CSI will have to reinvest 80 percent of its earnings for 5 years. Starting in year 6, however, it will again be able to pay out 60 percent of earnings. What will be CSI's stock price once this announcement is made and its consequences for CSI are known?

5 Why Net Present Value Leads to Better Investment Decisions than Other Criteria

In the first four chapters we have introduced, at times surreptitiously, most of the basic principles of the investment decision. In this chapter we consolidate that knowledge. We also take a critical look at other criteria that companies sometimes use to make investment decisions.

5-1 A REVIEW OF THE BASICS

Vegetron's financial manager is wondering how to analyze a proposed $1 million investment in a new venture called project X. He asks what you think.

Your response should be as follows: "First, forecast the cash flows generated by project X over its economic life. Second, determine the appropriate opportunity cost of capital. This should reflect both the time value of money and the risk involved in project X. Third, use this opportunity cost of capital to discount the future cash flows of project X. The sum of the discounted cash flows is called present value (PV). Fourth, calculate *net* present value (NPV) by subtracting the $1 million investment from PV. Invest in project X if its NPV is greater than zero."

However, Vegetron's financial manager is unmoved by your sagacity. He asks why NPV is so important.

You reply: "Let us look at what is best for Vegetron stockholders. They want you to make their Vegetron shares as valuable as possible.

"Right now Vegetron's total market value (price per share times the number of shares outstanding) is $10 million. That includes $1 million cash we can invest in project X. The value of Vegetron's other assets and opportunities must therefore be $9 million. We have to decide whether it is better to keep the $1 million cash and reject project X or to spend the cash and accept project X. Let us call the value of the new project PV. Then the choice is as follows:

	MARKET VALUE, MILLIONS OF DOLLARS	
Asset	Reject Project X	Accept Project X
Cash	1	0
Other assets	9	9
Project X	0	PV
	10	9 + PV

Clearly project X is worthwhile if its present value, PV, is greater than $1 million—that is, if net present value is positive."

Financial manager: "How do I know that the PV of project X will actually show up in Vegetron's market value?"

Your reply: "Suppose we set up a new, independent firm X, whose only asset is project X. What would be the market value of firm X?

"Investors would forecast the dividends firm X would pay and discount those dividends by the expected rate of return of securities having risks comparable to firm X. We know that stock prices are equal to the present value of forecasted dividends.

"Since project X is firm X's only asset, the dividend payments we would expect firm X to pay are exactly the cash flows we have forecasted for project X. Moreover, the rate investors would use to discount firm X's dividends is exactly the rate we should use to discount project X's cash flows.

"I agree that firm X is entirely hypothetical. But if project X is accepted, investors holding Vegetron stock will really hold a portfolio of project X and the firm's other assets. We know the other assets are worth $9 million considered as a separate venture. Since asset values are additive, we can easily figure out the portfolio value once we calculate the value of project X as a separate venture.

"By calculating the present value of project X, we are replicating the process by which the common stock of firm X would be valued in capital markets."

Financial manager: "The one thing I don't understand is where the discount rate comes from."

Your reply: "I agree that the discount rate is difficult to measure precisely. But it is easy to see what we are *trying* to measure. The discount rate is the opportunity cost of investing in the project rather than in the capital market. In other words, instead of accepting a project, the firm can always give the cash to the shareholders and let them invest it in financial assets.

"Figure 5-1 shows the trade-off. The opportunity cost of taking the project is the return shareholders could have earned had they invested the funds on their own. When we discount the project's cash flows by the expected rate of return on comparable financial assets, we are measuring how much investors would be prepared to pay for your project."

"But which financial assets?" Vegetron's financial manager queries. "The fact that investors expect only 12 percent on AT&T stock does not mean that we should purchase Fly-by-Night Electronics if it offers 13 percent."

Your reply: "The opportunity-cost concept makes sense only if assets of equiv-

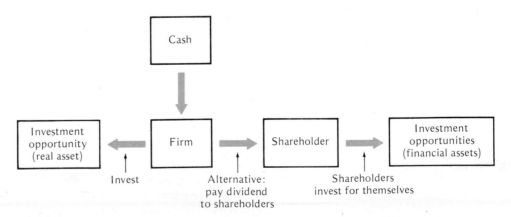

FIGURE 5-1
The firm can either keep and reinvest cash or return it to investors. (Arrows represent possible cash flows or transfers.) If cash is reinvested, the opportunity cost is the expected rate of return that shareholders could have obtained by investing in financial assets.

alent risk are compared. In general, you should identify financial assets with risks equivalent to the project under consideration, estimate the expected rate of return on these assets, and use this rate as the opportunity cost."

5-2   NET PRESENT VALUE'S COMPETITORS

Let us hope that the financial manager is by now convinced of the correctness of the net present value rule. But it is possible that the manager has also heard of some alternative investment criteria and would like to know why you do not recommend any of them. Just so that you are prepared, we will now look at the four most popular alternatives to the NPV rule. These are:

1. Payback
2. Average return on book value
3. Internal rate of return
4. Profitability index

As we look at these alternative criteria, it is worth keeping in mind the following key features of the net present value rule. First, the NPV rule recognizes that *a dollar today is worth more than a dollar tomorrow*, because the dollar today can be invested to start earning interest immediately. Any investment rule which does not recognize the *time value of money* cannot be sensible. Second, net present value depends solely on the *forecasted cash flows* from the project and the *opportunity cost of capital*. Any investment rule which is affected by the manager's tastes, the company's choice of accounting method, the profitability of the company's existing business, or the profitability of other independent projects will lead to inferior decisions. Third, *because present values are all measured in today's dollars, you can add them up*. Therefore, if you have two projects A and B, the net present value of the combined investment is

$$NPV(A + B) = NPV(A) + NPV(B)$$

This additivity property has important implications. Suppose project B has a negative NPV. If you tack it onto project A, the joint project (A + B) will have a lower NPV than A on its own. Therefore, you are unlikely to be misled into accepting a poor project (B) just because it is packaged with a good one (A). As we shall see, the alternative measures do not have this additivity property. If you are not careful, you may be tricked into deciding that a package of a good and a bad project is better than the good project on its own.

5-3   PAYBACK

Companies frequently require that the initial outlay on any project should be recoverable within some specified cutoff period. The **payback** period of a project is found by counting the number of years it takes before cumulative forecasted cash flows equal the initial investment. Consider projects A and B:

Project	CASH FLOWS, DOLLARS				Payback Period, Years	NPV at 10 Percent
	C_0	C_1	C_2	C_3		
A	−2,000	+2,000	0	0	1	−182
B	−2,000	+1,000	+1,000	+5,000	2	+3,492

Project A involves an initial investment of $2000 ($C_0 = -2000$) followed by a single cash inflow of $2000 in year 1. Suppose the opportunity cost of capital is 10 percent. Then project A has an NPV of $-\$182$:

$$NPV(A) = -2000 + \frac{2000}{1.10} = -\$182$$

Project B also requires an initial investment of $2000 but produces a cash inflow of $1000 in years 1 and 2 and $5000 in year 3. At a 10 percent opportunity cost of capital project B has an NPV of $+\$3492$:

$$NPV(B) = -2000 + \frac{1000}{1.10} + \frac{1000}{(1.10)^2} + \frac{5000}{(1.10)^3} = +\$3492$$

Thus the net present value rule tells us to reject project A and accept project B.

The Payback Rule

Now let us look at how rapidly each project pays back its initial investment. With project A you take 1 year to recover your $2000; with project B you take 2 years. If the firm used the payback *rule* with a cutoff period of 1 year, it would accept only project A; if it used the payback rule with a cutoff period of 2 or more years, it would accept both A and B. Therefore, regardless of the choice of cutoff period, the payback rule gives a different answer from the net present value rule.

The reason for the difference is that payback gives equal weight to all cash flows before the payback date and no weight at all to subsequent flows. For example, the following three projects all have a payback period of 2 years:

| | CASH FLOW, DOLLARS | | | | | |
Project	C_0	C_1	C_2	C_3	NPV at 10 Percent	Payback Period, Years
B	−2,000	+1,000	+1,000	+5,000	3,492	2
C	−2,000	0	+2,000	+5,000	3,409	2
D	−2,000	+1,000	+1,000	+100,000	74,867	2

The payback rule says that these projects are all equally attractive. But project B has a higher NPV than project C for *any* positive interest rate ($1000 in each of years 1 and 2 is more valuable than $2000 in year 2). And project D has a higher NPV than either B or C.

In order to use the payback rule a firm has to decide on an appropriate cutoff date. If it uses the same cutoff regardless of project life, it will tend to accept too many short-lived projects and too few long-lived ones. If, on average, the cutoff periods are too long, it will accept some projects with negative NPVs; if, on average, they are too short, it will reject some projects that have positive NPVs.

Many firms that use payback choose the cutoff period essentially by guesswork. It is possible to do better than that. If you know the typical pattern of cash flows, then you can find the cutoff period that would come closest to maximizing net present value.[1] However, this "optimal" cutoff point works only for those projects that have "typical" patterns of cash flows. So it is still better to use the net present value rule.

Discounted Payback

Some companies discount the cash flows before they compute the payback period. The **discounted payback rule** asks, "How many periods does the project have to last in order to make sense in terms of net present value?" This modification to the payback rule surmounts the objection that equal weight is given to all flows before the cutoff date. However, the discounted payback rule still takes no account of any cash flows after the cutoff date.

Suppose there are two mutually exclusive investments, A and B. Each requires a $20,000 investment and is expected to generate a level stream of cash flows starting in year 1. The cash flow for investment A is $6500 and lasts for 6 years. The cash flow for B is $6000 but lasts for 10 years. The appropriate discount rate for each project is 10 percent. Investment B is clearly a better investment on the basis of net present value:

$$\text{NPV(A)} = -20{,}000 + \sum_{t=1}^{6} \frac{6500}{(1.10)^t} = + \$8309$$

$$\text{NPV(B)} = -20{,}000 + \sum_{t=1}^{10} \frac{6000}{(1.10)^t} = +\$16{,}867$$

Yet A has higher cash receipts than B in each year of its life, and so obviously it has the shorter discounted payback. The discounted payback of A is a bit less than 4 years, since the present value of $6500 at 10 percent for 4 years is $20,604. The discounted payback of B is a bit more than 4 years, since the present value of $6000 for 4 years is $19,019.

Discounted payback is a whisker better than undiscounted payback. It recognizes that a dollar at the beginning of the payback period is worth more than a dollar at the end of the payback period. This helps, but it may not help much. The discounted payback rule still depends on the choice of an arbitrary cutoff date and it still ignores all cash flows after that date.

5-4 AVERAGE RETURN ON BOOK VALUE

Some companies judge an investment project by looking at its **book rate of return**. To calculate book rate of return it is necessary to divide the average forecasted profits of a project after depreciation and taxes by the average book value of the investment. This ratio is then measured against the book rate of return for the firm as a whole or, against some external yardstick, such as the average book rate of return for the industry.

[1] If the inflows are, on average, spread equally over the life of the project, the optimal cutoff for the payback rule is

$$\text{Optimal cutoff period} = \frac{1}{r} - \frac{1}{r(1 + r)^n}$$

where n denotes the project life. This expression for the optimal payback was first noted in M. J. Gordon, "The Pay-Off Period and the Rate of Profit," *Journal of Business*, **28**: 253–260 (October 1955).

TABLE 5-1a
Computing the average book rate of return on an investment of $9000 in project A

	CASH FLOW, DOLLARS		
Project A	Year 1	Year 2	Year 3
Revenue	12,000	10,000	8,000
Out-of-pocket cost	6,000	5,000	4,000
Cash flow	6,000	5,000	4,000
Depreciation	3,000	3,000	3,000
Net income	3,000	2,000	1,000

$$\text{Average book rate of return} = \frac{\text{average annual income}}{\text{average annual investment}} = \frac{2,000}{4,500} = .44$$

Table 5-1a shows projected income statements for project A over its 3-year life. Its average net income is $2000 per year (we assume for simplicity that there are no taxes). The required investment is $9000 at $t = 0$. This amount is then depreciated at a constant rate of $3000 per year. So the book value of the new investment will decline from $9000 in year 0 to zero in year 3:

	Year 0	Year 1	Year 2	Year 3
Gross book value of investment	$9,000	$9,000	$9,000	$9,000
Accumulated depreciation	0	3,000	6,000	9,000
Net book value of investment	$9,000	$6,000	$3,000	$ 0

Average net book value = $4,500

The average net income is $2000, and the average net investment is $4500. Therefore, the average book rate of return is 2000/4500 = .44. Project A would be undertaken if the firm's target book rate of return were less than 44 percent.[2]

This criterion suffers from several serious defects. First, because it considers only the *average* return on book investment, there is no allowance for the fact that immediate receipts are more valuable than distant ones. Whereas payback gives no weight to the more distant flows, return on book gives them too much weight. Thus in Table 5-1b we can introduce two projects, B and C, which have the same average book investment, the same average book income, and the same average book profitability as project A. Yet A clearly has a higher NPV than B or C because a greater proportion of the cash flows for project A occur in the early years.

Notice also that the average return on book depends on accounting income; it is not based on the cash flows of a project. Cash flows and accounting income are often very different. For example, the accountant labels some cash outflows *capital investment* and others *operating expenses*. The operating expenses are, of course, deducted immediately from each year's income. The capital expenditures are depreciated according to an arbitrary schedule chosen by the accountant. Then the depreciation charge is deducted from each year's income. Thus the average return on book depends on which items the accountant treats as capital investments and how rapidly they are depreciated. However, the accountant's decisions have noth-

---

[2] There are many variants on this rule. For example, some companies measure the *accounting return on cost*, that is, the ratio of average profits before depreciation but after tax to the initial cost of the asset.

TABLE 5-1b
Projects A, B, and C all cost $9000 and produce an average income of $2000. Therefore, they all have a 44 percent book rate of return

	Project	Year 1	Year 2	Year 3
		CASH FLOW, DOLLARS		
A	Cash flow	6,000	5,000	4,000
	Net income	3,000	2,000	1,000
B	Cash flow	5,000	5,000	5,000
	Net income	2,000	2,000	2,000
C	Cash flow	4,000	5,000	6,000
	Net income	1,000	2,000	3,000

ing to do with the cash flow[3] and therefore should not affect the decision to accept or reject.

A firm that uses average return on book has to decide on a yardstick for judging a project. This decision is also arbitrary. Sometimes the firm uses its current book return as a yardstick. In this case companies with high rates of return on their existing business may be led to reject good projects, and companies with low rates of return may be led to accept bad ones.

Payback is a bad rule. Average return on book is probably worse. It ignores the opportunity cost of money and is not based on the cash flows of a project, and the investment decision may be related to the profitability of the firm's existing business.

5-5 INTERNAL (OR DISCOUNTED CASH FLOW) RATE OF RETURN

Whereas payback and average return on book are ad hoc rules, internal rate of return has a much more respectable ancestry and is recommended in many finance texts. If, therefore, we dwell more on its deficiencies, it is not because they are more numerous but because they are less obvious.

In Chapter 2 we noted that net present value could also be expressed in terms of rate of return, which would lead to the following rule: "Accept investment opportunities offering rates of return in excess of their opportunity costs of capital." That statement, properly interpreted, is absolutely correct. However, interpretation is not always easy for long-lived investment projects.

There is no ambiguity in defining the true rate of return of an investment that generates a single payoff after 1 period:

$$\text{Rate of return} = \frac{\text{payoff}}{\text{investment}} - 1$$

Alternatively, we could write down the NPV of the investment and find that discount rate which makes NPV = 0.

$$\text{NPV} = C_0 + \frac{C_1}{1 + \text{discount rate}} = 0$$

[3] Of course, the depreciation method used for tax purposes does have cash consequences which should be taken into account in calculating NPV.

implies

$$\text{Discount rate} = \frac{C_1}{-C_0} - 1$$

Of course C_1 is the payoff and $-C_0$ the required investment, and so our two equations say exactly the same thing. *The discount rate that makes NPV = 0 is also the rate of return.*

Unfortunately, there is no wholly satisfactory way of defining the true rate of return of a long-lived asset. The best available concept is the so-called **discounted-cash-flow (DCF) rate of return** or **internal rate of return (IRR)**. The internal rate of return is used frequently in finance. It can be a handy measure, but, as we shall see, it can also be a misleading measure. You should, therefore, know how to calculate it and how to use it properly.

The internal rate of return is defined as the rate of discount which makes NPV = 0. This means that to find the IRR for an investment project lasting T years, we must solve for IRR in the following expression:

$$\text{NPV} = C_0 + \frac{C_1}{1 + \text{IRR}} + \frac{C_2}{(1 + \text{IRR})^2} + \cdots + \frac{C_T}{(1 + \text{IRR})^T} = 0$$

Actual calculation of IRR usually involves trial and error. For example, consider a project which produces the following flows:

CASH FLOWS, DOLLARS		
C_0	C_1	C_2
−4,000	+2,000	+4,000

The internal rate of return is IRR in the equation

$$\text{NPV} = -4000 + \frac{2000}{1 + \text{IRR}} + \frac{4000}{(1 + \text{IRR})^2} = 0$$

Let us arbitrarily try a zero discount rate. In this case NPV is not zero but +$2000:

$$\text{NPV} = -4000 + \frac{2000}{1.0} + \frac{4000}{(1.0)^2} = +\$2000$$

The NPV is positive; therefore, the IRR must be greater than zero. The next step might be to try a discount rate of 50 percent. In this case net present value is −$889:

$$\text{NPV} = -4000 + \frac{2000}{1.50} + \frac{4000}{(1.50)^2} = -\$889$$

The NPV is negative; therefore, the IRR must be less than 50 percent. In Figure 5-2 we have plotted the net present values implied by a range of discount rates. From this we can see that a discount rate of 28 percent gives the desired net present value of zero. Therefore IRR is 28 percent.

The easiest way to calculate IRR, if you have to do it by hand, is to plot three or four combinations of NPV and discount rate on a graph like Figure 5-2, connect the points with a smooth line, and read off the discount rate at which NPV = 0. It is of course quicker and more accurate to use a computer or a specially programmed calculator, and this is what most companies do.

FIGURE 5-2
This project costs $4000 and then produces cash inflows of $2000 in year 1 and $4000 in year 2. Its internal rate of return (IRR) is 28 percent, the rate of discount at which NPV is zero.

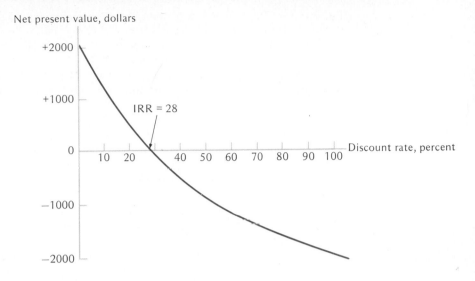

Now, the *rule* for capital budgeting on the basis of internal rate of return is to accept an investment project if the opportunity cost of capital is less than the internal rate of return. You can see the reasoning behind this idea if you look again at Figure 5-2. If the opportunity cost of capital is less than the 28 percent IRR, then the project has a *positive* NPV when discounted at the opportunity cost of capital. If it is equal to the IRR, the project has a *zero* NPV. And if it is greater than the IRR, the project has a *negative* NPV. Therefore, when we compare the opportunity cost of capital with the IRR on our project, we are effectively asking whether our project has a positive NPV. This is true not only for our example. The rule will give the same answer as the net present value rule *whenever the NPV of a project is a smoothly declining function of the discount rate.*[4]

Many firms use internal rate of return as a criterion in preference to net present value. We think that this is a pity. Although, properly stated, the two criteria are formally equivalent, the internal rate of return rule contains several pitfalls.

Pitfall 1—Lending or Borrowing?

Not all cash-flow streams have NPVs that decline as the discount rate increases. Consider the following projects A and B:

| Project | CASH FLOW, DOLLARS | | IRR, Percent | NPV at 10 Percent |
	C_0	C_1		
A	−1,000	+1,500	+50	+364
B	+1,000	−1,500	+50	−364

---

[4] Here is a word of caution. Some people confuse the internal rate of return and the opportunity cost of capital because both appear as discount rates in the NPV formula. The internal rate of return is a *profitability measure* which depends solely on the amount and timing of the project cash flows. The opportunity cost of capital is a *standard of profitability* for the project which we use to calculate how much the project is worth. The opportunity cost of capital is established in capital markets. It is the expected rate of return offered by other assets equivalent in risk to the project being evaluated.

Each project has an IRR of 50 percent. (In other words, $-1000 + 1500/1.50 = 0$ *and* $+1000 - 1500/1.50 = 0$.)

Does this mean that they are equally attractive? Clearly not, for in the case of A, where we are initially paying out $1000, we are *lending* money at 50 percent; in the case of B, where we are initially receiving $1000, we are *borrowing* money at 50 percent. When we lend money, we want a *high* rate of return; when we borrow money, we want a *low* rate of return.

If you plot a graph like Figure 5-2 for project B, you will find that NPV increases as the discount rate increases. Obviously the internal rate of return rule, as we stated it above, won't work in this case; we have to look for an IRR *less* than the opportunity cost of capital.

This is straightforward enough, but now look at project C:

	CASH FLOWS, DOLLARS					
Project	C_0	C_1	C_2	C_3	IRR, Percent	NPV at 10 Percent
C	+1,000	−3,600	+4,320	−1,728	+20	−.75

It turns out that project C has zero NPV at a 20 percent discount rate. If the opportunity cost of capital is 10 percent, that means the project is a good one. Or does it? In part, project C is like borrowing money, because we receive money now and pay it out in the first period; it is also partly like lending money because we pay out money in period 1 and recover it in period 2. Should we accept or reject? The only way to find the answer is to look at the net present value. Figure 5-3 shows that the NPV of our project *increases* as the discount rate increases. If the opportunity cost of capital is 10 percent (i.e., less than the IRR), the project has a very small negative NPV and we should reject.

Pitfall 2— Multiple Rates of Return

Project C had a unique IRR, but this will not generally be the case when there is more than one change in the sign of the cash flows. Consider, for example, project D. It costs $4000 and brings you in $25,000 in the first year. Then in year 2 you have to pay out $25,000. (There are many projects which have terminal cash outflows. For example, if you strip-mine coal, you may have to invest substantial amounts to reclaim the land after the coal is mined.)

	CASH FLOWS, DOLLARS				
Project	C_0	C_1	C_2	IRR, Percent	NPV at 10 Percent
D	−4,000	+25,000	−25,000	25 *and* 400	−1,934

Note there are *two* discount rates that make NPV = 0. That is, *each* of the following statements holds:

$$\text{NPV} = -4000 + \frac{25,000}{1.25} - \frac{25,000}{(1.25)^2} = 0$$

FIGURE 5-3
The net present value of project C increases as the discount rate increases.

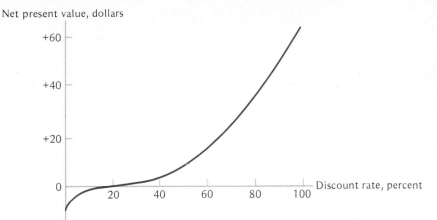

Net present value, dollars

and

$$NPV = -4000 + \frac{25,000}{5} - \frac{25,000}{(5)^2} = 0$$

In other words the investment has an IRR of both 25 *and* 400 percent. Figure 5-4 shows how this comes about. As the discount rate increases, NPV initially rises and then declines. The reason for this is the double change in the sign of the cash-flow stream. There can be as many different internal rates of return for a project as there are changes in the sign of the cash flows.[5]

---

[5] By Descartes' "rule of signs" there can be as many different solutions to a polynomial as there are changes of sign. For a discussion of the problem of multiple rates of return see J. H. Lorie and L. J. Savage, "Three Problems in Rationing Capital," *Journal of Business*, **28**: 229–239 (October 1955); and E. Solomon, "The Arithmetic of Capital Budgeting," *Journal of Business*, **29**: 124–129 (April 1956).

FIGURE 5-4
Project D has two internal rates of return. NPV = 0 when the discount rate is 25 percent and when it is 400 percent.

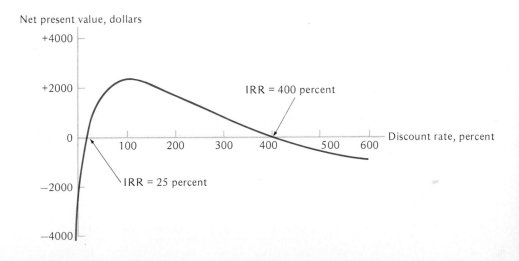

Net present value, dollars

As if this is not difficult enough, there are also cases in which *no* internal rate of return exists. For example, project E has a positive net present value at all discount rates.

| | CASH FLOWS, DOLLARS | | | | |
Project	C_0	C_1	C_2	IRR, Percent	NPV at 10 Percent
E	+1,000	−3,000	+2,500	none	+339

A number of adaptations of the IRR rule have been devised for such cases. Not only are they inadequate, they are unnecessary, for the simple solution is to use net present value.

Pitfall 3—Mutually Exclusive Projects

Firms often have to choose from among several alternative ways of doing the same job or using the same facility. In other words, they need to choose from among **mutually exclusive projects**. Here too the IRR rule can be misleading.

Consider projects F and G:

| | CASH FLOWS, DOLLARS | | | |
Project	C_0	C_1	IRR, Percent	NPV at 10 Percent
F	−10,000	+20,000	100	+8,182
G	−20,000	+35,000	75	+11,818

Perhaps project F is a manually controlled machine tool and project G is the same tool with the addition of computer control. Both are good investments, but G has the higher NPV and is, therefore, better. However, the IRR rule seems to indicate that if you have to choose, you should go for F since it has the higher IRR. If you follow the IRR rule, you have the satisfaction of earning a 100 percent rate of return; if you follow the NPV rule, you are $11,818 richer.

You can salvage the IRR rule in these cases by looking at the internal rate of return on the incremental flows. Here is how to do it. First, consider the smaller project (F in our example). It has an IRR of 100 percent, which is well in excess of the 10 percent opportunity cost of capital. You know, therefore, that F is acceptable. You now ask yourself whether it is worth making the additional $10,000 investment in G. The incremental flows from undertaking G rather than F are as follows:

| | CASH FLOWS, DOLLARS | | | |
Project	C_0	C_1	IRR, Percent	NPV at 10 Percent
G−F	−10,000	+15,000	50	+3,636

FIGURE 5-5
The IRR of project H exceeds that of project I, but the net present value of project I is higher *only* if the discount rate is less than 15.6 percent.

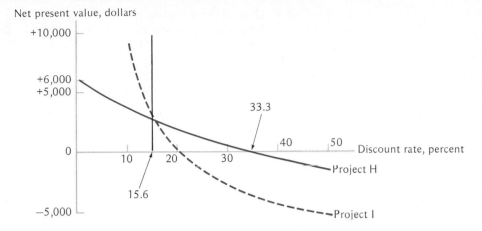

The IRR on the incremental investment is 50 percent, which is also well in excess of the 10 percent opportunity cost of capital. So you should prefer project G to project F.[6]

Unless you look at the incremental expenditure, IRR is unreliable in ranking projects of different scale. It is also unreliable in ranking projects which offer different patterns of cash flow over time. For example, suppose the firm can take project H *or* project I but not both (ignore J for the moment):

| | CASH FLOWS, DOLLARS | | | | | | IRR, | NPV at |
Project	C_0	C_1	C_2	C_3	C_4	C_5	Etc.	Percent	10 Percent
H	−9,000	+6,000	+5,000	+4,000	0	0	. . .	33	3,592
I	−9,000	+1,800	+1,800	+1,800	+1,800	+1,800	. . .	20	9,000
J		−6,000	+1,200	+1,200	+1,200	+1,200	. . .	20	6,000

Project H has a higher IRR, but project I has the higher NPV. Figure 5-5 shows why the two rules give different answers. The solid line gives the net present value of project H at different rates of discount. Since a discount rate of 33 percent produces a net present value of zero, this is the internal rate of return for project H. Similarly, the dashed line shows the net present value of project I at different discount rates. The IRR of project I is 20 percent. (We assume project I's cash flows continue indefinitely.) Note that project I has a higher NPV so long as the opportunity cost of capital is less than 15.6 percent.

The reason that IRR is misleading is that the total cash inflow of project I is larger but tends to occur later. Therefore, when the discount rate is low, I has the higher NPV; when the discount rate is high, H has the higher NPV. (You can see from Figure 5-5 that the two projects have the *same* NPV when the discount rate is 15.6 percent.) The internal rates of return on the two projects tell us that at a discount rate of 20 percent I has a zero NPV (IRR = 20 percent) and H has a

[6] You may, however, find that you have jumped out of the frying pan into the fire. The series of incremental cash flows may involve several changes in sign. In this case there are likely to be multiple IRRs and you wll be forced to use the NPV rule after all.

positive NPV. Thus if the opportunity cost of capital were 20 percent, investors would place a higher value on the shorter-lived project H. But in our example the opportunity cost of capital is not 20 percent but 10 percent. Investors are prepared to pay relatively high prices for longer-lived securities, and so they will pay a relatively high price for the longer-lived project. At a 10 percent cost of capital, an investment in I has an NPV of $9000 and an investment in H has an NPV of only $3592.[7]

This is a favorite example of ours. We have gotten many businesspeople's reaction to it. When asked to choose between H and I, many choose H. The reason seems to be the rapid payback generated by project H. In other words, they believe that if they take H, they will also be able to take a later project like J (note that J can be financed using the cash flows from H), whereas if they take I, they won't have money enough for J. In other words they implicitly assume that it is a *shortage of capital* which forces the choice between H and I. When this implicit assumption is brought out, they usually admit that I is better if there is no capital shortage.

But the introduction of capital constraints raises two further questions. The first stems from the fact that most of the executives preferring H to I work for firms that would have no difficulty raising more capital. Why would a manager at G.M., say, choose H on the grounds of limited capital? G.M. can raise plenty of capital and can take project J regardless of whether H or I is chosen; therefore J should not affect the choice between H and I. The answer seems to be that large firms usually impose capital budgets on divisions and subdivisions as a part of the firm's planning and control system. Since the system is complicated and cumbersome, the budgets are not easily altered, and so they are perceived as real constraints by middle management.

The second question is this. If there is a capital constraint, either real or self-imposed, should IRR be used to rank projects? The answer is no. The problem in this case is to find that package of investment projects which satisfies the capital constraint and has the largest net present value. The IRR rule will not identify this package. As we will show in Chapter 6, the only practical way to do so is to use the technique of linear programming.

When we have to choose between projects H and I, it is easiest to compare the net present values. But if your heart is set on the IRR rule, you can use it as long as you look at the internal rate of return on the incremental flows. The procedure is exactly the same as we showed above. First, you check that project H has a satisfactory IRR. Then you look at the return on the additional investment in I.

	CASH FLOWS, DOLLARS							IRR,	NPV at
Project	C_0	C_1	C_2	C_3	C_4	C_5	Etc.	Percent	10 Percent
I–H	0	−4,200	−3,200	−2,220	+1,800	+1,800	...	15.6	+5,408

The IRR on the incremental investment in I is 15.6 percent. Since this is greater than the opportunity cost of capital, you should undertake I rather than H.

---

[7] It is often suggested that the choice between the net present value rule and the internal rate of return rule should depend on the probable reinvestment rate. This is wrong. The prospective return on another *independent* investment should *never* be allowed to influence the investment decision. For a discussion of the reinvestment assumption see A. A. Alchian, "The Rate of Interest, Fisher's Rate of Return over Cost and Keynes' Internal Rate of Return." *American Economic Review,* **45:** 938–942 (December 1955).

Pitfall 4—What Happens When We Can't Finesse the Term Structure of Interest Rates?

We have simplified our discussion of capital budgeting by assuming that the opportunity cost of capital is the same for all the cash flows, C_1, C_2, C_3, etc. Now this is not the right place to discuss the term structure of interest rates, but we must point out certain problems with the IRR rule that crop up when short-term interest rates are different from long-term rates.

Remember our most general formula for calculating net present value:

$$\text{NPV} = C_0 + \frac{C_1}{1 + r_1} + \frac{C_2}{(1 + r_2)^2} + \cdots$$

In other words, we discount C_1 at the opportunity cost of capital for 1 year, C_2 at the opportunity cost of capital for 2 years, and so on. The IRR rule tells us to accept a project if the IRR is greater than the opportunity cost of capital. But what do we do when we have several opportunity costs? Do we compare IRR with r_1, r_2, r_3, ... ? Actually we would have to compute a complex weighted average of these rates to obtain a number comparable to IRR.

What does this mean for capital budgeting? It means trouble for the IRR rule whenever the term structure of interest rates becomes important.[8] In a situation where it is important, we have to compare the project IRR with the expected IRR (yield to maturity) offered by a traded security that (1) is equivalent in risk to the project and (2) offers the same time pattern of cash flows as the project. Such a comparison is easier said than done. It is much better to forget about IRR and just calculate NPV.

Many firms use the IRR, thereby implicitly assuming that there is no difference between short-term and long-term rates of interest. They do this for the same reason that we have so far finessed the term structure: simplicity.[9]

The Verdict on IRR

We have given four examples of things that can go wrong with IRR. We gave only one example of what could go wrong with payback or return on book. Does this mean that IRR is four times worse than the other two rules? Quite the contrary. There is little point in dwelling on the deficiencies of payback or return on book. They are clearly ad hoc rules which often lead to silly conclusions. The IRR rule has a much more respectable ancestry. It is a less easy rule to use than NPV, but, used properly, it gives the same answer. Now that you know the pitfalls, you should be able to use it properly.

5-6   PROFITABILITY INDEX OR BENEFIT-COST RATIO

The **profitability index** (or **benefit-cost ratio**) is the present value of forecasted future cash flows divided by the initial investment:

$$\text{Profitability index} = \frac{\text{PV}}{- C_0}$$

The profitability-index *rule* tells us to accept all projects with an index greater than 1. If the profitability index is greater than 1, the present value PV is greater than

---

[8] The source of the difficulty is that the IRR is a derived figure without any simple economic interpretation. If we wish to define it, we can do no more than say that it is the discount rate which applied to all cash flows makes NPV = 0. The IRR is a complex average of the separate interest rates. The problem here is not that the IRR is a nuisance to calculate but that it is not a very useful number to have.

[9] In Chapter 9, we will look at some special cases in which it would be misleading to use the same discount rate for both short-term and long-term cash flows.

the initial investment $-C_0$ and so the project must have a positive net present value. The profitability index, therefore, leads to exactly the same decisions as net present value.[10]

However, like internal rate of return, the profitability index can be misleading when we are obliged to choose between two mutually exclusive investments. Consider the following two projects:

| | CASH FLOWS, DOLLARS | | | | |
Project	C_0	C_1	PV at 10 Percent	Profitability Index	NPV at 10 Percent
K	−100	+200	182	1.82	82
L	−10,000	+15,000	13,636	1.36	3,636

Both are good projects, as the profitability index correctly indicates. But suppose the projects are mutually exclusive. We *should* take L, the project with the higher NPV. Yet the profitability index gives K the higher ranking.

As with internal rate of return, you can always solve such problems by looking at the profitability index on the *incremental* investment. In other words, you first check that project K is worthwhile; then you calculate the profitability index on the $9900 additional investment in L.

| | CASH FLOWS, DOLLARS | | | | |
Project	C_0	C_1	PV at 10 Percent	Profitability Index	NPV at 10 Percent
L−K	−9,900	+14,800	13,454	1.36	3,554

The profitability index on the additional investment is greater than 1, so you know that L is the better project.

Of our four rules the profitability index most closely resembles net present value. In the next chapter we will encounter a rather special case in which the profitability index is the more useful rule. But for most purposes it is safer to work with net present values that add up, rather than with profitability indexes that do not.

5-7   SUMMARY

If you are going to persuade your company to use the net present value rule, you must be prepared to explain why other rules do *not* give correct decisions. That is why we have devoted this chapter to four alternative investment criteria.

Some companies use the payback method to make investment decisions. In other words, they accept only those projects that recover their initial investment within some specified period. Payback is an ad hoc rule. It ignores the order in

---

[10] Some companies do not discount the benefits or costs before calculating the profitability index. The less said about these companies, the better.

which cash flows come within the payback period, and it ignores subsequent cash flows entirely. It therefore takes no account of the opportunity cost of capital.

The simplicity of payback makes it an easy device for *describing* investment projects. Managers talk casually about "quick payback" projects in the same way that investors talk about "high P/E" common stocks. The fact that managers talk about the payback periods of projects does not mean that the payback rule governs their decisions. Some managers *do* use payback in judging capital investments. Why they rely on such a grossly oversimplified concept is a puzzle.

Some firms use average return on book value. In this case the company must decide which cash payments are capital expenditures and must pick appropriate depreciation schedules. It must then calculate the ratio of average income to the average book value of the investment and compare it with the company's target return. Average return on book is another ad hoc method. Since it ignores whether the income occurs next year or next century, it takes no account of the opportunity cost of money.

The internal rate of return (IRR) is defined as the rate of discount at which a project would have zero NPV. It is a handy measure and widely used in finance; you should therefore know how to calculate it. The IRR rule states that companies should accept any investment offering an IRR in excess of the opportunity cost of capital. The IRR rule is, like net present value, a technique based on discounted cash flows. It will, therefore, give the correct answer if properly used. The problem is that it is easily misapplied. There are four things to look out for:

1. *Lending or borrowing?* If a project offers positive cash flows followed by negative flows, NPV *rises* as the discount rate is increased. You should accept such projects if their IRR is *less* than the opportunity cost of capital.
2. *Multiple rates of return.* If there is more than one change in the sign of the cash flows, the project may have several IRRs or no IRR at all.
3. *Mutually exclusive projects.* The IRR rule may give the wrong ranking of mutually exclusive projects that differ in economic life or in scale of required investment. If you insist on using IRR to rank mutually exclusive projects, you must examine the IRR on each additional unit of investment.
4. *Short-term interest rates may be different from long-term rates.* The IRR rule requires you to compare the project's IRR with the opportunity cost of capital. But sometimes there is an opportunity cost of capital for 1-year cash flows, a different cost of capital for 2-year cash flows, and so on. In these cases there is no simple yardstick for evaluating the IRR of a project.

The fourth rule uses the profitability index, or benefit-cost ratio. It says that companies should accept projects only if the ratio of the discounted future cash flows to the initial investment is greater than 1. This is just a roundabout way of saying that companies should accept projects with positive NPVs. The only drawback with using ratios is that you cannot add them up in the same way as you can add up values. Therefore you have to be careful when you are using this rule to choose between two projects.

This is a good point at which to stress political realities. Some people believe the earth is flat. It may be easier to persuade such people to accept the idea that the earth may be slightly curled at the corners than to convince them that it is completely round. When you become president or treasurer, we are sure you will use net present value. But if the current management has an inalienable attachment to payback, you can still hope to make a substantial improvement by persuading them to use different cutoff periods for projects with different lives and to change to discounted payback.

If we are going to the expense of collecting forecasts, we might as well use them properly. Ad hoc criteria should therefore have no role in our firm's decisions, and the net present value rule should be employed in preference to other techniques using discounted cash flows. Having said that, we must be careful not to exaggerate the payoff of proper technique. Technique is important, but it is by no means the only determinant of the success of a capital expenditure program. If the forecasts of cash flows are biased, even the most careful application of the net present value rule may fail.

FURTHER READING

Most capital budgeting texts contain a discussion of alternative budgeting criteria. See, for example:

H. Bierman, Jr., and S. Smidt: *The Capital Budgeting Decision*, 6th ed., The Macmillan Company, New York, 1984.

Classic articles on the internal rate of return rule include:

J. H. Lorie and L. J. Savage: "Three Problems in Rationing Capital," *Journal of Business*, **28:** 229–239 (October 1955).

E. Solomon: "The Arithmetic of Capital Budgeting Decisions," *Journal of Business*, **29:** 124–129 (April 1956).

A. A. Alchian: "The Rate of Interest, Fisher's Rate of Return over Cost and Keynes' Internal Rate of Return," *American Economic Review*, **45:** 938–942 (December 1955).

For a discussion of the profitability index, see:

B. Schwab and P. Lusztig: "A Comparative Analysis of the Net Present Value and the Benefit-Cost Ratios as Measures of the Economic Desirability of Investment," *Journal of Finance*, **24:** 507–516 (June 1969).

QUIZ

1. What is the opportunity cost of capital supposed to represent? Give a concise definition.

2. (*a*) What is the payback period on each of the following projects?

| | CASH FLOWS, DOLLARS | | | | |
Project	C_0	C_1	C_2	C_3	C_4
A	−5,000	+1,000	+1,000	+3,000	0
B	−1,000	0	+1,000	+2,000	+3,000
C	−5,000	+1,000	+1,000	+3,000	+5,000

(*b*) *Given* that you wish to use the payback rule with a cutoff period of 2 years, which projects would you accept?

(*c*) If you use a cutoff period of 3 years, which projects would you accept?

(*d*) If the opportunity cost of capital is 10 percent, which projects have positive NPVs?

(*e*) "Payback gives too much weight to cash flows that occur after the cutoff date." True or false?

(*f*) "If a firm uses a single cutoff period for all projects, it is likely to accept too many short-lived projects." True or false?

3. A machine costs $8000 and is expected to produce profit before depreciation of $2500 in each of years 1 and 2 and $3500 in each of years 3 and 4. Assuming that the machine is depreciated at a constant rate of $2000 a year and that there are no taxes, what is the average return on book?

4. True or false? Why?

    (*a*) "The average return on book rule gives too much weight to the later cash flows."   *True*

    (*b*) "If companies use their existing return on book as a yardstick for new investments, successful companies will tend to undertake too much investment."   *False*

5. (*a*) Calculate the net present value of the following project for discount rates of 0, 50, and 100 percent.

CASH FLOWS, DOLLARS		
C_0	C_1	C_2
−6,750	+4,500	+18,000

    (*b*) What is the IRR of the project?

6. Consider projects A and B:

Project	C_0	C_1	C_2	IRR, Percent
	CASH FLOWS, DOLLARS			
A	−4,000	+2,410	+2,930	21
B	−2,000	+1,310	+1,720	31

    (*a*) The opportunity cost of capital is less than 10 percent. Use the IRR rule to determine which project or projects you should accept (i) if you can undertake both, and (ii) if you can undertake only one.

    (*b*) Suppose that project A has an NPV of $690 and project B has an NPV of $657. What is the NPV of the $2000 incremental investment in A?

7. Consider the following projects:

Project	C_0	C_1	C_2
	CASH FLOW, DOLLARS		
A	−1,600	+1,200	+1,440
B	−2,100	+1,440	+1,728

    (*a*) Calculate the profitability index for A and B assuming a 20 percent opportunity cost of capital.

    (*b*) Use the profitability-index rule to determine which project(s) you should accept (i) if you could undertake both, and (ii) if you could undertake only one.

8. Projects C and D both involve the same outlay and offer the same IRR which exceeds the opportunity cost of capital. The cash flows generated by project C are larger than those of D but tend to occur later. Which project has the higher NPV?

9. You have the chance to participate in a project that produces the following cash flows:

CASH FLOWS, DOLLARS		
C_0	C_1	C_2
+5,000	+4,000	−11,000

The internal rate of return is 13 percent. If the opportunity cost of capital is 10 percent, would you accept the offer?

QUESTIONS AND PROBLEMS

1. Consider the following projects:

Project	CASH FLOWS, DOLLARS					
	C_0	C_1	C_2	C_3	C_4	C_5
A	−1,000	+1,000	0	0	0	0
B	−2,000	+1,000	+1,000	+4,000	+1,000	+1,000
C	−3,000	+1,000	+1,000	0	+1,000	+1,000

(a) If the opportunity cost of capital is 10 percent, which projects have a positive NPV?
(b) Calculate the payback period for each project.
(c) Which project(s) would a firm using the payback rule accept if the cutoff period were 3 years?

2. Project A (shown in Table 5-1a) has undergone some revisions. The initial investment has been reduced to $6000, and the firm proposes to depreciate this investment by $2000 a year. Operating costs unfortunately have increased by $1000 a year. If the opportunity cost of capital is 7 percent, how do these changes alter the NPV of the project? How do they affect the average return on book?

3. Consider a project with the following cash flows:

C_0	C_1	C_2
−100	+200	−75

(a) How many internal rates of return does this project have?
(b) The opportunity cost of capital is 20 percent. Is this an attractive project? Briefly explain.

4. Respond to the following comments:
(a) "We like to use payback principally as a way of coping with risk."
(b) "The great merit of the IRR rule is that one does not have to think about what is an appropriate discount rate."

5. The payback rule is still used by many firms despite its acknowledged theoretical shortcomings. Why do you think this is so?

6. Unfortunately, your chief executive officer refuses to accept any investments in plant expansion that do not return their original investment in 4 years or

less. That is, he insists on a *payback rule* with a *cutoff period* of 4 years. As a result, attractive long-lived projects are being turned down.

The CEO is willing to switch to a *discounted payback rule* with the same 4-year cutoff period. Would this be an improvement? Explain.

7. Consider the following two mutually exclusive projects:

time disparity

	CASH FLOWS, DOLLARS			
Project	C_0	C_1	C_2	C_3
A	− 100	+ 60	+ 60	0
B	− 100	0	0	+ 140

(a) Calculate the NPV of each project for discount rates of 0, 10, and 20 percent. Plot these on a graph with NPV on the vertical axis and discount rate on the horizontal.

(b) What is the approximate IRR for each project?

(c) In what circumstances should the company accept project A?

(d) Calculate the NPV of the incremental investment (B − A) for discount rates of 0, 10, and 20 percent. Plot these on your graph. Show that the circumstances in which you would accept A are also those in which the IRR on the incremental investment is less than the opportunity cost of capital.

8. Mr. Cyrus Clops, the president of Giant Enterprises, has to make a choice between two possible investments:

	CASH FLOWS, THOUSANDS OF DOLLARS			IRR, Percent
Project	C_0	C_1	C_2	
A	− 400	+ 241	+ 293	21
B	− 200	+ 131	+ 172	31

The opportunity cost of capital is 9 percent. Mr. Clops is tempted to take B, which has the higher IRR.

(a) Explain to Mr. Clops why this is not the correct procedure.

(b) Show him how to adapt the IRR rule to choose the best project.

(c) Show him that this project also has the higher NPV.

9. The Titanic Shipbuilding Company has a noncancelable contract to build a small cargo vessel. Construction involves a cash outlay of $250,000 at the end of each of the next 2 years. At the end of the third year the company will receive payment of $650,000. The company can speed up construction by working an extra shift. In this case there will be a cash outlay of $550,000 at the end of the first year followed by a cash payment of $650,000 at the end of the second year. Use the IRR rule to show the (approximate) range of opportunity costs of capital at which the company should work the extra shift.

10. Look again at projects A and B on page 73. Assume that the projects are mutually exclusive and that the opportunity cost of capital is 20 percent.

(a) Calculate the profitability index for each project.

(b) Show how the profitability-index rule can be used to select the superior project.

6 Making Investment Decisions with the Net Present Value Rule

We hope that by now you are convinced that wise investment decisions are based on the net present value rule. In this chapter we can think about how to apply the rule to practical investment problems. Our task is threefold. The first issue is to decide what should be discounted. We know the answer in principle: discount cash flows. But useful forecasts of cash flows do not arrive on a silver platter. Often the financial manager has to make do with raw data supplied by specialists in product design, production, marketing, and so on, and must check such information for relevance, completeness, consistency, and accuracy and then pull everything together into a usable forecast.

Our second task is to explain how the net present value rule should be used when there are project interactions. These occur when a decision about one project cannot be separated from a decision about another. Project interactions can be extremely complex. We will make no attempt to analyze every possible case. But we will work through most of the simple cases, as well as a few examples of medium complexity.

Our third task is to develop procedures for coping with capital rationing or other situations in which resources are strictly limited. There are two aspects to this problem. One is computational. Resource constraints often create problems of such complexity that a hunt-and-peck search for the right answer cannot cope with the vast number of alternatives. Linear programming can solve this problem and help the financial manager handle some project interactions at the same time. The other part of the problem is deciding whether capital rationing really exists and whether it invalidates net present value as a criterion for capital budgeting. Our discussion of these issues will take us back to the first principles outlined in Chapter 2.

6-1 WHAT TO DISCOUNT

Up to this point we have been concerned mainly with the mechanics of discounting and with the various methods of project appraisal. We have had almost nothing to say about the problem of *what* one should discount. When you are faced with this problem, you should always stick to three general rules:

1. Only cash flow is relevant.
2. Always estimate cash flows on an incremental basis.
3. Be consistent in your treatment of inflation.

We will discuss each of these rules in turn.

Only Cash Flow Is Relevant

The first and most important point is that the net present value rule is stated in terms of cash flows. Cash flow is the simplest possible concept; it is just the difference between dollars received and dollars paid out. Many people nevertheless confuse cash flow with accounting profits.

Accountants *start* with "dollars in" and "dollars out," but in order to obtain accounting income they adjust these data in two important ways. First, they try to show profit as it is *earned* rather than when the company and the customer get around to paying their bills. Second, they sort cash outflows into two categories: current expenses and capital expenses. They deduct current expenses when calculating profit but do *not* deduct capital expenses. Instead they "depreciate" capital expenses over a number of years and deduct the annual depreciation charge from profits. As a result of these procedures, profits include some cash flows and exclude others, and are reduced by depreciation charges, which are not cash flows at all.

It is not always easy to translate the customary accounting data back into actual dollars—dollars you can buy beer with. If you are in doubt about what is a cash flow, simply count the dollars coming in and take away the dollars going out. Don't assume without checking that you can find cash flow by simple manipulation of accounting data.

You should always estimate cash flows on an after-tax basis. Some firms do not deduct tax payments. They try to offset this mistake by discounting the cash flows before taxes at a rate higher than the opportunity cost of capital. Unfortunately, there is no reliable formula for making such adjustments to the discount rate.

You should also make sure that cash flows are recorded *only when they occur* and not when the work is undertaken or the liability incurred. For example, taxes should be discounted from their actual payment date, not from the time when the tax liability is recorded in the firm's books.

Estimate Cash Flows on an Incremental Basis

The value of a project depends on *all* the additional cash flows that follow from project acceptance. Here are some things to watch for when you are deciding which cash flows should be included:

Do Not Confuse Average with Incremental Payoffs. Most managers naturally hesitate to throw good money after bad. For example, they are reluctant to invest more money in a losing division. But occasionally you will encounter "turnaround" opportunities in which the *incremental* NPV on investment in a loser is strongly positive.

Conversely, it does not always make sense to throw good money after good. A division with an outstanding past profitability record may have run out of good opportunities. You would not pay a large sum for a 20-year-old horse, sentiment aside, regardless of how many races that horse had won or how many champions it had sired.

Here is another example illustrating the difference between average and incremental returns. Suppose that a railroad bridge is in urgent need of repair. With the bridge the railroad can continue to operate; without the bridge it can't. In this case the payoff from the repair work consists of all the benefits of operating the railroad. The incremental NPV of the investment may be enormous. Of course, these benefits should be net of all other costs and all subsequent repairs; otherwise the company may be misled into rebuilding an unprofitable railroad piece by piece.

Include All Incidental Effects.   It is important to include all incidental effects on the remainder of the business. For example, a branch line for a railroad may have a negative NPV when considered in isolation, but still be a worthwhile investment when one allows for the additional traffic that it brings to the main line.

Do Not Forget Working Capital Requirements.   **Net working capital** (often referred to simply as *working capital*) is the difference between a company's short-term assets and liabilities. The principal short-term assets are cash, accounts receivable (customers' unpaid bills), and inventories of raw materials and finished goods. The principal short-term liabilities are accounts payable (bills that *you* have not paid). Most projects entail an additional investment in working capital. This investment should, therefore, be recognized in your cash-flow forecasts. By the same token, when the project comes to an end, you can usually recover some of the investment. This is treated as a cash inflow.

Forget Sunk Costs.   Sunk costs are like spilt milk: They are past and irreversible outflows. Because sunk costs are bygones, they cannot be affected by the decision to accept or reject the project, and so they should be ignored.

This fact is often forgotten. For example, in 1971 Lockheed sought a federal guarantee for a bank loan to continue development of the TriStar airplane. Lockheed and its supporters argued it would be foolish to abandon a project on which nearly $1 billion had already been spent. Some of Lockheed's critics countered that it would be equally foolish to continue with a project that offered no prospect of a satisfactory return on that $1 billion. Both groups were guilty of the so-called *sunk-cost fallacy*; the $1 billion was irrecoverable and, therefore, irrelevant.[1]

Include Opportunity Costs.   The cost of a resource may be relevant to the investment decision even when no cash changes hands. For example, suppose a new manufacturing operation uses land which could otherwise be sold for $100,000. This resource is not free: it has an opportunity cost, which is the cash it could generate for the company if the project were rejected and the resource sold or put to some other productive use.

This example prompts us to warn you against judging projects on the basis of "before versus after." The proper comparison is "with or without." A manager comparing before versus after might not assign any value to the land because the firm owns it both before and after:

Before	Take Project	After	Cash Flow, Before versus After
Firm owns land	$\longrightarrow$	Firm still owns land	0

---

[1] U. E. Reinhardt provides an analysis of the value of the TriStar in 1971: "Break-Even Analysis for Lockheed's TriStar: An Application of Financial Theory," *Journal of Finance* **28**: 821–838 (September 1973). Reinhardt does not fall into the sunk-cost fallacy.

The proper comparison, which is with or without, is as follows:

Before	Take Project	After	Cash Flow, with Project
Firm owns land	$\longrightarrow$	Firm still owns land	0
	Do Not Take Project	After	Cash Flow, without Project
	$\longrightarrow$	Firm sells land for $100,000	$100,000

Comparing the two possible "afters," we see that the firm gives up $100,000 by undertaking the project. This reasoning still holds if the land will not be sold but is worth $100,000 to the firm in some other use.

Sometimes opportunity costs may be very difficult to estimate;[2] however, where the resource can be freely traded, its opportunity cost is simply equal to the market price. Why? It cannot be otherwise. If the value of a parcel of land to the firm is less than its market price, the firm will sell it. On the other hand the opportunity cost of using land in a particular project cannot exceed the cost of buying an equivalent parcel to replace it.

Beware of Allocated Overhead Costs.   We have already mentioned that the accountant's objective in gathering data is not always the same as the investment analyst's. A case in point is the allocation of overhead costs. Overheads include such items as supervisory salaries, rent, heat, and light. These overheads may not be related to any particular project, but they have to be paid for somehow. Therefore, when the accountant assigns costs to the firm's projects, a charge for overhead is usually made. Now our principle of incremental cash flows says that in investment appraisal we should include only the *extra* expenses that would result from the project. A project may generate extra overhead expenses—and then again it may not. We should be cautious about assuming that the accountant's allocation of overheads represents the true extra expenses that would be incurred.

Treat Inflation Consistently

Interest rates are usually quoted in *nominal* rather than *real* terms. In other words, if you buy a Treasury bill the government promises to pay you, say, $10,000. It makes no promises about what $10,000 will buy. Investors take that into account when they decide what is a fair rate of interest.

For example, suppose that the rate of interest on a 1-year United States Treasury bill is 8 percent and that next year's inflation is expected to be 6 percent. If you buy the bill, you get back principal and interest in period 1 dollars, which are worth 6 percent less than current dollars:

Invest Current Dollars		Receive Period 1 Dollars	Result
$10,000	$\longrightarrow$	$10,800	8% *nominal* rate of return

[2] They may be so difficult to estimate that it is often preferable just to note their existence rather than attempt to quantify them.

How much actual purchasing power is represented by the $10,800 return? Let us measure units of purchasing power in terms of current dollars. We convert period 1 dollars into current dollars by dividing by 1.06 (1 plus the expected inflation rate):[3]

$$\text{Purchasing power of} \atop \text{10,800 period 1 dollars} = \text{number of current} \atop {\text{dollars having same} \atop \text{purchasing power}} = \frac{10,800}{1.06} = \$10,188.68$$

This is the *real* payoff to the bill holder:

Invest Current Dollars	Expected Real Value of Period 1 Receipts	Result
$10,000 $\longrightarrow$	$10,188.68	Expected real rate of return is .0187, or about 1.9%

Thus we could say "The bill offers an 8 percent nominal rate of return" *or* "It offers a 1.9 percent expected real rate of return." Note that the nominal rate is certain but the real rate is only expected. The actual real rate cannot be calculated until period 1 arrives and the inflation rate is known.

If the discount rate is stated in nominal terms, then consistency requires that cash flows be estimated in nominal terms, taking account of trends in selling price, labor and materials cost, etc. This calls for more than simply applying a single assumed inflation rate to all components of cash flow. Labor cost per hour of work, for example, normally increases at a faster rate than the consumer price index because of improvements in productivity and increasing real wages throughout the economy. Tax shields on depreciation do not increase with inflation; they are constant in nominal terms because tax law in the United States allows only the original cost of assets to be depreciated.

Of course, there is nothing wrong with discounting real cash flows at a real discount rate, although this is not commonly done. Here is a simple example showing the equivalence of the two methods.

Suppose your firm usually forecasts cash flows in nominal terms and discounts at a 15 percent nominal rate. In this particular case, however, you are given project cash flows estimated in real terms, that is, current dollars:

REAL CASH FLOWS, THOUSANDS OF DOLLARS			
C_0	C_1	C_2	C_3
−100	+35	+50	+30

It would be inconsistent to discount these real cash flows at 15 percent. You have two alternatives: Either restate the cash flows in nominal terms and discount at 15 percent, or restate the discount rate in real terms and use this to discount the real cash flows. We will now show you that both methods produce the same answer.

---

[3] A 6 percent inflation rate means that $1.00 now has the same purchasing power as $1.06 next year. Thus, the real purchasing power of $10,800 next year is $10,800/1.06. Real purchasing power is measured in terms of today's dollars.

Assume that inflation is projected at 10 percent a year. Then the first cash flow for year 1, which is \$35,000 in current dollars, will be $35,000 \times 1.10 = \$38,500$ in year 1 dollars. Similarly the cash flow for year 2 will be $50,000 \times (1.10)^2 = \$60,500$ in year 2 dollars, and so on. If we discount these nominal cash flows at the 15 percent nominal discount rate, we have

$$NPV = -100 + \frac{38.5}{1.15} + \frac{60.5}{(1.15)^2} + \frac{39.9}{(1.15)^3} = 5.5, \text{ or } \$5500$$

Instead of converting the cash-flow forecasts into nominal terms, we could convert the discount rate into real terms by using the following relationship:

$$Real discount rate = \frac{1 + \text{nominal discount rate}}{1 + \text{inflation rate}} - 1$$

In our example this gives

$$Real discount rate = \frac{1.15}{1.10} - 1 = .045, \text{ or } 4.5\%$$

If we now discount the real cash flows by the real discount rate, we have an NPV of \$5500, just as before:

$$NPV = -100 + \frac{35}{1.045} + \frac{50}{(1.045)^2} + \frac{30}{(1.045)^3} = 5.5, \text{ or } \$5500$$

Note that the real discount rate is approximately equal to the *difference* between the nominal discount rate of 15 percent and the inflation rate of 10 percent. Discounting at 5 percent would give NPV = \$4600—not exactly right, but close.

The message of all this is quite simple. Discount nominal cash flows at a nominal discount rate. Discount real cash flows at a real rate. Obvious as this rule is, it is sometimes violated. For example, in 1974 there was a political storm in Ireland over the government's acquisition of a stake in Bula Mines. The price paid by the government reflected an assessment of £40 million as the value of Bula Mines; however, one group of consultants thought that the company's value was only £8 million and others thought that it was as high as £104 million. Although these valuations used different cash-flow projections, a significant part of the difference in views seemed to reflect confusion about real and nominal discount rates.[4]

6-2 EXAMPLE—IM&C PROJECT

As the newly appointed financial manager of International Mulch and Compost Company (IM&C), you are about to analyze a proposal for marketing guano as a garden fertilizer. (IM&C's planned advertising campaign features a rustic gentleman who steps out of a vegetable patch singing, "All my troubles have guano way.")[5]

You are given the forecasts shown in Table 6-1. The project requires an investment of \$10 million in plant and machinery (line 1). This machinery can be dismantled and sold for net proceeds estimated at \$1 million in year 7 (line 1, column 7). This amount is the plant's *salvage value*.

---

[4] In some cases it is unclear what procedure was used. At least one expert seems to have discounted nominal cash flows at a real rate. For a review of the Bula Mines controversy see E. Dimson and P. R. Marsh, *Cases in Corporate Finance*, Wiley International, London, 1987.

[5] Sorry.

TABLE 6-1

IM&C's guano project—initial projections (figures in thousands of dollars)

Period	0	1	2	3	4	5	6	7
1. Capital investment	10,000							−1,000*
2. Accumulated depreciation		1,583	3,167	4,750	6,333	7,917	9,500	0
3. Year-end book value	10,000	8,417	6,833	5,250	3,667	2,083	500	0
4. Working capital		500	1,065	2,450	3,340	2,225	1,130	0
5. Total book value (3 + 4)	10,000	8,917	7,898	7,700	7,007	4,308	1,630	0
6. Sales		475	10,650	24,500	33,400	22,250	11,130	
7. Cost of goods sold		761	6,388	14,690	20,043	13,345	6,678	
8. Other costs†	4,000	2,000	1,000	1,000	1,000	1,000	1,000	
9. Depreciation		1,583	1,583	1,583	1,583	1,583	1,583	
10. Pretax profit (6 − 7 − 8 − 9)	−4,000	−3,869	1,679	7,227	10,774	6,322	1,869	500‡
11. Tax at 34%	−1,360	−1,315	571	2,457	3,663	2,149	635	170
12. Profit after tax (10 − 11)	−2,640	−2,554	1,108	4,770	7,111	4,173	1,234	330

*Salvage value.
†Start-up costs in years 0 and 1, and general and administrative costs in years 1 through 6.
‡The difference between the salvage value and the ending book value of $500 is a taxable profit.

Whoever prepared Table 6-1 depreciated the capital investment over 6 years to an arbitrary salvage value of $500,000, which is less than your forecast of salvage value. *Straight-line depreciation* was assumed. Under this method annual depreciation equals a constant proportion of the initial investment less salvage value ($9.5 million). If we call the depreciable life T, then the straight-line depreciation in year t is:

$$\text{Depreciation in year } t = \frac{1}{T} \times \text{depreciable value} = \frac{1}{6} \times 9.5 = \$1.583 \text{ million}$$

Lines 6 to 12 in Table 6-1 show a simplified income statement for the guano project. This might be taken as a starting point for estimating cash flow. However, you discover that all figures submitted to you are based on costs and selling prices prevailing in year zero. IM&C's production managers realize there will be inflation, but they have assumed that prices can be raised to cover increasing costs. Thus they claim that inflation won't affect the real value of the project.

Though this line of argument sounds plausible, it will get you into trouble. First, opportunity costs of capital are usually expressed as *nominal* rates. You cannot use a nominal rate to discount real cash flows. Second, not all prices and costs increase at the same rate. For example, the tax savings provided by depreciation are unaffected by inflation, since the Internal Revenue Service allows you to depreciate only the original cost of the equipment regardless of what happens to prices after the investment is made. On the other hand, wages generally increase faster than the inflation rate. Labor cost per ton of guano will rise in real terms unless technological advances allow more efficient use of labor.

Assume that future inflation is forecasted at 10 percent a year. Table 6-2 restates Table 6-1 in nominal terms assuming just for simplicity that sales, investment, operating costs, and required working capital appreciate at this general rate. You can see, however, that depreciation is not affected by inflation.

TABLE 6-2
IM&C's guano project—revised projections reflecting inflation (figures in thousands of dollars)

Period	0	1	2	3	4	5	6	7
1. Capital investment	10,000							−1,949*
2. Accumulated depreciation		1,583	3,167	4,750	6,333	7,917	9,500	0
3. Year-end book value	10,000	8,417	6,833	5,250	3,667	2,083	500	0
4. Working capital		550	1,289	3,261	4,890	3,583	2,002	0
5. Total book value (3 + 4)	10,000	8,967	8,122	8,511	8,557	5,666	2,502	0
6. Sales		523	12,887	32,610	48,901	35,834	19,717	
7. Cost of goods sold		837	7,729	19,552	29,345	21,492	11,830	
8. Other costs	4,000	2,200	1,210	1,331	1,464	1,611	1,772	
9. Depreciation		1,583	1,583	1,583	1,583	1,583	1,583	
10. Pretax profit (6 − 7 − 8 − 9)	−4,000	−4,097	2,365	10,144	16,509	11,148	4,532	1,449†
11. Tax at 34%	−1,360	−1,393	804	3,449	5,613	3,790	1,541	493
12. Profit after tax (10 − 11)	−2,640	−2,704	1,561	6,695	10,896	7,358	2,991	956

*Salvage value.
†The difference between the salvage value and the ending book value of $500 is a taxable profit.

Table 6-3 derives cash-flow forecasts from the investment and income data given in Table 6-2. Cash flow from operations is defined as sales less cost of goods sold, other costs, and taxes.[6] The remaining cash flows include the changes in working capital, the initial capital investment, and the final recovery of salvage value. If, as you expect, the salvage value turns out higher than the depreciated value of the machinery, you will have to pay tax on the difference. So you must also include this figure in your cash-flow forecast.

[6] Sales revenue may not represent actual cash inflow. Costs may not represent cash outflows. This is why change in working capital must be taken into account, as it is in Table 6-3. The "Further Note on Estimating Cash Flow" in Section 6-2 discusses the relationship between operating cash flow and change in working capital in more detail.

TABLE 6-3
IM&C's guano project—cash-flow analysis (figures in thousands of dollars)

Period	0	1	2	3	4	5	6	7
1. Sales		523	12,887	32,610	48,901	35,834	19,717	
2. Cost of goods sold		837	7,729	19,552	29,345	21,492	11,830	
3. Other costs	4,000	2,200	1,210	1,331	1,464	1,611	1,772	
4. Tax on operations	−1,360	−1,393	804	3,449	5,613	3,790	1,541	
5. Cash flow from operations (1 − 2 − 3 − 4)	−2,640	−1,121	3,144	8,278	12,479	8,941	4,574	
6. Change in working capital		−550	−739	−1,972	−1,629	1,307	1,581	2,002
7. Capital investment and disposal	−10,000							1,456*
8. Net cash flow (5 + 6 + 7)	−12,640	−1,671	2,405	6,306	10,850	10,248	6,155	3,458
9. Present value at 20%	−12,640	−1,393	1,670	3,649	5,232	4,118	2,061	965
Net present value = $3,662								

*Salvage value of $1,949 less tax of $493 on the difference between salvage value and ending book value.

IM&C estimates the nominal opportunity cost of capital for projects of this type as 20 percent. When all cash flows are added up and discounted, the guano project is seen to offer a net present value of about $3.6 million:

$$NPV = -12,640 - \frac{1671}{1.20} + \frac{2405}{(1.20)^2} + \frac{6306}{(1.20)^3} + \frac{10,850}{(1.20)^4} + \frac{10,248}{(1.20)^5}$$

$$+ \frac{6155}{(1.20)^6} + \frac{3458}{(1.20)^7} = +3622, \quad or \quad \$3,622,000$$

Separating Investment and Financing Decisions

Our analysis of the guano project takes no notice of how that project is financed. It may be that IM&C would decide to finance partly by debt, but, if it did, we would not subtract the debt proceeds from the required investment, nor would we recognize interest and principal payments as cash outflows. We would treat the project as if it were all equity-financed, treating all cash outflows as coming from stockholders and all cash inflows as going to them.

We approach the problem in this way so that we can separate the analysis of the investment decision from the financing decision. Then, when we have calculated NPV, we can undertake a separate analysis of financing. Financing decisions and their possible interaction with investment decisions are covered later in the book.

*A Further Note on Estimating Cash Flow

Now here is an important point. You can see from line 6 of Table 6-3 that working capital increases in the early and middle years of the project. Why is this? There are several possibilities.

1. Sales recorded on the income statement overstate actual cash receipts from guano shipments because customers are slow to pay their bills. Therefore, accounts receivable increase.
2. Projected operating costs understate cash outlays for raw materials and production. Therefore inventory increases.
3. An offsetting effect occurs if payments for materials and services used in guano production are delayed. In this case accounts payable will increase.

Thus a detailed cash-flow forecast for, say, year 3 might look like Table 6-4.

TABLE 6-4

Details of cash-flow forecast for IM&C's guano project in year 3 (figures in thousands of dollars)

Cash Flows	Data from Forecasted Income Statement	Working Capital Changes
Cash inflow	= Sales	− Increase in accounts receivable
$31,110	= 32,610	− 1,500
Cash outflow	= Cost of goods sold, other costs and taxes	+ Increase in inventory net of increase in accounts payable
$24,804	= (19,552 + 1,331 + 3,449)	+ (972 − 500)
Net cash flow	= Cash inflow	− Cash outflow
$6,306	= 31,110	− 24,804

Instead of worrying about changes in working capital, you could estimate cash flow directly by counting up the dollars coming in and taking away the dollars going out. But you would still need to put together a projected income statement to estimate taxes.

A Further Note on Depreciation

Depreciation is a noncash expense; it is important only because it reduces taxable income. It provides an annual *tax shield* equal to the product of depreciation and the marginal tax rate:

$$\text{Tax shield} = \text{depreciation} \times \text{tax rate}$$
$$= 1583 \times .34 - 538, \text{ or } \$538,000$$

The present value of the tax shields ($538,000 for 6 years) is $1,789,000 at a 20 percent discount rate.[7]

Now if IM&C could just get those tax shields sooner, they would be worth more, right? Fortunately tax law allows corporations to do just that: It allows *accelerated depreciation*.

[7] By discounting the depreciation tax shields at 20 percent, we assume that they are as risky as the other cash flows. Since they depend only on tax rates, depreciation method, and IM&C's ability to generate taxable income, they may well be less risky. In some contexts—the analysis of financial leases, for example—depreciation tax shields are treated as safe, nominal cash flows and discounted at an after-tax borrowing or lending rate. See Chapter 26.

TABLE 6-5
Tax depreciation allowed under the accelerated cost recovery system
(figures in percent of depreciable investment)

	TAX DEPRECIATION SCHEDULES BY RECOVERY PERIOD CLASS					
Year(s)	3-Year	5-Year	7-Year	10-Year	15-Year	20-Year
1	33.33	20.00	14.29	10.00	5.00	3.75
2	44.45	32.00	24.49	18.00	9.50	7.22
3	14.81	19.20	17.49	14.40	8.55	6.68
4	7.41	11.52	12.49	11.52	7.70	6.18
5		11.52	8.93	9.22	6.93	5.71
6		5.76	8.93	7.37	6.23	5.28
7			8.93	6.55	5.90	4.89
8			4.45	6.55	5.90	4.52
9				6.55	5.90	4.46
10				6.55	5.90	4.46
11				3.29	5.90	4.46
12					5.90	4.46
13					5.90	4.46
14					5.90	4.46
15					5.90	4.46
16					2.99	4.46
17–20						4.46
21						2.25

Notes: 1. Tax depreciation is lower in the first year because assets are assumed to be in service for only 6 months.
  2. Real property is depreciated straight-line over 27.5 years for residential property and 31.50 years for nonresidential property.

The current rules for tax depreciation were set by the Tax Reduction Act of 1986, which established a modified accelerated cost recovery system. Table 6-5 summarizes the tax depreciation schedules. Note that there are six schedules, one for each recovery period class. Most industrial equipment falls into the 5- and 7-year classes. To keep things simple, we will assume that all the guano project's investment goes into 5-year assets. Thus, IM&C can write off 20 percent of its depreciable investment in year 1, as soon as the assets are placed in service, then 32 percent of depreciable investment in year 2, and so on. Here are the tax shields for the guano project:

Year	1	2	3	4	5	6
Tax depreciation (ACRS percentage × depreciable investment)	2,000	3,200	1,920	1,152	1,152	576
Tax shield (tax depreciation × tax rate, $T = .34$)	680	1,088	653	392	392	196

The present value of these tax shields is $2,112,000, about $323,000 higher than under the straight-line method.

Table 6-6 recalculates the guano project's impact on IM&C's future tax bills, and Table 6-7 shows revised after-tax cash flows and present value. This time we have incorporated realistic assumptions about taxes as well as inflation. We of course arrive at a higher NPV than in Table 6-3, because that table ignored the additional present value of accelerated depreciation.

There is one possible additional problem lurking in the woodwork behind Table 6-6: it is the *alternative minimum tax*, which can limit or defer the tax shields of accelerated depreciation or other *tax preference items*. Because the alternative minimum tax is an important motive for leasing, we discuss it in Chapter 26, rather than here. But make a mental note not to sign off on a capital budgeting analysis without checking whether your company is subject to the alternative minimum tax.

TABLE 6-6

Tax payments on IM&C's guano project (figures in thousands of dollars)

Period	0	1	2	3	4	5	6	7
1. Sales*		523	12,887	32,610	48,901	35,834	19,717	
2. Cost of goods sold*		837	7,729	19,552	29,345	21,492	11,830	
3. Other costs*	4,000	2,200	1,210	1,331	1,464	1,611	1,772	
4. Tax depreciation		2,000	3,200	1,920	1,152	1,152	576	
5. Pretax profit (1 − 2 − 3 − 4)	−4,000	−4,514	748	9,807	16,940	11,579	5,539	1,949[†]
6. Taxes at 34%[‡]	−1,360	−1,535	254	3,334	5,760	3,937	1,883	663

*From Table 6-2.

[†]Salvage value is zero, for tax purposes, after all tax depreciation has been taken. Thus, IM&C will have to pay tax on the full salvage value of 1,949.

[‡]A negative tax payment means a cash *inflow*, assuming IM&C can use the tax loss on its guano project to shield income from other projects.

TABLE 6-7
IM&C's guano project—revised cash-flow analysis (figures in thousands of dollars)

Period	0	1	2	3	4	5	6	7
1. Sales*		523	12,887	32,610	48,901	35,834	19,717	
2. Cost of goods sold*		837	7,729	19,552	29,345	21,492	11,830	
3. Other costs*	4,000	2,200	1,210	1,331	1,464	1,611	1,772	
4. Tax†	−1,360	−1,535	254	3,334	5,760	3,937	1,883	663
5. Cash flow from operations (1 − 2 − 3 − 4)	−2,640	−979	3,694	8,393	12,332	8,794	4,232	−663
6. Change in working capital		−550	−739	−1,972	−1,629	1,307	1,581	2,002
7. Capital investment and disposal	−10,000							1,949*
8. Net cash flow (5 + 6 + 7)	−12,640	−1,529	2,955	6,421	10,703	10,101	5,813	3,288
9. Present value at 20%	−12,640	−1,274	2,052	3,716	5,162	4,059	1,947	918
Net present value = +3,940								

*From Table 6-2.
†From Table 6-6.

A Final Comment on Taxes

Almost every large corporation keeps two separate sets of books, one for its stockholders and one for the Internal Revenue Service. It is common to use straight-line depreciation on the stockholder books and accelerated depreciation on the tax books. The IRS doesn't object to this, and it makes the firm's reported earnings higher than if accelerated depreciation is used everywhere. There are many other differences between tax books and shareholder books.

The financial analyst must be careful to remember which set of books he or she is looking at. In capital budgeting only the tax books are relevant, but to an outside analyst only the shareholder books are available.

A Final Comment on Project Analysis

Let's review. Several pages ago, you embarked on an analysis of IM&C's guano project. It appeared, at first, that you had all the facts you needed in Table 6-1, but many of those numbers had to be thrown away because they didn't reflect expected inflation. So you worked out revised projections and calculated project net present value. However, then you remembered accelerated depreciation; you turned wearily back to your worksheets and finally obtained decent estimates of cash flow and NPV.

You were lucky to get away with just two NPV calculations. In real situations, it often takes several tries to purge all inconsistencies and mistakes. Then there are "what if" questions. For example: What if inflation rages at 15 percent per year, rather than 10? What if technical problems delay start-up to year 2? What if gardeners prefer chemical fertilizers to your natural product?

You won't truly understand the guano project until these questions are answered. *Project analysis* is more than one or two NPV calculations, as we will see in Chapter 10.

However, before you become too deeply immersed in guano, we should now turn to the subject of project interactions.

6-3 PROJECT INTERACTIONS

Almost all decisions about capital expenditure involve "either-or" choices. The firm can build either a 90,000-square-foot warehouse or a 100,000-square-foot warehouse in one of several locations. It can heat it either by oil or by natural gas, and so on. These mutually exclusive options are simple examples of *project interactions*.

Project interactions can arise in countless ways. The literature of operations research and industrial engineering sometimes addresses cases of extreme complexity and difficulty. We will concentrate on five simple but important cases.

Case 1—Optimal Timing of Investment

The fact that a project has a positive NPV does not mean that it is best undertaken now. It might be even more valuable if undertaken in the future. Similarly, a project with a currently negative NPV might become a valuable opportunity if we wait a bit. Thus *any* project has two mutually exclusive alternatives: do it now, or wait and invest later.

The question of optimal timing of investment is not difficult under conditions of certainty. We first examine alternative dates (t) for making the investment and calculate its net *future* value as of each date. Then, in order to find which of the alternatives would add most to the firm's *current* value, we must work out

$$\frac{\text{Net future value as of date } t}{(1 + r)^t}$$

For example, suppose you own a large tract of inaccessible timber. In order to harvest it, you have to invest a substantial amount in access roads and other facilities. The longer you wait, the higher the investment required. On the other hand, lumber prices will rise as you wait, and the trees will keep growing, although at a gradually decreasing rate.

Let us suppose that the net value of the harvest at different future dates is as follows:

Year of Harvest	0	1	2	3	4	5
Net *future* value, thousands of dollars	50	64.4	77.5	89.4	100	109.4
Change in value from previous year, %		+28.8	+20.3	+15.4	+11.9	+9.4

As you can see, the longer you defer cutting the timber, the more money you will make. However, your concern is with the date that maximizes the the net *present* value of your investment. You therefore need to discount the net future value of the harvest back to the present. Suppose the appropriate discount rate is 10 percent. Then if you harvest the timber in year 1, it has a net *present* value of $58,500:

$$\text{NPV if harvested in year 1} = \frac{64.4}{1.10} = 58.5, \text{ or } \$58,500$$

The net present value (at $t = 0$) for other harvest dates is as follows:

Year of Harvest	0	1	2	3	4	5
Net present value, thousands of dollars	50	58.5	64.0	67.2	68.3	67.9

The optimal point to harvest the timber is year 4 because this is the point that maximizes NPV.

Notice that before year 4 the net future value of the timber increases by more than 10 percent a year: The gain in value is greater than the cost of the capital that is tied up in the project. After year 4 the gain in value is still positive but less than the cost of capital. You maximize the net present value of your investment if you harvest your timber as soon as the rate of increase in value drops below the cost of capital.[8]

The problem of optimal timing of investment under uncertainty is, of course, much more complicated. An opportunity not taken at $t = 0$ might be either more or less attractive at $t = 1$; there is rarely any way of knowing for sure. Perhaps it is better to strike while the iron is hot even if there is a chance it will become hotter. On the other hand, if you wait a bit you might obtain more information and avoid a bad mistake.[9]

Case 2— Choosing between Long- and Short-Lived Equipment

Suppose the firm is forced to choose between two machines, A and B. The two machines are designed differently but have identical capacity and do exactly the same job. Machine A costs $15,000 and will last 3 years. It costs $4000 per year to run. Machine B is an "economy" model costing only $10,000, but it will last only 2 years, and costs $6000 per year to run. These are real cash flows: The costs are forecasted in dollars of constant purchasing power.[10]

Because the two machines produce exactly the same product, the only way to choose between them is on the basis of cost. Suppose we compute the present value of cost:

Machine	COSTS, THOUSANDS OF DOLLARS				Present Value at 6%; Thousands of Dollars
	C_0	C_1	C_2	C_3	
A	+15	+4	+4	+4	25.69
B	+10	+6	+6		21.00

Should we take machine B, the one with the lower present value of costs? Not necessarily, because B will have to be replaced a year earlier than A. In other words, there is a future investment decision contingent on today's choice of A or B.

So, a machine with total PV (costs) of $21,000 spread over 3 years (0, 1, and 2) is not necessarily better than a competing machine with PV (costs) of $25,690

---

[8] Our timber-cutting example conveys the right idea about investment timing, but it misses an important practical point: The sooner you cut the first crop of trees, the sooner the second crop can start growing. Thus, the value of the second crop depends on when you cut the first. This more complex and realistic problem might be solved in one of two ways:

1. Find the cutting dates that maximize the present value of a series of harvests, taking account of the different growth rates of young and old trees.
2. Repeat our calculations, counting the future market value of cut-over land as part of the payoff to the first harvest. The value of cut-over land includes the present value of all subsequent harvests.

The second solution is far simpler if you can figure out what cut-over land will be worth.

[9] H. Bierman and S. Smidt discuss the tree-cutting problem in *The Capital Budgeting Decision*, 5th ed., New York: The Macmillan Company, 1980, pp. 439–444.

[10] The following calculations are best done in real terms. Of course we must be consistent and use a real discount rate. We will assume it is 6 percent.

spread over 4 years (0 to 3). Somehow we have to convert total PV (costs) to a cost *per year*.

Suppose the financial manager is asked to *rent* machine A to the plant manager actually in charge of production. There will be three equal rental payments starting in year 1. Obviously the financial manager has to make sure that the rental payments are worth $25,690, the total PV (costs) of machine A. This fair rental payment, which is usually called the *equivalent annual cost*, turns out to be 9.61 or $9610 per year:

	CASH FLOWS, THOUSANDS OF DOLLARS				NPV at 6%, Thousands of Dollars
	C_0	C_1	C_2	C_3	
Machine A	+15	+4	+4	+4	25.69
Equivalent annual cost		+9.61	+9.61	+9.61	25.69

The fair rental payment, or equivalent annual cost, is an annuity which has exactly the same life and present value as machine A. How did we know that the right cash flow from the annuity is 9.61? It was easy! We set the NPV of the annuity equal to the present value of A and solved for the payment of the annuity:

$$PV \text{ of annuity} = PV \text{ of cash outflows of } A = 25.69$$

$$= \text{annuity payment} \times 3\text{-year annuity factor}$$

Therefore the annuity payment equals the present value divided by the annuity factor, which is 2.673 for 3 years and a 6 percent cost of capital.[11]

$$\text{Annuity payment} = \frac{25.69}{2.673} = 9.61$$

If we make a similar calculation for machine B, we get:

	COSTS, THOUSANDS OF DOLLARS			Present Value at 6%, Thousands of Dollars
	C_0	C_1	C_2	
Machine B	+10	+6	+6	21.00
Equivalent 2-year annuity		+11.45	+11.45	21.00

We see that machine A is better, because its equivalent annual cost is less ($9610 versus $11,450 for machine B). In other words, machine A could be rented to the production manager for less than machine B.

Our rule for comparing assets of different lives is, therefore, as follows. Select the machine that has the lowest equivalent annual cost. The equivalent annual cost is simply the net present value of the cost divided by the annuity factor.

Now any rule this simple cannot be completely general. The rule implicitly assumes that like will be replaced with like—that no cheaper machine will come along in year 2 or 3. Suppose, for example, that machine C will arrive in year 2 with equivalent annual cost of only $5000. We would then have to consider

[11] This factor can be obtained from a present value table or from the annuity formula given in Section 3-2.

scrapping or selling machine A at year 2 (more on this decision below). The financial manager could not choose between machines A and B in year 0 without taking a detailed look at what each machine could be replaced with.

Finally, remember why equivalent annual costs are necessary in the first place. The reason is that A and B will be replaced at different future dates. The choice between them therefore affects future investment decisions. If subsequent decisions are not affected by the initial choice—for example, because neither machine will be replaced—then we do *not need to take future decisions into account.*[12]

Case 3—Deciding When to Replace an Existing Machine

The previous example took the life of each machine as fixed. In practice the point at which equipment is replaced reflects economic considerations rather than total physical collapse. *We* must decide when to replace. The machine will rarely decide for us.

Here is a common problem. You are operating an elderly machine that is expected to produce a net cash *inflow* of $4000 in the coming year and $4000 next year. After that it will give up the ghost. You can replace it now with a new machine, which costs $15,000 but is much more efficient and will provide a cash inflow of $8000 a year for 3 years. You want to know whether you should replace your equipment now or wait a year.

We can calculate the NPV of the new machine and also its equivalent annual cash flow, that is, the 3-year annuity that has the same net present value:

	CASH FLOWS, THOUSANDS OF DOLLARS				NPV at 6%, Thousands of Dollars
	C_0	C_1	C_2	C_3	
New machine	−15	+8	+8	+8	6.38
Equivalent 3-year annuity		+2.387	+2.387	+2.387	6.38

In other words, the cash flows of the new machine are equivalent to an annuity of $2387 per year. So we can equally well ask at what point we would want to replace our old machine with a new one producing $2387 a year. When the question is put this way, the answer is obvious. As long as your old machine can generate a cash flow of $4000 a year, who wants to put in its place a new one that generates only $2387 a year?

It is a simple matter to incorporate salvage values into this calculation. Suppose that the current salvage value is $8000 and next year's value is $7000. Let's see where you come out next year if you wait and then sell. On the one hand you gain $7000, but you lose today's salvage value *plus* a year's return on that money. That is, $8000 × 1.06 = $8480. Your net loss is $8480 − $7000 = $1480, which only partly offsets the operating gain. You should not replace yet.

Remember that the logic of such comparisons requires that the new machine should be the best of the available alternatives and that it in turn will be replaced at the optimal point.

---

[12] However, if neither machine will be replaced, then we would have to consider the extra revenue generated by machine A in its third year, when it will be operating but B will not.

Case 4—Cost of Excess Capacity

Any firm with a computer encounters many proposals for using it. Recently installed computers tend to have excess capacity, and, since the immediate marginal cost of using such computers seems to be negligible, management often encourages new uses. Sooner or later, however, the load on the machine will increase to a point at which management must either terminate the uses they originally encouraged or invest in another computer several years earlier than they had planned. Such problems can be avoided if a proper charge is made for the use of spare capacity.

Suppose we have a new investment project which requires heavy use of the computer. The effect of adopting the project is to bring the purchase date of a new computer forward from year 4 to year 3. This new computer has a life of 5 years, and at a discount rate of 6 percent the present value of the cost of buying and operating it is $500,000.

We begin by converting the $500,000 present value of cost of the computer to an equivalent annual cost of $118,700 for each of 5 years.[13] Of course, when the new computer in turn wears out, we will replace it with another. So we face the prospect of computing expenses of $118,700 a year. If we undertake the new project, the series of expenses begins in year 4; if we do not undertake it, the series begins in year 5. The new project, therefore, results in an *additional* computing cost of $118,700 in year 4. This has a present value of $118,700/(1.06)^4$, or about $94,000. This cost is properly charged against the new project. When we recognize it, the NPV of the project may prove to be negative. If so, we still need to check whether it is worthwhile undertaking the project now and abandoning it later, when the excess capacity of the present computer disappears.

Case 5—Fluctuating Load Factors

Although a $10 million warehouse may have a positive net present value, it should be built only if it has a higher NPV than a $9 million alternative. In other words, the NPV of the $1 million *marginal* investment required to buy the more expensive warehouse must be positive.

One case in which this is easily forgotten is when equipment is needed to meet fluctuating demand. Consider the following problem. A widget manufacturer operates two machines, each of which has a capacity of 1000 units a year. They have an indefinite life and no salvage value, and so the only costs are the operating expenses of $2 per widget. Widget manufacture, as everyone knows, is a seasonal business, and widgets are perishable. During the fall and winter, when demand is high, each machine produces at capacity. During the spring and summer, each machine works at 50 percent of capacity. If the discount rate is 10 percent and the machines are kept indefinitely, the present value of the costs is $30,000:

	Two Old Machines
Annual output per machine	750 units
Operating cost per machine	2 × 750 = $1,500
PV operating cost per machine	1,500/.10 = $15,000
PV operating cost of two machines	2 × 15,000 = $30,000

The company is considering whether to replace these machines with newer equipment. The new machines have a similar capacity, and so two would still be needed to meet peak demand. Each new machine costs $6000 and lasts indefi-

[13] The present value of $118,700 for 5 years discounted at 6 percent is $500,000.

nitely. Operating expenses are only $1 per unit. On this basis the company cal-
culates that the present value of the costs of two new machines would be $27,000:

	Two New Machines
Annual output per machine	750 units
Capital cost per machine	$6,000
Operating cost per machine	$1 \times 750 = \$750$
PV total cost per machine	$6,000 + 750/.10 = \$13,500$
PV total cost of two machines	$2 \times 13,500 = \$27,000$

Therefore, it scraps both old machines and buys two new ones.

The company was quite right in thinking that two new machines are better
than two old ones, but unfortunately it forgot to investigate a third alternative; to
replace just one of the old machines. Since the new machine has low operating
costs, it would pay to operate it at capacity all year. The remaining old machine
could then be kept simply to meet peak demand. The present value of the costs
under this strategy is $26,000:

	One Old Machine	One New Machine
Annual output per machine	500 units	1,000 units
Capital cost per machine	0	$6,000
Operating cost per machine	$2 \times 500 = \$1,000$	$1 \times 1,000 = \$1,000$
PV total cost per machine	$1,000/.10 = \$10,000$	$6,000 + 1,000/.10 = \$16,000$
PV total cost of both machines		$26,000

Replacing one machine saves $4000; replacing two machines saves only $3000.
The net present value of the *marginal* investment in the second machine is $-\$1000$.

6-4 CHOOSING THE CAPITAL EXPENDITURE PROGRAM WHEN RESOURCES ARE LIMITED

The entire discussion of methods of capital budgeting rests on the proposition that
the wealth of a firm's shareholders is highest if the firm accepts *every* project that
has a positive net present value. Suppose, however, that there are limitations on
the investment program that prevent the company from undertaking all such projects. If this is the case, we need a method of selecting the package of projects that
is within the company's resources yet gives the highest possible net present value.

Profitability Index under Capital Rationing

Let us start with a very simple example. Suppose that there is a 10 percent opportunity cost of capital, that our company has total resources of $10 million, and
that it has the following opportunities:

Project	CASH FLOWS, MILLIONS OF DOLLARS			NPV at 10%, Millions of Dollars	Profitability Index
	C_0	C_1	C_2		
A	-10	$+30$	$+5$	21	3.1
B	-5	$+5$	$+20$	16	4.2
C	-5	$+5$	$+15$	12	3.4

The firm has sufficient resources to invest either in project A or in projects B and C. Although individually B and C have lower net present values than project A, when taken together they have the higher net present value. It is clear, therefore, that we cannot choose between projects solely on the basis of individual net present values. When funds are limited, we need to concentrate on getting the biggest bang for our buck. In other words, we must pick the projects that offer the highest ratio of present value to initial outlay. This ratio is simply the profitability index, or benefit-cost ratio, that we described in Chapter 5:

$$\text{Profitability index} = \frac{\text{present value}}{\text{investment}}$$

Of our three projects, B has the highest profitability index and C the next highest. Therefore, if our budget limit is $10 million, we should accept these two projects.

Unfortunately, there are some limitations to these simple ranking methods. One of the most serious is that they break down whenever more than one resource is rationed. For example, suppose that a $10 million budget limit applies to cash flows in *each* of years 0 and 1 and that our menu is expanded as follows:

Project	CASH FLOWS, MILLIONS OF DOLLARS			NPV at 10%, Millions of Dollars	Profitability Index
	C_0	C_1	C_2		
A	-10	$+30$	$+5$	21	3.1
B	-5	$+5$	$+20$	16	4.2
C	-5	$+5$	$+15$	12	3.4
D	0	-40	$+60$	13	1.4

One strategy is to accept projects B and C; however, if we do this, we cannot also accept D, which costs more than our budget limit for period 1. An alternative is to accept project A in period 0. Although this has a lower net present value than the combination of B and C, it provides a $30 million positive cash flow in period 1. With that added to the $10 million budget we can also afford to undertake D. A and D have *lower* profitability indexes than B and C, but they have a *higher* total net present value.

The reason that ranking on the profitability index fails in this example is that resources are constrained in each of two periods. In fact, this ranking method is inadequate whenever there is *any* other constraint on the choice of projects. This means that it cannot cope with cases in which two projects are mutually exclusive or in which one project is dependent on another.

*Some More Elaborate Capital Rationing Models

The simplicity of the profitability-index method may sometimes outweigh its limitations. For example, it may not pay to worry about expenditures in subsequent years if you have only a hazy notion of future capital availability or investment opportunities. But there are also circumstances in which the limitations of the profitability-index method are intolerable. For such occasions we need a more general method for solving the capital rationing problem.

We begin by restating the problem just described. Suppose that we were to accept proportion x_A of project A in our example. Then the net present value of our investment in the project would be $21x_A$. Similarly, the net present value of our investment in project B can be expressed as $16x_B$, and so on. Our objective is to select the set of projects with the highest *total* net present value. In other words we wish to find the values of x that maximize

$$\text{NPV} = 21x_A + 16x_B + 12x_C + 13x_D$$

Our choice of projects is subject to several constraints. First, total cash outflow in period 0 must not be greater than \$10 million. In other words,

$$10x_A + 5x_B + 5x_C + 0x_D \leq 10$$

Similarly, total outflow in period 1 must not be greater than \$10 million.

$$-30x_A - 5x_B - 5x_C + 40x_D \leq 10$$

Finally, we cannot invest a negative amount in a project and we cannot purchase more than one of each. Therefore we have

$$0 \leq x_A \leq 1, \quad 0 \leq x_B \leq 1, \ldots$$

Collecting all these conditions, we can summarize the problem as follows:

Maximize $21x_A + 16x_B + 12x_C + 13x_D$

Subject to

$$10x_A + 5x_B + 5x_C + 0x_D \leq 10$$

$$-30x_A - 5x_B - 5x_C + 40x_D \leq 10$$

$$0 \leq x_A \leq 1, \quad 0 \leq x_B \leq 1, \ldots$$

One way to tackle such a problem is to keep selecting different values for the x's, noting which combination both satisfies the constraints and gives the highest net present value. But it's smarter to recognize that the equations above constitute a linear programming (LP) problem. It can be handed to a computer equipped to solve LPs.

The answer given by the LP method is somewhat different from the one we obtained earlier. Instead of investing in one unit of project A and one of project D, we are told to take half of project A, all of project B, and three-quarters of D. The reason is simple. The computer is a dumb, but obedient, pet, and since we did not tell it that the x's had to be whole numbers, it saw no reason to make them so. By accepting "fractional" projects, it is possible to increase NPV by \$2.25 million. For many purposes this is quite appropriate. If project A represents an investment in 1000 square feet of warehouse space or in 1000 tons of steel plate, it might be feasible to accept 500 square feet or 500 tons, and quite reasonable to assume that cash flow would be reduced proportionately. If, however, project A is a single crane or oil well, such fractional investments make little sense.

When fractional projects are not feasible, we can use a form of linear programming known as *integer* (or *zero-one*) *programming*, which limits all the x's to integers. Unfortunately, integer programs are less common and more awkward to use.

Uses of Capital Rationing Models

Linear programming models seem tailor-made for solving capital budgeting problems when resources are limited. Why then are they not universally accepted either in theory or in practice? One reason is that these models are often not cheap to use. We know of an oil company that spent over \$4 million in one year on an investment planning model using integer programming. While linear programming is considerably cheaper in terms of computer time, it cannot be used when large, indivisible projects are involved.

Second, as with any sophisticated long-range planning tool there is the general problem of getting good data. It is just not worth applying costly, sophisticated methods to poor data. Furthermore, these models are based on the assumption that all future investment opportunities are known. In reality, the discovery of investment ideas is an unfolding process.

Our most serious misgivings center on the basic assumption that capital is limited. When we come to discuss company financing, we shall see that most firms do not face capital rationing and can raise very large sums of money on fair terms. Why then do many company presidents tell their subordinates that capital is limited? If they are right, the capital market is seriously imperfect. What then are they doing maximizing NPV?[14] We might be tempted to suppose that if capital is not rationed, they do not *need* to use the LP model and, if it is rationed, then surely they *ought* not to use it. But that would be too quick a judgment. Let us look at this problem more deliberately.

Soft Rationing.   Many firms' capital constraints are "soft." They reflect no imperfections in capital markets. Instead they are provisional limits adopted by management as an aid to financial control.

Some ambitious divisional managers habitually overstate their investment opportunities. Rather than trying to distinguish which projects really are worthwhile, headquarters may find it simpler to impose an upper limit on divisional expenditures and thereby force the divisions to set their own priorities. In such instances budget limits are a rough but effective way of dealing with biased cash-flow forecasts. In other cases management may believe that very rapid corporate growth could impose intolerable strains on management and the organization. Since it is difficult to quantify such constraints explicitly, the budget limit may be used as a proxy.

Because such budget limits have nothing to do with any inefficiency in the capital market, there is no contradiction in using an LP model in the division to maximize net present value subject to the budget constraint. On the other hand, there is not much point in elaborate selection procedures if the cash-flow forecasts of the division are seriously biased.

Even if capital is not rationed, other resources may be. The availability of management time, skilled labor, or even other capital equipment often constitutes an important constraint on a company's growth. In the appendix to this chapter we show you how the programming model that we have described can be extended to incorporate such constraints. And we also show how they may be used to cope with project interactions.

Hard Rationing.   Soft rationing should never cost the firm anything. If capital constraints become tight enough to hurt—in the sense that projects with significant positive NPVs are passed up—then the firm raises more money and loosens the constraint. But what if it *can't* raise more money—what if it faces *hard* rationing?

Hard rationing implies market imperfections, but that does not necessarily mean we have to throw away net present value as a criterion for capital budgeting. It depends on the nature of the imperfection.

[14] Don't forget that we had to assume perfect capital markets to derive the NPV rule.

Arizona Aquaculture, Inc. (AAI), borrows as much as the banks will lend it, yet it still has good investment opportunities. This is not hard rationing so long as AAI can issue stock. But perhaps it can't. Perhaps the founder and majority shareholder vetoes the idea from fear of losing control of the firm: Perhaps a stock issue would bring costly red tape or legal complications.[15]

This does not invalidate the NPV rule. AAI's *shareholders* can borrow or lend, sell their shares, or buy more. They have free access to security markets. The type of portfolio they hold is independent of AAI's financing or investment decisions. The only way AAI can help its shareholders is to make them richer. Thus AAI should invest its available cash in the package of projects having the largest aggregate net present value.

A barrier between the firm and capital markets does not undermine net present value so long as the barrier is the *only* market imperfection. The important thing is that the firm's *shareholders* have free access to well-functioning capital markets.

The method of net present value *is* undermined when imperfections restrict shareholders' portfolio choice. Suppose that Nevada Aquaculture, Inc. (NAI), is solely owned by its founder, Alexander Turbot. Mr. Turbot has no cash or credit remaining, but he is convinced that expansion of his operation is a high-NPV investment. He has tried to sell stock but has found that prospective investors, skeptical of prospects for fish farming in the desert, offer him much less than he thinks his firm is worth. For Mr. Turbot capital markets hardly exist. It makes little sense for him to discount the prospective cash flows at a market opportunity cost of capital.

6-5 SUMMARY

By now present value calculations should be a matter of routine. However, forecasting cash flows will never be routine. It will always be a skilled, hazardous occupation. Mistakes can be minimized by following three rules.

1. Concentrate on cash flows after taxes. Be wary of accounting data masquerading as cash-flow data.
2. Always judge investments on an incremental basis. Tirelessly track down all cash-flow consequences of your decision.
3. Treat inflation consistently. Discount nominal cash-flow forecasts at nominal rates and real forecasts at real rates.

We might add a fourth rule: Recognize project interactions. Decisions involving only a choice of accepting or rejecting a project rarely exist, since capital projects can rarely be isolated from other projects or alternatives. The simplest decision normally encountered is accept or reject or delay. A project having a positive NPV if undertaken today may have a still higher NPV if undertaken tomorrow.

Another kind of project interaction stems from *capital rationing*. If capital is strictly limited, then acceptance of project A may preclude acceptance of B. If capital is limited in only one period, the objective of the firm shifts from maximizing NPV to maximizing NPV *per dollar of capital*. Projects can be ranked by their profitability index, and top-ranked projects chosen until funds are exhausted. This procedure fails when capital is rationed in more than one period or when there

---

[15] A majority owner who is "locked in" and has much personal wealth tied up in AAI may be effectively cut off from capital markets. The NPV rule may not make sense to such an owner, though it will to the other shareholders.

are other constraints on project choice. The only general solution is linear or integer programming.

"Hard" capital rationing always reflects a market imperfection—a barrier between the firm and capital markets. If that barrier also implies that the firm's shareholders lack free access to a well-functioning capital market, the very foundations of net present value crumble. Fortunately, hard rationing is rare for corporations in the United States. Many firms do use "soft" capital rationing however. That is, they set up self-imposed limits as a means of financial planning and control.

This chapter is concerned with the mechanics of applying the net present value rule in practical situations. All our analysis boils down to two simple themes. First, be careful about the definition of alternative projects. Make sure you are comparing like with like. Second, make sure that your calculations include all incremental cash flows.

APPENDIX   SOME EMBELLISHMENTS TO THE CAPITAL RATIONING MODEL

In Section 6-4 we showed that when capital is rationed you can set up the investment decision as a linear programming problem. In this appendix we describe some embellishments to these models, and we show how you can use them to cope with other resource constraints and project interactions.

Cash Carry-Forward

A plant manager who is forced to return the unspent part of an annual capital allocation may be goaded into a substantial year-end investment in pink carpeting for the foundry floor or other equally silly assets. (How can you argue for a high budget next year if there's money left over this year?) Headquarters can alleviate this problem by permitting the manager to carry forward any unspent balance. (Then the manager could at least wait until January and get a better selection of carpet colors.) Let us take the sample problem that we described in Section 6-4. To incorporate the possibility of cash carry-forward, we simply need to add another term to our spending constraint. Let s denote funds transferred from year 0 to year 1 and let them earn interest at the rate r. Then we can rewrite our constraint for year 0 as

$$10x_A + 5x_B + 5x_C + 0x_D + s = 10$$

Similarly, the constraint for year 1 becomes

$$-30x_A - 5x_B - 5x_C + 40x_D \leq 10 + (1 + r)s$$

Since carrying forward a negative amount is equivalent to borrowing, we will probably wish to add the constraint $s \geq 0$.

Mutually Exclusive Projects

Suppose now that projects B and C are mutually exclusive. We can take care of this in an *integer* program by specifying that our *total* investment in the two projects cannot be greater than 1.

$$x_B + x_C \leq 1, \qquad x_B, x_C = 0 \ or \ 1$$

In other words, if x_B is 1, x_C must be 0; if x_C is 1, x_B must be 0.

Contingent Projects

Suppose next that project D is an attachment to project A, and we cannot accept D *unless* we also accept A. In this case we need to add

$$x_D - x_A \leq 0 \qquad x_D, x_A = 0 \ or \ 1$$

In other words, if x_A is 1, x_D can be 0 *or* 1; but if x_A is 0, x_D must likewise be 0.

Constraints on Nonfinancial Resources

Money may not be the only scarce resource. Each of our projects may require services from a 12-person technical design department. If project A would employ three designers, project B two, and so on, we would need to add a constraint like

$$3x_A + 2x_B + 8x_C + 3x_D \leq 12$$

Constraints on Nonfinancial Output

Sometimes it is appropriate to place constraints on the total increase in physical capacity. Suppose that projects A and C produce four and three units, respectively, of the same product. If the company is unable to sell more than five units, it is necessary to add

$$4x_A + 3x_C \leq 5$$

We could go on—but you get the idea.

FURTHER READING

There are several good general texts on capital budgeting that cover project interactions. Two examples are:

E. L. Grant, W. G. Ireson, and R. S. Leavenworth, *Principles of Engineering Economy*, 7th ed., Ronald Press, New York, 1982.

H. Bierman and S. Smidt, *The Capital Budgeting Decision*, 6th ed., The Macmillan Company, New York, 1984.

Terborgh treats decisions involving machine replacement in detail.

G. W. Terborgh, *Business Investment Management*, Machinery and Allied Products Institute and Council for Technological Advancement, 1967.

The classic treatment of linear programming applied to capital budgeting is:

H. M. Weingartner, *Mathematical Programming and the Analysis of Capital Budgeting Problems*, Prentice-Hall, Inc., Englewood Cliffs, N.J., 1963.

There is a long scholarly controversy on whether capital constraints invalidate the NPV rule. Weingartner has reviewed this literature.

H. M. Weingartner, "Capital Rationing: n Authors in Search of a Plot," *Journal of Finance*, **32:** 1403–1432 (December, 1977).

Reinhardt provides an interesting case study of a capital investment decision in:

U. E. Reinhardt, "Break-Even Analysis for Lockheed's TriStar: An Application of Financial Theory," *Journal of Finance*, **32:** 821–838 (September 1973).

QUIZ

1. Which of the following should be treated as incremental cash flows when deciding whether to invest in a new manufacturing plant? The site is already owned by the company, but existing buildings would need to be demolished.

(a) The market value of the site and existing buildings
(b) Demolition costs and site clearance
(c) The cost of a new access road put in last year
(d) Lost earnings on other products due to executive time spent on the new facility
(e) A proportion of the cost of leasing the president's jet airplane
(f) Future depreciation of the new plant
(g) The reduction in the corporation's tax bill resulting from tax depreciation of the new plant
(h) The initial investment in inventories of raw materials
(i) Money already spent on engineering design of the new plant

2. M. Loup Garou will be paid 100,000 French francs 1 year hence. This is a nominal flow, which he discounts at a 15 percent nominal discount rate:

$$PV - \frac{100,000}{1.15} = 86,957 \text{ francs}$$

The inflation rate is 10 percent.

Calculate the present value of M. Garou's payment using the equivalent *real* cash flow and *real* discount rate. (You should get exactly the same answer as he did.)

3. Machines A and B are mutually exclusive and are expected to produce the following cash flows:

Machine	C_0	C_1	C_2	C_3
		CASH FLOWS, THOUSANDS OF DOLLARS		
A	−100	+110	+121	—
B	−120	+110	+121	+133

The opportunity cost of capital is 10 percent.
(a) Calculate the NPV of each machine.
(b) Use present value tables to calculate the equivalent annual cash flow from each machine.
(c) Which machine should you buy?

4. Machine C was purchased 5 years ago for $200,000 and produces an annual cash flow of $80,000. It has no salvage value but is expected to last another 5 years. The company can replace machine C with machine B (see question 3 above) *either* now *or* at the end of 5 years. Which should it do?

5. Suppose you have the following investment opportunites, but only $100,000 available for investment. Which projects should you take?

Project	NPV	Investment
1	5,000	10,000
2	5,000	5,000
3	10,000	90,000
4	15,000	60,000
5	15,000	75,000
6	3,000	15,000

6. What is the difference between "hard" and "soft" capital rationing? Does soft rationing mean the manager should stop trying to maximize NPV? How about hard rationing?

QUESTIONS AND PROBLEMS

1. When appraising mutually exclusive projects, many companies calculate the projects' equivalent annual costs and rank the projects on this basis. Why is this necessary? Why not just compare the projects' NPVs?

2. Calculate the NPV of some personal investment decision, such as buying a washing machine instead of using the laundromat, insulating the attic, or replacing the car. Ignore the extra convenience of the new asset. Just focus on the cash costs and benefits.

3. Discuss the following statement: "We don't want individual plant managers to get involved in the firm's tax position. So instead of telling them to discount after-tax cash flows at 10 percent, we just tell them to take the pretax cash flows and discount at 15 percent. With a 34 percent tax rate, 15 percent pretax generates approximately 10 percent after tax."

4. Discuss the following statement: "We like to do all our capital budgeting calculations in real terms. It saves making any forecasts of the inflation rate."

5. A project requires use of spare computer capacity. If the project is not terminated, the company will need to buy an additional disk at the end of year 2. If it is terminated, the disk will not be required until the end of year 4. If disks cost $10,000 and last 5 years, and if the opportunity cost of capital is 10 percent, what is the present value of the cost of this extra usage if the project is terminated at the end of year 2? What if the project continues indefinitely?   ⌐no additional cost!

6. Mrs. T. Potts, the treasurer of Ideal China, has a problem. The company has just ordered a new kiln for $400,000. Of this sum, $50,000 is described by the supplier as "installation cost." Mrs. Potts does not know whether the Internal Revenue Service will permit the company to treat this cost as a current expense or as a capital investment. In the latter case, the company could depreciate the $50,000 using the 5-year tax depreciation schedule. If the tax rate is 34 percent and the opportunity cost of capital is 5 percent, what is the present value of the tax shield in either case?

7. You own 500 acres of timberland, with young timber worth $40,000 if logged now. This represents 1000 cords of wood worth $40 per cord net of costs of cutting and hauling. A paper company has offered to purchase your tract for $140,000. Should you accept the offer? You have the following information:
(*a*)

Years	Yearly Growth Rate of Cords per Acre
1–4	16%
5–8	11
9–13	4
14 and subsequent years	1

(*b*) You expect price per cord to increase at 4 percent per year indefinitely.
(*c*) The cost of capital is 9 percent. Ignore taxes.

(d) The market value of your land would be $100 per acre if you cut and removed the timber this year. The value of cut-over land is also expected to grow at 4 percent per year indefinitely.

8. The Borstal Company has to choose between two machines which do the same job but have different lives. The two machines have the following costs:

Year	Machine A	Machine B
0	$40,000	$50,000
1	10,000	8000
2	10,000	8000
3	10,000 + replace	8000
4		8000 + replace

pg 107–108

These costs are expressed in real terms.

(a) Suppose you are Borstal's financial manager. If you had to buy one or the other machine, and rent it to the production manager for that machine's economic life, what annual rental payment would you have to charge? Assume a 6 percent real discount rate and ignore taxes.

(b) Which machine should Borstal buy?

(c) Usually the rental payments you derived in part (a) are just hypothetical—a way of calculating and interpreting equivalent annual cost. Suppose you actually do buy one of the machines and rent it to the production manager. How much would you actually have to charge in each future year if there is steady 8 percent per year inflation? (*Note:* The rental payments calculated in part (a) are real cash flows. You would have to mark those payments up to cover inflation.)

9. What biases or errors might be introduced by using nominal cash flows and discount rates to calculate equivalent annual costs? Think of situations like that described in problem 8 above.

√10. Borghia Pharmaceuticals has $1 million allocated for capital expenditures. Which of the following projects should the company accept to stay within the $1 million budget? How much does the budget limit cost the company in terms of its market value? The opportunity cost of capital for each project is 11 percent.

giving up 55,000 of mkt value by not taking)

Project	Investment, Thousands of Dollars	NPV, Thousands of Dollars	IRR, %
1	300	66	17.2
2	200	−4	10.7
3	250	43	16.6
4	100	14	12.1
5	100	7	11.8
6	350	63	18.0
7	400	48	13.5

11. The *Financial Analysts Journal* currently offers the following subscription options: 1 year, $48; 2 years, $84; 3 years, $108. These rates are expected to increase at the general rate of inflation. What is your optimal strategy assuming you intend to be a permanent subscriber? Make other assumptions as appropriate.

12. The president's executive jet is not fully utilized. You judge that its use by other officers would increase direct operating costs by only $20,000 a year and would save $100,000 a year in airline bills. On the other hand, you believe that with the increased use the company will need to replace the jet at the end of 3 years rather than 4. A new jet costs $1.1 million and (at its current low rate of use) has a life of 6 years. Assume that the company does not pay taxes and the opportunity cost of capital is 12 percent. Should you try to persuade the president to allow other officers to use the plane?

13. A project requires an initial investment of $100,000 and is expected to produce a cash inflow before tax of $26,000 per year for 5 years. Company A has substantial accumulated tax losses and is unlikely to pay taxes in the foreseeable future. Company B pays corporate taxes at a rate of 34 percent

TABLE 6-8
Cash flows and present value of Reliable Electric's proposed investment
(See problem 15. Annual cash flows in thousands of dollars)

	1988	1989	1990	1991–1998
1. Capital expenditure	−10,400			
2. Research and development	−2,000			
3. Working capital	−4,000			
4. Revenue		8,000	16,000	40,000
5. Operating costs		−4,000	−8,000	−20,000
6. Overhead		−800	−1,600	−4,000
7. Depreciation		−1,040	−1,040	−1,040
8. Interest		−2,160	−2,160	−2,160
9. Income	−2,000	0	3,200	12,800
10. Tax	0	0	408	4,352
11. Net cash flow	−16,400	0	2,792	8,448
Net present value = +14,374				

Notes:
1. *Capital expenditure:* $8 million for new machinery and $2.4 million for a warehouse extension. The full cost of the extension has been charged to this project, although only about half of the space is currently needed. SInce the new machinery will be housed in an existing factory building, no charge has been made for land and building.
2. *Research and development:* $1.82 million spent in 1987. This figure was corrected for 10 percent inflation from the time of expenditure to date. Thus 1.82 × 1.1 = $2 million.
3. *Working capital:* Initial investment in inventories.
4. *Revenue:* These figures assume sales of 2000 motors in 1989, 4000 in 1990, and 10,000 per year from 1991 through 1998. The initial unit price of $4000 is forecasted to remain constant in real terms.
5. *Operating costs:* These include all direct and indirect costs. Indirect costs (heat, light, power, fringe benefits, etc.) are assumed to be 200 percent of direct labor costs. Operating costs per unit are forecasted to remain constant in real terms at $2000.
6. *Overhead:* Marketing and administrative costs, assumed equal to 10 percent of revenue.
7. *Depreciation:* Straight-line for 10 years.
8. *Interest:* Charged on capital expenditure and working capital at Reliable's current borrowing rate of 15 percent.
9. *Income:* Revenue less the sum of research and development, operating costs, overhead, depreciation, and interest.
10. *Tax:* Thirty-four percent of income. However, income is negative in 1988. This loss is carried forward and deducted from taxable income in 1990.
11. *Net cash flow:* Assumed equal to income less tax.
12. *Net present value:* NPV of net cash flow at a 15 percent discount rate.

and can depreciate the investment for tax purposes using the 5-year tax depreciation schedule.

Suppose the opportunity cost of capital is 8 percent.

(a) Calculate project NPV for each company.

(b) What is the IRR of the after-tax cash flows for each company? What does comparison of the IRRs suggest is the effective corporate tax rate?

14. A widget manufacturer currently produces 200,000 units a year. It buys widget lids from an outside supplier at a price of $2 a lid. The plant manager believes that it would be cheaper to make these lids rather than buy them. Direct production costs are estimated to be only $1.50 a lid. The necessary machinery would cost $150,000. This investment could be written off for tax purposes using the 7-year tax depreciation schedule. The plant manager estimates that the operation would require additional working capital of $30,000 but argues that this sum can be ignored since it is recoverable at the end of the 10 years. If the company pays tax at a rate of 34 percent and the opportunity cost of capital is 15 percent, would you support the plant manager's proposal? State clearly any additional assumptions that you need to make.

15. Reliable Electric is considering a proposal to manufacture a new type of industrial electric motor which would replace most of its existing product line. A research breakthrough has given Reliable a 2-year lead on its competitors. The project proposal is summarized in Table 6-8.

(a) Read the notes to the table carefully. Which entries make sense? Which do not? Why or why not?

(b) What additional information would you need to contruct a version of Table 6-8 that makes sense?

(c) Construct such a table and recalculate NPV. Make additional assumptions as necessary.

PART TWO

RISK

7 Introduction to Risk, Return, and the Opportunity Cost of Capital

We have managed six chapters without directly addressing the problem of risk, but now the jig is up. We can no longer be satisfied with vague statements like: "The opportunity cost of capital depends on the risk of the project." We need to know how risk is defined and what the links are between risk and the opportunity cost of capital.

These topics will occupy the next three chapters. This chapter provides a general overview of the subject. We begin by looking at past returns from investments with different degrees of risk. We then discuss how risk is defined and measured, and finally we introduce an important theory linking risk and expected return.

If you are to use these ideas with any confidence, you need a deeper understanding of their foundations. Therefore, in Chapter 8, we shall review theory and evidence more carefully. You also need to be able to apply the ideas in practical situations, so in Chapter 9 we will describe in some detail how you can estimate the discount rate for an investment project.

7-1 SIXTY YEARS OF CAPITAL MARKET HISTORY IN ONE EASY LESSON

Financial analysts are blessed with an enormous quantity of data on security prices and returns. For example, the University of Chicago's Center for Research in Security Prices (CRSP) has developed a file of prices and dividends for each month since 1926 for every stock that has been listed on the New York Stock Exchange (NYSE). Other files give data for stocks that are traded on the American Stock Exchange and the over-the-counter market; data for bonds, for options, and so on. But this is supposed to be one easy lesson. We will, therefore, concentrate on a study by Ibbotson Associates which measures the historical performance of four portfolios of securities:

1. A portfolio of Treasury bills—that is, United States government debt securities maturing in less than 1 year
2. A portfolio of long-term United States government bonds
3. A portfolio of long-term corporate bonds[1]
4. Standard and Poor's Composite Index, which represents a portfolio of common stocks of 500 large firms

These portfolios offer different degrees of risk. Treasury bills are about as safe an investment as you can get. There is no risk of default and their short maturity means that the prices of Treasury bills are relatively stable. In fact, an investor who wishes to lend money for, say, 6 months can achieve a perfectly certain payoff by

---

[1] The two bond portfolios were revised each year in order to maintain a constant maturity.

TABLE 7-1

Average rates of return on common stocks, corporate bonds, government bonds, and Treasury bills, 1926–1985 (figures in percent per year)

Portfolio	Average Annual Rate of Return (Nominal)	Average Annual Rate of Return (Real)	Average Risk Premium (Extra Return versus Treasury Bills)
Common stocks	12.0	8.8	8.4
Corporate bonds	5.1	2.1	1.7
Government bonds	4.4	1.4	1.0
Treasury bills	3.5	.4	0

Source: R. G. Ibbotson and R. A. Sinquefield, *Stocks, Bonds, Bills and Inflation,* 1982, updated in *Stocks, Bonds, Bills, and Inflation: 1986 Yearbook,* Ibbotson Associates, Chicago, 1986.

purchasing a Treasury bill maturing in 6 months. However, the investor cannot lock in a *real* rate of return: There is still uncertainty about inflation.

By switching to long-term government bonds, the investor acquires an asset whose price fluctuates as interest rates vary. (Bond prices fall when interest rates rise, and rise when interest rates fall.) An investor who switches from government to corporate bonds accepts an additional *default* risk. An investor who shifts from corporate bonds to common stocks has a direct share in the risks of the enterprise.

Ibbotson Associates calculated a rate of return for each of these portfolios for each year from 1926 to 1985. This rate of return reflects both cash receipts— dividends or interest—and the capital gain or loss realized during the year. Averages of the 60 annual rates of return for each portfolio are shown in Table 7-1.[2] You can see that these returns coincide with our intuitive risk ranking. The safest investment, Treasury bills, also gave the lowest rate of return—3.5 percent a year in *nominal* terms and .4 percent in *real* terms. In other words, the average rate of inflation over this period was about 3 percent per year.

Long-term government bonds gave slightly higher returns than Treasury bills. Corporate bonds gave still higher returns. Common stocks were in a class by themselves. Investors who accepted the extra risk of common stocks received on average a premium of 8.4 percent a year over the return on Treasury bills.

You may ask why we look back 60 years to measure average rates of return. The reason is that annual rates of return for common stocks fluctuate so much that averages taken over short periods are meaningless. Our only hope of gaining insights from historical rates of return is to look at a very long period.[3]

Using Historical Evidence to Evaluate Today's Cost of Capital

Suppose there is a capital investment project which you *know*—don't ask how— has the same risk as Standard and Poor's Composite Index. We will say that it has the same degree of risk as the *market portfolio,* although this is speaking a bit loosely, because the index does not include all risky securities. What rate should you use to discount this project's forecasted cash flows?

Clearly you should use the currently expected rate of return on the market

[2] These are arithmetic averages. Ibbotson Associates simply added up the 60 annual returns and divided by 60. The arithmetic average return is higher than the compound annual return over the period. For example, suppose the market doubles in value one year and halves the next. Since you are back where you started, the compound annual return is zero. But the arithmetic average return is $(+100 - 50)/2 = +25$ percent. When estimating discount rates you are interested in the arithmetic average return.

[3] However, the average risk premiums are similar for the postwar period—the last 40 years or so.

portfolio: that is the return investors would forgo by investing in the proposed project. Let us call this market return r_m. One way to estimate r_m is to assume that the future will be like the past and that today investors expect to receive the same "normal" rates of return revealed by the averages shown in Table 7-1. In this case, you would set r_m at 12.0 percent, the average of past market returns.

Unfortunately, this is *not* the way to do it. The normal value of r_m is not likely to be stable over time. Remember that it is the sum of the risk-free interest rate r_f and a premium for risk. We know r_f varies over time. For example, as we edit this chapter in April 1987, Treasury bills yield 5.6 percent, more than 2.0 percentage points above the 3.5 average return of Ibbotson Associates' Treasury bill portfolio.

What if you were called upon to estimate r_m in 1987? Would you have said 12.0 percent? That would have squeezed the risk premium by 2.1 percentage points. A more sensible procedure is to take the current interest rate on Treasury bills plus 8.4 percent, the average *risk premium* shown in Table 7-1. With a rate of 5.6 percent for Treasury bills, that gives

$$r_m(1987) = r_f(1987) + \text{normal risk premium}$$

$$= .056 + .084 = .140, \text{ or } 14\%$$

The crucial assumption here is that there is a normal, stable risk premium on the market portfolio, so that the expected *future* risk premium can be measured by the average past risk premium. One could quarrel with this assumption, but at least it yields estimates of r_m that seem sensible.[4]

You now have a couple of benchmarks. You know the discount rate for safe projects and you know the rate for "average-risk" projects. But you *don't* know yet how to estimate discount rates for assets that do not fit these simple cases. In order to do that you have to learn (1) how to measure risk and (2) the relationship between risks borne and risk premiums demanded.

7-2   MEASURING PORTFOLIO RISK

Figure 7-1 shows the 60 annual rates of return calculated by Ibbotson Associates for Standard and Poor's Composite Index. The fluctuations in year-to-year returns are remarkably wide. The highest annual return was 54.0 percent in 1933—a partial rebound from the stock market crash of 1929–1932. On the other hand, there were losses exceeding 25 percent in 4 years, the worst being the -43.3 percent return in 1931.

Another way of presenting these data is by a histogram or frequency distribution. This is done in Figure 7-2, where the variability of year-to-year returns on the market portfolio shows up in the wide "spread" of outcomes.

Variance and Standard Deviation

The standard statistical measures of spread are **variance** and **standard deviation.** The variance of the market return is the expected squared deviation from the expected return. In other words,

$$\text{Variance } (\tilde{r}_m) = \text{the expected value of } (\tilde{r}_m - r_m)^2$$

[4] For example, estimates of r_m by this procedure are consistent with long-run average rates of return actually earned in the nonfinancial sector of the United States economy. See D. M. Holland and S. C. Myers, "Trends in Corporate Profitability and Capital Costs in the United States," in D. M. Holland (ed.), *Measuring Profitability and Capital Costs*, Lexington Books, Lexington, Mass., 1984.

Rate of return,
percent

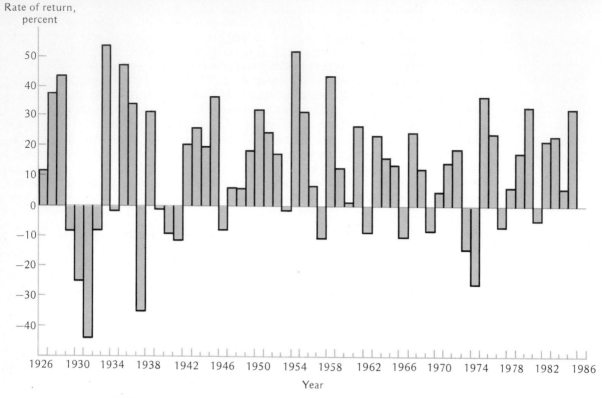

FIGURE 7-1
The stock market has been a profitable but extremely variable investment. [*Source:* R. G. Ibbotson and R. A. Sinquefield, *Stocks, Bonds, Bills and Inflation,* 1982, updated in Ibbotson Associates, *Stocks, Bonds, Bills, and Inflation: 1986 Yearbook,* Chicago, 1986.]

where $\tilde{r}_m$ is the actual return and r_m is the expected return.[5] The standard deviation is simply the square root of the variance:

$$\text{Standard deviation of } \tilde{r}_m = \sqrt{\text{variance } (\tilde{r}_m)}$$

Standard deviation is often denoted by σ and variance by σ^2.

Here is a very simple example showing how variance and standard deviation are calculated. Suppose you are offered the chance to play the following game. You start by investing \$100. Then two coins are flipped. For each head that comes up you get back your starting balance *plus* 20 percent, and for each tail that comes

---

[5] Here is a technical point. When variance is estimated from a sample of observed returns, we add up the squared deviations and divide by $N - 1$, where N is the number of observations. We divide by $N - 1$ rather than N to correct for what is called *the loss of a degree of freedom.* The formula is

$$\text{Variance } (\tilde{r}_m) = \frac{1}{N - 1} \sum_{t=1}^{N} (\tilde{r}_{mt} - r_m)^2$$

where

$\tilde{r}_{mt}$ = market return in period t

r_m = mean of the values of $\tilde{r}_{mt}$

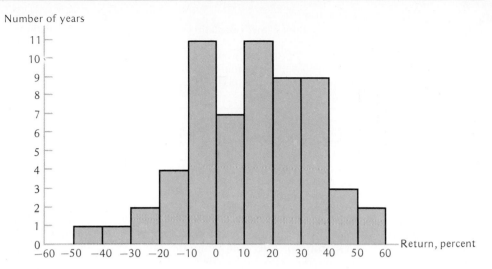

FIGURE 7-2
Histogram of the annual rates of return from the stock market in the United States, 1926–1985, showing the wide spread of returns from investment in common stocks. [*Source:* R. G. Ibbotson and R. A. Sinquefield, *Stocks, Bonds, Bills and Inflation,* 1982, updated in Ibbotson Associates, *Stocks, Bonds, Bills, and Inflation: 1986 Yearbook,* Chicago, 1986.]

up you get back your starting balance *less* 10 percent. Clearly there are four equally likely outcomes:

- Head + head: you gain 40 percent
- Head + tail: you gain 10 percent
- Tail + head: you gain 10 percent
- Tail + tail: you lose 20 percent

There is a chance of 1 in 4, or .25, that you will make 40 percent; a chance of 2 in 4, or .5, that you will make 10 percent; and a chance of 1 in 4, or .25, that you will lose 20 percent. The game's expected return is, therefore, a weighted average of the possible outcomes:

$$\text{Expected return} = (.25 \times 40) + (.5 \times 10) + (.25 \times -20) = +10\%$$

Table 7-2 shows that the variance of the percentage returns is 450. Standard deviation is the square root of 450 or 21. This figure is in the same units as the rate of return, so that we can say that the game's variability is 21 percent.

One way of defining uncertainty is to say that more things can happen than will happen. The risk of an asset can be completely expressed, as we first did for the coin-tossing game, by writing all possible outcomes and the probability of each one. For real assets this is cumbersome and often impossible. Therefore we use variance or standard deviation to summarize the spread of possible outcomes.[6]

These measures are natural indexes of risk.[7] If the outcome of the coin-tossing

[6] Which of the two we use is solely a matter of convenience. Since standard deviation is in the same units as the rate of return, it is generally more convenient to use standard deviation. However, when we are talking about the *proportion* of risk that is due to some factor, it is usually less confusing to work in terms of the variance.

[7] As we explain in Chapter 8, standard deviation and variance are the correct measures of risk if the returns on stocks are normally distributed.

TABLE 7-2
The coin-tossing game: calculating variance and standard deviation

(1) Percent Rate of Return $\tilde{r}$	(2) Deviation from Expected Return $\tilde{r} - r$	(3) Squared Deviation $(\tilde{r} - r)^2$	(4) Probability	(5) Probability $\times$ Squared Deviation
+40	+30	900	.25	225
+10	0	0	.5	0
−20	−30	900	.25	225

$$\text{Variance} = \text{expected value of } (\tilde{r} - r)^2 = \overline{450}$$
$$\text{Standard deviation} = \sqrt{\text{variance}} = \sqrt{450} = 21$$

game had been certain, the standard deviation would have been zero. The actual standard deviation is positive because we *don't* know what will happen.

Or think of a second game, the same as the first except that each head means a 35 percent gain and each tail means a 25 percent loss. Again, there are four equally likely outcomes:

- Head + head: you gain 70 percent
- Head + tail: you gain 10 percent
- Tail + head: you gain 10 percent
- Tail + tail   you lose 50 percent

For this game the expected return is 10 percent, the same as the first game's. But its standard deviation is double that of the first game, 42 versus 21 percent. By this measure the second game is twice as risky as the first.

Measuring Variability

In principle you could estimate the variability of any portfolio of stocks or bonds by the procedure that we have just described. You would identify the possible outcomes, assign a probability to each outcome, and grind through the calculations. But where do the probabilities come from? You can't look them up in the newspaper; newspapers seem to go out of their way to avoid definite statements about prospects for securities. We once saw an article headlined "Bond Prices Possibly Set to Move Sharply Either Way." Stockbrokers are much the same. Yours may respond to your query about possible market outcomes with a statement like this:

> *"The market currently appears to be undergoing a period of consolidation. For the intermediate term, we would take a constructive view provided economic recovery continues. The market could be up 20 percent a year from now, perhaps more if inflation moderates. On the other hand. . ."*

The Delphic oracle gave advice, but no probabilities.

Most financial analysts start by observing past variability. Of course, there is no risk in hindsight, but it is reasonable to assume that portfolios with histories of high variability also have the least predictable future performance.

The annual standard deviations and variances observed for our four portfolios over the 1926–1985 period were:[8]

---

[8] Ibbotson Associates, op. cit. Notice that when we are discussing the riskiness of *bonds* we must be careful to specify the time period. Long-term government bonds are risk-free to anyone who holds them to maturity.

Portfolio	Standard Deviation σ	Variance σ^2
Treasury bills	3.4	11.6
Long-term government bonds	8.2	67.2
Corporate bonds	8.3	68.9
Common stocks	21.2	449.4

You may find it interesting to compare the coin-tossing game and the stock market as alternative investments. The stock market generated an average annual return of 12.0 percent with a standard deviation of 21.2 percent. The game offers 10 and 21 percent, respectively—slightly lower return, and about the same variability. Your gambling friends may have come up with a crude representation of the stock market.

Of course there is no reason why the market's variability should stay the same over a full 60-year period. For example, it is less now than in the Great Depression of the 1930s, but for the most part the degree of year-to-year variability has been reasonably stable at least since the 1950s. Here are standard deviations of the returns on Ibbotson Associates' market portfolio for successive 10-year periods starting in 1926:

Period	Market Standard Deviation σ_m
1926–1935	33.5
1936–1945	23.9
1946–1955	18.1
1956–1965	16.5
1966–1975	19.7
1976–1985	14.2

How Diversification Reduces Risk

We can calculate our measures of variability just as well for individual securities as for portfolios of securities. Of course, 60-year averages are less interesting for specific companies than for the market portfolio—it is a rare company that faces the same business risks today as it did in 1926.

Table 7-3 presents estimated standard deviations for 10 well-known common stocks for a recent 5-year period.[9] The stocks in the left-hand column are "blue-chips," issued by big, established companies; those in the right-hand column are for smaller firms in the same industries.

Do the standard deviations given in Table 7-3 look "high" to you? They should. Remember that the market portfolio's standard deviation was 21.2 percent over the 1926–1985 period. Of our individual stocks only Exxon, Bristol Myers, and General Mills had lower standard deviations than the market portfolio. Most stocks

---

[9] These estimates are derived from *monthly* rates of return. Five annual observations are insufficient for estimating variability. We converted the monthly variance into an annual variance by multiplying by 12. That is, the variance of the monthly return is about one-twelfth of the annual variance. The longer you hold a security or portfolio, the more risk you have to bear.

This conversion assumes that successive monthly returns are statistically independent. This is, in fact, a good assumption, as we will show in Chapter 13.

Because variance is approximately proportional to the length of time interval over which a security or portfolio return is measured, standard deviation is about proportional to the square root of the interval.

TABLE 7-3
Standard deviations for selected common stocks, 1981–1986 (figures in percent per year)

Stock	Standard Deviation	Stock	Standard Deviation
AT&T	23.1	MCI Communications	48.4
Digital Equipment	35.4	Compaq Computer	57.3
Bristol Myers	20.3	Genentech	54.1
Exxon	17.7	Mesa Petroleum	50.9
General Mills	20.4	Holly Sugar	40.8

Source: Merrill Lynch, Pierce, Fenner & Smith, Inc., "Security Risk Evaluation," October 1986.

are substantially more variable than the market portfolio and only a handful are less variable.

This raises an important question: "The market portfolio is made up of individual stocks, so why doesn't its variability reflect the average variability of its components?" The answer is that *diversification reduces variability.*

Even a little diversification can provide a substantial reduction in variability. Suppose you form portfolios of differing size from a sample of stocks and then calculate the standard deviation of returns from each of these portfolios. You can see from Figure 7-3 that diversification can almost halve the variability of returns. But you can get most of this benefit with relatively few stocks: The improvement is slight when the number of securities is increased beyond, say, 15.

Diversification works because prices of different stocks do not move exactly together. Statisticians make the same point when they say that stock price changes are imperfectly correlated. Look, for example, at Figure 7-4. You can see that an investment in *either* Bristol Myers *or* Holly Sugar would have been very variable. But there were many occasions on which a decline in the value of one stock was canceled out by a rise in the price of the other.[10] Therefore there was an opportunity to reduce your risk by diversification. Figure 7-4 shows that if you had divided your funds evenly between the two stocks, the variability of your portfolio would have been substantially less than the average variability of the two stocks.

The risk that can potentially be eliminated by diversification is called **unique risk.**[12] Unique risk stems from the fact that many of the perils that surround an individual company are peculiar to that company and perhaps its immediate competitors. But there is also some risk that you can't avoid however much you diversify. This risk is generally known as **market risk.**[13] Market risk stems from the fact that there are other economy-wide perils which threaten all businesses. That is why stocks have a tendency to "move together." And that is why investors are exposed to "market uncertainties" no matter how many stocks they hold.

In Figure 7-5 we have divided the risk into its two parts—unique risk and market risk. If you only have a single stock, unique risk is very important, but once you have a portfolio of 10 or more stocks, diversification has done the bulk

[10] The two stocks' returns were essentially uncorrelated over this period.

[11] For the 3 years from 1983 to 1985, the standard deviations of Bristol Myers and Holly Sugar were 20.6 and 38.8 percent, respectively. The standard deviation of a portfolio half invested in each was about 22 percent.

[12] Unique risk is often called *unsystematic risk, residual risk, specific risk,* or *diversifiable risk.*

[13] Market risk is often called *systematic risk* or *undiversifiable risk.*

FIGURE 7-3
Diversification reduces risk
(standard deviation) rapidly at
first, then more slowly.

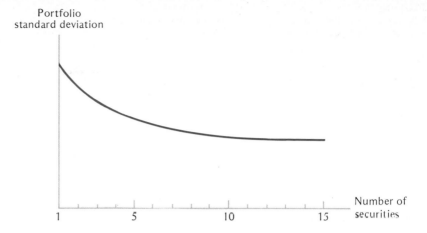

of its work. For a reasonably well-diversified portfolio, only market risk matters.
Therefore, the predominant source of uncertainty for a diversified investor is that
the market will rise or plummet, carrying the investor's portfolio with it.

7-3   HOW INDIVIDUAL SECURITIES AFFECT PORTFOLIO RISK

In the last section we presented some data on the variability of 10 individual
securities. Compaq Computer had the highest standard deviation and Exxon the

FIGURE 7-4
The variability of a
portfolio with equal
holdings in Bristol
Myers and Holly
Sugar would have
been less than the
average variability of
the individual stocks.

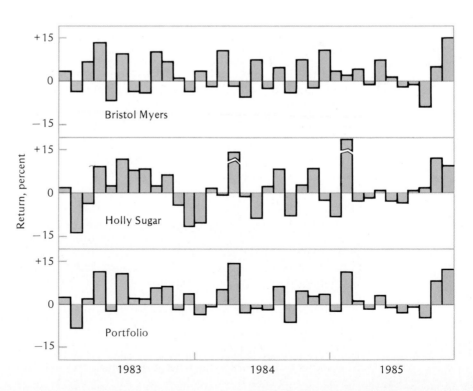

FIGURE 7-5
Diversification eliminates unique
risk. But there is some risk that
diversification *cannot* eliminate. This
is called *market risk.*

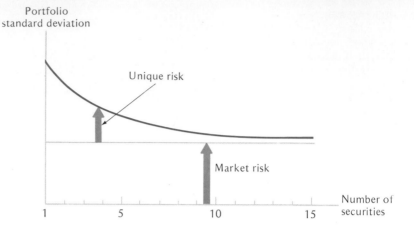

lowest. If you had held Compaq Computer on its own, the spread of possible
returns would have been three times greater than if you had held Exxon on its
own. But that is not a very interesting fact. Wise investors don't put all their eggs
into just one basket: They reduce their risk by diversification. They are therefore
interested in the effect that each stock will have on the risk of their portfolio. This
brings us to one of the principal themes of this chapter: **The risk of a well-
diversified portfolio depends on the market risk of the securities included in the portfolio.** Tattoo that statement on your forehead if you can't
remember it any other way. It is one of the most important ideas in this book.

**Market Risk
Is Measured
by Beta**

If you want to know the contribution of an individual security to the risk of a
well-diversified portfolio, it is no good thinking about how risky that security is if
held in isolation—you need to measure its *market* risk, and that boils down to
measuring how sensitive it is to market movements. This sensitivity of an investment's return to market movements is usually called its beta (β).

The steeply sloping line in Figure 7-6*a* shows how the outlook for stock A is
affected by market movements. Each extra 1 percent rise in the market results in
a further 2 percent rise in the price of stock A. Thus A has a beta of 2.0.

The gently sloping line in Figure 7-6*b* shows that the return on stock B is not
so sensitive to the market. Each extra 1 percent rise in the market produces only
an extra .5 percent rise in the price of B. Thus B has a beta of .5.[14]

A diversified portfolio of high-beta stocks is more risky than a diversified portfolio of low-beta stocks. For example, Figure 7-7 shows the performance of two
mutual funds—the Keystone S-1 Fund and the Keystone S-4 Fund. Both funds
were well-diversified and therefore had little unique risk. Yet the S-4 Fund was
about twice as variable as the S-1 Fund. The reason is that the stocks in the S-4
Fund were very sensitive to market changes: They had on average a beta of 1.4.
The standard deviation of a well-diversified portfolio of stocks with a beta of 1.4
would be 1.4 times that of the market portfolio. The stocks in the S-1 Fund were
less affected by market movements—they had on average a beta of .8. The standard

---

[14] Beta is measured by the slope of the lines in Figure 7-6*a* and *b*. For simplicity, we have drawn these
lines so that they pass through the intercept; i.e., both stocks are expected to give a zero return when
the market gives a zero return. This is not generally true, as we will explain in Chapter 8.

FIGURE 7-6a
The expected return on stock A changes by
2 percent for each extra 1 percent return on
the market. Its beta is therefore 2.0.

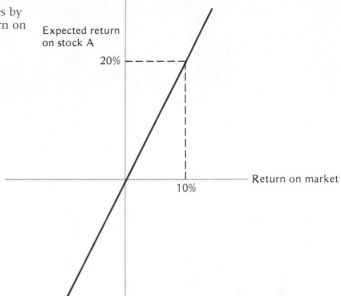

deviation of a well-diversified portfolio of stocks with a beta of .8 is .8 times the standard deviation of the market portfolio.[15] Of course on average stocks have a beta of 1.0. A well-diversified portfolio of such stocks would therefore have the same standard deviation as the market portfolio.

We repeat the general point: *The risk of a well-diversified portfolio depends on the*

---

[15] This statement is exactly true if the "well-diversified" portfolio is *perfectly* correlated with the market—that is, if the correlation coefficient between the portfolio and the market returns is +1.0. The statement is only approximately true for the Keystone funds because their returns were not perfectly correlated with the market. The correlation coefficients were .82 and .90 for the S-1 and S-4 funds, respectively.

FIGURE 7-6b
The expected return on stock B changes by
.5 percent for each extra 1 percent return on
the market. Its beta is therefore .5.

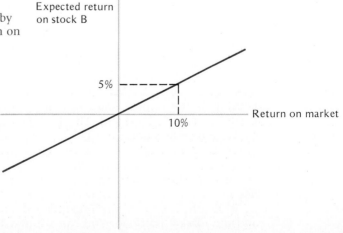

FIGURE 7-7
These two mutual funds are both well-diversified, but the S-4 Fund is about twice as variable as S-1. This is because it is more sensitive to market movements.

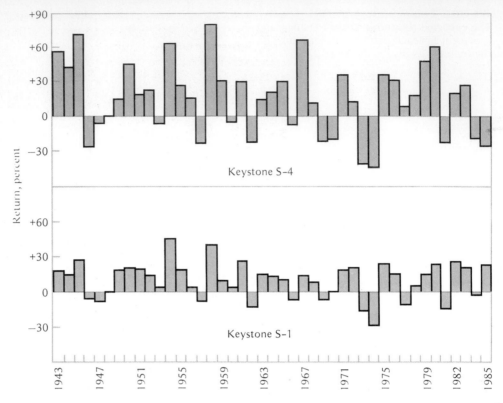

average beta of the securities included in the portfolio. Thus a security's contribution to portfolio risk depends on the security's beta.

The practical problems of estimating and using betas are taken up in Chapter 9. However, you may find it interesting to look at Table 7-4, which shows how past market movements have affected the 10 stocks that we discussed earlier. General Mills had the lowest beta: Its stock price was about half as sensitive as the average stock to market movements. Genentech was at the other extreme: Its price was almost twice as sensitive as the average stock to market movements.

7-4   RELATIONSHIP BETWEEN RISK AND RETURN

At the beginning of this chapter, we looked at the returns on selected investments. The least risky investment was U.S. Treasury bills. Since the return on Treasury bills is fixed, it is unaffected by what happens to the market. Thus the beta of Treasury bills is zero. The *most* risky investment that we considered was the market portfolio of common stocks. This has average market risk: Its beta is 1.0.

Wise investors don't run risks just for fun. They are playing with real money. Therefore they require a higher return from the market portfolio than from Treasury bills. The difference between the return on the market and the interest rate is termed the *market risk premium.* Over the past 60 years the average market risk premium $(r_m - r_f)$ has been 8.4 percent per year.

In Figure 7-8 we have plotted the risk and expected return from Treasury bills and the market portfolio. You can see that Treasury bills have a beta of zero and

TABLE 7-4
Betas for selected common stocks, 1981–1986

Stock	Beta	Stock	Beta
AT&T	.81	MCI Communications	1.52
Digital Equipment	1.21	Compaq Computer	1.73
Bristol Myers	.91	Genentech	1.95
Exxon	.71	Mesa Petroleum	.68
General Mills	.57	Holly Sugar	.62

Source: Merrill Lynch, Pierce, Fenner & Smith, Inc., "Security Risk Evaluation," October 1986.

a risk premium of zero.[16] The market portfolio has a beta of 1.0 and an expected risk premium of $r_m - r_f$. This gives us two benchmarks for the expected risk premium. But what is the expected risk premium when beta is not zero or one?

In the mid-1960s three economists—Jack Treynor, William Sharpe, and John Lintner—produced an answer to this question.[17] Their answer is known as the *capital asset pricing model.* The model's message is both startling and simple. In a competitive market, the expected risk premium varies in direct proportion to beta. This means that in Figure 7-8, all investments must plot along the sloping line, known as the *security market line.* The expected risk premium on an investment with a beta of .5 is, therefore, *half* the expected risk premium on the market; and the expected risk premium on an investment with a beta of 2.0 is *twice* the expected risk premium on the market. We can write this relationship as:

[16] The return on Treasury bills is fixed regardless of how much the market rises or falls. Therefore, the bills have a beta of zero. Remember also that the risk premium is the difference between the investment's expected return and the risk-free rate. For Treasury bills, the difference is zero.

[17] See W. F. Sharpe, "Capital Asset Prices: A Theory of Market Equilibrium Under Conditions of Risk," *Journal of Finance* **19:** 425–442 (September 1964); J. Lintner, "The Valuation of Risk Assets and the Selection of Risky Investments in Stock Portfolios and Capital Budgets," *Review of Economics and Statistics* **47:** 13–37 (February 1965); Treynor's article has not been published.

FIGURE 7-8
The capital asset pricing model states that the expected risk premium on each investment is proportional to its beta. This means that each investment should lie on the sloping security market line connecting Treasury bills and the market portfolio.

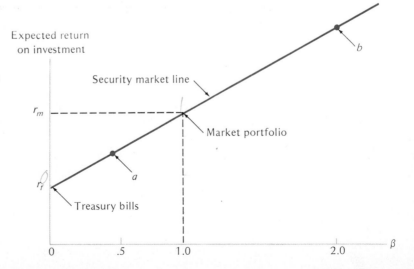

Expected risk premium on stock = beta × expected risk premium on market

$$r - r_f = \beta(r_m - r_f)$$

We have given you a bald statement of the capital asset pricing model. We will now give you a glimpse of where that formula came from and how it can be used to estimate the cost of capital. Then in the next two chapters we will examine both topics in more detail.

One investment strategy is to (1) decide what proportion of your money you are prepared to put at risk, and then (2) invest this sum in the market portfolio. If you have any money left over, you can *lend* it at a fixed rate of interest; if you don't have enough money, you can *borrow* the balance at a fixed rate of interest.

For example, suppose that you invest 50 percent of your money in the market portfolio and lend the balance. Then the beta of your investment would be midway between the beta of the market (β_m = 1.0) and the beta of the loan (β_f = .0):

$$\begin{pmatrix} \text{Beta of} \\ \text{investment} \end{pmatrix} = \begin{pmatrix} \text{proportion} \\ \text{in market} \end{pmatrix} \times \begin{pmatrix} \text{beta of} \\ \text{market} \end{pmatrix} + \begin{pmatrix} \text{proportion} \\ \text{in loan} \end{pmatrix} \times \begin{pmatrix} \text{beta of} \\ \text{loan} \end{pmatrix}$$

$$\beta = (.5 \times 1.0) + (.5 \times 0)$$

$$= .5$$

The expected risk premium on your investment would also be midway between the expected risk premium on the market ($r_m - r_f$) and the expected risk premium on the loan (zero):

$$\begin{pmatrix} \text{Expected risk premium} \\ \text{on investment} \end{pmatrix} = \begin{pmatrix} \text{proportion} \\ \text{in} \\ \text{market} \end{pmatrix} \times \begin{pmatrix} \text{expected} \\ \text{risk} \\ \text{premium} \\ \text{on market} \end{pmatrix}$$

$$+ \begin{pmatrix} \text{proportion} \\ \text{in loan} \end{pmatrix} \times \begin{pmatrix} \text{expected} \\ \text{risk} \\ \text{premium} \\ \text{on loan} \end{pmatrix}$$

$$r - r_f = (.5 \times (r_m - r_f)) + (.5 \times 0)$$

$$= .5(r_m - r_f)$$

In Figure 7-8, we have marked this investment strategy with the letter *a*.

If you are more audacious, you might choose to invest all your own money and an equal amount of borrowed money in the market portfolio. In this case, the beta of your investment would be twice the beta of the market.[18]

$$\begin{pmatrix} \text{Beta of} \\ \text{investment} \end{pmatrix} = \begin{pmatrix} \text{proportion} \\ \text{in market} \end{pmatrix} \times \begin{pmatrix} \text{beta of} \\ \text{market} \end{pmatrix} + \begin{pmatrix} \text{proportion} \\ \text{in loan} \end{pmatrix} \times \begin{pmatrix} \text{beta of} \\ \text{loan} \end{pmatrix}$$

$$\beta = (2.0 \times 1.0) + (-1.0 \times 0)$$

$$= 2.0$$

[18] Notice that the "proportion in loan" is negative. Borrowing money is equivalent to lending a negative amount.

The expected risk premium on your investment would also be twice the expected risk premium on the market:

$$\begin{array}{rcl} \text{Expected risk premium} \\ \text{on investment} \end{array} = \left(\begin{array}{c} \text{proportion} \\ \text{in} \\ \text{market} \end{array} \times \begin{array}{c} \text{expected} \\ \text{risk} \\ \text{premium} \\ \text{on market} \end{array} \right)$$

$$+ \left(\begin{array}{c} \text{proportion} \\ \text{in loan} \end{array} \times \begin{array}{c} \text{expected} \\ \text{risk} \\ \text{premium} \\ \text{on loan} \end{array} \right)$$

$$r - r_f = [2.0 \times (r_m - r_f)] + (-1.0 \times 0)$$

$$= 2.0(r_m - r_f)$$

In Figure 7-8, we have marked this investment strategy with the letter b.

These two examples illustrate that you can obtain *any* position along the security market line simply by investing a proportion of your money in the market portfolio and borrowing or lending the balance. The portfolios along the line set a standard for your other investments: You will be willing to hold them only if they offer equally good prospects.[19] Thus the required risk premium for any investment is given by the security market line:

$$r - r_f = \beta(r_m - r_f)$$

Using the Capital Asset Pricing Model to Calculate Expected Returns

In Chapter 4, we explained that the price of a common stock is equal to the discounted value of the expected dividend and end-of-period price:

$$P_0 = \frac{DIV_1 + P_1}{1 + r}$$

We defined the discount rate r as the expected return offered by other equally risky stocks. The capital asset pricing model allows us to be more specific about this discount rate.

In order to figure out the returns that investors are expecting from particular stocks, we need three numbers — r_f, $(r_m - r_f)$, and β. In April 1987, the interest rate on Treasury bills (r_f) was 5.6 percent. From past evidence, we would judge that $r_m - r_f$ is about 8.4 percent. Finally, in Table 7-4, we gave you estimates of the betas of 10 stocks. Table 7-5 puts these numbers together to give an estimate of the expected return from each stock. Let's take Exxon as an example:

$$\text{Expected rate of return} = r = r_f + \beta(r_m - r_f)$$

$$= .056 + .71(.084)$$

$$= .116, \text{ or } 11.6 \text{ percent}$$

You can also use the capital asset pricing model to find the discount rate for a new capital investment. For example, suppose that you are analyzing a proposal

---

[19] Suppose you could find a stock with a negative beta. Its expected risk premium would be negative; i.e., it would offer a *lower* expected return than Treasury bills. There is a good reason for this. A stock with a negative beta would be very desirable. If you invested in both the stock and the market portfolio in the proper proportions, you could reduce risk dramatically.

TABLE 7-5

These estimates of the returns *expected* by investors in early 1987 were based on the capital asset pricing model. We assumed that the interest rate $r_f = 5.6$ percent and the expected market risk premium $r_m - r_f = 8.4$ percent

Stock	Beta (β)	Expected Return $r_f + \beta(r_m - r_f)$
AT&T	.81	12.4
Digital Equipment	1.21	15.8
Bristol Myers	.91	13.2
Exxon	.71	11.6
General Mills	.57	10.4
MCI Communications	1.52	18.4
Compaq Computer	1.73	20.1
Genentech	1.95	22.0
Mesa Petroleum	.68	11.3
Holly Sugar	.62	10.8

by Digital Equipment Corporation to expand its capacity. At what rate should you discount the forecasted cash flows? According to Table 7-5 investors are looking for a return of 15.8 percent from businesses with the risk of Digital Equipment. So the cost of capital for a further investment in the same business is 15.8 percent.[20]

In practice, choosing a discount rate is seldom so easy. (After all, you can't expect to be paid a fat salary just for plugging numbers into a formula.) For example, you must learn how to adjust for the extra risk caused by company borrowing and how to estimate the discount rate for projects that do not have the same risk as the company's existing business. There are also tax issues. But these refinements can wait until later.[21]

7-5 DIVERSIFICATION AND VALUE ADDITIVITY

We have seen that diversification reduces risk and, therefore, makes sense for individual investors. But does it also make sense for the firm? Is a diversified firm more attractive to investors than an undiversified one? If it is, we have an *extremely* disturbing result. If diversification is an appropriate corporate objective, the financial manager faces a problem of horrendous complexity, for each project would need to be analyzed as a potential addition to the firm's portfolio of projects. The value of the diversified package would be greater than the sum of the parts. Present values would no longer add.

Diversification is undoubtedly a good thing, but that does not mean that firms

---

[20] Remember that instead of investing in plant and machinery, the firm could return the money to the shareholder. The opportunity cost of investing is the return that shareholders could expect to earn by buying financial assets. This expected return depends on the market risk of the assets, not on their unique risk.

[21] Tax issues arise because a corporation must pay tax on income from an investment in Treasury bills or other interest-paying securities. It turns out that the correct discount rate for risk-free investments is the *after-tax* Treasury rate. We come back to this point in Chapters 19 and 26.

Various other points on the practical use of betas and the capital asset pricing model are covered in Chapter 9.

should practice it. If investors were *not* able to hold a large number of securities, then they might want firms to diversify for them. But investors *can* diversify.[22] In many ways they can do so more easily than firms. Individuals can invest in the steel industry this week and pull out the next week. A firm cannot do that. To be sure, the individual would have to pay brokerage fees on the purchase and sale of steel company shares, but think of the time and expense for a firm to acquire a steel company or to start up a new steel-making operation.

You can probably see where we are heading. If investors can diversify on their own account, they will not pay any *extra* for firms that diversify. And if they have a sufficiently wide choice of securities, they will not pay any *less* because they are unable to invest separately in each factory. Therefore, in countries like the United States, which have large and competitive capital markets, diversification does not add to a firm's value or subtract from it. The total value is the sum of its parts.

This conclusion is important for corporate finance, because it justifies adding present values. The concept of value additivity is so important that we will give a formal definition of it. If the capital market establishes a value PV(A) for asset A and PV(B) for B, the market value of a firm that holds only these two assets is:

$$PV(AB) = PV(A) + PV(B)$$

A three-asset firm combining assets A, B, and C would be worth PV(ABC) = PV(A) + PV(B) + PV(C), and so on for any number of assets.

We have relied on intuitive arguments for value additivity. But the concept is a general one that can be proved formally by several different routes.[23] The concept of value additivity seems to be widely accepted, for thousands of managers add thousands of present values daily, usually without thinking about it.

*Value Additivity and the Capital Asset Pricing Model—An Example

The capital asset pricing model states that investors do not demand extra expected return just to cover a firm's *unique* risk. The only risk that investors care about is the risk that they *cannot* diversify away—that is, the *market* risk. But the firm can't diversify away market risk. Therefore, diversification by the firm has no impact on the opportunity cost of capital.

Here's an example which illustrates how value additivity works in the context of betas and the capital asset pricing model. Suppose we have two projects, A and B. Each offers $100 cash flow at year 1, and zero cash flow in all subsequent years. The beta for project A is $\beta_A = 1.0$. The beta for project B is $\beta_B = 2.0$. We will assume a risk-free rate of $r_f = 10$ percent and a market risk premium of $r_m - r_f = 8$ percent. The capital asset pricing model gives the following opportunity costs of capital for the two projects:

$$r = r_f + \beta(r_m - r_f)$$

$$r_A = .10 + 1.0(.08) = .18$$

$$r_B = .10 + 2.0(.08) = .26$$

[22] One of the simplest ways for an individual to diversify is to buy shares in a mutual fund which holds a diversified portfolio.

[23] You may wish to refer to the appendix to Chapter 33, which discusses diversification and value additivity in the context of mergers.

The present values of the two projects are therefore:

$$PV_A = \frac{100}{1 + r_A} = \frac{100}{1.18} = 84.75$$

$$PV_B = \frac{100}{1 + r_B} = \frac{100}{1.26} = 79.37$$

We can also consider a project AB formed by combining A and B. Here is what we know so far:

Project	Cash Flow	Beta	Opportunity Cost of Capital	Present Value
A	100	1.0	.18	84.75
B	100	2.0	.26	79.37
AB	200	?	?	?

Value additivity tells us that PV(AB) = PV(A) + PV(B). That implies

$$PV(AB) = 84.75 + 79.37 = 164.12$$

We'll now show that the capital asset pricing model gives exactly that answer.

First, calculate the beta of project AB. It's a weighted average of β_A and β_B, with weights determined by the present values of the two projects.[24]

$$\beta_{AB} = \beta_A \frac{PV(A)}{PV(AB)} + \beta_B \frac{PV(B)}{PV(AB)}$$

$$= 1.0 \frac{84.75}{164.12} + 2.0 \frac{79.37}{164.12}$$

$$= 1.484$$

Calculate the opportunity cost of capital for AB.

$$r_{AB} = r_f + \beta_{AB}(r_m - r_f)$$

$$= .10 + 1.484(.08)$$

$$= .2187$$

Calculate the present value of AB:

$$PV_{AB} = \frac{200}{1 + r_{AB}} = \frac{200}{1.2187} = 164.12$$

Thus everything works out. If we had started with beta (1.484) for a project AB, without knowing the present values of A and B as separate assets, we would have valued AB correctly.

Of course, in practice, you aren't handed any of the betas. You have to estimate them. We will discuss how betas are estimated in Chapter 9.

---

[24] This numerical example uses a beta calculated to three decimal places and an opportunity cost of capital calculated to four places. We do this so that rounding errors do not fog over the example's conceptual point. In real life, you will be lucky to pin down betas and costs of capital to two decimal places.

7-6 SUMMARY

Our review of capital market history showed that the returns received by investors have varied according to the risks they have borne. At one extreme, very safe securities like U.S. Treasury bills have provided an average return over half a century of only 3.5 percent a year. The riskiest securities that we looked at were common stocks. They have provided an average return of 12.0 percent, a premium of more than 8 percent over the safe rate of interest.

This gives us two benchmarks for the opportunity cost of capital. If we are evaluating a safe project, we discount at the current risk-free rate of interest. If we are evaluating a project of average risk, we discount at the expected return on the average common stock, which historical evidence suggests is between 8 and 9 percent above the risk-free rate. That still leaves us with a lot of assets that don't fit these simple cases. Before we can deal with them, we need to learn how to measure risk.

Risk is best judged in a portfolio context. Most investors do not put all their eggs in one basket: They diversify. Thus the effective risk of any security cannot be judged by an examination of that security alone. Part of the uncertainty about the security's return is diversified away when the security is grouped with others in a portfolio.

Risk in investment means that future returns are unpredictable. This spread of possible outcomes is usually measured by standard deviation. The standard deviation of the *market portfolio*—generally represented by the Standard and Poor's Composite Index—is around 20 percent a year.

Most individual stocks have higher standard deviations than this, but much of their variability represents *unique* risk that can be eliminated through diversification. Diversification cannot eliminate *market* risk. Diversified portfolios are exposed to variations in the general level of the market.

A security's contribution to the risk of a well-diversified portfolio depends on the security's reaction to a general market decline. This sensitivity to market movements is known as *beta* (β). Beta measures the amount that investors expect the stock price to change for each additional 1 percent change in the market. The average beta of all stocks is 1.0. A stock with a beta greater than 1 is unusually sensitive to market movements. A stock with a beta below 1 is unusually insensitive to market movements. The standard deviation of a well-diversified portfolio is proportional to its beta. Thus a diversified portfolio invested in stocks with a beta of 2.0 will have twice the risk of a diversified portfolio invested in stocks with a beta of 1.0.

We looked at the relationship between risk and return in a well-functioning capital market, and presented a model of risk and return known as the *capital asset pricing model*. Its message is simple: If investors can invest some fraction of their money in the market portfolio and borrow or lend the balance, they can obtain any point on the security market line, as shown in Figure 7-8. In that case, an investor should be willing to hold a security with a particular beta only if it offers an equally good return. Therefore, all securities should plot along this line. Another way to say the same thing is that the expected risk premium should increase in proportion to the security's beta:

$$\text{Expected risk premium} = \text{beta} \times (\text{expected market risk premium})$$

$$r - r_f = \beta(r_m - r_f)$$

One theme of this chapter is that diversification is a good thing *for the investor.* This does not imply that *firms* should diversify. Corporate diversification is redundant if investors can diversify on their own account, though it does not hurt if it does not noticeably reduce the range of choices open to investors. Since diversification does not affect the firm's value, present values add even when risk is explicitly considered. This property of well-functioning capital markets is called *value additivity.*

FURTHER READING

There are two valuable records of the performance of United States securities since 1926.

Ibbotson Associates: *Stocks, Bonds, Bills and Inflation: 1986 Yearbook,* Ibbotson Associates, Chicago, 1985.

L. Fisher and J. H. Lorie: *A Half Century of Returns on Stocks and Bonds,* University of Chicago, Graduate School of Business, Chicago, 1977.

Merton discusses the problems encountered in measuring average returns from historical data:

R. C. Merton, "On Estimating the Expected Return on the Market: An Exploratory Investigation," *Journal of Financial Economics,* **8:** 323–361 (December 1980).

Most investment texts devote a chapter or two to the distinction between market and unique risk and to the effect of diversification on risk. See, for example:

J. H. Lorie, P. Dodd and M. Hamilton Kimpton: *The Stock Market: Theories and Evidence,* 2d ed., Richard D. Irwin, Inc., Homewood, Ill., 1985.

W. F. Sharpe: *Investments,* 3d ed., Prentice-Hall, Inc., Englewood Cliffs, N.J., 1985.

An important analysis of the degree to which stocks move together is:

B. F. King, "Market and Industry Factors in Stock Price Behavior," *Journal of Business,* Security Prices: A Supplement, **39:** 179–190 (January 1966).

There have been several studies of the way that standard deviation is reduced by diversification. Our diagrams are based on:

W. H. Wagner and S. C. Lau, "The Effect of Diversification on Risk," *Financial Analysts Journal,* **27:** 48–53 (November–December 1971).

Formal proofs of the value additivity principle can be found in:

S. C. Myers, "Procedures for Capital Budgeting under Uncertainty," *Industrial Management Review,* **9:** 1–20 (Spring 1968).

L. D. Schall, "Asset Valuation, Firm Investment and Firm Diversification," *Journal of Business,* **45:** 11–28 (January 1972).

QUIZ

1. (*a*) What was the average annual return on United States common stocks from 1926–1985 (approximately)?
    (*b*) What was the average difference between this return and the return on Treasury bills?
    (*c*) What was the average return on Treasury bills in real terms?
    (*d*) What was the standard deviation of annual returns on the market index?
    (*e*) Was this market standard deviation more or less than that on most individual stocks?

2. Fill in the missing words:

Risk is usually measured by the variance of returns or the _____ , which is simply the square root of the variance. As long as the stock price changes are not perfectly _____ , the risk of a diversified portfolio is _____ than the average risk of the individual stocks.

The risk that can be eliminated by diversification is known as _____ risk. But diversification cannot remove all risk; the risk that it cannot eliminate is known as _____ risk.

The theory linking risk and expected return is known as the _____ _____ _____ model. It states that all stocks lie along the _____ line. A risk-free stock has a beta of _____ and, therefore, its expected return is equal to the _____ . A stock that contributes an average amount of risk has a beta of _____ and, therefore, its expected return is equal to the expected return on the _____ .

3. True or false?

(a) Investors prefer diversified companies because they are less risky.

(b) The capital asset pricing model implies that, if you could find an investment with a negative beta, its expected return would be less than the interest rate.

(c) The expected return on an investment with a beta of 2.0 is twice as high as the expected return on the market.

(d) If stocks were perfectly positively correlated, diversification would not reduce risk.

(e) The contribution of a stock to the risk of a well-diversified portfolio depends on its market risk.

(f) If a stock lies below the security market line, it is undervalued.

(g) A well-diversified portfolio with a beta of 2.0 is twice as risky as the market portfolio.

(h) An undiversified portfolio with a beta of 2.0 is less than twice as risky as the market portfolio.

4. What is the beta of each of the stocks shown in Table 7-6?

5. The standard deviation of the market return is about 20 percent.

(a) What is the standard deviation of returns on a well-diversified portfolio with a beta of 1.5?

(b) What is the standard deviation of returns on a well-diversified portfolio with a beta of 0?

(c) A well-diversified portfolio has a standard deviation of 15 percent. What is its beta?

TABLE 7-6
See Quiz, question 4

Stock	Expected Stock Return if Market Return is −10%	Expected Stock Return if Market Return Is +10%
A	0	+20
B	−20	+20
C	−30	0
D	+15	+15
E	+10	−10

(*d*) A poorly diversified portfolio has a standard deviation of 20 percent. What can you say about its beta?

6. A portfolio contains equal investments in 10 stocks. Five have a beta of 1.2; the remainder have a beta of 1.4. The portfolio beta is which of the following?
   (*a*) 1.3
   (*b*) Greater than 1.3 because the portfolio is not completely diversified
   (*c*) Less than 1.3 because diversification reduces beta

7. During the past 5 years, the stock of General American Fish (GAF) has moved as follows:

Year	1	2	3	4	5
Price change, %	+20	−10	−30	+5	+15

   (*a*) Calculate the variance and standard deviation of the returns of GAF.
   (*b*) Is this standard deviation higher or lower than that of the market?

8. Suppose that the Treasury bill rate is 4 percent and the expected return on the market is 10 percent. Using the information in Table 7-4:
   (*a*) Calculate the expected return from Compaq Computer.
   (*b*) Find the highest expected return that is offered by one of these stocks.
   (*c*) Find the lowest expected return that is offered by one of these stocks.
   (*d*) Would Digital Equipment offer a higher or lower expected return if the interest rate were 6 percent rather than 4 percent? Assume the expected market return stays at 10 percent.
   (*e*) Would General Mills offer a higher or lower expected return if the interest rate were 6 percent?

9. The capital asset pricing model states that a stock has the same market risk and expected return as:
   (*a*) A portfolio with proportion β invested in Treasury bills and $1 - \beta$ in the market
   (*b*) A portfolio with β invested in the market and $1 - \beta$ in Treasury bills
   (*c*) A portfolio evenly divided between the market and Treasury bills
   Which is the correct answer?

10. Here is another question on the capital asset pricing model. Stock A has a beta of .5 and investors expect it to return 7 percent. Stock B has a beta of 1.5 and investors expect it to return 15 percent. What is the expected return on the market and the risk premium on the market?

QUESTIONS AND PROBLEMS

1. The Treasury bill rate is 4 percent and the expected return on the market portfolio is 12 percent. On the basis of the capital asset pricing model:
   (*a*) Draw a graph similar to Figure 7-8 showing how expected return varies with beta.
   (*b*) What is the risk premium on the market?
   (*c*) What is the required return on an investment with a β of 1.5?
   (*d*) If an investment with a β of .8 offers an expected return of 9.8 percent, does it have a positive NPV?
   (*e*) If the market expects a return of 11.2 percent from stock X, what is its beta?

2. Estimate the returns expected by investors *today* for the 10 stocks in Table 7-4. Plot the expected returns against beta as in Figure 7-8.

3. A company is deciding whether to make a stock issue to raise money for an investment project which has the same risk as the market and an expected return of 20 percent. If the risk-free rate is 10 percent and the expected return on the market is 15 percent, the company should go ahead
   (a) Unless the company's beta is greater than 2.0
   (b) Unless the company's beta is less than 2.0
   (c) Whatever the company's beta
   Which answer is correct? Say briefly why.

4. The stock of United Merchants has a beta of 1.0 and very high unique risk. If the expected return on the market is 20 percent, the expected return on United will be
   (a) 10 percent if the interest rate is 10 percent
   (b) 20 percent
   (c) More than 20 percent because of the high unique risk
   (d) Indeterminate unless you also know the interest rate
   Which is the right answer? Say *briefly* why.

5. The expected return on a stock is frequently written as $r = \alpha + \beta r_m$, where r_m is the expected return on the market. The capital asset pricing model says that in equilibrium
   (a) $\alpha = 0$
   (b) $\alpha = r_f$ (the risk-free rate of interest)
   (c) $\alpha = (1 - \beta)r_f$
   (d) $\alpha = (1 - r_f)\beta$
   Which is correct?

6. Estimate the expected return from the stock market in the United States over the next year. Subtract the current dividend yield to give you a rough estimate of the expected capital appreciation.

7. "The job of financial managers is to select a portfolio of projects offering the maximum return for the minimum risk. In principle, this means that they have to think about how the returns on each pair of projects are correlated." Explain why this is or is not true.

8 More about the Relationship between Risk and Return

In Chapter 7, we began to come to grips with the relationship between risk and expected return. Here is the story so far.

What makes an investment in the stock market risky is that there is a spread of possible outcomes. The usual measure of this spread is the standard deviation or variance.

The risk of any stock can be broken into two parts. There is the *unique risk* that is peculiar to that stock, and there is the *market risk* that stems from market-wide variations. Investors can eliminate unique risk by holding a well-diversified portfolio, but they cannot eliminate market risk. *All* the risk of a fully diversified portfolio is market risk.

A stock's contribution to the risk of a fully diversified portfolio depends on its sensitivity to market changes. This sensitivity is generally known as *beta*. A security with a beta of 1.0 has average market risk—a well-diversified portfolio of such securities has the same standard deviation as the market index. A security with a beta of .5 has below-average market risk—a well-diversified portfolio of these securities tends to move half as far as the market moves and has half the market's standard deviation.

Since investors can diversify away unique risk, they will not demand a higher return from stocks that have above-average unique risk. But they *will* demand higher return from stocks with above-average *market* risk. The capital asset pricing model states that the expected risk premium from any investment should vary in direct proportion to its market risk.

In this chapter, we shall see how this relationship between risk and return stems from the efforts of each investor to choose a sensible portfolio.

8-1 HARRY MARKOWITZ AND THE BIRTH OF PORTFOLIO THEORY

Most of the ideas in Chapter 7 date back to an article written in 1952 by Harry Markowitz.[1] Markowitz drew attention to the common practice of portfolio diversification and showed exactly how an investor can reduce the standard deviation of portfolio returns by choosing stocks that do not move exactly together. But Markowitz did not stop there—he went on to work out the basic principles of portfolio construction. These principles are the foundation for most of what we can say about the relationship between risk and return.

Let us begin with Figure 8-1, which shows a histogram of the daily returns on General Foods stock. On this histogram we have superimposed a bell-shaped **normal distribution**. Strikingly similar, are they not? And we have not cheated in

---

[1] H. M. Markowitz, "Portfolio Selection," *Journal of Finance*, **7:** 77–91 (March 1952).

FIGURE 8-1
Daily price changes
for General Foods
from 1983 to 1985
are approximately
normally distributed.

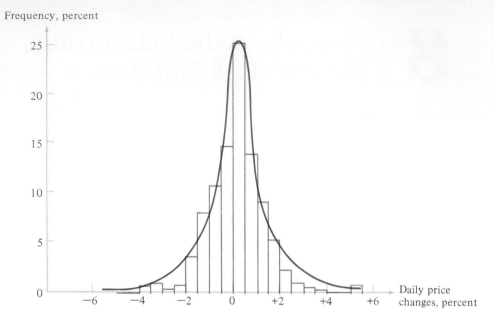

our choice of stock. When measured over short intervals, the past rates of return on almost any stock conform closely to a normal distribution.[2]

One important feature of a normal distribution is that it can be completely defined by two numbers. One is the average or "expected" return; the other is the variance or standard deviation. Now you can see why in Chapter 7 we discussed the calculation of expected return and standard deviation. They are not just arbitrary measures: if returns are normally distributed, they are the *only* two measures that an investor need consider.

Figure 8-2 pictures the distribution of possible returns from two investments. Both offer an expected return of 10 percent, but A has much the wider spread of possible outcomes. Its standard deviation is 30 percent; the standard deviation of B is 15 percent. Most investors dislike uncertainty and would therefore prefer B to A.

Figure 8-3 pictures the distribution of returns from two other investments. This time both have the *same* standard deviation but the expected return is 20 percent from stock C and only 10 percent from stock D. Most investors like high expected returns and would therefore prefer C to D.

**Combining
Stocks into
Portfolios**

Suppose that you are wondering whether to invest in the shares of Boeing or Eastman Kodak. You decide that Boeing offers an expected return of 21 percent and Kodak an expected return of 15 percent. After looking back at the past variability of the two stocks, you also decide that the standard deviation of returns is 40 percent for Boeing and 20 percent for Kodak. Figure 8-4 illustrates the choice

[2] There is, however, one qualification. If you were to measure returns over *long* intervals, the distribution would be skewed. You would encounter returns greater than 100 percent but none less than −100 percent.

FIGURE 8-2
These two investments both have an *expected* return of 10 percent; but because investment A has the greater spread of *possible* returns, it is more risky than B. We can measure this spread by the standard deviation. Investment A has a standard deviation of 30 percent; B, 15 percent. Most investors would prefer B to A.

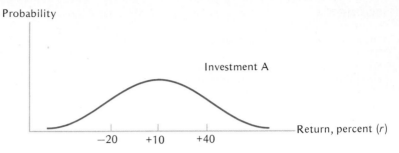

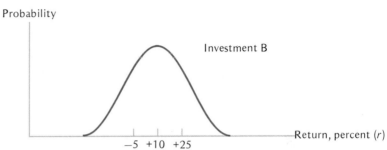

that you confront. Boeing offers the higher expected return but it is considerably more risky.

There is no reason that you should restrict yourself to holding only one stock. For example, you might consider investing 33 percent of your portfolio in the shares of Boeing and the remainder in Eastman Kodak. The expected return on

FIGURE 8-3
The standard deviation of possible returns is 15 percent for both these investments, but the expected return from C is 20 percent compared with an expected return from D of only 10 percent. Most investors would prefer C to D.

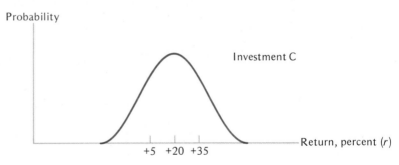

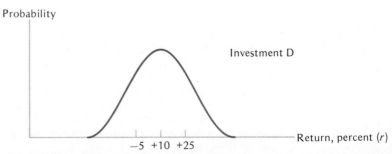

FIGURE 8-4
Here is a plot of the expected returns and standard deviations for just two stocks. Boeing has an expected return of 21 percent and a standard deviation of 40 percent. Kodak has an expected return of 15 percent and a standard deviation of 20 percent.

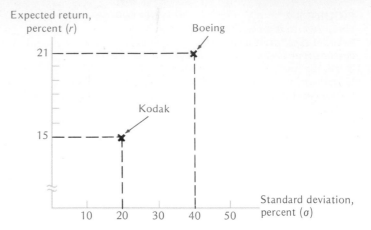

this portfolio is simply a weighted average of the expected returns on the individual stocks:

$$\text{Expected portfolio return} = (.33 \times 21) + (.67 \times 15) = 17 \text{ percent}$$

Calculating the expected portfolio return is easy. The hard part is to work out the risk of your portfolio. Your first inclination may be to assume that it is a weighted average of the standard deviations of the individual holdings—that is, $(.33 \times 40) + (.67 \times 20) = 26.7$ percent. But that would be correct only if the prices of the two stocks moved in perfect lockstep. In any other circumstances, diversification would reduce the risk below 26.7 percent.

The exact procedure for calculating the variance of a two-stock portfolio is given in Figure 8-5. You need to fill in four boxes. To complete the top left box, you weight the variance of the returns on stock 1 (σ_1^2) by the *square* of the proportion invested in it (x_1^2). Similarly, to complete the bottom right box, you weight the variance of the returns on stock 2 (σ_2^2) by the *square* of the proportion invested in stock 2 (x_2^2).

The entries in these diagonal boxes depend on the variances of stocks 1 and 2; the entries in the other two boxes depend on their *covariance*. As you might guess, the covariance is a measure of the degree to which the two stocks "covary." The covariance is equal to the product of the correlation coefficient ρ_{12} and the two standard deviations:

$$\text{Covariance between stocks 1 and 2} = \sigma_{12} = \rho_{12}\sigma_1\sigma_2$$

For the most part stocks tend to move together. In this case the correlation coefficient ρ_{12} is positive and therefore the covariance σ_{12} is also positive. If the prospects of the stocks were wholly unrelated, both the correlation coefficient and the covariance would be zero; and if the stocks tended to move in opposite directions, the correlation coefficient and the covariance would be negative. Just as you weighted the variances by the square of the proportion invested, so you must weight the covariance by the *product* of the two proportionate holdings x_1 and x_2.

FIGURE 8-5
The variance of a two-stock portfolio is the sum of these four boxes. x_i = proportion invested in stock i; σ_i^2 = variance of return on stock i; σ_{ij} = covariance of returns on stocks i and j ($\rho_{ij}\sigma_i\sigma_j$); ρ_{ij} = correlation between returns on stocks i and j.

	Stock 1	Stock 2
Stock 1	$x_1^2\sigma_1^2$	$x_1x_2\sigma_{12} = x_1x_2\rho_{12}\sigma_1\sigma_2$
Stock 2	$x_1x_2\sigma_{12} = x_1x_2\rho_{12}\sigma_1\sigma_2$	$x_2^2\sigma_2^2$

Once you have completed these four boxes, you simply add up the entries in order to obtain the portfolio variance:

$$\text{Portfolio variance} = (x_1^2\sigma_1^2) + (x_2^2\sigma_2^2) + 2(x_1x_2\rho_{12}\sigma_1\sigma_2)$$

The portfolio standard deviation is of course the square root of the variance.

Now you can try putting in some figures for Boeing and Eastman Kodak. We said earlier that if the two stocks were perfectly correlated, the standard deviation of the portfolio would lie 33 percent of the way between the standard deviations of the two stocks. Let us check that out by filling in the boxes with $\rho_{12} = +1$.

Boeing SD = 40
K = 20

	Boeing	Kodak
Boeing	$x_1^2\sigma_1^2 = (.33)^2 \times 1600$	$x_1x_2\rho_{12}\sigma_1\sigma_2 = .33 \times .67 \times 1 \times 40 \times 20$
Kodak	$x_1x_2\rho_{12}\sigma_1\sigma_2 = .33 \times .67 \times 1 \times 40 \times 20$	$x_2^2\sigma_2^2 = (.67)^2 \times 400$

The variance of your portfolio would be the sum of these entries:

$$\begin{aligned}\text{Portfolio variance} &= [(.33)^2 \times 1600] + [(.67)^2 \times 400] \\ &\quad + 2[.33 \times .67 \times 1 \times 40 \times 20] \\ &= 707.6\end{aligned}$$

The standard deviation would be $\sqrt{707.6} = 26.7$ percent, one third of the way between 20 and 40.

Diversification reduces risk only when the correlation is less than 1. The greatest diversification payoff comes when the two stocks are *negatively* correlated. Unfortunately, this almost never occurs with real stocks, but just for illustration, let us assume it for Boeing and Eastman Kodak. As long as we are being unrealistic, we might as well go whole hog and assume perfect negative correlation ($\rho_{12} = -1$). In this case:

$$\begin{aligned}\text{Portfolio variance} &= [(.33)^2 \times 1600] + [(.67)^2 \times 400] \\ &\quad + 2[.33 \times .67 \times (-1) \times 40 \times 20] \\ &= 0\end{aligned}$$

FIGURE 8-6
The curved line illustrates how expected
return and standard deviation change as
you hold different combinations of two
stocks. For example, if you invest 33
percent of your money in Boeing and
the remainder in Kodak, your expected
return is 17 percent, which is 33 percent of the way between the expected
returns on the two stocks. The standard
deviation is 22 percent, which is *much
less* than 33 percent of the way between
the standard deviations on the two
stocks. This is because diversification
reduces risk.

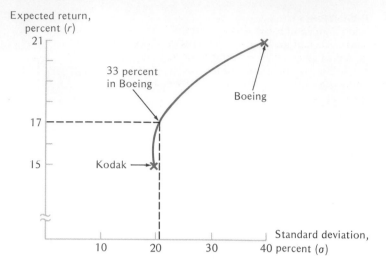

When there is perfect negative correlation, there is always a portfolio strategy
(represented by a particular set of portfolio weights) which will completely eliminate risk.[3]

In practice, Boeing and Kodak neither move in perfect lockstep nor do they
move in opposite directions. If the past experience is any guide, the correlation
between the two stocks is about .4. If we go through the same exercise again with
$\rho_{12} = +.4$, we find:

$$\text{Portfolio variance} = [(.33)^2 + 1600] + [(.67)^2 \times 400]$$
$$+ 2[.33 \times .67 \times .4 \times 40 \times 20]$$
$$= 495$$

The standard deviation is $\sqrt{495} = 22$ percent. The risk is now *less* than 33 percent
of the way between 20 and 40—in fact, only a trifle more than investing in Kodak
alone.

We can also use these formulas to calculate the expected return and risk of
other combinations of Boeing and Eastman Kodak. In Figure 8-6, we have assumed a correlation of .4 and we have plotted the expected return and risk that
you could achieve by different combinations of these two stocks.

Which of these combinations is best? That depends partly on your stomach. If
you want to stake all on getting rich quickly, you would do best to put all your
funds in Boeing. If you want a more peaceful life, you should invest part of your
money in Kodak—to minimize risk you should keep a small investment in Boeing.

**Choosing
Portfolios
from Many
Stocks**

These methods for calculating expected portfolio return and risk can easily be
extended to portfolios containing three or more securities. The expected return is
always just a weighted average of the expected returns on the individual stocks.
To calculate the variance of the portfolio, we just have to fill in more boxes. Each
of those along the diagonal—the shaded boxes in Figure 8-7—contains the vari-

[3] Since the standard deviation of Boeing is twice that of Kodak, you need to invest twice as much in
Kodak to eliminate risk in this two-stock portfolio.

FIGURE 8-7
To find the variance of an *N*-stock portfolio we must add up a matrix like this. The diagonal boxes contain variance terms $(x_i^2 \sigma_i^2)$ and the off-diagonal boxes contain covariance terms $(x_i x_j \sigma_{ij})$.

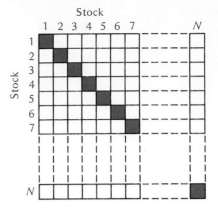

ance of the stock weighted by the square of the proportion invested in the stock. Each of the other boxes contains the covariance between that pair of securities, weighted by the product of the proportions invested. The portfolio variance is the sum of all these boxes.

Figure 8-8 shows how your choice is enlarged when you have a larger selection of securities. Each cross represents the combination of risk and return offered by a different individual security. By mixing these securities in different proportions, you can reduce your risk and obtain an even wider selection of risk and expected return. For example, the range of attainable combinations might look something like the broken-egg-shaped area in Figure 8-8. Since you wish to increase expected return and reduce standard deviation, you will be interested only in those portfolios that lie along the heavy solid line. Markowitz called them *efficient portfolios*. Whether you want to choose the minimum risk portfolio (portfolio A) or the maximum expected return portfolio (portfolio B) or some other efficient portfolio depends on how much you dislike taking risk.

The problem of finding these efficient portfolios is similar to a problem that we encountered in Chapter 6. There we wanted to deploy a limited amount of capital in a mixture of projects to give the highest total NPV. Here we want to deploy a

FIGURE 8-8
Each cross shows the expected return and standard deviation from investing in a single stock. The broken-egg-shaped area shows the possible combinations of expected return and standard deviation if you invest in a *mixture* of stocks. If you like high expected returns and dislike high standard deviations, you will prefer portfolios along the heavy line. These are *efficient* portfolios.

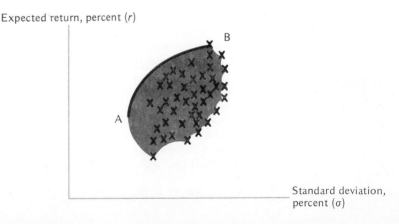

limited amount of capital to give the highest expected return for a given standard deviation. In principle both problems can be solved by a hunt-and-peck procedure—but only in principle. To solve the capital-rationing problem in practice, we can employ linear programming techniques; to solve the portfolio problem, we can employ a variant of linear programming known as *quadratic programming*. If we estimate the expected return and standard deviation for each stock in Figure 8-8, and also the correlation between each pair of stocks, then we can use a standard computer program to calculate the set of efficient portfolios.

Limits to Diversification

When we showed you in Figure 8-7 how to calculate the risk of a portfolio, did you notice how much more important the covariances become as we add securities to the portfolio? When there are just two securities, there is an equal number of variance boxes and covariance boxes. When there are many securities, the number of covariances is much larger than the number of variances. Thus the variability of a well-diversified portfolio reflects mainly the covariances.

Suppose we are dealing with portfolios in which equal investments are made in each of N stocks. The proportion invested in each stock is, therefore, $1/N$. So in each variance box we have $(1/N)^2$ times the variance and in each covariance box we have $(1/N)^2$ times the covariance. There are N variance boxes and $N^2 - N$ covariance boxes. Therefore

$$\text{Portfolio variance} = N\left(\frac{1}{N}\right)^2 \times \text{average variance}$$

$$+ (N^2 - N)\left(\frac{1}{N}\right)^2 \times \text{average covariance}$$

$$= \frac{1}{N} \times \text{average variance} + \left(1 - \frac{1}{N}\right) \times \text{average covariance}$$

Notice that as N increases, the portfolio variance steadily approaches the average covariance. If the average covariance were zero, it would be possible to eliminate *all* risk by holding sufficient securities. Unfortunately common stocks move together, not independently. Thus most of the stocks that the investor can actually buy are tied together in a web of positive covariances which set the limit to the benefits of diversification. In Chapter 7, we referred to the risk that cannot be diversified away as *market risk*. Now you can understand the precise meaning of that term. Market risk is the average covariance of all securities. This is the bedrock risk remaining after diversification has done its work.

Contribution to Portfolio Risk

If we want to know the contribution of an individual security to the risk of a portfolio, it is no good thinking about the risk of that security if it is held in isolation. We need to take account of how it covaries with the other stocks in the portfolio.

Look again at Figure 8-7. The sum of all the boxes in the first row shows the contribution of stock 1 to portfolio risk; the sum of the boxes in the second row shows the contribution of stock 2; and so on. This means that contribution of stock 1 to portfolio risk depends on its market value (x_1) and its average covariance with all the stocks in the portfolio $\left(\sum_{j=1}^{N} x_j \sigma_{1j}\right)$. To put it another way, the risk that stock 1 contributes to the portfolio depends on its relative market value (x_1) and its covariance with the portfolio (σ_{1p}):

$$\text{Contribution to risk} = x_1\sigma_{1p}$$

If you want to measure the *proportion* of the risk contributed by stock 1, you can express these measures as a proportion of the portfolio risk (σ_p^2):

$$\frac{\textit{Proportionate } \text{contribution}}{\text{to portfolio risk}} = \frac{x_1\sigma_{1p}}{\sigma_p^2}$$

Obviously the *total* proportion of risk accounted for by all stocks in the portfolio must equal 1.0.

The ratio σ_{1p}/σ_p^2 is the sensitivity of stock 1 to changes in the value of the portfolio. If this ratio is greater than 1, then stock 1 is unusually sensitive to changes in portfolio value. A marginal increase in your holding would, therefore, increase portfolio risk. If the ratio is less than 1, then stock 1 is relatively insensitive to changes in portfolio value. In this case, a marginal increase in your holding would reduce portfolio risk.

Suppose that the portfolio is the market portfolio. Then the ratio σ_{1p}/σ_p^2 is the stock's *beta*, which we discusssed, but never properly defined, in Chapter 7. Beta is simply a measure of the stock's marginal contribution to the risk of the market portfolio. Stocks with betas greater than 1 have an above-average impact on the market's risk; stocks with betas less than 1 have a below-average impact.

Borrowing and Lending

We have talked about efficient common stock portfolios but we must also take account of the possibility that you can lend and borrow money at some risk-free rate of interest r_f. If you invest part of your money in Treasury bills (i.e., lend money) and place the remainder in common stock portfolio S, you can obtain any combination of expected return and risk along the straight line joining r_f and S in Figure 8-9. Since borrowing is merely negative lending, you can extend the range of possibilities to the right of S by borrowing funds at an interest rate of r_f and investing them as well as your own money in portfolio S.

Let us put some numbers on this. Suppose that portfolio S has an expected return of 15 percent and a standard deviation of 16 percent. Treasury bills offer

FIGURE 8-9
Lending and borrowing extend the range of investment possibilities. If you invest in portfolio S and lend or borrow at the risk-free interest rate, r_f, you can achieve any point along the straight line from r_f through S. This gives you a higher expected return for any level of risk than if you just invest in common stocks.

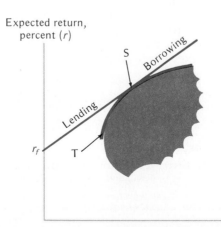

an interest rate (r_f) of 5 percent and are risk-free (i.e., their standard deviation is zero). If you invest half your money in portfolio S and lend the remainder at 5 percent, the expected return on your investment is halfway between the expected return on S and the expected return on Treasury bills:

$$r = (\tfrac{1}{2} \times \text{expected return on S}) + (\tfrac{1}{2} \times \text{interest rate}) = 10\%$$

And since Treasury bills are risk-free, the standard deviation of your investment is half the standard deviation of S:[4]

$$\sigma = (\tfrac{1}{2} \times \text{standard deviation of S}) + (\tfrac{1}{2} \times \text{standard deviation of bills})$$

$$= 8\%$$

Or suppose you decide to go for the big time: you borrow at the Treasury bill rate an amount equal to your initial wealth and invest everything in portfolio S. You have twice your own money invested in S but you have to *pay* interest on the loan. Therefore your expected return is:

$$r = (2 \times \text{expected return on S}) - (1 \times \text{interest rate}) = 25\%$$

But now you have doubled your exposure to the risks of portfolio S:

$$\sigma = (2 \times \text{standard deviation of S}) - (1 \times \text{standard deviation of bills})$$

$$= 32\%$$

You can see from Figure 8-9 that when you lend a portion of your money you end up partway between r_f and S; if you can borrow money at the risk-free rate, you can extend your possibilities beyond S. You can also see that regardless of what level of risk you choose, you can get the highest expected return by a mixture of portfolio S and borrowing or lending. There is no reason ever to hold, say, portfolio T.

This means that we can separate the investor's job into two stages. First, the "best" portfolio of common stocks must be selected—S in our example.[5] Second, this portfolio must be blended with borrowing or lending to obtain an exposure to risk that suits the investor's particular tastes. Each investor, therefore, should put money into just two benchmark investments—a risky portfolio S and a risk-free loan (borrowing or lending).[6]

What does portfolio S look like? If you have better information than your rivals, you will want it to include relatively large investments in the stocks you think are undervalued. But in a competitive market you are unlikely to have a monopoly on good ideas. In that case there is no reason to hold a different portfolio of common stocks from anybody else. In other words, the market portfolio would be the most efficient portfolio for you. That is why many professional investors invest in a market-index portfolio and why most others hold well-diversified portfolios.

---

[4] If you want to check this, write down the formula for the standard deviation of a two-stock portfolio:

$$\text{Standard deviation} = \sqrt{x_1^2\sigma_1^2 + x_2^2\sigma_2^2 + 2x_1x_2\rho_{12}\sigma_1\sigma_2}$$

Now see what happens when security 2 is riskless—that is, $\sigma_2 = 0$.

[5] Portfolio S is the point of tangency to the set of efficient portfolios. It offers the highest expected risk premium ($r - r_f$) per unit of standard deviation (σ).

[6] This so-called *separation theorem* was first pointed out by J. Tobin, in "Liquidity Preference as Behavior Toward Risk," *Review of Economic Studies*, **25**: 65–86 (February 1958).

8-2   THE RELATIONSHIP BETWEEN RISK AND RETURN

We have now suggested four basic principles of portfolio selection:

1. Investors like high expected return and low standard deviation. Common stock portfolios that offer the highest expected return for a given standard deviation are known as *efficient portfolios*.
2. If you want to know the marginal impact of a stock on the risk of a portfolio, you must look not at the risk of that stock in isolation, but at its contribution to portfolio risk. That contribution depends on the stock's sensitivity to changes in the value of the portfolio.
3. A stock's sensitivity to changes in the value of the *market* portfolio is known as *beta*. Beta, therefore, measures the marginal contribution of a stock to the risk of the market portfolio.
4. If investors can borrow and lend at the risk-free rate of interest, then they should always hold a mixture of the risk-free investment and one particular common stock portfolio. The composition of this stock portfolio depends only on investor's assessment of the prospects for each stock and not on their attitude to risk. If they have no superior information, they should hold the same stock portfolio as everybody else—in other words, they should hold the market portfolio.

We now need to consider the implications of these ideas for the way that securities are priced. We discussed this topic briefly in Chapter 7 when we described the capital asset pricing model. This model states that in competitive markets, the expected returns on each stock must plot along the security market line, as shown in Figure 8-10.

To see why stocks should lie along the security market line, imagine that you are choosing a portfolio. Some stocks will add to the risk of the portfolio and you will, therefore, buy them only if they also increase the expected return. Others will reduce portfolio risk and you may, therefore, be prepared to buy them even if they also reduce the portfolio's expected return. If the portfolio you have chosen is efficient, each of your investments must work equally hard for you. So, if one stock has a greater marginal effect on the risk of the portfolio than another stock, it must also have proportionately greater expected return. This means that if you plot each stock's expected return against its marginal contribution to the risk of your efficient portfolio, you will find that the stocks lie along a straight line, as in

FIGURE 8-10
The capital asset pricing model states that the security market line describes the relationship between a stock's expected return and its beta. Note: The beta of the market portfolio is the average beta of all stocks, i.e., 1.0.

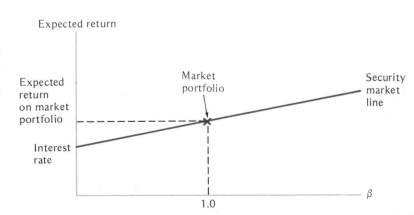

FIGURE 8-11
If a portfolio is efficient, each stock
should lie along a straight line linking
the stock's expected return with its
marginal contribution to the portfolio's
risk.

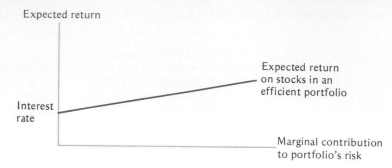

Figure 8-11. This is *always* the case: if a portfolio is efficient, there must be a
straight-line relationship between each stock's expected return and its marginal
contribution to portfolio risk. The converse is also true: if there is not a straight-
line relationship, the portfolio is not efficient.

Now you can see that Figures 8-10 and 8-11 are identical *if* the efficient portfolio in Figure 8-11 is the market portfolio. (Remember that the beta of a stock
measures its marginal contribution to the risk of the market portfolio.) So, the
capital asset pricing model boils down to the statement that the market portfolio
is efficient. As we have already seen, this will be so if each investor has the same
information and faces the same opportunities as everyone else. In these circumstances, each investor should hold the same portfolio as everyone else—in other
words, each should hold the market portfolio.

**What Would
Happen If a
Stock Did Not
Lie on the
Market Line?**

Imagine that you encounter stock A in Figure 8-12. Would you buy it? We hope
not—if you want an investment with a beta of .5, you could get a higher expected
return by investing half your money in Treasury bills and half in the market
portfolio. If everybody shares your view of the stock's prospects, the price of A
will have to fall until the expected return matches up to what you could get
elsewhere.

FIGURE 8-12
In equilibrium no stock can lie below the security market line. For
example, instead of buying stock A,
investors would prefer to lend part
of their money and put the balance
in the market portfolio. And, instead of buying stock B, they
would prefer to borrow and invest
in the market portfolio.

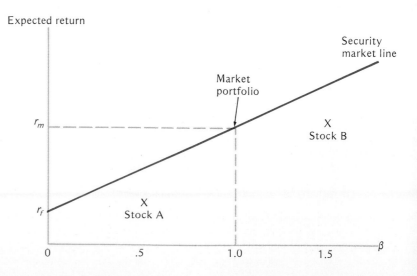

What about stock B in Figure 8-12? Would you be tempted by its high return? You wouldn't if you are smart. You could get a higher expected return for the same beta by borrowing 50 cents for every dollar of your own money and investing in the market portfolio. Again, if everybody agrees with your assessment, the price of stock B cannot be an equilibrium price. It will have to fall until the expected return on B is equal to the expected return on the levered investment in the market.

We think we have made our point. An investor can always obtain an expected risk premium of $\beta(r_m - r_f)$ by holding a mixture of the market portfolio and a risk-free loan. So in well-functioning markets nobody will hold a stock that offers an expected risk premium of *less* than $\beta(r_m - r_f)$. But what about the other possibility? Are there stocks that offer a higher expected risk premium? If we take all stocks together, we have the market portfolio. Its beta is 1.0 and its expected risk premium is:

$$\text{Expected market risk premium} = \beta(r_m - r_f) = r_m - r_f$$

Since stocks *on average* offer an expected risk premium of $\beta(r_m - r_f)$ and since none offers a *lower* expected risk premium, then there can't be any that offer a *higher* premium. The expected risk premium on each and every stock is:

$$r - r_f = \beta(r_m - r_f)$$

8-3 VALIDITY AND ROLE OF THE CAPITAL ASSET PRICING MODEL

Any economic model is a simplified statement of reality. We need to simplify in order to interpret what is going on around us. But we also need to know how much faith we can place in our model.

Let us begin with some matters on which there is broad agreement. First, few people quarrel with the idea that investors require some extra return for taking on risk. That is why common stocks have given on average a higher return than U.S. Treasury bills. Who would want to invest in risky common stocks if they offered only the *same* expected return as bills? We wouldn't and we suspect you wouldn't either.

Second, investors do appear to be concerned principally with those risks that they cannot eliminate by diversification. If this were not so, we should find that stock prices increase whenever two companies merge to spread their risks. And we should find that investment companies which invest in the shares of other firms are more highly valued than the shares they hold. But we don't observe either phenomenon. Diversifying mergers don't increase stock prices, and investment companies are no more highly valued than the shares they hold.

The capital asset pricing model captures these ideas in a simple way. That is why many financial managers find it the most convenient tool for coming to grips with the slippery notion of risk. And it is why economists often use the capital asset pricing model to demonstrate important ideas in finance even when there are other ways to prove these ideas. In years to come economists will develop better models of risk and return, but it is doubtful whether they will ever develop a simpler and more intuitively appealing model.

Tests of the Capital Asset Pricing Model

The ultimate test of any model is whether it fits the facts. Unfortunately there are two problems in testing the capital asset pricing model. First, it is concerned with *expected* returns, whereas we can observe only *actual* returns. Second, the market

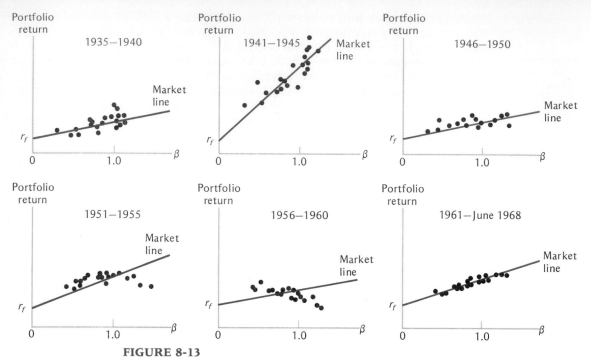

FIGURE 8-13
The capital asset pricing model states that the *expected* return from any investment should lie on the market line. The dots show the *actual* returns from portfolios with different betas. [*Source:* Results supplied by E. F. Fama and J. D. MacBeth. See their paper, "Risk, Return and Equilibrium: Empirical Tests," *Journal of Political Economy,* **81**:607–636 (May 1973).]

portfolio should include all risky investments, whereas most market indexes contain only a sample of common stocks.[7]

No study has properly tackled the second problem, but a paper by Fama and MacBeth avoids the main pitfalls that come from having to work with actual rather than expected returns. Fama and MacBeth grouped all New York Stock Exchange stocks into 20 portfolios. They then plotted the estimated beta of each portfolio in one 5-year period against the portfolio's average return over a subsequent 5-year period.[8] Figure 8-13 shows what they found. You can see that the estimated beta of each portfolio told investors quite a lot about its future return.

If the capital asset pricing model is correct, investors would not have expected any of these portfolios to perform better or worse than a comparable package of Treasury bills and the market portfolio. Therefore, the expected return on each portfolio, given the market return, should plot along the sloping lines in Figure 8-13. Notice that the *actual* returns on Fama and MacBeth's portfolios do plot

[7] See, e.g., R. Roll, "A Critique of the Asset Pricing Theory's Tests; Part 1: On Past and Potential Testability of the Theory," *Journal of Financial Economics,* **4:** 129–176 (March 1977).

[8] Fama and MacBeth first estimated the beta of each stock during one period and then formed portfolios on the basis of these estimated betas. Next, they reestimated the beta of each portfolio by using the returns in the subsequent period. This ensured that the estimated betas for each portfolio were largely unbiased and free from error. Finally, these portfolio betas were plotted against returns in an even later period. E. F. Fama and J. D. MacBeth, "Risk, Return and Equilibrium: Empirical Tests," *Journal of Political Economy,* **81:** 607–636 (May 1973).

roughly along these lines. That is encouraging, but we should like to know why the portfolios don't plot *exactly* along the lines. Is it because the capital asset pricing model is only a rough approximation to real markets? Or is it because the tests are not appropriate? (Remember that Fama and MacBeth are looking at *actual* returns, whereas the capital asset pricing model is concerned with expectations; also, Fama and MacBeth did not include *all* risky assets in their market index.) Unfortunately, nobody knows which explanation is correct. Betas that are calculated using a stock market index seem to tell us something about expected return, but we can't be sure what we would find if we were able to calculate betas using the full market portfolio of *all* risky assets.

The capital asset pricing model also predicts that beta is the *only* reason that expected returns differ. But we shall present some evidence in Chapter 13 that the average return on small-firm stocks has been substantially higher than the return on large-firm stocks. If investors *expected* the returns to depend on firm size, then the simple version of the capital asset pricing model cannot be the whole truth.

Assumptions behind the Capital Asset Pricing Model

In getting to the capital asset pricing model we made a number of assumptions that we did not fully spell out. For example, we assumed that investment in U.S. Treasury bills is risk-free. It is true that there is little chance of default with Treasury bills, but they don't guarantee a *real* return. There is still the risk of inflation. Another assumption was that investors can *borrow* money at the same rate of interest as they can lend. Generally borrowing rates are higher than lending rates.

It turns out that many of these assumptions are not crucial and with a little pushing and pulling it is possible to modify the capital asset pricing model to handle them. The really important assumption behind the model is that investors are content to invest their money in a limited number of benchmark portfolios such as Treasury bills and the market portfolio. As long as that is the case, we can express a security's expected return in terms of the expected return on these portfolios.[9]

*Arbitrage Pricing Theory

The capital asset pricing model may reign today, but no one regards it as Ultimate Truth. A new model will take the throne sooner or later, but we can't say now which model that will be. It may be one of the existing extensions or generalizations of the simple capital asset pricing model,[10] or it may be something completely new.

Most existing theories have a clear family resemblance. However, one theory, Steven Ross's *arbitrage pricing theory*,[11] comes from a different family entirely. We will briefly sketch Ross's approach.

[9] See, e.g., M. C. Jensen (ed.): *Studies in the Theory of Capital Markets*, Frederick A. Praeger, Inc., New York, 1972. In the introduction to his book, Jensen provides a very useful summary of some of these variations on the capital asset pricing model. In each case, the definition of market risk or of the two benchmark portfolios changes, but the general form of the model does not change. For practical purposes, none of these alternative forms is as widely used as the standard model.

[10] Two prominent contenders are R. C. Merton, "An Intertemporal Capital Asset Pricing Model," *Econometrica*, **41:** 867–887 (September 1973), and D. T. Breeden, "An Intertemporal Asset Pricing Model with Stochastic Consumption and Investment Opportunites," *Journal of Financial Economics* **7:** 265–296 (September 1979).

[11] S. A. Ross, 'The Arbitrage Theory of Capital Asset Pricing," *Journal of Economic Theory* **13:** 341–360 (December 1976).

The capital asset pricing model follows from an analysis of how investors can construct efficient portfolios. Arbitrage pricing theory skips this step and starts instead by *assuming* that each stock's return depends on several independent influences or "factors." Moreover, the return *must* obey the following simple relationship:

$$\text{Expected return on stock} = a + b_1(\text{factor 1}) + b_2(\text{factor 2}) + b_3(\text{factor 3}) + \cdots$$

The theory doesn't say what the factors are: there could be an oil price factor, an interest rate factor, and so on. The return on the market portfolio *might* serve as one factor, but then again it might not.

Some stocks will be more sensitive to a particular factor than others. Exxon would be more sensitive to an oil factor than, say, Quaker Oats. If factor 1 picks up unexpected changes in oil prices, b_1 would be higher for Exxon.

Now think of a portfolio whose expected return depended on factor 1 *only*. Buying this portfolio is like buying the factor; think of the return on this "pure play" portfolio as the return on the factor itself. Each of the other factors has its own pure play portfolio and thus its own return.

The arbitrage pricing model states that, if there are sufficient stocks, it must be possible to construct a diversified portfolio that has zero sensitivity to each factor. Such a portfolio would be effectively risk-free and, therefore, it should offer a zero risk premium. The model also states that each stock's risk premium should depend on two things: first, the risk premiums associated with each factor, and, second, the stock's sensitivity to each of the factors (i.e., the stock's b_1, b_2, b_3, etc.). Thus, the formula is:

$$\text{Risk premium on stock} = r - r_f = b_1(r_{\text{factor 1}} - r_f) + b_2(r_{\text{factor 2}} - r_f) + \cdots$$

What would happen if the expected risk premium on a stock were lower than this? In that case, Ross argues, there would be a money machine. Investors would sell the stock and buy a package of other fairly priced stocks with the same average sensitivity to each factor. The new portfolio would be equally exposed to changes in oil prices, interest rates, and so on, but it would offer a higher expected return.

What if the expected risk premium were higher? Then smart investors would sell other stocks and rush to buy this one. The pressure of their demand would force up the price and force down the return and risk premium, until Ross's equation held.

Will the arbitrage pricing theory provide a better handle on expected returns? That depends partly on whether it is possible to (1) identify the factors affecting stock returns and (2) measure the expected return on each of these factors as well as the sensitivity of stocks to them. Research on these issues is at a very early stage. Until these practical problems are solved, the capital asset pricing model, or another model drawn from its family, is likely to remain the dominant theory of risk and return.[12]

---

[12] To understand the relationship between the arbitrage pricing model and the capital asset pricing model, think of a set of portfolios each of which is a "pure play" on a single factor. Perhaps the expected return on portfolio 1 depends only on an oil price factor, the expected return on portfolio 2 depends only on an inflation factor, and so on. If the expected risk premium on each of these "pure play" portfolios is proportional to the portfolio's market risk (beta), then the arbitrage pricing model and the capital asset pricing model are equivalent. In other words, they would both indicate the same expected return on any stock. You can, therefore, think of the capital asset pricing model as a special case of Ross's more general model.

8-4 SUMMARY

In the first part of this chapter, we described some basic principles of portfolio selection. We suggested that most investors would like to increase the expected return on their portfolios and to reduce the standard deviation of the return. A portfolio that gives the highest expected return for a given standard deviation, or the lowest standard deviation for a given expected return, is known as an efficient portfolio. Working out the expected return on a portfolio is easy; simply take a weighted average of the expected returns on the individual stocks. The standard deviation of the portfolio return is more complicated to calculate because it depends on the standard deviation of each stock and the correlation between each pair of stocks.

Investors who are restricted to holding common stocks should choose an efficient portfolio that suits their attitude to risk. But investors who can also borrow and lend at the risk-free rate of interest should choose the "best" common stock portfolio *regardless* of their attitude to risk. Having done that, they can then set the risk of their overall portfolio by deciding what proportion of their money they are willing to invest in stocks. For an investor who has only the same opportunities and information as everybody else, the best stock portfolio is the same as the best stock portfolio for other investors. In other words, he or she should invest in a mixture of the market portfolio and a risk-free loan (i.e., borrowing or lending).

A stock's marginal contribution to portfolio risk is measured by its sensitivity to changes in the value of the portfolio. If a portfolio is efficient, there will be a straight-line relationship between each stock's expected return and its marginal contribution to the risk of the portfolio. The marginal contribution of a stock to the risk of the *market portfolio* is measured by *beta*. So if the market portfolio is efficient, there will be a straight-line relationship between the expected return and beta of each stock. That is the fundamental idea behind the capital asset pricing model.

The capital asset pricing model is the best-known model of risk and return. A number of modifications have been proposed to cope with such complexities as different borrowing and lending rates. The arbitrage pricing model offers an alternative theory of risk and return. All financial economists, however, agree on two basic ideas: (1) investors require extra expected return for taking on risk, and (2) they appear to be concerned predominantly with the risk that they cannot eliminate by diversification.

FURTHER READING

The pioneering article on portfolio selection is:

   H. M. Markowitz: "Portfolio Selection," *Journal of Finance,* **7:** 77–91 (March 1952).

There are a number of textbooks on portfolio selection which explain both Markowitz's original theory and some ingenious simplified versions. See, for example:

   E. J. Elton and M. J. Gruber: *Modern Portfolio Theory and Investment Analysis,* 2d ed., John Wiley & Sons, New York, 1984.
   H. Levy and M. Sarnat: *Portfolio and Investment Selection: Theory and Practice,* Prentice-Hall International, Englewood Cliffs, N.J., 1984.

Of the three pioneering articles on the capital asset pricing model, Jack Treynor's has never been published. The other two articles are:

   W. F. Sharpe: "Capital Asset Prices: A Theory of Market Equilibrium under Conditions of Risk," *Journal of Finance,* **19:** 425–442 (September 1964).

J. Lintner: "The Valuation of Risk Assets and the Selection of Risky Investments in Stock Portfolios and Capital Budgets," *Review of Economics and Statistics*, **47:** 13–37 (February 1965).

The subsequent literature on the capital asset pricing model is enormous. The following book provides a collection of some of the more important articles plus a very useful survey by Jensen:

M. C. Jensen (ed): *Studies in the Theory of Capital Markets*, Frederick A. Praeger, Inc., New York, 1972.

Another very good survey article is:

F. Modigliani and G. A. Pogue: "An Introduction to Risk and Return," *Financial Analysts Journal*, **30:** 68–80 (March–April 1974); 69–88 (May–June 1974).

There have been a number of tests of the capital asset pricing model. Some of the more important tests are:

E. F. Fama and J. D. MacBeth: "Risk, Return and Equilibrium: Empirical Tests," *Journal of Political Economy*, **81:** 607–636 (May 1973).

F. Black, M. C. Jensen, and M. Scholes, "The Capital Asset Pricing Model: Some Empirical Tests," in M. C. Jensen (ed.): *Studies in the Theory of Capital Markets*, Frederick A. Praeger, Inc., New York, 1972.

M. R. Gibbons: "Multivariate Tests of Financial Models," *Journal of Financial Economics*, **10:** 3–27 (March 1982).

For a critique of empirical tests of the model, see:

R. Roll: "A Critique of the Asset Pricing Theory's Tests; Part I: On Past and Potential Testability of the Theory," *Journal of Financial Economics*, **4:** 129–176 (March 1977).

Two alternative models of asset prices are described in:

D. T. Breeden: "An Intertemporal Asset Pricing Model with Stochastic Consumption and Investment Opportunities," *Journal of Financial Economics*, **7:** 265–296 (September 1979).

S. A. Ross: "The Arbitrage Theory of Capital Asset Pricing," *Journal of Economic Theory*, **13:** 341–360 (December 1976).

Several attempts have been made both to test the arbitrage pricing model and to identify the principal factors. Here are three examples:

R. Roll and S. A. Ross, "An Empirical Investigation of the Arbitrage Pricing Theory," *Journal of Finance*, **35:** 1073–1103 (December 1980).

N-F. Chen, "Some Empirical Tests of the Theory of Arbitrage Pricing," *Journal of Finance*, **38:** 1393–1414 (December 1983).

N-F. Chen, R. Roll, and S. A. Ross, "Economic Forces and the Stock Market: Testing the APT and Alternative Pricing Theories," *Journal of Business*, **59:** 383–403 (July 1986).

QUIZ

1. Figures 8-14 and 8-15 purport to show the range of attainable combinations of expected return and standard deviation.
   (*a*) Which diagram is incorrectly drawn and why?
   (*b*) Which is the efficient set of portfolios?
   (*c*) If r_f is the rate of interest, mark with an X the optimal stock portfolio.
2. For each of the following pairs of investments, state which would always be preferred by a rational investor (assuming that these are the *only* investments

FIGURE 8-14
See
Quiz,
question
1.

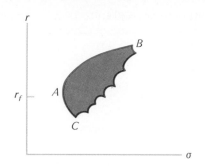

FIGURE 8-15
See
Quiz,
question
1.

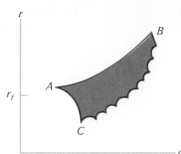

that are available to the investor):
(a) Portfolio A r = 18 percent σ = 20 percent
    Portfolio B r = 14 percent σ = 20 percent
(b) Portfolio C r = 15 percent σ = 18 percent
    Portfolio D r = 13 percent σ = 8 percent
(c) Portfolio E r = 14 percent σ = 16 percent
    Portfolio F r = 14 percent σ = 10 percent
3. To calculate the variance of a three-stock portfolio you need to add nine boxes:

Use the same symbols that we used in this chapter; e.g., x_1 = proportion invested in stock 1 and σ_{12} = covariance between stocks 1 and 2. Now complete the nine boxes.
4. Consider the following four portfolios:
   (a) 50 percent in Treasury bills, 50 percent in share W
   (b) 50 percent in share W, 50 percent in share X, where the returns on W and X are perfectly positively correlated
   (c) 50 percent in share X, 50 percent in share Y, where the returns are uncorrelated
   (d) 50 percent in share Y, 50 percent in share Z, where the returns are perfectly negatively correlated
   In which of these cases would the standard deviation of the portfolio lie exactly midway between that of the two securities?
5. In which of the following situations would you get the largest reduction in risk by spreading your investment across two stocks:
   (a) When the two shares are perfectly correlated
   (b) When there is no correlation
   (c) When there is modest negative correlation
   (d) When there is perfect negative correlation

6. (*a*) Plot the following risky portfolios on a graph:

Portfolio	A	B	C	D	E	F	G	H
Expected return, r, percent	10	12.5	15	16	17	18	18	20
Standard deviation, σ, percent	23	21	25	29	29	32	35	45

(*b*) Five of these portfolios are efficient and three are not. Which are *in*efficient ones?

(*c*) Suppose you can also borrow and lend at an interest rate of 12 percent. Which of the above portfolios is best?

(*d*) Suppose you are prepared to tolerate a standard deviation of 25 percent. What is the maximum expected return that you can achieve if you cannot borrow or lend?

(*e*) What is your optimal strategy, if you can borrow or lend at 12 percent and are prepared to tolerate a standard deviation of 25 percent? What is the maximum expected return that you can achieve?

QUESTIONS AND PROBLEMS

1. (*a*) List four common stocks that are likely to have very high standard deviations and four stocks that are likely to have very low standard deviations.

(*b*) List four pairs of securities that are likely to be highly correlated and four pairs that are likely to be relatively uncorrelated.

2. Enter in Figure 8-16 the characteristic line for (*a*) a portfolio that is evenly divided between Treasury bills and the market index, and (*b*) a portfolio that is financed half by borrowing and is entirely invested in the market index.

3. Last week Prudence Puffin analyzed three common stock portfolios. She remembers that portfolio X offered an expected return of 10 percent and standard deviation of 10 percent, and that portfolio Y offered an expected return of 14 percent and standard deviation of 20 percent. Unfortunately, all that she can remember about portfolio Z is that it is the best of the three portfolios as

FIGURE 8-16
See Questions and Problems, 2.

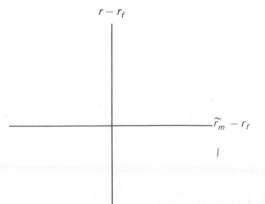

long as the interest rate is between 5 and 9 percent. Otherwise she would do better to invest in one of the other two portfolios and borrow or lend the balance of her money.

(a) What are the expected return and standard deviation of portfolio Z?

(b) When should Ms. Puffin invest in portfolio X and portfolio Y?

4. "There's upside risk and downside risk. Standard deviation doesn't distinguish between them." Do you think the speaker has a fair point?

5. Respond to the following comments:

(a) "Risk is not variability. If I know a stock is going to fluctuate between $10 and $20, I can make myself a bundle."

(b) "There are all sorts of risk in addition to beta risk. There's the risk that we'll have a downturn in demand, there's the risk that my best plant manager will drop dead, there's the risk of a hike in steel prices. You've got to take all things into consideration."

(c) "Risk to me is the probability of loss."

(d) "Those guys who suggest beta is a measure of risk make the big assumption that betas don't change."

6. "There may be some truth in the capital asset pricing model, but over the past year many stocks gave a substantially higher return than the capital asset pricing model predicted and many others gave a substantially lower return." Is this a valid criticism of the model?

7. Sketch the efficient set of common stock portfolios. Show the combinations of expected return and risk that you could achieve if you could borrow and lend at the same risk-free rate of interest. Now show the combinations of expected return and risk that you could achieve if the rate of interest is higher for borrowing than for lending.

8. Look back at the calculation for Boeing and Kodak in Section 8-1. Recalculate the expected portfolio return and standard deviation for different values of x_1 and x_2 assuming $\rho_{12} = 0$. Plot the efficient frontier as in Figure 8-6.
Repeat the exercise for $\rho_{12} = +1$ and for $\rho_{12} = -1$.

9. Here are some historical data on the risk characteristics of Kodak and Polaroid:

	Kodak	Polaroid
β (beta)	.59	1.15
Yearly standard deviation of return	19.8	34.0

The standard deviation of the return on the market was 22 percent.

(a) Assume the correlation coefficient of Kodak's return versus Polaroid's is .40. What is the standard deviation of a portfolio half invested in Polaroid and half in Kodak?

(b) What is the standard deviation of a portfolio one-third invested in Kodak, one-third in Polaroid, and one-third in Treasury bills?

(c) What is the standard deviation if the portfolio is split equally between Kodak and Polaroid and financed at 50 percent margin—that is, the investor puts up only 50 percent of the total amount and borrows the balance from the broker?

(d) What is the *approximate* standard deviation of a portfolio composed of 100 stocks with β's of .59, like Kodak? How about 100 stocks like Polaroid? (*Hint:* Part (d) should not require anything but the simplest arithmetic to answer.)

10. Mark Harrywitz proposes to invest in two shares, X and Y. He expects a return of 12 percent from X and 8 percent from Y. The standard deviation of the returns is 8 percent for X and 5 percent for Y. The correlation coefficient between the returns is .2.

(*a*) Compute the expected return and standard deviation of the following portfolios:

Portfolio	Percent in X	Percent in Y
1	50	50
2	25	75
3	75	25

(*b*) Sketch the set of portfolios composed of X and Y.

(*c*) Suppose that Mr. Harrywitz can also borrow or lend at an interest rate of 5 percent. Show on your sketch how this alters his opportunities. Given that he can borrow or lend, what proportions of the common stock portfolio should be invested in X and Y?

11. You believe that there is a 40 percent chance that stock A will decline by 10 percent and a 60 percent chance that it will rise by 20 percent. Correspondingly, there is a 30 percent chance that stock B will decline by 10 percent and a 70 percent chance that it will rise by 20 percent. The correlation coefficient between the two stocks is .7. Calculate the expected return, the variance, and the standard deviation for each stock. Then calculate the covariance between their returns.

12. Hilda Hornbill has invested 60 percent of her money in share A and the remainder in share B. She assesses their prospects as follows:

	A	B
Expected return, %	15	20
Standard deviation, %	20	22
Correlation between returns	.5	

(*a*) What is the expected return and standard deviation of returns on her portfolio?

(*b*) How would your answer be changed if the correlation coefficient were 0 or −.5?

(*c*) Is Ms. Hornbill's portfolio better or worse than one invested entirely in share A or is it not possible to say?

13. An individual invests 60 percent of his funds in stock I and the balance in stock J. The standard deviation of returns on I is 10 percent and on J it is 20 percent. Calculate the variance of portfolio returns assuming

(*a*) The correlation between the returns is 1.0

(*b*) The correlation is .5.

(*c*) The correlation is 0.

14. (*a*) How many variance terms and how many covariance terms do you need to sum to calculate the risk of a 100-share portfolio?

(*b*) Suppose all stocks had a standard deviation of 30 percent and a correlation with each other of .4. What is the standard deviation of the returns on a portfolio that has equal holdings in 100 stocks?

(c) What is the standard deviation of a fully diversified portfolio of such stocks?

15. Suppose that the standard deviation σ of returns from a typical share is about .25 (or 25 percent) a year. The correlation ρ between the returns of a typical pair of shares is about .3. Calculate the variance and standard deviation of the returns on a portfolio that has equal investments in two shares, three shares, and so on up to ten shares.

Use your estimates to draw two graphs like Figure 7-3. How large is the underlying market risk that cannot be diversified away?

✓ 16. The market portfolio has a standard deviation of 20 percent and the covariance between the returns on the market and those on stock Z is 800.

(a) What is the beta of stock Z?

? (b) What would be the standard deviation of a fully diversified portfolio of such stocks?

(c) What is the average beta of all stocks?

(d) If the market portfolio gave a 5 percent higher return than you expected, by how much is the return on portfolio Z likely to exceed your expectations?

17. It is often useful to know how well your portfolio is diversified. Two measures have been suggested:

(a) The variance of the returns of a fully diversified portfolio as a proportion of the variance of the returns on *your* portfolio.

(b) The number of shares in a portfolio that (i) has the same risk as yours, (ii) is invested in "typical" shares, and (iii) has equal amounts invested in each share.

Suppose that you hold eight stocks. All are fairly typical—they have a standard deviation σ of .40 a year and the correlation ρ between each pair is .3. Of your fund, 20 percent is invested in one stock, 20 percent in a second, and the remaining 60 percent is spread evenly over a further six stocks.

Calculate each of the above two measures of portfolio diversification.

.36

.5625

.16

9 Capital Budgeting and the Capital Asset Pricing Model

Long before the development of capital asset pricing theory, smart financial managers adjusted for risk in capital budgeting. They realized intuitively that, if other things are equal, risky projects are less desirable than safe ones. Therefore they demanded a higher rate of return from risky projects or they based their decisions on conservative estimates of the cash flows.

Various rules of thumb are often used to make these risk adjustments. For example, many companies estimate the rate of return required by investors in their securities and use this **company cost of capital** to discount the cash flows on all new projects. Since investors require a higher rate of return from a very risky company, such a firm will have a higher company cost of capital and will set a higher discount rate for its new investment opportunities.

You can use the capital asset pricing model as a rule of thumb for estimating the company cost of capital. For instance, we showed in Table 7-5 that the stock of Digital Equipment Corporation (DEC) had a beta of 1.21 at the end of 1986. The corresponding expected rate of return was .158, or about 16 percent. Therefore, according to the company cost of capital rule, DEC should have been using a 16 percent discount rate to compute project net present values.[1]

This is a step in the right direction. Even though we can't measure betas or the market risk premium with absolute precision, it is still reasonable to assert that DEC faced more risk than the average firm and, therefore, should have demanded a higher rate of return from its capital investments.

But the company cost of capital rule can also get a firm into trouble if the new projects are more or less risky than its existing business. Each project should be evaluated at *its own* opportunity cost of capital. This is a clear implication of the value-additivity principle introduced in Chapter 7. For a firm composed of assets A and B, firm value is

Firm value = PV(AB) = PV(A) + PV(B) = sum of separate asset values

Here PV(A) and PV(B) are valued just as if they were mini-firms in which stockholders could invest directly. Note: Investors would value A by discounting its forecasted cash flows at a rate reflecting the risk of A. They would value B by discounting at a rate reflecting the risk of B. The two discount rates will, in general, be different.

If the firm considers investing in a third project C, it should also value C as if it were a mini-firm. That is, it should discount the cash flows of C at the expected rate of return investors would demand to make a separate investment in C. *The true cost of capital depends on the use to which the capital is put.*

[1] DEC did not use any significant amount of debt financing. Thus its cost of capital is the rate of return investors expect on its common stock. The complications caused by debt are discussed later in this chapter.

FIGURE 9-1
A comparison between the company cost of capital rule and the required return under the capital asset pricing model. DEC's company cost of capital is about 16 percent. This is the correct discount rate only if the project beta is 1.21. In general, the correct discount rate increases as project beta increases. DEC should accept projects with rates of return above the security market line relating required return to beta.

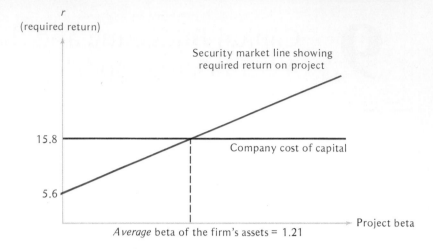

Capital asset pricing theory tells us to invest in any project offering a return that more than compensates for the *project's beta*. This means that DEC should have accepted any project above the upward-sloping market line in Figure 9-1. If the project had a high beta, DEC needed a higher prospective return than if the project had a low beta. Now contrast this with the company cost of capital rule, which is to accept any project *regardless of its beta* as long as it offers a higher return than the *company's* cost of capital. In terms of Figure 9-1 it tells DEC to accept any project above the horizontal cost-of-capital line—that is, any project offering a return of more than 16 percent.

It is clearly silly to suggest that DEC should demand the same rate of return from a very safe project as from a very risky one. If DEC used the company cost of capital rule, it would reject many good low-risk projects and accept many poor high-risk projects. It is also silly to suggest that, just because AT&T has a low company cost of capital, it is justified in accepting projects that DEC would reject. If you followed such a rule to its seemingly logical conclusion, you would think it possible to enlarge the company's capital investment opportunities by investing a large sum in Treasury bills. That would make the common stock safe and create a low company cost of capital.[2]

The notion that each company has some individual discount rate or cost of capital is widespread, but far from universal. Many firms require different returns from different categories of investment. Discount rates might be set, for example, as follows:

Category	Discount Rate, Percent
Speculative ventures	30
New product	20
Expansion of existing business	15 (company cost of capital)
Cost improvement, known technology	10

---

[2] If the present value of an asset depended on the identity of the company that bought it, present values would not add up. Remember that a good project is a good project is a good project.

Our object in this chapter is to show you how to use beta and the capital asset pricing model to help cope with risk in practical capital-budgeting situations. The main problem is to estimate the discount rate, which by the capital asset pricing model is:

$$r = r_f + (\text{project beta})(r_m - r_f)$$

And in order to calculate that discount rate you have to figure out the project beta. It is a difficult problem; so much so that many people hope it will go away if they ignore it. They may go away but unfortunately the problem won't—any investment decision contains an *implicit* assumption about project risk.

We will start by reconsidering the problems you would encounter in using beta to estimate a company's cost of capital. It turns out that beta is difficult to measure accurately for an individual firm: Much greater accuracy can be achieved by looking at an average of similar companies. But then we have to define *similar*. Among other things we will find that a firm's borrowing policy affects its stock's beta. It would be misleading, for example, to average the betas of Navistar, which is a heavy borrower, and General Motors, which is not.

The company cost of capital is the correct discount rate for projects that have the same risk as the company's existing business but *not* for those that are safer or riskier than the company's average. The problem is to judge the relative risks of the projects available to the firm. In order to handle that problem, we will need to dig a little deeper and look at what features make some investments riskier than others. After you know *why* AT&T stock has less market risk than, say, MCI Communications, you will be in a better position to judge the relative risks of capital investment opportunities.

There is still another complication: Project betas can shift over time. Some projects are safer in youth than in old age, others are riskier. In this case, what do we mean by *the* project beta? There may be a separate beta for each year of the project's life. To put it another way, can we jump from the capital asset pricing model, which looks out one period into the future, to the discounted-cash-flow formula that we developed in Chapters 2 to 6 for valuing long-lived assets? Most of the time it is safe to do so, but you should be able to recognize and deal with exceptions.

As you have no doubt guessed, capital asset pricing theory supplies no mechanical formula for measuring and adjusting for risk in capital budgeting. These tasks of financial management will be among the last to be automated. The best a financial manager can do is to combine an understanding of theory with good judgment and a good nose for hidden clues. Therefore don't be discouraged if we dwell on the problems of using the theory. Do you want to be a dilettante who is interested solely in the theory, or a professional who looks to theory for help but not always a final answer? If it's the latter, then press on.

9-1 MEASURING BETAS

Suppose that you were considering an across-the-board expansion by your firm. Such an investment would have about the same degree of risk as the existing business. Therefore you should discount the projected flows at the company cost of capital. To estimate that, you could begin by estimating the beta of the company's stock.

An obvious way to measure the beta of a stock is to look at how its price has responded in the past to market movements. For example, in Figure 9-2 we have plotted monthly rates of return from AT&T and Inland Steel against market returns

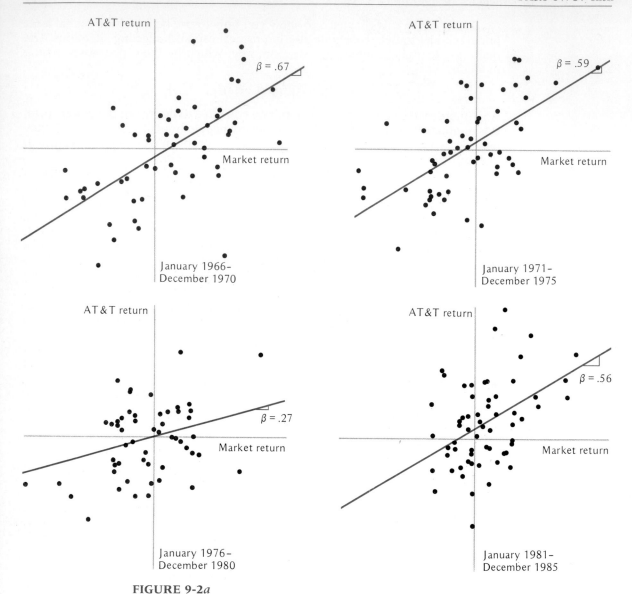

FIGURE 9-2a
We can use data on past prices to obtain an estimate of AT&T's beta. Notice that it is consistently less than 1.

for the same months. In each case we have fitted a line through the points. Beta is the slope of the line. It varied from one period to the other, but there is little doubt that Inland's beta was greater than AT&T's. If you had used the past beta of either stock to predict its future beta, you would, in most cases, not have been too far off. The only real surprise was AT&T's very low beta between 1976 and 1980.

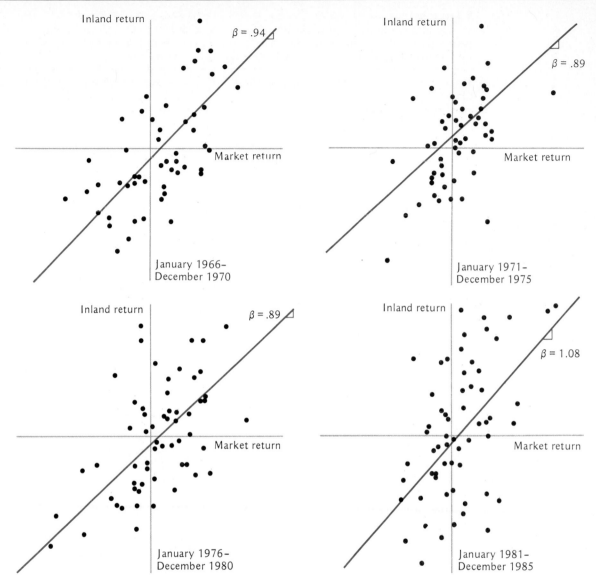

FIGURE 9-2b
Here is a similar exercise for Inland Steel. Notice that Inland's estimated beta is consistently greater than AT&T's.

Stability of Betas over Time

Of course, evidence from two (carefully selected) stocks is not worth much, but betas appear to be reasonably stable. An extensive study of stability was provided by Sharpe and Cooper.[3] They divided stocks into 10 classes according to the estimated beta in that period. Each class contained one-tenth of the stocks in the

[3] W. F. Sharpe and G. M. Cooper, "Risk-Return Classes of New York Stock Exchange Common Stocks, 1931–1967," *Financial Analysts Journal*, **28:** 46–54, 81 (March–April 1972).

TABLE 9-1
Sharpe and Cooper divided stocks into risk classes according to their betas in one 5-year period (class 10 contains high betas, class 1 contains low betas). They then looked at how many of these stocks were in the same risk class 5 years later.

Risk Class	Percent in Same Risk Class 5 Years Later	Percent within One Risk Class 5 Years Later
10	35	69
9	18	54
8	16	45
7	13	41
6	14	39
5	14	42
4	13	40
3	16	45
2	21	61
1	40	62

sample. The stocks with the lowest betas went into class 1. Class 2 contained stocks with slightly higher betas, and so on. They then looked at the frequency with which stocks jumped from one class to another. The more jumps, the less stability. You can see from Table 9-1 that there is a marked tendency for stocks with very high or very low betas to stay that way. If you are willing to stretch the definition of *stable* to include a jump to an adjacent risk class, then from 40 to 70 percent of the betas were stable over the subsequent 5 years.

One reason that these estimates of beta are only imperfect guides to the future is that the stocks may genuinely change their market risk. However, a more important reason is that the betas in any one period are just estimates based on a limited number of observations. If good company news coincides by chance with high market returns, the stock's beta will appear higher than if the news coincides with low market returns. We can twist this the other way around. If a stock appears to have a high beta, it may be because it genuinely does have a high beta, or it may be because we have overestimated it.

This explains some of the fluctuation in betas observed by Sharpe and Cooper. Suppose a company's true beta really is stable. Its apparent (estimated) beta will fluctuate from period to period due to random measurement errors. So the stability of true betas is probably better than Sharpe and Cooper's results seem to imply.

Using a Beta Book

Because of the investment community's interest in market risk, beta estimates of varying quality are regularly published by a number of brokerage and advisory services. Table 9-2 shows an extract from one of the better-known services. Look more closely at Digital Equipment Corporation (DEC), one of the stocks in Table 9-2. Merrill Lynch recorded the change in the price of DEC stock and in the level of the market (represented by Standard and Poor's Composite Index) in each month during a 5-year period. That made 60 monthly observations. DEC's beta of 1.21 was estimated by "straight" regression, that is, by using a standard least-squares regression program to find the line of "best fit."[4]

---

[4] Although it is easy in principle to find a line of best fit, there are some tricks to finding the best time span over which to measure returns, to dealing with stocks that only trade infrequently, and so on. Some "beta services" are much more careful than others.

TABLE 9-2

A page from Merrill Lynch's "beta book"

MLPF&S, INC. --- MARKET SENSITIVITY STATISTICS

TKR SYMB	SECURITY NAME	09/86 CLOSE PRICE	BETA	ALPHA	R-SQR	RESID STD DEV-N	STD.ERR OF BETA	STD.ERR OF ALPHA	ADJUSTED BETA	NUMBER OF OBSERV
DTE1	DETROIT EDISON CO PFD CONV	93.250	.40	.56	.09	4.96	.15	.67	.60	60
DVP	DEVELOPMENT CORP AMER	12.125	1.50	-.56	.30	9.54	.29	1.28	1.33	60
DIN	DEVON RESOURCE INVS DEPOSITA	5.875	.86	-4.68	.04	12.42	.68	3.48	.90	14
DVRY	DEVRY INC	9.500	.62	-.79	.08	7.92	.33	1.43	.75	33
DLCF	DEVELCON ELECTRS LTD	3.438	.21	-4.36	.03	16.28	.69	3.11	.48	30
DWY	DEWEY ELECTRS CORP	3.750	.91	2.29	.02	19.54	.60	2.63	.94	60
DXON	DEXON INC	1.000	2.99	-.98	.12	31.64	.98	4.26	2.32	60
DEX	DEXTER CORP	29.750	.98	.01	.23	7.35	.23	.99	.99	60
DIA9	DI AN CTLS INC	1.313	.28	-.02	.01	18.11	.56	2.44	.52	60
DIG	DI GIORGIO CORP	24.375	.93	.64	.27	6.32	.19	.85	.95	60
DIGN	DIAGNON CORP	1.688	.25	-1.23	.03	20.82	.85	3.49	.50	38
DINO	DIAGNOSTIC INC	7.250	.88	7.28	.01	36.76	1.13	4.95	.92	60
DPC2	DIAGNOSTIC PRUDS CORP	23.000	1.69	.37	.31	10.35	.35	1.55	1.46	51
DRS1	DIAGNOSTIC RETRIEVAL	7.500	1.08	.40	.09	13.10	.40	1.76	1.05	60
DBH	DIAMOND BATHURST INC	16.000	2.07	1.28	.27	13.43	.55	2.28	1.71	37
DMD	DIAMOND CRYSTAL SALT CO	32.500	.37	1.76	.03	7.14	.22	.96	.58	60
DIA	DIAMOND SHAMROCK CORP	10.875	.90	-2.24	.23	6.82	.21	.92	.94	60
SLF	DIANA CORP	11.000	.56	1.48	.04	10.11	.31	1.36	.71	60
DNIC	DIASONICS INC	3.375	1.55	-4.67	.12	15.80	.61	2.50	1.36	43
DXTK	DIAGNOSTEK INC	2.063	1.27	1.67	.00	29.88	1.27	5.82	1.18	29
DBRL	DIBRELL BROS INC	25.000	.95	1.77	.16	8.77	.27	1.18	.96	60
DICN	DICEON ELECTRS INC	19.750	1.12	.13	.13	11.29	.46	2.00	1.08	34
DKJN	DICKEY-JOHN CORP	11.500	.70	-.69	.07	9.87	.30	1.33	.80	60
DCOM	DICOMED CORP	2.250	2.11	-3.22	.31	12.95	.40	1.74	1.74	60
DBD	DIEBOLD INC	39.500	.72	.24	.10	8.51	.26	1.15	.82	60
DIGI	DIGICON INC	.500	1.19	-6.22	.11	13.78	.42	1.84	1.13	60
DILD	DIGILOG INC	6.000	1.11	-.39	.06	16.44	.51	2.21	1.07	60
DEC	DIGITAL EQUIP CORP	89.875	1.21	.21	.23	8.97	.28	1.21	1.14	60
DGPD	DIGITAL PRODS CORP	2.313	.98	-1.88	.02	21.11	.65	2.84	.99	60
DGTD	DIGITECH INC	5.625	3.69	6.73	.08	45.78	1.88	8.00	2.78	35

BASED ON S&P 500 INDEX, USING STRAIGHT REGRESSION   PAGE 46

Source: Merrill Lynch, Pierce, Fenner & Smith, Inc., "Security Risk Evaluation." October 1986.

The other information in Table 9-2 is also interesting.

Alpha. Figure 9-3 shows the line that Merrill Lynch's regression program fitted to the plot of price changes on DEC and the market. Beta is then the slope of the line and alpha (α) is the intercept. DEC's alpha was .21.

Alpha is a rate of price appreciation. Its units are percent per period (in this case percent per month since the line was fitted to monthly data). The alpha of .21 is approximately equal to 12 $\times$ .21, or 2.5 percent per year. From Figure 9-3 we see that alpha was the average rate of price appreciation earned by DEC stockholders when investors in the market as a whole earned nothing. Investors in some of the other stocks listed in Table 9-2 were not so lucky. What about the future? Will DEC continue to offer this rate of appreciation? Possibly, but you should not bet on it. The most likely outcome is that the return (price appreciation plus dividend yield) will simply compensate for the market risk.

R-Squared and Residual Standard Deviation. The column headed *R-SQR* shows the proportion of the total variance of DEC stock price changes that can be explained by market movements. That is, 23 percent of its risk is market risk, and 77 percent is unique risk.

The next column is the amount of unique or diversifiable risk, measured as a standard deviation: 8.97 percent per month for DEC, equivalent to 31 percent per year. This is the standard deviation of the unique price change, that part of the actual change that was not explained by the change in the market index.[5]

Standard Errors of Alpha and Beta. Merrill Lynch's betas are simply *estimates* based on 60 particular months. Therefore, we would like to have an idea of the extent of possible error in these estimates. The column labeled *STD. ERR. OF BETA* provides this information. Statisticians set up a *confidence interval* of the estimated

[5] From these two columns we can figure out the *total* risk of DEC stock. The unique variance is the square of the unique standard deviation: $(8.97)^2 = 80.5$ per month. We know this amounts to 77 percent of the total variance, so total variance must be 80.5/.77, or 104.5 per month. The total variance per year is therefore 104.5 $\times$ 12 = 1254 and the standard deviation per year is $\sqrt{1254} = 35.4$.

FIGURE 9-3
Results of regressing DEC's price changes on the market changes for 60 months ending in October 1986. The slope of the fitted line is beta. The intercept is alpha.

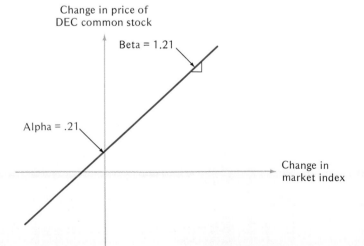

value plus or minus two standard errors. Thus the confidence interval for DEC's beta is between 1.21 plus or minus (2 × .28). If you state that the *true* beta for DEC was between .65 and 1.77, you have a 95 percent chance of being right. You have to do the best you can when estimating risk, but never forget the huge margin for error when estimating beta for individual stocks.[6]

Similarly, the standard error of alpha tells us to be cautious about inferring anything as to DEC's "true" or "normal" alpha. All we can say is that DEC stockholders did well in this particular period.

Adjusted Beta.   Merrill Lynch uses an adjustment formula which gives better predictions than the unadjusted figures listed under *BETA*. The formula pushes high betas down toward 1.0 and low betas up toward 1.0. DEC's adjusted beta is 1.14.

Adjusted betas are tricky to work with, and the Bayesian statistics needed to understand them are beyond the scope of this book. Thus we will stick to "raw" betas.

Industry Betas and the Divisional Cost of Capital	That concludes our lesson on how to estimate and predict betas for individual stocks. You should now understand the basic idea of how to estimate a stock's beta by fitting a line to past data, and you should be able to read and understand a publication like Merrill Lynch's "beta book." Bear in mind that such estimates should enable you to pick up major differences in market risk, but they do not allow you to draw fine distinctions. The reason is that you are exposed to potentially large estimate errors when you estimate betas of individual stocks from a limited sample of data. Fortunately these errors tend to cancel out when you estimate betas of *portfolios.* Suppose that you were to compute the average of the betas of 100 common stocks. The standard error of the average would be about one-tenth of the average standard error of the 100 individual betas.[7] That is why it is often easier to estimate *industry betas* than betas for individual firms.

If DEC is contemplating an across-the-board expansion, it would be reasonable to discount the cash flows at the company cost of capital. To estimate this company cost of capital, DEC could use its stock beta or, better still, the average beta of several similar computer manufacturers.[8] Suppose, however, that DEC proposed instead to invest in the production of computer-controlled machine tools. The company cost of capital is not likely to be the right discount rate for its new machine tool division. For such a venture the company needs an estimate of the division's cost of capital. This is where the notion of an industry beta comes into its own. Probably the best way to estimate the discount rate for such an expansion is to use the beta of a portfolio of firms in the machine tool industry.

Thus we can think of *divisional* costs of capital as a way station between company and project costs of capital. Company costs of capital are nearly useless for diversified firms. If DEC's machine tool venture becomes at all significant, DEC's beta will not measure the risk of *either* the machine tool *or* the computer businesses.

---

[6] The wide confidence interval exaggerates the uncertainty about DEC's true beta. For example, Digital's beta has been consistently above 1.0 for nearly 20 years. Unless its business changes drastically, it is hard to believe that its true beta is substantially less than 1.0.

[7] If the observations are independent, the standard error of the estimated mean declines in proportion to the square root of the number of observations.

[8] But we would have to adjust the observed betas for differences in the debt policies of the firms. This is explained in the next section.

TABLE 9-3
Industry betas

Industry	Beta
Electronic components	1.49
Crude petroleum and natural gas	1.07
Retail department stores	.95
Petroleum refining	.95
Motor vehicle parts	.89
Chemicals	.88
Metal mining	.87
Food	.84
Trucking	.83
Textile mill products	.82
Paper and allied products	.82
Retail grocery stores	.76
Airlines	.75
Steel	.66
Railroads	.61
Natural gas transmission	.52
Telephone companies	.50
Electric utilities	.46

Note: These are *asset* betas. The effect of financial leverage on beta has been removed.
Source: U.S. Federal Energy Regulatory Commission, Testimony of Gerald A. Pogue, Williams Pipe Line Co., Docket Nos. OR79-1, et al., p. 74.

It will just measure the average risk of the two divisions. A company cost of capital based on DEC's beta will almost inevitably be too high for one division and too low for the other.

In Table 9-3 we set out some estimates of industry betas. They range from a high of 1.49 for electronic components to a low of .46 for electric utilities. You can see why diversified companies should set different discount rates for their different activities.

9-2 HOW TO ESTIMATE PHILADELPHIA ELECTRIC'S COST OF CAPITAL—AN EXAMPLE

In Chapter 4 we showed you how to use the constant-growth DCF formula to estimate market capitalization rates for common stocks.[9] That is essentially the same problem we are discussing here: The market capitalization rate for DEC's stock is also its company cost of capital. The constant-growth formula and the capital asset pricing model are two different ways of getting a handle on the same problem.[10]

Remember that we faced many of the same difficulties there as we do here. In

[9] See Section 4-3.

[10] In Chapter 4 we pointed out that the constant-growth formula will not give you very good estimates of the required rate of return for stocks with rapid or unstable growth. But in other cases, the constant-growth formula could give you a useful check on the estimate of r that you get from the capital asset pricing formula.

particular, the constant-growth DCF formula is less reliable for an individual firm than for a sample of comparable-risk firms. We, therefore, suggested that the financial analyst might "take a large sample of equivalent-risk securities, measure r for each, and average." We gave an example in which the constant-growth DCF formula was applied to a sample of large electric utilities.

Table 9-4 shows estimates of beta and the standard errors of these estimates for the common stocks of 23 large utilities. Most of the standard errors are less than DEC's, but they are still large enough to preclude a precise estimate of any particular utility's beta (look at the standard error for Central Maine Power). But our confidence about the average beta of the 23 utilities is much better.

Are these utility stocks really equivalent-risk securities? Judging from Table 9-4, that appears to be a reasonable assumption. Much of the spread of estimated betas could be attributed to random measurement errors. It would be hard to reject the hypothesis that the "true" beta was the same for each of the firms.

Let us consider how a financial manager at, say, Philadelphia Electric might have used the information in Table 9-4 to figure out the firm's cost of capital. There are two clues to the true beta of this stock: the direct estimate of .51 and the average estimate for the industry of .45. Fortunately, these two pieces of evidence are in broad agreement, so let us suppose for the moment that our financial manager takes the easy way out and elects to use the figure of .51. In early 1987 the risk-free rate of interest r_f was 5.6 percent. Therefore if the financial manager had accepted our estimate of 8.4 percent for the risk premium on the market, the

TABLE 9-4
Betas for 23 large electric utilities, 1981–1986

Firm	Beta	Standard Error
Baltimore Gas & Electric	.30	.15
Boston Edison	.33	.15
Carolina Power & Light	.52	.15
Central Hudson Gas & Electric	.44	.19
Central Maine Power	.37	.30
Cincinnati Gas & Electric	.65	.24
Cleveland Electric	.36	.18
Commonwealth Edison	.58	.16
Consolidated Edison	.33	.15
Dayton Power & Light	.40	.28
Delmarva Power & Light	.35	.15
Detroit Edison	.40	.15
Florida Progress	.51	.13
Houston Industries	.54	.15
Idaho Power	.42	.13
Indianapolis Power & Light	.49	.14
Northeast Utilities	.50	.16
Pacific Gas & Electric	.44	.16
Pennsylvania Power & Light	.46	.19
Philadelphia Electric	.51	.19
Public Service Corporation of Colorado	.45	.14
Souther California Edison	.56	.15
Utah Power & Light	.38	.13
Average	.45	

Source: Merrill Lynch, Pierce, Fenner & Smith, Inc., "Security Risk Evaluation," October 1986.

conclusion would be that the expected rate of return on Philadelphia Electric stock was about 10 percent:[11]

$$r = r_f + \beta(r_m - r_f)$$

$$= .056 + .51(.084) = .099, \text{ or about } 10\%$$

Is that the company cost of capital? Unfortunately not. There is one more step.

The cost of capital is a hurdle rate for capital-budgeting decisions. It depends on the *business risk* of the firm's investment opportunities. The risk of a common stock reflects the business risk of the real assets held by the firm. But shareholders also bear *financial risk* to the extent that the firm issues debt to finance its real investments. The more a firm relies on debt financing, the riskier its common stock is.

We did not have to worry about this in DEC's case, because DEC had essentially no debt. But electric utilities use a great deal: Their outstanding debt is typically worth more than their outstanding equity.

Borrowing is said to create *financial leverage* or *gearing*. Financial leverage pushes the firm's common stock or *equity beta* above its *asset* beta. Which beta should we use?

Asset Betas and Equity Betas

Think again of what the *company* cost of capital is and what it is used for. We *define* it as the opportunity cost of capital for the firm's existing assets; we *use* it to value new assets which have the same risk as the old ones. The right beta for calculating the company cost of capital is the beta of the firm's existing assets, its *asset beta*.

Think of a simple balance sheet with assets on the left and debt and equity on the right.

Asset value	Debt value	(D)
	Equity value	(E)
Asset value	Firm value	(V)

Note that the values of debt and equity add up to firm value ($D + E = V$), and that firm value equals asset value.

---

[11] This is really a discount rate for near-term cash flows since it rests on a risk-free interest rate measured by the yield on Treasury bills with maturities of less than 1 year. Is this, you may ask, the right discount rate for cash flows from an asset with, say, a 10- or 20-year expected life?

Well, now that you mention it, possibly not. Longer-term Treasury bonds yielded about 7.5 percent in early 1987, which suggests that investors expected the (short-term) risk-free rate of interest to rise. (We explain this statement in Chapter 23.)

The risk-free rate could be defined as a long-term Treasury bond yield. If you do this, however, you should subtract the risk premium of Treasury bonds over bills, which we gave as 1.0 percent in Table 7-1. This gives a rough-and-ready estimate of the expected yield on short-term Treasury *bills* over the life of the bond:

$$\frac{\text{Expected average}}{\text{T-bill rate}} = \frac{\text{T-bond}}{\text{yield}} - \frac{\text{premium of}}{\text{bonds over bills}}$$

$$= 7.5 - 1.0 = 6.5$$

This figure could in turn be used as an expected average future r_f in the capital asset pricing model. For Philadelphia Electric,

$$r = r_f + \beta(r_m - r_f)$$

$$= .065 + .51(.084) = .108, \text{ or about } 11\%$$

Stockholders own the firm's equity but they can't claim all the asset value; they have to share it with debtholders. The debtholders receive part of the cash flows generated by the firm's assets, and they may bear part of the asset's risks. (For example, if the assets turn out to be worthless, there will be no cash to pay stockholders *or* debtholders.) But debtholders of big firms such as Philadelphia Electric bear much less risk than stockholders. Debt betas are typically close to zero—close enough that for large blue-chip companies many financial analysts just assume $\beta_{\text{debt}} = 0$.[12] But we want the asset beta, β_{asset}. How do we get it?

Suppose you bought *all* the firm's securities—100 percent of the debt and 100 percent of the equity. You would own the assets lock, stock, and barrel. You wouldn't have to share the firm's asset value with anyone; every dollar of cash the firm pays out would be paid out to you. You wouldn't share the risks with anyone else, either; you bear them all. Thus the beta of your debt plus equity portfolio would equal the firm's asset beta.

The beta of this hypothetical portfolio is just a weighted average of the debt and equity betas.[13]

$$\beta_{\text{asset}} = \beta_{\text{portfolio}} = \beta_{\text{debt}} \frac{\text{debt}}{\text{debt} + \text{equity}} + \beta_{\text{equity}} \frac{\text{equity}}{\text{debt} + \text{equity}}$$

Calculating Philadelphia Electric's Asset Beta and Company Cost of Capital

Now that we know how to derive the beta of a firm's assets from the beta of its stock, we can return to the problem of figuring out Philadelphia Electric's company cost of capital. We have already estimated its common stock beta at .51. In early 1987 common stock accounted for about 46 percent of the market value of Philadelphia Electric's securities. The remaining 54 percent consisted of debt and preferred stock. To keep matters simple we will just lump the preferred stock in with the debt and assume both are risk-free.[14] This gives us the following estimates for the beta of Philadelphia Electric's assets:

$$\beta_{\text{asset}} = \beta_{\text{debt}} \frac{\text{debt}}{\text{debt} + \text{equity}} + \beta_{\text{equity}} \frac{\text{equity}}{\text{debt} + \text{equity}}$$

$$= 0(.54) + .51(.46) = .235$$

Of course this is a very low number. The reason it is so low is that Philadelphia Electric's stock beta is low (only .51) despite its heavy use of debt and correspondingly high financial risk. When the financial risk is removed, we find the remaining business risk to be small.

With a risk-free rate of 5.6 percent and an expected market risk premium of 8.4 percent, Philadelphia Electric's cost of capital is

$$r = r_f + \beta_{\text{asset}} (r_m - r_f)$$

$$= .056 + .235(.084) = .076, \text{ or } 7.6\%$$

[12] This assumption should be challenged in periods of volatile interest rates, when prices of long-term corporate and government bonds can fluctuate dramatically. There were periods in the early 1980s when bond betas were as high as .3 to .4.

[13] Here we ignore certain tax complications. If debt interest generates valuable tax savings, then the formula for β_{asset} changes somewhat.

[14] We will discuss preferred stock in Chapter 14. For now all you need to know is that it is less risky than common stock but more risky than debt.

This estimate is probably low, because we arbitrarily assumed Philadelphia Electric's debt was totally risk-free. If we had used $\beta_{debt} = .2$,

$$\beta_{asset} = \beta_{debt} \frac{debt}{debt + equity} + \beta_{equity} \frac{equity}{debt + equity}$$

$$= .2(.54) + .51(.46)$$

$$= .34$$

$$r = r_f + \beta_{asset}(r_m - r_f)$$

$$= .056 + .34(.084) = .085, \text{ or } 8.5\%$$

Business and Financial Risk

A firm's asset beta reflects its *business risk*. The *difference* between its equity and asset beta reflects *financial risk*. More debt means more financial risk.

What would happen if Philadelphia Electric decided to use more debt and correspondingly less equity? It would not affect the firm's *business* risk. There would be no change in the firm's asset beta, and no change in the beta of a portfolio of *all* the firm's debt and equity securities. The *equity* beta would change, however.

Let's go back to our formula for β_{asset},

$$\beta_{asset} = \beta_{debt} \frac{debt}{debt + equity} + \beta_{equity} \frac{equity}{debt + equity}$$

and solve the formula for β_{equity}:

$$\beta_{equity} = \beta_{asset} + (\beta_{asset} - \beta_{debt}) \frac{debt}{equity}$$

If we assume Philadelphia Electric's debt is risk-free, we have

$$\beta_{equity} = .235 + (.235 - 0) \frac{.54}{.46} = .51,$$

which is, of course, the figure we started with from Table 9-4.

But if the company switched to 75 percent debt, β_{equity} would go up to .94:

$$\beta_{equity} = .235 + (.235 - 0) \frac{.75}{.25} = .94$$

We would expect to find this number in a future edition of Merrill Lynch's beta book. On the other hand, if Philadelphia Electric paid off all its debt, we would expect to find:

$$\beta_{equity} = \beta_{asset} + (\beta_{asset} - \beta_{debt}) \frac{debt}{equity}$$

$$= .235 + (.235 - 0) \frac{0}{1.0}$$

$$= .235$$

With no debt, the firm's asset and equity betas would be exactly the same.

In general, the observed equity beta depends on the firm's asset beta, β_{asset}, the spread between the asset and debt betas, $\beta_{asset} - \beta_{debt}$, and the ratio of debt to equity. Figure 9-4 plots the relationship assuming risk-free debt ($\beta_{debt} = 0$).

FIGURE 9-4

Effect of financial leverage on β_{equity}, the beta of the firm's common stock. The higher the debt-equity ratio, the higher β_{equity}. When the firm uses no debt (D/E = 0), $\beta_{equity} = \beta_{asset}$; β_{asset} measures the business risk of the firm's assets. Note that this figure is drawn assuming risk-free debt ($\beta_{debt} = 0$).

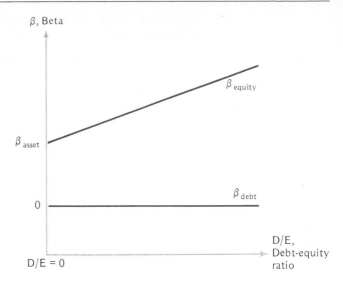

In many ways we have given an oversimplified version of how financial leverage affects equity risks and returns. We have said nothing about taxes, for example. The finer points can wait. For now, there are really just two points to remember. First, *financial leverage creates financial risk.* The beta of the firm's stock increases in proportion to the amount borrowed. Second, *asset betas can always be calculated as a weighted average of the betas of the various debt and equity securities issued by the firm.* Of course, it is the asset beta that is relevant in capital budgeting decisions, not the beta of the firm's stock.[15]

9-3 SETTING DISCOUNT RATES WHEN YOU CAN'T USE A BETA BOOK

Stock or industry betas provide a rough guide to the risk typically encountered in various lines of business. But an asset beta for, say, the steel industry can take us only so far. Not all investments made in the steel industry are "typical." What other kinds of evidence about business risk might a financial manager examine?

In some cases the asset is publicly traded. If so, we can simply estimate its beta from past price data. For example, suppose a firm wants to analyze the risks of holding a large inventory of copper. Because copper is a standardized, widely traded commodity, it is possible to calculate rates of return from holding copper and to calculate a copper beta.[16]

What should a manager do if the asset has no such convenient price record? What if the proposed capital investment is not close enough to business as usual to justify using a company or divisional cost of capital?

---

[15] Incidentally, financial risk has been removed from the figures shown in Table 9-3; they are estimated industry *asset* betas.

[16] You may encounter an interesting statistical problem. Because trading in copper is less active than in the stock market, changes in copper prices may tend to lag changes in the value of the market portfolio. You may therefore uncover the full market risk of copper only when rates of return on copper are related to previous market rates of return. This problem is often called a *Fisher effect*, after Lawrence Fisher of the University of Chicago, who first called attention to it. Watch out for it anytime you are working with price data taken from a "thin" market.

These cases clearly call for judgment. For managers making that kind of judgment, we offer two pieces of advice.

1. *Avoid fudge factors.* Don't give in to the temptation to add fudge factors to the discount rate to offset things that could go wrong with the proposed investment. Adjust cash flow forecasts first.
2. *Think about the determinants of asset betas.* Often the characteristics of high- and low-beta assets can be observed when the beta itself cannot be.

Let us expand on each of these points.

Avoiding Fudge Factors in Discount Rates

We have defined risk from the investor's viewpoint, as the standard deviation of portfolio return or the beta of a common stock or other security. But in everyday usage "risk" simply equals "bad outcome." People think of the "risks" of a project as a list of things that can go wrong. For example,

- A geologist looking for oil worries about the "risk of a dry hole."
- A pharmaceutical manufacturer worries about the "risk" that a new drug which cures baldness may not be approved by the Food and Drug Administration.
- The owner of a hotel in a politically unstable part of the world worries about the "political risk" of expropriation.

Managers often add fudge factors to discount rates to offset worries such as these.

This sort of adjustment makes us nervous. First, the bad outcomes we cited appear to reflect unique (that is, diversifiable) risks which would not affect the expected rate of return demanded by investors. Second, the need for a discount rate adjustment usually arises because managers fail to give bad outcomes their due weight in cash-flow forecasts. The managers then try to offset that mistake by adding a fudge factor to the discount rate.

Example.   Project Z will produce just one cash flow, forecasted at $1 million at year 1. It's regarded as average risk, suitable for discounting at a 10 percent company cost of capital:

$$PV = \frac{C_1}{1 + r} = \frac{1,000,000}{1.1} = \$909,100$$

But now you discover that the company's engineers are behind schedule in making the technology required for the project work. They're "confident" it will work, but admit to a small chance that it won't. You still see the *most likely* outcome as $1 million, but you also see some chance that project Z will generate *zero* cash flow next year.

Now the project's prospects are clouded by your new worry about technology. It must be worth less than the $909,100 you calculated before that worry arose. But how much less? There is *some* discount rate (10 percent plus a fudge factor) which will give the right value, but we don't know what that adjusted discount rate is.

We suggest you reconsider your original $1 million forecast for project Z's cash flow. Project cash flows are supposed to be *unbiased* forecasts, which give due weight to all possible outcomes, favorable and unfavorable. Managers making unbiased forecasts are correct on average. Sometimes their forecasts will turn out high, sometimes low, but their errors will average out over many projects.

If you forecast cash flow of $1 million for projects like Z, you will overestimate the average cash flow, because every now and then you will hit a zero. Those zeros should be "averaged in" to your forecasts.

For many projects, the most likely cash flow is also the unbiased cash flow. If there are three possible outcomes, for example, with the probabilities shown below, the unbiased forecast is $1 million. (The unbiased forecast is the sum of the probability-weighted cash flows.)

Possible Cash Flow	Probability	Probability-Weighted Cash Flow	Unbiased Cash Flow
1.2	.25	.3	
1.0	.50	.5	1.0, or $1 million
.8	.25	.2	

This might describe the initial prospects of project Z. But if technological uncertainty introduces the chance of a zero cash flow, the unbiased forecast could drop to $833,300:

Possible Cash Flow	Probability	Probability-Weighted Cash Flow	Unbiased Forecast
1.2	.25	.3	
1.0	.333	.333	.833, or $833,000
.8	.25	.2	
0	.167	0	

Present value is:

$$PV = \frac{.833}{1.1} = .757, \text{ or } \$757,000$$

Now, of course, you can figure out the right fudge factor to add to the discount rate to apply to the original $1 million forecast to get the right answer. But you have to think through possible cash flows in order to get that fudge factor, and once you have thought through the cash flows you don't need the fudge factor.

Managers often work out a range of possible outcomes for major projects, sometimes with explicit probabilities attached. We give more elaborate examples and further discussion in Chapter 10. But even when a range of outcomes and probabilities is not explicitly written down, the manager can still consider the good and bad outcomes as well as the most likely one. When the bad outcomes outweigh the good, the cash-flow forecast should be reduced until balance is regained.

Step 1, then, is to do your best to make unbiased forecasts of a project's cash flows. Step 2 is to consider whether *investors* would regard the project as more or less risky than typical for a company or division. Here our advice is to search for characteristics of the asset that are associated with high or low betas. We wish we had a more fundamental scientific understanding of what these characteristics are. We see business risks surfacing in capital markets, but as yet there is no completely satisfactory theory describing how those risks are generated. Nevertheless, some things are known.

**What
Determines
Asset Betas?**

Cyclicality. Many people intuitively associate risk with the variability of book, or accounting, earnings. But much of this variability reflects diversifiable or unique risk. Lone prospectors in search of gold look forward to extremely uncertain future earnings, but whether or not they strike it rich is unlikely to depend on the performance of the market portfolio. Even if they do find gold, they do not bear much market risk. Therefore, an investment in gold has a high standard deviation but a relatively low beta.

What really counts is the strength of the relationship between the firm's earnings and the aggregate earnings on all real assets. We can measure this either by the *accounting beta* or by the *cash-flow beta*. These are just like a real beta except that changes in book earnings or cash flow are used in place of rates of return on securities. We would predict that firms with high accounting or cash-flow betas should also have high stock betas—and the prediction is correct.[17]

This means that cyclical firms—firms whose revenues and earnings are strongly dependent on the state of the business cycle—tend to be high-beta firms. Thus you should demand a higher rate of return from investments whose performance is strongly tied to the performance of the economy.

*Operating Leverage. We have already seen that financial leverage—in other words, the commitment to fixed debt charges—increases the beta of an investor's portfolio. In just the same way, operating leverage—in other words, the commitment to fixed *production* charges—must add to the beta of a capital project. Let's see how this works.

The cash flows generated by any productive asset can be broken down into revenue, fixed costs, and variable costs

$$\text{Cash flow} = \text{revenue} - \text{fixed cost} - \text{variable cost}$$

Costs are variable if they depend on the rate of output. Examples are raw materials, sales commissions, and some labor and maintenance costs. Fixed costs are cash outflows that occur regardless of whether the asset is active or idle—property taxes, for example, or the wages of workers under contract.

We can break down the asset's present value in the same way:

$$\text{PV(asset)} = \text{PV(revenue)} - \text{PV(fixed cost)} - \text{PV(variable cost)}$$

Or equivalently:

$$\text{PV(revenue)} = \text{PV(fixed cost)} + \text{PV(variable cost)} + \text{PV(asset)}$$

Those who *receive* the fixed costs are like debtholders in the project. Those who receive the net cash flows from the asset are like holders of levered equity in PV(revenue).

We can now figure out how the asset's beta is related to the betas of the values of revenue and costs. We just use our previous formula with the betas relabeled:

$$\beta_{\text{revenue}} = \beta_{\text{fixed cost}} \frac{\text{PV(fixed cost)}}{\text{PV(revenue)}} + \beta_{\text{variable cost}} \frac{\text{PV(variable cost)}}{\text{PV(revenue)}}$$
$$+ \beta_{\text{asset}} \frac{\text{PV(asset)}}{\text{PV(revenue)}}$$

---

[17] For example, see W. H. Beaver and J. Manegold, "The Association between Market-Determined and Accounting-Determined Measures of Systematic Risk: Some Further Evidence," *Journal of Financial and Quantitative Analysis,* **10:** 231–284 (June 1975).

In other words, the beta of the value of the revenues is simply a weighted average of the beta of its component parts. Now the fixed-cost beta is zero by definition: Whoever receives the fixed costs holds a safe asset. The betas of the revenues and variable costs should be approximately the same, because they respond to the same underlying variable, the rate of output. Therefore, we can substitute β_{revenue} for $\beta_{\text{variable cost}}$ and solve for the asset beta. Remember that $\beta_{\text{fixed cost}} = 0$.

$$\beta_{\text{asset}} = \beta_{\text{revenue}} \frac{PV(\text{revenue}) - PV(\text{variable cost})}{PV(\text{asset})}$$

$$= \beta_{\text{revenue}} \left[1 + \frac{PV(\text{fixed cost})}{PV(\text{asset})} \right]$$

Thus, given the cyclicality of revenues (reflected in β_{revenue}), asset beta is proportional to the ratio of the present value of fixed costs to the present value of the project.

Now you have a rule of thumb for judging the relative risks of alternative designs or technologies for producing the same project. Other things being equal, the alternative with the higher ratio of fixed costs to project value will have the higher project beta.

Firms or assets whose costs are mostly fixed are said to have high *operating leverage*. As we have seen, the analogy between financial and operating leverage is almost exact. The beta of the stock increases in proportion to the ratio of debt to equity, and the beta of the asset increases in proportion to the ratio of the value of the fixed costs to the value of the asset. Empirical tests confirm that companies with high operating leverage actually do have high betas.[18]

Searching for Clues

Recent research suggests a variety of other factors that affect an asset's beta.[19] But going through a long list of these possible determinants would take us too far afield.

You cannot hope to estimate the relative risk of assets with any precision, but good managers examine any project from a variety of angles and look for clues as to its riskiness. They know that high market risk is a characteristic of cyclical ventures and of projects with high fixed costs. They think about the major uncertainties affecting the economy and consider how projects are affected by these uncertainties.[20]

9-4　*ANOTHER LOOK AT DISCOUNTED CASH FLOW

We have spent the bulk of this chapter discussing how you might estimate the risk and required return on a project. We now have to worry a little about what happens as risk changes over the life of a project.

[18] See B. Lev, "On the Association between Operating Leverage and Risk," *Journal of Financial and Quantitative Analysis*, **9**: 627–642 (September 1974), and G. N. Mandelker and S. G. Rhee, "The Impact of the Degrees of Operating and Financial Leverage on Systematic Risk of Common Stock," *Journal of Financial and Quantitative Analysis*, **19**: 45–57 (March 1984).

[19] This work is reviewed in G. Foster, *Financial Statement Analysis*, 2d ed., Prentice-Hall, Inc., Englewood Cliffs, N.J., 1986, Chapter 10.

[20] Sharpe's article on a "multi-beta" interpretation of market risk offers a useful way of thinking about these uncertainties and tracing out their impact on a firm's or project's risk. W. F. Sharpe, "The Capital Asset Pricing Model: A 'Multi-Beta' Interpretation," in H. Levy and M. Sarnat (eds.), *Financial Decision Making Under Uncertainty*, New York, Academic Press, 1977.

We have implied that an expected rate of return calculated from the capital asset pricing model

$$r = r_f + \beta(r_m - r_f)$$

could be plugged into the standard discounted cash flow formula as

$$PV = \sum_{t=1}^{T} \frac{C_t}{(1 + r)^t} = \sum_{t=1}^{T} \frac{C_t}{[1 + r_f + \beta(r_m - r_f)]^t}$$

You should not take that step without thinking about it first. In capital budgeting we must usually value cash flows extending over several future periods. The discounted cash flow formula does this in one step, but the capital asset pricing model looks at rates of return and prices over one period at a time.

One-period projects pose no problems:

$$PV = \frac{C_1}{1 + r} = \frac{C_1}{1 + r_f + \beta(r_m - r_f)}$$

Longer-lived assets likewise pose no problem if you have an estimate of PV_1, future value 1 period hence

$$PV_0 = \frac{C_1 + PV_1}{1 + r} = \frac{C_1 + PV_1}{1 + r_f + \beta(r_m - r_f)}$$

But suppose that your company is evaluating the construction of a hydroelectric dam and asks your advice on how to calculate its present value. Would you tell it not to bother about anything other than the cash flow in the first period and the end-of-period value? Of course not. The end-of-period value depends on the cash flow in later periods. You would want a formula that explicitly took this into account.

When this problem arose in Chapter 3 we solved it by expressing PV_1 as $(C_2 + PV_2)/(1 + r)$, and substituting until all future PVs were eliminated and PV_0 was tied only to the asset's cash-flow stream. This is formally correct only if we *know* that the discount rates that will prevail in future periods will be the same as this year's. Among other things,[21] this requires the asset's beta to be constant over the asset's entire future life. Only under that crucial assumption is it strictly proper to write down the discounted cash flow formula with a single discount rate for all future cash flows.

What does that assumption mean in practical terms? In order to answer that question we must develop alternative formulas for calculating present value when beta and r *do* vary.

*Certainty Equivalents

Let us start again with a single future cash flow C_1. If C_1 is certain, its present value is found by discounting at the risk-free rate r_f:

$$PV = \frac{C_1}{1 + r_f}$$

[21] See E. F. Fama, "Risk-Adjusted Discount Rates and Capital Budgeting under Uncertainty," *Journal of Financial Economics,* **5:** 3–24 (August 1977); or S. C. Myers and S. M. Turnbull, "Capital Budgeting and the Capital Asset Pricing Model: Good News and Bad News," *Journal of Finance,* **32:** 321–332 (May 1977).

If the cash flow is risky, the normal procedure is to discount its forecasted (expected) value at a *risk-adjusted discount rate r* which is greater than r_f.[22]

Another approach is to ask, "What is the smallest *certain* return for which I would exchange the risky cash flow $\tilde{C}_1$?" This is called the *certainty equivalent of* $\tilde{C}_1$, denoted by CEQ_1.

Suppose that the forecasted value of the risky cash flow is $1000, but that you would be willing to trade it for a safe cash flow of as little as $800. Then $800 is the certainty equivalent of the risky cash flow. You are indifferent between an $800 *safe* return and an *expected*, but risky, cash flow of $1000.

What is the present value of the $1000 forecasted cash flow? It must be the same as the present value of a certain $800, because by definition you are indifferent between the two flows. Suppose the risk-free rate of interest is $r_f = .08$. Then

$$\text{PV of forecasted \$1000 cash flow} = \frac{CEQ_1}{1 + r_f} = \frac{800}{1.08} = \$740.74$$

You could have gotten the same answer by discounting $1000 at a risk-adjusted rate. We can figure out what the proper discount rate is. If

$$PV = \frac{1000}{1 + r} = \$740.74$$

then $r = .35$, or 35 percent.

Now we have two equivalent expressions for PV.[23]

$$PV = \frac{C_1}{1 + r} = \frac{CEQ_1}{1 + r_f}$$

As long as you look only one period into the future, the two formulas are exactly the same. But there are important differences when the concept of certainty equivalents is applied to cash flows generated by long-lived assets.[24]

---

*Certainty Equivalent and Risk-Adjusted Discount Rate Formulas for Long-Lived Assets

We can easily extend the concept of certainty equivalents to long-lived assets:

$$PV = \sum_{t=1}^{T} \frac{CEQ_t}{(1 + r_f)^t} = \sum_{t=1}^{T} \frac{a_t C_t}{(1 + r_f)^t}$$

---

[22] The quantity r can be less than r_f for assets with negative betas. But the betas of the assets which corporations hold are almost always positive.

[23] CEQ_1 can be calculated directly from the capital asset pricing model. The formula is:

$$CEQ_1 = C_1 - \lambda \, \text{cov} \, (\tilde{C}_1, \tilde{r}_m)$$

where cov $(\tilde{C}_1, \tilde{r}_m)$ is the covariance between the dollar cash flow $(\tilde{C}_1)$ and the return on the market portfolio $(\tilde{r}_m)$, and

$$\lambda = \frac{r_m - r_f}{\sigma_m^2}$$

Here $r_m - r_f$ is the expected risk premium on the market portfolio; σ_m^2 is the variance of the market return. The quantity λ is often referred to as the *market price of risk*. In the appendix to this chapter we show you where this formula for CEQ_1 comes from.

[24] The risk-adjusted discount rate formula can always be applied to long-lived assets if a different discount rate is used for each period's cash flow. But that approach does not help explain the assumption required for use of a constant risk-adjusted rate.

where a_t is the ratio of the certainty equivalent of a cash flow to its expected value ($a_t = \text{CEQ}_t/C_t$). Normally a_t will be positive, but less than 1.0.[25]

When we discount at a constant risk-adjusted rate r, we are implicitly making a special assumption about the coefficients a_t. Consider an asset offering cash flows in two periods. If the certainty equivalent and risk-adjusted discount rate formulas are really equivalent, they should give the same present value for *each* cash flow:

$$\frac{C_1}{1 + r} = \frac{a_1 C_1}{1 + r_f} \quad \text{and} \quad \frac{C_2}{(1 + r)^2} = \frac{a_2 C_2}{(1 + r_f)^2}$$

But this implies that

$$a_1 = \frac{1 + r_f}{1 + r} \quad \text{and} \quad a_2 = \left(\frac{1 + r_f}{1 + r}\right)^2 = (a_1)^2$$

In general, you are justified in using a constant risk-adjusted discount rate r to value the cash flow for each period only if the value of a_t decreases over time at a constant rate. The formula is

$$a_t = \left(\frac{1 + r_f}{1 + r}\right)^t = (a_1)^t$$

*Using Risk-
Adjusted
Discount
Rates—An
Example

Consider a project requiring $350 today ($t = 0$) and offering expected cash flows of $100 per year for 5 years. The risk-free rate is 4 percent, the market risk premium is 9 percent, and the estimated beta is .67; therefore the financial manager settles on a discount rate of

$$r = r_f + \beta(r_m - r_f)$$
$$= .04 + .67(.09) = .10, \text{ or } 10\%$$

The project's net present value is calculated as

$$\text{NPV} = \text{PV} - 350 = \sum_{t=1}^{5} \frac{100}{(1.10)^t} - 350 = \$29$$

What is the financial manager implicitly assuming about the values of a_t? The answer is given by Table 9-5. By using a constant discount rate the financial manager is effectively making a much larger deduction for risk from the later cash flows. The larger deduction is reflected in lower values for a_t. Notice also that a_t decreases at a constant compound rate of about 5.5 percent per year.

It is usually reasonable to assume that risk increases at a constant rate. For example, if you are willing to assume that beta is constant in each future period, then the risk borne *per period* will be constant but cumulative risk will grow steadily as you look further into the future.

*When You
Cannot Use a
Single Risk-
Adjusted
Discount Rate
for Long-
Lived Assets

Here is a disguised, simplified, and somewhat exaggerated version of an actual project proposal that one of the authors was asked to analyze. The scientists at Vegetron have come up with an electric mop, and the firm is ready to go ahead with pilot production and test marketing. The preliminary phase will take a year and cost $125,000. Management feels that there is only a 50 percent chance that

[25] The quantity a_t would be greater than 1.0 for negative-beta assets.

TABLE 9.5
Example showing certainty equivalents implied by use of constant risk-adjusted discount rate

Period	Expected Cash Flow $= C_t$	Present Value Using 10% Risk-Adjusted Discount Rate, $PV = C_t/(1.10)^t$	Certainty Equivalent CEQ_t Implied by Use of 10% Discount Rate, $CEQ_t = C_t \left(\dfrac{1 + r_f}{1 + r} \right)^t$	a_t, Ratio of CEQ_t to C_t	Present Value of CEQs at 4% Risk-Free Rate
0	-350	-350	-350	1.00	-350
1	100	91	95	0.945	91
2	100	83	89	0.894	83
3	100	75	85	0.845	75
4	100	68	80	0.799	68
5	100	62	76	0.755	62
	Net present value =	29			29

Note: By using a constant risk-adjusted discount rate of 10 percent the financial manager is implicitly making larger deductions for risk from the later cash flows. Notice that discounting the cash flows at 10 percent *or* the certainty equivalents at 4 percent would give NPV = 29.

pilot production and market tests will be successful. If they are, then Vegetron will build a $1 million plant which would generate an expected annual cash flow in perpetuity of $250,000 a year after taxes. If they are not successful, the project will have to be dropped.

The expected cash flows (in thousands of dollars) are

$$C_0 = -125$$

$$C_1 = 50\% \text{ chance of } -1000 \text{ and } 50\% \text{ chance of } 0$$

$$= .5(-1000) + .5(0) = -500$$

$$C_t, \text{ for } t = 2, 3, \ldots$$

$$= 50\% \text{ chance of } 250 \text{ and } 50\% \text{ chance of } 0$$

$$= +.5(250) + .5(0) = 125$$

Management has little experience with consumer products and considers this a project of extremely high risk:[26] Therefore, they discount the cash flows at 25 percent, rather than Vegetron's normal 10 percent standard:

$$NPV = -125 - \frac{500}{1.25} + \sum_{t=2}^{\infty} \frac{125}{(1.25)^t} = -125, \text{ or } -\$125,000$$

This seems to show that the project is not worthwhile.

Management's analysis is open to criticism if the first year's experiment resolves a high proportion of the risk. If the test phase is a failure, then there's no risk at all—the project is *certain* to be worthless. If it is a success, there could well be only normal risk from there on. That means there is a 50 percent chance that in 1 year Vegetron will have the opportunity to invest in a project of *normal* risk, for which

[26] We will assume they mean high *market* risk, and that the difference between 25 and 10 percent is *not* a fudge factor introduced to offset optimistic cash-flow forecasts.

the *normal* discount rate of 10 percent would be appropriate. Thus they have a 50 percent chance to invest $1 million in a project with a net present value of $1.5 million:

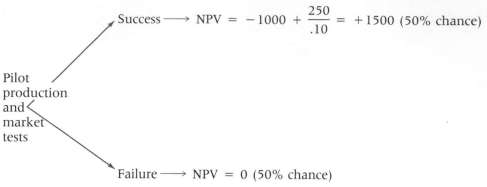

$$\text{Success} \longrightarrow \text{NPV} = -1000 + \frac{250}{.10} = +1500 \ (50\% \text{ chance})$$

Pilot production and market tests

$$\text{Failure} \longrightarrow \text{NPV} = 0 \ (50\% \text{ chance})$$

Thus, we could view the project as offering an expected payoff of $.5(1500) + .5(0) = 750$ or $750,000 at $t = 1$ on a $125,000 investment at $t = 0$. Of course, the certainty equivalent of the payoff is less than $750,000, but a_1 would have to be very small to justify rejecting the project. For example, if the CEQ is half the expected value ($a_1 = .5$), and the risk-free rate is 7 percent, the project is worth $225,500:

$$\text{NPV} = C_0 + \frac{a_1 C_1}{1 + r_f}$$

$$= -125 + \frac{.5(750)}{1.07} = 225.5, \text{ or } \$225,500$$

Not bad for a $125,000 investment—and quite a change from the negative NPV that management got by discounting all future cash flows at 25 percent.

A Common Mistake

You sometimes hear people say that because distant cash flows are "riskier," they should be discounted at a higher rate than earlier cash flows. That's quite wrong: *Any* risk-adjusted discount rate automatically recognizes the fact that more distant cash flows have more risk. The reason is that the discount rate compensates for the risk borne *per period*. The more distant the cash flows, the greater the number of periods and the larger the *total* risk adjustment.

9-5 SUMMARY

In Chapter 8 we set out some basic principles for valuing risky assets. In this chapter we have tried to show you how to apply these principles to practical situations.

The problem is easiest when you believe that the project has the same market risk as the company's existing assets. In this case, the required return would be equal to the required return on the company's securities. This is often called the *company's cost of capital.* Capital asset pricing theory states that the required return on any asset depends on its beta:

$$r = r_f + \beta(r_m - r_f)$$

Therefore to figure out the company's cost of capital you need to find the beta of its assets.

A good place to start is with the beta of the company's stock. The most common way to estimate the beta of a stock is to figure out how the stock price has responded to market changes in the past. Of course, this will only give you an estimate of the stock's true beta. You may get a more reliable figure if you take an average of the estimated betas for a group of similar companies.

Suppose that you now have an estimate of the stock's beta. Can you plug that into the capital asset pricing formula to find the company cost of capital? No, the stock beta may reflect both business and financial risk. Whenever a company borrows money, it increases the beta (and the expected return) of its stock. Therefore, to calculate the company cost of capital, you must first adjust the beta of the stock to remove the effect of this financial risk.

The company cost of capital is the correct discount rate for projects that have the same risk as the company's existing business. Many firms, however, use the company cost of capital to discount the forecasted cash flows on all new projects. This is a dangerous procedure. It is *project risk* that counts.

We cannot give you a neat formula that will allow you to estimate project betas, but we can give you some clues. First, avoid adding fudge factors to discount rates to offset worries about bad project outcomes. Adjust cash-flow forecasts to give due weight to bad outcomes as well as good; *then* ask whether the chance of bad outcomes adds to the project's market risk. Second, you can often identify the characteristics of a high- or low-beta project even when project beta cannot be calculated directly. For example, you can try to figure out how far the cash flows are affected by the overall performance of the economy: Cyclical investments are generally high-beta investments. Another thing you should look at is the project's operating leverage: Fixed production charges work like fixed debt charges; that is, they increase beta.

There is one more fence to jump. The capital asset pricing model values only the cash flow for the first period (C_1). But most projects go on producing cash flows for several years. It would be very convenient if you could use the capital asset pricing model risk-adjusted rate r to discount each of these cash flows:

$$\text{PV} = \sum_{t=1}^{T} \frac{C_1}{(1 + r)^t} = \sum_{t=1}^{T} \frac{C_t}{[1 + r_f + \beta(r_m - r_f)]^t}$$

If you do this, you are implicitly assuming that cumulative risk increases at a constant rate as you look further out into the future. That assumption is usually reasonable. The assumption is precisely true when the project's future beta will be constant, that is, when risk *per period* will be constant.

It is the exceptions that prove the rule. You should therefore be on the alert for projects where risk very clearly does *not* increase steadily. In these cases, you should break the project into segments within which the same discount rate can be reasonably used. Or you should use the certainty-equivalent version of the DCF model which allows you to make separate risk adjustments to each period's cash flow.

As we pointed out in Chapter 8, the capital asset pricing model is probably not the ultimate truth about risk and return in capital markets. New, and presumably better, theories are emerging as research continues. But the capital asset pricing model is a useful rule of thumb, and a good vehicle for presenting basic concepts. That is why we have devoted this chapter to its application to capital budgeting problems.

Finally, remember that the most fundamental principle presented in this chapter does not depend on the capital asset pricing model. The principle is:

> *Each project should be evaluated at its own opportunity cost of capital; the
> true cost of capital depends on the use to which the capital is put.*

This follows from value additivity. The capital asset pricing model implies value
additivity, but value additivity holds as well under other theories of asset valuation.

APPENDIX   USING THE CAPITAL ASSET PRICING MODEL TO CALCULATE CERTAINTY EQUIVALENTS

When calculating present value you can take account of risk in either of two ways.
You can discount the expected cash flow C_1 by the risk-adjusted discount rate r:

$$PV = \frac{C_1}{1 + r}$$

Alternatively, you can discount the certainty equivalent cash flow CEQ_1 by the
risk-free rate of interest r_f:

$$PV = \frac{CEQ_1}{1 + r_f}$$

In this appendix we show how you can derive CEQ_1 from the capital asset pricing
model.

We know from our present value formula that $1 + r$ equals the expected dollar
payoff on the asset divided by its present value:

$$1 + r = \frac{C_1}{PV}$$

The capital asset pricing model also tells us that $1 + r$ equals

$$1 + r = 1 + r_f + \beta(r_m - r_f)$$

Therefore,

$$\frac{C_1}{PV} = 1 + r_f + \beta(r_m - r_f)$$

In order to find beta, we calculate the covariance between the asset return and
the market return and divide by the market variance:

$$\beta = \frac{\text{cov }(\tilde{r}, \tilde{r}_m)}{\sigma_m^2} = \frac{\text{cov }[(\tilde{C}_1/PV - 1, \tilde{r}_m)]}{\sigma_m^2}$$

The quantity $\tilde{C}_1$ is the future cash flow and is, therefore, uncertain. But PV is the
asset's present value: It is *not* unknown and, therefore, does not "covary" with
$\tilde{r}_m$. Therefore, we can rewrite the expression for beta as

$$\beta = \frac{\text{cov }(\tilde{C}_1, \tilde{r}_m)}{PV \; \sigma_m^2}$$

Substituting this expression back into our equation for C_1/PV gives

$$\frac{C_1}{PV} = 1 + r_f + \frac{\text{cov }(\tilde{C}_1, \tilde{r}_m)}{PV} \cdot \frac{r_m - r_f}{\sigma_m^2}$$

The expression $(r_m - r_f)/\sigma_m^2$ is the expected risk premium on the market per unit
of variance. It is often known as the *market price of risk* and is written as λ (lambda).

Thus

$$\frac{C_1}{PV} = 1 + r_f + \frac{\lambda \; cov \; (\tilde{C}_1, \; \tilde{r}_m)}{PV}$$

Multiplying through by PV and rearranging, gives

$$PV = \frac{C_1 - \lambda \; cov \; (\tilde{C}_1, \; \tilde{r}_m)}{1 + r_f}$$

This is the certainty-equivalent form of the capital asset pricing model. It tells us that, if the asset is risk-free, cov $(\tilde{C}_1 \; \tilde{r}_m)$ is zero and we simply discount C_1 by the risk-free rate. But, if the asset is risky, we must discount the certainty equivalent of C_1. The deduction that we make from C_1 depends on the market price of risk and on the covariance between the cash flows on the project and the return on the market.

FURTHER READING

There is a good review article by Rubinstein on the application of the capital asset pricing model to capital investment decisions:

M. E. Rubinstein: "A Mean-Variance Synthesis of Corporate Financial Theory," *Journal of Finance,* **28:** 167–182 (March 1973).

For evidence on the stability of betas estimated from past stock price data, see:

M. E. Blume: "On the Assessment of Risk," *Journal of Finance,* **26:** 1–10 (March 1971).
W. F. Sharpe and G. M. Cooper: "Risk-Return Classes of New York Stock Exchange Common Stocks, 1931–1967," *Financial Analysts Journal,* **28:** 46–54, 81 (March–April 1972).

There have been a number of studies of the relationship between accounting data and beta. Many of these are reviewed in:

G. Foster: *Financial Statement Analysis,* 2d ed., Prentice-Hall, Inc., Englewood Cliffs, N.J. 1986.

For some ideas on how one might break down the problem of estimating beta, see:

W. F. Sharpe: "The Capital Asset Pricing Model: A 'Multi-Beta' Interpretation," in H. Levy and M. Sarnat (eds.), *Financial Decision Making Under Uncertainty,* New York, Academic Press, 1977.

The assumptions required for use of risk-adjusted discount rates are discussed in:

E. F. Fama: "Risk-Adjusted Discount Rates and Capital Budgeting under Uncertainty," *Journal of Financial Economics,* **5:** 3–24 (August 1977).
S. C. Myers and S. M. Turnbull: "Capital Budgeting and the Capital Asset Pricing Model: Good News and Bad News," *Journal of Finance,* **32:** 321–332 (May 1977).

The relationship between the certainty equivalent and risk-adjusted discount rate valuation formulas was first discussed by:

A. A. Robichek and S. C. Myers, "Conceptual Problems in the Use of Risk-Adjusted Discount Rates," *Journal of Finance,* **21:** 727–730 (December 1966).

QUIZ

1. Suppose a firm uses its company cost of capital to evaluate all capital projects. What kinds of mistakes will it make?

2. A project costs $100,000 and offers a single $150,000 cash flow 1 year hence. The project beta is 2.0 and the market risk premium $(r_m - r_f)$ is 8 percent. Look up current risk-free interest rates in the *Wall Street Journal* or another newspaper. Use the capital asset pricing model to find the opportunity cost of capital and the present value of the project.

3. Look again at Table 9-2 and the row of statistics shown for Diamond Shamrock Corp. Define and interpret each of these statistics.

4. A company is financed 40 percent by risk-free debt. The interest rate is 10 percent, the expected market return is 20 percent, and the stock's beta is .5. What is the company cost of capital?

5. The total market value of the common stock of the Okenfenokee Real Estate Company is $6 million, and the total value of its debt is $4 million. The treasurer estimates that the beta of the stock is currently 1.5 and that the expected risk premium on the market is 10 percent. The Treasury bill rate is 8 percent.
(a) What is the required return on Okenfenokee stock?
(b) What is the beta of the company's existing portfolio of assets?
(c) Estimate the company's cost of capital.
(d) Estimate the discount rate for an expansion of the company's present business.
(e) Suppose the company wants to diversify into the manufacture of rose-colored spectacles. The beta of unleveraged optical manufacturers is 1.2. Estimate the required return on Okenfenokee's new venture.

6. A geologist fears that a new oil well will be a dry hole. He therefore discounts the well's forecasted cash flows at 30 percent rather than the oil company's 10 percent overall cost of capital. Is this good discounting practice? Can you suggest a better approach?

*7. Which of these companies is likely to have the higher company cost of capital?
(a) A's sales force is paid a fixed annual rate; B's is paid on a commission basis.
(b) C produces machine tools; D produces breakfast cereal.

*8. Select the appropriate phrase from within each pair of brackets:
"In calculating PV there are two ways to adjust for risk. One is to make a deduction from the expected cash flows. This is known as the *certainty-equivalent method*. It is usually written as PV = $[CEQ_t/(1 + r_f)^t; CEQ_t/(1 + r_m)^t]$. The certainty-equivalent cash flow, CEQ_t, can be written as $a_t C_t$, where a_t is [greater than 1; less than 1]. Another way to allow for risk is to discount the expected cash flows at a rate of r. If we use the capital asset pricing model to calculate r, r is $[r_f + \beta r_m; r_f + \beta(r_m - r_f); r_m + \beta(r_m - r_f)]$. This method is *exact* for a one-period project. It is exact for a long-lived project only if the values of a_t [increase at a constant rate; are constant; decrease at a constant rate]. For the majority of projects, the use of a single discount rate, r, is probably a perfectly acceptable approximation.

*9. A project has a forecasted cash flow of $110 in year 1 and $121 in year 2. The interest rate is 5 percent, the estimated risk premium on the market is 10 percent, and the project has a beta of .5. If you use a constant risk-adjusted discount rate, what is
(a) The present value of the project?
(b) The certainty-equivalent cash flows in years 1 and 2?
(c) The ratio (a_t) of the certainty-equivalent cash flows to the expected cash flows in years 1 and 2?

QUESTIONS AND PROBLEMS

1. Look at Table 9-2.
   (a) How much did Digiloc's price tend to change in an unchanged market?
   (b) Which stock had price changes that were most closely related with the market? What proportion of the stock's risk was market risk, and what proportion was unique risk?
   (c) What is the confidence interval on Digiloc's beta?
   (d) Why is the adjusted beta for Diasonics lower than the unadjusted beta?
   (e) What is the total risk of Diebold, Inc., *per year?*
2. Explain the estimate of alpha for Diebold, Inc., in Table 9-2. Why is this not a good guide to the stock's future alpha? What is your best forecast of alpha?
3. (a) Nero Violins has the following capital structure:

Security	Beta	Total Market Value, Thousands of Dollars
Debt	0	100
Preferred stock	.20	40
Common stock	1.20	200

   What is the firm's asset beta (that is, the beta of its stock if it were all-equity-financed)?
   (b) Assume the capital asset pricing model is correct. What discount rate should Nero set for investments that expand the scale of its operations without changing its asset beta? Assume any new investment is all-equity-financed. Plug in numbers that are reasonable today. Specify two discount rates, one real and one nominal.
4. Amalgamated Products has three operating divisions:

Division	Percent of Firm Value
Food	50
Electronics	30
Chemicals	20

   In order to estimate the cost of capital for each division, Amalgamated has identified the following three principal competitors:

	Estimated Equity Beta	Debt/(Debt + Equity)
United Foods	.8	.3
General Electronics	1.6	.2
Associated Chemicals	1.2	.4

   (a) Assuming that the debt of these firms is risk-free, estimate the asset beta for each of Amalgamated's divisions.
   (b) Amalgamated's· debt to debt plus equity ratio is .4. If your estimates of divisional betas are right, what is Amalgamated's equity beta?

(c) Assume that the risk-free interest rate is 7 percent and the expected return on the market index is 15 percent. Estimate the cost of capital for each of Amalgamated's divisions.

(d) How much would your estimates of each division's cost of capital change if you assumed that each company's debt had a beta of .2?

5. Calculate the financial leverage for any three companies in Table 9-2 (other than DEC), and estimate the opportunity cost of capital for a "typical" investment by each firm.

6. "The errors in estimating beta are so great that you might just as well assume that all betas are 1.0." Do you agree?

7. Mom and Pop Groceries has just dispatched a year's supply of groceries to the government of the Central Antarctic Republic. Payment of $250,000 will be made 1 year hence after the shipment arrives by snow train. Unfortunately there is a good chance of a coup d'état, in which case the new government will not pay. Mom and Pop's controller therefore decides to discount the payment at 40 percent, rather than the company's 12 percent cost of capital.

(a) What's wrong with using a 40 percent rate to offset "political risk"?

(b) How much is the $250,000 payment really worth if the odds of a coup d'état are 25 percent?

8. Here is a more challenging problem involving cash-flow forecasts, discount rates, and fudge factors. An oil company executive is considering investing $10 million in one or both of two wells: *Well 1* is expected to produce oil worth $3 million per year for 10 years; *well 2* is expected to produce $2 million for 15 years. These are *real* (inflation-adjusted) cash flows.

The beta for *producing* wells is .9. The market risk premium is 8 percent, the nominal risk-free interest rate is 6 percent, and expected inflation is 4 percent.

The two wells are intended to develop a previously discovered oil field. Unfortunately there is still a 20 percent chance of a dry hole in each case. A dry hole means zero cash flows and complete loss of the $10 million investment.

Ignore taxes and make further assumptions as necessary.

(a) What is the correct real discount rate for cash flows from developed wells?

(b) The oil company executive proposes to add 20 percentage points to the real discount rate to offset the risk of a dry hole. Calculate the NPV of each well with this adjusted discount rate.

(c) What do *you* say the NPVs of the two wells are?

(d) Is there any *single* fudge factor that could be added to the discount rate for developed wells that would yield the correct NPV for both wells? Explain.

*9. A project has the following forecasted cash flows:

CASH FLOWS,
THOUSANDS OF DOLLARS

C_0	C_1	C_2	C_3
-100	$+40$	$+60$	$+50$

The estimated project beta is 1.5. The market return r_m is 16 percent, and the risk-free rate r_f is 7 percent.

(a) Estimate the opportunity cost of capital and the project's present value (using the same rate to discount each cash flow).

(b) What are the certainty-equivalent cash flows in each year?

(c) What is the ratio (a_t) of the certainty-equivalent cash flow to the expected cash flow in each year?

(d) Explain why this ratio declines.

*10. Recalculate Table 9-5 assuming that:

(a) Expected cash flow is $150 per year for 5 years.

(b) The risk-free rate of interest is 5 percent.

(c) The market risk premium is 9 percent.

(d) The estimated beta is 1.2.

*11. The McGregor Whiskey Company is proposing to market diet scotch. The product will first be test-marketed for 2 years in Southern California at an initial cost of $500,000. This test launch is not expected to produce any profits but should reveal consumer preferences. There is a 60 percent chance that demand will be satisfactory. In this case, McGregor will spend $5 million to launch the scotch nationwide and will receive an expected annual profit of $700,000 in perpetuity. If demand is not satisfactory, diet scotch will be withdrawn.

Once consumer preferences are known, the product will be subject to an average degree of risk, and therefore, McGregor requires a return of 12 percent on its investment. However, the initial test-market phase is viewed as much riskier, and McGregor demands a return of 40 percent on this initial expenditure.

What is the NPV of the diet scotch project?

12. "For a high-beta project, you should use a high discount rate to value positive cash flows and a low discount rate to value negative cash flows." Is this statement correct? Should the sign of the cash flow affect the appropriate discount rate?

PART THREE

PRACTICAL PROBLEMS IN CAPITAL BUDGETING

10 A Project Is Not a Black Box

A *black box* is something that we accept and use but do not understand. For most of us a computer is a black box. We may know what it is supposed to do, but we do not understand how it works and, if something breaks, we cannot fix it.

We have been treating capital projects as black boxes. In other words, we have talked as if managers are handed unbiased cash-flow forecasts and their only task is to assess risk, choose the right discount rate, and crank out net present value. Actual financial managers won't rest until they understand what makes the project tick and what could go wrong with it. Remember Murphy's law, "If anything can go wrong, it will," and O'Reilly's corollary, "at the worst possible time."

Even if the project's risk is wholly diversifiable, you still need to understand why the venture could fail. Once you know that, you can decide whether it is worth trying to resolve the uncertainty. Maybe further expenditure on market research would clear up these doubts about acceptance by consumers, maybe another drill hole would give you a better idea of the size of the ore body, and maybe some further work on the test bed would confirm the durability of those welds. If the project really has a negative NPV, the sooner you can identify it, the better. And even if you decide that it is worth going ahead on the basis of present information, you do not want to be caught by surprise if things subsequently go wrong. You want to know the danger signals and the actions you might take.

In short, managers avoid black boxes whenever they can, and they reward whoever can help them look inside. Consequently, consultants and academics have developed procedures for what we will call *project analysis*. We will discuss several of the procedures in this chapter, mainly sensitivity analysis, break-even analysis, Monte Carlo simulation, and decision trees. There is no magic in these techniques, just computer-assisted common sense. You don't need a license to use them.

Some analysts have proposed these techniques not only for project analysis but also as a supplement or replacement for net present value. You can imagine our reaction to that. Their proposals seem to reflect a belief that net present value cannot cope with risk. But we have seen that it can cope.

10-1 SENSITIVITY ANALYSIS

Uncertainty means that more things can happen than will happen. Therefore, whenever you are confronted with a cash-flow forecast, you should try to discover what else can happen.

Put yourself in the well-heeled shoes of the treasurer of the Jalopy Motor Company. You are considering the introduction of a small electrically powered car for city use. Your staff members have prepared the cash-flow forecasts shown in

TABLE 10-1
Preliminary cash-flow forecasts in millions of dollars for
Jalopy Motor's electric car project

	Year 0	Years 1–10
Investment	150	
1. Revenue		375
2. Variable cost		300
3. Fixed cost		30
4. Depreciation		15
5. Pretax profit (1 − 2 − 3 − 4)		30
6. Tax		15
7. Net profit (5 − 6)		15
8. Operating cash flow (4 + 7)		30
Net cash flow	−$150	$30

Assumptions:
Investment is depreciated over 10 years straight line.
Income is taxed at a rate of 50 percent.

Table 10-1. Since NPV is positive at the 10 percent opportunity cost of capital, it appears to be worth going ahead.

$$\text{NPV} = -150 + \sum_{t=1}^{10} \frac{30}{(1.10)^t} = \$34.3 \text{ million}$$

Before you decide, you want to delve into these forecasts[1] and identify the key variables that determine whether the project succeeds or fails. It turns out that the marketing department has estimated revenue as follows:

Unit sales = new product's share of market × size of car market
= .01 × 10 million = 100,000 cars

Revenue = unit sales × price per unit
= 100,000 × 3750 = $375 million

The production department has estimated variable costs per unit as $3000. Since projected volume is 100,000 cars per year, *total* variable cost is $300 million. Fixed costs are $300 million per year. The initial investment can be depreciated on a straight-line basis over the 10-year period, and profits are taxed at a rate of 50 percent.

These seem to be the important things you need to know, but look out for unidentified variables. Perhaps there are patent problems, or perhaps you will need to invest in service stations that will recharge the car batteries. The greatest dangers often lie in these *unknown* unknowns, or "unk-unks," as scientists call them.

Having found no unk-unks (no doubt you'll find them later), you conduct a **sensitivity analysis** with respect to market size, market share, and so on. In order to do this, the marketing and production staffs are asked to give optimistic

[1] Bear in mind, when you are working with cash-flow forecasts, the distinction between the expected value and the most likely (or modal) value. Present values are concerned with *expected* cash flows— that is, the weighted average of the possible cash flows. If the distribution of possible outcomes is skewed, the expected cash flow will not be the same as the most likely cash flow.

TABLE 10-2
To undertake a sensitivity analysis of the electric car project, we set each variable *in turn* at its most pessimistic or optimistic value and recalculate the net present value of the project

Variable	RANGE			NET PRESENT VALUE, MILLIONS OF DOLLARS		
	Pessimistic	Expected	Optimistic	Pessimistic	Expected	Optimistic
Market size	9 million	10 million	11 million	+11	+34	+57
Market share	.004	.01	.016	−104	+34	+173
Unit price	$3,500	3,750	3,800	−42	+34	+50
Unit variable cost	$3,600	3,000	2,750	−150	+34	+111
Fixed cost	$40 million	30 million	20 million	+4	+34	+65

and pessimistic estimates for the underlying variables. These are set out in the left-hand columns of Table 10-2. The right-hand side shows what happens to the project's net present value if the variables are set *one at a time* to their optimistic and pessimistic values. Your project appears to be by no means a sure thing. The most dangerous variables appear to be market share and unit variable cost. If market share is only .004 (and all other variables are as expected), then the project has an NPV of − $104 million. If unit variable cost is $3600 (and all other variables are as expected), then the project has an NPV of − $150 million.

Value of Information

Now you can check whether an investment of time or money could resolve some of the uncertainty *before* your company parts with the $150 million investment. Suppose that the pessimistic value for unit variable cost partly reflects the production department's worry that a particular machine will not work as designed and that the operation will have to be performed by other methods at an extra cost of $200 per unit. The chance that this will occur is only 1 in 10. But, if it did occur, the extra $200 unit cost would reduce after-tax cash flow by

Unit sales × additional unit cost × (1 − tax rate)
$$= 100,000 \times 200 \times .50 \times \$10 \text{ million}$$

It would reduce the net present value of your project by

$$\sum_{t=1}^{10} \frac{10}{(1.10)^t} = \$61.4 \text{ million}$$

Suppose further that a $100,000 pretest of the machine will reveal whether it will work or not and allow you to clear up the problem. It clearly pays to invest $100,000 to avoid a 10 percent probability of $61.4 million loss. You are ahead by − 100,000 + .10 × 61,400,000 = $6,040,000.

On the other hand, the value of additional information about market size is small. Because the project is acceptable even under pessimistic assumptions about market size, you are unlikely to be in trouble if you have misestimated that vari-able.[2]

Limits to Sensitivity Analysis

Sensitivity analysis boils down to expressing cash flows in terms of unknown variables and then calculating the consequences of misestimating the variables. It forces the manager to identify the underlying variables, indicates where additional information would be most useful, and helps to expose confused or inappropriate forecasts.

One drawback to sensitivity analysis is that it always gives somewhat ambig-uous results. For example, what exactly does *optimistic* or *pessimistic* mean? The marketing department may be interpreting the terms in a different way from the production department. Ten years from now, after hundreds of projects, hindsight may show that the marketing department's pessimistic limit was exceeded twice as often as the production department's; but what you may discover 10 years hence is no help now. One solution is to ask the two departments for a *complete* description of the various odds. However, it is far from easy to extract a forecaster's subjective notion of the complete probability distribution of possible outcomes.[3]

Another problem with sensitivity analysis is that the underlying variables are likely to be interrelated. What sense does it make to look at the effect in isolation of an increase in market size? If market size exceeds expectations, it is likely that demand will be stronger than you anticipated and unit prices will be higher. And why look in isolation at the effect of an increase in price? If inflation pushes prices to the upper end of our range, it is quite probable that costs will also be inflated. And so on.

Sometimes the analyst can get around the problem by defining underlying variables so that they are roughly independent. But you cannot push *one-at-a-time* sensitivity analysis too far. It is impossible to obtain expected, optimistic, and pessimistic values for total *project* cash flows from the information in Table 10-2.

Examining the Project under Different Scenarios

If the variables are interrelated, it may help to consider some alternative plausible combinations. For example, perhaps the company economist is worried about the possibility of another sharp rise in world oil prices. The direct effect of this would be to encourage the use of electrically powered cars. The popularity of "compacts" after the oil price increases in the 1970s leads you to estimate that an immediate 20 percent price rise in oil would enable you to capture an extra .3 percent of the automobile market. On the other hand, the economist also believes that higher oil prices would prompt a world recession and at the same time stimulate inflation. In that case, market size might be in the region of 8 million cars and both prices and cost might be 15 percent higher than your initial estimates. Table 10-3 shows that this scenario of higher oil prices and recession would on balance help your new venture. Its net present value would increase to $65 million.

[2] Of course, these are very simple examples. The derivation of optimal rules for investing in information is a well-developed part of Bayesian statistics. See H. Raiffa, *Decision Analysis: Introductory Lectures on Choices under Uncertainty*, Addison-Wesley Publishing Company, Inc., Reading, Mass., 1968; and H. Raiffa and R. Schlaifer, *Applied Statistical Decision Theory*, Division of Research, Graduate School of Business Administration, Harvard University, Boston, 1961.

[3] If you doubt this, try some simple experiments. Ask the person who repairs your television to state a numerical probability that your set will work for at least 1 more year. Or construct your own subjective probability distribution of the number of telephone calls you will receive next week. That ought to be easy. Try it.

TABLE 10-3
How the net present value of the electric car project would be affected by higher oil prices and a world recession

	CASH FLOWS YEARS 1–10, MILLIONS OF DOLLARS	
	Base Case	High Oil Prices and Recession Case
1. Revenue	375	449
2. Variable cost	300	359
3. Fixed cost	30	35
4. Depreciation	15	15
5. Pretax profit (1 − 2 − 3 − 4)	30	40
6. Tax	15	20
7. Net profit (5 − 6)	15	20
8. Net cash flow (4 + 7)	+30	35
Present value of cash flows	+184	+215
Net present value	+34	+65

	ASSUMPTIONS	
	Base Case	High Oil Prices and Recession Case
Market size	10 million	8 million
Market share	.01	.013
Unit price	$3,750	$4,313
Unit variable cost	$3,000	$3,450
Fixed cost	$30 million	$35 million

Managers often find it helpful to look at how their project would fare under different scenarios. It allows them to look at different but *consistent* combinations of variables. Forecasters generally prefer to give an estimate of revenues or costs under a particular scenario than to give some absolute optimistic or pessimistic value.

Break-Even Analysis

When we undertake a sensitivity analysis of a project or when we look at alternative scenarios, we are asking how serious it would be if sales or costs turn out to be worse than we forecasted. Managers sometimes prefer to rephrase this question and ask how bad sales can get before the project begins to lose money. This exercise is known as **break-even analysis**.

In the left-hand portion of Table 10-4 we set out the revenues and costs of the electric car project under different assumptions about annual sales.[4] In the right-hand portion of the table we discount these revenues and costs to give us the *present value* of the inflows and the *present value* of the outflows. *Net* present value is of course the difference between these numbers.

You can see that NPV is strongly negative if the company does not produce a single car. It is just positive if (as expected) the company sells 100,000 cars and is strongly positive if it sells 200,000 cars. Clearly the *zero*-NPV point occurs a little under 100,000 cars.

---

[4] Notice that if the project makes a loss, this loss can be used to reduce the tax bill on the rest of the company's business. In this case the project produces a tax saving—the tax outflow is negative.

TABLE 10-4
NPV in millions of dollars of electric car project under different assumptions about unit sales

Unit Sales, Thousands of Cars	INFLOWS Revenue Years 1–10	OUTFLOWS YEAR 0 Investment	OUTFLOWS YEARS 1–10 Variable Costs	Fixed Costs	Taxes	PV Inflows	PV Outflows	NPV
0	0	150	0	30	−22.5	0	196	−196
100	375	150	300	30	15	2,304	2,270	34
200	750	150	600	30	52.5	4,608	4,344	264

In Figure 10-1 we have plotted the present value of the inflows and outflows under different assumptions about annual sales. The two lines cross when sales are 85,000 cars. This is the point at which the project has zero NPV. As long as sales are greater than 85,000, the project has a positive NPV.

Instead of working with the present values of the inflows and outflows, we could work equally well with the equivalent annual revenues and costs. The annual cost of the project includes the recurring costs (variable costs, fixed costs, and taxes) *plus* the equivalent annual cost of the $150 million initial investment. To calculate the equivalent annual cost of the initial investment we divide the investment by the 10-year annuity factor:

$$\text{Equivalent annual cost of investment} = \frac{\text{Investment}}{\text{10-year annuity factor}}$$

$$= \frac{150}{6.145} = \$24.4 \text{ million}$$

FIGURE 10-1
A break-even chart showing the present value of Jalopy's cash inflows and outflows under different assumptions about unit sales. NPV is zero when sales are 85,000.

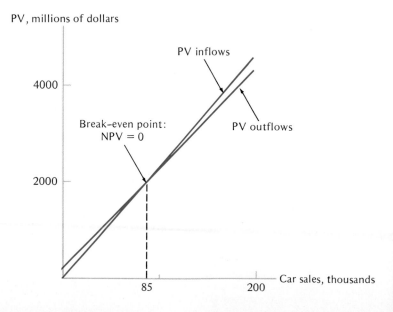

TABLE 10-5
Equivalent annual cash flow from the electric car project under different assumptions about unit sales (millions of dollars)

Unit Sales, Thousands of Cars	INFLOWS Revenues	EQUIVALENT ANNUAL OUTFLOW Initial Investment	Variable Costs	Fixed Costs	Taxes	Total	Net Equivalent Annual Flow
0	0	24.4	0	30	−22.5	31.9	−31.9
100	375	24.4	300	30	15	369.4	5.6
200	750	24.4	600	30	52.5	706.9	43.1

In Table 10-5 we show the equivalent annual revenues and costs under our three assumptions about unit sales. The final column of this table shows the difference between the annual revenues and costs. As long as this is positive, the project has a positive NPV.

In Figure 10-2 we have plotted the equivalent annual revenues and costs against different levels of sales. As you would expect, it tells exactly the same story as Figure 10-1. The two lines cross when sales are 85,000 cars. At this point, equivalent annual revenues equal equivalent annual costs and the project has zero NPV.

It really makes no difference whether we work with present values or equivalent annual revenues and costs. The two methods give identical answers. Very frequently, however, managers do not use either method: instead, they calculate the break-even point in terms of accounting profits. Table 10-6 shows the effect on Jalopy's after-tax profit of differences in electric car sales. Once again, in Figure 10-3 we have plotted revenues and costs against unit sales. But the story this time is different. Figure 10-3, which is based on accounting profits, shows a break-even point of 60,000 cars; Figures 10-1 and 10-2, which are based on present values

FIGURE 10-2
We can redraw our break-even chart in terms of Jalopy's equivalent annual revenues and costs. The net equivalent annual flow is zero when sales are 85,000.

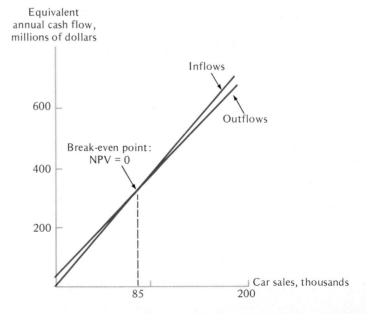

TABLE 10-6
Effect of the electric car project on accounting profit under different assumptions about unit sales (millions of dollars)

Unit Sales, Thousands of Cars	Revenue	Variable Costs	Fixed Costs	Depreciation	Taxes	Total Costs	Profit after Tax
0	0	0	30	15	−22.5	22.5	−22.5
100	375	300	30	15	15	360	15
200	750	600	30	15	52.5	697.5	52.5

and equivalent annual flows, both show a break-even point of 85,000 cars. Why the difference?

When we work in terms of accounting profit, we deduct depreciation of $15 million each year to cover the cost of the initial investment. If Jalopy sells 60,000 cars a year, revenues will be sufficient both to pay operating costs and to recover the initial outlay of $150 million. But they will *not* be sufficient to repay the *opportunity cost* of that $150 million. If we allow for the fact that the $150 million could have been invested elsewhere to earn 10 percent, the annual cost of the investment is not $15 million but $24.4 million.

Companies that break even on an accounting basis are really making a loss—they are losing the opportunity cost of their investment. Reinhardt has described a dramatic example of this mistake.[5] In 1971 Lockheed managers found themselves having to give evidence to Congress on the viability of the company's L-1011 TriStar program. They argued that the program appeared to be "commercially attractive" and that TriStar sales would eventually exceed the break-even point of about 200 aircraft. But in calculating this break-even point, Lockheed appears to

[5] U. E. Reinhardt, "Break-Even Analysis for Lockheed's TriStar: An Application of Financial Theory," *Journal of Finance*, **28**: 821–838 (September 1973).

FIGURE 10-3
Sometimes break-even charts are constructed in terms of accounting numbers. After-tax profit is zero when sales are 60,000.

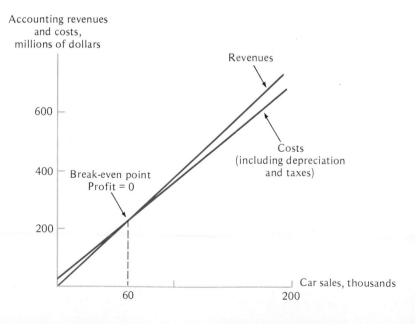

have ignored the opportunity cost of the huge $1 billion capital investment on this project. Had it allowed for this cost, the break-even point would probably have been nearer to 500 aircraft.

10-2 MONTE CARLO SIMULATION

Sensitivity analysis allows you to consider the effect of changing one variable at a time. By looking at the project under alternative scenarios, you can consider the effect of a *limited number* of plausible combinations of variables. **Monte Carlo simulation** is a tool for considering *all* possible combinations. It therefore enables you to inspect the entire distribution of project outcomes. Its use in capital budgeting is principally associated with David Hertz[6] and McKinsey and Comany, the management consultants. As we shall see, it is a controversial method.

Imagine that you are a gambler at Monte Carlo. You know nothing about the laws of probability (few gamblers do), but a friend has suggested to you a complicated strategy for playing roulette. Your friend has not actually tested the strategy but is confident that it will *on the average* give you a 2½ percent return for every 50 spins of the wheel. Your friend's optimistic estimate for any series of 50 spins is a profit of 55 percent; your friend's pessimistic estimate is a loss of 50 percent. How can you find out whether these really are the odds? An easy but possibly expensive way is to start playing and record the outcome at the end of each series of 50 spins. After, say, 100 series of 50 spins each, plot a frequency distribution of the outcomes and calculate the average and upper and lower limits. If things look good, you can then get down to some serious gambling.

An alternative is to tell a computer to simulate the roulette wheel and the strategy. In other words, you could instruct the computer to draw numbers out of its hat to determine the outcome of each spin of the wheel and then to calculate how much you would make or lose from the particular gambling strategy.

That would be an example of Monte Carlo simulation. In capital budgeting we replace the gambling strategy with a model of the project, and the roulette wheel with a model of the world in which the project operates. Let's see how this might work with our project for an electrically powered car.

Simulating the Electric Car Project

Step 1: Modeling the Project. The first step in any simulation is to give the computer a precise model of the project. For example, the sensitivity analysis of the car project was based on the following implicit model of cash flow:

Cash flow = (revenues − costs − depreciation) × (1 − tax rate)
            + depreciation

Revenues = market size × market share × unit price

Costs = (market size × market share × variable unit cost) + fixed cost

This model of the project was all that you needed for the simpleminded sensitivity analysis that we described above. But if you wish to simulate the whole project, you need to think about how the variables are interrelated.

For example, consider the first variable—market size. The marketing department has estimated a market size of 10 million cars in the first year of the project's life, but of course you do not *know* how things will work out. Actual market size

[6] See D. B. Hertz, "Investment Policies that Pay Off," *Harvard Business Review*, **46:** 96–108 (January–February 1968).

will exceed or fall short of expectations by the amount of the department's error in the forecast:

$$\text{Market size, year 1} = \text{expected market size, year 1} \times \left(1 + \begin{array}{c} \text{proportionate} \\ \text{forecast error,} \\ \text{year 1} \end{array} \right)$$

You *expect* the forecast error to be zero but it could turn out to be positive or negative.

You can write the market size in the second year in exactly the same way:

$$\text{Market size, year 2} = \text{expected market size, year 2} \times \left(1 + \begin{array}{c} \text{proportionate} \\ \text{forecast error,} \\ \text{year 2} \end{array} \right)$$

But at this point you must consider how the expected market size in year 2 is affected by what happens in year 1. If car sales are below expectations in year 1, it is likely that they will continue to be below in subsequent years. Suppose that a shortfall in sales in year 1 would lead you to revise down your forecast of sales in year 2 by a like amount. Then

$$\text{Expected market size, year 2} = \text{actual market size, year 1}$$

Now you can rewrite the market size in year 2 in terms of the actual market size in the previous year plus a forecast error:

$$\text{Market size, year 2} = \text{market size, year 1} \times \left(1 + \begin{array}{c} \text{proportionate} \\ \text{forecast error,} \\ \text{year 2} \end{array} \right)$$

In the same way you can describe the expected market size in year 3 in terms of market size in year 2 and so on.

This set of equations illustrates how you can describe interdependence between different *periods*. But you also need to allow for interdependence between different *variables*. For example, the price of electrically powered cars is likely to increase with general inflation and with market size. Suppose that these are the only uncertainties and that a 10 percent shortfall in market size would lead you to predict a 3 percent reduction in price. Then you could model the first year's price as follows:

$$\text{Price, year 1} = \text{expected price, year 1} \times \left(1 + \begin{array}{c} \text{error in} \\ \text{inflation} \\ \text{forecast,} \\ \text{year 1} \end{array} + \begin{array}{c} .3 \times \text{error in} \\ \text{market size} \\ \text{forecast,} \\ \text{year 1} \end{array} \right)$$

Then, if these variations in the inflation rate and market size exert a permanent effect on price, you can define the second year's price as

$$\text{Price, year 2} = \text{expected price, year 2} \times \left(1 + \begin{array}{c} \text{error in} \\ \text{inflation} \\ \text{forecast,} \\ \text{year 2} \end{array} + \begin{array}{c} .3 \times \text{error in} \\ \text{market size} \\ \text{forecast,} \\ \text{year 2} \end{array} \right)$$

$$= \text{actual price, year 1} \times \left(1 + \begin{array}{c} \text{error in} \\ \text{inflation} \\ \text{forecast,} \\ \text{year 2} \end{array} + \begin{array}{c} .3 \times \text{error in} \\ \text{market size} \\ \text{forecast,} \\ \text{year 2} \end{array} \right)$$

The complete model of your project would include a set of equations for each of the variables—market size, price, market share, unit variable cost, and fixed cost. You can imagine that even if you allow for only a few interdependencies between variables and across time, the result would be quite a complex list of equations.[7] Perhaps that is not a bad thing if it forces you to understand what the project is all about. Model building is like spinach: you may not like the taste, but it is good for you.

Step 2: Specifying Probabilities.   Remember the procedure for simulating the gambling strategy? The first step was to specify the strategy, the second was to specify the numbers on the roulette wheel, and the third was to tell the computer to select these numbers at random and calculate the results of the strategy:

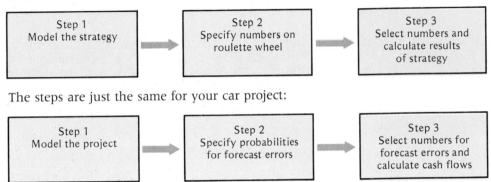

The steps are just the same for your car project:

Figure 10-4 illustrates how you might go about specifying your possible errors in forecasting market size. You *expect* market size to be 10 million cars. You obviously don't think that you are underestimating or overestimating market size; therefore your expected forecast error is zero. On the other hand, the marketing department has given you a range of possible estimates. Market size could be as low as 9 million cars or as high as 11 million cars. Thus the forecast error has an expected value of 0 and a range of plus or minus 10 percent.

You need to draw up similar patterns of the possible forecast errors for each of the other variables that are in your model.[8]

Step 3: Simulate the Cash Flows.   The computer now *samples* from the distribution of the forecast errors, calculates the resulting cash flows for each period, and records them. After many iterations you begin to get accurate estimates of the probability distributions of the project cash flows.[9]

Figure 10-5 shows the output of some actual simulations of the Jalopy Motor Company project. You can see that in the first year the expected cash flow is about $31 million and that there is a 95 percent chance that the cash flow will fall within the range of $4 million to $57 million.

[7]Specifying the interdependencies is the hardest and most important part of a simulation. If all components of project cash flows were unrelated, simulation would rarely be necessary.

[8] Figure 10-4 asserts that you are less likely to have made a large forecast error than a small forecast error. More precisely, it says that the probability of a possible error declines in proportion to the absolute size of the error. But forecast errors do not always fit this pattern. For example, the marketing department may feel that it is equally likely that market size will fall anywhere within the range of 9 million to 11 million cars.

[9] Accurate only to the extent that your model and the probability distributions of the forecast errors are accurate. Remember the GIGO principle: "Garbage in, garbage out."

FIGURE 10-4
Distribution of errors in forecasting market size. The expected error is 0, but the error could be as large as plus or minus 10 percent.

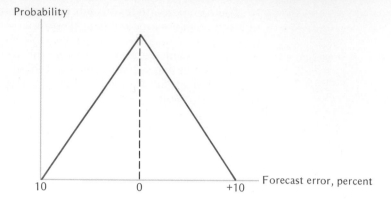

Have you noticed one slightly curious feature of this result? Our simulations tell us that the expected cash flow in each year is about $31 million, but the new products group told you that the expected cash flow was $30 million. They evidently arrived at this figure by taking the expected sales, multiplying by the expected profit per unit, and deducting the expected fixed cost and tax:

$$\text{Expected sales (units)} \times \left(\begin{array}{c} \text{expected} \\ \text{expected unit price} - \text{variable} \\ \text{unit cost} \end{array} \right)$$

$$- \text{ expected fixed costs } - \text{ expected tax}$$

$$100{,}000(3750 - 3000) - 30 \text{ million} - 15 \text{ million} = \$30 \text{ million}$$

Unfortunately, there was an error in the logic of the new products group. The expected revenues are *not* equal to the expected unit sales times the expected unit price unless sales and price are unrelated. If that sounds odd to you, consider the following example. Suppose a firm is equally likely to sell 100 items at a price of

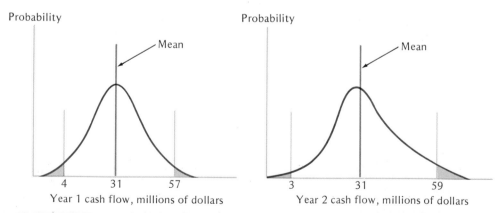

Year 1 cash flow, millions of dollars   Year 2 cash flow, millions of dollars

FIGURE 10-5
An example of the simulation output for the first 2 years of the electric car project. It provides cash-flow forecasts (i.e., the means of the simulated distributions) as well as some idea of the predictability. The outer pairs of vertical lines include 95 percent of the simulated cash flows.

$1 each or 300 items at a price of $3 each. Its expected unit sales are (100 × 300)/2 = 200, and the expected price is (1 + 3)/2 = $2. The expected unit sales times the expected price is, therefore, 200 × 2 = $400. But the expected *revenue* is [(100 × 1) + (300 × 3)]/2 = $500.

Similarly in the case of Jalopy Motors, price tends to go up and down with sales volume. Therefore the calculations of the new products group have *underestimated* the expected cash flow. Simulation therefore has given us one useful piece of information: project NPV is

$$-150 + \sum_{t=1}^{10} \frac{31}{(1.10)^t} = \$40 \text{ million}$$

Assessing Simulation: You Pay for What You Get	Simulation, though costly and complicated, has the obvious merit of compelling the forecaster and the decision maker to face up to uncertainty and to interdependencies.

Once you have constructed your model, it is simple to analyze what would happen if you were able to narrow down the range of uncertainty about any of the variables. You may also be able to use it to explore the effect of modifications to the project.

All this makes simulation sound like a panacea for the world's ills. But, as usual, you pay for what you get. In fact you sometimes pay for *more* than you get.

It is not just a matter of the time and money spent in building the model. It is extremely difficult to estimate interrelationships between variables and the underlying probability distributions, even when you are trying to be honest. But in capital budgeting, forecasters are seldom impartial and the probability distributions on which the simulation is based can be highly biased.

In practice, a simulation that attempts to be realistic will also be very complex. That usually means the decision maker delegates the task of constructing the model to management scientists or consultants. The danger here is that, even if the builders understand their creation, the decision maker cannot and therefore does not rely on it. This is a common but ironic experience: the model that was intended to open up black boxes ends up creating another one.

Misusing Simulation	The financial manager, like a detective, must use every clue. Simulation should be regarded as one of several ways to obtain information about expected cash flows and risk. But the final investment decision involves only one number, net present value.

Some of the early champions of simulation made much greater claims for the method. They started with the premise that net present value cannot in itself reflect risk properly and, therefore, they bypassed that last crucial step.

In this alternative approach the financial manager is given distributions not of cash flows but of NPVs or internal rates of return. Now that may sound attractive—isn't a whole distribution of NPVs better than a single number? But we shall see that this "more is better" reasoning leads the financial manager into a trap.

First, we should explain what is meant by a distribution of NPVs. The cash flows for each iteration of the simulation model are translated into a net present value by *discounting at the risk-free rate*. Why are they not discounted at the opportunity cost of capital? Because, if you know what that is, you don't need a simulation model, except perhaps to help forecast cash flows. The risk-free rate is used to avoid prejudging risk.

FIGURE 10-6
Some advocates of simulation propose that the financial manager should be presented with a distribution of "NPVs" like this one of the electric car project.

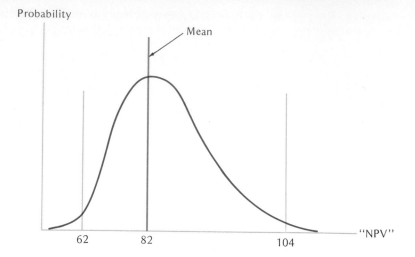

Look at Figure 10-6, which shows the distribution of NPVs for the Jalopy Motor project. The "expected NPV" includes no allowance for risk. Risk is reflected in the dispersion of the NPV distribution. Thus the term *net present value* takes on a very different meaning from the usual one. If an asset has a number of possible "present values," it makes little sense to associate PV with *the* price the asset would sell at in a competitive capital market.[10]

The "risk" of this distribution ignores the investors' opportunity to diversify. Moreover, it is sensitive to the definition of the project. If two unrelated projects are combined, the "risk" of the NPV of the combined projects will be less than the average "risk" of the NPVs of the two separate projects. That not only offends the value additivity principle, but it also encourages sponsors of marginal projects to beat the system by submitting joint proposals.

Finally, it is very difficult to interpret a distribution of NPVs. Since the risk-free rate is not the opportunity cost of capital, there is no economic rationale for the discounting process. Because the whole edifice is arbitrary, managers can only be told to stare at the distribution until inspiration dawns. No one can tell them how to decide or what to do if inspiration never dawns.

Some of these difficulties can be dodged by presenting a distribution of internal rates of return. This avoids the arbitrary discount rate at the cost of introducing all the problems associated with the internal rate of return. Moreover, the manager is again left staring at the distribution with no guidance concerning the acceptable balance of expected return and variance of return.[11]

10-3 DECISION TREES AND SUBSEQUENT DECISIONS

If financial managers treat projects as black boxes, they may be tempted to think only of the first accept-reject decision and to ignore the subsequent investment

[10] The only interpretation we can put on these bastard NPVs is the following: suppose all uncertainty about the project's ultimate cash flows were resolved the day after the project is undertaken. On that day the project's opportunity cost of capital would fall to the risk-free rate. The distribution of NPVs represents the distribution of possible project values on that second day of the project's life.

[11] He or she might use the standard deviation of the IRR as a proxy for the relative risk of projects in the same line of business, however.

decisions that may be tied to it. But if subsequent investment decisions depend on those made today, then today's decision may depend on what you plan to do tomorrow.

An Example: Vegetron

We have already solved in the last chapter a simple sequential decision problem, Vegetron's electric mop project. The problem was the following one:

> *The scientists at Vegetron have come up with an electric mop and the firm is ready to go ahead with pilot production and test marketing. The preliminary phase will take a year and cost $125,000. Management feels that there is only a 50–50 chance that the pilot production and market tests will be successful. If they are, then Vegetron will build a $1 million plant which will generate an expected annual cash flow in perpetuity of $250,000 a year after taxes. If they are not successful, Vegetron will not continue with the project.*

Of course Vegetron *could* go ahead even if the tests fail. Let's suppose that in that case the $1 million investment would generate only $75,000 per year.

Financial managers often use **decision trees** for analyzing projects involving sequential decisions. Figure 10-7 displays the electric mop problem as a decision tree. You can think of it as a game between Vegetron and fate. Each square represents a separate decision point for Vegetron; each circle represents a decision point for fate. Vegetron starts the play at the left-hand box. If Vegetron decides to test, then fate casts the enchanted dice and decides the result of the tests. If the tests are successful—there is a probability of ½ that they will be—then the firm

FIGURE 10-7
The electric mop example from Chapter 9 expressed as a decision tree. This is a project involving sequential decisions. The investment in testing generates the opportunity to invest in full-scale production. (All figures are in thousands; probabilities are in parentheses.)

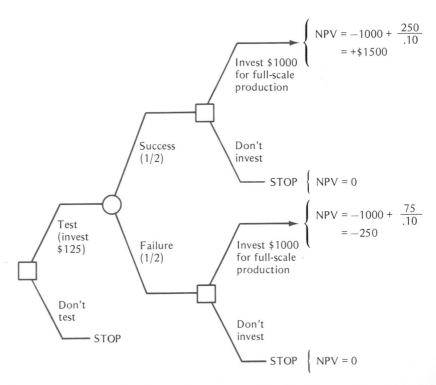

Invest $1000 for full-scale production
$$NPV = -1000 + \frac{250}{.10}$$
$$= +\$1500$$

Success (1/2)

Don't invest
STOP $NPV = 0$

Test (invest $125)

Failure (1/2)

Invest $1000 for full-scale production
$$NPV = -1000 + \frac{75}{.10}$$
$$= -250$$

Don't test
STOP

Don't invest
STOP $NPV = 0$

faces a second decision: invest $1 million in a project offering a $1.5 million net present value or stop. If the tests fail, Vegetron has a similar choice but the investment yields a net present value of −$250,000.

It is obvious what the second-stage decisions will be: invest if the tests are successful and stop if they fail. The net present value of stopping is zero, so the decision tree boils down to a simple problem: should Vegetron invest $125,000 now to obtain a 50 percent chance of $1.5 million a year later?

*A Tougher Example: Magna Charter

Magna Charter is a new corporation formed by Agnes Magna to provide an executive flying service for the southeastern United States. The founder thinks there will be a ready demand from businesses that cannot justify a full-time company plane but nevertheless need one from time to time. However, the venture is not a sure thing. There is a 40 percent chance that demand in the first year will be low. If it is low, there is a 70 percent chance that it will remain low in subsequent years. On the other hand, if the initial demand is high, there is an 80 percent chance that it will stay high.

The immediate problem is to decide what kind of plane to buy. A brand-new turboprop costs $400,000. A used piston-engine plane costs only $200,000 but has less capacity and customer appeal. Moreover, the piston-engine plane is an old design and likely to depreciate rapidly. Ms. Magna thinks that next year secondhand piston aircraft will be available for only $100,000.

That gives Ms. Magna an idea: why not start out with one piston plane and buy another if demand is still high? It will cost only $100,000 to expand. If demand is low, Magna Charter can sit tight with one small, relatively inexpensive aircraft.

Figure 10-8 displays these choices. The square on the left marks the company's initial decision to purchase a turboprop for $400,000 or a piston aircraft for $200,000. After the company has made its decision, fate decides on the first year's demand. You can see in parentheses the probability that demand will be high or low, and you can see the expected cash flow for each combination of aircraft and demand level. At the end of the year the company has a second decision to make if it has a piston-engine aircraft: it can either expand or sit tight. This decision point is marked by the second square. Finally fate takes over again and selects the level of demand for year 2. Again you can see in parentheses the probability of high or low demand. Notice that the probabilities for the second year depend on the first-period outcomes. For example, if demand is high in the first period, then there is an 80 percent chance that it will also be high in the second. The chance of high demand in *both* the first and second periods is .6 × .8 = .48. After the parentheses we again show the profitability of the project for each combination of aircraft and demand level. You can interpret each of these figures as the present value at the end of year 2 of the cash flows for that and all subsequent years.

The problem for Ms. Magna is to decide what to do today. We solve that problem by thinking first what she would do next year. This means that we start at the right side of the tree and work backward to the beginning on the left.

The only decision that Ms. Magna needs to make next year is whether to expand if purchase of a piston-engine plane is succeeded by high demand. If she expands, she invests $100,000 and receives a payoff of $800,000 if demand continues to be high and $100,000 if demand falls. So her *expected* payoff is

(Probability high demand × payoff with high demand)

+ (probability low demand × payoff with low demand)

= (.8 × 800) + (.2 × 100) = $660,000

FIGURE 10-8
Decision tree for Magna Charter. Should it buy a new turboprop or a smaller, secondhand piston-engine plane? A second piston plane can be purchased in year 1 if demand turns out to be high. (All figures are in thousands.)

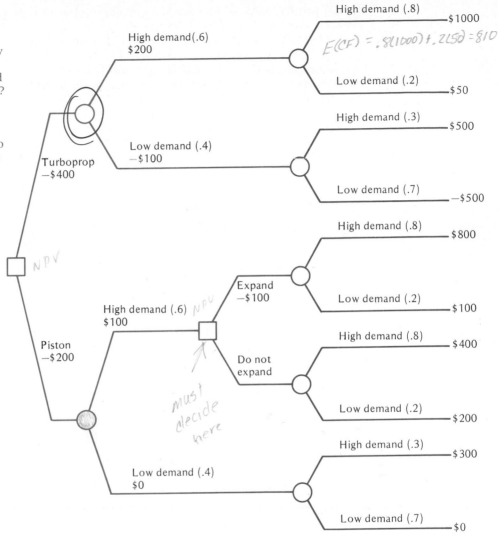

If the opportunity cost of capital for this venture is 10 percent,[12] then the net present value of expanding, computed as of year 1, is

$$NPV = -100 + \frac{660}{1.10} = +500, \text{ or } \$500,000$$

If Ms. Magna does *not* expand, the expected payoff is

(Probability high demand × payoff with high demand)

+ (probability low demand × payoff with low demand)

= (.8 × 400) + (.2 × 200) = $360,000

---

[12] We are guilty here of assuming away one of the most difficult questions. Just as in the Vegetron mop case, the most risky part of Ms. Magna's venture is likely to be the initial prototype project. Perhaps we should use a lower discount rate for the second piston-engine plane than for the first.

The net present value of *not* expanding, computed as of year 1, is

$$NPV = 0 + \frac{360}{1.10} = +327, \text{ or } \$327,000$$

Expansion obviously pays if market demand is high.

Now that we know what Magna Charter ought to do if faced with the expansion decision, we can "roll back" to today's decision. If the first piston-engine plane is bought, Magna can expect to receive cash worth $600,000 in year 1 if demand is high and cash worth $82,000 if it is low:

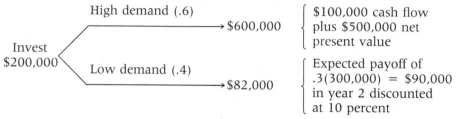

The net present value of the investment in the piston-engine plane is therefore $157,000:

$$NPV = -200 + \frac{.6(600) + .4(82)}{1.10} = +\$157,000$$

If Magna buys the turboprop, there are no future decisions to analyze, and so there is no need to roll back. We just calculate expected cash flows and discount:

$$NPV = -400 + \frac{.6(200) + .4(-100)}{1.10}$$

$$+ \frac{.6[.8(1000) + .2(50)] + .4[.3(500) + .7(-500)]}{(1.10)^2}$$

$$= -400 + \frac{80}{1.10} + \frac{406}{(1.10)^2} = +8, \text{ or } \$8000$$

Thus the investment in the piston-engine plane has an NPV of $157,000; the investment in the turboprop has an NPV of $8000. The piston-engine plane is the better bet. Note, however, that the choice would seem much closer if we forgot to take account of the option to expand. In that case the NPV of the piston-engine plane would drop from $157,000 to $63,000:

$$NPV = -200 + \frac{.6(100) + .4(0)}{1.10}$$

$$+ \frac{.6[.8(400) + .2(200)] + .4[.3(300) + .7(0)]}{(1.10)^2}$$

$$= +63, \text{ or } \$63,000$$

The value of the *option to expand* is, therefore,

$$157 - 63 = +94, \text{ or } \$94,000$$

---

*Bailing Out   If the option to expand has value, how about the option to *contract* or to abandon the venture entirely?

We have assumed that Magna Charter can buy a secondhand piston-engine plane for $100,000 in year 1. We can also assume that it could sell one for the same amount. That is exactly what it should do if it buys the piston-engine plane and encounters low demand: $100,000 cash received from the sale of the plane now is obviously better than a 30 percent chance of a recovery in demand and $300,000 a year later.

Let's suppose that the turboprop could be sold for $300,000 in year 1. Again, it obviously makes sense to sell if demand is low.

But now we must think again about the decision to buy the piston-engine plane. If Magna Charter can "bail out" of either investment, why not take the turboprop and shoot for the big payoff?

Figure 10-9 represents Magna Charter's decision problem with the abandonment options included. First, we figure out the net present value of buying the

FIGURE 10-9
Revised decision tree for Magna Charter, taking account of the possibility of abandoning the business if demand turns out to be low. (All figures are in thousands.)

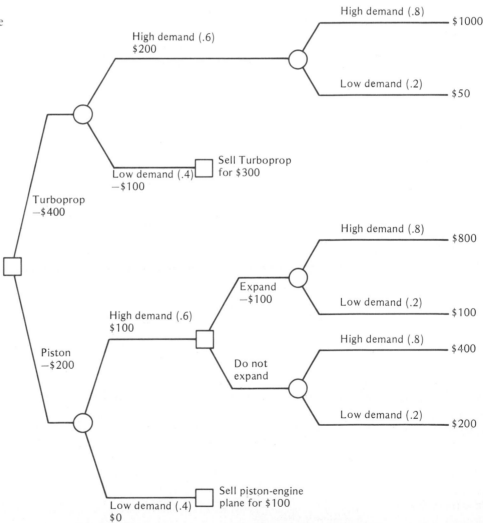

turboprop. This reduces to a simple 1-period problem:

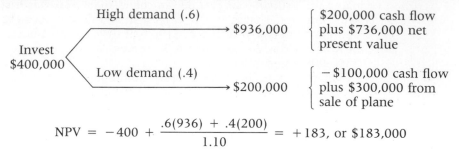

$$NPV = -400 + \frac{.6(936) + .4(200)}{1.10} = +183, \text{ or } \$183{,}000$$

Thus, when we allow for the possibility of abandonment, the net present value of the turboprop investment increases from $8000 to $183,000. The value of the *option to abandon* is

Value of abandonment option = NPV with abandonment − NPV without
abandonment

$$= 183 - 8$$

$$= 175, \text{ or } \$175{,}000$$

Now we figure out the net present value of buying the piston-engine plane with the abandonment option included. The payoffs for this plane are as follows:

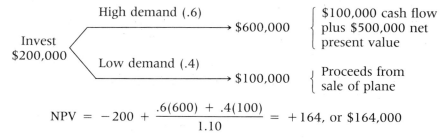

$$NPV = -200 + \frac{.6(600) + .4(100)}{1.10} = +164, \text{ or } \$164{,}000$$

With the abandonment option the piston-engine plane is worth $164,000; without it, the plane is worth $157,000. Therefore the value of the abandonment option is

$$164 - 157 = 7, \text{ or } \$7000$$

It is a good thing we remembered the possibility of reselling the aircraft. When we include the value of the abandonment option, the turboprop has an NPV of $183,000 and the piston-engine plane has an NPV of only $164,000.

Abandonment Value and Capital Budgeting	Abandonment value—the value of the option to bail out of a project—is a simple idea that has surprisingly broad practical implications. In a way it is just common sense; disaster, like a cat, is always waiting to pounce, and so you must always be prepared to cut and run. Some assets are easier to bail out of than others: Tangible assets are usually easier to sell than intangible ones.[13] It helps to have active secondhand markets,

---

[13] This is of course not always the case. Some tangible assets you have to *pay* to get rid of—worn-out refrigerators, for instance.

which really only exist for standardized, widely used items. Real estate, airplanes, trucks, and certain machine tools are likely to be relatively easy to sell. The knowledge accumulated by Vegetron's research and development program, on the other hand, is a specialized intangible asset and probably would not have a significant abandonment value.

In the worst case a firm's stockholders can bail out by going bankrupt. It may sound strange to say that an investor is helped by the possibility of bankruptcy, but it is true. Investors in corporations have *limited liability*: they risk only the money they invest. From their point of view there is a limit to the money the firm can lose; they always have the option of walking away from the firm and leaving its problems in the hands of the creditors and the bankruptcy courts.[14]

Expansion value can be just as important as abandonment value. When things turn out well, the quicker and easier the business can be expanded, the better. The best of all possible worlds occurs when good luck strikes and you find that you can expand quickly *but your competitors cannot.*

Pro and Con Decision Trees

Our examples of abandonment and expansion are extreme simplifications of the sequential decision problems that financial managers face. But they make an important general point. If today's decisions affect what you can do tomorrow, then tomorrow's decisions have to be analyzed before you can act rationally today.

Any cash flow forecast rests on some assumption about the firm's future investment and operating strategy. Often that assumption is implicit. Decision trees force the underlying strategy into the open. By displaying the links between today's and tomorrow's decisions, they help the financial manager to find the strategy with the highest net present value.[15]

The trouble with decision trees is that they get so _____ complex so _____ quickly (insert your own expletives). What will Magna Charter do if demand is neither high nor low but just middling? In that event Ms. Magna might sell the turboprop and buy a piston-engine plane, or she might defer expansion and abandonment decisions until year 2. Perhaps middling demand requires a decision about a price cut or an intensified sales campaign.

There are other possibilities. Perhaps there is uncertainty about future prices of secondhand aircraft. If so, abandonment will depend not just on the level of demand but also on the level of secondhand prices. What is more, secondhand prices are likely to be depressed if demand is low and buoyant if demand is high.

We could draw a new decision tree covering this expanded set of events and decisions. Try it if you like: you'll see how fast the circles, squares, and branches accumulate.

Life is complex, and there is very little we can do about it. It is therefore unfair to criticize decision trees because they can become complex. Our criticism is reserved for analysts who let the complexity become overwhelming. The point of decision trees is to allow explicit analysis of possible future events and decisions. They should be judged not on their comprehensiveness but on whether they show the most important links between today's and tomorrow's decisions. Decision trees

---

[14] We will discuss bankruptcy in Chapters 18 and 30.

[15] Some analysts go further than that. Like the early advocates of simulation models, they start with the premise that net present value cannot take account of risk. They, therefore, propose that the decision tree should be used to calculate a *distribution* of "NPVs" or internal rates of return for each possible sequence of company decisions. That may sound like a gingerbread house, but you should know by now that there is a witch inside.

used in real life will be more complex than Figures 10-8 and 10-9, but they will nevertheless display only a small fraction of possible future events and decisions. Decision trees are like grapevines: they are productive only if they are vigorously pruned.

Our analysis of the Magna Charter project begged an important question. The option to expand enlarged the spread of possible outcomes and therefore increased the risk of investing in a piston aircraft. Conversely, the option to bail out narrowed the spread of possible outcomes. So it reduced the risk of investment. We should have used different discount rates to recognize these changes in risk, but decision trees do not tell us how to do this. In fact, decision trees don't tell us how to value options at all; they are just a convenient way to summarize cash-flow consequences. But the situation is not hopeless. Modern techniques of option valuation are beginning to help value these investment options. We will describe these techniques in Chapters 20 and 21.

Decision Trees and Monte Carlo Simulation

We have said that any cash-flow forecast rests on assumptions about future investment and operating strategy. Think back to the Monte Carlo simulation model that we constructed for the Jalopy Motor Company. What strategy was that based on? We don't know. Inevitably Jalopy will face decisions about pricing, production, expansion, and abandonment, but the model builder's assumptions about these decisions are buried in the model's equations. At some point the model builder may have explicitly identified a future strategy for Jalopy, but it is clearly not the optimal one. There will be some runs of the model when nearly everything goes wrong and when in real life Jalopy would abandon to cut its losses. Yet the model goes on period after period, heedless of the drain on Jalopy's cash resources. The most unfavorable outcomes reported by the simulation model would never be encountered in real life.

On the other hand, the simulation model probably understates the project's potential value if nearly everything goes right: there is no provision for expanding to take advantage of good luck.

Most simulation models incorporate a "business as usual" strategy, which is fine as long as there are no major surprises. The greater the divergence from expected levels of market growth, market share, cost, etc., the less realistic is the simulation. Therefore the extreme high and low simulated values—the "tails" of the simulated distributions—should be treated with extreme caution. Don't take the area under the tails as realistic probabilities of disaster or bonanza.

10-4 SUMMARY

There is more to capital budgeting than grinding out calculations of net present value. If you can identify the major uncertainties, you may find that it is worth undertaking some additional preliminary research that will *confirm* whether the project is worthwhile. And even if you decide that you have done all you can to resolve the uncertainties, you still want to be aware of the potential problems. You do not want to be caught by surprise if things go wrong: you want to be ready to take corrective action.

There are three ways in which companies try to identify the principal threats to a project's success. The simplest is to undertake a sensitivity analysis. In this case the manager considers in turn each of the determinants of the project's success and estimates how far the present value of the project would be altered by taking a very optimistic view or a very pessimistic view of that variable.

Sensitivity analysis of this kind is easy, but it is not always helpful. Variables do not usually change one at a time. If costs are higher than you expect, it is a good bet that prices will be higher also. And if prices are higher, it is a good bet that sales volume will be lower. If you don't allow for the dependencies between the swings and the merry-go-rounds, you may get a false idea of the hazards of the fairground business. Many companies try to cope with this problem by examining the effect on the project of alternative plausible combinations of variables. In other words, they will estimate the net present value of the project under different scenarios and compare this estimate with the base case.

In a sensitivity analysis you change variables one at a time: when you analyze scenarios, you look at a limited number of alternative combinations of variables. If you want to go whole hog and look at *all* possible combinations of variables, then you will probably need to use Monte Carlo simulation to cope with the complexity. In that case you must construct a complete model of the project and specify the probability distribution of each of the determinants of cash flow. You can then ask the computer to select a random number for each of these determinants and work out the cash flows that would result. After the computer has repeated this process a hundred or so times, you should have a fair idea of the expected cash flow in each year and the spread of possible cash flows.

Simulation can be a very useful tool. The discipline of building a model of the project can in itself lead you to a deeper understanding of the project. And once you have constructed your model, it is a simple matter to see how the outcomes would be affected by altering the scope of the project or the distribution of any of the variables. There are of course limits to what you can learn from simulations. A marine engineer uses a tank to simulate the performance of alternative hull designs but knows that it is impossible to fully replicate the conditions that the ship will encounter. In the same way, the financial manager can learn a lot from "laboratory" tests but cannot hope to build a model that accurately captures all the uncertainties and interdependencies that really surround a project.

Books about capital budgeting sometimes create the impression that, once the manager has made an investment decision, there is nothing to do but sit back and watch the cash flows unfold. In practice, companies are constantly modifying their operations. If cash flows are better than anticipated, the project may be expanded; if they are worse, it may be contracted or abandoned altogether. Good managers take account of these options when they value a project. One convenient way to analyze them is by means of a decision tree. You identify the principal things that could happen to the project and the main counteractions that you might take. Then, working back from the future to the present, you can calculate which action you *should* take in each case. Once you know that, it is easy to work out how much the value of the project is increased by these opportunities to react to changing circumstances.

Many of the early articles on simulation and decision trees were written before we knew how to introduce risk into calculations of net present value. Their authors believed that these techniques might allow the manager to make investment decisions without estimating the opportunity cost of capital and calculating net present value. Today we know that simulation and decision analysis cannot save you from having to calculate net present value. The value of these techniques is to help the manager go behind the cash-flow forecast; they help the manager to understand what could go wrong and what opportunities are available to modify the project. That is why we described them as tools to open up black boxes.

FURTHER READING

For an excellent case study of break-even analysis, see:

U. E. Reinhardt: "Break-Even Analysis for Lockheed's TriStar: An Application of Financial Theory," *Journal of Finance,* **28:** 821–838 (September 1973).

The principal exponent of simulation in investment appraisal is David Hertz. See:

D. B. Hertz: "Investment Policies that Pay Off," *Harvard Business Review,* **46:** 96–108 (January–February 1968).

D. B. Hertz: "Risk Analysis in Capital Investment," *Harvard Business Review,* **42:** 95–106 (January–February 1964).

Lewellen and Long are generally against simulation. See, however, Myers's "Postscript."

W. G. Lewellen and M. S. Long: "Simulation vs. Single-Value Estimates in Capital Expenditure Analysis," *Decision Sciences,* **3:** 19–34 (1972).

S. C. Myers, "Postscript: Using Simulation for Risk Analysis," in S. C. Myers, ed., *Modern Developments in Financial Management,* Praeger Publishers, Inc., New York, 1976.

The use of decision trees in investment appraisal is discussed in:

J. Magee: "How to Use Decision Trees in Capital Investment," *Harvard Business Review,* **42:** 79–96 (September–October 1964).

R. F. Hespos and P. A. Strassmann: "Stochastic Decision Trees for the Analysis of Investment Decisions," *Management Science,* **11:** 244–259 (August 1965).

Hax and Wiig discuss how Monte Carlo simulation and decision trees were used in an actual capital budgeting decision:

A. C. Hax and K. M. Wiig: "The Use of Decision Analysis in Capital Investment Problems," *Sloan Management Review,* **17:** 19–48 (Winter 1976).

The abandonment option in capital budgeting was first analyzed by:

A. A. Robichek and J. C. Van Horne: "Abandonment Value in Capital Budgeting," *Journal of Finance,* **22:** 577–590 (December 1967).

QUIZ

1. Define and briefly explain each of the following terms or procedures:
   (*a*) Project analysis
   (*b*) Sensitivity analysis
   (*c*) Break-even analysis
   (*d*) Monte Carlo simulation
   (*e*) Decision tree
   (*f*) Abandonment value
   (*g*) Expansion value

2. What is the NPV of the electric car project under the following scenario?

   - Market size   11 million
   - Market share   .01
   - Unit price $4000
   - Unit variable cost $3600
   - Fixed cost $20 million

3. Jalopy Motor is considering an alternative production method for its electric car. It would require an additional investment of $150 million but would reduce variable costs by $40 million a year.
   (*a*) What is the NPV of this alternative scheme?
   (*b*) Draw break-even charts for this alternative scheme along the lines of Figures 10-1 and 10-3.

(c) Explain how you would interpret the break-even figures.
4. Summarize the problems that a manager would encounter in interpreting a standard sensitivity analysis, such as the one shown in Table 10-2. Which of these problems are alleviated by examining the project under alternative scenarios?
5. True or false?
(a) Project analysis is unnecessary for projects with asset betas that are equal to zero.
(b) Sensitivity analysis can be used to identify the variables most crucial to a project's success.
(c) Sensitivity analysis gives "optimistic" and "pessimistic" values for project cash flow and NPV.
(d) The break-even sales level of a project is higher when *break-even* is defined in terms of NPV rather than accounting income.
(e) Monte Carlo simulation can be used to help forecast cash flows.
(f) Monte Carlo simulation eliminates the need to estimate a project's opportunity cost of capital.
(g) Decision trees are useful when future investment decisions may depend on today's decision.
(h) High abandonment value increases NPV, other things being equal.
6. Suppose a manager has already estimated a project's cash flows, calculated its NPV, and done a sensitivity analysis like the one shown in Table 10-2. List the additional steps required to carry out a Monte Carlo simulation of project cash flows.
7. Use a decision tree to show that it pays Jalopy Motor to conduct a pretest of the suspect machine (see Section 10-1).
8. Big Oil is wondering whether to drill for oil in Westchester County. The prospects are as follows:

Depth of Well, Feet	Total Cost, Millions of Dollars	Cumulative Probability of Finding Oil	PV of Oil (If Found), Millions of Dollars
1000	2	.5	5
2000	2.5	.6	4.5
3000	3	.7	4

Draw a decision tree showing the successive drilling decisions to be made by Big Oil. How deep should it be prepared to drill?

QUESTIONS AND PROBLEMS

1. Your staff has come up with the following revised estimates for the electric car project:

	Pessimistic	Expected	Optimistic
Market size	8 million	10 million	12 million
Market share	.004	.01	.016
Unit price	$3,000	$3,750	$4,000
Unit variable cost	$3,500	$3,000	$2,750
Fixed cost	$50 million	$30 million	$10 million

Conduct a sensitivity analysis. What are the principal uncertainties in the project?

2. Amalgamated Boot is proposing to replace its old shoe-making machinery with more modern equipment. The new equipment costs $10 million and the company expects to sell its old equipment for $1 million. The attraction of the new machinery is that it is expected to cut manufacturing costs from their current level of $8 a pair to $4. However, as the following table shows, there is some uncertainty both about future sales and about the performance of the new machinery:

	Pessimistic	Expected	Optimistic
Sales (millions of pairs)	.4	.5	.7
Manufacturing cost with new machinery (dollars per pair)	6	4	3
Economic life of new machinery (years)	7	10	13

Conduct a sensitivity analysis of the replacement decision assuming a discount rate of 12 percent. Amalgamated does not pay taxes.

3. Use a computer spreadsheet program to perform a sensitivity analysis of the IM&C guano project in Section 6-2. Examine the effect of differences in:
   (a) the inflation rate
   (b) the project life
   (c) working capital requirements
   (d) sales
   (e) operating costs
   (f) the discount rate

*4. Agnes Magna has found some errors in her data (see Section 10-3). The corrected figures are as follows:
   Price of turbo, year 0 = $350,000
   Price of piston, year 0 = $180,000
   Price of turbo, year 1 = $300,000
   Price of piston, year 1 = $150,000
   Discount rate = 8 percent
   Redraw the decision tree with the changed data. Calculate the value of the option to expand. Recalculate the value of the abandonment option. Which plane should Ms. Magna buy?

*5. Ms. Magna has thought of another idea. Perhaps she should buy a piston-engine plane now. Then, if demand is high in the first year, she can sell it and buy a turboprop. Redraw Figure 10-8 to incorporate this possibility. What should Ms. Magna do?

6. For what kinds of capital investment projects do you think Monte Carlo simulation would be most useful? For example, can you think of some industries in which this technique would be particularly attractive? Would it be more useful for large-scale investments than small ones? Discuss.

7. You own an unused gold mine that will cost $100,000 to reopen. If you open the mine, you expect to be able to extract 1000 ounces of gold a year for each of 3 years. After that, the deposit will be exhausted. The gold price is currently $500 an ounce, and each year the price is equally likely to rise or fall by $50 from its level at the start of the year. The extraction cost is $460 an ounce and the discount rate is 10 percent.

(a) Should you open the mine now or delay in the hope of a rise in the gold price?

(b) What difference would it make to your decision if you could costlessly (but irreversibly) shut down the mine at any stage?

8. Read and criticize the Hax-Wiig article mentioned in the "Further Reading" for this chapter. Are all of their recommendations consistent with finance theory?

9. You are considering a new consulting service. There is a 60 percent chance the demand will be high in the first year. If it is high, there is an 80 percent chance that it will continue high indefinitely. If demand is low in the first year, there is a 60 percent chance that it will continue low indefinitely.

   If demand is high, forecasted revenue is $90,000 a year; if demand is low, forecasted revenue is $70,000 a year. You can cease to offer the service at any point, in which case, of course, revenues are zero. Costs other than computing are forecasted at $50,000 a year regardless of demand. These costs also can be terminated at any point. You have a choice on computing costs. One possibility is to buy your own minicomputer. This involves an initial outlay of $200,000 and no subsequent expenditure. If has an economic life of 10 years and no salvage value. The alternative is to rent computer time as you need it. In this case computer costs are 40 percent of revenues.

   Assume that the computing decision cannot be reversed (i.e., if you buy a computer, you cannot resell it; if you do *not* buy it today, you cannot do so later).

   There are no taxes and the opportunity cost of capital is 10 percent.

   Draw a decision tree showing the alternatives. Is it better to buy a computer or rent?

   State clearly any additional assumptions that you need to make.

11 Where Positive Net Present Values Come From

We have now spent several chapters explaining exactly how to calculate net present values but we have had little to say about the forecasts that are the basis of every investment decision. But good investment decisions require good cash-flow forecasts. If financial managers are to get the kinds of forecasts that they need, they must understand how those forecasts are produced. What can financial managers do to ensure that everybody is acting consistently? It is impossible to make rational investment choices if each forecaster is employing different assumptions about the prospects for the economy. How also should financial managers cope with biased or exaggerated forecasts? It's easy if the biases can be identified before the fact, but that is rarely possible. Perhaps crude rules of thumb, like payback, can protect against forecasting disasters. Is there any way to distinguish NPVs that are truly positive from those that are merely overoptimistic? We suggest that managers should ask some probing questions about the possible source of economic gains.

11-1 INCONSISTENT ATTITUDES AND ASSUMPTIONS

Inconsistent recommendations and forecasts can crop up in various ways. For example, some managers are more averse to risk than others and they may let their attitudes toward risk interfere with their judgment of what is a good project. Managers of divisions that have assured good performance are more likely to propose high-risk projects than managers of faltering divisions with an uncertain future. Also a large division is more likely than a small division to risk a $1 million loss. Such a loss might merely dent the profits of the larger division, but it could throw the managers of the small division out of work.

A manager's attitude to risk will partly depend on the way that his or her performance is measured and rewarded. A good measurement and reward system should have some tolerance for mistakes and should be able to discriminate between good decisions and lucky ones. Ideally, managers would be rewarded for good decisions thwarted by bad luck and penalized for bad decisions rescued by good luck.

That takes us back to an issue that we touched on in Chapter 2: if shareholders want managers to act in their interests, they must provide managers with the right incentives.

Another danger is that investment proposals may be based on inconsistent assumptions. For example, suppose the manager of your furniture division is bullish on housing starts but the manager of your appliance division is bearish. This inconsistency makes the projects of the furniture division look better than those of the appliance division. Senior management ought to negotiate a consensus estimate and make sure that all NPVs are recomputed using that joint estimate. Then a rational decision can be made.

This is why many firms begin the capital-budgeting process by establishing forecasts of economic indicators like inflation and the growth in national income, as well as forecasts of particular items that are important to the firm's business, such as housing starts or the price of raw materials. These forecasts can then be used as the basis for all project analyses.

11-2 THE PROBLEMS OF BIAS AND ERRORS

Overoptimism and exaggeration appear to be very common in financial forecasts. For example, a study by one company of 50 projects showed that the actual present value of "cost reduction" projects was 10 percent above the forecast, whereas for "sales expansion" projects the actual present value was 40 percent *below* the forecast, and for "new products" it was 90 percent *below*.[1] Perhaps these results were not typical, but it looks as if management was receiving grossly biased forecasts on any project that involved expansion.

You will probably never be able to eliminate bias completely, but if you are aware of why bias occurs, you are at least part of the way there. Project sponsors are likely to overstate their case deliberately only if you, the financial manager, encourage them to do so. For example, if they believe that success depends on having the largest division rather than the most profitable one, they will propose large expansion projects that they do not truly believe have positive NPVs. Or, if they believe that you won't listen to them unless they paint a rosy picture, you will be presented with many rosy pictures. Or, if you invite each division to compete for limited resources, you will find that each attempts to outbid the other for those resources. The fault in such cases is your own—it is only because you are holding up the hoop that others try to jump through it.

Our development of the net present value rule assumed implicitly that you are supplied with unbiased cash-flow forecasts. If the forecasts are biased, the net present value rule may lead to wrong decisions. If you are aware that a forecaster always doubles the original figure, you can correct for this bias. But what do you do when you do not know forecasters' idiosyncracies or when they play games with you? In that case, you may find that ad hoc procedures sometimes provide better protection against the effects of bias than the net present value rule.

Suppose, for example, that a divisional manager is congenitally overoptimistic. Simple application of the net present value rule would lead to too much investment by that division: the company may, therefore, do better to pretend that capital is limited and confine the division's spending to some arbitrary amount.[2] That *forces* the divisional manager to define priorities. Or suppose that forecasters' biases are stronger for more distant cash flows—it's much easier to put on the rose-colored glasses if you're forecasting 10 or 15 years into the future. The net present value rule will then give long-term forecasts more weight than they deserve. The financial manager might do better to use a payback criterion that places *no* weight on them.

[1] Cited in J. L. Bower, *Managing the Resource Allocation Process*, Division of Research, Graduate School of Business Administration, Harvard University, Boston, 1970.

[2] Of course it may also encourage divisions to compete even more strongly to get a large allocation of funds to invest.

These two examples illustrate that, unless the forecasts are corrected for bias, the ad hoc criterion can *sometimes* give the better result. The converse is also true: a company that uses an ad hoc criterion may *sometimes* find that it pays to use biased forecasts.[3] Two wrongs do not make a right, but they may come closer than a right and a wrong combined.

We should stress that we are *not* recommending the use of ad hoc criteria. The essential point is that improvements in one aspect of the decision-making process must take account of deficiencies in other areas.

Errors in Forecasting

Let us suppose that you have persuaded all your project sponsors to give honest forecasts. You have eliminated the problem of overoptimism but the forecasts still contain errors. Some errors will be positive and some negative; the average error will be zero. But that is little consolation because you only want to accept projects with *truly* superior profitability.

Think, for example, of what would happen if you were to jot down your estimates of the cash flows from operating various items of equipment. You would probably find that about half *appeared* to have positive net present values. This may not be because you personally possess any superior skill in operating jumbo jets or running a chain of laundromats but because you have introduced a large amount of error into your estimates of the cash flows. The more projects you contemplate, the more likely you are to uncover projects that *appear* to be extremely worthwhile. Indeed, if you were to extend your activities to making cash-flow estimates of other companies, you would also find a number of *apparently* attractive merger candidates. In some of these cases you may have genuine information and the proposed investment really may have a positive NPV. But in many other cases the investment only looks good because you have made a forecasting error.

11-3 LOOK FIRST AT MARKET VALUES

What can you do to prevent forecast errors from swamping genuine information? We suggest that you begin by looking at market values.[4]

The following parable should help to illustrate what we mean by this. Your local Cadillac dealer is announcing a special offer. For $25,001 you not only get a brand new Cadillac, you also get the chance to shake hands with your favorite movie star. You wonder how much you are paying for that handshake. There are two possible approaches to the problem. You could evaluate the worth of the Cadillac's power steering, disappearing windshield wipers, and other features and conclude that the Cadillac is worth $26,000. This would seem to suggest that the dealership is willing to pay $999 to have a movie star shake hands with you. Alternatively, you might note that the market price for Cadillacs is worth $25,000,

---

[3] We stress the word sometimes. In very many circumstances use of an ad hoc criterion makes matters worse. For a discussion of the interactions between criterion, forecasting ability, and bias, see P. R. Marsh and R. A. Brealey, ''The Use of Imperfect Forecasts in Capital Investment Decisions,'' *Proceedings of the European Finance Association, 1976*, North-Holland, Amsterdam, 1976.

[4] Black also makes a similar suggestion in a paper that outlines a number of general rules for investment decisions. See F. Black, ''Corporate Investment and Discounting Rules,'' unpublished paper, Sloan School of Management, MIT, February 1983.

so that you are paying $1 for the handshake. As long as there is a competitive market for Cadillacs, the latter approach is more appropriate.

Whenever security analysts value a company's stock, they are also faced with the task of valuing a package. They must evaluate all the information that is known to the market about a company *and* they must evaluate the information that is known only to them. The information that is known to the market is the Cadillac; the private information is the handshake with the movie star. Investors have already evaluated the information that is generally known. Security analysts do not need to evaluate this information again. They can *start* with the market price of the stock and concentrate on valuing their private information.

While lesser mortals would instinctively accept the Cadillac's market value of $25,000, the financial manager is trained to enumerate and value all the costs and benefits from an investment, and is therefore tempted to substitute his or her own opinion for the market's. Unfortunately this approach increases the chance of error. Many capital assets are traded in a competitive market and so it makes sense to *start* with the market price and then ask why these assets should earn more in your hands than those of your rivals.

For example, we encountered a department store chain that estimated the present value of the expected cash flows from each proposed store, including the price at which it could eventually sell the store. Although the firm took considerable care with these estimates, it was disturbed to find that the conclusions were heavily influenced by the forecasted selling price of each store. Thus, despite the fact that the firm disclaimed any particular real estate expertise, it discovered that its investment decisions were unintentionally dominated by its assumptions about future real estate prices. Thereafter, whenever he was faced with a proposal to open a new store, the financial manager always checked the decision by asking the following question: "Let us assume that the property is fairly priced. What is the evidence that it is best suited to one of our department stores rather than to some other use?" In asking himself this question the financial manager was observing the eternal wisdom:

> *If an asset is worth more to others than it is to you, then beware of bidding for the asset against them.*

Let us take the department store problem a little further. Suppose that the new store costs $100 million and you forecast that it will generate income of $8 million a year for 10 years. Real estate prices are estimated to grow by 3 percent a year, so the expected value of the store at the end of 10 years is $100 \times (1.03)^{10} = \$134$ million. At a discount rate of 10 percent, your proposed department store has an NPV of $1 million:

$$\text{NPV} = -100 + \frac{8}{1.10} + \frac{8}{(1.10)^2} + \cdots + \frac{8 + 134}{(1.10)^{10}} = \$1 \text{ million}$$

It is helpful to imagine such a business as divided into two parts—a real estate subsidiary which buys the building and a retailing subsidiary that rents and operates it. Then figure out how much the real estate subsidiary would have to charge.

In some cases a fair rental can be estimated from real estate transactions. For example, we might observe that similar retail space recently rented for $10 million a year. In that case we would conclude that our department store was an unattractive use for the site. Once the site was acquired, it would be better to rent it out at $10 million than to use it for a store generating only $8 million.

You can also estimate a fair rent even if similar real estate transactions are not available. Suppose that the cost of capital for the $100 million invested in real estate is 10 percent. The real estate subsidiary expects to earn 3 percent in the form of capital appreciation and, therefore, the immediate rental yield must be $10 - 3 = 7$ percent. Thus, for the first year the retailing subsidiary should pay a rent of $.07 \times 100 = \$7$ million; in the second year the rent should be $.07 \times 103 = \$7.21$ million; and so on. We can now calculate the NPV of the retailing subsidiary's new department store, remembering that it now rents the store instead of buying it:

$$NPV = \frac{8 - 7}{1.10} + \frac{8 - 7.21}{(1.10)^2} + \cdots + \frac{8 - 8.87}{(1.10)^9} + \frac{8 - 9.13}{(1.10)^{10}}$$

$$= \$1 \text{ million}$$

The answer's the same as before,[5] but we can now see that our forecasts don't stack up. During the last 5 years of the project's life the income from the store fails to cover the rental charge. If the forecasted income levels and growth in real estate prices are correct, we should terminate the project in year 5. But that brings us back to the key question: Do we believe that a department store will continue to be the best use for the site?[6] If we do, then we must be ignoring potential growth in income from the store. Another possibility is that real estate prices are expected to grow by less than 3 percent a year. But that would imply that initial rents are higher; if so, the store might not be a positive NPV investment for any project life.

Here is another example of how market prices can help you make better decisions. Kingsley Solomon is considering a proposal to open a new gold mine. He estimates that the mine will cost $200 million to develop and that in each of the next 10 years it will produce .1 million ounces of gold at a cost, after mining and refining, of $200 an ounce. Although the extraction costs can be be predicted with reasonable accuracy, Mr. Solomon is much less confident about future gold prices. His best guess is that the price will rise by 5 percent per year from its current level of $400 an ounce. At a discount rate of 10 percent, this gives the mine an NPV of $-\$10$ million.

$$NPV = -200 + \frac{.1(420 - 200)}{1.10} + \frac{.1(441 - 200)}{(1.10)^2} + \cdots + \frac{.1(652 - 200)}{(1.10)^{10}}$$

$$= -\$11 \text{ million}$$

Therefore the gold mine project is rejected.

Unfortunately, Mr. Solomon did not look at what the market was telling him. What is the present value of an ounce of gold? Clearly, if the gold market is functioning properly, it is the current price—$400 an ounce. Gold does not produce any income, so $400 is the discounted value of the expected future

---

[5] It has to be. Since the real estate subsidiary simply earns its cost of capital, all the NPV goes to the retailing subsidiary.

[6] It is possible but unlikely that the project is expected to terminate early because the real estate is expected to become too expensive for a department store. A more likely reason for shifting location is that the productivity of the initial site declines and the store is induced to move to a newer, more productive site.

gold price.[7] Since the mine is expected to produce a total of 1 million ounces (.1 million ounces per year for 10 years), the present value of the revenue stream is $1 \times 400 = \$400$ million.[8] We assume that 10 percent is an appropriate discount rate for the relatively certain extraction costs. Thus

$$\text{NPV} = -\text{ initial investment} + \text{PV revenues} - \text{PV costs}$$

$$= -200 + 400 - \sum_{t=1}^{10} \frac{.1 \times 200}{(1.10)^t} = \$77 \text{ million}$$

It looks as if Kingsley Solomon's mine is not such a bad bet after all.

Mr. Solomon's gold was just like anyone else's gold. So there was no point in trying to value it separately. By taking the present value of the gold sales as given, Mr. Solomon was able to focus on the crucial issue: Were the extraction costs sufficiently low to make the venture worthwhile? That brings us to another of those fundamental truths:

> *If others are producing an article profitably and (like Mr. Solomon) you can make it more cheaply, then you don't need any NPV calculations to know that you are probably on to a good thing.*

We confess that our example of King Solomon's mine is somewhat special. Unlike gold, most commodities are not kept solely for investment purposes, and therefore you cannot automatically assume that today's price is equal to the present

---

[7] Investing in an ounce of gold is like investing in a stock that pays no dividends: the investor's return comes entirely as capital gains. Look back at Section 4-2, where we showed that P_0, the price of the stock today, depends on DIV_1 and P_1, the expected dividend and price for next year, and the opportunity cost of capital r:

$$P_0 = \frac{\text{DIV}_1 + P_1}{1 + r}$$

But for gold $\text{DIV}_1 = 0$, so

$$P_0 = \frac{P_1}{1 + r}$$

In words, *today's price is the present value of next year's price.* Therefore we don't have to know either P_1 or r to find the present value. Also, since $\text{DIV}_2 = 0$,

$$P_1 = \frac{P_2}{1 + r}$$

and we can express P_0 as

$$P_0 = \frac{P_1}{1 + r} = \frac{1}{1 + r}\left(\frac{P_2}{1 + r}\right) = \frac{P_2}{(1 + r)^2}$$

In general,

$$P_0 = \frac{P_t}{(1 + r)^t}$$

This holds for any asset which pays no dividends, is traded in a competitive market, and costs nothing to store. Storage costs for gold or common stocks are very small compared to asset value.

Storage costs would have to be treated as negative dividends. The owner of a warehouse full of butter would have to pay out cash for use of the warehouse, refrigeration, and so on.

[8] We assume that the extraction rate does not vary with the gold price. If it does, you would need to read Chapters 20 and 21 before you could value the mine.

value of the future price.[9] But when you do have the market value of an asset, *use it*, at least as a starting point for your analysis.

One more example. Suppose that an oil company is contemplating an additional investment in tankers. Tankers are freely traded in a competitive market. Therefore the present value of a tanker to the oil company is equal to the tanker's price *plus* any extra gains that are likely to come from having the oil company, rather than another owner, operate the vessel.

11-4 FORECASTING ECONOMIC RENTS

We recommend that financial managers ask themselves whether an asset is more valuable in their hands than another's. A bit of classical microeconomics can help to answer that question. When an industry settles into long-run competitive equilibrium, all its assets are expected to earn their opportunity cost of capital—no more and no less. If they earned more, firms in the industry would expand, or firms outside the industry would try to enter it.

Profits that *more* than cover the opportunity cost of capital are known as *economic rents*. These rents may be either temporary (in the case of an industry that is not in long-run equilibrium) or persistent (in the case of a firm with some degree of monopoly or market power).[10] The NPV of an investment is simply the discounted value of the economic rents that it will produce. Therefore when you are presented with a project that appears to have a positive NPV, don't just accept the calculations at face value. They may reflect simple estimate errors in forecasting cash flows. Probe behind the cash-flow estimates and *try to identify the source of economic rents*. A positive NPV for a new project is only believable if *you* believe that your company has some special advantage.

Such advantages can arise in several ways. You may be smart or lucky enough to be first to the market with a new, improved product for which customers are prepared to pay premium prices (until your competitors enter and squeeze out excess profits). You may have a patent, proprietary technology, or production cost advantage that competitors cannot match, at least for several years. You may have some valuable contractual advantage, for example the distributorship for gargle blasters in France (see Section 11-5 below).

Thinking about competitive advantage can also help ferret out negative NPV calculations that are negative by mistake. If you are the lowest-cost producer of a profitable product in a growing market, then you should invest to expand along with the market. If your calculations show a negative NPV for such an expansion, then you have probably made a mistake.

---

[9] However, Hotelling has pointed out that if there are constant returns to scale in mining any mineral, the expected rise in the price of the mineral *less* extraction costs should equal the cost of capital. If the expected growth were faster, everyone would want to postpone extraction; if it were slower, everyone would want to exploit the resource today. In this case the value of a mine would be independent of when it was exploited and you could value it by calculating the value of the mineral at today's price less the current cost of extraction. If (as is usually the case in practice), there are declining returns to scale, the expected price rise net of costs must be less than the cost of capital. For a review of Hotelling's principle, see S. Devarajan and A. C. Fisher, ''Hotelling's 'Economics of Exhaustible Resources': Fifty Years Later,'' *Journal of Economic Literature,* **19:** 65–73 (March 1981). And for an application to the problem of valuing mineral deposits, see M. H. Miller and C. W. Upton, ''A Test of the Hotelling Valuation Principle,'' *Journal of Political Economy,''* **93:** 1–25 (1985).

[10] Temporary rents are often called *quasi rents*.

*11-5 EXAMPLE—MARVIN ENTERPRISES DECIDES TO EXPLOIT A NEW TECHNOLOGY

To illustrate some of the problems involved in predicting economic rents, let us leap forward to the 21st century and look at the decision by Marvin Enterprises to exploit a new technology.[11]

One of the most unexpected developments of these years was the remarkable growth of a completely new industry. By 2013, annual sales of gargle blasters totaled $1.68 billion, or 240 million units. Although it controlled only 10 percent of the market, Marvin Enterprises was among the most exciting growth companies of the decade. Marvin had come late into the business, but it had pioneered the use of integrated microcircuits to control the genetic engineering processes used to manufacture gargle blasters. This development had enabled producers to cut the price of gargle blasters from $9 to $7 and had thereby contributed to the dramatic growth in the size of the market. The estimated demand curve in Figure 11-1 shows just how responsive demand is to such price reductions.

Table 11-1 summarizes the cost structure of the old and new technologies. While companies with the new technology were earning 20 percent on their initial investment, those with first-generation equipment had been hit by the successive price cuts. Since all of Marvin's investment was in the 2009 technology, it had been particularly well placed during this period.

Rumors of new developments at Marvin had been circulating for some time and the total market value of Marvin's stock had risen to $460 million by January 2014. At that point Marvin called a press conference to announce another technological breakthrough. Management claimed that their new third-generation process involving mutant neurons enabled the firm to reduce capital costs to $10 and manufacturing costs to $3 a unit. Marvin proposed to capitalize on this invention by embarking on a huge $1 billion expansion program that would add 100 million units to capacity. The company expected to be in full operation within 12 months.

[11] We thank Stewart Hodges for permission to adapt this example from a case prepared by him, and the BBC for permission to use the term *gargle blasters*.

FIGURE 11-1
The demand "curve" for gargle blasters shows that for each $1 cut in price there is an increase in demand of 80 million units.

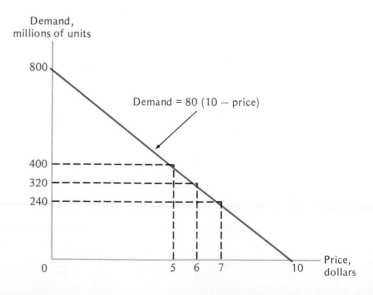

TABLE 11-1
Size and cost structure of the gargle blaster industry before Marvin announced its expansion plans

Technology	CAPACITY, MILLIONS OF UNITS		Capital Cost per Unit, Dollars	Manufacturing Cost per Unit, Dollars	Salvage Value per Unit, Dollars
	Industry	Marvin			
First generation (2001)	120	....	17.50	5.50	2.50
Second generation (2009)	120	24	17.50	3.50	2.50

Note: Selling price is $7 per unit. One "unit" means one gargle blaster.

Before deciding to go ahead with this development, Marvin had undertaken extensive calculations on the effect of the new investment. The basic assumptions were as follows:

1. The cost of capital was 20 percent.
2. The production facilities had an indefinite physical life.
3. The demand curve and the costs of each technology would not change.
4. There was no chance of a fourth-generation technology in the foreseeable future.
5. The corporate income tax, which had been abolished in 2004, was not likely to be reintroduced.

Marvin's competitors greeted the news with varying degrees of concern. There was general agreement that it would be 5 years before any of them would have access to the new technology. On the other hand, many consoled themselves with the reflection that Marvin's new plant could not compete with fully depreciated existing plant.

Suppose that you were Marvin's financial manager. Would you have agreed with the decision to expand? Do you think it would have been better to go for a larger or smaller expansion? How do you think Marvin's announcement is likely to affect the price of its stock?

You have a choice. You can go on *immediately* to read *our* solution to these questions. But you will learn much more if you stop and work out your own answer first. Try it.

*Forecasting Prices of Gargle Blasters

Up to this point in any capital budgeting problem we have always given you the set of cash-flow forecasts. In the present case you have to *derive* those forecasts.

The first problem is to decide what is going to happen to the price of gargle blasters. Marvin's new venture will increase industry capacity to 340 million units. From the demand curve in Figure 11-1, you can see that the industry can sell this number of gargle blasters only if the price declines to $5.75:

$$\text{Demand} = 80(10 - \text{price})$$

$$= 80(10 - 5.75) = 340 \text{ million units}$$

If the price falls to $5.75, what will happen to companies with the 2001 technology? They also have to make an investment decision: Should they stay in business or should they sell their equipment for its salvage value of $2.50 per unit? With a 20 percent opportunity cost of capital, the NPV of staying in business is

$$\text{NPV} = -\text{investment} + \text{PV(price} - \text{manufacturing cost)}$$

$$= -2.50 + \frac{5.75 - 5.50}{.20} = -\$1.25 \text{ per unit}$$

Smart companies with 2001 equipment will, therefore, see that it is better to sell off capacity. No matter what their equipment originally cost or how far it is depreciated, it is more profitable to sell the equipment for $2.50 per unit than to operate it and lose $1.25 per unit.

As capacity is sold off, the supply of gargle blasters will decline and the price will rise. An equilibrium is reached when the price gets to $6. At this point 2001 equipment has a zero NPV:

$$\text{NPV} = -2.50 + \frac{6.00 - 5.50}{.20} = \$0 \text{ per unit}$$

How much capacity will have to be sold off before the price reaches $6? You can check that by going back to the demand curve:

$$\text{Demand} = 80(10 - \text{price})$$

$$= 80(10 - 6) = 320 \text{ million units}$$

Therefore Marvin's expansion will cause the price to settle down at $6 a unit and will induce first-generation producers to withdraw 20 million units of capacity.

But after 5 years Marvin's competitors will also be in a position to build third-generation plants. As long as these plants have positive NPVs, companies will increase their capacity and force prices down once again. A new equilibrium will be reached when the price reaches $5. At this point, the NPV of new third-generation plants is zero and there is no incentive for companies to expand further:

$$\text{NPV} = -10 + \frac{5.00 - 3.00}{.20} = \$0 \text{ per unit}$$

Looking back once more at our demand curve, you can see that with a price of $5 the industry can sell a total of 400 million gargle blasters:

$$\text{Demand} = 80(10 - \text{price}) = 80(10 - 5) = 400 \text{ million units}$$

The effect of the third-generation technology is, therefore, to cause industry sales to expand from 240 million units in 2013 to 400 million 5 years later. But that rapid growth is no protection against failure. By the end of 5 years any company that has only first-generation equipment will no longer be able to cover its manufacturing costs and will be *forced* out of business.

*The Value of Marvin's New Expansion

We have shown that the introduction of third-generation technology is likely to cause gargle blaster prices to decline to $6 for the next 5 years and to $5 thereafter. We can now set down the expected cash flows from Marvin's new plant:

	Year 0 (Investment)	Years 1–5 (Revenue − Manufacturing Cost)	Year 6, 7, 8, . . . (Revenue − Manufacturing Cost)
Cash flow, per unit, dollars	− 10	6 − 3 = 3	5 − 3 = 2
Cash flow, 100 million units, millions of dollars	− 1,000	600 − 300 = 300	500 − 300 = 200

Discounting these cash flows at 20 percent gives us

$$\text{NPV} = -1000 + \sum_{t=1}^{5} \frac{300}{(1.20)^t} + \frac{1}{(1.20)^5} \left(\frac{200}{.20} \right) = \$299 \text{ million}$$

It looks as if Marvin's decision to go ahead was correct. But there is something we have forgotten. When we evaluate an investment, we must consider *all* incremental cash flows. One effect of Marvin's decision to expand is to reduce the value of its existing 2009 plant. If Marvin decided not to go ahead with the new technology, the $7 price of gargle blasters would hold until Marvin's competitors start to cut prices in 5 years' time. Marvin's decision, therefore, leads to an immediate $1 cut in price. This reduces the present value of its 2009 equipment by

$$24 \text{ million} \times \sum_{t=1}^{5} \frac{1.00}{(1.20)^t} = \$72 \text{ million}$$

Considered in isolation, Marvin's decision has an NPV of $299 million. But it also reduces the value of existing plant by $72 million. The net present value of Marvin's venture is, therefore, 299 − 72 = $227 million.

*Alternative Expansion Plans

Marvin's expansion has a positive NPV, but perhaps Marvin could do better to build a larger or smaller plant. You can check that by going through the same calculations as above. First you need to estimate how the additional capacity will affect gargle blaster prices. Then you can calculate the net present value of the new plant and the change in the present value of the existing plant. The total NPV of Marvin's expansion plan is

Total NPV = NPV of new plant + change in PV of existing plant

We have undertaken these calculations and plotted the results in Figure 11-2. You can see how total NPV would be affected by a smaller or larger expansion.

When the new technology becomes generally available in 2019, firms will construct a total of 280 million units of new capacity.[12] But Figure 11-2 shows that it would be foolish for Marvin to go that far. If Marvin added 280 million units of new capacity in 2014, the discounted value of the cash flows from the new plant would be zero *and* the company would have reduced the value of its

[12] Total industry capacity in 2019 will be 400 million units. Of this, 120 million units is second-generation capacity, and the remaining 280 million units is third-generation capacity.

FIGURE 11-2
Effect on net present value
of alternative expansion
plans. Marvin's 100-mil-
lion-unit expansion has a
total NPV of $227 million
(total NPV = NPV new
plant + change in PV ex-
isting plant = 299 − 72
= 227). Total NPV is
maximized if Marvin
builds 200 million units of
new capacity. If Marvin
builds 280 million units of
new capacity, total NPV is
− $144 million.

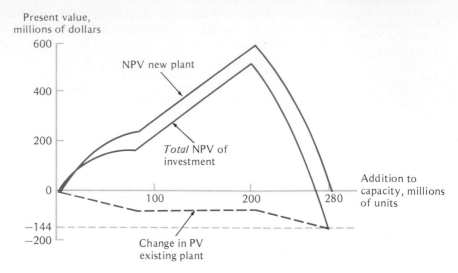

old plant by $144 million. To maximize NPV Marvin should construct 200 million
units of new capacity and set the price just below $6 to drive out the 2001 man-
ufacturers. Output is, therefore, less and price is higher than either would be under
free competition.[13]

*The Value of Marvin Stock

Let us think about the effect of Marvin's announcement on the value of its common
stock. Marvin has 24 million units of second-generation capacity. In the absence
of any third-generation technology, gargle blaster prices would hold at $7 and
Marvin's existing plant would be worth

$$PV = 24 \text{ million} \times \frac{7.00 - 3.50}{.20}$$

$$= \$420 \text{ million}$$

Marvin's new technology reduces the price of gargle blasters initially to $6 and
after 5 years to $5. Therefore the value of existing plant declines to

$$PV = 24 \text{ million} \times \left[\sum_{t=1}^{5} \frac{6.00 - 3.50}{(1.20)^t} + \frac{5.00 - 3.50}{.20 \times 1.20^5} \right]$$

$$= \$252 \text{ million}$$

---

[13] Notice that we are assuming that all customers have to pay the same price for their gargle blasters.
If Marvin could charge each customer the maximum price which that customer would be willing to
pay, output would be the same as under free competition. Such direct price discrimination is illegal
and in any case difficult to enforce. But firms do search for indirect ways to differentiate between
customers. For example, stores often offer free delivery which is equivalent to a price discount for
customers who live at an inconvenient distance. Publishers differentiate their products by selling hard-
back copies to libraries and paperbacks to impecunious students. In the early years of electronic cal-
culators, manufacturers put a high price on their product. Although buyers knew that the price would
be reduced in a year or two, the additional outlay was more than compensated for by the convenience
of having the machines for the extra time.

But the *new* plant makes a net addition to shareholders' wealth of $299 million. So after Marvin's announcement its stock will be worth

$$252 + 299 = \$551 \text{ million}^{14}$$

Now here is an illustration of something we talked about in Chapter 4. Before the announcement, Marvin's stock was valued in the market at $460 million. The difference between this figure and the value of the existing plant represented the present value of Marvin's growth opportunities (PVGO). The market valued Marvin's ability to stay ahead of the game at $40 million even before the announcement. After the announcement PVGO rose to $299 million.[15]

The Lessons of Marvin Enterprises

Marvin Enterprises may be just a piece of science fiction, but the problems that it confronts are very real. Whenever IBM considers a new generation of computers or Polaroid thinks about developing a new camera, these firms must face up to exactly the same issues as Marvin. We have tried to illustrate the *kind* of questions that you should be asking when presented with a set of cash-flow forecasts. Of course no economic model is going to predict the future with accuracy. Perhaps Marvin can hold the price above $6. Perhaps competitors will not appreciate the rich pickings to be had in the year 2004. In that case, Marvin's expansion would be even more profitable. But would you want to *bet* $1 billion on such possibilities? We don't think so.

Investments often turn out to earn far more than the cost of capital because of a favorable surprise. This surprise may in turn create a temporary opportunity for further investments earning more than the cost of capital. But anticipated and more prolonged rents will naturally lead to the entry of rival producers. That is why you should be suspicious of any investment proposal that predicts a stream of economic rents into the indefinite future. Try to estimate *when* competition will drive the NPV down to zero and think what that implies for the price of your product.

Many companies try to identify the major growth areas in the economy and then concentrate their investment in these areas. But the sad fate of first-generation gargle blaster manufacturers illustrates how rapidly existing plants can be made obsolete by changes in technology. It is fun being in a growth industry when you are at the forefront of the new technology, but a growth industry has no mercy on technological laggards.

You can expect to earn economic rents only if you have some superior resource such as management, sales force, design team, or production facilities. Therefore, rather than trying to move into growth areas, you would be better to identify your firm's comparative advantages and try to capitalize on them. Unfortunately, superior profits will not accrue to the firm unless it can also avoid paying the full value of the superior resources. For example, the Boeing 757 is a much more efficient plane to operate than older aircraft. But that does not mean that the

---

[14] In order to finance the expansion Marvin is going to have to sell $1000 million of new stock. Therefore the *total* value of Marvin's stock will rise to $1551 million. But investors who put up the new money will receive shares worth $1000 million. The value of Marvin's old shares after the announcement is therefore $551 million.

[15] Notice that the market value of Marvin stock will be greater than $551 million if investors expect the company to expand again within the 5-year period. In other words, PVGO after the expansion may still be positive. Investors may expect Marvin to stay one step ahead of its competitors, or to successfully apply its special technology in other areas.

airlines which operate the 757 can expect to earn supernormal profits. The greater efficiency is likely to be reflected in the price that Boeing charges for the 757. An airline will earn superior profits (that is, economic rents) only if the 757 is more valuable to it than other operators.[16]

We do not wish to imply that good investment opportunities don't exist. For example, such opportunities frequently arise because the firm has invested money in the past which gives it the option to expand cheaply in the future. Perhaps the firm can increase its output just by adding an extra production line, whereas its rivals would need to construct an entire new factory. In such cases, you must take into account not only *whether* it is profitable to exercise your option, but also *when* it is best to do so.

Marvin also reminded us of project interactions, which we first discussed in Chapter 6. When you estimate the incremental cash flows from a project, you must remember to include the project's impact on the rest of the business. By introducing the new technology immediately, Marvin reduced the value of its existing plant by $72 million. Sometimes the losses on existing plants may completely offset the gains from a new technology. That is why we sometimes see established, technologically advanced companies deliberately slowing down the rate at which they introduce new products.

Notice that Marvin's economic rents were equal to the difference between its costs and those of the marginal producer. The costs of the marginal 2001-generation plant consisted of the manufacturing costs plus the opportunity cost of not selling the equipment. Therefore, if the salvage value of the 2001 equipment were higher, Marvin's competitors would incur higher costs and Marvin could earn higher rents. We took the salvage value as given, but it in turn depends on the cost savings from substituting outdated gargle blaster equipment for some other asset. In a well-functioning economy, assets will be used so as to minimize the *total* cost of producing the chosen set of outputs. The economic rents earned by any asset are equal to the total extra costs that would be incurred if that asset were withdrawn.

Here's another point about salvage value which takes us back to our discussion of Magna Charter in the last chapter. A high salvage value gives the firm an option to abandon a project if things start to go wrong. However, if competitors *know* that you can bail out easily, they are more likely to enter your market. If it is clear that you have no alternative but to stay and fight, they will be more cautious about competing.

When Marvin announced its expansion plans, many owners of first-generation equipment took comfort in the belief that Marvin could not compete with their fully depreciated plant. Their comfort was misplaced. Regardless of past depreciation policy, it paid to scrap first-generation equipment rather than keep it in production. Do not expect that numbers in your balance sheet can protect you from harsh economic reality.

11-6 SUMMARY

It helps to use present value when making investment decisions, but that is not the whole story. Good investment decisions depend both on a sensible criterion

---

[16] The rent that you earn because equipment is worth more to you than your rivals is known as "consumer surplus." If Boeing were able to charge each customer the maximum price that it was prepared to pay, no airline could expect to earn a consumer surplus from operating the 757, and Boeing would capture all the benefits.

and on sensible forecasts. In this chapter, we have looked at some of the things financial managers can do to get the forecasts they need.

One source of trouble is inconsistency in the macroeconomic assumptions that underlie the forecasts. If cash-flow forecasts for one project assume no inflation and those for another project are based on a 5 percent inflation rate, meaningful comparisons between these projects are impossible. The financial manager must, therefore, ensure that all forecasts within the company are based on a consistent view.

The net present value criterion is concerned with *expected* cash flows. But many of the cash-flow forecasts that the financial manager receives are likely to be biased. Companies employ a variety of ad hoc ways for limiting the worst effects of bias. For example, if the head office believes that each division is submitting overoptimistic forecasts, it can force the divisions to be more selective by imposing capital rationing. A financial manager who does away with these ad hoc rules without tackling the underlying problem may well bring about worse investment decisions. That is why the manager must think about how project sponsors can be encouraged to give fair and honest forecasts and how cases of overoptimism or exaggeration can be identified.

Projects may look attractive for two reasons: (1) there may be some errors in the sponsor's forecasts, and (2) the company can genuinely expect to earn excess profit from the project. Good managers, therefore, try to ensure that the odds are stacked in their favor by expanding in areas in which the company has a comparative advantage. We like to put this another way by saying that good managers try to identify projects which will generate "economic rents."

Our story of Marvin Enterprises illustrates the origin of rents and how they determine a project's cash flows and net present value.

Any present value calculation, including our calculation for Marvin Enterprises, is subject to error. That's life: there's no other sensible way to value most capital investment projects. But some assets, such as gold, real estate, crude oil, ships, airplanes, and financial assets such as stocks and bonds, are traded in reasonably competitive markets. When you have the market value of such an asset, *use it*, at least as a starting point for your analysis.

FURTHER READING

Most microeconomics texts contain a discussion of the determinants of economic rents. See, for example,

> S. Fischer and R. Dornbusch: *Introduction to Microeconomics*, McGraw-Hill Book Company, New York, 1983.

For an interesting analysis of the likely effect of a new technology on the present value of existing assets, see

> S. P. Sobotka and C. Schnabel: "Linear Programming as a Device for Predicting Market Value: Prices of Used Commercial Aircraft, 1959–65," *Journal of Business*, **34:** 10–30 (January 1961).

QUIZ

1. You have inherited 250 acres of prime Iowa farmland. There is an active market in land of this type, and similar properties are selling for $1000 per acre. Net cash returns per acre are $75 per year. These cash returns are ex-

pected to remain constant in real terms. How much is the land worth? A local banker has advised you to use a 12 percent discount rate.

2. True or false?
   (*a*) A firm that earns the opportunity cost of capital is earning economic rents.
   (*b*) A firm that invests in positive NPV ventures expects to earn economic returns.
   (*c*) Financial managers should try to identify areas where their firm can earn economic rents, because it's there that positive NPV projects are likely to be found.
   (*d*) Economic rent is the equivalent annual cost of operating capital equipment.

3. Demand for concave utility meters is expanding rapidly, but the industry is highly competitive. A utility meter plant costs $50 million to set up and it has an annual capacity of 500,000 meters. The production cost is $5 per meter, and this cost is not expected to change. If the machines have an indefinite physical life and the cost of capital is 10 percent, what is the price of a utility meter?
   (*a*) $5
   (*b*) $10
   (*c*) $15

4. The following comment appeared in *Aviation Week and Space Technology*, July 25, 1966: "Alitalia has decided against ordering an advanced-technology jet transport. The carrier's analysis, in common with some other airlines, indicates that it can operate fully depreciated Douglas DC-8's at fare levels competitive with a Boeing 747. This is because seat or ton-mile costs of a fully depreciated current generation subsonic jet may not differ greatly from the advanced-technology jet." Discuss whether the low depreciation charge on a DC-8 justifies the continued use of that plane. Under what circumstances would it pay to operate 747s?

5. If a capital equipment producer brings out a new, more efficient product, who is likely to get the benefits? In what circumstances would purchase of the new equipment be a positive NPV investment?

QUESTIONS AND PROBLEMS

1. Suppose that you are considering investing in an asset for which there is a reasonably good secondary market. Specifically, you're Delta Airlines and the asset is a Boeing 757—a very widely used airplane. How does the presence of a secondary market simplify your problem in principle? Do you think these simplifications could be realized in practice? Explain.

2. Photographic laboratories recover and recycle the silver used in photographic film. Stikine River Photo is considering purchase of improved equipment for their lab at Telegraph Creek. Here is the information they have:
   (*a*) The equipment costs $100,000.
   (*b*) It will cost $80,000 per year to run.
   (*c*) It has an economic life of 10 years but can be depreciated over 5 years by the straight line method (see Section 6-2).
   (*d*) It will recover an additional 5000 ounces of silver per year.
   (*e*) Silver is selling for $20 per ounce. Over the past 10 years, the price of silver has appreciated by 4.5 percent per year in real terms. Silver is traded in an active, competitive market.

(*f*) Stikine's marginal tax rate is 34 percent. Assume United States tax law.

(*g*) Stikine's company cost of capital is 8 percent in real terms.

What is the NPV of the new equipment? Make additional assumptions as necessary.

3. Does it make any difference whether a capital equipment producer sells equipment or rents it out? Does it affect the producer's willingness to bring out new products?

4. The manufacture of polysyllabic acid is a competitive industry. Most plants have an annual output of 100,000 tons. Operating costs are 90 cents a ton and the sales price is $1 a ton. A 100,000-ton plant costs $100,000, has an indefinite life, and a scrap value of $60,000.

   Phlogiston, Inc., proposes to invest $100,000 in a plant that employs a new low-cost process to manufacture polysyllabic acid. The plant has the same capacity as existing units, but operating costs are 85 cents a ton. Phlogiston estimates that it has 2 years' lead over each of its rivals in use of the process but is unable to build any further plants itself before year 2. Also it believes that demand over the next 2 years is likely to be sluggish and that its new plant will therefore cause temporary overcapacity.

   You can assume that there are no taxes, and that the cost of capital is 10 percent.

   (*a*) By the end of year 2 the prospective increase in acid demand will require the construction of several new plants using the Phlogiston process. What is the likely NPV of such plants?

   (*b*) What would be the present value of each of these new plants?

   (*c*) What does that imply for the price of polysyllabic acid in year 3 and beyond?

   (*d*) Would you expect existing plant to be scrapped in year 2? How would your answer differ if scrap value were $40,000 or $80,000?

   (*e*) The acid plants of United Alchemists, Inc. have been fully depreciated. Can it operate them profitably after year 2?

   (*f*) Acidosis, Inc. purchased a new plant last year for $100,000 and is writing it down by $10,000 a year. Should it scrap this plant in year 2?

   (*g*) What would be the present value of Phlogiston's venture?

5. The Cambridge Opera Association has come up with a unique door prize for its December (1988) fund-raising ball: Twenty door prizes will be distributed, each one a ticket entitling the bearer to receive a cash award from the Association on December 30, 1989. The cash award is to be determined by calculating the ratio of the level of the Standard and Poor's composite stock price index on December 30, 1989, to its level on June 30, 1989, and multiplying by $100. Thus, if the index turns out to be 125 on June 30, 1989, and 150 on December 30, 1989, the payoff will be $100 \times (150/125) = \$120$.

   After the ball, a black market springs up in which the tickets are traded. What will the tickets sell for on January 1, 1989? On June 30, 1989? Assume the risk-free interest rate is 10 percent per year. Also, assume the Cambridge Opera Association will be solvent at year-end 1989 and will in fact pay off on the tickets. Make other assumptions as necessary.

   Would ticket values be different if the tickets' payoffs depended on the Dow Jones Industrial Index rather than the Standard and Poor's composite?

6. You are asked to value a large building in northern New Jersey. The valuation is needed for a bankruptcy settlement. Here are the facts:

   (*a*) The settlement *requires* that the building's value equal the present value of the *net cash proceeds* the railroad would receive if it cleared the building and sold it for its highest and best nonrailroad use, which is as a warehouse.

(b) The building has been appraised at $1 million. This figure is based on actual recent selling prices of a sample of similar New Jersey buildings used as, or available for use as, warehouses.

(c) If rented out today as a warehouse, the building could generate $80,000 per year. This cash flow is calculated *after* out-of-pocket operating expenses, and *after* real estate taxes of $50,000 per year:

Gross rents	$180,000
Operating expenses	50,000
Real estate taxes	50,000
Net	$ 80,000

Gross rents, operating expenses, and real estate taxes are uncertain but are expected to grow with inflation.

(d) However, it would take 1 year and $200,000 to clear out the railroad equipment and prepare the building for use as a warehouse. This expenditure would be spread evenly over the next year.

(e) The property will be put on the market when ready for use as a warehouse. Your real estate advisor says that properties of this type take, on average, 1 year to sell after they are put on the market. However, the railroad could rent out the building as a warehouse while waiting for it to sell.

(f) The opportunity cost of capital for investment in real estate is 8 percent in *real* terms.

(g) Your real estate advisor notes that selling prices of comparable buildings in northern New Jersey have declined, in real terms, at an average rate of 2 percent per year over the last 10 years.

(h) A 5 percent sales commission would be paid by the railroad at the time of the sale.

(i) The railroad pays no income taxes. It would have to pay property taxes.

*7. The world airline system is composed of the routes X and Y, each of which requires 10 aircraft. These routes can be serviced by three types of aircraft—A, B, and C. There are 5 A-type aircraft available, 10 B-type, and 10 C-type. These aircraft are identical except for their operating costs which are as follows:

	ANNUAL OPERATING COST, THOUSANDS OF DOLLARS	
Aircraft Type	Route X	Route Y
A	15	15
B	25	20
C	45	35

The aircraft have a useful life of 5 years and a salvage value of $10,000.

The aircraft owners do not operate the aircraft themselves but rent them out to the operators. Owners act competitively to maximize their rental income, and operators attempt to minimize their operating costs. Air fares are also competitively determined.

Assume the cost of capital is 10 percent.

(a) Which aircraft would be used on which route and how much would each aircraft be worth?

(*b*) What would happen to usage and prices of each aircraft if the number of A-type aircraft increased to 10?

(*c*) What would happen if the number of A's increased to 15?

(*d*) What would happen if the number of A's increased to 20?

State any additional assumptions you need to make.

*8. Taxes are a cost and, therefore, changes in tax rates can affect consumer prices, project lives, and the value of existing firms. The following (quite hard) problem illustrates this. It also illustrates that tax changes that appear to be ''good for business'' do not always increase the value of existing firms. Indeed, unless new investment incentives increase consumer demand, they can only work by obsoleting existing equipment.

The manufacture of bucolic acid is a competitive business. Demand is steadily expanding and new plants are constantly being opened. Expected cash flows from an investment in plant are as follows:

	0	1	2	3
1. Initial investment	100			
2. Revenues		100	100	100
3. Cash operating costs		50	50	50
4. Tax depreciation		33.33	33.33	33.33
5. Income pre-tax		16.67	16.67	16.67
6. Tax at 40%		6.67	6.67	6.67
7. Net income		10	10	10
8. After tax salvage				15
9. Cash flow (7+8+4−1)	−100	+43.33	+43.33	+58.33
NPV at 20% = 0				

Assumptions:
1. Tax depreciation is straight line over 3 years.
2. Pre-tax salvage value is 25 in year 3, and 50 if the asset is scrapped in year 2.
3. Tax on salvage value is 40 percent of the difference between salvage value and depreciated investment.
4. The cost of capital is 20 percent.

(*a*) What is the value of a 1-year old plant? Of a 2-year old plant?

(*b*) Suppose that the government now changes tax depreciation to allow a 100 percent writeoff in year 1. How does this affect the value of existing 1- and 2-year-old plants? Existing plants must continue using the original tax depreciation schedule.

(*c*) Would it now make sense to scrap existing plants when they are 2 rather than 3 years old?

(*d*) How would your answers change if the corporate income tax were abolished entirely?

12 Organizing Capital Expenditure and Evaluating Performance Afterward

Our task up to this point has been to show how a firm *should* set its capital budget. In this chapter we discuss how this is done in practice. We give particular attention to how capital budgeting is organized and to the administrative problems that inevitably crop up.

A good capital budgeting system does more than just make accept-reject decisions on individual projects. It must tie into the firm's long-range planning process—the process that decides what lines of business the firm concentrates in and sets out plans for financing, production, marketing, research and development, etc. It must also tie into a procedure for measurement of performance. Otherwise the firm has no way of knowing how its decisions about capital expenditure finally turn out. Measurement of performance occupies a substantial part of this chapter. The pitfalls in measuring profitability are serious but not as widely recognized as they should be.

12-1 CAPITAL BUDGETS AND PROJECT AUTHORIZATIONS

For most sizable firms the first step in the investment process is the preparation of an annual **capital budget**, which is a list of planned investment projects and a breakdown of planned investment outlays by plant and division. (In this chapter we will think of plants as building blocks for divisions, and divisions as building blocks for firms. That is arbitrary: there may be more than two layers. Also, divisions are often organized by product line, region, or some other business unit.) In principle, the capital budget should be a list of all positive-NPV opportunities open to the firm.

Most firms let project proposals bubble up from plants for review by division management, and from divisions for review by senior management. The administrative process typically works as follows.

Plant managers identify "interesting" opportunities, analyze them, and decide which ones are really worthwhile. Proposed expenditures for these projects are then submitted to division managers for further review. Some of the proposals by the plants do not "make the cut" at the divisional level. But divisional management may add its own ideas, usually new, larger ventures, like manufacturing a new product, that plant managers could not be expected to initiate. The lists of the divisions are forwarded to the corporate controller, who prunes and consolidates them into a proposed company budget. For very large diversified firms there may be several intermediate review stages.

The resulting budget is a list of proposed new projects for the coming year and of any projects from former years that are incomplete. Supporting information is usually provided on standard forms, supplemented by descriptive memoranda for larger projects. Since approval of the budget rarely confers authority to spend money, backup information is not as detailed at this stage as it is later. Projects below a specified size are typically not even listed separately, but simply included under a blanket approval for a given division or plant. In many companies the budget also contains rough estimates of likely expenditures over a 5-year period.

The suggested budget is then reviewed by senior management and staff specializing in planning and financial analysis. It may be considered initially by a committee that includes the president, treasurer, and controller. Usually there are negotiations between the firm's senior management and its divisional management, and perhaps there will also be special analyses of major outlays or ventures into new areas, before the budget is submitted to the board for approval. Once approved, the budget generally remains the basis for planning over the ensuing year. In a few firms, however, it is updated each quarter.

Because each proposal in the budget requires subsequent specific authorization, the use of a budget involves some duplication of effort. But it allows information exchange up and down the management hierarchy before attitudes have hardened and personal commitments have been made. The danger with the whole procedure is loss of flexibility. There is a tendency for most projects to appear for the first time in the annual budget, and in some companies it is difficult to initiate project ideas at any other time of year.

Project Authorizations

The approval of a capital budget rarely confers authority to undertake the expenditures listed in the budget. Most companies stipulate that formal **appropriation requests** should be prepared for each proposal. The requests are accompanied by more or less elaborate backup, depending on the project's size, novelty, and strategic importance. Also, the type of backup information required depends on project category. Some firms use a fourfold breakdown:

1. Safety or environmental outlays required by law or company policy—e.g., for pollution-control equipment
2. Maintenance or cost reduction—e.g., machine replacement
3. Capacity expansion in existing businesses
4. Investment for new products or ventures

The information requirements for projects differ across these categories:

1. Pollution control does not have to pay its own way. The main issue is whether standards are met at minimum present value of cost. The decision is likely to hinge on engineering analyses of alternative technologies.
2. Engineering analysis is also important in machine replacement, but new machines have to pay their own way. In category 2 above the firm faces the classical capital budgeting problems described in Chapter 6.
3. Projects in category 3 are less straightforward capital budgeting problems; these decisions may hinge on forecasts of demand, of possible shifts in technology, and of competitors' strategies.
4. Projects in category 4 are most likely to depend on intangibles. The first projects in a new area may not have positive NPVs if they are considered in isolation, yet the firm may go ahead in order to establish a position in a market and pave the way for profitable future projects. The first projects are not taken for their own sake, but because they give the firm a valuable *option* to undertake follow-on projects. Thus, for projects in category 4, cash-flow forecasts may be less important than the issue of whether the firm enjoys some technological or other advantage which promises to generate economic rents for the firm. That issue becomes the main focus of project analysis.

Most large companies have manuals providing checklists to make sure that all relevant costs and alternatives are considered. The manual may contain instructions showing how to forecast cash flows and how to compute NPV, internal rate of return, or other measures of project value. Sometimes the manual also specifies the opportunity cost of capital.

Though appropriation requests may be prepared by the project originator, the plant manager is usually responsible for submitting them. These requests come up through the ranks of operating management for approval at each succeeding level. If the project is large, the request may be checked at some stage by staff accountants, engineers, and economists. The number of hurdles the proposal must pass depends on the magnitude of the expenditure involved.

Because the investment decision is central to the development of the firm, authorization tends to be reserved for senior management. Almost all companies set ceilings on the size of capital projects that divisional managers can authorize without specific approval from their superiors. Moreover, the ceilings are surprisingly low. Scapens and Sale surveyed 203 larger firms, with average capital budgets of $130 million per year, and found that the average ceiling for individual projects was only $136,000.[1] When you consider that a large company may generate thousands of authorization requests each year, the limited extent of delegation is striking.

Bottom-up versus Top-down

We have pictured the capital investment process as if all proposals bubbled up from the bottom of the organization. That is never the whole story. The managers of plants A and B cannot be expected to see the potential economies of scale of closing their plants and consolidating production at a new plant C. We expect divisional management to propose plant C. Similarly, divisions 1 and 2 may not be eager to give up their own data processing operations to a large, central computer. That proposal would come from senior management.

The final capital budget must also reflect strategic choices made by senior management. Strategic planning attempts to identify the businesses in which the firm has a real competitive advantage. It also attempts to identify businesses to sell or liquidate as well as declining businesses that should be allowed to run down. Strategic planning is really capital budgeting on a grand scale.

In many firms strategic plans impose a strong top-down input to capital budgeting decisions. Projects that appear to have negative NPVs may be accepted if they help to establish the firm in a business with good long-run potential. Similarly, projects that appear to have positive NPVs may be rejected if the firm plans to run down this part of its business. Of course, if a "declining" business continually generates high-NPV projects, the strategic planners ought to think again—perhaps the business isn't declining.

The Decision Criteria Firms Actually Use

We know that companies use a number of different criteria for project selection. Table 12-1 shows the results of a survey by Schall, Sundem, and Geijsbeek of the relative popularity of different techniques. Notice the popularity of theoretically inappropriate techniques like payback and book rate of return, usually in combination with IRR, NPV, or both. But comparison of this study with earlier ones confirms that the sophisticated techniques are gaining.

---

[1] R. W. Scapens and J. T. Sale, "Performance Measurement and Formal Capital Expenditure Controls in Divisionalized Companies," *Journal of Business Finance and Accounting*, **8:** 389–420 (Autumn 1981).

TABLE 12-1
This survey of capital investment procedures shows that many firms use more than one investment criterion and that they frequently employ theoretically inappropriate criteria

Payback	Return on Book	IRR	NPV	Percentage of Firms Using Each Combination of Criteria
x	x	x	x	17
x	x	x		14
x	x		x	9
x		x	x	9
	x	x	x	2
x	x			8
x		x		8
x			x	7
		x	x	7
	x		x	4
	x	x		2
		x		6
	x			4
			x	2
x				2

Source: L. D. Schall, G. L. Sundem, and W. R. Geijsbeek, "Survey and Analysis of Capital Budgeting Methods," *Journal of Finance,* **33:** 281–287 (March 1978), table 1, p. 282.

Of course, the use of intelligent techniques does not guarantee intelligent decisions. You can have good techniques and poor judgment or vice versa. Often operating managers display considerable conceptual confusion on financial issues. One encounters such statements as "We do all three (book rate of return, payback, and internal rate of return) and may decide that one is more relevant than the other," or "We don't use present value becausing it can't handle uncertainty." Even when companies do impose theoretically justifiable criteria, their application is often imperfect. For example, a British survey noted that almost half of the companies producing cash-flow estimates treated depreciation as a cash outflow.[2] Many American companies think they can ignore inflation in cash-flow forecasts because "on the average revenues increase to cover inflated costs."

There is ignorance in the world. But before we get too smug, let's stop and think of other explanations. There are, in fact, several.

The Role of Judgment.   Businesspeople often act smarter than they talk. (For students and scholars it is the other way around.) They may make correct decisions but they may not be able to explain them in the language of finance and economics. Many decisions are fundamentally intuitive. If *intuitive* sounds capricious, replace the word with *informed judgment.* As we argued in Chapter 11: if a firm enjoys an advantage that promises to generate economic rents in a stable or growing business, it probably should press on regardless of calculated payback or present value. Experience helps in identifying such opportunities.

Of course, this is not a complete answer. Few decisions are totally judgmental. In principle, if *any* quantitative measure of project value affects a decision, it should be present value, not payback or return on book.

[2] See L. E. Rockley, *Investment for Profitability: An Analysis of the Policies and Practices of UK and International Companies,* Business Books Ltd., London, 1973.

Communication.　Payback is the easiest way to *communicate* an idea of project profitability. It is important to have one measure everyone can understand, because capital budgeting is a process of discussion and negotiation involving people from all parts of the firm. Insisting that everyone commenting on a project do so in terms of NPV may cut off those who don't understand NPV, but who nevertheless can contribute useful information.

There is a law at work here which we can also observe working in television, publishing, and many other areas: a wider audience demands simpler concepts and language. Perhaps we could have sold more copies of this book by making it easier.

Rewards to Managers.　Plant and divisional managers are concerned for their own futures. Sometimes their interests conflict with stockholders'. New plant managers, for example, naturally want to demonstrate good performance right away in order to move up the corporate ladder. Perhaps they will propose quick-payback projects even if NPV is sacrificed. If their performance is judged on book earnings, they will be attracted by projects whose accounting results look good. Even if managers propose the right (NPV-maximizing) projects, we can understand their concern for payback and book return.

The problem lies in the way many firms measure performance and reward managers. Don't expect them to concentrate only on NPV if you always demand quick results or if you will reward them later on the basis of book return. More on this later in the chapter.

12-2　PROBLEMS AND SOME SOLUTIONS

Problems of Cooperation

Valuing capital investment opportunities is hard enough when you can do the entire job yourself. In real life it is a cooperative effort. Although cooperation brings more knowledge and intelligence to bear, it brings its own problems. Some are unavoidable—just another cost of doing business. Some can be alleviated by adding checks and balances to the capital investment process.

Many of the problems stem from sponsors' eagerness to obtain approval for their favorite projects. As the proposal proceeds up the organization, alliances are formed. Preparation of the request inevitably involves discussions and compromises which limit subsequent freedom of action. Thus once a division has screened its plants' proposals, the plants unite in competing against "outsiders."

This competition among divisions can be put to good use if it forces division managers to develop better justifications for what they want to do. But the competition has its costs as well. Several thousand appropriation requests may reach the senior management level each year, all of them essentially sales documents presented by united fronts and designed to persuade. Alternative schemes have been filtered out at an earlier stage. The danger is that senior management cannot obtain (let alone absorb) the information to evaluate each project rationally.

The dangers are illustrated by the following practical question: "Should we establish a definite opportunity cost of capital for computing the NPV of projects in our furniture division?" The answer in theory is a clear yes, providing that the projects of the division are all in the same risk class. Remember that most project analysis is done at the plant or divisional level. Only a small proportion of project ideas analyzed survives for submission to top management. Plant and division managers cannot judge projects correctly unless they know the true opportunity cost of capital.

Suppose senior management settles on 12 percent. That helps plant managers make rational decisions. But it also tells them exactly how optimistic they have to be to get their pet project accepted. Brealey and Myers's second law states that the proportion of proposed projects having a positive estimated NPV is independent of top management's estimate of the opportunity cost of capital.[3] If the law is true, top management is better off concealing its estimates of the cost of capital, asking instead for NPVs calculated for a range of different discount rates, and applying the right rate when the final decision is made.

A firm that accepts poor information at the top faces two consequences. First, senior management cannot evaluate individual projects. In a study by Bower of a large multidivisional company, projects that had the approval of a division general manager were seldom turned down by his or her group of divisions, and those reaching the executive committee were almost never rejected. Second, the only effective control available to management is to impose expenditure limits on individual plants or divisions. The effect is to force the subunits to choose among projects and to encourage the divisions to compete for funds. The firm ends up using capital rationing as a way of decentralizing decisions.

Of course, capital rationing is not the only solution. Firms can improve the quality of information flowing to the top by setting up corporate capital budgeting staffs to enforce consistency, uncover unspecified assumptions, and undertake sophisticated analyses of major projects.

These analysts may also have to ferret out local managers who are evading the controls in the capital investment process. For example, managers may be permitted to approve projects only up to a certain value. But this authority may become infinite if each project can be broken down into a large number of small parts. The following story illustrates this problem:

> *Our [top managers] like to make all the major capital decisions. They think they do, but I've just seen one case where a division beat them.*
>
> *I received for editing a capital request from the division for a large chimney. I couldn't see what anyone could do with just a chimney so I flew out for a visit. They've built and equipped a whole plant on plant expense orders. The chimney is the only indivisible item that exceeded the $50,000 limit we put on the expense orders. Apparently they learned informally that a new plant wouldn't be favorably received, and since they thought the business needed it, and the return would justify it, they built the damn thing.[4]*

This embarrassment might have been avoided if the firm had imposed a limit on individual discretionary expenditures and *also* on the total amount of such expenditures by each manager in any one year.

A similar difficulty stems from the imprecise concept of a capital expenditure. It may not be material whether a firm purchases or leases a piece of equipment: the subsequent effect on operating cash flows is similar. Clearly management's interest is in controlling the acquisition of any important asset whether it be leased or purchased. It also wants to control acquisition not only of tangible assets, but also of intangible ones such as a patent or a long-term contract. Authorization

---

[3] There is no first law. We thought that "second law" sounded better. There *is* a third law, but that is for another chapter.

[4] Cited in J. L. Bower, *Managing the Resource Allocation Process: A Study of Corporate Planning and Investment*, Division of Research, Graduate School of Business Administration, Harvard University, Boston, 1970, p. 15.

procedures should be broadly construed and should not encourage the inefficient substitution of one kind of asset for another.

Another problem is to ensure that the authorization request draws attention to all likely contingent expenditures. Too often, seemingly small and innocuous investments are the first step in a chain of economically dependent investments. Management should be aware of the full consequences of letting a plant or division get its foot in the door.

Some Partial Solutions

We risk overemphasizing the problems and underemphasizing the ability of organizations to cope with them. They cope because people are sensible and because informal communication and negotiation reinforce formal procedures. There are also formal solutions, most of them mentioned in passing as we discussed the problems. Now we will present them in a more organized way.

Corporate Staff.　Corporate staff can be assigned to enforce consistency in project analyses, check the assumptions behind cash-flow forecasts, and undertake special analyses. Large corporations often have special staff departments devoted mainly to these tasks.

Budgeting and Planning.　The capital budget is a part of a broader budgeting and planning cycle. The firm has to set operating budgets for plants and divisions and also plan marketing, research, financing, and long-term growth. Capital investments have to make sense in terms of these other plans.

Strategic Choices.　We referred to strategic planning as *capital budgeting on a grand scale*. It attempts to identify the businesses which offer the best long-run opportunities and to develop a plan for achieving success in those businesses.

Strategic planning deals in intangibles. Present values are rarely calculated explicitly. But the goal is clear: to identify areas where the firm has a competitive advantage. Firms which emphasize strategic planning are doing just what we recommended in Chapter 11: looking for the sources of economic rents as a check against bias and exaggeration in cash flow forecasts.

A firm's capital investment choices should reflect both "bottom-up" and "top-down" processes—capital budgeting and strategic planning, respectively. The two processes should complement one another. Plant and division managers, who do most of the work in bottom-up capital budgeting, may not see the forest for the trees. Strategic planners may have a mistaken view of the forest because they do not look at the trees one by one.

Strategic planning is more important in some industries than in others. It is not important for oil exploration companies, which have to analyze prospects one by one. It is important in industries where tomorrow's opportunities are created by today's investments and where success depends on intangible assets like technology, product design, and reputation, or on elaborate marketing and distribution systems. Intangible assets are hard to evaluate in a purely bottom-up process.

Decentralization.　Most decisions on significant capital outlays are reserved for top management. At least this is the formal process. The real decisions may be made further down in the organization. Senior management may have limited effective control over project-by-project decisions because of lack of information at the top.

When this happens capital investment decisions are effectively decentralized regardless of what formal procedures specify. Many firms force divisions to set their own priorities by setting rigid constraints on the capital expenditures of the divisions. Other firms are less rigid: they accept decentralization; they relax and enjoy it, keeping control by budgeting, planning, and monitoring the overall operations of the divisions.

But decentralization can only work if plant and division managers are rewarded for doing the right things. The way performance is measured and rewarded affects the kinds of projects that are proposed. Capital tends to flow more easily to divisions that seem to perform well.

Therefore any discussion of the capital expenditure process has to consider what happens *after* the project is accepted. That is our next topic.

12-3 EVALUATING PERFORMANCE

Most firms have formal procedures for evaluating the performance of their capital investments. There are three aspects to performance measurement. First, companies need to monitor projects under construction to ensure that there are no serious delays or cost overruns. Second, companies generally conduct a post-mortem on major projects shortly after they have begun to operate. These investigations are known as **postaudits**. They help to identify problems that need fixing, to check the accuracy of forecasts, and to suggest questions that should have been asked before the project was undertaken. Postaudits pay off mainly by helping managers do a better job when they come to analyze the next round of investment proposals. Finally, there is ongoing performance measurement, which is done through the firm's accounting and control system. We will explain how that system should work to support the capital investment process and why it sometimes fails.

Controlling Projects in Progress

Control over projects in progress is an essential follow-up to a decision to authorize expenditure. The authorization usually specifies how much money may be spent and when. Control is established by accounting procedures for recording expenditures as they occur. Typically, companies will permit up to 10 percent expenditure overruns, but beyond that the sponsor is required to submit a supplemental appropriation request. To ensure that the money is not diverted to other uses, the sponsor is also required to submit a revised appropriation request if there is any significant change in the nature of the project.

In order to avoid delays, a few companies attempt to set limits to the length of time before construction begins. Almost all firms require the sponsor to submit a formal notice of completion, so that the accumulated costs can be transferred to the permanent accounts and any unspent cash can be recovered rather than kept in a hidden kitty for miscellaneous uses.

These procedures are necessary aspects of control. More general information on progress is usually contained in monthly or quarterly status reports.

Postaudits

Postaudits of capital expenditures are now undertaken in most large firms. Not all projects are audited, and those that are, are usually audited only once. A few firms require further audits for "problem" projects. The most common time for audit is 1 year after construction or installation is completed.

The audit is usually the responsibility of the corporation's controller and is handled by the internal auditing department. Because this department may be ill-equipped to assess technical issues, the task is sometimes jointly assigned to accounting and engineering departments. Sometimes the audit is delegated to plants, and not infrequently it is assigned to the project originator. The scope for conflicts of interest in such cases is obvious.

It is a sensible precaution to check on the progress of recent investments. Otherwise problems may go undetected and uncorrected. Postaudits can also provide useful insights to the next round of decision making on capital investments. After a postaudit the controller may say, "We should have anticipated the extra working capital needed to support the project." Next time working capital will get the attention it deserves.

The postaudit is sometimes also used to monitor the quality of forecasts made by project proposers. However, it is worth sounding a note of caution here. The audit is usually taken far too soon after installation to provide any clear assessment of the project's success. And, since the forecasters rarely specify the economic assumptions behind their forecasts, it is hard to measure whether they really got it right or whether they were bailed out by a buoyant economy. Finally, the number of audited projects is so small and their authorship so imprecise that it is difficult to associate forecasting ability with a particular type of project or proposer.

Of course, the mere threat of postaudit may spur the forecaster to greater accuracy. But it can work the other way around. Many managers make conservative forecasts in the belief that what matters is to beat one's forecasts. In other cases the threat of audit may cause risky projects to be suppressed altogether.

Problems in Measuring Incremental Cash Flows after the Fact

Often postaudits cannot measure all cash flows generated by a project. It may be impossible to split the project away from the rest of the business.

Suppose you have just taken over a trucking firm which operates a package delivery service for local stores. You decide to try to revitalize the business by cutting costs and improving service. This requires three investment projects:

1. Buy five new trucks
2. Construct two additional dispatching centers
3. Buy a small computer to keep track of packages and schedule trucks

A year later you try a postaudit of the computer. You verify that it is working properly and check actual costs of purchase, installation, and training against projections. But how do you identify the incremental cash *inflows* generated by the computer? No one has kept records of the extra gas that *would have* been used, or the number of packages that *would have* been lost, had the computer not been installed. You may be able to verify that service is better, but how much of the improvement comes from the new trucks, how much from the dispatching centers, and how much from the computer? It is impossible to say. The only meaningful way to judge the success or failure of your revitalization program is to examine the delivery business as a whole.

Evaluating Operating Performance

Think again of your package delivery business. We could measure its performance in two ways:

1. *Actual versus projected.* We could compare actual operating earnings or cash flow with what you predicted.
2. *Actual profitability versus an absolute standard of profitability.* We could also compare actual profitability against an absolute standard of profitability. Ideally we

would like to know the present value of that business's future cash flow relative to the parent firm's current investment in it. The current investment is the value of the assets now committed to the business if they were put to the best alternative use.

The first measure is easy to understand and implement. The second is full of pitfalls, as we will now see.

Accounting Rate of Return as a Performance Measure

Let us think for a moment about how profitability should be measured in principle. It is easy enough to compute the true, or "economic," rate of return for a common stock that is continuously traded. We just record cash receipts (dividends) for the year, add the change in price over the year, and divide by the beginning price:

$$\text{Rate of return} = \frac{\text{cash receipts } + \text{ change in price}}{\text{beginning price}}$$

$$= \frac{C_1 + (P_1 - P_0)}{P_0}$$

The numerator of the expression for rate of return (cash flow plus change in value) is called **economic income**:

$$\text{Economic income} = \text{cash flow} + \text{change in present value}$$

Any reduction in present value represents **economic depreciation**; any increase in present value represents *negative* economic depreciation. Therefore

$$\text{Economic depreciation} = \text{reduction in present value}$$

and

$$\text{Economic income} = \text{cash flow} - \text{economic depreciation}$$

The concept works for any asset. Rate of return equals cash flow plus change in value divided by starting value. The return on the package delivery service for 1984 is

$$\text{Rate of return} = \frac{C_{1984} + (\text{PV}_{1984} - \text{PV}_{1983})}{\text{PV}_{1983}}$$

where PV_{1983} and PV_{1984} indicate the present values of the business at the ends of 1983 and 1984.

The only hard part in measuring economic income and return is calculating present value. You can observe market value if shares in the asset are actively traded, but few plants, divisions, or capital projects have *their own* shares traded in the stock market. You can observe the present market value of *all* the firm's assets but not of any one of them taken separately.

Accountants rarely even attempt to measure present value. Instead they give us net book value (BV), which is original cost less depreciation computed according to some arbitrary schedule. Many companies use the book value to calculate the book return on investment (ROI):

$$\text{Book income} = \text{cash flow} - \text{book depreciation}$$

$$= C_1 + (\text{BV}_1 - \text{BV}_0)$$

Therefore

$$\text{Book ROI} = \frac{C_1 + (\text{BV}_1 - \text{BV}_0)}{\text{BV}_0}$$

If book depreciation and economic depreciation are different (they are rarely the same), then the book profitability measures will be wrong; that is, they will not measure true profitability. (In fact, it is not clear that accountants should even *try* to measure true profitability. They could not do so without heavy reliance on subjective estimates of value. Perhaps they should stick to supplying objective information, and leave the estimation of value to managers and investors.)

12-4 EXAMPLE—MEASURING THE PROFITABILITY OF THE NODHEAD SUPERMARKET

Supermarket chains invest heavily in building and equipping new stores. The regional manager of a chain is about to propose investing $1 million in a new store in Nodhead. Projected cash flows are:

Year	1	2	3	4	5	6	After Year 6
Cash flow, in thousands of dollars	100	200	250	298	298	298	0

Of course real supermarkets last more than 6 years. But these numbers are realistic in one important sense: it may take 2 or 3 years for a new store to catch on—that is, to build up a substantial, habitual clientele. Thus cash flow is low for the first few years even in the best locations.

We will assume the opportunity cost of capital is 10 percent. The Nodhead store's NPV at 10 percent is zero. It is an acceptable project, but not an unusually good one:

$$\text{NPV} = -1000 + \frac{100}{1.10} + \frac{200}{(1.10)^2} + \frac{250}{(1.10)^3} + \frac{298}{(1.10)^4} + \frac{298}{(1.10)^5} + \frac{298}{(1.10)^6} = 0$$

It is not hard to forecast economic income and rate of return. Table 12-2 shows the calculations. From the cash-flow forecasts we can forecast present value at the start of periods 1 to 6. Cash flow plus *change* in present value equals economic income. Rate of return equals economic income divided by start-of-period value.

Of course, these are forecasts. Actual future cash flows and values will be higher or lower. Table 12-2 shows that investors *expect* to earn 10 percent in each year of the store's 6-year life. In other words, investors expect to earn the opportunity cost of capital each year from holding this asset.[5]

Table 12-3 shows the store's forecasted *book* profitability assuming straight-line depreciation over its 6-year life. The book ROI is lower than the true return for the first 2 years and higher afterward.[6] The error can be traced to the use of straight-

---

[5] This is a general result. Forecasted profitability always equals the discount rate used to calculate the estimated future present values.

[6] The errors in book ROI always catch up with you in the end. If the firm chooses a depreciation schedule that overstates a project's return in some years, it must also understate the return in other years. In fact, you can think of a project's IRR as a kind of average of the book returns. It is not a simple average, however. The weights are the project's book values discounted at the IRR. See J. A. Kay, "Accountants, Too, Could Be Happy in a Golden Age: The Accountant's Rate of Profit and the Internal Rate of Return," *Oxford Economic Papers*, **28:** 447–460 (1976).

TABLE 12-2
Forecasted economic income and rate of return for the proposed Nodhead store.
Economic income equals cash flow plus change in present value. Rate of return equals
economic income divided by value at start of year.

| | YEAR | | | | | |
	1	2	3	4	5	6
Cash flow	100	200	250	298	298	298
Present value, at *start* of year, 10 percent discount rate	1,000	1,000	901	741	517	271
Present value at *end* of year, 10 percent discount rate	1,000	901	741	517	271	0
Change in value during year	0	−99	−160	−224	−246	−271
Economic income	100	101	90	74	52	27
Rate of return	.10	.10	.10	.10	.10	.10
Economic depreciation	0	99	160	224	246	271

Note: There are minor rounding errors in some annual figures.

line depreciation, which overstates economic depreciation at first and understates it later on. Note that any kind of accelerated depreciation would make the errors worse. Economic depreciation is *decelerated* in this case.

Book Earnings versus True Earnings

At this point the regional manager steps up on stage for the following soliloquy:

> *"The Nodhead store's a decent investment. I really should propose it. But if we go ahead, I won't look very good at next year's performance review. And what if I also go ahead with the new stores in Russet, Gravenstein, and Sheepnose? Their cash-flow patterns are pretty much the same. I could actually appear to lose money next year. The stores I've got won't earn enough to cover the initial losses on four new ones.*
>
> *"Of course, everyone knows new supermarkets lose money at first. The loss would be in the budget. My boss will understand—I think. But what about her boss? What if the board of directors starts asking pointed questions about profitability in my region? I'm under a lot of pressure to generate better earnings. Pamela Quince, the upstate manager, got a bonus for generating a 40 percent increase in book ROI. She didn't spend much on expansion. . . ."*

The regional manager is getting conflicting signals. On the one hand he is told to find and propose good investment projects. *Good* is defined by discounted cash flow. On the other hand, he is also urged to increase book earnings. But the two goals conflict because book earnings do not measure true earnings. The greater the pressure for immediate book profits, the more the regional manager is tempted to forgo good investments or to favor quick-payback projects over longer-lived projects, even if the latter have higher NPVs.

TABLE 12-3
Forecasted book income and ROI for the proposed Nodhead store. Book ROI is lower than the economic rate of return for the first 2 years and higher thereafter

	YEAR					
	1	2	3	4	5	6
Cash flow	100	200	250	298	298	298
Book value at start of year, straight-line depreciation	1,000	833	667	500	333	167
Book value at end of year, straight-line depreciation	833	667	500	333	167	0
Change in book value during year	−167	−167	−167	−167	−167	−167
Book income	−67	+33	+83	+131	+131	+131
Book ROI	−.067	+.04	+.124	+.262	+.393	+.784
Book depreciation	167	167	167	167	167	167

Does ROI Give the Right Answer in the Long Run?

Some people downplay the problem we have just described. Is a temporary dip in book profits a major problem? Don't the errors wash out in the long run, when the region settles down to a steady state with an even mix of old and new stores?

It turns out that the errors diminish but do *not* exactly offset. The simplest steady-state condition occurs when the firm does not grow, but reinvests just enough each year to maintain earnings and asset values. Table 12-4 shows steady-state book ROIs for a regional division which opens one store a year. For simplicity we assume the division starts from scratch and that each store's cash flows are carbon copies of the Nodhead store. The true rate of return on each store is, therefore, 10 percent. But, as Table 12-4 demonstrates, steady-state book ROI, at 12.6 percent, overstates the true rate of return. Therefore, you cannot assume that the errors in book ROI will wash out in the long run.

Thus we still have a problem even in the long run. The extent of error depends on how fast the business grows. We have just considered one steady state with a zero growth rate. Think of another firm with a 5 percent steady-state growth rate. Such a firm would invest $1000 the first year, $1050 the second, $1102.50 the third, and so on. Clearly the faster growth means more new projects relative to old ones. The greater weight given to young projects, which have low book ROIs, the lower the business's apparent profitability. Figure 12-1 shows how this works out for a business composed of projects like the Nodhead store. Book ROI will either overestimate or underestimate the true rate of return unless the amount that the firm invests each year grows at the same rate as the true rate of return.[7]

Book measures of profitability can be wrong or misleading because:

1. Errors occur at different stages of project life. Book measures are likely to understate true profitability for new projects and overstate it for old ones.

[7] This also is a general result. Biases in steady-state book ROIs disappear when the growth rate equals the true rate of return. This was discovered by E. Solomon and J. Laya, "Measurement of Company Profitability: Some Systematic Errors in Accounting Rate of Return," in A. A. Robichek (ed.), *Financial Research and Management Decisions*, John Wiley & Sons, Inc., New York, 1967, pp. 152–183.

TABLE 12-4
Book ROI for a group of stores like the Nodhead store. The steady-state book ROI overstates .the 10 percent *economic* rate of return.

	YEAR					
	1	2	3	4	5	6
Book income for store						
1	−67	+33	+83	+131	+131	+131
2		−67	+33	+83	+131	+131
3			−67	+33	+83	+131
4				−67	+33	+83
5					−67	+33
6						−67
TOTAL BOOK INCOME	−67	−34	+49	180	311	442
Book value for store						
1	1,000	833	667	500	333	167
2		1,000	833	667	500	333
3			1,000	833	667	500
4				1,000	833	667
5					1,000	833
6						1,000
TOTAL BOOK VALUE	1,000	1,833	2,500	3,000	3,333	3,500
Book ROI for all stores = total book income / total book value	−.067	−.019	+.02	+.06	+.093	**+.126***

Note: Book income = cash flow + change in book value during year.
*Steady-state book ROI.

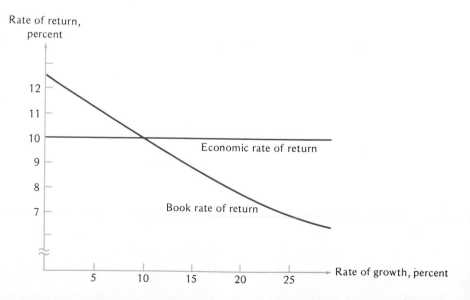

FIGURE 12-1
The faster a firm grows, the lower its book rate of return, providing true profitability is constant. This graph is drawn for a firm composed of identical projects all like the Nodhead store (Table 12-2), but growing at a constant compound rate.

2. Errors also occur when firms or divisions have a balanced mix of old and new projects. Our "steady-state" analysis shows this.

3. Errors occur because of inflation, basically because inflation shows up in revenue faster than it shows up in costs. For example, a firm owning a plant built in 1970 will, under standard accounting procedures, calculate depreciation in terms of the plant's original cost in 1970 dollars. The plant's output is sold for current dollars. This is why the U.S. National Income and Product Accounts report corporate profits calculated under replacement cost accounting. This procedure bases depreciation not on the original cost of firms' assets, but on what it would cost to replace the assets at current prices.

4. Book measures are often confused by "creative accounting." Some firms pick and choose among available accounting procedures, or even invent new ones, in order to make their income statements and balance sheets look good. This was done with particular imagination in the "go-go years" of the mid-1960s.

Investors and financial managers, having been burned by inflation and creative accounting, have learned not to take accounting profitability at face value. Yet many people do not realize the depth of the problem. They think that if firms adopted inflation accounting and eschewed creative accounting, everything would be all right except perhaps for temporary problems with very old or very young projects. In other words, they worry about reasons 3 and 4, and a little about reason 1, but not at all about 2. We think reason 2 deserves more attention.

12-5 WHAT CAN WE DO ABOUT BIASES IN ACCOUNTING PROFITABILITY MEASURES?

The dangers in judging profitability by accounting measures are clear from this chapter's discussion and examples. To be forewarned is to be forearmed. But we can say something beyond just "be careful."

It is natural for firms to set an absolute standard of profitability for plants or divisions. Ideally that standard should be the opportunity cost of capital for investment in the plant or division. But if performance is measured by book ROI, then the standard should be adjusted to reflect accounting biases.

This is easier said than done, because accounting biases are notoriously hard to measure in complex practical situations. Thus, many firms end up asking not "Did the widget division earn more than its cost of capital last year?" but "Was the widget division's book ROI typical of a successful firm in the widget industry?" The underlying assumptions are (1) similar accounting procedures are used by other widget manufacturers and (2) that successful widget companies earn their cost of capital.

There are some simple accounting changes that could reduce biases in book ROI. Remember that the biases all stem from *not* using economic depreciation. Therefore why not switch to economic depreciation? The main reason is that each asset's present value would have to be reestimated every year. Imagine the confusion if this were attempted. You can understand why accountants set up a depreciation schedule when an investment is made and then stick to it apart from exceptional circumstances. But why restrict the choice of depreciation schedules to the old standbys, straight-line, double-declining balance, and sum-of-the-years' digits? Why not specify a depreciation pattern that at least matches *expected* economic depreciation? For example, the Nodhead store could be depreciated according to the expected economic depreciation schedule shown in Table 12-2. This would avoid any systematic biases.[8] It would break no law or accounting standard. This step seems so simple and effective that we are at loss to explain why firms have not adopted it.[9]

Much of the pressure for good book earnings comes from the top management. Chief executives have good reasons to shoot for good short-run earnings. Probably their bonuses depend on it. The market watches current earnings per share (partly because it isn't allowed to look over top management's shoulder at the 5-year plan). Is it surprising that top management does not always jump happily into high-NPV projects that will depress next year's earnings per share?

We do not mean to imply that chief executives typically sacrifice long-run value for immediate earnings. But they at least *worry* about earnings, and their worries affect attitudes and decisions down the line.

We think managers worry too much. They are uptight about book earnings. They often picture investors as mindless creatures who respond only to the latest earnings announcement. Investors are more sophisticated than that. Polaroid Corporation provides a good example. Its earnings dropped sharply in the early 1970s because of heavy development expenditures on the SX-70 instant camera, which was successfully introduced in 1973. If investors looked only at the latest earnings announcement they would have concluded that Polaroid was in big trouble in 1972. In fact they understood *why* earnings were low and acted accordingly.

Financial managers can help investors do better by *not* playing the earnings game. That is, they should not hire creative accountants or emphasize book earnings while downplaying more fundamental information about their firm's performance. The firm that brags only about its book earnings will be judged on its book earnings.

12-6   SUMMARY

We began this chapter by describing how capital budgeting is organized and ended by exposing serious biases in accounting measures of financial performance. Inevitably such discussions stress the mechanics of organization, control, and accounting. It is harder to talk about the informal procedures that reinforce the formal ones. But remember that it takes informal communication and personal initiative to make capital budgeting work. Also, the accounting biases are partly or wholly alleviated because managers and stockholders are smart enough to look behind reported book earnings.

Formal capital-budgeting systems usually have four stages:

1. Preparation of a *capital budget* for the firm. This is a plan for capital expenditure by plant, division, or other business unit.
2. *Project authorizations* give authority to go ahead with specific projects.
3. Procedures for *control of projects under construction* warn if projects are behind schedule or costing more than planned.
4. *Postaudits* check on the progress of recent investments.

The formal criteria used in project evaluation are a mixture of modern rules like net present value and internal rate of return, and old-fashioned rules like payback and average return on book. The old rules survive partly because everyone

---

[8] Using expected economic depreciation will not generate book ROIs that are exactly right unless realized cash flows exactly match forecasted flows. But we expect forecasts to be right on average.

[9] This procedure has been suggested by several authors, most recently by Zvi Bodie in "Compound Interest Depreciation in Capital Investment," *Harvard Business Review*, **60:** 58–60 (May–June 1982).

understands them; they provide a common language for discussing the project. They also survive because of the way performance is evaluated and rewarded. If managers are expected to generate quick results, and results are measured as contribution to book earnings, then management is naturally interested in payback and book return.

Most specific project proposals originate at the plant or division level. If the project doesn't cost much, it may be approved by middle management. But the final say on major capital outlays belongs to top management. The desire of top management to retain control of capital budgeting is understandable. But the chief executive cannot undertake a detailed analysis of every project he or she approves. Information at the top is often limited; project proposals may be designed more to persuade than inform.

Top management copes by relying on staff financial analysts, by making capital budgeting part of a broader budgeting and planning process, and by keeping the capital budgeting process flexible and open to informal communication.

Capital budgeting is not entirely a bottom-up process. Strategic planners practice "capital budgeting on a grand scale" by attempting to identify those businesses in which the firm has a special advantage. Project proposals that support the firm's accepted overall strategy are much more likely to have clear sailing as they come up through the organization.

Usually the plant or division proposing a capital investment will be responsible for making the project work. A project's sponsors are naturally concerned that the project performs well, and also that it *appears* to perform well. Thus the way the firm evaluates operating performance can affect the kinds of projects that middle managers are willing to propose.

There are two approaches to performance measurement. The first and easier is to compare actual cash flow with projected cash flow. The second is to compare actual profitability with the opportunity cost of capital. Both approaches are needed.

The second approach is the difficult and dangerous one. Most firms measure performance in terms of accounting or book profitability. Unfortunately book income and ROI are often seriously biased measures of true profitability and thus should not be directly compared to the opportunity cost of capital.

In principle true or economic income is easy to calculate: you just subtract economic depreciation from the asset's cash flow for the period you are interested in. Economic depreciation is simply the decrease in the asset's present value during the period. (If the asset's value increases, then economic depreciation is negative.)

Unfortunately we can't ask accountants to recalculate each asset's present value every time income is calculated. But it does seem fair to ask why they don't try at least to match book depreciation schedules to typical patterns of economic depreciation.

FURTHER READING

The most extensive study of the capital budgeting process is:

J. L. Bower: *Managing the Resource Allocation Process*, Division of Research, Graduate School of Business Administration, Harvard University, Boston, 1970.

Scapens and Sale's article is a more up-to-date survey of current practice.

R. W. Scapens and J. T. Sale: "Performance Measurement and Formal Capital Expenditure Controls in Divisionalized Companies," *Journal of Business Finance and Accounting*, **8**: 389–420 (Autumn 1981).

There are many surveys of capital budgeting criteria. Two good ones are:

> L. D. Schall, G. L. Sundem, and W. R. Geijsbeek: "Survey and Analysis of Capital Budgeting Methods," *Journal of Finance*, **33:** 281–287 (March 1978).
> T. Klammer: "Empirical Evidence of the Adoption of Sophisticated Capital Budgeting Techniques," *Journal of Business*, **45:** 387–397 (July 1972).

Swalm and Weingartner discuss some of the incentive problems arising in corporations:

> R. O. Swalm: "Utility Theory: Insights into Risk-Taking," *Harvard Business Review*, **44:** 123–136 (November–December 1966).
> H. M. Weingartner: "Some New Views on the Payback Period and Capital Budgeting," *Management Science*, **15:** B594–607 (August 1969).

Biases in book ROI and procedures for reducing the biases are discussed by:

> E. Solomon and J. Laya: "Measurement of Company Profitability: Some Systematic Errors in the Accounting Rate of Return," in A. A. Robichek (ed.), *Financial Research and Management Decisions*, John Wiley & Sons, Inc., New York, 1967, pp. 152–183.
> F. M. Fisher and J. I. McGowan: "On the Misuse of Accounting Rates of Return to Infer Monopoly Profits," *American Economic Review*, **73:** 82–97 (March 1983).
> J. A. Kay, "Accountants, Too, Could Be Happy in a Golden Age: The Accountant's Rate of Profit and the Internal Rate of Return," *Oxford Economic Papers*, **28:** 447–460 (1976).
> Z. Bodie, "Compound Interest Depreciation in Capital Investment," *Harvard Business Review*, **60:** 58–60 (May–June 1982).

QUIZ

1. True or false?
   (*a*) The approval of a capital budget allows managers to go ahead with any projects included in the budget.
   (*b*) In most companies the controller authorizes all appropriation requests for capital expenditures.
   (*c*) Typically, companies will permit up to 10 percent expenditure overruns, but beyond that the sponsor is required to submit a supplemental appropriation request.
   (*d*) Most firms use several criteria for project selection.
   (*e*) Postaudits are usually undertaken about 5 years after project completion.
   (*f*) Setting capital budgets and project authorizations is a bottom-up process. Strategic planning, insofar as it affects capital investment decisions, is a top-down process.

2. Fill in the blanks:
   A project's economic income for a given year equals the project's _____ less its _____ depreciation. Book income is typically _____ than economic income early in the project's life and _____ than economic income later in its life.

3. Consider the following project:

Period	0	1	2	3
New cash flow	−100	0	78.55	78.55

The internal rate of return is 20 percent. The NPV, assuming a 20 percent opportunity cost of capital, is exactly zero. Calculate the expected *economic* income and economic depreciation in each year.

4. True or false?
   (a) Book profitability measures are biased measures of true profitability for individual assets. However, these biases "wash out" when firms hold a balanced mix of old and new assets.
   (b) Accountants do not allow firms to pick and choose among accounting procedures to make their income statements look good.
   (c) Rapid inflation means that book ROIs overstate true, real rates of return, because book depreciation is based on assets' original costs.
   (d) Systematic biases in book profitability would be avoided if companies used depreciation schedules which matched expected economic depreciation. However, few, if any, firms have done this.

QUESTIONS AND PROBLEMS

1. Discuss the value of postaudits. Who should conduct them? When? Should they consider solely financial performance? Should they be confined to the larger projects?
2. Rework Table 12-4 assuming that the firm's investment expands by 10 percent per year; i.e., it invests $1 million in year 0, $1.10 million in year 1, etc. Then rework the table assuming a 20 percent annual expansion. How does the bias in the steady-state book ROI vary with the rate of expansion?
3. Suppose that the cash flows from Nodhead's new supermarket are as follows:

Year	0	1	2	3	4	5	6
Cash flows, thousands of dollars	−1,000	+298	+298	+298	+138	+138	+138

   (a) Recalculate economic depreciation. Is it accelerated or decelerated?
   (b) Rework Tables 12-2 and 12-3 to show the relationship between the "true" rate of return and book ROI in each year of the project's life.
   (c) Redraw Figure 12-1 to show how the bias in steady-state ROI varies with the rate of firm growth.
4. Consider an asset with the following cash flows:

Year	0	1	2	3
Cash flows, millions of dollars	−12	+5.20	+4.80	+4.40

   The firm uses straight-line book depreciation. Thus, for this project, it writes off $4 million per year in years 1, 2, and 3. The discount rate is 10 percent.
   (a) Show that economic depreciation equals book depreciation.
   (b) Show that the book rate of return is the same in each year.
   (c) Show that the project's book profitability is its true profitability.
   Notice that you've just illustrated an interesting theorem: if the book rate of return is the same in each year of a project's life, the book rate of return equals the IRR.
5. For internal accounting purposes, many firms charge each subsidiary or division for the cost of the capital that it uses. Income after deduction of this charge is usually known as *residual income*.

What do you think are the advantages and disadvantages of such a system? How would you measure residual income?

6. Many accountants believe that instead of showing the written-down book value of the company's assets, the balance sheet should show the "written-down replacement cost." What is meant by this statement? Do you agree?

7. A project is expected to produce the following cash flows:

C_0	C_1	C_2	C_3
-900	$+300$	$+400$	$+500$

(a) Find the IRR of the project.

(b) Calculate the accounting return in each year assuming straight-line depreciation.

(c) In footnote 6, we stated that the IRR is a weighted average of the accounting returns where the weights are equal to the book values (at start of year) discounted by the IRR. Show that this is true for the above project.

8. Here is a harder question. It is often said that book income is overstated when there is rapid inflation because book depreciation understates true depreciation. What definition of *true depreciation* is implicit in this statement? Does *true depreciation* equal *economic depreciation* as we have defined the latter term?

9. Instead of looking at past market returns for a guide to the cost of capital, some financial managers look at past accounting returns. What do you think are the advantages and disadvantages of doing this?

10. The following are extracts from two newsletters sent to a stockbroker's clients:

Investment Letter—March 1987

Kipper Parlors was founded earlier this year by its president, Mr. Albert Herring. It plans to open a chain of kipper parlors where young people can get together over a kipper and a glass of wine in a pleasant, intimate atmosphere. In addition to the traditional grilled kipper, the parlors serve such delicacies as Kipper Schnitzel, Kipper Grandemere, and (for dessert) Kipper Sorbet.

The economics of the business are simple. Each new parlor requires an initial investment in fixtures and fittings of $200,000 (the property itself is rented). These fixtures and fittings have an estimated life of 5 years and are depreciated straight-line over that period. Each new parlor involves significant start-up costs and is not expected to reach full profitability until its fifth year. Profits per parlor are estimated as follows:

	YEAR AFTER OPENING				
	1	2	3	4	5
Profit	0	40	80	120	170
Depreciation	40	40	40	40	40
Profit after depreciation	-40	0	40	80	130
Book value at start of year	200	160	120	80	40
Return on investment percent	-20	0	33	100	325

Kipper has just opened its first parlor and plans to open one new parlor each year. Despite the likely initial losses (which simply reflect start-up costs), our calculations show a dramatic profit growth and a long-term return on investment that is substantially higher than Kipper's 20 percent cost of capital.

The total market value of Kipper stock is currently only $250,000. In our opinion, this does not fully reflect the exciting growth prospects and we strongly recommend clients to buy.

Investment Letter—April 1987

Albert Herring, president of Kipper Parlors, yesterday announced an ambitious new building plan. Kipper plans to open two new parlors next year, three the year after, and so on.

We have calculated the implications of this for Kipper's earnings per share and return on investment. The results are extremely disturbing and under the new plan, there seems to be no prospect of Kipper *ever* earning a satisfactory return on capital.

Since March, the value of Kipper's stock has fallen by 40 percent. Any investor who did not heed our earlier warnings should take the opportunity to sell the stock now.

Compare Kipper's accounting and economic income under the two expansion plans. How does the change in plan affect the company's return on investment? What is the present value of Kipper stock? Ignore taxes in your calculations.

PART FOUR

FINANCING DECISIONS AND
MARKET EFFICIENCY

13 Corporate Financing and the Six Lessons of Market Efficiency

Up to this point we have concentrated almost exclusively on the left-hand side of the balance sheet—the firm's capital expenditure decision. Now we move to the right-hand side and to the problems involved in providing finance for the capital expenditures. To put it crudely, you've learned how to spend money—now learn how to raise it.

Of course, we haven't totally ignored financing in our discussion of capital budgeting. But we made the simplest possible assumption: all-equity financing. That means we assumed the firm raises its money by selling stock and then invests the proceeds in real assets. Later, when those assets generate cash flows, the cash is either returned to stockholders or invested in a second generation of real assets. Stockholders supply all of the firm's capital, bear all the business risks, and receive all the rewards.

Now we are turning the problem around. We take the firm's present portfolio of real assets and its future investment strategy as given, and then determine what the best financing strategy is. We will analyze trade-offs between different financing alternatives. For example,

- Should the firm reinvest most of its earnings in the business or should it pay them out as dividends?
- If the firm needs more money, should it issue more stock or should it borrow?
- Should it borrow short-term or long-term?
- Should it borrow by issuing a normal long-term bond or a convertible bond (i.e., a bond which can be exchanged by the bondholders for common stock of the firm)?

There are countless other financing trade-offs, as you will see.

The purpose of holding the firm's capital budgeting decision constant is to separate those decisions from the financing decision. Strictly speaking, this assumes that capital budgeting and financing decisions are *independent*. In many circumstances this is a quite reasonable assumption. The firm is generally free to change its capital structure by repurchasing one security and issuing another. In that case there is no need to associate a particular investment project with a particular source of cash. The firm can think first about what projects to accept and second about how they should be financed.

Sometimes decisions about capital structure depend on project choice or vice versa, and in those cases the investment and financing decisions have to be considered jointly. However, we defer discussion of such interactions of financing and investment decisions until later in the book.

13-1   WE ALWAYS COME BACK TO NPV

Although it is helpful to separate investment and financing decisions, there are basic similarities in the criteria for making them. The decisions to purchase a machine tool or to sell a bond each involve valuation of a risky asset. The fact that one asset is real and the other financial doesn't matter. In both cases we end up computing net present value.

The phrase *net present value of borrowing* may seem odd to you. But the following example should help to explain what we mean. As part of its policy of encouraging small business, the government offers to lend your firm $100,000 for 10 years at an interest rate of 3 percent. This means that the firm is liable for interest payments of $3000 in each of the years 1 through 10 and that it is responsible for repaying the $100,000 in the final year. Should you accept the offer?

We can compute the NPV of the loan agreement in the usual way. The one difference is that the first cash flow is *positive* and the subsequent flows *negative:*

$$\text{NPV} = \text{amount borrowed} - \text{present value of interest}$$
$$\text{payments} - \text{present value of loan repayment}$$

$$= +100,000 - \left[\sum_{t=1}^{10} \frac{3000}{(1 + r)^t} \right] - \frac{100,000}{(1 + r)^{10}}$$

The only missing variable is r, the opportunity cost of capital. You need that to value the liability created by the loan. We reason this way. The government's loan to you is a financial asset: a piece of paper representing your promise to pay $3000 per year plus the final repayment of $100,000. How much would that paper sell for if freely traded in capital markets? It would sell for the present value of those cash flows, discounted at r, the rate of return offered by other securities of equivalent risk. Now, the class of equivalent-risk securities includes other bonds issued by your firm, so that all you have to do to determine r is to answer this question: "What interest rate would my firm have to pay to borrow money directly from the capital markets rather than from the government?"

Suppose that this rate is 10 percent. Then

$$\text{NPV} = +100,000 - \left[\sum_{t=1}^{10} \frac{3000}{(1.10)^t} \right] - \frac{100,000}{(1.10)^{10}}$$

$$= +100,000 - 56,988 = +\$43,012$$

Of course, you don't need any arithmetic to tell you that borrowing at 3 percent is a good deal when the fair rate is 10 percent. But the NPV calculation tells you just how much that opportunity is worth ($43,012).[1] It also brings out the essential similarity of investment and financing decisions.

Differences between Investment and Financing Decisions

In some ways investment decisions are simpler than financing decisions. The number of different financing instruments (that is, securities) is continually expanding. You will have to learn the major families, genera, and species. You should also be aware of the major financial institutions which provide financing for business firms. Finally, the vocabulary of financing has to be acquired. You will learn about *tombstones, red herrings, balloons, sinking funds,* and many other exotic beasts—behind each of these terms lies an interesting story.

---

[1] We ignore here any tax consequences of borrowing. We show in Chapter 19 how a taxpaying firm should value a subsidized loan.

There are also ways in which financing decisions are much easier than investment decisions. First, financing decisions do not have the same degree of finality as investment decisions. They are easier to reverse. In other words, their abandonment value is higher.

Second, it's harder to make or lose money by smart or stupid financing strategies. In other words, it is difficult to find financing schemes with NPVs significantly different from zero. That reflects the nature of the competition.

When the firm looks at capital investment decisions, it does *not* assume that it is facing perfect, competitive markets. It may have only a few competitors that specialize in the same line of business in the same geographical area. And it may own some unique assets that give it an edge over its competitors. Often these assets are intangible items, like patents, expertise, reputation, or market position. All this opens up the opportunity of making superior profits and of finding projects with positive NPVs. It also makes it difficult to tell whether any specific product has a positive NPV or not.

In financial markets your competition is all other corporations seeking funds, to say nothing of the state, local, and federal governments, financial institutions, individuals, and foreign firms and governments that also come to Wall Street, London, or Tokyo for financing. The investors who supply financing are comparably numerous, and they are smart: Money attracts brains. The financial amateur often views capital markets as *segmented,* that is, broken down into distinct sectors. But money moves between those sectors, and it moves fast.

Remember that a good financing decision generates a positive NPV. It is one in which the amount of cash raised exceeds the value of the liability created. But turn that statement around. If selling a security generates a positive NPV for you, it must generate a negative NPV for the buyer. Thus, the loan we discussed was a good deal for your firm, but a negative NPV investment from the government's point of view. By lending at 3 percent it offered a $43,012 subsidy.

What are the chances that your firm could consistently trick or persuade investors into purchasing securities with negative NPVs to them? Pretty low. In general, firms should assume that the securities they issue are fairly priced.

Efficient Capital Markets

We are leading up to the fundamental financial concept of **efficient capital markets.** *If capital markets are efficient, then purchase or sale of any security at the prevailing market price is never a positive-NPV transaction.*

Does that sound like a sweeping statement? It is. That is why we have devoted all the rest of this chapter to the history, logic, and tests of the efficient-market hypothesis.

You may ask why we start our discussion of financing issues with this conceptual point, before you have even the most basic knowledge about securities, issue procedures, and financial institutions. We do it this way because financing decisions seem overwhelmingly complex if you don't learn to ask the right questions. We are afraid you might flee from confusion to the myths that often dominate popular discussion of corporate financing.

You need to understand the efficient-market hypothesis, not because it is *universally* true, but because it leads you to ask the right questions.

13-2   WHAT IS AN EFFICIENT MARKET?

When economists say that the security market is efficient, they are not talking about whether the filing is up-to-date or whether desktops are tidy. They mean that information is widely and cheaply available to investors and that all relevant and ascertainable information is already reflected in security prices. That is why purchases or sales in an efficient market cannot be positive-NPV transactions.

A Startling Discovery: Price Changes Are Random

As is so often the case with important ideas, this concept of efficient markets was a by-product of a chance discovery. In 1953 the Royal Statistical Society met in London to discuss a rather unusual paper.[2] Its author, Maurice Kendall, was a distinguished statistician and the subject was the behavior of stock and commodity prices. Kendall had been looking for regular price cycles but to his surprise he could not find them. Each series appeared to be "a 'wandering' one, almost as if once a week the Demon of Chance drew a random number . . . and added it to the current price to determine the next week's price." In other words, prices seemed to follow a *random walk.*

If you are not sure what we mean by *random walk,* you might like to think of the following example. You are given $100 to play a game. At the end of each week a coin is tossed. If it comes up heads, you win 3 percent of your investment; if it is tails, you lose 2.5 percent. Therefore your capital at the end of the first week is either $103.00 or $97.50. At the end of the second week the coin is tossed again. Now the possible outcomes are:

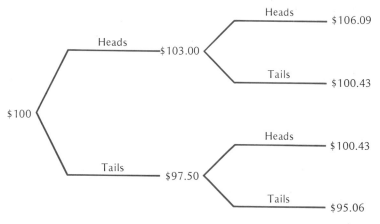

This process is a random walk with a positive drift of .25 percent per week.[3] It is a random walk because successive changes in value are independent. That is, the odds each week are 50 percent, regardless of the value at the start of the week or of the pattern of heads and tails in the previous weeks.

If you find it difficult to believe that there are no patterns in share price changes, look at the two charts in Figure 13-1. One of these charts shows the outcome from playing our game for 5 years; the other shows the actual performance of the Standard and Poor's Index for a 5-year period. Can you tell which one is which?

[2] See M. G. Kendall, "The Analysis of Economic Time-Series, Part I. Prices," *Journal of the Royal Statistical Society,* **96:** 11–25 (1953).

[3] The drift is equal to the expected outcome:

$$\frac{1}{2}(3) + \frac{1}{2}(-2.5) = .25\%$$

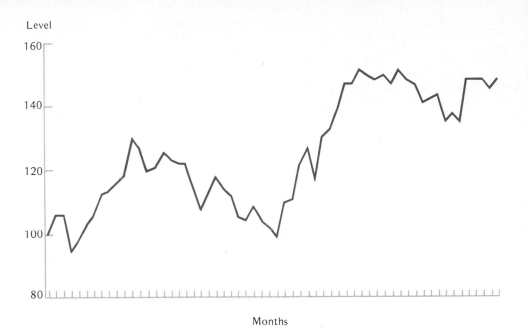

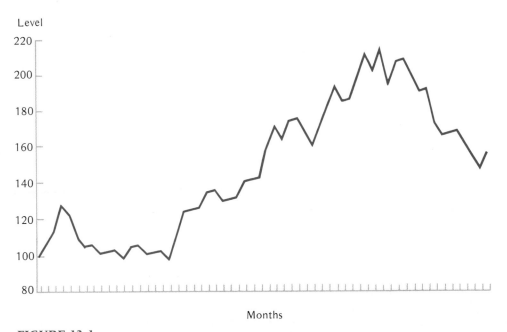

FIGURE 13-1
One of these charts shows the Standard and Poor's Index for a 5-year period. The other shows the results of playing our coin-tossing game for 5 years. Can you tell which is which?

FIGURE 13-2
Each point shows a pair of returns for General Foods stock on 2 successive days during 1983, 1984, or 1985. For example, the circled point records a return of −1.3 percent on January 12, 1983, and a −4.2 percent return the following day. This scatter diagram shows no significant relationship between returns on successive days.

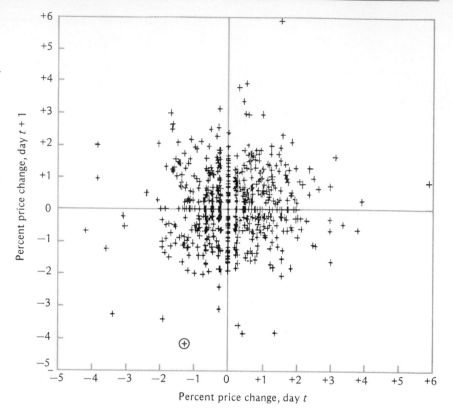

We will give you the answer in a moment.[4]

When Maurice Kendall suggested that stock prices follow a random walk, he was implying that the price changes are as independent of one another as the gains and losses in our game. To most economists this was a startling and bizarre idea. In fact the idea was *not* completely novel. It had been proposed in an almost forgotten doctoral thesis written 53 years earlier by a Frenchman, Louis Bachelier.[5] Bachelier's suggestion was original enough, but his accompanying development of the mathematical theory of random processes anticipated by 5 years Einstein's famous work on the random motion of colliding gas molecules.

Kendall's work did not suffer the neglect of Bachelier's. As computers and data became more readily available, economists and statisticians rapidly amassed a large volume of supporting evidence. Let us look very briefly at the kinds of tests that they have used.

[4] A similar comparison between cumulated random numbers and actual price series was first suggested by H. V. Roberts, "Stock Market 'Patterns' and Financial Analysis: Methodological Suggestions," *Journal of Finance,* **14:** 1–10 (March 1959).

[5] See L. Bachelier, *Theorie de la Speculation,* Gauthier-Villars, Paris, 1900. Reprinted in English (A. J. Boness, trans.) in P. H. Cootner (ed.), *The Random Character of Stock Market Prices,* M.I.T. Press, Cambridge, Mass., 1964, pp. 17–78. During the 1930s the food economist Holbrook Working had also noticed the random behavior of commodity prices. See H. Working, "A Random Difference Series for Use in the Analysis of Time Series," *Journal of the American Statistical Association,* **29:** 11–24 (March 1934).

Suppose that you wished to assess whether there is any tendency for price changes to persist from one day to the next. You might begin by drawing a scatter diagram of changes on successive days. Figure 13-2 is an example of such a diagram. Each cross shows the change in the price of General Foods stock on successive days. The percentage price change was −1.3 percent on January 12, 1983, and −4.2 percent the next day. This gives the circled point in the southwest quadrant of Figure 13-2. If there was a systematic tendency for a negative price change to be followed by another negative one, there would be many points in the southwest quadrant and few in the southeast quadrant. It is obvious from a glance that there is very little pattern in these price movements, but we can test this more precisely by calculating the coefficient of correlation between each day's price change and the next. If price movements persisted, the correlation would be significantly positive; if there was no relationship, it would be 0. In our example, the correlation was +.07—there was a negligible tendency for price rises to be followed by further rises.

Figure 13-2 showed the behavior of only one stock but our finding is typical. Researchers have looked at daily changes, weekly changes, monthly changes; they have looked at many different stocks in many different countries and for many different periods; they have calculated the coefficient of correlation between these price changes; they have looked for runs of positive or negative price changes; they have examined some of the so-called *technical rules* that have been used by some investors to exploit the "patterns" they claim to see in past stock prices. With remarkable unanimity researchers have concluded that there is no useful information in the sequence of past changes in stock price. As a result, many of the researchers have become famous. None has become rich.

Which Was the Real Standard & Poor's?

The answer to the puzzle in Figure 13-1 is that the top chart shows the real Standard and Poor's Index for the years 1980 through 1984; the lower chart is a series of cumulated random numbers. Of course, 50 percent of you will have guessed right but we bet it was just a guess.

A Theory to Fit the Facts

We have mentioned that the initial reaction to the random-walk finding was surprise. It was in fact several years before economists appreciated that this price behavior is exactly what one should expect in any competitive market.

Suppose, for example, that you wish to sell an antique painting at an auction but you have no idea of its value. Can you be sure of receiving a fair price? The answer is that you can if the auction is sufficiently competitive. In other words, you need to satisfy yourself that it is to be properly conducted,[6] that there is no substantial cost involved in submitting a bid, and that the auction is attended by a reasonable number of skilled potential bidders, each of whom has access to the available information. In this case, no matter how ignorant *you* may be, competition among experts will ensure that the price you realize fully reflects the value of the painting.

In just the same way, competition among investment analysts will lead to a stock market in which prices at all times reflect true value. But what do we mean by *true value*? It is a potentially slippery phrase. True value does not mean ultimate *future* value—we do not expect investors to be fortune-tellers. It means an equi-

---

[6] That includes no collusion among bidders.

FIGURE 13-3

Cycles self-destruct as soon as they are recognized by investors. The stock price instantaneously jumps to the present value of the expected future price.

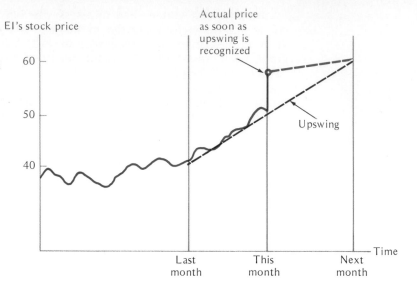

librium price which incorporates *all* the information available to investors at that point in time. That was our definition of an efficient market.

Now you can begin to see why price changes in an efficient market are random. If prices always reflect all relevant information, then they will change only when new information arrives. But new information *by definition* cannot be predicted ahead of time (otherwise it would not be new information). Therefore price changes cannot be predicted ahead of time. To put it another way, if stock prices already reflect all that is predictable, then stock price *changes* must reflect only the unpredictable. The series of price changes must be random.[7]

Suppose, however, that competition among research analysts was not so strong and that there were predictable cycles in stock prices. Investors could then make superior profits by trading on the basis of these cycles. Figure 13-3, for example, shows a 2-month upswing for Establishment Industries (EI). The upswing started last month, when EI's stock price was $40, and it is expected to carry the stock price to $60 next month. What will happen when investors perceive this bonanza? It will self-destruct. Since EI stock is a bargain at $50, investors will rush to buy. They will stop buying only when the stock offers a normal rate of return. Therefore, as soon as a cycle becomes apparent to investors, they immediately eliminate it by their trading.

Two types of investment analyst help to make price changes random. Many analysts study the company's business and try to uncover information about its profitability that will shed new light on the value of the stock. These analysts are often called *fundamental analysts*. Competition in fundamental research will tend to ensure that prices reflect *all* relevant information and that price changes are

---

[7] When economists speak of stock prices as following a random walk, they are being a little imprecise. A statistician reserves the term *random walk* to describe a series that has a constant expected change each period and a constant degree of variability. But market efficiency does not imply that expected risks and expected returns cannot shift over time.

unpredictable. The other analysts study the past price record and look for cycles. These analysts are called *technical analysts*. Competition in technical research will tend to ensure that current prices reflect all information in the past sequence of prices and that future price changes cannot be predicted from past prices.

Three Forms of the Efficient-Market Theory

Harry Roberts has defined three levels of market efficiency.[8] The first is the case in which prices reflect all information contained in the record of past prices. Roberts called this a *weak* form of efficiency. The random-walk research shows that the market is *at least* efficient in this weak sense.

The second level of efficiency is the case in which prices reflect not only past prices but all other published information. Roberts called this a *semistrong* form of efficiency. Researchers have tested this by looking at specific items of news such as announcements of earnings and dividends, forecasts of company earnings, changes in accounting practices, and mergers.[9] Most of this information was rapidly and accurately impounded in the price of the stock.[10]

Finally, Harry Roberts envisaged a *strong* form of efficiency in which prices reflect not just public information but *all* the information that can be acquired by painstaking fundamental analysis of the company and the economy. In such a case, the stock market would be like our ideal auction house: Prices would *always* be fair and *no* investor would be able to make consistently superior forecasts of stock prices. Most tests of this view have involved an analysis of the performance of professionally managed portfolios. These studies have concluded that, after taking account of differences in risk, no group of institutions has been able to outperform the market consistently and that even the differences between the performance of individual funds are no greater than you would expect from chance.[11]

---

[8] See H. V. Roberts, "Statistical Versus Clinical Prediction of the Stock Market." Unpublished paper presented to the Seminar on the Analysis of Security Prices, University of Chicago, May 1967.

[9] See, for example, R. Ball and P. Brown, "An Empirical Evaluation of Accounting Income Numbers," *Journal of Accounting Research,* **6:** 159–178 (Autumn 1968); R. R. Pettit, "Dividend Announcements, Security Performance, and Capital Market Efficiency," *Journal of Finance,* **27:** 993–1007 (December 1972); G. Foster, "Stock Market Reaction to Estimates of Earnings per Share by Company Officials," *Journal of Accounting Research,* **11:** 25–37 (Spring 1973); R. S. Kaplan and R. Roll, "Investor Evaluation of Accounting Information: Some Empirical Evidence," *Journal of Business,* **45:** 225–257 (April 1972); G. Mandelker, "Risk and Return: The Case of Merging Firms," *Journal of Financial Economics,* **1:** 303–335 (December 1974).

[10] The price reaction to news appears to be almost immediate. For example, within 5 to 10 minutes of earnings or dividend announcements appearing on the broad tape, most of the price adjustment has occurred and any remaining gain from acting on the news is less than the transaction costs. See J. M. Patell and M. A. Wolfson, "The Intraday Speed of Adjustment of Stock Prices to Earnings and Dividend Announcements," *Journal of Financial Economics,* **13:** 223–252 (June 1984). The price reaction to the sale of a large block of stock seems to be equally rapid. See L. Dann, D. Mayers, and R. Raab, "Trading Rules, Large Blocks, and the Speed of Adjustment," *Journal of Financial Economics,* **4:** 3–22 (January 1977).

[11] The classic study was M. C. Jensen, "The Performance of Mutual Funds in the Period 1945–64," *Journal of Finance,* **23:** 389–416 (May 1968). More recent studies include T. Kim, "An Assessment of the Performance of Mutual Fund Management: 1969–1975," *Journal of Financial and Quantitative Analysis,* **13:** (September 1978); J. C. Bogle and J. M. Twardowski, "Institutional Investment Performance Compared: Banks, Investment Counselors, Insurance Companies, and Mutual Funds," *Financial Analysts Journal,* **36:** 33–41 (January–February 1980); and S. J. Kon and F. C. Jen, "The Investment Performance of Mutual Funds: An Empirical Investigation of Timing, Selectivity and Market Efficiency," *Journal of Business,* **52:** 263–289 (1979).

TABLE 13-1
On average the stocks of small companies have
outperformed those of large companies

	AVERAGE ANNUAL RETURN	
	Small Firm Stocks	Standard & Poor's Index
1926–35	12.5%	10.8%
1936–45	28.6	11.1
1946–55	13.1	17.9
1956–65	17.7	12.2
1966–75	9.3	5.0
1976–86	26.9	15.5
Average 1926–86	18.2%	12.1%

Source: R. G. Ibbotson and R. A. Sinquefield, *Stocks, Bonds, Bills and Inflation,* 1982, updated in Ibbotson Associates, *Stocks, Bonds, Bills, and Inflation: 1987 Yearbook,* Ibbotson Associates, Chicago, 1987.

Although few simple economic ideas are as well supported by the evidence as the efficient-market theory, it would be wrong to pretend that there are no puzzles or apparent exceptions. For instance, New York Stock Exchange specialists seem to have made consistently superior profits; so do company managers when they deal in their own company's stock.[12] These are two cases that don't seem to square well with the strong form of the efficient-market theory.

It is not so surprising that insiders make superior profits, but there are other phenomena that take rather more explaining. For example, Table 13-1 shows the average return on an index of small company stocks and on the Standard and Poor's Index which is mainly composed of large company stocks. During the past 61 years the substantially higher returns of the small company stocks have far outweighed their extra risk. Also the magnitude of this size effect seems to differ both by months of the year and days of the week. In particular much of the superior performance is concentrated during the first week of January.[13]

We believe that there is now widespread agreement that capital markets function well. So nowadays when economists come across instances where this apparently isn't true, they don't throw the efficient-market hypothesis onto the economic garbage heap. Instead they ask whether there isn't some missing ingredient that their theories ignore. Thus, despite the apparent superior performance of small company stocks, no economist has to our knowledge been tempted to make a king-size investment in such stocks. Instead economists have assumed that investors aren't stupid and have looked at whether small-firm stocks suffer from some other defect, such as a lack of easy marketability, that is not allowed for in our theories or tests.

[12] See V. Niederhoffer and M. F. M. Osborne, "Market Making and Reversal on the Stock Exchange," *Journal of the American Statistical Association,* **61:** 897–916 (December 1966); J. Jaffe, "The Effect of Regulation Changes on Insider Trading," *Bell Journal of Economics and Management Science,* **5:** 93–121 (Spring 1974); and H. N. Seyhun, "Insiders' Profits, Costs of Trading, and Market Efficiency," *Journal of Financial Economics,* **16:** 189–212 (June 1986).

[13] A readable summary of these size and seasonal effects is given by D. B. Keim, "The CAPM and Equity Return Regularities," *Financial Analysts Journal,* **42:** 19–34 (May–June 1986).

Some Misconceptions

The efficient-market hypothesis is frequently misinterpreted. One common error is to think it implies perfect forecasting ability. In fact it implies only that prices reflect all available information. In the same vein, some have suggested that prices cannot represent fair value because they go up and down. The answer, however, is that they would not represent fair value *unless* they went up and down. It is because the future is so uncertain and people are so often surprised that prices fluctuate. (Of course, when we look *back,* nothing seems quite so surprising: It is easy to convince ourselves that we really knew all along how prices were going to change.) A rather different temptation is to believe that the inability of institutions to achieve superior portfolio performance is an indication that their portfolio managers are incompetent. This is incorrect. Market efficiency exists only because competition is keen and managers are doing their job.

Another error is to think that the random behavior of stock prices implies that the stock market is irrational. *Randomness* and *irrationality* are not synonymous. Stock price changes are random because investors are rational and competitive.

When we talk about an efficient market, we mean that the market is functioning well and prices are fair.[14] For the financial manager the concept of market efficiency entails six main lessons. Let us consider them in turn and at the same time introduce briefly some of the issues we shall be discussing in subsequent chapters.

13-3 THE FIRST LESSON OF MARKET EFFICIENCY: MARKETS HAVE NO MEMORY

The weak form of the efficient-market hypothesis states that the sequence of past price changes contains no information about future changes. Economists express the same idea more concisely when they say that the market has no memory. Sometimes financial managers *seem* to act as if this were not the case. For example, they are often reluctant to issue stock after a fall in price. They are inclined to wait for a rebound. Similarly, managers favor equity rather than debt financing after an abnormal price rise. The idea is to "catch the market while it is high." But we know that the market has no memory and the cycles that financial managers seem to rely on do not exist.

Sometimes a financial manager will have inside information indicating that the firm's stock is overpriced or underpriced. Suppose, for example, that there is some good news which the market does not know but you do. The stock price will rise sharply when the news is revealed. Therefore, if the company sold shares at the current price, it would be offering a bargain to new investors at the expense of present stockholders.

Naturally managers are reluctant to sell new shares when they have favorable inside information. But such inside information has nothing to do with the history of the stock price. Your firm's stock could be selling now at half its price of a year

---

[14] Everyone thinks they know a duck when they see one, but it is hard to come up with a satisfactory definition. It is rather like that with efficient markets. We have talked about "well-functioning" markets and "fair" markets without ever saying what this means. Fama defined efficient markets in terms of the difference between the actual price and the price that investors expected given a particular set of information. An efficient market, Fama argues, is one in which the expected value of this difference is zero. [See E. F. Fama, "Efficient Capital Markets: A Review of Theory and Empirical Work," *Journal of Finance*, **25:** 383–417 (May 1970).] Rubinstein defines an efficient market as one in which prices would not be altered if everyone revealed all that they knew. [See M. Rubinstein, "Securities Market Efficiency in an Arrow-Debreu Economy," *American Economic Review*, **65:** 812–824 (December 1975).]

ago and yet you could have special information suggesting that it is *still* grossly overvalued. Or it may be undervalued at twice last year's price.

13-4 THE SECOND LESSON OF MARKET EFFICIENCY: TRUST MARKET PRICES

In an efficient market you can trust prices. They impound all available information about the value of each security.

This means that in an efficient market there is no way for most investors to achieve consistently superior rates of return. To do so, you not only need to know more than *anyone* else; you need to know more than *everyone* else. This message is important for the financial manager who is responsible for the firm's exchange rate policy or for its purchases and sales of debt. If you operate on the basis that you are smarter than others at predicting currency changes or interest rate moves, you will trade a consistent financial policy for an elusive will-o'-the wisp.

The company's assets may also be directly affected by management's faith in its investment skills. For example, one company will often purchase another simply because its management thinks that the stock is undervalued. On approximately half the occasions the stock of the acquired firm really will be undervalued. But on the other half it will be overvalued. On average the value will be correct, so that the acquiring company is playing a fair game except for the costs of acquisition.

Example: Northwestern Bell's Bond Repurchase Offer

Here is another instance in which the financial manager should trust market prices. In early 1977 four AT&T subsidiaries offered to repurchase outstanding bonds which had been issued in 1974 at a time of high interest rates. The bonds of one issue by Northwestern Bell carried a *coupon rate* of 10 percent and had a *maturity* of 40 years. In other words, Northwestern Bell had promised to pay the bondholder $100 a year for every $1000 borrowed. These interest payments were to continue for 40 years, until 2014, at which time the original amount borrowed was to be repaid.

The bonds had a zero NPV *at the time of issue.* The fair interest rate at that time was 10 percent:

$$\text{NPV at time of issue} = +1000 - \sum_{t=1}^{40} \frac{100}{(1.10)^t} - \frac{1000}{(1.10)^{40}} = 0$$

$$= \frac{\text{amount}}{\text{borrowed}} - \frac{\text{present value of}}{\text{interest payments}} - \frac{\text{present value of}}{\text{loan repayment}}$$

By January 1977 interest rates on newly issued bonds had dropped to approximately 8.2 percent. As a result, the market value of the Northwestern Bell bonds on January 20 had risen to $1130. Northwestern Bell would clearly have gained by handing back to each bondholder the original amount borrowed ($1000 a bond) and canceling the debt issue. But the company had no right to do so, at least not in 1977. The firm did have the option to repurchase or "call" the bonds in 1979 at a price of $1085.70, but that option was no help in 1977.[15]

Northwestern Bell offered to repurchase the bonds for $1160, in effect offering

---

[15] But the call option explains why the bonds sold at only $1130 and not at the present value of $100 per year for 37 years followed by a final payment of $1000. Investors anticipated that the bonds would be retired before maturity.

bondholders a bonus of $30 per bond for agreeing to retire the issue. Bondholders were naturally happy to accept the unexpected $30 bonus, and 80 percent of the issue was retired.

Why did Northwestern Bell do it? The stated reason was to reduce interest charges. These interest charges amounted to $15 million a year on the old bonds. Notice that the company could have financed the repurchase by issuing 1160/1000 × $150 million, or $174 million, of fresh debt at an interest rate of 8.2 percent. Therefore instead of paying out $15 million as interest, it would have had to pay out only .082 × 174 = $14.3 million, a saving of $700,000 per year.

But what was the NPV of this venture? The company was investing $1160 per bond to eliminate a liability with a market value of $1130. In an efficient market the price of the bonds must represent their true value. Therefore the NPV of the transaction was −$30 per bond.

Northwestern Bell was right. The bond repurchase did reduce interest charges. But our analysis shows that this was no justification for the transaction in an efficient market. Why didn't the firm wait and call the bonds in 1979 at the lower price of $1085.70 stated in the bond contract? Northwestern Bell's managers were not stupid. Thus we suspect that there was some other reason for the repurchase.[16] Our point is that the *stated* reason was clearly wrong in an efficient bond market.

13-5 THE THIRD LESSON OF MARKET EFFICIENCY: THERE ARE NO FINANCIAL ILLUSIONS

In an efficient market there are no financial illusions. Investors are unromantically concerned with the firm's cash flows and the portion of those cash flows to which they are entitled.

Stock Splits and Dividends

We can illustrate our third lesson by looking at the effect of stock splits and stock dividends. Every year hundreds of companies increase the number of shares in issue either by subdividing the stock that is already outstanding or by distributing more shares of stock as dividends. For a large company, the administrative costs of such action may exceed $1 million. Yet it does not affect in any other way the company's cash flows nor the proportion of these cash flows attributable to each shareholder. You may think that you are better off, but that is an illusion.

Suppose the stock of Chaste Manhattan Finance Company is selling for $210 per share. A 3-for-1 split would replace each outstanding share with three new shares.[17] Chaste would probably arrange this by printing two new shares for each original share and distributing the new shares to its stockholders as a "free gift." After the split we would expect each share to sell for 210/3 = $70. Dividends per share, earnings per share, and all other "per share" variables would be one-third their previous levels.

---

[16] Taxes are one possibility. Since Northwestern Bell could claim the difference between the $1160 cost of repurchase and the $1000 face value of each bond as a loss for tax purposes, the firm's income taxes for 1977 were reduced by 48 percent of $160. Thus the effective repurchase cost was $1083.20, not $1160. For a discussion of the tax consequences of refunding debt, see J. D. Finnerty, "Refunding High-Coupon Debt," *Midland Corporate Finance Journal,* **3:** 59–74 (Winter, 1986).

[17] There are some confusing transatlantic differences in terminology. In the United Kingdom such increases usually take the form of a "scrip issue." A 2-for-1 scrip issue (i.e., two new shares in addition to one old) is equivalent to a 3-for-1 stock split.

A variety of justifications have been proposed for splits and stock dividends. One endorsement came from the president of a large American corporation, who observed that stock dividends "give shareholders a reasonable hedge against inflation and let them participate in the increase in book value." "On the other hand," he warned, "it would be silly to declare [them] if not earned because that would just lower the book value." A further argument was proposed by the chairman of another company, who suggested that paying a stock dividend would provide investors with "a greater return while at the same time conserving cash to finance the company's anticipated growth."[18] A third and disarmingly simple explanation was offered by a textbook which observed that stockholders like stock splits because they expect them to be followed by more stock splits. Claims such as these contrast strongly with the efficient-markets notion that investors are concerned solely with their share of the company's cash flows.

Of course extremely high stock prices are inconvenient for small investors. In June 1987 shares in Nippon Telegraph and Telephone were trading at 2.85 million yen each, or about $20,000. That is a nuisance if you have only $1000 to invest. A stock split by Nippon Telegraph and Telephone could therefore have significant convenience value. But convenience value does not justify the many companies that split their shares when they are selling for less than $100.[19]

Calculating Abnormal Returns

We can check whether investors are fooled by stock splits by looking at whether there are any abnormal changes in the stock price at the time of the split. First, however, we must explain how you can use some of the ideas in Chapter 9 to identify these abnormal price movements.[20] In Chapter 9 we introduced you to Merrill Lynch's "beta book." This contains two measures of each stock's performance. Alpha (α) describes how much on average the stock price moved when the market was unchanged. Beta (β) describes the average additional return for each 1 percent change in the market index. For example, Table 9-2 showed that DEC's stock price rose on average by .21 percent per month when the market was unchanged ($\alpha = .21$), and it rose a further 1.21 percent for each 1 percent change in the market index ($\beta = 1.21$).[21] Now suppose that you were interested in the performance of DEC's stock in January 1987, when the market rose 13.2 percent. On past evidence you would judge that the expected change in the stock price that month was

---

[18] Cited in J. E. Walter, *Dividend Policy and Enterprise Valuation,* Wadsworth Publishing Company, Inc., Belmont, Calif., 1967.

[19] Lakonishok and Lev provide some evidence that many companies do split their stock in order to keep the price in a desirable trading range. See J. Lakonishok and B. Lev, "Stock Splits and Stock Dividends: Why, Who and When," *Journal of Finance,* forthcoming.

[20] There is more to being a good car driver than knowing which way to turn the steering wheel. Similarly, if you want a good estimate of the abnormal return, you need to know more about how to calculate it than the brief overview that we provide. We suggest that you consult S. J. Brown and J. B. Warner, "Measuring Security Price Performance," *Journal of Financial Economics,* **8:** 205–258 (1980).

[21] It is important when estimating α and β that you choose a period in which you believe the stock behaved normally. If its performance was abnormal, then estimates of α and β cannot be used to measure the returns that investors expected. As a precaution ask yourself whether your estimates of expected returns *look* sensible.

FIGURE 13-4

Changes in stock price at the time of a stock split. The changes are adjusted for both general market movements and the increase in the number of shares. Notice the rise before the split and the absence of abnormal changes after the split. [*Source:* E. Fama, L. Fisher, M. Jensen, and R. Roll, "The Adjustment of Stock Prices to New Information," *International Economic Review*, **10** (February 1969), fig. 2b, p. 13.]

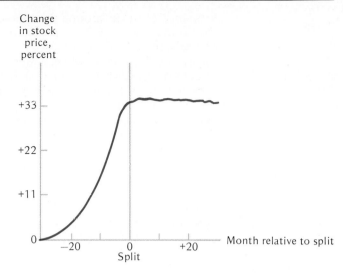

$$\text{Expected price change} = .21 + (1.21 \times \text{market change})$$
$$= .21 + (1.21 \times 13.2) = 16.2\%$$

In fact DEC's stock price rose by 38.5 percent in January 1987. Its abnormal price change was, therefore,

$$\text{Abnormal price change} = \text{actual change} - \text{expected change}$$
$$= 38.5 - 16.2 = 22.3\%$$

This 22.3 percent rise in DEC's stock price was over and above the normal rise in such market conditions.[22]

Now we can look at the abnormal price movements that generally take place around the time of a stock split. Figure 13-4 summarizes the results of an important study of splits during the period 1926 to 1960.[23] It shows the abnormal per-

---

[22] You will generally get a fairly similar answer if you use the capital asset pricing model to measure abnormal returns. This states that the expected return for DEC stock is

$$\text{Expected return} = r_f + \beta(r_m - r_f)$$

The market return (r_m) in January 1987 was equal to the 13.2 percent change in the index plus the .25 percent monthly dividend yield. The interest rate (r_f) was 5.5 percent a year, or about .45 percent a month. Therefore,

$$\text{Expected return} = .45 + 1.21 (13.45 - .45) = 16.2\%$$

$$\text{Abnormal return} = \text{actual return} - \text{expected return}$$
$$= 38.5 - 16.2 = 22.3\%$$

Note that, since DEC did not pay a dividend, *return* and *price change* are identical.

[23] See E. F. Fama, L. Fisher, M. Jensen, and R. Roll, "The Adjustment of Stock Prices to New Information," *International Economic Review*, **10:** 1–21 (February 1969). Later researchers have discovered that shareholders make abnormal gains both when the split or stock dividend is announced and when it takes place. Nobody has offered a convincing explanation for the latter phenomenon. See, for example, M. S. Grinblatt, R. W. Masulis, and S. Titman, "The Valuation Effects of Stock Splits and Stock Dividends," *Journal of Financial Economics*, **13:** 461–490 (December 1984).

formance of stocks around the time of the split after adjusting for the increase in the number of shares.[24] Notice the rise in price before the split. The announcement of the split would have occurred in the last month or two of this period. That means the decision to split is both the consequence of a rise in price and the cause of a further rise. It looks as if shareholders are not as hard headed as we have been making out: They do seem to care about form as well as substance. However, during the subsequent year two-thirds of the splitting companies announced above-average increases in cash dividends. Usually such an announcement would cause an unusual rise in the stock price, but in the case of the splitting companies there was no such occurrence at any time after the split. Indeed, the stocks of those companies that did *not* increase their dividends by an above-average amount declined in value to levels prevailing well before the split. The apparent explanation is that the split was accompanied by an explicit or implicit promise of a subsequent dividend increase, and the rise in price at the time of the split had nothing to do with a predilection for splits as such but with the information that it was thought to convey.[25] A stock split seems an expensive way to send the message, however.

Accounting Changes

There are other occasions on which managers seem to assume that investors suffer from financial illusion. For example, some firms devote enormous ingenuity to the task of manipulating earnings reported to stockholders. This is done by "creative accounting"—that is, by choosing accounting methods which stabilize and increase reported earnings. Presumably firms go to this trouble because management believes that stockholders take the figures at face value. Leonard Spacek, a leading accountant, echoed this belief in the following complaint.[26]

> Let us assume that you sincerely want to report the profits in the way you feel fairly presents the true results of your company's business. This is an admirable and objective motive; but when you do this, you find that your competitor shows a relatively more favorable profit result than you do. This creates a demand for the competitor's stock, while yours lags behind. You put your analyst to work, and you find that if your competitor followed the same accounting practices you do, your results would be better than his. You show this analysis to your complaining stockholders. Naturally, they ask, "If this is true, and if your competitor's accounting practices are generally accepted, too, why not change your accounting practices and thus improve your profits?" At that point you try to explain why your accounting is much more factual and reliable than your competitor's. Your stockholders listen, but nothing you can say will convince them that they should give up a 20 percent, 50 percent, or 100 percent possible increase in the market value just because you like certain accounting practices better than others.

Is Spacek right? Can the firm increase its market value by creative accounting? Or are the firm's shares traded in an efficient, well-functioning market, in which investors can see through such financial illusions?

[24] By this we mean that the study looked at the change in the shareholders' wealth. A decline in the price of Chaste Manhattan stock from $210 to $70 at the time of the split would not affect shareholders' wealth.

[25] This does not imply that investors like high-dividend payouts for their own sake. It could be that dividend increases are valued only because they are a sign of company prosperity. We will discuss this point in Chapter 16.

[26] See L. Spacek, "Business Success Requires an Understanding of Unsolved Problems of Accounting and Financial Reporting." Address before the financial accounting class, Graduate School of Business Administration, Harvard University, September 25, 1959.

FIGURE 13-5
Kaplan and Roll's study shows that investors are not misled by accounting changes that are designed to inflate earnings. (Changes in price of the firms' stock are adjusted for general market movements.) [*Source:* R. S. Kaplan and R. Roll, "Investor Evaluation of Accounting Information: Some Empirical Evidence," *Journal of Business,* **45** (April 1972), fig. 1c, p. 239. © 1972 by the University of Chicago. All rights reserved.]

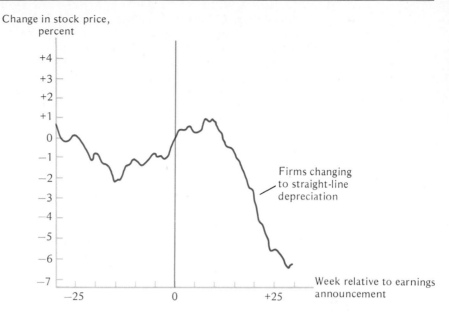

A number of researchers have tried to resolve this question by looking at how the market reacts when companies change their accounting methods. For example, Kaplan and Roll have studied what happens to stock prices when companies boost their reported profits by switching from accelerated depreciation to straight-line depreciation.[27] This switch is purely cosmetic. It reduces the reported depreciation charge but it does not affect the company's tax bill—the tax authorities allow firms to use accelerated depreciation for tax purposes and straight-line depreciation for reporting purposes.

Figure 13-5 shows the results of Kaplan and Roll's study. The preliminary announcement of increased earnings seems to prompt a slight abnormal rise in the stock price but this could simply be because investors were not informed at that stage of the accounting change. Within 3 months of the earnings announcement investors appear to have concluded that the accounting cosmetics were a sign of weakness rather than strength.

This result not only suggests the futility of earnings manipulation. It also raises some more basic questions about the role of accounting conventions. Jack Treynor illustrates the problem with the fable of nail soup:

> There was once a band of itinerant soldiers who, when they had difficulty persuading townsmen to feed them, hit upon the following solution. They set a large pot of water to boiling and then, when all the townsmen were watching curiously, dropped in a nail and announced with much licking of lips that they were making nail soup. The townsmen were assured that there would be enough soup for everybody. When one of the soldiers allowed that a few carrots actually improved the flavor of nail soup, a townsman dashed off to fetch some carrots. When it was observed that tomatoes made a wonderful garnish for nail soup, another townsman quickly pro-

[27] See R. S. Kaplan and R. Roll, "Investor Evaluation of Accounting Information: Some Empirical Evidence," *Journal of Business,* **45**: 225–257 (April 1972).

duced some tomatoes. Soon the nail soup contained beef stock, turnips and onions. Before the soup was served, the nail was removed. But the townsmen continued to regard the soup as nail soup.

Nail soup was nourishing, but not because of the nail. Earnings have information content, but not because of the ingredients that have been the main concern of the APB.[28] Accountants painstakingly put the nail into the soup; analysts painstakingly take it out, all the while believing they are really supping on nail soup. The overall process may seem unnecessarily complicated since the same result could have been obtained without the nail.[29]

13-6   THE FOURTH LESSON OF MARKET EFFICIENCY: THE DO-IT-YOURSELF ALTERNATIVE

In an efficient market investors will not pay others for what they can do equally well themselves. As we shall see, many of the controversies in corporate financing center on how well individuals can replicate corporate financial decisions. For example, companies often justify mergers on the grounds that they produce a more diversified and hence more stable firm. But if investors can hold the stocks of both companies, why should they thank the companies for diversifying? It is much easier and cheaper for them to diversify than it is for the firm.

The financial manager needs to ask the same question when considering whether it is better to issue debt or common stock. If the firm issues debt, it will create financial leverage. As a result, the stock will be more risky and it will offer a higher expected return. But stockholders can obtain financial leverage without the firm's issuing debt. They can issue debt on their own account. The problem for the financial manager is, therefore, to decide whether the company can issue debt more cheaply than the individual shareholder.

13-7   THE FIFTH LESSON OF MARKET EFFICIENCY: SEEN ONE STOCK, SEEN THEM ALL

The elasticity of demand for any article measures the percentage change in the quantity demanded for each percentage addition to the price. If the article has close substitutes, the elasticity will be strongly negative; if not, it will be near zero. For example, coffee, which is a staple commodity, has a demand elasticity of about $-.2$. This means that a 5 percent increase in the price of coffee changes sales by $-.2 \times .05 = -.01$; in other words it reduces demand by only 1 percent. Consumers are likely to regard different *brands* of coffee as much closer substitutes for each other. Therefore the demand elasticity for a particular brand could be in the region of, say, -2.0. A 5 percent increase in the price of Maxwell House relative to that of Nescafe would in this case reduce demand by 10 percent.

Investors don't buy a stock for its unique qualities; they buy it because it offers the prospect of a fair return for its risk. This means that stocks should be like *very* similar brands of coffee, almost perfect substitutes for each other. Therefore, the demand for the company's stock should be very elastic. If its prospective risk

---

[28] APB = Accounting Principles Board

[29] See J. L. Treynor, "Discussion: Changes in Accounting Techniques and Stock Prices," *Empirical Research in Accounting: Selected Studies,* 1972, Institute for Professional Accounting, Graduate School of Business, University of Chicago, Chicago, 1972, p. 43.

premium is lower relative to its risk than other stocks, *nobody* will want to hold that stock. If it is higher, *everybody* will want to hold it.

Suppose that you want to sell a large block of stock. Since demand is elastic, you naturally conclude that you need only cut the offering price very slightly to sell your stock. Unfortunately that doesn't necessarily follow. When you come to sell your stock, other investors may suspect that you want to get rid of it because you know something they don't. Therefore they will revise their assessment of the stock's value downward. Demand is still elastic but the whole demand curve moves down. Elastic demand does not imply that stock prices never change; it *does* imply that you can sell large blocks of stock at close to the market price *as long as you can convince other investors that you have no private information.*

Here is one case that supports this view. In June 1977 the Bank of England offered its holding of BP shares for sale at 845 pence each. The bank owned nearly 67 million shares of BP so that the total value of the holding was £564 million, or about $970 million. It was a huge sum to ask the public to find.

Anyone who wished to apply for BP stock had nearly 2 weeks within which to do so.[30] Just before the bank's announcement the price of BP stock was 912 pence. Over the next 2 weeks the price drifted down to 898 pence, largely in line with the British equity market. Therefore by the final application date, the discount being offered by the bank was only 6 percent. In return for this discount, any applicant had to raise the necessary cash, taking the risk that the price of BP would decline before the result of the application was known, and had to pass over to the Bank of England the next dividend on BP.

If Maxwell House coffee is offered at a discount of 6 percent, the demand is unlikely to be overwhelming. But the discount on BP stock was enough to bring in applications for $4.6 billion worth of stock, 4.7 times the amount on offer.

We admit that this case was unusual in some respects, but an important study by Myron Scholes of a large sample of secondary offerings confirmed the ability of the market to absorb blocks of stock.[31] The average effect of the offerings was to reduce the stock price slightly, but the decline was almost independent of the amount offered. Scholes's estimate of the demand elasticity for a company's stock was -3000. Of course this figure was not meant to be precise and some researchers have argued that demand is not as elastic as Scholes's study suggests.[32] However there seems to be widespread agreement with the general point that you can sell large quantities of stock at close to the market price as long as other investors do not deduce that you have some private information.

Here again we encounter an apparent contradiction with practice. Many corporations seem to believe that the demand elasticity is not only low, but that it varies with the stock price, so that when the price is relatively low new stock can be sold only at a substantial discount. State and federal regulatory commissions, which set the prices charged by telephone companies, electric companies, and other utilities, often allow 10 percent higher earnings to compensate the firm for price "pressure." This pressure is the decline in the firm's stock price that is supposed to occur when new shares are offered to investors. Yet Paul Asquith and

---

[30] However, applicants were required to put up only £3 per share on application and the remainder at a later date.

[31] See M. Scholes, "The Market for Securities: Substitution versus Price Pressure and the Effects of Information on Share Prices," *Journal of Business,* **45:** 179–211 (April 1972). A secondary distribution is a large block of stock sold off the floor of the exchange.

[32] For example, see W. H. Mikkelson and M. M. Partch, "Stock Price Effects and Costs of Secondary Distributions," *Journal of Financial Economics,* **14:** 165–194 (1985).

David Mullins, who searched for evidence of pressure, found that new stock issues by utilities drove down their stock prices on average by only .9 percent.[33] We will come back to the subject of pressure when we discuss stock issues in Chapter 15.

13-8 THE SIXTH LESSON OF MARKET EFFICIENCY: READING THE ENTRAILS

If the market is efficient, prices impound all available information. Therefore, if only we can learn to read the entrails, security prices can tell us a lot about the future. For example, in Chapter 27 we will show how information in the company's accounts can help the financial manager to estimate the probability of bankruptcy. But of course these accounts are only one of many sources of information available to investors. The return offered by the company's bonds and the performance of its common stock are, therefore, just as good indicators of bankruptcy as accounting data.[34]

Here is another example. The National Bureau of Economic Research has identified a series of leading indicators of economic activity. Since stock prices are heavily influenced by economic prospects, it is not surprising that they earn relatively high marks as a leading indicator.[35] In other words, the stock market represents an informed consensus about the nation's economic prospects.

Suppose that investors are confident that interest rates are going to rise over the next year. In that case, they will prefer to wait before, they enter into long-term loans. Any firm that wants to borrow long-term money today will have to offer the inducement of a higher rate of interest. In other words, the long-term rate of interest will have to be higher than the 1-year rate. Differences between the long-term interest rate and the short-term rate tell you something about what investors expect to happen to short-term rates in the future.[36]

13-9 SUMMARY

The patron saint of the Bolsa (stock exchange) in Barcelona, Spain, is Nuestra Senora de la Esperanza—Our Lady of Hope. She is the perfect patron, for we all hope for superior returns when we invest. But competition between investors will tend to produce an efficient market. In such a market, prices will rapidly impound any new information, and it will be very difficult to make consistently superior returns. We may indeed *hope,* but all we can rationally *expect* in an efficient market is that we shall obtain a return that is just sufficient to compensate us for the time value of money and for the risks we bear.

The efficient-market hypothesis comes in three different flavors. The weak form of the hypothesis states that prices efficiently reflect all the information contained in the past series of stock prices. In this case it is impossible to earn superior returns

[33] See P. Asquith and D. W. Mullins, "Equity Issues and Offering Dilution," *Journal of Financial Economics,* **15:** 61–89 (January–February 1986).

[34] See W. H. Beaver, "Market Prices, Financial Ratios and the Prediction of Failure," *Journal of Accounting Research,* **6:** 179–192 (Autumn 1968).

[35] See G. H. Moore and J. Shiskin, *Indicators of Business Expansion and Contraction,* National Bureau of Economic Research, New York, 1967. However, you should be cautious about placing too much faith in any such leading indicators. We are reminded of Paul Samuelson's quip that stock prices have predicted 7 of the past 5 recessions.

[36] We will discuss the relationship between short-term and long-term interest rates in Chapter 23. Notice, however, that in an efficient market the difference between the prices of *any* short-term and long-term contracts always says something about how participants expect prices to move.

simply by looking for patterns in stock prices—in other words, price changes are random. The semistrong form of the hypothesis states that prices reflect all published information. That means it is impossible to make consistently superior returns just by reading the newspaper, looking at the company's annual accounts, and so on. The strong form of the hypothesis states that stock prices effectively impound all available information. It tells us that inside information is hard to find because in pursuing it you are in competition with thousands, perhaps millions, of active, intelligent, and greedy investors. The best you can do in this case is to assume that securities are fairly priced and to hope that one day Nuestra Senora will reward your humility.

The concept of an efficient market is astonishingly simple and remarkably well-supported by the facts. Less than 20 years ago any suggestion that security investment is a fair game was generally regarded as bizarre. Today it is not only widely accepted in business schools, but it also permeates investment practice and government policy toward the security markets.

For the corporate treasurer who is concerned with issuing or purchasing securities the efficient-market theory has obvious implications. In one sense, however, it raises more questions than it answers. The existence of efficient markets does not mean that the financial manager can let financing "take care of itself." It provides only a starting point for analysis. It is time to get down to details about securities, issue procedures, and financial institutions. We start in Chapter 14.

FURTHER READING

A good review article on market efficiency is:

E. F. Fama, "Efficient Capital Markets: A Review of Theory and Empirical Work," *Journal of Finance,* **25:** 383–417 (May 1970).

There are several books of readings that contain a selection of the classic articles on the subject. See, for example:

P. H. Cootner (ed.), *The Random Character of Stock Market Prices,* M.I.T. Press, Cambridge, Mass., 1964.

J. H. Lorie and R. A. Brealey (eds.), *Modern Developments in Investment Management,* 2d ed., Dryden Press, Hinsdale, Ill., 1978.

A useful collection of recent work on possible exceptions to the efficient-market theory is contained in:

"Symposium on Some Anomalous Evidence on Capital Market Efficiency," a special issue of the *Journal of Financial Economics,* **6** (June 1977).

QUIZ

1. Stock prices appear to behave as though successive values
   (*a*) Are random numbers
   (*b*) Follow regular cycles
   (*c*) Differ by a random number
   Which (if any) of these statements are true?

2. Supply the missing words: "There are three forms of the efficient-market hypothesis. Tests of randomness in stock prices provide evidence for the _____ form of the hypothesis. Tests of stock price reaction to well-publicized news provide evidence for the _____ form and tests of the performance of professionally managed funds provide evidence for the _____ form. Market efficiency results from competition between investors. Many investors search for new information about the company's business that would help them to value the stock more accurately. This is known as _____ research. Such research helps to ensure that prices reflect all available information: In other words, it helps to keep the market efficient in the _____ form. Other investors study past stock prices for recurrent patterns that would allow them to make superior profits. This is know as _____ research. Such research helps to ensure that prices reflect all the information contained in past stock prices: ·In other words, it helps to keep the market efficient in the _____ form.

3. Which of the following statements (if any) are true? The efficient-market hypothesis assumes:
   (a) That there are no taxes
   (b) That there is perfect foresight
   (c) That successive price changes are independent
   (d) That investors are irrational
   (e) That there are no transaction costs
   (f) That forecasts are unbiased

4. The stock of United Boot is priced at $400 and offers a dividend yield of 2 percent. The company has a 2-for-1 stock split.
   (a) Other things equal, what would you expect to happen to the stock price?
   (b) Other things equal, what would you expect to happen to the dividend yield?
   (c) In practice would you expect the stock price to fall by more or less than this amount?
   (d) Suppose a few months later United Boot announces a rise in dividends that is exactly in line with that of other companies. Would you expect the announcement to lead to a slight abnormal rise in the stock price, a slight abnormal fall, or no change?

5. True or false?
   (a) Financing decisions are less easily reversed than investment decisions.
   (b) Financing decisions don't affect the total size of the cash flows; they just affect who receives the flows.
   (c) Tests have shown that there is almost perfect negative correlation between successive price changes.
   (d) The semistrong form of the efficient-market hypothesis states that prices reflect all publicly available information.
   (e) In efficient markets the expected return on each stock is the same.
   (f) Myron Scholes's study of the effect of secondary distributions provided evidence that the demand schedule for a single company's shares is highly elastic.

QUESTIONS AND PROBLEMS

1. How would you respond to the following comments?
   (a) "Efficient market, my eye! I know of lots of investors who do crazy things."
   (b) "Efficient market? Balderdash! I know at least a dozen people who have made a bundle in the stock market."
   (c) "The trouble with the efficient-market theory is that it ignores investors' psychology."
   (d) "Despite all the limitations, the best guide to a company's value is its written-down book value. It is much more stable than market value, which depends on temporary fashions."

2. Respond to the following comments:
   (a) "The random-walk theory with its implication that investing in stocks is like playing roulette is a powerful indictment of our capital markets."
   (b) "If everyone believes you can make money by charting stock prices, then price changes won't be random."
   (c) "The random-walk theory implies that events are random but many events are not random—if it rains today, there's a fair bet that it will rain again tomorrow."

3. Which of the following observations *appear* to indicate <u>market</u> <u>inefficiency</u>? Explain whether the inefficiency is weak, semistrong, or strong. (*Note:* If the market is not weak-form-efficient, it is said to be *weak-form-inefficient;* if it is not semistrong-form-efficient, it is *semistrong-form-inefficient,* and so on.)
   (a) Tax-exempt municipal bonds offer lower pretax returns than taxable government bonds.
   Strong ✓(b) Managers make superior returns on their purchases of their company's stock.
   (c) There is a positive relationship between the return on the market in one quarter and the change in aggregate corporate profits in the next quarter.
   weak ✓(d) There is disputed evidence that stocks which have appreciated unusually in the recent past continue to do so in the future.
   (e) The stock of an acquired firm tends to appreciate in the period before the merger announcement.
   Semi ✓(f) Stocks of companies with unexpectedly high earnings *appear* to offer high returns for several months after the earnings announcement.
   (g) Very risky stocks on the average give higher returns than safe stocks.

4. Look again at Figure 13-4.
   (a) Is the steady rise in the stock price before the split evidence of market inefficiency?
   (b) How do you think those stocks performed that did *not* increase their dividends by an above-average amount?

5. Stock splits are important because they convey information. Can you suggest some other financial decisions that convey information?

6. Estimate the *abnormal* return in each of the past 3 months for one of the stocks shown in Table 9-2.

7. Select a small sample of mutual funds and estimate whether they have been able to achieve consistently abnormal returns. (*Hint:* Funds may have different degrees of risk.)

8. It is sometimes suggested that low price-earnings stocks are generally underpriced. Describe a possible test of this view. Be as precise as possible.

9. "If a project provides an unusually high rate of return in one year, it will probably do so again in the next year." Does this statement make sense if you use the definition of economic rate of return that we gave in Chapter 12?

10. "Long-term interest rates are at record highs. Most companies, therefore, find it cheaper to finance with common stock or relatively inexpensive short-term bank loans." Discuss.

11. "If the efficient-market hypothesis is true, then it makes no difference what securities a company issues. All are fairly priced." Does this follow?

12. "If the efficient-market hypothesis is true, the pension fund manager might as well select a portfolio with a pin." Explain why this is not so.

13. Bond dealers buy and sell bonds at very low spreads. Used car dealers buy and sell cars at very wide spreads. What has this got to do with the strong form of the efficient-market hypothesis?

14. In May 1987 Citicorp announced that it was bolstering its loan loss reserves by $3 billion in order to reflect its exposure to Third World borrowers. Consequently, second-quarter earnings were transformed from a $.5 billion profit to a $2.5 billion loss.

In after-hours trading the price of Citicorp stock fell sharply from its closing level of $50 but next day when the market had had a chance to digest the news, the price recovered to $53. Other bank stocks fared less well and *The Wall Street Journal* reported that Citicorp's decision "triggered a big sell-off of international banking stocks that roiled stock markets around the world."

Comment on the Citicorp action varied. The bank's chairman claimed that "it significantly strengthens the institution" and analysts and bankers suggested that it was a notable step toward realism. For example, one argued that it was the recognition of the problem that made the difference, while another observed that the action "is merely recognizing what the stock market has been saying for several months: that the value of the sovereign debt of the big US money center banks is between 25% and 50% less than is carried in their books." The *London Financial Times* made the more cautionary comment that Citicorp had "simply rearranged its balance sheet not strengthened its capital base" and the Lex column described the move as an "outsize piece of cosmetic self-indulgence rather than a great stride towards the reconstruction of Third World debt." A lead article in the same paper stated that "even if all this means that Citicorp shareholders are $3 billion poorer today, the group as a whole is better placed to absorb whatever shocks lie ahead."

There was also considerable discussion of the implications for other banks. As one analyst summed up, "There's no question that the market will put higher confidence in those institutions that can reserve more fully."

Discuss the general reaction to the Citicorp announcement. It is not often that a company announces a $2.5 billion loss in one quarter and its stock price rises. Do you think that the share price reaction was consistent with an efficient market?

An Overview of Corporate Financing

This chapter begins our analysis of long-term financing decisions—a task we will not complete until Chapter 26. We will devote considerable space in these chapters to the classic finance problems of dividend policy and the use of debt versus equity financing. Yet to concentrate on these problems alone would miss the enormous *variety* of financing instruments that are used by companies today.

Look, for example, at Table 14-1. It shows the many long-term securities issued by Occidental Petroleum in the 1970s and 1980s. Yet Occidental has not come close to exhausting the different kinds of securities.

This chapter introduces you to the principal families of securities and it explains how they are used by corporations. We also draw attention to some interesting aspects of the behavior of firms issuing these securities.

14-1 COMMON STOCK

Definitions

Table 14-2 shows the common equity of Occidental as it was reported in the company's books at the end of 1986.

The maximum number of shares that can be issued is known as the *authorized share capital*—for Occidental, it is 400 million shares. This maximum is specified in the firm's articles of incorporation and can be increased only with the permission of the stockholders. Occidental has already issued 164,729,000 shares, and so it can issue just over 235 million more without the stockholders' approval.

All the issued shares are held by investors. These shares are said to be *issued and outstanding*. Sometimes a company will repurchase some of its previously issued shares. These shares are held in the company's treasury until it cancels or resells them. Treasury shares are said to be *issued but not outstanding*. The cost of the repurchased shares is subtracted from stockholders' equity.[1]

The issued shares are entered in the company's books at their par value. Each share has a par value of $.20. Thus, the total book value of the issued shares is

$$164{,}729{,}000 \times \$.20 = \$32{,}946{,}000$$

---

[1] Suppose Occidental spends $9 million to repurchase 300,000 shares at $30 per share. Then shareholders' equity in Table 14-2 would be reduced by subtracting:

  Treasury shares, at cost   (9,000)

  The number of outstanding shares would be 164,729 − 300 = 164,429 and treasury shares would be 300.

TABLE 14-1

Large firms often use many different kinds of securities. Look at the long-term securities that have been issued by Occidental Petroleum. There have been several issues of most of these security types.

Stock:
   Common stock
   Cumulative preferred stock
   Convertible cumulative preferred stock
Long-term debt:
   Sinking fund debentures
   Convertible subordinated debentures
   Zero coupon notes and bonds
   Secured notes
   Unsecured notes
   Revolving credit notes
   Eurocurrency notes
   Eurodollar revolving credit notes
Warrants

Note: Warrants are not shown on balance sheet.

Par value has little economic significance.[2] Some companies issue shares with no par value. In this case, the stock is listed in the accounts at an arbitrarily determined figure.

The price of new shares sold to the public almost always exceeds the par value. The difference is entered in the company's accounts as additional paid-in capital or capital surplus. Thus, when Occidental sold an additional 37,950,000 shares in March 1987, the common stock account was increased by 37,950,000 × $.20 = $7,590,000. The remainder of the $1.1 billion issue was added to additional paid-in capital.

Recently Occidental has paid out a large fraction of its earnings as dividends. The remainder was retained in the business and used to finance new investment. The cumulative amount of retained earnings is $1,047,034.

[2] Because some states do not allow companies to sell shares below par value, par value is generally set at a low figure.

TABLE 14-2

Book value of common stockholders' equity of Occidental Petroleum, December 31, 1986 (figures in thousands)

Common shares ($.20 par value per share)	32,946
Additional paid-in capital	2,914,213
Retained earnings	1,047,034
Currency translation adjustment	(17,768)
	$3,976,425

Note:
Shares

Authorized shares	400,000
Issued and outstanding shares	164,729

Finally, the common stock account shows a minor adjustment for currency translation losses stemming from Occidental's foreign operations. We'd rather not get into foreign exchange accounting here. Let's move on.

Stockholders' Rights

The common stockholders are the owners of the corporation. They therefore have a general *preemptive right* to anything of value that the company may wish to distribute. They also have the ultimate control of the company's affairs. In practice this control is limited to a right to vote, either in person or by proxy, on appointments to the board of directors and a number of other matters.

If the corporation's articles specify a *majority voting* system, each director is voted upon separately and stockholders can cast one vote for each share that they own. If the articles permit *cumulative voting*, the directors are voted upon jointly and the stockholders can, if they want, allot all their votes to just one candidate.[3] Cumulative voting makes it easier for a minority group among the stockholders to elect directors representing the group's interests. That is why minority groups devote so much of their efforts to campaigning for cumulative voting.

The issues on which stockholders are asked to vote are rarely contested, particularly in the case of large, publicly traded firms. Occasionally there are *proxy contests* in which the firm's existing management and directors compete with outsiders for control of the corporation. But the odds are stacked against the outsiders, for the insiders can get the firm to pay all the costs of presenting their case and obtaining votes.

Most companies issue just one class of common stock. Occasionally, however, a firm may have two classes outstanding, which differ in their right to vote and receive dividends. Suppose that a firm needs fresh equity capital but its present stockholders do not want to relinquish their control of the firm. The existing shares could be labeled class A, and class B shares issued to outside investors. The class B shares could have limited voting privileges, although they would probably sell for less as a result.[4]

The New York Stock Exchange (NYSE) has traditionally stood for "one share, one vote." Unlike the American Stock Exchange and the over-the-counter market, the NYSE has turned down companies attempting to list two or more share classes with different voting rights. But the NYSE is under pressure from companies which want to deter hostile takeover bids by concentrating voting power in a class of stock which can be held in friendly hands. These companies feel they deserve protection against "corporate raiders" and "takeover pirates." On the other hand, perhaps these pirates capture only the slower ships; many investors believe that the takeover specialists prey mostly on entrenched management teams that are not doing a good job for their stockholders.

---

[3] For example, suppose there are five directors to be elected and you own 100 shares. You therefore have a total of $5 \times 100 = 500$ votes. Under the majority voting system, you can cast a maximum of 100 votes for any one candidate. Under a cumulative voting system you can cast all 500 votes for your favorite candidate.

[4] R. C. Lease, J. J. McConnell, and W. H. Mikkleson have studied companies with two classes of publicly traded shares. They found that the class with superior voting rights almost always traded at the higher price. Typical premiums were on the order of 2 to 4 percent. See "The Market Value of Control in Publicly Traded Corporations," *Journal of Financial Economics*, **11:** 439–471 (April 1983), especially table 4, pp. 460–461.

14-2   A FIRST LOOK AT CORPORATE DEBT

When they borrow money, companies promise to make regular interest payments and to repay the principal (i.e., the original amount borrowed) according to an agreed schedule. However, this liability is limited. Stockholders have the right to default on any debt obligation, handing over the corporation's assets to the lenders. Clearly they will choose to do this only if the value of the assets is less than the amount of the debt.

Because lenders are not regarded as proprietors of the firm, they do not normally have any voting power. The company's payments of interest are regarded as a cost and are deducted from taxable income. Thus interest is paid from *before-tax* income. In contrast, dividends on common stock are paid out of *after-tax* income. Therefore the government provides a tax subsidy on the use of debt which it does not provide on equity.

Debt Comes in Many Forms

Some orderly scheme of classification is essential to cope with the almost infinite variety of corporate debt claims. We will spend several chapters in Part Seven examining the various features of corporate debt. But here is a preliminary guide to the major distinguishing characteristics.

Maturity.   **Funded** debt is any obligation repayable more than 1 year from the date of issue. Debt due in less than 1 year is termed **unfunded** and is carried on the balance sheet as a current liability.

Unfunded debt is often described as short-term debt and funded debt is described as long-term—although it is clearly artificial to call a 364-day note short-term and a 366-day note long-term (except on leap years).

There are corporate bonds of nearly every conceivable maturity. The Canadian Pacific Railroad has issued perpetuities, bonds with no specified maturity. They may survive forever. At the other extreme we find firms borrowing literally overnight. We describe how this is done in Chapter 32.

Repayment Provision.   Long-term loans are commonly repaid in a steady, regular way, perhaps after an initial grace period. For publicly traded bonds this is done by means of a **sinking fund.** Each year the firm pays a sum of cash into a sinking fund which is then used to repurchase and retire the bonds.

Most firms issuing debt to the public reserve the right to **call** the debt—that is, to repay and retire all the bonds in a given issue before the final maturity date. Call prices are specified when the debt is originally issued. Usually lenders are given at least 5 years of call protection. During this period the firm cannot call the bonds.

Seniority.   Some debt instruments are **subordinated.** In the event of default the subordinated lender gets in line behind the firm's general creditors. The subordinated lender holds a junior claim and is paid after all senior creditors are satisfied.

When you lend money to a firm you can assume that you hold a senior claim unless the debt agreement says otherwise. However, this does not always put you at the front of the line, for the firm may have set aside some of its assets specifically for the protection of other creditors. That brings us to our next classification.

Security. We have used the word *bond* to refer to all kinds of corporate debt, but in some contexts it means **secured** debt; often *bonds* are secured by mortgages on plant and equipment, and unsecured long-term claims are called *debentures*.[5] In the event of default, the bondholders have first claim on the mortgaged assets; investors holding debentures have a general claim on the unmortgaged assets but only a junior claim on the mortgaged assets.

Default Risk. Seniority and security do not guarantee payment. A bond can be senior and secured, but still as risky as a vertiginous tightrope walker—it depends on the value and risk of the issuing firm's assets.

A debt security is **investment grade** if it qualifies for one of the top four ratings from the Moody's or Standard and Poor's ratings services. (We describe the rating criteria in Chapter 23.) Below-investment-grade debt is traded in the so-called **junk bond market.**

Some junk debt issues are "fallen angels," securities issued as investment grade which later fell from grace. But in the late 1970s, a *new issue* junk bond market was created. Companies discovered a pool of investors willing to accept unusually high default risks in exchange for high promised yields. New issues of junk bonds were about $1 billion in 1977 and $20 billion by 1985.[6] Many of these issues were made on short notice to finance mergers and acquisitions.

Floating versus Fixed Rates. The interest payment or *coupon* on most long-term debt is fixed at the time of issue. If a $1000 bond is issued when long-term interest rates are 10 percent, the firm continues to pay $100 per year regardless of how interest rates fluctuate.

Loan agreements negotiated with banks usually incorporate a **floating rate.** For example, your firm may be offered a loan at "1 percent above prime." The **prime rate,** which is the interest rate the bank charges on loans to its most creditworthy customers, is adjusted up or down as interest rates on traded securities change. Therefore when the prime rate changes the interest on your floating-rate loan also changes.

Floating interest rates are not necessarily tied to the prime rate. LIBOR, the London interbank borrowing rate, is a common base. Yields on various Treasury securities are also frequently used.

Country and Currency. Many large firms in the United States, particularly those having significant overseas operations, borrow abroad. If such a firm wants long-term debt, it will probably borrow by an issue of **eurobonds** sold simultaneously in several countries; if it wants unfunded debt, it will probably obtain a **eurodollar** loan from a bank.

Corporations in the United States sometimes issue bonds denominated in foreign currencies. Often their overseas subsidiaries borrow directly from banks in the countries in which the subsidiaries are operating. Cross-currency borrowing

---

[5] The terminology can be confusing. A *debenture* in the United States signifies unsecured debt; in Great Britain it usually refers to *secured* debt.

[6] See R. A. Taggart, "The Growth of the 'Junk' Bond Market and Its Role in Financing Takeovers," Working Paper, National Bureau of Economic Research, Cambridge, Mass., September 1986, table 2.

also occurs the other way around. That is, foreign corporations will offer debt denominated in dollars in the United States.

A Debt by Any Other Name

The word *debt* sounds straightforward, but companies enter into a number of financial arrangements that look suspiciously like debt but are treated differently in the accounts. Some of these obligations are easily identifiable. For example, accounts payable are simply obligations to pay for goods that have already been delivered. Other arrangements are not so easily detected. For example, instead of borrowing money to buy equipment, many companies **lease** or rent it on a long-term basis. As we will show in Chapter 26, such arrangements are economically equivalent to secured long-term debt.

14-3   PREFERRED STOCK

In the chapters that follow we shall have much more to say about common stock and debt. **Preferred stock,** on the other hand, accounts for only a small part of new issues, and so it will occupy less time later on. However, we shall see that it is a useful method of financing in mergers and certain other special situations.

Preferred stock is legally an equity security. Despite the fact that it offers a fixed dividend like debt, payment of the dividend is almost invariably within the complete discretion of the directors. The only stipulation is that no dividends may be paid on the common until after the preferred dividend has been paid. For some older issues the firm could pay common dividends *without* making up preferred dividends that had been skipped in previous years. This gave an opportunity for considerable abuse. Therefore, almost all new issues specifically provide that the obligation should be cumulative, so that the firm must pay *all* past preferred dividends before common stockholders get a cent.

Like common stock, preferred stock does not have a final repayment date. However, roughly half the issues make some provision for periodic retirement and in many cases companies have an option to repurchase or call preferred stock at a specified price. If the company goes out of business, the claim of the preferred stock is junior to that of any debt but senior to that of common stock.

The contract which sets out the terms of the preferred stock also imposes restrictions on the company, including some limits on payments to common stockholders either as dividends or through repurchase of the common stock. These restrictions may also stipulate that the company cannot make any payments to common stockholders unless it is able to maintain a minimum level of common equity and a minimum ratio of working capital to debt and preferred. Other clauses typically require that further issues of securities must have the consent of two-thirds of the preferred shareholders unless the ratio of equity to all debt and preferred stock exceeds a specified minimum.

Preferred stock rarely confers full voting privileges. However, almost always the consent of two-thirds of the preferred holders must be obtained on all matters affecting the seniority of their claim. Most issues also provide the holder with some voting power if the preferred dividend is skipped.

Unlike interest payments on debt, the preferred dividend is not an allowable deduction from taxable corporate income. Thus the dividend is paid from after-tax income. For most industrial firms this is a serious deterrent to issuing preferred. Regulated public utilities, which can take tax payments into account when negotiating the rates they charge customers, can effectively pass the tax disadvantage of preferred stock on to the consumer. As a result, a large fraction of the dollar value of new offerings of nonconvertible preferred stock consists of issues by utilities.

Preferred stock does have one important tax advantage, however. If one corporation buys another's stock, only 20 percent of the dividends received are treated as taxable income to the corporation. This rule applies to common as well as preferred dividends, but it is most important for preferred issues.

Suppose that your firm has surplus cash to invest. If it buys a bond, interest income will be taxed at the full marginal rate (34 percent). If it buys a preferred share, it owns an asset like a bond (the preferred dividends can be viewed as "interest"), but the effective tax rate is only 20 percent of 34 percent, $.34 \times .20 = .068$, about 7 percent. It is no surprise to find that most preferred shares are held by corporations.[7]

14-4   CONVERTIBLE SECURITIES

Corporations often issue securities with terms that can be altered subsequently at the option of the firm, the holder of the security, or both. We have already seen one example, the call option on corporate bonds, which allows the firm to retire a bond issue before its maturity date.

Options often have a substantial effect on value. The most dramatic example is provided by a **warrant,** which is *nothing but* an option. The owner of a warrant can purchase a set number of common shares at a set price on or before a set date. For example, in June 1987 you could have purchased a Navistar International "Series A" warrant for $4⅞. That security gave the right to purchase one share of Navistar common stock for an *exercise price* of $5 per share at any time before December 15, 1993. Navistar had two other warrants outstanding—Series B and C—with different exercise prices and expiration dates.

Warrants are often sold as part of a package of other securities. Thus, the firm might make a "combination offer" of bonds and warrants. Notice incidentally that, although the bonds are shown in the company's balance sheet as a liability, the warrants are only mentioned in the notes to the accounts.

A **convertible** bond gives its owner the option to exchange the bond for a predetermined number of common shares. The convertible bondholder hopes that the issuing company's share price will zoom up so that the bond can be converted for a big profit. But if the shares zoom down, there is no obligation to convert; the bondholder remains just that. A convertible is therefore like a package of a corporate bond and a warrant.[8] There is one principal difference. When the owners of a convertible wish to exercise their option to buy shares, they do not pay cash—they just give up the bond.

These examples do not exhaust the options encountered by the financial manager. Far from it: We will see in Chapter 20 that *all* corporate securities can be analyzed in terms of options. In fact, once you read that chapter and learn how to analyze options, you will find that they are all around you.

---

[7] In Chapter 32, we will describe *floating-rate preferreds,* securities designed as temporary parking places for corporations' excess cash. These securities' dividends change with short-term interest rates, in the same way as coupon payments on floating-rate debt.

[8] Convertible preferred is also issued, usually to finance mergers.

14-5 VARIETY'S THE VERY SPICE OF LIFE

We have indicated several dimensions along which corporate securities can be classified. The financial manager has at least that many alternatives in designing corporate securities. As long as you can convince investors of its attractions, you can issue a convertible, callable, subordinated, floating-rate bond denominated in deutsche marks. Rather than combining features of existing securities, you may create an entirely new one. We can imagine a copper mining company issuing preferred shares on which the dividend fluctuates with the world copper price. We know of no such security, but it is perfectly legal to issue it and—who knows?—it might generate considerable interest among investors.

Variety is intrinsically good. People have different tastes, levels of wealth, rates of tax, and so on. Why not offer them a choice? Of course the problem is the expense of designing and marketing new securities. But if you can think of a new security that will appeal to investors, you may be able to issue it on especially favorable terms and thus increase the value of your company.

Financial market innovation in the 1980s has been unusually fast and extensive. New varieties of debt seem to appear almost daily. In addition, there has been a remarkable growth in the use of *derivative instruments*. These securities are side bets on interest rates, exchange rates, commodity prices, and so on. Firms do not issue these securities to raise money; they buy or sell them to protect against adverse changes in various external factors.

Here are four types of side bets that have experienced rapid growth in the last decade.

Traded Options.   An option gives the firm the right (but not the obligation) to buy or sell an asset in the future at a price that is agreed upon today. We have already seen that the firm sometimes issues options either on their own or tacked on to other securities. But in addition, there is a huge volume of dealing in options that are created by specialized options exchanges. Trading in stock options took off in 1973 when the Chicago Board Options Exchange was established. Now you can deal in options to buy or sell common stocks, bonds, currencies, and commodities. We describe options and their applications in Chapters 20 and 21.

Futures.   A futures contract is an order that you place in advance to buy or sell an asset or commodity. The price is fixed when you place the order but you don't pay for the asset until the delivery date. Futures markets have existed for a long time in commodities such as wheat, soybeans, and copper. The major development of the 1970s occurred when the futures exchanges began to trade contracts on financial assets, such as bonds, currencies, and stock market indexes. Within 10 years, the worldwide volume of transactions in these financial futures increased from zero to more than $10 *trillion* a year.

Forwards.   Futures contracts are standardized products bought and sold on organized exchanges. A forward contract is a tailor-made futures contract that is not traded on an organized exchange. For example, firms that need to protect themselves against a change in the exchange rate have usually bought or sold forward currency through a bank. Since 1983, banks have also been prepared to enter into forward contracts to borrow or lend money. If you buy a forward rate agreement (FRA), you agree to borrow in the future at a rate that is fixed today; if you sell an FRA, you agree to lend in the future at a preset rate.

Swaps.   Suppose that you would like to swap your dollar debt for deutsche mark debt. In this case, you can arrange for a bank to pay you each year the dollars that are needed to service your dollar debt, and in exchange you agree to pay the bank the cost of servicing a deutsche mark loan. Such an arrangement is known as a *currency swap.*

Companies also enter into *interest rate swaps.* For example, the bank might agree to pay you each year the cost of servicing a fixed-rate loan, and in return you agree to pay the bank the cost of servicing a similar floating-rate loan.

We discuss swaps, as well as forward and futures contracts, in Chapter 25.

The Process of Innovation

Developing a new financial instrument is like developing any other product. Initially, the emphasis is on creativity and experiment. Then, as the market develops, the focus switches to low-cost methods of volume production. Finally, it becomes economic to offer the customer optional extras.

For example, when swaps were invented, banks were unwilling to take one side of the swap for their own accounts. They acted solely as arrangers and looked about for another firm that was prepared to take on the other side of the bargain. No two swaps were alike, and they could take weeks to fix up. By 1986, banks were prepared to take on the risks of swaps themselves, documentation was standardized, and you could arrange a swap within hours. Banks were also beginning to work on the problem of making it easy for one party to resell his or her side of the swap to someone else. Perhaps by the time you read this chapter, there will be a regular market for trading swaps. As swaps have become more standardized and cheaper to arrange, banks have also been able to offer extra features. For example, you can now buy a forward swap and even an option on a swap (or "swaption").

What are the causes of financial innovation? One answer is taxes and regulation. In the following chapters, we shall come across a number of cases where taxes and government regulation have in effect subsidized innovation. But why do many new instruments survive long after the initial government stimulus has been removed? And why has so much innovation occurred in the last 10 years? Taxes and regulation have been around for much longer than that.

A second important motive for innovation is to widen investor choice. In particular, the sharp recent fluctuations in exchange rates and interest rates have increased the demand by firms and investors for ways to hedge themselves against such hazards.

But this still cannot be the entire explanation. For example, firms have long been able to protect themselves against exchange rate changes by buying or selling forward currency through a bank. So why are traded currency futures needed as well? The answer is that many of these new financial instruments are low-cost ways to mass-produce a particular service. These low production costs reflect improvements in telecommunications and computing which make it possible to disseminate prices and execute orders rapidly throughout the world.

There have also been developments in the design of instruments and trading systems. For example, if you sell a commodity future and don't buy it back, you will eventually have to deliver that commodity to the buyer. This would not be possible with many financial futures (try delivering a stock market index to someone). The novel feature of these contracts is that instead of delivering the asset at maturity, you just settle up the profit or loss in cash.

That completes our tour of corporate securities and derivative instruments. You may feel like the tourist who has just emerged from 12 cathedrals in 5 days. But there will be plenty of time in later chapters for reflection and analysis.

14-6   PATTERNS OF CORPORATE FINANCING

Let us now turn to Table 14-3, which summarizes the relative importance of alternative sources of capital for corporations in the United States. The most striking aspect of this table is the dominance of internally generated cash (line 7), defined as cash flow from operations less cash dividends paid to stockholders.[9] Internally generated cash normally covers a majority of firms' capital requirements: It fell below half of total expenditures only in 1973 and 1974. During the 1980s, however, internally generated cash covered more than 60 percent of total requirements. The proportion not covered by internal sources is the financial deficit, shown in line 8.

Do Firms Rely Too Heavily on Internal Funds?

As we have already noted, retained earnings are additional capital invested by shareholders—they represent, in effect, a compulsory issue of shares. A firm which retains $1 million could have paid out the cash as dividends and then sold new common shares to raise additional capital. In the same way, any reinvestment of dollars labeled "depreciation" amounts to investing dollars that could have been paid to investors. The opportunity cost of capital ought not to depend on whether the project is financed by depreciation, retained earnings, or a new stock issue.

Some people have been distressed by the heavy reliance on internal funds. Gordon Donaldson, in a field survey of corporate debt policies, encountered several firms which acknowledged "that it was their long-term object to hold to a rate of growth which was consistent with their capacity to generate funds internally." A number of other firms appeared to apply more stringent criteria to expenditure proposals that might require outside finance. Donaldson pointed out that depending on retained earnings is the line of least resistance for most companies; it allows them to avoid "the glare of publicity and shareholder attention" which accompanies a public issue. His concern may well be justified, but there may be other, less sinister explanations.[10]

William Baumol has expressed a slightly different concern about the use of retained earnings. He argued as follows:

> . . . A very substantial proportion of American business firms manage to avoid the *direct* disciplining influences of the securities market, or at least to evade the type of discipline which can be imposed by the provision of funds to inefficient firms only on extremely unfavorable terms. A company which makes no direct use of the stock market as a source of capital can, apparently, proceed to make its decisions confident in its immunity

---

[9] In Table 14-3, internally generated cash was calculated by adding depreciation to retained earnings. Depreciation is a noncash expense. Thus, retained earnings understates the cash flow available for reinvestment.

[10] See G. Donaldson, *Corporate Debt Capacity,* Division of Research, Graduate School of Business Administration, Harvard University, Boston, 1961, chap. 3, especially pp. 51–56. One less sinister explanation would be the following: As we suggested in Chapter 11, if management has to invest on the basis of several biased cash-flow forecasts, it may well use such simple capital-rationing schemes as a crude guide to an appropriate rate of expansion.

TABLE 14-3
Sources and uses of funds in nonfinancial corporations

	1967	1968	1969	1970	1971	1972	1973	1974	1975	1976
	SOURCES AND USES, PERCENT OF TOTAL[a]									
Uses:										
1. Capital expenditures	65	63	63	72	62	60	58	66	76	67
2. Investment in inventories	9	6	7	3	4	5	7	9	−6	8
3. Investment in liquid assets	2	5	0[b]	0[b]	7	6	7	3	13	7
4. Investment in accounts receivable	9	17	19	8	11	18	22	18	4	10
5. Other	15	9	11	16	16	10	7	4	13	7
6. Total expenditures	100	100	100	100	100	100	100	100	100	100
Sources:										
7. Internally generated cash	62	56	51	55	56	56	49	46	76	68
8. Financial deficit (6 − 7) = required external financing	38	44	49	45	44	44	51	54	24	32
Financial deficit covered by:										
9. Net stock issues	2	0	3	5	9	7	4	2	6	5
10. Net increase in long-term debt	22	20	18	27	23	10	7	12	18	13
11. Net increase in short-term debt	6	8	11	6	3	11	19	24	−5	8
12. Increase in accounts payable	7	15	17	7	9	15	21	16	4	5
	EXPENDITURE AND DEFICIT, BILLIONS OF DOLLARS									
Total expenditures	98	111	121	107	131	151	187	184	157	207
Financial deficit	37	49	59	48	58	66	96	99	37	65

	1977	1978	1979	1980	1981	1982	1983	1984	1985	1986
	SOURCES AND USES, PERCENT OF TOTAL[a]									
Uses:										
1. Capital expenditures	63	61	68	73	75	85	66	67	74	77
2. Investment in inventories	7	7	3	0[b]	3	−6	0[b]	11	1	1
3. Investment in liquid assets	1	5	5	6	5	10	13	5	3	11
4. Investment in accounts receivable	14	18	21	14	7	−5	16	11	8	2
5. Other	15	8	3	7	10	16	5	7	13	10
6. Total expenditures	100	100	100	100	100	100	100	100	100	100
Sources:										
7. Internally generated cash	64	58	58	60	66	74	69	68	75	79
8. Financial deficit (6 − 7) = required external financing	36	42	42	40	34	26	31	32	25	21
Financial deficit covered by:										
9. Net stock issues	1	0[b]	−2	4	−3	3	7	−16	−17	−18
10. Net increase in long-term debt	13	11	9	12	9	10	7	14	21	23
11. Net increase in short-term debt	14	16	20	12	19	11	7	27	14	15
12. Increase in accounts payable	9	16	16	12	8	2	10	7	7	0
	EXPENDITURE AND DEFICIT, BILLIONS OF DOLLARS									
Total expenditures	259	317	338	334	364	328	414	477	468	452
Financial deficit	94	134	141	134	125	86	128	151	115	94

[a] Columns may not add up to 100 percent because of rounding.
[b] Less than .5 percent.
[c] Net income plus depreciation less cash dividend paid to stockholders.
Source: Board of Governors of the Federal Reserve System, Division of Research and Statistics, *Flow of Funds Accounts,* various issues.

FIGURE 14-1
Companies are generally short of funds just after the peak of a boom. They need new funds least just after the bottom of a slump.

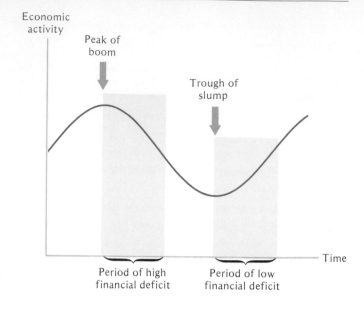

from this type of punishment by the impersonal mechanism of the stock exchange.[11]

In this passage Baumol echoes a widespread belief that internal funds are allocated by management, whereas external funds are somehow allocated by investors. It is not obvious this is true. For example, if the authorized capital is sufficient, a company can *always* raise money by the sale of shares as long as it sets the price sufficiently low. Any discipline, therefore, must exist solely in the manager's mind.

The subject is not one on which we can take a strong stand. Donaldson's diagnosis of management's motives is by no means implausible, but equally we have no good reason to suppose that managers would invest more wisely if they were forced to use the capital market more frequently.[12]

When Do Firms Need External Finance?

Line 8 of Table 14-3 shows that corporations have incurred a financial deficit in every year since 1965. Thus they have been persistent sellers of financial assets.

The financial deficit is linked to the general level of economic activity. Figure 14-1 illustrates this. In general, the deficit is lowest when the economy is pulling out of a recession. At this point companies are operating well below capacity, and so even a small increase in sales can produce a sharp improvement in profits and retained earnings. But the *need* for funds does not increase so sharply. As long as companies have significant spare capacity, management is unlikely to authorize

[11] Reprinted by permission of the publisher from *The Stock Market and Economic Efficiency* by W. J. Baumol (New York, Fordham University Press, 1965), copyright © 1965 by Fordham University Press; p. 70. Another related concern is commonly expressed by left-wing politicians in Great Britain. They argue that since retained earnings provide the bulk of industry's capital needs, the securities markets serve little function. Of course, the individual shareholders are happy for the firm to plow back their money *only* because the securities markets allow them to sell their stock if they need liquidity.

[12] Even if Donaldson is right, how do we know whether managers impose too high a standard for external capital or too low a one for retained earnings?

major investment in new plant. Furthermore, the pickup in sales may reduce inventories, which releases cash.

The financial deficit is usually largest when economic activity begins to turn down. The decline in sales brings about a fall in retained earnings but the high level of investment in plant and inventory continues until firms have managed to adjust their spending to the gathering recession.

It is natural to associate bad times with a shortage of funds. But for corporations as a whole the opposite relationship holds.

Timing Debt and Equity Issues

A further interesting aspect of Table 14-3 is the extent of the year-to-year variation in stock issues. Compare 1977, 1983, and 1986:

Net Stock Issues	1977	1983	1986
As percent of total corporate sources of funds	1	7	−18
As percent of financial deficit	2.8	23	−86
Absolute amount, in billions	$2.7	28.3	−80.8

In 1977 issues of equity amounted to only $2.7 billion. In 1983, just 6 years later, $28.3 billion was issued. In 1986, stock issues were *negative* to the tune of $80.8 billion.

Some companies did raise new money by stock issues in 1986. But this new supply was overwhelmed by the unprecedented scale of stock repurchases made by companies which bought back their own shares, or purchased and retired *other* companies' shares in the course of mergers and acquisitions.[13]

Now 1986 was clearly an exceptional year. What can we say about behavior in the longer run?

Several things seem to be happening simultaneously: First, we would expect firms to seek a balance of debt and equity.

If debt weighs too heavily in their capital structure, they acquire equity by retaining earnings or issuing stock. If the debt ratio is too low, they favor debt over equity. But firms are never precisely on target. They are continually buffeted by changing business conditions. They always move toward the targets but they hardly ever get there. Because the adjustment process is slow, it does not preclude substantial short-term fluctuations in capital structure and in external financing by corporations.

Some of the fluctuations in stock issues can be explained by managers' attempts to time these issues. Studies by Taggart and others in the United States and by Marsh in Great Britain show that stock is more likely to be issued after stock prices have risen.[14] The rational explanation for this is that an increase in the stock price signals expanded investment opportunities, and the need to finance these investments really prompts the stock issues. Unfortunately the rational explanation doesn't explain all the facts. It tells us why firms raise more money *in total* when stock prices are historically high but it does not tell us why they issue only more

---

[13] We discuss share repurchases in Chapter 16, and mergers and acquisitions in Chapter 33.

[14] R. A. Taggart, "A Model of Corporate Financing Decisions," *Journal of Finance,* **32:** 1467–1484 (December 1977); P. Asquith and D. W. Mullins, Jr., "Equity Issues and Offering Dilution," *Journal of Financial Economics,* **15:** 16–89 (January–February 1986). P. Marsh, "The Choice Between Equity and Debt: An Empirical Study," *Journal of Finance,* **37:** 121–144 (March 1982).

equity and not more debt. If anything, a company should be even more ready to issue debt at such times, because the company's higher market value and enhanced prospects increase its "debt capacity." Yet Marsh finds exactly the opposite behavior: Debt issues do *not* respond to high stock prices, other things being equal. Firms in effect substitute equity for debt issues at precisely the time they should find it easier to borrow more.

Why should managers act in this way? Do they believe that equity is cheap when stock prices are historically high? As we pointed out in Chapter 13, in an efficient market buying or selling stock is a zero-NPV transaction regardless of whether the price is historically high or historically low.

We don't know why managers tend to issue equity rather than debt after a rise in the stock price. It may reflect confused interpretations of price-earnings and market-book ratios. Some financial managers still think that a high P/E indicates a low rate of return demanded by stockholders and a good time to issue equity. Many of the same managers worry that selling stock at low prices relative to book value will "dilute" earnings per share. These managers defer issues when stock price is low, and their stored-up demand for fresh equity is released after prices rise.

The Dilution Fallacy

The popular P/E fallacies were amply described in Chapter 4. But we haven't yet dissected the dilution fallacy.

The imagined dangers of dilution are dramatized by the sad tale of Quangle Hats. Quangle's profitability is as follows:

- Book net worth $100,000
- Number of shares   1,000
- Book value per share $100,000/1,000 = $100
- Net earnings $8,000
- Earnings per share $8,000/1,000 = $8.00
- Price-earnings ratio   10
- Stock price   10 × $8.00 = $80.00
- Total market value $80,000

The total amount of money that has been put up by Quangle's stockholders is $100,000—$100 per share. But that investment is earning only $8 per share—an 8 percent book return. Investors evidently regard this return as inadequate, for they are willing to pay only $80 per share for Quangle stock.

Now suppose that Quangle raises $10,000 by issuing 125 additional shares at the market price of $80 per share—suppose also that the $10,000 is invested to earn a return of 8 percent. In that case, we would expect investors to continue to pay $10 for each $1 of Quangle's earnings. Now we have:

	Before the Issue	After the Issue
Book net worth	$100,000	$110,000
Number of shares	1,000	1,125
Book value per share	$100,000/1,000 = $100	$110,000/1,125 = $97.78
Net earnings	$8,000	8% of book net worth = $8,800
Earnings per share	$8,000/1,000 = $8.00	$8,800/1,125 = $7.82
Price-earnings ratio	10	10
Stock price	10 × $8.00 = $80.00	10 × $7.82 = $78.20
Total market value	$80,000	$88,000

We note that selling stock below book *does* decrease book value per share and stock price as well.

But there are two things wrong with our example. First, we assumed investors could be tricked into paying $80 for shares shortly destined to be worth $78.20. Actually, if Quangle wishes to raise $10,000, it will have to offer shares *worth* $10,000. And since we know that aggregate market value after the stock issue is $88,000, the *original* 1000 shares must end up with an aggregate value of $78,000. The price per share will therefore be $78,000/1,000 = $78 and the firm will have to issue $10,000/78 = 128 shares to raise the capital it requires.

Many financial analysts would stop at this point, satisfied that they had "proved" the folly of selling stock for less than book value. But there is a second thing wrong with our example: We never questioned Quangle's decision to expand. It is raising $10,000 and getting only $8000 in additional market value. In other words, the market's verdict is that expansion has an NPV of −$2000. Note that this is exactly the loss suffered by the original shareholders.

What if the investment earned a *10* percent return? In that case the issue of shares would cause the firm's market value to increase by $10,000 to $90,000, and the earnings per share and stock price would be unchanged. Quangle could therefore raise $10,000 by selling only $10,000/80 = 125 new shares.

The point is simple. There is no harm whatsoever in selling stock at prices below book value per share, as long as investors know that you can earn an adequate rate of return on the new money. If the firm has good projects and needs equity capital to finance them, then "dilution" should not bar it from going to the market.

Has Capital Structure Changed?

In 1974 *Business Week* devoted a special edition to "The Debt Economy," which described a United States in which everybody appeared to be a borrower and there was not a lender in sight. Prominent among these borrowers were American corporations, which, it was pointed out, had tripled their debt in the previous 15 years. With typical understatement, *Business Week* concluded that this debt imposed "an ominously heavy burden with the world as it is today—ravaged by inflation, threatened with economic depression, torn apart by the massive redistribution. . . ." Twelve years later, *Business Week* found little consolation in the fall in inflation: "In a disinflationary environment, U.S. companies and individuals are finding it increasingly tough to manage the mountainous debt they've amassed."[15]

Is there really a trend to heavier reliance on debt financing? This is a hard question to answer in general, because financing policy varies so much from industry to industry and firm to firm. But a few statistics will do no harm as long as you keep these difficulties in mind.

Table 14-4 shows the aggregate balance sheet of all manufacturing corporations in the United States in 1986. If all manufacturing corporations were merged into one gigantic firm, Table 14-4 would be its balance sheet.

The table shows that manufacturing corporations had total book assets of $2005.5 billion. On the right-hand side of the balance sheet, we find total long-term liabilities of $599.2 billion and stockholders' equity of $891.1 billion.

What was the debt ratio of manufacturing corporations in the United States in

[15] Reprinted from the October 12, 1974, issue of *Business Week*, p. 45, and the August 4, 1986, issue, p. 24, by special permission; © 1974, 1986 by McGraw-Hill, Inc., New York, NY 10020. All rights reserved.

TABLE 14-4
Aggregate balance sheet for manufacturing corporations in the United States, 1986
(figures in billions)

Current assets[a]		$ 808.4	Current liabilities[a]	$ 515.2
Fixed assets[b]	$1,320.1		Long-term debt	410.9
Less depreciation	587.0		Other long-term liabilities[c]	188.3
Net fixed assets		733.1	Total long-term liabilities	599.2
Other long-term assets		464.0	Stockholders' equity	891.1
Total assets		2,005.5	Total liabilities and stockholders' equity	2,005.5

[a] See Table 29-1, Section 29-1, for a breakdown of current assets and liabilities.
[b] Includes land, mineral rights, and construction in progress, as well as plant and equipment.
[c] Includes deferred taxes and several miscellaneous categories.
Source: U.S. Federal Trade Commission, *Quarterly Financial Report for Manufacturing, Mining and Trade Corporations,* Third Quarter, 1986, p. 56.

1986? It depends on what you mean by *debt*. If all liabilities are counted as debt, the debt ratio is .56:

$$\frac{\text{Debt}}{\text{Total assets}} = \frac{515.2 + 599.2}{2005.5} = .56$$

This measure of debt includes both current liabilities and long-term obligations. Sometimes financial analysts look at the proportions of debt and equity in long-term financing. The proportion of debt in long-term financing is

$$\frac{\text{Long-term liabilities}}{\text{Long-term liabilities + stockholders' equity}} = \frac{599.2}{599.2 + 891.1} = .40$$

Figure 14-2 plots these two ratios from 1954 to 1986. There is a clear upward shift from the 1950s to the 1980s. By these measures corporations are "using more debt." We do not know whether the shift to more debt is permanent or why it has occurred. However, it is worth noting that the rate of inflation began to accelerate in the late 1960s, and remained high (by standards in the United States) through the 1970s. Rapid inflation means that the *book* value of corporate assets falls behind the actual value of those assets. If corporations are borrowing against *actual* value, it would not be surprising to observe rising ratios of debt to book asset values.

To illustrate, suppose that you bought a house 10 years ago for $30,000. You financed the purchase in part with a $15,000 mortgage, 50 percent of the purchase price. Today the house is worth $60,000. Suppose that you repay the remaining balance of your original mortgage and take out a new mortgage for $30,000, which is again 50 percent of current market value. Your *book* debt ratio would be 100 percent. The reason is that the book value of the house is its *original* cost of $30,000 (we assume no depreciation). An analyst having only book values to work with would conclude that you had decided to "use more debt"—10 years ago your book debt ratio was only 50 percent. But you have no more debt relative to the actual value of your house.

Figure 14-3 shows debt as a fraction of the total inflation-adjusted value of

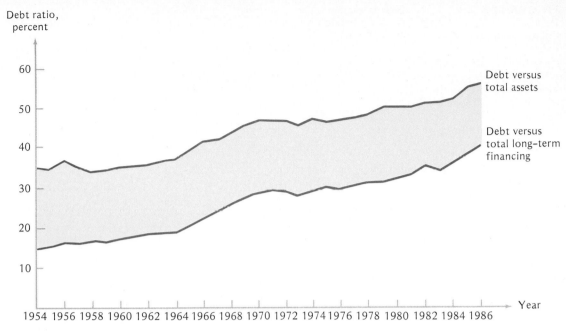

FIGURE 14-2
Average debt ratios for manufacturing corporations in the United States have increased in the postwar period. However, note that these ratios compare debt with the *book* value of total assets and total long-term financing. The actual value of corporate assets is higher as a result of inflation. (*Source:* U.S. Federal Trade Commission, *Quarterly Report for Manufacturing, Mining and Trade Corporations,* various issues.)

assets held by United States corporations.[16] Since inflation-adjusted values exceed book values, we would expect these debt ratios to be lower than the ones in the top line of Figure 14-2, and so they are. But you can still see the same upward trend since the 1940s and 1950s.

Should we be worried? It's true that higher debt ratios mean that more companies will fall into financial distress if a serious recession hits the economy. But all companies have to live with this risk to some degree, and it does not follow that less risk is better. Finding the optimal debt ratio is like finding the optimal speed limit: We can agree that accidents at 30 miles per hour are less dangerous, other things equal, than accidents at 60, but we do not therefore set the national speed limit at 30. Speed has benefits as well as risks. So does debt, as we will see in Chapter 18.

There is no God-given, correct debt ratio, and if there were it would change. It may be that the recent wave of financial innovation, by giving firms easier access to financial markets and the ability to hedge operating risks, has made higher debt ratios possible without increasing the risks or costs of financial distress. Note, too,

---

[16] These debt ratios are estimates for all nonfinancial corporations, not just manufacturing corporations, as in Figure 14-2. Comparable figures for manufacturing are not readily available, but manufacturing corporations generally carry less debt than all nonfinancial corporations.

FIGURE 14-3

Debt as a fraction of total inflation-adjusted asset values of U.S. nonfinancial corporations. The 1900–1958 series was prepared by Raymond Goldsmith, the 1952–1978 series by George Von Furstenburg. Note the upward trend since the 1940s, and the high debt ratios in the early 1900s. (*Source:* R. A. Taggart, Jr., "Secular Patterns in the Financing of U.S. Corporations," in B. F. Friedman, ed., *Corporate Capital Structures in the United States,* University of Chicago Press, Chicago, 1985, fig. 1.3, p. 25.)

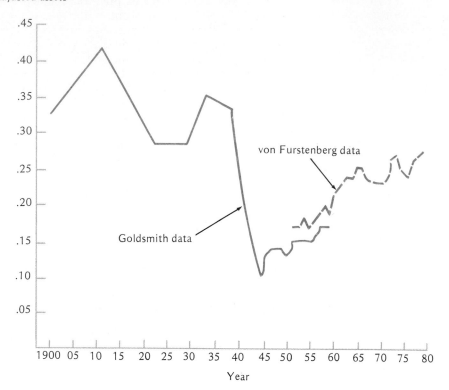

that debt ratios in the 1980s, though higher than in the early postwar period, are still lower than in the first third of this century. They are also lower than in most other countries. Successful companies in Germany, for example, often operate at debt levels much higher than United States companies are accustomed to.

14-7 SUMMARY

Financing is principally a marketing problem. The company tries to split the cash flows generated by its assets into different streams that will appeal to investors with different tastes, wealth, and tax rates. In this chapter we have introduced you to the principal sources of finance and outlined their relative importance.

The simplest and most important source of finance is shareholders' equity, raised either by stock issues or retained earnings.

The next most important source of finance is debt. Debtholders are entitled to a fixed regular payment of interest and the final repayment of principal. But the company's liability is not unlimited. If it cannot pay its debts, it can file for bankruptcy. The usual result is that the debtholders then take over and operate the company's assets.

Note that the tax authorities treat interest payments as a cost. That means the company can deduct interest when calculating its taxable income. Interest is paid from pretax income. Dividends and retained earnings come from after-tax income.

The third source of finance is preferred stock. Preferred is like debt in that it promises a fixed dividend payment, but payment of this dividend is within the discretion of the directors. They must, however, pay the dividend on the preferred before they are allowed to pay a dividend on the common stock. Lawyers and tax experts treat preferred as part of the company's equity. That means preferred dividends must be paid out of after-tax income. This is one reason that preferred is less popular than debt. Preferred shares play various specialized roles, however. For example, they are widely used by regulated utility companies, who can pass on the cost of preferred dividends to their customers.

The fourth source of finance consists of options. These are not recorded separately in the company's balance sheet. The simplest option is the warrant which gives its holder the right to buy a share at a set price by a set date. Warrants are often sold in combination with other securities and are merely recorded in a note to the accounts. Convertible bonds are securities that give their holder the right to convert the bond into shares. They are therefore like a mixture of straight debt and a warrant.

Corporations also trade in a variety of derivative securities to hedge their exposure to external risks, including fluctuations in commodity prices, interest rates, and foreign exchange rates. Derivative securities include traded options, futures and forward contracts, and swaps.

The large volume of trade in these derivative instruments reflects a wave of recent innovation in world financial markets. The innovation was stimulated by changes in taxes and government regulation; by demand from corporations and investors for new instruments to hedge against increasingly volatile interest and exchange rates; and by improvements in telecommunications and computing, which make it possible to execute transactions cheaply and quickly throughout the world.

Table 14-3 summarized the ways in which companies raise and spend money. Have another look at it and try to get some feel for the numbers. Notice that:

1. Internally generated cash is the principal source of funds. Some people worry about that; they think that if management does not have to go to the trouble of raising the money, it won't think so hard when it comes to spending it.
2. Internally generated cash does not provide all the money companies need. The deficit is particularly large after a period of buoyant sales; this is the time when companies tend to come to the capital markets for more money.
3. There are cycles in company financing. Sometimes companies prefer to issue debt, sometimes equity. In part this reflects their attempt to keep to a target debt-equity ratio. But it also looks as if companies try to make equity issues after a market rise. Nobody knows why they do this. There does not seem any reason to do so in an efficient market. An equity issue is a zero-NPV transaction regardless of whether the stock price has just risen or fallen.

Table 14-4 and Figures 14-2 and 14-3 show the net effect of this fund raising on the aggregate balance sheet of corporations in the United States. Debt ratios have generally increased over the postwar period. Some find this cause for concern. But successful companies in many other countries, Germany for example, operate at debt ratios much higher than United States companies would think prudent.

FURTHER READING

Donaldson describes a survey of corporate attitudes to different sources of finance in:

> G. Donaldson: *Corporate Debt Capacity,* Division of Research, Graduate School of Business Administration, Harvard University, Boston, 1961.

Some common concerns about the role of the capital market in providing funds for industry are set out in:

> W. J. Baumol: *The Stock Market and Economic Efficiency,* Fordham University Press, New York, 1965.

Taggart and Marsh provide some evidence on why and when companies use different sources of finance:

> R. A. Taggart: "A Model of Corporate Financing Decisions," *Journal of Finance,* **32:** 1467–1484 (December 1977).
>
> P. Marsh: "The Choice between Equity and Debt: An Empirical Study," *Journal of Finance,* **37:** 121–144 (March 1982).

Taggart describes long-term trends in corporate financing in:

> R. A. Taggart: "Secular Patterns in the Financing of Corporations," in B. M. Friedman, ed., *Corporate Capital Structures in the United States,* University of Chicago Press, Chicago, 1985.

QUIZ

1. The authorized share capital of the Alfred Cake Company is 100,000 shares. The equity is currently shown in the company's books as follows:

- Common stock ($.50 par value) $40,000
- Additional paid-in capital   10,000
- Retained earnings   30,000
- Common equity   80,000
- Treasury stock (2,000 shares)   5,000
- Net common equity $75,000

   (*a*) How many shares are issued?

   (*b*) How many are outstanding?

   (*c*) Explain the difference between your answers to (*a*) and (*b*).

   (*d*) How many more shares can be issued without the approval of shareholders?

   (*e*) Suppose that the company issues 10,000 shares at $2 a share. Which of the above figures would be changed?

2. If there are 10 directors to be elected and a shareholder owns 80 shares, indicate the maximum number of votes that he or she can cast for a favorite candidate under:

   (*a*) Majority voting

   (*b*) Cumulative voting

3. Fill in the blanks using the terms listed at the end of this question.

   (*a*) Debt maturing in more than 1 year is often called _____ debt.

   (*b*) An issue of bonds that is sold simultaneously in several countries is called a _____ .

   (*c*) If a lender ranks behind the firm's general creditors in the event of default, his or her loan is said to be _____ .

   (*d*) Unsecured bonds are usually termed _____ bonds.

   (*e*) In many cases, a firm is obliged to make regular contributions to a _____ which is then used to repurchase bonds.

(*f*) Most bonds give the firm the right to repurchase or _____ the bonds at specified prices.

(*g*) The rate that banks charge to their most creditworthy customers is generally termed the _____ .

(*h*) The interest rate on bank loans is often tied to short-term interest rates. These loans are usually called _____ loans.

(*i*) A long-term, noncancellable rental agreement is called a _____ .

(*j*) A _____ bond can be exchanged for shares of the issuing corporation.

(*k*) A _____ gives its owner the right to buy shares in the issuing company at a predetermined _____ .

lease, funded, floating-rate, eurobond, exercise price, commercial paper, convertible, term loan, subordinated, call, sinking fund, prime rate, debentures, mortgage bond, senior, unfunded, eurodollar rate, warrant

4. The figures in the following table are in the wrong order. Can you place them in their correct order?

	Percent of Total Sources in 1986
Internally generated cash	6
Financial deficit	− 18
Net share issues	79
Debt issues	21

5. True or false?

(*a*) Firms sell forward contracts primarily to raise money for new capital investment.

(*b*) Firms trade in futures contracts to hedge their exposure to unexpected changes in interest rates, foreign exchange rates, or commodity prices.

(*c*) The recent wave of financial innovation was partly caused by deregulation of financial markets.

(*d*) In several recent years, nonfinancial corporations in the United States have repurchased more stock than they have issued.

(*e*) Firms are more likely to issue equity than debt after stock prices have fallen.

(*f*) A corporation pays tax on only 20 percent of the common or preferred dividends it receives from other corporations.

(*g*) Therefore a large fraction of preferred shares are held by corporations.

QUESTIONS AND PROBLEMS

1. "It is frequently held that the cost of funds on the security market falls whenever stock prices rise, just as the yield of a bond varies inversely with its price. One would think that it pays management to turn to the market for funds whenever the cost of stock market capital, thus interpreted, falls sufficiently."[17] Discuss.

2. It is sometimes suggested that since retained earnings provide the bulk of industry's capital needs, the securities markets are largely redundant. Do you agree?

[17] W. J. Baumol, op. cit., p. 71.

3. Can you think of any new kinds of security that might appeal to investors? Why do you think they have not been issued?
4. Look back at Table 14-2.
    (a) Suppose that Occidental issues 15,000 shares at $40 a share. Rework Table 14-2 to show the company's equity after the issue.
    (b) Suppose that Occidental *subsequently* repurchases 10,000 shares at $45 a share. Rework Table 14-2 to show the effect of the further change.
5. The shareholders of the Pickwick Paper Company need to elect five directors. There are 100,000 shares outstanding. How many shares do you need to own to *ensure* that you can elect at least one director if:
    (a) The company has majority voting?
    (b) It has cumulative voting?
6. Compare the yields on preferred stocks with those on corporate bonds. Can you explain the difference?
7. Who are the main holders and issuers of preferred stock? Explain why?
8. Briefly explain the chief difference between a forward and a futures contract.
9. Work out the financing proportions given in Table 14-3 for a particular industrial company—General Mills, for example—for some recent year.
10. Here is recent financial data on Pisa Construction, Inc.

    - Stock price = $40
    - Number shares = 10,000
    - Book net worth = $500,000
    - Market value of firm = $400,000
    - Earnings per share = $4
    - Return on investment = 8 percent

    Pisa has not performed spectacularly to date. However, it wishes to issue new shares to obtain $80,000 to finance expansion into a promising market. Pisa's financial advisers think a stock issue is a poor choice because, among other reasons, "sale of stock at a price below book value per share can only depress the stock price and decrease shareholders' wealth." To prove the point they construct the following example: "Suppose 2000 new shares are issued at $40 and the proceeds invested. (Neglect issue costs.) Suppose return on investment doesn't change. Then

$$\text{Book net worth} = \$580,000$$

$$\text{Total earnings} = .08\,(580,000) = \$46,400$$

$$\text{Earnings per share} = \frac{46,400}{12,000} = \$3.87$$

    Thus, EPS declines, book value per share declines, and share price will decline proportionately to $38.70."
    Evaluate this argument with particular attention to the assumptions implicit in the numerical example.

15

How Corporations Issue Securities

In Chapter 11 we encountered Marvin Enterprises, one of the most remarkable growth companies of the twenty-first century. It was founded by George and Mildred Marvin, two high school dropouts, together with their chum Charles P. (Chip) Norton. To get the company off the ground the three entrepreneurs relied on their own savings together with personal loans from a bank. However, the company's rapid growth meant that they had soon borrowed to the hilt and needed more equity capital. Equity investment in young private companies is generally known as **venture capital.** Such venture capital may be provided by specialist venture capital partnerships, by investment institutions, or by wealthy individuals who are prepared to back an untried company in exchange for a piece of the action. In the first part of this chapter we will explain how companies like Marvin go about raising venture capital.

Venture capital companies aim to help growing firms over that awkward adolescent period before they are large enough to "go public." For a successful firm such as Marvin there is likely to come a time when it needs to tap a wider source of capital and therefore decides to make its first public issue of common stock. The first public issue of a security by a company is known as an **unseasoned** issue. We will describe in the next section of the chapter what is involved in an unseasoned issue of stock.

A company's first public offering is rarely also its last. In Chapter 14 we saw that corporations face a persistent financial deficit which they meet by selling securities. We will look therefore at how established public corporations go about raising more capital.

If a stock or bond is sold publicly, it can then be traded on the securities markets. But sometimes investors intend to hold onto their securities and are not concerned about whether they can sell them. In these cases there is little advantage to a public issue, and the firm may prefer to place the securities directly with one or two financial institutions. At the end of this chapter we will discuss the choice between a public offer and a private placement.

15-1 VENTURE CAPITAL

On April 1, 2003, George and Mildred Marvin met with Chip Norton in their research lab (which also doubled up as a bicycle shed) to celebrate the incorporation of Marvin Enterprises. The three entrepreneurs had raised $100,000 from savings and personal bank loans and had purchased 1 million shares in the new company. At this *zero stage* investment, the company's assets were $90,000 in the bank ($10,000 had been spent for legal and other expenses of setting up the company), plus the *idea* for a new product, the household gargle blaster. George

Marvin was the first to see that the gargle blaster, up to that point an expensive curiosity, could be commercially produced using microgenetic refenestrators.

Marvin Enterprises's bank account steadily drained away as design and testing proceeded. Local banks did not see Marvin's idea as adequate collateral, so a transfusion of equity capital was clearly needed. Preparation of a *business plan* was a necessary first step. The plan was a confidential document describing the proposed product, its potential market, the underlying technology, and the resources—time, money, employees, plant and equipment—needed for success.

Most entrepreneurs are able to spin a plausible yarn about their company. But it is as hard to convince a venture capitalist that your business plan is sound as it is to get a first novel published. Marvin's management were able to point to the fact that they were prepared to put their money where their mouths were. Not only had they staked all their savings in the company but they were mortgaged to the hilt. This *signaled* their faith in the business.[1]

First Meriam Venture Partners were impressed with Marvin's presentation and agreed to buy 1 million new shares for $1 each. After this *first-stage* financing, the company's market value balance sheet looked like this:

Marvin Enterprises First-Stage Balance Sheet
(market values in millions)

Cash from new equity	$1	$1	New equity from venture capital
Other assets, mostly intangible	1	1	Original equity held by entrepreneurs
Value	$2	$2	Value

By accepting a $2 million *after-the-money* valuation, First Meriam implicitly put a $1 million value on the entrepreneurs' idea and their commitment to the enterprise. They also handed the entrepreneurs a $900,000 paper gain over their original $100,000 investment. In exchange, the entrepreneurs gave up half their company and accepted First Meriam's representatives to the board of directors.[2]

The success of a new business depends critically on the effort put in by the managers. So venture capital firms try to structure a deal so that management has a strong incentive to work hard. For example, any entrepreneur who demands a water-tight employment contract and a fat salary is not going to find it easy to raise venture capital. The Marvin team agreed to put up with modest salaries and, therefore, they could cash in only from appreciation of their stock. If Marvin failed they would get nothing, because First Meriam actually bought *preferred* stock designed to convert automatically into common stock when and if Marvin Enterprises succeeded in an initial public offering or consistently generated more than a target

---

[1] For a formal analysis of how management's investment in the business can provide a reliable signal of the company's value, see H. E. Leland and D. H. Pyle, "Informational Asymmetries, Financial Structure, and Financial Intermediation," *Journal of Finance*, **32:** 371–387 (May 1977).

[2] Venture capital investors do not necessarily demand a majority on the board of directors. Whether they do depends, for example, on how mature the business is and on what fraction of it they own. A common compromise gives an equal number of seats to the founders and to outside investors; the two parties then agree to one or more additional directors to serve as tie-breakers in case a conflict arises. Regardless of whether they have a majority of directors, venture capital companies are seldom silent partners; their judgment and contacts can often prove useful to a relatively inexperienced management team.

level of earnings. This raised even further the stakes for the company's management.[3]

Venture capitalists rarely give a young company all the money it will need all at once. At each stage they give enough to reach the next major checkpoint. Thus in spring 2005, having designed and tested a prototype, Marvin Enterprises was back asking for more money for pilot production and test marketing. Its *second-stage* financing was $4 million, of which $1.5 million came from First Meriam, its original backers, and $2.5 million from two other venture capital partnerships and wealthy individual investors. The balance sheet just after the second stage was as follows:

Marvin Enterprises Second-Stage Balance Sheet
(market values in millions)

Cash from new equity	$ 4	$ 4	New equity, second stage
Fixed assets	1	5	Equity from first stage
Other assets, mostly intangible	9	5	Original equity held by entrepreneurs
Value	$14	$14	Value

Now the after-the-money valuation was $14 million. First Meriam marked up its original investment to $5 million, and the founders noted an additional $4 million paper gain.

Does this begin to sound like a (paper) money machine? It was so only with hindsight. At stage one it wasn't clear whether Marvin would ever get to stage two: if the prototype hadn't worked, First Meriam could have refused to put up more funds and effectively closed the business down.[4] Or they could have advanced stage two money in a smaller amount on less favorable terms. The board of directors could also have fired George, Mildred, and Chip and gotten someone else to try to develop the business.

For every 10 first-stage venture capital investments, only two or three may survive as successful, self-sufficient businesses, and one may pay off big as Marvin Enterprises did.[5] From these statistics come two rules for success in venture capital investment. First, don't shy away from uncertainty; accept a low probability of success. But don't buy into a business unless you can see the *chance* of a big, public

---

[3] Notice there is a trade-off here. Marvin's management is being asked to put all its eggs into one basket. That creates pressure for managers to work hard but it also means that they take on risk that they could have diversified away.

The problem of ensuring that managers act in the interests of investors is sometimes referred to as an *agency* problem. For a discussion of these issues see M. C. Jensen and W. H. Meckling, "Theory of the Firm: Managerial Behavior, Agency Costs and Capital Structure," *Journal of Financial Economics*, **3**: 305–360 (1976).

[4] If First Meriam had refused to invest at stage two, it would have been an exceptionally hard sell convincing another investor to step in in its place. The other outside investors knew they had less information about Marvin than First Meriam and would have read its refusal as a bad omen for Marvin's prospects.

[5] One study of venture capital investments between 1960 and 1975 found that about one in six were total failures. On the other hand, thanks to a few outstanding successes the average return after costs was about 19 percent a year. See B. Huntsman and J. P. Hoban, Jr., "Investment in New Enterprise: Some Empirical Observations on Risk, Return, and Market Structure," *Financial Management*, **9**:44–51 (Summer 1980).

FIGURE 15-1
Capital commitments to independent private venture capital funds. (Figures in billions.) (*Source:* Venture Economics, Inc., Wellesley, Mass. Reproduced with permission.)

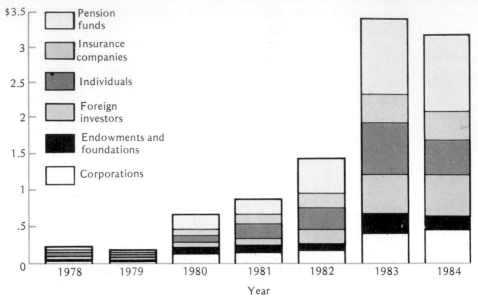

company in a profitable market. There's no sense taking a long shot unless it pays off big if you win. Second, cut your losses; identify losers early, and if you can't fix the problem—by replacing management, for example—throw no good money after bad.

For Marvin, fortunately, everything went like clockwork. Third-stage financing was arranged,[6] full-scale production began on schedule, and gargle blasters were acclaimed by music critics worldwide. Marvin Enterprises "went public" on February 3, 2009. Once its shares were traded, the paper gains earned by First Meriam and the company's founders turned into fungible wealth.

Before we get on to this initial public offering, a word on the venture capital market in the 1980s.

Entrepreneurs have generated a continuous flow of successful new corporations for at least a century. Some of the new companies managed to grow by their own bootstraps, by borrowing and generating funds internally. Others sought out equity investment, often from wealthy families or established firms. So venture capital has been around for some time.

But by the 1980s the United States had a well-developed venture capital *market,* in which specialists set up partnerships, pooled funds from a variety of investors, *sought out* fledgling companies to invest in, and then worked with these companies as they tried to grow into publicly traded firms. As Figure 15-1 shows, the amounts raised by these partnerships grew rapidly to over $3 billion in 1983 and 1984. Note the large amounts contributed by pension funds and foreign investors.

Governments around the world seem to believe that, unless they intervene, profitable new ventures are likely to fail for lack of finance. They therefore look for ways to provide subsidized finance for young companies. In the United States

---

[6] Later-stage financing is often called *mezzanine financing,* in contrast to financing by those investors who get in on the "ground floor."

the government provides cheap loans to Small Business Investment Companies (SBICs) who then relend the money to deserving entrepreneurs. SBICs occupy a small, specialized niche in the venture capital market.

15-2   THE INITIAL PUBLIC OFFERING

Very few new businesses make it big, but venture capitalists keep sane by forgetting about the many failures and reminding themselves of the success stories—the investors who got in on the ground floor of firms like DEC, Teledyne, and Lotus Development Corporation.[7] When First Meriam invested in Marvin Enterprises, it was not looking for a high income stream from the investment; instead it was hoping for rapid growth that would allow Marvin to "go public" and give First Meriam an opportunity to cash in on some of its gains.

By 2009 Marvin had grown to the point at which it needed substantial new capital to implement its second-generation production technology. At this point it decided to make an initial public offering of stock. This was to be partly a **primary** offering—that is, new shares were to be sold to raise additional cash for the company. It was also to be partly a **secondary** offering—that is, the venture capitalists and the company's founders were looking to sell some of their existing shares.

Often when companies go public, the issue is solely intended to raise new capital for the company. But there are also occasions when no new capital is raised and all the shares on offer are being sold by existing shareholders. In fact some of the biggest initial public offerings occur when governments sell off their shareholdings in companies. For example, the United States government made a secondary issue of $1.6 billion when it divested Conrail.[8]

Arranging a Public Issue[9]

Once Marvin had taken the decision to go public, the next task was to select the underwriters. Underwriters act as financial midwives to a new issue. Usually they play a triple role—first providing the company with procedural and financial advice, then buying the issue, and finally reselling it to the public. After some discussion Marvin settled on Klein Merrick as the lead underwriter. Klein Merrick would be responsible for forming and managing a syndicate of underwriters who would buy and resell the issue.

Together with Klein Merrick and firms of lawyers and accountants, Marvin prepared a **registration statement** for submission to the Securities and Exchange Commission.[10] This statement is required for any public issue of securities. It is a detailed and sometimes cumbersome document which presents information about the proposed financing and the firm's history, existing business, and plans for the

---

[7] The founder of Lotus took a finance class from one of the authors. Within 5 years he had become a multimillionaire. Perhaps that will make you feel better about the cost of this book.

[8] Even the Conrail issue looks tiny compared with the secondary offering by the Japanese government of $12.6 billion of the stock of Nippon Telegraph and Telephone or the $9 billion offering by the British government of British Gas.

[9] For an excellent case study of how one company went public see B. Uttal, "Inside the Deal That Made Bill Gates $350,000,000," *Fortune,* July 21, 1986.

[10] The rules governing the sale of securities derive principally from the Securities Act of 1933. Some issues are exempted from the registration requirement. The principal exemptions are so-called *Regulation A* issues involving less than $1.5 million and loans maturing within 9 months.

future.[11] The SEC studies this document and sends the company a "deficiency memorandum" requesting any changes. Finally an amended statement is filed with the SEC.[12]

Marvin was not allowed to sell securities during this waiting period nor could it engage in any unusual publicity that might affect the sale. However, management did make a number of presentations to institutional investors and the underwriters began to sound out the interest of potential buyers.

The first part of the registration statement was distributed by the company in the form of a preliminary **prospectus.** Such a prospectus is generally known as a *red herring* because of the statement printed in red ink denying that the company is trying to sell securities before the registration is effective. In Appendix B to this chapter we have reproduced the prospectus for Marvin's first public issue of stock. Most prospectuses would go into much more detail on each topic, but this example should serve to give you a feel for the mixture of valuable information and re-dundant qualification that characterizes these documents. The Marvin prospectus also illustrates how the SEC takes care to ensure that investors' eyes are opened to the dangers of purchase (see "Certain Considerations" of the prospectus). Some investors have joked that if they read prospectuses carefully, they would never dare buy any new issue.

After registration, Marvin issued a final prospectus which differed from the preliminary one only by the addition of the final offering price and a few minor changes required by the SEC. Marvin was obliged to send this prospectus to all purchasers and to all those who were offered securities through the mail.

Marvin had other tasks before it was able to go public. It needed to appoint a **registrar** to record any issues of stock and to prevent any unauthorized issue. It appointed a **transfer agent** to look after the transfer of the newly issued securities. Finally it checked that the issue complied with the so-called "blue-sky" laws of each state that regulate sales of securities within the state.[13]

Pricing a New Issue	During the registration period Marvin and its underwriters began to firm up the issue price. First they looked at the price-earnings ratios of the shares of Marvin's principal competitors. Then they worked through a number of discounted cash-flow calculations like the ones we described in the appendix to Chapter 4 and in Chapter 11. Most of the evidence pointed to a market value of around $90 a share.

While Marvin's management were anxious to secure the highest possible price |

---

[11] Fortunately, the amount of detail is considerably less than it used to be. (A registration statement filed by Republic Steel in 1934 comprised 19,897 pages!) Now a complete registration statement might run to 50 pages or so, and some are much shorter. For example, a solid public company may not be required to reprint the standard financial data published in its most recent annual report. These data are "incorporated by reference," i.e., by simply referring to them in the registration statement.

The example of the Republic Steel registration statement is cited in P. M. Van Arsdell, *Corporate Finance,* Ronald Press Co., New York, 1958.

[12] Occasionally the SEC will issue a "stop order" to prevent the sale until its requests have been complied with. Note incidentally that the SEC's concern is solely with disclosure and it has no power to prevent an issue as long as there has been proper disclosure.

[13] In 1980 when Apple Computer Inc. made its first public issue, the Massachusetts state government decided the offering was too risky for its residents and therefore barred sale of the shares to individual investors in the state. The state relented later, after the issue was out and the price had risen. Needless to say, this action was not acclaimed by Massachusetts investors.

States do not usually reject security issues by honest firms through established underwriters. We cite the example to illustrate the potential power of state securities laws, and to show why underwriters keep careful track of them.

for their stock, the underwriters were more cautious. Not only would they be left with any unsold stock if they overestimated investor demand; they also argued that some degree of underpricing was needed to tempt investors to buy the stock.

Immediately after the company received clearance from the SEC, Marvin and the underwriters agreed on an issue price of $80 a share. On February 3, 2009, Marvin finally went public and the underwriters began to telephone interested buyers of the stock. The issue proved popular with investors; the underwriters had no difficulty selling the stock at the issue price. By the end of the first week, the shares were trading at a price of $95. The issue brought the Marvin management team $16 million in cash before their share of the costs, and the 800,000 shares that they retained were worth $800,000 \times 95 - \$76$ million.

Costs of a Public Issue

Marvin's issue created substantial administrative costs. Preparation of the registration statement and prospectus involved management, legal counsel, and accountants, as well as the underwriters and their advisers. In addition, the firm had to pay fees for registering the new securities, printing and mailing costs, and so on. You can see from the first page of the Marvin prospectus (Appendix B) that these administrative and registration costs amounted in total to $820,000.

The second major cost of the Marvin issue was underwriting. Underwriters make their profit by buying the issue from the company at a discount from the price at which they resell it to the public. In Marvin's case this discount, or *spread*, amounted to $4.5 million, which was equivalent to 6.25 percent of the total amount of the issue.

Marvin's issue was costly in yet another way. Since the offering price was *less* than the true value of the issued securities, investors who bought the issue got a bargain at the expense of the firm's original stockholders.

These costs of *underpricing* are hidden but nevertheless real. For initial public offerings they generally exceed the other issue costs. Whenever any company goes public, it is very difficult for the underwriter to judge how much investors will be willing to pay for the stock. A number of researchers have tried to measure underwriters' success in gauging the value of such issues. With remarkable unanimity they have found that on average investors who buy at the issue price realize very high returns over the following weeks. For example, a study by Jay Ritter of approximately 5000 new issues from 1960 to 1982 indicated average underpricing of 19 percent.

This underpricing does not imply that any investor can expect to become wealthy by purchasing unseasoned stock from the underwriters, for if the issue is attractive, the underwriters will not have enough stock to go around. In order to get stock at the issue price investors would probably have to be prepared to pay for it indirectly, for example, by allocating more brokerage business to the underwriter than they otherwise would. Therefore underpricing helps underwriters. It reduces the risk of underwriting and gains them the gratitude of investors who buy the issue. Does that mean the underwriter earns excessive profits? Possibly, but not necessarily. If the business is sufficiently competitive, underwriters will take all these hidden benefits into account when they negotiate the spread.

Suppose that you could always be sure of getting your fair share of any issue that you applied for without having to ingratiate yourself with the investment banker. Does that mean that you could make handsome profits on average by applying for an equal amount of each issue? Unfortunately, no. If an issue is cheap, it is also likely to be oversubscribed; if it is dear, it is likely to be undersubscribed. So you will receive a small proportion of the cheap issues and a large proportion of the dear ones. If you are smart, you will play the game only if there is substantial underpricing on the average.[14]

Many investment bankers and institutional investors argue that underpricing is in the interests of the issuing firm. They say that a low offering price on the initial offer raises the price of the stock when it is subsequently traded in the market and enhances the firm's ability to raise further capital. At least one industrialist has accepted this argument, for writing some time after his company went public the president described the pricing decision as follows:

> *Our underwriting group suggested a price of $15. The general market was strong ... when our registration statement was filed and we felt that the public might well pay $17 or $18 for our stock rather than $15. Our underwriters were strong in their desire to have the stock sold at $15 a share on the basis that this was a proper price for the stock. They pointed out that the after-market was important and that the price could decline if the stock was overpriced. Having practiced law for many years ..., it was always my opinion that clients should not second-guess their counselors. I had to follow the same rules in accepting the advice of our investment bankers. And how right our underwriting group was! Within six months our stock rose from $15 a share to $50. Would the stock have had this dramatic increase if the initial price had been $17 or $18? There may have been some who felt that it was overpriced initially and would not have been in the market for our stock. Suffice it to say that the overall result was extremely good. It points out the importance of working with competent investment bankers who guide you in these matters.[15]*

Contentment at selling an article for one-third of its ultimate worth is a rare quality.

15-3 GENERAL CASH OFFERS BY PUBLIC COMPANIES

After its initial public offering Marvin Enterprises continued to grow and, like most growing companies, it needed from time to time to make further issues of debt and equity. But at this point we will leave Marvin and review in general terms the procedures involved in these periodic security issues.

Any issue of securities needs to be formally approved by the firm's board of directors. If the stock issue requires an increase in the company's authorized capital, it also needs the consent of the stockholders.

Public companies can issue securities either by making a general cash offer to investors at large or by making a rights issue that is limited to existing stockholders. We will concentrate in this chapter on the mechanics of the general cash offer, which is used for virtually all debt issues and most equity issues. However, although rights issues have become a rarity in the United States, they are widespread in other countries and you should know how they work. Therefore in Appendix

---

[14] For a discussion of this point, see K. Rock, "Why New Issues Are Underpriced," *Journal of Financial Economics*, **15:** 187–212 (January–February 1986).

[15] From E. L. Winter, *A Complete Guide to Making a Public Offering.* © 1962, published by Prentice-Hall, Inc., Englewood Cliffs, N.J. Here's another example. In 1987 the British company Sock Shop International went public at 125p a share. First-day dealings were at a price of 205p. The company's chairman was reported to be "ecstatic" about the market's reaction. She dismissed suggestions that the issue was underpriced by saying that had the shares been more expensive, the company would "quite justifiably" have been accused of overpricing. See *Financial Times*, May 15, 1987.

A to this chapter we describe rights issues and we look at some interesting and controversial questions about their use.

General Cash Offers and Shelf Registration

When a public company makes a general cash offer of debt or equity, it goes through the same procedure as when it first went public. In other words, it registers the issue with the SEC and then sells it to an underwriter (or a syndicate of underwriters), who in turn offers the securities to the public.

In 1982 the SEC issued its Rule 415, which allows large companies to file a single registration statement covering financing plans for up to 2 years into the future. The actual issue, or issues, can be done with scant additional paperwork, whenever the firm needs the cash or thinks it can issue securities at an attractive price. This is called *shelf registration*—the registration statement is "put on the shelf," to be taken down and used as needed.

Think of how you as financial manager might use shelf registration. Suppose that your company is likely to need up to $200 million of new long-term debt over the next year or so. It can file a shelf registration for that amount. It then has prior approval to issue up to $200 million of debt, but it isn't obligated to issue a penny. Nor is it required to work through any *particular* underwriters—the registration statement may name one or more underwriters the firm thinks it may work with, but others can be substituted later.

Now you can sit back and issue debt as needed, in bits and pieces if you like. Suppose Merrill Lynch comes across an insurance company with $10 million ready to invest in corporate bonds. Your phone rings. It's Merrill Lynch offering to buy $10 million of your bonds, priced to yield, say, 12½ percent. If you think that's a good price, the financial manager says "OK" and the deal is done, subject to only a little additional paperwork. Merrill Lynch then resells the bonds to the insurance company, it hopes at a slightly higher price than it paid for them, thus earning an intermediary's profit.

Here is another possible deal. Suppose that you think you see a window of opportunity in which interest rates are "temporarily low." You invite bids for $100 million of bonds. Some bids may come from large investment bankers acting alone, others from ad hoc syndicates. But that's not your problem; if the price is right, you just take the best deal offered.

Thus shelf registration gives firms several different things that they did not have previously:

1. Securities can be issued in dribs and drabs without incurring excessive transaction costs.
2. Securities can be issued on short notice.
3. Security issues can be timed to take advantage of "market conditions" (although any financial manager who can *reliably* identify favorable market conditions could make a lot more money by quitting and becoming a bond or stock trader instead).
4. The issuing firm can make sure that underwriters compete for its business. It can in effect auction off securities.

Underwriters do compete. Although several large investment banking houses lobbied hard against Rule 415 when the SEC was considering it, once the rule was approved, they played the new game with gusto. As an attorney who works with them observed, "If the SEC passed a rule saying you had to do underwriting in

Watertown, NY, in the snow stark naked, these guys would take the first plane up."[16]

Not all companies eligible for shelf registration actually use it for all their public issues. Sometimes they believe they can get a better deal by making one large issue through traditional channels, especially when the security to be issued has some unusual feature or when the firm believes it needs the investment banker's counsel or stamp of approval on the issue. Shelf registration is thus less often used for issues of common stock or convertible securities than for garden variety corporate bonds.

International Security Issues

Well-established companies are not restricted to the capital market in the United States; they can also raise money in the international capital markets. We saw in Chapter 14 that this can mean one of two things. Either the company makes a foreign bond issue in another country's market (in which case it is subject to the laws and customs of that country), or it makes an issue of eurobonds which are offered internationally.[17] The procedures for making a eurobond issue are broadly similar to the procedures for a domestic bond issue in the United States. Here are two points to note:

1. As long as the bond issue is not publicly offered in the United States, it does not have to be registered with the SEC. Therefore, the borrower saves the costs of registration. However, it must still produce a prospectus or offering circular.[18]
2. Frequently a eurobond issue takes the form of a *bought deal,* in which case one or a few underwriters buy the entire issue. Bought deals allow companies to issue bonds at very short notice.

The Costs of the General Cash Offer

Whenever a firm makes a cash offer, it incurs substantial administrative costs. Also the firm needs to compensate the underwriters by selling them securities below the price that they expect to receive from investors. Tables 15-1 and 15-2 show the average underwriting and administrative costs for United States domestic stock and debt issues.[19] Two aspects of the data are of immediate interest. (Ignore for the moment the data on rights issues.)

First, it is more expensive to issue common stock than the same amount of debt. For example, a large issue of common stock might involve total expenses (administrative costs and underwriters' compensation) of 4 percent. A comparable debt issue would cost only about 1 percent. This difference partly reflects the greater administrative costs of stock issues, but it is chiefly because underwriters require compensation for the greater risks they bear in buying and reselling stock.

Second, a large part of the issue cost is fixed. Therefore there are economies of scale in issuing securities: Costs may absorb 15 percent of a $1 million underwritten stock issue but only 4 percent of a $500 million issue.

---

[16] Quoted in Tim Carrington, "New Ball Game: Investment Bankers Enter a New Era," *The Wall Street Journal,* June 21, 1982, p. 10.

[17] Occasionally companies in the United States may make an overseas issue of equity, either to tap a wider market or to avoid registration requirements. For example, in 1982 International Signal and Control went public not by issuing stock in the United States but by selling it in London.

[18] If the issue is not registered, it cannot be sold to investors in the United States until it has "come to rest," or about 90 days after the sale has been completed.

[19] The figures do not capture *all* administrative costs. For example, they do not include management time spent on the issue.

TABLE 15-1

Issue costs as a percent of proceeds for registered issues of common stock during 1971–1975

Size of Issue (Millions of Dollars)	GENERAL UNDERWRITTEN CASH OFFERS			UNDERWRITTEN RIGHTS ISSUES		
	Underwriters' Compensation (Percent)	Other Expenses (Percent)	Total Cost (Percent)	Underwriters' Compensation (Percent)	Other Expenses (Percent)	Total Cost (Percent)
.50–.99	7.0	6.8	13.7	3.4	4.8	8.2
1.00–1.99	10.4	4.9	15.3	6.4	4.2	10.5
2.00–4.99	6.6	2.9	9.5	5.2	2.9	8.1
5.00–9.99	5.5	1.5	7.0	3.9	2.2	6.1
10.00–19.99	4.8	.7	5.6	4.1	1.2	5.4
20.00–49.99	4.3	.4	4.7	3.8	.9	4.7
50.00–99.99	4.0	.2	4.2	4.0	.7	4.7
100.00–500.00	3.8	.1	4.0	3.5	.5	4.0
Average	5.0	1.2	6.2	4.3	1.7	6.1

Source: C. W. Smith, "Alternative Methods for Raising Capital: Rights versus Underwritten Offerings," *Journal of Financial Economics,* **5:** 273–307 (December 1977), table 1, p. 277.

*Market
Reaction to
Stock Issues

Because stock issues usually throw a large additional supply of shares onto the market, it is widely believed that they must temporarily depress the stock price. If the proposed issue is very large, the price pressure may, it is thought, be so severe as to make it almost impossible to raise new money. If so, the firm effectively faces capital rationing.

This belief in price pressure implies that after the decline in price the company's shares can be bought for less than their true value. It is therefore inconsistent with market efficiency. The alternative view stresses that investors buy stocks because they offer a fair reward for their risk. If the stock price fell solely because of increased supply, then that stock would offer a reward which was *more* than

TABLE 15-2

Average underwriting and administrative costs for underwritten public issues of bonds, 1960–1969

Size of Issue (Millions of Dollars)	Underwriters' Compensation (Percent)	Other Expenses (Percent)
Under .50	13.6	6.2
.50–.99	7.7	5.2
1.00–1.99	6.4	3.0
2.00–4.99	4.6	1.7
5.00–9.99	1.6	.9
10.00–19.99	1.2	.6
20.00–49.99	1.1	.4
50.00 and above	.8	.3

Source: R. Hillstrom and R. King (eds.), *1960–69: A Decade of Corporate and International Finance,* Investment Dealers Digest, Inc., New York, p. 18.

commensurate with the risk, and investors would be attracted to it as donkeys to a thistle. This is what Myron Scholes found when he looked at sales by investors of large blocks of stock (see Section 13-7); demand for the stock was responsive to very small changes in the stock's price, though the information conveyed by the block sale led to a small and permanent decline in price.

Economists who have studied new issues of common stock have generally found that announcement of the issue *does* result in a decline in the stock price. For industrial issues in the United States this decline amounts to about 3 percent.[20] While this may not sound overwhelming, the fall in market value is equivalent to nearly a third of the new money raised by the issue.

What's going on here? Is the price of the stock simply depressed by the prospect of the additional supply? It is possible,[21] but there are several alternative explanations. Here is one. . . .

Suppose that managers know that their stock is undervalued. If the company sells new stock at this low price, it will favor the new shareholders at the expense of the old. In these circumstances managers might be prepared to forgo the new investment rather than sell shares at too low a price.[22]

If managers know that the stock is *over*valued, the position is reversed. If the company sells new shares at the high price, it will help its existing shareholders at the expense of the new ones. Managers might be prepared to issue stock even if the new cash was just put in the bank.

Of course investors are not stupid. They can predict that managers are more likely to issue stock when they think it is overvalued and therefore they mark the price of the stock down accordingly. Thus the decline in the price of the stock at the time of the new issue may have nothing to do with the increased supply but simply with the information that the issue provides.[23]

15-4   THE ROLE OF THE UNDERWRITER

We now need to look more carefully at the part played by the underwriters during a public offer. We have described them as playing a triple role—providing advice, buying a new issue from the company, and reselling it to the public. In return they receive a payment in the form of a *spread*—that is, they are allowed to buy

---

[20] See, for example, P. Asquith and D. W. Mullins, "Equity Issues and Offering Dilution," *Journal of Financial Economics,* **15:** 61–90 (January–February 1986); R. W. Masulis and A. N. Korwar, "Seasoned Equity Offerings: An Empirical Investigation," *Journal of Financial Economics,* **15:** 91–118 (January–February 1986); W. H. Mikkelson and M. M. Partch, "Valuation Effects of Security Offerings and the Issuance Process," *Journal of Financial Economics,* **15:** 31–60 (January–February 1986). There appears to be a smaller price decline for utility issues. Also Marsh observed a smaller decline for rights issues in the United Kingdom; see P. R. Marsh, "Equity Rights Issues and the Efficiency of the UK Stock Market," *Journal of Finance,* **34:** 839–862 (September 1979).

[21] If the fall is due to price pressure, we would expect a recovery when the issue was digested, but none of the studies showed such a recovery. Also, with the exception of the Asquith and Mullins study, all the studies cited in footnote 20 found that the price decline was unrelated to the size of the issue. This doesn't fit with the notion of price pressure.

[22] Of course, if managers could convince shareholders that the stock was undervalued, then the problem would go away. But managers might find it difficult to demonstrate that their information was genuine or they might be reluctant to give out too much information in case it helped the firm's competitors.

[23] This explanation was developed in S. C. Myers and N. S. Majluf, "Corporate Financing and Investment Decisions When Firms Have Information that Investors Do Not Have," *Journal of Financial Economics,* **13:** 187–222 (1984).

the shares for less than the *offering price* at which the securities are sold on to investors. In the more risky cases the underwriter usually receives some extra noncash compensation, such as warrants to buy additional stock. Occasionally, where a new issue of common stock is regarded as particularly risky, the underwriter may be unwilling to enter into a fixed commitment and will handle the issue only on a "best efforts" or an "all-or-none" basis. *Best efforts* means that the underwriter promises to sell as much of the issue as possible but does not guarantee the sale of the entire issue. *All or none* means that if the entire issue cannot be sold at the offering price, the deal is called off and the issuing company receives nothing.

If the issue is large, a group of underwriters will usually get together to form a syndicate to handle the sale. In this case one underwriter acts as syndicate manager and for this job keeps about 20 percent of the spread. A further 20 to 30 percent of the spread is used to pay those members of the group who buy the issue. The remaining 50 to 60 percent goes to the larger number of firms that provide the sales force for the issue.[24]

The National Association of Security Dealers (NASD) requires that the underwriting syndicate sell the issue at the stated offering price. However, the underwriter is generally allowed to support the market by repurchasing shares at the market price.[25] (Look, for example, at the second page of the Marvin prospectus.) We have no information about the effects of such stabilizing transactions. But, if capital markets are efficient, then transactions affect prices only insofar as they are thought to convey information. In that case the underwriters' efforts at stabilization cannot have a lasting effect on prices.

In any case, if the issue obstinately remains unsold and the market price falls substantially below the offering price, the underwriters have no alternative but to break the syndicate. The members then dispose of their commitments individually as best they can.

Most companies raise new capital only occasionally, but underwriters are in the business all the time. Established underwriters are, therefore, careful of their reputation and will not handle a new issue unless they believe the facts have been presented fairly to investors. Thus, in addition to handling the sale of an issue, the underwriters in effect give their seal of approval to it. This implied endorsement may be worth quite a bit to a company that is coming to the market for the first time.

| **Who Are the Underwriters?** | Since underwriters play such a crucial part in new issues, we should look at who they are. Several thousand investment banks, security dealers, and brokers are at least sporadically involved in underwriting. However, the market for the larger issues is dominated by the major investment banking firms, which enjoy great prestige, experience, and financial resources. Table 15-3 lists some of the largest underwriting firms. |

For each public issue a "tombstone" advertisement is published that lists the names of all the underwriters. In Figure 15-2 we reproduce the tombstone for the initial public offering by Conrail, which involved over a hundred underwriters.

[24] Sometimes, instead of a formal selling group, a selling discount will be offered to any member of the National Association of Security Dealers.

[25] In such cases syndicate members could escape their obligation by selling their shares in the market to the principal underwriter. To prevent this, a record is kept so that syndicate members whose shares end up in the hands of the principal underwriter lose that part of their selling concession.

TABLE 15-3
Managing underwriters listed in order of
total value of issues underwritten in 1986

Salomon Brothers
First Boston
Merrill Lynch
Goldman Sachs
Drexel Burnham Lambert
Morgan Stanley
Shearson Lehman Brothers
Kidder Peabody
Bear Stearns
Paine Webber

Source: "1987 Corporate Sweepstakes," *Institu-*
tional Investor **21:** (March 1987).

The ordering of the names on the tombstone reflects a well-established hierarchy
among underwriters. The most important underwriters are listed in alphabetical
order at the top of the list. Then come the second-rankers, and so on.

Firms guard their ranking with remarkable possessiveness. Those that struggle
to attain a particular ranking often have to consent to being listed "out of order."
But the old regime does change. Firms with strong sales forces, such as Merrill
Lynch, have over the years increased their participation and improved their ranking. At the same time the large, traditional houses such as Morgan Stanley have
responded to the need for greater distribution capacity by forming loose networks
of regional firms.

Since a eurobond issue is marketed internationally, a eurobond underwriting
syndicate is not restricted to investment banks in the United States. As you can
see from Table 15-4, foreign banks are major players in this market; among these

TABLE 15-4
Managing underwriters of eurobonds in order of
total value underwritten January–June 1987
(Note that rankings are based on issues by both
American and non-American issuers)

Nomura Securities
Daiwa Securities
Yamaichi Securities
Deutsche Bank
Credit Suisse First Boston
Nikko Securities
Morgan Guaranty
Salomon Brothers
S. G. Warburg
Banque Paribas
Industrial Bank of Japan
Morgan Stanley
Union Bank of Switzerland
Dresdner Bank
Swiss Bank Corporation

Source: IDD Information Services, cited in A. Nicoll and
C. Pearson, "Profit Ranked Above League Rating," *Fi-*
nancial Times, July 2, 1987, p. 33.

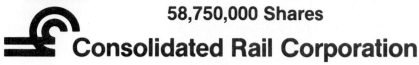

58,750,000 Shares

Consolidated Rail Corporation

Common Stock
(par value $1.00 per share)

The shares are being sold by the United States Government pursuant to the Conrail Privatization Act. The Company will not receive any proceeds from the sale of the shares.

52,000,000 Shares

This portion of the offering is being offered in the United States and Canada by the undersigned.

Goldman, Sachs & Co.

The First Boston Corporation

Merrill Lynch Capital Markets

Morgan Stanley & Co.
Incorporated

Salomon Brothers Inc

Shearson Lehman Brothers Inc.

Alex. Brown & Sons   Dillon, Read & Co. Inc.   Donaldson, Lufkin & Jenrette   Drexel Burnham Lambert   Hambrecht & Quist   E. F. Hutton & Company Inc.
Incorporated   Securities Corporation   Incorporated   Incorporated

Kidder, Peabody & Co.   Lazard Frères & Co.   Montgomery Securities   Prudential-Bache Capital Funding   Robertson, Colman & Stephens
Incorporated

L. F. Rothschild, Unterberg, Towbin, Inc.   Smith Barney, Harris Upham & Co.   Wertheim Schroder & Co.   Dean Witter Reynolds Inc.
Incorporated

William Blair & Company   J. C. Bradford & Co.   Dain Bosworth   A. G. Edwards & Sons, Inc.   McDonald & Company   Oppenheimer & Co., Inc.
Incorporated   Incorporated   Securities Inc.

Piper, Jaffray & Hopwood   Prescott, Ball & Turben, Inc.   Thomson McKinnon Securities Inc.   Wheat, First Securities, Inc.
Incorporated

Advest, Inc.   American Securities Corporation   Arnold and S. Bleichroeder, Inc.   Robert W. Baird & Co.   Bateman Eichler, Hill Richards
Incorporated   Incorporated

Sanford C. Bernstein & Co., Inc.   Blunt Ellis & Loewi   Boettcher & Company, Inc.   Burns Fry and Timmins Inc.   Butcher & Singer Inc.   Cowen & Company
Incorporated

Dominion Securities Corporation   Eberstadt Fleming Inc.   Eppler, Guerin & Turner, Inc.   First of Michigan Corporation   First Southwest Company

Furman Selz Mager Dietz & Birney   Gruntal & Co., Incorporated   Howard, Weil, Labouisse, Friedrichs   Interstate Securities Corporation
Incorporated   Incorporated

Janney Montgomery Scott Inc.   Johnson, Lane, Space, Smith & Co., Inc.   Johnston, Lemon & Co.   Josephthal & Co.   Ladenburg, Thalmann & Co. Inc.
Incorporated   Incorporated

Cyrus J. Lawrence   Legg Mason Wood Walker   Morgan Keegan & Company, Inc.   Moseley Securities Corporation   Needham & Company, Inc.
Incorporated   Incorporated

Neuberger & Berman   The Ohio Company   Rauscher Pierce Refsnes, Inc.   The Robinson-Humphrey Company, Inc.   Rothschild Inc.   Stephens Inc.

Stifel, Nicolaus & Company   Sutro & Co.   Tucker, Anthony & R. L. Day, Inc.   Underwood, Neuhaus & Co.   Wood Gundy Corp.
Incorporated   Incorporated   Incorporated

This special bracket of minority-owned and controlled firms assisted the Co-Lead Managers in the United States Offering pursuant to the Conrail Privatization Act.

AIBC Investment Services Corporation   Daniels & Bell, Inc.   Doley Securities, Inc.

WR Lazard Securities Corporation   Pryor, Govan, Counts & Co., Inc.   Muriel Siebert & Co., Inc.

6,750,000 Shares

This portion of the offering is being offered outside the United States and Canada by the undersigned.

Goldman Sachs International Corp.

First Boston International Limited

Merrill Lynch Capital Markets

Morgan Stanley International

Salomon Brothers International Limited

Shearson Lehman Brothers International

Algemene Bank Nederland N.V.   Banque Bruxelles Lambert S.A.   Banque Nationale de Paris   Cazenove & Co.   The Nikko Securities Co., (Europe) Ltd.

Nomura International   N. M. Rothschild & Sons   J. Henry Schroder Wagg & Co.   Société Générale   S. G. Warburg Securities
Limited   Limited

Arab Banking Corporation (ABC)   Banque Paribas Capital Markets Limited   Caisse Nationale de Crédit Agricole
Capital Markets Group

Compagnie de Banque et d'Investissements, CBI   Crédit Lyonnais   Daiwa Europe   IMI Capital Markets (UK) Ltd.   Joh. Berenberg, Gossler & Co.
Limited

Leu Securities Limited   Morgan Grenfell & Co.   Peterbroeck, van Campenhout & Cie SCS   Swiss Volksbank
Limited

Vereins- und Westbank   J. Vontobel & Co Ltd   M.M. Warburg-Brinckmann, Wirtz & Co.   Westdeutsche Landesbank   Yamaichi International (Europe)
Aktiengesellschaft   Girozentrale   Limited

April 1987

FIGURE 15-2
"Tombstone" advertisements such as this list the underwriters to a new issue.

foreign banks the Japanese have been increasing their share of the business very aggressively. Also, the London branches of American commercial banks are involved in underwriting eurobond issues, whereas their parents in the United States are prohibited by the Glass-Steagall Act from underwriting domestic bond issues.

Choosing an Underwriter

Many companies develop a well-established relationship with a particular investment banker, who underwrites the firm's security issues and provides other financial services.[26] Utility holding companies are an exception, for they are generally required to choose underwriters by competitive bids (although sometimes, when a holding company faces "unsettled market conditions," the SEC relents and allows negotiation). Utilities that are not organized as holding companies can do as they like.

The competition is real. Utilities almost always get at least two bids. For smaller issues, where fewer firms are needed to form a syndicate, four or five bids may be made. But does the competition make a difference?

It does seem to reduce the spreads charged by underwriters. For example, a study by Bhagat and Frost of 479 utility stock issues between 1973 and 1980 found average spreads of 3.9 percent for negotiated issues and 3.1 percent for competitive ones.[27] Yet negotiated underwriting is used by almost all firms that have a choice. Why?

Underwriters argue that negotiated offerings allow them to allocate more time to marketing the issue—for example, identifying large buyers, and recruiting "salespeople" in brokers' local offices. This marketing is most effective if done well before the issue date. Under competitive bidding, a syndicate does not put the same effort into marketing because the investment is wasted if the syndicate does not win. Therefore it has to attract buyers by underpricing the issue rather than by sales expertise.

If the underwriters are right, we ought to observe that competitive offerings cause a larger temporary price decline around the offering date. There is less unanimity as to whether this is in fact the case. Bhagat and Frost's study found the reverse: There was on average *less* underpricing for competitive offerings, though there was a much greater variation in the degree of underpricing.[28]

This is a controversial issue and we suspect that Bhagat and Frost's study may not be the final word on it. There is no evidence that companies are on average losing out from competitive bidding and, according to Bhagat and Frost's calculations, they may be reducing their costs substantially.

15-5   THE PRIVATE PLACEMENT

Whenever a company makes a public offering, it is obliged to register the issue with the SEC. It could avoid this costly process by selling the security privately.

[26] We described above how companies, after they have gone public, sometimes use a process of "shelf registration" to raise further capital. In these cases the company is not tied to a particular underwriter.

[27] S. Bhagat and P. A. Frost, "Issuing Costs to Existing Shareholders in Competitive and Negotiated Underwritten Public Utility Equity Offerings," *Journal of Financial Economics,* **15:** 233–259 (January–February 1986).

[28] Looking at an earlier period, Logue and Jarrow found a greater degree of underpricing for competitive issues, which almost offset the benefits of the lower underwriting spread. See D. E. Logue and R. A. Jarrow, "Negotiation vs. Competitive Bidding in the Sale of Securities by Public Utilities," *Financial Management,* **7:** 31–39 (Autumn 1978).

TABLE 15-5
A comparison of debt financing in public and private markets, 1976–1980. In some years
the total amount of private placements nearly matches the amount raised by public issues
(figures in billions, numbers of issues in parentheses)

	UTILITIES		INDUSTRIALS		TOTAL[a]	
	Private	Public	Private	Public	Private	Public
1976	$2.2	8.2	10.6	8.4	20.5	31.9
	(109)	(128)	(540)	(99)	(963)	(454)
1977	1.9	8.3	13.8	4.9	23.7	27.6
	(97)	(113)	(810)	(88)	(1,290)	(448)
1978	2.0	7.7	12.3	4.1	21.7	23.4
	(123)	(92)	(731)	(106)	(1,323)	(364)
1979	3.8	9.2	7.9	6.5	19.5	28.9
	(127)	(98)	(661)	(109)	(1,209)	(343)
1980	1.7	13.1	6.9	15.2	14.5	41.6
	(76)	(138)	(494)	(212)	(933)	(517)

[a] Includes issues by transportation, finance, and other companies in addition to issues by utilities and
　industrials.
Source: Compiled from issues listed in the *Investment Dealers Digest,* by G. D. Hawkins, "Essays on Non-
　Publicly Issued Debt: Revolving Credit Agreements and the Pricing of Privately Placed Debt," un-
　published Ph.D. dissertation, MIT, 1982, table I, p. 57.

There are no hard and fast definitions of a private placement, but the SEC has
insisted that the security should be sold to no more than a dozen or so knowl-
edgeable investors.

One of the disadvantages of a private placement is that the investor cannot
easily resell the security. For the common stock investor this drawback looms large,
so that *letter stock,* as it is called,[29] is rarely issued except by small, closely held
companies. Liquidity is less important to institutions such as life insurance companies, which invest huge amounts of money in corporate debt for the "long haul."
Consequently, an active private placement mechanism has evolved for corporate
debt. The size of this market is illustrated by Table 15-5, which shows the numbers
of public and private offerings and the aggregate amounts raised through each
channel from 1976 to 1980. You can see that private placements outnumbered
public issues, although the public issues were generally larger. Also note that
private placements were used more by industrial firms than utilities.

Often the privately placed debt is negotiated directly between the company and
the lender. If the issue is too large to be absorbed by one institution, the company
generally employs an investment banker to draw up the prospectus and identify
possible buyers.

As you would expect, it costs less to arrange a private placement than to make
a public issue. Unfortunately, we have no up-to-date statistics on issue costs for
private placements, but we do know that underwriting costs are substantially lower
than, say, the figures shown for public debt issues in Table 15-2. This is a particular
advantage for companies making smaller issues.

Another advantage of the private placement is that the debt contract can be
custom-tailored for firms with special problems or opportunities. The relationship

[29] So-called because the SEC requires a letter from the buyer confirming that the stock is not bought
for resale.

between borrower and lender is much more intimate. Imagine a $20 million debt issue privately placed with an insurance company and compare it with an equivalent public issue held by 200 anonymous investors. The insurance company can justify a more thorough investigation of the company's prospects and therefore may be more willing to accept unusual terms or conditions.[30] Renegotiating the debt contract in response to unexpected developments is also extremely cumbersome for a public issue but relatively easy for a private placement.

Therefore, it is not surprising that private placements occupy a particular niche in the corporate debt market, namely loans to small and medium-sized firms. These are the firms that face the highest issue costs in public issues, that require the most detailed investigation, and that may require specialized, flexible loan arrangements.[31]

Of course these advantages are not free. Lenders in private placements have to be compensated for the risks they face and for the costs of research and negotiation. They also have to be compensated for holding an illiquid asset. All these factors are rolled into the interest rate paid by the firm. It is difficult to generalize about the differences in interest rates between private placements and public issues, but a typical differential is on the order of 50 basis points or .50 percentage points.

15-6 SUMMARY

In this chapter we have summarized the various procedures for issuing corporate securities. We first looked at how infant companies raise venture capital to carry them through to the point at which they can make their first public issue of stock. We then looked at how companies can make further public issues of securities by a general cash offer. Finally, we reviewed the procedures for a private placement. It is always difficult to summarize a summary. Instead we will attempt to state the most important implications for the financial manager who must decide how to raise capital.

1. *Larger is cheaper.* There are always economies of scale in issuing securities. It is cheaper to go to the market once for $100 million than to make two trips for $50 million each. Consequently firms "bunch" security issues. That may often mean relying on short-term financing until a large issue is justified. Or it may mean issuing more than is needed at the moment in order to avoid another issue later.

2. *There are no issue costs for retained earnings.* There are significant costs associated with any stock issue. But stock issues can be avoided to the extent that the firm can plow back its earnings. Why then do we observe firms paying generous cash dividends *and* issuing stock from time to time? Why don't they cut the dividend, reduce new issues, and thereby avoid paying underwriters, lawyers, and accountants? This is a question to which we will return in Chapter 16.

3. *Private placements for the small, risky, and unusual.* We do not mean that large, safe, and conventional firms should rule out private placements. Enormous amounts of capital are sometimes raised by this method. For example, AT&T once borrowed $500 million in a single private placement. But the special

---

[30] Of course debt with the same terms could be offered publicly but then 200 separate investigations would be required—a much more expensive proposition.

[31] However, many large companies use private placements too. Gregory Hawkins examined a sample of large firms listed in the 1977 *Moody's Industrial Manual.* Eighty percent of the firms that had made public debt issues had *also* borrowed privately. See G. D. Hawkins, op. cit., table II, p. 62.

advantages of private placement stem from avoiding registration expenses and a more direct relationship with the lender. These are not worth as much to blue-chip borrowers.

4. *Watch out for underpricing.* Underpricing is a hidden cost to the existing shareholders. Fortunately, it is usually serious only for companies who are selling stock to the public for the first time.

5. *New issues may depress the stock price.* The extent of this price pressure varies, but for industrial issues in the United States the fall in the value of the existing stock may amount to a significant proportion of the money raised. We think that the likely explanation for this pressure is the information the market reads into the company's decision to issue stock.

6. *Shelf registration often makes sense for debt issues by blue-chip firms.* Shelf registration reduces the time taken to arrange a new issue, it increases flexibility, and it may cut underwriting costs. It seems best suited for debt issues by large firms that are happy to switch between investment banks. It seems least suited for issues of unusually risky or complex securities or for issues by small companies who are likely to benefit from a close relationship with an investment bank.

APPENDIX A   THE PRIVILEGED SUBSCRIPTION OR RIGHTS ISSUE

In the United States most new issues of common stock are offered to investors at large. However, occasionally companies make a rights issue that is restricted to existing shareholders. In many other countries the rights issue is the most common or only method for issuing stock. In this appendix we look at how rights issues work and how much they cost.

Firms' articles of incorporation sometimes state that shareholders have a *preemptive right* to subscribe to new offerings. A strict interpretation of preemptive rights would place intolerable restrictions on management's freedom of action, and so it is not surprising that these rights have been interpreted in a limited way. First, they usually apply to issues of common stock, to convertible securities, and to voting preferred stock, but not to issues of debt. Second, they do not apply to issues of stock to employees, nor to stock which has been repurchased from shareholders and then held in the company treasury for subsequent resale. The last exemption will seem strange to those who believe that the life history of a particular share is an irrelevant bygone.

How Rights Issues Work

Here is an example of how rights issues work. In June 1977, American Electric Power Co. issued $198 million of common stock by a rights issue. The preliminary stages of the issue, including registration requirements, were the same as for any other public issue. The only difference lay in selling procedures. Shareholders were sent warrants showing that they owned one "right" for each share that they held. Eleven of these rights entitled a shareholder to buy one additional share at a subscription price of $22 at any time within 24 days of the offer date.[32]

Shareholders could sell, exercise, or throw away these rights. Those who didn't sell should have postponed any exercise decision until the end of the 24-day

---

[32] A rights issue that gives the shareholder one right for each share held is known as a "New York" right. In the United States, almost all issues are New York rights. But in some countries, such as the United Kingdom, you need one right to purchase one new share. This is known as a "Philadelphia right." If AEP were a company in the United Kingdom, the shareholder would need to own 11 shares in order to receive one right and this right would be correspondingly 11 times more valuable.

TABLE 15-6
Issue price in a rights offering does not affect the shareholder's wealth

	1 for 11 at $22	1 for 5½ at $11
Before issue		
Number of shares held	11	11
Share price (rights on)	$24.00	$24.00
Value of holding	$264.00	$264.00
After issue		
Number of new shares	1	2
Amount of new investment	$22.00	2 × $11 = $22
Total value of holding	$286.00	$286.00
Total number of shares	12	13
New share price (ex-rights)	$286/12 = $23.83	$286/13 = $22
Value of a right	$24 − 23.83 = $.17	$24 − 22 = $2

period. At that point, they should have taken advantage of the opportunity to buy stock at $22 if, and only if, the stock price was at least $22.

To guard against the danger that the price might end up below the subscription price, AEP arranged for the issue to be underwritten. Instead of actually buying the issue as in the cash offer, the underwriters were paid a *standby fee* of $900,000. In return, they stood ready to buy all unsubscribed shares at the subscription price less an additional *take-up fee* of $.287 per share purchased.[33] Most rights issues have standby underwriting, but occasionally companies save the underwriting fee by choosing a low subscription price and crossing their fingers that the market price won't fall below the subscription price.

As it turned out, AEP's stock price was $24⅜ at the end of the 24 days. Although this was above the $22 subscription price, holders of about 10 percent of the stock failed to exercise their rights. We must attribute this lapse to either ignorance or vacations.[34]

How a Rights Issue Affects the Stock Price

The left-hand portion of Table 15-6 shows the case of a stockholder who owned 11 shares of AEP stock just prior to the rights issue. The price of the stock at that time was about $24, and so this stockholder's total holding was worth $24 × 11, or $264. The AEP offer gave the opportunity to purchase one additional share for $22. Put yourself in the stockholder's shoes. If you buy the new share immediately, your holding increases to 12 shares and, other things being equal, the value of the 12 shares is $264 + $22 = $286. The price per share after the issue would no longer be $24, but $286/12 = $23.83.

---

[33] You can think of standby underwriting as providing shareholders with an option. In return for paying the standby fee, they can sell their stock to the underwriters at the issue price. We will tell you how to value such options in Chapter 20.

[34] Despite this shortfall, AEP did not have to turn to its underwriters. AEP's shareholders had been given an oversubscription privilege, which allowed them to buy unsubscribed shares at the subscription price ($22). As it turned out, AEP had no trouble selling the unsubscribed shares to shareholders who applied for extra shares. Of course, these shareholders profited at the expense of the vacationers and *incognoscenti*.

The only difference between the old $24 shares and the new $23.83 shares is that the former carried rights to subscribe to the issue. Therefore the old shares are generally termed *rights-on* shares and the new shares are termed *ex-rights* shares. The 17-cent difference in price between the two shares represents the price of one right. We can confirm that this is the correct price of the right by imagining a second investor who had no stock in AEP, but wishes to acquire some. One way to do this would be to buy 11 rights at 17 cents each and then exercise them at a further cost of $22. The total cost of this investor's share would be $11 \times \$.17 + \$22 = \$23.87$, which, save for rounding error, is the same outlay required to buy one of the new shares directly.

Inside the back cover of this book we have listed the formulas for calculating the value of a right and the corresponding ex-rights price.

Issue Price Is Irrelevant As Long As the Rights Are Exercised

It should be clear on reflection that AEP could have raised the same amount of money on a variety of terms. For example, instead of a 1-for-11 at $22, it could have made a 1-for-5½ at $11. In this case it would have sold twice as many shares at half the price. If we now work through the arithmetic again in the right-hand portion of Table 15-6, we can see that the issue price is irrelevant in a rights offering. After all, it cannot affect the real plant and equipment owned by the company or the proportion of these assets to which each shareholder is entitled. Therefore the only thing a firm ought to worry about in setting the terms of a rights issue is the possibility that the stock price will fall below the issue price. If that happens, shareholders will not take up their rights and the whole issue will be torpedoed. You can avoid this danger by arranging a standby agreement with the underwriter. But standby agreements tend to be expensive. It may be cheaper just to set the issue price low enough to foreclose the possibility of failure.

The Choice between the Cash Offer and the Rights Issue

You now know about the two principal forms of public issue—the cash offer to all investors and the rights issue to existing shareholders. The former method is used for almost all debt issues and unseasoned stock issues and many seasoned stock issues. Rights issues are largely restricted to seasoned stock issues.

One essential difference between the two methods is that in a rights offering the issue price is largely irrelevant. Shareholders can sell their new stock or their rights in a free market. Therefore, they can expect to receive a fair price. In a cash offer, however, the issue price may be important. If the company sells stock for less than the market would bear, the buyer has made a profit at the expense of existing shareholders. Although this danger creates a natural presumption in favor of the rights issue, it can be argued that underpricing is a serious problem only in the case of the unseasoned issue of stock in which a rights issue is not a feasible alternative.

In practice, most companies in the United States that have used rights issues in recent years have been regulated utilities. Some firms whose stockholders have enjoyed preemptive rights have cajoled their stockholders into giving them up. For example, consider the following appeal made in 1976 by Consolidated Edison to its stockholders:

> Expenses involved in a pre-emptive Common Stock rights offering are significantly greater than expenses involved in a direct offering of Common Stock to the public due to additional printing and mailing costs, expenses

associated with the handling of rights and the processing of subscriptions, higher underwriters' commissions and the longer time required for consummation of the financing. Thus, if the amendment is adopted, the Company will be able to obtain the amount of capital needed through the issuance of fewer shares. Over a period of time this will result in slightly less dilution, higher equity value per share, and better earnings per share.[35]

What are the major points in this argument?

1. *Higher expenses?* Take another look at Table 15-1. Rights issues seem no more expensive than general cash offers. AEP didn't think its offer was expensive.[36] Note also that underwriters' compensation is a major part of the costs of rights issues, and that rights issues don't have to be underwritten as long as the exercise price is set well below the stock price. *Nonunderwritten* rights issues might be significantly *cheaper* than general cash offers.[37]
2. *Longer time required?* Perhaps an extra month—rarely an important consideration.
3. *Fewer shares issued?* You should know the argument against that one by now.

In short, the arguments that firms make for avoiding rights issues don't make sense. We don't know why they use cash offers. Perhaps there are hidden reasons, but until they are uncovered we don't think you should rule out rights issues.

---

[35] We are indebted to Clifford Smith for finding the quotation from Consolidated Edison.

[36] "Some financial executives dismiss rights offerings as expensive and cumbersome. American Electric, according to Gerald P. Maloney, senior vice president for finance, has found them to be neither.

  'The underwriting costs on the utility's last offering totaled $1.1 million,' Mr. Maloney said in an interview the other day, 'only six-tenths of the total amount of money involved.'

  'We think that's very inexpensive,' he continued. He estimated that underwriting costs would have amounted to '3 or 4 percent' if the company had bypassed shareholders and gone directly to the public."

  From Richard Phalon, "Personal Investing—American Electric's Rights Offering," *The New York Times,* July 9, 1977, p. 15.

[37] Clifford Smith, who prepared Table 15-3, also calculated costs for a small sample of nonunderwritten rights issues, and found average issue costs of only 2.5 percent.

APPENDIX B   MARVIN'S NEW ISSUE PROSPECTUS[38]

PROSPECTUS

900,000 Shares
Marvin Enterprises Inc.
Common Stock ($.10 par value)

Of the 900,000 shares of Common Stock offered hereby, 500,000 shares are being sold by the Company and 400,000 shares are being sold by the Selling Stockholders. See "Principal and Selling Stockholders." The Company will not receive any of the proceeds from the sale of shares by the Selling Stockholders.

Before this offering there has been no public market for the Common Stock. **These securities involve a high degree of risk. See "Certain Considerations."**

THESE SECURITIES HAVE NOT BEEN APPROVED OR DISAPPROVED BY THE SECURITIES AND EXCHANGE COMMISSION NOR HAS THE COMMISSION PASSED ON THE ACCURACY OR ADEQUACY OF THIS PROSPECTUS. ANY REPRESENTATION TO THE CONTRARY IS A CRIMINAL OFFENSE.

	Price to Public	Underwriting Discount	Proceeds to Company (1)	Proceeds to Selling Stockholders (1)
Per share	$80.00	$5.00	$75.00	$75.00
Total (2)	$72,000,000	$4,500,000	$37,500,000	$30,000,000

(1) Before deducting expenses payable by the Company estimated at $820,000, of which $455,555 will be paid by the Company and $364,445 by the Selling Stockholders.
(2) The Company has granted to the Underwriters an option to purchase up to an additional 50,000 shares at the initial public offering price, less the underwriting discount, solely to cover over-allotment.

The Common Stock is offered subject to receipt and acceptance by the Underwriters, to prior sale, and to the Underwriters' right to reject any order in whole or in part and to withdraw, cancel, or modify the offer without notice.

Klein Merrick Inc.   **February 3, 2009**

---

[38] Most prospectuses have content similar to that of the Marvin prospectus but go into considerably more detail. Also we have omitted from the Marvin prospectus the list of underwriters and Marvin's financial statements.

Prospectus Summary

The following summary information is qualified in its entirety by the detailed information and financial statements appearing elsewhere in this Prospectus.

The Offering

Common Stock offered by the Company.......................... 500,000 shares
Common Stock offered by the Selling Stockholders .... 400,000 shares
Common Stock to be outstanding after this offering............. 4,100,000 shares

Use of Proceeds

For the construction of new manufacturing facilities and to provide working capital.

The Company

Marvin Enterprises Inc. designs, manufactures, and markets gargle blasters for domestic use. Its manufacturing facilities employ integrated microcircuits to control the genetic engineering processes used to manufacture gargle blasters.

The Company was organized in Delaware in 2003.

Use of Proceeds

The net proceeds of this offering are expected to be $37,044,445. Of the net proceeds, approximately $27.0 million will be used to finance expansion of the Company's principal manufacturing facilities. The balance will be used for working capital.

Certain Considerations

Investment in the Common Stock involves a high degree of risk. The following factors should be carefully considered in evaluating the Company:

Substantial Capital Needs   The Company will require additional financing to continue its expansion policy. The Company believes that its relations with its lenders are good, but there can be no assurance that additional financing will be available in the future.

Licensing   The expanded manufacturing facilities are to be used for the production of a new imploding gargle blaster. An advisory panel to the U.S. Food and Drug Administration (FDA) has recommended approval of this product for the U.S. market but no decision has yet been reached by the full FDA committee.

Dividend Policy

The company has not paid cash dividends on its Common Stock and does not anticipate that dividends will be paid on the Common Stock in the foreseeable future.

Management

The following table sets forth information regarding the Company's directors, executive officers, and key employees.

Name	Age	Position
George Marvin	32	President, Chief Executive Officer, & Director
Mildred Marvin	28	Treasurer & Director
Chip Norton	30	General Manager

George Marvin—George Marvin established the Company in 2003 and has been its Chief Executive Officer since that date. He is a past president of the Institute of Gargle Blasters.

Mildred Marvin—Mildred Marvin has been employed by the Company since 2003.

Chip Norton—Mr. Norton has been General Manager of the Company since 2003. He is a former vice president of Amalgamated Blasters, Inc.

Executive Compensation

The following table sets forth the cash compensation paid for services rendered for the year 2008 by the Executive officers:

Name	Capacity	Cash Compensation
George Marvin	President and Chief Executive Officer	$200,000
Mildred Marvin	Treasurer	$120,000
Chip Norton	General Manager	$120,000

Certain Transactions

At various times between 2005 and 2007 First Meriam Venture Partners invested a total of $8.5 million in the Company. In connection with this investment, First Meriam Venture Partners was granted certain rights to registration under the Securities Act of 1933, including the right to have their shares of Common Stock registered at the Company's expense with the Securities and Exchange Commission.

Principal and Selling Stockholders

The following table sets forth certain information regarding the beneficial ownership of the Company's voting Common Stock as of the date of this prospectus by (i) each person known by the Company to be the beneficial owner of more than 5% of its voting Common Stock, and (ii) each director of the Company who beneficially owns voting Common Stock. Unless otherwise indicated, each owner has sole voting and dispositive power over his shares.

| | COMMON STOCK | | | | |
| Name of Beneficial Owner | SHARES BENEFICIALLY OWNED PRIOR TO OFFERING | | Shares to Be Sold | SHARES BENEFICIALLY OWNED AFTER OFFER (1) | |
	Number	Percent		Number	Percent
George Marvin	337,500	9.4	60,000	277,500	6.8
Mildred Marvin	337,500	9.4	60,000	277,500	6.8
Chip Norton	250,000	6.9	80,000	170,000	4.1
First Meriam Venture Partners	1,700,000	47.2	—	1,700,000	41.5
TFS Investors	260,000	7.2	—	260,000	6.3
Centri-Venture Partnership	260,000	7.2	—	260,000	6.3
Henry Pobble	180,000	5.0	—	180,000	4.4
Georgina Sloberg	200,000	5.6	200,000	—	—

(1) Assuming no exercise of the Underwriters' over-allotment option.

Description of Capital Stock

The Company's authorized capital stock consists of 10,000,000 shares of voting Common Stock.

As of the date of this Prospectus, there are 10 holders of record of the Common Stock.

Under the terms of one of the Company's loan agreements, the Company may not pay cash dividends on Common Stock except from net profits without the written consent of the lender.

Underwriting

Subject to the terms and conditions set forth in the Underwriting Agreement, the Company has agreed to sell to each of the Underwriters named below, and each of the Underwriters, for whom Klein Merrick Inc. are acting as Representatives, has severally agreed to purchase from the Company, the number of shares set forth opposite its name below.

Underwriters   **Number of Shares to Be Purchased**

[Table of underwriters omitted.]

In the Underwriting Agreement, the several Underwriters have agreed, subject to the terms and conditions set forth therein, to purchase all shares offered hereby if any such shares are purchased. In the event of a default by any Underwriter, the Underwriting Agreement provides that, in certain circumstances, purchase commitments of the nondefaulting Underwriters may be increased or the Underwriting Agreement may be terminated.

There is no public market for the Common Stock. The price to the public for the Common Stock was determined by negotiation between the Company and the Underwriters and was based on, among other things, the Company's financial and operating history and condition, its prospects and the prospects for its industry in general, the management of the Company, and the market prices of securities for companies in businesses similar to that of the Company.

Legal Matters

The validity of the shares of Common Stock offered by the Prospectus is being passed on for the Company by Thatcher, Kohl, and Lubbers and for the Underwriters by Hawke and Mulroney.

Experts

The consolidated financial statements of the Company have been so included in reliance on the reports of Hooper Firebrand, independent accountants, given on the authority of that firm as experts in auditing and accounting.

Financial Statements

[Text and tables omitted.]

FURTHER READING

Two useful works on investment banking are:

I. Friend et al., *Investment Banking and the New Issues Market*, The World Publishing Company, Cleveland, 1967.

C. W. Smith, "Investment Banking and the Capital Acquisition Process," *Journal of Financial Economics*, **15:** 3–29 (January–February 1986).

The best sources of material on venture capital are the specialized journals. See, for example, recent issues of Venture Capital Journal.

There has been a number of studies of the market for unseasoned issues of common stock. Two good articles to start with are:

K. Rock, "Why New Issues Are Underpriced," *Journal of Financial Economics*, **15:** 187–212 (January–February 1986).

J. R. Ritter, "The 'Hot Issue' Market of 1980," *Journal of Business*, **57:** 215–240 (1984).

The first two articles both find a significant and permanent fall in price after an industrial stock issue in the United States. The Marsh paper, using data from the United Kingdom, finds only a negligible fall in price:

P. Asquith and D. W. Mullins, "Equity Issues and Offering Dilution," *Journal of Financial Economics*, **15:** 61–90 (January–February 1986).

R. W. Masulis and A. N. Korwar, "Seasoned Equity Offerings: An Empirical Investigation," *Journal of Financial Economics*, **15:** 91–118 (January–February 1986).

P. R. Marsh, "Equity Rights Issues and the Efficiency of the UK Stock Market," *Journal of Finance*, **34:** 839–862 (September 1979).

Smith, in the following article, argues that the cheapest way to issue stock is to offer it by a rights issue to existing stockholders. Hansen and Pinkerton disagree:

C. W. Smith, "Alternative Methods for Raising Capital: Rights versus Underwritten Offerings," *Journal of Financial Economics* **5**: 273–307 (December 1977).

R. S. Hansen and J. M. Pinkerton, "Direct Equity Financing: A Resolution of a Paradox," *Journal of Finance* **37**: 651–666 (June 1982).

A good analysis of the relative merits of negotiated underwriting and competitive bidding is given in:

S. Bhagat and P. A. Frost, "Issuing Costs to Existing Shareholders in Competitive and Negotiated Underwritten Public Utility Equity Offerings," *Journal of Financial Economics*, **15**: 213–232 (January–February 1986).

The following collection contains several articles on the issue of international securities:

A. M. George and I. H. Giddy (eds.), *International Finance Handbook*, Volume 1, John Wiley & Sons, New York, 1983.

For an analysis of the role of private placements see:

E. Shapiro and C. R. Wolf, *The Role of Private Placements in Corporate Finance*, Division of Research, Graduate School of Business Administration, Harvard University, Boston, 1972.

QUIZ

1. Beside each of the following issue methods we have listed two issues. Choose the one most likely to employ that method.
   (*a*) Rights issue (issue of seasoned stock/issue of unseasoned stock)
   (*b*) Competitive general cash offer (bond issue by industrial company/bond issue by utility holding company)
   (*c*) Private placement (issue of seasoned stock/bond issue by industrial company)
   (*d*) Shelf registration (issue of unseasoned stock/bond issue by a large industrial company)

2. Each of the following terms is associated with one of the events beneath. Can you match them up?
   (*a*) Company registrar
   (*b*) Best efforts
   (*c*) Tombstone
   (*d*) Red herring
   (*e*) Shelf registration
   (*f*) Letter stock
   (A) The company issues a preliminary prospectus.
   (B) Some issues are privately placed and exempted from registration.
   (C) An advertisement is published in the financial press listing members of the underwriting syndicate.
   (D) A trust company is appointed to ensure that no unauthorized shares are issued.
   (E) The underwriter accepts responsibility only to *try* to sell the issue.
   (F) Several tranches of the same security may be sold under the same registration.

3. State for each of the following pairs of issues which you would expect to involve the lower proportionate underwriting and administrative costs, other things equal:
   (*a*) A large issue/a small issue
   (*b*) A bond issue/a common stock issue
   (*c*) A large negotiated bond issue/a large competitive bond issue
   (*d*) A small private placement of bonds/a small general cash offer of bonds

4. Look back at Marvin's initial public offering:
   (*a*) If there is unexpectedly heavy demand for the issue, how many extra shares can the underwriters buy?
   (*b*) How many shares are to be sold in the primary offering? How many will be sold in the secondary offering?
   (*c*) What with the benefit of hindsight was the degree of underpricing? How does that compare with the average degree of underpricing found by Ritter?
   (*d*) There are three kinds of cost to Marvin's new issue—underwriting expense, administrative costs, and underpricing. What was the *total* dollar cost of the Marvin issue?

5. You need to choose between issuing
   (*a*) *A public issue of $10 million face value of 10-year debt.* The interest rate on the debt would be 8.5 percent and the debt would be issued at face value. The underwriting spread would be 1.5 percent and other expenses would be $80,000.
   (*b*) *A private placement of $10 million face value of 10-year debt.* The interest rate on the private placement would be 9 percent but the total issuing expenses would be only $30,000.
   (A) What is the difference in the proceeds to the company net of expenses?
   (B) Other things equal, which is the better deal?
   (C) What other factors beyond the interest rate and issue costs would you wish to consider before deciding between the two offers?

6. Associated Breweries is planning to market unleaded beer. To finance the venture it proposes to make a rights issue at $10 of 1 new share for each 2 shares held. (The company currently has outstanding 100,000 shares priced at $40 a share.) Assuming that the new money is invested to earn a fair return, give values for the following:
   (*a*) Number of rights needed to purchase one share
   (*b*) Number of of new shares
   (*c*) Amount of new investment
   (*d*) Total value of company after issue
   (*e*) Total number of shares after issue
   (*f*) Rights-on price
   (*g*) Ex-rights price
   (*h*) Price of a right

QUESTIONS AND PROBLEMS

1. In some countries initial public offerings of common stock are sold by auction. Another procedure is for the underwriter to advertise the issue publicly and invite orders for shares at the issue price. If the applications exceed the number of shares on offer, then they are scaled down in proportion; if there are too few applications, any unsold shares are left with the underwriters. Compare these procedures with the initial public offering in the United States. Can you think of any better ways to sell new shares?

2. (*a*) Why do venture capital companies prefer to advance money in stages? If you were the management of Marvin Enterprises, would you have been happy with such an arrangement? With the benefit of hindsight did First Meriam gain or lose by advancing money in stages?
   (*b*) The price at which First Meriam would advance more money to Marvin was not fixed in advance. But Marvin could have given First Meriam an *option* to buy more shares at a preset price. Would this have been better?

(c) At the second stage Marvin could have raised money from another venture capital company in preference to First Meriam. To protect themselves against this, venture capital firms sometimes demand first refusal on new capital issues. Would you recommend this arrangement?

3. "For small issues of common stock, the costs of flotation amount to about 15 percent of the proceeds. This means that the opportunity cost of external equity capital is about 15 percentage points higher than that of retained earnings." Does this follow?

4. Do you think that there could be a shortage of finance for new ventures? Should the government help to provide such finance and, if so, how?

5. Get hold of a copy of the prospectus for a recent issue of securities. How do the issue costs compare with (a) those of the Marvin issue, (b) those shown in Tables 15-1 and 15-2? Can you suggest reasons for the difference?

6. In 1988 Pandora, Inc. makes a rights issue at $5 a share of one new share for every four shares held. Before the issue there were 10 million shares outstanding and the share price was $6.
   (a) What is the total amount of new money raised?
   (b) How many rights are needed to buy one new share?
   (c) What is the value of one right?
   (d) What is the prospective ex-rights price?
   (e) How far could the total value of the company fall before shareholders would be unwilling to take up their rights?

7. Problem 6 contains details of a rights offering by Pandora. Suppose that the company had decided to issue new stock at $4. How many new shares would it have needed to raise the same sum of money? Recalculate the answers to questions (b) to (e) in problem 6. Show that Pandora's shareholders are just as well off if it issues the shares at $4 a share rather than the $5 assumed in problem 6.

8. Construct a simple numerical example to show the following:
   (a) Existing shareholders are made worse off when a company makes a cash offer of new stock below the market price.
   (b) Existing shareholders are *not* made worse off when a company makes a rights issue of new stock below the market price even if the stockholders do not wish to take up their rights.

*9. There are three reasons that a common stock issue might cause a fall in price—(a) demand for the company's stock is inelastic, (b) the issue causes price pressure until it has been digested, and (c) management has information that stockholders do not have. Explain these reasons more fully. Which do you find most plausible? Is there any way that you could seek to test whether you are right?

10. (a) "A signal is credible only if a false signal is costly." Explain why management's willingness to invest in Marvin's equity rather than its debt was a credible signal. Was their willingness to accept only a part of the venture capital that would eventually be needed also a credible signal?
    (b) "When managers take their reward in the form of increased leisure or executive jets, the cost is borne by the shareholders." Explain how First Meriam's financing package avoided this problem.

PART FIVE

DIVIDEND POLICY AND CAPITAL STRUCTURE

16 The Dividend Controversy

In this chapter we explain how companies set their dividend payments and we discuss the controversial question of how dividend policy affects value.

Why should you care about the answer to this question? Of course, if you are responsible for deciding on your company's dividend payment, you will want to know how it affects value. But there is a more general reason than that. We have up to this point assumed that the company's investment decision is independent of its financing policy. In that case a good project is a good project is a good project, no matter who undertakes it or how it is ultimately financed. If dividend policy does not affect value, that is still true. But perhaps it *does* affect value. In that case the attractiveness of a new project may depend on where the money is coming from. For example, if investors prefer companies with high payouts, companies might be reluctant to take on investments financed by retained earnings.

The first step toward understanding dividend policy is to recognize that the phrase means different things to different people. Therefore we must start by defining what *we* mean by it.

A firm's decisions about dividends are often mixed up with other financing and investment decisions. Some firms pay low dividends because management is optimistic about the firm's future and wishes to retain earnings for expansion. In this case the dividend is a by-product of the firm's capital budgeting decision. Suppose, however, that the future opportunities evaporate, that a dividend increase is announced, and that the stock price falls. How do we separate the impact of the dividend increase from the impact of investors' disappointment at the lost growth opportunities?

Another firm might finance capital expenditures largely by borrowing. This releases cash for dividends. In this case the firm's dividend is a by-product of the borrowing decision.

We must isolate dividend policy from other problems of financial management. The precise question we should ask is: "What is the effect of a change in cash dividends paid, *given the firm's capital budgeting and borrowing decisions*?" Of course the cash used to finance a dividend increase has to come from somewhere. If we fix the firm's investment outlays and borrowing, there is only one possible source—an issue of stock. Thus we define *dividend policy* as the trade-off between retaining earnings on the one hand and paying out cash and issuing new shares on the other.

This trade-off may seem artificial at first, for we do not observe firms scheduling a stock issue with every dividend payment. But there are many firms that pay dividends and also issue stock from time to time. They could avoid the stock issues by paying lower dividends. Many other firms restrict dividends so that they *do not* have to issue shares. They could issue stock occasionally and increase the dividend. Both groups of firms are facing the dividend policy trade-off.

16-1 HOW DIVIDENDS ARE PAID

The dividend is set by the firm's board of directors. The announcement states that the payment will be made to all those stockholders who are registered on a particular "record date." Then about 2 weeks later dividend checks are mailed to stockholders.

Shares are normally bought and sold "with dividend" until a few days before the record date. But investors who buy with dividend do not have to worry if their shares are not registered in time. The dividend must be paid over to them by the seller. Similarly, investors who buy a share "ex dividend" are obliged to return the dividend if they receive it.

Some Legal Limitations on Dividends

Suppose that an unscrupulous board decided to sell all the firm's assets and distribute the money as dividends. That would not leave anything in the kitty to pay the company's debts. Therefore, bondholders often guard against this danger by placing a limit on dividend payments.

State law also helps to protect the company's creditors against excessive dividend payments. Most states prohibit a company from paying dividends if doing so would make the company insolvent.[1] In addition state law distinguishes between a company's "legal" (or "stated") capital and "surplus." Legal capital generally consists of the par value of all outstanding shares; where there is no par value, it consists of part or all the receipts from the issue of shares. Surplus is what remains after legal capital is subtracted from book net worth. Companies are allowed to pay a dividend out of surplus but they may not distribute legal capital.[2]

Par value and legal capital rarely have much economic significance. Par value is often arbitrarily set at $1 per share. The laws restricting payment of legal capital probably serve a purpose, however. They give most corporations a large degree of flexibility in deciding what to pay out, but they help prevent unscrupulous firms from escaping their creditors.

Dividends Come in Many Forms

Most dividends are paid in the form of cash. *Regular cash dividends* are usually paid quarterly, but a few companies declare them monthly, semiannually, or annually.[3] The term *regular* merely indicates that the company expects that it will be able to maintain the payment in the future. If the company does not want to give that kind of assurance, it usually declares both a regular and an *extra dividend.* Investors understand that the extra dividend may not be repeated. Finally, the term *special dividend* tends to be reserved specifically for payments that are unlikely to be repeated.

---

[1] The statutes define insolvency in different ways. In some cases, it just means an inability to meet immediate obligations; in other cases, it means a deficiency of assets compared with all outstanding fixed liabilities.

[2] Companies with wasting assets, such as mining companies, may be an exception to this rule. They may be allowed to distribute legal capital to the extent of the depletion. Also, in some states companies may distribute current profits even though previous losses may have impaired legal capital.

[3] Many companies have automatic dividend reinvestment plans. The usual procedure is for the corporation to send the dividends of the participating stockholders directly to the trust department of a bank, which then purchases stock on behalf of shareholders in the open market. However, some firms issue new shares directly to stockholders who wish to reinvest dividends. Often the new shares are issued at a 5 percent discount from market price; the firm offers this sweetener because it saves the underwriting costs of a regular share issue. Sometimes 10 percent or more of total dividends will be reinvested under such plans.

Paying a dividend reduces the amount of retained earnings shown on the firm's balance sheet. However, if all retained earnings are "used up," and if funds are not needed for the protection of creditors, the company may be permitted to pay a *liquidating dividend*. Because such payments are regarded as a return of capital, they are not taxed as income.

Dividends are not always in the form of cash. Frequently companies declare *stock dividends*. For example, General Tire has paid a yearly stock dividend of 2 percent for more than a decade. That means it sends each shareholder two extra shares for every 100 shares that he or she currently owns. You can see that a stock dividend is very much like a stock split. Both increase the number of shares, and both reduce value per share, other things equal. Neither makes anybody better off. The distinction between the two is a technical one. A stock dividend is shown in the accounts as a transfer from retained earnings to equity capital, whereas a split is shown as a reduction in the par value of each share.

There are also other types of noncash dividends. For example, companies sometimes send shareholders a sample of their product. The British company Dominion International (formerly Dundee Crematorium) offers its more substantial shareholders a discount cremation. Needless to say, you are not *required* to receive this dividend.

Share Repurchase

When a firm wants to pay cash to its shareholders, it usually declares a cash dividend. But an alternative and increasingly popular method is to repurchase its own stock. In the period 1973–1974 the government imposed a limit on dividends but it forgot to impose a limit on share repurchase. Many firms discovered share repurchase for the first time and the total value of repurchases swelled to about a fifth of the value of dividend payments. IBM was one of the firms to repurchase its stock in 1977. As IBM's rapid expansion of the 1960s slowed down, the company found itself with more cash than it needed. Therefore in 1977 IBM gave back $1.4 billion to its stockholders by repurchasing shares.

In the 1980s, repurchases seemed almost an everyday event. For example, Ford Motor Company repurchased roughly 30 million shares for about $1.2 billion. Ralston Purina repurchased more than 40 percent of its shares. From 1984 to 1986, Merck & Company repurchased 13 million shares for $907 million. Its cash dividends for that period were only $738 million.

The biggest and most dramatic repurchases came in the oil industry, where cash resources generally outran good capital investment opportunities. Exxon is in first place, having spent more than $7 billion on shares repurchased through year-end 1986.

There are three principal methods of repurchase: (1) Many repurchased shares are acquired in the open market. This activity is regulated by the SEC, which requires that the purchases cannot coincide with issues of stock or private negotiations to buy stock. The SEC also sets guidelines for how the repurchases are carried out: For example, repurchases cannot exceed a stated proportion of trading in the company's stock. (2) The second method is by a general tender offer either to all shareholders or just to small shareholders.[4] In this case the firm usually engages an investment banker to manage the tender and pays a special commission to brokers who persuade shareholders to accept the offer. (3) Finally, repurchase may take place by direct negotiation with a major shareholder. The most notorious

---

[4] The costs of printing and mailing annual reports, dividend checks, etc., are the same for small stockholders as for large ones. Firms often try to reduce these costs by buying out small holdings.

instances are *greenmail* transactions, in which the target of a takeover attempt buys off the hostile bidder. Bidders accumulate shares in the target company in the course of the takeover battle. "Greenmail" means that these shares are repurchased by the target at a price which makes the bidder happy to agree to leave the target alone. This price does not always make the target's *shareholders* happy, as we point out in Chapter 33.

Reacquired shares are seldom deregistered and canceled. Instead they are kept in the company's treasury and then resold when the company needs money. Stockholders are not required to authorize these resales of treasury stock and they do not enjoy preemptive rights on such stock.

Stockholders who sell shares back to their firm pay tax only on capital gains realized in the sale, although the Internal Revenue Service has attempted to prevent firms from disguising dividends as repurchases; for example, proportional or regular repurchases are liable to be treated as dividend payments. The U.S. tax authorities should be less concerned with this distinction now that dividends and capital gains are taxed at the same rate.[5]

16-2 HOW DO COMPANIES DECIDE ON DIVIDEND PAYMENTS?

Lintner's Model

In the mid-1950s John Lintner conducted a classic series of interviews with corporate managers about their dividend policies.[6] His description of how dividends are determined can be summarized in four "stylized facts":[7]

1. Firms have long-run target dividend payout ratios.
2. Managers focus more on dividend changes than on absolute levels. Thus, paying a $2.00 dividend is an important financial decision if last year's dividend was $1.00, but no big deal if last year's dividend was $2.00.
3. Dividend changes follow <u>shifts</u> in long-run, sustainable earnings. Managers "smooth" dividends. Transitory earnings changes are unlikely to affect dividend payouts.
4. Managers are reluctant to make dividend changes that might have to be reversed. They are particularly worried about having to rescind a dividend increase.

Lintner developed a simple model which is consistent with these facts and explains dividend payments well. Here it is: Suppose that a firm always stuck to its target payout ratio. Then the dividend payment in the coming year (DIV_1) would equal a constant proportion of earnings per share (EPS_1):

$$DIV_1 = \text{target dividend}$$
$$= \text{target ratio} \times EPS_1$$

The dividend *change* would equal

$$DIV_1 - DIV_0 = \text{target change}$$
$$= \text{target ratio} \times EPS_1 - DIV_0$$

---

[5] We discuss tax issues further in Section 16-5.

[6] J. Lintner, "Distribution of Incomes of Corporations among Dividends, Retained Earnings, and Taxes," *American Economic Review,* **46:** 97–113 (May 1956).

[7] The stylized facts are given by Terry A. Marsh and Robert C. Merton, "Dividend Behavior for the Aggregate Stock Market," *Journal of Business* **60:** 1–40 (January 1987). See pp. 5–6. We have paraphrased and embellished.

A firm that always stuck to its payout ratio would have to change its dividend whenever earnings changed. But the managers in Lintner's survey were reluctant to do this. They believed that shareholders prefer a steady progression in dividends. Therefore even if circumstances appeared to warrant a large increase in their company's dividend, they would move only partway toward their target payment. Their dividend changes therefore seemed to conform to the following model:

$$DIV_1 - DIV_0 = \text{adjustment rate} \times \text{target change}$$

$$= \text{adjustment rate} \times (\text{target ratio} \times EPS_1 - DIV_0)$$

The more conservative the company, the more slowly it would move toward its target and, therefore, the *lower* would be its adjustment rate.

Lintner's simple model suggests that the dividend depends in part on the firm's current earnings and in part on the dividend for the previous year, which in turn depends on that year's earnings and the dividend in the year before. Therefore if Lintner is correct, we should be able to describe dividends in terms of a weighted average of current and past earnings.[8] The probability of an increase in the dividend rate should be greatest when *current* earnings have increased; it should be somewhat less when only the earnings from the previous year have increased and so on. An extensive study by Fama and Babiak confirmed this hypothesis.[9]

The Information Content of Dividends

We have suggested above that the dividend payment depends on both last year's dividend and this year's earnings. This simple model seems to provide a fairly good explanation of how companies decide on the dividend rate, but it is unlikely to be the whole story. For example, we would also expect managers to take future prospects into account when setting the payment. And that is what we find. When companies pay dividends lower than our simple model suggests, earnings on the average subsequently decline. When they pay dividends higher than the model suggests, earnings on the average subsequently rise by an abnormal amount.[10] Since dividends anticipate future earnings, it's no surprise to find that announcements of dividend increases are usually taken as good news (stock price typically

---

[8] This can be demonstrated as follows: Dividends per share in time t are

$$DIV_t = aT(EPS_t) + (1 - a)DIV_{t-1} \qquad (1)$$

where a is the adjustment rate and T the target payout ratio. But the same relationship holds in $t - 1$:

$$DIV_{t-1} = aT(EPS_{t-1}) + (1 - a)DIV_{t-2} \qquad (2)$$

Substitute for DIV_{t-1} in (1):

$$DIV_t = aT(EPS_t) + aT(1 - a)(EPS_{t-1}) + (1 - a)^2 DIV_{t-2}$$

We can make similar substitutions for DIV_{t-2}, DIV_{t-3}, etc., thereby obtaining

$$DIV_t = aT(EPS_t) + aT(1 - a)(EPS_{t-1}) + aT(1 - a)^2(EPS_{t-2}) + \cdots + aT(1 - a)^n(EPS_{t-n})$$

[9] E. F. Fama and H. Babiak, "Dividend Policy: An Empirical Analysis," *Journal of the American Statistical Association,* **63:** 1132–1161 (December 1968), p. 1134.

[10] See, for example, R. Watts, "The Information Content of Dividends," *Journal of Business,* **46:** 191–211 (April 1973), for an analysis of information effects in the United States.

rises), and that dividend cuts are bad news (stock price typically falls).[11] But the stock price changes don't prove that investors like higher dividends for their own sake. A dividend increase may be important only as a sign of higher earnings.

Do you remember from Chapter 13 that stock splits lead to stock price increases? That is not because splits create value, but because they signal future prosperity, specifically increased dividends. Now we see that dividend increases in turn may be important mostly as signals of future earnings. (Finally, we could say that *earnings* are important because they tell investors something about the *true* measures of corporate prosperity: cash flow and the extent of positive-NPV capital investment opportunities.)

Market efficiency means that all information available to investors is quickly and accurately impounded in stock prices. It does not imply that fundamental information about a company's operations or prospects is always cheaply or easily obtained. Investors therefore seize on any clue. That is why stock prices respond to stock splits, dividend changes, and other actions or announcements which reveal managements' optimism or pessimism about their firms' futures.

16-3 CONTROVERSY ABOUT DIVIDEND POLICY

Now we turn to the controversial question of how dividend policy affects value. One endearing feature of economics is that it can always accommodate not just two, but three opposing points of view. And so it is with the controversy about dividend policy. On the right there is a conservative group which believes that an increase in dividend payout increases firm value. On the left, there is a radical group which believes that an increase in payout reduces value. And in the center there is a middle-of-the-road party which claims that dividend policy makes no difference.

The middle-of-the-road party was founded in 1961 by Miller and Modigliani (always referred to as *MM* or *M* and *M*), when they published a theoretical paper showing the irrelevance of dividend policy in a world without taxes, transaction costs, or other market imperfections.[12] By the standards of 1961 MM were leftist radicals, because at that time most people believed that even under idealized assumptions increased dividends made shareholders better off.[13] But now MM's proof is generally accepted as correct, and the argument has shifted to whether

---

[11] For example, Paul Asquith and David W. Mullins, who examined firms that paid cash dividends for the first time (or the first time in at least 10 years), found that stock price rose by 3.7 percent on average at the announcement. See "The Impact of Initiating Dividend Payments on Shareholders' Wealth," *Journal of Business,* **56:** 77–96 (January 1983).

Terry E. Dielman and Henry R. Oppenheimer examined a sample of firms that cut or omitted dividends. For firms that cut dividends by more than 25 percent, stock price fell by 7.7 percent on average. Stock price fell by 8.1 percent on average when dividends were omitted altogether. See "An Examination of Investor Behavior During Periods of Large Dividend Changes," *Journal of Financial and Quantitative Analysis,* **19:** 208 (June 1984), table 2.

Stock price changes in both studies were corrected for market movements by the methods explained in Chapter 13, Section 13-5. Dielman and Oppenheimer also tried more elaborate statistical procedures with essentially consistent results.

[12] M. H. Miller and F. Modigliani: "Dividend Policy, Growth and the Valuation of Shares," *Journal of Business,* **34:** 411–433 (October 1961).

[13] Not *everybody* believed dividends make shareholders better off. MM's arguments were anticipated in 1938 in J. B. Williams, *The Theory of Investment Value,* Harvard University Press, Cambridge, Mass., 1938. Also, a proof very similar to MM's was developed by J. Lintner in "Dividends, Earnings, Leverage, Stock Prices and the Supply of Capital to Corporations," *Review of Economics and Statistics,* **44:** 243–269 (August 1962).

taxes or other market imperfections alter the situation. In the process MM have been pushed toward the center by a new leftist party which argues for *low* dividends. The leftists' position is based on MM's argument modified to take account of taxes and costs of issuing securities. The conservatives are still with us, relying on essentially the same arguments as in 1961.

We begin our discussion of dividend policy with a presentation of MM's original argument. Then we will undertake a critical appraisal of the positions of the three parties. Perhaps we should warn you before we start that our own position has traditionally been marginally leftist. But now, after the 1986 Tax Reform Act, we have joined the middle-of-the-roaders.

Dividend Policy Is Irrelevant in Perfect Capital Markets

In their classic 1961 article MM argued as follows: Suppose your firm has settled on its investment program. You have worked out how much of this program can be financed from borrowing, and you plan to meet the remaining funds requirement from retained earnings. Any surplus money is to be paid out as dividends.

Now think what happens if you want to increase the dividend payment without changing the investment and borrowing policy. The extra money must come from somewhere. If the firm fixes its borrowing, the only way it can finance the extra dividend is to print some more shares and sell them. The new stockholders are going to part with their money only if you can offer them shares that are worth as much as they cost. But how can the firm do this when its assets, earnings, investment opportunities and, therefore, market value are all unchanged? The answer is that there must be a *transfer of value* from the old to the new stockholders. The new ones get the newly printed shares, each one worth less than before the dividend change was announced, and the old ones suffer a capital loss on their shares. The capital loss borne by the old shareholders just offsets the extra cash dividend they receive.

Figure 16-1 shows how this transfer of value occurs. Our hypothetical company pays out a third of its total value as a dividend and it raises the money to do so by selling new shares. The capital loss suffered by the old stockholders is represented by the reduction in the size of the shaded boxes. But that capital loss is

FIGURE 16-1
This firm pays out a third of its worth as a dividend and raises the money by selling new shares. The transfer of value to the new stockholders is equal to the dividend payment. The total value of the firm is unaffected.

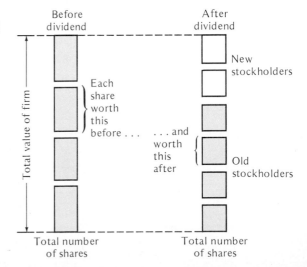

exactly offset by the fact that the new money raised (the white boxes) is paid over to them as dividends.

Does it make any difference to the old stockholders that they receive an extra dividend payment plus an offsetting capital loss? It might if that were the only way they could get their hands on cash. But as long as there are efficient capital markets, they can raise the cash by selling shares. Thus the old shareholders can "cash in" either by persuading the management to pay a higher dividend or by selling some of their shares. In either case there will be a transfer of value from old to new shareholders. The only difference is that in the former case this transfer is caused by a dilution in the value of each of the firm's shares, and in the latter case it is caused by a reduction in the number of shares held by the old shareholders. The two alternatives are compared in Figure 16-2.

Because investors do not need dividends to get their hands on cash, they will not pay higher prices for the shares of firms with high payouts. Therefore firms ought not to worry about dividend policy. They should let dividends fluctuate as a by-product of their investment and financing decisions.

Dividend Irrelevance—An Illustration

Consider the case of Rational Demiconductor, which at this moment has the following balance sheet:

Rational Demiconductor's Balance Sheet (Market Values)

Cash ($1,000 held for investment)	$1,000	$0	Debt
Fixed assets	$9,000	$10,000 + NPV	Equity
Investment opportunity ($1,000 investment required)	NPV		
Total asset value	$10,000 + NPV	$10,000 + NPV	Value of firm

Rational Demiconductor has $1000 cash earmarked for a project requiring $1000 investment. We do not know how attractive the project is, and so we enter it at NPV; after the project is undertaken it will be worth $1000 + NPV. Note that the balance sheet is constructed with market values; equity equals the market value of the firm's outstanding shares (price per share times number of shares outstanding). It is not necessarily equal to book net worth.

Now Rational Demiconductor uses the cash to pay a $1000 dividend to its stockholders. The benefit to them is obvious: $1000 of spendable cash. It is also obvious that there must be a cost. The cash is not free.

Where does the money for the dividend come from? Of course, the immediate source of funds is Rational Demiconductor's cash account. But this cash was ear-

FIGURE 16-2
Two ways of raising cash for the firm's original shareholders. In each case the cash received is offset by a decline in the value of the old stockholders' claim on the firm. If the firm pays a dividend, each share is worth less because more shares have to be issued against the firm's assets. If the old stockholders sell some of their shares, each share is worth the same but the old stockholders have fewer shares.

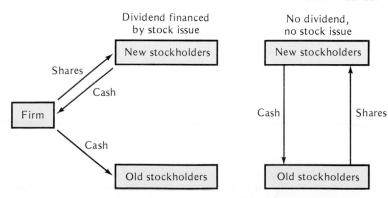

marked for the investment project. Since we want to isolate the effects of dividend policy on shareholders' wealth, we assume that the company *continues* with the investment project. That means that $1000 cash must be raised by new financing. This could consist of an issue of either debt or stock. Again, we just want to look at dividend policy for now, and we defer discussion of the debt-equity choice until Chapters 17 and 18. Thus Rational Demiconductor ends up financing the dividend with a $1000 stock issue.

Now we examine the balance sheet after the dividend is paid, the new stock sold, and the investment undertaken. Because Rational Demiconductor's investment and borrowing policies are unaffected by the dividend payment, its *overall* market value must be unchanged at $10,000 + NPV.[14] We know also that if the new stockholders pay a fair price, their stock is worth $1000. That leaves us with only one missing number—the value of the stock held by the original stockholders. It is easy to see that this must be

$$\text{Value of original stockholders' shares} = \text{value of company} - \text{value of new shares}$$
$$= (10,000 + \text{NPV}) - 1000$$
$$= \$9000 + \text{NPV}$$

The old shareholders have received a $1000 cash dividend and incurred a $1000 capital loss. Dividend policy doesn't matter.

By paying out $1000 with one hand and taking it back with the other, Rational Demiconductor is recycling cash. To suggest that this makes shareholders better off is like advising a cook to cool the kitchen by leaving the refrigerator door open.

Of course, our proof ignores taxes, issue costs, and a variety of other complications. We will turn to those items in a moment. The really crucial assumption in our proof is that the new shares are sold at a fair price. The shares sold to raise $1000 must actually be *worth* $1000.[15] In other words, we have assumed efficient capital markets.

Calculating Share Price

We have assumed that Rational Demiconductor's new shares can be sold at a fair price, but what is that price and how many new shares are issued?

Suppose that before this dividend payout the company had 1000 shares outstanding and that the project had an NPV of $2000. Then the old stock was worth in total $10,000 + NPV = $12,000, which works out at $12,000/1000 = $12 per share. After the company has paid the dividend and completed the financing, this old stock is worth $9000 + NPV = $11,000. That works out at $11,000/1000 = $11 per share. In other words, the price of the old stock falls by the amount of the $1 per share dividend payment.

Now let us look at the new stock. Clearly, after the issue this must sell at the same price as the rest of the stock. In other words, it must be valued at $11. If the new stockholders get fair value, the company must issue $1000/$11 or 91 new shares in order to raise the $1000 that it needs.

Share Repurchase

We have seen that any increased cash dividend payment must be offset by a stock issue if the firm's investment and borrowing policies are held constant. In effect

[14] All other factors that might affect Rational Demiconductor's value are assumed constant. This is not a necessary assumption, but it simplifies the proof of MM's theory.

[15] The "old" shareholders get all the benefit of the positive NPV project. The "new" shareholders require only a fair rate of return. They are making a zero NPV investment.

the stockholders finance the extra dividend by selling off part of their ownership of the firm. Consequently, the stock price falls by just enough to offset the extra dividend.

This process can also be run backward. With investment and borrowing policy given, any *reduction* in dividends must be balanced by a reduction in the number of shares issued or by repurchase of previously outstanding stock. But if the process has no effect on stockholders' wealth when run forward, it must likewise have no effect when run in reverse. We will confirm this by another numerical example.

Suppose that a technical discovery reveals that Rational Demiconductor's new project is not a positive NPV venture, but a sure loser. Management announces that the project is to be discarded, and that the $1000 earmarked for it will be paid out as an extra dividend of $1 per share. After the dividend payout, the balance sheet is:

Rational Demiconductor's Balance Sheet (Market Values)

Cash	$0	$0	Debt
Existing fixed assets	$9,000	$9,000	Equity
New project	$0		
Total asset value	$9,000	$9,000	Total firm value

Since there are 1000 shares outstanding, the stock price is $10,000/1000 = $10 before the dividend payment and $9000/1000 = $9 *after* the payment.

What if Rational Demiconductor uses the $1000 to repurchase stock instead? As long as the company pays a fair price for the stock, the $1000 buys $1000/$10 = 100 shares. That leaves 900 shares worth 900 × $10 = $9000.

As expected, we find that switching from cash dividends to share repurchase has no effect on shareholders' wealth. They forgo a $1 cash dividend but end up holding shares worth $10 instead of $9.

Note that when shares are repurchased the transfer of value is in favor of those stockholders who do not sell. They forgo any cash dividend but end up owning a larger slice of the firm. In effect they are using their share of Rational Demiconductor's $1000 distribution to buy out some of their fellow shareholders.

16-4   THE RIGHTISTS

Much of traditional finance literature has advocated high payout ratios. Here, for example, is a statement of the rightist position made by Graham and Dodd in 1951:

> . . . the considered and continuous verdict of the stock market is overwhelmingly in favor of liberal dividends as against niggardly ones. The common stock investor must take this judgment into account in the valuation of stock for purchase. It is now becoming standard practice to evaluate common stock by applying one multiplier to that portion of the earnings paid out in dividends and a much smaller multiplier to the undistributed balance.[16]

[16] These authors later qualified this statement, recognizing the willingness of investors to pay high price-earnings multiples for growth stocks. But otherwise they have stuck to their position. We quoted their 1951 statement because of its historical importance. Compare B. Graham and D. L. Dodd, *Security Analysis: Principles and Techniques,* 3d ed., McGraw-Hill Book Company, New York, 1951, p. 432, with B. Graham, D. L. Dodd, and S. Cottle, *Security Analysis: Principles and Techniques,* 4th ed., McGraw-Hill Book Company, New York, 1962, p. 480.

Another author has written a book urging the government to enforce full distribution of earnings on the grounds that it "would almost certainly double or treble (within a short period) the market value of equities."[17]

This belief in the importance of dividend policy is common in the business and investment communities. Stockholders and investment advisers continually pressure corporate treasurers for increased dividends. When we had wage-price controls in the United States in 1974, it was deemed necessary to have dividend controls as well. As far as we know, no labor union objected that "dividend policy is irrelevant." After all, if wages are reduced, the employee is worse off. Dividends are the shareholders' wages, and so if the payout ratio is reduced the shareholder is worse off. Therefore fair play requires that wage controls be matched by dividend controls. Right?

Wrong! You should be able to see through that kind of argument by now. But let us turn to some of the more serious arguments for a high-payout policy.

Do MM Ignore Risk?

One of the most common and immediate objections to MM's argument about the irrelevance of dividends is that dividends are cash in hand while capital gains are at best in the bush. It may be true that the recipient of an extra cash dividend forgoes an equal capital gain, but if the dividend is safe and the capital gain is risky, isn't the stockholder ahead?

It's true that dividends are more predictable than capital gains. Managers can stabilize dividends but they cannot control stock price. From this it seems a small step to conclude that increased dividends make the firm less risky.[18] But the important point is, once again, that as long as investment policy and borrowing are held constant, a firm's *overall* cash flows are the same regardless of payout policy. The risks borne by *all* the firm's stockholders are likewise fixed by its investment and borrowing policies, and unaffected by dividend policy.[19]

A dividend increase creates a transfer of ownership between "old" and "new" stockholders. The old stockholders—those who receive the extra dividend and do not buy their part of the stock issue undertaken to finance the dividend—find their stake in the firm reduced. They have indeed traded a safe receipt for an uncertain future gain. But the reason their money is safe is not because it is special "dividend money," but because it is in the bank. If the dividend had not been increased, the stockholders could have achieved an equally safe position just by selling shares and putting the money in the bank.

If we really believed that old stockholders are better off by trading a risky asset for cash, then we would also have to argue that the new stockholders—those who trade cash for the newly issued shares—are worse off. But this doesn't make sense: the new stockholders are bearing risk, but they are getting paid for it. They are

---

[17] See A. Rubner, *The Ensnared Shareholder*, Macmillan International Ltd., London, 1965, p. 139.

[18] By analogy one could presumably argue that interest payments are even more predictable, so that a company's risk would be diminished by increasing the proportion of receipts paid out as interest.

[19] There are a number of variations of the "bird-in-the-hand" argument. Perhaps the most persuasive is found in M. J. Gordon, "Dividends, Earnings and Stock Prices," *Review of Economics and Statistics*, **41:** 99–105 (May 1959). He reasoned that investors run less risk if the firm pays them cash now rather than retaining and reinvesting it in the hope of paying higher future dividends. But careful analysis of Gordon's argument—see M. J. Brennan, "A Note on Dividend Irrelevance and the Gordon Valuation Model," *Journal of Finance*, **26:** 1115–1122 (December 1971), for example—shows that he was really talking about changes in *investment* policy, not dividend policy.

willing to buy because the new shares are priced to offer a return adequate to cover the risk.

MM's argument for the irrelevance of dividend policy does not assume a world of certainty: It assumes an efficient capital market. Market efficiency means that the transfers of value created by shifts in dividend policy are carried out on fair terms. And since the *overall* value of (old and new) stockholders' equity is unaffected, nobody gains or loses.

Market Imperfections

We believe—and it is widely believed—that MM's conclusions follow from their assumption of perfect and efficient capital markets. Nobody claims their model is an exact description of the so-called "real world." Thus the dividend controversy finally boils down to arguments about imperfections, inefficiencies, or whether stockholders are fully rational.[20]

There is a natural clientele for high-payout stocks. For example, some financial institutions are legally restricted from holding stocks lacking established dividend records. Trusts and endowment funds may prefer high-dividend stocks because dividends are regarded as spendable "income," whereas capital gains are "additions to principal," which cannot be spent.[21]

There is also a natural clientele of investors who look to their stock portfolios for a steady source of cash to live on. In principle this cash could be easily generated from stocks paying no dividends at all; the investor could just sell off a small fraction of his or her holdings from time to time. But it is simpler and cheaper for AT&T to send a quarterly check than for its stockholders to sell, say, one share every 3 months. AT&T's regular dividends relieve many of its shareholders of transaction costs and considerable inconvenience.

Those advocating generous dividends might go on to argue that a regular cash dividend relieves stockholders of the risk of having to sell shares at "temporarily depressed" prices. Of course, the firm will have to issue shares eventually to finance the dividend, but (the argument goes) the firm can pick the *right time* to sell. If firms really try to do this and if they are successful—two big *ifs*—then stockholders of high-payout firms do indeed get something for nothing.

There is another line of argument that you can use to justify high payouts. Think of a market in which investors receive very little reliable information about a firm's earnings. Such markets exist in some European countries where a passion for secrecy and a tendency to construct many-layered corporate organizations produce asset and earnings figures that are next to meaningless. Some people say that, thanks to creative accounting, the situation is little better in the United States. How does an investor in such a world separate marginally profitable firms from the real money makers? One clue is dividends. A firm which reports good earnings and pays a generous dividend is putting its money where its mouth is.[22] We can

---

[20] Psychologists' experiments show that human beings are not 100 percent rational decision makers. Shefrin and Statman use some of the psychologists' results to argue that investors may have an irrational preference for cash dividends. See H. Shefrin and M. Statman, "Explaining Investor Preference for Cash Dividends," *Journal of Financial Economics,* **13:** 253–282 (June 1984).

[21] Most colleges and universities are legally free to spend capital gains from their endowments, but this is rarely done.

[22] Of course, firms can cheat in the short run by overstating earnings and scraping up cash to pay a generous dividend. But it is hard to cheat in the long run, for a firm that is not making money will not have the cash flow to pay out. Financing dividends by issuing stock is self-defeating, for it ultimately reduces dividends per share and thereby reveals that the initial dividend was not supported by earnings.

understand why investors would favor firms with established dividend records. We can also see how the information content of dividends would come about. Investors would refuse to believe a firm's reported earnings announcements unless they were backed up by an appropriate dividend policy.

MM regard the informational content of dividends as a temporary thing. A dividend increase signals management's optimism about future earnings, but investors will be able to *see for themselves* whether the optimism is justified. The jump in stock price that accompanies an unexpected dividend increase *would have happened anyway* as information about future earnings came out through other channels. Therefore, MM expect to find changes in dividends associated with stock price movements, but no permanent relationship between stock price and the firm's long-run target payout ratio. MM believe management should be concerned with dividend *changes*, but not with the average *level* of payout.

16-5   TAXES AND THE RADICAL LEFT

The left-wing dividend creed is simple: Whenever dividends are taxed more heavily than capital gains, firms should pay the lowest cash dividend they can get away with. Available cash should be retained and reinvested or used to repurchase shares.

The Tax Reform Act of 1986 undercut the leftists' arguments. Before the reform, investors paid up to a 50 percent tax on dividends, versus a maximum 20 percent tax on capital gains. Since the reform, dividends and capital gains are taxed at the same rate, which is 28 percent for the highest-earning investors.[23]

The leftists' arguments nevertheless deserve a closer look. First, it's important to understand their historical contribution to the dividend controversy. Second, capital gains are taxed at relatively low rates in many countries (Great Britain, for example), and may regain their favored tax treatment in the United States when its tax code changes yet again. Third, capital gains retain some tax advantages even under the Tax Reform Act.

We will explain these remaining tax advantages in a moment, after we set out the leftist argument in more detail.

---

[23] But some individuals are subject to a 5 percent surcharge, that is, a $28 + 5 = 33$ percent marginal rate. Here are two examples of marginal rates by income bracket:

Marginal Tax Rates	INCOME BRACKET	
	Single	Married, Joint Return
15%	0–$17,850	0–$29,750
28	17,850–43,150	29,750–71,900
28 + 5 = 33	43,150–89,560	71,900–149,250
28	Over 89,560	Over 149,250

There are different schedules for married taxpayers filing separately and for single taxpayers who are heads of households.

The 5 percent surcharge offsets the advantage given by the low 15 percent rate on the first block of income. The starting point for the surcharge will be indexed for inflation starting in 1989.

How Taxes Affect Values

Corporations can transmute dividends into capital gains by shifting their dividend policies. When dividends are more heavily taxed than capital gains, such financial alchemy should be welcomed by any taxpaying investor. That is the basic point made by the leftist party when it argues for low dividend payout.

If dividends are taxed more heavily than capital gains, investors should pay more for stocks with low dividend yields. In other words, they should accept a lower *pretax* rate of return from securities offering returns in the form of capital gains rather than dividends. Table 16-1 illustrates this. The stocks of firms A and B are equally risky. Investors expect A to be worth $112.50 per share next year. The share price of B is expected to be only $102.50, but a $10 dividend is also forecast, and so the total pretax payoff is the same, $112.50.

Yet we find B's stock selling for less than A's and therefore offering a higher pretax rate of return. The reason is obvious: Investors prefer A because its return comes in the form of capital gains. Table 16-1 shows that A and B are equally attractive to investors who pay a 50 percent tax on dividends and a 20 percent tax on capital gains (the maximum marginal rates prior to tax reform). Each offers a 10 percent return after all taxes. The difference between the stock prices of A and B is exactly the present value of the extra taxes the investors face if they buy B.[24]

The management of B could save these extra taxes by eliminating the $10 dividend and using the released funds to repurchase stock instead. Its stock price should rise to $100 as soon as the new policy is announced.

Why Pay Any Dividends at All?

Why then should *any* firm *ever* pay a cash dividend when dividends are taxed more heavily than capital gains? If cash is to be distributed to stockholders, isn't share repurchase the best channel for doing so? The leftist position seems to call not just for low payout by firm B, but for *zero* payout whenever capital gains have a tax advantage.

Few leftists would go quite that far. A firm which eliminates dividends and starts repurchasing stock on a regular basis may find that the Internal Revenue Service would recognize the repurchase program for what it really is and would tax the payments accordingly. That is why financial managers have never announced that they are repurchasing shares to save stockholders taxes; they give some other reason.[25]

The low-payout party has nevertheless maintained that the market rewards firms which have low-payout policies. They have claimed that firms which paid dividends and as a result had to issue shares from time to time were making a serious mistake. Any such firm was essentially financing its dividends by issuing stock; it should have cut its dividends at least to the point at which stock issues were unnecessary. This would not only have saved taxes for shareholders; it would also have avoided the transaction costs of the stock issues.[26]

---

[24] Michael Brennan has modeled what happens when you introduce taxes into an otherwise perfect market and found that the capital asset pricing model continues to hold, but on an *after-tax* basis. Thus, if A and B have the same beta, they should offer the same after-tax rate of return. The spread between pretax and posttax returns is determined by a weighted average of investors' tax rates. See M. J. Brennan, "Taxes, Market Valuation and Corporate Financial Policy," *National Tax Journal,* **23:** 417–427 (December 1970).

[25] They might say, "Our stock is a good investment," or, "We want to have the shares available to finance acquisitions of other companies." What do you think of these rationales?

[26] These costs can be substantial. Refer back to Chapter 15, especially Table 15-1.

TABLE 16-1
Effects of a shift in dividend policy when dividends are taxed more heavily than capital gains. The high-payout stock (firm B) must sell at a lower price in order to provide the same after-tax return.

	Firm A (No Dividend)	Firm B (High Dividend)
Next year's price	$112.50	$102.50
Dividend	$0	$10.00
Toal pretax payoff	$112.50	$112.50
Today's stock price	$100	$96.67
Capital gain	$12.50	$5.83
Before-tax rate of return (percent)	$\frac{12.5}{100} \times 100 = 12.5$	$\frac{15.83}{96.67} \times 100 = 16.4$
Tax on dividend at 50 percent	$0	$.50 \times 10 = \$5.00$
Tax on capital gain at 20 percent	$.20 \times 12.50 = \$2.50$	$.20 \times 5.83 = \$1.17$
Total after-tax income (dividends plus capital gains less taxes)	$(0 + 12.50)$ $-2.50 = \$10.00$	$(10.00 + 5.83)$ $-(5.00 + 1.17) = \$9.66$
After-tax rate of return (percent)	$\frac{10}{100} \times 100 = 10.0$	$\frac{9.66}{96.67} \times 100 = 10.0$

Empirical Evidence on Dividends and Taxes

It is hard to deny that taxes are important to investors. You can see that in the bond market. Interest on municipal bonds is not taxed, and so municipals sell at low pretax yields. Interest on federal government bonds is taxed, and so these bonds sell at higher pretax yields. It does not seem likely that investors in bonds just forget about taxes when they enter the stock market. Thus, we would expect to find an historical tendency for high-dividend stocks to sell at lower prices and therefore to offer higher yields, just as in Table 16-1.

Unfortunately, there are difficulties in measuring this effect. For example, suppose that Stock A is priced at $100 and is expected to pay a $5 dividend. The *expected* yield is, therefore, $5/100 = .05$, or 5 percent. The company now announces bumper earnings and a $10 dividend. Thus with the benefit of hindsight, A's *actual* dividend yield is $10/100 = .10$, or 10 percent. If the unexpected increase in earnings causes a rise in A's stock price, we will observe that a high actual yield is accompanied by a high actual return. But that would not tell us anything about whether a high *expected* yield was accompanied by a high *expected* return. In order to measure the effect of dividend policy, we need to estimate the dividends that investors expected.

A second problem is that nobody is quite sure what is meant by high dividend yield. For example, utility stocks have generally offered high yields. But did they have a high yield all year, or only in months or on days that dividends are paid? Perhaps for most of the year, they had zero yields and were perfect holdings for the highly taxed individuals.[27] Of course, high-tax investors did not want to hold a stock on the days dividends were paid, but they could sell their stock temporarily to a security dealer. Dealers are taxed equally on dividends and capital gains, and therefore should not have demanded any extra return for holding stocks over the

---

[27] Suppose there are 250 trading days in a year. Think of a stock paying quarterly dividends. We could say that the stock offers a high dividend yield on 4 days, but a zero dividend yield on the remaining 246 days.

TABLE 16-2
Some tests of the effect of yield on returns: A positive implied tax rate on dividends means that investors require a higher pretax return from high-dividend stocks.

Test	Test Period	Interval	Implied Tax Rate (Percent)	Standard Error of Tax Rate
Brennan	1946–1965	Monthly	34	12
Black & Scholes (1974)	1936–1966	Monthly	22	24
Litzenberger & Ramaswamy (1979)	1936–1977	Monthly	24	3
Litzenberger & Ramaswamy (1982)	1940–1980	Monthly	14–23	2–3
Rosenberg & Marathe (1979)	1931–1966	Monthly	40	21
Bradford & Gordon (1980)	1926–1978	Monthly	18	2
Blume (1980)	1936–1976	Quarterly	52	25
Miller & Scholes (1982)	1940–1978	Monthly	4	3
Stone & Bartter (1979)	1947–1970	Monthly	56	28
Morgan (1982)	1946–1977	Monthly	21	2

Sources: M. J. Brennan: "Dividends and Valuation in Imperfect Markets: Some Empirical Tests," unpublished paper, not dated.
F. Black and M. Scholes: "The Effects of Dividend Yield and Dividend Policy on Common Stock Prices and Returns," *Journal of Financial Economics,* **1:** 1–22 (May 1974).
R. H. Litzenberger and K. Ramaswamy: "The Effect of Personal Taxes and Dividends on Capital Asset Prices: Theory and Empirical Evidence," *Journal of Financial Economics,* **7:** 163–195 (June 1979).
R. H. Litzenberger and K. Ramaswamy: "The Effects of Dividends on Common Stock Prices: Tax Effects or Information Effects," *Journal of Finance,* **37:** 429–443 (May 1982).
B. Rosenberg and V. Marathe: "Tests of Capital Asset Pricing Model Hypotheses," in H. Levy (ed.), *Research in Finance I,* Greenwich, Conn.: JAI Press (1979).
D. F. Bradford and R. H. Gordon: "Taxation and the Stock Market Valuation of Capital Gains and Dividends," *Journal of Public Economics,* **14:** 109–136 (1980).
M. E. Blume: "Stock Returns and Dividend Yields: Some More Evidence," *Review of Economics and Statistics,* 567–577 (November 1980).
M. H. Miller and M. Scholes: "Dividends and Taxes: Some Empirical Evidence," *Journal of Political Economy,* 90: (1982).
B. K. Stone and B. J. Bartter: "The Effect of Dividend Yield on Stock Returns: Empirical Evidence on the Relevance of Dividends," W.P.E.-76-78, Atlanta, Ga.: Georgia Institute of Technology.
I. G. Morgan: "Dividends and Capital Asset Prices," *Journal of Finance,* **37:** 1071–1086 (September 1982).

dividend period.[28] If shareholders could pass stocks freely between each other at the time of the dividend payment, we should not observe any tax effects at all.

Given these difficulties in measuring the relationship between expected yield and return, it is not surprising that different researchers have come up with different results. Table 16-2 summarizes some of the findings. Notice that in each of these tests the estimated tax rate was positive. In other words, high-yielding stocks appeared to have lower prices and to offer higher returns. However, while the dividends-are-bad school could claim that the weight of evidence is on its side,

---

[28] The stock could also be sold to a corporation, which could "capture" the dividend and then resell the shares. Corporations are natural buyers of dividends, because they pay tax only on 20 percent of dividends received from other corporations. (We say more on the taxation of intercorporate dividends later in this section.)

the contest is by no means over. Many respected scholars, including Merton Miller and Myron Scholes, were unconvinced. They stressed the difficulty of measuring dividend yield properly and proving the link between dividend yield and expected return.[29]

Dividends and Capital Gains under the 1986 Tax Reform Act

But all this evidence has more historical than current interest, now that dividends and capital gains are taxed at the same rate.

Tax law is still on the leftists' side in one respect, however. Taxes on dividends have to be paid immediately, but taxes on capital gains can be deferred until shares are sold and capital gains are realized. Stockholders can choose when to sell their shares and thus when to pay the capital gains tax. The longer they wait, the less the present value of the capital gains tax liability.[30] Thus there is one group of investors—individual investors who can hold on to their shares—who may still prefer capital gains to dividends, although less so than before the Tax Reform Act.

These motives are less important for financial institutions, many of which operate free of all taxes, and therefore have no tax reason to prefer capital gains to dividends, or vice versa. Pension funds are untaxed, for example.

Only corporations have a tax reason to *prefer* dividends. They pay corporate income tax on only 20 percent of any dividends received. Thus the effective tax rate on dividends received by large corporations is 20 percent of 34 percent (the marginal corporate tax rate), or 6.8 percent. But they have to pay a 34 percent tax on the full amount of any realized capital gain.

Although the dividend affects the shareholder's tax liability, it does not in general alter the taxes that must be paid by the company itself. Corporate income tax has to be paid regardless of whether the company distributes or retains its profits. There is one exception. If the Internal Revenue Service (IRS) can prove that earnings are retained solely to avoid any taxes on dividends, it can levy an additional tax on the excess retentions. However, public companies are almost always able to justify their retentions to the IRS.

The implications of the Tax Reform Act for dividend policy are pretty simple. Capital gains still have tax advantages to many investors because they can be deferred; but once realized, they are no longer taxed at a lower rate than dividends. Thus, the leftist case for minimizing cash dividends, though not demolished, is significantly undercut. At the same time, the middle-of-the-road party has come into its own.

---

[29] Miller reviews several of the studies cited in Table 16-2 in "Behavioral Rationality in Finance: The Case of Dividends," *Journal of Business,* **59:** S451–S468 (October 1986).

[30] When securities are sold, capital gains tax is paid on the difference between the selling price and the initial purchase price or *basis.* Thus, shares purchased in 1985 for $20, and sold for $30 in 1988, would generate $10 per share in capital gains and a tax of $2.80 at a 28 percent marginal rate.

Suppose the investor now decides to defer sale for 1 year. Then, if the interest rate is 8 percent, the present value of the tax, viewed from 1988, falls to $2.80/(1.08) = $2.59. That is, the *effective* capital gains rate is 25.9 percent. The longer sale is deferred, the lower the effective rate.

The effective rate falls to zero if the investor dies before selling, because the investor's heirs get to "step up" the basis without recognizing any taxable gain. Suppose the price is still $30 when the investor dies. The heirs could sell for $30 and pay no tax, because they could claim a $30 basis. The $10 capital gain would escape tax entirely.

16-6   THE MIDDLE-OF-THE-ROADERS

The middle-of-the-road party, which is principally represented by Miller, Black, and Scholes, maintains that a company's value is not affected by its dividend policy.[31] We have already seen that this would be the case if there were no impediments such as transaction costs or taxes. The middle-of-the-roaders are aware of these phenomena, but nevertheless raise the following disarming question: If companies could increase their share price by distributing more or less cash dividends, why have they not already done so? Perhaps dividends are where they are because no company believes that it could increase its stock price simply by changing its dividend policy.

This "supply effect" is not inconsistent with the existence of a clientele of investors who demand low-payout stocks. Firms recognized that clientele long ago. Enough firms may have switched to low-payout policies to satisfy fully the clientele's demand. If so, there is no incentive for *additional* firms to switch to low-payout policies.

Miller, Black, and Scholes similarly recognize possible "high-payout clienteles," but argue that they are satisfied also. If all clienteles are satisfied, their demands for high or low dividends have no effects on prices or returns. It doesn't matter which clientele a particular firm chooses to appeal to. If the middle-of-the-road party is right, we should not expect to observe any general association between dividend policy and market values, and the value of any individual company would be independent of its choice of dividend policy.

The middle-of-the-roaders stress that companies would not have generous payout policies unless they believed that this was what investors wanted. But this does not answer the question, "Why *should* so many investors want high payouts?"

Before the Tax Reform Act, this was the chink in the armor of the middle-of-the-roaders. If high dividends bring high taxes, it's difficult to believe that investors got what they wanted. The response of the middle-of-the-roaders was to argue that there were plenty of wrinkles in the tax system which determined stockholders could use to avoid paying taxes on dividends. For example, instead of investing directly in common stocks, they could do so through a pension fund or insurance company, which received more favorable tax treatment.

Since 1986, the tax disadvantage of dividends has largely disappeared in the United States, so it is easier to suppose that there is a substantial clientele of investors who are content to receive high dividends. That is why there have been many new converts to the middle-of-the-road cause.

Has this Tax Reform Act led to a change in corporate and investor attitudes to dividends? Corporations *believe* that it has led to a pressure for higher payouts, but we still need to wait before we can tell whether there has been a shift in payouts or investors' required returns. Meanwhile, we may gain some clues from the experience of other countries that have changed tax rates on dividends relative to capital gains. In Canada, for example, dividend payouts increased after a capital gains tax was introduced and dividend tax rates were cut for many investors.[32]

---

[31] F. Black and M. S. Scholes, "The Effects of Dividend Yield and Dividend Policy on Common Stock Prices and Returns," *Journal of Financial Economics,* **1:** 1–22 (May 1974); M. H. Miller and M. S. Scholes, "Dividends and Taxes," *Journal of Financial Economics,* **6:** 333–364 (December 1978), and M. H. Miller, "Behavioral Rationality in Finance: The Case of Dividends," *Journal of Business,* **59:** S451–S468 (October 1986).

[32] The Canadian experience is summarized in our Canadian edition, especially pp. 360–369, 372–374. See R. Brealey, S. Myers, G. Sick, and R. Whaley, *Principles of Corporate Finance,* McGraw-Hill Ryerson, Ltd., Toronto, 1986. Also, see I. G. Morgan, "Dividends and Stock Price Behavior in Canada," *Journal of Business Administration,* **12:** 91–106 (Fall 1980).

16-7   SUMMARY

Dividends come in many forms. The most common is the regular cash dividend, but sometimes companies pay an extra or special cash dividend, and sometimes they pay a dividend in the form of stock. A firm is not free to pay whatever dividends it likes. It may have promised its bondholders not to declare large dividends, and it is also prevented by state law from paying dividends if it is insolvent or if it has insufficient surplus.

As an alternative to dividend payments, the company can repurchase its own stock. Although this has the same effect of distributing cash to shareholders, the Internal Revenue Service taxes shareholders only on the capital gains that they may realize as a result of the repurchase.

When managers decide on the dividend, their primary concern seems to be to give shareholders a "fair" level of dividends. Most managers have a conscious or subconscious long-term target payout rate. If firms simply applied the target payout rate to each year's earnings, dividends could fluctuate wildly. Managers therefore try to smooth dividend payments by moving only partway toward the target payout in each year. Also they don't just look at past earnings performance: They try to look into the future when they set the payment. Investors are aware of this and they know that a dividend increase is often a sign of optimism on the part of management.

If we hold the company's investment policy constant, then dividend policy is a trade-off between cash dividends and the issue or repurchase of common stock. Should firms retain whatever earnings are necessary to finance growth and pay out any residual as cash dividends? Or should they increase dividends and then (sooner or later) issue stock to make up the shortfall of equity capital? Or should they reduce dividends below the "residual" level and use the released cash to repurchase stock?

If we lived in an ideally simple and perfect world, there would be no problem, for the choice would have no effect on market value. The controversy centers on the effects of dividend policy in our flawed world. A common—though by no means universal—view in the investment community is that high payout enhances share price. There are natural clienteles for high-payout stocks. But we find it difficult to explain a *general* preference for dividends other than in terms of an irrational prejudice. The case for "liberal dividends" depends largely on a wealth of tradition.

The most obvious and serious market imperfection has been the different tax treatment of dividends and capital gains. Before the Tax Reform Act of 1986, dividends were taxed at rates up to 50 percent, but capital gains rates topped out at only 20 percent. Thus investors should have required a higher before-tax return on high-payout stocks to compensate for their tax disadvantage. High-income investors should have held mostly low-payout stocks.

This view has a respectable theoretical basis. It is supported by some evidence that gross returns have, on the average, reflected the tax differential. The weak link is the theory's silence on the question of why companies continued to distribute such large sums contrary to the preferences of investors.

The third view of dividend policy starts with the notion that the actions of companies *do* reflect investors' preferences; the fact that companies pay substantial dividends is the best evidence that investors want them. If the supply of dividends exactly meets the demand, no single company could improve its market value by changing its dividend policy. Although this explains corporate behavior, it is at a cost, for we cannot explain why dividends are what they are and not some other amount.

These theories are too incomplete and the evidence is too sensitive to minor changes in specification to warrant any dogmatism. Our sympathies, however, lie with the third, middle-of-the-road view. Our recommendations to companies would emphasize the following points. First, there is little doubt that sudden shifts in dividend policy can cause abrupt changes in stock price. The principal reason is the information that investors read into the company's actions, although some casual evidence suggests that there may be other less rational explanations.[33] Given such problems, there is a clear case for smoothing dividends, for example, by defining the firm's target payout and making relatively slow adjustments toward it. If it is necessary to make a sharp dividend change, the company should provide as much forewarning as possible and take care to ensure that the action is not misinterpreted.

Subject to these strictures, we believe that, at the very least, a company should adopt a target payout that is sufficiently low as to minimize its reliance on external equity. Why pay out cash to stockholders if that requires issuing new shares to get the cash back? It's better to hold on to the cash in the first place.

FURTHER READING

Lintner's classic analysis of how companies set their dividend payments is provided in:

> J. Lintner: "Distribution of Incomes of Corporations among Dividends, Retained Earnings, and Taxes," *American Economic Review,* **46:** 97–113 (May 1956).

There have been a number of tests of how well Lintner's model describes dividend changes. One of the best known is:

> E. F. Fama and H. Babiak: "Dividend Policy: An Empirical Analysis," *Journal of the American Statistical Association,* **63:** 1132–1161 (December 1968).

Marsh and Merton have reinterpreted Lintner's findings and used them to explain the aggregate dividends paid by United States corporations:

> T. A. Marsh and R. C. Merton, "Dividend Behavior for the Aggregate Stock Market," *Journal of Business,* **60:** 1–40 (January 1987).

The pioneering article on dividend policy in the context of a perfect capital market is:

> M. H. Miller and F. Modigliani: "Dividend Policy, Growth and the Valuation of Shares," *Journal of Business,* **34:** 411–433 (October 1961).

There are several interesting models explaining the information content of dividends. Two influential examples are:

> S. Bhattacharya, "Imperfect Information, Dividend Policy and the Bird in the Hand Fallacy," *Bell Journal of Economics and Management Science,* **10:** 259–270 (Spring 1979).
> M. H. Miller and K. Rock, "Dividend Policy Under Asymmetric Information," *Journal of Finance,* **40:** 1031–1052 (September 1985).

The most powerful advocacy of the "dividends are good" case is Gordon's. Brennan discusses the source of the differences between Gordon and MM.

---

[33] For example, in an article in *Fortune* Carol Loomis tells the story of General Public Utilities ("A Case for Dropping Dividends," *Fortune,* June 15, 1968, pp. 181 ff.). In 1968 its management decided to reduce its cash dividend to avoid a stock issue. Despite the company's assurances, it encountered considerable opposition. Individual shareholders advised the president to see a psychiatrist, institutional holders threatened to sell their stock, the share price fell nearly 10 percent, and eventually GPU capitulated.

M. J. Gordon, "Dividends, Earnings and Stock Prices," *Review of Economics and Statistics,* **41:** 99–105 (May 1959).

M. J. Brennan: "A Note on Dividend Irrelevance and the Gordon Valuation Model," *Journal of Finance,* **26:** 1115–1122 (December 1971).

The effect of differential rates of tax on dividends and capital gains is analyzed rigorously in the context of the capital asset pricing model in:

M. J. Brennan: "Taxes, Market Valuation and Corporate Financial Policy," *National Tax Journal,* **23:** 417–427 (December 1970).

The argument that dividend policy is irrelevant even in the presence of taxes is presented in:

F. Black and M. S. Scholes: "The Effects of Dividend Yield and Dividend Policy on Common Stock Prices and Returns," *Journal of Financial Economics,* **1:** 1–22 (May 1974).

M. H. Miller and M. S. Scholes: "Dividends and Taxes," *Journal of Financial Economics,* **6:** 333–364 (December 1978).

A brief review of some of the empirical evidence is contained in:

R. H. Litzenberger and K. Ramaswamy: "The Effects of Dividends on Common Stock Prices: Tax Effects or Information Effects," *Journal of Finance,* **37:** 429–443 (May 1982).

Merton Miller reviews research on the dividend controversy in:

M. H. Miller, "Behavioral Rationality in Finance: The Case of Dividends," *Journal of Business,* **59:** S451–S468 (October 1986).

QUIZ

1. In 1987 Maytag Co. paid a regular quarterly dividend of $.40 a share.
   (*a*) Match each of the following sets of dates:

(A) May 14, 1987	(a) Record date
(B) May 25, 1987	(b) Payment date
(C) May 26, 1987	(c) Ex-dividend date
(D) June 1, 1987	(d) Last with-dividend date
(E) June 15, 1987	(e) Declaration date

   (*b*) On one of these dates the stock price is likely to fall by about the value of the dividend. Why?
   (*c*) The stock price in early January was $50. What was the prospective dividend yield?
   (*d*) The earnings per share for 1987 were forecast at around $3.40. What was the percentage payout rate?
   (*e*) Suppose that in 1987 the company paid a 10 percent stock dividend. What would be the expected fall in the stock price?
2. Which of the following statements are false?
   (*a*) A company may not generally pay a dividend out of legal capital.
   (*b*) A company may not generally pay a dividend if it is insolvent.
   (*c*) Realized long-term gains are taxed at the marginal rate of income tax.
   (*d*) Nevertheless, the *effective* tax rate on capital gains can be less than the tax rate on dividends.
   (*e*) Corporations are taxed on only 50 percent of dividends received from other corporations.

3. Here are several "facts" about typical corporate dividend policies. Which of the "facts" are true and which false? Write out a corrected version of any false statements.

(a) Most companies set a target dividend payout ratio.

(b) They set each year's dividend equal to the target payout ratio times that year's earnings.

(c) Managers and investors seem more concerned with dividend changes than dividend levels.

(d) Managers often increase dividends temporarily when earnings are unexpectedly high for a year or two.

4. Between 1964 and 1982 one could explain 80 percent of the variation in GM's dividend changes by the following equation:

$$\text{DIV}_t - \text{DIV}_{t-1} = 1.66 + .77 \,(.35\ \text{EPS}_t - \text{DIV}_{t-1})$$

What do you think was

(a) GM's target payout ratio?

(b) The rate at which dividends adjusted toward the target?

5. Suppose the Miller-Modigliani (MM) theory of dividend policy is correct. How would a government-imposed dividend freeze affect

(a) Stock prices?

(b) The volume of capital investment?

6. Stock price usually rises when there is an unexpected dividend increase, and falls when there is an unexpected dividend cut. Why?

7. How did the Tax Reform Act of 1986 affect the taxation of dividends and capital gains? Are there any investors left who could have a rational tax reason to prefer capital gains? Other things equal, how should the tax law changes affect prices and expected rates of return on high- versus low-payout stocks?

QUESTIONS AND PROBLEMS

1. Look in a recent issue of *The Wall Street Journal* at "Dividend News" and choose a company reporting a regular dividend.

(a) How frequently does the company pay a regular dividend?

(b) What is the amount of the dividend?

(c) By what date must your stock be registered for you to receive the dividend?

(d) How many weeks later is the dividend paid?

(e) Look up the stock price and calculate the annual yield on the stock.

2. Respond to the following comment: "It's all very well saying that I can sell shares to cover cash needs, but that may mean selling at the bottom of the market. If the company pays a regular dividend, investors avoid that risk."

3. "Dividends are the shareholder's wages. Therefore, if a government adopts an income policy which restricts increases in wages, it should in all logic restrict increases in dividends." Does this make sense?

4. Refer to the first balance sheet prepared for Rational Demiconductor on page 364. Again it uses cash to pay a $1000 cash dividend, planning to issue stock to recover the cash required for investment. But this time catastrophe hits before the stock can be issued. A new pollution control regulation increases manufacturing costs to the extent that the value of Rational Demiconductor's

existing business is cut in half, to $4500. The NPV of the new investment opportunity is unaffected, however. Show that dividend policy is still irrelevant.

5. "Risky companies tend to have lower target payout ratios and more gradual adjustment rates." Explain what is meant by this statement. Why do you think it is so?

6. Consider the following two statements: "Dividend policy is irrelevant." "Stock price is the present value of expected future dividends" (see Chapter 4). They *sound* contradictory. This question is designed to show that they are fully consistent.

   The current price of the shares of Charles River Mining Corporation is $50. Next year's earnings and dividends per share are $4 and $2, respectively. Investors expect perpetual growth at 8 percent per year. The expected rate of return demanded by investors is $r = 12$ percent.

   We can use the perpetual-growth model

$$P_0 = \frac{DIV}{r - g} = \frac{2}{.12 - .08} = 50$$

   Suppose that Charles River Mining announces that it will switch to a 100 percent payout policy, issuing shares as necessary to finance growth. Use the perpetual-growth model to show that current stock price is unchanged.

7. The expected pretax return on three stocks is divided between dividends and capital gains in the following way:

Stock	Expected Dividend	Expected Capital Gain
A	$0	$10
B	5	5
C	10	0

   (a) If each stock is priced at $100, what are the expected net returns on each stock to (i) a pension fund, (ii) a corporation paying tax at 34 percent, (iii) an individual paying tax at 28 percent on investment income and 28 percent on capital gains, and (iv) a security dealer paying tax at 34 percent on investment income and capital gains?

   (b) Suppose that before the 1986 Tax Reform Act stocks A, B, and C were priced to yield an 8 percent *after-tax* return to individual investors paying 50 percent tax on dividends and 20 percent tax on capital gains. What would A, B, and C each sell for?

8. Answer the following question twice, once assuming current tax law, and once assuming tax law prior to the Tax Reform Act of 1986.

   Suppose all investments offered the same expected return *before* tax. Consider two equally risky shares, Hi and Lo. Hi shares pay a generous dividend and offer low expected capital gains. Lo shares pay low dividends and offer high expected capital gains. Which of the following investors would prefer the Lo shares? Which would prefer the Hi shares? Which wouldn't care? Explain.

   (a) A pension fund
   (b) An individual
   (c) A corporation

(*d*) A charitable endowment

(*e*) A security dealer

Assume that any stock purchased will be sold after 1 year.

9. An article on stock repurchase in the *Los Angeles Times* noted that "An increasing number of companies are finding that the best investment they can make these days is in themselves." Discuss this view. How is the desirability of repurchase affected by company prospects and the price of its stock?

10. Adherents of the "dividends-are-good" school sometimes point to the fact that stocks with high yields tend to have above-average price-earnings multiples. Is this evidence convincing? Discuss.

11. For each of the following four groups of companies, state whether you would expect them to distribute a relatively high or low proportion of current earnings and whether you would expect them to have a relatively high or low price-earnings ratio.

(*a*) High-risk companies

(*b*) Companies that have recently experienced an unexpected decline in profits

(*c*) Companies that expect to experience a decline in profits

(*d*) "Growth" companies with valuable future investment opportunities

12. "Many companies use stock repurchase to increase earnings per share. For example, suppose that a company is in the following position:

- Net profit $10 million
- Number of shares before repurchase   1 million
- Earnings per share $10
- Price-earnings ratio   20
- Share price $200

The company now repurchases 200,000 shares at $200 a share. The number of shares declines to 800,000 shares and the earnings per share increase to $12.50. Assuming the price-earnings ratio stays at 20, the share price must rise to $250.00." Discuss.

13. (*a*) The Horner Pie Company pays a quarterly dividend of $1. Suppose that the stock price is expected to fall on the ex-dividend date by 90 cents. Would you prefer to buy on the with-dividend date or the ex-dividend date if you were (i) a tax-free investor, (ii) an investor with a marginal tax rate of 40 percent on income and 16 percent on capital gains?

(*b*) In a study of ex-dividend behavior Elton and Gruber estimated that the stock price fell on the average by 85 percent of the dividend. Assuming that the tax rate on capital gains was 40 percent of the rate on income tax, what did Elton and Gruber's result imply about investors' marginal rate of income tax?

(*c*) Elton and Gruber also observed that the ex-dividend price fall was different for high-payout stocks and for low-payout stocks. Which group would you expect to show the larger price fall?

(*d*) Would the fact that investors can trade stocks freely around the ex-dividend date alter your interpretation of Elton and Gruber's study?

(*e*) Suppose Elton and Gruber repeat their tests for the period 1988–1990, after the 1986 Tax Reform Act. How would you expect their results to change?

14. The middle-of-the-road party holds that dividend policy doesn't matter because the *supply* of high-, medium- and low-payout stocks has already adjusted

to satisfy investors' demands. Investors who like generous dividends hold stocks which give them all they want. Investors who want capital gains see a surfeit of low-payout stocks to choose from. Thus, high-payout firms cannot gain by transforming to low-payout firms or vice versa.

Suppose this was the way it was just before the Tax Reform Act of 1986. How would you expect the 1986 tax changes to affect the total cash dividends paid by United States corporations and the proportion of high- versus low-payout companies? Would dividend policy still be irrelevant after any dividend supply adjustments are completed? Explain.

17 Does Debt Policy Matter?

A firm's basic resource is the stream of cash flows produced by its assets. When the firm is financed entirely by common stock, all those cash flows belong to the stockholders. When it issues both debt and equity securities, it undertakes to split up the cash flows into two streams, a relatively safe stream that goes to the debt-holders and a more risky one that goes to the stockholders.

The firm's mix of different securities is known as its **capital structure.** The choice of capital structure is fundamentally a marketing problem. The firm can issue dozens of distinct securities in countless combinations but it attempts to find the particular combination that maximizes its overall market value.

Are these attempts worthwhile? We must consider the possibility that *no* combination has any greater appeal than any other. Perhaps the really important decisions concern the company's assets, and decisions about capital structure are mere details—matters to be attended to but not worried about.

Modigliani and Miller (MM), who showed that dividend policy doesn't matter in perfect capital markets, also showed that financing decisions don't matter in perfect markets.[1] Their famous "proposition I" states that a firm cannot change the *total* value of its securities just by splitting its cash flows into different streams: The firm's value is determined by its real assets, not by the securities it issues. Thus capital structure is irrelevant as long as the firm's investment decisions are taken as given.

MM's proposition I allows complete separation of investment and financing decisions. It implies that any firm could use the capital budgeting procedures presented in Chapters 2 to 12 without worrying about where the money for capital expenditures comes from. In those chapters, we assumed all-equity financing without really thinking about it. If proposition I holds, that is exactly the right approach.

We believe that in practice capital structure *does* matter, but we nevertheless devote all of this chapter to MM's argument. If you don't fully understand the conditions under which MM's theory holds, you won't fully understand why one capital structure is better than another. The financial manager needs to know what kinds of market imperfection to look for.

In Chapter 18 we will undertake a detailed analysis of the imperfections that are most likely to make a difference, including taxes, the costs of bankruptcy, and the costs of writing and enforcing complicated debt contracts. We will also argue

---

[1] MM's paper [F. Modigliani and M. H. Miller, "The Cost of Capital, Corporation Finance and the Theory of Investment," *American Economic Review,* **48:** 261–297 (June 1958)] was published in 1958, but their basic argument was anticipated in 1938 by J. B. Williams and to some extent by David Durand. See J. B. Williams, *The Theory of Investment Value,* Harvard University Press, Cambridge, Mass., 1938, and D. Durand, "Cost of Debt and Equity Funds for Business: Trends and Problems of Measurement," in *Conference on Research in Business Finance,* National Bureau of Economic Research, New York, 1952.

that it is naive to suppose that investment and financing decisions can be completely separated.

But in this chapter we isolate the decision about capital structure by holding the decision about investment fixed. We also assume that dividend policy is irrelevant.

17-1 THE EFFECT OF LEVERAGE IN A COMPETITIVE TAX-FREE ECONOMY

We have referred to the firm's choice of capital structure as a *marketing problem*. The financial manager's problem is to find the combination of securities that has the greatest overall appeal to investors—the combination that maximizes the market value of the firm. Before tackling this problem, we ought to make sure that a policy which maximizes firm value also maximizes the wealth of the shareholders.

Let D and E denote the market values of the outstanding debt and equity of the Wapshot Mining Company. Wapshot's 1000 shares sell for $50 apiece. Thus

$$E = 1000 \times 50 = \$50,000$$

Wapshot has also borrowed $25,000, and so V, the aggregate market value of all Wapshot's outstanding securities, is

$$V = D + E = \$75,000$$

Wapshot's stock is known as *levered equity*. Its stockholders face the benefits and costs of *financial leverage*, or *gearing*. Suppose that Wapshot "levers up" still further by borrowing an additional $10,000 and paying the proceeds out to shareholders as a special dividend of $10 per share. This substitutes debt for equity capital with no impact on Wapshot's assets.

What will Wapshot's equity be worth after the special dividend is paid? We have two unknowns, E and V:

Old debt	$25,000⎫	
New debt	$10,000⎭	$35,000 = D
Equity		? = E
Firm value		? = V

If V is $75,000 as before, then E must be $V - D = 75,000 - 35,000 = \$40,000$. Stockholders have suffered a capital loss which exactly offsets the $10,000 special dividend. But if V *increases* to, say, $80,000 as a result of the change in capital structure, then $E = \$45,000$ and the stockholders are $5000 ahead. In general, any increase or decrease in V caused by a shift in capital structure accrues to the firm's stockholders. We conclude that a policy which maximizes the market value of the firm is also best for the firm's stockholders.

This conclusion rests on two important assumptions: first, that Wapshot can ignore dividend policy and, second, that after the change in capital structure the old and new debt is *worth* $35,000.

Dividend policy may or may not be relevant, but there is no need to repeat the discussion of Chapter 16. We need only note that shifts in capital structure sometimes force important decisions about dividend policy. Perhaps Wapshot's cash dividend has costs or benefits which should be considered in addition to any benefits achieved by its increased financial leverage.

Our second assumption that old and new debt ends up worth $35,000 seems innocuous. But it could be wrong. Perhaps the new borrowing has increased the risk of the old bonds. If the holders of old bonds cannot demand a higher rate of interest to compensate for the increased risk, the value of their investment is reduced. In this case Wapshot's stockholders gain at the expense of the holders of old bonds even though the overall value of the debt and equity is unchanged.

But this anticipates issues better left to Chapter 18. In this chapter we will assume that any issue of debt has no effect on the market value of existing debt.[2]

Enter Modigliani and Miller

Let us accept that the financial manager would like to find the combination of securities that maximizes the value of the firm. How is this done? MM's answer is that the financial manager should stop worrying: In a perfect market any combination of securities is as good as another. The value of the firm is unaffected by its choice of capital structure.

You can see this by imagining two firms that generate the same stream of operating income and differ only in their capital structure. Firm U is unlevered. Therefore the total value of its equity E_U is the same as the total value of the firm V_U. Firm L, on the other hand, is levered. The value of its stock is, therefore, equal to the value of the firm less the value of the debt: $E_L = V_L - D_L$.

Now think which of these firms you would prefer to invest in. If you don't want to take much risk, you can buy common stock in the unlevered firm U. For example, if you buy 1 percent of firm U's shares, your investment is $.01 V_U$ and you are entitled to 1 percent of the gross profits:

Dollar Investment	Dollar Return
$.01V_U$	.01 Profits

Now compare this with an alternative strategy. This is to purchase the same fraction of both the debt and the equity of firm L. Your investment and return would then be as follows:

	Dollar Investment	Dollar Return
Debt	$.01D_L$	.01 Interest
Equity	$.01E_L$	.01 (Profits − interest)
Total	$.01 (D_L + E_L)$ $= .01 \ V_L$	.01 Profits

Both strategies offer the same payoff: 1 percent of the firm's profits. In well-functioning markets two investments that offer the same payoff must have the same cost. Therefore $.01 \ V_U$ must equal $.01 \ V_L$: The value of the unlevered firm must equal the value of the levered firm.

Suppose that you are willing to run a little more risk. You decide to buy 1 percent of the outstanding shares in the *levered* firm. Your investment and return are now as follows:

Dollar Investment	Dollar Return
$.01E_L$ $= .01(V_L - D_L)$	.01 (Profits − interest)

[2] See E. F. Fama, "The Effects of a Firm's Investment and Financing Decisions." *American Economic Review* **68**: 272–284 (June 1978), for a rigorous analysis of the conditions under which a policy of maximizing the value of the firm is also best for the stockholders.

But there is an alternative strategy. This is to borrow $.01D_L$ on your own account and purchase 1 percent of the stock of the *unlevered* firm. In this case, your borrowing gives you an immediate cash *inflow* of $.01D_L$, but you have to pay interest on your loan equal to 1 percent of the interest that is paid by firm L. Your total investment and return are, therefore, as follows:

	Dollar Investment	Dollar Return
Borrowing	$- .01D_L$	$- .01$ Interest
Equity	$.01V_U$	$.01$ Profits
Total	$.01(V_U - D_L)$	$.01$ (Profits $-$ interest)

Again both strategies offer the same payoff: 1 percent of profits after interest. Therefore, both investments must have the same cost. The quantity $.01 (V_U - D_L)$ must equal $.01(V_L - D_L)$ and V_U must equal V_L.

It does not matter whether the world is full of cautious investors, incautious investors, or a mixture of each. All would agree that the value of the unlevered firm U must be equal to the value of the levered firm L. As long as investors can borrow or lend on their own account on the same terms as the firm, they can "undo" the effect of any changes in the firm's capital structure. This is the basis for MM's famous proposition I: "The market value of any firm is independent of its capital structure."

The Law of the Conservation of Value

MM's argument that debt policy is irrelevant is an application of an astonishingly simple idea. If we have two streams of cash flow, A and B, then the present value of $A + B$ is equal to the present value of A plus the present value of B. We met this principle of *value additivity* in our discussion of capital budgeting, where we saw that in perfect capital markets the present value of two assets combined is equal to the sum of their present values considered separately.

In the present context we are not combining assets, but splitting them up. But value additivity works just as well in reverse. We can slice a cash flow into as many parts as we like; the values of the parts will always sum back to the value of the unsliced stream. (Of course, we have to make sure that none of the stream is lost in the slicing. We cannot say, "The value of a pie is independent of how it is sliced," if the slicer is also a nibbler.)

This is really a *law of conservation of value.* The value of an asset is preserved regardless of the nature of the claims against it. Thus proposition I: Firm value is determined on the *left-hand* side of the balance sheet by real assets—not by the proportions of debt and equity securities issued by the firm.

The simplest ideas often have the widest application. For example, we could apply the law of conservation of value to the choice between issuing preferred stock, common stock, or some combination. The law implies that the choice is irrelevant, assuming perfect capital markets and providing that the choice does not affect the firm's investment, borrowing, and operating policies. If the total value of the equity "pie" (preferred and common combined) is fixed, the firm's owners (its common stockholders) do not care how this pie is sliced.

The law also applies to the *mix* of debt securities issued by the firm. The choices of long-term versus short-term, secured versus unsecured, senior versus subordinated, and convertible versus nonconvertible debt all should have no effect on the overall value of the firm.

TABLE 17-1

Macbeth Spot Removers is entirely equity-financed. Although it *expects* to have an income of $1500 a year in perpetuity, this income is not certain. This table shows the return to the stockholder under different assumptions about operating income. We assume no taxes.

Data				
Number of shares	1,000			
Price per share	$10			
Market value of shares	$10,000			

Outcomes				
Operating income, dollars	500	1,000	**1,500**	2,000
Earnings per share, dollars	.50	1.00	**1.50**	2.00
Return on shares, percent	5	10	**15**	20
			Expected outcome	

Combining assets and splitting them up will not affect values as long as they do not affect an investor's choice. When we showed that capital structure does not affect choice, we implicitly assumed that both companies and individuals can borrow and lend at the same risk-free rate of interest. As long as this is so, individuals can "undo" the effect of any changes in the firm's capital structure.

In practice corporate debt is not risk-free and firms cannot escape with rates of interest appropriate to a government security. Some people's initial reaction is that this alone invalidates MM's proposition. It is a natural mistake, but capital structure can be irrelevant even when debt is risky.

If a company borrows money, it does not *guarantee* repayment: It repays the debt in full only if its assets are worth more than the debt obligation. The shareholders in the company, therefore, have limited liability.

Many individuals would like to borrow with limited liability. They might, therefore, be prepared to pay a small premium for levered shares *if the supply of levered shares was insufficient to meet their needs.*[3] But there are literally thousands of common stocks of companies that borrow. Therefore it is unlikely that an issue of debt would induce them to pay a premium for *your* shares.[4]

An Example of Proposition I	Macbeth Spot Removers is reviewing its capital structure. Table 17-1 shows its current position. The company has no leverage and all the operating income is paid as dividends to the common stockholders (we assume still that there are no

[3] Of course individuals could *create* limited liability if they chose. In other words, the lender could agree that borrowers need repay their debt in full only if the assets of company X are worth more than a certain amount. Presumably individuals don't enter into such arrangements because they can obtain limited liability more simply by investing in the stocks of levered companies.

[4] Capital structure is also irrelevant if each investor holds a fully diversified portfolio. In that case he or she owns all the risky securities offered by a company (both debt and equity). But anybody who owns *all* the risky securities doesn't care about how the cash flows are divided between different securities.

taxes). The expected earnings and dividends per share are $1.50, but this figure is by no means certain—it could turn out to be more or less than $1.50. The price of each share is $10. Since the firm expects to produce a level stream of earnings in perpetuity, the expected return on the share is equal to the earnings-price ratio, $1.50/10.00 = .15$ or 15 percent.[5]

Ms. Macbeth, the firm's president, has come to the conclusion that shareholders would be better off if the company had equal proportions of debt and equity. She therefore proposes to issue $5000 of debt at an interest rate of 10 percent and use the proceeds to repurchase 500 shares. To support her proposal, Ms. Macbeth has analyzed the situation under different assumptions about operating income. The results of her calculations are shown in Table 17-2.

In order to see more clearly how leverage would affect earnings per share, Ms. Macbeth has also produced Figure 17-1. The solid line shows how earnings per share would vary with operating income under the firm's current all-equity financing. It is, therefore, simply a plot of the data in Table 17-1. The dotted line shows how earnings per share would vary given equal proportions of debt and equity. It is, therefore, a plot of the data in Table 17-2.

Ms. Macbeth reasons as follows: "It is clear that the effect of leverage depends on the company's income. If income is greater than $1000, the return to the equity holder is *increased* by leverage. If it is less than $1000, the return is *reduced* by leverage. The return is unaffected when operating income is exactly $1000. At this point the return on the market value of the assets is 10 percent, which is exactly equal to the interest rate on the debt. Our capital structure decision, therefore, boils down to what we think about income prospects. Since we expect operating income to be above the $1000 break-even point, I believe we can best help our shareholders by going ahead with the $5000 debt issue."

[5] See Chapter 4, Section 4.

TABLE 17-2
Macbeth Spot Removers is wondering whether to issue $5000 of debt at an interest rate of 10 percent and repurchase 500 shares. This table shows the return to the shareholder under different assumptions about operating income.

Data	
Number of shares	500
Price per share	$10
Market value of shares	$5,000
Market value of debt	$5,000
Interest at 10 percent	$500

Outcomes				
Operating income, dollars	500	1,000	**1,500**	2,000
Interest, dollars	500	500	**500**	500
Equity earnings, dollars	0	500	**1,000**	1,500
Earnings per share, dollars	0	1	**2**	3
Return on shares, percent	0	10	**20**	30
			Expected outcome	

FIGURE 17-1
Borrowing increases Macbeth's EPS (earnings per share) when operating income is greater than $1000 and reduces EPS when operating income is less than $1000. Expected EPS rise from $1.50 to $2.

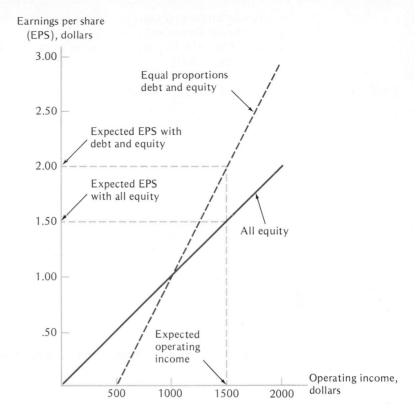

As financial manager of Macbeth Spot Removers, you reply as follows: "I agree that leverage will help the shareholder as long as our income is greater than $1000. But your argument ignores the fact that Macbeth's shareholders have the alternative of borrowing on their own account. For example, suppose that a person borrows $10 and then invests $20 in two unlevered Macbeth shares. This person has to put up only $10 of his or her own money. The payoff on the investment varies with Macbeth's operating income, as shown in Table 17-3. This is exactly the same set of payoffs as the investor would get by buying one share in the levered company. (Compare the last two lines of Tables 17-2 and 17-3.) Therefore a share in the levered company must also sell for $10. If Macbeth goes ahead and borrows,

TABLE 17-3
Individual investors can replicate Macbeth's leverage.

	OPERATING INCOME, DOLLARS			
	500	1,000	**1,500**	2,000
Earnings on two shares, dollars	1	2	**3**	4
Less interest at 10 percent, dollars	1	1	**1**	1
Net earnings on investment, dollars	0	1	**2**	3
Return on $10 investment, percent	0	10	**20**	30
			Expected outcome	

it will not allow investors to do anything that they could not do already, and so it will not increase value."

The argument that you are using is exactly the same as MM used to prove proposition I.

17-2   HOW LEVERAGE AFFECTS RETURNS

Implications of Proposition I

Consider now the implications of proposition I for the expected returns on Macbeth stock:

	Current Structure: All Equity	Proposed Structure: Equal Debt and Equity
Expected earnings per share	$1.50	$2.00
Price per share	$10.00	$10.00
Expected return on share, percent	15	20

Leverage increases the expected stream of earnings per share, but *not* the share price. The reason is that the change in the expected earnings stream is exactly offset by a change in the rate at which the earnings are capitalized. The expected return on the share (which for a perpetuity is equal to the earnings-price ratio) increases from 15 to 20 percent. We now show how this comes about.

The expected return on a firm's assets r_A is equal to the expected operating income divided by the total market value of the firm's securities:

$$\text{Expected return on assets} = r_A = \frac{\text{expected operating income}}{\text{market value of all securities}}$$

We have seen that in perfect capital markets the company's borrowing decision does not affect *either* the firm's operating income *or* the total market value of its securities. Therefore the borrowing decision also does not affect the expected return on the firm's assets r_A.

Suppose that an investor holds all of a company's debt and all its equity. This investor would be entitled to all the firm's operating income; therefore, the expected return on the portfolio would be equal to r_A.

The expected return on a portfolio is equal to a weighted average of the expected returns on the individual holdings. Therefore the expected return on a portfolio consisting of *all* the firm's securities is

$$\begin{array}{c}\text{Expected return}\\\text{on assets}\end{array} = \left(\begin{array}{c}\text{proportion}\\\text{in debt}\end{array} \times \begin{array}{c}\text{expected}\\\text{return on}\\\text{debt}\end{array}\right) + \left(\begin{array}{c}\text{proportion}\\\text{in equity}\end{array} \times \begin{array}{c}\text{expected}\\\text{return on}\\\text{equity}\end{array}\right)$$

$$r_A = \left(\frac{D}{D + E} \times r_D\right) + \left(\frac{E}{D + E} \times r_E\right)$$

We can rearrange this equation to obtain an expression for r_E, the expected return on the equity of a levered firm:

$$\begin{array}{c}\text{Expected return}\\\text{on equity}\end{array} = \begin{array}{c}\text{expected}\\\text{return on}\\\text{assets}\end{array} + \begin{array}{c}\text{debt-}\\\text{equity}\\\text{ratio}\end{array} \times \left(\begin{array}{c}\text{expected}\\\text{return on}\\\text{assets}\end{array} - \begin{array}{c}\text{expected}\\\text{return on}\\\text{debt}\end{array}\right)$$

$$r_E = r_A + \frac{D}{E}(r_A - r_D)$$

Proposition II

This is MM's proposition II: The expected rate of return on the common stock of a levered firm increases in proportion to the debt-equity ratio (D/E), expressed in market values; the rate of increase depends on the spread between r_A, the expected rate of return on a portfolio of all the firm's securities, and r_D, the expected return on the debt. Note that $r_E = r_A$ if the firm has no debt.

We can check out this formula for Macbeth Spot Removers. Before the decision to borrow

$$r_E = r_A = \frac{\text{expected operating income}}{\text{market value of all securities}}$$

$$= \frac{1500}{10,000} = .15, \text{ or } 15\%$$

If the firm goes ahead with its plan to borrow, the expected return on assets r_A is still 15 percent. The expected return on equity is

$$r_E = r_A + \frac{D}{E}(r_A - r_D)$$

$$= .15 + \frac{5000}{5000}(.15 - .10)$$

$$= .20, \text{ or } 20\%$$

The general implications of MM's proposition II are shown in Figure 17-2. The figure assumes that the firm's bonds are essentially risk-free at low debt levels. Thus r_D is independent of D/E and r_E increases linearly as D/E increases. As the firm borrows more, the risk of default increases and the firm is required to pay higher rates of interest. Proposition II predicts that when this occurs the rate of increase in r_E slows down. This is also shown in Figure 17-2. The more debt the firm has, the less sensitive r_E is to further borrowing.

Why does the slope of the r_E line in Figure 17-2 taper off as D/E increases? Essentially because holders of risky debt bear some of the firm's business risk. As

FIGURE 17-2
MM's proposition II. The expected return on equity r_E increases linearly with the debt-equity ratio so long as debt is risk-free. But if leverage increases the risk of the debt, debtholders demand a higher return on the debt. This causes the rate of increase in r_E to slow down.

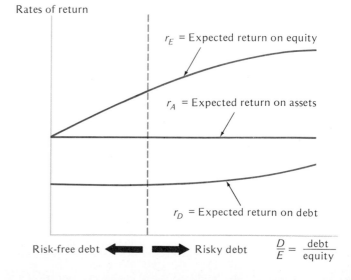

the firm borrows more, more of that risk is transferred from stockholders to bond-holders.

The Risk-Return Trade-off

Proposition I says that financial leverage has no effect on shareholders' wealth. Proposition II says that the rate of return they can expect to receive on their shares increases as the firm's debt-equity ratio increases. How can shareholders be indifferent to increased leverage when it increases expected return? The answer is that any increase in expected return is exactly offset by an increase in risk and therefore in shareholders' *required* rate of return.

Look at what happens to the risk of Macbeth shares if it moves to equal debt-equity proportions. Table 17-4 shows how a shortfall in operating income affects the payoff to the shareholders.

You can see that the debt-equity proportion does not affect the *dollar* risk borne by equityholders. Suppose operating income drops from $1500 to $500. Under all-equity financing, equity earnings drop by $1 per share. There are 1000 outstanding shares, and so *total* equity earnings fall by $1 × 1000 = $1000. With 50 percent debt, the same drop in operating income reduces earnings per share by $2. But there are only 500 shares outstanding, and so total equity income drops by $2 × 500 = $1000, just as in the all-equity case.

However, the debt-equity choice does amplify the spread of *percentage* returns. If the firm is all-equity-financed, a decline of $1000 in the operating income reduces the return on the shares by 10 percent. If the firm issues risk-free debt with a fixed interest payment of $500 a year, then a decline of $1000 in the operating income reduces the return on the shares by 20 percent. In other words, the effect of leverage is to double the amplitude of the swings in Macbeth's shares. Whatever the beta of the firm's shares before the refinancing, it would be twice as high afterward.

Just as the expected return on the firm's assets is a weighted average of the expected return on the individual securities, so likewise is the beta of the firm's assets a weighted average of the betas of the individual securities:[6]

$$\text{Beta of assets} = \left(\begin{matrix} \text{proportion} \\ \text{of debt} \end{matrix} \times \begin{matrix} \text{beta of} \\ \text{debt} \end{matrix} \right) + \left(\begin{matrix} \text{proportion} \\ \text{of equity} \end{matrix} \times \begin{matrix} \text{beta of} \\ \text{equity} \end{matrix} \right)$$

$$\beta_A = \left(\frac{D}{D + E} \times \beta_D \right) + \left(\frac{E}{D + E} \times \beta_E \right)$$

[6] This equation should look familiar. We used it in Section 9-2 to work out how a change in leverage would affect the beta of Philadelphia Electric stock.

TABLE 17-4
Leverage increases the risk of Macbeth shares.

		OPERATING INCOME	
		$500	$1500
All equity:	Earnings per share, dollars	.50	1.50
	Return on shares, percent	5	15
50 percent debt:	Earnings per share, dollars	0	2.00
	Return on shares, percent	0	20

FIGURE 17-3
If Macbeth is unlevered, the expected return on its equity equals the expected return on its assets. Leverage increases both the expected return on equity (r_E) and the risk of equity (β_E).

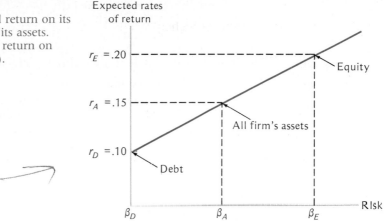

We can rearrange this equation also to give an expression for β_E, the beta of the equity of a levered firm:

$$\text{Beta of equity} = \frac{\text{beta of}}{\text{assets}} + \frac{\text{debt-equity}}{\text{ratio}} \times \left(\frac{\text{beta of}}{\text{assets}} - \frac{\text{beta of}}{\text{debt}} \right)$$

$$\beta_E = \beta_A + \frac{D}{E}(\beta_A - \beta_D)$$

Now you can see why investors require higher returns on levered equity. The required return simply rises to match the increased risk.

In Figure 17-3, we have plotted the expected returns and the risk of Macbeth's securities, assuming that the interest on the debt is risk-free.[7]

17-3 THE TRADITIONAL POSITION

What did financial experts think about debt policy before MM? It is not easy to say because with hindsight we see that they did not think too clearly.[8] However, a "traditional" position has emerged in response to MM. In order to understand it, we have to discuss the **weighted-average cost of capital.**

The expected return on a portfolio of all the company's securities is often referred to as the *weighted-average cost of capital:*[9]

$$\text{Weighted-average cost of capital} = r_A = \left(\frac{D}{V} \times r_D \right) + \left(\frac{E}{V} \times r_E \right)$$

The weighted-average cost of capital is used in capital budgeting decisions to find the net present value of projects that would not change the business risk of the firm.

---

[7] In this case $\beta_D = 0$ and $\beta_E = \beta_A + (D/E)\beta_A$.

[8] Financial economists in the year 2000 may remark on Brealey and Myers's blind spots and clumsy reasoning. On the other hand, they may not remember us at all.

[9] Remember that in this chapter we ignore taxes. In Chapter 19, we shall see that the weighted-average cost of capital formula needs to be amended when debt interest can be deducted from taxable profits.

For example, suppose that a firm has $2 million of outstanding debt and 100,000 outstanding shares selling at $30 per share. Its current borrowing rate is 8 percent and the financial manager thinks that the stock is priced to offer a 15 percent return, therefore $r_E = .15$. (The hard part is estimating r_E, of course.) This is all we need to calculate the weighted-average cost of capital:

$$D = \$2 \text{ million}$$
$$E = 100,000 \text{ shares} \times \$30 \text{ per share} = \$3 \text{ million}$$
$$V = D + E = 2 + 3 = \$5 \text{ million}$$

$$\text{Weighted-average cost of capital} = \left(\frac{D}{V} \times r_D\right) + \left(\frac{E}{V} \times r_E\right)$$

$$\left(\frac{2}{5} \times .08\right) + \left(\frac{3}{5} \times .15\right)$$

$$= .122, \text{ or } 12.2\%$$

Note that we are still assuming that proposition I holds. If it doesn't, we can't use this simple weighted average as the discount rate even for projects that do not change the firm's business "risk class." As we will see in Chapter 19, the weighted-average cost of capital is at best a starting point for setting discount rates.

Two Warnings

Sometimes the objective in financing decisions is stated not as "maximize overall market value" but as "minimize the weighted-average cost of capital." These are equivalent objectives under the simplifying assumptions we have made so far. If MM's proposition I does *not* hold, then the capital structure that maximizes the value of the firm also minimizes the weighted-average cost of capital, *provided* that operating income is independent of capital structure. Remember that the weighted-average cost of capital equals the expected operating income divided by the market value of all securities. Anything that increases the value of the firm reduces the weighted-average cost of capital if operating income is constant. But if operating income is varying too, all bets are off.

In Chapter 18 we will show that financial leverage can affect operating income in several ways. Therefore maximizing the value of the firm is *not* always equivalent to minimizing the weighted-average cost of capital.

Warning 1. Shareholders want management to increase the firm's value. They are more interested in being rich than in owning a firm with a low weighted-average cost of capital.

Warning 2. Trying to minimize the weighted-average cost of capital seems to encourage logical short circuits like the following. Suppose that someone says: "Shareholders demand—and deserve—higher expected rates of return than bond-holders do. Therefore debt is the cheaper capital source. We can reduce the weighted-average cost of capital by borrowing more." But this doesn't follow if the extra borrowing leads stockholders to demand a still higher expected rate of return. According to MM's proposition II the "cost of equity capital" r_E increases by just enough to keep the weighted-average cost of capital constant.

This is not the only logical short circuit you are likely to encounter. We have cited two more in question 5 at the end of this chapter.

<table>
<tr><td>

**Rates of
Return on
Levered
Equity—The
Traditional
Position**

</td><td>

You may ask why we have even mentioned the weighted-average cost of capital at this point if it is often wrong or confusing as a financial objective. We had to because the traditionalists accept this objective and argue their case in terms of it.

The logical short circuit we just described rested on the assumption that r_E, the expected rate of return demanded by stockholders, does not rise as the firm borrows more. Suppose, just for the sake of argument, that this is true. Then r_A, the weighted-average cost of capital, must decline as the debt-equity ratio rises.

Take Figure 17-4, for example, which is drawn on the assumption that shareholders demand 12 percent no matter how much debt the firm has, and that bondholders always want 8 percent. The weighted-average cost of capital starts at 12 percent and ends up at 8. Suppose that this firm's operating income is a level, perpetual stream of $100,000 a year. Then firm value starts at

</td></tr>
</table>

$$V = \frac{100,000}{.12} = \$833,333$$

and ends up at

$$V = \frac{100,000}{.08} = \$1,250,000$$

The gain of $416,667 falls into the stockholders' pockets.[10]

Of course this is absurd: A firm that reaches 100 percent debt *has to be bankrupt.* If there is *any* chance that the firm could remain solvent, then the equity retains some value, and the firm cannot be 100 percent debt-financed. (Remember that we are working with the *market* values of debt and equity.)

But if the firm is bankrupt and its original shares are worthless pieces of paper, then its *lenders are its new shareholders.* The firm is back to all-equity financing! We

---

[10] Note that Figure 17-4 relates r_E and r_D to D/V, the ratio of debt to firm value, rather than to the debt-equity ratio D/E. In this figure we wanted to show what happens when the firm is 100 percent debt-financed. At that point $E = 0$ and D/E is infinite.

FIGURE 17-4
If the expected rate of return demanded by stockholders r_E is unaffected by financial leverage, then the weighted average cost of capital r_A declines as the firm borrows more. At 100 percent debt r_A equals the borrowing rate r_D. Of course this is an absurd and totally unrealistic case.

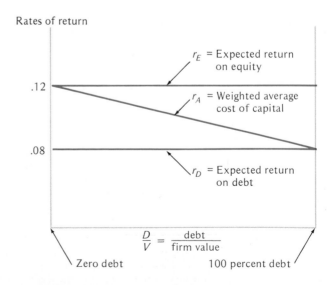

assumed that the original stockholders demanded 12 percent—why should the new ones demand any less? They have to bear all of the firm's business risk.[11]

The situation described in Figure 17-4 is just impossible.[12] However, it is possible to stake out a position somewhere *between* Figures 17-3 and 17-4. That is exactly what the traditionalists have done. Their hypothesis is shown in Figure 17-5. They hold that a moderate degree of financial leverage may increase the expected equity return r_E although not to the degree predicted by MM's proposition II. But irresponsible firms that borrow *excessively* find r_E shooting up faster than MM predict. Consequently, the weighted-average cost of capital r_A declines at first, then rises. Its minimum point is the point of optimal capital structure. Remember that minimizing r_A is equivalent to maximizing overall firm value if, as the traditionalists assume, operating income is unaffected by borrowing.

Two arguments might be advanced in support of the traditional position. First, it could be that investors don't notice or appreciate the financial risk created by "moderate" borrowing, although they wake up when debt is "excessive." If so, investors in moderately leveraged firms may accept a lower rate of return than they really should.

That seems naive.[13] The second argument is better. It accepts MM's reasoning as applied to perfect capital markets, but holds that actual markets are imperfect. Imperfections may allow firms that borrow to provide a valuable service for investors. If so, levered shares might trade at premium prices compared to their theoretical values in perfect markets.

Suppose that corporations can borrow more cheaply than individuals. Then it would pay investors who want to borrow to do so indirectly by holding the stock of levered firms. They would be willing to live with expected rates of return that do not fully compensate them for the business and financial risk they bear.

Is corporate borrowing really cheaper? It's hard to say. Interest rates on home mortgages are not too different from rates on high-grade corporate bonds.[14] Rates on margin debt (borrowing from a stockbroker with the investor's shares tendered as security) are not too different from the rates firms pay banks for short-term loans.

There are some individuals who face relatively high interest rates, largely because of the costs lenders incur in making and servicing small loans. There are economies of scale in borrowing. A group of small investors could do better by borrowing via a corporation, in effect pooling their loans and saving transaction costs.[15]

---

[11] We ignore the costs, delays, and other complications of bankruptcy. They are discussed in Chapter 18.

[12] This case is often termed the *net-income* (NI) approach because investors are assumed to capitalize income *after* interest at the same rate regardless of financial leverage. In contrast, MM's approach is a net-operating-income (NOI) approach, because the value of the firm is fundamentally determined by operating income, the total dollar return to *both* bondholders and stockholders. This distinction was emphasized by Durand in his important, pre-MM paper (op. cit.).

[13] This first argument may reflect a confusion between financial risk and the risk of default. Default is not a serious threat when borrowing is moderate; stockholders worry about it only when the firm goes "too far." But stockholders bear financial risk—in the form of increased volatility of rate of return and higher beta—even when the chance of default is nil. We demonstrated this in Figure 17-3.

[14] One of the authors once obtained a home mortgage at a rate one-half percentage point *less* than the contemporaneous yield on long-term AT&T bonds.

[15] Even here there are alternatives to borrowing on personal account. Investors can draw down their savings accounts or sell a portion of their investment in bonds. The impact of reductions in lending on the investor's balance sheet and risk position is exactly the same as increases in borrowing.

FIGURE 17-5
The dashed lines show MM's view of the effect of leverage on the expected return on equity r_E and the weighted-average cost of capital r_A. (See Figure 17-2.) The solid lines show the traditional view. Traditionalists say that borrowing at first increases r_E more slowly than MM predict but that r_E shoots up with excessive borrowing. If so, the weighted-average cost of capital can be minimized if you use just the right amount of debt.

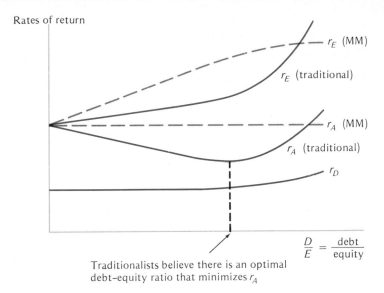

Rates of return

r_E (MM)

r_E (traditional)

r_A (MM)

r_A (traditional)

r_D

$$\frac{D}{E} = \frac{\text{debt}}{\text{equity}}$$

Traditionalists believe there is an optimal debt–equity ratio that minimizes r_A

But suppose that this class of investors is large, both in number and in the aggregate wealth it brings to capital markets. Shouldn't the investors' needs be fully satisfied by the thousands of levered firms already existing? Is there really an unsatisfied clientele of small investors standing ready to pay a premium for one more firm that borrows?

Maybe the market for corporate leverage is like the market for automobiles. Americans need millions of automobiles and are willing to pay thousands of dollars apiece for them. But that doesn't mean that you could strike it rich by going into the automobile business. You're at least 50 years too late.

Where to Look for Violations of MM's Propositions

MM's propositions depend on perfect capital markets. Here we are using the phrase *perfect capital markets* a bit loosely, for scholars have argued about the *degree* of perfection necessary for proposition I. (We remember an off-the-cuff comment made many years ago by Ezra Solomon: "A perfect capital market should be *defined* as one in which the MM theory holds.")

We believe capital markets are generally well-functioning, but they are not 100 percent perfect 100 percent of the time. Therefore, MM must be wrong some times in some places. The financial manager's problem is to figure out when and where.

That is not easy. Just finding market imperfections is insufficient.

Consider that traditionalists' claim that imperfections make borrowing costly and inconvenient for many individuals. That creates a clientele for whom corporate borrowing is better than personal borrowing. That clientele would, in principle, be willing to pay a premium for the shares of a levered firm.

But maybe they don't *have* to pay a premium. Perhaps smart financial managers long ago recognized this clientele and shifted the capital structures of their firms to meet its needs. The shifts would not have been difficult or costly to make. But if the clientele is now satisfied it is no longer willing to pay a premium for levered shares. Only the financial managers who *first* recognized the clientele extracted any advantage from it.

Today's Unsatisfied Clienteles Are Probably Interested in Exotic Securities

So far we have made little progress in identifying cases where firm value might plausibly depend on financing. But our examples illustrate what smart financial managers look for. They look for an *unsatisfied* clientele, investors who want a particular kind of financial instrument but because of market imperfections can't get it or can't get it cheaply.

MM's proposition I is violated when the firm, by imaginative design of its capital structure, can offer some *financial service* that meets the needs of such a clientele. Either the service must be new and unique, or the firm must find a way to provide some old service more cheaply than other firms or financial intermediaries can.

Now, is there an unsatisfied clientele for garden-variety debt or levered equity? We doubt it. But perhaps you can invent an exotic security and uncover a latent demand for it.

AT&T's Stillborn Savings Bonds

On October 9, 1970, a front-page article appeared in *The Wall Street Journal* with the headline "AT&T Mulls Offering Ma Bell Savings Bonds Similar to Treasury's." The reporter quoted "sources" at AT&T who described the terms of the possible issue. The bonds would be sold directly to investors in $100 denominations through 2000 AT&T business offices. They would yield at least 6.5 percent. Investors would not receive cash interest payments. Instead, the value of the bonds would appreciate over time, in the same way that a savings deposit grows when you leave the interest to accumulate. Thus, at a 6.5 percent yield you might purchase a 10-year bond for $100 and 10 years later cash it in for

$$\text{Future value} = \$100(1.065)^{10} = \$187.71$$

This was an almost exact copy of a United States savings bond, except that the interest rate was higher. At the time, United States savings bonds offered only 5 percent, or 5.5 percent if held for a full 10 years.

AT&T's motives were clear. It was borrowing billions of dollars yearly, and at that time its newly issued bonds were yielding about 8.6 percent. Borrowing at 6.5 percent would have been a big improvement.

And there was a natural market for AT&T savings bonds: an unsatisfied clientele of investors who found it difficult to take advantage of the high yields offered in the bond market. There were billions of dollars on deposit in bank savings accounts and savings and loan associations. The *maximum* rate offered on these accounts was 6 percent on deposits committed for a 2-year period. Most of the deposits yielded only about 5 percent.

Why didn't depositors cash in and invest in higher-yielding securities? Even the most conservative investor could obtain a 7.3 percent yield in 7-year United States notes: Corporate bonds yielded 8 percent and up. Many depositors did cash in.[16] But many did not, partly from inertia and unfamiliarity with the bond market, and partly because buying bonds is inconvenient if you only have a few hundred or a few thousand dollars to invest. The minimum denomination for a corporate bond is $1000. Ten thousand dollars is more common.

AT&T savings bonds would have offered such investors an easy, convenient way to earn 6.5 percent or more. At the same time they would have saved AT&T a lot of money. It was a great idea.

---

[16] This is called *disintermediation* (probably the longest word in this book). The investor who withdraws funds from a savings account and invests directly in securities is reducing the role of financial intermediation. The intermediary (the savings institution) is no longer used as a vehicle for investment.

What created this opportunity? What explained the spread between bond rates and yields on savings accounts? The most important cause was restrictions imposed by the federal government on interest rates offered to small investors. The government was trying to protect savings institutions by limiting competition for their depositors' money. The fear was that depositors would run off in search of higher yields, causing a cash drain that savings institutions would not be able to meet, cutting off the supply of funds from those institutions for new real estate mortgages, and knocking the housing market for a loop. The savings institutions could not compete by offering higher interest rates on deposits—even if the government had allowed them to—because most of their past deposits had been locked up in fixed-rate mortgages issued when interest rates were lower.

These regulations helped the savings institutions, and may have helped the housing market, but they were grossly unjust to small investors, who lost billions in interest income. We have never been able to understand why there was no political pressure to compensate small investors for the cost of these restrictions, or why consumer advocates never took up the small investor's cause.

Anyway, it was no surprise to find both savings institutions and the federal government arrayed against AT&T's plan. AT&T capitulated and its idea died a quiet death.

But if we believe the idea would have worked, then we have found a counter-example to MM's proposition I. AT&T could have increased its overall market value by issuing savings bonds rather than garden-variety debt and equity.

Imperfections and Opportunities

The most serious capital market imperfections are often those created and protected by government. But even these tend to erode. An imperfection which supports a violation of MM's proposition I *also* creates a money-making opportunity. Firms and financial intermediaries will find some way to reach the clientele of investors that the imperfection is frustrating. When they finally get low-cost access to that clientele, MM's proposition is restored.

Thus money-market funds were invented in the mid-1970s and offered to individual investors in competition with conventional savings accounts. Money-market funds are mutual funds invested in Treasury bills, commercial paper, and other high-grade, short-term debt instruments. Any saver with a few thousand dollars to invest can gain access to these instruments through a money fund, yet the investor can withdraw funds anytime by writing a check against his or her money-fund balance. A money-market fund thus resembles a checking or savings account which pays close to market interest rates.[17] These money-market funds have become enormously popular. By early 1987, their assets had increased to about $230 billion.

The money fund is one of many financial inventions which have extended the menu of opportunities open to investors. Another is the *floating-rate note*, first issued on a large scale, and with terms designed to appeal to individual investors, by Citicorp on July 30, 1974. Floating-rate notes are medium-term debt securities whose interest payments "float" with short-term interest rates. On the Citicorp issue, for example, the coupon rate used to calculate each semiannual interest payment was set at one percentage point above the contemporaneous yield on Treasury bills. The holder of the Citicorp note was therefore hedged against fluc-

---

[17] Money funds offer rates slightly lower than on the securities they invest in. This spread covers the funds' operating costs and profits.

tuating interest rates, because Citicorp sent a larger semiannual check when interest rates rose (though, of course, a smaller check when rates fell).

Citicorp evidently found an untapped clientele of investors, for it was able to raise $650 million in the first offering, and within 5 months an additional $650 million of floating-rate notes was issued by other companies. By the mid-1980s about $43 billion of floating-rate securities was outstanding.[18]

What about the savings institutions? During the 1970s, more and more of their depositors' money left for money funds, floating-rate notes, and other high-yielding investments. The institutions were forced to compete, so they gradually edged up the rates paid to investors willing to salt money away for a few years. They provided extra services in place of higher interest rates. Many offered "free gifts"—toasters, radios, hair dryers—to new depositors. But as they competed, and as money funds and other high-yielding instruments became more easily available, the protection given by government restrictions on savings account rates became less and less helpful. Finally the restrictions were lifted, and savings institutions met their competition head on.[19]

In short, there are many more options open to the small investor now than there were in 1970. AT&T's savings bonds might work today, but there is no longer any special clientele who would buy them on terms attractive to AT&T. If *you* ever find an unsatisfied clientele, do something about it right away, or capital markets will evolve and steal it from you.

17-4 SUMMARY

At the start of this chapter we characterized the firm's financing decision as a marketing problem. Think of the financial manager as taking all the firm's real assets and selling them to investors as a package of securities. Some financial managers choose the simplest package possible: all-equity financing. Some end up issuing dozens of debt and equity securities. The problem is to find the particular combination that maximizes the market value of the firm.

Modigliani and Miller's (MM's) famous proposition I states that no combination is better than any other—that the firm's overall market value (the value of all its securities) is independent of capital structure. Firms that borrow do offer investors a more complex menu of securities, but investors yawn in response. The menu is redundant. Any shift in capital structure can be duplicated or "undone" by investors. Why should they pay extra for borrowing indirectly (by holding shares in a levered firm) when they can borrow just as easily and cheaply on their own accounts?

MM agree that borrowing increases the expected rate of return on shareholders' investment. But it also increases the risk of the firm's shares. MM show that the risk increase exactly offsets the increase in expected return, leaving stockholders no better or worse off.

Proposition I is an extremely general result. It applies not just to the debt-equity

---

[18] A good review of the development of the floating-rate market is Richard S. Wilson, "Domestic Floating-Rate and Adjustable-Rate Debt Securities," in F. J. Fabozzi and I. M. Pollack, eds., *Handbook of Fixed Income Securities*, 2d ed., Dow Jones–Irwin, Homewood, Ill., 1987.

[19] By 1986, interest rates on regular savings accounts were still limited by government regulation, but banks and savings institutions were free to create other accounts at unrestricted rates. For example, most banks offered "money-market accounts," which closely resembled money-market funds. Thus the remaining restrictions had little practical effect.

trade-off but to *any* choice of financing instruments. For example, MM would say that the choice between long-term and short-term debt has no effect on firm value.

The formal proofs of proposition I all depend on the assumption of perfect capital markets.[20] MM's opponents, the "traditionalists," argue that market imperfections make personal borrowing excessively costly, risky, and inconvenient for some investors. This creates a natural clientele willing to pay a premium for shares of levered firms. The traditionalists say that firms should borrow to realize the premium.

But this argument is incomplete. There may be a clientele for levered equity, but that is not enough; the clientele has to be *unsatisfied*. There are already thousands of levered firms available for investment. Is there still an unsatiated clientele for garden-variety debt and equity? We doubt it.

Proposition I is violated when financial managers find an untapped demand and satisfy it by issuing something new and different. The argument between MM and the traditionalists finally boils down to whether this is difficult or easy. We lean toward MM's view: Finding unsatisfied clienteles and designing exotic securities to meet their needs is a game that's fun to play but hard to win.

APPENDIX MM AND THE CAPITAL ASSET PRICING MODEL

We showed in Section 17-2 that, as the firm increases its leverage, the expected equity return goes up in lockstep with beta of the equity. Given this, it should be no surprise to find that we can use the capital asset pricing model to derive MM's proposition I. The following demonstration has been simplified by assuming that the firm can issue risk-free debt.

The firm is initially all-equity-financed. Its expected end-of-period value is V_1, which we take to include any operating income for the initial period. We now draw on the certainty-equivalent form of the capital asset pricing model which we derived in the appendix to Chapter 9. This states that the present value of the firm is

$$V = E = \frac{V_1 - \lambda \text{Cov} (\tilde{V}_1, \tilde{r}_m)}{1 + r_f}$$

where λ is the market price of risk $(r_m - r_f)/\sigma_m^2$.

Now suppose that the firm borrows D at the risk-free rate of interest and distributes the proceeds to stockholders. They get D dollars now but next year they will have to repay the debt with interest. Therefore instead of receiving V_1 at the end of the year, they can expect to receive only $V_1 - (1 + r_f)D$. The present value of their levered equity is therefore

$$E = \frac{V_1 - (1 + r_f)D - \lambda \text{ Cov} [\tilde{V}_1 - (1 + r_f)D, \tilde{r}_m]}{1 + r_f}$$

But since $(1 + r_f)D$ is known, it has no effect on the covariance. When debt is risk-free, stockholders have to bear *all* the risk associated with V_1. Therefore, we

---

[20] Proposition I can be proved umpteen different ways. The references at the end of this chapter include several more abstract and general proofs. Our formal proofs have been limited to MM's own arguments and (in the appendix) a proof based on the capital asset pricing model.

substitute Cov $(\tilde{V}_1, \tilde{r}_m)$ for Cov $[\tilde{V}_1 - (1 + r_f)D, \tilde{r}_m]$. This gives us

$$E = \frac{V_1 - (1 + r_f)D - \lambda \text{ Cov } (\tilde{V}_1, \tilde{r}_m)}{1 + r_f}$$

$$= \frac{V_1 - \lambda \text{ Cov } (\tilde{V}_1, \tilde{r}_m)}{1 + r_f} - D$$

To calculate the value of the *firm* we add the value of the debt D. This gives

$$V = \frac{V_1 - \lambda \text{ Cov } (\tilde{V}_1, \tilde{r}_m)}{1 + r_f}$$

The value of the levered firm is identical to the value of the unlevered firm.

FURTHER READING

The pioneering work on the theory of capital structure is:

F. Modigliani and M. H. Miller: "The Cost of Capital, Corporation Finance and the Theory of Investment," *American Economic Review*, **48:** 261–297 (June 1958).

However, Durand deserves credit for setting out the issues that MM later solved:

D. Durand: "Cost of Debt and Equity Funds for Business: Trends and Problems in Measurement," in *Conference on Research in Business Finance*, National Bureau of Economic Research, New York, 1952, pp. 215–247.

A somewhat difficult article which analyzes capital structure in the context of capital asset pricing theory is:

R. S. Hamada: "Portfolio Analysis, Market Equilibrium and Corporation Finance," *Journal of Finance*, **24:** 13–31 (March 1969).

More abstract and general theoretical treatments can be found in:

J. E. Stiglitz: "On the Irrelevance of Corporate Financial Policy," *American Economic Review*, **64:** 851–866 (December 1974).

E. F. Fama: "The Effects of a Firm's Investment and Financing Decisions," *American Economic Review*, **68:** 272–284 (June 1978).

QUIZ

1. Assume a perfectly competitive market with no corporate or personal taxes. Companies A and B each earn gross profits of P and differ only in their capital structure—A is wholly equity-financed and B has debt outstanding on which it pays a certain $100 of interest each year. Investor X purchases 10 percent of the equity of A.
   (*a*) What profits does X obtain?
   (*b*) What alternative strategy would provide the same result?
   (*c*) Suppose investor Y purchases 10 percent of the equity of B. What profits does Y obtain?
   (*d*) What alternative strategy would provide the same result?
2. Ms. Kraft owns 50,000 shares of the common stock of Copperhead Corporation with a market value of $2 per share, or $100,000 overall. The company is currently financed as follows:

	Book Value
Common stock	$2,000,000
(8 million shares)	
Short-term loans	$2,000,000

Copperhead now announces that it is replacing $1 million of short-term debt with an issue of common stock. What action can Ms. Kraft take to ensure that she is entitled to exactly the same proportion of profits as before? (Ignore taxes.)

3. The common stock and debt of Northern Sludge are valued at $50 million and $30 million, respectively. Investors currently require a 16 percent return on the common stock and an 8 percent return on the debt. If Northern Sludge issues an additional $10 million of common stock and uses this money to retire debt, what happens to the expected return on the stock? Assume that the change in capital structure does not affect the risk of the debt and that there are no taxes. If the risk of the debt did change, would your answer underestimate or overestimate the expected return on the stock?

4. Company C is financed entirely by common stock and has a β of 1.0. The stock has a price-earnings multiple of 10 and is priced to offer a 10 percent expected return. The company decides to repurchase half the common stock and substitute an equal value of debt. If the debt yields a risk-free 5 percent,

   (a) Give:

      (i) The beta of the common stock after the refinancing
      (ii) The beta of the debt
      (iii) The beta of the company (i.e., stock and debt combined)

   (b) Give:

      (i) The required return on the common stock before the refinancing
      (ii) The required return on the common stock after the refinancing
      (iii) The required return on the debt
      (iv) The required return on the company (i.e., stock and debt combined) after the refinancing

   (c) Assume that the operating profit of firm C is expected to remain constant. Give:

      (i) The percentage increase in earnings per share
      (ii) The new price-earnings multiple

5. Suppose that Macbeth Spot Removers issues $2500 of debt and uses the proceeds to repurchase 250 shares.

   (a) Rework Table 17-2 to show how earnings per share and share return now vary with operating income.
   (b) If the beta of Macbeth's assets is .8 and its debt is risk-free, what would be the beta of the equity after the increased borrowing?

6. True or false? Explain briefly.

   (a) Stockholders always benefit from an increase in company value.
   (b) MM's proposition I assumes that actions which maximize firm value also maximize shareholder wealth.
   (c) The reason that borrowing increases equity risk is because it increases the probability of bankruptcy.
   (d) If firms did not have limited liability, the risk of their assets would be increased.
   (e) If firms did not have limited liability, the risk of their equity would be increased.

FIGURE 17-6
See quiz question 7.

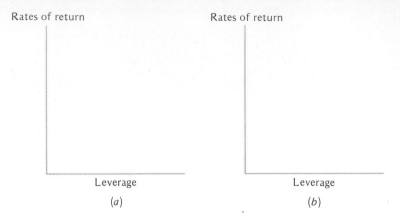

(f) Borrowing does not affect the return on equity if the return on the firm's assets is equal to the interest rate.

(g) As long as the firm is certain that the return on assets will be higher than the interest rate, an issue of debt makes the shareholders better off.

(h) MM's proposition I implies that an issue of debt increases expected earnings per share and leads to an offsetting fall in the price-earnings ratio.

(i) MM's proposition II assumes increased borrowing does not affect the interest rate on the firm's debt.

(j) Borrowing increases firm value if there is a clientele of investors with a reason to prefer debt.

7. Note the two blank graphs in Figure 17-6. On graph (a), assume MM are right, and plot the relationship between financial leverage and (i) the rates of return on debt and equity and (ii) the weighted-average cost of capital. Then fill in graph (b) assuming the traditionalists are right.

QUESTIONS AND PROBLEMS

 1. Companies A and B differ only in their capital structure. A is financed 30 percent debt and 70 percent equity: B is financed 10 percent debt and 90 percent equity. The debt of both companies is risk-free.

(a) Mr. X owns 1 percent of the common stock of A. What other investment package would produce identical cash flows for Mr. X?

(b) Mrs. Y owns 2 percent of the common stock of B. What other investment package would produce identical cash flows for Mrs. Y?

(c) Show that neither Mr. X nor Mrs. Y would invest in the common stock of B if the *total* value of company A were less than that of B.

2. Hubbard's Pet Foods is financed 80 percent by common stock and 20 percent by bonds. The expected return on the common stock is 12 percent and the rate of interest on the bonds is 6 percent. Assuming that the bonds are default-free, draw a graph that shows the expected return of Hubbard's common stock r_E and the expected return on the package of common stock and bonds r_A for different debt-equity ratios.

3. Here is a limerick:

There once was a man named Carruthers,
Who kept cows with miraculous udders.
He said, "Isn't this neat?
They give cream from one teat,
And skim milk from each of the others!"

What is the analogy between Mr. Carruthers's cows and firms' financing decisions? What would MM's proposition I, suitably adapted, say about the value of Mr. Carruthers's cows? Explain.

4. "MM totally ignore the fact that as you borrow more, you have to pay higher rates of interest." Explain carefully whether this is a valid objection.

5. Indicate what's wrong with the following arguments:
    (a) "As the firm borrows more and debt becomes risky, both stock- and bond-holders demand higher rates of return. Thus by *reducing* the debt ratio we can reduce *both* the cost of debt and the cost of equity, making everybody better off."
    (b) "Moderate borrowing doesn't significantly affect the probability of financial distress or bankruptcy. Consequently moderate borrowing won't increase the expected rate of return demanded by stockholders."

6. Each of the following statements is false or at least misleading. Explain why in each case.
    (a) "A capital investment opportunity offering a 10 percent DCF rate of return is an attractive project if it can be 100 percent debt-financed at an 8 percent interest rate."
    (b) "The more debt the firm issues, the higher the interest rate it must pay. That is one important reason why firms should operate at conservative debt levels."

7. Can you invent any new kinds of debt that might be attractive to investors? Why do you think they have not been issued?

8. It has been suggested that one disadvantage of common stock financing is that share prices tend to decline in recessions, thereby increasing the cost of capital and deterring investment. Discuss this view. Is it an argument for greater use of debt financing?

9. People often convey the idea behind MM's proposition I by various supermarket analogies, for example, "The value of a pie should not depend on how it is sliced," or, "The cost of a whole chicken should equal the cost of assembling one by buying two drumsticks, two wings, two breasts, and so on."

    Actually proposition I doesn't work in the supermarket. You'll pay less for an uncut whole pie than for a pie assembled from pieces purchased separately. Supermarkets charge more for chickens after they are cut up.

    Why? What costs or imperfections cause proposition I to fail in the supermarket? Are these costs or imperfections likely to be important for corporations issuing securities on the United States or world capital market? Explain.

18 How Much Should a Firm Borrow?

In Chapter 17 we found that debt policy rarely matters in well-functioning capital markets. Few financial managers would accept that conclusion as a practical guideline. If debt policy doesn't matter, then they shouldn't worry about it—financing decisions should be delegated to underlings. Yet financial managers do worry about debt policy. This chapter explains why.

If debt policy were *completely* irrelevant, then actual debt ratios should vary randomly from firm to firm and industry to industry. Yet almost all airlines, utilities, banks, and real estate development companies rely heavily on debt. And so do many firms in capital-intensive industries like steel, aluminum, chemicals, and mining. On the other hand, it is rare to find a drug company or advertising agency that is not predominantly equity-financed. Glamorous "growth" companies like Genentech, Hewlett-Packard, and Digital Equipment Corporation rarely use much debt despite rapid expansion and often heavy requirements for capital.

The explanation of these patterns lies partly in the things we left out of the last chapter. We ignored taxes. We assumed bankruptcy was cheap, quick, and painless. It isn't, and there are costs associated with financial distress even if legal bankruptcy is ultimately avoided. We ignored potential conflicts of interest between the firm's security holders. For example, we did not consider what happens to the firm's "old" creditors when new debt is issued or when a shift in investment strategy takes the firm into a riskier business. We ignored the possible *interactions* of investment and financing decisions.

Now we will put all these things back in: taxes first, then the costs of bankruptcy and financial distress. This will lead us to conflicts of interest and to possible interactions of financing and investment decisions. In the end we will have to admit that debt policy *does* matter.

However, we will *not* throw away the MM theory we developed so carefully in Chapter 17. We're shooting for a theory combining MM's insights *plus* the effects of taxes, costs of bankruptcy and financial distress, and various other complications. We're not dropping back to the traditional view based on imperfections in the capital market. Instead, we want to see how well-functioning capital markets *respond* to taxes and the other things covered in this chapter.

After finishing with theory, we will have a look at the evidence. We will point out the variables that seem to explain differences in financial leverage from company to company, and the instances in which increases in financial leverage seem to be good news to investors. Finally, we will attempt to draw the theory and evidence together in a checklist for financial managers to use when choosing their firms' debt-equity ratios.

TABLE 18-1

The tax deductibility of interest increases the total income that can be
paid out to bondholders and stockholders

	Income Statement of Firm U	Income Statement of Firm L
Earnings before interest and taxes	$1,000	$1,000.00
Interest paid to bondholders	0	80.00
Pretax income	1,000	920.00
Tax at 34 percent	340	312.80
Net income to stockholders	$ 660	$ 607.20
Total income to both bondholders and stockholders	$0 + 660 = $660	$80 + 607.20 = $687.20
Interest tax shield (.34 × interest)	$0	$27.20

18-1 CORPORATE TAXES

Debt financing has one important advantage under the corporate income tax system in the United States. The interest that the company pays is a tax-deductible
expense. Dividends and retained earnings are not. Thus the return to bondholders
escapes taxation at the corporate level.

Table 18-1 shows simple income statements for firm U, which has no debt,
and firm L, which has borrowed $1000 at 8 percent. The tax bill of L is $27.20
less than that of U. This is the *tax shield* provided by the debt of L. In effect the
government pays 34 percent of the interest expense of L. The total income that L
can pay out to its bondholders and stockholders increases by that amount.

Tax shields can be valuable assets. Suppose that the debt of L is permanent.
(That is, it plans to refinance its present debt obligations when they mature and
to keep "rolling over" its debt obligations indefinitely.) It looks forward to a permanent stream of cash flows of $27.20 per year. The risk of these flows is likely
to be less than the risk of the operating assets of L. The tax shields depend only
on the corporate tax rate[1] and on the ability of L to earn enough to cover interest
payments. Now the corporate tax rate has been pretty stable. (It did fall from 46
to 34 percent after the Tax Reform Act of 1986, but that was the first material
change since the 1950s.) And the ability of L to earn its interest payments must
be reasonably sure—otherwise it could not have borrowed at 8 percent.[2] Therefore
we should discount the interest tax shields at a relatively low rate.

But what rate? The most common assumption is that the risk of the tax shields
is the same as that of the interest payments generating them. Thus we discount at
8 percent, the expected rate of return demanded by investors who are holding the
firm's debt:

$$\text{PV tax shield} = \frac{27.20}{.08} = \$340$$

---

[1] Always use the marginal corporate tax rate, not the average rate. For large corporations the marginal
tax rate was 34 percent when this chapter was written (1987). Average rates were often much less
than that because of accelerated depreciation and various other adjustments.

[2] If the income of L does not cover interest in some future year, the tax shield is not necessarily lost.
L can "carry back" the loss and receive a tax refund up to the amount of taxes paid in the previous 3
years. If L has a string of losses, and thus no prior tax payments that can be refunded, then losses can
be "carried forward" and used to shield income in subsequent years. Losses can be carried forward for
up to 15 years.

In effect the government itself assumes 34 percent of the $1000 debt obligation of L.

Under these assumptions, the present value of the tax shield is independent of the return on the debt r_D. It equals the corporate tax rate T_c times the amount borrowed D:

$$\text{Interest payment} = \text{return on debt} \times \text{amount borrowed}$$

$$= r_D \times D$$

$$\text{PV tax shield} = \frac{\text{corporate tax rate} \times \text{expected interest payment}}{\text{expected return on debt}}$$

$$= \frac{T_c\,(r_D D)}{r_D} = T_c D$$

Of course PV tax shield is less if the firm does not plan to borrow permanently, or if it may not be able to use the tax shields in the future.

How Do Interest Tax Shields Contribute to the Value of Stockholders' Equity?

MM's proposition I amounts to saying that "the value of a pie does not depend on how it is sliced." The pie is the firm's assets, and the slices are the debt and equity claims. If we hold the pie constant, then a dollar more of debt means a dollar less of equity value.

But there is really a third slice, the government's. Look at Table 18-2: It shows an *expanded* balance sheet with *pretax* asset value on the left, and the value of the government's tax claim recognized as a liability on the right. MM would still say that the value of the pie—in this case *pretax* asset value—is not changed by slicing. But anything the firm can do to reduce the size of the government's slice obviously makes stockholders better off. One thing it can do is to borrow money, which reduces its tax bill, and as we saw in Table 18-1, increases the cash flows to debt and equity investors. The *after-tax* value of the firm (the sum of its debt and equity values as shown in a normal market value balance sheet) goes up by PV tax shield.

Recasting Merck's Capital Structure

Merck & Co. is a large, successful firm that uses essentially no long-term debt. Table 18-3a shows simplified book and market value balance sheets for Merck as of year-end 1986.

Suppose that you had been Merck's financial manager in 1986 with complete responsibility for its capital structure. You decide to borrow $1 billion on a permanent basis and use the proceeds to repurchase shares.

Table 18-3b shows the new balance sheets. The book version simply has $1000 million more long-term debt and $1000 million less equity. But we know that Merck's assets must be worth more, for its tax bill has been reduced by 34 percent of the interest on the new debt. In other words, Merck has a new asset, PV tax shield, which is worth $T_c D = .34 \times 1000 = \$340$ million. If the MM theory holds *except* for taxes, firm value must increase by $340 million to $18,359 million. Merck's equity ends up worth $16,239 million.

Now you have repurchased $1000 million worth of shares but Merck's equity value has dropped by only $660 million. Therefore Merck's stockholders must be $340 million ahead. Not a bad day's work.[3]

---

[3] Notice that as long as the bonds are sold at a fair price, all the benefits from the tax shield go to the shareholders.

TABLE 18-2
Normal and expanded market value balance sheets. In a normal balance sheet assets are valued after-tax. In the expanded balance sheet, assets are valued pretax and the value of the government's tax claim is recognized on the right-hand side. Interest tax shields are valuable because they reduce the government's claim.

NORMAL BALANCE SHEET (MARKET VALUES)		
Asset value (present value of after-tax cash flows)		Debt
		Equity
	Total assets	Total liabilities

EXPANDED BALANCE SHEET (MARKET VALUES)		
Pretax asset value (present value of *pretax* cash flows)		Debt
		Government's claim (present value of future taxes)
		Equity
	Total pretax assets	Total liabilities

TABLE 18-3a
Simplified balance sheets for Merck & Co., December 31, 1986 (figures in millions)

BOOK VALUES			
Net working capital	$ 1,094	$ 168	Long-term debt
Long-term assets	2,594	952	Other long-term liabilities
		2,569	Equity
Total assets	$ 3,688	$ 3,688	Total liabilities

MARKET VALUES			
Net working capital	$ 1,094	$ 168	Long-term debt
Market value of long-term assets	16,925	952	Other long-term liabilities
		16,899	Equity
Total assets	$18,019	$18,019	Total liabilities

Notes
1. Market value is assumed to equal book value for net working capital, long-term debt, and other long-term liabilities. Equity is entered at actual market value: number of shares times closing price on December 31, 1986. The difference between the market and book values of long-term assets is equal to the difference between the market and book values of equity.
2. The market value of the long-term assets includes the tax shield on the existing debt. This tax shield is worth $.34 \times \$168 = \$57$ million.
3. Book value of liabilities does not add because of rounding.

TABLE 18-3b
Balance sheets for Merck & Co., with additional $1 billion of long-term debt substituted for stockholders' equity (figures in millions)

BOOK VALUES

Net working capital	$ 1,094	$ 1,168	Long-term debt
			Other long-term
Long-term assets	2,594	952	liabilities
		1,569	Equity
Total assets	$ 3,688	$ 3,688	Total liabilities

MARKET VALUES

Net working capital	1,094	1,168	Long-term debt
Market value of			Other long-term
long-term assets	16,925	952	liabilities
Present value			
of additional			
tax shields	340	16,239	Equity
Total assets	$18,359	$18,359	Total liabilities

Notes
1. The figures in Table 18-3b for net working capital, long-term assets, and other long-term liabilities are identical to those in Table 18-3a.
2. Present value of tax shields assumed equal to corporate tax rate (34 percent) times amount of additional debt obligation.

MM and Taxes

We have just developed a version of MM's proposition I as "corrected" by them to reflect corporate income taxes.[4] The new proposition is

$$\text{Value of firm} = \text{value if all-equity-financed} + \text{PV tax shield}$$

In the special case of permanent debt,

$$\text{Value of firm} = \text{value if all-equity-financed} + T_c D$$

Our imaginary financial surgery on Merck provides the perfect illustration of the problems inherent in this "corrected" theory. That $340 million windfall came too easily; it seems to violate the law that "there is no such thing as a money machine." And if Merck's stockholders would be richer with $1168 million of corporate debt, why not $2268 or $3688 million?[5] Our formula implies that firm value and stockholders' wealth continue to go up as D increases. The implied optimal debt policy is embarrassingly extreme; all firms should be 100 percent debt-financed.

MM were not that fanatical about it. No one would expect the formula to apply at extreme debt ratios. But that does not explain why firms like Merck not only

---

[4] MM's original article [F. Modigliani and M. H. Miller, "The Cost of Capital, Corporation Finance and the Theory of Investment," *American Economic Review*, **48**: 261–297 (June 1958) recognized interest tax shields, but did not value them properly. They put things right in their 1963 article "Corporate Income Taxes and the Cost of Capital: A Correction," *American Economic Review*, **53**: 433–443 (June 1963).

[5] The last figure would correspond to a 100 percent book debt ratio. But Merck's market value would be $19,216 million according to our formula for firm value. Merck's common shares would have an aggregate value of $14,576 million.

exist, but thrive with no debt at all. It is hard to believe that the management of Merck is simply missing the boat.

Therefore we have argued ourselves into a corner. There are just two ways out:

1. Perhaps a fuller examination of the United States system of corporate *and personal* taxation will uncover a tax disadvantage of corporate borrowing, offsetting the present value of the corporate tax shield.
2. Perhaps firms that borrow incur other costs—bankruptcy costs, for example—offsetting the present value of the tax shield.

We will now explore these two escape routes.

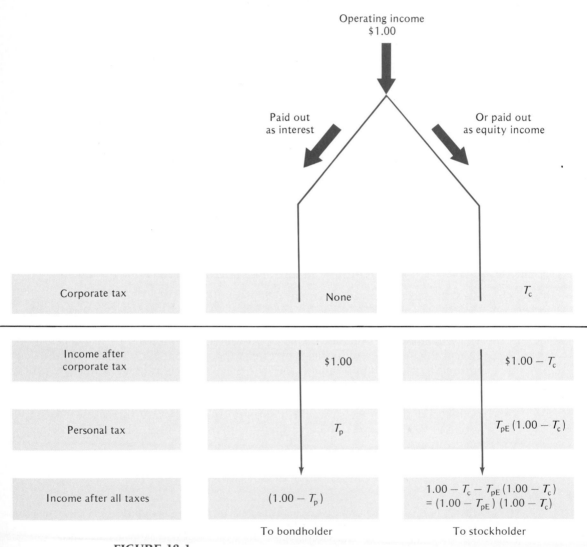

FIGURE 18-1
The firm's capital structure determines whether operating income is paid out as interest or equity income. Interest is taxed only at the personal level. Equity income is taxed at both the corporate and the personal levels. However, T_{pE}, the personal tax rate on equity income, can be less than T_p, the personal tax rate on interest income.

18-2 CORPORATE AND PERSONAL TAXES

When personal taxes are introduced, the firm's objective is no longer to minimize the *corporate* tax bill; the firm should try to minimize the present value of *all* taxes paid on corporate income. "All taxes" include *personal* taxes paid by bondholders and stockholders.

Figure 18-1 illustrates how corporate and personal taxes are affected by leverage. Depending on the firm's capital structure, a dollar of operating income will accrue to investors either as debt interest or equity income (dividends or capital gains). That is, the dollar can go down either branch of Figure 18-1.

Notice that Figure 18-1 distinguishes between T_p, the personal tax rate on interest, and T_{pE}, the effective personal rate on equity income. The two rates are equal if equity income comes entirely as dividends. But T_{pE} can be less than T_p if equity income comes as capital gains. Before the 1986 Tax Reform Act, capital gains were taxed at a top rate of 20 percent, versus a top rate of 50 percent on dividends and interest. Since the act, *realized* capital gains are taxed at the same rate as dividends and interest—a top rate of 28 percent.[6] However, capital gains taxes can be deferred until shares are sold, so the top *effective* capital gains rate can be less than 28 percent.

The firm's objective should be to arrange its capital structure so as to maximize after-tax income. You can see from Figure 18-1 that corporate borrowing is better if $1 - T_p$ is more than $(1 - T_{pE}) \times (1 - T_c)$; otherwise it is worse. Corporate debt policy is irrelevant if

$$1 - T_p = (1 - T_{pE}) \times (1 - T_c)$$

We seem to have a simple, practical decision rule. Arrange the firm's capital structure to shunt operating income down that branch of Figure 18-1 where the tax is least. We will now try a couple of back-of-the-envelope calculations to see what that rule could imply.

Debt Policy When Interest and Equity Income Are Taxed at the Same Personal Rate

We start with the case in which debt and equity income are taxed at the same personal rate. This case fits current United States tax law if all equity income comes as dividends or if all capital gains are immediately realized. We calculate income after all taxes assuming the top-bracket personal tax rate of 28 percent:

	Interest	Equity Income
Income before tax	$1.00	$1.00
Less corporate tax at $T_c = .34$	0	.34
Income after corporate tax	1.00	.66
Less personal tax at $T_p = T_{pE} = .28$	.28	.185
Income after all taxes	$ .72	$ .475

Advantage to debt = $.245

---

[6] See Chapter 16, Section 16-5, for details. Note that we are simplifying by ignoring *corporate* investors, for example banks, that pay top rates of 34 percent. Of course, banks shield their interest income by borrowing on their own account.

Debt comes out ahead by about 25 cents on the dollar, so there is still a strong tax advantage to borrowing.

In fact, the value of this advantage is exactly as MM calculated it. The existence of personal taxes does not reduce the tax advantages of corporate borrowing *provided* that all kinds of personal income are taxed at the same rate.

Look back at the example in Table 18-1. Firm U is unlevered; firm L has borrowed $1000 at 8 percent. The annual corporate tax shield produced by L's borrowing is .34 × 80 = $27.20 a year. Therefore, the total income to investors is increased by that $27.20.

In Table 18-4 we have added *personal* taxes to Table 18-1 on the assumption that the income of both bondholders and stockholders is taxed at a rate of 28 percent. Notice that investors in firm L have to pay personal tax on their extra income of $27.20. Thus their after-tax income is increased by $27.20 (1 − .28) = $19.58.

We assumed that the debt of L is permanent. What is the present value of $19.58 per annum in perpetuity? Since this cash flow is computed *after personal taxes*, we have to discount at an opportunity cost of capital *likewise computed after personal taxes*. The stockholders of L can obtain 8 percent before tax, but only 8(1 − .28) = 5.76 percent after tax. Thus

$$\text{PV tax shield (after personal tax)} = \frac{19.58}{.0576} = \$340$$

But this is the same answer we got before, when we ignored personal taxes en-

TABLE 18-4
Personal income taxes reduce, but do not eliminate, the annual tax shield generated by corporate borrowing, assuming that equity and interest income are subject to the same personal income tax rate

	Firm U	Firm L
Total income to both bondholders and stockholders (before personal tax; see Table 18-1)	$0 + $660 = $660	$80 + $607.20 = $687.20
Tax shield generated by interest on corporate debt	0	$ 27.20
Tax paid by bondholders (28% marginal rate)	0	$.28 × $80 = $ 22.40
Tax paid by stockholders (28% marginal rate)	$.28 × $660 = $184.80	$.28 × $607.20 = $170.02
Total personal tax paid	$184.80	$192.42
Total after-tax income to both bondholders and stockholders	$660 − $184.80 = $475.20	$687.20 − $192.42 = $494.78
Tax shield remaining after personal taxes		$494.78 − $475.20 = $ 19.58

tirely. The cash flow due to the corporate income tax shield is 28 percent less when personal taxes are recognized, but so is the opportunity cost of capital.[7]

In short, MM's "corrected" theory of debt and taxes does not have to assume away personal taxes. It only requires that debt and equity income be taxed at the same rate.

Debt Policy When Interest Is Taxed at a Higher Rate Than Equity Income

Let's now go to the other extreme. Before the 1986 Tax Reform Act, the corporate tax rate was 46 percent, and interest and dividends were taxed at rates up to 50 percent. The top capital gains rate was 20 percent. The *effective* rate was less than 20 percent because capital gains taxes can be deferred until shares are sold.

Suppose that all equity income comes as unrealized capital gains, and that T_{pE} turns out to be zero. If T_p, the tax rate on interest, is .50, then

	Interest	Equity Income
Income before tax	$1.00	$1.00
less corporate tax at $T_c = .46$	0	.46
Income after corporate tax	1.00	.54
Personal tax at $T_p = .5$ and $T_{pE} = 0$	.50	0
Income after all taxes	$ .50	$ .54

Advantage to equity = $.04

Now *equity* has a small advantage; it's worth paying the 46 percent corporate rate to escape the 50 percent personal tax on interest.

These back-of-the-envelope calculations show some possible outcomes but they don't tell the financial manager what to do, for in real life it isn't clear which investors' tax rates should be used. What's T_{pE}, for example? The shareholder roster of a large corporation may include tax-exempt investors (such as pension funds or university endowments) as well as millionaires. All possible tax brackets will be mixed together. And it's the same with T_p, the personal tax rate on interest. The large corporation's "typical" bondholder might be a tax-exempt pension fund but many taxpaying investors also hold corporate debt.

*Merton Miller's "Debt and Taxes"

How does capital structure affect firm value when investors have different tax rates? There is one model that may help us find the answer. It was put forward in "Debt and Taxes," Merton Miller's 1976 Presidential Address to the American Finance Association.[8]

[7] In general, if investors are willing to lend at a prospective return *before* personal taxes of r_D, then they must also be willing to accept a return *after* personal taxes of $r_D(1 - T_p)$, where T_p is the marginal rate of personal tax. Thus we can compute the value after personal taxes of the tax shield on permanent debt:

$$\text{PV tax shield} = \frac{T_c \times (r_D D) \times (1 - T_p)}{r_D \times (1 - T_p)} = T_c D$$

This brings us back to our previous formula for firm value:

Value of firm = value if all-equity-financed + $T_c D$

[8] M. H. Miller, "Debt and Taxes," *Journal of Finance,* **32:** 261–276 (May 1977). Some of the issues and ideas in Miller's paper were also discussed in D. Farrar and L. L. Selwyn, "Taxes, Corporate Financial Policy and the Returns to Investors," *National Tax Journal,* **20:** 144–154 (December 1967) and in some unpublished papers by Fischer Black.

Miller was considering debt policy before the 1986 Tax Reform Act. He started by assuming a simple world in which all equity income comes as unrealized capital gains, and nobody pays any tax on equity income; T_{pE} is zero for all investors. But the rate of tax on bond interest depends on the investor's tax bracket. Tax-exempt institutions do not pay any tax on interest; for them T_p is zero. At the other extreme, millionaires pay tax at a rate of 50 percent on bond interest; for them T_p is .50. Most investors fall somewhere between these two extremes.

Suppose that companies are initially financed entirely by equity. If financial managers are on their toes, this cannot represent a stable situation. Think of it in terms of Figure 18-1. If every dollar goes down the equity branch, there are no taxes paid at the personal level (remember $T_{pE} = 0$). Thus the financial manager need consider only corporate taxes, which we know create a strong incentive for corporate borrowing.

As companies begin to borrow, some investors have to be persuaded to hold corporate debt rather than common stock. There should be no problem in persuading tax-exempt investors to hold debt. They do not pay any personal taxes regardless of whether they hold bonds or stocks. Thus, the initial impact of borrowing is to save corporate taxes and to leave personal taxes unchanged.

But as companies borrow more, they need to persuade taxpaying investors to migrate from stocks to bonds. Therefore they have to offer a bribe in the form of a higher interest rate on their bonds. Companies can afford to bribe investors to migrate as long as the corporate tax saving *is greater than* the personal tax loss. But there is no way that companies can bribe millionaires to hold their bonds. The corporate tax saving cannot compensate for the extra personal tax that those millionaires would need to pay. Thus the migrations stop when the corporate tax saving *equals* the personal tax loss. This point occurs when T_p, the personal tax rate of the migrating investor, equals the corporate tax rate T_c.

Let us put some numbers on this. The corporate tax rate T_c is 46 percent. We continue to assume that T_{pE}, the effective rate of tax on equity income, is zero for all investors. In this case, companies will bribe investors with tax rates below 46 percent to hold bonds. But there is nothing to be gained (or lost) by persuading investors with tax rates *equal* to 46 percent to hold bonds. In the case of these investors $1 of operating income will produce income after all taxes of $.54, regardless of whether the dollar is interest or equity income:

	Income Remaining after All Taxes
Income paid out as interest	$1 - T_p = 1 - .46 = \$.54$
Income paid out as equity income	$(1 - T_{pE})(1 - T_c) = (1 - 0)(1 - .46) = \$.54$

In this equilibrium taxes determine the aggregate amount of corporate debt but not the amount issued by any particular firm. The debt-equity ratio for corporations as a whole depends on the corporate tax rate and the funds available to individual investors in the various tax brackets. If the corporate tax rate is increased, migration starts again, leading to a higher debt-equity ratio for companies as a whole. If personal tax rates are increased, the migration reverses, leading to a lower debt-equity ratio. If *both* personal and corporate tax rates are increased by the same amount—10 percentage points, say—there is no migration and no change. That explains why there was no substantial increase in the debt-equity ratio when the corporate income tax rose drastically at the start of World War II. Personal tax rates were simultaneously increased by about the same amount.

The companies in our example that first sold bonds to tax-exempt investors may have gained an advantage. But once the "low" taxpayers have invested in bonds and the migrations have stopped, no single firm can gain an advantage by borrowing more or suffer any penalty by borrowing less. Therefore there is no such thing as an optimal debt-equity ratio *for any single firm*. The market is interested only in the *total* amount of debt. No single firm can influence that.

One final point about Miller's tax equilibrium: Because he assumes equity returns escape personal tax ($T_{pE} = 0$), investors are willing to accept lower rates of return on low-risk common stocks than on debt. Consider a safe (zero-beta) stock. The standard capital asset pricing model would give an expected return of $r = r_f$, the risk-free interest rate (see Chapter 7, Section 7-4). But the investor migrating from equity to debt gives up r and earns $r_f(1 - T_p)$, the *after-tax* interest rate. In equilibrium, the migrating investor is content with either debt or equity, so $r = r_f(1 - T_p)$. Moreover, that investor's T_p equals the corporate rate T_c. Therefore, $r = r_f(1 - T_c)$. If we accept Miller's argument lock, stock, and barrel, the security market line should pass through the after-tax risk-free interest rate.

*Miller's Model Before and After the 1986 Tax Reform Act

Miller's model was not intended as a detailed description of the United States tax system, but as a way of illustrating how corporate and personal taxes could cancel out and leave firm value independent of capital structure. Nevertheless, the model's predictions are plausible only if the effective tax rate on equity income is substantially lower than on interest, as it was before the 1986 Tax Reform Act. Under today's tax system, it's hard to see how Miller's model could work out as he originally intended. Even if there were no tax advantage to borrowing before the 1986 tax law changes, there ought to be one now.

Let's try one more numerical example. Suppose half of equity income comes as dividends and half as capital gains. Capital gains are deferred for long enough that their effective rate is half the statutory rate, that is one-half of 28, or 14 percent. Thus the effective rate on equity income is an average of the dividend and capital gains rates, or 21 percent.

	Interest	Equity Income
Income before tax	$1.00	$1.00
Less corporate tax at $T_c = .34$	0	.34
Income after corporate tax	1.00	.66
Less personal tax at $T_p = .28$ and $T_{pE} = .21$	.28	.139
Income after all taxes	$ .72	$ .521

Advantage to debt = $.199

The advantage to debt financing is about 20 cents on the dollar.

Some questions about Miller's model were raised even before the tax changes. For example, if we take his argument literally, tax-exempt institutions such as pension funds ought to invest only in bonds and highly taxed individuals ought to invest only in equities. But we haven't observed any obvious clienteles of this kind.

FIGURE 18-2

It pays companies to borrow as long as the corporate tax saving exceeds the extra personal tax paid by the marginal lender. MM and Miller disagree only about how the extra personal tax varies with total company borrowing.

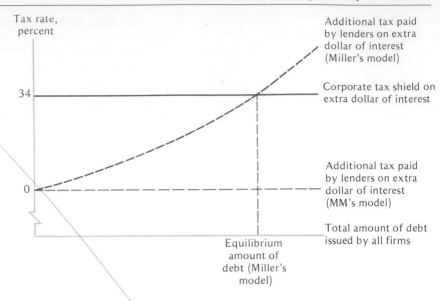

*A Possible Compromise Theory?

The majority of financial managers and economists believe our tax system favors corporate borrowing. Before Miller's paper, they had fallen into the habit of calculating the tax advantage of financial leverage as T_cD, the present value of the tax shields generated by a perpetual stream of corporate interest payments. When pressed they admitted that this is a first approximation only, and they professed a willingness to consider personal taxes too, if only they had a sensible model showing them how to do it.

Enter Miller's model, which recognizes that investors have different personal tax rates, but which says financial managers ought to forget about taxes entirely in choosing between debt and equity. Yet the model is probably oversimplified and not a plausible fit to today's tax law.

Here is a compromise theory which attempts to combine the best features of the MM and Miller positions. We start with Figure 18-2.

Both MM and Miller would agree that there is a corporate tax shield on debt that is equal to 34 percent of the interest payments. The corporate tax shield is shown by the solid horizontal line in Figure 18-2. It pays companies to issue more debt as long as this corporate tax shield exceeds the personal tax cost to the marginal lender. This tax cost is the difference between that lender's personal tax rate T_p and the effective rate T_{pE} the lender would pay on equity income.

The disagreement between MM and Miller centers on the additional personal taxes paid by debt versus equity investors. MM implicitly assume that personal taxes are the same on debt and equity. In this case the corporate tax shield *always* exceeds the extra taxes paid by the marginal lender, and companies should borrow to the hilt.

Miller assumes that investors are subject to different tax rates. Therefore, as the total amount of corporate debt increases, investors with higher tax rates must be bribed to hold debt. In this case the tax cost to the marginal lender is shown by the broken *upward-sloping* line in Figure 18-2.[9] The equilibrium amount of debt

---

[9] We have arbitrarily shown this as a smooth curve. In practice there would be a series of steep sections and plateaus.

FIGURE 18-3
If companies cannot be sure of taxable profits in the future, the expected corporate tax saving will be less, and less debt will be issued.

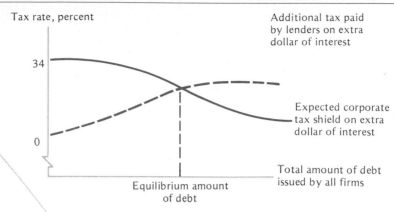

in Miller's model is reached when the corporate tax benefit to the borrower equals the personal tax cost to the marginal lender. As long as all companies pay the same rate of tax, it is immaterial which firms supply this debt.

But how could the additional tax paid by lenders ever reach 34 cents per dollar, much less rise above that point, when the marginal tax rate is 28 percent for the wealthiest investors? It seems that the corporate tax shield line has to come down in order for our compromise theory to work.

Perhaps we should reconsider the assumption that the corporate tax shield on debt is a constant 34 percent regardless of the amount borrowed. In practice few firms can be *sure* they will show a taxable profit in the future. If a firm shows a loss and cannot carry the loss back against past taxes, its interest tax shield must be carried forward with the hope of using it later. The firm loses the time value of money while it waits. If its difficulties are deep enough, the wait may be permanent and the interest tax shield lost forever.

Notice also that borrowing is not the only way to shield income against tax. Firms have accelerated write-offs for plant and equipment. Investment in many intangible assets can be expensed immediately. So can contributions to the firm's pension fund. The more that firms shield income in these other ways, the lower the expected tax shield from borrowing.[10]

If there is a chance that firms will make a loss, the *expected* corporate tax shield is less than 34 percent. The more that firms borrow, the higher the probability of loss and therefore the lower the expected tax shield.[11] In Figure 18-3 we have redrawn the corporate tax shield line to recognize this. The expected tax shield starts close to 34 percent but it declines as more debt is issued. We continue to represent the extra personal tax payments on debt interest by an upward-sloping line, but we assume that line tops out at 28 percent, the maximum personal rate. The total amount of debt that will be issued is again given by the point at which the tax benefit to the marginal borrower equals the tax payment by the marginal lender, but this equilibrium differs from Miller's model in three ways.

[10] For a discussion of the effect of these other tax shields on company borrowing see H. DeAngelo and R. Masulis, "Optimal Capital Structure Under Corporate and Personal Taxation," *Journal of Financial Economics,* **8:** 5–29 (March 1980).

[11] For some evidence on the average marginal tax rate of United States firms see J. J. Cordes and S. M. Sheffrin, "Taxation and the Sectoral Allocation of Capital in the U.S.," *National Tax Journal,* **34:** 419–432 (1981).

First, if companies cannot be sure they can take full advantage of the corporate tax shield, the total amount of debt issued will be less than in Miller's model. (The intersection in Figure 18-3 is farther left than in Figure 18-2.)

Second, since companies cannot be sure of benefiting from the corporate tax shield, they will not be prepared to pay such a high rate of interest on the debt. (The intersection in Figure 18-3 is lower than in Figure 18-2.)

Third, since companies have different expected tax rates, the corporate tax shields are worth more to some firms than to others. For example, look at Figure 18-4. The lower line depicts the expected corporate tax saving from an additional dollar of interest payments for the Drop Forge and Basic Slag Company. Drop Forge has large accumulated tax loss carry-forwards and uncertain prospects. So there is little chance that it will be able to use any corporate tax shield. Since the expected tax saving is less than the extra personal tax payment by the marginal lender, borrowing has a negative net present value for Drop Forge. By contrast the upper line shows the expected corporate tax saving from an additional dollar of interest payments for Con Gas, a company whose income is relatively high and stable. Since the expected corporate tax saving exceeds the lender's expected personal tax payment, borrowing is a positive-NPV activity for Con Gas. But the more Con Gas borrows, the greater the chance that it will incur future losses. This places a limit on the amount of borrowing that the company should undertake.

To maximize value, Con Gas should borrow until the expected tax saving on its last dollar of interest is equal to the extra personal tax payment by the lender. The shaded area in Figure 18-4 shows the total net benefit each year to Con Gas.

We don't pretend that this is the whole story. Our point is that there may be an intermediate position if you are not prepared to go out on a limb for either MM or Miller. Our own view is that there is a moderate tax advantage to corporate borrowing, at least for companies that are reasonably sure they can use the corporate tax shields. For companies that do not expect to be able to use the corporate tax shields we believe there is a moderate tax disadvantage.

FIGURE 18-4
Drop Forge is unlikely to earn taxable profits and therefore should not borrow. Con Gas should borrow until the expected corporate tax saved on extra borrowing equals the personal tax paid by the lender. (Note: the personal tax paid by lenders is unaffected by the debt ratio of an individual company.)

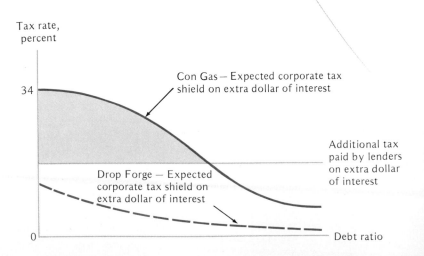

18-3 COSTS OF FINANCIAL DISTRESS

Financial distress occurs when promises to creditors are broken, or honored with difficulty. Sometimes financial distress leads to bankruptcy. Sometimes it means only that the firm skates on thin ice.

As we will see, financial distress is costly. Investors know that levered firms may fall into financial distress, and they worry about it. That worry is reflected in the current market value of the levered firm's securities. Thus, the value of the firm is

$$\begin{array}{c} \text{Value} \\ \text{of firm} \end{array} = \begin{array}{c} \text{value if} \\ \text{all-equity-financed} \end{array} + \text{PV tax shield} - \begin{array}{c} \text{PV costs of} \\ \text{financial distress} \end{array}$$

The costs of financial distress depend on the probability of distress and the magnitude of costs encountered if distress occurs.

Figure 18-5 shows how the trade-off between the tax benefits and the costs of distress determines optimal capital structure. PV tax shield initially increases as the firm borrows more. At moderate debt levels the probability of financial distress is trivial, and so PV cost of financial distress is small and tax advantages dominate. But at some point the probability of financial distress increases rapidly with additional borrowing; the costs of distress begin to take a substantial bite out of firm value. Also, if the firm can't be sure of profiting from the corporate tax shield, the tax advantage of debt is likely to dwindle and eventually disappear. The theoretical optimum is reached when the present value of tax savings due to additional borrowing is just offset by increases in the present value of costs of distress.

Costs of financial distress covers several specific items. Now we identify these costs and try to understand what causes them and why they cannot be avoided.

Bankruptcy Costs

You rarely hear anything nice said about corporate bankruptcy. But there is some good in almost everything. Corporate bankruptcies occur when stockholders exercise their *right to default*. That right is valuable; when a firm gets into trouble, limited liability allows stockholders simply to walk away from it, leaving all its

---

FIGURE 18-5
The value of the firm is equal to its value if all-equity financed plus PV tax shield minus PV costs of financial distress. The manager should choose the debt ratio that maximizes firm value.

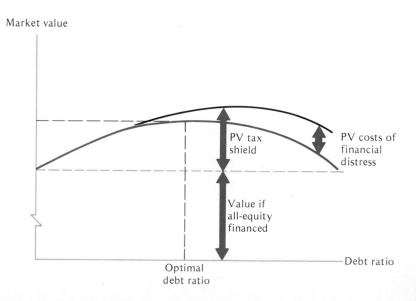

troubles to its creditors. The former creditors become the new stockholders, and the old stockholders are left with nothing.

In our legal system all stockholders automatically enjoy limited liability. But suppose that this were not so. Suppose that there were two firms with identical assets and operations. Each firm has debt outstanding and each has promised to repay $1000 (principal and interest) next year. But only one of the firms, Ace Limited, enjoys limited liability. The other firm, Ace Unlimited, does not; its stockholders are personally liable for its debt.

Figure 18-6 compares next year's possible payoffs to the creditors and stockholders of these two firms. The only differences occur when next year's asset value turns out to be less than $1000. Suppose that next year the assets of each company are worth only $500. In this case Ace Limited defaults. Its stockholders walk away; their payoff is zero. Bondholders get the assets worth $500. But Ace Unlimited's stockholders can't walk away. They have to cough up $500, the difference between asset value and the bondholders' claim. The debt is paid whatever happens.

Suppose that Ace Limited does go bankrupt. Of course, its stockholders are disappointed that their firm is worth so little, but that is an operating problem having nothing to do with financing. Given poor operating performance, the right to go bankrupt—the right to default—is a valuable privilege. As Figure 18-6 shows, Ace Limited's stockholders are in better shape than Unlimited's are.

FIGURE 18-6
Comparison of limited and unlimited liability for two otherwise identical firms. If the two firms' asset values are less than $1000, Ace Limited stockholders default and its bondholders take over the assets. Ace Unlimited stockholders keep the assets, but they must reach into their own pockets to pay off its bondholders. The total payoff to both stockholders and bondholders is the same for the two firms.

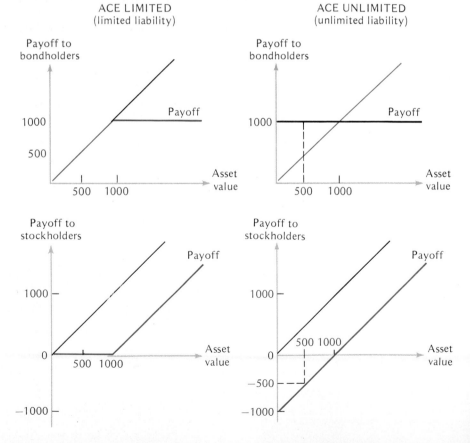

The example illuminates a mistake people often make in thinking about the costs of bankruptcy. Bankruptcies are thought of as corporate funerals. The mourners (creditors and especially shareholders) look at their firm's present sad state. They think of how valuable their securities used to be and how little is left. Moreover, they think of the lost value as a cost of bankruptcy. That is the mistake. The decline in the value of assets is what the mourning is really about. That has no necessary connection with financing. The bankruptcy is merely a legal mechanism for allowing creditors to take over when the decline in the value of assets triggers a default. Bankruptcy is not the *cause* of the decline in value. It is the result.

Be careful not to get cause and effect reversed. When a person dies, we do not cite the implementation of his or her will as the cause of death.

We said that bankruptcy is a legal mechanism allowing creditors to take over when a firm defaults. Bankruptcy costs are the costs of using this mechanism. There are no bankruptcy costs at all shown in Figure 18-6. Note that only Ace Limited can default and go bankrupt. But, regardless of what happens to asset value, the *combined* payoff to the bondholders and stockholders of Ace Limited is always the same as the *combined* payoff to the bondholders and stockholders of Ace Unlimited. Thus the overall market values of the two firms now (this year) must be identical. Of course, Ace Limited's *stock* is worth more than Ace Unlimited's stock because of Ace Limited's right to default. Ace Limited's *debt* is worth correspondingly less.

Our example was not intended to be strictly realistic. Anything involving courts and lawyers cannot be free. Suppose that court and legal fees are $200 if Ace Limited defaults. The fees are paid out of the remaining value of Ace's assets. Thus if asset value turns out to be $500, creditors end up with only $300. Figure 18-7 shows next year's *total* payoff to bondholders and stockholders net of this bankruptcy cost. Ace Limited, by issuing risky debt, has given lawyers and the court system a claim on the firm if it defaults. The present market value of the firm is reduced by the present value of this claim.

It is easy to see how increased leverage affects the present value of the costs of financial distress. If Ace borrows more, it must promise more to bondholders. This increases the probability of default and the value of the lawyers' claim. It increases PV costs of financial distress and reduces Ace's present market value.

FIGURE 18-7
Total payoff to Ace Limited security holders. There is a $200 bankruptcy cost in the event of default (shaded area).

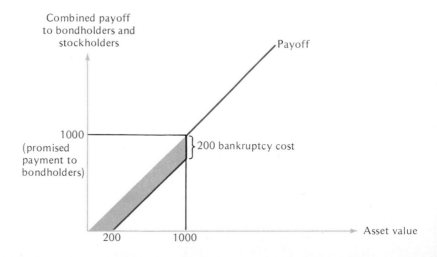

The costs of bankruptcy come out of stockholders' pockets. Creditors foresee the costs and foresee that *they* will pay them if default occurs. For this they demand compensation in advance in the form of higher payoffs when the firm does *not* default. That is, they demand a higher promised interest rate. This reduces the possible payoffs to stockholders and reduces the present market value of their shares.

Evidence on Bankruptcy Costs

Bankruptcy costs can add up fast. *Aviation Week and Space Technology* reported in 1984 that legal and professional fees of the Braniff International Corporation bankruptcy were $12 million; legal fees in the Continental Airlines bankruptcy were running $2 million per month.[12] Daunting as these numbers may seem, they are not a large fraction of these airlines' *asset* values. For example, in 1984 it cost about $95 million to buy *one* airplane, a Boeing 747.

J. B. Warner has reported legal and administrative costs of 11 railroad bankruptcies.[13] The average cost was about $2 million spread over many years. (On average, it took 13 years before the railroads were reorganized and released from the bankruptcy courts. For one railroad it took 23 years.)

Two million dollars is not small change. But, on average, the costs were only 5.3 percent of the overall market value of the railroads' debt and equity securities, estimated just before bankruptcy. The costs declined to 1.4 percent of overall market value estimated 5 years prior to bankruptcy, when the railroads were in better health. That is a small number. Suppose that you are the financial manager of a railroad facing a 20 percent chance of bankruptcy in 5 years.[14] Using Warner's results, you guesstimate the present value of bankruptcy costs as follows:

$$\begin{array}{c} \text{Expected} \\ \text{cost} \end{array} = \begin{array}{c} \text{probability} \\ \text{of bankruptcy} \end{array} \times \begin{array}{c} \text{cost of bankruptcy as proportion} \\ \text{of firm's current market value} \end{array}$$

$$= .2 \times .014 \text{ (value of firm)} = .0028 \text{ (value of firm)}$$

Discount back 5 years at, say, 8 percent:

$$\text{PV costs of bankruptcy} = \frac{.0028}{(1.08)^5} \text{(value of firm)} = .0019 \text{ (value of firm)}$$

Trivial. Of course, Warner's data apply only to railroads. Legal and administrative costs could be a larger proportion of firm value for, say, a sample of manufacturing firms.[15]

Direct versus Indirect Costs of Bankruptcy

So far we have discussed the *direct* (that is, legal and administrative) costs of bankruptcy. There are indirect costs too, which are nearly impossible to measure. But we have circumstantial evidence indicating their importance.

The indirect costs reflect the difficulties of running a railroad—or any com-

---

[12] *Aviation Week and Space Technology,* April 23, 1984, p. 35.

[13] J. B. Warner, "Bankruptcy Costs: Some Evidence," *Journal of Finance,* **26:** 337–348 (May 1977).

[14] Investors weren't able to predict the railroad bankruptcies 5 years before they happened. We are assuming that railroads like the ones that Warner examined had a 20 percent chance of going bankrupt in 5 years. That is one guess, but any other guess will do for present purposes.

[15] Bankruptcy costs are likely to be larger for *small* firms; there are economies of scale in going bankrupt, as in many other economic endeavors.

pany—while it is going through bankruptcy. Management's effort to prevent further deterioration in the firm's business are often undermined by the delays and legal tangles that go with bankruptcy as a legal process.

The Penn Central Railroad went under in June 1970. Four years later, with bankruptcy proceedings nowhere near completion, *Business Week* published an article called "Why the Penn Central Is Falling Apart." Here are some excerpts.

> As its creditors hound it—some of them want to shut it down to get back their money—the railroad must continue operations at a time when it can barely keep running without pouring in huge sums to rebuild its facilities. Those sums, however, will not be available until the railroad shows that it can be reorganized.

Penn Central could have raised money by selling off some of its assets, but its creditors naturally oppose this:

> . . . Scores of other problems arise from a lack of money. Agonizingly for everyone on the Penn Central, there is a tremendous source of capital that cannot be touched. For example, just about every abandoned mine branch in the Allegheny Mountains is chock full of old Penn Central cars destined for scrap. With today's scrap prices, they are a potential gold mine. But the creditors will not allow this asset to be turned into cash that will be reinvested in the estate, since that estate is eroding day by day.

The creditors' interest also got in the way of sensible maintenance:

> And the creditors' problems do not stop there. Between Indianapolis and Terre Haute, the former Pennsylvania and New York Central RRs had double-track, high-speed main lines rarely more than three miles apart. After the merger, most traffic was routed over the old New York Central route and the Pennsy line's second track was picked up. There are still 11 mi. of double track on the old Pennsy, though, and the 132-lb. rail is in excellent shape. It is desperately needed on the old New York Central line where double traffic and deferred maintenance have left much of that stretch with 10 mph speed limits.

The obvious thing is to use the good rail on the Penn Central line. Unfortunately,

> . . . the rail belongs to a Pennsy subsidiary, itself in reorganization, and the creditors will not permit the asset to be moved to a subsidiary of the New York Central except for "cash on the barrel," which, of course, is unavailable.[16]

We do not know what the sum of direct and indirect costs of bankruptcy amounts to. We suspect it is a significant number, particularly for large firms for which proceedings would be lengthy and complex. Perhaps the best evidence is the reluctance of creditors to force bankruptcy. In principle, they would be better off to end the agony and seize the assets as soon as possible. Instead creditors often overlook defaults in the hope of nursing the firm over a difficult period. They do

---

TABLE 18-5
Texaco's stock price dropped by $3.375 when its bankruptcy filing was announced.
Pennzoil was Texaco's largest creditor; its stock price dropped too, by $15.125.
The combined market value of the two firms' stock fell $1445 million.

	SHARE PRICE			Number of Shares (Millions)	Change in Value (Millions)
	Friday April 10, 1987	Monday April 13, 1987	Change		
Texaco	$31.875	$28.50	− $ 3.375	242	− $ 817
Pennzoil	92.125	77.00	− 15.125	41.5	−628
Total					−$1445

this in part to avoid costs of bankruptcy.[17] There is an old financial saying, "Borrow $1000 and you've got a banker. Borrow $10,000,000 and you've got a partner."

Here is one final piece of evidence on the direct plus indirect costs of bankruptcy. On April 10, 1987, Texaco filed for bankruptcy, surprising most investors and financial analysts. Texaco's biggest creditor was Pennzoil, to whom it owed $10.5 billion in damages stemming from Texaco's 1984 takeover of Getty Oil.[18] Texaco had been negotiating with Pennzoil, trying to cut a deal in which Pennzoil would give up its claim—which Texaco was contesting—in exchange for an immediate cash settlement. When these negotiations broke down, Texaco turned to the bankruptcy court.

Table 18-5 reports that Texaco stock fell from $31.875 to 28.50 after the announcement, a fall of $817 million in Texaco's equity value. At the same time Pennzoil's equity value fell by $628 million. We do not know how Texaco's other creditors fared, but the value of their claims cannot have increased. Therefore, bankruptcy reduced the market value of (the claims on) Texaco's assets by at least $817 plus 628 or $1445 million, roughly $1.5 billion. We can take this loss as the stock market's estimate of the present value of the direct and indirect costs of the Texaco bankruptcy.

But how could bankruptcy cost $1.5 *billion?* Texaco's business operations were healthy and profitable, and thus unlikely to encounter the sort of problems that plagued Penn Central. We are at a loss to explain how a stock market could rationally forecast bankruptcy costs as large as those implied by Table 18-5.

Perhaps our readers can help. We hereby offer a free, autographed copy of this book to the reader who submits the most sensible or ingenious interpretation.

---

[17] There is another reason. Creditors are not always given absolute priority in bankruptcy. Absolute priority means that creditors must be paid in full before stockholders receive a cent. Sometimes reorganizations are negotiated which provide "something for everyone," even though creditors are *not* paid in full. Thus creditors can never be sure how they will fare in bankruptcy.

[18] Pennzoil thought it had struck a deal to buy Getty when Texaco arrived with a higher bid. Texaco finally won, but Pennzoil sued, arguing that Texaco had broken up a valid contract between Pennzoil and Getty. The court agreed and ordered Texaco to pay over $11.1 billion. This amount was reduced on appeal, but *with interest* the damages still amounted to $10.5 billion by April 1987.

Financial Distress without Bankruptcy

Not every firm which gets into trouble goes bankrupt. As long as the firm can scrape up enough cash to pay the interest on its debt, it may be able to postpone bankruptcy for many years. Eventually the firm may recover, pay off its debt, and escape bankruptcy altogether.

When a firm is in trouble, both bondholders and stockholders want it to recover, but in other respects their interests may be in conflict. In times of financial distress the security holders are like many political parties—united on generalities but threatened by squabbling on any specific issue.

Financial distress is costly when these conflicts of interest get in the way of proper operating, investment, and financing decisions. Stockholders are tempted to forsake the usual objective of maximizing the overall market value of the firm and to pursue narrower self-interest instead. They are tempted to play games at the expense of their creditors. We will now illustrate how such games can lead to costs of financial distress.

Here is the Circular File Company's present book balance sheet:

Circular File Company
(book values)

Net working capital	$ 20	$ 50	Bonds outstanding
Fixed assets	80	50	Common stock
Total assets	$100	$100	Total liabilities

We will assume there is only one share and one bond outstanding. The stockholder is also the manager. The bondholder is somebody else.

Here is its balance sheet in market values—a clear case of financial distress, since the face value of Circular's debt ($50) exceeds the firm's market value ($30):

Circular File Company
(market values)

Net working capital	$20	$25	Bonds outstanding
Fixed assets	10	5	Common stock
Total assets	$30	$30	Total liabilities

If the debt matured today, Circular's owner would default, leaving the firm bankrupt. But suppose that the bond actually matures 1 year hence, that there is enough cash for Circular to limp along for 1 year, and that the bondholder cannot "call the question" and force bankruptcy before then.

The 1-year grace period explains why the Circular share still has value. Its owner is betting on a stroke of luck that will rescue the firm, allowing it to pay off the debt with something left over. The bet is a long shot—the owner wins only if firm value increases from $30 to more than $50.[19] But the owner has a secret weapon: He controls investment and operating strategy.

---

[19] We are not concerned here with how to work out whether $5 is a fair price for stockholders to pay for the bet. We will come to that in Chapter 20 when we discuss the valuation of options.

Risk Shifting: The First Game

Suppose that Circular has $10 cash. The following investment opportunity comes up:

Now	Possible Payoffs Next Year
	$120 (10% probability)
Invest $10	
	$0 (90% probability)

This is a wild gamble and probably a lousy project. But you can see why the owner would be tempted to take it anyway. Why not go for broke? Circular will probably go under anyway, and so the owner is essentially betting with the bondholder's money. But the owner gets most of the loot if the project pays off.

Suppose that the project's NPV is − $2 but that it is undertaken anyway, thus depressing firm value by $2. Circular's new balance sheet might look like this:

Circular File Company
(market values)

Net working capital	$10	$20	Bonds outstanding
Fixed assets	18	8	Common stock
Total assets	$28	$28	Total liabilities

Firm value falls by $2, but the owner is $3 ahead because the bond's value has fallen by $5. The $10 cash that used to stand behind the bond has been replaced by a very risky asset worth only $8.

Thus a game has been played at the expense of Circular's bondholder. The game illustrates the following general point. Stockholders of levered firms gain when business risk increases. Financial managers who act strictly in their shareholders' interests (and *against* the interests of creditors) will favor risky projects over safe ones. They may even take risky projects with negative NPVs.

This warped strategy for capital budgeting clearly is costly to the firm and to the economy as a whole. Why do we associate the costs with financial distress? Because the temptation to play is strongest when the odds of default are high. Exxon would never invest in our negative-NPV gamble. Its creditors are not vulnerable to this type of game.

Refusing to Contribute Equity Capital: The Second Game

We have seen how stockholders, acting in their immediate, narrow self-interest, may take projects which reduce the overall market value of their firm. These are errors of commission. Conflicts of interest may also lead to errors of omission.

Assume that Circular cannot scrape up any cash, and therefore cannot take that wild gamble. Instead a *good* opportunity comes up: a relatively safe asset costing $10 with a present value of $15 and NPV = + $5.

This project will not in itself rescue Circular, but it is a step in the right direction. We might therefore expect Circular to issue $10 of new stock and to go ahead with the investment. Suppose that two new shares are issued to the original owner for $10 cash. The project is taken. The new balance sheet might look like this:

Circular File Company
(market values)

Net working capital	$20	$33	Bonds outstanding
Fixed assets	25	12	Common stock
Total assets	$45	$45	Total liabilities

The total value of the firm goes up by $15 ($10 of new capital and $5 NPV). Notice that the Circular bond is no longer worth $25, but $33. The bondholder receives a capital gain of $8 because the firm's assets include a new, safe asset worth $15. The probability of default is less and the payoff to the bondholder if default occurs is larger.

The stockholder loses what the bondholder gains. Equity value goes up not by $15, but by $15 − $8 = $7. The owner puts in $10 of fresh equity capital but gains only $7 in market value. Going ahead is in the firm's interest, but not the owner's.

Again, our example illustrates a general point. If we hold business risk constant, any increase in firm value is shared among bondholders and stockholders. The value of any investment opportunity *to the firm's stockholders* is reduced because project benefits must be shared with bondholders. Thus it may not be in the stockholders' self-interest to contribute fresh equity capital even if that means forgoing positive-NPV investment opportunities.

This problem theoretically affects all levered firms, but it is most serious when firms land in financial distress. The greater the probability of default, the more bondholders have to gain from investments which increase firm value.

And Three More Games, Briefly

As with other games, the temptation to play is particularly strong in financial distress.

1. *Cash in and Run:* Stockholders may be reluctant to put money into a firm in financial distress, but they are happy to take the money out—in the form of a cash dividend, for example. The market value of the firm's stock goes down by less than the amount of the dividend paid, because the decline in *firm* value is shared with creditors. This game is just "refusing to contribute equity capital" run in reverse.

2. *Playing for Time:* When the firm is in financial distress, creditors would like to salvage what they can by forcing the firm to settle up. Naturally, stockholders want to delay this as long as they can. There are various devious ways of doing this, for example through accounting changes designed to conceal the true extent of trouble, by encouraging false hopes of spontaneous recovery, or by cutting corners on maintenance, research and development, etc., in order to make this year's operating performance look better.

3. *Bait and Switch:* This game is not always played in financial distress, but it is a quick way to get *into* distress. You start with a conservative policy, issuing a limited amount of relatively safe debt. Then you suddenly switch and issue a lot more. That makes all your debt risky, imposing a capital loss on the "old" bondholders. Their capital loss is the stockholders' gain.

**What the
Games Cost**

Why should anyone object to these games so long as they are played by consenting adults? Because playing them means poor decisions about investment and operations.

The more the firm borrows, the greater the temptation to play the games (assuming the financial manager acts in the stockholders' interest). The increased odds of poor decisions in the future prompt investors to mark down the present market value of the firm. The fall in value comes out of stockholders' pockets. Potential lenders, realizing that games may be played at their expense, protect themselves by demanding better terms.

Therefore it is ultimately in the stockholders' interest to avoid temptation. The easiest way to do this is to limit borrowing to levels at which the firm's debt is safe or close to it.

But suppose that the tax advantages of debt spur the firm on to a high debt ratio and a significant probability of default or financial distress. Is there any way to convince potential lenders that games will not be played? The obvious answer is to give lenders veto power over potentially dangerous decisions.

There we have the ultimate economic rationale for all that fine print backing up corporate debt. Debt contracts almost always limit dividends or equivalent transfers of wealth to stockholders; the firm may not be allowed to pay out more than it earns, for example. Additional borrowing is almost always limited. For example, many companies are prevented by existing bond indentures from issuing any additional long-term debt unless their ratio of earnings to interest charges exceeds 2.0.

Sometimes firms are restricted from selling assets or making major investment outlays except with the lenders' consent. The risks of "playing for time" are reduced by specifying accounting procedures and by giving lenders access to the firm's books and its financial forecasts.

Of course fine print cannot be a complete solution for firms that insist on issuing risky debt. The fine print has its own costs; you have to spend money to save money. Obviously a complex debt contract costs more to negotiate than a simple one. Afterward it costs the lender more to monitor the firm's performance. Lenders anticipate monitoring costs and demand compensation in the form of higher interest rates; thus the monitoring costs are ultimately paid by stockholders.

Perhaps the most severe costs of the fine print stem from the constraints it places on operating and investment decisions. For example, an attempt to prevent the "risk shifting" game may also prevent the firm from pursuing *good* investment opportunities. At the minimum there are delays in clearing major investments with lenders. In some cases lenders may veto high-risk investments even if net present value is positive. Lenders can lose from risk shifting even when the firm's overall market value increases. In fact, the lenders may try to play a game of their own, forcing the firm to stay in cash or low-risk assets even if good projects are forgone.

Thus, debt contracts cannot cover every possible manifestation of the games we have just discussed. Any attempt to do so would be hopelessly expensive and doomed to failure in any event. Human imagination is insufficient to conceive of all the possible things that could go wrong. We will always find surprises coming at us on dimensions we never thought to think about.

We hope we have not left the impression that managers and stockholders always succumb to temptation unless restrained. Usually they refrain voluntarily, not only from a sense of fair play, but also on pragmatic grounds: A firm or individual that makes a killing today at the expense of a creditor will be coldly received when the time comes to borrow again. Aggressive game playing is done only by out-and-out crooks and by firms in extreme financial distress. Firms limit borrowing precisely because they don't wish to land in distress and be exposed to the temptation to play.

Costs of Distress Vary with Type of Asset

Suppose your firm's only asset is a large downtown hotel, mortgaged to the hilt. The recession hits, occupancy rates fall, and the mortgage payments cannot be met. The lender takes over and sells the hotel to a new owner and operator. You use your firm's stock certificates for wallpaper.

What is the cost of bankruptcy? In this example, probably very little. The value of the hotel is, of course, much less than you hoped, but that is due to the lack of guests, not to the bankruptcy. The direct bankruptcy costs of Heartbreak Hotel are restricted to items such as legal and court fees, real estate commissions, and the time the lender spends sorting things out.

Suppose we repeat the story of Heartbreak Hotel for Fledgling Electronics. Everything is the same, except for the underlying real assets—not real estate but a high-tech going concern, a growth company whose most valuable assets are technology, investment opportunities, and its employees' human capital.

If Fledgling gets into trouble, the stockholders may be reluctant to put up money to cash in on its growth opportunities. Failure to invest is likely to be much more serious for Fledgling than for a company like Heartbreak Hotel.

If Fledgling finally defaults on its debt, the lender would find it much more difficult to cash in by selling off the assets. Many of them are intangibles which have value only as a part of a going concern.

Could Fledgling be kept as a going concern through default and reorganization? It may not be as hopeless as putting a wedding cake through a car wash, but there are a number of serious difficulties. First the odds of defections by key employees are higher than if the firm had never gotten into financial trouble. Special guarantees may have to be given to customers who are doubtful whether the firm will be around to service its products. Aggressive investment in new products and technology will be difficult; each class of creditors will have to be convinced that it is in their interest for the firm to invest new money in risky ventures.

Our examples of the hotel and electronics firm illustrate that the values of some assets can pass through bankruptcy and reorganization largely unscathed; the values of other assets are likely to be considerably diminished. The losses are greatest for the intangible assets that are linked to the health of the firm as a going concern—for example, technology, human capital, and brand image. That may be why debt ratios are low in the pharmaceutical industry, where value depends on continued success in research and development, and in many service industries where value depends on human capital. We can also understand why highly profitable growth companies, such as Hewlett-Packard or Digital Equipment Corporation, use mostly equity finance.[20]

The moral of these examples is: *Do not think only about the probability that borrowing will bring trouble. Think also of the value that may be lost if trouble comes.*

---

[20] Recent empirical research confirms that firms holding largely intangible assets borrow less. See M. Long and I. Malitz, "The Investment-Financing Nexus: Some Empirical Evidence," *Midland Corporate Finance Journal,* **3:** 53–59 (Fall 1985); and S. Williamson, "The Moral Hazard Theory of Corporate Capital Structure: Empirical Tests," unpublished Ph.D. dissertation, MIT, November 1981.

18-4 EXPLAINING FINANCING CHOICES

Financial managers often think of the firm's debt-equity decision as a trade-off between interest tax shields and the costs of financial distress. Of course, there is controversy about how valuable interest tax shields are and what kinds of financial trouble are most threatening, but these disagreements are only variations on a theme. Thus, Figure 18-5 illustrates the debt-equity trade-off.

This *trade-off theory* of capital structure recognizes that target debt ratios may vary from firm to firm. Companies with safe, tangible assets and plenty of taxable income to shield ought to have high target ratios. Unprofitable companies with risky, intangible assets ought to rely primarily on equity financing.

If there were no costs of adjusting capital structure, then each firm should always be at its target debt ratio. However, there are costs, and therefore delays, in adjusting to the optimum. Firms cannot immediately offset the random events that bump them away from their capital structure targets, so we should see random differences in actual debt ratios among firms having the same target debt ratio.

All in all, this trade-off theory of capital structure choice tells a comforting story. Unlike the "corrected" MM theory, which seemed to say that firms should take on as much debt as possible, it avoids extreme predictions and rationalizes moderate debt ratios.

But what are the facts? Can the trade-off theory of capital structure explain how companies actually behave?

The answer is "yes and no." On the "yes" side, the trade-off theory successfully explains many industry differences in capital structure. High-tech growth companies, for example, whose assets are risky and mostly intangible, normally use relatively little debt. Airlines can and do borrow heavily because their assets are tangible and relatively safe.[21]

The trade-off theory also helps explain what kinds of companies "go private" in **leveraged buyouts (LBOs).** LBOs are acquisitions of public companies by private investors who finance a large fraction of the purchase price with debt. The target companies for LBO takeovers are usually mature "cash cow" businesses with established markets for their products, but little in the way of high-NPV growth opportunities. That makes sense by the trade-off theory, because these are exactly the kind of companies that *ought* to have high debt ratios.

The trade-off theory also says that companies saddled with extra heavy debt—too much to pay down with a couple of years' internally generated cash—should issue stock, constrain dividends, or sell off assets to raise cash to rebalance capital structure. Here again, we can find plenty of confirming examples. When Texaco bought Getty Petroleum in January 1984, it borrowed $8 billion from a consortium of banks to help finance the acquisition. (The loan was arranged and paid over to Texaco within 2 weeks!) By the end of 1984, it had raised about $1.8 billion to pay down this debt, mostly by selling assets and forgoing dividend increases. Chrysler, when it emerged from near-bankruptcy in 1983, sold $432 million of new common stock to help regain a conservative capital structure.[22]

---

[21] We are not suggesting that all airline *companies* are safe; many are not. But air*craft* can support debt where air*lines* cannot. If Fly-by-Night Airlines fails, its planes retain their value in another airline's operations. There's a good secondary market in used aircraft, so a loan secured by aircraft can be well-protected even if made to an airline flying on thin ice (and in the dark).

[22] Note that Chrysler issued stock *after* it emerged from financial distress. It did not *prevent* financial distress by raising equity money when trouble loomed on its horizon. Why not? Refer back to "Refusing to Contribute Equity Capital: The Second Game" in Section 18-3 of this chapter.

On the "no" side, there are other things the trade-off theory cannot explain. It cannot explain why some of the most successful companies thrive with little debt. Think of Merck, which as Table 18-3a shows, is basically all-equity-financed. Granted, Merck's most valuable assets are intangible, the fruits of its pharmaceutical research and development. We know that intangible assets and conservative capital structures tend to go together. But Merck also has a very large corporate income tax bill ($360 million in 1986) and the highest possible credit rating. It could borrow enough to save tens of millions of tax dollars without raising a whisker of concern about possible financial distress.

Merck illustrates an odd fact about real-life capital structures: The most profitable companies generally borrow the least.[23] Here the trade-off theory fails, for it predicts exactly the reverse: Under the trade-off theory, high profits should mean more debt-servicing capacity and more taxable income to shield, and should give a *higher* target debt ratio.[24]

A Pecking Order Theory

There is an alternative story which could explain the inverse relationship between profitability and debt ratios. It goes like this.[25]

1. Firms prefer internal finance.
2. They adapt their target dividend payout ratios to their investment opportunities, while trying to avoid sudden changes in dividends.
3. Sticky dividend policies, plus unpredictable fluctuations in profitability and investment opportunities, mean that internally generated cash flow is sometimes more than capital expenditures and at other times less. If it is more, the firm pays off debt or invests in marketable securities. If it is less, the firm first draws down its cash balance or sells its marketable securities.
4. If external finance is required, firms issue the safest security first. That is, they start with debt, then possibly hybrid securities such as convertible bonds, then perhaps equity as a last resort.

In this story, there is no well-defined target debt-equity mix, because there are two kinds of equity, internal and external, one at the top of the pecking order and one at the bottom. Each firm's observed debt ratio reflects its cumulative requirements for external finance.

The pecking order explains why the most profitable firms generally borrow less—not because they have low target debt ratios, but because they don't need outside money. Less profitable firms issue debt because they do not have internal funds sufficient for their capital investment program, and because debt financing is first on the pecking order of *external* financing.

The pecking order theory rests on (1) sticky dividend policy, (2) a preference for internal funds, and (3) an aversion to issuing equity. We will not revisit divi-

---

[23] For example, Carl Kester, in a study of the financing policies of firms in the United States and in Japan, found that in each country, high book profitability was the most statistically significant variable distinguishing low- from high-debt companies. See "Capital and Ownership Structure: A Comparison of United States and Japanese Manufacturing Corporations," *Financial Management*, **15:** 5–16 (Spring 1986).

[24] Here we mean debt as a fraction of the book or replacement value of the company's assets. Profitable companies might not borrow a greater fraction of their market value. Higher profits imply higher market value as well as stronger incentives to borrow.

[25] The description is paraphrased from S. C. Myers, "The Capital Structure Puzzle," *Journal of Finance*, **39:** 581–582 (July 1984). For the most part, this section follows Myers's arguments.

dend policy, which occupied Chapter 16, but items (2) plus (3) deserve a further word.

Some think that financial managers do not strive for optimal financing decisions, but simply finance by the line of least resistance. If so, internal funds would be their first choice. Internal funds relieve financial managers of contact with outside investors and the "disciplining influences of the securities market." If these comfortable people have to seek external financing, debt is next on the line of least resistance. Who wants to face "the glare of publicity and public attention generated by a stock issue?"[26]

However, a pecking order might also spring from fully rational economic motives, for example, from differences in *issue costs*. Internal funds of course have no issue costs, but if outside money is needed, issue costs are less for debt than for equity. Thus, it makes sense to use retained earnings, rather than external equity, and to build up *financial slack*, in the form of cash, marketable securities, or unused debt capacity, to reduce the odds that a future stock issue will be necessary.

Financial managers also worry about the adverse *signal* transmitted to investors when equity is issued. Remember from Chapter 15 that stock issues are bad news to investors: The announcement of a stock issue drives down stock price. Issuing debt, on the other hand, seems to be no news at all, or at worst a trifling disappointment.[27] You can appreciate why financial managers, who would rather not see stock price fall, would put debt ahead of equity in the pecking order.[28]

18-5 CHOOSING THE FIRM'S DEBT-EQUITY RATIO

A Checklist

important

It should be clear that there are no simple answers to the capital structure decision. For example, we can't say that more debt is always better. Debt may be better than equity in some cases, worse in others. We suggest, however, that you use a four-dimensional checklist when thinking about capital structure. These dimensions are taxes, risk, asset type, and the need for financial slack.

1. *Taxes:* If your company is in a taxpaying position, an increase in leverage reduces the income tax paid by the company and increases the tax paid by investors. If the company has large accumulated losses, an increase in leverage cannot reduce corporate taxes but does increase personal taxes.

Of course you are not just interested in whether the company is currently paying taxes but whether it will do so throughout the life of the debt. Firms with high and stable income streams are more likely to remain in a taxpaying position, but even they may be unable to take full advantage of the interest tax shields if they borrow too much; hence our recommendation that there is a tax advantage to borrowing for companies that are reasonably sure that they can use the interest tax shields and a disadvantage for those that are unlikely to use them.

Remember also that borrowing is not the only way to shield income. For example, accelerated write-offs of plant and equipment can be used to reduce corporate taxes.

---

[26] See Chapter 14, Section 14-6.

[27] For example, see B. E. Eckbo, "Valuation Effects of Corporate Debt Offerings," *Journal of Financial Economics*, **15:** 119–151 (January–February 1986).

[28] We have not given a full account of the theoretical underpinnings of the pecking order theory. There is more to it than "managers who would rather not see stock price fall." The theory was developed in S. C. Myers and N. S. Majluf, "Corporate Financing and Investment Decisions When Firms Have Information Investors Do Not Have," *Journal of Financial Economics*, **13:** 187–222 (June 1984).

2. *Risk:* With or without bankruptcy, financial distress is costly. Other things equal, distress is more likely for firms with high business risk. That is why such firms generally issue less debt.

3. *Asset Type:* The costs of distress are likely to be greater for firms whose value depends on growth opportunities or intangible assets. These firms are more likely to forgo profitable investment opportunities and, if default occurs, their assets may erode rapidly. Hence firms whose assets are weighted toward intangible assets should borrow significantly less, on average, than firms holding assets you can kick.

4. *Financial Slack:* In the long run, a company's value rests more on its capital investment and operating decisions than on financing. Therefore, you want to make sure your firm has sufficient financial slack, so that financing is quickly accessible when good investment opportunities arise. Financial slack is most valuable to firms that have ample positive-NPV growth opportunities. That is another reason why growth companies usually aspire to conservative capital structures.

Planning Ahead

When you issue debt, you need to persuade the lenders that you will be able to repay their loan. Therefore companies seeking debt financing usually draw up a set of pro forma income statements and balance sheets. These are simply your best forecasts of the firm's profits, assets, and liabilities.

You may find when you do this that the firm is unlikely to generate sufficient cash internally to repay the loan. That is not in itself a cause for alarm—remember that most growing firms run a financial deficit and are, therefore, repeatedly raising new capital. But such a result should prompt you to ask two questions. First, "Can the maturity of the proposed loan be extended so that the firm *can* repay the loan out of income?" Second, "Is the firm likely to be *able* to raise the additional debt or equity that it will need to repay the proposed loan?"

Most managers are not only interested in the expected outcome; they also want to know what could happen if things go wrong. The techniques that we used in Chapter 10 for examining a single project can also be used to examine the firm as a whole. For example, before their firm issues a large amount of debt, many financial managers conduct a break-even analysis. In other words, they look at how far sales or profits could decline without imperiling the firm's ability to service the loan. Or they look at how well the firm would fare under alternative plausible scenarios. Or they use Monte Carlo simulation to estimate the whole distribution of financial consequences.

The capital structure decision cannot be made in a vacuum. It has to form part of a sensible financial plan that takes into account future investment opportunities, the firm's dividend policy, and so on. That is why the financial manager needs to think about the effects of an issue of debt or equity on future income and balance sheets.

Pro forma income statements and balance sheets will indicate future financing needs. But they won't tell you much about whether you will be able to raise the necessary money. In other words, they won't tell you when you are bankrupt. Remember that bankruptcy occurs when the market value of the firm is less than the payments that have to be made on the debt. When this happens, the shares are worthless and the shareholders have no incentive to put up any further capital. If you want to estimate the risk of bankruptcy, you need to estimate the distribution of future company values. Here again you may find it useful to use simulation to estimate the odds that the market value of the company will be less than the payments that need to be made on the debt.

18-6 SUMMARY

Our goal in this chapter was to build a theory of optimal capital structure combining MM's insights with an analysis of taxes and financial distress.

The value of the firm equals

Value if all-equity-financed + PV tax shield − PV costs of financial distress

The cost of financial distress can be broken down as follows:

1. Bankruptcy costs
   (a) Direct costs such as court fees
   (b) Indirect costs reflecting the difficulty of managing a company undergoing reorganization
2. Costs of financial distress short of bankruptcy
   (a) Conflicts of interest between bondholders and stockholders of firms in financial distress may lead to poor operating performance and investment decisions. Stockholders acting in their narrow self-interest can gain at the expense of creditors by playing "games" which reduce the overall value of the firm.
   (b) The fine print in debt contracts is designed to prevent these games. But fine print increases the costs of writing, monitoring, and enforcing the debt contract.

The value of the tax shield is more controversial. Let us define the net tax shield as T^* times the interest payment on the debt $r_D D$. To calculate present value, this tax shield is usually discounted at the borrowing rate r_D. In the special case of permanent debt

$$\text{PV tax shield} = \frac{T^*(r_D D)}{r_D} = T^* D$$

The problem is to identify T^*.

Most economists have become accustomed to thinking only of the corporate tax advantages of debt. Because firms do not pay corporate tax on any profits that are paid out as interest, interest payments provide a corporate tax shield. If this is the only tax consequence of debt, then for a taxpaying company the net tax saving T^* is simply the marginal corporate tax rate.

The principal difficulty with this view is that many firms seem to thrive with no debt at all despite the strong inducement to borrow. Miller has presented an alternative theory which may explain this. He argued that the net tax saving T^* is really zero when personal taxes as well as corporate taxes are considered. Interest income is not taxed at the corporate level but is taxed at the personal level. Equity income is taxed at the corporate level but may largely escape personal taxes if it comes in the form of capital gains.

In Miller's theory, the supply of corporate debt expands as long as the corporate tax rate exceeds the personal tax rate of the investors absorbing the increased supply. The supply which equates these two tax rates establishes an optimal debt ratio for the aggregate of corporations. But, if the total supply of debt suits investors' needs, any single taxpaying firm must find that debt policy does not matter.

The Tax Reform Act of 1986 has to some extent undercut Miller's argument by cutting back the extra personal taxes paid on interest income versus taxes paid on equity income (dividends and capital gains). But there is probably still a personal tax disadvantage to debt which to some degree offsets its corporate tax advantage.

We suggest that borrowing may make sense for some firms but not for others. If a firm can be fairly sure of earning a profit, there is likely to be a net tax saving from borrowing. In these cases T^* is greater than zero but less than .34. However for firms that are unlikely to earn sufficient profits to benefit from the corporate tax shield, there is little, if any, net tax advantage to borrowing. For these firms T^* could even be negative.

There is no neat formula that you can plug in to find the optimal capital structure. But we recommend that you employ a four-dimensional checklist of taxes, risk, asset type, and the need for financial slack. This provides a framework for making sensible borrowing decisions.

We have portrayed the capital structure choice as a trade-off of the tax advantages of borrowing against the costs of financial distress. Corporations are supposed to pick a target capital structure that maximizes firm value. Firms with safe, tangible assets and plenty of taxable income to shield ought to have high targets. Unprofitable companies with risky, intangible assets ought to rely primarily on equity financing.

This "trade-off theory" of capital structure successfully explains many industry differences in capital structure, but it does not explain why the most profitable firms *within* an industry generally have the most conservative capital structures. (Under the trade-off theory, high profitability should mean high debt capacity *and* a strong corporate tax incentive to use that capacity.)

There is an alternative "pecking order" theory, which states that firms use internal finance when available, and choose debt over equity when external finance is needed. This could explain why less profitable firms borrow more—not because they have higher target debt ratios, but because they need more external financing, and because debt is next in the pecking order when internal funds are exhausted. A pecking order in financing could reflect managers' attempts to minimize issue costs and to avoid the adverse signals conveyed to investors when equity issues are announced.

The pecking order theory stresses the value of financial slack. Without financial slack, the company may be caught at the bottom of the pecking order, and may be forced to choose between issuing undervalued shares or passing over a positive-NPV investment opportunity.

FURTHER READING

Modigliani and Miller's analysis of the present value of interest tax shields at the corporate level is in:

F. Modigliani and M. H. Miller, "Corporate Income Taxes and the Cost of Capital: A Correction," *American Economic Review,* **53:** 433–443 (June 1963).

F. Modigliani and M. H. Miller, "Some Estimates of the Cost of Capital to the Electric Utility Industry, 1954–57," *American Economic Review,* **56:** 333–391 (June 1966).

The following articles consider personal as well as corporate taxes:

D. Farrar and L. L. Selwyn, "Taxes, Corporate Financial Policy and the Returns to Investors," *National Tax Journal,* **20:** 144–154 (December 1967).

M. H. Miller, "Debt and Taxes," *Journal of Finance,* **32:** 261–276 (May 1977).

Miller's theory is extended to include depreciation and other tax shields in:

> H. DeAngelo and R. Masulis, "Optimal Capital Structure Under Corporate Taxation," *Journal of Financial Economics*, **8:** 5–29 (March 1980).

Estimates of bankruptcy costs are presented in:

> J. B. Warner, "Bankruptcy Costs: Some Evidence," *Journal of Finance*, **32:** 337–348 (May 1977).

The following four articles analyze the conflicts of interest between bondholders and stockholders, and their implications for financing policy. (Do not read the fourth article until you have read Chapter 20.)

> M. J. Gordon, "Towards a Theory of Financial Distress," *Journal of Finance*, **26:** 347–356 (May 1971).
>
> M. C. Jensen and W. H. Meckling, "Theory of the Firm: Managerial Behavior, Agency Costs and Ownership Structure," *Journal of Financial Economics*, **3:** 305–360 (October 1976).
>
> S. C. Myers, "Determinants of Corporate Borrowing," *Journal of Financial Economics*, **5:** 146–175 (1977).
>
> D. Galai and R. W. Masulis, "The Option Pricing Model and the Risk Factor of Stock," *Journal of Financial Economics*, **3:** 53–82 (January–March 1976).

For an interesting survey of the capital structure controversy, see:

> R. H. Gordon and B. G. Malkiel, "Corporation Finance," in H. J. Aaron and J. A. Pechman (eds.), *How Taxes Affect Economic Behavior*, The Brookings Institution, Washington, D.C., 1981.

Donaldson has described how corporations set their borrowing targets. He also suggests how these targets can be set more intelligently.

> G. Donaldson, *Corporate Debt Capacity: A Study of Corporate Debt Policy and the Determination of Corporate Debt Capacity*, Division of Research, Graduate School of Business Administration, Harvard University, Boston, 1962.
>
> G. Donaldson, *Strategy for Financial Mobility*, Division of Research, Graduate School of Business Administration, Harvard University, Boston, 1969.

Myers describes the pecking order theory, which is in turn based on work by Myers and Majluf:

> S. C. Myers, "The Capital Structure Puzzle," *Journal of Finance*, **39:** 575–592 (July 1984).
>
> S. C. Myers and N. S. Majluf, "Corporate Financing and Investment Decisions When Firms Have Information Investors Do Not Have," *Journal of Financial Economics*, **13:** 187–222 (June 1984).

The January–February 1986 issue of the Journal of Financial Economics *(vol. 15, no. 1/2) collects a series of empirical studies on the stock price impacts of debt and equity issues and capital structure changes.*

QUIZ

1. Compute the present value of interest tax shields generated by these three debt issues. Consider corporate taxes only. The marginal tax rate is $T_c = .34$.
   (*a*) A $1000, 1-year loan at 8 percent.
   (*b*) A 5-year loan of $1000 at 8 percent. Assume no principal is repaid until maturity.
   (*c*) A $1000 perpetuity at 7 percent.
2. Here are book and market value balance sheets of the United Frypan Company:

Book					Market				
Net working capital	20	Debt	40		Net working capital	20	Debt	40	
Long-term assets	80	Equity	60		Long-term assets	140	Equity	120	
	100		100			160		160	

Assume that MM's theory holds with taxes. There is no growth and the $40 of debt is expected to be permanent. Assume a 40 percent corporate tax rate.

(a) How much of the firm's value is accounted for by the debt-generated tax shield?

(b) How much better off will UF's shareholders be if the firm borrows $20 more and uses it to repurchase stock?

(c) Now suppose that Congress passes a law which eliminates the deductibility of interest for tax purposes after a grace period of 5 years. What will be the new value of the firm, other things equal? (Assume an 8 percent borrowing rate.)

3. Suppose that, in an effort to reduce the federal deficit, Congress increases the top personal tax rate on interest and dividends to 38 percent, but retains a 28 percent tax rate on realized capital gains. The corporate income tax rate stays at 34 percent. Compute the total corporate plus personal taxes paid on debt versus equity income if (a) all capital gains are realized immediately and (b) capital gains are deferred forever. Capital gains are half of equity income.

*4. Suppose that the rate of corporate income tax is reduced to 24 percent. What would Miller predict about (a) the aggregate supply of corporate debt and (b) corporate debt policy?

5. "The firm can't use interest tax shields unless it has (taxable) income to shield." What does this statement imply for the debt policy? Explain briefly.

6. Let us go back to Circular File's market value balance sheet:

Net working capital	$20	$25	Bonds outstanding
Fixed assets	10	5	Common stock
Total assets	$30	$30	Total liabilities

Who gains and who loses from the following maneuvers?

(a) Circular scrapes up $5 in cash and pays a cash dividend.

(b) Circular halts operations, sells its fixed assets, and converts net working capital into $20 cash. Unfortunately the fixed assets fetch only $6 on the secondhand market. The $26 cash is invested in Treasury bills.

(c) Circular encounters an acceptable investment opportunity, NPV = 0, requiring an investment of $10. The firm borrows to finance the project. The new debt has the same security, seniority, etc., as the old.

(d) Suppose that the new project has NPV = +$2 and is financed by an issue of preferred stock.

(e) The lenders agree to extend the maturity of their loan from 1 year to 2 in order to give Circular a chance to recover.

7. What types of firms would be likely to incur heavy costs in the event of bankruptcy or financial distress? What types would incur relatively light costs? Give a few examples of each type.

8. The conventional theory of optimal capital structure states that firms trade off corporate interest tax shields against the possible costs of financial distress due to borrowing. What does this theory predict about the relationship between book profitability and target book debt ratios? Is the theory's prediction consistent with the facts?

9. What is meant by the "pecking order" theory of capital structure? Could this theory explain the observed relationship between profitability and debt ratios? Explain briefly.

QUESTIONS AND PROBLEMS

1. Montmorency Inc. has assets of $100 million and these are expected to remain unchanged in real terms. Assume that the real interest rate is 5 percent, the corporate tax rate is 34 percent, and debt interest is paid at the end of each year. If debt is a constant 30 percent of the value of the assets, what is PV tax shield
   (a) If there is no expected inflation?
   (b) If expected inflation is 10 percent a year?
2. "The trouble with MM's argument is that it ignores the fact that individuals can deduct interest for personal income tax." Show why this is not an objection. What difference would it make if individuals were not allowed to deduct interest for personal tax?
3. Look back at the Merck example in Section 18-1. Suppose that Merck moves to a 40 percent book debt ratio by issuing debt and using the proceeds to repurchase shares. Assume that MM's theory holds except for taxes. Now reconstruct Table 18-2b to reflect the new capital structure. Before it changes its capital structure, Merck has 136 million shares outstanding. What is the stock price before and after the change?
4. Calculate the tax shield for an actual United States company assuming
   (a) Debt is permanent.
   (b) MM arc right.
   How would the stock price change if the company announced tomorrow that it intended to replace all its debt with equity?
*5. Explain the implications of Miller's capital structure theory for the debt policy of:
   (a) A company that pays corporate income tax.
   (b) A company that is not in a taxpaying position.
   (c) A company that is paying taxes now, but is unsure that it will have taxable income in the future.

   Assume 1985 tax rates for the United States: 46 percent for corporations, personal rates of up to 50 percent for dividends and interest, and effective personal rates of, say, 10 percent on capital gains.
*6. Imagine the following very simple world. There are three groups of investors with the following tax rates:

Group	Tax Rate, Percent
A	60
B	40
C	0

They can choose from perpetual municipal bonds, perpetual corporate bonds, and common stock. Municipals and common stock attract no personal tax. Interest from corporate bonds attracts personal tax but is deductible for corporate tax. The corporate tax rate is 50 percent. Interest payments on municipals total $20 million. Cash flow (before interest and taxes) from corporations totals $300 million. Each group starts with the same amount of money. Regardless of what changes are made in capital structure, the three groups always invest the same amount, and they require a minimum return of 10 percent after taxes on any security.

(*a*) Suppose that companies are financed initially by common stock. Company X now decides to allocate $1 million of its pretax cash flows to interest payments on debt. Which group or groups of investors will buy this debt? What will be the rate of interest? What will be the effect on the value of Company X?

(*b*) Other companies have followed the example of X and interest payments now total $150 million. At this point company Y decides to allocate $1 million to interest payments on debt. Which group or groups will buy this debt? What will be the rate of interest? What will be the effect on the value of company Y?

(*c*) Total interest payments have somehow risen to $250 million. Now company Z substitutes common stock for debt, thereby *reducing* interest payments by $1 million. Which group or groups will sell their debt to Z? At what rate of interest can Z repurchase the debt? What will be the effect on Z's value?

(*d*) What is the equilibrium capital structure? Which groups will hold which securities? What is the rate of interest? What is the total value of all companies? Show that in equilibrium even an unlevered company has no incentive to issue debt. Similarly show that even a company with above-average leverage has no incentive to reduce its debt.

*7. Here is a difficult problem. What difference does the deduction for depreciation make to Miller's equilibrium? Try recalculating the equilibrium in problem 6, assuming that companies can deduct depreciation of:

(*a*) $100 million.

(*b*) $50 million.

*8. The expected return on (risk-free) equity is 14 percent and the interest rate is 20 percent.

(*a*) What is the implied personal tax rate of the marginal lender? (Assume that equity income is free of personal tax.)

(*b*) Company A has large depreciation tax shields and uncertain income. As a result, A's expected marginal rate of corporate tax is 40 percent if it finances solely with equity. For every 5 percent increase in A's debt ratio, A's marginal tax rate is expected to decline by 2 percent. How much should A borrow?

9. Look at some real companies with different types of assets. What operating problems would each encounter in the event of financial distress? How well would the assets keep their value?

10. The Salad Oil Storage Company (SOS) has financed a large part of its facilities with long-term debt. There is a significant risk of default, but the company is not on the ropes yet. Explain:

(*a*) Why SOS stockholders could lose by investing in a positive-NPV project financed by an equity issue.

(*b*) Why SOS stockholders could gain by investing in a negative-NPV project financed by an equity issue.

(*c*) Why SOS stockholders could gain from paying out a large cash dividend. How might the firm's adherence to a target debt ratio mitigate some or all of the problems noted above?

√ **11.** (*a*) Who benefits from the "fine print" in bond contracts when the firm gets into financial trouble? Give a one-sentence answer.

    (*b*) Who benefits from the fine print when the bonds are issued? Suppose the firm is offered the choice of issuing (1) a bond with standard restrictions on dividend payout, additional borrowing, etc., and (2) a bond with minimal restrictions, but a much higher interest rate? Suppose the interest rates on both (1) and (2) are fair from the viewpoint of lenders. Which bond would you expect the firm to issue? Why?

12. Explain why stock price falls when equity issues are announced but not when debt issues are announced. *Hint:* You'll find part of the answer in Chapter 15, Section 15-3.

13. "I was amazed to find that the announcement of a stock issue drives down the value of the issuing firm by *30 percent,* on average, of the proceeds of the issue. That issue cost dwarfs the underwriter's spread and the administrative costs of the issue. It makes common stock issues prohibitively expensive."

    (*a*) You are contemplating a $100 million stock issue. On past evidence, you anticipate that announcement of this issue will drive down stock price by 3 percent and that the market value of your firm will fall by 30 percent of the amount to be raised. On the other hand, additional equity funds are necessary to fund an investment project which you believe has a positive NPV of $40 million. Should you proceed with the issue?

    (*b*) Is the fall in market value on announcement of a stock issue an *issue cost* in the same sense as an underwriter's spread? Respond to the quote which begins this question.

Use your answer to (*a*) as a numerical example to explain your response to (*b*).

14. Ronald Masulis[29] has analyzed the stock price impact of *exchange offers* of debt for equity or vice versa. In an exchange offer, the firm offers to trade freshly issued securities for seasoned securities in the hands of investors. Thus, a firm that wanted to move to a higher debt ratio could offer to trade new debt for outstanding shares. A firm that wanted to move to a more conservative capital structure could offer to trade new shares for outstanding debt securities.

    Masulis found that debt for equity exchanges were good news (stock price increased on announcement) and equity for debt exchanges were bad news.

    (*a*) Are these results consistent with the "trade-off" theory of capital structure?

    (*b*) Are the results consistent with the evidence that investors regard announcements of (i) stock issues as bad news, (ii) stock repurchases as good news, and (iii) debt issues as no news, or at most trifling disappointments?

    (*c*) How could Masulis's results be explained?

---

[29] R. W. Masulis, "The Effects of Capital Structure Change on Security Prices: A Study of Exchange Offers," *Journal of Financial Economics,* **8:** 139–177 (June 1980), and "The Impact of Capital Structure Change on Firm Value," *Journal of Finance,* **38:** 107–126 (March 1983).

Interactions of Investment and Financing Decisions

We first addressed problems of capital budgeting in Chapter 2. At that point we had said hardly a word about financing decisions; we proceeded under the simplest possible assumption about financing, namely, all-equity financing. We were really assuming an idealized Modigliani-Miller (MM) world in which all financing decisions are irrelevant. In a strict MM world, firms can analyze real investments as if they are to be all-equity-financed; the actual financing plan is a mere detail to be worked out later.

Under MM assumptions, decisions to spend money can be separated from decisions to raise money. In this chapter we reconsider the capital budgeting decision when investment and financing decisions *interact* and cannot be separated.

In the early chapters you learned how to value a capital investment opportunity by a four-step procedure:

1. Forecast the project's incremental after-tax cash flow.
2. Assess the project's risk.
3. Estimate the opportunity cost of capital, that is, the expected rate of return offered to investors by the equivalent-risk investments traded in capital markets.
4. Calculate NPV using the discounted cash flow formula.

In effect, we were thinking of each project as a mini-firm, and asking, "How much would that mini-firm be worth if we spun it off as a separate, all-equity-financed enterprise? How much would investors be willing to pay for shares in the project?"

Of course, this procedure rests on the concept of *value additivity*. In well-functioning capital markets the market value of the firm is the sum of the present value of all the assets held by the firm[1]—the whole equals the sum of the parts. If value additivity did *not* hold, then the value of the firm with the project could be more or less than the sum of the separate value of the project and the value of the firm without the project. We could not determine the project's contribution to firm value by evaluating it as a separate mini-firm.

In this chapter we stick with the value-additivity principle, but extend it to include value contributed by financing decisions as well as value contributed by investment decisions. That leads us to a simple and straightforward approach to analyzing the interactions of financing and investment decisions. The idea is to start by estimating the project's "base-case" value as an all-equity-financed mini-

---

[1] *All assets* means intangible as well as tangible assets. For example, a going concern is usually worth more than a haphazard pile of tangible assets. Thus, the aggregate value of a firm's tangible assets often falls short of its market value. The difference is accounted for by going-concern value or by other intangible assets such as accumulated technical expertise, an experienced sales force, or valuable growth opportunities.

firm, and then to adjust this project's base-case NPV to account for the project's impact on the firm's capital structure. Thus

Adjusted NPV (ANPV, or just APV for short) = base-case NPV

+ NPV of financing decisions caused by project acceptance

Once you identify and value the side effects of financing a project, calculating its APV (adjusted net present value[2]) is no more than addition or subtraction.

There is another way to capture financing side effects. This alternative procedure is more widely used than APV, and it *looks* simpler: You just change the discount rate for the project's cash flows. We will discuss the pros and cons of the adjusted discount rate after you master APV.

We conclude the chapter by reexamining a basic and apparently simple issue: What should the discount rate be for a risk-free project? Once we recognize the tax deductibility of debt interest, we will find that all risk-free, or *debt-equivalent*, cash flows can be evaluated by discounting at the *after-tax* interest rate.

19-1   THE ADJUSTED PRESENT VALUE RULE

The adjusted present value rule is easiest to understand in the context of simple numerical examples. We start by analyzing a project under base-case assumptions, and then consider possible financing side effects of accepting the project.

The Base Case

The APV method begins by valuing the project as if it were a mini-firm financed solely by equity. Consider a project to produce solar water heaters. It requires a $10 million investment and offers a level after-tax cash flow of $1.8 million per year for 10 years. The opportunity cost of capital is 12 percent, which reflects the project's business risk. Investors would demand a 12 percent expected return to invest in the mini-firm's shares.

Thus the mini-firm's base-case NPV is

$$\text{NPV} = -10 + \sum_{t=1}^{10} \frac{1.8}{(1.12)^t} = + \$.17 \text{ million, or } \$170,000$$

Considering the project's size, this figure is not significantly greater than zero. In a pure MM world where no financing decision matters, the financial manager would lean toward taking the project but would not be heartbroken if the project were discarded.

Issue Costs

But suppose that the firm actually has to finance the $10 million investment by issuing stock (it will not have to issue stock if it rejects the project) and that issue costs soak up 5 percent of the gross proceeds of the issue. That means the firm has to issue $10,526,000 in order to obtain $10,000,000 cash. The $526,000 difference goes to underwriters, lawyers, and others involved in the issue process.

The project's APV is calculated by subtracting the issue cost from base-case NPV:

APV = base-case NPV − issue cost = +170,000 − 526,000 = −$356,000

The firm would reject the project because APV is negative.

---

[2] APV is sometimes called *valuation by components*.

Additions to the Firm's Debt Capacity

Consider a different financing scenario. Suppose that the firm has a 50 percent target debt ratio. Its policy is to limit debt to 50 percent of its assets. Thus, if it invests more, it borrows more; in this sense investment adds to the firm's debt capacity.[3]

Is debt capacity worth anything? The most widely accepted answer is "yes" because of the tax shields generated by interest payments on corporate borrowing. (You may wish to look back to our discussion of debt and taxes in Chapter 18.) For example, MM's original theory states that the value of the firm is independent of its capital structure *except* for the present value of interest tax shields:

$$\text{Firm value} = \text{value with all-equity financing} + \text{PV tax shield}$$

This theory tells us to compute the value of the firm in two steps: First compute its base-case value under all-equity financing, and then add the present value of taxes saved due to a departure from all-equity financing. This procedure is like an APV calculation for the firm as a whole.

We can repeat the calculation for a particular project. For example, suppose that the solar heater project increases the firm's assets by $10 million and therefore prompts it to borrow $5 million more. To keep things simple, we assume that this $5 million loan is repaid in equal installments, so that the amount borrowed declines with the depreciating book value of the solar heater project. We also assume that the loan carries an interest rate of 8 percent. Table 19-1 shows how the value of the interest tax shields is calculated. This is the value of the additional

---

[3] *Debt capacity* is potentially misleading because it seems to imply an absolute limit to the amount the firm is *able* to borrow. That is not what we mean. The firm limits borrowing to 50 percent of assets because that is its financing rule. It could borrow more if it wanted to.

TABLE 19-1

Calculating the present value of interest tax shields on debt supported by the solar heater project (figures in thousands)

Year	Debt Outstanding at Start of Year	Interest	Interest Tax Shield	Present Value of Tax Shield
1	$5,000	$400	$136	$126
2	4,500	360	122	105
3	4,000	320	109	87
4	3,500	280	95	70
5	3,000	240	82	56
6	2,500	200	68	43
7	2,000	160	54	32
8	1,500	120	41	22
9	1,000	80	27	14
10	500	40	14	6
			Total	$561

Assumptions:
1. Marginal tax rate = .34; tax shield = .34 × interest.
2. Debt principal repaid at end of year in ten $500,000 installments.
3. Interest rate on debt is 8 percent.
4. Present value calculated at the 8 percent borrowing rate. The assumption here is that the tax shields are just as risky as the interest payments generating them.

debt capacity contributed to the firm by the project. We obtain APV by adding this amount to the project's NPV:

$$APV = \text{base-case NPV} + \text{PV tax shield}$$
$$= +\ 170,000 + 561,000 = \$731,000$$

The Value of Interest Tax Shields

In Table 19-1, we boldly assumed that the firm could fully capture interest tax shields of 34 cents on the dollar discounted back to the present. The true value of the tax shield is almost surely less:

1. You can't use tax shields unless you pay taxes, and you don't pay taxes unless you make money. Few firms can be *sure* that future profitability will be sufficient to use up the interest tax shields.
2. The government takes two bites out of corporate income: the corporate tax and the tax on bondholders' and stockholders' personal income. The corporate tax favors debt; the personal tax favors equity.

In Chapter 18, we argued that the effective tax shield on interest was probably not 34 percent ($T_c = .34$), but some lower figure, call it T^*. We were unable to pin down an exact figure for T^* (some respected scholars have argued that $T^* = 0$).

Suppose, for example, that we believe $T^* = .20$. We can easily recalculate the APV of the solar heater project. Just multiply the present value of the interest tax shields by 20/34. The bottom line of Table 19-1 drops from $561,000 to $561,000(20/34) = \$330,000$. APV drops to:

$$APV = \text{base-case NPV} + \text{PV tax shield}$$
$$= +170,000 + 330,000 = \$500,000$$

Review of the Adjusted Present Value Approach

If the decision to invest in a capital project has important side effects on other financial decisions made by the firm, those side effects should be taken into account when the project is evaluated.

The idea behind APV is "divide and conquer." The approach does not attempt to capture all the side effects in a single calculation. A series of present value calculations is made instead. The first establishes a base-case value for the project: Its value as a separate, all-equity-financed mini-firm. Then each side effect is traced out and the present value of its cost or benefit to the firm is calculated. Finally, all the present values are added together to estimate the project's total contribution to the value of the firm. Thus, in general,

$$\text{Project APV} = \text{base-case NPV} + \frac{\text{sum of the present values of the side}}{\text{effects of accepting the project}}$$

The wise financial manager will want to see not only the adjusted present value, but also where that value is coming from. For example, suppose that base-case NPV is positive but the benefits are outweighed by the costs of issuing stock to finance the project. That should prompt the manager to look around to see if the project can be rescued by an alternative financing plan.

19-2 ADJUSTED DISCOUNT RATES—AN ALTERNATIVE TO ADJUSTED PRESENT VALUE

Calculating APV is not mathematically difficult, but tracing out and evaluating a project's financial side effects takes financial sophistication. Many firms use a simpler procedure. They adjust the discount rate rather than adjusting present value. This allows them to calculate net present value only once, rather than the two or more times required by APV. They set the discount rate for project acceptance equal to an *adjusted cost of capital* which reflects the opportunity cost of capital *and* the project's financing side effects.

Example: The Geothermal Project

We will explain the adjusted-cost-of-capital approach with an even simpler numerical example. The project calls for tapping geothermal energy to supply heat and air conditioning for a shopping center. The investment required is $1 million. Once installed the project will save $220,000 per year after taxes. To keep the arithmetic simple, we will assume the saving continues indefinitely. The business risk of the venture requires a 20 percent discount rate—this is r, the opportunity cost of capital. Thus the project's base-case NPV is just positive:

$$\text{Base-case NPV} = -1,000,000 + \frac{220,000}{.20}$$

$$= +\$100,000$$

We assume that the project has one financing side effect. It expands the firm's borrowing power by $400,000. The project lasts indefinitely, and so we treat it as supporting perpetual debt. In other words, the firm is assumed to borrow $400,000 against the project, and to maintain that borrowing come hell or high water. If the borrowing rate is 14 percent and the net tax shield per dollar of interest is $T^* = .34$, the project supports debt which generates interest tax shields of $.34 \times .14 \times 400,000 = \$19,000$ per year forever. The present value of these tax shields is $19,000/.14 = 135,700$. Thus the geothermal project's APV is:

$$\text{APV} = \text{base-case NPV} + \text{PV tax shield}$$

$$= + 100,000 + 135,700 = +\$235,700$$

The geothermal project looks even better when its contribution to corporate debt capacity is recognized.

The present value of the interest tax shield is $+\$135,700$. Therefore the geothermal project would still be acceptable even if base-case NPV were as low as $-135,700$. What does that imply for the minimum acceptable *income* from the project? To answer that question, we set base-case NPV at $-\$135,700$ and solve for the project's annual income:

$$\begin{array}{l}\text{Minimum acceptable} \\ \text{base-case NPV}\end{array} = -1,000,000 + \frac{\text{annual income}}{.20}$$

$$= -135,700$$

$$\text{Annual income} = .2(1,000,000 - 135,700) = \$172,900$$

Thus, the minimum acceptable income from the project is $172,900 a year and the minimum acceptable IRR is $172,900/1,000,000 = .173$ or 17.3 percent.[4] This is the lowest return that the firm would be willing to accept from projects like this one; it is the IRR at which APV is zero.

Suppose that we encounter another perpetuity. Its opportunity cost of capital is also $r = .20$, and it also expands the firm's borrowing power by 40 percent of the investment. We know that if such a project offers an IRR greater than 17.3 percent, it will have a positive APV. Therefore, we could shorten the analysis by just discounting the project's cash inflows at 17.3 percent.[5] This discount rate is often called the adjusted cost of capital. It reflects both the project's business risk and its contribution to the firm's debt capacity.

We will denote the adjusted cost of capital by r^*. To calculate r^*, we find the minimum acceptable internal rate of return—the IRR at which APV = 0. The rule is

Accept projects which have a positive NPV at the adjusted cost of capital r^*.

A General Definition of the Adjusted Cost of Capital

We now have two concepts of the cost of capital:

Concept 1. The Opportunity Cost of Capital (r): The expected rate of return offered in capital markets by equivalent-risk assets. This depends on the risk of the project's cash flows.

Concept 2. The Adjusted Cost of Capital (r*): An adjusted opportunity cost or hurdle rate that reflects the financing side effects of an investment project.

Some people just say "cost of capital." Sometimes their meaning is clear in context. At other times, they don't know which concept they are referring to and that can sow widespread confusion.

When financing side effects are important, you should accept projects with positive APVs. But if you know the adjusted discount rate, you don't have to calculate APV; you just calculate NPV at the adjusted rate. If we could find a simple, universally correct method for calculating r^*, we would be all set. Unfortunately, there is no such method. There are some useful shorthand formulas, however.

MM's Formula. One formula for calculating r^* was suggested by Modigliani and Miller (MM).[6] MM's formula is

$$r^* = r(1 - T^*L)$$

where r is the opportunity cost of capital and L is the project's marginal contribution to the firm's debt capacity as a proportion of the project's present value. The value of L may be higher than the firm's overall debt ratio or lower than the

---

[4] Since the project produces a level stream of cash flows in perpetuity, IRR equals cash flow divided by investment.

[5] Remember that forecasted project cash flows do *not* reflect the tax shields generated by any debt the project may support.

[6] The formula first appeared in F. Modigliani and M. H. Miller, "Corporate Income Taxes and the Cost of Capital: A Correction," *American Economic Review,* **53:** 433–443 (June 1963). It is explained more fully in M. H. Miller and F. Modigliani, "Some Estimates of the Cost of Capital to the Electric Utility Industry: 1954–1957," *American Economic Review,* **56:** 333–391 (June 1966). In these articles, MM assumed that T^* equals the corporate tax rate T_c.

firm's overall debt ratio. Remember, T^* reflects the net tax saving attached to a dollar of future interest payments.

Example. The contribution of the geothermal project to the firm's debt capacity is \$400,000. Therefore $L = .40$. The project's opportunity cost of capital is $r = .20$ and we continue to assume that $T^* = .34$. We worked out earlier that the project's adjusted cost of capital was $r^* = .173$. That is precisely what we get using the MM formula:

$$r^* = r(1 - T^*L)$$
$$= .20[1 - .34(.4)] = .173, \text{ or } 17.3\%$$

How Reliable Is MM's Formula? The MM formula works for the geothermal project or for any other project that is expected to (1) generate a level, perpetual cash flow and (2) support permanent debt. The formula is exactly right only if these two assumptions are met. Assets offering perpetual cash-flow streams are like abominable snowmen: often referred to but seldom seen. But MM's formula still works reasonably well for projects with limited lives or irregular cash-flow streams. Using the formula to calculate the present value of these projects will typically result in an error of 2 to 6 percent.[7] This is not too bad when you consider that a biased cash-flow forecast could put project value off the mark by plus or minus 20 percent.

What Happens When Future Debt Levels Are Uncertain

We wish we could stop at this point and go on to something easier. But conscience won't allow it. Any capital budgeting procedure that assumes debt levels are fixed when a project is undertaken is grossly oversimplified. For example, we assumed that the geothermal project contributed \$400,000 to the firm's debt capacity—not just when the project is undertaken, but "from here to eternity." That amounts to saying that the future value and risk of the project will not change—a strong assumption indeed. Suppose the price of oil shoots up unexpectedly a year after the project is undertaken; since the geothermal project *saves* oil, its cash flow and value shoot up too. Suppose the project's value doubles. In that case, won't its contribution to debt capacity also double, to \$800,000? It works the other way too: If the oil price falls out of bed, the contribution to debt capacity tumbles.

Suppose the firm's rule is not "Always borrow \$400,000," but "Always borrow 40 percent of the geothermal project's value." Then if project value increases, the firm borrows more. If it decreases, it borrows less. Under this policy, you can no longer discount future interest tax shields at the borrowing rate because the shields are no longer certain. Their size depends on the amount actually borrowed and, therefore, on the actual future value of the project.

When the firm adjusts its borrowing to keep a constant debt proportion, it can often be a wearisome task to calculate the project's APV. Fortunately, James Miles and Russell Ezzell have derived an adjusted discount rate formula for this problem.[8]

$$r^* = r - Lr_DT^*\left(\frac{1 + r}{1 + r_D}\right)$$

[7] See S. C. Myers, "Interactions of Corporate Financing and Investment Decisions—Implications for Capital Budgeting," *Journal of Finance,* **29:** 1–25 (March 1974).

[8] J. Miles and R. Ezzell, "The Weighted Average Cost of Capital, Perfect Capital Markets, and Project Life: A Clarification," *Journal of Financial and Quantitative Analysis,* **15:** 719–730 (September 1980).

where r_D is the borrowing rate. For the geothermal project, we would calculate an adjusted cost of capital of:

$$r^* = .20 - .4(.14)(.34) \left(\frac{1.2}{1.14}\right) = .18, \text{ or } 18\%$$

Discounting the project's cash flows at 18% gives a net present value of

$$NPV = -1,000,000 + \frac{220,000}{.18}$$

$$= +\$222,200$$

The Miles-Ezzell formula works only for firms that maintain a constant debt proportion, but in these cases, it is exact for any cash-flow pattern or project life.[9] It is also much easier to use than the adjusted-present-value method.

How Useful Are Adjusted-Cost-of-Capital Formulas?

We now have two adjusted-cost-of-capital formulas. The major *conceptual* difference between the two formulas lies in their assumptions about the amount of debt the firm can or will issue against the project. MM assume this amount is fixed. Miles and Ezzell assume it will vary with the project's future value. Miles and Ezzell's assumption is more attractive theoretically, but on the other hand, we have to admit that firms' debt policies are sticky: We don't see firms issuing or retiring debt every time their stock price goes up or down. So the truth may be somewhere in between.

Truth's exact location may not be so important. The geothermal and solar heater projects were attractive regardless of which method or formula we used. This is one illustration of Brealey and Myers's Third Law: *You can make a lot more money on the left-hand side of the balance sheet than on the right*. That is, there's more value to be gained by good investment decisions than by good financing decisions.

Nevertheless, it's important to understand the assumptions underlying the formulas and their relationship to the more general APV rule. Both formulas assume that financing affects firm value only through interest tax shields. This is a bold simplification. Most financial scholars and practitioners agree that the tax shields have value—although even this is controversial, as we saw in Chapter 18. But practically no one believes that interest tax shields are the *only* thing governing the financing decision. The decision to accept a project may lead to a stock issue and to issue costs. It may force the firm to shift its dividend policy, or it may enable the firm to make use of an advantageous financial lease or government-subsidized financing. The adjusted-cost-of-capital formulas assume that side effects like these do not exist, or, if they do exist, that they do not matter.

Of course firms can, if they wish, derive more complicated formulas for calculating the adjusted cost of capital in cases where these kinds of financing side effects do matter. But such effects are rarely worth the trouble. It is much simpler to calculate the net present value of side effects separately and then work out the adjusted present value.[10]

---

[9] Remember that the MM formula was exact, given its assumption about debt policy, only for perpetuities.

[10] Of course you can still use the MM formula or the Miles and Ezzell formula to take account of the interest tax shields and then add on the present value of any other financing side effects.

19-3 THE WEIGHTED-AVERAGE-COST-OF-CAPITAL FORMULA

Bear with us; we have still another formula. This one does not require an estimate of T^*, the *net* tax advantage of corporate borrowing, but only T_c, the marginal tax rate. Unfortunately, the formula applies to the firm as a whole, not necessarily to any specific project.

We refer to the *weighted-average cost of capital.* Sometimes we call it the *textbook formula,* since many other textbooks have put heavy emphasis on it. The formula is[11]

$$r^* = r_D(1 - T_c)\frac{D}{V} + r_E\frac{E}{V}$$

where r^* = the adjusted cost of capital
   r_D = the firm's current borrowing rate
   T_c = the marginal *corporate* income tax rate—*not* the effective rate T^* used in Sections 19-1 and 19-2
   r_E = the expected rate of return on the firm's stock (which depends on the firm's business risk *and* its debt ratio)
   D,E = the market values of currently outstanding debt and equity
   $V = D + E$ = the total market value of the firm

The first thing to notice about the weighted-average formula is that all variables in it refer to the firm as a whole. As a result the formula gives the right discount rate only for projects that are just like the firm undertaking them. The formula works for the "average" project. It is incorrect for projects that are safer or riskier than the average of the firm's existing assets. It is incorrect for projects whose acceptance would lead to an increase or decrease in the firm's debt ratio.

The idea behind the weighted-average formula is simple and intuitively appealing. If the new project is profitable enough to pay the (after-tax) interest on the debt used to finance it, and also to generate a superior expected rate of return on the equity invested in it, then it must be a good project. What is a "superior" equity return? One that exceeds r_E, the expected rate of return required by investors in the firm's shares. Let us see how this idea leads to the weighted-average formula.

Suppose that the firm invests in a new project which is expected to produce the same yearly income in perpetuity. If the firm maintains the same debt ratio, the amount of debt used to finance the project is

$$\text{Firm's debt ratio} \times \text{investment} = \frac{D}{V} \times \text{investment}$$

Similarly, the equity used to finance the project is

$$\text{Firm's equity ratio} \times \text{investment} = \frac{E}{V} \times \text{investment}$$

---

[11] If $T_c = 0$, the weighted-average cost of capital simplifies to

$$r_D\frac{D}{V} + r_E\frac{E}{V}$$

This is exactly the formula that we introduced in Chapter 17, where we ignored taxes. As we pointed out in that chapter, MM's proposition I implies that this weighted average is independent of the debt ratio D/V. If MM's proposition fails because of market imperfections, the firm can try to seek the debt ratio D/V which minimizes r^*. See Chapter 17, Section 17-3.

If the project is worthwhile, the income must cover after-tax interest charges and provide an acceptable return to equityholders. The after-tax interest costs on the additional debt are equal to

$$\text{After tax interest rate} \times \text{value of debt} = r_D(1 - T_c) \times \frac{D}{V} \times \text{investment}$$

The minimum acceptable income to equityholders is

$$\text{Expected return on equity} \times \text{value of equity} = r_E \times \frac{E}{V} \times \text{investment}$$

Therefore, for the project to be acceptable, its income *must exceed*:

$$r_D(1 - T_c) \times \frac{D}{V} \times \text{investment} + r_E \times \frac{E}{V} \times \text{investment}$$

This brings us back to the weighted-average formula. Just divide through by the initial investment:

$$\frac{\text{Income}}{\text{Investment}} \text{ must exceed } r_D(1 - T_c)\frac{D}{V} + r_E\frac{E}{V}$$

Note that the ratio of the project's annual income to investment is just the project's return. Therefore our formula gives the minimum acceptable rate of return from the project.

We have derived the textbook formula only for firms and projects offering perpetual cash flows. But Miles and Ezzell have shown that the formula works for any cash-flow pattern if the firm adjusts its borrowing to maintain a constant debt ratio D/V, regardless of whether things turn out well or poorly. When the firm departs from this policy, the textbook formula is only approximately correct.

Now We Apply the Textbook Formula to the Geothermal Project

Imagine the geothermal project set up as an independent, one-asset firm which we'll call Geothermal, Inc. Once the project is built, Geothermal's market value will be worth the initial investment of $1,000,000 plus the project's APV.

In Section 19-2, we calculated that if Geothermal maintains a constant debt ratio of 40 percent, the APV is $222,200. Thus Geothermal's balance sheet should turn out as follows:

Geothermal, Inc.
(market values)

Assets (initial investment + APV)	1,222,200	488,900	Debt (D) (40% of firm value)
		733,300	Equity (E) (60% of firm value)
	1,222,200	1,222,200	

Each year the equityholders expect to receive the cash flow from the investment, *(C) less* the interest payment on debt $(r_D D)$, *plus* the interest tax shield $(T_c r_D D)$:

$$\text{Expected equity income} = C - r_D D + T_c r_D D$$

$$= 220{,}000 - .14(488{,}900) + .34(.14)(488{,}900)$$

$$= 174{,}800$$

The expected rate of return on equity is equal to the expected equity income divided by the equity value:

$$\text{Expected equity return} = r_E = \frac{\text{expected equity income}}{\text{equity value}}$$

$$= \frac{174{,}800}{733{,}300} - .238, \text{ or } 23.8\%$$

Now suppose Geothermal unexpectedly encounters another investment opportunity. The second is a clone of the first in all dimensions save profitability: It has the same business risk and the same time pattern of cash flows. Geothermal therefore plans to borrow 40 percent of the project's value.

If management has forgotten the calculations we did in Section 19-2, it can use the textbook formula to find the appropriate adjusted discount rate.

$$r^* = r_D (1 - T_c) \frac{D}{V} + r_E \frac{E}{V}$$

$$= .14(1 - .34)(.4) + .238(.6)$$

$$= .18, \text{ or } 18\%$$

That's exactly the same figure that we got earlier using the Miles and Ezzell formula.

Using the Textbook Formula

One of the handy features of the textbook formula is that you can often use stock market data to get an estimate of r_E, the expected rate of return demanded by investors in the company's stock. With that estimate, the textbook r^* is not too hard to calculate, because the borrowing rate r_D and the debt and equity ratios D/V and E/V can be directly observed or estimated without too much trouble.[12]

The textbook r^* is a *company* adjusted cost of capital. Strictly speaking, it works only for projects that are carbon copies of the firm's existing assets, both in business risk and financing. Often it is used as a companywide benchmark discount rate; the benchmark is adjusted upward for unusually risky projects and downward for unusually safe ones.

You can also calculate the textbook r^* for *industries*. Suppose that a pharmaceutical company has a subsidiary which produces specialty chemicals. What discount rate is better for the subsidiary's projects—the company r^* or a weighted-average cost of capital for a portfolio of "pure play" specialty chemical companies?

---

[12] Most corporate debt is not actively traded, so its market value cannot be observed directly. But you can usually value a nontraded debt security by looking to securities which *are* traded and which have approximately the same default risk and maturity. See Chapter 23.

The latter rate is better in principle, and also in practice if good data are available for firms with operations and markets similar to the subsidiary's.

An Application to the Railroad Industry

In mid-1974 the assets of the Penn Central Railroad were taken over by Conrail, a new, federally sponsored corporation. Since Penn Central had declared bankruptcy in 1971, the assets taken by Conrail really belonged to the railroad's creditors. Congress set up a special court to determine fair compensation.

Although the Penn Central system was generating hair-curling losses overall, some of its freight lines were potentially profitable. In 1978 one of the authors was asked to estimate a discount rate for valuing the cash flows these lines would have produced, had Conrail not taken them over. He was asked to assume that these freight lines would have had the same business risk and financing as the railroad industry generally. That sounded like a job for the textbook formula. An extensive investigation boiled down to the following calculation:

$$r^*(\text{in mid-1974}) = r_D(1 - T_c)D/V + r_E E/V$$

$$= .087(1 - .5)(.45) + .16(.55)$$

$$= .1076, \text{ or about } 10\frac{3}{4}\%$$

The formula's components were derived as follows:

$r_D = .087$, a weighted average of bond yields for 10 major railroads in mid-1974

$T_c = .50$. The corporate income tax rate in mid-1974 was 48 percent. Two percentage points were added to cover state income taxes.

$D/V = .45$. The estimated average market debt-to-value ratio for 10 major railroads. Thus $E/V = .55$.

$r_E = .16$. Railroad stocks on average appeared to have about the same risk as the market portfolio. Their betas averaged out close to 1.0. Thus $r_E = r_M$. The 16 percent market return equals the sum of the Treasury bill yield in mid-1974 plus the historical risk premium on the market portfolio.

Of course each of these numbers was to some extent controversial. Other expert witnesses used the same textbook formula to arrive at substantially different answers. Anyone brave enough to estimate a discount rate in public can expect controversy.

Mistakes People Make in Using the Weighted-Average Formula

The real danger with the weighted-average formula is that it tempts people to make logical errors. For example, manager Q, who is campaigning for a pet project, might look at the formula

$$r^* = r_D(1 - T_c)\frac{D}{V} + r_E \frac{E}{V}$$

and think, "Aha! My firm has a good credit rating. It could borrow, say, 90 percent of the project's cost if it likes. That means $D/V = .9$ and $E/V = .1$. My firm's borrowing rate r_D is 8 percent and the required return on equity r_E is 15 percent. Therefore

$$r^* = .08(1 - .34)(.9) + .15(.1) = .063$$

or 6.3 percent. When I discount at that rate, my project looks great."

Q is wrong on several counts. First, the weighted-average formula works only for projects that are carbon copies of the firm. The firm isn't 90 percent debt-financed.

Second, the immediate source of funds for a project has no necessary connection with the hurdle rate for the project. What matters is the project's overall contribution to the firm's borrowing power. A dollar invested in Q's pet project will not increase the firm's debt capacity by 90 cents. If it borrows 90 percent of the project's cost, it is really borrowing in part against its *existing* assets. Any advantage from financing the new project with more debt than normal should be attributed to the old projects, not to the new one.

Third, even if the firm were willing and able to lever up to 90 percent debt, its cost of capital would not decline to 6.3 percent (as Q's naive calculation predicts). You cannot increase the debt ratio without creating financial risk for stockholders and thereby increasing r_E, the expected rate of return they demand from the firm's common stock. Going to 90 percent debt would certainly increase the borrowing rate too.

19-4 DISCOUNTING SAFE, NOMINAL CASH FLOWS

Suppose you're considering purchase of a $100,000 machine. The manufacturer sweetens the deal by offering to finance the purchase by lending you $100,000 for 5 years, with annual interest payments of 5 percent. You would have to pay 13 percent to borrow from a bank. Your marginal tax rate is 30 percent ($T_c = .3$).

How much is this loan worth? If you take it, the cash flows are:

Period	0	1	2	3	4	5
Cash flow (in thousands)	$100	−5	−5	−5	−5	−105
Tax shield		+1.5	+1.5	+1.5	+1.5	+1.5
After-tax cash flow	$100	−3.5	−3.5	−3.5	−3.5	−103.5

What is the right discount rate?

Here you are discounting *safe, nominal* cash flows—safe because your company must commit to pay if it takes the loan,[13] and nominal because the payments would be fixed regardless of future inflation. Now, the correct discount rate for safe, nominal cash flows is your company's *after-tax, un*subsidized borrowing rate.[14] In this case $r^* = r_D(1 - T_c) = .13(1 - .3) = .091$. Therefore:

$$\text{NPV} = +100 - \frac{3.5}{1.091} - \frac{3.5}{(1.091)^2} - \frac{3.5}{(1.091)^3} - \frac{3.5}{(1.091)^4} - \frac{103.5}{(1.091)^5}$$

$$= +21.73, \text{ or } \$21,730$$

The manufacturer has effectively cut the machine's purchase price from $100,000 to ($100,000 − $21,730) = $78,270. You can now go back and recalculate the

---

[13] In theory, "safe" means literally risk-free, like the cash returns on a Treasury bond. In practice, it means that the risk of not paying or receiving a cash flow is small.

[14] In Section 13-1, we calculated the NPV of subsidized financing using the *pretax* borrowing rate. Now you can see that was a mistake. Using the pretax rate implicitly defines the loan in terms of its pretax cash flows, violating a rule promulgated way back in Section 6-1: *Always* estimate cash flows on an after-tax basis.

machine's NPV using this fire-sale price, or you can use the NPV of the subsidized loan as one element of the machine's adjusted present value.

A General Rule

Clearly, we owe an explanation of why $r^* = r_D(1 - T_c)$ for safe, nominal cash flows. It's no surprise that r^* depends on r_D, the unsubsidized borrowing rate, for that is investors' opportunity cost of capital, the rate they would demand from your company's debt. But why should r_D be converted to an *after-tax* figure?

Let's simplify by taking a *1-year* subsidized loan of $100,000 at 5 percent. The cash flows, in thousands, are:

Period	0	1
Cash flow	$100	−105
Tax shield		+1.5
After-tax cash flow	$100	−103.5

Now ask, "What is the maximum amount X that could be borrowed for 1 year through regular channels if $103,500 is set aside to service the loan?" The cash flows of this *equivalent loan* are:

Period	0	1
Cash flow	X	$-(1+r_D)X = -1.13X$
Tax shield		$+T_c r_D X = .039X$
After-tax cash flow		$-[1+r_D(1-T_c)]X = -1.091X$

In other words, you will need 109.1 percent of the amount borrowed to pay back principal plus after-tax interest changes. If $1.091X = 103,500$, $X = 94,867$. Now if you can borrow $100,000 by a subsidized loan, but only $94,867 through normal channels, the difference ($5133) is money in the bank. Therefore, it must also be the NPV of this one-period subsidized loan.

When you discount a safe, nominal cash flow at an after-tax borrowing rate, you are implicitly calculating the equivalent loan, the amount you could borrow through normal channels using the cash flow as debt service. Note that:

$$\begin{matrix} \text{Equivalent} \\ \text{loan} \end{matrix} = PV \begin{pmatrix} \text{cash flow} \\ \text{available for} \\ \text{debt service} \end{pmatrix} = \frac{103,500}{1.091} = 94,867$$

In some cases, it may be easier to think of taking the lender's side of the equivalent loan rather than the borrower's. For example, you could ask, "How much would my company have to invest today in order to cover next year's debt service on the subsidized loan?" The answer is $94,867: If you lend that amount at 13 percent, you will earn 9.1 percent after tax, and therefore have $94,867(1.091) = 103,500$. By this transaction, you can in effect cancel, or "zero out," the future obligation. If you can borrow $100,000 and then set aside only $94,867 to cover all the required debt service, you clearly have $5133 to spend as you please. That amount is the NPV of the subsidized loan.

Therefore, regardless of whether it's easier to think of borrowing or lending, the correct discount rate for safe, nominal cash flows is an after-tax interest rate.[15]

In some ways, this is an obvious result once you think about it. Companies are free to borrow or lend money. If they *lend,* they receive the after-tax interest rate on their investment; if they *borrow* in the capital market, they pay the after-tax interest rate. Thus, the opportunity cost to companies of investing in debt-equivalent cash flows is the after-tax interest rate. This is the adjusted cost of capital for debt-equivalent cash flows.

Some Further Examples

Here are some further examples of debt-equivalent cash flows:

Payout Fixed by Contract. Suppose you sign a maintenance contract with a truck leasing firm, which agrees to keep your leased trucks in good working order for the next 2 years in exchange for 24 fixed monthly payments. These payments are debt-equivalent flows.[16]

Depreciation Tax Shields. Capital projects are normally valued by discounting the total after-tax cash flows they are expected to generate. Depreciation tax shields contribute to project cash flow, but they are not valued separately; they are just folded into project cash flows along with dozens, or hundreds, of other specific inflows and outflows. The project's opportunity cost of capital reflects the average risk of the resulting aggregate.

However, suppose we ask what depreciation tax shields are worth *by themselves.* For a firm that's sure to pay taxes, depreciation tax shields are a safe, nominal flow. Therefore, they should be discounted at the firm's after-tax borrowing rate.[17]

Suppose we buy an asset with a depreciable basis of $200,000, which can be depreciated by the 5-year tax depreciation schedule (see Table 6-5). The resulting tax shields are:

Period	1	2	3	4	5	6
Percentage deductions	20	32	19	11.5	11.5	6
Dollar deductions (in thousands)	$40	64	38	23	23	12
Tax shields at $T_c = .30$	$12	19.2	11.4	6.9	6.9	3.6

The after-tax discount rate is $r_D(1 - T_c) = .13(1 - .3) = .091$. (We continue to assume a 13 percent pretax borrowing rate and a 30 percent marginal tax rate.) The present value of these shields is:

---

[15] Borrowing and lending rates should not differ by much if the cash flows are truly safe—that is, if the chance of default is small. Usually your decision will not hinge on the rate used. If it does, ask which offsetting transaction—borrowing or lending—seems most natural and reasonable for the problem at hand. Then use the corresponding interest rate.

[16] We assume you are locked into the contract. If it can be canceled without penalty, you may have a valuable option.

[17] The depreciation tax shields are cash inflows, not outflows as for the contractual payout or the subsidized loan. For safe, nominal inflows, the relevant question is, "How much could the firm borrow today if it uses the inflow for debt service?" You could also ask, "How much would the firm have to lend today to generate the same future inflow?"

$$PV = \frac{12}{1.091} + \frac{19.2}{(1.091)^2} + \frac{11.4}{(1.091)^3} + \frac{6.9}{(1.091)^4} + \frac{6.9}{(1.091)^5} + \frac{3.6}{(1.091)^6}$$

$$= +47.4, \text{ or } \$47,400$$

*Adjusted Discount Rates for Debt-Equivalent Cash Flows

You may have wondered whether our procedure for valuing debt-equivalent cash flows is consistent with the adjusted-discount-rate approaches presented earlier in this chapter. Yes, they are consistent, as we will now illustrate.

Remember from Chapter 18, Section 18-2, that the value of corporate interest tax shields depends on the personal tax rates paid by debt and equity investors. No one knows for sure what the relevant personal rates actually are. The polar views are those of Modigliani and Miller (MM), on the one hand, and Miller on the other. MM assume that investors face the same tax rate on debt and equity income, so that only corporate taxes need be considered; in that case, $T^* = T_c$. But Miller argues that debt investors pay higher effective tax rates than equity investors, so much so that any advantage of the corporate interest tax shield is entirely offset, and $T^* = 0$.

Let's look at a very simple numerical example from each viewpoint. Our problem is to value a $1 million payment to be received from a blue-chip company 1 year hence. After taxes at 34 percent, the cash inflow is $660,000. The payment is fixed by contract.

Since the contract generates a debt-equivalent flow, the opportunity cost of capital is the rate investors would demand on a 1-year note issued by the blue-chip company, which happens to be 8 percent. For simplicity, we'll assume this is your company's borrowing rate too. Our valuation rule for debt-equivalent flows is therefore to discount at $r^* = r_D(1 - T_c) = .08(1 - .34) = .053$:

$$PV = \frac{660,000}{1.053} = \$626,800$$

Valuing Debt-Equivalent Cash Flows under MM Assumptions. Now let's see how MM would address this same problem. The opportunity cost of capital is still $r_D = .08$, or 8 percent. With $T^* = T_c$, the MM adjusted-cost-of-capital formula is $r^* = r_D(1 - T_cL)$.

What is L? In Section 19-2, we defined it as a project's "marginal contribution to the firm's debt capacity," expressed as a fraction of project value, which is normally well below 1. But the debt capacity of a safe cash flow is 100 percent of its value, because the firm could "zero out" the cash flow by taking out an equivalent loan with the same after-tax debt service. Thus, we can think of "debt capacity" as the offsetting equivalent loan. Since the equivalent loan has exactly the same present value as the debt-equivalent flow, $L = 1$.

The MM adjusted-cost-of-capital formula for debt-equivalent cash flows therefore boils down to the same after-tax borrowing rate we used to discount the $660,000 inflow:

$$r^* = r(1 - T_cL) = r_D(1 - T_c) = .08(1 - .34) = .053$$

We get the same result from the Miles-Ezzell formula. With $r = r_D$ and $L = 1$:

$$r^* = r - Lr_DT_c\left(\frac{1+r}{1+r_D}\right)$$

$$= r_D - 1 \times r_DT_c\left(\frac{1+r_D}{1+r_D}\right)$$

$$= r_D - r_DT_c = r_D(1 - T_c)$$

Let's also try an APV calculation under MM assumptions. This is a two-part calculation. First, the $660,000 inflow is discounted at the opportunity cost of capital, 8 percent. Second, we add the present value of interest tax shields on debt supported by the project. Since the firm can borrow 100 percent of the cash flow's value, the tax shield is r_DT_cAPV, and APV is:

$$\text{APV} = \frac{660,000}{1.08} + \frac{.08(.34)\text{APV}}{1.08}$$

Solving for APV, we get $626,900, which save for a rounding error,[18] is the same answer we obtained by discounting at the after-tax borrowing rate.

Thus our valuation rule for debt-equivalent flows is a special case of the APV rule once we adopt MM's assumptions about debt and taxes.

Valuing Debt-Equivalent Cash Flows under Miller's Assumptions. But suppose that you share Miller's view that there is no tax advantage to debt, so that $T^* = 0$. That would seem to imply that debt-equivalent cash flows should be discounted at the *pretax* borrowing rate. For example, if we set $T^* = 0$ in the MM adjusted-cost-of-capital formula, $r^* = r(1 - T^*L) = r(1 - 0 \times L) = r$, the opportunity cost of capital, which we would normally set at $r = r_D$ for debt-equivalent flows.

However, the reason why $T^* = 0$ in Miller's theory is that debt investors' personal tax rate equals the corporate rate ($T_p = T_c$), while the effective tax rate on equity income is zero ($T_{pE} = 0$). (See Chapter 18, Section 18-2.) Thus debt investors demand a higher pretax rate of return on safe investments than equity investors do. For example, if the after-personal-tax return on debt is $0.8(1 - .34) = .053$, or 5.3 percent, then investors will also be content with a 5.3 percent rate of return on a safe, *untaxed* equity investment.

Therefore, equity investors' opportunity cost of capital for a safe cash flow is the *after-tax* interest rate: $r = r_D(1 - T_p) = r_D(1 - T_c)$.

Thus, although $T^* = 0$ in Miller's world, we nevertheless end up discounting debt-equivalent flows at $r_D(1 - T_c)$, because that is the rate the firm's stockholders demand.

19-5 SUMMARY

Investment decisions always have side effects on financing: Every dollar spent has to be raised somehow. Sometimes the side effects are irrelevant or at least unimportant. In an ideal world with no taxes, transaction costs, or other market imperfections, only investment decisions would affect firm value. In such a world firms could analyze all investment opportunities as if they were all-equity financed.

---

[18] The after-tax borrowing rate is actually $r^* = .0528$. Rounding to .053 reduces PV to $626,800 from the correct figure, $626,900.

Firms would decide which assets to buy and then worry about getting the money to pay for them. No one would worry about where the money might come from, because debt policy, dividend policy, and all other financing choices would have no impact on stockholders' wealth.

The side effects cannot be ignored in practice. Therefore in this chapter we showed you how they should be taken into account.

The technique is simple. We first calculate the present value of the project as if there are no important side effects. Then we adjust present value to calculate the project's total impact on firm value. The rule is to accept the project if adjusted net present value (APV) is positive:

$$\text{Accept project if APV} = \text{base-case NPV} + \begin{array}{c}\text{present value}\\ \text{of financing}\\ \text{side effects}\end{array} > 0$$

The base-case NPV is the project's NPV computed assuming all-equity financing and perfect capital markets. Think of it as the project's value if it were set up as a separate mini-firm. You would compute the mini-firm's value by forecasting its cash flows and discounting at the opportunity cost of capital for the project. The cash flows should be net of the taxes that an all-equity-financed mini-firm would pay.

Financing side effects are evaluated one by one and their present values added to or subtracted from base-case NPV. We looked at several cases:

1. *Issue costs.* If accepting the project forces the firm to issue securities, then the present value of issue costs should be subtracted from base-case NPV.
2. *Interest tax shields.* Debt interest is a tax-deductible expense. Most people believe that interest tax shields contribute to firm value. Thus a project that prompts the firm to borrow more generates additional value. The project's APV is increased by the present value of interest tax shields on debt the project supports.
3. *Special financing.* Sometimes special financing opportunities are tied to project acceptance. For example, the government might offer subsidized financing for socially desirable projects. You simply compute the present value of the financing opportunity and add it to base-case NPV.

Remember not to confuse *contribution to corporate debt capacity* with the immediate source of funds for investment. For example, a firm might, as a matter of convenience, borrow $1 million for a $1 million research program. But the research would be unlikely to contribute $1 million in debt capacity; a large part of the $1 million new debt would be supported by the firm's other assets.

Also remember that *debt capacity* is not meant to imply an absolute limit on how much the firm *can* borrow. The phrase refers to how much it *chooses* to borrow. Normally the firm's optimal debt level increases as its assets expand; that is why we say that a new project contributes to corporate debt capacity.

Calculating APV may require several steps: one step for base-case NPV, and one for each financing side effect. Many firms try to calculate APV in a single calculation. They do so by the following procedure. After-tax cash flows are forecasted in the usual way—that is, as if the project is all-equity-financed. But the discount rate is adjusted to reflect the financing side effects. If the discount rate is adjusted correctly, the result is APV:

$$\begin{array}{c}\text{NPV at adjusted}\\ \text{discount rate}\end{array} = \text{APV} = \begin{array}{c}\text{NPV at opportunity}\\ \text{cost of capital}\end{array} + \begin{array}{c}\text{present value of}\\ \text{financing side effects}\end{array}$$

Unfortunately, there is no formula for adjusting the discount rate that is simple and generally correct. However, there are two useful rules of thumb. The first is the Modigliani-Miller (MM) formula:

$$r^* = r(1 - T^*L)$$

Here r is the opportunity cost of capital and r^* is adjusted cost of čapital. The quantity T^* is the net tax saving per dollar of interest paid, and L is the proportional contribution made by the project to corporate borrowing power. MM's formula is strictly correct only for projects offering level, perpetual cash-flow streams and supporting permanent debt. But the errors from applying it to other types of projects are not serious.

Miles and Ezzell have developed another formula,

$$r^* = r - Lr_DT^* \left(\frac{1 + r}{1 + r_D} \right)$$

This formula assumes the firm will adjust its borrowing to follow every fluctuation in future project value. If this assumption is right, the formula works for projects of any maturity or cash-flow pattern.

The Miles-Ezzell formula typically gives adjusted discount rates slightly higher than MM's. The truth is probably somewhere in between. However, both formulas assume that the present value of additional interest tax shields is the *only* side effect of accepting the project.

To apply the MM and Miles-Ezzell formulas, you need to know r, the cost of capital for an all-equity-financed project. If you don't know r, you may be able to calculate the adjusted cost of capital using the weighted-average or textbook formula:

$$r^* = r_D(1 - T_c) \frac{D}{V} + r_E \frac{E}{V}$$

Here r_D and r_E are the expected rates of return demanded by investors in the firm's bonds and stock, respectively. The quantities D and E are the current *market values* of debt and equity, and V is the total market value of the firm ($V = D + E$).

Strictly speaking, this formula only works for projects that are carbon copies of the existing firm—projects with the same business risk that will be financed to maintain the firm's current, market debt ratio. But firms can use it as a benchmark rate, to be adjusted upward for especially risky projects and downward for especially safe ones.

Finally, we offered a simple valuation rule for safe, nominal cash flows: Simply discount at the after-tax interest rate.

Remember that each of these formulas rests on special assumptions. When you encounter a project that seriously violates these assumptions, you should go back to APV.

FURTHER READING

For a discussion of adjusted present value, see Myers's article and the subsequent comments:

S. C. Myers: "Interactions of Corporate Financing and Investment Decisions—Implications for Capital Budgeting," *Journal of Finance,* **29:** 1–25 (March 1974).

S. Bar-Yosef: "Interactions of Corporate Financing and Investment Decisions—Implications for Capital Budgeting: Comment," *Journal of Finance,* **32:** 211–217 (March 1977), followed by Myers's "Reply."

D. Ashton and D. Atkins: "Interactions of Corporate Financing and Investment Decisions—Implications for Capital Budgeting: A Further Comment," *Journal of Finance,* **33:** 1447–1453 (December 1978).

Formulas for the adjusted discount rate are explained in:

F. Modigliani and M. H. Miller: "Corporate Income Taxes and the Cost of Capital: A Correction," *American Economic Review,* **53:** 433–443 (June 1963).

M. H. Miller and F. Modigliani: "Some Estimates of the Cost of Capital to the Electric Utility Industry: 1954–1957," *American Economic Review,* **56:** 333–391 (June 1966).

J. Miles and R. Ezzell: "The Weighted Average Cost of Capital, Perfect Capital Markets and Project Life: A Clarification," *Journal of Financial and Quantitative Analysis,* **15:** 719–730 (September 1980).

There have been dozens of articles on the weighted-average cost of capital and other issues discussed in this chapter. Here are two representative ones:

M. J. Brennan: "A New Look at the Weighted-Average Cost of Capital," *Journal of Business Finance,* **5:** 24–30 (1973).

D. R. Chambers, R. S. Harris, and J. J. Pringle: "Treatment of Financing Mix in Analyzing Investment Opportunities," *Financial Management,* **11:** 24–41 (Summer 1982).

The valuation rule for safe, nominal cash flows is developed in:

R. S. Ruback, "Calculating the Market Value of Risk-Free Cash Flows," *Journal of Financial Economics,* **15:** 323–339 (March 1986).

QUIZ

1. A project costs $1 million and has a base-case NPV of exactly zero (NPV = 0). What is the project's APV in the following cases?
   (a) If the firm invests, it has to raise $500,000 by stock issue. Issue costs are 15 percent of *net* proceeds.
   (b) The firm has ample cash on hand. But if it invests, it will have access to $500,000 of debt financing at a subsidized interest rate. The present value of the subsidy is $175,000.
   (c) If the firm invests, its debt capacity increases by $500,000. The present value of interest tax shields on this debt is $76,000.
   (d) If the firm invests, it issues equity, as in (a), and borrows, as in (c).

2. Consider the APV of the solar heater project, as calculated in Table 19-1. How would the APV change if the net tax shield per dollar of interest is not $T_c = .34$, but $T^* = .10$?

3. Consider a project lasting 1 year only. The initial outlay is $1000 and the expected inflow is $1200. The opportunity cost of capital is $r = .20$. The borrowing rate is $r_D = .10$ and the net tax shield per dollar of interest is $T^* = .20$.
   (a) What is the project's base-case NPV?
   (b) What is its APV if the firm borrows 30 percent of the project's required investment?

4. Calculate the adjusted cost of capital for the one-period project discussed in Quiz question 3, just above.
   (a) First, use the MM formula.
   (b) Then use the Miles-Ezzell formula.
   (c) Calculate the project's NPV using the discount rates you calculated in (a) and (b).

5. Calculate the weighted-average cost of capital for Federated Junkyards of America, using the following information.

   - Debt: $75,000,000 outstanding, at book value. The debt is trading at 90 percent of par. The yield to maturity is 16 percent.
   - Equity: 2,500,000 shares selling at $42 per share. Assume the expected rate of return on Federated's stock is 25 percent.
   - Taxes: Federated's marginal tax rate is $T_c = .23$.

6. The textbook formula seems to imply that debt is "cheaper" than equity—i.e., that a firm with more debt could use a lower discount rate r^*. Does this make sense? Explain briefly.

7. You are considering a 5-year lease of office space for R&D personnel. Once signed, the lease cannot be canceled. It would commit your firm to six annual $100,000 payments, with the first payment due immediately. What is the present value of the lease if your company's borrowing rate is 9 percent and its tax rate is 34 percent? Note: The lease payments would be tax-deductible.

QUESTIONS AND PROBLEMS

1. Consider another perpetual project like the geothermal project in Section 19-2. Its initial investment is $1,000,000 and the expected cash inflow is $85,000 a year in perpetuity. The opportunity cost of capital with all-equity financing is 10 percent, and the project allows the firm to borrow an additional $400,000 at 7 percent. Assume the net tax advantage to borrowing is 30 cents per dollar of interest paid ($T^* = .30$). What is the project's APV?

2. Suppose the project described in problem 1 is to be undertaken by a university. Funds for the project will be withdrawn from the university's endowment, which is invested in a widely diversified portfolio of stocks and bonds. However, the university can also borrow at 7 percent.

   Suppose the university treasurer proposes to finance the project by issuing $400,000 of perpetual bonds at 7 percent, and by selling $600,000 worth of common stocks from the endowment. The expected return on the common stocks is 10 percent. He therefore proposes to evaluate the project by discounting at a weighted-average cost of capital, calculated as:

   $$r^* = r_D \frac{D}{V} + r_E \frac{E}{V}$$

   $$= .07 \left(\frac{400,000}{1,000,000} \right) + .10 \left(\frac{600,000}{1,000,000} \right)$$

   $$= .088, \text{ or } 8.8\%$$

   What's right or wrong with the treasurer's approach? Should the university invest? Should it borrow?

3. Digital Organics has the opportunity to invest $1 million now ($t = 0$) and expects after-tax returns of $600,000 in $t = 1$ and $700,000 in $t = 2$. The project will last for 2 years only. The appropriate cost of capital is 12 percent with all-equity financing, the borrowing rate is 8 percent, and DO's target debt ratio for a project of this type is .3. Assume debt tax shields have a net value of 30 cents per dollar of interest paid. Calculate the project's APV using each of the following methods.

(*a*) Use the procedure followed in Table 19-1, where debt ratios were assumed fixed in terms of book values.

(*b*) Discount project cash flows at an adjusted rate derived from the Miles-Ezzell formula.

(*c*) Use an adjusted rate derived from the MM formula.

4. Refer again to Quiz question 3 for this chapter. Suppose the firm borrows 30 percent of the project's *value*.

(*a*) What is the project's APV?

(*b*) What is the minimum acceptable rate of return for projects of this type?

(*c*) Show that your answer to (*b*) is consistent with the Miles-Ezzell formula.

5. List the assumptions underlying the MM adjusted-discount-rate formula. Derive the formula algebraically for a perpetual project. Then try to derive it for a one-period project like the one described in Quiz question 3. Keep MM's other assumptions intact. *Hint:* You will end up with the Miles-Ezzell formula. In other words, their formula works for one-period projects; MM's does not.

6. The Bunsen Chemical Company is currently at its target debt ratio of 40 percent. It is contemplating a $1 million expansion of its existing business. This expansion is expected to produce a cash inflow of $130,000 a year in perpetuity.

   The company is uncertain whether to undertake this expansion and how to finance it. The two options are a $1 million issue of common stock or a $1 million issue of 20-year debt. The flotation costs of a stock issue would be around 5 percent of the amount raised and the flotation costs of a debt issue would be around 1½ percent.

   Bunsen's financial manager, Miss Polly Ethylene, estimates that the required return on the company's equity is 14 percent, but she argues that the flotation costs increase the cost of new equity to 19 percent. On this basis, the project does not appear viable.

   On the other hand, she points out that the company can raise new debt on a 7 percent yield which would make the cost of new debt 8½ percent. She therefore recommends that Bunsen should go ahead with the project and finance it with an issue of long-term debt.

   Is Miss Ethylene right? How would you evaluate the project?

7. Can you explain why we use the marginal corporate tax rate (T_c) in the textbook formula, but the *net* tax shield per dollar of interest (T^*) in the MM and Miles-Ezzell formulas?

8. Suppose you wanted to figure out the *opportunity* cost of capital (r) for the railroad industry in mid-1974. You have an estimate of r^*, the adjusted discount rate: 10¾ percent as reported in Section 19-3. *Hint:* We presented two formulas linking r and r^*.

9. Suppose the firm issues not just debt and equity, but preferred stock also. How would this change the weighted-average cost of capital formula? How would it change the MM and Miles-Ezzell formulas?

10. Consider a different financing scenario for the solar water heater project discussed in Section 19-1. The project requires $10 million and has a base-case NPV of $170,000. Suppose the firm happens to have $5 million in the bank which could be used for the project.

    The government, eager to encourage solar energy, offers to help finance the project by lending $5 million at a subsidized rate of 5 percent. The loan calls for the firm to pay the government $647,500 annually for 10 years (this amount includes both principal and interest).

(a) What is the value of being able to borrow from the government at 5 percent? Assume the company's normal borrowing rate is 8 percent and the corporate tax rate is 34 percent.

(b) Suppose the company's normal debt policy is to borrow 50 percent of the book value of its assets. It calculates the present value of interest tax shields by the procedure shown in Table 19-1 and includes this present value in APV. Should it do so here, given the government's offer of cheap financing?

(c) Suppose instead that the firm normally borrows 30 percent of the *market* value of its assets. Does this change your answer to part (b)? *Hint:* The Miles-Ezzell formula can be used to calculate project APV in this case; that formula does not capture the value of the subsidized loan, however.

PART SIX

OPTIONS

20 Corporate Liabilities and the Valuation of Options

The world's largest securities market in terms of the dollar value of securities traded is the New York Stock Exchange. Which do you think is the second largest—the American Exchange, London, Tokyo? The answer is none of these—it is the Chicago Board Options Exchange (CBOE). The CBOE is a success story in finance. It was founded in 1973. Within 5 years investors were trading options to buy or sell more than 10 million shares daily.

Option trading now takes place on a number of exchanges. In addition to options on individual common stocks, there are also options on stock indexes, bonds, commodities, and foreign exchange. A list of the principal traded options is given in Table 20-1.

Option trading is a specialized business and its devotees speak a language of their own. They talk of calls, puts, straddles, butterflies, deep-in-the-money options, and naked options. We will not tell you the meaning of *all* these terms but by the time you have finished this chapter you should know the principal kinds of option and how to value them.

Why should a financial manager of an industrial company be interested in such matters? Because managers routinely use currency commodity, and interest rate options, and they also come up against a variety of corporate investment and financing problems which have options embedded in them.

Many capital investment proposals include an option to buy additional equipment at some future date. For instance, the company may invest in a patent that allows it to exploit a new technology or it may purchase adjoining land that gives it an opportunity to expand. In each case the company is paying money today for the opportunity to make a further investment. To put it another way, it is acquiring *growth opportunities*. We discussed these options in Chapter 4, and in Chapter 10 we showed how you can use decision trees to analyze Magna Charter's options to expand a project or abandon it. We return to Magna Charter in the next chapter, when we show you how to calculate the value of the abandonment option using option pricing theory.

Here is another disguised option. You are considering the purchase of a tract of desert land that is known to contain gold deposits. Unfortunately, the cost of extraction is higher than the current price of gold. Does that mean the land is almost worthless? Not at all. You are not obliged to mine the gold, but the land gives you the option to do so. Of course, if you know that the gold price will remain below the extraction cost, then the option is worthless. But if there is uncertainty about future gold prices, you could be lucky and make a killing.[1]

---

[1] In Chapter 11 we valued King Solomon's gold mine by calculating the value of the gold in the ground and then subtracting the value of the extraction costs. That is strictly correct only if we *know* that the gold will be mined. Otherwise the value of the mine is increased by the value of the option to leave the gold in the ground if its price is less than the extraction cost.

TABLE 20-1
Some options and the exchanges on which they are traded

U.S. common stocks   AMEX, CBOE, NYSE, PSE, PhilSE
U.S. stock market indexes   AMEX, CBOE, IMM,^{f} NASDAQ, NYFE,^{f} NYSE, PSE, PhilSE

U.S. Treasury bonds and notes   CBT^f
Eurodollar deposits   IMM,^{f} LIFFE^f

Australian dollars   SFE^f
Canadian dollars   CBOE,* ME, PhilSE, VSE
Deutsche marks   CBOE,* IMM,^{f} EOE, LSE, ME, PhilSE
Dutch florin   EOE
Ecu (European currency unit)   EOE
French franc   CBOE,* PhilSE
Pound sterling   CBOE,* IMM,^{f} EOE, LIFFE, LSE, ME, PhilSE
Swiss franc   CBOE,* IMM,^{f} ME, PhilSE
Yen   CBOE,* PhilSE

Gold   COMEX,^{f} EOE, MCE,^{f} ME, VSE
Silver   CBT,^{f} COMEX,^{f} EOE, TFE, VSE
Gold and silver index   PhilSE

Cattle   CME^f
Corn   CBT^f
Cotton   NYCE^f
Hogs   CME^f
Soybeans   CBT,^{f} MCE^f
Sugar   CSCE^f
Wheat   KC,^{f} MCE,^{f} MPLS^f

Key:
   AMEX   American Stock Exchange
   CBOE   Chicago Board Options Exchange
   CBT   Chicago Board of Trade
   CME   Chicago Mercantile Exchange
   COMEX   Commodity Exchange, New York
   CSCE   Coffee, Sugar, and Cocoa Exchange, New York
   EOE   European Options Exchange
   IMM   International Monetary Market (at CME)
   KC   Kansas City Board of Trade
   LIFFE   London International Financial Futures Exchange
   LSE   London Stock Exchange
   MCE   MidAmerica Commodity Exchange
   MPLS   Minneapolis Grain Exchange
   ME   Montreal Exchange
   NASDAQ   National Association of Securities Dealers Automated Quotations
   NYCE   New York Cotton Exchange
   NYFE   New York Futures Exchange
   NYSE   New York Stock Exchange
   PSE   Pacific Stock Exchange
   PhilSE   Philadelphia Stock Exchange
   SFE   Sydney Futures Exchange
   TFE   Toronto Futures Exchange
   VSE   Vancouver Stock Exchange

---

^{f}denotes option on a future
*European option
Note: futures are orders to buy an asset at a future date. They are described in Chapter 25.

In Chapters 14 and 15 we discussed a variety of options associated with new financing. For example:

1. Warrants and convertible securities give their holders an option to exchange their securities for common stock.

2. Rights issues give the existing shareholders an option to buy the new issue.
3. A call option on a bond gives the company the right to repurchase the bond before maturity.

In fact, whenever a company borrows it creates an option. The reason is that the borrower is not *compelled* to repay the debt at maturity. If the value of the company's assets is less than the amount of the debt, the company will choose to default on the payment and the bondholders will get to keep the company's assets. Thus, when the firm borrows, the lender effectively acquires the company and the shareholders obtain the option to buy it back by paying off the debt. This is an extremely important insight. It means that anything that we can learn about traded call options applies equally to corporate liabilities.[2]

Our primary goal in this chapter is to tell you how options work and how they are valued. We are asking you to invest to acquire several important ideas. The return to this investment comes primarily in later chapters, where these concepts are applied to a variety of corporate financial problems.

20-1 CALLS, PUTS, AND SHARES

In Chapter 13 we met Louis Bachelier, who in 1900 first suggested that security prices follow a random walk. Bachelier also devised a very convenient shorthand to illustrate the effects of investing in options.[3] Let us use this shorthand to compare three possible investments—buying a call option, buying a put option, and buying the share itself.

A **call option** gives its owner the right to buy stock at a specified "exercise" or "striking" price. In some cases, the option can be exercised only on one particular day and it is then conventionally known as a European call; in other cases, it can be exercised on or before that day and it is then known as an American call. We shall initially concentrate on the conceptually simpler European option, but almost all our remarks apply equally well to its American cousin. Figure 20-1a shows the possible values just before expiration of a call option that is exercisable at $100. If the share price at that time turns out to be less than this figure, nobody will pay $100 to obtain the share via the call option. Our call option will in that case be valueless and we will throw it away. On the other hand, if the share price turns out to be greater than $100, it will pay us to exercise our option to buy the share. In this case the option will be worth the market price of the share minus the $100 that we must pay to acquire it.

Now let us look at a European **put option** with the same exercise price. Whereas the call gives us the right to *buy* a share for $100, the comparable put gives us the right to *sell* it for $100. Therefore the circumstances in which the put will be valuable are just the opposite of those in which the call will be valuable. We can see this from Figure 20-1b. If the share price immediately before expiration turns out to be *greater* than $100, nobody will want to sell the share at that price. Our put option will be worthless. Conversely, if the share price turns out to be *less* than $100, it will pay to buy the share and then take advantage of the option to sell it for $100. In this case, the value of the put option at expiration is the differ-

---

[2] This relationship was first recognized by Fischer Black and Myron Scholes, in "The Pricing of Options and Corporate Liabilities," *Journal of Political Economy*, **81**: 637–654 (May–June 1973).

[3] L. Bachelier, *Théorie de la Speculation*, Gauthier-Villars, Paris, 1900. Reprinted in English in P. H. Cootner (ed.), *The Random Character of Stock Market Prices*, M.I.T. Press, Cambridge, Mass., 1964.

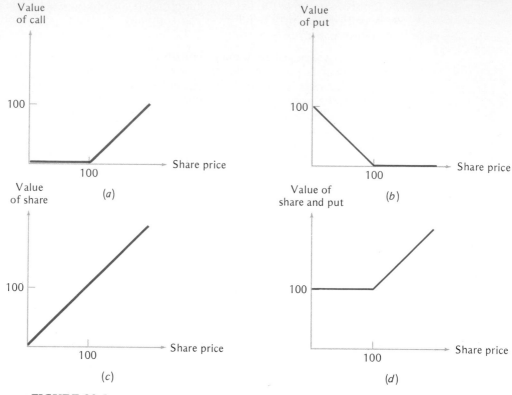

FIGURE 20-1
Payoffs to owners of calls, puts, and shares (shown by the heavy lines) depend on the share price. (*a*) Result of buying call exercisable at $100. (*b*) Result of buying put exercisable at $100. (*c*) Result of buying share. (*d*) Result of buying share *and* put option exercisable at $100; this is equivalent to owning a call and having $100 in the bank.

ence between the $100 proceeds of the sale and the market price of the share. For example, if the share is worth $60, the put is worth $40:

$$\text{Value of put option at expiration} = \text{exercise price} - \text{market price of the share}$$

$$= \$100 - \$60$$

$$= \$40$$

Our third investment consists of the share itself. Figure 20-1*c* betrays few secrets when it shows that the value of this investment is always exactly equal to the market value of the share.

| Selling Calls, Puts, and Shares | Let us now look at the position of an investor who *sells* these investments. The individual who sells, or "writes," a call promises to deliver shares if asked to do so by the call buyer. In other words, the buyer's asset is the seller's liability. If at expiration the share price is below the exercise price, the buyer will not exercise the call and the seller's liability will be zero. If it rises above the exercise price, the |

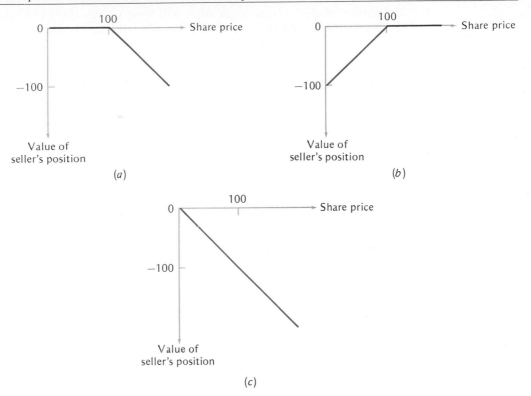

FIGURE 20-2
Payoffs to sellers of calls, puts, and shares (shown by the heavy lines) depend on the share price. (*a*) Result of selling call exercisable at $100. (*b*) Result of selling put exercisable at $100. (*c*) Result of selling share short.

buyer will exercise and the seller will give up the shares. The seller loses the difference between the share price and the exercise price received from the buyer.

Suppose that the exercise price is $100 and the stock price turns out to be $150. The call option will be exercised. The seller is forced to sell stock worth $150 for only $100 and therefore loses $50. Of course the buyer gains $50.

In general, the seller's loss is the buyer's gain, and vice versa. Figure 20-2*a* shows the payoffs to the seller. Note that Figure 20-2*a* is just Figure 20-1*a* drawn upside down.

In just the same way we can depict the position of an investor who sells, or "writes," a put by standing Figure 20-1*b* on its head. The seller of the put has agreed to pay $100 for the share if the put buyer should request it. Clearly the seller will be safe as long as the share price remains above $100 but will lose money if the share price falls below this figure. The worst thing that can happen is for the stock to be worthless. The seller would then be obliged to pay $100 for a stock worth $0. The "value" of the option position would be − $100.

Finally, Figure 20-2*c* shows the position of someone who sells the stock short. Short sellers sell stock which they do not yet own. There is a saying on Wall Street:

> *He who sells what isn't his'n*
> *Buys it back or goes to prison.*

Eventually, therefore, the short seller will have to buy the stock back. The short seller will make a profit if it has fallen in price and a loss if it has risen.[4] You can see that Figure 20-2c is simply an upside-down Figure 20-1c.

20-2 HOLDING CALLS, PUTS, AND SHARES IN COMBINATION

We now return to the option buyer and see what happens when we add two investments together. Suppose, for example, that our portfolio contains *both* the share and an option to sell (put) it for $100. We can read off the value of each of these holdings from panels *b* and *c* in Figure 20-1. Notice that if the share price rises above $100, the put option will be worthless and the value of our portfolio will be equal to that of the share. Conversely, if the share price falls below $100, the decline in the value of the share will be exactly offset by the rise in that of the put. In Figure 20-1d we have plotted the total value of these two holdings.

This diagram tells us something about the relationship between a call option and a put option. We can see why if we compare it with Figure 20-1a. Regardless of the share price, the final value of our combined investment in the share and the put is exactly $100 greater than that of a simple investment in the call. In other words, if you (1) buy the call and (2) put aside enough money to pay the $100 exercise price on the expiration date, you have the same investment as someone who buys the share and also an option to sell it for $100. At the expiration date both strategies give the investor the choice between $100 cash or owning the share. Since the two packages give *identical* payoffs, they should at all times sell for the same price. This gives us a fundamental relationship for European options

Value of call + present value of exercise price = value of put + share price

To repeat, this relationship holds because the payoff of

[Buy call, invest present value of exercise price in safe asset[5]]

is identical to the payoff of

[Buy put, buy share]

Here is a slightly different example. Suppose that you want to invest in a particular stock but you have no cash on hand. However, you know you will receive $100 3 months hence. Therefore you borrow the present value of $100 from your bank and invest that amount in the stock. We assume that is enough to buy one share. At the end of 3 months your payoff is the share price less the $100 owed the bank. Now compare this with an alternative strategy to *buy* a 3-month call option with an exercise price of $100 and to *sell* a 3-month put option with an exercise price of $100. The final value of such a package would be equal to the sum of Figure 20-1a and b. Figure 20-3 shows that this sum is always equal to the market price of the share less $100. It is not difficult to see why. If the share price rises, we would exercise our call and pay $100 to obtain the share; if it goes down, the other person would exercise it and sell us a share for $100. In either case, we would pay $100 and acquire the share. Since our two investment

---

[4] Selling short is not as simple as we have described it. For example, a short seller usually has to put up margin, that is, deposit cash or securities with the broker. This assures the broker that the short seller will be able to repurchase the stock when the time comes to do so.

[5] This present value is calculated at the *risk-free rate of interest*. It is the amount you would have to invest today in Treasury bills to realize the exercise price on the option's expiration date.

FIGURE 20-3
Result of buying a call *and* selling a put, each exercisable at $100. Whatever happens to the share price, you end up paying $100 and acquiring the share at the expiration date of the option. You could achieve the same outcome by buying the share and borrowing the present value of $100, to be repaid on the expiration date.

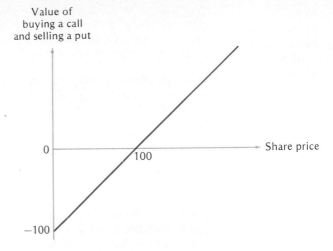

strategies have exactly the same consequences, they should have exactly the same value. In other words, we have the following rearrangement of our earlier equation:

Value of call − value of put = share price − present value of exercise price

which holds because

[Buy call, sell put]

is identical to

[Buy share, borrow present value of exercise price[6]]

Of course there are many ways to express the basic relationship between share price, call and put values, and the present value of the exercise price. Each expression implies two investment strategies that give identical results.

One more example. Solve the basic relationship for the value of a put:

Value of put = value of call − value of share + present value of exercise price

From this expression you can deduce that

[Buy put]

is identical to

[Buy call, sell share, invest present value of exercise price]

In other words, if puts were not available you could create them by buying shares, selling calls, and borrowing.

Maneuvers such as these are called *option conversions*. Calls can be converted into puts, or vice versa, by taking the appropriate position in the share and borrowing or lending. As a result, we do not need calls, puts, shares, *and* borrowing or lending in this world (and we hope not in the next). Given any three of these investment opportunities we can always construct the fourth.

---

[6] Again, present value is computed at the risk-free rate of interest. In other words, the comparison assumes that you are certain to pay off the loan.

***The
Difference
between Safe
and Risky
Bonds**

In Chapter 18 we discussed the plight of Circular File Company, which borrowed $50 per share. Unfortunately the firm fell on hard times and the market value of its assets fell to $30. Circular's bond and stock prices fell to $25 and $5, respectively. Circular's *market* value balance sheet is now:

Circular File Company (market values)			
Asset value	$30	$25	Bonds
		5	Stock
	$30	$30	Firm value

If Circular's debt were due and payable now, the firm could not repay the $50 it originally borrowed. It would default, bondholders receiving assets worth $30 and shareholders receiving nothing. The reason Circular stock is worth $5 is that the debt is *not* due now but rather is due a year from now. A stroke of good fortune could increase firm value enough to pay off the bondholders in full, with something left over for the stockholders.

Let us go back to a statement that we made at the start of the chapter. Whenever a firm borrows, the lender effectively acquires the company and the shareholders obtain the option to buy it back by paying off the debt. The stockholders have in effect purchased a call option on the assets of the firm. The bondholders have sold them this call option. Thus the balance sheet of Circular File can be expressed as follows:

Circular File Company (market values)			
Asset value	$30	$25	Bond value = asset value − value of call
		5	Stock value = value of call
	$30	$30	Firm value = asset value

If this still sounds like a strange idea to you, try drawing one of M. Bachelier's position diagrams for Circular File. It should look like Figure 20-4. If the future value of the assets is less than $50, Circular will default and the stock will be

FIGURE 20-4
The value of Circular's common stock is the same as the value of a call option on the firm's assets with an exercise price of $50.

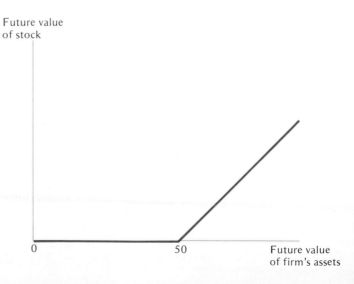

worthless. If the value of the assets exceeds $50, the stockholders will receive asset value *less* the $50 paid over to the bondholders. The payoffs in Figure 20-4 are identical to a call option on the firm's assets, with an exercise price of $50.

Now look again at the basic relationship between calls and puts:

Value of call + present value of exercise price = value of put + value of share

To apply this to Circular File, we have to interpret "value of share" as "asset value," because the common stock is a call option on the firm's assets. Also, "present value of exercise price" is the present value of receiving the promised payment of $50 to bondholders *for sure* next year. Thus

Value of call + present value of promised payment to bondholders
= value of put + asset value

Now we can solve for the value of Circular bonds. This is equal to the firm's asset value less the value of the shareholders' call option on these assets:

Bond value = asset value − value of call
= present value of promised payment to bondholders − value of put

Circular's bondholders have in effect (1) bought a safe bond, and (2) given the shareholders the option to sell them the firm's assets for the amount of the debt. You can think of the bondholders as receiving the $50 promised payment but they have given the shareholders the option to take the $50 back in exchange for the assets of the company. If firm value turns out to be less than the $50 that is promised to bondholders, the shareholders will exercise their put option.

Circular's risky bond is equal to a safe bond less the value of the shareholders' option to default. To value this risky bond we need to value a safe bond and then subtract the value of the default option. The default option is equal to a put option on the firm's assets.

In the case of Circular File the option to default is extremely valuable because default is likely to occur. At the other extreme, the value of AT&T's option to default is trivial compared to the value of AT&T's assets. Default on AT&T bonds is possible but extremely unlikely. Option traders would say that for Circular File the put option is "deep in the money" because today's asset value ($30) is well below the exercise price ($50). For AT&T the put option is well "out of the money" because the value of AT&T's assets substantially exceeds the value of AT&T debt.

We know that Circular's stock is equivalent to a call option on the firm's assets. It is also equal to (1) owning the firm's assets, (2) borrowing the present value of $50 with the obligation to repay regardless of what happens, but also (3) buying a put on the firm's assets with an exercise price of $50.

We can sum up by presenting Circular's balance sheet in terms of asset value, put value, and the present value of a sure $50 payment:

Circular File Company (market values)			
Asset value	$30	$25	Bond value = present value of promised payment − value of put
		5	Stock value = asset value − present value of promised payment + value of put
	$30	$30	Firm value = asset value

Again you can check this with a position diagram. The colored line in Figure 20-5 shows the payoffs to Circular's bondholders. If the firm's assets are worth

FIGURE 20-5
You can also think of Circular's bond (the colored line) as equivalent to a risk-free bond (the upper black line) *less* a put option on the firm's assets with an exercise price of $50 (the lower black line).

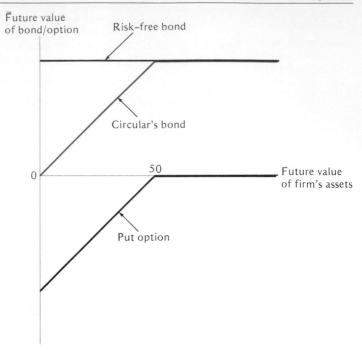

more than $50, the bondholders are paid off in full; if the assets are worth less than $50, the firm defaults and the bondholders receive the value of the assets. You could get an identical payoff pattern by buying a safe bond (the upper black line) and selling a put option on the firm's assets (the lower black line).

*Spotting the Option

Options rarely come with a large label attached. Often the trickiest part of the problem is to identify the option. For example, we suspect that until it was pointed out, you did not realize that every risky bond contains a hidden option.

When you are not sure whether you are dealing with a put or a call or a complicated blend of the two, it is a good precaution to draw a position diagram. Here is an example.

The Flatiron and Mangle Corporation has offered its president Ms. Higden the following incentive scheme. If at the end of the year the price of the stock has risen by a minimum of 20 percent from its present level of $100, Ms. Higden will receive $100,000. Otherwise she will receive nothing.

You can think of Ms. Higden as owning 100,000 tickets each of which pays $1 if the stock price exceeds $120. Figure 20-6 shows the payoffs from just one of these tickets. The payoffs are not the same as those of the simple put and call options that we drew in Figure 20-1 but it is possible to find a combination of options that almost exactly replicates Figure 20-6. Before going on to read the answer, see if you can spot it yourself (if you are someone who enjoys puzzles of the 'make-a-triangle-from-just-two-matchsticks' type, this one should be a walkover).

The answer is in Figure 20-7. The solid black line represents the purchase of a call option with an exercise price of 119.5 and the dotted line the sale of another

FIGURE 20-6
The payoff from one of Ms. Higden's "tickets" depends on Flatiron's stock price.

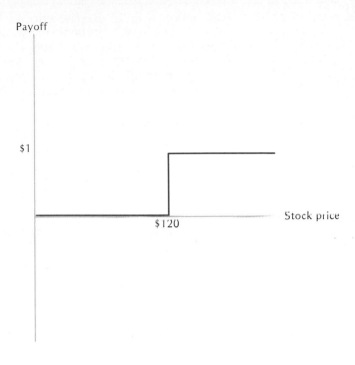

FIGURE 20-7
The solid black line shows the payoff from buying a call with an exercise price of 119.5. The dotted black line shows the *sale* of a call with an exercise price of 120.5. The combined purchase and sale (shown by the colored line) closely resembles one of Ms. Higden's "tickets."

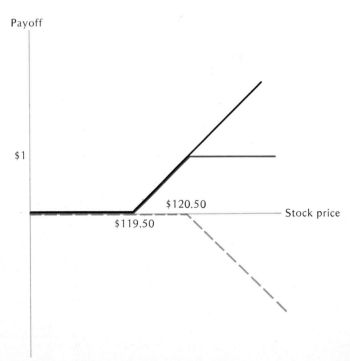

call option with an exercise price of 120.5. The colored line shows the payoffs from a combination of the purchase and the sale—almost identical to the payoffs from each of Ms. Higden's tickets.

Thus if we wish to know how much the incentive scheme is costing the company we need to calculate the difference between the value of 100,000 call options with an exercise price of 119.5 and the value of 100,000 calls with an exercise price of 120.5.[7]

We could have made the incentive scheme depend in a much more complicated way on the stock price. For example, it could pay $100,000 if the stock price is between $120 and $140 and nothing in any other circumstances. (Don't ask why anyone would want to offer such an arrangement—perhaps there's some tax angle.) You could still have represented this scheme as a combination of options. In fact, we can state a general theorem:

> *Any set of contingent payoffs—that is, payoffs which depend on the value of some other asset—can be valued as a mixture of simple options on that asset.*

For instance, if you needed to value a capital project that would pay off $2 million if the price of copper was less than $1500 but only $1 million if the price was greater than $1500, you could use option theory to do so.

20-3   WHAT DETERMINES OPTION VALUES?

So far we have said nothing about how the market value of options is determined. We do know what an option is worth when it matures, however. Consider, for example, our earlier case of an option to buy stock at $100. If the stock price is below $100 at the expiration date, the call will be worthless; if the stock price is above $100, the call will be worth $100 less than the value of the stock. In terms of Bachelier's position diagram, the relationship is depicted by the heavy line in Figure 20-8.

[7] The fact that Figure 20-7 is not quite identical to Figure 20-6 means that the value is not exact, but we can make the approximation as close as we choose. For example, for greater accuracy we could calculate the difference between the value of 1 million calls with an exercise price of 119.95 and 1 million calls with an exercise price of 120.05.

FIGURE 20-8
Value of a call before its expiration date (dashed line). The value depends on the stock price. It is always worth more than its value if exercised now (heavy line). It is never worth more than the stock price itself.

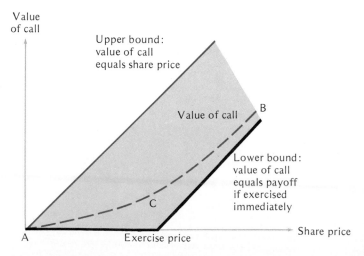

Even before maturity the price of the option can never remain *below* the heavy line in Figure 20-8. For example, if our option were priced at $50 and the stock at $200, it would pay any investor to buy the option, exercise it for an additional $100, and then sell the stock. That would give a money machine with a profit of $50. The demand for options from investors using the money machine would quickly force the option price up at least to the heavy line in the figure. For options that still have some time to run, the heavy line is therefore a *lower* limit on the market price of the option.

The diagonal line in Figure 20-8 is the *upper* limit to the option price. Why? Because the stock gives a higher ultimate payoff, whatever happens. If at the option's expiration the stock price ends up above the exercise price, the option is worth the stock price *less* the exercise price. If the stock price ends up below the exercise price, the option is worthless, but the stock's owner still has a valuable security. Let P be the stock price at the option's expiration date, and assume the option's exercise price is $100. Then the extra dollar returns realized by stockholders are:

	Stock Payoff	Option Payoff	Extra Payoff from Holding Stock Instead of Option
Option exercised (P greater than $100)	P	$P - 100$	$100
Option expires unexercised (P less than or equal to $100)	P	0	P

If the stock and the option have the same price, everyone will rush to sell the option and buy the stock. Therefore, the option price must be somewhere in the shaded region of Figure 20-8. In fact, it will lie on a curved, upward-sloping line like the dashed curve shown in the figure. This line begins its travels where the upper and lower bounds meet (at zero). Then it rises, gradually becoming parallel to the upward-sloping part of the lower bound. This line tells us an important fact about option values: *the value of an option increases as stock price increases*, if the exercise price is held constant.

That should be no surprise. Owners of call options clearly hope for the stock price to rise, and are happy when it does. But let us look more carefully at the shape and location of the dashed line. Three points, *A*, *B*, and *C*, are marked on the dashed line. As we explain each point you will see why the option price has to behave as the dashed line predicts.

Point *A*: *When the stock is worthless the option is worthless*. A stock price of zero means that there is no possibility the stock will ever have any future value.[8] If so, the option is sure to expire unexercised and worthless, and it is worthless today.

Point *B*: *When the stock price becomes large, the option price approaches the stock price less the present value of the exercise price*. Notice that the dashed line representing the option price in Figure 20-8 eventually becomes parallel to the ascending heavy line representing the lower bound on the option price. The reason is as follows: the higher the stock price, the higher the probability that the option will eventually be exercised. If the stock price is high enough, exercise becomes a virtual certainty;

---

[8] If a stock *can* be worth something in the future, then investors will pay *something* for it today, although possibly a very small amount.

the probability that the stock price will fall below the exercise price before the option expires becomes trivially small.

If you own an option which you *know* will be exchanged for a share of stock, you effectively own the stock now. The only difference is that you don't have to pay for the stock (by handing over the exercise price) until later, when formal exercise occurs. In these circumstances, buying the call is equivalent to buying the stock but financing part of the purchase by borrowing. The amount implicitly borrowed is the present value of the exercise price. The value of the call is therefore equal to the stock price less the present value of the exercise price.

This brings us to another important point about options. Investors who acquire stock by way of a call option are buying on installment credit. They pay the purchase price of the option today, but they do not pay the exercise price until they actually take up the option. This delayed payment is particularly valuable if interest rates are high and the option has a long maturity. With an interest rate r_f and the time to maturity t, then we would expect the value of the option to depend on the *product*[9] of r_f and t: *the value of an option increases with both the rate of interest and the time to maturity*.

Point *C*: *the option price always exceeds its minimum value* (except when stock price is zero). We have seen that the dashed and heavy lines in Figure 20-8 coincide when stock price is zero (point *A*), but elsewhere the lines diverge; that is, the option price must exceed the minimum value given by the heavy line. The reason for this can be understood by examining point *C*.

At point *C*, the stock price exactly equals the exercise price. The option is therefore worthless if exercised today. However, suppose that the option will not expire until 3 months hence. Of course we do not know what the stock price will be at the expiration date. There is roughly a 50 percent chance that it will be higher than the exercise price, and a 50 percent chance that it will be lower. The possible payoffs to the option are therefore:

Outcome	Payoff
Stock price rises (50 percent probability)	Stock price less exercise price (option is exercised)
Stock price falls (50 percent probability)	Zero (option expires worthless)

If there is a positive probability of a positive payoff, and if the worst payoff is zero, then the option must be valuable. That means the option price at point *C* exceeds its lower bound, which at point *C* is zero. In general, the option prices will exceed their lower-bound values as long as there is time left before expiration.

One of the most important determinants of the *height* of the dashed curve (i.e., of the difference between actual and lower-bound value) is the likelihood of substantial movements in the stock price. An option on a stock whose price is unlikely to change by more than 1 or 2 percent is not worth much; an option on a stock whose price may halve or double is very valuable.

Panels *a* and *b* in Figure 20-9 illustrate this point. The panels compare the payoffs at expiration of two options with the same exercise price and the same stock price. The panels assume that stock price equals exercise price (like point *C* in Figure 20-8), although this is not a necessary assumption. The only difference

---

[9] Using continuous compounding, the present value of the exercise price is (exercise price $\times e^{-r_f t}$). The discount factor $e^{-r_f t}$ depends on the product of r_f and t.

FIGURE 20-9

Call options are written against the shares of (*a*) firm X and (*b*) firm Y. In each case, the current share price equals the exercise price, so that each option has a 50 percent chance of ending up worthless (if the share price falls) and a 50 percent chance of ending up "in the money" (if the share price rises). However, the chance of a *large* payoff is *greater* for the option on firm Y's share, because Y's stock price is more volatile and therefore has more "upside potential."

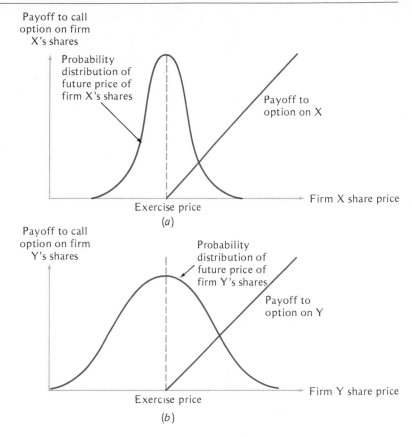

is that the price of stock Y at its option's expiration date (Figure 20-9*b*) is much harder to predict than the price of stock X at its option's expiration date. You can see this from the probability distributions superimposed on the figures.

In both cases there is roughly a 50 percent chance that the stock price will decline and make the options worthless, but if the prices of stocks X and Y rise, the odds are that Y will rise more than X. Thus there is a larger chance of a big payoff from the option on Y. Since the chance of a zero payoff is the same, the option on Y is worth more than the option on X. Figure 20-10 illustrates this: the higher curved line belongs to the option on Y.

The probability of large stock price changes during the remaining life of an option depends on two things: (1) the variance (i.e., volatility) of the stock price *per period* and (2) the number of periods until the option expires. If there are *t* remaining periods, and the variance per period is σ^2, the value of the option should depend on cumulative variability $\sigma^2 t$.[10] Other things equal, you would like to hold an option on a volatile stock (high σ^2). Given volatility, you would like to hold

---

[10] Here is an intuitive explanation. If the stock price follows a random walk (see Section 13-2), successive price changes are statistically independent. The cumulative price change before expiration is the sum of *t* random variables. The variance of a sum of independent random variables is the sum of the variances of those variables. Thus, if σ^2 is the variance of the daily price change, and there are *t* days until expiration, the variance of the cumulative price change is $\sigma^2 t$.

FIGURE 20-10

Values of calls on shares of firm X and shares of firm Y. The call on Y's shares is worth more because Y's shares are more volatile (see Figure 20-9). The higher curved line describes the value of a call on Y's shares; the lower curved line describes the value of a call on X's shares.

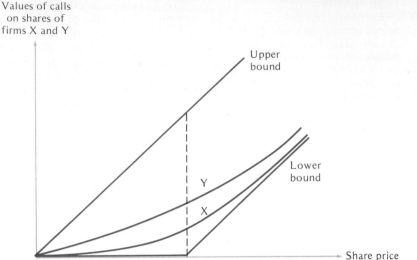

Values of calls on shares of firms X and Y

Upper bound

Lower bound

Y

X

Exercise price

Share price

an option with a long life ahead of it (large t). Thus the value of an option increases *with both the variability of the share and the time to maturity.*

It's a rare person who can keep all these properties straight at first reading. Therefore, we have summed them up in Table 20-2.

20-4 AN OPTION-VALUATION MODEL

We would now like to replace the qualitative statements of Table 20-2 with an exact option-valuation model—a formula we can plug numbers into and get a definite answer. The search for that formula went on for years before Fischer Black and Myron Scholes finally found it. Before we show you what they found, we should say a few words to explain why the search was so difficult.

TABLE 20-2
What the price of a call option depends on

1. If the following variables *increase,*	the changes in the call option price are:
Stock price (P)	positive
Exercise price (EX)	negative
Interest rate (r_f)	positive
Time to expiration (t)	positive
Volatility of stock price (σ)	positive

2. Other properties:
   a. <u>Upper bound.</u> The option price is always less than the stock price.
   b. <u>Lower bound.</u> The option price never falls below the payoff to immediate exercise ($P -$ EX or zero, whichever is larger).
   c. If the stock is worthless, the option is worthless.
   d. As the stock price becomes very large, the option price approaches the stock price less the present value of the exercise price.

Why Discounted Cash Flow Won't Work for Options

Our standard operating procedure of (1) forecasting expected cash flow and (2) discounting at the opportunity cost of capital is not helpful for options. The first step is messy but feasible. Finding *the* opportunity cost of capital is impossible, because the risk of an option changes every time the stock price moves,[11] and we know it *will* move along a random walk through the option's lifetime.

When you buy a call you are *taking a position* in the stock but putting up less of your own money than if you had bought the stock directly. Thus an option is always riskier than the underlying stock. It has a higher beta and a higher standard deviation of return.

How much riskier the option is depends on the stock price relative to the exercise price. An option that is in the money (stock price greater than exercise price) is safer than one that is out of the money (stock price less than exercise price). Thus a stock price increase raises the option's price *and* reduces its risk. When the stock price falls, the option's price falls *and* its risk increases. That is why the expected rate of return investors demand from an option changes day by day, or hour by hour, every time the stock price moves.

We repeat the general rule: the higher the stock price relative to the exercise price, the safer the option, although the option is always riskier than the stock. The option's risk changes every time the stock price changes.

Constructing Option Equivalents from Common Stocks and Borrowing

If you've digested what we've said so far, you can appreciate why options are hard to value by standard discounted cash flow formulas, and why a rigorous option-valuation technique eluded economists for many years. The breakthrough came when Black and Scholes exclaimed "Eureka! We have found it![12] The trick is to set up an *option equivalent* by combining common stock investment and borrowing. The net cost of buying the option equivalent must equal the value of the option."

We will show you how this works with a simple numerical example. We will work out the value of a 1-year option to buy the stock of Wombat Corporation at an exercise price of $160. To keep matters simple, we will assume that Wombat stock can do only two things over the coming year—either the price will fall to $110 from its current level of $140 or it will rise to $210. We will also assume that the 1-year rate of interest is 10 percent.

If Wombat's stock price falls to $110, the call option will be worthless, but if the price rises to $210, the option will be worth $210 - 160 = 50. The possible payoffs to the option are therefore:

	Stock Price = $110	Stock Price = $210
1 call option	$0	$50

Now compare these payoffs with those that you would get if you bought one share of stock and borrowed $100 from the bank:

	Stock Price = $110	Stock Price = $210
1 share of stock	$110	$210
Repayment of loan + interest	−110	−110
Total payoff	$ 0	$100

[11] It also changes over time even with the stock price constant.

[12] We do not know whether Black and Scholes, like Archimedes, were sitting in bathtubs at the time.

Notice that the payoffs from the levered investment in the stock are identical to the payoffs from *two* call options. Therefore, both investments must have the same value:

$$\text{Value of 2 calls} = \text{value of share} - \$100 \text{ bank loan}$$

$$= 140 - 100 = \$40$$

$$\text{Value of 1 call} = \$20$$

Presto! You've valued a call option.

To value the Wombat option we borrowed money and bought stock in such a way that we exactly replicated the payoff from a call option. The number of shares that are needed to replicate one call is often called the **hedge ratio** or **option delta**. In our Wombat example two calls are replicated by a levered position in one share. The option delta is, therefore, 1/2.

You have learned not only to value a simple option. You have also learned that you can replicate an investment in the option by a levered investment in the underlying asset. Thus, if you can't buy or sell an option on an asset, you can create a homemade option by a replicating strategy.

*The Risk-Neutral Method

Notice why the Wombat call option has to sell for $20. If the option price is higher than $20, you could make a certain profit by buying one share of stock, selling two call options, and borrowing $100. Similarly, if the option price is less than $20, you could make an equally certain profit by selling the stock, buying two calls, and lending the balance. In either case there would be a money machine.

If there's a money machine, everyone scurries to take advantage of it. So when we say that the option price must be $20 or otherwise there would be a money machine, we did not have to know anything about investor attitudes to risk. The price would have to be the same whether investors detested risk or could not care a jot.

This suggests an alternative way to calculate the value of the Wombat option. We can *pretend* that all investors are *indifferent* about risk, work out the expected future value of the option in such a world, and discount it back at the risk-free interest rate to give the current value. Let us check that this method gives the same answer.

If investors are indifferent to risk, the expected return on the stock must be equal to the rate of interest:

$$\text{Expected return on Wombat stock} = 10 \text{ percent per annum}$$

We know that Wombat stock can either rise by 50 percent to $210 or fall by 21.5 percent to $110. We can, therefore, calculate the probability of a price rise in our hypothetical risk-neutral world:

$$\text{Expected return} = (\text{probability of rise}) \times 50$$

$$+ (1 - \text{probability of rise}) \times (-21.5)$$

$$= 10 \text{ percent}$$

Therefore,

$$\text{Probability of rise} = .44, \text{ or } 44 \text{ percent}$$

We know that if the stock price rises, the Wombat call option will be worth $50; if it falls, the call will be worth nothing. Therefore, the expected value of the call option is:

$$(\text{Probability of rise} \times 50) + ((1 - \text{probability of rise}) \times 0)$$

$$= (.44 \times 50) + (.56 \times 0)$$

$$= \$22$$

And the current value of the call is

$$\frac{\text{Expected future value}}{1 + \text{interest rate}} = \frac{22}{1.10} = \$20$$

Exactly the same answer that we got earlier!

We now have two ways to calculate the value of an option:

1. Find the combination of stock and loan that replicates an investment in the option. Since the two strategies give identical payoffs in the future, they must sell for the same price today.
2. Pretend that investors do not care about risk, so that the expected return on the stock is equal to the interest rate. Calculate the expected future value of the option in this risk-neutral world and discount it at the interest rate.

Valuing Options That Last for More than One Period

Our example of the Wombat call option is fanciful in one important respect: there will be more than two possible prices for Wombat's stock at the end of the year. We could make the problem slightly more realistic by assuming that there were two possible changes in the stock price in each 6-month period. That would give a wider range of end-year prices. It would still be possible to construct a series of levered investments in the stock that would give exactly the same prospects as the option.[13]

There is no reason that we should stop at 6-month periods. We could go on to take shorter and shorter intervals, with each interval showing two possible changes in Wombat's stock price. Eventually we would reach a situation in which Wombat's stock price was changing continuously and generating a continuum of possible year-end prices. We could still replicate the call option by a levered investment in the stock, but we would need to adjust the degree of leverage continuously as the year went by.

Calculating the value of this levered investment may sound like a hopelessly tedious business, but Black and Scholes derived a formula that does the trick. This unpleasant-looking formula is:

$$\text{Present value of call option} = PN(d_1) - EXe^{-r_f t}N(d_2)$$

where

$$d_1 = \frac{\log(P/EX) + r_f t + \sigma^2 t/2}{\sigma\sqrt{t}}$$

$$d_2 = \frac{\log(P/EX) + r_f t - \sigma^2 t/2}{\sigma\sqrt{t}}$$

$$N(d) = \text{cumulative normal probability density function}[14]$$

[13] We will work through a two-period example in the next chapter.

[14] That is, $N(d)$ is the probability that a normally distributed random variable $\tilde{x}$ will be less than or equal to d. $N(d_1)$ in the Black-Scholes formula is the option delta. Thus the formula tells us that the value of a call is equal to an investment of $N(d_1)$ in the common stock less borrowing of $EXe^{-r_f t}N(d_2)$.

$$EX = \text{exercise price of option}$$
$$t = \text{time to exercise date}$$
$$P = \text{price of stock now}$$
$$\sigma^2 = \text{variance per period of (continuously compounded)}$$
$$\text{rate of return on the stock}$$
$$r_f = \text{(continuously compounded) risk-free rate of interest}$$

For our purposes the precise formula is less important than the terms that appear in it. Notice that the willingness of individuals to bear risk does not affect value, nor does the expected return on the stock.[15] The value of the option increases with the level of the stock price relative to the exercise price (P/EX), the time to expiration times the interest rate ($r_f t$), and the time to expiration times the stock's variability ($\sigma^2 t$).

Using the Black-Scholes Formula

Does the Black-Scholes option-valuation formula seem a little removed from the real world? It should not. Every day dealers on the options exchanges use this formula to make huge trades. These dealers are not for the most part trained in the formula's mathematical derivation; they just use a specially programmed calculator or a set of tables to find the value of the option.

Appendix Tables 6 and 7 allow you to use the Black-Scholes formula to value a variety of simple options. In order to use the tables, follow these four steps:

Step 1. Multiply the standard deviation of the proportionate changes in the asset's value by the square root of time to the option's expiration. For example, suppose that you wish to value a 4-year option on the stock of Ragwort Corporation and that the standard deviation of the continuously compounded stock price changes is 40 percent per year.

$$\text{Standard deviation} \times \sqrt{\text{time}} = .40 \times \sqrt{4} = .80$$

Step 2. Calculate the ratio of the asset value to the present value of the option's exercise price. For example, suppose that Ragwort's stock price is currently $140, that the option's exercise price is $160, and that the interest rate is 12.47 percent. Then

$$\frac{\text{Asset value}}{\text{PV(exercise price)}} = 140 \div \frac{160}{(1.1247)^4} = 1.4$$

Step 3. Now turn to Table 6 and look up the entry corresponding to the numbers that you calculated in steps 1 and 2. You can see that a 4-year call option on Ragwort stock would be worth 43.1 percent of the stock price, or $60.34.

If you want to know the value of a put option with the same exercise price, then you can use the simple relationship that we derived in Section 20-2:

$$\text{Value of put} = \text{value of call} + \text{PV(exercise price)} - \text{stock price}$$

$$= 60.34 + \frac{160}{(1.1247)^4} - 140 = \$20.34$$

---

[15] Although the expected return affects the price of the stock, it does not affect the *relative* value of the stock and option.

Step 4. Table 7 tells you the option delta. For example, if you look up the equivalent entry in Table 7, you see that the Ragwort call option has a delta of .79. This means that instead of buying a call for $60.34, you could achieve the same result by buying .79 shares of stock (at a cost of .79 × 140 = $110.60) and borrowing the balance (110.60 − 60.34 = $50.26).[16]

To find the option delta for the put, you simply subtract 1 from the entry in Table 7. In our example

$$\text{Put option delta} = \text{call option delta} - 1$$

$$= .79 - 1 = -.21$$

In other words, instead of *paying out* $20.34 to buy a Ragwort put option, you could *sell* .21 shares of stock (for a cash inflow of .21 × 140 = $29.40) and buy a Treasury bill with the available cash (20.34 + 29.40 = $49.74).

20-5 SUMMARY

If you have managed to reach this point, you are probably in need of a rest and a stiff gin and tonic. So we will summarize what we have learned so far and take up the subject of options again in the next chapter when you are rested (or drunk).

There are two basic types of option. An American call is an option to buy an asset at a specified exercise price on or before a specified exercise date. Similarly, an American put is an option to sell the asset at a specified price on or before a specified date. European calls and puts are exactly the same except that they cannot be exercised *before* the specified exercise date. Calls and puts are the basic building blocks that can be combined to give any pattern of payoffs.

What determines the value of a call option? Common sense tells us that it ought to depend on three things:

1. In order to exercise an option you have to pay the exercise price. Other things being equal, the less you are obliged to pay, the better. Therefore, the value of an option increases with the ratio of the asset price to the exercise price.
2. You do not have to pay the exercise price until you decide to exercise the option. Therefore, an option gives you a free loan. The higher the rate of interest and the longer the time to maturity, the more this free loan is worth. Therefore the value of an option increases with the interest rate multiplied by the time to maturity.
3. If the price of the asset falls short of the exercise price, you won't exercise the option. You will, therefore, lose 100 percent of your investment in the option no matter how far the asset depreciates below the exercise price. On the other hand, the more the price rises *above* the exercise price, the more profit you will make. Therefore the option holder does not lose from increased variability if things go wrong, but gains if they go right. The value of an option increases with the variance per period of the stock return multiplied by the number of periods to maturity.

We showed you how to value an option on a stock when there are only two possible changes in the stock price in each subperiod. Black and Scholes have also derived a formula that gives the value of an option when there is a continuum of possible future stock prices. Tables in the Appendix should allow you to apply this formula to a number of simple option problems.

---

[16] Of course, as time passes and the share price changes, the option delta changes. Therefore, you will need to keep adjusting your levered holding in Ragwort stock.

Unfortunately, not all option problems are simple. Therefore, in the next chapter we will look at some of the complications and work through several examples of moderate complexity.

FURTHER READING

The classic articles on option valuation are:

F. Black and M. Scholes: "The Pricing of Options and Corporate Liabilities," *Journal of Political Economy*, **81**: 637–654 (May–June 1973).

R. C. Merton: "Theory of Rational Option Pricing," *Bell Journal of Economics and Management Science*, **4**: 141–183 (Spring 1973).

There are also a number of good texts on option valuation. They include:

J. Cox and M. Rubinstein, *Options Markets*, Prentice-Hall, Inc., Englewood Cliffs, N.J., 1985.

R. Jarrow and A. Rudd, *Option Pricing*, Dow Jones–Irwin, Inc., Homewood, Ill., 1983.

QUIZ

1. Complete the following passage: A _____ option gives its owner the opportunity to buy a stock at a specific price which is generally called the _____ price. A _____ option gives its owner the opportunity to sell stock at a specified _____ price.

   Options that can be exercised only at maturity are called _____ options.

   The common stock of firms that borrow is a _____ option. Stockholders effectively sell the firm's _____ to _____ , but retain the option to buy the _____ back. The exercise price is the _____ .

2. Fill in the blanks:
   (a) A firm that issues warrants is selling a _____ option.
   (b) A firm that enters a standby agreement whereby the underwriter to a rights issue guarantees to take up any unwanted stock acquires a _____ option.
   (c) Rights are _____ options on the issuing firm's stock.
   (d) An oil company acquires mining rights to a silver deposit. It is not obligated to mine the silver, however. The company has effectively acquired a _____ option, where the exercise price is the cost of opening the mine.
   (e) Some preferred shareholders have the right to redeem their shares at par value after a specified date. (If they hand over their shares, the firm sends them a check equal to the shares' par value.) These shareholders have a _____ option.
   (f) An executive who qualifies for a stock option plan acquires a _____ option.
   (g) An investor who buys stock in a levered firm acquires a _____ option on the firm's assets.
   (h) A firm buys a standard machine with a ready secondhand market. The secondhand market gives the firm a _____ option.

3. Note Figure 20-11a and 20-11b. Match each figure with one of the following positions:
   (a) Call buyer
   (b) Call seller
   (c) Put buyer
   (d) Put seller

FIGURE 20-11
See Quiz,
question 3.

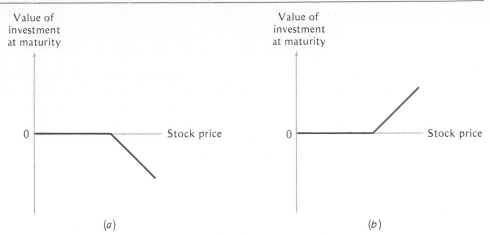

(a) (b)

4. Suppose that you hold a share of stock and a put option on that share. What is the payoff when the option expires if
   (a) The stock price is below the exercise price?
   (b) The stock price is above the exercise price?
5. There is a another strategy involving calls and borrowing and lending which gives the same payoffs as the strategy described in question 4. What is the alternative strategy?
6. What is the lower bound to the price of a call option? What is the upper bound?
7. What is a call option worth if:
   (a) The stock price is zero?
   (b) The stock price is extremely high relative to the exercise price?
8. How does the price of a call option respond to the following changes, other things equal? Does the call price go up or down?
   (a) Stock price increases.
   (b) Exercise price is increased.
   (c) Risk-free interest rate increases.
   (d) Expiration date of the option is extended.
   (e) Volatility of the stock price falls.
   (f) Time passes, so the option's expiration date comes closer.
9. "An option is always riskier than the stock it is written on." True or false? How does the risk of an option change when the stock price changes?
10. Why can't you value options using a standard discounted cash flow formula?
11. Use Appendix Table 6 to value the following options.
   (a) A call option written on a stock selling for $60 per share with a $60 exercise price. The stock's standard deviation is 6 percent per month. The option matures in 3 months. The risk-free interest rate is 1 percent per month.
   (b) A put option written on the same stock at the same time, with the same exercise price and expiration date.
   Now for each of these options use Table 7 to calculate the combination of stock and risk-free asset that would replicate the option.
12. Imagine that the range of future prices for Wombat stock widens to $100 to $220 (see Section 20-4). Recalculate the value of the call option using (a) the replicating-portfolio method (b) the risk-neutral method. Explain intuitively why the option value increases.

QUESTIONS AND PROBLEMS

1. Look up the terms of actual call and put options on stocks, currencies, etc. Plot their payoffs at maturity using diagrams like those in Figures 20-1 and 20-2.

2. Explain why the value of a call depends on each of the following:
   (a) The *product* of volatility per period and time to maturity.
   (b) The *product* of the risk-free interest rate and time to maturity.

3. Look at actual trading prices of call options on stocks to check whether they behave as the theory presented in this chapter predicts. For example:
   (a) Follow several options as they approach maturity. How would you expect their prices to behave? Do they actually behave that way?
   (b) Compare two call options written on the same stock with the same maturity but different exercise prices.
   (c) Compare two call options written on the same stock with the same exercise price but different maturities.

*4. Indicate how the value of Circular File common stock (see Section 20-2) would change if:
   (a) The value of the firm's assets increases.
   (b) The maturity of its debt is extended.
   (c) The assets become safer (less volatile).
   (d) The risk-free rate of interest increases (hold the value of the firm's assets constant).

5. The Rank and File Company is considering a rights issue to raise $50 million. An underwriter offers to "stand by" (i.e., to guarantee the success of the issue by buying any unwanted stock at the issue price). The underwriter's fee is $2 million.
   (a) What kind of option does Rank and File acquire if it accepts the underwriter's offer?
   (b) What determines the value of the option?
   (c) How would you calculate whether the underwriter's offer is a fair deal?

6. Indicate which *one* of the following statements is correct:
   (a) Value of put + present value of exercise price = value of call + share price
   ✓(b) Value of put + share price = value of call + present value of exercise price
   (c) Value of put − share price = present value of exercise price − value of call
   (d) Value of put + value of call = share price − present value of exercise price

   The correct statement equates the value of two investment strategies. Plot the payoffs to each strategy as a function of the stock price. Show that the two strategies give identical payoffs.

7. The price of Backwoods Chemical Company stock on January 20 is $90 per share. Three call options are trading on the stock, one maturing on April 20, one on July 20, and one on October 20. All three options have the same $100 exercise price. The standard deviation of Backwoods stock is 42 percent per year. The risk-free interest rate is 11 percent per year. What are the three call options worth?

8. The common stock of Triangular File Company is selling at $90. A 26-week call option written on Triangular File's stock is selling for $8. The call's exercise price is $100. The risk-free interest rate is 10 percent per year.

(a) Suppose that puts on Triangular stock are not traded, but you want to buy one. How would you do it?

(b) Suppose that puts *are* traded. What should a 26-week put with an exercise price of $100 sell for?

(c) Test the option conversion formula you used to answer (a) and (b) by using it to explain the relative prices of traded puts and calls.

*9. Refer again to the Circular File balance sheet given in Section 20-2. Suppose that the United States government suddenly offers to guarantee the $50 principal payment due bondholders next year and also to guarantee the interest payment due next year. (In other words, if firm value falls short of the promiscd interest and principal payment, the government will make up the difference.) This offer is a complete surprise to everyone. The government asks nothing in return, and so its offer is cheerfully accepted.

(a) Suppose that the promised interest rate on Circular's debt is 10 percent. The rate on 1-year United States government notes is 8 percent. How will the guarantee affect bond value?

(b) The guarantee does *not* affect the value of Circular stock. Why? (*Note:* There could be some effect if the guarantee allows Circular to avoid costs of financial distress or bankruptcy. See Section 18-3.)

(c) How will the value of the firm (debt plus equity) change?

Now suppose that the government offers the same guarantee for *new* debt issued by *Rectangular* File Company. Rectangular's assets are identical to Circular's, but Rectangular has no existing debt. Rectangular accepts the offer and uses the proceeds of a $50 debt issue to repurchase or retire stock.

Will Rectangular stockholders gain from the opportunity to issue the guaranteed debt? By how much, approximately? (Ignore taxes.)

10. How would you use Appendix Table 6 to estimate the volatility of a common stock on which call options are written and actively traded?

11. Use Table 7 to show how the option delta changes as the stock price rises relative to the exercise price. Explain intuitively why this is the case. (What would happen to the option delta if the exercise price of an option was zero? What would happen if the exercise price became indefinitely large?)

12. Use either the replicating-portfolio method or the risk-neutral method to value a put option on Wombat stock (see Section 20-4) with an exercise price of $160. Use the conversion formula that we derived in Section 20-2 to check your answer.

13. Is it more valuable to own an option to buy a portfolio of stocks or a portfolio of options to buy each of the individual stocks? Say briefly why.

14. Discuss briefly the relative risk of the following positions:

(a) Buy stock and a put option on the stock.

(b) Buy stock.

(c) Buy call.

(d) Buy stock and sell call option on the stock.

(e) Buy bond.

(f) Buy stock, buy put, and sell call.

(g) Sell put.

*15. In Section 20-2 we suggested a more complicated payment scheme for Ms. Higden ($100,000 only if the stock price is between $120 and $140).

(a) Draw a position diagram showing the payoffs from such a scheme.

(b) Show that this scheme is a combination of simple options.

(c) Assume that the current stock price is $100, the standard deviation of the stock price is 30 percent a year, and the rate of interest is 10 percent. What is the value of this incentive scheme?

16. A very difficult question: Use our conversion formula (see Section 20-2) and the one-period binomial model to show that the option delta for a put option is equal to the option delta for a call option minus one.

17. Option traders often refer to straddles and butterflies. Here is an example of each:

    Straddle Buy call with exercise price of $100 and simultaneously buy put with exercise price of $100.

    Butterfly Simultaneously buy one call with exercise price of $100, sell two calls with exercise price of $110, and buy one call with exercise price of $120.

    Draw position diagrams for the straddle and butterfly, showing the payoffs from the investor's net position. Each strategy is a bet on variability. Explain briefly the nature of this bet.

21 Applications of Option Pricing Theory

This chapter brings the first reward to your investment in learning about options. We start by describing two common but important *real options* found in capital investment projects.

- The option to *wait* (and learn) before investing
- The option to make *follow-on* investments if the immediate investment project succeeds

Real options such as these allow managers to add value to their firms, by acting to amplify good fortune or to mitigate loss. Managers often speak of these options diffusely; for example, they may refer to "intangibles" rather than to puts or calls. But when they review major investment proposals, these option "intangibles" are often the key to their decisions.

In the first section of this chapter you will learn what real options are and why they can tip capital investment decisions one way or the other.[1] You will also see that real options are more complex than traded puts and calls. Therefore, we will move on to some of the practical problems of applying the option pricing models described in Chapter 20. You will also learn to recognize some of the more complicated options for which the simple pricing models *don't* work. In these cases you can obtain a numerical value by setting up a computer to crunch numbers, although we will not get into that kind of number crunching here.

21-1 REAL OPTIONS AND THE VALUE OF MANAGEMENT

Timing of Capital Investment

Optimal investment timing is easy when there is no uncertainty. You just calculate project NPV at various future investment dates and pick the date that gives the highest current value.[2] Unfortunately, this simple rule breaks down in the face of uncertainty.

Suppose you have a project which could be a big winner or a big loser. The project's upside outweighs its downside, and it has a positive NPV if undertaken today. However, the project is not "now or never." Should you invest right away or wait? It's hard to say: If the project is truly a winner, waiting means loss or deferral of its early cash flows. But if it turns out a loser, waiting could prevent a bad mistake.

In Chapter 6 we sidestepped this problem of optimal investment timing under

---

[1] Some options encountered in corporate *financing* decisions are covered in the next and several subsequent chapters.

[2] See Chapter 6, Section 6-3.

uncertainty. Now we have the tools to confront it head on, because the opportunity to invest in a positive-NPV project is equivalent to an in-the-money call option. Optimal investment timing means exercising that call at the best time.

Example.   We'll suppose the project we've been discussing involves construction of a malted herring factory for $100 million. As most of our readers will know, the demand for malted herring fluctuates widely, depending on the price of competing fertilizers.

Assume first that construction of the plant is a now-or-never opportunity. That's the same as having an about-to-expire call option on the factory with an exercise price equal to the $100 million investment required to build it. If the present value of the plant's forecasted cash flows exceeds $100 million, the call option's payoff is the project NPV. But if project NPV is negative, the call option's payoff is zero, *because in that case the firm will not make the investment.* We've plotted these payoffs in Figure 21-1.

Now suppose that you could choose to delay construction of the plant for up to 2 years. Even though the project may have a zero or negative NPV *if undertaken today,* your call option has value because 2 years gives room for hope that the volatile malted herring market will take off. We have shown a possible range of values as the curved line in Figure 21-1.

The decision to launch or defer investment in the malted herring factory amounts to deciding whether to exercise the call option immediately or to wait and possibly exercise later.[3] Naturally this involves a trade-off. You are reluctant to exercise, because if you do so you can no longer take advantage of the volatility of the project's future value. Remember, option holders like volatility because it generates upside potential and the option contract limits loss. On the other hand, as long as the project has a positive NPV, you are eager to exercise in order to get your hands on the cash inflows. If the cash flows (and NPV) are high enough, you will gladly exercise your call before its time is up.

The cash inflows from an investment project play the same role as dividend payments on a stock. When a stock does not pay dividends, an American call option is *always* worth more alive than dead, and should never be exercised early. But payment of a dividend before the option matures reduces the ex-dividend price and the possible payoffs to the call option at maturity. Think of the extreme case: If a company pays out all of its assets in one bumper dividend, then afterward stock price must be zero and the call worthless. Therefore, any in-the-money call would be exercised just before this liquidating dividend.

Dividends do not always prompt early exercise, but if they are sufficiently large, call option holders capture them by exercising just before the ex-dividend date. We see managers acting in the same way: When project's forecasted cash flows are sufficiently large, they "capture" the cash flows by investing right away.[4] But when forecasted cash flows are small, they are inclined to hold on to their call rather than investing, even when project NPV is positive. This explains why managers are sometimes reluctant to commit to positive-NPV projects. This caution is rational so long as the option to wait is open and sufficiently valuable.

---

[3] We are now thinking of American options. European options cannot be exercised before maturity.

[4] In this case the call's value equals its lower-bound value because it is exercised immediately; the two lines in Figure 21-1 touch where project PV is high enough to trigger immediate investment. At this or still higher PV, the value of a *European* call option, which could *not* be exercised immediately, would lie *below* the value of a now-or-never investment.

FIGURE 21-1

The opportunity to invest in the malted herring factory amounts to a call option. If investment is now or never, the call's payoffs are shown by the heavy line. If investment can be postponed, the call option is valuable even if project NPV is zero or negative. Compare Figure 20-8.

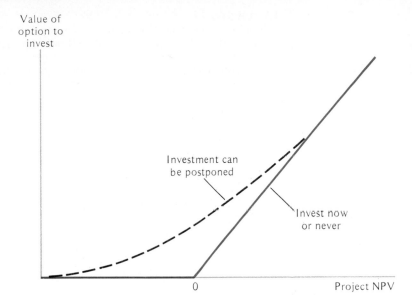

Suppose, for example, that our malted herring factory is expected to produce a level stream of real cash flows for 10 years. There is considerable uncertainty about each year's cash flow: By waiting a year you will get information that could lead you to revise your cash flow forecasts by 20 percent up or down. So if you postpone investment, you may avoid making a bad mistake. On the other hand, you miss out on 1 year's cash flow. In this case the benefits of waiting outweigh the cost as long as the project NPV is less than $8.7 million. Table 21-1 shows the

TABLE 21-1

Investment of $100 million in the malted herring factory should be postponed unless NPV is greater than the critical values shown (figures in millions of dollars)

Uncertainty of Annual Cash Flows, Plus or Minus	PROJECT LIFE (YEARS)						
	4	5	6	7	8	9	10
10%	.0	.0	.0	.0	.0	.0	.0
20	.0	.0	.0	2.9	5.3	7.1	8.7
30	.0	4.2	9.1	12.9	15.9	18.4	20.5
40	5.3	13.6	20.0	25.0	29.0	32.4	35.1
50	14.3	25.5	33.3	40.0	45.5	50.0	53.8

Assumptions:
1. Expected cash flow stream is level in real terms.
2. Cost of malted herring factory is level in real terms.
3. Project termination date is fixed regardless of when investment is made.
4. Real interest rate is zero.
5. Forecasted real cash flows follow a simple binomial process; e.g., forecasts are revised up or down each year by 30 percent.

TABLE 21-2
Summary of cash flows and financial analysis of the Mark I microcomputer. (Figures in millions. After-tax operating cash flow is negative in 1982 because of R&D costs.)

Year	1982	1983	1984	1985	1986	1987
After-tax operating cash flow	−200	+110	+159	+295	+185	0
Capital investment	250	0	0	0	0	0
Increase in working capital	0	50	100	100	−125	−125
Net cash flow (1)-(2)-(3)	−450	+60	+59	+195	+310	+125
NPV at 20% = −$46.45, about −$46 million						

critical values at which you should postpone investment for a variety of project lives and levels of cash-flow uncertainty.[5] As you would expect, the greater the uncertainty and the longer the remaining life of the project, the more incentive there is to delay.

Follow-on Investment Opportunities

It is 1982. You are assistant to the chief financial officer (CFO) of Blitzen Computers, an established computer manufacturer casting a profit-hungry eye on the rapidly developing personal computer market. You arc helping the CFO evaluate the proposed introduction of the Blitzen Mark I Micro.

The Mark I's forecasted cash flows and NPV are shown in Table 21-2. Unfortunately the Mark I can't meet Blitzen's customary 20 percent hurdle rate, and has a $46 million negative NPV, contrary to top management's strong gut feeling that Blitzen ought to be in the personal computer market.

> *"The Mark I just can't make it on financial grounds," the CFO says, "but we've got to do it for strategic reasons. I'm recommending we go ahead."*

> *"But you're missing the all-important financial advantage, Chief," you reply.*

> *"Don't call me Chief. What financial advantage?"*

> *"If we don't launch the Mark I, it will probably be too expensive to enter the micro market later, when Apple, IBM, and others are firmly established. If we go ahead, we have the opportunity to make follow-on investments which could be extremely profitable. The Mark I gives not only its own cash flows, but a call option to go on with a Mark II micro. That call option is the real source of strategic value."*

> *"So it's strategic value by another name. That doesn't tell me what the Mark II investment's worth. The Mark II could be a great investment or a lousy one—we haven't got a clue."*

---

[5] These values were calculated on a personal computer using the binomial method described in Section 21-3.

TABLE 21-3
Calculating what the option to invest in the Mark II microcomputer could be worth

Assumptions
1. The decision to invest in the Mark II must be made after 3 years, in 1985.
2. The Mark II investment is double the scale of the Mark I (note the expected rapid growth of the industry). Investment required is $900 million (the exercise price), which is taken as fixed.
3. Forecasted cash inflows of the Mark II are also double those of the Mark I, with present value of about $800 million in 1985 and $800/(1.2)^3 = \$463$ million in 1982.
4. The future value of the Mark II cash flows is highly uncertain. This value evolves like a stock price with a standard deviation of 35 percent per year. (Many high-tech stocks have standard deviations higher than 35 percent.)

Interpretation
The opportunity to invest in the Mark II is a 3-year call option on an asset worth $463 million with a $900 million exercise price.

Valuation
See Appendix Table 6:

$$\text{Standard deviation} \times \sqrt{\text{time}} = .35\sqrt{3} = .61$$

$$\frac{\text{Asset value}}{\text{PV (exercise price)}} = \frac{463}{900/(1.1)^3} = .68$$

$$\frac{\text{Call value}}{\text{Asset value}} = .119 \quad \text{(closest figure from Appendix Table 6)}$$

$$\text{Call value} = .119 \times 463 = 55.1, \text{ or about } \$55 \text{ million}$$

"That's exactly when a call option is worth the most," *you point out perceptively.* *"The call lets us invest in the Mark II if it's great, and walk away from it if it's lousy."*

"So what's it worth?"

"Hard to say precisely, but I've done a back-of-the-envelope calculation that suggests the value of the option to invest in the Mark II could more than offset the Mark I's $46 million negative NPV. [The calculations are shown in Table 21-3.] If the option to invest is worth $55 million, the total value of the Mark I is its own NPV, − $46 million, plus the $55 million option attached to it, or + $9 million."

"You're just overestimating the Mark II," *the CFO says gruffly.* *"It's easy to be optimistic when an investment is three years away."*

"No, no," *you reply patiently.* *"The Mark II is expected to be no more profitable than the Mark I—just twice as big, and therefore twice as bad in terms of discounted cash flow. I'm forecasting it to have a **negative** NPV of about $100 million. But there's a **chance** the Mark II could be extremely valuable indeed. The call option allows Blitzen to cash in on those upside outcomes. The chance to cash in could be worth $55 million.*

"Of course the $55 million is only a trial calculation, but it illustrates how valuable follow-on investment opportunities can be, especially when uncertainty is high and the product market is growing rapidly. Moreover, the Mark II will give us a call on the Mark III, the Mark III on the Mark IV, and so on. My calculations don't take subsequent calls into account."

"I think I'm beginning to understand a little bit of corporate strategy," *mumbles the CFO.*

Real Options and the Value of Management

Discounted cash flow (DCF) implicitly assumes that firms hold real assets passively. It ignores the options found in real assets—options that sophisticated managers can act to take advantage of. You could say that DCF does not reflect the value of management.

Remember that the DCF valuation method was originally developed for bonds and common stocks. Investors in these securities are necessarily passive: With rare exceptions, there is nothing investors can do to improve the interest rate they are paid or the dividend they receive. A bond or common stock can be sold, of course, but that merely substitutes one passive investor for another.

Options, and securities such as convertible bonds which contain options, are fundamentally different. Investors who hold options do not have to be passive. They are given a right to make a decision, which they can exercise to capitalize on good fortune or to mitigate loss. The right clearly has value whenever there is uncertainty. However, calculating that value is not a simple matter of discounting. Option pricing theory tells us what the value is, but the necessary formulas do not look like DCF.

Now consider the firm as an investor in *real* assets. Management can *add value* to those assets by responding to changing circumstances—by *acting* to take advantage of good fortune or to mitigate loss.

Management has the opportunity to act because many capital investment opportunities have valuable real options embedded in them, options which management can exercise when it is in the firm's interest to do so. Discounted cash flow misses this extra value because it implicitly treats the firm (and its management) as a passive investor.

21-2 SOME PRACTICAL PROBLEMS IN VALUING OPTIONS

In the last chapter you learned two equivalent ways to calculate the value of an option:

1. Find the combination of stock and loan that replicates an investment in the option. Since the two strategies give identical payoffs in the future, they must sell for the same price today.
2. Pretend that investors are unconcerned about risk, so that the expected return on the stock is equal to the interest rate. Calculate the expected future value of the option in this risk-neutral world and discount it at the interest rate.

We began in Chapter 20 by applying these ideas to value a very simple option on the stock of Wombat Corporation. We assumed that the option on Wombat stock lasted only one period and that in this period the stock price could vary in one of only two ways. We then remarked that the time to maturity could be divided into a number of subperiods in *each* of which the stock price can vary in one of two ways. As the intervals get shorter and shorter you approach a situation where the stock price is changing continuously and there is a continuum of possible stock prices at the option's maturity. For this case Black and Scholes devised their famous short-cut option-valuation formula.

We now turn again to these option pricing models. First we warm up with an example which should help to reinforce what you learned in the last chapter.

Valuing the Abandonment Put—An Example

In Chapter 10 we introduced you to that airborne pioneer Agnes Magna, who was pondering the purchase of a turboprop for her new airline. If the airline gets off to a good start and demand is high, Ms. Magna calculates that she will have a business worth $736,000 by the end of the first year. If things don't work out, she will face the prospect of a stream of losses worth $-\$182,000$ at the end of the first year. Thus at the end of the year she will own a very valuable asset or an expensive liability.

Ms. Magna estimates that there is a 60 percent chance that the business will be successful and therefore calculates its *expected* value in year 1 as $(.6 \times 736) + (.4 \times -182) = \$369,000$. She discounts this at a 10 percent cost of capital to give a present value of $369/1.1 = \$335,000$.[6]

Note that these calculations do not allow for the possibility of abandonment. If the business does not take off in the first year, Ms. Magna would do better to sell the turboprop for $300,000, rather than face a stream of future losses. What is the value of this option to bail out? In Chapter 10 we tried to answer that question using standard discounted cash flow (DCF) techniques. We know now that you cannot use standard DCF where there is an option involved, because the discount rate changes as the value of the underlying asset changes. To value Ms. Magna's option to abandon, you need to value a 1-year put option with an exercise price of $300,000.

You require the following information to value the put (figures in thousands):

- Present value of business without option to abandon $= \$335$
- Exercise price $= \$300$
- Maturity $= 1$ year
- Interest rate $= 5\%$
- Future value of business with high demand $= +\$736$
- Future value with low demand $= -\$182$

Since Ms. Magna can foresee only two outcomes, this problem is tailor-made for the *binomial* method that we used in Chapter 20 to value the Wombat option. Here is a chance to show that you haven't forgotten it.

We start by *pretending* that Ms. Magna is indifferent about risk. In this case she would be content if the business just offered the 5 percent risk-free rate of interest. We know that the value of the business will either go from $335,000 to $736,000, a rise of 120 percent, or it will go to $-\$182,000$, a fall of 154 percent. We can therefore calculate the probability that value will rise in our hypothetical risk-neutral world:

$$\frac{\text{Expected}}{\text{return}} = \left(\begin{array}{c}\text{probability}\\\text{of rise}\end{array}\right) \times 120 + \left(1 - \begin{array}{c}\text{probability}\\\text{of rise}\end{array}\right) \times (-154)$$

$$= .05, \text{ or } 5\%$$

Therefore, the probability of rise equals .58, or 58 percent.[7]

We know that if the business is successful, the option to abandon will be worthless. If it is unsuccessful, Ms. Magna will sell the turboprop and save herself

---

[6] This is not the *total* value of the business to Ms. Magna, since she also expects to earn some income during the first year. This income does not affect the value of the option to abandon at the end of the first year and so we ignore it here.

[7] Remember that these probabilities are not true probabilities; they are the probabilities that would exist if investors were risk-neutral. We know that the *actual* probability of high demand is .6.

$300 - (-182) = \$482,000$. Therefore the expected future value of the option to abandon is

$$\left(\begin{matrix}\text{Probability} \\ \text{of rise}\end{matrix}\right) \times 0 + \left(1 - \begin{matrix}\text{probability} \\ \text{of rise}\end{matrix}\right) \times 482$$

$$= (.58 \times 0) + (.42 \times 482) = 202, \text{ or } \$202,000$$

And the current value of the option to abandon is

$$\frac{\text{Expected future value}}{1 + \text{interest rate}} = \frac{202}{1.05} = 192, \text{ or } \$192,000$$

Thus recognizing the option to abandon increases the value of Ms. Magna's business by \$192,000:

$$\begin{matrix}\text{Value of business} \\ \text{with abandonment} \\ \text{option}\end{matrix} = \begin{matrix}\text{value of business} \\ \text{without abandonment} \\ \text{option}^8\end{matrix} + \begin{matrix}\text{value} \\ \text{of} \\ \text{option}\end{matrix}$$

$$= 335 + 192 = 527, \text{ or } \$527,000$$

Unfortunately the option valuation methods given in Chapter 20 cannot be used for most abandonment puts. There will be complications. For example, the exercise price will change over time and will rarely be known in advance. In general, the option to abandon is like an American option on a dividend-paying stock, in which both the dividend payments and exercise price are uncertain. A number-crunching computer is usually needed to get a numerical value.

But before we get on to more complicated cases, we offer one more real option, which is really an abandonment put in disguise.

The Value of Flexibility

Suppose you must choose between two technologies for production of a brand-new product, a Wankel-engined outboard motor.

1. Technology A uses computer-controlled machinery custom-designed to produce the complex shapes required for Wankel engines in high volumes and at low cost. But if the Wankel motor doesn't sell, this equipment will be worthless.
2. Technology B uses standard machine tools. Labor costs are much higher, but the tools can be sold or shifted to another use if the motor doesn't sell.

Technology A looks better in a discounted cash flow analysis of the new product, because it was designed to have the lowest possible cost at the planned production volume. Yet you can sense the advantage of technology B's flexibility if you are not sure whether the new outboard will sink or swim in the marketplace.

In many practical cases like this one, managers ignore technology A's better discounted cash flow value and choose technology B instead for its "intangible" flexibility advantage. But we can make the value of this flexibility more concrete by modeling it as a put option.

A put option on a stock is an insurance policy which pays off when the stock price ends up below the put's exercise price. Technology B provides the same kind of insurance policy: If the outboard's sales are sufficiently disappointing, you can abandon the machinery and realize its value. This value is the exercise price of the

---

[8] We should also add in the value of any income received in the first year.

FIGURE 21-2
The possible stock prices of Buffelhead.
Figures in parentheses show the values
of a 1-year call option with an exercise
price of 165.

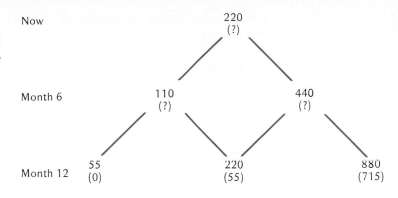

abandonment put. The payoff to this put is the difference between its exercise price
and the value of the Wankel motor project if it could *not* be abandoned.

21-3 VALUING OPTIONS THAT LAST FOR MORE THAN ONE PERIOD

In both the Wombat and the Magna Charter examples we imagined that there are
only two possible prices for the asset at the option's expiration. We will now show
you how to apply the binomial method when the period to expiration is divided
into a number of subperiods.

Suppose that in each of the next two 6-month periods the price of Buffelhead
Corporation's stock could either double or halve. The current stock price is 220
and the interest rate is 21 percent a year or 10 percent for 6 months. What is the
value of a 1-year call option on Buffelhead with an exercise price of 165?

Figure 21-2 shows the possible future stock prices. By the end of the year the
price could be 55, 220, or 880—quite a range. Underneath each year-end stock
price we show in brackets the associated value of the call option. Thus, if the stock
price turns out to be 55, the option will be worthless; at the other extreme, if the
price is 880, the option will be worth

$$\text{Stock price} - \text{exercise price} = 880 - 165 = 715$$

We now use the risk-neutral trick to work out option values at the end of the
first 6 months. If investors are risk-neutral, the expected return on the stock must
be equal to the interest rate. So[9]

$$\begin{pmatrix}\text{Probability} \\ \text{of rise}\end{pmatrix} \times 100 + \begin{pmatrix}1 - \text{probability} \\ \text{of rise}\end{pmatrix} \times (-50) = 10$$

$$\text{Probability of rise} = .4$$

---

[9] The general formula for calculating the probability of a rise is

$$p = \frac{r - d}{u - d}$$

where p = probability of rise
r = interest rate
u = upside change
d = downside change

Thus in the Buffelhead case

$$p = \frac{10 - (-50)}{100 - (-50)} = .4$$

**Option
Values after
6 Months**

First we calculate option values after 6 months. We know that, if the stock price in month 6 is 440, there is a .4 chance that the option will be worth 715 at the end of the year and a .6 chance that it will be worth 55. Thus

Expected value of option at end of year $= (.4 \times 715) + (.6 \times 55) = 319$

And

$$\text{Value at month } 6 = \frac{319}{1.10} = 290$$

Similarly, if the stock price at month 6 is 110, the option could turn out to be worth 55 with a probability of .4, or zero with a probability of .6. In this case

Expected option value at end of year $= (.4 \times 55) + (.6 \times 0) = 22$

and the option value at month 6 is $22/1.1 = 20$.

**Option Value
Now**

We can now get rid of two of the question marks in Figure 21-2. Figure 21-3 shows that if the stock price in month 6 is 440, the option value is 290 and, if the stock price is 110, the option price is 20. It now remains only to work back to the value of the option today.

The expected value of the option in month 6 is

$$\begin{pmatrix} \text{Probability} \\ \text{of rise} \end{pmatrix} \times 290 + \begin{pmatrix} 1 - \text{probability} \\ \text{of rise} \end{pmatrix} \times 20 = 128$$

Therefore, the value today is

$$\frac{\text{Expected option payoff}}{1 + \text{interest rate}} = \frac{128}{1.1} = 116.4$$

It took us longer to value an option with two periods to run, but the principle is exactly the same as for the Wombat option and you don't need any more advanced mathematics than multiplication and division.[10]

**Calculating
the Option
Delta**

At the end of the 6 months the value of the Buffelhead call option could be either 290 or 20. The spread of possible option values is, therefore, $290 - 20 = 270$. Similarly the spread of possible stock prices is $440 - 110 = 330$. Thus for each $1 change in the stock price the option price changes $270/330 = \$.818$.

---

[10] We did not need to go through the intermediate stage of calculating the value of the option at month 6. Imagine you are in period zero. One year hence there is a $.6 \times .6 = .36$ chance that the stock price will be 55, a $2 \times .6 \times .4 = .48$ chance that it will be 220, and a $.4 \times .4 = .16$ chance that it will be 880. The value of the option at year-end would be 0, 55, and 715, respectively. Thus

Expected value of option at end of year $= (.36 \times 0) + (.48 \times 55) + (.16 \times 715) = 140.8$

The value of the option today is $140.8/1.1^2 = 116.4$. We showed the intermediate steps only because in some cases (e.g., when there are intermediate dividend payments) you need to check that it is not worth exercising before maturity. More about that in the next section.

FIGURE 21-3
We have worked back from the month-12 option values to calculate the values of the Buffelhead call option in month 6.

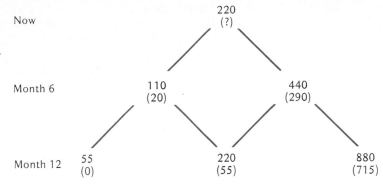

This tells us the option delta:

$$\text{Option delta} = \frac{\text{spread of possible option prices}}{\text{spread of possible stock prices}}$$

$$= \frac{270}{330} = .818$$

In other words, you can replicate an investment in the option by buying .818 units of stock and borrowing the balance. Let's check that this works:

		CASH FLOW NEXT PERIOD IF	
	Cash Flow Now	Stock Price Falls	Stock Price Rises
Buy option	−116.4	+20	+290
Equals			
Buy .818 shares	−180	+90	+360
Borrow balance	+ 63.6	− 70	− 70
	−116.4	+20	+290

The General Binomial Method

In the last chapter when we valued the Wombat call option, we assumed that the option lasted only one period and during that period there were only two ways that the stock price could change. In the Buffelhead example we divided the life of the option into two subperiods during each of which the stock price could change in only two ways. In each case we were using the *binomial method* to value the option.

There is no reason to stop at two subperiods. You could go on to take shorter and shorter intervals in each of which there are only two possible changes in the stock price. For example, you might choose to divide the year into 12 subintervals of 1 month each. That would give 13 possible year-end prices. You could still use the binomial method to work progressively back from the final date to the present. It may sound long-winded, but with a computer you can whisk through options with many periods to run.

TABLE 21-4

As the number of intervals is increased, you must adjust the range of possible stock price changes to keep the same standard deviation. But you will get increasingly close to the Black-Scholes measure of the value of the Buffelhead option ($115.83)

Number of Intervals in a Year ($1/h$)	Upside Change (u)	Downside Change (d)	Estimated Option Value
1	+166.4%	−62.5%	$126.92
2	+100	−50	116.35
12	+32.7	−24.6	116.84
52	+14.6	−12.7	115.66

Black-Scholes value = 115.83

Note: The standard deviation is $\sigma = .98$ and the interest rate is 21 percent.

Since stock prices could take on an almost limitless number of future values, the binomial method is likely to give a more realistic and accurate measure of the option's value if you work with a large number of subperiods. But that raises an important question: How do we pick sensible values for the range of possible stock price changes? Fortunately there is a neat little formula that can help:

$$\text{Upside change} \quad = u = e^{(\sigma\sqrt{h})} - 1$$

$$\text{Downside change} = d = e^{(-\sigma\sqrt{h})} - 1$$

where e = the base for natural logs = 2.718
       σ = the standard deviation of (continuously compounded) annual returns
       h = the interval as a fraction of a year

For example, suppose you know that the standard deviation of annual returns of Buffelhead stock is 98 percent ($\sigma = .98$). The left-hand columns in Table 21-4 show the up and down moves in the stock price that are consistent with this standard deviation.

As the number of intervals is increased, the values that you obtain from the binomial method should get closer and closer to the Black-Scholes value. In fact you can think of the Black-Scholes formula as a shortcut alternative to the binomial method as the number of intervals gets very large. For the Buffelhead option the Black-Scholes formula gives a value of $115.83. The right-hand column of Table 21-4 shows that if you chop the period to expiration into 52 weekly subperiods, the binomial method gives a good approximation to the Black-Scholes value.

If the Black-Scholes formula is more accurate and quicker to use than the binomial method, why trouble with the binomial method at all? The answer is that there are circumstances in which you *cannot* use the Black-Scholes formula but where the binomial method will still give you a good measure of an option's value. We will tell you about these complications in the next section.

21-4 SOME COMPLICATIONS

You now know how to value a (relatively) simple option. Unfortunately, many of the options that you are likely to encounter will not be simple. In this section we discuss some of the more frequent complications.

European versus American Options

In the last chapter we distinguished between a European option, which can be exercised on only one date, and an American option which can be exercised at any time before that date. We know that the value of a call option increases with time to maturity. So, if you exercised an American call option early, you would needlessly reduce its value. Since an American call should not be exercised until its final date, its value is the same as that of a European call, and the Black-Scholes formula applies to both options.[11]

If we wish to find the value of a European put, we can use a formula that we developed in the last chapter:

$$\text{Value of put} = \text{value of call} - \text{value of stock} + \text{PV(exercise price)}$$

Unfortunately this procedure is not exactly right for an American put, because it can sometimes pay to exercise a put before maturity in order to reinvest the exercise price. For example, suppose that immediately after buying an American put the stock price falls to zero. In this case there is no advantage to holding on to the option since it *cannot* become more valuable. It is better to exercise the put and invest the exercise money. Such an option is worth more dead than alive.

An American put is always more valuable than a European put. In our extreme example the difference is equal to the present value of the interest that you could earn on the exercise price. In all other cases the difference is less.

Because the Black-Scholes formula does not allow for early exercise, it cannot be used to value an American put exactly. But you can use the step-by-step binomial method as long as you check at each point whether the option is worth more dead than alive.

Example. The stock price of American Cyanide is currently 100, but by the end of 6 months could fall to 80 or rise to 115. Now suppose you have a put option on the stock with an exercise price of 110. The 6-month rate of interest is 5 percent. Here are the possible values of the stock and the option:

We first calculate the probability of a stock rise in a risk-neutral world:

$$(\text{Probability of rise} \times 15) + (1 - \text{probability of rise}) \times (-20) = 5$$

$$\text{Probability of rise} = .71$$

Next we calculate the expected payoff if you hold on to the option until maturity and discount this payoff at 5 percent:

$$\text{PV option} = \frac{(.71 \times 0) + (.29 \times 30)}{1.05} = 8.3$$

However, if we exercise the option immediately, the option is worth $110 - 100 = 10$. Obviously we will follow the strategy that makes the option most valuable.

---

[11] Exercising before maturity would effectively reduce t, the time until maturity, and therefore reduce value.

Dividends

We noted early in the chapter that a call option's value is reduced when dividends are paid on the underlying stock. But our discussion of the Black-Scholes and binomial methods has so far ignored dividends altogether.

Here are some ways to handle dividends:

1. The simplest case is a *European* call on an asset that pays dividends. You can use the Black-Scholes formula to value this option but you must first calculate the present value of dividend payments over the asset's life and deduct this figure from the current stock price.
2. We have already seen that when the stock does not pay dividends, an American call option is *always* worth more alive than dead. That way you both keep your option open *and* earn interest on your exercise money. Even when there are dividends, you should never exercise early if the dividend payment that you would gain is smaller than the interest that you would lose by having to pay the exercise price early. However, if the dividend is sufficiently large, you might want to capture it by exercising your option just before the ex-dividend date.

   There is a rough-and-ready way to value an American call with known dividends. You first use the Black-Scholes formula to calculate the value of the option, assuming that you hold it to maturity (remembering, of course, to deduct the present value of the dividends from the share price). Next, pretending that the option matures just before the last ex-dividend date, you again use the Black-Scholes formula to work out the value of the option. In the same way, you can calculate the Black-Scholes values for all the other ex-dividend dates. Obviously, if you have to decide today the date at which you can exercise your option, you will pick the one that maximizes the option's value. This figure is often known as the "pseudo Black-Scholes" value.
3. The pseudo Black-Scholes value tells you the value of an American call option on a dividend-paying stock when you have to specify the exercise date ahead of time. But one of the nice features of an American option is that you can wait and see when the best time to exercise is. Thus the pseudo Black-Scholes value will always be an underestimate of the true value of an American call on a dividend-paying stock.

   You can get a more accurate measure of the value of an American call on a dividend-paying stock by using the step-by-step binomial method. In this case you must check at each stage whether the option is more valuable if exercised just before the ex-dividend date or if you hold it for at least one more period.

One bonus of using the binomial method is that you do not have to assume that the dividends are known ahead of time. Instead you can assume that they also depend on the level of the stock price. For example, you could value a call on a stock where the dividends are a constant proportion of the stock price.

*Currency Options

Here is an interesting example of an option on a dividend-paying asset. Suppose that in June 1986 you are offered a 1-year call option to buy sterling at the current exchange rate of $1.50; i.e., $1.50 = £1. You have the following information:

- Maturity of option $t = 1$
- Exercise price $E = \$1.50$
- Current price of sterling $P = \$1.50$
- Standard deviation of exchange rate changes $\sigma = .10$
- Dollar interest rate $r_\$ = .075$
- Sterling interest rate $r_£ = .095$

If you buy sterling, you can invest it to earn interest at 9.5 percent. By buying the option rather than sterling itself you miss out on this "dividend." Therefore, to value the call option you must first reduce the current price of sterling by the amount of the lost interest:[12]

$$\text{Adjusted price of sterling} = P^* = \frac{\text{current price}}{1 + r_£} = \frac{1.50}{1.095} = \$1.37$$

Now you can apply the Black-Scholes formula:

$$\text{Standard deviation} \times \sqrt{\text{time}} = .10\sqrt{1} = .10$$

$$\frac{\text{Price}}{\text{PV (exercise price)}} = \frac{P^*}{E/(1 + r_\$)} = \frac{1.37}{150/1.075} = .98$$

Using the call option tables in Appendix Table 6 gives

$$\text{Value of call} = .031 \times P^* = .031 \times 1.37 = .042$$

that is, 4.2 cents per pound. An option to purchase £1 million on these terms would be worth \$42,000.

*21-5 HEDGING AND VOLATILITY

To use the Black-Scholes formula you need to know:

1. The asset value divided by the present value of the exercise (P/PV(E)).
2. The variability of the asset returns over the life of the option ($\sigma\sqrt{t}$).

The difficult problem is to forecast variability. If you get it wrong, you get the option delta and the option value wrong too.

For example, suppose you decide to buy delta units of an asset, sell a call option, and borrow the balance. As time goes by and the price of the asset changes, you recalculate delta and adjust your holding in the asset. Your net position will be perfectly protected against changes in the price of the asset *as long as you use a correct measure of variability to calculate the option delta.* If you *mis*estimate variability, your position will not be free of risk and you could either make or lose money.

Here is a simple example. The current stock price is \$100 and over the next period you believe that the price will either decline to \$80 or rise to \$120.

Current price: 100

Possible prices
next period: 80   120

A call on the stock has an exercise price of \$100 and to keep the arithmetic easy we will assume the interest rate is zero. If the market shares your assessment of

[12] Note that current price − PV(interest) = $P - \dfrac{r_£ P}{1 + r_£} = \dfrac{P}{1 + r_£}$.

stock price variability, the call option will be priced at $10. At the end of the period it will be worth $0 (if the stock price falls) or $20 (if the stock price rises).

Option price:

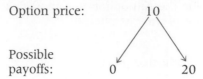

Possible payoffs: 0   20

You calculate that the option delta is .5. So you should be fully protected if you hold .5 units of stock, sell a call, and borrow the balance. Your cash flows under these circumstances are shown below:

	Initial Outlay	END OF YEAR	
		Stock Price Falls	Stock Price Rises
Buy .5 units of stock	−50	+40	+60
Borrow $40	+40	−40	−40
Sell 1 call	+10	0	−20
Net cash flow	0	0	0

But suppose that your estimate of stock price variability is wrong: In fact the price will either fall to $60 or rise to $140.

Current price:

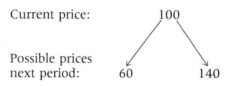

Possible prices next period: 60   140

The *actual* return on your portfolio is, therefore,

	Initial Outlay	END OF YEAR	
		Stock Price Falls	Stock Price Rises
Buy .5 units of stock	−50	+30	+70
Borrow $40	+40	−40	−40
Sell 1 call	+10	0	−40
Net cash flow	0	−10	−10

Thus, regardless of the direction of the stock price change, your future cash flows are *negative*. If variability turns out to be *lower* than your forecast, your "hedged" portfolio would again not be hedged. But in this case the future cash flows on the portfolio would be positive regardless of whether the stock price rises or falls. In order to be perfectly hedged, so that net cash flow "zeroes out" next period, you must base your measure of the option delta on a correct estimate of future variability.

Changing Volatility

The Black-Scholes option formula assumes that variability of the underlying asset does not change. In practice that is rarely the case. Look, for example, at Figure

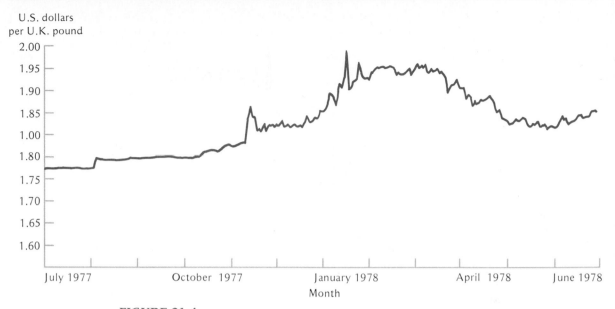

U.S. dollars
per U.K. pound

FIGURE 21-4
This graph of the dollar-sterling exchange rate shows that sterling was less variable from July to October 1977 than from November on.

21-4, which shows the dollar-sterling exchange rate in 1977 and 1978. Sterling was clearly much less variable at the beginning of this period than it was later.

Suppose you correctly forecast the variability of the daily exchange rate changes during this period. This gives you a single measure of the typical variability of sterling, but obviously it doesn't recognize that sterling was less variable early in this period and more variable later. You now use this measure of "average" variability to calculate the delta of a 1-year call option on sterling. You then sell the call, buy delta units of sterling, and borrow the balance. Every day as time passes and the value of sterling changes, you recalculate the option delta and you adjust your investment in sterling.

The dotted line in Figure 21-5 shows what happens to the value of your levered purchase of sterling and the solid line shows what happens to the value of the option that you have sold. In order to protect yourself against changes in the value of sterling, the two values should always be equal.

In the first part of the period sterling had below-average variability; in the second part it had above-average variability. Since you ignored this when calculating the option delta, your combined position in sterling and the option will not be risk-free: It will make money in the first part of the period and lose it again in the second part. Over the full 12 months your portfolio is almost perfectly protected against exchange rate changes; that is, the levered position in sterling is almost exactly equal to the value of the option that you have sold.

The moral of the story is this: If you can predict the asset's price variability over the life of the option and if you then use this figure to maintain a hedged portfolio, you will be almost perfectly protected against risk *as long as you maintain the hedged position until the option matures*. However, you will be perfectly hedged at all intermediate points only if variability is constant.

U.S. dollars

FIGURE 21-5
The solid line shows the value of a 1-year call option on sterling maturing at the end of June 1978. The dotted line shows the value of a levered purchase of delta units of sterling. The changing variability of sterling was ignored when calculating delta. Nevertheless over the year as a whole the value of the levered investment in sterling is almost exactly equal to the value of the option. (We thank Ian Cooper and Evi Kaplanis for supplying this example.)

Transaction Costs

The Black-Scholes model assumes that stock prices are continuously changing. Therefore, to maintain a *perfectly* hedged portfolio or to *exactly* replicate an option by a portfolio of shares plus borrowing or lending, you must recalculate the option delta every nanosecond and adjust your holding correspondingly. Not only would this be tiresome, but also you would suffer very large transactions costs. In practice, therefore, you are faced with a trade-off. If you adjust your position less frequently, the transaction costs will be reduced, but you will be less well hedged.

Rather than mechanically adjusting your portfolio at regular intervals, it may be more efficient to adjust only when the option delta has changed by some minimum amount. That will ensure that you make transactions when they are most needed.

21-6 USING OPTIONS TO INSURE AGAINST RISK

Options are simply a way to trade variability. If you buy a naked call option, you take on variability. At the other extreme, if you hold delta units of the asset, sell a call, and borrow the balance, you have transferred all risk to other investors.

Firms rarely want to eliminate *all* the uncertainty of owning an asset, but they may want to insure themselves against extreme loss. Options can provide home-made insurance. For example, suppose you buy an asset and a put option on the asset. If the value of the asset rises, the firm continues to hold it. If the value declines, the firm can exercise the put option and walk away with the exercise price.

Imagine that your firm has tendered for a large construction contract in Canada. Payment will be in Canadian dollars, but you will not know for several months whether your tender is successful. By that time the value of the Canadian dollar may have declined and your contract may no longer be profitable.

In order to limit this exchange risk, the firm can take out a put option on the Canadian dollar. If you get the contract and the Canadian dollar depreciates, the profit on the put should offset the reduction in the value of the contract. If you *don't* get the contract and the Canadian dollar depreciates, you walk away with a profit on the put.

The firm's purchase of a put option provides insurance against a fall in the exchange rate. Of course insurance doesn't come free; the price you pay for the put is the insurance premium. If the Canadian dollar appreciates, you have with hindsight bought unnecessary insurance.

Here is another example of how options may be used to insure against loss. Imagine that you have a bill outstanding for $100,000. In the meantime you have invested in a diversified portfolio of common stocks. Your worry is that by the time the bill becomes due, the value of your portfolio may have taken a nosedive.

Wouldn't it be nice if you could insure yourself against loss on the stock portfolio? Fortunately, you can. You can take out a put option on the market index with an exercise price equal to the current level of the index. If the market rises, you let the put option lapse; if the market falls, you exercise. As long as your portfolio moves in line with the market, any loss on your portfolio is exactly offset by a profit on the put.

Let us put some numbers on this. We assume that over the next year stock prices could either fall by 23 percent or rise by 43 percent. The cost of a 1-year put option on a $100,000 investment in the index is $10,455. This is the premium that you need to pay to insure against loss.

Here are the possible cash flows from your investments:

	Initial Outlay	END OF YEAR	
		Stock Prices Fall	Stock Prices Rise
Common stocks	− $100,000	+ $ 77,000	+ $143,000
Put option	− 10,455	+ 23,000	0
Total cash flow	− $110,455	+ $100,000	+ $143,000

Any losses that you incur on your common stock portfolio are exactly offset by the profits on the put option.

Even if the options on the index don't exist, you can invent them.[13] In our example you could achieve exactly the same total cash flow by reducing your investment in common stocks to $65,150 and placing $45,305 in a bank deposit yielding 10 percent. The possible cash flows from your investments would be:[14]

	Initial Outlay	END OF YEAR	
		Stock Prices Fall	Stock Prices Rise
Common stocks	− $ 65,150	$ 50,165	+ $ 93,165
Bank deposit at 10%	− 45,305	49,835	+ 49,835
Total cash flow	− $110,455	+ $100,000	+ $143,000

---

[13] A homemade option may be the only answer if the returns on your portfolio are not closely correlated with returns on the index.

[14] This is exactly the same as the cost of holding $100,000 of common stocks and buying a put. Thus we know that the put is fairly priced at $10,455.

We should remind you that in practice an investment in common stocks usually has many more than two possible outcomes. In this case, as time passes and prices change, the option delta will change and you will need to keep adjusting your balance between stocks and bank deposits. That takes us back to the discussion in the last section. The trick is to get a good estimate of variability when estimating the option delta and to strike a sensible balance between replicating the option exactly and minimizing transaction costs.

21-7 SUMMARY

In Chapter 20 you learned the basics of option valuation. Now you should be able to recognize the real and financial options corporations encounter and to handle option-valuation problems of moderate complexity.

We described three important real options.

1. *The option to wait* (and learn) before investing amounts to owning a call option on the investment project. The call is exercised when the firm commits to the project. But often it's better to defer a positive-NPV project in order to keep the call alive. Deferral is most attractive when uncertainty is great and immediate project cash flows—which are lost or postponed by waiting—are small.
2. *The option to make follow-on investments.* Companies often cite "strategic" value when taking negative-NPV projects. A close look at the projects' payoffs reveals a call option on follow-on projects in addition to the immediate projects' cash flows. Today's investments can generate tomorrow's opportunities.
3. *The option to abandon.* The option to abandon a project provides partial insurance against failure. This is a put option; the put's exercise price is the value of the project's assets if sold or shifted to a more valuable use.

We used the abandonment problem as an example to review and extend the binomial option-valuation methods introduced in Chapter 20.

The binomial method of option valuation assumes that the time to the option's maturity can be divided into a number of subintervals in each of which there are only two possible price changes. In the last chapter we valued an option with only one period to expiration. Here we showed you how to value an option with many periods to expiration. You can think of the Black-Scholes formula as a shortcut solution when there is an indefinite number of these subperiods.

There are several complications that you need to keep in mind. When valuing an American put option you should consider whether it would pay to exercise it early. Also you may need to recognize that the call option holder misses out on any dividends on the stock.

Options are a means for trading variability. For example, if you buy delta units of an asset, sell a call, and borrow the balance, you are perfectly hedged against changes in the value of the asset. However, in constructing option hedges a good estimate of delta is essential. Also you will need to adjust your hedge over time. If you adjust too frequently, you will incur high transaction costs. If you forget to adjust, your hedge will become less and less effective.

Firms often use options to provide insurance against loss. We looked at how currency options can be used to insure against exchange rate loss and how stock index options can be used to insure against losses in the stock market.

FURTHER READING

The spring 1987 issue of the Midland Corporate Finance Journal *contains several articles on real options and capital investment decisions. See also Kester for a discussion of options and corporate strategy:*

W. C. Kester, "Today's Options for Tomorrow's Growth," *Harvard Business Review,* **62**:153–160 (March–April 1984).

Mason and Merton review a range of option applications to corporate finance:

S. P. Mason and R. C. Merton, "The Role of Contingent Claims Analysis in Corporate Finance," in E. I. Altman and M. G. Subrahmanyam (eds.), *Recent Advances in Corporate Finance,* Richard D. Irwin, Inc., Homewood, Ill., 1985.

Brennan and Schwartz have worked out an interesting application to natural resource investments.

M. J. Brennan and E. S. Schwartz, "Evaluating Natural Resource Investments," *Journal of Business,* **58**:135–157 (April 1985).

The texts given under Further Reading in Chapter 20 can be referred to for further discussion of the binomial method and the practical complications of applying option pricing theory.

QUIZ

1. Describe the real option in each of the following cases.
    (a) Backwoods Chemical postpones a major plant expansion. The expansion has positive NPV on a discounted cash flow basis, but top management wants to get a better fix on product demand before proceeding.
    (b) Western Telecom commits to production of digital switching equipment specially designed for the European market. The project has a negative discounted cash flow NPV, but is justified by the need for a strong market position in the rapidly growing, and potentially very profitable, market.
    (c) Western Telecom vetos a fully integrated, automated production line for the new digital switches. It relies on standard, less expensive equipment. The automated line is more efficient overall, according to a discounted cash flow analysis.
2. Backwoods Chemical's stock price changes only once a month: Either it goes up by 20 percent or it falls by 10 percent. Its price now is 40. The interest rate is 12.7 percent per year, or about 1 percent per month.
    (a) What is the value of a 1-month call option with an exercise price of 40?
    (b) What is the option delta?
    (c) Show how the payoffs of this call option can be replicated by buying Backwoods stock and borrowing.
    (d) What is the value of a 2-month call option with an exercise price of 40?
    (e) What is the option delta of the 2-month call over the first 1-month period?
3. "The Black-Scholes formula gives the same answer as the binomial method when _____ ." Fill in the blank and briefly explain.
4. For which of these options *might* it be rational to exercise before maturity? Say briefly why or why not.
    (a) American put on a nondividend-paying stock.
    (b) American call—the dividend payment is $5 per annum, the exercise price is $100, and the interest rate is 10 percent.

(c) American call—the interest rate is 10 percent and the dividend payment is 5 percent of future stock price. *Hint:* Stock price may rise or fall.

(d) American call on deutsche marks.

5. Suppose a stock price can go up by 15 percent or down by 10 percent over the next period. You own a one-period put on the stock. The interest rate is 10 percent, and the current stock price is 60.

(a) What exercise price leaves you indifferent between holding the put or exercising it now?

(b) How does this "break-even" exercise price change if the interest rate is increased?

6. Dr. Livingstone I. Presume holds £600,000 in East African gold stocks. Bullish as he is on gold mining, he requires absolute assurance that at least £500,000 will be available in 6 months to fund an expedition. Describe two ways for Dr. Presume to achieve this goal. There is an active market for puts and calls on East African gold stocks, and the sterling rate of interest is 12.4 percent per year.

QUESTIONS AND PROBLEMS

1. Describe each of the following situations in the language of options.

(a) Drilling rights to undeveloped heavy crude oil in Southern California. Development and production of the oil now is a negative-NPV endeavor. (The break-even oil price is $32 per barrel, versus a spot price of $20.) However, the decision to develop can be put off for up to 5 years. Development costs are expected to increase by 5 percent per year.

(b) A restaurant producing net cash flows, after all out-of-pocket expenses, of $700,000 per year. There is no upward or downward trend in the cash flows, but they fluctuate, with an annual standard deviation of 15 percent. The real estate occupied by the restaurant is owned, not leased, and could be sold for $5 million. Ignore taxes.

(c) A variation on part (b): Assume the restaurant faces known fixed costs of $300,000 per year incurred so long as the restaurant is operating. Thus

$$\text{Net cash flow} = \begin{array}{c} \text{revenue} \\ \text{less variable} \\ \text{costs} \end{array} - \text{fixed costs}$$

$$\$700,000 = 1,000,000 - 300,000$$

The annual standard deviation of the forecast error of revenue less variable costs is 10.5 percent. The interest rate is 10 percent. Ignore taxes.

(d) The British-French treaty giving a concession to build a railroad link under the English Channel also requires the concessionaire to propose by the year 2000 to build a "drive-through link" if "technical and economic conditions permit . . . and the increase in traffic shall justify it without undermining the expected return on the first [rail] link." Other companies will not be permitted to build a link before the year 2020.

2. Perform a sensitivity analysis on Table 21-2. The CFO would like to know how the present value of the option on the Mark II depends on

(a) The degree of uncertainty (standard deviation)

(b) The forecasted NPV of the Mark II

(c) The rate of growth of the micro market (which determines the possible *scale* of the Mark II project)

3. You own a 1-year call option on 1 acre of Los Angeles real estate. The exercise price is $2 million, and the current, appraised market value of the land is $1.7 million. The land is currently used as a parking lot, generating just enough money to cover real estate taxes. Over the last 5 years, similar properties have appreciated by 20 percent per year. The annual standard deviation is 15 percent and the interest rate 12 percent. How much is your call worth? Use the Black-Scholes formula and Appendix Table 6.

4. A variation on question 3: Suppose the land is occupied by a warehouse, generating rents of $150,000 after real estate taxes and all other out-of-pocket costs. The value of the land plus warehouse is again $1.7 million. Other facts are as in question 3. You have a *European* call option. What is it worth?

5. Revalue the Magna Charter option to abandon (see Section 21-2) using the Black-Scholes model. Assume a standard deviation of project returns of 80 percent. What does the Black-Scholes model assume about the distribution of project returns? How good is this assumption in the present case?

6. The price of Wigeon Corp. stock is 100. During each of the next two 6-month periods the price may either rise by 25 percent or fall by 20 percent. At month 6 the company will pay a dividend equal to 20 percent of the cum-dividend stock price. The interest rate is 10 percent per 6-month period. What is the value of a one year American call option with an exercise price of 80?

7. In Section 21-3 we calculated the option delta for the first 6 months of the Buffelhead option.
   (*a*) Now calculate the option delta for the second 6 months if (i) the stock price rises to $440; (ii) the stock price falls to $110.
   (*b*) How does the call option delta vary with the level of the stock price? Explain, intuitively, why.
   (*c*) Suppose that in month 6 the Buffelhead stock price is $110. How at that point could you replicate an investment in the stock by a combination of call options and risk-free lending? Show that your strategy does indeed produce the same returns as an investment in the stock.

8. Recalculate the value of the Buffelhead option (see Section 21-3) assuming that the option is American and that at the end of the first 6 months the company pays a dividend equal to 9 percent of the stock price. (Thus the price at the end of the year is either double or half the *ex*-dividend price in month 6.) How would your answer change if the option were European?

9. Suppose that you have an option which allows you to sell Buffelhead stock in month 6 for $165 *or* to buy it in month 12 for $165 (see Section 21-3). What is the value of this unusual option?

10. The current price of Northern Airlines stock is $100. During each 6-month period it will either rise by 10 percent or fall by 10 percent. The interest rate is 5 percent per 6-month period.
    (*a*) Calculate the value of a 1-year European put option on Northern stock with an exercise price of 102.
    (*b*) Recalculate the value of the Northern put option, assuming that it is an American option.

11. The current price of United Carbon (UC) stock is $200. The standard deviation is 22.3 percent a year and the interest rate is 21 percent a year. A 1-year call option on UC has an exercise price of $180.
    (*a*) Use the Black-Scholes model to value the call option on UC.
    (*b*) Use the formula given in Section 21-3 to calculate the up and down moves that you would use if you valued the UC option with the one-period

binomial method. Now value the option using the one-period binomial method.

(c) Now recalculate the up and down moves and revalue the option using the two-period binomial method.

(d) Use your answer to part (c) to calculate the option delta (i) today, (ii) next period if the stock price rises, and (iii) next period if the stock price falls. Show at each point how you would replicate a call option with a levered investment in the company's stock.

12. Options have many uses. They allow you (a) to take a levered position in the asset, (b) to sell the asset short, (c) to insure against a fall in the value of the asset, (d) to hedge against any changes in the asset value and (e) to bet on the asset's variability. Explain *how* you can use options in these ways. Are there other means to achieve the same ends?

13. Suppose you construct an option hedge by buying a levered position in delta shares of stock and selling one call option. As the share price changes the option delta changes and you will need to adjust your hedge. You can minimize the cost of adjustments if changes in the stock price have only a small effect on the option delta. Construct an example to show whether the option delta is likely to vary more if you hedge with an in-the-money option, an at-the-money option, or an out-of-the-money option.

14. Suppose you expect to need a new plant ready to produce turbo-encabulators in 36 months. If design A is chosen, construction must begin immediately. Design B is more expensive, but you can wait 12 months before breaking ground. Figure 21-6 shows the cumulative present value of construction costs

FIGURE 21-6
Cumulative construction cost of the two plant designs. Plant A takes 36 months to build, plant B only 24. But plant B costs more.

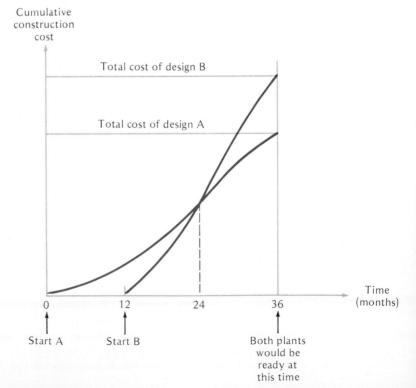

for the two designs up to the 36-month deadline. Assume that the designs, once built, are equally efficient and have equal production capacity.

A standard discounted cash flow analysis ranks design A ahead of design B. But suppose the demand for turbo-encabulators falls and the new factory is not needed; then, as Figure 21-6 shows, the firm is better off with design B provided the project is abandoned before month 24.

Describe this situation as the choice between two (complex) call options. Then describe the same situation in terms of (complex) abandonment put options. The two descriptions should imply identical payoffs to each design, given optimal exercise strategies.

15. In August 1986 Salomon Brothers issued 4-year Standard & Poor's 500 Index Subordinated Notes (SPINS). These pay no interest but at maturity the investor receives the face value plus a possible bonus. This bonus is equal to $1000 times the proportionate appreciation in the market index.
   (a) What would be the value of SPINS if issued today?
   (b) If Salomon Brothers wished to hedge itself against a rise in the market index, how should it do so?

22 Warrants and Convertibles

Many debt issues are either packages of bonds and warrants or convertibles. The warrant gives its owner the right to buy other company securities. A convertible bond gives its owner the right to exchange the bond for other securities.

There is also convertible preferred stock—it is often used to finance mergers, for example. Convertible preferred gives its owner the right to exchange the preferred share for other securities.

What are these strange hybrids, and how should you value them? Why are they issued? We will answer each of these questions in turn.

22-1 WHAT IS A WARRANT?

A significant proportion of private placement bonds and a smaller proportion of public issues are sold with warrants. In addition, warrants are sometimes attached to issues of preferred stock or given to investment bankers as compensation for underwriting services.

In July 1983, MCI Communications raised a record $1 billion by selling packages of bonds and warrants. The package consisted of one $9\frac{1}{2}$ percent subordinated note due 1993 plus 18 warrants. Each warrant gave the right to buy one share of common stock for $55 at any time before August 1988. Since the price of the common at time of issue was $42, this exercise price was 31 percent above the initial share price. The package, or "unit," was issued at $1000.

Occasionally bonds and warrants can be traded only as a package, but the MCI warrants were detachable. This means that they could be traded separately as soon as the issue was distributed.

The warrant holder was not entitled to vote or to receive dividends. But the exercise price of the warrant was adjusted for any stock dividends or stock splits. For example, when MCI subsequently split its stock 2 for 1, it also split the warrants 2 for 1 and reduced the exercise price per warrant to $55/2 = \$27.50$.

The MCI issue had two special features. First, instead of paying out $55 in cash to exercise the warrant, the holder can choose instead to hand over bonds with a face value of $55. If the bond is worth less than $1000, it pays to hand over the bond; if it is worth more than $1000, it is better to use cash.

Second, after 1986 the company has the right to repurchase each warrant for $17 as long as the stock price exceeds $82.50. By announcing that it intends to repurchase, the company can effectively force the warrant holders to exercise.[1]

---

[1] The MCI warrant is fairly standard but you do occasionally encounter "funnies." For example, Emerson Electric has issued a warrant where the owner gets some money back if the warrant is *not* exercised. There are also "income warrants" that make a regular interest payment.

FIGURE 22-1
Relationship between warrant value and stock price. The heavy line is the lower limit for warrant value. Warrant value falls to the lower limit just before the option expires. Before expiration, warrant value lies on a curve like the one shown here.

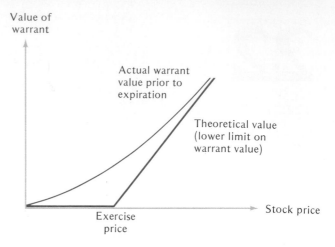

Value of warrant

Actual warrant value prior to expiration

Theoretical value (lower limit on warrant value)

Exercise price

Stock price

Valuing Warrants

As a trained option spotter (having read Chapter 20), you have probably already classified the MCI warrant as a 5-year American call option exercisable at $55. You can depict the relationship between the value of the warrant and the value of the common stock with our standard option shorthand, as in Figure 22-1. The lower limit on the value of the warrant is the heavy line in the figure.[2] If the price of MCI stock is less than $55, the lower limit on the warrant price is zero; if the price of the stock is greater than $55, the lower limit is equal to the stock price minus $55. Investors in warrants sometimes refer to this lower limit as the *theoretical* value of the warrant. It is a misleading term because both theory and practice tell us that before the final exercise date the value of the warrant should lie *above* the lower limit, on a curve like the one shown in Figure 22-1.

The height of this curve depends on two things. As we explained in Section 20-3, it depends on the variance of the stock returns per period (σ^2) times the number of periods before the option expires ($\sigma^2 t$). It also depends on the rate of interest times the length of the option period ($r_f t$). Of course as time runs out on a warrant, its price snuggles closer and closer to the lower bound. On the final day of its life, its price hits the lower bound.

Two Complications: Dividends and Dilution

If the warrant has no unusual features[3] and the stock pays no dividends, then the value of the option can be estimated from the Black-Scholes formula described in Section 20-4.

But there is a problem when warrants are issued against dividend-paying stocks. The warrant holder is not entitled to dividends. In fact the warrant holder loses every time a cash dividend is paid, because the dividend reduces stock price and thus reduces the value of the warrant. It may pay to exercise the warrant before maturity in order to capture the extra income.[4]

---

[2] Do you remember why this is a lower limit? What would happen if, by some accident, the warrant price was *less* than the stock price minus $55? (See Section 20-3.)

[3] We have already seen that in the case of the MCI warrant there *are* some special features. The holder has the option to pay the exercise money in cash or in bonds and the company has the option to repurchase the warrants. Thus there are two mini-options hidden inside the main option.

[4] This cannot make sense unless the dividend payment is larger than the interest that could be earned on the exercise price. By *not* exercising, the warrant holder keeps the exercise price and can put this money to work.

Remember that the Black-Scholes option-valuation formula assumes that the stock pays no dividends. Thus it will not give the theoretically correct value for a warrant issued by a dividend-paying firm. However, we showed in Chapter 21 how you can use the one-step-at-a-time binomial method to value options on dividend-paying stocks.

Another complication is that exercising the warrants increases the number of shares. Therefore, exercise means that the firm's assets and profits are spread over a larger number of shares. For example, MCI's net income in 1984 was $59 million and it had 234 million shares outstanding.[5] So earnings per share were $59/234 = \$.25$. If the warrants had been exercised in 1984, there would have been $234 + 36 = 270$ million shares outstanding. Unless net income was increased by the influx of cash from exercise, earnings per share would have fallen to $59/270 = \$.22$. Firms with significant amounts of warrants or convertible issues outstanding are now required to report earnings on a "fully diluted" basis.

This problem of *dilution* never arises with call options. If you buy or sell an option on the Chicago Board Options Exchange, you have no effect on the number of shares outstanding.

Example: Valuing United Glue's Warrants	United Glue has just issued a $2 million package of debt and warrants. Here are some basic data that we can use to value the warrants:

- Number of shares outstanding $= N = 1$ million
- Current stock price $= P = \$12$
- Number of warrants issued per share outstanding $= q = .10$
- Total number of warrants issued $= Nq = 100,000$
- Exercise price of warrants $= EX = \$10$
- Time to expiration of warrants $= t = 4$ years
- Annual standard deviation of stock price changes $= \sigma = .40$
- Rate of interest $= r = 10$ percent

Suppose that without the warrants the debt is worth $1.5 million. Then investors must be paying $.5 million for the warrants:

$$\frac{\text{Cost of}}{\text{warrants}} = \frac{\text{total amount}}{\text{of financing}} - \frac{\text{value of loan}}{\text{without warrants}}$$

$$500,000 = 2,000,000 \quad - 1,500,000$$

$$\text{Each warrant costs investors } \frac{500,000}{100,000} = \$5$$

The following table shows the market value of United's assets and liabilities both before and after the issue:

Before the issue:

Market Value Balance Sheet
(in millions)

Existing assets	$16	$ 4	Existing loans
			Common stock (1 million shares) at $12 a share)
		12	
Total	$16	$16	Total

[5] Adjusted for the 2-for-1 stock split in 1983.

After the issue:

Market Value Balance Sheet
(in millions)

Existing assets	$16	$ 4	Existing loans
New assets financed			New loan without
by debt and warrants	2	1.5	warrants
		5.5	Total debt
		.5	Warrants
		12	Common stock
		12.5	Total equity
Total	$18	$18	Total

Now let us take a stab at checking whether the warrants are really worth the $500,000 that investors are paying for them. Remember that the warrant is a call option to buy United stock. The stock does not pay a dividend. Therefore we can use the call option tables in Appendix Table 6 to value the warrants. First we need two items of data:

$$\text{Standard deviation} \times \text{square root of time} = \sigma\sqrt{t} = .40\sqrt{4} = .80$$

$$\frac{\text{Share price divided by PV (exercise money)}}{} = \frac{P}{PV(EX)} = \frac{12}{10/(1.1)^4} = 1.75$$

From Appendix Table 6, we find

$$\frac{\text{Call option value}}{\text{Share price}} = \frac{C}{P} = .511$$

Therefore,

$$\text{Call option value} = .511 \times \text{share price} = .511 \times 12 = \$6.13$$

Thus the warrant issue looks to be a good deal for investors and a bad deal for United. Investors are paying $5 a share for warrants that are worth $6.13.

*How the Value of United Warrants Is Affected by Dilution

Unfortunately, our calculations for United warrants do not tell the whole story. Remember that when investors exercise a traded call or put option, there is no change in either the company's assets or the number of shares outstanding. But, if United's warrants are exercised, the number of shares outstanding will increase by $Nq = 100,000$. Also the assets will increase by the amount of the exercise money ($Nq \times EX = 100,000 \times \$10 = \$1$ million). In other words, there will be dilution. We need to allow for this dilution when we value the warrants.

Let us call the value of United's equity V:

$$\text{Value of equity} = V = \text{value of United's total assets} - \text{value of debt}$$

If the warrants are exercised, equity value will increase by the amount of the exercise money to $V + NqEX$. At the same time the number of shares will increase to $N + Nq$. So the share price after the warrants are exercised will be

$$\text{Share price after exercise} = \frac{V + NqEX}{N + Nq}$$

At maturity the warrant holder can choose to let the warrants lapse or to exercise them and receive the share price less the exercise price. Thus the value of the warrants will be the share price minus the exercise price or zero, whichever is the higher. Another way to write this is

$$\text{Warrant value at maturity} = \text{maximum} \left(\frac{\text{share}}{\text{price}} - \frac{\text{exercise}}{\text{price,}} \; \text{zero} \right)$$

$$= \text{maximum} \left(\frac{V + NqEX}{N + Nq} - EX, \; 0 \right)$$

$$= \text{maximum} \left(\frac{V/N - EX}{1 + q}, \; 0 \right)$$

$$= \frac{1}{1 + q} \, \text{maximum} \left(\frac{V}{N} - EX, \; 0 \right)$$

This tells us the effect of dilution on the value of United's warrants. The warrant value is the value of $1/(1 + q)$ call options written on the stock of an alternative firm with the same total equity value V, *but with no outstanding warrants*. The alternative firm's stock price would be equal to V/N—that is, the total value of United's equity (V) divided by the number of shares outstanding (N).[6] The stock price of this alternative firm is more variable than United's stock price. So when we value the call option on the alternative firm, we must remember to use the standard deviation of the changes in V/N.

Now we can recalculate the value of United's warrants allowing for dilution. First, we find the value of one call option on the stock of an alternative firm with a stock price of V/N:

$$\text{Current equity value of alternative firm} = V = \frac{\text{value of United's}}{\text{total assets}} - \frac{\text{value of}}{\text{loans}}$$

$$= 18 - 5.5 = \$12.5 \text{ million}$$

$$\text{Current share price of alternative firm} = \frac{V}{N} = \frac{12.5 \text{ million}}{1 \text{ million}} = \$12.50$$

To use the option table we calculate

$$\text{Share price divided by PV(exercise price)} = 12.50 \div \frac{10}{(1.1)^4} = 1.83$$

---

[6] The modifications to allow for dilution when valuing warrants were originally proposed in F. Black and M. Scholes, ''The Pricing of Options and Corporate Liabilities,'' *Journal of Political Economy*, **81:** 637–654 (May–June 1973), pp. 648, 649. Our exposition follows a discussion in D. Galai and M. I. Schneller, ''Pricing of Warrants and the Valuation of the Firm,'' *Journal of Finance*, **33:** 1333–1342 (December 1978).

Also, suppose the standard deviation of the share price changes of the alternative firm is σ* = .41.[7] Then

$$\frac{\text{Standard}}{\text{deviation}} \times \frac{\text{square root}}{\text{of time}} = \sigma^* \times \sqrt{t} = .41 \times \sqrt{4} = .82$$

Using a little interpolation in Appendix Table 6, we find

$$\frac{\text{Call option value}}{\text{share price}} = \frac{C}{P} = .53 \text{ (approximately)}$$

Therefore,

$$\frac{\text{Value of call on}}{\text{alternative firm}} = \frac{C}{P} \times \frac{V}{N} = .53 \times 12.50 = \$6.63$$

The value of United warrants is equal to

$$\frac{1}{1 + q} \times \frac{\text{value of call on}}{\text{alternative firm}} = \frac{1}{1.1} \times 6.63 = \$6.02$$

This is a somewhat lower value than we computed when we ignored dilution, but still a bad deal for United.

It may sound from all this as if you need to know the value of United warrants to compute their value. This is not so. The formula does not call for warrant value but for V, the value of United's equity (that is, the shares *plus* warrants). Given equity value, the formula calculates how the overall value of equity should be split up between stock and warrants. Thus, suppose that United's underwriter advises that $500,000 extra can be raised by issuing a package of bonds and warrants rather than the bonds alone. Is this a fair price? You can check using the Black-Scholes formula with the adjustment for dilution.

Finally, notice that these modifications are necessary to apply the Black-Scholes formula to value a warrant. They are not needed by the warrant holder, who must decide whether to exercise at maturity. If at maturity the price of the stock exceeds the exercise price of the warrant, the warrant holder will of course exercise.

---

[7] How in practice could we compute σ*? It would be easy if we could wait until the warrants had been trading for some time. In that case σ* could be computed from the returns on a package of *all* the company's shares and warrants. In the present case we need to value the warrants *before* they start trading. We argue as follows. The standard deviation of the *assets* before the issue is equal to the standard deviation of a package of the common stock and the existing loans. For example, suppose that the company's debt is risk-free and that the standard deviation of stock returns *before* the bond-warrant issue is 38 percent (slightly lower than the standard deviation of the common stock after the issue). Then we calculate the standard deviation of the initial assets as follows:

$$\frac{\text{Standard deviation}}{\text{of initial assets}} = \frac{\text{proportion in}}{\text{common stock}} \times \frac{\text{standard deviation}}{\text{of common stock}}$$

$$= \frac{12}{16} \times 38 = 28.5\%$$

Now suppose that the assets after the issue are equally risky. Then

$$\frac{\text{Standard deviation of}}{\text{assets after issue}} = \frac{\text{proportion of equity}}{\text{after issue}} \times \frac{\text{standard deviation}}{\text{of equity } (\sigma^*)}$$

$$28.5 = \frac{12.5}{18} \times \frac{\text{standard deviation}}{\text{of equity } (\sigma^*)}$$

Standard deviation of equity (σ*) = 41%

Warrants on Bonds

Most warrants are changeable into common stock, but some companies have issued warrants on bonds.[8] For example, in 1982 Citicorp sold 100,000 warrants which gave the option to buy 11 percent 7-year Citicorp notes at any time within the next 3 years.

The Black-Scholes option model assumes that the price of the underlying asset is free to wander randomly, so that the further you look out into the future, the wider is the range of possible prices. But the price of a bond is not free to wander in this happy-go-lucky fashion; as maturity approaches, bond price gets pulled back to its face value. Because bonds have a date with destiny, the Black-Scholes model gives only a rough estimate of the value of a short-term warrant on a bond and a worse estimate of the value of a long-term warrant on a bond. In these cases you need to use an option valuation model that recognizes the way that bond prices vary over time.[9]

22-2 WHAT IS A CONVERTIBLE BOND?

The convertible bond is a close relative of the bond-warrant package. Also, many companies choose to issue convertible preferred as an alternative to issuing packages of preferred stock and warrants. We will concentrate on convertible bonds. But almost all our comments also apply to convertible preferred issues.

In 1983 MCI issued not only warrants, but also $400 million of 7¾ percent convertible bonds due in 2003.[10] These could be converted at any time into 19.18 shares of common stock. In other words, the owner had a 20-year option to return the bond to MCI and receive 19.18 shares of MCI stock in exchange. The number of shares for each bond is called the bond's *conversion ratio*. The conversion ratio of the MCI bond was 19.18.

In order to receive 19.18 shares of MCI stock you had to surrender bonds with a face value of $1000. Therefore in order to receive one share, you had to surrender a face amount of $1000/19.18 = 52.13. This figure is called the *conversion price*. Anybody who bought the bond at $1000 in order to convert it into 19.18 shares paid the equivalent of $52.13 per share.

At the time of issue the price of MCI stock was $44. Therefore the conversion price was 19 percent higher than the stock price.

Convertibles are usually protected against stock splits or stock dividends. When MCI split its stock 2 for 1, the conversion ratio was increased to 38.37 from 19.18. Thus the conversion price dropped to $1000/38.37 = 26.06.

The MCI convertible is a fairly typical issue, but you do come across more complicated cases. Often the conversion price is stepped up over time, and Litton Industries once issued a convertible in which the conversion price was stepped

---

[8] Now and then you encounter "option warrants" that give you a choice between buying equity or debt. One or two companies have also issued warrants that give the holder the right to buy some commodity.

[9] The following authors have developed more elaborate versions of the Black-Scholes model that can be used for pricing warrants on bonds: G. Courtadon, "The Pricing of Options on Default-Free Bonds," *Journal of Financial and Quantitative Analysis*, **17:** 75–100 (March 1982); and M. J. Brennan and E. S. Schwartz, "Alternative Methods for Valuing Debt Options," *Finance*, **4:** 119–137 (October 1983).

[10] The MCI issue was a convertible subordinated debenture. The term *subordinated* indicates that the bond is a junior debt—its holders will be at the bottom of the heap of creditors in the event of default. A *debenture* is simply an unsecured bond. Therefore there are no specific assets that have been reserved to pay off the holders in the event of default. There is more about these terms in Section 24-3.

down.[11] Also in the last few years it has been increasingly common for firms to issue convertibles that can be exchanged for other bonds. So-called "flip-flop" bonds give the investor the option to change back and forth several times.

Valuing Convertible Bonds

The owner of a convertible owns a bond and a call option on the firm's stock. So does the owner of a bond-warrant package. There are differences, of course, the most important being the requirement that a convertible owner give up the bond in order to exercise the call option. The owner of a bond-warrant package can (generally) exercise the warrant for cash and keep the bond. Nevertheless, understanding convertibles is easier if you analyze them first as bonds and then as call options.

The price of a convertible bond depends on its *bond value* and its *conversion value*. The bond value is what the bond would sell for if it could *not* be converted. The conversion value is what the bond would sell for if it had to be converted immediately.

How would we compute the bond value of the MCI convertible? This clearly depends on the general level of interest rates and investors' perceptions of the risk of default. Suppose that we catch this convertible at a time when similar nonconvertible issues are yielding 13 percent. Also suppose that the MCI convertible has a remaining maturity of 20 years. Then its bond value is found by discounting the $73.4 coupon and the final $1000 principal repayment at 13 percent:

$$\text{Bond value} = \sum_{t=1}^{20} \frac{\$73.4}{(1.13)^t} + \frac{\$1000}{(1.13)^{20}} = \$602$$

Bond value establishes a lower bound, or "floor," to the price of a convertible issue. But the height of the floor depends on how well the issuing firm is doing. If it falls on hard times the bonds may not be worth very much. Figure 22-2a illustrates this by plotting bond value against firm value. Note that low firm values and low bond prices go together; so the "floor" can have a nasty slope. In the worst case, when the firm is worthless, its bonds are also worthless. On the other hand, bond value increases if the firm does well. The upper limit to the bond value is what it would be worth if the probability of default were zero.

Conversion value is the value of the bond if holders converted immediately. Investors usually calculate conversion value by multiplying the stock price by the number of shares into which each bond can be converted. The MCI bond can be converted into 38.37 shares. Thus, if the stock price is $20, conversion value is $38.37 \times \$20 = \$767$. Figure 22-2b shows that conversion value rises in line with the value of the firm.

A convertible can *never sell for less* than its conversion value. If it did, smart investors would buy the convertible, exchange it for stock, and sell the stock. Their profit would be equal to the difference between the conversion value and the price of the convertible.

Therefore there are *two* lower bounds to the price of any convertible: its bond value and its conversion value. The heavy line in Figure 22-2c shows their combined effect. When the firm does well, conversion value exceeds bond value; the

[11] Convertibles are usually issued at their face value, that is, 100 percent of par. Since they consist of a bond plus an option, the underlying bond at issue is worth less than 100. Thus the value of the bond can be expected to increase between issue and maturity. This means that for most convertibles the value of the bond that must be surrendered (i.e., the exercise price of the option) increases over time. For very low coupon convertibles these changes in exercise price can be dramatic.

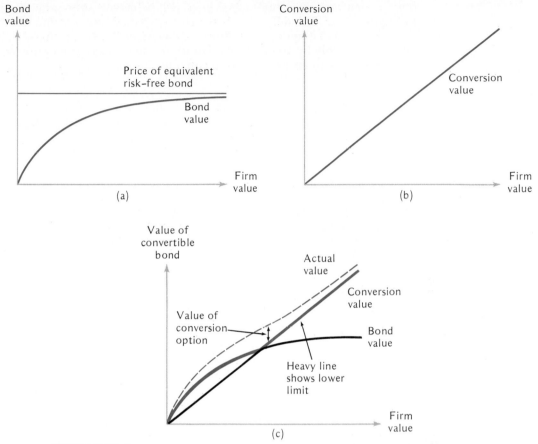

FIGURE 22-2

(*a*) As the market value of the firm increases, debt is better secured and bond prices rise. Thus if the firm does extremely well, the bond value of a convertible approaches the price of an equivalent nonconvertible bond with no risk of default. On the other hand, bond values fall sharply if the firm's value falls to a very low level. (*b*) Conversion value (the value of a convertible bond if converted immediately) rises in proportion to firm value. (*c*) Value of a convertible bond as a function of firm value. The heavy line shows the lower limit to the value of a convertible bond: either bond value or conversion value, whichever is larger. The actual value of the bond exceeds the lower limit (except at maturity). The difference between the dashed line and the heavy line is the value of the conversion option.

investor would choose to convert if forced to make an immediate choice. Thus the convertible's value must at least equal its conversion value.

Bond value exceeds conversion value when the firm does poorly and firm value is low. The owners of the convertible issue would hold onto their bonds if forced to make an immediate decision for or against conversion. In this case bond value is the effective lower bound.

Of course convertible bondholders *do not have to make a now-or-never choice for or against conversion.* They can wait and then, with the benefit of hindsight, take whatever course turns out to give them the highest payoff. Thus a convertible is always worth *more* than its lower-bound value (except when time runs out at the bond's maturity). Its actual selling price will behave as shown by the dashed line in Figure 22-2c. The difference between the dashed line and the lower bound is the value of a call option on the firm. Remember, however, that this option can be exercised only by giving up the bond. In other words, the option to convert is a call option with an exercise price equal to the bond value.

Dividends and Dilution Revisited

If you want to value a convertible, it is easiest to break the problem down into two parts. First estimate bond value, then add the value of the conversion option.

When you value the conversion option, you need to look out for the same things that make warrants more tricky to value than traded options. For example, you must remember that the convertible owner is missing out on the dividends on the common stock. If these dividends are higher than the interest on the bonds, it may pay to convert before the final exercise date in order to pick up the extra cash income.

Dilution may also be important. If the bonds are converted, the company saves on its interest payments and is relieved of having to eventually repay the loan; on the other hand, net profits have to be divided among a larger number of shares.[12] Companies are obliged to show in their financial statements how earnings would be affected by conversion.[13]

Forcing Conversion

Companies usually retain an option to buy back or "call" the convertible bond at a preset price. If the company calls the bond, the owner has a brief period, usually about 30 days, within which to convert the bond or surrender it. If the bond is surrendered, the investor receives the call price in cash.

Calling the bond obviously does not affect the total size of the company pie, but it can affect the size of the individual slices. In other words, conversion has no effect on the total value of the firm's assets, but it does affect how asset value is *distributed* among the different classes of security holders. Therefore, if you want to maximize your shareholders' slice of the pie, you must minimize the convertible bondholders'. That means you must not call the bonds if they are worth *less* than the call price, for that would be giving the bondholders an unnecessary present. Similarly, you must not allow the bonds to remain uncalled if their value is *above* the call price, for that would not be minimizing the value of the bonds. This gives a rule for calling a convertible bond: *Call the bond when, and only when, its value reaches the call price.*

Managers are fickle creatures. No sooner do they issue convertibles than they seem to want to get rid of them. They often complain of "overhanging" convertibles—that is, ones that are not being converted. They feel that overhanging convertibles limit their freedom of action. In view of these complaints, you might expect that managers would be only too eager to call their convertibles. But Ingersoll has found that in practice it is just the reverse. Firms seldom call their

---

[12] Thus investors are imprecise when they calculate conversion value as the share price times the number of shares into which each bond is converted. A convertible bond actually gives an option to acquire a fraction of the "new equity"—the equity *after* conversion. When conversion occurs the *total* value of equity (price per share times number of outstanding shares) is increased because one of the firm's debt liabilities is extinguished. On the other hand, the number of shares is increased. If conversion is worthwhile, price per share is less than it would be if the conversion option did not exist. Any formal valuation model for convertible bonds has to take this effect into account. The adjustments would be similar to those for warrants, presented earlier in this chapter.

[13] These "diluted" earnings take into account the extra shares, but not the savings in interest payments.

TABLE 22-1
Convertible bonds outstanding in June 1987 with high conversion values
relative to call price

Issuing Firm	Coupon	Maturity	Call Price	Conversion Value
Altec Corp.	15.00	1995	105.87	281⅛
Ashland Oil	4.75	1993	101.15	187⅞
Baxter Travenol	4.75	2001	101.45	195⅛
Black & Decker	4.00	1992	100.00	227⅜
Hercules, Inc.	6.50	1999	102.60	166¾
Kellwood Co.	9.00	1999	107.00	343⅜
MacMillan, Inc.	4.00	1992	100.00	497⅜
McDonnell-Douglas	4.47	1991	100.00	223⅝
Pfizer, Inc.	4.00	1997	101.00	274⅛
Ralston Purina	5.76	2000	102.30	525⅞

Notes:
1. Data as of June 1987, from Moody's Bond Record.
2. All issues are convertible subordinated debentures.
3. Coupons, call prices, and conversion values are given as percentages of par value.

convertibles until they are worth *more* than their call price. For example, Ingersoll looked at 124 firms that called their convertible bonds between 1968 and 1975. All but six delayed the call too long, and the typical company waited until conversion value was 44 percent above the call price.[14]

Table 22-1 shows several convertible issues outstanding in 1987. Each of the issues has conversion value well above the current call price. Therefore these companies could have called the bonds and forced conversion. Finance theory implies that they should have done so. The reason for firms' reluctance to call convertibles is not known.[15]

Of course Table 22-1 is not a random sample of convertible issues. We chose extreme cases to illustrate a point. We could have presented another table of convertible issues with conversion values well below call prices.

22-3 THE DIFFERENCE BETWEEN WARRANTS AND CONVERTIBLES

We have dwelt on the basic similarity between warrants and convertibles. Now let us look at some of the differences.

1. *Warrants are usually issued privately.* Packages of bonds with warrants or preferred stock with warrants tend to be more common in private placements. By contrast most convertible bonds are issued publicly.

---

[14] J. E. Ingersoll, "An Examination of Corporate Call Policies on Convertible Securities," *Journal of Finance,* **32:** 463–478 (May 1977).

[15] Here is one ingenious explanation. Imagine two firms, each with a convertible bond that is selling above its call price. The manager of the first firm believes his stock is undervalued. He will therefore be confident that the bond will be converted eventually and will conclude that there is little to be lost by not forcing conversion now. The manager of the second firm believes her stock is *over*valued. So she can help her shareholders by forcing conversion before the stock price falls. Of course investors will realize that managers of overvalued stocks have the greater incentive to force conversion and will mark down the price of the stock when the bond is called. The managers of the undervalued firms will prefer not to be tarred with the same brush and will therefore not force conversion even though they would otherwise do so. See M. Harris and A. Raviv, "A Sequential Signalling Model of Convertible Debt Call Policy," *Journal of Finance,* **40:** 1263–1282 (December 1985).

2. *Warrants can be detached.* When you buy a convertible, the bond and the option are bundled up together. You cannot sell them separately. This may be inconvenient. If your tax position or attitude to risk inclines you to bonds, you may not want to hold options as well. Sometimes warrants are also "nondetachable." But usually you can keep the bond and sell the warrant.

3. *Warrants may be issued on their own.* Warrants do not have to be issued in conjunction with other securities. Often they are used to compensate investment bankers for underwriting services. Many companies also give their executives long-term options to buy stock. These executive stock options are not usually called warrants but that is exactly what they are. Companies can also sell warrants on their own directly to investors, though they rarely do so.

4. *Warrants are exercised for cash.* When you convert a bond, you simply exchange your bond for common stock. When you exercise warrants, you generally put up extra cash, though occasionally you have to surrender the bond or can choose to do so. This means that bond-warrant packages and convertible bonds usually have different effects on the company's cash flow and on its capital structure.

5. *A package of bonds and warrants may be taxed differently.* There are some tax differences between warrants and convertibles. Suppose that you are wondering whether to issue a convertible bond at 100. You can think of this convertible as a package of a straight bond worth, say, 90 and an option worth 10. If you issue the bond and option separately, the IRS will note that the bond is issued at a discount and that its price will rise by 10 points over its life. They will allow you, the issuer, to spread this prospective price appreciation over the life of the bond and deduct it from your taxable profits. They will also allocate the prospective price appreciation to the taxable income of the bondholder. Thus, by issuing a package of bonds and warrants rather than a convertible, you may reduce the tax paid by the issuing company and increase the tax paid by the investor.[16]

22-4 WHY DO COMPANIES ISSUE WARRANTS AND CONVERTIBLES?

You hear many arguments for issuing warrants and convertibles but most of them have a "Heads I win, tails you lose" flavor. For example, here is one such argument:[17]

> *A company that wishes to sell common stock must usually offer the new stock at 10 percent to 20 percent below the market price for the flotation to be a success.[18] However, if warrants are sold for cash, exercisable at 20 percent to 50 percent above the market price of the common, the result will be equivalent to selling common stock at a premium rather than a discount; and if the warrants are never exercised, the proceeds from their sale will become a clear profit to the company.*

There is something that you should find immediately suspicious about an argument like this. If the shareholder inevitably wins, the warrant holder must inev-

---

[16] See J. D. Finnerty, "The Case for Issuing Synthetic Convertible Bonds," *Midland Corporate Finance Journal,* **4:** 73–82 (Fall 1986).

[17] See S. T. Kassouf: *Evaluation of Convertible Securities,* Analytical Investors, New York, 1966, p. 6. We hasten to add that Kassouf's lapse is *not* characteristic of him. He is a respected scholar who has made important contributions to finance.

[18] This is an overestimate of the discount associated with seasoned issues. See Section 15-3.

itably lose. But that doesn't make sense. Surely there must be some price at which it pays to buy warrants.

Suppose that your company's stock is priced at $100 and that you are considering an issue of warrants exercisable at $120. You believe that you can sell these warrants at $10. If the stock price subsequently fails to reach $120, the warrants will not be exercised. You will have sold warrants for $10 each, which with the benefit of hindsight proved to be worthless to the buyer. If the stock price reaches $130, say, the warrants will be exercised. Your firm will have received the initial payment of $10 *plus* the exercise price of $120. On the other hand, it will have issued to the warrant holders stock worth $130 per share. The net result is a standoff. You have received a payment of $130 in exchange for a liability worth $130.

Think now what happens if the stock price rises above $130. Perhaps it goes to $200. In this case the warrant issue will end up producing a loss of $70. This is not a cash outflow but an opportunity loss. The firm receives $130, but in this case it could have sold stock for $200. On the other hand, the warrant holders gain $70: They invest $130 in cash to acquire stock that they can sell, if they like, for $200.

Our example is oversimplified—for instance, we have kept quiet about the time value of money and risk—but we hope it has made the basic point. When you sell warrants, you are selling options and getting cash in exchange. Options are valuable securities. If they are properly priced this is a fair trade—in other words, it is a zero NPV transaction.

You can see why the quotation is misleading. When it refers to "selling stock at a premium," the implicit comparison is with the market value of the stock today. The relevant comparison is with what it may be worth tomorrow.

Managers often use similar arguments to justify the sale of convertibles. For example, several surveys have revealed two main motives for their use. A large number of managers look on convertibles as "cheap debt." A somewhat higher proportion regard them as a deferred sale of stock at an attractive price.[19]

We have seen that a convertible is like a package of a straight bond and an option. The difference between the market value of the convertible and that of the straight bond is therefore the price investors place on the call option. The convertible is "cheap" only if this price overvalues the option.

What then of the other managers—those who regard the issue as a deferred sale of common stock? A convertible bond gives you the right to buy stock by giving up a bond.[20] Bondholders may decide to do this, but then again they may not. Thus issues of a convertible bond *may* amount to a deferred stock issue. But if the firm *needs* equity capital, a convertible issue is an unreliable way of getting it.

Taken at their face value the motives of management are irrational. Convertibles are not just cheap debt nor are they a deferred sale of stock. But we suspect that these simple phrases encapsulate some more complex and rational motives.

Notice that convertibles tend to be issued by the smaller and more speculative

---

[19] See, for example, E. F. Brigham: "An Analysis of Convertible Debentures: Theory and Some Empirical Evidence," *Journal of Finance*, **21:** 35–54 (March 1966).

[20] That is much the same as already having the stock together with the right to sell it for the convertible's bond value. In other words, instead of thinking of a convertible as a bond plus a call option, you could think of it as the stock plus a put option. Now you see why it is wrong to think of a convertible as equivalent to the sale of stock; it is equivalent to the sale of both stock *and* a put option. If there is any possibility that investors will want to hold onto their bond, the put option will have some value.

firms. They are almost invariably unsecured and generally subordinated.[21] Now put yourself in the position of a potential investor. You are approached by a small firm with an untried product line that wants to issue some junior unsecured debt. You know that if things go well, you will get your money back, but if they do not, you could easily be left with nothing. Since the firm is in a new line of business, it is difficult to assess the chances of trouble. Therefore you don't know what the fair rate of interest is. Also you may be worried that once you have made the loan, management will be tempted to run extra risks. It may borrow additional senior debt or it may decide to expand its operations and go for broke on your money. In fact, if you charge a very high rate of interest, you could be encouraging this to happen.

What can management do to protect you against a wrong estimate of the risk and to assure you that its intentions are honorable? In crude terms, it can give you a piece of the action. You don't mind the company running unanticipated risks as long as you share in the gains as well as the losses.[22]

Convertible securities and warrants make sense whenever it is unusually costly to assess the risk of debt or whenever investors are worried that management may not act in the bondholders' interest.

The relatively low coupon rate on convertible bonds may also be a convenience for rapidly growing firms facing heavy capital expenditures. They may be willing to give up the conversion option to reduce immediate cash requirements for debt service. Without the conversion option, lenders might demand extremely high (promised) interest rates to compensate for the probability of default. This would not only force the firm to raise still more capital for debt service, but also increase the risk of financial distress. Paradoxically, lenders' attempts to protect themselves against default may actually increase the probability of financial distress by increasing the burden of debt service on the firm.[23]

22-5 SUMMARY

Instead of issuing straight bonds, companies may sell either packages of bonds and warrants or convertible bonds.

A warrant is just a long-term call option issued by the company. You already know a good deal about valuing call options. You know from Chapter 20 that call options must be worth at least as much as the stock price less the exercise price. You know that their value is greatest when they have a long time to expiration, when the underlying stock is risky, and when the interest rate is high.

Warrants are somewhat trickier to value than the call options that are traded on the options exchanges. First, because they are long-term options, it is important to recognize that the warrant holder does not receive any dividends. Second, dilution must be allowed for.

A convertible bond gives its holder the right to swap the bond for common stock. The rate of exchange is usually measured by the *conversion ratio*—that is,

---

[21] The MCI convertible was a subordinated debenture. See footnote 10.

[22] See M. J. Brennan and E. S. Schwartz, "The Case for Convertibles," *Chase Financial Quarterly*, **1:** 27–46 (Spring 1982).

[23] This fact led to an extensive body of literature on "credit rationing." A lender rations credit if it is irrational to lend more to a firm regardless of the interest rate the firm is willing to *promise* to pay. Whether this can happen in efficient, competitive capital markets is controversial. We give an example of credit rationing in Chapter 32. For a review of this literature see E. Baltensperger, "Credit Rationing: Issues and Questions," *Journal of Money, Credit and Banking*, **10:** 170–183 (May 1978).

the number of shares that the investor gets for each bond. Sometimes the rate of exchange is expressed in terms of the *conversion price*—that is, the face value of the bond that must be given up in order to receive one share.

Convertibles are like a package of a bond and a call option. When you evaluate the conversion option you must again remember that the convertible holder does not receive dividends and that conversion results in dilution of the common stock. There are two other things to watch out for. One is the problem of default risk. If the company runs into trouble, you may have not only a worthless conversion option, but also a worthless bond. Second, the company may be able to force conversion by calling the bond. It should do this as soon as the market price of the convertible reaches the call price. Many companies do not call their bonds until well after this point. Nobody knows why.

You hear a variety of arguments for issuing warrants or convertibles. Convertible bonds and bonds with warrants are almost always junior bonds and are frequently issued by risky companies. We think that this says something about the reasons for their issue. Suppose that you are lending to an untried company. You are worried that the company may turn out to be riskier than you thought or that it may issue additional senior bonds. You can try to protect yourself against such eventualities by imposing very restrictive conditions on the debt, but it is often simpler to say that you don't mind the company taking some extra risk as long as you get a piece of the action. The convertible and bond-warrant package give you a chance to participate in the firm's successes as well as its failures. They diminish the possible conflicts of interest between bondholder and stockholder.

FURTHER READING

The items listed in Chapter 20 under ''Further Reading'' are also relevant to this chapter, in particular Black and Scholes's discussion of warrant valuation.

Ingersoll's work represents the ''state of the art'' in valuing convertibles:

J. E. Ingersoll: "A Contingent Claims Valuation of Convertible Securities," *Journal of Financial Economics*, **4:** 289–322 (May 1977).

Ingersoll also examines corporate call policies on convertible bonds in:

J. E. Ingersoll: "An Examination of Corporate Call Policies on Convertible Securities," *Journal of Finance*, **32:** 463–478 (May 1977).

Brennan and Schwartz's paper was written about the same time as Ingersoll's and reaches essentially the same conclusions. They also present a general procedure for valuing convertibles.

M. J. Brennan and E. S. Schwartz: "Convertible Bonds: Valuation and Optimal Strategies for Call and Conversion," *Journal of Finance*, **32:** 1699–1715 (December 1977).

Two useful articles on warrants are:

E. S. Schwartz: "The Valuation of Warrants: Implementing a New Approach," *Journal of Financial Economics*, **4:** 79–93 (January 1977).

D. Galai and M. A. Schneller: "Pricing of Warrants and the Value of the Firm," *Journal of Finance*, **33:** 1333–1342 (December 1978).

For a nontechnical discussion of the pricing of convertibles and the reasons for their use, see:

M. J. Brennan and E. S. Schwartz: "The Case for Convertibles," *Chase Financial Quarterly*, **1:** 27–46 (Spring 1982).

QUIZ

1. Associated Elk warrants entitle the owner to buy one share at $40.
   (a) What is the "theoretical" value of the warrant if the stock price is
      (i) $20?
      (ii) $30?
      (iii) $40?
      (iv) $50?
      (v) $60?
   (b) Plot the theoretical value of the warrant against the stock price.
   (c) Suppose the stock price is $60 and the warrant price is $5. What would you do?

2. In 1972 B. F. Goodrich issued 1.5 million warrants. Each warrant could have been exercised before 1979 at a price of $30 per share. Suppose that the stock price were $20.
   (a) Did the warrant holder have a vote?
   (b) Did the warrant holder receive dividends?
   (c) If the stock were split 3 for 1, how would the exercise price have been adjusted?
   (d) Suppose that, instead of reducing the exercise price after a 3-for-1 split, the company gave each warrant holder the right to buy *three* shares at $30 apiece. Would this have had the same effect?
   (e) What was the "theoretical" value of the warrant?
   (f) Prior to maturity, was the warrant worth more or less than the "theoretical" value?
   (g) *Other things being equal,* would the warrant have been more or less valuable if:
      (i) The company increased its rate of dividend payout?
      (ii) The interest rate declined?
      (iii) The stock became riskier?
      (iv) The company extended the exercise period?
      (v) The company reduced the exercise price?
   (h) A few companies issue perpetual warrants (that is, warrants with no final exercise date). Suppose that the Goodrich warrant were perpetual. In what circumstances might it make sense for investors to exercise their warrant?

3. Amalgamated Sludge has outstanding 10 million warrants, each of which may be converted into one share of common stock. Assume
   Net income = $40 million
   Number of shares outstanding = 20 million
   (a) Calculate earnings per share.
   (b) Calculate earnings per share on a fully diluted basis.

4. Suppose that Maple Aircraft has issued a 4¾ percent convertible subordinated debenture due 1998. The conversion price is $47.00 and the debenture is callable at 102.75. The market price of the convertible is 91 percent of face value and the price of the common is $41.50. Assume the value of the bond in the absence of a conversion feature is about 65 percent of face value.
   (a) What is the conversion ratio of the debenture?
   (b) If the conversion ratio were 50, what would be the conversion price?
   (c) What is the conversion value?
   (d) At what stock price is the conversion value equal to the bond value?
   (e) Can the market price be less than the conversion value?

(f) How much is the convertible holder paying for the option to buy one share of common stock?

(g) By how much does the common have to rise by 1998 to justify conversion?

(h) When should Maple call the debenture?

QUESTIONS AND PROBLEMS

1. Refer again to the MCI warrant discussed in Section 22-1. When the warrants were issued, MCI had 117 million shares and 18 million warrants outstanding. The warrant's exercise price was $55. Shortly after the issue the MCI stock was split 2 for 1 and the terms of the warrants were adjusted to reflect this.

   (a) After the stock split how many shares and warrants were outstanding?

   (b) What would be the exercise price of the warrants after the split? Would this also be adjusted?

   (c) Suppose that when the warrants expired, the stock price was $35. What would be the value of the warrants at that point?

   (d) Suppose that the stock price was $35 a year *before* expiration. Would the warrants have sold for more or less than your answer to (c)? Would they have sold for their theoretical value? Explain.

   (e) In 1984 MCI's undiluted earnings were $.25 per share. Calculate its diluted earnings per share.

*2. How would you use the Black-Scholes formula to compute the value of the MCI warrant immediately after its issue, assuming a stock price of $42 and a warrant price of $15? Begin by ignoring the problem of dilution. Then go on to describe how dilution would affect your calculations.

3. Occasionally firms extend the life of warrants that would otherwise expire unexercised. What is the cost of doing this?

*4. Here's a question on dilution. The Electric Bassoon Company has outstanding 2000 shares with a total market value of $20,000 *plus* 1000 warrants with a total market value of $5000. Each warrant gives its holders the option to buy one share at $20.

   (a) To value the warrants, you first need to value a call option on an alternative share. What is the current price of this alternative share? How might you calculate its standard deviation?

   (b) Suppose that the value of a call option on this alternative share were $6. Calculate whether the Electric Bassoon warrants were undervalued or overvalued.

5. The Surplus Value Company had $10 million (face value) of convertible bonds outstanding in 1990. Each bond has the following features:

   - Conversion price $25
   - Current call price   105 (percent of face value)
   - Current trading price   130 (percent of face value)
   - Maturity   2000
   - Current stock price $30 (per share)
   - Interest rate   10 (coupon as percent of face value)

   (a) What is the bond's conversion value?

   (b) Can you explain why the bond is selling above conversion value?

   (c) Should Surplus call? What will happen if it does so?

6. Growth-Tech has issued $10 million of a 10 percent subordinated convertible debenture. Assume:

   - Net income = $50 million
   - Number of shares outstanding = 2.5 million
   - Conversion ratio = 50
   - Tax rate = 50 percent

   (a) Calculate earnings per share.
   (b) Calculate earnings per share on a fully diluted basis.
7. Associated Elk warrants have an exercise price of $40. The share price is $50. The dividend on the stock is $3 and the interest rate is 10 percent.
   (a) Would you exercise your warrants now or later? State why.
   (b) If the dividend increased to $5, it could pay to exercise now if the stock price had low variability and it could be better to exercise later if the stock price had high variability. Explain why.
8. "The company's decision to issue warrants should depend on the management's forecast of likely returns on the stock." Do you agree?
9. In each case, state which of the two securities is likely to provide the higher return:
   (a) When the stock price rises (stock *or* convertible bond?).
   (b) When interest rates fall (straight bond *or* convertible bond?).
   (c) When the specific risk of the stock decreases (straight bond *or* convertible bond?).
   (d) When the dividend on the stock increases (stock *or* convertible bond?).
10. Towncorp has issued 3-year warrants to buy 12 percent perpetual debentures at a price of 120 percent. The current interest rate is 12 percent and the standard deviation of returns on the bond is 20 percent. Use the Black-Scholes model to obtain a rough estimate of the value of Towncorp warrants.
11. Moose Stores has outstanding 1 million shares of common stock with a total market value of $40 million. It now announces a rights issue of 1 million warrants at $5 each. Each warrant entitles the owner to buy one Moose share for a price of $30 at any time within the next 5 years. Moose Stores has stated that it will not pay a dividend within this period.

    The standard deviation of the returns on Moose's equity is 20 percent a year, and the interest rate is 8 percent.
    (a) What is the market value of each warrant?
    (b) What is the market value of each share after the warrant issue? (*Hint:* The value of the shares is equal to the total value of the equity less the value of the warrants.)
12. Look again at question 11. Suppose that Moose now forecasts the following dividend payments:

End of Year:	Dividend
1	$2.00
2	3.00
3	4.00
4	5.00
5	6.00

Reestimate the market values of the warrant and stock.

13. Occasionally it is said that issuing convertible bonds is better than issuing stock when the firm's shares are undervalued. Suppose that the financial manager of the Butternut Furniture Company does in fact have inside information indicating that the Butternut stock price is too low. Butternut's future earnings will in fact be higher than investors expect. Suppose further that the inside information cannot be released without giving away a valuable competitive secret. Clearly, selling shares at the present low price would harm Butternut's existing shareholders. Will they also lose if convertible bonds are issued? If they do lose in this case, is the loss more or less than if common stock is issued?

Now suppose that investors forecast earnings accurately, but still undervalue the stock because they overestimate Butternut's actual business risk. Does this change your answers to the questions posed in the preceding paragraph? Explain.

14. Banks or insurance companies sometimes negotiate "equity kickers" when lending money. The firm pays interest and also gives warrants to the lender. Thus the lender has an equity interest in the firm (via the warrants) and shares in the rewards if the firm is successful. Of course, in negotiating the loan, the lender always has the alternative of forgoing the warrants and demanding a higher interest rate instead. What are the advantages of the "equity kicker" arrangement compared to this alternative? In what circumstances would use of the equity kicker be most sensible?

15. Rupert Thorndike, the autocratic CEO of Thorndike Oil, was found dead this morning in a pool of blood on his office floor. He had been shot through the head. Yesterday Thorndike had flatly rejected an offer by T. Spoone Dickens to buy all of Thorndike Oil's assets for $1 billion cash, effective January 1, 1989. With Thorndike out of the way, Dickens's offer will be immediately accepted.

The immediate suspects were Thorndike's two nieces, Doris and Patsy, and his nephew John.

Thorndike Oil's capital structure is as follows:

- *Debt:* $250 million face value, issued in 1965 at a coupon rate of 5 percent, with market value of 60 percent of face value. This debt will be paid off at par if Dickens's offer goes through.
- *Stock:* 30 million shares closing yesterday at $10 per share.
- *Warrants:* Warrants to buy an additional 20 million shares at $10 per share, expiring December 31, 1988. The last trade of the warrants was at $1 per warrant.

Here are Doris, John, and Patsy's stakes in Thorndike Oil:

	Debt (Market Value)	Stock (Number of Shares)	Warrants (Number)
Doris	$6 million	1 million	0
John	0	.5 million	2 million
Patsy	0	1.5 million	1 million

Which niece or nephew stood to gain most (in portfolio value) by eliminating old Thorndike and allowing Dickens's offer to succeed? Explain. Make additional assumptions if you find them necessary.

PART SEVEN

DEBT FINANCING

23

Valuing Risky Debt

How do you estimate the present value of a company's bonds? The answer is simple. You take the cash flows and discount them at the opportunity cost of capital. Therefore if a bond produces cash flows of C dollars per year for N years and is then repaid at its face value ($1000), the present value is

$$\text{PV} = \frac{C}{1 + r_1} + \frac{C}{(1 + r_2)^2} + \cdots + \frac{C}{(1 + r_N)^N} + \frac{\$1000}{(1 + r_N)^N}$$

where $r_1, r_2, \ldots, r_N$ are the appropriate discount rates for the cash flows to be received by the bond's owner in years $1, 2, \ldots, N$.

That is correct as far as it goes but it does not tell us anything about what *determines* the discount rates. For example:

1. In 1945, U.S. Treasury bills offered a return of .4 percent: In May 1987 they offered a return of 5.4 percent. Why does the same security offer radically different yields at different points in time?
2. In May 1987 the U.S. Treasury could borrow for 1 year at an interest rate of about 7 percent: But it had to pay a rate of nearly 9 percent for 20-year loans. Why do bonds maturing at different dates offer different rates of interest? In other words, why is there a *term structure* of interest rates?
3. In May 1987 the United States government could issue long-term bonds at a rate of nearly 9 percent. You could not have borrowed at that rate. Why not? What explains the premium you have to pay?

These questions lead to deep issues which will keep economists simmering for years. But we can give general answers and at the same time present some fundamental ideas.

Why should the financial manager care about these ideas? Who needs to know how bonds are priced as long as the bond market is active and efficient? Efficient markets protect the ignorant trader. If it is necessary to check whether the price is right for a proposed bond issue, you can check the prices of similar bonds. There is no need to worry about the historical behavior of interest rates, about the term structure, or about the other issues discussed in this chapter.

We do not believe that ignorance is desirable even when it is harmless. At least you ought to be able to read *The Wall Street Journal* and talk to investment bankers. More important, you will encounter many problems of bond pricing where there are no similar instruments already traded. How do you evaluate a private placement with a custom-tailored repayment schedule? How about financial leases? In Chapter 26 we will see that they are essentially debt contracts, but often extremely complicated ones, for which traded bonds are not close substitutes. You will find that the terms, concepts, and facts presented in this chapter are essential to the analysis of these and other practical problems in financing covered in later chapters.

We start, therefore, with our first question: "Why does the general level of interest rates change over time?"

23-1   THE CLASSICAL THEORY OF INTEREST

Real Interest Rates

Suppose that everyone knows that there is not going to be any inflation. If so, all interest rates are *real* rates—they include no premium for anticipated inflation. What are the essential determinants of the rate of interest in such a world? The classical economist's answer to this question is summed up in the title of Irving Fisher's great book: *The Theory of Interest: As Determined by Impatience to Spend Income and Opportunity to Invest It.*[1] The real interest rate, according to Fisher, is the price which equates the supply and demand for capital. The supply depends on people's willingness to save—that is, to postpone consumption.[2] The demand depends on the opportunities for productive investment.

For example, suppose that investment opportunities generally improve. Firms have more good projects, and so are willing to invest more at any interest rate. Therefore, the rate has to rise to induce individuals to save the additional amount that firms want to invest.[3] Conversely, if investment opportunities deteriorate, there will be a fall in the real interest rate.

Fisher's theory emphasizes that the real rate of interest depends on real phenomena. A high aggregate willingness to save may be associated with such factors as high aggregate wealth (because wealthy people usually save more), an uneven distribution of wealth (an even distribution would mean few rich people, who do most of the saving), and a high proportion of middle-aged people (the young don't need to save and the old don't want to—"You can't take it with you"). Correspondingly, a high propensity to invest may be associated with a high level of industrial activity or major technological advances.

Inflation and Interest Rates

Now let us see what Irving Fisher had to say about the effect of inflation on interest rates. Suppose that consumers are equally happy with 100 apples today or 105 apples in a year's time. The real, or "apple," rate of interest is 5 percent. Suppose also that I know the price of apples will increase over the year by 10 percent. Then I will part with $100 today if I am repaid $115 at the end of the year. That $115 is needed to buy me 5 percent more apples than I can get for my $100 today. In other words, the nominal, or "money," rate of interest must equal the real, or "apple," rate plus the prospective rate of inflation. A change of one percentage point in the expected inflation rate produces a change of one percentage point in the nominal interest rate. That is Fisher's theory: A change in the expected inflation will cause the same change in the nominal interest rate.[4]

---

[1] Augustus M. Kelley, Publishers, New York, 1965; originally published in 1930.

[2] Some of this saving is done indirectly. For example, if you hold 100 shares of GM stock, and GM retains earnings of $1 per share, GM is saving $100 on your behalf.

[3] We assume that investors save more as interest rates rise. It doesn't *have* to be that way; here is an example of how a higher interest rate could mean *less* saving. Suppose that you need $10,000 20 years hence for your children's college expenses. How much will you have to set aside today to cover this obligation? The answer is the present value of $10,000 after 20 years, or $10,000/(1 + r)^{20}$. The higher the r, the lower the present value and the less you have to set aside.

[4] The apple example was taken from R. Roll, "Interest Rates on Monetary Assets and Commodity Price Index Changes," *Journal of Finance*, **27**: 251–278 (May 1972).

In principle, there is no upper limit to the real rate of interest. But is there any lower limit? For example, is it possible for the money rate of interest to be 5 percent and the expected rate of inflation to be 10 percent, thus giving a negative real interest rate? If this happens, you may be able to make money in the following way. You borrow $100 at an interest rate of 5 percent and you use the money to buy apples. You store the apples and sell them at the end of the year for $110, which leaves you enough to pay off your loan plus $5 for yourself.

Since easy ways to make money are rare, we can conclude that, if it doesn't cost anything to store goods, the money rate of interest is unlikely to be less than the expected rise in prices. But many goods are even more expensive to store than apples, and others cannot be stored at all (you can't store haircuts, for example). For these goods, the money interest rate can be less than the expected price rise.

Comment.   If you look back to our discussion of inflation and discount rates in Section 6-1, you will see that our apple example is a bit oversimplified. If apples cost $1.00 apiece today and $1.10 next year, you need $1.10 \times 105 = \$115.50$ next year to buy 105 apples. The money interest rate is 15.5 percent, not 15.

The exact formula relating real and money rates is

$$1 + r_{money} = (1 + r_{real})(1 + i)$$

where i is the expected inflation rate. Thus

$$r_{money} = r_{real} + i + i(r_{real})$$

In our example, the money rate should be

$$r_{money} = .05 + .10 + .10(.05) = .155$$

When we said the money rate should be 15 percent, we ignored the "cross-product" term $i(r_{real})$. This is a common rule of thumb, because the cross-product is usually small. But there are countries where i is large (sometimes 100 percent per year or more). In such cases it pays to use the full formula.

Back to Fisher's Theory.   Not all economists would agree with Fisher that the real rate of interest is unaffected by the inflation rate. For example, if changes in prices are associated with changes in the level of industrial activity, then in inflationary conditions I might want more or less than 105 apples in a year's time to compensate me for the loss of 100 today.

We wish we could show you the past behavior of interest rates and *expected* inflation. Instead, we have done the next best thing and plotted in Figure 23-1 the return on U.S. Treasury bills against the *actual* inflation. Notice that between 1926 and 1986 the return on Treasury bills has been below the inflation rate about as often as it has been above. The average real interest rate during this period was .5 percent. Since 1981 the return on bills has been significantly higher than inflation. If you knew for sure whether these positive real rates will persist, you could make yourself a bundle and retire to the Caribbean.

Fisher's theory states that changes in anticipated inflation produce corresponding changes in the rate of interest. But there is little evidence of this in the 1930s and 1940s. During this period, the return on Treasury bills scarcely changed even though inflation fluctuated sharply. Either these changes in inflation were unanticipated or Fisher's theory was wrong. Since the early 1950s, there appears to have been a closer relationship between interest rates and inflation in the United

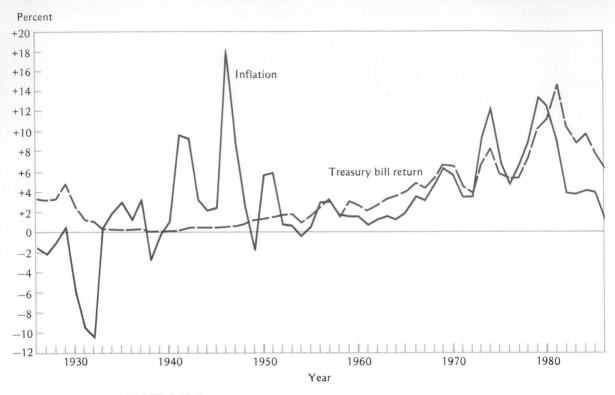

FIGURE 23-1
The return on U.S. Treasury bills and the rate of inflation 1926–1986. (*Source:* R. G. Ibbotson and R. A. Sinquefield, *Stocks, Bonds, Bills, and Inflation,* 1982, updated in *Stocks, Bonds, Bills, and Inflation: 1987 Yearbook,* Ibbotson Associates, Chicago, 1987.)

States.[5] Therefore, it is worth looking more carefully at how well Fisher's theory has worked in these recent years.

Eugene Fama has suggested that one way to test Fisher's theory is to twist it around and measure whether the inflation rate can be forecasted by subtracting a constant real rate from the observed nominal rate. That is, if Fisher's theory is right,

$$\frac{\text{Nominal}}{\text{interest rate}} = \frac{\text{real}}{\text{interest rate}} - \frac{\text{inflation rate}}{\text{forecasted by investors}}$$

or

$$\frac{\text{Inflation rate}}{\text{forecasted by investors}} = \frac{\text{nominal}}{\text{interest rate}} - \frac{\text{real}}{\text{interest rate}}$$

Of course, investors cannot predict the actual inflation rate perfectly—there will be a random forecast error. But in an efficient market, we expect them to be right on the average. Thus, the forecast error should be zero on the average.

---

[5] This probably reflects government policy, which before 1951 stabilized nominal interest rates. The 1951 "accord" between the Treasury and the Federal Reserve system permitted more flexible nominal interest rates after 1951.

Suppose that each quarter we observe the nominal return on Treasury bills and the *actual* rate of inflation. We fit the following equation to these data:

Actual
inflation = $a + b$ (nominal interest rate) + random forecasting error
rate

If Fisher is correct, the coefficient b should be close to 1.0 and the constant term a should be equal to minus the real interest rate.

We estimated b for 1953 to 1986 as .82, which is a little less than we should expect if Fisher is right *and* if the real interest rate is constant.[6]

Before leaving this topic, we must add two qualifications. First, the real interest rate is really an *expected* rate. When you buy a Treasury bill and hold it to maturity, you know what the dollar payoff will be, but the *real* payoff is uncertain because future inflation is not wholly predictable. Thus, to be perfectly precise, we should define the real interest rate as follows:

Real interest rate = *expected* real rate of return from
U.S. Treasury bills

= nominal rate of return on Treasury bills
− *expected* rate of inflation

Second, Nelson and Schwert, and Hess and Bicksler, have pointed out that the (expected) real interest rate *does* vary over time. Indeed we have seen that the real rate appears to have been unusually high since 1981. If that is so, Fama's test may be inappropriate.[7]

Until these problems have been resolved, we recommend that you look on Fisher's theory simply as a useful rule of thumb. Thus, if the expected inflation rate changes, your best bet is that there will be a corresponding change in the interest rate.

23-2   TERM STRUCTURE AND YIELDS TO MATURITY

We turn now to the relationship between short-term and long-term rates of interest. Suppose that we have a simple loan which pays $1 at time 1. The present value of this loan is

$$PV = \frac{1}{1 + r_1}$$

Thus we discount the cash flow at r_1, the rate appropriate for a one-period loan. This rate is fixed today; it is often called today's one-period **spot rate.**

If we have a loan which pays $1 at both time 1 and time 2, present value is

$$PV = \frac{1}{1 + r_1} + \frac{1}{(1 + r_2)^2}$$

[6] Fama fitted his equation to data for the period 1953 to 1971. His estimate of b was .98, which is almost identical to the figure that Fisher would predict. See E. F. Fama: "Short-Term Interest Rates as Predictors of Inflation," *American Economic Review,* **65:** 269–282 (June 1975).

[7] C. R. Nelson and G. Schwert, "Short-Term Interest Rates as Predictors of Inflation: On Testing the Hypothesis that the Real Rate of Interest Is Constant," *American Economic Review,* **67:** 478–486 (June 1977); P. Hess and J. Bicksler, "Capital Asset Prices versus Time Series Models as Predictors of Inflation," *Journal of Financial Economics,* **2:** 341–360 (December 1975).

Thus the first period's cash flow is discounted at today's one-period spot rate and the second period's flow is discounted at today's two-period spot rate. The series of spot rates r_1, r_2, etc., is one way of expressing the **term structure** of interest rates.

Yield to Maturity

Rather than discounting each of the payments at a different rate of interest, we could find a single rate of discount that would produce the same present value. Such a rate is known as the **yield to maturity,** though it is in fact no more than our old acquaintance, the internal rate of return (IRR), masquerading under another name. If we call the yield to maturity y, we can write the present value as

$$PV = \frac{1}{1 + y} + \frac{1}{(1 + y)^2}$$

All you need to calculate y is the price of a bond, its annual payment, and its maturity. You can then rapidly work out the yield with the aid of a preprogrammed calculator or you can find it in a set of bond tables.

Look at Table 23-1, which contains eight pages from a mini-book of bond tables. Each page shows yields for bonds with a particular coupon. For example, suppose that you have an 8 percent bond maturing in 10 years and priced at 85. (Bond prices are quoted as percentages of the bond's face value.) Look at the fourth page of our mini-bond tables. This shows yields for bonds with an 8 percent coupon. If you run your eye down the column for 10 years, you will see that a bond priced at 87.54 yields 10 percent and a bond priced at 77.06 yields 12 percent. Obviously the yield on your bond lies somewhere in between, about 10.5 percent.

Real books of bond tables contain several hundred pages, each crammed with bond prices for different combinations of coupon, yield, and maturity, but in all other respects, they are the same as our mini-book of Table 23-1.

An Example. The yield to maturity is unambiguous and easy to calculate. It is the stock in trade of any bond dealer. By now, however, you should have learned to treat any internal rate of return with suspicion.[8] The more closely we examine the yield to maturity, the less informative it is seen to be. Here is an example.

It is 1990. You are contemplating an investment in U.S. Treasury bonds. You come across the following quotations for two bonds:

Bond	Price	Yield to Maturity, Percent (IRR)
5s of '95	85.21	8.78
10s of '95	105.43	8.62

The phrase "5s of '95" means a bond maturing in 1995 paying annual interest amounting to 5 percent of the bond's face value. The interest payment is called *coupon* payment. Bond investors would say that these bonds have a 5 percent coupon. Face value plus interest are paid back at maturity, 1995. The price of each bond is quoted as a percent of face value. Therefore, if face value is $1000, you would have to pay $852.10 to buy the bond and your yield would be 8.78 percent.

---

[8] See Section 5-5.

TABLE 23-1
Each page of this mini-book of bond tables shows bond prices for a different coupon level

COUPON = 5%					PAGE 1
			YEARS		
Yield	6	8	10	12	14
6.0%	95.02	93.72	92.56	91.53	90.62
8.0	85.92	82.52	79.61	77.13	75.01
10.0	77.84	72.91	68.84	65.50	62.75
12.0	70.66	64.63	59.86	56.07	53.08
14.0	64.26	57.49	52.33	48.39	45.38

COUPON = 6%					PAGE 2
			YEARS		
Yield	6	8	10	12	14
6.0%	100.00	100.00	100.00	100.00	100.00
8.0	90.61	88.35	86.41	84.75	83.34
10.0	82.27	78.32	75.08	72.40	70.20
12.0	74.85	69.68	65.59	62.35	59.78
14.0	68.23	62.21	57.62	54.12	51.45

COUPON = 7%					PAGE 3
			YEARS		
Yield	6	8	10	12	14
6.0%	104.98	106.28	107.44	108.47	109.38
8.0	95.31	94.17	93.20	92.38	91.67
10.0	86.71	83.74	81.31	79.30	77.65
12.0	79.04	74.74	71.33	68.62	66.48
14.0	72.20	66.94	62.92	59.86	57.52

COUPON = 8%					PAGE 4
			YEARS		
Yield	6	8	10	12	14
6.0%	109.95	112.56	114.88	116.94	118.76
8.0	100.00	100.00	100.00	100.00	100.00
10.0	91.14	89.16	87.54	86.20	85.10
12.0	83.23	79.79	77.06	74.90	73.19
14.0	76.17	71.66	68.22	65.59	63.59

COUPON = 9%					PAGE 5
			YEARS		
Yield	6	8	10	12	14
6.0%	114.93	118.84	122.32	125.40	128.15
8.0	104.69	105.83	106.80	107.62	108.33
10.0	95.57	94.58	93.77	93.10	92.55
12.0	87.42	84.84	82.80	81.17	79.89
14.0	80.14	76.38	73.51	71.33	69.66

(continued)

TABLE 23-1
Continued

COUPON = 10%   PAGE 6

			YEARS		
Yield	6	8	10	12	14
6.0%	119.91	125.12	129.75	133.87	137.53
8.0	109.39	111.65	113.59	115.25	116.66
10.0	100.00	100.00	100.00	100.00	100.00
12.0	91.62	89.89	88.53	87.45	86.59
14.0	84.11	81.11	78.81	77.06	75.73

COUPON = 11%   PAGE 7

			YEARS		
Yield	6	8	10	12	14
6.0%	124.89	131.40	137.19	142.34	146.91
8.0	114.08	117.48	120.39	122.87	124.99
10.0	104.43	105.42	106.23	106.90	107.45
12.0	95.81	94.95	94.27	93.72	93.30
14.0	88.09	85.83	84.11	82.80	81.79

COUPON = 12%   PAGE 8

			YEARS		
Yield	6	8	10	12	14
6.0%	129.86	137.68	144.63	150.81	156.29
8.0	118.77	123.30	127.18	130.49	133.33
10.0	108.86	110.84	112.46	113.80	114.90
12.0	100.00	100.00	100.00	100.00	100.00
14.0	92.06	90.55	89.41	88.53	87.86

Letting 1990 be $t = 0$, 1991 be $t = 1$, etc., we have the following discounted cash flow calculation:[9]

			CASH FLOWS				
Bond	C_0	C_1	C_2	C_3	C_4	C_5	Yield in Percent
5s of '95	−852.11	+50	+50	+50	+50	+1,050	8.78
10s of '95	−1,054.29	+100	+100	+100	+100	+1,100	8.62

Although the two bonds mature at the same date, they presumably were issued at different times, the 5s when interest rates were low, and the 10s when interest rates were high.

[9] Coupon payments are actually made semiannually—the owners of the 5s of '95 would receive $25 every 6 months. Thus our calculations are a little bit off what you would get from using bond tables like Table 23-1. Also, the yields shown are rounded, not exact.

TABLE 23-2
Calculating present value of two bonds when long-term interest rates are higher than short-term rates

		PRESENT VALUE CALCULATIONS			
		5s OF '95		10s OF '95	
Period	Interest Rate	C_t	PV at r_t	C_t	PV at r_t
$t = 1$	$r_1 = .05$	$ 50	$ 47.62	$ 100	$ 95.24
$t = 2$	$r_2 = .06$	50	44.50	100	89.00
$t = 3$	$r_3 = .07$	50	40.81	100	81.63
$t = 4$	$r_4 = .08$	50	36.75	100	73.50
$t = 5$	$r_5 = .09$	1,050	682.43	1,100	714.92
	Totals	$1,250	$852.11	$1,500	$1,054.29

Are the 5s of '95 a better buy? Is the market making a mistake by pricing these two issues at different yields? The only way you will know for sure is to calculate the bonds' present values using spot rates of interest r_1 for 1991, r_2 for 1992, etc. This is done in Table 23-2.

The important assumption in Table 23-2 is that long-term interest rates are higher than short-term interest rates. We have assumed that the 1-year interest rate is $r_1 = .05$, the 2-year rate is $r_2 = .06$, and so on. When each year's cash flow is discounted at the rate appropriate to that year, we see that each bond's present value is exactly equal to the quoted price. Thus each bond is *fairly priced.*

Why do the 5s have a higher yield? Because for each dollar that you invest in the 5s you receive relatively little cash inflow in the first 4 years and a relatively high cash inflow in the final year. Therefore, although the two bonds have identical maturity dates, the 5s provide a greater proportion of their cash flows in 1995. In this sense the 5s are a longer-term investment than the 10s. Their higher yield to maturity just reflects the fact that long-term interest rates are higher than short-term rates.

Problems with Yield to Maturity

With this in mind, we can sum up the problems with the yield to maturity.

First, when a bond's yield to maturity is calculated, the *same* rate is used to discount *all* payments to the bondholder. The bondholder may actually demand different rates of return (r_1, r_2, etc.) for different periods. Unless two bonds offer exactly the same pattern of cash flows, they are likely to have different yields to maturity. Therefore the yield to maturity on one bond can offer only a rough guide to the appropriate yield on another.

Second, yields to maturity do not determine bond prices. It is the other way around. The demand by companies for capital and the supply of savings by individuals combine to determine the spot rates r_1, r_2, etc. These rates then determine the value of any package of future cash flows. Finally, *given* the value, we can compute the yield to maturity. We cannot, however, derive the appropriate yield to maturity *without* first knowing the value. We cannot, for example, assume that the yield should be the same for two bonds with the same maturity unless they also happen to have the same coupon.

The yield to maturity is a complicated average of spot rates of interest. Suppose that r_2 is greater than r_1. Then the yield on a 2-year coupon bond must lie between r_1 and r_2. In this case, the yield on the 2-year bond provides an underestimate of the 2-year spot rate. Of course, if r_2 is less than r_1, it would be the other way around—the yield on the 2-year bond would overestimate the 2-year spot rate. Sometimes these differences can be dramatic. For example, in Britain in 1977 the 20-year spot rate of interest r_{20} was nearly 20 percent. But the *yield* on high-coupon bonds maturing in 20 years was only about 13 percent. The reason was that short-term spot rates of interest were much lower than 20 percent. The yield on 20-year bonds was an average of short-term and long-term rates.[10]

In Chapter 5 we asserted that one problem with internal rates of return is that they don't add up. In other words, even if you know the return on A and the return on B, you cannot generally work out the return on A + B. Let us illustrate. Suppose your portfolio is evenly divided between two bonds both priced at 100. Bond A is a 1-year bond with a 10 percent coupon and therefore yields 10 percent. Bond B is a 2-year bond with an 8 percent coupon and therefore yields 8 percent. You might think that the yield on your portfolio would be halfway between at 9 percent. You would be wrong. The yield is 8.68 percent. In other words

$$200 = \frac{110 + 8}{1.0868} + \frac{108}{1.0868^2}$$

Thus it is dangerous to rely on the yield to maturity—like most averages, it hides much of the interesting information.

*Measuring the Term Structure

If you just want a quick, summary measure of the return offered on a bond, look at the yield to maturity. But if you want to understand why different bonds sell at different prices, you need to dig deeper and estimate the spot rates of interest. That is not something most bond analysts do at the moment. Here's your chance to be ahead of the game.

Look back at Table 23-2, which shows how investors value the 5 percent bonds of '95. Five years before maturity each bond is like a package of five mini-bonds. The package contains one mini-bond paying $50 at $t = 1$, another $50 at $t = 2$, and so on up to the fifth mini-bond, which pays $1050 at $t = 5$.

To calculate the spot rates of interest, we must first work out the price of each mini-bond. For example, in 1990, you could buy the following packages:

1. Invest $1704.22 to buy *two* 5s of '95.
2. Invest $1054.29 to buy *one* 10s of '95.

Each package provides a $100 cash flow for 4 years. But in year 5, when both bonds mature, the first package gives 2 × 1050 = $2100, and the second package gives 1 × 1100 = $1100. Thus, the only cash-flow advantage of package 1 occurs in year 5. It costs $649.92 more to buy package 1 (1704.22 − 1054.29 = $649.93), but you gain $1000 in year 5 (2100 − 1100 = $1000).

Investors must be indifferent between the two packages—if they were not, they would dump one bond and buy the other, and the bond prices would change. Thus an extra $1000 received in year 5 must be worth $649.93 now:

$$PV(\$1000 \text{ in year } 5) = \$649.93$$

---

[10] For a good analysis of the relationship between the yield to maturity and spot interest rates, see S. M. Schaefer, "The Problem with Redemption Yields," *Financial Analysts Journal*, **33**: 59–67 (July–August 1977).

But this present value depends on the 5-year spot rate r_5:

$$PV = \frac{1000}{(1 + r_5)^5} = 649.93$$

Solving for r_5, we find that it equals .09, or 9 percent.

In this example, we had two bonds with the same 5-year maturity, but different coupons. This allowed us to work out the price of a mini-bond that made a payment only in year 5 and this in turn gave us the 5-year spot rate. In order to work out the exact prices of mini-bonds and spot prices for all other periods, we would need a complete series of matching bonds. In practice, we are never so fortunate, but as long as we have a fair spread of coupons and maturities, we can get quite satisfactory estimates of the spot rates.[11] For example, the solid line in Figure 23-2 shows some estimates by BARRA of spot interest rates in February 1987.

In 1982, several investment bankers came up with a novel idea. They reasoned that many investors would welcome the opportunity to buy individual minibonds rather than the complete package. So the banks bought U.S. Treasury bonds and reissued their own separate mini-bonds each of which made only one payment.[12] If you've got a smart idea, you can be sure that others will soon clamber on to your bandwagon. It was therefore not long before the Treasury issued its own mini-bonds, known as "stripped" bonds.[13]

These developments give you another way to measure spot interest rates. Simply look at the interest rate on each of these mini-bonds. For example, the broken line in Figure 23-2 shows the rates of interest on Treasury stripped bonds.

*Pricing Bonds of Different Maturity

Do you remember how we valued options? The profit or loss on an option depends only on what happens to the underlying stock. You can, therefore, create a mixture of a risk-free loan and the stock which gives exactly the same payoffs as the option. If both packages give the same payoff, they must sell for the same price.

We can use a similar idea to check that bonds of different maturity are consistently priced. For example, suppose that the price of each bond depends only on what happens to the short-term rate of interest. Then you could exactly duplicate the payoffs on any bond by holding a mixture of two other bonds. If both investments give the same payoff, you know that they should sell for the same price. If they don't, you unload the expensive investment and buy the cheap one. Investors are now starting to use these ideas to price different bonds.

23-3 EXPLAINING THE TERM STRUCTURE

The term structure in Figure 23-2 is upward-sloping. In other words, long rates of interest are higher than short rates. This is the more common pattern but some-

---

[11] You may also have to adjust for the fact that low-coupon bonds, because they sell at a discount, get a tax break relative to high-coupon bonds. Part of the expected return from the low-coupon bond comes as capital gain because the discount diminishes over time. Also, bonds may have differing call provisions (see Section 24-4).

[12] These mini-bonds have a variety of exotic names. The Merrill Lynch issues are known as TIGRs (Treasury Investment Growth Receipts). Those issued by Salomon Brothers are known as CATS (Certificates of Accrual on Treasury Securities).

[13] The Treasury continued to auction coupon bonds in the normal way but investors could exchange them at the Federal Reserve Bank for stripped bonds.

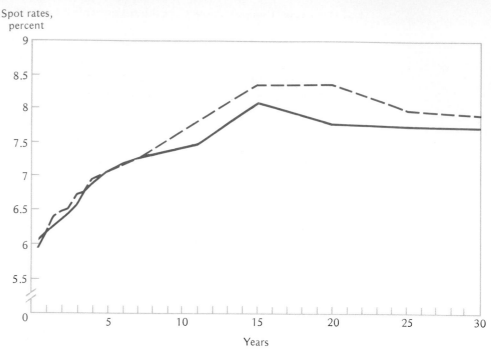

Spot rates, percent

FIGURE 23-2
Estimated spot rates on U.S. Treasury securities, February 1987. The solid line gives estimates made by BARRA. The broken line shows rates on U.S. Treasury "strips."

times it is the other way around, with short rates higher than long rates. Why do
we get these shifts in term structure?

**Ms. Long's
Problem**

Let us look at a simple example. Ms. Long wants to invest $1000 for 2 years. Two
strategies open to her are described in Table 23-3. Strategy L1 is to put the money
in a 1-year bond at an interest rate of r_1. At the end of the year she must then
take her money and find another 1-year bond. Let us call the rate of interest
on this second bond $_1r_2$—that is, the spot rate of interest at time 1 on a loan
maturing at time 2.[14] As Table 23-3 shows, the final payoff to this strategy is
$1000(1 + r_1)(1 + {_1}r_2)$.

Of course Ms. Long cannot know for sure what the one-period spot rate of
interest $_1r_2$ will be next year. Suppose that she *expects* it to be 11 percent. That is,
$E(_1r_2) = .11$. The current one-period spot rate is 10 percent. The expected final
payoff is

$$1000(1 + r_1)[1 + E(_1r_2)] = 1000(1.10)(1.11) = \$1221$$

Instead of making two separate investments of 1 year each, Ms. Long could
invest her money today in a bond that pays off in year 2 (strategy L2 in Table

[14] Be careful to distinguish $_1r_2$ from r_2, the spot interest rate on a 2-year bond held from time 0 to time
2. The quantity $_1r_2$ is a *1-year* spot rate established at time 1.

TABLE 23-3
Two investment strategies for Ms. Long, who wants to invest $1,000 for 2 years.

Strategy	Now	Year 1	Year 2 (Final Payoff)
L1 Invest in two 1-year bonds	$1,000	→ Invest in first bond yielding r_1 $1,000(1 + r_1)$ → Invest in second bond yielding $_1r_2$	$1,000(1 + r_1)(1 + {_1}r_2)$
L2 Invest in one 2-year bond	$1,000	→ Invest in bond yielding r_2	$1,000(1 + r_2)^2$
Strategy L2 can be expressed as	$1,000	→ Invest for 1 year at r_1 $1,000(1 + r_1)$ → Invest for second year at implicit forward rate f_2	$1,000(1 + r_1)(1 + f_2)$

23-3). That is, she would invest at the *2-year* spot rate r_2, and receive a final payoff of $1000(1 + r_2)^2$. If $r_2 = .105$, the payoff is $1000(1.105)^2 = \$1221$.

Now look below the dashed line in Table 23-3. The table shows that strategy L2 can be reinterpreted as investing for 1 year at the spot rate r_1 and for the second year at a **forward rate** f_2. The forward rate is the extra return that Ms. Long gets by lending for 2 years rather than 1. This forward rate is *implicit* in the 2-year spot rate r_2. It is also *guaranteed:* By buying the 2-year bond, Ms. Long can "lock in" an interest rate of f_2 for the second year.

Suppose that the 2-year spot rate is 10.5 percent as before. Then the forward rate f_2 must be 11 percent. By definition, this forward rate is the implicit interest rate in the second year of the 2-year loan:

$$(1 + r_2)^2 = (1 + r_1)(1 + f_2)$$

$$(1.105)^2 = (1.10)(1 + f_2)$$

$$f_2 = \frac{(1.105)^2}{1.10} - 1 = .11$$

or 11 percent.[15] The 2-year spot rate of 10.5 percent is an average of the 10 percent 1-year spot rate and the 11 percent forward rate.

What should Ms. Long do? One possible answer is that she should follow the strategy that gives the highest *expected* payoff. That is, she should compare:

Expected Payoff to Strategy L1	To	(Certain) Payoff to Strategy L2
$1,000(1 + r_1)[1 + E({_1}r_2)]$	to or to	$1,000(1 + r_2)^2$ $1,000(1 + r_1)(1 + f_2)$

Strategy L1 gives the higher expected return if $E({_1}r_2)$, the expected future spot rate, exceeds the forward rate f_2 implicit in the 2-year spot rate r_2. In our numerical

[15] Actually 11.002 percent. We rounded.

example, with $r_1 = .10$, $r_2 = .105$, and $E(_1r_2) = .11$, the two strategies give the same expected return:

Strategy	Payoff
L1	$1,000(1.10)(1.11) = \$1,221$ (expected)
L2	$1,000(1.105)^2 = \$1,221$ (certain)

Mr. Short's Problem

Now let us look at the decision faced by Mr. Short. He also has $1000 to invest, but he wants it back in 1 year. An obvious strategy is to invest in a 1-year bond. In this case his payoff is $1000(1 + r_1)$. This is strategy S1 in Table 23-4. A second strategy (S2 in the table) is to buy a 2-year bond and sell it after 1 year. The sale price will be the bond's present value in year 1. At that time, the bond will have 1 year to maturity. Its present value will be equal to its year 2 payoff $1000(1 + r_2)^2$ discounted at $_1r_2$, the one-period spot rate prevailing in year 1:

$$\text{PV of 2-year bond at year 1} = \frac{1000(1 + r_2)^2}{1 + {_1r_2}}$$

We know from Ms. Long's problem that the two-period rate r_2 can be expressed in terms of the one-period spot rate r_1 and the forward rate f_2. Thus

$$\text{PV of 2-year bond at year 1} = \frac{1000(1 + r_1)(1 + f_2)}{1 + {_1r_2}}$$

Of course Mr. Short cannot predict the future spot rate, and therefore he cannot predict the price at year 1 of the 2-year bond. But if $r_2 = .105$, and he expects the spot rate to be $_1r_2 = .11$, then the expected price is

$$\frac{1000(1.105)^2}{1.11} = \frac{1221}{1.11} = \$1100$$

What should Mr. Short do? Suppose that he prefers the strategy that gives the highest expected payoff. Then he should compare:[16]

[16] Here we are making an approximation because the expected payoff of S2 in $t = 1$ is not exactly equal to $[1000(1 + r_2)^2]/[1 + E(_1r_2)]$. We should calculate the expected price of the 2-year bond at $t = 1$. Call this $\tilde{P}$. By definition

$$\tilde{P} = \frac{100(1 + r_2)^2}{1 + {_1\tilde{r}_2}}$$

and

$$E(\tilde{P}) = E\left[\frac{1000(1 + r_2)^2}{1 + {_1\tilde{r}_2}}\right]$$

But

$$E\left[\frac{1000(1 + r_2)^2}{1 + {_1\tilde{r}_2}}\right]$$

is only approximately equal to

$$\frac{1000(1 + r_2)^2}{1 + E(_1\tilde{r}_2)}$$

In general, for any positive random variable $\tilde{x}$, $E(1/\tilde{x})$ is greater than $1/E(\tilde{x})$. This is called *Jensen's inequality*. Ignoring Jensen's inequality can be dangerous if the variance of $\tilde{x}$ is large.

(Certain) Payoff to Strategy S1	To	Expected Payoff to Strategy S2
$1000(1 + r_1)$	to	$\dfrac{1,000(1 + r_2)^2}{1 + E(_1r_2)}$
	or to	$\dfrac{1,000(1 + r_1)(1 + f_2)}{1 + E(_1r_2)}$

Strategy S2 is better if the forward rate f_2 exceeds the expected future spot rate $E(_1r_2)$. If Mr. Short faces the same interest rates as Ms. Long [$r_1 = .10$, $r_2 = .105$, $E(_1r_2) = .11$, $f_2 = .11$], the two strategies give the same expected return:

Strategy	Payoff
S1	$1,000(1.10) = \$1,100$ (certain)
S2	$\dfrac{1,000(1.105)^2}{1.11} = \dfrac{1,000(1.10)(1.11)}{1.11} = \$1,100$ (expected)

The Expectations Hypothesis

You can see that if the world is made up of people like Ms. Long and Mr. Short, all trying to maximize their expected return, then 1-year and 2-year bonds can exist side by side only if

$$f_2 = E(_1r_2)$$

This condition was satisfied in our numerical example—both f_2 and $E(_1r_2)$ equaled 11 percent. But what happens if the forward rate exceeds the expected future spot rate? Then both Long and Short prefer investing in 2-year bonds. If the world were entirely made up of expected-return maximizers, and f_2 exceeds $E(_1r_2)$, no one would be willing to hold 1-year bonds. On the other hand, if the forward rate were less than the expected future spot rate, no one would be willing to hold 2-year bonds. Since investors *do* hold both 1-year and 2-year bonds, it follows that forward rates of interest must equal expected future spot rates (providing that investors are interested only in expected return).

TABLE 23-4
Two investment strategies for Mr. Short, who wants to invest $1,000 for 1 year

Strategy	Now		Year 1 (Final Payoff)
S1 Invest in 1-year bond	$1,000	$\xrightarrow{\text{Invest at } r_1}$	$1,000(1 + r_1)$
S2 Invest in 2-year bond, but sell in year 1	$1,000	$\xrightarrow[\substack{\text{Invest, sell} \\ \text{for PV at} \\ \text{year 1}}]{}$	$\dfrac{1,000(1 + r_2)^2}{1 + _1r_2}$

This is the **expectations hypothesis** of the term structure.[17] It says that the *only* reason for an upward-sloping term structure is that investors expect future spot rates to be higher than current spot rates; the *only* reason for a declining term structure is that investors expect spot rates to fall below current levels. The expectations hypothesis also implies that investing in short-term bonds (as in strategies L1 and S1) gives exactly the same expected return as investing in long-term bonds (as in strategies L2 and S2).

The Liquidity- Preference Theory

One problem with the expectations theory is that it says nothing about risk. Look back for a moment at our two simple cases. Ms. Long wants to invest for 2 years. If she buys a 2-year bond, she can nail down her final payoff today. If she buys a 1-year bond, she knows her return for the first year but she does not know at what rate she will be able to reinvest her money. If she does not like this uncertainty, she will tend to prefer the 2-year bond, and she will hold the 1-year bond only if

$$E(_1r_2) \text{ is greater than } f_2$$

What about Mr. Short? He wants to invest for 1 year. If he invests in a 1-year bond, he can nail down his payoff today. If he buys the 2-year bond, he will have to sell it next year at an unknown price. If he does not like this uncertainty, he will prefer the 1-year investment, and he will hold 2-year bonds only if

$$E(_1r_2) \text{ is less than } f_2$$

Here we have the basis for the **liquidity-preference** theory of term structure.[18] Other things equal, Ms. Long will prefer to invest in 2-year bonds and Mr. Short in 1-year bonds. If more companies want to issue 2-year bonds than there are Ms. Longs to hold them, they will need to offer a bonus to tempt some of the Mr. Shorts to hold them. Conversely, if more companies want to issue 1-year bonds than there are Mr. Shorts to hold them, they will need to offer a bonus to tempt some of the Ms. Longs to hold them.

Any bonus shows up as a difference between forward rates and expected future spot rates. This difference is usually called the **liquidity premium.**

Advocates of the liquidity-preference theory believe that for the most part there is a shortage of lenders like Ms. Long. In this case the liquidity premium is positive and the forward rate will exceed the expected spot rate. A positive liquidity premium rewards investors for lending long by offering them higher long-term rates of interest. Thus, if this view is right, the term structure should be upward-sloping more often than not. Of course, if future spot rates are expected to fall, the term structure could be downward-sloping and *still* reward investors for lending long. But the liquidity-preference hypothesis would predict a less dramatic downward slope than the expectations hypothesis would.

---

[17] The expectations hypothesis is usually attributed to Lutz and Lutz. See F. A. Lutz and V. C. Lutz, *The Theory of Investment in the Firm*, Princeton University Press, Princeton, N.J., 1951.

[18] The liquidity-preference hypothesis is usually attributed to Hicks. See J. R. Hicks, *Value and Capital: An Inquiry into Some Fundamental Principles of Economic Theory*, 2d ed., Oxford University Press, Oxford, 1946. For a theoretical development, see R. Roll, *The Behavior of Interest Rates: An Application of the Efficient Market Model to U.S. Treasury Bills*, Basic Books, Inc., New York, 1970.

Introducing Inflation

We argued above that Ms. Long could nail down her return by investing in 2-year bonds. What do we mean by that? If the bonds are issued by the U.S. Treasury, she can be virtually certain that she will be paid the promised number of dollars. But she cannot be certain what that money will buy. The expectations theory and the liquidity-preference theory of term structure implicitly assume that future inflation rates are known. Let us consider the opposite case in which the *only* uncertainty about interest rates stems from uncertainty about inflation.[19]

Suppose that Irving Fisher is right and short rates of interest always incorporate fully the market's latest views about inflation. Suppose also that the market learns more as time passes about the likely inflation rate in a particular year. Perhaps today it has only a very hazy idea about inflation in year 2, but in a year's time it expects to be able to make a much better prediction.

Because future inflation rates are never known with certainty, neither Ms. Long nor Mr. Short can make a completely risk-free investment. But since they expect to learn a good deal about the inflation rate in year 2 from experience in year 1, next year they will be in a much better position to judge the appropriate interest rate in year 2. It is therefore more risky for either of them to make a forward commitment to lend in year 2. Even Ms. Long, who wants to invest for 2 years, would be incurring unnecessary risk by buying a 2-year bond. Her least risky strategy is to invest in successive 1-year bonds. She does not know what her reinvestment rate will be, but at least she knows that it will incorporate the latest information about inflation in year 2.

Of course this means that borrowers must offer some incentive if they want investors to lend long. Therefore the forward rate of interest f_2 must be greater than the expected spot rate $E(_1r_2)$ by an amount that compensates investors for the extra inflation risk.

Example. Suppose that the real interest rate is always 2 percent. Nominal interest rates therefore equal 2 percent plus the expected rate of inflation. Suppose that the *expected* inflation rate is 8 percent for both year 1 and year 2. However, inflation may accelerate to 10 percent in year 1, or it may decrease to 6 percent. To keep things simple, assume that the actual inflation rate for year 1 continues for year 2:

	Actual Inflation in Year 1	Actual Inflation in Year 2
Expected inflation rate = .08	.10	.10
	.08	.08
	.06	.06

Each outcome has a probability of 1/3.

Now reconsider Ms. Long's problem. Suppose that she can lend for either 1 or 2 years at 10 percent (the 2 percent real rate plus the 8 percent expected inflation rate). If she invests in a 1-year bond, she will get 1000(1.1) = $1100 in year 1. This amount is reinvested, but at what rate? The answer is that the future spot

[19] The following is based on R. A. Brealey and S. M. Schaefer, "Term Structure and Uncertain Inflation," *Journal of Finance,* **32:** 277–290 (May 1977).

rate $_1r_2$ will be 2 percent plus the inflation rate experienced in year 1 and projected for year 2:

Actual Inflation Rate	Spot Interest Rate in Year 1
.10	.12
.08	.10
.06	.08

Thus the final payoffs to lending short are:

	Year 1	Reinvest at	Final Payoff in Year 2
Invest for first year at $r_1 = .10$	$1,100 1,100 1,100	$_1r_2 = .12$ $_1r_2 = .10$ $_1r_2 = .08$	$1,232 1,210 1,188

Note that this strategy gives high payoffs when inflation turns out high.

Now Ms. Long could lock in a $1210 payoff in year 2 by purchasing a 2-year bond at 10 percent $[1000(1 + r_2)^2 = 1000(1.1)^2 = \$1210]$. But this would not lock in her *real* return. In fact lending short is the *safer* strategy when the final payoffs are converted back to current dollars:

Strategy	Final Payoffs	Inflation Rate	Inflation-Adjusted Payoffs[a]
Buy 2-year bond	$1,210 1,210 1,210	.10 .08 .06	$1,000 1,037 1,077
Buy 1-year bond	1,232 1,210 1,188	.10 .08 .06	1,018 1,037 1,057

[a] The inflation-adjusted payoffs are calculated by dividing by $(1 + i)^2$. In this case i is the actual inflation rate.

A Comparison of Theories of Term Structure

We have described three views about why long and short interest rates differ. The first view, the expectations theory, is somewhat extreme and not fully supported by the facts. For example, if we look back over the period 1926–1986, we find that the average annual return was 4.7 percent on long-term U.S. Treasury bonds and 3.5 percent on short-term Treasury bills.[20] Perhaps short-term interest rates did not go up as much as investors expected, but it seems more likely that investors wanted a higher expected return for holding long bonds, and that on the average they got it. If so, the expectations theory is wrong.

The expectations theory states that if the forward rate of interest is 1 percent above the spot rate of interest, then your best estimate is that the spot rate of interest will rise by 1 percent. In a study of the U.S. Treasury bill market between 1959 and 1982, Eugene Fama found that a forward premium *does* on average

---

[20] These are nominal rates of return from Ibbotson Associates, op. cit.

precede a rise in the spot rate but the rise is less than the expectations theory would predict.[21]

The expectations theory has few strict adherents, but Fama's study confirms that long-term interest rates reflect, in part, investors' expectations about future short-term rates.

Our other two theories both suggest that long-term bonds ought to offer some additional return to compensate for their additional risk. The liquidity-preference theory supposes that risk comes solely from uncertainty about the underlying real rates. This may be a fair approximation in periods of price stability such as the 1960s. The inflation-premium theory supposes that the risk comes solely from uncertainty about the inflation rate, which may be a fair approximation in periods of fluctuating inflation such as the 1970s.

If short-term rates of interest are significantly lower than long-term rates, it is often tempting to borrow short-term rather than long-term. Our discussion of term structure theories should serve to warn against such naive strategies. One reason for higher long rates could be that short rates are expected to rise in the future. Also, investors who buy long bonds may be accepting liquidity or inflation risks for which they correctly want compensation. You should borrow short when the term structure is upward sloping only if you feel that investors are *overestimating* future increases in interest rates or *overestimating* the risks of lending long.

If the risk of bond investment comes primarily from uncertainty about the real rate, then the safest strategy for investors is to hold bonds that match their liabilities. For example, the firm's pension fund generally has long-term liabilities. The liquidity-preference theory, therefore, implies that the pension fund should favor long-term bonds. If the risk comes from uncertainty about the inflation rate, then the safest strategy is to hold short bonds. For example, most pension funds have real liabilities that depend on the level of wage inflation. The inflation-premium theory implies that, if a pension fund wants to minimize risk, it should favor short-term bonds.

23-4 ALLOWING FOR THE RISK OF DEFAULT

You should by now be familiar with some of the basic ideas about why interest rates change and why short rates may differ from long rates. It only remains to consider our third question: "Why do some borrowers have to pay a higher rate of interest than others?"

The answer is obvious: "Bond prices go down, and interest rates go up, when the probability of default increases." But when we say "interest rates go up," we mean *promised* interest rates. If the borrower defaults, the *actual* interest rate paid to the lender is less than the promised rate. The *expected* interest rate may go up with increasing probability of default, but this is not a logical necessity.

These points can be illustrated by a simple numerical example. Suppose that the interest rate on 1-year, *risk-free* bonds is 9 percent. Backwoods Chemical Company has issued 9 percent notes with face values of $1000, maturing in 1 year. What will the Backwoods notes sell for?

The answer is easy—if the notes are risk-free, just discount principal ($1000) and interest ($90) at 9 percent:

$$\text{PV of notes} = \frac{\$1000 + 90}{1.09} = \$1000$$

---

[21] See E. F. Fama, "The Information in the Term Structure," *Journal of Financial Economics*, **13**: 509–528 (December 1984).

Suppose instead that there is a 20 percent chance that Backwoods will default. If default does occur, holders of its notes receive nothing. In this case, the possible payoffs to the noteholder are:

	Payoff	Probability
Full payment	$1,090	.8
No payment	0	.2

The expected payment is .8($1090) + .2($0) = $872.

We can value the Backwoods notes like any other risky asset, by discounting their expected payoff ($872) at the appropriate opportunity cost of capital. We might discount at the risk-free interest rate (9 percent) if Backwoods's possible default is totally unrelated to other events in the economy. In this case the default risk is wholly diversifiable, and the beta of the notes is zero. The notes would sell for

$$\text{PV of notes} = \frac{\$872}{1.09} = \$800$$

An investor who purchased these notes for $800 would receive a *promised* yield of about 36 percent:

$$\text{Promised yield} = \frac{\$1090}{\$800} - 1 = .363$$

That is, an investor who purchased the notes for $800 would earn a 36.3 percent rate of return *if* Backwoods does not default. Bond traders therefore might say that the Backwoods notes "yield 36 percent." But the smart investor would realize that the notes' *expected* yield is only 9 percent, the same as on risk-free bonds.

This of course assumes that risk of default with these notes is wholly diversifiable, so that they have no market risk. In general, risky bonds do have market risk (that is, positive betas) because default is more likely to occur in recessions when all businesses are doing poorly. Suppose that investors demand a 2 percent risk premium and an 11 percent expected rate of return. Then the Backwoods notes will sell for 872/1.11 = $785.59 and offer a promised yield of (1090/785.59) − 1 = .388, or about 39 percent.

You rarely see traded bonds offering 39 percent yields. But at one point in 1970 an LTV issue (the 5s of 1988) sold for 20 percent of face value and offered a promised yield to maturity of about 27 percent.[22] Needless to say, the expected yield on this issue was much less than 27 percent. The bonds sold at such a low price because the odds of default seemed high. As it turned out, however, the bondholders were lucky: The threat of default receded and the bondholders received a substantial capital gain. In 1985 the bonds sold at 91 percent of par, more than four times their value in 1970. Unfortunately the bondholders' joy was short-lived: LTV finally declared bankruptcy in 1986. By April 1987 the price of the bonds had fallen back to 31 percent of face value.

---

[22] That is, if

$$\text{Price (percent of par)} = 20 = \sum_{t=1}^{18} \frac{5}{(1 + y)^t} + \frac{100}{(1 + y)^{18}}$$

then *y*, the yield to maturity, equals about .27. This calculation assumes annual, instead of semiannual, coupon payments.

Bond Ratings

The relative quality of most traded bonds can be judged from bond ratings given by Moody's and Standard and Poor's. For example, Moody's classifies several thousand bond issues into the categories described in Table 23-5.

Bonds rated Baa or above are known as *investment-grade* bonds. Commercial

TABLE 23-5
Key to Moody's bond ratings

Aaa
Bonds which are rated **Aaa** are judged to be of the best quality. They carry the smallest degree of investment risk and are generally referred to as "gilt edge." Interest payments are protected by a large or by an exceptionally stable margin, and principal is secure. While the various protective elements are likely to change, such changes as can be visualized are most unlikely to impair the fundamentally strong position of such issues.

Aa
Bonds which are rated **Aa** are judged to be of high quality by all standards. Together with the **Aaa** group they comprise what are generally known as high-grade bonds. They are rated lower than the best bonds because margins of protection may not be as large as in **Aaa** securities, or fluctuation of protective elements may be of greater amplitude, or there may be other elements present which make the long-term risks appear somewhat larger than in **Aaa** securities.

A
Bonds which are rated **A** possess many favorable investment attributes and are to be considered as upper-medium-grade obligations. Factors giving security to principal and interest are considered adequate but elements may be present which suggest a susceptibility to impairment sometime in the future.

Baa
Bonds which are rated **Baa** are considered as medium-grade obligations; i.e., they are neither highly protected nor poorly secured. Interest payments and principal security appear adequate for the present but certain protective elements may be lacking or may be characteristically unreliable over any great length of time. Such bonds lack outstanding investment characteristics and in fact have speculative characteristics as well.

Ba
Bonds which are rated **Ba** are judged to have speculative elements; their future cannot be considered as well assured. Often the protection of interest and principal payments may be very moderate and thereby not well safeguarded during both good and bad times over the future. Uncertainty of position characterizes bonds in this class.

B
Bonds which are rated **B** generally lack characteristics of the desirable investment. Assurance of interest and principal payments or of maintenance of other terms of the contract over any long period of time may be small.

Caa
Bonds which are rated **Caa** are of poor standing. Such issues may be in default or there may be present elements of danger with respect to principal or interest.

Ca
Bonds which are rated **Ca** represent obligations which are speculative in a high degree. Such issues are often in default or have other marked shortcomings.

C
Bonds which are rated **C** are the lowest-rated class of bonds, and issues so rated can be regarded as having extremely poor prospects of ever attaining any real investment standing.

Source: Moody's Investor Services.

banks and many pension funds and other financial institutions are not allowed to invest in bonds unless they are investment-grade.[23]

Bond ratings are judgments about firms' financial and business prospects. If there is insufficient information to permit a judgment, the bond will not be rated. There is no fixed formula by which ratings are calculated. Nevertheless, investment bankers, bond portfolio managers, and others who follow the bond market closely can get a fairly good idea of how a bond will be rated by looking at a few key numbers such as the firm's debt-equity ratio, the variability of its income, and the size of issue.

Since bond ratings reflect the probability of default, it is not surprising that there is also a close correspondence between a bond's rating and its promised yield. For example, in the postwar period the promised yield on Aaa industrials has been on average about .9 percent less than on Baa's. (In 1932 the differential was as large as 4.3 percent.)

Once Moody's or Standard and Poor's rates a bond, the rating is not changed unless there is a significant shift in the company's financing or prospects. But the rating agencies do change their minds when conditions warrant it.

In July 1965 the issue of an additional $175 million of New York City bonds led Moody's to down-rate the city's debt from A to Baa. As a result a city official complained that the rating services were "causing leading cities to be shortchanged out of hundreds of millions of dollars in unwarranted interest charges." Suggested remedies included the idea that a federal agency be established that could rate municipal bonds "more objectively." Ten years later, after New York had nearly defaulted, Moody's was again the subject of criticism—this time for overoptimistic ratings. "Moody's," complained one senator, "continued to signal 'All is well,' " even while the city "was floundering on the financial rocks and was being abandoned by its crew of bankers and money men." A bond rater's lot is not a happy one.

*Option Pricing and Risky Debt

In Section 20-2 we showed that holding a corporate bond is equivalent to lending money with no chance of default *but* at the same time giving stockholders a put option on the firm's assets. When a firm defaults, its stockholders are in effect exercising their put. The put's value is the value of limited liability—of stockholders' right to walk away from their firm's debts in exchange for handing over the firm's assets to its creditors. To summarize,

$$\text{Bond value} = \begin{array}{c} \text{bond value} \\ \text{assuming no chance} \\ \text{of default} \end{array} - \text{value of put}$$

Thus, valuing bonds should be a two-step process. The first step is easy: Calculate the bond's value assuming no default risk. (Discount promised interest and principal payments at the yield on comparable United States government issues.) Second, calculate the value of a put written on the firm's assets, where the maturity of the put equals the maturity of the bond, and the exercise price of the put equals the promised payments to bondholders.

Owning a corporate bond is *also* equivalent to owning the firm's assets *but* giving a call option on these assets to the firm's stockholders.

$$\text{Bond value} = \text{asset value} - \text{value of call on assets}$$

---

[23] Investment-grade bonds can usually be entered at face value on the books of banks and life insurance companies.

Thus you can also calculate a bond's value, given the value of the firm's assets, by valuing a call on these assets, and subtracting the call value from the asset value. (The call value is just the value of the firm's common stock.)

Therefore, if you can value puts and calls on a firm's assets, you can value its debt.[24]

In practice, this is a good bit more difficult than it sounds. The put or call you have to value is usually not the simple option described in Chapter 20, but a much more complex one. Suppose, for example, that Backwoods Chemical issues a 10-year bond which pays interest annually. We can still think of Backwoods stock as a call option which can be exercised by making the promised payments. But in this case there are 10 payments rather than just 1. To value Backwoods stock we would have to value 10 sequential call options. The first option can be exercised by making the first interest payment when it comes due. By exercise the stockholders obtain a second call option, which can be exercised by making the second interest payment. The reward to exercising is that the stockholders get a third call option, and so on. Finally, in year 10 the stockholders can exercise the tenth option. By paying off both the principal and the last year's interest the stockholders regain unencumbered ownership of Backwoods's assets.

Of course if the firm does not make any of these payments when due, bondholders take over and stockholders are left with nothing. In other words, by not exercising one call option, stockholders give up all subsequent call options.

Valuing Backwoods stock when the 10-year bond is issued is equivalent to valuing the first of the 10 call options. But you cannot value the first option without valuing the nine following ones.[25] Even this example understates the practical difficulties, because large firms may have dozens of outstanding debt issues with different interest rates and maturities, and before the current debt matures they may make further issues. But do not lose heart. Computers can solve these problems, more or less by brute force, even in the absence of simple, exact valuation formulas.

Figure 23-3 shows a simple application. The figure is designed to give you some feel for the effect of default risk on (promised) bond yields. It takes a company with average operating risk and shows how the interest rate should increase with the amount of bonds that are issued and their maturity. You can see, for example, that, if the company raises 20 percent of its capital in the form of 20-year bonds, it should pay about one-half of a percentage point above the government borrowing rate to compensate for the default risk. Companies with more leverage or with longer-maturity bonds ought to pay higher premia.[26]

In practice, interest-rate differentials tend to be greater than those shown in Figure 23-3. High-grade corporate bonds typically offer promised yields about one percentage point greater than U.S. Treasury bonds. Does this mean that these companies are paying too much for their debt?

Probably not; there are a number of other possible explanations. For example, notice that Figure 23-3 makes several artificial assumptions. One assumption is

---

[24] However, option valuation procedures cannot value the *assets* of the firm. Puts and calls must be valued as a proportion of asset value. For example, note that the Black-Scholes formula (Section 20-4) requires stock price in order to compute the value of a call option.

[25] The other approach to valuing Backwoods's debt (subtracting put value from risk-free bond value) is no easier. The analyst would be confronted by not one simple put, but a package of 10 sequential puts.

[26] But beyond a certain point (not shown in Figure 23-3), the yield premia begin to decline with increasing maturity.

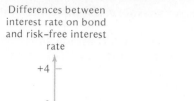

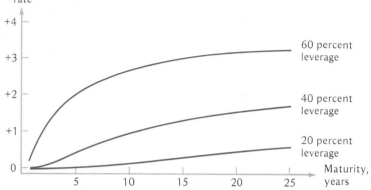

FIGURE 23-3
How the interest rate on risky corporate debt changes with leverage and maturity. These curves are calculated using option pricing theory under the following simplifying assumptions: (1) The risk-free interest rate is constant for all maturities. (2) The standard deviation of the return on the company's assets is 25 percent per annum. (3) No dividends are paid. (4) Debt is in the form of discount bonds (i.e., only one payment is made, at maturity). (5) Leverage is the ratio of the *market* value of the debt to the *market* value of the debt plus equity.

that the company does not pay dividends. If it does regularly pay out part of its assets to stockholders, there may be substantially fewer assets to protect the bondholder in the event of trouble. In this case, the market may be quite justified in requiring a higher yield on the company's bonds. Also, most publicly issued corporate bonds are less easily marketable than Treasury bonds, which trade every day in huge quantities. Lawrence Fisher has conducted an important study of the corporate bond market in which he concluded that differences in marketability were a principal reason for differences in interest rates.[27]

*Valuing Government Loan Guarantees

In the summer of 1971 Lockheed Corporation was in trouble. It was nearly out of cash after absorbing heavy cost overruns on military contracts and, at the same time, committing more than $800 million[28] to the development of the L1011 TriStar airliner. Introduction of the TriStar had been delayed by unexpected problems with its Rolls-Royce engines, and it would be many years before the company could recoup its investment in the plane. Lockheed was on the brink of bankruptcy. (Rolls-Royce was itself driven to the brink by the costs of fixing the engine problems. It was taken over by the British government.)

After months of suspense and controversy, the United States government rescued Lockheed by agreeing to guarantee up to $250 million of new bank loans.

---

[27] L. Fisher, "Determinants of Risk Premiums on Corporate Bonds," *Journal of Political Economy*, **67:** 212–237 (June 1959).

[28] See U. Reinhardt, "Break-Even Analysis for Lockheed's TriStar: An Application of Financial Theory," *Journal of Finance*, **28:** 821–838 (September 1973).

If Lockheed had defaulted on these loans, the banks could have gotten their money back directly from the government.

From the banks' point of view, these loans were as safe as Treasury notes. Thus, Lockheed was assured of being able to borrow up to $250 million at a favorable rate.[29] This assurance in turn gave Lockheed's banks the confidence to advance the rest of the money the firm needed.

The loan guarantee was a helping hand—a subsidy—to bring Lockheed through a difficult period. What was it worth? What did it cost the government?

This loan guarantee did not turn out to cost the government anything, because Lockheed survived, recovered, and paid off the loans the government guaranteed. Does that mean that the value of the guarantee to Lockheed was also zero? Does it mean the government absorbed no risks when it gave the guarantee in 1971, when Lockheed's survival was still uncertain? Of course not. The government absorbed the risk of default. Obviously the banks' loans to Lockheed were worth more with the guarantee than they would have been without it.

The present value of a loan guarantee is the amount lenders would be willing to pay to relieve themselves of all risk of default on an otherwise equivalent unguaranteed loan. It is the difference between the present value of the loan with the guarantee and its present value without the guarantee. A guarantee can clearly have substantial value on a large loan when the chance of default by the firm is high.

It turns out that a loan guarantee can be valued as a put on the firm's assets, where the put's maturity equals the loan's maturity, and its exercise price equals the interest and principal payments promised to lenders. We can easily show the equivalence by starting with the definition of the value of the guarantee.

$$\text{Value of guarantee} = \text{value of guaranteed loan} - \text{loan value without the guarantee}$$

Without a guarantee, the loan becomes an ordinary debt obligation of the firm. We know from Section 20-2 that

$$\text{Value of ordinary loan} = \text{value assuming no chance of default} - \text{value of put}$$

The loan's value, assuming no chance of default, is exactly its guaranteed value. Thus the put value equals the difference between the values of a guaranteed and an ordinary loan. This is exactly the value of the loan guarantee.

Thus option pricing theory should lead to a way of calculating the actual cost of the government's many loan guarantee programs. This will be a healthy thing. The government's possible liability under existing guarantee programs is enormous: For example, in 1987 $4 billion in loans to shipowners had been guaranteed under the so-called Title IX program to support shipyards in the United States.[30] This program is one of dozens. Yet the true cost of these programs is not widely recognized. Because loan guarantees involve no immediate outlay, they do not appear in the federal budget. Members of Congress sponsoring loan guarantee programs do not, as far as we know, present careful estimates of the value of the

---

[29] Lockheed paid the current Treasury bill rate plus a fee of roughly 2 percent to the government.

[30] The actual figure on March 31, 1987 was $4,497,365,297.98. We rounded.

programs to business and the present value of the programs' cost to the public. But this may change as option pricing theory is applied to the valuation of risky debt.

23-5 SUMMARY

Efficient debt management presupposes that you understand how bonds are valued. That means you need to consider three problems:

1. What determines the general level of interest rates?
2. What determines the difference between long-term and short-term rates?
3. What determines the difference between the interest rates on company and government debt?

Here are some things to remember.

The rate of interest depends on the demand for savings and the supply. The *demand* comes from firms who wish to invest in new plant and equipment. The *supply* of savings comes from individuals who are willing to consume tomorrow rather than today. The equilibrium interest rate is the rate which produces a *balance* between the demand and supply.

The best-known theory about the effect of inflation on interest rates is that suggested by Irving Fisher. He argued that the nominal, or money, rate of interest is equal to the expected real rate plus the expected inflation rate. If the expected inflation rate increases by 1 percent, so too will the money rate of interest. During the past 30 years Fisher's simple theory has not done a bad job of explaining changes in short-term interest rates in the United States.

The value of any bond is equal to the cash payments discounted at the spot rates of interest. For example the value of a 10-year bond with a 5 percent coupon equals

$$\text{PV(percent of face value)} = \frac{5}{1 + r_1} + \frac{5}{(1 + r_2)^2} + \cdots + \frac{105}{(1 + r_{10})^{10}}$$

Bond dealers generally look at the yield to maturity on a bond. This is simply the internal rate of return y, the discount rate at which

$$\text{Bond price} = \frac{5}{1 + y} + \frac{5}{(1 + y)^2} + \cdots + \frac{105}{(1 + y)^{10}}$$

The yield to maturity y is a complex average of the spot interest rates r_1, r_2, etc. Like most averages it can be a useful summary measure but it can also hide a lot of interesting information. We would like you to use some of the new techniques that produce estimates of the spot rates of interest.

The one-period spot rate r_1 may be very different from the two-period spot rate r_2. In other words, investors often want a different annual rate of interest for lending for 1 year than for 2 years. Why is this? The *expectations theory* says that bonds are priced so that the expected rate of return from investing in bonds over any period is independent of the maturity of the bonds held by the investor. The expectations theory predicts that r_2 will exceed r_1 *only* if *next* year's one-period interest rate is expected to rise.

The *liquidity-preference* theory points out that you are not exposed to risks of changing interest rates and changing bond prices if you buy a bond that matures exactly when you need the money. However, if you buy a bond that matures *before* you need the money, you face the risk that you may have to reinvest your savings at a low rate of interest. And, if you buy a bond that matures *after* you need the money, you face the risk that the price will be low when you come to sell it. Investors don't like risk and they need some compensation for taking it. Therefore when we find that r_2 is generally higher than r_1, it may mean that investors have relatively short horizons and have to be offered an inducement to hold long bonds.

No bonds are risk-free in real terms. If inflation rates are uncertain, the safest strategy for an investor is to keep investing in short bonds and to trust that the rate of interest on the bonds will vary as inflation varies. Therefore another reason why r_2 may be higher than r_1 is that investors have to be offered an inducement to accept additional inflation risk.

Finally, we come to our third question: "What determines the difference between interest rates on company and government debt?" Company debt sells at a lower price than government debt. This discount represents the value of the company's option to default. We showed you how the value of this option varies with the degree of leverage and the time to maturity. Moody's and Standard and Poor's rate company bonds according to their default risk, and the price of the bonds is closely related to these ratings.

FURTHER READING

The classic work on interest rates is:

Irving Fisher: *The Theory of Interest: As Determined by Impatience to Spend Income and Opportunity to Invest It*, Augustus M. Kelley, Publishers, New York, 1965. Originally published in 1930.

Fisher's work also anticipated Lutz and Lutz's expectations hypothesis of the term structure of interest rates.

F. A. Lutz and V. C. Lutz: *The Theory of Investment of the Firm*, Princeton University Press, Princeton, N.J., 1951.

The liquidity-premium hypothesis is due to Hicks, and our description of the effect of inflation on term structure is taken from Brealey and Schaefer.

J. R. Hicks: *Value and Capital: An Inquiry into Some Fundamental Principles of Economic Theory*, 2d ed., Oxford University Press, Oxford, 1946.

R. A. Brealey and S. M. Schaefer: "Term Structure and Uncertain Inflation," *Journal of Finance*, **32:** 277–290 (May 1977).

Good reviews of the term structure literature may be found in Nelson and Roll.

C. R. Nelson: "The Term Structure of Interest Rates: Theories and Evidence," in J. L. Bicksler, ed., *Handbook of Financial Economics*, North-Holland Publishing Company, Amsterdam, 1980.

R. Roll: *The Behavior of Interest Rates: An Application of the Efficient Market Model to U. S. Treasury Bills*, Basic Books, Inc., Publishers, New York, 1970.

Dobson, Sutch, and Vanderford review empirical tests of term structure theories. Two more recent tests of term structure theories are provided by Fama.

S. Dobson, R. Sutch, and D. Vanderford: "An Evaluation of Alternative Empirical Models of the Term Structure of Interest Rates," *Journal of Finance*, **31:** 1035–1066 (September 1976).

E. F. Fama, "The Information in the Term Structure," *Journal of Financial Economics*, **13:** 509–528 (December 1984).

E. F. Fama, "Term Premiums in Bond Returns," *Journal of Financial Economics*, **13:** 529–546 (December 1984).

Here are three papers which discuss measurement of the term structure:

W. Carleton and I. Cooper: "Estimation and Uses of the Term Structure of Interest Rates," *Journal of Finance,* **31:** 1067–1084 (September 1976).

J. McCulloch: "Measuring the Term Structure of Interest Rates," *Journal of Business,* **44:** 19–31 (January 1971).

S. M. Schaefer: "Measuring a Tax Specific Term Structure of Interest Rates in the Market for British Government Securities," *Economic Journal,* **91:** 415–438 (June 1981).

The Brennan and Schwartz paper is a readable description of how "no-arbitrage" conditions can be used to derive consistent relationships between bond prices.

M. J. Brennan and E. S. Schwartz: "Bond Pricing and Market Efficiency," *Financial Analysts Journal,* **38:** 49–56 (September–October 1982).

Fama's tests indicate that the expected real rate of interest was essentially constant between 1953 and 1971. However, if you read Fama's paper, you should also read the replies by Hess and Bicksler and by Nelson and Schwert.

E. F. Fama: "Short-Term Interest Rates as Predictors of Inflation," *American Economic Review,* **65:** 269–282 (June 1975).

P. Hess and J. Bicksler: "Capital Asset Prices versus Time Series Models as Predictors of Inflation," *Journal of Financial Economics,* **2:** 341–360 (December 1975).

C. R. Nelson, and G. Schwert: "Short-Term Interest Rates as Predictors of Inflation: On Testing the Hypothesis That the Real Rate of Interest Is Constant," *American Economic Review,* **67:** 478–486 (June 1977).

The classic empirical study on valuing risky debt is by Lawrence Fisher. Robert Merton has shown how option pricing theory can be applied to risky debt.

L. Fisher: "Determinants of Risk Premiums on Corporate Bonds," *Journal of Political Economy,* **67:** 212–237 (June 1959).

R. Merton: "On the Pricing of Corporate Debt: The Risk Structure of Interest Rates," *Journal of Finance,* **29:** 449–470 (May 1974).

Evidence on long-run average bond returns may be found in:

Ibbotson Associates, *Stocks, Bonds, Bills, and Inflation: 1987 Yearbook,* Ibbotson Associates, Chicago, 1987.

QUIZ

1. The real interest rate is determined by the demand and supply for capital. Draw a diagram showing how the demand by companies for capital and the supply of capital by investors vary with the interest rate. Use this diagram to show:
   (a) What will happen to the amount of investment and saving if firms' investment prospects improve? How will the equilibrium interest rate change?
   (b) What will happen to the amount of investment and saving if individuals' willingness to save increases at each possible interest rate? How will the equilibrium interest rate change? Assume firms' investment opportunities do not change.

2. (a) What is the formula for the value of a 2-year, 5 percent bond in terms of spot rates?
   (b) What is the formula for its value in terms of yield to maturity?
   (c) If the 2-year spot rate is higher than the 1-year rate, is the yield to maturity greater or less than the 2-year spot rate?
   (d) In each of the following sentences choose the correct term from within the parentheses:

"The (yield-to-maturity/spot-rate) formula discounts all cash flows from one bond at the same rate even though they occur at different points in time." "The (yield-to-maturity/spot-rate) formula discounts all cash flows received at the same point in time at the same rate even though the cash flows may come from different bonds."

3. Use Table 23-1 to check your answers to the following:
    (a) If interest rates rise, do bond prices rise or fall?
    (b) If the bond yield is greater than the coupon, is the price of the bond greater or less than 100?
    (c) If the price of a bond exceeds 100, is the yield greater or less than the coupon?
    (d) Do high-coupon bonds sell at higher or lower prices than low-coupon bonds?

4. Use Table 23-1 to answer the following questions:
    (a) What is the yield to maturity on a 7 percent, 8-year bond selling at 74¾?
    (b) What is the approximate price of a 5 percent, 9-year bond yielding 10 percent?
    (c) A 9 percent, 12-year bond yields 14 percent. If the yield remains unchanged, what will be its price 2 years hence? What will the price be if the yield falls to 10 percent?

5. (a) Suppose that the 1-year spot rate of interest at time 0 is 1 percent and the 2-year spot rate is 3 percent. What is the forward rate of interest for year 2?
    (b) What does the expectations theory of term structure say about the relationship between this forward rate and the 1-year spot rate at time 1?
    (c) Over a very long period of time, the term structure in the United States has been, on average, upward-sloping. Is this evidence for or against the expectations theory?
    (d) What does the liquidity-preference theory say about the relationship between the forward rate and the 1-year spot rate at time 1?
    (e) If the liquidity-preference theory is a good approximation and you have to meet long-term liabilities (college tuition for your children, for example), is it safer to invest in long-term or short-term bonds? Assume inflation is predictable.
    (f) If the inflation-premium theory is a good approximation and you have to meet long-term real liabilities, is it safer to invest in long-term or short-term bonds?
    (g) What does the inflation-premium theory say about the relationship between the forward rate and the 1-year spot rate at time 1?

6. (a) State the four Moody's ratings which are generally known as "investment-grade" ratings.
    (b) Other things equal, would you expect the yield to maturity on a corporate bond to increase or decrease with:
        (i) The company's business risk?
        (ii) The expected rate of inflation?
        (iii) The risk-free rate of interest?
        (iv) The degree of leverage?

*7. (a) How in principle would you calculate the value of a government loan guarantee?
    (b) The difference between the price of a government bond and a simple corporate bond is equal to the value of an option. What is this option and what is its exercise price?

QUESTIONS AND PROBLEMS

1. Why might Fisher's theory about inflation and interest rates *not* be true?

2. You have estimated spot interest rates as follows:

Year	Spot Rate, Percent
1	$r_1 = 5.00$
2	$r_2 = 5.40$
3	$r_3 = 5.70$
4	$r_4 = 5.90$
5	$r_5 = 6.00$

   (a) What are the discount factors for each date (that is, the present value of $1 paid in year t)?
   (b) What are the forward rates for each period?
   (c) Calculate the PV of the following Treasury notes.
       (i)   5 percent, 2-year note
       (ii) 5 percent, 5-year note
       (iii) 10 percent, 5-year note
   (d) Explain intuitively why the yield to maturity on the 10 percent bond is less than on the 5 percent bond.

3. Look at the spot interest rates shown in problem 2. Suppose that someone told you that the 6-year spot interest rate was 4.80 percent. Why would you not believe him? How could you make money if he was right? What is the minimum sensible value for the 6-year spot rate?

4. Look just one more time at the spot interest rates shown in problem 2. What can you deduce about the 1-year spot interest rate in 4 years if:
   (a) The expectations theory of term structure is right?
   (b) The liquidity-preference theory of term structure is right?
   (c) The term structure contains an inflation uncertainty premium?

5. Assume the term structure of interest rates is upward-sloping, as in Figure 23-2. How would you respond to the following comment? "The present term structure of interest rates makes short-term debt more attractive to corporate treasurers. Firms should avoid new long-term debt issues."

6. It has been suggested that the Fisher theory is a tautology. If the real rate of interest is defined as the difference between the nominal rate and the expected inflation rate, then the nominal rate *must* equal the real rate plus the expected inflation rate. In what sense is Fisher's theory *not* a tautology?

7. Look up prices of 10 U.S. Treasury bonds with different coupons and different maturities. Use bond tables to calculate how their prices would change if their yields to maturity increased by one percentage point. Are long-term bonds or short-term bonds most affected by the change in yields? Are high-coupon bonds or low-coupon bonds most affected?

*8. Look up prices of 10 corporate bonds with different coupons and maturities. Be sure to include some low-rated bonds on your list. Now estimate what these bonds would sell for if the United States government had guaranteed them. Calcuulate the value of the guarantee for each bond. Can you explain the differences between the 10 guarantee values?

9. Look in a recent issue of *The Wall Street Journal* at New York Stock Exchange bonds.
   (a) The yield shown in *The Wall Street Journal* is the current yield—that is, the coupon divided by price. Calculate the yield to maturity for a long-dated AT&T issue (assume annual interest payments).

(b) How much higher is the yield on the AT&T bond than the yield on a Treasury bond with a similar maturity?

(c) Glance quickly through the list of bonds and find one with a very high current yield. Calculate the yield to maturity on this bond.

(d) Why is the yield to maturity on this bond so high?

(e) Would the expected return be more or less than the yield to maturity?

10. Under what conditions can the expected real interest rate be negative?

11. Bond-rating services usually charge corporations for rating their bonds.

(a) Why do they do this, rather than charge those investors who use the information?

(b) Why will a company pay to have its bonds rated even when it knows that the service is likely to assign a below-average rating?

(c) A few companies are not willing to pay for their bonds to be rated. What can investors deduce about the quality of these bonds?

*12. A 6 percent, 6-year bond yields 12 percent and a 10 percent, 6-year bond yields 8 percent. Calculate the 6-year spot rate. (Assume annual coupon payments.)

*13. In 1982 Merrill Lynch TIGRs were priced as follows:

Maturity	Price
2000	10.540%
2001	9.314
2002	8.231
2003	8.038
2004	7.137
2005	6.337
2006	5.626

TIGRs are "zero-coupon" securities which make only one payment at maturity.

(a) Estimate the spot rates of interest.

(b) Estimate the forward rates of interest.

(c) If the expectations theory of term structure is correct, what is the expected 1-year rate of interest in 2005?

14. Are high-coupon bonds more likely to yield more than low-coupon bonds when the term structure is upward-sloping or when it is downward-sloping?

*15. Look back to the first Backwoods Chemical example at the start of Section 23-4. Suppose that the firm's book balance sheet is:

Backwoods Chemical Company
(Book values)

Net working capital	$ 400	$1,000	Debt
Net fixed assets	1,600	1,000	Equity (net worth)
Total assets	$2,000	$2,000	Total liabilities and net worth

The debt has a 1-year maturity and a promised interest rate of 9 percent. Thus, the promised payment to Backwoods's creditors is $1090. The market value of the assets is $1200 and the standard deviation of asset value is 45 percent per year. The risk-free interest rate is 9 percent. Use Appendix Table 6 to value the Backwoods debt and equity.

24 The Many Different Kinds of Debt

In Chapter 14 we introduced you to some of the different kinds of debt. For example, we saw that debt may be short-term or long-term, it may consist of straight bonds or it may be convertible into common stock, it may be issued domestically or sold overseas, and so on.

As financial manager, you need to choose the type of debt that makes sense for your company. We begin our analysis of this problem by looking in this chapter at the different kinds of straight bonds. After describing the form of the debt contract, we will examine the differences between senior and junior bonds and between secured and unsecured bonds. Then we will describe how bonds are repaid by means of a sinking fund and how the borrower or the lender may have an option for early repayment. Finally, we will look at some of the restrictive provisions that seek to prevent the company from doing anything that would reduce the value of the bonds.

We will not only describe the different features of corporate debt, but also try to say *why* sinking funds, repayment options, and the like exist. They are not simply matters of custom; there are generally good economic reasons for their use.

Debt may be sold to the public by means of a general cash offer or may be placed privately with a limited number of financial institutions. One important kind of private debt is the bank term loan. This may run from 1 to 8 years, which is rather shorter than most bonds. We will discuss these term loans in more detail in Chapter 32 when we describe short-term bank lending.

Another form of private debt is project finance. This is the glamorous part of the debt market. The words "project finance" always conjure up images of multi-million-dollar loans to finance mining ventures in exotic parts of the world. We examine project finance in Appendix B to this chapter. You'll find there's something to the popular image, but it's not the whole story.

Finally, there is a large market for standard long-term private placement bonds. These private placements are closely related to the publicly issued bonds that we look at in this chapter. Whether you decide to make a private placement or a public issue will depend partly on the relative issue costs, for a public issue involves higher fixed costs but a lower rate of interest.[1] But your choice should not depend solely on these costs. There are three other ways in which the private placement bond may differ from its public counterpart.

First, if you place an issue privately with one or two financial institutions, it may be necessary to sign only a simple promissory note. This is simply an IOU which lays down certain conditions that the borrower must observe. However, when you make a public issue of debt, you must worry about who is to represent

[1] See Section 15-5.

the bondholders in any subsequent negotiations and what procedures are needed for paying interest and principal. Therefore the contractual arrangement has to be that much more complicated.

The second characteristic of publicly issued bonds is that they are highly standardized products. They *have* to be—investors are constantly buying and selling them without checking the fine print in the agreement. This is not so necessary in private placements. They are not regularly traded; they are bought and held by large institutions that are well-equipped to evaluate any unusual features. Furthermore, because private placements involve lower fixed issue costs, they tend to be issued by smaller companies. These are just the companies that most need custom-tailored debt.

All bond agreements seek to protect the lender by imposing a number of conditions on the borrower. In the case of private placements these restrictions may be severe. For example, if the borrower wishes to issue any more bonds, the firm may need the permission of the existing bondholders. Because there are only one or two lenders involved, this permission is usually easily obtained. That would not be possible with publicly issued debt. Therefore the limitations tend to be less stringent in the case of public issues.

We are not going to discuss private placement bonds separately in this chapter, because the greater part of what we have to say about public issues is also true of private placements. Just bear the following in mind:

1. The private placement contract is simpler than the public issue contract.
2. The private placement contract is more likely to have nonstandard features.
3. The private placement contract often imposes more stringent conditions on the borrower, but it is more easily renegotiated.

24-1 DOMESTIC BONDS, FOREIGN BONDS, AND EUROBONDS

In the United States a borrower can either make an issue in the domestic market or raise the money overseas. One way to do the latter is to make a so-called **foreign bond** issue. In this case it issues bonds on a foreign capital market just like any local firm. The bond must of course be denominated in the local currency and the terms must conform to local custom. For American borrowers the most important markets for foreign bonds have been Switzerland and, to a lesser extent, Japan.

Foreign bonds are issued nationally and are subject to local regulations. There is also an international market for long-term debt known as the **eurobond** market. A eurobond is a bond that is sold simultaneously in a number of foreign countries by an international syndicate of underwriters. Although eurobonds may be sold throughout the world, eurobond underwriters and dealers are mainly located in London and they include the London branches of United States, European, and Japanese commercial and investment banks.

Eurobond issues are generally made in currencies that are actively traded, fully convertible, and relatively stable. The United States dollar has been the most popular choice, followed by the Japanese yen and the deutsche mark. In the last few years there has also been a growing market in ECU bonds. An ECU, or European Currency Unit, is simply a basket of currencies that is used as the benchmark for the European Monetary System.[2] Occasionally, when a eurobond has been de-

---

[2] When an ECU bond matures, lenders don't receive a mixture of currencies. They take payment in the currency of their choice at the current exchange rate for ECUs.

nominated in a weak currency the holder has been given an option to ask for payment to be made in another currency. There are also dual currency bonds that pay interest in one currency and principal in another.

The eurobond market grew up during the 1960s because the United States government imposed an interest-equalization tax on the purchase of foreign securities and because it discouraged American corporations from exporting capital. Therefore both European and American multinationals were forced to tap an international market for capital. The interest-equalization tax was removed in 1974 and there are no longer any controls on capital exports.[3] Since firms in the United States can now choose whether to borrow in New York or London, the interest rates in the two markets are usually fairly similar. However, the eurobond market is not directly subject to regulation by the United States authorities and therefore the financial manager always needs to be alert to small differences in the costs of borrowing in one market rather than another.

24-2 THE BOND CONTRACT

Indenture, or Trust Deed

As we have seen, a private issue of debt typically consists of a simple promissory note or IOU. The contract in any public issue of bonds in the United States usually takes the form of an **indenture,** or **trust deed,** between the borrower and a trust company. The trust company is the representative of the bondholders. It must see that the terms of the indenture are observed, administer any sinking fund, and look after the bondholders' interests in the event of default.

A copy of the bond indenture is included in the registration statement. It is a turgid legal document,[4] and its main provisions are summarized in the prospectus to the issue.[5] To give you some feel for these provisions, Appendix A to this chapter contains details of an issue of bonds by Potomac Electric Power (Pepco). The appendix has two parts. The second part provides information that is common to all bonds that may be issued by Pepco under the same indenture. The first part is the prospectus supplement, which describes the specific issue of bonds. If the company wishes to issue a second series of bonds under the same indenture, it will need to provide a separate prospectus supplement.

We will use the prospectus to illustrate some of the features of the bond contract. As you look at it, you might consider whether even these summary documents are not unduly obscure. In particular, like most legal documents, they review only the conditions and safeguards that exist and do nothing to draw your attention to any omissions or unusual features.

---

[3] Also, until 1984 the United States imposed a withholding tax on interest payments to foreign investors. Investors could avoid this tax by buying a eurobond issued in London rather than a similar bond issued in New York.

[4] For example, the indenture for one J. C. Penney bond states: "In any case where several matters are required to be certified by, or covered by an opinion of, any specified Person, it is not necessary that all such matters be certified by, or covered by the opinion of, only one such Person, or that they be certified or covered by only one document, but one such Person may certify or give an opinion with respect to some matters and one or more other such Persons as to other matters, and any such Person may certify or give an opinion as to such matters in one or several documents." Try saying that three times fast.

[5] Private placements are often accompanied by an *offering memorandum,* which is similar to a prospectus.

**The Bond
Terms**

The first page of the Pepco prospectus contains a table showing the price and cost of the issue. Notice two things about the price. First, although bonds have a face value of $1000, their prices are always shown as a percentage of face value. Second, the bond price is quoted net of *accrued interest.* This means that the bond buyer must pay not only the quoted price, but also the amount of any future interest that may have accrued. Since the proposed delivery date (November 13) was almost 2 weeks into the first interest period, accrued interest was approximately $2/52 \times 11.25 = .43$ percent. Therefore, the buyer would have had to pay a price of 99.50 percent plus .43 percent of accrued interest.[6]

The bonds were offered to the public at a price of 99.50 percent but Pepco sold the issue to the underwriters at 99.099 percent. The difference represented the underwriters' commission or spread. Of the total sum raised, $74,324,250 went to the company and $300,750 went to the underwriters.

Since the bonds were offered to the public at a price of 99.50 percent, investors who hold the bond to maturity will receive a capital gain over the 30 years of .50 percent. The bulk of their return is provided by the regular interest payment. This interest is payable semiannually at a rate of 11.25 percent per annum; thus, every 6 months investors receive interest of $11.25/2 = 5.625$ percent. A comparable eurobond would generally pay interest annually.[7]

Sometimes bonds are sold at a discount on their face value, so that investors receive a significant part of their return in the form of capital appreciation.[8] The ultimate is the zero coupon bond, which pays no interest at all; in this case all the return consists of price appreciation.[9]

The Pepco interest payment is fixed for the life of the bond, but in some issues the payment varies with the general level of interest rates. For example, the payment may be tied to the U.S. Treasury bill rate or to the London interbank offered rate (LIBOR), which is the rate at which banks lend eurodollars to one another. These floating-rate notes (FRNs) are particularly common in the eurobond market.

Until 1974 floating-rate notes were relatively rare in the United States market. In that year Citicorp issued $850 million of FRNs. These notes had a special attraction for Citicorp. Since they were a long-term debt of the bank holding company, the terms of the offer were not subject to Regulation Q, which placed a ceiling on the rate that banks could pay for time deposits. Eventually Regulation Q was repealed, but by that time banks and industrial firms had found other attractions to floating-rate notes.[10]

[6] The exact method of calculating accrued interest depends on the market. In some bond markets calculations are based on the assumption that a year is composed of twelve 30-day months; in other markets calculations recognize the actual number of days in each calendar month.

[7] In Table 23-1 we showed you an extract from a book of yields to maturity. These yields were semiannually compounded; in other words, they are equal to twice the 6-month yield. Because eurobonds pay interest annually, it is conventional to quote yields to maturity on eurobonds on an *annually* compounded basis. Remember this when comparing yields on different bonds.

[8] A zero coupon is often called a "pure discount bond." Any bond that is issued at a discount is known as an original issue discount (OID) bond.

[9] The ultimate of ultimates was an issue on behalf of a charity of a perpetual zero coupon bond.

[10] In 1985 a change in government regulation again led Citicorp to make an issue of floating-rate notes. The SEC required that investments made by money-market funds must have an average maturity of no more than 120 days, where maturity was defined as "the period until the next readjustment of the interest rate." Citicorp therefore reset the interest rate on the notes each *week.* SEC regulations also required that money-market funds should only buy debt due within 1 year. The Citicorp notes had a maturity of 364 days, but each quarter the notes were automatically extended unless the investor requested otherwise. Therefore the notes could be held by money-market funds even though the final repayment could be extended indefinitely.

Often floating-rate notes specify a minimum (or "floor") interest rate or, less frequently, they specify a maximum (or "cap") on the rate.[11] You may also come across "collars," which stipulate both a maximum and a minimum payment or "drop-locks," which provide that, if the rate falls to a specified trigger point, the payment is then fixed for the remainder of the bond's life.

The regular interest payment on a bond is like a hurdle that the company must keep jumping.[12] If the company ever fails to pay the interest on its debt, lenders can demand their money back instead of waiting until matters may have deteriorated further. Thus interest payments provide additional protection for lenders.[13]

Registered and Bearer Bonds

A small paragraph in the main Pepco prospectus also states that the bonds are to be issued in denominations of $1000 in *registered* form. This means that the company's registrar will record the ownership of each bond and the company will then pay directly to each owner both the interest and the final $1000 principal.

Sometimes a bond issue may be in registered form with coupons. This means that the owner must claim each interest payment by detaching a coupon from the bond certificate and forwarding it to the company. On other occasions, the bond may be in *bearer* form. In this case, the certificate constitutes the primary evidence of ownership, so that the bondholder must send in coupons to claim interest and must send the certificate itself to claim the final repayment of principal. Eurobonds almost invariably give the owner the alternative of holding them in bearer form. However, since the ownership of such bonds cannot be traced, the IRS has tried to deter United States residents from holding them.[14]

24-3 SECURITY AND SENIORITY

Almost all debt issues by industrial and financial companies are general unsecured obligations. Longer-term unsecured issues are usually called **debentures;**[15] shorter-term issues are usually termed **notes.** Occasionally unsecured issues may be guaranteed by another company and many private placements are guaranteed by the company's management. It does not necessarily matter in these cases that the manager is not personally wealthy—the guarantee serves as an important signal of the manager's confidence and is a fine incentive.

---

[11] Instead of issuing a straight (uncapped) FRN, a company will sometimes issue a capped FRN and at the same time sell the cap to another investor. The first investor receives a coupon payment up to the specified maximum and the second investor receives any interest in excess of this maximum.

[12] There is one type of bond where the borrower is obliged to pay interest only if it is covered by the year's earnings. These so-called income bonds have largely been issued as part of railroad reorganizations. For a discussion of the attractions of income bonds, see J. J. McConnell and G. G. Schlarbaum: "Returns, Risks, and Pricing of Income Bonds, 1956–1976 (Does Money Have an Odor?)," *Journal of Business*, **54:** 33–64 (January 1981).

[13] See F. Black and J. C. Cox: "Valuing Corporate Securities: Some Effects of Bond Indenture Provisions," *Journal of Finance*, **31:** 351–367 (May 1976). Black and Cox point out that the interest payment would be a trivial hurdle if the company could sell assets to make the payment. Such sales are, therefore, prohibited.

[14] United States residents cannot generally deduct capital losses on bearer bonds. Also, payments on such bonds cannot be made to a bank account in the United States.

[15] There are international differences in terminology. In Great Britain *debenture* usually signifies a bond that has a *prior* claim on the firm's assets.

Like most domestic issues by utility and railroad companies, the Pepco issue is a secured obligation. This means that if the company defaults on the debt, the trustee or lender may take possession of the relevant assets. If these are insufficient to satisfy the claim, the remaining debt will have a general claim alongside any unsecured debt against the other assets of the firm.

The vast majority of secured debt consists of **mortgage bonds** like the Pepco issue. Some of these mortgages are "closed," so that no more bonds may be issued against the mortgage. However, usually there is no specific limit to the amount of bonds that may be secured (in which case the mortgage is said to be "open") or there is a specific limit which has not been reached (in which case the mortgage is said to be "limited, open end"). If you look at the final page of the prospectus, you will see that the mortgage securing the Pepco bond is limited open end.

Mortgage bonds sometimes provide a claim against a specific building, but like the Pepco bond they are more often secured on almost all the company's property.[16] The issuer undertakes to insure this property and to keep it in good repair. Frequently the indenture will provide for a fixed annual contribution for such maintenance, with any unspent balance being used to redeem bonds. Of course the value of any mortgage depends not only on how well the property is maintained but also on whether it has value in alternative uses. A custom-built machine for producing buggy whips will not be worth much if the market for buggy whips dries up.

Collateral trust bonds closely resemble mortgage bonds except that in this case the claim is against securities held by the corporation. Generally these bonds are issued by holding companies—that is, firms whose main assets consist of common stock in a number of subsidiaries. The problem for the lender is that this stock is junior to *all* other claims on the assets of the subsidiaries, and so the collateral trust bond will usually include detailed restrictions on the freedom of the subsidiaries to issue debt or preferred stock.

The third principal form of secured debt is the **equipment trust certificate.** This is most frequently used to finance new railroad rolling stock. Under this arrangement a trustee obtains formal ownership of the equipment. The railroad makes a down payment of 10 to 25 percent of the cost and the balance is provided by a package of trust certificates with different maturities that might typically run from 1 to 15 years. Only when all these debts have finally been paid off does the railroad become the formal owner of the equipment. Because the trustee holds the title to the pledged equipment and can immediately repossess it in the event of default, equipment trust certificates offer good security to their holders. Bond rating agencies such as Moody's or Standard and Poor's, therefore, usually rate equipment trust certificates one grade higher than the railroad's regular debt.

Bonds may be senior claims or they may be subordinated to the senior bonds or to *all* other creditors.[17] If the firm defaults, the senior bonds come first in the pecking order. For example, a company may issue first and second mortgage bonds. The first mortgage bonds have the first claim against the assets, then come the second mortgage bonds.

---

[16] Many mortgage bonds are secured not only by existing property but also by "after-acquired" property. However, if the company buys only property that is already mortgaged, the bondholder would have only a junior claim on the new property. Therefore, mortgage bonds with after-acquired property clauses also restrict the extent to which the company can purchase additional mortgaged property.

[17] If a bond does not specifically state that it is junior, you can assume that it is senior.

24-4 REPAYMENT PROVISIONS

**Sinking
Funds**

Many bonds include provisions for part of the issue to be repaid on a regular basis before maturity. The usual arrangement is for the company to make a regular payment into a *sinking fund*. This payment can be in the form either of cash or of bonds that the company has bought back in the marketplace. If payment is in cash, then the trustee will select bonds by lottery and use the cash to redeem them at par.[18]

For most publicly issued bonds, the borrower can *choose* between repurchasing the bonds in the market or calling them at par.[19] If the price of the bond is low, the firm will satisfy the sinking fund requirement by buying bonds in the market; if the price is high, it will call the bonds by lottery. This option tends to reduce the value of sinking fund bonds.

Generally, there is a mandatory fund which *must* be satisfied and an optional fund which can be satisfied if the borrower chooses. Utility first mortgage bonds often have a wholly optional fund, and the Pepco bond has no sinking fund at all. A number of private placements (particularly those in extractive industries) require a payment only when net income exceeds some specified level.[20]

Most "sinkers" begin to operate after about 10 years. For lower-quality issues the payments are usually sufficient to redeem the entire issue in equal installments over the life of the bond. In contrast, high-quality bonds often have light sinking fund requirements with large "balloon" payments at maturity. Generally, bonds may be redeemed for the sinking fund at par but some issues provide for a gently declining schedule of repayment prices.[21]

We saw earlier that interest payments provide a regular test of the company's solvency. Sinking funds provide an additional hurdle that the firm must keep jumping. If it cannot pay the cash into the sinking fund, the lenders can demand their money back. That is why long-dated, low-quality issues usually involve larger sinking funds.

Unfortunately, a sinking fund is no test of solvency *if the firm is allowed to repurchase bonds in the market*. Since the *market* value of the debt must always be less than the value of the firm, you can never be driven into default by repurchasing your debt in the market. So in this case the sinking fund is like a hurdle that gets progressively lower as the hurdler gets weaker.

---

[18] Every investor dreams of buying up the entire supply of a sinking fund bond that is selling way below face value and then forcing the company to buy the bonds back at face value. "Cornering the market" in this way is fun to dream about but difficult to do. For a discussion, see K. B. Dunn and C. S. Spatt, "A Strategic Analysis of Sinking Fund Bonds," *Journal of Financial Economics*, **13**: 399–424 (September 1984).

[19] If the bonds are privately placed, the company cannot repurchase the bonds in the marketplace—it must call them at par. Similarly, equipment trust certificates consist of a package of bonds that mature in successive years. Such bonds are usually called *serial bonds*. A package of serial bonds is rather like a sinking fund bond. Both provide regular repayments of the debt. But the serial bond does not give the borrower the option to buy the bonds in the marketplace—the borrower *must* redeem the bonds at par.

[20] Strictly speaking, the private placement arrangement for regular repayment does not involve establishment of a sinking fund.

[21] Some bonds have a *purchase fund*. In this case the company agrees to put aside money which is to be used to repurchase bonds in the market only if the price is below par.

Pepco has an option to buy back, or "call," the entire bond issue. If it does so, it is required to pay a premium which declines from 10.75 percent in the first year to zero in the year 2006. Pepco is subject to a particular limitation on the use of this call option. Until 1990 the company is prohibited from calling the bond in order to replace it with new debt yielding less than the 11.36 percent yield on the original bond.

These repayment provisions are typical of long-term bonds. Most such issues mature in 25 or 30 years, are callable at a premium that is initially roughly equal to the coupon, and are "nonrefundable" (NR) for 10 to 15 years "below interest cost." Medium-term loans are either wholly noncallable (NC) or are nonrefundable below interest cost for most of their lives.

The option to call the bond is obviously attractive to the issuer. If interest rates decline and bond prices rise, the issuer has the opportunity to repurchase the bonds below their true value. For example, suppose that by 2000 yields on investment-quality bonds have fallen to 7 percent. An 11.25 percent bond with 15 years to run would be worth 139.1 percent, or $1391. The call provision allows Pepco to repurchase bonds that are worth $1391 for only $1032.20. Or the company can, if it chooses, hold on and hope to do even better by calling the bonds in 2001.

How does Pepco know when to call its bonds? The answer is simple. Other things equal, if it wishes to maximize the value of its stock, it must minimize the value of its bond. Therefore, it should never call the bond if its market value is less than the call price, for that would just be giving a present to the bondholders. Equally, it *should* call the bond if it is worth *more* than the call price.

Of course, investors take the call option into account when they buy or sell the bond. They know that the company will call the bond as soon as it is worth more than the call price. Therefore no investor will be willing to pay more than the call price for the bond. The market price of the bond may, therefore, reach the call price but it will not rise above it. This gives the company the following rule for calling its bonds: *Call the bond when, and only when, the market price reaches the call price.*[22]

If we know how bond prices behave over time, we can modify our basic option-valuation model of Chapter 20 to give us the value of the callable bond, *given* that investors know the company will call the issue as soon as the market price reaches the call price. For example, look at Figure 24-1. It illustrates the relationship between the value of a straight 8 percent 5-year bond and the value of a callable 8 percent 5-year bond. Suppose that the value of the straight bond is very low. In this case there is little likelihood that the company will ever wish to call its bonds. (Remember that it will call the bonds only if they are worth more than the call price.) Therefore the value of the callable bond will be almost identical to the value of the straight bond. Now suppose that the straight bond is worth exactly 100. In this case there is a good chance that the company will wish at some time to call its bonds. Therefore the value of our callable bond will be slightly less than that of the straight bond. If interest rates decline further, the price of the straight will move above 100. But nobody will ever pay *more* than 100 for the callable bond.

---

[22] See M. J. Brennan and E. S. Schwartz, "Savings Bonds, Retractable Bonds, and Callable Bonds," *Journal of Financial Economics,* **5:** 67–88 (1977). Of course this assumes that the bond is correctly priced, that investors are acting rationally, and that investors expect the *firm* to act rationally. Also, we ignore some complications. First, you may not wish to call a bond if you are prevented by a nonrefunding clause from issuing new debt. Second, the call premium is a tax-deductible expense for the company but is taxed as a capital gain to the bondholder. Third, there are other possible tax consequences to both the company and the investor from replacing a low-coupon bond with a higher-coupon bond. Fourth, there are costs to calling and reissuing debt.

FIGURE 24-1
Relationship between the value of a callable bond and that of a straight (noncallable) bond. Assumptions: (1) Both bonds have an 8 percent coupon and a 5-year maturity. (2) The callable bond may be called at any time before maturity. (3) The short-term interest rate follows a random walk, and the expected returns on bonds of all maturities are equal. [*Source:* M. J. Brennan and E. S. Schwartz, "Savings Bonds, Retractable Bonds, and Callable Bonds," *Journal of Financial Economics* **5:** 67–88 (1977).]

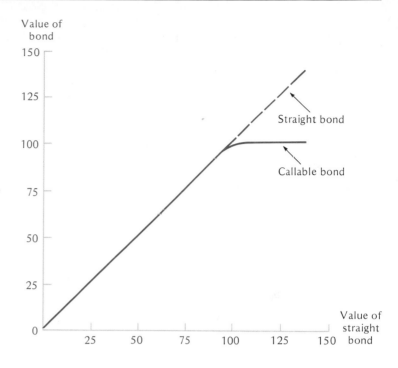

Extendable and Retractable Bonds	Occasionally you may come across bonds that give the *investor* the repayment option. Extendable bonds give investors the option to extend the bond's life, and retractable bonds give them the option to demand early repayment. The Belgian government once issued a bond that gave both borrower *and* lender the right to demand early repayment at the bond's face value.

24-5   RESTRICTIVE COVENANTS

The difference between a corporate bond and a comparable Treasury bond is that the company has an option to default—the government supposedly doesn't. That is a valuable option. If you don't believe us, think about whether (other things equal) you would prefer to be a shareholder in a company with limited liability or in a company with unlimited liability. Of course the answer is that you would prefer to have the option to walk away from your debts. Unfortunately, every silver lining has its cloud and the drawback to having a default option is that corporate bondholders expect to be compensated for giving it to you. That is why corporate bonds sell at lower prices and therefore higher yields than government bonds.[23]

Investors know that there is a risk of default when they buy a corporate bond. But they still want to make sure that the company plays fair. They don't want it to gamble with their money or to take any other unreasonable risks. Therefore,

---

[23] In Chapters 20 and 23 we showed that this option to default is equivalent to a put option on the assets of the firm.

the bond agreement includes a number of restrictive covenants to prevent the company from purposely increasing the value of its default option.[24]

When Pepco issued its bonds, the company had a total market value of $2730 million and total senior debt of $1113 million. This meant that the value of the company could fall by about 59 percent before Pepco would want to default.

Suppose that immediately after issuing the 11.25 percent bonds, Pepco announces a further $200 million bond issue. The company now has a market value of $2930 million and senior debt of $1313 million. The point at which it would want to exercise its default option is 45 percent of the value of the assets. The original bondholders are slightly worse off. If they had known about the new issue, they would not have been willing to pay quite such a high price for their bonds.

The reason that the new issue hurts the original bondholders is that it alters the *ratio* of senior debt to company value. They would not object to the issue if the company kept the ratio the same by simultaneously issuing common stock. Therefore, the bond agreement generally states that the company may issue more senior debt only if the ratio of senior debt to the net asset value is within a specified limit.

Why don't companies limit *subordinated* as well as senior debt? The answer is that the subordinated debtor does not get *any* money until the senior bondholders have been paid in full.[25] The senior bondholders, therefore, view subordinated bonds in much the same way that they view equity: They would be happy to see an issue of either. Of course, the converse is not true. Holders of subordinated debt *do* care both about the total amount of debt and about the proportion that is senior to their claim. As a result, the indenture for an issue of subordinated debt generally includes a restriction on both total debt and senior debt.

Another worry for all bondholders is that the company may issue more secured debt than they had anticipated. An issue of mortgage bonds usually imposes a limit on the amount of secured debt. This is not necessary when you are issuing unsecured debentures. As long as the debenture holders are given equal treatment, they do not care how much you mortgage your assets. Therefore the bond agreement for a debenture issue usually includes a so-called **negative pledge clause,** in which the debenture holders simply say, "Me too."[26]

During the 1950s and 1960s many companies found that they could circumvent some of these restrictions if instead of borrowing money to buy an asset, they entered into a long-term agreement to rent or lease it. For the debtholder this arrangement is very similar to secured borrowing. Therefore indentures began to include limitations on leasing.

Leases are an example of a hidden debt. After their fingers had been burned, bondholders began to impose restrictions on leases. But you want to shut the stable door *before* your fingers have been burned. Perhaps, therefore, lenders should be placing restrictions on other kinds of hidden debt such as some of the project

---

[24] We described in Section 18-3 some of the games that managers could play at the expense of the bondholders.

[25] In practice the courts do not always observe the strict rules of precedence. Therefore the subordinated debtholder may receive *some* payment even when the senior debtholder is not fully paid off.

[26] "Me too" is not acceptable legal jargon. Instead the bond agreement usually says something like, "The company will not issue, assume, or guarantee any debt secured by a lien upon any principal property without providing that the (existing) securities shall be secured equally and ratably." Notice that, if the firm *does* subsequently issue secured debt, this negative pledge clause allows the debenture holders to demand repayment. But it does not invalidate the security given to the other debtholders.

financings that we describe in Appendix B to this chapter, or such as unfunded pension liabilities, which we describe in Chapter 35.

We have talked about how an unscrupulous borrower can try to increase the value of the default option by issuing more debt. But that is not the only way that it can exploit its existing bondholders. For example, we know that the value of an option is affected by dividend payments. If the company pays out large dividends to its shareholders and doesn't replace the cash by an issue of stock, there is less asset value available to cover the debt. Therefore many bond issues restrict the amount of dividends that the company may pay.[27]

Positive Covenants

The restrictions on new debt issues or dividend payments prevent the company from doing things that would benefit the shareholders at the expense of the bondholders, but they don't make the bonds safe. Therefore lenders also seek to protect themselves by arrangements that give them the chance to demand repayment at the first sign of trouble. For example, bank loans sometimes specify that the bank can demand repayment if there is a "material adverse change" which impairs the borrower's ability to repay the loan.[28]

We have already seen that lenders impose a number of hurdles which the company must keep jumping. The most obvious of these hurdles are the regular interest payments and sinking fund contributions. If these obligations are not met, the loan becomes repayable immediately. That is why the company will always try to make the payment if it possibly can. Another, rather different hurdle is the repayment of other outstanding debt. Many issues contain a *cross-default* clause. This says that the company is in default if it fails to meet its obligations on any of its debt issues. Thus a cross-default clause may enable the lender to get out from under before the firm has missed a payment on that particular loan.

Most indentures also include so-called *positive* covenants, which impose certain duties on the borrower. In the case of public bond issues these affirmative covenants are generally fairly innocuous. For example, the company may be obliged to furnish bondholders with a copy of its annual accounts. If it doesn't do so, it is in default on the bonds.

Many privately placed issues impose much more onerous affirmative covenants. The most common of these are covenants to maintain at all times some minimum level of working capital or of net worth. If the amount of working capital or net worth is a good guide to the value of the company, the lenders are putting a ceiling on the amount they can lose.

We do not want to give the impression that the lenders are constantly seeking an opportunity to cry "default" and then demand their money back. If the company does default, the lenders have the *right* to claim repayment but they will not generally do so. The more usual result is that the lenders or the trustee will seek a detailed explanation from the company and discuss possible changes in its oper-

---

[27] Usually these restrictions prohibit the company from paying dividends if their cumulative amount would exceed the sum of (1) cumulative net income, (2) the proceeds from the sale of stock or conversion of debt, and (3) a dollar amount equal to about 1 year's dividend.

[28] "Material adverse change" is usually not specifically defined—the clause protects the lender in scenarios where the borrower falls into default without triggering specific covenants. Of course this clause might be a dangerous weapon in the hands of a short-sighted and unscrupulous lender, who could pretend to see an adverse change and try to extort a higher interest rate by threatening to demand immediate repayment. Fortunately, few if any financial institutions play this game. They would be sued for trying it, and their reputation for *not* taking unfair advantage of their customers is a valuable business asset.

ating policy. It is only as a last resort that lenders demand early repayment and force the company into bankruptcy.

24-6   INNOVATION IN THE BOND MARKET

Domestic bonds, foreign bonds, and eurobonds; fixed-rate and floating-rate bonds; coupon bonds and zeros; callable, extendable, and retractable bonds; secured and unsecured bonds; senior and junior bonds—you might think that all this would give you as much choice as you need. Yet almost every day some new type of bond seems to be issued. The following paragraphs present a few examples of unusual bonds that were issued in 1985 and 1986.

A liquid yield option note (LYON) is a callable and retractable, convertible zero coupon bond (and you can't get anything much more complicated than that). In 1985 Waste Management Inc. issued the first LYON at a price of 25 percent. It was a 16-year zero coupon bond that was convertible at any time into a fixed number of shares. The bondholder had an annual option to sell the bond back to the company for cash and in addition Waste Management had the option to *call* the bond for cash. The exercise price of the company's call option was set initially below the exercise price of the investors' put option. However, both prices were increased each year and from year 10 onward the two options had the same exercise price.[29]

In January 1986 the Student Loan Marketing Association (Sallie Mae) issued the first yen bond to have so-called harmless warrants. The bond was a $6\frac{1}{2}$ percent 5-year bond, which after 3 years could be called by the company at its face value. The warrants gave the investor the option to acquire an identical bond except that it was noncallable. During the first 3 years these warrants could be exercised only by surrendering the original bond and thereafter they had to be exercised by paying cash.

Notice that investors will want to exercise their warrants to buy the *new* bonds for cash only if interest rates fall. But these are exactly the circumstances that Sallie Mae will want to call the *old* bonds. So what's special about a bond with harmless warrants? The package of bonds and warrants is effectively the same as a non-callable 5-year bond.

One month later Sallie Mae issued an even more unusual bond—a reverse floater. The interest rate on this bond was set at $17\frac{1}{4}$ percent less the London interbank offered rate (LIBOR). Thus, if the general level of interest rates rose, the payment on the Sallie Mae issue fell. However, it was not allowed to fall below zero.[30]

Companies in the United States do not have a monopoly on creativity. For example, Swedish Export Credit (SEK) issued a 5-year yen bond with an 8 percent coupon. The issue came in two tranches. For one tranche the final repayment is

---

[29] To complicate matters, investors could not exercise their put option until 1988. In contrast Waste Management could exercise its call option beginning in 1986, but it was prohibited from doing so in the first 2 years if the price of the common stock was below a specified minimum. If the bond is called, investors have a final chance to decide whether to convert into common stock. For an interesting discussion of the Waste Management LYON see J. McConnell and E. S. Schwartz, "Taming LYONS," *Journal of Finance,* **41**: 561–576 (July 1986).

[30] In October 1986 Hong Kong Mass Transit Railway went one better and offered a 5-year United States dollar floater with warrants. The warrants had a maturity of 1 year and gave the holder the right to buy a 5-year, Hong Kong dollar, reverse floater paying 15.15 percent *less* the short-term Hong Kong interest rate (HIBOR).

TABLE 24-1
GMAC's original issue discount bonds were expected to appreciate by an increasing percentage amount each year, but the IRS allowed GMAC to deduct the same *dollar* amount each year from taxable income

Year	(1) PV at Start of Year	(2) Change in PV During Year	(3) Allowable Tax Write-Off
1	$252.5	$37.3	$74.75
2	289.8	42.8	74.75
3	332.5	49.1	74.75
4	381.6	56.3	74.75
5	437.9	64.6	74.75
6	502.5	74.1	74.75
7	576.6	85.1	74.75
8	661.7	97.6	74.75
9	759.4	112.0	74.75
10	871.4	128.6	74.75
Total		$747.5	$747.50

60 percent of face value if the Japanese stock market index declines. For each percentage point rise in the market index the final repayment is increased by .75 percentage points, but the most that you can get back is 110.6 percent of face value. The second tranche of the issue was similar except that it pays 110.6 percent of face value if the market does *not* rise. For each percentage point rise in the market index, the final repayment is *reduced* by .75 percentage points with a minimum repayment of 60 percent of face value.[31]

The Causes of Innovation

It is often difficult to foresee which new securities will become popular and which will never get off the ground. However, Merton Miller believes that government often has a crucial role to play. He compares government regulation and tax with the grain of sand that irritates the oyster and produces the pearl.[32] Let's look in some detail at how one quirk in the tax rules brought about a new type of bond.

Example. In June 1981 General Motors Acceptance Corporation issued $750 million of 10-year zero coupon notes. The issue price was $252.50 for each note. Thus the investor faced a prospective fourfold increase in value over 10 years, which is equivalent to a compound return of about 14.8 percent a year.

Table 24-1 shows the expected yearly change in the value of the GMAC notes. In year 1, the prospective appreciation is .148 × 252.5 = $37.3. At the start of year 2, the expected value of the notes is 252.5 + 37.3 = $289.8. Thus the appreciation in year 2 is .148 × 289.8 = $42.8, and so on. Of course, the total appreciation over the 10 years is 1000 − 252.5 = $747.5.

The attraction to GMAC of zero coupon debt arose from an IRS mistake. The IRS correctly recognized that even if debt does not pay interest, it is still costly to

[31] Issues like the SEK issue are generally known as "bull-bear" bonds.

[32] See M. H. Miller, "Financial Innovation: The Last Twenty Years and the Next," *Journal of Financial and Quantitative Analysis,* **21:** 459–471 (December 1986).

the issuer. Therefore, it allowed the company to deduct a portion of the original issue discount from taxable income. But in calculating this deduction, the IRS employed simple, rather than compound, interest. Thus GMAC was permitted to deduct the same amount in each year, 747.5/10 = $74.75.

If you compare columns 2 and 3 of Table 24-1, you will see that in the early years of the loan's life, GMAC could deduct more than the cost of the loan from its taxable income. For example, in year 1 each note *cost* GMAC $37.3, or 14.8 percent of the amount of the loan. However, when calculating taxable profits GMAC was allowed to deduct $74.75, or 29.6 percent of the amount of the loan. From year 7 onward, the deduction is less than the cost of the loan but, other things equal, GMAC benefited from having the extra tax shield in the early years.

Of course, this is not the whole story. Just as the IRS pretended that GMAC paid interest of $74.75 a year, so it pretended that the noteholders received interest of $74.75 a year. But, as long as GMAC notes were bought by tax-exempt investors, this was no disadvantage.[33]

The tax advantage to zero coupon bonds led to a flurry of issues in 1981. By 1982, the IRS had become sufficiently concerned about the loss of revenue that it began to use compound interest to calculate the tax deduction. From that point on, the tax incentive to issue zero coupon debt disappeared. Companies continued to issue zero coupon debt but at a much slower rate than before.[34]

The Gains from Innovation

Initially the benefits of zero coupon debt went to those investment banks that were smart enough to devise and market the idea, and to issuers such as GMAC. But, remember, there was an advantage to zero coupon debt only if the marginal investor had a lower tax rate than the borrower. This takes us back to the capital structure controversy of Chapter 18. As long as only a few companies issued zero coupons, there were enough tax-exempt investors who were happy to hold them. But, as more such debt was issued, those companies who came late on the scene faced higher rates of interest. Thus, as soon as everyone had cottoned on to the idea, all the benefits went to the tax-exempt investors in the form of this higher interest rate.[35]

The lesson is a simple one. Investment banks and companies can be sure of benefiting from an innovation only if they are early in the field. Once the market is in equilibrium, all the benefits go to the players that are in short supply (in our example, the tax-exempt investors).

Lasting Innovations

You can think of the IRS as subsidizing the development of zero coupon bonds. But the important and worthwhile innovations are those that survive once such subsidies have been removed. Some endure because they reduce costs. Often an idea starts as a one-off deal between a bank and its customer. As demand grows, the tailor-made product is replaced by tradeable securities that perform a similar function. Such a process is known as "securitization."

---

[33] Zero coupon bonds were popular with the Japanese, since the Japanese tax authorities treated the price appreciation as a capital gain. This ruling was changed in 1985.

[34] For a further analysis of the tax incentives for OID debt, see D. Pyle, "Is Deep Discount Debt Financing a Bargain?," *Chase Financial Quarterly,* **1:** 39–61 (1981).

[35] We may oversimplify: If tax-exempt investors foresee that further issues are going to force up the interest rate on zero coupon bonds, they may be reluctant to buy the early issues at the lower interest rate.

There are economies of scale in the securities markets just as there are in other businesses, and this creates a continuing pressure for standardization. In the next chapter we shall see how the increased volatility of interest rates and exchange rates brought about a demand for low-cost ways to hedge these risks. The huge volume of potential business made it possible to offer standardized futures contracts at very low cost.[36]

Innovations also survive because they widen investor choice. When economists smile in their sleep, they are probably dreaming of a complete capital market in which there are as many different securities as there are possible future states of the world. Such a market would give investors the widest possible choice and allow them to select portfolios that would protect them against any combination of hazards.

Of course complete markets are just make-believe, but we do observe a constant demand for new securities to protect against new dangers. For example, in countries such as Israel or Brazil that suffer from persistent inflation, investors don't want bonds that offer a fixed money return; they want ones that give a fixed *real* return. Therefore, in these countries payments on most debt are indexed to the rate of inflation. Indexed bonds are rare in the United States, but whenever inflation rears its head, so do proponents of indexed bonds.

Instead of being tied to the general rate of inflation, payments are sometimes indexed to the price of a particular commodity. French Rail, for example, has issued a bond which is linked to the price of rail travel and which therefore resembles a long-term transferable season ticket. A few companies in the United States have also sought to limit shareholders' risk by tying bond payments to the price of a particular commodity. For instance, in June 1986 Standard Oil issued a zero coupon note maturing in 1992. At maturity the lenders are repaid at least the $1000 face value. In addition, they are entitled to a bonus equal to 200 times the amount by which the oil price exceeds $25 a barrel.[37] The Standard Oil bond gives the firm protection against the vagaries of oil prices. If the price of oil is low in 1992, so is the company's income. However, this is partly mitigated by the fact that the cost of its debt is also low.

24-7 SUMMARY

Now that you have read this chapter, you should have a fair idea of what you are letting yourself in for when you make a public issue of bonds. You can make an issue of bonds in the domestic United States market or you can do so in a foreign bond market or in the eurobond market. Eurobonds are bonds that are marketed simultaneously in a number of foreign countries, usually by the London branches of international banks and security dealers.

The detailed bond agreement is set out in the indenture between your company and a trustee, but the main provisions are summarized in the prospectus to the issue.

The indenture states whether the bonds are senior or subordinated and whether they are secured or unsecured. Most bonds are unsecured debentures or notes.

---

[36] For a general discussion of the way that market innovations have stemmed from a drive for more efficient ways to provide a financial service, see I. A. Cooper, "Innovations: New Market Instruments," *Oxford Review of Economic Policy,* **2:** 1–17 (1986).

[37] However, the bonus could not be greater than 200 × $15 = $3000 per bond. In the same month Standard Oil also issued a 4½-year note. The bonus on this note was equal to 170 times the amount by which the oil price exceeded $25 a barrel.

This means that they are general claims on the corporation. The principal exceptions are utility first mortgage bonds, collateral trust bonds, and equipment trust certificates. In the event of a default the trustee to these issues can repossess the company's assets in order to pay off the debt.

Most long-term bond issues have a *sinking fund*. This means that the company must set aside enough money each year to retire a specified number of bonds. A sinking fund reduces the average life of the bond and (as long as the company is not allowed to repurchase bonds in the marketplace) it provides a yearly test of the company's ability to service its debt. It therefore protects the bondholders against the risk of default.

Most long-dated bonds may be called at a premium which is initially equal to the coupon and which declines progressively to zero. There is one common limitation to this right—companies are generally prohibited from calling the bond in the first few years if they intend to replace it with another bond at a lower rate of interest. The option to call the bond may be very valuable: If interest rates decline and bond values rise, you may be able to call a bond that would be worth substantially more than the call price. Of course, if investors know that you may call the bond, the call price will act as a ceiling on the market price. Your best strategy, therefore, is to call the bond as soon as the market price hits the call price. You are unlikely to do better than that.

The bond indenture also lays down certain conditions. Here are some examples of things the company must *not* do.

1. Issues of senior bonds usually prohibit the company from issuing further senior or junior debt if the ratio of senior debt to net tangible assets would exceed a specified maximum.
2. Issues of subordinated bonds usually also prohibit the company from issuing further senior or junior debt if the ratio of *all* debt to net tangible assets would exceed a specified maximum.
3. Unsecured bonds incorporate a *negative pledge* clause, which prohibits the company from securing additional debt without giving equal treatment to the existing unsecured bonds.
4. Many bonds place a limit on the company's dividend payments.

Conditions that require the company to take positive steps to protect the bondholders are known as *positive covenants*. In public bond issues these conditions are generally innocuous. The really important positive covenants are those that give the bondholder the chance to claim a default and get money out while the company still has a substantial value. For example, some bond issues require the company to maintain a minimum level of working capital or net worth. Since a deficiency in either is a good indication of financial weakness, this condition is tantamount to giving the bondholders the right to demand their money back as soon as life appears hazardous.

Private placements are less standardized than public issues and they impose more stringent covenants. Otherwise they are close counterparts of publicly issued bonds.

There is an enormous variety of bond issues, and new forms of bonds are spawned almost daily. By a principle of natural selection some of these new instruments become popular and may even replace existing species. Others are ephemeral curiosities. We don't know all the reasons for the success of some innovations but we suggest that many new securities owe their origin to tax rules and government regulation. The lasting innovations are those that reduce costs or widen investor choice.

APPENDIX A   EXCERPTS FROM A PROSPECTUS FOR A BOND ISSUE

Prospectus Supplement

(To Prospectus Dated October 9, 1985)
$75,000,000
Potomac Electric Power Company

First Mortgage Bonds, 11¼% Series due 2015

The New Bonds will mature on November 1, 2015. Interest on the New Bonds is payable semi-annually on May 1 and November 1 beginning May 1, 1986. The New Bonds will be redeemable, in whole or in part, on not less than 30 days notice at the option of the Company and at the redemption prices set forth herein; provided, however, that none of the New Bonds shall be redeemed prior to November 1, 1990, if such redemption is for the purpose or in anticipation of refunding such New Bonds through the use, directly or indirectly, of funds borrowed by the Company at an effective interest cost of less than 11.36% per annum. See "Description of the New Bonds—Redemption of New Bonds" herein.

Application will be made to list the New Bonds on the New York Stock Exchange.

THESE SECURITIES HAVE NOT BEEN APPROVED OR DISAPPROVED BY THE SECURITIES AND EXCHANGE COMMISSION NOR HAS THE COMMISSION PASSED UPON THE ACCURACY OR ADEQUACY OF THIS PROSPECTUS SUPPLEMENT OR THE PROSPECTUS. ANY REPRESENTATION TO THE CONTRARY IS A CRIMINAL OFFENSE.

	Price to Public (1)	Underwriting Discount	Proceeds to Company (1) (2)
Per Bond	99.500%	.401%	99.099%
Total	$74,625,000	$300,750	$74,324,250

(1) Plus accrued interest from November 1, 1985, to date of delivery.
(2) Before deduction of expenses payable by the Company, estimated to be $490,000.

The New Bonds are offered subject to receipt and acceptance by the Underwriters, to prior sale and to the Underwriters' right to reject any order in whole or in part and to withdraw, cancel or modify the offer without notice. It is expected that delivery of the New Bonds will be made at the office of Salomon Brothers, Inc, One New York Plaza, New York, New York or through the facilities of The Depository Trust Company on or about November 13, 1985.

Salomon Brothers Inc

> **The First Boston Corporation**

> > **Kidder, Peabody & Co.**
> > Incorporated

> > > **Merrill Lynch Capital Markets**

> > > > **PaineWebber**
> > > > Incorporated

> > > > > **Prudential-Bache**
> > > > > Securities

The date of this Prospectus Supplement is October 28, 1985.

IN CONNECTION WITH THIS OFFERING, THE UNDERWRITERS MAY OVER-ALLOT OR EFFECT TRANSACTIONS WHICH STABILIZE OR MAINTAIN THE MARKET PRICE OF THE NEW BONDS OFFERED HEREBY AT A LEVEL ABOVE THAT WHICH MIGHT OTHERWISE PREVAIL IN THE OPEN MARKET. SUCH TRANSACTIONS MAY BE EFFECTED ON THE NEW YORK STOCK EXCHANGE OR OTHERWISE. SUCH STABILIZING, IF COMMENCED, MAY BE DISCONTINUED AT ANY TIME.

THE ISSUE IN BRIEF

The following is a summary of certain pertinent facts, and is qualified in its entirety by detailed information and financial statements appearing elsewhere in this Prospectus Supplement or the Prospectus to which it is attached, or in documents incorporated in the Prospectus by reference. See ''Incorporation of Certain Documents by Reference.''

THE OFFERING

Company .... Potomac Electric Power Company
Securities Offered .... $75,000,000 First Mortgage Bonds, 11¼% Series due 2015
Interest Payment Dates ...... May 1 and November 1, commencing May 1, 1986
Application for Listing .... New York Stock Exchange
Redemption .... ''Redemption of New Bonds''

THE COMPANY

Business and Service Area... Generation, transmission, distribution and sale of electricity in the Washington metropolitan area
1984 Fuel Mix .... Coal 89%; Oil 11%

For selected financial information and the Company's ratio of earnings to fixed charges see ''Selected Financial Information'' and ''Ratio of Earnings to Fixed Charges.''

DESCRIPTION OF THE NEW BONDS

The following description of the particular terms of the New Bonds offered hereby supplements the description of the general terms and provisions of the New Bonds set forth in the Prospectus, to which description reference is hereby made. See ''Description of Bonds and Mortgage.''

General. The New Bonds offered hereby, of which $75 million principal amount will be issued, will be due November 1, 2015, and will bear interest at the rate set forth in the title thereof, payable semiannually on May 1 and November 1 in each year, commencing May 1, 1986.

Redemption of New Bonds. The New Bonds offered hereby are to be redeemable prior to maturity, in whole or in part, at any time upon at least 30 days notice, at the election of the Company, at the redemption prices (in terms of percentage of principal amount) set forth in the following table, together, in each case, with accrued interest to the redemption date; *provided, however,* that prior to November 1, 1990 the Company may not redeem any of such New Bonds from or in anticipation of moneys borrowed having an effective interest cost (computed in accordance with generally accepted financial practice) of less than 11.36%, the interest cost to the Company of such New Bonds.

If Redeemed During the 12 Month Period Ending November 1	Redemption Price Expressed as Percentage of the Principal Amount of Bonds	If Redeemed During the 12 Month Period Ending November 1	Redemption Price Expressed as Percentage of the Principal Amount of Bonds
1986	110.75%	1997	104.84%
1987	110.21	1998	104.30
1988	109.67	1999	103.76
1989	109.14	2000	103.22
1990	108.60	2001	102.69
1991	108.06	2002	102.15
1992	107.52	2003	101.61
1993	106.99	2004	101.07
1994	106.45	2005	100.54
1995	105.91	2006 and	
1996	105.37	thereafter	100.00

UNDERWRITING

Subject to the terms and conditions set forth in the Underwriting Agreement, the Company has agreed to sell to each of the Underwriters named below, and each of the Underwriters has severally agreed to purchase, the principal amount of the New Bonds set forth opposite its name below:

Underwriters	Principal Amount of New Bonds
Salomon Brothers, Inc.	$12,500,000
The First Boston Corporation	12,500,000
Kidder, Peabody & Co. Incorporated	12,500,000
Merrill Lynch, Pierce, Fenner & Smith Incorporated...............	12,500,000
PaineWebber Incorporated	12,500,000
Prudential-Bache Securities Inc.....................................	12,500,000
Total	$75,000,000

The Underwriting Agreement provides that the several obligations of the Underwriters are subject to certain conditions precedent and that the Underwriters will be obligated to purchase all of the New Bonds if any are purchased.

The Company has been advised by the Underwriters that they propose initially to offer the New Bonds to the public at the public offering price set forth on the cover page of this Prospectus Supplement, and to certain dealers at such price less a concession not in excess of .30% of the principal amount of the New Bonds. The Underwriters may allow and such dealers may reallow a concession not in excess of .25% of the principal amount of the New Bonds to certain other dealers. After the initial public offering, the public offering price and such concessions may be changed.

The Underwriting Agreement provides that, subject to certain conditions, the Company will indemnify the several Underwriters and their controlling persons against certain liabilities, including liabilities under the Securities Act of 1933, arising out of or based upon, among other things, any untrue statement or alleged untrue statement of a material fact contained in the Registration Statement, the Prospectus or this Prospectus Supplement, or the documents incorporated by reference therein, or the omission or alleged omission to state therein a material fact required to be stated therein or necessary to make the statements therein, in light of the circumstances under which they were made, not misleading.

POTOMAC ELECTRIC POWER COMPANY

FIRST MORTGAGE BONDS

Potomac Electric Power Company (the "Company") may offer from time to time up to $150,000,000 aggregate principal amount of its First Mortgage Bonds (The "New Bonds"), which may be offered as separate series in amounts, at prices and on terms to be determined by market conditions at the time of sale. The aggregate principal amount, rate (or method of calculation) and time of payment of interest, maturity, offering price, any redemption terms or other specific terms of the series of New Bonds in respect of which this Prospectus is being delivered are set forth in the accompanying Prospectus Supplement (the "Prospectus Supplement").

The Company may sell the New Bonds through underwriters designated by the Company, or dealers, directly to a limited number of institutional purchasers or through agents. See "Plan of Distribution". The Prospectus Supplement sets forth the names of such underwriters, dealers or agents, if any, any applicable commissions or discounts and the net proceeds to the Company from such sale.

THESE SECURITIES HAVE NOT BEEN APPROVED OR DISAPPROVED BY THE SECURITIES AND EXCHANGE COMMISSION NOR HAS THE COMMISSION PASSED UPON THE ACCURACY OR ADEQUACY OF THIS PROSPECTUS. ANY REPRESENTATION TO THE CONTRARY IS A CRIMINAL OFFENSE.

The date of this Prospectus is October 9, 1985.

THE COMPANY

Potomac Electric Power Company (the "Company") is engaged in the generation, transmission, distribution and sale of electric energy in the Washington metropolitan area, including the District of Columbia, major portions of Montgomery and Prince George's Counties in Maryland, and a small portion of Arlington County in Virginia. It also supplies, at wholesale, most of the electricity distributed in Calvert, Charles and St. Mary's Counties in southern Maryland. During 1984, approximately 53% of its revenue was derived from Maryland, 45% from the District of Columbia and 2% from Virginia. Approximately 17% and 4% of such revenue were derived from departments of the United States and District of Columbia governments, respectively.

The Company's principal executive offices are located at 1900 Pennsylvania Avenue, N.W., Washington, D.C. 20068 and its telephone number is (202) 872-2456.

USE OF PROCEEDS

The proceeds from the sale of the New Bonds will be applied to refund the Company's senior securities: long-term debt retirements, preferred and preference stock redemptions and contractual sinking fund requirements. Proceeds may be used to pay off short-term debt incurred to fund the above-mentioned senior security retirements or may be temporarily placed in short-term investments pending the application of the proceeds as stated above.

The Company does not plan to use the proceeds to support its ongoing construction program which will be financed through internally generated funds and short-term borrowings.

PLAN OF DISTRIBUTION

The Company may sell the New Bonds in any of three ways: (i) through underwriters or dealers; (ii) directly to a limited number of institutional purchasers or to a single purchaser; or (iii) through agents. The Prospectus Supplement with respect to any New Bonds being offered thereby sets forth the terms of the offering of such New Bonds, including the name or names of any underwriters, the purchase price of such New Bonds and the proceeds to the Company from such sale, any underwriting discounts and other items constituting underwriters' compensation, any initial public offering price and any discounts or concessions allowed or reallowed or paid to dealers and any securities exchanges on which such New Bonds may be listed.

If underwriters are used in the sale, the New Bonds will be acquired by the underwriters for their own account and may be resold from time to time in one or more transactions, including negotiated transactions, at a fixed public offering price or at varying prices determined at the time of sale. The New Bonds may be either offered to the public through underwriting syndicates represented by the underwriter or underwriters to be designated by the Company, or directly by one or more of such firms. Unless otherwise set forth in the Prospectus Supplement, the obligations of the underwriters to purchase the New Bonds offered thereby will be subject to certain conditions precedent, and the underwriters will be obligated to purchase all such New Bonds if any are purchased. Any initial public offering price and any discounts or concessions allowed or reallowed or paid to dealers may be changed from time to time.

New Bonds may be sold directly by the Company or through agents designated by the Company from time to time. The Prospectus Supplement sets forth the name of any agent involved in the offer or sale of the New Bonds in respect of which the Prospectus Supplement is delivered as well as any commission payable by the Company to such agent. Unless otherwise indicated in the Prospectus Supplement, any such agent is acting on a best efforts basis for the period of its appointment.

If so indicated in the Prospectus Supplement, the Company will authorize agents, underwriters or dealers to solicit offers by certain specified institutions to purchase the New Bonds from the Company at the public offering price set forth in the Prospectus Supplement pursuant to delayed delivery contracts providing for payment and delivery on a specified date in the future. Such contracts will be subject to those conditions set forth in the Prospectus Supplement, and the Prospectus Supplement will set forth the commission payable for solicitation of such contracts.

Agents and underwriters may be entitled under agreements entered into with the Company to indemnification by the Company against certain civil liabilities, including liabilities under the Securities Act of 1933, or to contribution with respect to payments which the agents or underwriters may be required to make in respect thereof. Agents and underwriters may be customers of, engage in transactions with, or perform services for the Company in the ordinary course of business.

. . . .

DESCRIPTION OF BONDS AND MORTGAGE

General. The New Bonds are to be issued under the Mortgage and Deed of Trust dated July 1, 1936, between the Company and The Riggs National Bank of Washington, D.C., as Trustee, as amended and supplemented and as to be supplemented by a separate supplemental indenture (the "Supplemental Indenture") each time New Bonds are offered under this Prospectus and the accompanying Prospectus Supplement. Said mortgage, as so amended and supplemented and to be supplemented, is herein sometimes called the "Mortgage". Copies of the documents currently constituting the Mortgage are exhibits to the Registration Statement, as is the form of the Supplemental Indenture.

Reference is made to the Prospectus Supplement which accompanies this Prospectus for the following terms and other information with respect to the New Bonds being offered thereby: (1) the designation and aggregate principal amount of such New Bonds; (2) the date on which such New Bonds will mature; (3) the rate per annum at which such New Bonds will bear interest, or the method of determining such rate; (4) the dates on which such interest will be payable; and (5) any redemption terms or other specific terms applicable to the New Bonds.

The New Bonds will be available only in fully registered form without coupons in the denominations of $1,000 or any multiple thereof. Both principal and interest on the New Bonds will be payable at the agencies of the Company, The Riggs National Bank of Washington, D.C. and Bankers Trust Company, New York, N.Y. The Company will not impose charges for any exchanges of New Bonds.

The Supplemental Indenture will contain no provision for an improvement and sinking fund or any maintenance and replacement requirement or dividend restriction; neither does the Mortgage and all indentures supplemental thereto relating to any outstanding Series of Bonds contain any such provisions; the supplemental indentures relating to certain outstanding Series of Bonds do, however, contain sinking fund provisions.

The following statements are outlines of certain provisions contained in the Mortgage and do not purport to be complete. They are qualified by express reference to the cited Sections and Articles of the Mortgage. Certain terms used are as defined in the Mortgage.

Security.   The New Bonds will be secured, together with all other Bonds now or hereafter issued under the Mortgage, by a valid and direct first lien (subject to certain leases, Permitted Liens and other minor matters) on substantially all the properties and franchises of the Company (the principal properties being its generating stations and its electric transmission and distribution systems), other than cash, accounts receivable and other liquid assets, securities (including securities evidencing investments in subsidiaries of the Company), leases by the Company as lessor, equipment and materials not installed as part of the fixed property, and electric energy and other materials, merchandise or supplies produced or purchased by the Company for sale, distribution or use. The Company's 9.72% undivided interest in a mine-mouth, steam-electric generating station, known as the Conemaugh Generating Station, which is located in Indiana County, Pennsylvania, and its associated transmission lines is that of a tenant in common with eight other utility owners. Substantially all of such Conemaugh transmission lines and of the transmission and distribution lines of less than 230,000 volts, portions of the 230,000 and 500,000 volt transmission lines and 13 substations are located on land owned by others or on public streets and highways.

The Mortgage contains provisions subjecting after-acquired property (subject to pre-existing and Permitted Liens) to the lien thereof. The lien on such property is, however, subject (except for property in Pennsylvania) to rights of persons having superior equities attaching prior to the recording or filing of an appropriate supplemental indenture.

Issuance of Additional Bonds. Additional Bonds ranking equally with the New Bonds may be issued in an aggregate amount of up to (i) 60% of the Net Bondable Value of Property Additions not subject to an Unfunded Prior Lien, (ii) the amount of cash deposited with the Trustee (which may thereafter be withdrawn on the same basis that Additional Bonds are issuable under (i) and (iii)), and (iii) the amounts of Bonds retired or to be retired (except out of trust moneys or by any sinking or analogous fund if the fund prevents such use) (Secs. 4, 6 and 7, Art. III; Sec. 4 Art. VIII).

Additional Bonds may not be issued unless Net Earnings of the Company Available for Interest and Property Retirement Appropriations (i.e., earnings before depreciation, amortization, income taxes and interest charges) during 12 of the immediately preceding 15 months shall have been at least twice the annual interest charges on all Bonds and Prior Lien Bonds then outstanding and then being issued, unless they are being issued on the basis of Bonds paid at or redeemed or purchased within two years of maturity or on the basis of Property Additions subject to an Unfunded Prior Lien (which simultaneously becomes a Funded Prior Lien) and the Bonds are issued within two years of the maturity of the Prior Lien Bonds secured by such Prior Lien (Secs. 3, 4 and 7, Art. III). Giving effect to the issuance of the New Bonds at an assumed rate of interest of 11% (and before giving effect to any interest reductions arising from debt refundings), such Net Earnings for the twelve months ended June 30, 1985 would be approximately 4.7 times the aggregate annual interest charges referred to above. Such coverage would permit issuance of approximately $1.25 billion of mortgage bonds (in addition to the New Bonds) at an assumed average interest rate of 11% per annum, against property additions or cash deposits, although only approximately $540 million of such additional bonds could currently be issued in compliance with unbonded net property addition limitations contained in the mortgage indenture.

So long as any New Bonds are outstanding, Property Additions constructed or acquired on or before December 31, 1946 may not be made the basis for the issue of Bonds, or the withdrawal of cash, or the reduction of cash required to be paid to the Trustee (Sec. 2, Part IV, Supplemental Indenture).

Prior Lien Bonds secured by an Unfunded Prior Lien may be issued under the circumstances and subject to the limitations contained in the Mortgage (Sec. 16, Art. IV)

After giving effect to the issuance of the New Bonds (which are to be issued against Property Additions), approximately $905 million of the Property Additions as of June 30, 1985 will remain available for the purposes permitted in the Mortgage, including the issuance of Bonds.

Release of Property. The Mortgage permits property to be released from the lien of the Mortgage upon compliance with the provisions thereof. Such provisions generally require that cash be deposited with the Trustee in an amount equal to the fair value of the property to be released. The Mortgage also contains certain requirements relating to the withdrawal of cash deposited to obtain a release of property. (Art. VII and Art. VIII.)

Modification of Mortgage. With the consent of 80% in amount of Bonds and of 80% in amount of Bonds of each series affected if less than all are affected, the Mortgage may be changed except to affect the terms of payment of the principal or interest on any Bond or to reduce the percentage of Bondholders required to effect any change (Sec. 6, Art. XV).

The Supplemental Indenture, however, provides that the foregoing percentages shall be reduced to 60% upon the consent or agreement to such change by 80% of outstanding Bonds. Purchasers of the New Bonds will be deemed to have agreed to such reduction pursuant to the terms of the Supplemental Indenture.

Events of Default. 25% in amount of Bonds, upon any Event of Default, may require the Trustee to accelerate maturity of the Bonds (although a majority in amount of Bonds may waive such default and rescind such acceleration if such default is cured) and to enforce the lien of the Mortgage upon being indemnified to its satisfaction (Sec 1 and 4, Art. IX).

A majority in amount of Bonds may direct proceedings for the sale of the trust estate, or for the appointment of a receiver or any other proceedings under the Mortgage, but have no right to involve the Trustee in any personal liability without indemnifying it to its satisfaction (Sec. 11, Art. IX).

Events of Default include failure to pay principal, failure for 30 days to pay interest or to satisfy any improvement, maintenance or sinking fund obligation, failure for 60 days (after notice by the Trustee or the holders of 15% in amount of Bonds) to perform any other covenant, and certain events in bankruptcy, insolvency or reorganization (Sec. 1, Art. IX).

The Mortgage does not require that periodic evidence be furnished to the Trustee as to the absence of default or as to compliance with the terms of the Mortgage.

APPENDIX B   PROJECT FINANCE

The privately placed loans that we have referred to in this chapter are direct obligations of the parent or one of its principal subsidiaries. In recent years there has been considerable interest in a new type of private loan that is tied as far as possible to the fortunes of a particular project and that minimizes the exposure of the parent. Such a loan is usually referred to as *project finance* and is the specialty of the large banks.

An Example from the Oil Industry

Let us look at how British Petroleum (BP) used project financing to pay for development of its huge Forties Field in the North Sea. Since BP needed to finance very large expenditures elsewhere in the world, management wanted to segregate the financing of the Forties Field project as far as possible from BP's other fund-raising activities. Ideally it would have liked to isolate its other business completely from the fate of the North Sea, but no bank could be expected to take the risk of lending solely on the security of a field that was not yet producing.

BP's solution is illustrated in Figure 24-2. A syndicate of 66 major banks agreed to lend a total of $945 million—the largest industrial bank loan in history. But instead of lending the money directly to BP, they lent it to a company called Norex, which was controlled by the banks. Norex in turn paid the money to BP Development, the subsidiary of BP that was responsible for developing the Forties Field. But Norex's payment to BP Development was not in the form of a loan; it was an advance payment for future deliveries of oil. In other words, in return for the money BP Development promised to deliver to Norex an agreed quantity of oil. Of course, the last thing the banks wanted was a load of oil on their doorsteps. Therefore, they also arranged for another BP subsidiary, BP Trading, to repurchase the oil from Norex at a prescribed price.

Payments to Norex had to be completed within 10 years. But, because a number of unpredictable factors affected the development of the Forties Field, the speed with which Norex was paid off was tied to the production rate of the field.

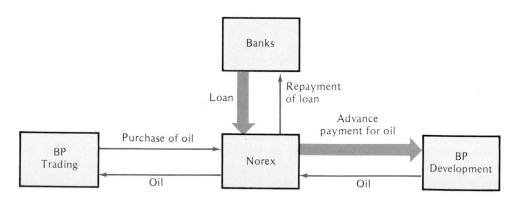

FIGURE 24-2
Financing for the Forties Field project. The banks made a loan to Norex, which then made an advance payment to BP Development for future deliveries of oil. This oil was resold to BP Trading at an agreed-on price. These payments by BP Trading allowed Norex to repay the banks. The heavy arrows show how the banks provided financing; the lighter arrows show how BP repaid the banks.

The banks consented to bear the ultimate risk that the oil reserves were insufficient to service their loan. However, they were protected against three other hazards. The first was the possible failure of BP Development to construct the necessary facilities. The agreement, therefore, specified in considerable detail the manner in which the field should be developed, and BP guaranteed that its subsidiary would carry out this plan.

The second danger was that the field might be depleted more rapidly than was envisaged. To protect the banks against this possibility BP guaranteed that each year the difference between the market value of the oil produced and the amount needed to service the loan should be paid into a "reclaim account," which could be drawn upon by Norex if the oil flow was subsequently reduced.

The third risk was that of force majeure. If it proved impossible to produce any oil before the end of 6 years and if the assessed reserves would have been adequate to service the loan, then Norex could claim repayment from a restitution account that was guaranteed by BP.

One effect of this complicated financing arrangement was that the banks accepted some of the risk associated with the Forties Field. For example, if the oil reserves were inadequate to service the banks' loan to Norex, the banks had no claim against BP's other assets. A second difference between the Forties project financing and a straight bank loan was that the project financing did not show up in BP's balance sheet as a debt. Instead, BP Trading's promise to repurchase the oil from Norex was recorded as a deferred liability against future oil delivery.

Project Finance— Some Common Features

The arrangement for the Forties Field project illustrates the most important features of project financing. The basic requirement of any project financing is that the project can be physically isolated from the parent and that it offers the lender tangible security. The additional research and legal costs also mean that project financing is economic only when the sums involved are very large. Most of the projects have been major mineral extraction and processing developments. Many have been located overseas and often they have been joint ventures.

Project finance is often provided in the form of a straight loan to the operating company. However, the BP Forties financing is an example of an alternative arrangement known as a *production payment*. In this case the banks do not lend to either the parent or the operating company. Instead they lend to an intermediate company (such as Norex) which is controlled by them. This company then uses the money to make an advance payment to the project's owner against future delivery of the product. When the product is delivered, the intermediate company can sell it and use the proceeds to repay the banks.

We can classify all project financings according to the contractual obligations of the project's owners. The purest, but least common, method of financing offers the lender "no recourse" against the owners at any stage. This notion of "no recourse" is somewhat imprecise, for the banks may well require a general assurance from the parent that it will do its best to ensure the success of the project. Although these "comfort letters" are usually too general to be sued upon, they do represent a potentially embarrassing commitment on the part of the parent.

One of the most common threats to a successful project loan is a serious delay in completion. Occasionally the project may even turn out to be technically infeasible. Our second class of loans, therefore, consists of those that are supported by a completion guarantee. Such a guarantee may be provided by the parent company or by an insurance company in the form of "completion bonding."

The third and largest group of project loans provides the lender with rather more recourse against the parent. For instance, we saw that BP promised to repurchase oil from Norex at a prescribed price. Here are three other examples of how the parent companies may provide some limited guarantees:

1. *The throughput arrangement.* Many oil pipeline loans involve a "throughput arrangement." This states that if other companies do not make sufficient use of the pipeline, the owners themselves will ship enough oil through it to provide the pipeline company with the cash that it needs to service the loan.
2. *The cost company arrangement.* Under a cost company arrangement the project's owners receive all the project's output free of charge. In exchange they agree to pay all operating costs including loan service. Thus the project has no net income, and each parent firm simply deducts from its own profits its share of the project's expenses.
3. *The cash deficiency arrangement.* Under this arrangement, the project's owners agree to provide the operating company with enough funds to maintain a certain level of working capital.

Regardless of the precise arrangement, it is important in any project financing that the payments on the loan should correspond as closely as possible to the ability of the project to generate earnings. For example, if the project's completion date is uncertain, the first payment date on the loan may simply be set at a specified number of months after completion. If the loan involves a large final payment, it is common to include an "earnings recapture" clause under which a proportion of any surplus earnings is applied to reduce the final payment. A lender who bears the risk of inadequate reserves will wish to ensure that the reserves are not depleted too rapidly. In these cases, therefore, it is common to assign a *proportion* of revenues to loan repayments rather than a fixed sum.

The Benefits of Project Finance

A number of motives have been suggested for the use of project finance rather than direct borrowing by the parent company. It is tempting to believe that the value of a project to the parent is enhanced if it can be made to stand alone as a self-financing entity, so that the parent benefits from its success and is isolated from its failure. Such a result is improbable. When we look at actual project loans, we find that not only is the parent rarely isolated from the vicissitudes of the project but the rate of interest on the project loan is directly related to the degree of support that the parent provides. However, project finance does allow the parent to transfer specific risks to the lenders. For example, if BP had borrowed on the general credit of the parent company, it would have remained exposed to the risk of inadequate North Sea reserves, whereas the Forties financing effectively provided insurance against this contingency. Correspondingly, with many loans for projects in politically unstable countries the lenders are taking on the risk of adverse government action. Many companies believe that expropriation by a foreign government is *less likely* when they raise money by a project financing. They argue that few governments would want to take an action that would anger a group of leading international banks.

A further motive that has been suggested for project financing is that it may not be shown as debt on the company's balance sheet. For example, we have already seen how BP's financing of the Forties Field showed up as a deferred liability against future deliveries. In some cases the owner's guarantees may not be shown on the balance sheet at all. In this case, the financing is said to be "off balance sheet.'' Of course this does not make any difference unless the lenders or shareholders do not recognize these hidden liabilities.

Project financing can often be costly to arrange, but sometimes the arrangement may be simpler than a direct loan. This is partly because the projects are often jointly owned by several parents, but it is also because the security for the lenders commonly derives as much from the contractual arrangements as from the tangible assets. For example, a bank's security for a pipeline loan depends on the existence of throughput arrangements, and its security for a tanker loan depends on the charter agreements. In such instances it may be simplest to tie the loan directly to these contracts.

FURTHER READING

Brennan and Schwartz and Kraus provide a general discussion of call provisions.

M. J. Brennan and E. S. Schwartz: ''Savings Bonds, Retractable Bonds and Callable Bonds,'' *Journal of Financial Economics,* **5:** 67–88 (1977).

A. Kraus: ''An Analysis of Call Provisions and the Corporate Refunding Decision,'' *Midland Corporate Finance Journal,* **1:** 46–60 (Spring 1983).

Smith and Warner provide an extensive survey and analysis of covenants.

C. W. Smith and J. B. Warner, ''On Financial Contracting: An Analysis of Bond Covenants,'' *Journal of Financial Economics,* **7:** 117–161 (June 1979).

The following booklets provide useful reviews of the variations in bond terms.

R. Mason: *Innovations in the Structures of International Securities,* Credit Suisse First Boston, London, September 1986.

The Salomon Brothers Global Fixed-Income Catalog, Salomon Brothers, Inc., September 1987.

QUIZ

1. Select the most appropriate term from within the parentheses:

(*a*) (High-grade utility bonds/Low-grade industrial bonds) generally have only light sinking fund requirements.

(*b*) (Short-dated notes/Long-dated debentures) are often noncallable.

(*c*) Collateral trust bonds are often issued by (utilities/industrial holding companies).

(*d*) (Utility bonds/Industrial bonds) are usually unsecured.

(*e*) Equipment trust certificates are usually issued by (railroads/financial companies).

2. (*a*) If interest rates rise, will callable or noncallable bonds fall more in price?

(*b*) The Belgian government has issued bonds that may be repaid after a specified date at the option of *either* the government or the bondholder. If each side acts rationally, what will happen on that date?

3. Which of the following sinking funds increase the value of a bond at the time of issue?

(*a*) An optional sinking fund operating by drawings at par

(*b*) A mandatory sinking fund operating by drawings at par *or* by purchases in the market

(*c*) A mandatory sinking fund operating by drawings at par

4. (*a*) As a senior debtholder would you like the company to issue more junior debt, would you prefer it not to do so, or would you not care?

    (*b*) You hold debt secured on the company's existing property. Would you like the company to issue more unsecured debt, would you prefer it not to do so, or would you not care?

  5. Use the Pepco prospectus (but not the text) to answer the following questions:

    (*a*) Who are the principal underwriters for the issue?

    (*b*) Who is the trustee for the issue?

    (*c*) How many dollars does the company receive for each debenture after deduction of *all* expenses?

    (*d*) Is the debenture "bearer" or "registered?"

    (*e*) Does the investor have to send in coupons in order to receive the regular interest payment?

    (*f*) At what price is the issue callable in 1989?

    (*g*) Can the company call the bond in 1989 and replace it with a debenture yielding 5 percent?

  6. Look at the Pepco prospectus:

    (*a*) How much would you have to pay to buy one bond delivered at the end of November, 1985? Don't forget to include accrued interest.

    (*b*) When is the first interest payment on the bond and what is the total amount of that payment?

    (*c*) On what date do the bonds finally mature and what is the principal amount of the bonds that is due to be repaid that date?

    (*d*) Suppose that the market price of the bonds rises to 102 and thereafter does not change. When should the company call the issue?

QUESTIONS AND PROBLEMS

  1. After a sharp change in interest rates, newly issued bonds generally sell at yields different from outstanding bonds of the same quality. One suggested explanation is that there is a difference in the value of the call provision. Explain how this could arise.

  2. Obtain a prospectus for a recent bond issue and compare the terms and conditions with the Pepco issue.

  3. What restrictions are usually imposed on a company's freedom to issue further debt? Be as precise as possible. Explain carefully the reasons for such restrictions.

  4. Explain carefully why senior and subordinated bond indentures place different restrictions on a company's freedom to issue additional debt.

  5. A retractable bond is a bond which may be repaid before maturity at the investor's option. Sketch a diagram similar to Figure 24-1 showing the relationship between the value of a straight bond and a retractable bond.

  6. What determines the value of an indexed bond? Should the rate of interest on an indexed bond be higher or lower than the expected real rate on a nominal bond?

  7. Explain carefully why bond indentures place limitations on the following actions:

    (*a*) Sale of the company's assets

    (*b*) Payment of dividends to shareholders

    (*c*) Issue of additional senior debt

  8. Look up the terms of a commodity-linked bond (e.g., the Standard Oil "oil bond" or the International Refining gold bond). Find out what has happened to these bonds as the commodity price has changed. Have these bonds increased shareholders' risk or reduced it?

9. Suppose that instead of issuing the original issue discount bonds, GMAC had raised the same amount of money by an issue of 14.80 percent 10-year notes at a price of $100.

(*a*) What face amount of notes would GMAC have needed to issue?

(*b*) Value the gain to GMAC from the issue of OID debt rather than the 14.80 percent notes. (You may assume either the MM or Miller theory of debt and taxes. See Sections 18-2 and 18-3.)

(*c*) Show that the gain to GMAC disappears if the annual tax deduction is calculated using compound interest rather than simple interest.

10. Does the issue of additional junior debt harm senior bondholders? Would your answer be the same if the junior debt matured *before* the senior debt? Explain.

11. Estimate the value of the Standard Oil "oil bond" (see Section 24-6).

12. State as precisely as you can the circumstances in which each of the options on Waste Management's LYONs will be exercised. What does this imply about the upper and lower limits on the price of the bond in each year?

13. In Section 24-6 we referred to Sallie Mae's upside-down floater. The payment on this bond is calculated by deducting LIBOR from 17¼ percent. The rate is not permitted to fall below zero. Explain how you would value such a security. (*Hint:* Find a package of other securities that would produce identical cash flows.) What does this tell you about the riskiness of Hong Kong Mass Transit Railway's warrants (see footnote 29).

14. Dorlcote Milling has outstanding a $1 million 3 percent mortgage bond maturing in 10 years. The coupon on any new debt issued by the company is 10 percent. The finance director, Mr. Tulliver, cannot decide whether there is a tax benefit to repurchasing the existing bonds in the marketplace and replacing them with new 10 percent bonds. What do you think? Start by assuming that all bondholders are tax-exempt. Then introduce Miller's idea that higher-rate taxpayers will gravitate to tax-efficient securities and force up their prices.

15. Look up a recent issue of an unusual bond in, say, a recent issue of the periodical *Euromoney*. Why do you think this bond was issued? What investors do you think it would appeal to? How would you value the unusual features?

16. In a number of countries such as France it is not uncommon for firms to band together to make a debt issue. A portion of the receipts is put aside in a safe government bond and the remainder is parceled out among the different issuers. Each firm is responsible for its portion of the total debt, but in the event of default by any one firm the lenders can draw on the money invested in the government bond. Do you think this is a good idea? How would you value this debt?

17. Some eurobonds involve payments in more than one currency. For example, in 1985 Anheuser-Busch issued a 10-year yen bond at a price of 101. The coupon payment is made in yen but the final repayment of principal is in dollars at an exchange rate of 208 yen to the dollar. How would you value such a bond?

25

Hedging Financial Risk

Most of the time we take risk as God-given. An asset or business has its beta, and that's that. Its cash flow is exposed to unpredictable changes in selling price, labor cost, tax rates, technology, and a long list of other variables. There's nothing the manager can do about it.

That's not wholly true. To some extent a manager can *select* the risks of an asset or business. Some risks can be *hedged* (i.e., offset) by trading in options, **futures,** or other financial instruments.[1]

Suppose your company harvests trees and manufactures building products. Here are some of its principal sources of risk:

- Selling prices of standardized products, such as:
  Lumber
- Exchange rates including:
  U.S. versus Canadian dollars, because some of your major competitors are Canadian
  U.S. dollars versus Japanese yen, because Japan is a major market for lumber and building products
- New housing starts in the United States, which (among other things) depend on:
  Mortgage interest rates
- Changes in the energy cost of running your factories, which largely reflect:
  Crude oil prices

All the risks shown in italics can be hedged. For example, you can cancel out the unpredictable fluctuations in the selling price of your lumber by trading in futures contracts. As Table 25-1 shows, there is a futures market for each of the variables in italics, and for many other commodities and financial instruments. You may also be able to use options and other securities to hedge risks.

This chapter will explain *how* firms can hedge out unpredictable fluctuations in many business and financial variables. But first we should give some of the reasons *why* they do it.

Like insurance, hedging is seldom free. Most businesses hedge to reduce risk, not to make money.[2]

Why then bother to hedge? For one thing, it makes financial planning easier and reduces the odds of an embarrassing cash shortfall. A shortfall might only

---

[1] Risks can also be *amplified* by trading, but operating managers do not usually speculate in this way. They leave speculation to professional traders.

[2] Hedging transactions are zero-NPV when trading is costless and markets are completely efficient. In practice the firm has to pay small trading costs. Sometimes also it may be less well informed than professional traders on the other side of the market.

TABLE 25-1

Some futures contracts and the exchanges on which they are traded

---

COMMODITY FUTURES

Barley (LGF,WPG)	Lumber (CME,ME)
Corn (CBT,MCE)	
Oats (CBT,MCE,WPG)	Aluminum (COMEX,LME)
Rye (WPG)	Copper (COMEX,LME,MCE)
Wheat (CBT,KC,LGF,MCE,MPLS,WPG)	Gold (CBT,COMEX,MCE)
	Lead (LME)
Flaxseed (WPG)	Nickel (LME)
Rapeseed (WPG)	Palladium (NYMEX)
Soybeans (CBT,MCE)	Platinum (MCE,NYMEX)
Soybean meal (CBT,MCE)	Silver (CBT,COMEX,LME,MCE)
Soybean oil (CBT)	Zinc (LME)
Cattle (CME,MCE)	Crude oil (NYMEX)
Hogs (CME,MCE)	Gas oil (IPE)
Pork bellies (CME)	Heating oil (NYMEX)
	Propane (CTN)
Cocoa (CSCE, LCE)	
Coffee (CSCE, LCE)	Freight rates (BIFFEX)
Orange Juice (CTN)	
Potatoes (LPFA, NYMEX)	Cotton (CTN)
Sugar (CSCE, LSFM)	Wool (SFE)
	Commodity Futures Index (NYFE)

FINANCIAL FUTURES

Canadian dollar (IMM,MCE)	U.S. Treasury bills (IMM,MCE)
Deutschemark (IMM,LIFFE,MCE)	U.S. Treasury notes (CBT)
European Currency Unit (CTN)	U.S. Treasury bonds (CBT,LIFFE,MCE)
French franc (IMM)	
Sterling (IMM,LIFFE,MCE)	Eurodollar deposits (IMM,LIFFE)
Swiss franc (IMM,LIFFE,MCE)	U.S. dollar CDs (IMM)
U.S. dollar index (CTN)	
Yen (IMM,LIFFE,MCE)	GNMA (CBT)
	U.S. municipal bond index (CBT)
U.S. stock market indexes (CBT,IMM,KC,NYFE,PhilSE)	
U.S. Consumer Price Index (CSCE)	

Key to abbreviations:

BIFFEX	Baltic International Freight Futures Exchange
CBT	Chicago Board of Trade
CME	Chicago Mercantile Exchange
COMEX	Commodity Exchange, New York
CSCE	Coffee, Sugar and Cocoa Exchange, New York
CTN	New York Cotton Exchange
IMM	International Monetary Market (at CME)
IPE	International Petroleum Exchange of London
KC	Kansas City Board of Trade
LCE	London Commodity Exchange
LGF	London Grain Futures Market
LIFFE	London International Financial Futures Exchange
LME	London Metal Exchange
LPFA	London Potato Futures Association
LSFM	London Sugar Futures Market
MCE	MidAmerica Commodity Exchange
ME	Montreal Exchange
MPLS	Minneapolis Grain Exchange
NYFE	New York Futures Exchange (unit of the New York Stock Exchange)
NYMEX	New York Mercantile Exchange
PhilSE	Philadelphia Stock Exchange
SFE	Sydney Futures Exchange
WPG	Winnipeg Commodity Exchange

mean an unexpected trip to the bank, but in extreme cases it could trigger financial distress or even bankruptcy. Why not reduce the odds of these awkward outcomes with a hedge?

In some cases hedging also makes it easier to decide whether an operating manager deserves a stern lecture or a pat on the back. Suppose your lumber export division shows a 60 percent profit increase in a period when the yen unexpectedly jumps by 12 percent against the U.S. dollar. How much of the increase is due to the exchange rate shift, and how much to good management? If the exchange rate was hedged, it's probably good management. If it was not, things have to be sorted out with hindsight, probably by asking, "What would profits have been *if* the yen had been hedged?"[3]

Finally, hedging extraneous events can help focus the operating manager's attention. We know we shouldn't worry about events outside our control, but most of us do anyway. It's naive to expect the sawmill manager not to worry about lumber prices if her bottom line and bonus depend on them. That worrying time would be better spent if the prices were hedged.[4]

In this chapter we are going to explain how to set up a hedge and we shall introduce you to some of the basic tools of hedging, including forward and futures contracts and swaps.

25-1 THE TECHNIQUE OF HEDGING

In Chapter 7 we saw how risk can be reduced by diversifying across a number of securities that are not closely correlated. The idea behind hedging is somewhat different. Ideally you want to find two investments that are *perfectly* correlated. You then buy one and sell the other so that the net position is absolutely safe. In practice the correlation is often not perfect, and therefore some residual risk remains despite the hedge.

Whether the correlation is perfect or not, the techniques for setting up a hedge are the same. Suppose that you already have a liability A. You now wish to hedge this liability by an offsetting purchase of asset B. The object is to minimize the uncertainty of your net position.

The size of your investment in B depends on how the values of A and B are related. Suppose, for example, you estimate that percentage changes in the value of A are related in the following way to percentage changes in the value of B

$$\begin{pmatrix} \text{Expected change in} \\ \text{value of A} \end{pmatrix} = a + \delta \begin{pmatrix} \text{change in value} \\ \text{of B} \end{pmatrix}$$

Delta (δ) measures the sensitivity of A to changes in the value of B. It is also equal to the hedge ratio—that is, the number of units of B which should be purchased to hedge the liability of A. You minimize risk if you offset your liability by the purchase of delta units of B.[5]

---

[3] Many large firms hedge away operating divisions' risk exposures by setting up internal, make-believe markets between the divisions and the treasurer's office. Trades in the internal markets are at real (external) market prices. The object is to relieve the operating manager of risks outside his or her control. The treasurer makes a separate decision on whether to hedge the *firm's* exposure.

[4] A Texas oilman who lost hundreds of millions in various ill-fated deals protested, "Why should I worry? Worry is for strong minds and weak characters." If there are any financial managers with weak minds and strong characters, we especially advise them to hedge whenever they can.

[5] Notice that A, the item that you wish to hedge, is the dependent variable. Delta is the sensitivity of A to changes in B.

Let us illustrate. Imagine that an investment dealer has sold short $12.5 million of IBM stock. If the market rises, it is likely that the price of IBM will rise also and the dealer will lose money on her sale of IBM. She can reduce this risk by making an offsetting purchase of the market portfolio. (In practice, rather than attempting to buy the market portfolio, she would buy an index future. More about that later.) To judge how much she should invest in the market, the dealer must first estimate the sensitivity of IBM's stock price to changes in the market index. On past evidence this relationship is as follows:

$$\left(\begin{array}{l}\text{Expected monthly change}\\\text{in value of IBM}\end{array}\right) = a + \delta \left(\begin{array}{l}\text{monthly change}\\\text{in market index}\end{array}\right)$$

$$= .78 + .72 \times \text{(change in market index)}$$

In this case the sensitivity of IBM's stock price is identical to our old friend, beta. To minimize risk the investment dealer should combine her short position in IBM with an offsetting investment of $.72 \times 12.5 = \$9$ million in the market portfolio.

Note that we said "minimize" risk, not "eliminate." Market movements explained only 28 percent of the variance of price changes in IBM stock.[6] Hedging with the market index cannot offset the remaining 72 percent, the unique, or diversifiable, risk of IBM stock. The correlation between the returns on the market index and the returns on a diversified portfolio of stocks is much higher than for IBM alone. If the market index is used to hedge a short position in a diversified portfolio, the proportionate reduction in risk is much greater.

Notice that our investment dealer hedges a $12.5 million short position by making a $9 million investment in the market portfolio. Although she is hedged against *changes* in the value of IBM stock, the value of her short position in IBM is not equal to the value of her investment in the market portfolio. To create a *zero-value hedge* the investment dealer would also need to set aside $3.5 million in a bank deposit:

Assets (Millions)		Liability (Millions)	
PV (market investment)	$ 9	PV(IBM stock)	$12.5
PV (bank deposit)	3.5		
	$12.5		$12.5

As time passes, the investment dealer is likely to find that the value of her assets is no longer equal to that of her liability. For example, suppose the market index falls 5 percent and the price of IBM stock rises 10 percent. (Remember the hedge is not perfect. IBM stock will not always move by .72 times the market change.) Now the value of the market investment is $8.55/13.75 = 62$ percent of the short position in IBM and the risk of her position is no longer minimized. She must invest $1.35 more in the market to regain the .72 hedge ratio.

Thus the investment dealer needs to follow a dynamic hedging strategy in which she periodically buys or sells the market portfolio to maintain the desired hedge ratio. Later in the chapter we will come across cases where the hedge ratio itself changes over time. Here, too, you will need to follow a dynamic hedging strategy.

---

[6] That is, $R^2 = .28$. See Chapter 9, Section 9-1.

TABLE 25-2
The first four columns show that the final cash flow accounts for only 63.2 percent of the present value of the 13¾s of 1991. The final column shows how to calculate a weighted average of the time to each cash flow. This average is the bond's duration

Year	C_t	PV(C_t) at 7.6%	Proportion of Total Value (PV(C_t)/V)	Proportion of Total Value × Time
1	$ 137.5	127.79	.102	.102
2	137.5	118.76	.095	.190
3	137.5	110.37	.088	.265
4	137.5	102.58	.082	.329
5	1,137.5	788.66	.632	3.159
		$V = 1,248.16$	1.000	Duration = 4.045 years

25-2 DURATION AND VOLATILITY

When we estimated the hedge ratio for our investment dealer, we relied on past history to tell us the sensitivity of IBM's stock price to changes in the value of the market. We will now see how a little theory can sometimes help to estimate the hedge ratio.

In July 1986 Treasury 13¾s of 1991 had a present value of 124.82 and yielded 7.6 percent. Table 25-2 shows where this present value comes from. Notice that the cash flow in year 5 accounts for only 63.2 percent of value. More than one-third of the value comes from earlier cash flows. Therefore, it is somewhat misleading to describe the bond as a 5-year bond; the average time to each cash flow is less than 5 years.

Bond analysts often use the term *duration* to describe the average time to each payment. If we call the total value of the bond V, then duration is calculated as follows:[7]

$$\text{Duration} = \left[\frac{\text{PV}(C_1)}{V} \times 1 \right] + \left[\frac{\text{PV}(C_2)}{V} \times 2 \right] + \left[\frac{\text{PV}(C_3)}{V} \times 3 \right] + \cdots$$

For the 13¾s of 1991,

$$\text{Duration} = (.102 \times 1) + (.095 \times 2) + (.088 \times 3) + \cdots$$

$$= 4.045 \text{ years}$$

The Treasury 8⅛s of 1991 have the same maturity as the 13¾s, but the first 4 years' coupon payments account for a smaller fraction of the bond's value. In this sense the 8⅛s are a longer bond than the 13¾s. The duration of the 8⅛s is 4.311 years.

Consider now what happens to the prices of our two bonds as interest rates change:

	13¾s OF 1991		8⅛s OF 1991	
	New Price	Change	New Price	Change
Yield falls .5%	127.19	+1.90%	104.19	+2.03%
Yield rises .5%	122.50	−1.86	100.10	−1.98
Difference	4.69	3.76%	4.09	4.01%

[7] We assume annual coupon payments. Actual payments are semiannual.

Thus a 1 percent variation in yield causes the price of the 13¾s to change by 3.76 percent. We can say that the 13¾s have a *volatility* of 3.76 percent.

Notice that the 8⅛ percent bonds have the greater volatility and they also have the longer duration. In fact a bond's volatility is directly related to its duration:

$$\frac{\text{Volatility}}{\text{(percent)}} = \frac{\text{duration}}{1 + \text{yield}}$$

In the case of the 13¾s,

$$\frac{\text{Volatility}}{\text{(percent)}} = \frac{4.045}{1.076} = 3.76$$

Volatility is a useful summary measure of the likely effect of a change in interest rates on a debt portfolio.

Example and Some Refinements

Potterton Leasing has just purchased some equipment and arranged to rent it out for $2 million a year over 8 years. At an interest rate of 12 percent, Potterton's rental income has a present value of $9.94 million:[8]

$$PV = \frac{2}{1.12} + \frac{2}{(1.12)^2} + \cdots + \frac{2}{(1.12)^8} = \$9.94 \text{ million}$$

The duration of the rental income is 3.9 years; that is,

$$\text{Duration} = \frac{1}{9.94}\left[\left(\frac{2}{1.12} \times 1\right) + \left(\frac{2}{1.12^2} \times 2\right) + \cdots + \left(\frac{2}{1.12^8} \times 8\right)\right]$$

$$= 3.9 \text{ years}$$

Potterton proposes to finance the deal by issuing a package of $1.91 million of 1-year debt and $8.03 million of 6-year debt, each with a 12 percent coupon. Think of its new asset (the stream of rental income) and the new liability (the issue of debt) as a package. Does Potterton stand to gain or lose on this package if interest rates change?

We can answer this question by calculating the duration of Potterton's new liability. The duration of the 1-year debt is 1 year and the duration of the 6-year debt is 4.6 years. The duration of the package of 1- and 6-year debt is a weighted average of the durations of the individual issues:

$$\begin{array}{l}\text{Durability of} \\ \text{liability}\end{array} = \left(\frac{1.91}{9.94} \times \begin{array}{l}\text{duration of} \\ \text{1-year debt}\end{array}\right) + \left(\frac{8.03}{9.94} \times \begin{array}{l}\text{duration of} \\ \text{6-year debt}\end{array}\right)$$

$$= (.192 \times 1) + (.808 \times 4.6) = 3.9 \text{ years}$$

Thus, both the asset (the lease) and the liability (the debt package) have a duration of 3.9 years. Therefore, both are affected equally by a change in interest rates. If rates rise, the present value of Potterton's rental income will decline, but the value of its debt obligation will also decline by the same amount. Rental income will decline, but the value of its debt obligation will also decline by the same amount. By equalizing the duration of the asset and the liability, Potterton has *immunized* itself against any change in interest rates. It looks as if Potterton's financial manager knows a thing or two about hedging.

---

[8] We ignore tax in this example.

TABLE 25-3
Potterton can hedge by issuing this sinking fund bond that pays out $2 million each year

Year	CASH FLOWS, IN MILLIONS							
	1	2	3	4	5	6	7	8
Balance at start of year	$9.94	9.13	8.23	7.22	6.08	4.81	3.39	1.79
Interest at 12%	1.19	1.10	.99	.87	.73	.58	.40	.21
Sinking fund payment	.81	.90	1.01	1.13	1.27	1.42	1.60	1.79
Interest plus sinking fund payment	$2.00	2.00	2.00	2.00	2.00	2.00	2.00	2.00

Notice several things about this example. First, the hedge ratio is measured by the ratio of the durations of the liability and the asset. Since both the lease and the debt package have the same duration, the hedge ratio is 1.0: Potterton minimizes uncertainty by ensuring that the amount of debt issued is equal to the present value of the rental payments ($9.94 million). Could Potterton have hedged itself simply by issuing 6-year debt? Certainly. The duration of the lease is 85 percent of the duration of the 6-year debt:

$$\frac{\text{Duration of lease}}{\text{Duration of 6-year debt}} = \frac{3.9}{4.6} = .85$$

Therefore Potterton could have hedged itself against changes in interest rates simply by issuing $.85 \times$ PV(lease) = $8.45 million of 6-year debt. If interest rates change, the change in the value of the lease will be equal to the change in the value of the debt issue. However, in this case the amount of the debt issue will not be equal to the value of the lease. To create a zero-value hedge, Potterton would also need to issue a further $9.94 - 8.45 = \$1.49$ million of very short-term debt with a duration of zero.

Second, notice that Potterton's debt package protects the firm only against an across-the-board change in interest rates. For example, if short-term and long-term interest rates do not move exactly together, Potterton would have to consider two volatility measures. It would need to ensure that its assets and liabilities were equally affected by changes in the short-term rate and also that they were equally affected by changes in the long rate.[9]

Third, as interest rates change and time passes, the duration of Potterton's asset may no longer be the same as that of its liability. Thus, to remain hedged against interest rate changes, Potterton must be prepared to keep adjusting the duration of its debt.

If Potterton is not disposed to follow this dynamic hedging strategy, it has an alternative. It can devise a debt issue whose cash flows exactly match the rental income from the lease. For example, suppose that it issues an 8-year sinking fund bond; the amount of the sinking fund is $810,000 in year 1 and the payment increases by 12 percent annually. Table 25-3 shows that the bond payments (interest plus sinking fund) are $2 million in each year.

---

[9] In practice short-term and long-term interest rates do not move in exact lockstep. In addition short rates vary *more* than long rates. Despite this, hedging policies based on a simple duration measure are hard to beat. (See J. Nelson and S. M. Schaefer, "The Dynamics of the Term Structure and Alternative Portfolio Immunization Strategies" in G. O. Bierwag, G. G. Kaufman, and A. Toevs, eds., *Innovations in Bond Portfolio Management: Duration Analysis and Immunization,* Greenwich, Conn.: JAI Press, 1983.) As so often in finance, simple rules are hard to beat.

Since the cash flows on the asset exactly match those on the liability, Potterton's financial manager can now relax. Each year the manager simply collects the $2 million rental income and hands it to the bondholders. Whatever happens to interest rates, the firm is always perfectly hedged.

Why would not Potterton's financial manager *always* prefer to construct matching assets and liabilities? One reason is that it may be relatively costly to devise a bond with a specially tailored pattern of cash flows. Another may be that Potterton is continually entering into new lease agreements and issuing new debt. In this case the manager can never relax; it may be simpler to keep the duration of the assets and liabilities equal than to maintain an exact match between the cash flows.

25-3 HEDGING WITH FUTURES

Before the harvest, a wheat farmer cannot be sure of the price at which he will be able to sell his crop. If he does not like this uncertainty, he can reduce it by selling wheat **futures.** In this case he agrees to deliver so many bushels of wheat in the future at a price that is set today. Do not confuse this futures contract with an option where the holder has a choice whether or not to make delivery; the farmer's futures contract is a firm promise to deliver wheat.

A miller is in the opposite position. She needs to *buy* wheat after the harvest. If she would like to fix the price of this wheat ahead of time, she can do so by *buying* wheat futures. In other words, she agrees to take delivery of wheat in the future at a price that is fixed today. The miller also does not have an option; if she holds the contract to maturity, she is obliged to take delivery.

Both the farmer and the miller have less risk than before.[10] The farmer has hedged risk by *selling* wheat futures; this is termed a *short hedge.* The miller has hedged risk by *buying* wheat futures; this is known as a *long hedge.*

Hedgers are not the only buyers and sellers of futures. The market also needs speculators who are prepared to take on risk. For example, if there is an excess of short hedgers like our farmer, the price of futures will be forced down until a sufficient number of speculators are prepared to buy in hope of a profit. If there is an excess of long hedgers like our miller, the futures price will rise until a sufficient number of speculators are prepared to sell wheat futures.

The price of wheat for immediate delivery is known as the **spot price.** When the farmer sells wheat futures, the price that he agrees to take for his wheat may be very different from the spot price. But as the date for delivery approaches, a futures contract becomes more and more like a spot contract and the price of the future gets closer and closer to the spot price.

The farmer may decide to wait until his futures contract matures and then deliver wheat to the buyer. In practice such delivery is very rare, for it is more convenient for the farmer to buy back the wheat futures just before maturity.[11] If he is properly hedged, any loss of his wheat crop will be exactly offset by the profit on his sale and subsequent repurchase of wheat futures.

---

[10] We are oversimplifying. The miller won't reduce risk if bread prices vary in proportion to the post-harvest wheat price. In this case the miller is in the hazardous position of having fixed her cost but not her selling price. This point is discussed in A. C. Shapiro and S. Titman, "An Integrated Approach to Corporate Risk Management," *Midland Corporate Finance Journal,* **3:**41–56 (Summer 1985).

[11] In the case of some of the financial futures described below, you *cannot* deliver the asset. At maturity the buyer simply receives (or pays) the difference between the spot price and the price at which he or she agreed to purchase the asset.

Commodity and Financial Futures

Futures contracts are bought and sold on organized futures exchanges. The first part of Table 25-1 lists the principal commodity futures contracts and the exchanges on which they are traded. Notice that our farmer and miller are not the only businesses that can hedge risk with commodity futures. The lumber company and the builder can hedge against changes in timber prices, the copper producer and cable manufacturer against changes in copper prices, the oil producer and the trucker against changes in gasoline prices, and so on.[12]

For many firms the wide fluctuations in interest rates and exchange rates have become at least as important a source of risk as changes in commodity prices. The financial futures listed in the second part of Table 25-1 allow firms also to hedge against these risks. Financial futures are similar to commodity futures but, instead of placing an order to buy or sell a commodity at a future date, you place an order to buy or sell a financial asset at a future date.

Financial futures have been a remarkably successful innovation. They were invented in 1976; within a few years, trading in financial futures significantly exceeded trading in commodity futures.

The Mechanics of Futures Trading

When you buy or sell a futures contract, the price is fixed today but payment is not made until later. You will, however, be asked to put up margin in the form of either cash or Treasury bills to demonstrate that you have the money to honor your side of the bargain. As long as you earn interest on the margined securities, there is no cost to you.

In addition, futures contracts are *marked to market*. This means that each day any profits or losses on the contract are calculated; you pay the Exchange any losses and receive any profits. For example, suppose that our farmer agreed to deliver 100,000 bushels of wheat at $2.50 a bushel. The next day the price of wheat futures declines to $2.45 a bushel. The farmer now has a profit on his sale of 100,000 × $.05 = $5000. The Exchange's clearinghouse therefore pays this $5000 to the farmer. You can think of the farmer as closing out his position every day and then opening up a new position. Thus after the first day the farmer has realized a profit of $5000 on his trade and now has an obligation to deliver wheat for $2.45 a bushel.

Of course our miller is in the opposite position. The fall in the futures price leaves her with a *loss* of 5 cents a bushel. She must, therefore, pay over this loss to the Exchange's clearinghouse. In effect the miller closes out her initial purchase at a 5-cent loss and opens a new contract to take delivery at $2.45 a bushel.

Spot and Futures Prices —Financial Futures

If you want to buy a security, you have a choice. You can buy it for immediate delivery at the spot price. Alternatively, you can place an order for later delivery; in this case you buy at the futures price. When you buy a financial future, you end up with exactly the same security that you would have if you bought in the spot market. However, there are two differences. First, you don't pay for the security "up front," and so you can earn interest on its purchase price. Second, you

---

[12] By the time you read this, the list of futures contracts will almost certainly be out of date. Unsuccessful contracts are regularly dropped and at any time the Exchanges are seeking approval for literally dozens of new contracts.

miss out on any dividends or interest that are paid in the interim. This tells us something about the relationship between the spot and futures prices:[13]

$$\frac{\text{Futures price}}{(1 + r_f)^t} = \frac{\text{spot}}{\text{price}} - \text{PV}\left(\begin{array}{l}\text{dividends or}\\ \text{interest payments}\\ \text{forgone}\end{array}\right)$$

Here r_f is the t-period risk-free interest rate.

Two examples will show how and why this formula works.

Example: Stock Index Futures.   Suppose 6-month stock index futures trade at 320.28 when the index is 314. The 6-month interest rate is 8.2 percent and the average dividend yield of stocks in the index is 4 percent per year. Are these numbers consistent?

Suppose you buy the futures contract and set aside the money to exercise it. At an 8.2 percent annual rate, you'll earn about 4 percent interest over the next 6 months. Thus you invest:

$$\frac{\text{Futures price}}{(1 + r_f)^t} = \frac{320.28}{1.04} = 307.96$$

What do you get in return? Everything you would have gotten by buying the index now at the spot price, except for the dividends paid over the next 6 months. If we assume for simplicity that a half-year's dividends are paid in month 6 (rather than evenly over 6 months), your payoff is:

$$\frac{\text{Spot}}{\text{price}} - \text{PV(dividends)} = 314 - \frac{314(.02)}{1.04}$$

$$= 307.96$$

You get what you pay for.

* Example: Foreign Exchange Futures.   Suppose that you decide to buy 1-year Swiss franc futures rather than buying spot francs. Since you don't take delivery of the francs for a year, you earn an extra year's interest on your dollars. On the other hand, you also miss the opportunity to earn a year's interest on the francs. That lost interest plays the same role as the lost dividends on the stock index contract. Thus, if $r_\$$ is the dollar interest rate,

$$\frac{\begin{array}{c}\text{Futures price}\\ \text{of Swiss francs}\end{array}}{1 + r_\$} = \frac{\text{spot}}{\text{price}} - \text{PV}\left(\begin{array}{l}\text{forgone}\\ \text{interest on}\\ \text{Swiss francs}\end{array}\right)$$

Now the interest forgone is at the Swiss franc rate r_{sf}, and

$$\text{PV}\left(\begin{array}{l}\text{forgone}\\ \text{interest}\end{array}\right) = \frac{r_{sf} \times \text{spot price}}{1 + r_{sf}}$$

---

[13] This relationship is strictly true only if the contract is not marked to market. Otherwise the value of the future depends on the path of interest rates up to the delivery date. In practice this qualification is usually unimportant. See J. C. Cox, J. E. Ingersoll, and S. A. Ross, "The Relationship between Forward and Futures Prices," *Journal of Financial Economics,* **9:**321–346 (1981).

TABLE 25-4
Spreads between spot and discounted futures prices reveal the difference between storage costs and convenience yield. These figures are based on 1-year futures contracts in mid-September 1987

Commodity	Futures Price	Futures Price Discounted*	Spot Price†	PV(Storage Costs) Less PV(Convenience Yield)‡
Cocoa, per ton	$196.4	181.9	184	−2.1 (−1.1%)
Coffee, per pound	1.246	1.154	1.163	.009 (−.8%)
Copper, per pound	.757	.701	.804	−.103 (−12.8%)
Corn, per bushel	1.895	1.755	1.63	+.125 (+7.7%)
Frozen orange juice, per pound	1.3125	1.215	1.368	−.153 (−11.2%)
Soybean oil, per pound	.1727	.16	.158	+.002 (+1.2%)

* Interest rate of 8 percent assumed.
† Spot prices assumed equal to prices of futures maturing in September 1987.
‡ Figures in parentheses are percentages of spot prices.

A bit of algebra gives:

$$\text{Futures price of Swiss francs} = \text{spot price} \times \left(\frac{1 + r_\$}{1 + r_{\text{sf}}}\right)$$

This relationship between the futures and spot prices of currency is an important one which we will come back to in Chapter 34, International Financial Management.

Spot and Futures Prices— Commodities

The difference between buying *commodities* today and commodity futures is more complicated. First, because payment is again delayed, the buyer of the future earns interest on her money. Second, she does not need to store the commodities and, therefore, saves warehouse costs, wastage, and so on. On the other hand, the futures contract gives no *convenience yield,* which is the value of being able to get your hands on the real thing. The manager of a supermarket can't burn heating oil futures if there's a sudden cold snap and he can't stock the shelves with orange juice futures if he runs out of inventory at 1 P.M. on a Saturday. All this means that for commodities,

$$\frac{\text{Futures price}}{(1 + r_f)^t} = \text{spot price} + \text{PV}\left(\text{storage costs}\right) - \text{PV}\left(\text{convenience yield}\right)$$

No one would be willing to hold the futures contract at a higher futures price or to hold the commodity at a lower futures price.[14]

You can't observe PV(storage costs) or PV(convenience yield) separately, but you can infer the difference between them by comparing the spot price to the discounted futures price. Table 25-4 does this for a half-dozen commodities in

[14] The futures price could be less than given by our formula if no one is willing to hold the commodity, that is, if inventories fall to zero or some absolute minimum.

September 1987. For copper and orange juice, the convenience yield outweighed the storage costs. For corn it was the other way around. For cocoa, soybean oil, and coffee, storage cost and convenience yield more or less balanced out.

Though interesting, these figures are not necessarily typical. Spreads between commodity spot and futures prices can bounce around. For example, convenience yields on oil and gasoline can rise to very high levels when troubles in the Middle East revive fears of an interruption of supply.

25-4   FORWARD CONTRACTS

Each day billions of dollars of futures contracts are bought and sold. This liquidity is possible only because futures contracts are standardized and mature on a limited number of dates each year.

Fortunately there is usually more than one way to skin a financial cat. If the terms of futures contracts do not suit your particular needs, you may be able to buy or sell a **forward contract.** Forward contracts are simply tailor-made futures contracts. For example, suppose that you know that at the end of 6 months you are going to need a 3-month loan. You can lock in the interest rate on that loan by buying a **forward rate agreement** (FRA) from a bank.[15] For example, the bank might offer to sell you a 6-month forward rate agreement on 3-month LIBOR at 7 percent. If at the end of 6 months the 3-month LIBOR rate is greater than 7 percent, the bank will pay you the difference: If the 3-month LIBOR is less than 7 percent, you pay the bank the difference.[16]

By far the largest volume of business in forward contracts occurs in the foreign exchange markets. Banks regularly buy and sell forward currency for dates up to 1 year ahead, and in the case of the major currencies they are increasingly prepared to enter into contracts for 5 years or more.

All this may make forwards sound more attractive than futures. However, banks charge a higher rate if you want to buy forward currency for odd amounts or for odd periods. And, if you change your mind and decide that you want to sell your forward contract, you must renegotiate with the bank.

Homemade Forward Contracts

Suppose that you borrow $90.91 for 1 year at 10 percent and lend $90.91 for 2 years at 12 percent. These interest rates are for loans made today; therefore, they are spot interest rates.

The cash flows on your transactions are as follows:

	YEAR		
	0	1	2
Borrow for 1 year at 10%	+90.91	−100	
Lend for 2 years at 12%	−90.91		+114.04
Net cash flow	0	−100	+114.04

---

[15] Notice that the party that profits from a rise in rates is described as the "buyer." In our example she is usually said to buy "6 against 9 months" money, meaning that the forward agreement is for a 3-month loan in 6 months' time.

[16] Unlike futures contracts, forwards are not marked to market. Thus all profits or losses are settled when the contract matures.

Notice that you do not have any net cash outflow today but you have contracted to pay out money in year 1. The interest rate on this forward commitment is 14.04 percent. To calculate this forward interest rate we simply worked out the extra return for lending for 2 years rather than 1:

$$\text{Forward interest rate} = \frac{(1 + 2\text{-year spot rate})^2}{1 + 1\text{-year spot rate}} - 1$$

$$= \frac{1.12^2}{1.10} - 1 = .1404, \text{ or } 14.04\%$$

In our example you manufactured a forward loan by borrowing short-term and lending long. But you can also run the process in reverse. If you wish to fix today the rate at which you borrow next year, you borrow long and lend short.

You can also construct a do-it-yourself forward contract to buy or sell foreign exchange. For example, suppose that you want to place an order today to buy Swiss francs in 1 year. The current (or spot) exchange rate is 1 franc = $.50, the 1-year dollar interest rate is 6 percent, and the 1-year franc interest rate is 4 percent. You now borrow $50 for 1 year, exchange these dollars into francs, and lend your francs for a year. Your cash flows are as follows:

	NOW		AFTER 1 YEAR	
	Dollars	Francs	Dollars	Francs
Borrow dollars at 6%	+50		−53	
Change dollars into francs	−50	+100		
Lend francs at 4%		−100		+104
Net cash flow	0	0	−53	+104

Your net cash flow today is zero but you have committed to pay out $53 at the end of the year and receive 104 francs. Thus you have constructed a homemade forward contract to buy Swiss francs at an exchange rate of 1 franc = 53/104 = $.51.

We stated in Section 25-3 that the 1-year futures price for Swiss francs is

$$\text{Spot price of francs} \times \frac{1 + \text{dollar interest rate}}{1 + \text{franc interest rate}}$$

That better turn out to equal $.51, the cost of our homemade forward contract. It does:

$$\begin{matrix}\text{Futures} \\ \text{price of} \\ \text{francs}\end{matrix} = .50 \times \frac{1.06}{1.04} = \$.51$$

What would happen if the price of futures were higher than this figure? Everyone would rush to sell futures, borrow dollars, and lend francs. If the futures price were lower, they would do the reverse. Sharp-eyed arbitrageurs with families to support are constantly on the lookout for such discrepancies.

If you can make your own forward contract, why does anyone bother to trade on the futures exchanges? The answer is, "Convenience and cost." Some of the most popular futures contracts are the interest rate and currency futures contracts that are closest to maturity. In principle these are the easiest to replicate but the huge volume of business in financial futures makes them a very low cost tool for hedging (or speculation).

25-5 SWAPS

Suppose that the Possum Company wishes to borrow deutsche marks to help finance its European operations. Since Possum is better known in the United States, the financial manager believes that the company can obtain more attractive terms on a dollar loan than on a deutsche mark loan. Therefore, the company issues $10 million of 5-year 12 percent notes in the United States. At the same time Possum arranges with a bank to **swap** its future dollar liability for deutsche marks. Under this arrangement the bank agrees to pay Possum sufficient dollars to service its dollar loan; in exchange Possum agrees to make a series of annual payments in deutsche marks to the bank.

Here are Possum's cash flows (in millions):

	YEAR 0		YEARS 1–4		YEAR 5	
	$	DM	$	DM	$	DM
1. Issue dollar loan	+ 10		− 1.2		− 11.2	
2. Swap dollars for deutsche marks (DM)	− 10	+ 20	+ 1.2	− 1.6	+ 11.2	− 21.6
3. Net cash flow	0	+ 20	0	− 1.6	0	− 21.6

The combined effect of Possum's two steps (line 3) is to convert a 12 percent dollar loan into an 8 percent deutsche mark loan. The device that makes this possible is the currency swap. You can think of the cash flows for the swap (line 2) as a series of forward currency contracts. In each of years 1 through 4 Possum agrees to purchase $1.2 million at a cost of 1.6 million deutsche marks; in year 5 it agrees to buy $11.2 million at a cost of 21.6 million deutsche marks.[17]

The bank's cash flows from the swap are the reverse of Possum's. It has undertaken to pay out dollars in the future and receive deutsche marks. Since the bank is now exposed to the risk that the deutsche mark will weaken unexpectedly against the dollar, it will try to hedge this risk by a series of futures or forward contracts or by swapping deutsche marks for dollars with another counterparty. As long as Possum and the other counterparty honor their promises, the bank is fully protected against risk. The recurring nightmare for swap managers is that one party will default, leaving the bank with a large unmatched position.

Swaps are not new. For many years the British government limited purchases of foreign currency to invest abroad. These restrictions led many British firms to arrange so-called back-to-back loans. The firm would lend sterling to a company in the United States and simultaneously borrow dollars which could then be used for foreign investment. In taking out the back-to-back loan the British firm agreed to make a series of future dollar payments in exchange for receiving a flow of sterling income.

In 1979 these limits on overseas investment were removed and British firms no longer needed to take out back-to-back loans. However, during the 1980s the banks did a respray job on the back-to-back loan and relaunched it as a swap. Swaps turned out to be very popular with corporate customers; in the first quarter of 1987, 70 percent of dollar eurobond issues were accompanied by a swap.[18]

---

[17] Usually in a currency swap the two parties make an initial payment to each other (i.e., Possum pays the bank $10 million and receives 20 million deutsche marks). However, this is not necessary, and in the case of swaps that are in the *same* currency no initial payments occur and there are no final principal repayments.

[18] See *Euromoney Corporate Finance,* May 1987, p. 70.

Swaps are not limited to future exchanges of currency. For example, firms often swap fixed-interest-rate loans for floating-rate loans. In this case one party promises to make a series of fixed annual payments in return for receiving a series of payments that are linked to the level of short-term interest rates. Sometimes also swaps are used to convert between floating-rate loans that are tied to different base rates. For example, a firm might wish to swap a series of payments that are linked to the prime rate for a series of payments that are linked to the Treasury bill rate. It is even possible to swap commodities. In this case you don't need to deliver the commodities, you just settle up any differences in their value.[19]

25-6 SUMMARY

As a manager, you are paid to take risks, but you are not paid to take *any* risks. Some are simply bad bets and others could jeopardize the success of the firm. In these cases you should look for ways to hedge.

The idea behind hedging is straightforward. You find two closely related assets. You then buy one and sell the other in proportions that minimize the risk of your net position. If the assets are *perfectly* correlated, you can make the net position risk-free.

The trick is to find the hedge ratio, or delta—that is, the number of units of one asset that is needed to offset changes in the value of the other asset. Sometimes the best solution is to look at how the prices of the two assets have moved together in the past. For example, suppose that a 1 percent change in the value of B has been accompanied on average by a 2 percent change in the value of A. Then delta equals 2.0; to hedge each dollar invested in A you need to sell $2 of B.

On other occasions a little theory can help to find delta. For example, we showed how the average life of a fixed income stream can be measured by its "duration." If you buy a bond to hedge a fixed money liability, delta depends on the relative durations of the liability and the bond.

If the value of the asset *equals* the value of the liability, the net investment in the hedge is zero. We described this as a "zero-value" hedge. You can always convert any hedge into a zero-value hedge. If the value of the asset is *less* than the value of the liability, you put the difference into a bank deposit. If the value of the asset *exceeds* the liability, you can convert to a zero-value hedge by borrowing from the bank.

Some hedging strategies are static. Once you have set up the hedge, you can take a long vacation, confident that the firm is well-protected. Most hedging strategies are dynamic. As time passes and prices change, you may need to rebalance your position to maintain the hedge.

Firms use a number of tools to hedge:

1. Futures contracts are advance orders to buy or sell an asset. The price is fixed today but payment does not occur until the delivery date. The futures markets allow firms to place advance orders for dozens of different commodities, securities, and currencies.

2. Futures contracts are highly standardized and are traded in huge volume on the futures exchanges. Instead of buying or selling a standardized futures contract, you may be able to arrange a tailor-made contract with a bank. These tailor-made futures contracts are usually called "forward" contracts. Firms regu-

---

[19] You also encounter forwards on swaps, options on swaps (or "swaptions"), callable swaps, and puttable swaps.

larly protect themselves against exchange rate changes by buying or selling forward currency contracts.

3. It is also sometimes possible to construct homemade forward contracts. For example, as an alternative to buying forward currency, you could borrow dollars, exchange them for foreign currency, and then lend the foreign currency until it is needed. This would have exactly the same cash-flow consequences as a purchase of forward currency.

4. In recent years firms have entered into a variety of swap arrangements. For example, you may arrange for the bank to make all the future payments on your dollar loan in exchange for paying the bank the cost of servicing a deutsche-mark loan. Swaps are like packages of forward contracts.

FURTHER READING

The following are general articles on corporate risk management:

R. W. Anderson and J. P. Danthine, "Cross Hedging," *Journal of Political Economy,* **89**:1182–1196 (1981).

A. C. Shapiro and S. Titman, "An Integrated Approach to Corporate Risk Management," *Midland Corporate Finance Journal,* **3**:41–56 (Summer 1985).

C. W. Smith and R. M. Stultz, "The Determinants of Firms' Hedging Policies," *Journal of Financial and Quantitative Analysis,* **20**:391–405 (December 1985).

The following book is a general study of market innovation but it includes very useful material on swaps, forward rate agreements, and so forth:

Bank for International Settlements, *Recent Innovations in International Banking,* Basel, April 1986.

Hodges and Schaefer's article provides an example of how to hedge interest rate risk with exactly matching portfolios. Schaefer's paper is a useful review of how duration measures are used to immunize fixed liabilities:

S. D. Hodges and S. M. Schaefer, "A Model for Bond Portfolio Improvement," *Journal of Financial and Quantitative Analysis,* **12:** 243–260 (1977).

S. M. Schaefer, "Immunisation and Duration: A Review of Theory, Performance and Applications," *Midland Corporate Finance Journal,* **3:** 41–58 (Autumn 1984).

For material on futures and swaps see:

S. Figlewski, K. John, and J. Merrick, *Hedging with Financial Futures for Institutional Investors: From Theory to Practice,* Ballinger Publishing Company, Cambridge, Mass., 1986.

C. W. Smith, C. W. Smithson, and L. M. Wakeman, "The Evolving Market for Swaps," *Midland Corporate Finance Journal,* **3:** 20–32 (Winter 1986).

S. K. Henderson and J. A. M. Price, *Currency and Interest Rate Swaps,* Butterworths & Co., London, 1984.

QUIZ

1. True or false?
   (a) A perfect hedge of asset A requires an asset B that's perfectly correlated with A.
   (b) Hedging transactions in an active futures market have zero or slightly negative NPVs.
   (c) Longer maturity bonds necessarily have longer durations.
   (d) The longer a bond's duration, the lower is its volatility.

(e) When you buy a futures contract, you pay now for delivery at a future date.

(f) The holder of a futures contract receives the convenience yield on the underlying commodity.

(g) The holder of a financial futures contract misses out on any dividend or interest payments made on the underlying security.

2. You own a $1 million portfolio of aerospace stocks with a beta of 1.2. You are enthusiastic about aerospace but uncertain about the prospects for the overall stock market. Explain how you could "hedge out" your market exposure by selling the market short. How much would you sell? How in practice would you go about "selling the market?"

3. Calculate the durations and volatilities of securities A, B, and C. Their cash flows are shown below. The interest rate is 8 percent.

	PERIOD		
	1	2	3
A	40	40	40
B	20	20	120
C	10	10	110

4. Suppose you have promised to pay out $100 in period 3. Explain how you could hedge the present value of this liability by investing in Security A from Quiz question 3. Could you also hedge by buying B or C?

5. Calculate the value of a 6-month futures contract on a Treasury bond. You have the following information:
   ▪ 6-month interest rate = 10 percent per year, or 4.9 percent for 6 months.
   ▪ Spot price of bond = 95.
   ▪ Coupon payments on the bond over the next 6 months have a present value of 4.

6. Calculate PV(convenience yield) for magnoosium scrap from the following information:
   ▪ Spot price = $2550 per ton.
   ▪ Futures price = $2408 for a 1-year contract.
   ▪ Interest rate = 12 percent.
   ▪ PV(storage costs) = $100 per year.

7. What is a currency swap? An interest-rate swap? Give one example of how each might be used.

QUESTIONS AND PROBLEMS

1. Legs Diamond owns shares in Vanguard Index Trust worth $1 million on July 15. (This trust is an index fund that tracks the Standard & Poor's 500.) He wants to cash in now but his accountant advises him to wait 6 months so as to defer a large capital gains tax. Explain to Legs how he can use stock index futures to hedge out his exposure to market movements over the next 6 months. Could Legs "cash in" without actually selling his shares? Explain.

2. Refer back to question 1. Suppose that the nearest index futures contract matures in 7 months rather than 6. Show how Legs Diamond can still use index futures to hedge his position. How would the maturity date affect the hedge ratio?

3. Price changes on two gold-mining stocks have shown strong positive correlation. Their historical relationship is

$$\begin{matrix} \text{Average} \\ \text{percentage} \\ \text{change in A} \end{matrix} = .001 + .75 \begin{pmatrix} \text{percentage} \\ \text{change in} \\ \text{B} \end{pmatrix}$$

Changes in B explain 60 percent of the variation of the changes in A ($R^2 = .6$).
(a) Suppose you own \$100,000 of A. How much of B should you sell to minimize the risk of your net position?
(b) What is the hedge ratio?
(c) How would you construct a zero-value hedge?
(d) Here is the historical relationship between A and gold prices:

$$\begin{matrix} \text{Average} \\ \text{percentage} \\ \text{change in A} \end{matrix} = -.002 + 1.2 \begin{pmatrix} \text{percentage} \\ \text{change in} \\ \text{gold price} \end{pmatrix}$$

If $R^2 = .5$, can you lower the risk of your net position by hedging with gold (or gold futures) rather than with stock B? Explain.

4. In Section 25-2, we stated that the duration of the 8⅛s of 1991 was 4.311 years. Construct a table like Table 25-2 to show that this is so.

5. In Section 25-2, we stated that the duration of Potterton's lease equals the duration of its debt.
(a) Show that this is so.
(b) Now suppose that the interest rate falls to 3 percent. Show how the value of the lease and the debt package are now affected by a .5 percent rise or fall in the interest rate. What would Potterton need to do to reestablish the interest-rate hedge?

6. Line 1 of the following table shows cash outflows that your company has just promised to make. Below that are the cash flows on a blue-chip corporate note. The interest rate is 10 percent. Your company can borrow at this rate if it wishes.

	YEAR			
	1	2	3	4
Liability in millions	0	0	- \$20	- \$20
Note's cash payments as percent of face value	12	12	12	112

(a) Calculate the durations of the liability and the note.
(b) How much must you invest in the note to hedge the liability?
(c) How would you construct a zero-value hedge?
(d) Would this hedge continue to protect your company
 (i) If interest rates dropped by 3 percent?
 (ii) If short-term interest rates fluctuate while longer-term rates remain basically constant?
 (iii) If interest rates remain the same but 2 years pass?
(e) Can you set up a hedge portfolio that relieves the financial manager of all the worries mentioned in (d)? Describe that portfolio.

TABLE 25-5
Spot and 6-month futures prices for selected commodities and securities

Commodity	Spot Price	Futures Price	Comments
Magnoosium, per ton	$ 2,550	$ 2,728.50	PV (storage costs) = PV (convenience yield)
Frozen Quiche, per pound	.50	.514	PV (storage costs) = .10 per pound; PV (convenience yield) = .05 per pound
Nevada Hydro 8s of 2002	77	78.39	4% semiannual coupon payment due just before futures contract expires
Costaguanan Pulgas (currency), in Pulgas per dollar	9,300	6,900	Costaguanan interest rate is 95% per year
Establishment industries common stock	95	97.54	Establishment pays dividends of $2 per quarter. Next dividend is paid 2 months from now
Cheap white wine, per 10,000 gallon tank	$12,500	$14,200	PV (convenience yield) = $250 per tank. Your company unexpectedly has surplus storage and can store 50,000 gallons at no cost

7. Explain the chief differences between futures and forward contracts, e.g., for foreign exchange.

8. In mid-September 1987, 6-month futures on the New York Stock Exchange Composite Index traded at 178.95. Spot was 175.79. Assume an interest rate of 7.8 percent. What was the PV of the average dividend yield on the stocks in this index?

9. Table 25-5 contains spot and 6-month futures prices for several commodities and financial instruments. There may be some money-making opportunities. See if you can find them, and explain how you would trade to take advantage of them. The interest rate is 14.5 percent, or 7 percent over the 6-month life of the contracts.

10. The following table shows gold futures prices for varying contract lengths. Gold is predominantly an investment good, not an industrial commodity. Investors hold gold because it diversifies their portfolios and because they hope its price will rise. They do not hold it for its convenience yield.

    Calculate the interest rate faced by traders in gold futures for each of the contract lengths shown below. The spot price is $456.90 per ounce.

	CONTRACT LENGTH (MONTHS)				
	1	3	9	15	21
Futures price	$458.90	464.50	483.30	503.90	525.70

11. The Commodities and Futures Trading Commission needs to be assured that new futures contracts serve the public interest. One of the tests that it applies is that the contract should provide price discovery—that is, the futures price should provide the public with new information on investors' forecasts of changes in spot prices. In justifying their proposals to trade index futures the

exchanges have argued that index futures provide information about investor views on future prices. Evaluate this claim.

12. Firms A and B face the following borrowing rates for making a 5-year fixed-rate debt issue in U.S. dollars or Swiss francs:

	U.S. Dollars	Swiss Francs
Firm A	10%	7%
Firm B	8	6

Suppose that A wishes to borrow U.S. dollars and B wishes to borrow Swiss francs. Show how a swap could be used to reduce the borrowing costs of each company. Assume a spot exchange rate of 2 Swiss francs per dollar.

13. "Last year we had a substantial income in sterling, which we hedged by selling sterling forward. In the event sterling rose and our decision to sell forward cost us a lot of money. I think that in future we should stop hedging our currency exposure." As financial manager, how would you respond to this chief executive's comment?

14. "Speculators want futures contracts to be incorrectly priced; hedgers want them to be correctly priced." Why?

15. Hoopoe Corp. wants to borrow 100 million U.S. dollars at a fixed rate with a maturity of 5 years. It calculates that it can make a eurobond issue with the following terms:

- Interest: $10\frac{5}{8}\%$ payable annually
- Maturity: 5 years
- Commissions: $1\frac{1}{8}\%$
- Agency fees: .15% on coupon
                     .075% on principal
- Issue expenses: .2%

A bank has presented Hoopoe with a proposal for a Swiss franc issue combined with a currency swap in U.S. dollars. The proposed terms for the Swiss franc issue are:

- Amount: 200 million Swiss francs
- Interest: $5\frac{3}{8}\%$ annually
- Maturity: 5 years
- Commissions: 2.8%
- Agency fees: .75% on coupon
                     .30% on principal
- Issue expenses: .2%

The counterparty of the swap would raise fixed dollars on the following terms:

- Amount: 100 million U.S. dollars (equivalent to 200 million Swiss francs)
- Interest: $10\frac{5}{8}\%$ annually
- Maturity: 5 years
- Commissions: 1.8%
- Agency expenses: .15% on coupon
                     .075% on principal
- Issue expenses: .2%

The counterparty would be happy with an all-in cost in Swiss francs of 6.4%.

(*a*) Which alternative should Hoopoe undertake? (Ignore credit risk in your analysis.)

(*b*) Suppose that you are the corporate finance manager of Hoopoe. Discuss the credit risk issues involved in the alternatives.

26 Leasing

Most of us occasionally rent a car, bicycle, or boat. Usually such personal rentals are short-lived—we may rent a car for a day or week. But in corporate finance longer-term rentals are common. A rental agreement that extends for a year or more and involves a series of fixed payments is called a **lease.**

Firms lease as an alternative to buying capital equipment. Computers are often leased; so are trucks, railroad cars, aircraft, and ships. Just about every kind of asset has been leased sometime by somebody, including electric power plants, nuclear fuel, handball courts, and zoo animals.

Every lease involves two parties. The *user* of the asset is called the *lessee.* The lessee makes periodic payments to the *owner* of the asset, who is called the *lessor.* For example, if you sign an agreement to rent an apartment for a year, you are the lessee and the owner is the lessor.

You often see references to the *leasing industry*. This refers to lessors. (Almost all firms are lessees to at least a minor extent.) Who are the lessors?

The largest group of lessors is equipment manufacturers. For example, GATX is the largest lessor of railcars (it leased about 44,200 cars at the end of 1986); IBM is the largest lessor of computers, and Xerox is the largest lessor of copiers.

Banks are the second largest group. They account for roughly one-third of the dollar volume of leased assets, versus about one-half for equipment manufacturers. Most of the remaining volume is accounted for by independent leasing companies.

The independent leasing companies offer a variety of services. Some act as lease brokers (arranging lease deals) as well as lessors. Others specialize in leasing automobiles, trucks, and standardized industrial equipment; they succeed because they can buy equipment in quantity, service it efficiently, and if necessary resell it at a good price. Independent computer leasing companies got started because some people believed that IBM's leasing charges were too high. Computer leasing companies bought equipment, mainly from IBM, and leased it to computer users at rates below IBM's.

26-1 WHAT IS A LEASE?

Leases come in many forms, but in all cases the lessee (user) promises to make a series of payments to the lessor (owner). The lease contract specifies the monthly or semiannual payments, with the first payment usually due as soon as the contract is signed. The payments are usually level, but their time pattern can be tailored to the user's needs. For example, suppose that a manufacturer leases a machine to produce a complex new product. There will be a year's "shakedown" period before volume production is possible. In this case, it might be possible to arrange for lower payments during the first year of the lease.

When a lease is terminated, the leased equipment reverts to the lessor. However, the lease agreement often gives the user the option to repurchase the equipment or take out a new lease.

Some leases are short-term and cancelable during the contract period at the option of the lessee: These are generally known as *operating leases.* Others extend over most of the estimated economic life of the asset and cannot be canceled or can be canceled only if the lessor is reimbursed for any losses: These are called *capital, financial,* or *full-payout leases.*[1]

Financial leases are a *source of financing.* Signing a financial lease contract is like borrowing money. There is an immediate cash inflow because the lessee is relieved of having to pay for the asset. But the lessee also assumes a binding obligation to make the payments specified in the lease contract. The user could have borrowed the full purchase price of the asset by accepting a binding obligation to make interest and principal payments to the lender. Thus the cash-flow consequences of leasing and borrowing are similar. In either case, the firm raises cash now and pays it back later. A large part of this chapter will be devoted to comparing leasing and borrowing as financing alternatives.

Leases also differ in the services provided by the lessor. Under a *full-service,* or *rental* lease, the lessor promises to maintain and insure the equipment and to pay any property taxes due on it. In a *net* lease, the lessee agrees to maintain the asset, insure it, and pay any property taxes. Most financial leases are net leases.

Most financial leases are arranged for brand new assets. The lessee identifies the equipment he or she would like to use, arranges for the leasing company to buy it from the manufacturer, and signs a contract with the leasing company. This is called a *direct* lease. In other cases, the firm sells an asset it already owns and leases it back from the buyer. These *sale and lease-back* arrangements are common in real estate. For example, firm X may wish to raise cash by selling a factory, but still retain use of the factory. It could do this by selling the factory for cash to a leasing company and simultaneously signing a long-term lease contract for the factory. Legal ownership of the factory passes to the leasing company but the right to use it stays with firm X.

You may also encounter *leveraged* leases. These are financial leases in which the lessor borrows part of the purchase price of the leased asset, using the lease contract as security for the loan. Leveraged lease deals are complicated, and so we defer discussion of them to the end of this chapter.

Example of a Financial Lease

Imagine yourself in the position of Thomas Pierce, III, president of Greymare Bus Lines. Your firm was established by your grandfather, who was quick to capitalize on the growing demand for transportation between Widdicombe and nearby townships. The company has owned all its vehicles from the time the company was formed; you are now reconsidering that policy. Your operating manager wants to buy a new bus costing $100,000. The bus will last only 6 years before going to the scrap yard. You are convinced that investment in the additional equipment is worthwhile. However, the representative of the bus manufacturer has pointed out that her firm would also be willing to lease the bus to you over 6 years for an annual payment of $20,600. Greymare would remain responsible for all maintenance, insurance, and operating expenses.

Table 26-1 shows the direct cash-flow consequences of signing the lease contract. (An important indirect effect is considered later.) The consequences are:

---

[1] In the shipping industry, a financial lease is often termed a *bareboat charter* or *demise hire.*

TABLE 26-1
Cash-flow consequences of the lease contract offered to Greymare Bus Lines
(figures in thousands)

	YEAR					
	0	1	2	3	4	5
Cost of new bus	+ 100					
Lost depreciation tax shield	− 6.8	− 10.88	− 6.53	− 3.92	− 3.92	− 1.96
Lease payment	− 20.6	− 20.6	− 20.6	− 20.6	− 20.6	− 20.6
Tax shield of lease payment	+ 7.0	+ 7.0	+ 7.0	+ 7.0	+ 7.0	+ 7.0
Cash flow of lease	+ 79.60	− 24.48	− 20.13	− 17.52	− 17.52	− 15.56

(handwritten note to left of Tax shield of lease payment row:) tax rate × lease pymt

(handwritten note below table:) tax rate × dep = tax shield

1. Greymare does not have to pay for the bus. This is equivalent to a cash inflow of $100,000.
2. Greymare no longer owns the bus, and so it cannot depreciate it. Therefore it gives up a valuable depreciation tax shield. In Table 26-1, we have assumed depreciation would be calculated using 5-year tax depreciation schedules. (See Table 6-5.)
3. Greymare must pay $20,600 per year for 6 years to the lessor. The first payment is due immediately.
4. However, these lease payments are fully tax-deductible. At a 34 percent marginal tax rate, the lease payments generate tax shields of $7000 per year. You could say that the after-tax cost of the lease payment is $20,600 − $7000 = $13,600.

We must emphasize that Table 26-1 assumes that Greymare will pay taxes at the full 34 percent marginal rate. If the firm were sure to lose money, and therefore pay no taxes, lines 2 and 4 would be left blank. The depreciation tax shields are worth nothing to a firm that pays no taxes, for example.

Table 26-1 also assumes the bus will be worthless when it goes to the scrap yard at the end of year 6. Otherwise there would be an entry for salvage value lost.

Who *Really* Owns the Leased Asset?

To a lawyer or a tax accountant, this would be a silly question: The lessor is clearly the *legal* owner of the leased asset. That is why the lessor is allowed to deduct depreciation from taxable income.

From an *economic* point of view, you might say that the *user* is the real owner, because in a *financial* lease, the user faces the risks and receives the rewards of ownership. If the new bus turns out to be hopelessly costly and unsuited for Greymare's routes, that is Greymare's problem, not the lessor's. If it turns out to be a great success, the profit goes to Greymare, not the lessor. The success or failure of the firm's business operations does not depend on whether the buses are financed by leasing or some other financial instrument.

In many respects, a financial lease is equivalent to a secured loan. The lessee must make a series of fixed payments and, if the lessee fails to do so, the lessor can repossess the asset. Thus we can think of a balance sheet like this:

GREYMARE BUS LINES
(figures in thousands of dollars)

Bus	100	100	Loan secured by bus
All other assets	1,000	450	Other loans
		550	Net worth
Total assets	1,100	1,100	Total liabilities and net worth

as being economically equivalent to a balance sheet like this:

GREYMARE BUS LINES
(figures in thousands of dollars)

Bus	100	100	Financial lease
All other assets	1,000	450	Other loans
		550	Net worth
Total assets	1,100	1,100	Total liabilities and net worth

Having said this, we must immediately add two qualifications. First, legal ownership can make a big difference when a financial lease expires, because the lessor gets the salvage value of the asset. Once a secured loan is paid off the user owns the asset free and clear.

Second, lessors and secured creditors may be treated differently in bankruptcy. If a company defaults on a lease payment, you might think that the lessor could pick up the leased asset and take it home. But if the bankruptcy court decides the asset is "essential" to the lessee's business, it "affirms" the lease. Then the bankrupt firm can continue to use the asset, *but* it must also continue to make the lease payments. This can be *good* news for the lessor: it is paid cash while other creditors cool their heels. Even secured creditors are not paid until the bankruptcy process works itself out.

If the lease is not affirmed but "rejected," the lessor can of course recover the leased asset. If it is worth less than the future payments the lessee had promised, the lessor can try to recoup this loss. But in this case the lender must get in line with the unsecured creditors.

Of course neither the lessor nor the secured lender can be sure it will come out whole. Our point is that lessors and secured creditors have different rights when the asset user gets into trouble.

Leasing and the Internal Revenue Service

We have already noted that the lessee loses the tax depreciation of the leased asset, but can deduct the lease payment in full. The *lessor*, as legal owner, uses the depreciation tax shield but must report the lease payments as taxable rental income.

However, the Internal Revenue Service is suspicious by nature, and it will not allow the lessee to deduct the entire lease payment unless it is satisfied that the arrangement is a genuine lease and not a disguised installment purchase or secured loan agreement. Here are examples of lease provisions that will arouse its suspicions.

1. Designating any part of the lease payment as "interest."
2. Giving the lessee the option to acquire the asset for, say, $1 when the lease expires. Such a provision would effectively give the asset's salvage value to the lessee.

3. Adopting a schedule of payments such that the lessee pays a large proportion of the cost over a short period and thereafter is able to use the asset for a nominal rent.
4. Including a so-called hell-or-high-water clause that obliges the lessee to make payments regardless of what subsequently happens to the lessor or the equipment.
5. Limiting the lessee's right to issue debt or pay dividends while the lease is in force.
6. Leasing "limited use" property—for example, leasing a machine or production facility custom-designed for the lessee's operations, and which therefore would have scant secondhand value.

Leasing and the Accountants

Until the end of 1976 financial leases were *off-balance-sheet financing*. That is, a firm could buy an asset, finance it through a financial lease, and show neither the asset nor the lease contract on its balance sheet. The firm was required only to add a brief footnote to its accounts describing its lease obligation. Accounting standards now require that all *capital* (financial) leases be *capitalized*.[2] That is, the present value of the lease payments must be calculated and shown alongside debt on the right-hand side of the balance sheet. The same amount must be shown as an asset on the left-hand side of the balance sheet.[3]

In order to implement this new requirement, the Financial Accounting Standards Board (FASB) had to come up with objective rules for distinguishing between operating and capital (financial) leases. They defined capital leases as leases which meet *any one* of the following requirements:

1. The lease agreement transfers ownership to the lessee before the lease expires.
2. The lessee can purchase the asset for a bargain price when the lease expires.
3. The lease lasts for at least 75 percent of the asset's estimated economic life.
4. The present value of the lease payments is at least 90 percent of the asset's value.

All other leases are operating leases as far as the accountants are concerned.

Many financial managers have tried to take advantage of this arbitrary boundary between operating and financial leases. Suppose that you wanted to finance a computer-controlled machine tool costing $1 million. The machine tool is expected to last for 12 years. You could sign a lease contract for 8 years, 11 months (just missing requirement 3) with lease payments having a present value of $899,000 (just missing requirement 4). You also make sure the lease contract avoids requirements 1 and 2. Result? You have off-balance-sheet financing. This lease would not have to be capitalized, although it is clearly a long-term, fixed obligation.

Now we come to the $64 question: "Why should anyone *care* whether financing is off balance sheet or on balance sheet?" Shouldn't the financial manager worry about substance rather than appearance?

---

[2] See "Accounting for Leases," *Statement of Financial Accounting Standards No. 13*, Financial Accounting Standards Board, Stamford, Conn., 1976.

[3] This "asset" is then amortized over the life of the lease. The amortization is deducted from book income, just as depreciation is deducted for a purchased asset.

When a firm obtains off-balance-sheet financing, the conventional measures of financial leverage, such as the debt-equity ratio, understate the true degree of financial leverage. Some believe that financial analysts do not always notice off-balance-sheet lease obligations (which are still referred to in footnotes) or the greater volatility of earnings that results from the fixed lease payments. They may be right, but we would not expect such an imperfection to be widespread.

When a company borrows money, it must usually consent to certain restrictions on future borrowing. Early bond indentures did not include any restrictions on financial leases. Therefore leasing was seen as a way to circumvent restrictive covenants. Loopholes such as these are easily stopped and most bond indentures now include limits on leasing.

Long-term lease obligations ought to be regarded as debt whether or not they appear on the balance sheet. Financial analysts may overlook moderate leasing activity, just as they overlook minor debts. But major lease obligations are generally recognized and taken into account.

In May 1979, *Business Week* described the financial problems facing San Diego Gas and Electric Company (SDG&E). A "cash squeeze" on the company led to the following sale and lease-back deal:

> In March [the company] sold a new generating unit for $132 million to a group of banks headed by Bank of America and then took a lease on the plant. . . . Its near-term profit picture has not been affected. But ultimately, the desperate measure will remove a huge asset from the utility's rate [i.e., asset] base, thus lowering potential profits and further weakening SDG&E's bond rating. "The rating agencies look at the $132 million obligation as if it were long-term debt," explains [Robert E. Morris, the company's president].[4]

26-2   WHY LEASE?

You hear many suggestions about why companies should lease equipment rather than buy it. Let us look at some sensible reasons·and then at one or two that are more dubious.

Sensible Reasons for Leasing

Short-Term Leases Are Convenient.   Suppose you want the use of a car for a week. You could buy one and sell it 7 days later, but that would be silly. Quite apart from the fact that registering ownership is a nuisance, you would spend some time selecting a car, negotiating purchase, and arranging insurance. Then at the end of the week you must negotiate resale, and cancel registration and insurance. When you need a car only for a short time, it clearly makes sense to rent it. You save the trouble of registering ownership and you know the effective cost. In the same way, it pays a company to lease equipment that it needs for only a short time. Of course this kind of lease is always an operating lease.

Cancelation Options Are Valuable.   Computers are frequently leased on a short-term cancelable basis. It is difficult to estimate how rapidly such equipment will become obsolete, because the technology of computers is advancing rapidly and somewhat unpredictably. Leasing with an option to cancel passes the risk of premature obsolescence from the user to the lessor. Usually the lessor is a computer

---

manufacturer or a computer leasing specialist, and therefore knows more about the risks of obsolescence than the user. Thus the lessor is better equipped than the user to bear these risks. It makes sense for the user to pay the lessor for the option to cancel. The payment comes in the form of higher lease payments.

Maintenance Is Provided.   Under a full-service lease, the user receives maintenance and other services. Many lessors are well equipped to provide efficient maintenance. However, bear in mind that these benefits will be reflected in higher lease payments.

Standardization Leads to Low Administrative and Transaction Costs.   Suppose that you operate a leasing company which specializes in financial leases for trucks. You are effectively lending money to a large number of firms (the lessees) which may differ considerably in terms of size and risk. But, because the underlying asset is in each case the same saleable item (a truck), you can safely "lend" the money (lease the truck) without conducting a detailed analysis of each firm's business. You can also use a simple, standard lease contract. This standardization makes it possible to "lend" small sums of money without incurring large investigative, administrative, or legal costs. Therefore leasing is often a relatively cheap source of cash for the small company. It offers long-term financing on a flexible, piecemeal basis, with lower transaction costs than in a private placement or a public bond or stock issue.

Tax Shields Can Be Used.   Sometimes lessors can make better use of depreciation tax shields generated by an asset than the asset's user. Therefore it may make sense for the leasing company to own the equipment and pass on some of the tax benefits to the lessee in the form of low lease payments. We will see exactly how this works in the next section of this chapter.

Avoiding the Alternative Minimum Tax.   Red-blooded financial managers want to earn lots of money for their shareholders but *report* low profits to the tax authorities. Tax law allows this. A firm may use straight-line depreciation in its annual report, but choose accelerated depreciation (and the shortest possible asset life) for its tax books. By this and other perfectly legal and ethical devices, profitable companies have occasionally managed to escape tax entirely. Almost all companies pay less tax than their public income statements suggest.[5]

But the 1986 Tax Reform Act has a trap for companies that shield too much income: the alternative minimum tax (AMT). Corporations must pay the AMT whenever it is higher than their tax computed in the regular way.

Here is how the AMT works. It requires a second calculation of taxable income, in which part of the benefit of accelerated depreciation and other tax-reducing items[6] is added back. The AMT is 20 percent of the result.

---

[5] Year-by-year differences between reported tax expense and taxes actually paid are explained in footnotes to the financial statements. The cumulative difference is shown on the balance sheet as a deferred tax liability. (Note that accelerated depreciation *postpones* tax; it does not eliminate tax.)

[6] Other items include some interest receipts from tax-exempt municipal securities and taxes deferred by use of completed contract accounting. (The completed contract method allows a manufacturer to postpone reporting taxable profits until a production contract is completed. Since contracts may span several years, this deferral can have a substantial positive NPV.) The list of tax-reducing items also includes a "BURPs", or "book unreported profits" adjustment, which depends on the difference between income reported to the Internal Revenue Service and the pretax *book* income reported to shareholders. Thus exposure to the AMT may be reduced by more conservative financial reporting.

Suppose Yuppytech Services would have $10 million in taxable income but for the AMT, which forces it to add back $9 million of tax privileges:

	Regular Tax	Alternative Minimum Tax
Income	$10	10 + 9 = 19
Tax rate	.34	.20
Tax	$ 3.4	$3.8

Yuppytech must pay $3.8 million, not $3.4.[7]

How can this painful payment be avoided? How about leasing? Lease payments are *not* on the list of items added back in calculating the AMT. If you lease rather than buy, tax depreciation is less and the AMT is less. There is a net gain if the *lessor* is not subject to the AMT and can pass back depreciation tax shields in the form of lower lease payments.

Some Dubious Reasons for Leasing

We have already mentioned one dubious reason for leasing, that is, leasing in order to obtain off-balance-sheet financing. Here are three more dubious reasons.

Leasing Affects Book Income.   Leasing can make the firm's balance sheet and income statement *look* better by increasing book income or decreasing book asset value, or both.

A lease which qualifies as off-balance-sheet financing[8] affects book income in only one way: The lease payments are an expense. If the firm buys the asset instead, and borrows to finance it, both depreciation and interest expense are deducted. Leases are usually set up so that payments in the early years are less than depreciation plus interest under the buy-and-borrow alternative. Consequently, leasing increases book income in the early years of an asset's life. The book rate of return can increase even more dramatically, because the book value of assets (the denominator in the book-rate-of-return calculation) is understated if the leased asset never appears on the firm's balance sheet.

Leasing's impact on book income should in itself have no effect on firm value. In efficient capital markets investors will look through the firm's accounting results to the true values of the asset and the liability incurred to finance it.

Leasing Avoids Capital Expenditure Controls.   In many companies lease proposals are scrutinized as carefully as capital expenditure proposals, but in others leasing may enable an operating manager to avoid the elaborate approval procedures needed to buy an asset. Although this is a dubious reason for leasing, it may be influential, particularly in the public sector. For example, city hospitals have sometimes found it politically more convenient to lease their medical equipment than to ask the city government to provide funds for purchase. Another example is provided by the United States Navy, which recently leased a fleet of new tankers and supply ships instead of asking Congress for the money to buy them.

---

[7] But Yuppytech can carry forward the $.4 million difference. If later years' AMTs are *lower* than regular taxes, the difference can be used as a tax credit. Suppose the AMT next year is $4 million and the regular tax is $5 million. Then Yuppytech pays only 5 − .4 = $4.6 million.

[8] It is difficult to generalize about the effects of leasing on book income when the leases are capitalized.

Leasing Preserves Capital.   Leasing companies provide "100 percent financing"; they advance the full cost of the leased asset. Consequently, they often claim that leasing preserves capital, allowing the firm to save its cash for other things.

But the firm can also "preserve capital" by borrowing money. If Greymare leases a $100,000 bus rather than buying it, it does conserve $100,000 cash. It could also (1) buy the bus for cash and (2) borrow $100,000 using the bus as security. Its bank balance ends up the same whether it leases or buys and borrows. It has the bus in either case, and it incurs a $100,000 liability in either case. What's so special about leasing?

26-3   VALUING FINANCIAL LEASES

Leasing does offer special advantages to some firms in some circumstances. However, there is no point in further discussion of these advantages until you know how to value financial lease contracts.

A First Pass at Valuing a Lease Contract

When we left Thomas Pierce III, president of Greymare Bus Lines, he had just set down in Table 26-1 the cash flows of the financial lease proposed by the bus manufacturer.

These cash flows are typically assumed to be about as safe as the interest and principal payments on a secured bond issued by the lessee. This assumption is reasonable for the lease payments because the lessor is effectively making a loan to the lessee. But the various tax shields might carry enough risk to deserve a higher discount rate. For example, Greymare might be confident it could make the lease payments, but not confident that it could earn enough taxable income to use these tax shields. In that case the cash flows generated by the tax shields would probably deserve a higher discount rate than the borrowing rate used for the lease payments.

A lessee might, in principle, end up using a separate discount rate for each line of Table 26-1, each rate chosen to fit the risk of that line's cash flow. But established, profitable firms usually find it reasonable to simplify by discounting the types of flows shown in Table 26-1 at a single rate based on the rate of interest the firm would pay if it borrowed rather than leased. We will assume Greymare's borrowing rate is 10 percent.

At this point we must go back to our discussion in Chapter 19 of debt-equivalent flows. When a company lends money, it pays tax on the interest it receives. Its net return is the after-tax interest rate. When a company borrows money, it can *deduct* interest payments from its taxable income. The net cost of borrowing is the after-tax interest rate. Thus the after-tax interest rate is the effective rate at which a company can transfer debt-equivalent flows from one time period to another. Therefore, to value the incremental cash flows stemming from the lease we need to discount them at the after-tax interest rate.

Since Greymare can borrow at 10 percent, we should discount the lease cash flows at $r^* = .10(1 - .34) = .066$, or 6.6 percent. This gives:

$$\text{NPV}_{\text{lease}} = +79.60 - \frac{24.48}{1.066} - \frac{20.13}{(1.066)^2} - \frac{17.52}{(1.066)^3} - \frac{17.52}{(1.066)^4} - \frac{15.56}{(1.066)^5}$$

$$= -.41, \text{ or } -\$410$$

Since the lease has a negative NPV, Greymare is better off buying the bus.

TABLE 26-2
Details of the equivalent loan for the lease offered to Greymare Bus Lines
(figures in thousands; cash outflows shown with negative sign)

	YEAR					
	0	1	2	3	4	5
Amount borrowed at year-end	80.01	60.81	44.70	30.13	14.60	0
Interest paid at 10%		− 8.00	− 6.08	− 4.47	− 3.01	− 1.46
Interest tax shield at 34%		+ 2.72	+ 2.07	+ 1.52	+ 1.02	+ .50
Interest paid after tax		− 5.28	− 4.01	− 2.95	− 1.99	− .96
Principal repaid		− 19.20	− 16.11	− 14.57	− 15.53	− 14.60
Net cash flow of equivalent loan	+ 80.01	− 24.48	− 20.12[a]	− 17.52	− 17.52	− 15.56

[a] This figure is .01 less than the lease cash flows given in Table 26-1 because of rounding.

**Why Leasing
Would Make
Greymare's
Shareholders
Worse Off**

In earlier chapters we have stated that a positive or negative NPV is not an abstract concept; in this case Greymare's shareholders really are $410 poorer if the company leases. Let us now check how this comes about.

Look once more at Table 26-1. The lease cash flows are:

	YEAR					
	0	1	2	3	4	5
Lease cash flows (thousands)	+ $79.60	− 24.48	− 20.13	− 17.52	− 17.52	− 15.56

The lease payments are contractual obligations like the principal and interest payments on secured debt. Thus you can think of the incremental lease cash flows in years 1 through 5 as the "debt service" of the lease. Table 26-2 shows a loan with *exactly* the same debt service as the lease. The initial amount of the loan is 80.01 thousand dollars. If Greymare borrowed this sum, it would need to pay interest in the first year of .10 × 80.01 = 8.00 and would *receive* a tax shield on this interest of .34 × 8.00 = 2.72. Greymare could then repay 19.20 of the loan, leaving a net cash outflow of 24.74 (exactly the same as for the lease) in year 1, and an outstanding debt at the start of year 2 of 60.81.

As you walk through the calculations in Table 26-2, you see that it costs exactly the same to service a loan that brings an immediate inflow of 80.01 as it does to service the lease, which brings in only 79.60. That is why we say that the lease has a net present value of 79.60 − 80.01 = − .41, or − $410. If Greymare leases the bus rather than raising an equivalent loan,[9] there will be $410 less in Greymare's bank account.

Our example illustrates two general points about leases and equivalent loans. First, if you can devise a borrowing plan that gives the same cash flow as the lease

[9] When we compare the lease to its equivalent loan, we do not mean to imply that the bus alone could support all of that loan. Some part of the loan would be supported by Greymare's other assets. Some part of the lease would likewise be supported by the other assets.

in every future period but a higher immediate cash flow, then you should not lease. If, however, the equivalent loan provides the same future cash outflows as the lease but a lower immediate inflow, then leasing is the better choice.

Second, our example suggests two ways to value a lease:

1. *Hard way:* Construct a table like Table 26-2 showing the equivalent loan.
2. *Easy way:* Discount the lease cash flows at the *after-tax* interest rate that the firm would pay on an equivalent loan. Both methods give the same answer—in our case an NPV of $-$410.

The Story So Far

We concluded that the lease contract offered to Greymare Bus Lines was *not* attractive because the lease provided $410 less financing than the equivalent loan. The underlying principle is as follows: A financial lease is superior to buying and borrowing if the financing provided by the lease exceeds the financing generated by the equivalent loan.

The principle implies this formula:

$$\frac{\text{Net value}}{\text{of lease}} = \frac{\text{initial financing}}{\text{provided}} - \sum_{t=1}^{N} \frac{\text{LCF}_t}{[1 + r(1 - T_c)]^t}$$

where LCF$_t$ is the cash outflow attributable to the lease in period t and N is the length of the lease. Initial financing provided equals the cost of the leased asset minus any immediate lease payment or other cash outflow attributable to the lease.

Notice that the value of the lease is its incremental value relative to borrowing via an equivalent loan. A positive lease value means that *if* you acquire the asset, lease financing is advantageous. It does not prove you should acquire the asset.

However, sometimes favorable lease terms rescue a capital investment project. Suppose that Greymare had decided *against* buying a new bus because the NPV of the $100,000 investment was $-$5000 assuming normal financing. The bus manufacturer could rescue the deal by offering a lease with a value of, say, $+$8000. By offering such a lease, the manufacturer would in effect cut the price of the bus to $92,000, giving the bus-lease package a positive value to Greymare. We could express this more formally by treating the lease's NPV as a favorable financing side effect which adds to project adjusted present value (APV):[10]

$$\text{APV} = \text{NPV of project} + \text{NPV of lease}$$

$$= -5000 + 8000 = +\$3000$$

Notice also that our formula applies to net financial leases. Any insurance, maintenance, and other operating costs picked up by the lessor have to be evaluated separately and added to the value of the lease. If the asset has salvage value at the end of the lease, that value should be taken into account also.

Suppose, for example, that the bus manufacturer offers to provide routine maintenance that would otherwise cost $3000 per year after tax. However, Mr. Pierce reconsiders and decides that the bus will probably be worth $10,000 after 6 years. (Previously he assumed the bus would be worthless at the end of the lease.) Then the value of the lease increases by the present value of the maintenance savings and decreases by the present value of the lost salvage value.

Maintenance and salvage value are harder to predict than the cash flows shown in Table 26-1, and so they normally deserve a higher discount rate. Suppose that

[10] See Chapter 19, Section 19-1.

Mr. Pierce uses 12 percent. Then the maintenance savings are worth

$$\sum_{t=0}^{5} \frac{3000}{(1.12)^t} = \$13,800$$

The lost salvage value is worth $\$10,000/(1.12)^5 = \$5700$.[11] Remember that we previously calculated the value of the lease as $-\$410$. The revised value is therefore $-\$410 + 13,800 - 5700 = \$7690$. Now the lease looks like a good deal.

26-4   WHEN DOES LEASING PAY?

We have examined the value of a lease from the viewpoint of the lessee. However, the lessor's criterion is simply the reverse. As long as lessor and lessee are in the same tax bracket, every cash outflow to the lessee is an inflow to the lessor, and vice versa. In our numerical example, the bus manufacturer would project cash flows in a table like Table 26-1, but with the signs reversed. The value of the lease to the bus manufacturer would be

$$\text{Value of lease to lessor} = -79.60 + \frac{24.48}{1.066} + \frac{20.13}{(1.066)^2} + \frac{17.52}{(1.066)^3} + \frac{17.52}{(1.066)^4} + \frac{15.56}{(1.066)^5}$$

$$= +.41, \text{ or } \$410$$

In this case, the values to lessee and lessor exactly offset $(-\$410 + \$410 = 0)$. The lessor can win only at the lessee's expense.

But both lessee and lessor can win if their tax rates differ. Suppose that Greymare paid no tax $(T_c = 0)$. Then the only cash flows of the bus lease would be

		YEAR				
	0	1	2	3	4	5
Cost of new bus	+100					
Lease payment	−20.6	−20.6	−20.6	−20.6	−20.6	−20.6

These flows would be discounted at 10 percent, because $r_D(1 - T_c) = r_D$ when $T_c = 0$. The value of the lease is

$$\text{Value of lease} = +100 - \sum_{t=0}^{5} \frac{20.6}{(1.10)^t}$$

$$= +100 - 98.69 = +1.31, \text{ or } \$1310$$

In this case there is a net gain of $\$410$ to the lessor (who has the 34 percent tax rate) *and* a net gain of $\$1310$ to the lessee (who pays zero tax). This mutual gain is at the expense of the government. On the one hand, the government gains from the lease contract because it can tax the lease payments. On the other hand, the contract allows the lessor to take advantage of depreciation and interest tax shields which are of no use to the lessee. However, because the depreciation is accelerated, and the interest rate is positive, the government suffers a net loss in the present value of its tax receipts as a result of the lease.

---

[11] For simplicity, we have assumed maintenance expenses are paid at the start of the year, and that salvage value is measured at the end of year 5.

Now you should begin to understand the circumstances in which the government makes a loss on the lease and the other two parties gain. Other things being equal, the potential gains to lessor and lessee are highest when:

1. The lessor's tax rate is substantially higher than the lessee's.
2. The depreciation tax shield is received early in the lease period.
3. The lease period is long and the lease payments are concentrated toward the end of the period.
4. The interest rate r_D is high—if it were zero there would be no advantage in present value terms to postponing tax.

26-5   EVALUATING A LARGE, LEVERAGED LEASE

Now let us try using our new-found knowledge to evaluate a large leasing deal. In 1971 Anaconda began to build a $138 million aluminum reduction mill at Sebree, Kentucky. The company's original intention was to finance the project largely by a private placement of debt, but, before it could do so, the Allende government expropriated Anaconda's Chilean copper mines and so provided the company with a $356 million tax-deductible loss.

Anaconda clearly was unlikely to pay taxes for a number of years. If it went ahead and bought the mill, it could not make immediate use of depreciation tax shields or of the 7 percent investment tax credit which was then available. By leasing the mill, however, Anaconda could pass on these benefits to someone who could use them.[12] It therefore decided to purchase only the real estate at Sebree and to pay $1.1 million to a leasing broker, U.S. Leasing International, to put together a leveraged lease for the $110.7 million of plant and equipment. Figure 26-1 shows how this was arranged. First Kentucky Trust Company issued $39 million of equity to a group of banks and finance companies and $72 million of debt to a group of insurance companies. It then used this money to purchase the mill and lease it to Anaconda. Anaconda agreed to make 40 lease payments, prepaid semiannually, over a 20-year period. The first 21 payments were set at $3.99 million each and the last 19 at $5.46 million each.

The $72 million loan was secured by a first claim on Anaconda's lease payments and by a mortgage on the plant. It was *not* guaranteed by First Kentucky or the equity investors. It was a *nonrecourse* loan: If Anaconda had defaulted on the lease payments, the insurance companies' only protection would have been the value of the mill and a general claim against Anaconda.

This is called a *leveraged* lease because part of the cost of the plant was raised by a loan secured by the asset and the lease payments. The lessor, First Kentucky Trust, really acted as an intermediary, receiving the lease payments from Anaconda, paying the debt service, and distributing what was left over to the equity investors. First Kentucky in effect financed the lease contract by selling off debt and equity claims against it.

But let's look at the lease contract itself from the lessor's viewpoint. The initial outlay was $110.7 million less the investment tax credit of $7.75 million and the initial prepaid lease payment. The major subsequent cash inflows were the 39

---

[12] The Anaconda lease was described in P. Vanderwicken, "Powerful Logic of the Leasing Boom," *Fortune,* **87:** 132–161 (November 1973). Our analysis of its present value is taken from S. C. Myers, D. A. Dill, and A. J. Bautista, "Valuation of Financial Lease Contracts," *Journal of Finance,* **31:** 799–819 (June 1976), and J. R. Franks and S. D. Hodges, "Valuation of Financial Lease Contracts: A Note," *Journal of Finance,* **33:** 647–669 (May 1978).

Figure 26-1

How Anaconda arranged a lease on its aluminum reduction mill. This is a leveraged lease because part of the cost of the plant was raised by borrowing.

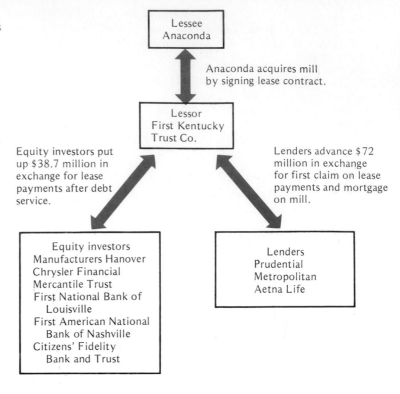

TABLE 26-3

Value of Anaconda lease to lessor (figures in millions of dollars)

Item	Present Value
1. Price	−110.7
2. Investment tax credit	+7.7
3. Depreciation tax shield	+44.3
4. After-tax lease payments	+60.8
5. Salvage value	+.9
Total value to *lessor*	+3.0

Notes:

1. Assumed tax rate is $T_c = .5$.
2. The adjusted discount rate for items 3 and 4 is 4.5625%. (The present values were actually calculated assuming semiannual cash flows and an equivalent semiannual rate.)
3. The discount rate for item 5 is 15%, our guesstimate of the average cost of capital for Anaconda's assets.
4. The depreciation schedule was based on an 11-year depreciable life and a 5% book salvage value. The double-declining-balance method was used for the first 2 years and then a switch was made to sum-of-the-years' digits. This appears to be the fastest write-off available under 1973 regulations.
5. The lessor's estimate of the plant's after-tax salvage value appears to be $10.9 million. This is not from the horse's mouth; it is inferred from other information.
6. In principle, ownership of the salvage value also creates debt capacity. We have not included an estimate of the NPV of this capacity to the lessors. It is in any event a small number.

Source: S. C. Myers, D. A. Dill, and A. J. Bautista, "Valuation of Financial Lease Contracts," *Journal of Finance,* **31:** 799–819 (June 1976), table 1, p. 809.

Figure 26-2
The value of the aluminum reduction mill to Anaconda increases rapidly as its "tax holiday" is extended. If the holiday extends for 15 years, the lease is worth about $36 million. [*Source:* J. R. Franks and S. D. Hodges, "Valuation of Financial Lease Contracts: A Note," *Journal of Finance,* **33:**667 (May 1978), Table 3]

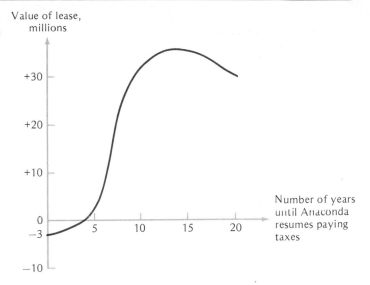

semiannual lease payments, the depreciation tax shields, and the salvage value in 1993.

As frequently happens in financial analysis, the hardest problem is to choose the right discount rate. Here is one way to look at it. The interest rate on the insurance companies' loan was 9.125 percent. Because this debt is also protected by the lessor's equity, the lease payments must be *riskier* than the debt. On the other hand, the depreciation tax shield must be *safer* than the lease payments, for once the contract is signed, the size of the shields is independent of Anaconda's fortunes. Since our formula calls for a single rate of discount for both the after-tax lease payments and the depreciation tax shield, we will compromise on a discount rate of 9.125 percent. The adjusted discount rate is 4.5625 percent. (The marginal tax rate at the time was approximately 50 percent.)

The present value calculations are set out in Table 26-3 along with a list of the other assumptions we have made. You can see that for the lessor the lease was moderately profitable: Its net value was roughly 3 percent of the plant's cost.

It is not so easy to evaluate the lease from Anaconda's side because we do not know when Anaconda expected to resume paying taxes. But we can work out how much the lease was worth to Anaconda under varying assumptions about its future tax position. The results are presented in Figure 26-2. Notice that if Anaconda paid taxes immediately, it would lose exactly the $3.0 million that the lessor gained. The break-even point comes after only 3 years, and thereafter the value of the lease arrangement to Anaconda rises rapidly to the maximum of about $35 million. It appears that the deal was a good one for Anaconda.

26-6 SUMMARY

A lease is just an extended rental agreement. The owner of the equipment (the *lessor*) allows the user (the *lessee*) to operate the equipment in exchange for regular lease payments.

There is a wide variety of possible arrangements. Short-term, cancelable leases are known as *operating leases:* In these cases the lessor bears the risk of obsolescence. Long-term, noncancelable leases are called *full payout, financial,* or *capital* leases: In these cases the lessee bears the risk of obsolescence. Operating leases make sense when you want to use the equipment for only a short time or where the lessor has some control over the obsolescence rate. Financial leases are *sources of financing* for assets the firm wishes to acquire and use for an extended period.

Many vehicle or office equipment leases include insurance and maintenance. They are *full-service* leases. If the lessee is responsible for insurance and maintenance, the lease is a *net* lease.

Frequently the lessor acquires the asset directly from the manufacturer. This is a *direct* lease. Sometimes the lessor acquires the asset from the user and then leases it back to the user. This is a *sale and lease-back*.

Most leases involve only the lessee and the lessor. But, if the asset is very costly, it may be convenient to arrange a *leveraged* lease, in which the cost of the leased asset is financed by issuing debt and equity claims against the asset and the future lease payments.

There are a number of reasons that companies sometimes prefer to lease equipment rather than buying it. For example, there may be good tax reasons. If the operator cannot use the depreciation tax shield, it makes sense to sell the equipment to someone who can. Also, the lessor may be better able to bear the risk of obsolescence, or be in a better position to resell secondhand assets. The lessor may be able to offer a very good deal on maintenance. Finally, it may be much less costly in time and effort to arrange a simple lease contract on a standard item of equipment than to arrange a normal loan.

A financial lease is like a secured bond. If a firm invests in bonds, it earns the after-tax interest rate on its investment; if it issues bonds, it pays the after-tax rate of interest on its debt. Therefore, the opportunity cost of lease financing is the after-tax rate of interest on the firm's bonds. To value the lease, we need to discount the incremental cash flows from leasing by the after-tax interest rate.

An equivalent loan to a lease is one that commits the firm to exactly the same future cash flows. When we calculate the net present value of the lease we are measuring the difference between the amount of financing provided by the lease and the financing provided by the equivalent loan:

$$\text{Value of lease} = \text{financing provided by lease} - \text{value of equivalent loan}$$

We can also analyze leases from the lessor's side of the transaction using the same approaches we developed for the lessee. If lessee and lessor are in the same tax bracket, they will receive exactly the same cash flows, but with signs reversed. Thus, the lessee can gain only at the lessor's expense, or vice versa. However, if the lessee's tax rate is lower than the lessor's, then both can gain at the federal government's expense.

Although this chapter was mostly devoted to financial leases, we included a few hints on analyzing operating leases. Remember that many operating leases have valuable options attached to them—for example, the right to renew the lease at a prespecified rate or to purchase the asset at a prespecified price.

FURTHER READING

The approach to lease valuation presented in this chapter is based on:

S. C. Myers, D. A. Dill, and A. J. Bautista: "Valuation of Financial Lease Contracts," *Journal of Finance,* **31:** 799–819 (June 1976).

J. R. Franks and S. D. Hodges: "Valuation of Financial Lease Contracts: A Note," *Journal of Finance,* **33:** 647–669 (May 1978).

Other useful works include Nevitt and Fabozzi's book and the theoretical discussions of Miller and Upton, and Lewellen, Long, and McConnell:

P. K. Nevitt and F. J. Fabozzi: *Equipment Leasing,* 3d ed., Dow Jones–Irwin, Inc., Homewood, Ill., 1988.

M. H. Miller and C. W. Upton: "Leasing, Buying and the Cost of Capital Services," *Journal of Finance,* **31:** 761–786 (June 1976).

W. G. Lewellen, M. S. Long, and J. J. McConnell: "Asset Leasing in Competitive Capital Markets," *Journal of Finance,* **31:** 787–798 (June 1976).

The options embedded in some lease contracts are discussed in:

T. E. Copeland and J. F. Weston: "A Note on the Evaluation of Cancellable Operating Leases," *Financial Management,* **11:** 68–72 (Summer 1982).

J. J. McConnell and J. S. Schallheim: "Valuation of Asset Leasing Contracts," *Journal of Financial Economics,* **12:** 237–261 (August 1983).

QUIZ

1. The following terms are often used to describe leases:
   (*a*) Direct
   (*b*) Full-service
   (*c*) Operating
   (*d*) Financial
   (*e*) Rental
   (*f*) Net
   (*g*) Leveraged
   (*h*) Sale and lease-back
   (*i*) Full-payout
   Match each of these terms with one of the following statements:
   (*A*) The initial lease period is shorter than the economic life of the asset.
   (*B*) The initial lease period is long enough for the lessor to recover the cost of the asset.
   (*C*) The lessor provides maintenance and insurance.
   (*D*) The lessee provides maintenance and insurance.
   (*E*) The lessor buys the equipment from the manufacturer.
   (*F*) The lessor buys the equipment from the prospective lessee.
   (*G*) The lessor finances the lease contract by issuing debt and equity claims against it.

2. Some of the following reasons for leasing are rational. Others are irrational, or assume imperfect or inefficient capital markets. Which of the following reasons are the rational ones?
   (*a*) The lessee's need for the leased asset is only temporary.
   (*b*) Specialized lessors are better able to bear the risk of obsolescence.
   (*c*) Leasing provides 100 percent financing and thus preserves capital.
   (*d*) Leasing allows firms with low marginal tax rates to "sell" depreciation tax shields.
   (*e*) Leasing increases earnings per share.
   (*f*) Leasing reduces the transaction cost of obtaining external financing.
   (*g*) Leasing avoids restrictions on capital expenditures.
   (*h*) Leasing can reduce the alternative minimum tax.

3. True or false?
   (*a*) Lease payments are usually made at the start of each period. Thus the first payment is usually made as soon as the lease contract is signed.

(b) Financial leases can still provide off-balance-sheet financing.

(c) The cost of capital for a financial lease is the interest rate the company would pay on a bank loan.

(d) An equivalent loan's principal plus after-tax interest payments exactly match the after-tax cash flows of the lease.

(e) A financial lease should not be undertaken unless it provides more financing than the equivalent loan.

(f) It makes sense for firms that pay no taxes to lease from firms that do.

(g) Other things equal, the net tax advantage to leasing increases as nominal interest rates increase.

4. Suppose that National Waferonics has before it a 4-year lease proposal for a machine it may invest in. The firm constructs a table like Table 26-1. The bottom line of its table shows the lease cash flows:

	YEAR			
	0	1	2	3
Lease cash flow	+ 62,000	− 26,800	− 22,200	− 17,600

These flows reflect the cost of the machine, depreciation tax shields and the after-tax lease payments. Ignore salvage value. Assume the firm could borrow at 10 percent and faces a 34 percent marginal tax rate.

(a) What is the value of the equivalent loan?

(b) What is the value of the lease?

(c) Suppose the machine's NPV under normal financing is − $5000. Should National Waferonics invest? Should it sign the lease?

QUESTIONS AND PROBLEMS

1. Look again at the bus lease described in Section 26-1 and Table 26-1.

(a) What is the value of the lease if Greymare's marginal tax rate is $T_c = .20$?

(b) What would the lease value be if Greymare had to use straight-line depreciation for tax purposes?

2. In Section 26-3 we showed that the lease offered to Greymare Bus Lines had a positive NPV of $1310 if Greymare paid no tax, and also a + $410 NPV to a lessor paying 34 percent tax. What is the minimum lease payment the lessor could accept under these assumptions? What is the maximum amount that Greymare could pay?

3. Recalculate the value of the lease to Greymare Bus Lines if the company pays no taxes until year 3. Calculate the lease cash flows by modifying Table 26-1. Remember that the after-tax borrowing rate for periods 1 and 2 differs from the rate for periods 3 through 5.

4. NNW Airlines proposes to lease a $10 million aircraft. The terms require six annual lease payments of $1.65 million prepaid. NNW pays tax at 34 percent and, if it purchases the aircraft, it can write it off over 5 years. The interest rate is 10 percent. Draw up a schedule like Table 26-1 showing the incremental cash flows from leasing. What is the equivalent loan? How does it change over the life of the lease?

Suppose the plane is expected to have a $4 million salvage value after 6 years, and that investors in airplanes require a 15 percent expected return. Should NNW accept the lease as offered?

5. Nodhead College needs a new computer. It can either buy it for $250,000 or lease it from Compulease. The lease terms require Nodhead to make six annual payments (prepaid) of $62,000. Nodhead pays no tax. Compulease pays tax at 34 percent. Compulease can depreciate the computer for tax purposes over 5 years. The computer will have no residual value at the end of year 5. The interest rate is 8 percent.

    (*a*) What is the NPV of the lease for Nodhead College?

    (*b*) What is the NPV for Compulease?

    (*c*) What is the overall gain to leasing?

6. Many companies calculate the internal rate of return of the incremental after-tax cash flows from leasing. What problems do you think this may give rise to? To what rate should the IRR be compared?

7. The overall gain to leasing is the sum of the lease's value to the lessee and its value to the lessor. Construct simple numerical examples showing how this gain is affected by:

    (*a*) The rate of interest

    (*b*) The choice of depreciation schedule

    (*c*) The difference between the tax rates of the lessor and lessee

    (*d*) The length of the lease

8. Discuss the following two opposite statements. Which do you think makes the most sense?

    (*a*) "Leasing is tax avoidance and should be legislated against."

    (*b*) "Leasing ensures that the government's investment incentives work. It does so by allowing companies in nontaxpaying positions to take advantage of depreciation allowances."

9. The Safety Razor Company has a large tax-loss carry-forward and does not expect to pay taxes for another 10 years. The company is therefore proposing to lease $100,000 of new machinery. The lease terms consist of eight equal lease payments prepaid annually. The lessor can write the machinery off over 7 years using the tax depreciation schedules given in Table 6-5. There is no salvage value at the end of the machinery's economic life. The tax rate is 34 percent and the rate of interest is 10 percent. Wilbur Occam, the president of Safety Razor, wants to know the maximum lease payment that his company should be willing to make and the minimum payment that the lessor is likely to accept. Can you help him? How would your answer differ if the lessor was obliged to use straight-line depreciation?

10. Here is a very hard question. Merton Miller argues that companies which pay corporate income tax should be indifferent between issuing debt and equity (see Section 18-2). Suppose that he is right. Then companies that do not pay income tax should prefer to issue equity rather than debt. They should also prefer to lease rather than issue debt. Does this mean that they should be indifferent between leasing and issuing equity?

PART EIGHT

FINANCIAL PLANNING

27 Analyzing Financial Performance

"Divide and conquer" is the only practical strategy for presenting a complex field like financial management. We have broken down the financial manager's job into a series of clearly but narrowly defined topics, including capital budgeting, dividend policy, stock issue procedures, debt policy, and leasing. In the end the financial manager has to consider the combined effects of these decisions on the firm as a whole.

In this chapter we look at how you can use financial data to analyze a firm's past performance and assess its current financial standing. For example, you may need to check whether your own firm's financial performance is in the ballpark of standard practice. Or you may wish to understand the policies of a competitor or to check on the financial health of a customer.

Understanding the past is a necessary prelude to contemplating the future. Therefore the other chapters in Part Eight are devoted to financial planning. Chapter 28 shows how managers use long-term financial plans to establish concrete goals and to anticipate surprises. Chapter 29 then discusses short-term planning, where the emphasis is on ensuring that the firm has enough cash to pay its bills and puts any spare cash to good use. Chapter 29 also serves as an introduction to Part Nine, which covers the management of the firm's short-term assets and liabilities.

But all that comes later. The business at hand is to analyze financial performance. We start with the time-honored method of financial ratio analysis. We discuss how ratios are used, and we note the limitations of the accounting data which most of the ratios are based on.

27-1 FINANCIAL RATIOS

We have all heard stories of financial whizzes who in minutes can take a company's accounts apart and find its innermost secrets in financial ratios. The truth, however, is that financial ratios are no substitute for a crystal ball. They are just a convenient way to summarize large quantities of financial data and to compare firms' performance. Ratios help you to ask the right questions; they seldom answer them.

Financial ratios fall into four groups: leverage ratios, liquidity ratios, profitability or efficiency ratios, and market value ratios. We will illustrate the most common measures in each group with the aid of the 1985 income statements and balance sheets of Goodyear.

In 1985 Goodyear had a reputation as a well-managed and technologically advanced company operating in what can only be described as a flat tire market. The fierce competition and declining profitability of Goodyear's traditional business had led it to diversify into oil and gas exploration and transmission. The year 1985

TABLE 27-1
Summary financial statements for the Goodyear Tire and Rubber
Company (figures in millions)

	1985	1984
*Balance sheet:**		
Cash and short-term securities	$ 139	$ 143
Receivables	957	1,370
Inventories	1,379	1,333
Other current assets	83	54
Total current assets	2,558	2,901
Plant and equipment	4,025	3,037
Other long-term assets	370	257
Total assets	$6,954	$6,194
Current liabilities	$1,607	$1,558
Long-term debt and capital leases	998	657
Other long-term liabilities	841	808
Shareholders' equity	3,507	3,171
Total liabilities	$6,954	$6,194
Income statement:		
Net sales	$9,585	
Cost of goods sold	7,635	
Other expenses	1,507	
Other income	118	
Earnings before interest and tax (EBIT)	561	
Interest	105	
Tax	155	
Net income	$ 301	
Other financial information:		
Depreciation	$ 301	
Current cost of inventories	1,774	
Market value of equity	3,378	
Market value of equity plus all other liabilities	6,825	
Current cost of plant and equipment	5,338	
Current cost for all assets	8,662	
Average number of shares (millions)	107.369	
Earnings per share (dollars)	$ 2.80	
Dividend per share (dollars)	1.60	
Share price (dollars)	31¼	

* Columns may not add because of rounding.

was a period of calm before the storm, for in 1986 Sir James Goldsmith's General Oriental Group made a takeover bid for the company. Goodyear survived by re-purchasing General Oriental's holding, but in fighting the bid it had to implement a number of major changes. In particular, it repurchased a further 40 percent of its stock for $2 billion and it financed this repurchase by an increase in debt. Also Goodyear agreed to sell off its aerospace business and the rest of its oil and gas operations. Thus the company's moves to diversify out of tires were reversed and its future cash flows were earmarked to pay off the large debt burden.

However, in 1985 all this was in the future and largely unforeseen. We start therefore by summarizing in Table 27-1 Goodyear's 1985 income statement and balance sheet.

Leverage Ratios

Suppose that you are a bank lending officer considering a possible loan to a company. One of the first things you will wish to know is what other debts that firm has. Our first set of ratios, therefore, summarizes the firm's financial leverage.

Debt Ratio. Financial leverage is usually measured by the ratio of long-term debt to total long-term capital. Since long-term lease agreements also commit the firm to a series of fixed payments, it makes sense to include the value of lease obligations with the long-term debt. Thus for Goodyear:

$$\text{Debt ratio} = \frac{\text{long-term debt} + \text{value of leases}}{\text{long-term debt} + \text{value of leases} + \text{equity}}$$

$$= \frac{998}{998 + 3507} = .22$$

Another way to express leverage is in terms of the company's debt-equity ratio:

$$\text{Debt-equity ratio} = \frac{\text{long-term debt} + \text{value of leases}}{\text{equity}}$$

$$= \frac{998}{3507} = .28$$

Notice that both these measures make use of book (i.e., accounting) values rather than market values.[1] The market value of the company finally determines whether debtholders get their money back, so you would expect analysts to look at the face amount of the debt as a proportion of the total market value of debt and equity. The main reason that they don't do this is that market values are often not readily available. Does it matter much? Perhaps not; after all, the market value includes the value of intangible assets generated by research and development, advertising, staff training, and so on. These assets are not readily saleable and, if the company falls on hard times, the value of these assets may disappear altogether. For some purposes, it may be just as well to follow the accountant and to ignore these intangible assets entirely.

Notice also that this measure of leverage takes account only of long-term debt obligations. Managers sometimes also define debt to include all liabilities other than equity:

$$\frac{\text{Total liabilities} - \text{equity}}{\text{Total liabilities}} = \frac{6954 - 3507}{6954} = .50$$

Times Interest Earned. Another measure of financial leverage is the extent to which interest is covered by earnings before interest and taxes (EBIT) plus depreciation. In the case of Goodyear:[2]

$$\text{Times interest earned} = \frac{\text{EBIT} + \text{depreciation}}{\text{interest}}$$

$$= \frac{561 + 301}{105} = 8.2$$

[1] In the case of leased assets the accountant tries to estimate the present value of the lease commitments. In the case of long-term debt he or she simply shows face value. This can sometimes be very different from present value. For example, the present value of low-coupon debt may be only a fraction of its face value.

[2] The numerator of "times interest earned" can be defined in several ways. Sometimes depreciation is excluded. Sometimes it is just net earnings plus interest—that is, earnings before interest *but after tax*. This last definition seems nutty to us, because the point of "times interest earned" is to assess the risk that the firm won't have enough money to pay interest. If EBIT falls below interest obligations, the firm won't have to worry about taxes. Interest is paid before the firm pays income taxes.

Often analysts use an average of earnings over several years. The idea here is to smooth out temporary peaks and troughs. However, we will see later that there is no significant tendency for earnings to bounce back after a fall or to sink back after a rise. The current level of earnings is generally likely to be a better guide to the future than some past average.

The regular interest payment is a hurdle that companies must keep jumping if they are to avoid default. The "times interest earned" ratio measures how much clear air there is between hurdle and hurdler. However, always bear in mind that such summary measures tell only a part of the story. For example, it would make sense to include other fixed charges such as regular repayments of existing debt or long-term lease payments.[3]

Earnings Variability. A large debt burden is a problem only if there is uncertainty about future earnings. You may, therefore, want to look at the variability of the company's earnings over time.

There is no generally accepted measure of earnings variability. But on the basis of the past 12 years we would conclude that 1 year in 2 the change in Goodyear's earnings will lie within the range of -15 percent to $+10$ percent. Statisticians would say that the *interquartile range* of earnings changes is $10 - (-15) = 25$ percent.[4]

Liquidity Ratios

If you are extending credit or lending to a company for a short period, you are not interested only in the total asset coverage of the debt. You want to know whether the company will be able to lay its hands on the cash to repay you. That is why credit analysts and bankers look at several measures of *liquidity*.

Another reason that managers focus on liquid assets is because the figures are more reliable. The book value of a catalytic cracker may be a poor guide to its true value, but at least you know what cash in the bank is worth.

Liquidity ratios also have some less desirable characteristics. Because short-term assets and liabilities are easily changed, measures of liquidity can rapidly become out of date. You might not know what that catalytic cracker is worth but you can be fairly sure that it won't disappear overnight. Also, companies generally choose a slack period for the end of their financial year. At these times the companies are likely to have more cash and less short-term debt than during busier seasons.

Net Working Capital to Total Assets. Current assets are those assets which the company expects to turn into cash in the near future; current liabilities are liabilities which it expects to meet in the near future. The difference between the current assets and current liabilities is known as net working capital. It roughly measures

[3] In 1985 Goodyear charged about $18 million of long-term lease payments to income and it repaid about $31 million of long-term debt. That gives

$$\frac{\text{EBIT + depreciation + capital lease payments}}{\text{Interest + repayments of long-term debt + capital lease payments}} = \frac{561 + 301 + 18}{105 + 31 + 18} = 5.7$$

[4] Since earnings may vary from negative to positive, you cannot simply calculate the standard deviation of percentage earnings changes. Using the interquartile range will usually, but not always, avoid this problem.

the company's potential reservoir of cash. Managers often express net working capital as a proportion of total assets:

$$\frac{\text{Net working capital}}{\text{Total assets}} = \frac{2558 - 1607}{6954} = .14$$

Current Ratio.   Another measure which serves a similar purpose is the current ratio:

$$\text{Current ratio} = \frac{\text{current assets}}{\text{current liabilities}} = \frac{2558}{1607} = 1.6$$

Changes in the current ratio can mislead. For example, suppose that a company borrows a large sum from the bank and invests it in marketable securities. If nothing else changes, net working capital is unaffected but the current ratio changes.

Quick (or Acid-Test) Ratio.   Some assets are closer to cash than others. If trouble comes, inventories may not sell at anything above fire-sale prices. (Trouble typically comes *because* the firm can't sell its finished product inventory for more than production cost.) Thus, managers often focus only on cash, marketable securities, and bills that customers have not yet paid:

$$\text{Quick ratio} = \frac{\text{cash} + \text{marketable securities} + \text{receivables}}{\text{current liabilities}}$$

$$= \frac{139 + 957}{1607} = .7$$

Cash Ratio.   A company's most liquid assets are its holdings of cash and marketable securities. That is why financial analysts also look at the cash ratio:

$$\text{Cash ratio} = \frac{\text{cash} + \text{marketable securities}}{\text{current liabilities}} = \frac{139}{1607} = .09$$

Of course, lack of cash may not matter if the firm can borrow on short notice. Who cares whether a firm has actually borrowed from the bank or whether it has a guaranteed line of credit that enables it to borrow if it chooses? None of the standard liquidity measures takes the firm's "reserve borrowing power" into account.

Interval Measure.   Instead of looking at a firm's liquid assets relative to its current liabilities, it may be useful to measure whether they are large relative to the firm's regular cash outgoings. One suggestion is the so-called interval measure:

$$\text{Interval measure} = \frac{\text{cash} + \text{marketable securities} + \text{receivables}}{\text{average daily expenditures from operations}}$$

$$= \frac{139 + 957}{(7635 + 1507) \div 365} = 44 \text{ days}$$

Thus Goodyear has sufficient liquid assets to finance operations for 44 days, even if it receives no further cash.

Financial analysts employ another set of ratios to judge how efficiently companies are using their assets. As we will see, there is a much greater degree of ambiguity in these ratios. For example, we can be fairly sure that it is safer to lend to a company that has relatively little leverage and a predominance of liquid assets. But how should the lender interpret the fact that a firm has a high profit margin? Perhaps it is in a low-volume, high-mark-up business. (Jewelers operate on higher profit margins than food wholesalers but they are not necessarily safer.) Or perhaps it is more vertically integrated than its rivals. Again, that is not necessarily safer. Perhaps it charges higher prices, which may be a bad sign if it is trying to expand sales volume. Or perhaps it has lower costs, which is a good sign. We think that you should use these profitability ratios to help you *ask* the important questions rather than to help answer them.

Sales to Total Assets.   The sales-to-assets ratio shows how hard the firm's assets are being put to use.

$$\frac{\text{Sales}}{\text{Average total assets}} = \frac{9585}{(6954 + 6194) \div 2} = 1.5$$

A high ratio could indicate that the firm is working close to capacity. It may prove difficult to generate further business without an increase in invested capital.

Sales to Net Working Capital.   Net working capital can be measured more accurately than other assets. Also the level of net working capital can be adjusted more rapidly to reflect temporary fluctuations in sales. Thus managers sometimes focus on how hard working capital has been put to use.

$$\frac{\text{Sales}}{\text{Average net working capital}} = \frac{9585}{(951 + 1343) \div 2} = 8.4$$

Net Profit Margin.   If you want to know the proportion of sales that finds its way into profits, you look at the profit margin. Thus

$$\text{Net profit margin} = \frac{\text{EBIT} - \text{tax}}{\text{sales}} = \frac{561 - 155}{9585}$$

$$= .042, \text{ or } 4.2\%$$

Inventory Turnover.   Managers sometimes look at the rate at which companies turn over their inventories. In Goodyear's case,

$$\text{Inventory turnover} = \frac{\text{cost of goods sold}}{\text{average inventory}}$$

$$= \frac{7635}{(1379 + 1333) \div 2} = 5.6$$

A high inventory turnover is often regarded as a sign of efficiency. But don't jump to conclusions—it may simply indicate that the firm is living from hand to mouth.

Average Collection Period.   The average collection period measures the speed with which customers pay their bills:

$$\text{Average collection period} = \frac{\text{average receivables}}{\text{average daily sales}}$$

$$= \frac{(957 + 1370) \div 2}{9585 \div 365} = 44 \text{ days}$$

A low ratio is again believed to indicate an efficient collection department, but it sometimes results from an unduly restrictive credit policy.[5]

Return on Total Assets.   Managers often measure the performance of a firm by the ratio of income to total assets. Income is usually defined as earnings before interest but after taxes. Also, since the assets are likely to change over the year, it is common to measure return on the average of the assets at the beginning and end of the year:[6]

$$\text{Return on total assets} = \frac{\text{EBIT} - \text{tax}}{\text{average total assets}}$$

$$= \frac{561 - 155}{(6954 + 6194) \div 2}$$

$$= .062, \text{ or } 6.2\%$$

Another measure focuses on the return on the firm's equity:

$$\text{Return on equity} = \frac{\text{earnings available for common}}{\text{average equity}}$$

$$= \frac{301}{(3507 + 3171) \div 2} = .090, \text{ or } 9.0\%$$

The assets in a company's books are valued on the basis of their original cost (less any depreciation). A high return on assets does not mean that you could buy the same assets today and get a high return. Nor does a low return on assets imply that the assets could be better employed elsewhere. Thus return on assets does not tell you whether the firm's assets are being used efficiently.

---

[5] If possible, it would make sense to divide average receivables by average daily *credit* sales. Otherwise a low ratio might simply indicate that only a small proportion of sales were made on credit.

[6] This measure is sometimes misleading if it is used to compare firms with different capital structures. The reason is that firms which pay more interest pay less taxes. Thus this ratio reflects differences in financial leverage as well as in operating performance. If you want a measure of operating performance alone, we suggest adjusting taxes by adding back interest tax shields (interest payments × marginal tax rate). This gives the taxes the firm would pay if all-equity-financed. Thus, using the 1985 tax rate of 46 percent,

$$\text{Return on total assets} = \frac{\text{EBIT} - (\text{tax} + \text{interest tax shields})}{\text{average total assets}}$$

$$= \frac{561 - (155 + 0.46 \times 105)}{(6954 + 6194) \div 2} = .054, \text{ or } 5.4\%$$

We could use this measure to compare the operating performance of two firms even if they had radically different debt ratios.

Sometimes net income after interest and taxes is used in the numerator. This is an odd measure; equity income ought to be compared with equity investment, not with total assets.

Some profitability or efficiency ratios can be linked in useful ways. For example, the return on assets depends on the firm's sales-to-assets ratio and profit margin:

$$\frac{\text{Income}}{\text{Assets}} = \frac{\text{sales}}{\text{assets}} \times \frac{\text{income}}{\text{sales}}$$

All firms would like to earn a higher return on assets, but their ability to do so is limited by competition. If the expected return on assets is fixed by competition, firms face a trade-off between the sales-to-assets ratio and the profit margin. Thus we find that fast-food chains, which turn over their capital frequently, also tend to operate on low profit margins. Hotels have relatively low sales-to-assets ratios but tend to compensate for this with higher margins.

Firms often seek to increase their profit margins by becoming more vertically integrated—for example, they may acquire a supplier or one of their sales outlets. Unfortunately, unless they have some special skill in running these new businesses, they are likely to find that any gain in profit margin is offset by a decline in the sales-to-assets ratio.

Payout Ratio.   The payout ratio measures the proportion of earnings that is paid out as dividends. Thus

$$\text{Payout ratio} = \frac{\text{dividend}}{\text{earnings per share}} = \frac{1.60}{2.80} = .57$$

We saw in Section 16-2 that managers don't like to cut dividends because of a shortfall in earnings. Therefore, if a company's earnings are particularly variable, management is likely to play safe by setting a low average payout ratio.

When earnings fall unexpectedly, the payout ratio is likely to rise temporarily. Likewise, if earnings are expected to rise next year, management may feel that it can pay slightly more generous dividends than it would otherwise have done.

Earnings not paid out as dividends are plowed back into the business.

$$\text{Proportion of earnings plowed back} = 1 - \text{payout ratio}$$

$$= \frac{\text{earnings} - \text{dividend}}{\text{earnings}}$$

If you multiply this figure by the return on equity, you can see how rapidly the shareholders' investment is growing as a result of plowback. Thus for Goodyear:

$$\text{Growth in equity from plowback} = \frac{\text{earnings} - \text{dividend}}{\text{earnings}} \times \frac{\text{earnings}}{\text{equity}}$$

$$= .43 \times .090 = .039, \text{ or } 3.9\%$$

If Goodyear can continue to earn 9.0 percent on its book equity and plow back 43 percent of earnings, both earnings and equity will grow at 3.9 percent a year.

Market Value Ratios

There is no law that prohibits the financial manager from introducing data which are not in the company accounts. For example, if you were analyzing a steel company, you might want to look at the cost per ton of steel produced or the sales per employee. Frequently managers find it helpful to look at ratios that combine accounting and stock market data. Here are four of these market-based ratios.

Price-Earnings Ratio. The price-earnings, or P/E, ratio is a common measure of the esteem in which the company is held by investors. In the case of Goodyear:[7]

$$\text{P/E ratio} = \frac{\text{stock price}}{\text{earnings per share}} = \frac{31.25}{2.80} = 11.2$$

What does it mean when a company's stock sells on a high or low P/E? To answer this question you may find it helpful to look back to a formula that we introduced in Chapter 4. If a company's dividends are expected to grow at a steady rate, then the current stock price is

$$P_0 = \frac{\text{DIV}_1}{r - g}$$

In this formula DIV_1 measures the expected dividend next year, r is the return that investors require from similar investments, and g is the expected rate of dividend growth. In order to find the P/E ratio, simply divide through by expected earnings per share:

$$\frac{P_0}{\text{EPS}_1} = \frac{\text{DIV}_1}{\text{EPS}_1} \times \frac{1}{r - g}$$

Thus a high P/E ratio may indicate that (1) investors expect high dividend growth (g); or (2) the stock has low risk and, therefore, investors are content with a low prospective return (r); or (3) the company is expected to achieve average growth while paying out a high proportion of earnings ($\text{DIV}_1/\text{EPS}_1$).

Dividend Yield. The stock's dividend yield is simply the expected dividend as a proportion of the stock price. Thus for Goodyear:

$$\text{Dividend yield} = \frac{\text{dividend per share}}{\text{stock price}} = \frac{1.60}{31\frac{1}{4}}$$

$$= .051, \text{ or } 5.1\%$$

Again it is helpful to consider a company with a steady expected growth in dividends. In this case

$$\text{Dividend yield} = \frac{\text{DIV}_1}{P_0} = r - g$$

Thus a high yield may indicate that investors expect low dividend growth or that investors require a high return.

Market-to-Book Ratio. The market-to-book ratio is the ratio of stock price to book value per share. For Goodyear:

$$\text{Market-to-book ratio} = \frac{\text{stock price}}{\text{book value per share}}$$

$$= \frac{31\frac{1}{4}}{3507 \div 107.369} = .96$$

---

[7] We use 1985 earnings per share and the price at the end of 1985. Since stockholders always look forward, not back, it would be better to use earnings that were forecasted for 1986. See Section 4-4.

Book value per share is just stockholders' book equity (net worth) divided by the number of shares outstanding. Book equity equals common stock plus retained earnings—the net amount that the firm has received from stockholders or reinvested on their behalf.[8] Thus Goodyear's market-to-book ratio of .96 means that the firm is worth 4 percent less than past and present shareholders have put into it.

Tobin's q.   The ratio of the market value of a company's debt and equity to the current replacement cost of its assets is often known as Tobin's q, after the economist James Tobin.[9] In the case of Goodyear:

$$q = \frac{\text{market value of assets}}{\text{estimated replacement cost}} = \frac{6825}{8662} = .79$$

This ratio is like the market-to-book ratio, but there are several important differences. The numerator of q includes all the firm's debt and equity securities, not just its common stock.[10] The denominator includes all assets, not just the firm's net worth. Also these assets are not entered at original cost, as shown in the firm's books, but at what it would cost to replace them. Since inflation has driven many assets' replacement cost well above original cost, the Financial Accounting Standards Board (FASB) recommended procedures that would take into account the impact of inflation. Until 1985 large companies were obliged to report these "current cost" adjustments. Since then it has become a voluntary inclusion in the firm's financial statements. Because Goodyear no longer reports the current cost of its assets, you would need to adjust historic asset costs for inflation before you could calculate q.

Tobin argued that firms have an incentive to invest when q is greater than 1 (i.e., when capital equipment is worth more than it costs to replace), and that they will stop investing only when q is less than 1 (i.e., when equipment is worth less than its replacement cost). When q is less than 1, it may be cheaper to acquire assets through merger rather than buying new assets. At these times investors sometimes joke that the cheapest place for a firm to buy assets is on Wall Street.

Of course it is possible to think of cases when the existing assets are worth much more than their cost but there is no scope for further profitable investment. Nevertheless, a high market value is usually a sign that investors believe there are good opportunities in your business.

We should also expect q to be higher for firms with a strong competitive advantage. Table 27-2 bears this out. The companies with the highest values of q tend to be those that have had very strong brand images or patent protection.

---

[8] Retained earnings are measured net of depreciation. They represent stockholders' new investment in the business over and above the amount needed to maintain the firm's existing stock of assets.

[9] J. Tobin, "A General Equilibrium Approach to Monetary Theory," *Journal of Money, Credit, and Banking*, **1:** 15–29 (February 1969).

   For estimates of q see R. H. Gordon and D. F. Bradford, "Taxation and the Stock Market Valuation of Capital Gains and Dividends: Theory and Empirical Results," *Journal of Public Economics*, **14:** (October 1980); G. von Furstenberg, "Corporate Investment: Does Market Valuation Really Matter?" *Brookings Papers on Economic Activity*, **2:** 347–397 (1977); and E. B. Lindberg and S. A. Ross, "Tobin's q Ratio and Industrial Organization," *Journal of Business*, **54:** 1–33 (January 1981).

[10] For a public company it is easy to compute the market value of the stock. Most of the other liabilities are not regularly traded but in these cases market value is likely to be much closer to book value. We have estimated the total market value of Goodyear by simply substituting in the balance sheet the market value of the equity rather than the book value.

TABLE 27-2
Average values of Tobin's *q*, 1960–1977

High *q*'s		Low *q*'s	
Avon Products	8.53	Cone Mills	.45
Polaroid	6.42	Holly Sugar	.50
Xerox	5.52	Federal Paper Board	.52
Searle	5.27	National Steel	.53
MMM	4.87	Graniteville	.55
Schering-Plough	4.30	Publicker Industries	.59
IBM	4.21	Medusa Corp.	.60
Coca-Cola	4.21	Lowenstein	.61
Smith Kline	4.19	U.S. Steel	.62
Eli Lilly	4.02	Dan River	.67

Source: E. B. Lindberg and S. A. Ross, "Tobin's *q* Ratio and Industrial Organization," *Journal of Business,* **54:** 1–33 (January 1981).

Those with the lowest values have generally been in highly competitive and shrinking industries.

Accounting Definitions

Many years ago a British bank chairman observed that not only did the bank's accounts show its true position but the actual situation was a little better still.[11] Since that time accounting standards have been much more carefully defined but companies still have considerable discretion in calculating profits and deciding what to show on the balance sheet. Thus, when you calculate financial ratios, you need to look below the surface and understand some of the decisions taken by the firm's accountants. Here are some examples.

1. In July 1985 Goodyear sold some of its natural gas and pipeline interests to Tenneco. Therefore, in addition to showing income of $2.80 a share from continuing operations, Goodyear's income statement included income of $.08 per share from these discontinued operations plus a capital gain from the sale of $.95 a share. If you want to measure sustainable income, it probably makes sense to focus, as we did, on the income from continuing operations.

2. Each year Goodyear sells some of its receivables to a wholly owned subsidiary, Goodyear Financial Corporation, which is financed partly by Goodyear's equity stake and partly by external borrowing. Since Goodyear does not consolidate the accounts of its finance subsidiary, the figures in Table 27-3 understate the group's total receivables by $789 million and its short-term debt by $581 million. (Current FASB proposals will, if adopted, require companies to consolidate the accounts of their finance subsidiaries.)

3. Some fixed obligations are not shown on the balance sheet but are simply recorded in the notes to the accounts. For example, the pensions that firms promise to their employees are like a debt, though they are not shown on the balance sheet. To pay these future pensions, companies make contributions to a pension fund. The pension fund's portfolio is one of the company's most important assets though it is also not shown on the balance sheet.

[11] Speech by the Chairman of the London and County Bank at the Annual Meeting, February 1901. Reported in *The Economist* 1901, p. 204, and cited in C. A. E. Goodhart, *The Business of Banking 1891–1914,* Weidenfeld (George) and Nicholson, Ltd., London, 1972, p. 15.

In Goodyear's case the pension scheme was $172 million in surplus—that is, the assets in the fund were worth $172 million more than the pension promises. For some companies it is the other way around. Therefore, some analysts argue that one could get a clearer picture of the company's financial position by including the pension scheme's assets and liabilities in the company's balance sheet. A step in this direction has been made by a recent ruling (FASB 87) that by 1989 companies will need to record any pension scheme deficit as an explicit balance-sheet liability.

Contributions to the firm's pension scheme are treated as an expense and therefore reduce the firm's earnings. In 1985 Goodyear reduced its pension expenses by $25 million despite offering an improvement in benefits. Much of this reduction came from a change in the actuarial assumptions that were used to calculate the amount of the pension liability. This gain had nothing to do with the operating cash flows and you certainly could not bet on it being repeated. If you want a measure of Goodyear's sustainable earnings, it might be better to exclude this reduction in pension costs.

4. Goodyear uses the last-in-first-out (LIFO) method for valuing some of its inventories. If the company draws on inventory that was bought in earlier years, the cost of goods sold will fall and income will rise. That is what happened in 1983. Goodyear reduced its inventory and therefore used up materials that were bought at lower prices in earlier years. This added $.15 a share to 1983 earnings. Goodyear was better off as a result of the inventory appreciation, but you certainly would not want to rely on that gain being repeated.

Choosing a Benchmark

We have shown you how to calculate the principal financial ratios for Goodyear. But you still need some way of judging whether a ratio is high or low.

A good starting point is to compare the 1985 ratios with the equivalent figures for Goodyear in earlier years.[12] For example, you can see from the first two columns of Table 27-3 that in 1985 Goodyear was less highly levered, it was operating on lower levels of working capital, and it was earning a somewhat lower return on its capital. Look also at the market ratios. One worrisome feature is that the market value of Goodyear's assets remains below replacement cost. This suggests that investors may need some persuading if Goodyear wishes to plow back substantial sums into the business.

When making comparisons of this kind remember our earlier warning about the need to dig behind the figures. For example, it turns out that a large part of the reduction in working capital simply reflects increased sales of receivables to Goodyear Financial. Also, how worrisome is that fall in profitability? Some part is due to a buildup in research and development expenditures; although this may reduce current earnings, it is an investment that should pay off in the future. You might also want to look at how income has been affected by changes in inventory profits or pension contributions. In sum, don't just measure whether Goodyear's financial ratios have changed; try to understand *why* they have changed.

It is also helpful to compare Goodyear's financial position with that of other firms. However, you would not expect companies in different industries to have

[12] Averages of ratios are somewhat odd animals. For example, you wouldn't want to take an average of P/E ratios if one company had negligible earnings. In Table 27-3 we have scaled all the data by dividing by the year's total assets. Then we have calculated the ratio of the average of one item to the average of the other item.

TABLE 27-3
Financial ratios for Goodyear and other tire and rubber companies

	GOODYEAR		OTHER COMPANIES IN THE TIRE AND RUBBER INDUSTRY
	1985	1980–1984	1985*
Leverage ratios:			
Debt ratio	.22	.27	.27
Total liabilities − equity / Total liabilities	.50	.53	.59
Times interest earned	8.2	5.4	1.7
Liquidity ratios:			
Net working capital to total assets	.14	.26	.16
Current ratio	1.6	2.0	1.5
Quick ratio	.7	1.1	1.0
Cash ratio	.09	.07	.19
Interval measure (days)	44	63	79
Profitability (or efficiency) ratios:			
Sales to total assets	1.5	1.7	1.4
Sales to net working capital	8.4	6.5	9.2
Net profit margin (percent)	4.2	5.2	− 1.0
Inventory turnover	5.6	5.1	6.8
Average collection period (days)	44	51	54
Return on total assets (percent)	6.2	8.5	− 1.4
Return on equity (percent)	9.0	11.3	− 9.0
Market value ratios:			
Price-earnings ratio	11.2	8.4	− †
Dividend yield (percent)	5.1	5.5	3.5
Market-to-book ratio	.96	.93	1.09
Tobin's q	.79	.75	.83

* B. F. Goodrich, Firestone, and Gencorp.
† Not meaningful: B. F. Goodrich and Firestone reported losses for 1985, giving a negative average price-earnings ratio.

similar financial ratios. For example, a tire manufacturer is unlikely to have the same profit margin as a jeweller or the same leverage as a finance company. It makes sense, therefore, to limit the comparison to other firms in the same industry. The third column of Table 27-3 shows the average financial ratios for other tire and rubber companies. But once again you should not stop there. For example, the difference in the return on assets stems largely from a difference in profit margins. Was this due to greater efficiency or to a difference in the type of business? You can obtain some clues by comparing the segment accounts, which break profitability down according to product and area of operation. Are there any indications that the difference in margins may be temporary? A closer examination of the cost of goods sold may help you decide.

Financial ratios for industries are published by the U.S. Department of Commerce, Dun and Bradstreet, Robert Morris Associates, and others. Table 27-4 gives the principal ratios for major industry groups. This should give you a feel for some of the differences between industries.

TABLE 27-4
Financial ratios for major industry groups, third quarter 1986

	All Manufacturing Corporations	Food and Kindred Products	Printing and Publishing	Chemical and Allied Products	Petroleum and Coal Products	Machinery Except Electrical	Electrical and Electronic Equipment	Retail Trade
Debt ratio*	.40	.49	.43	.39	.49	.29	.29	.45
Net working capital to total assets	.15	.11	.19	.12	.02	.23	.20	.21
Current ratio	1.57	1.45	1.84	1.52	1.13	1.92	1.64	1.74
Quick ratio	.95	.83	1.43	.96	.67	1.16	.93	.77
Sales to total assets	1.12	1.49	1.29	.95	.61	.97	1.11	2.04
Net profit margin, %†	3.7	4.7	5.7	4.8	2.3	2.6	3.1	2.9
Inventory turnover	6.3	9.0	12.4	6.3	9.6	4.8	4.6	6.9
Return on total assets, %†	4.1	7.0	7.4	4.5	1.4	2.5	3.5	5.9
Return on equity, %‡	8.5	15.5	19.9	15.4	1.0	5.9	7.1	10.4
Dividend payout ratio	.64	.47	.24	.65	6.37	.68	.79	.41

* Long-term debt includes capitalized leases, and also deferred income taxes.
† Reflects operating income only.
‡ Reflects nonoperating as well as operating income.
Source: United States Department of Commerce, *Quarterly Financial Report for Manufacturing, Mining and Trade Corporations*, Third Quarter, 1986.

Which Financial Ratios?

Be selective in your choice of financial ratios, because many ratios tell you similar things. For example, Table 27-5 shows the correlation between nine financial ratios.[13] Notice that the correlation between the debt-equity ratio and the long-term debt-equity ratio is .8. This suggests that you may not need to calculate both these ratios. Conversely, there is almost no relationship between a firm's current ratio and the return on equity. You can get additional information by looking at both figures.

27-2 THE EARNINGS RECORD

Figure 27-1 summarizes Goodyear's earnings record over the past 10 years. To interpret this record you need to take into account what was happening to other companies. The reason for this is that Goodyear is affected by the state of the economy as a whole and by the prosperity of its particular industry. The importance of these external influences on a company's income is shown in Table 27-6. On average an estimated 17 percent of the yearly variation in income is due to changes in the aggregate income of all corporations. A further 26 percent is explained by changes in the industry's income.

---

[13] The correlations are rank correlations. In other words, they measure whether a company's ranking in terms of one ratio corresponds to its ranking in terms of another ratio.

TABLE 27-5
Correlations between different financial ratios; all industries 1975

	Long-Term Debt-Equity Ratio	Debt-Equity Ratio	Times Interest Earned	Current Ratio	Quick Ratio	Interval Measure	Return on Assets	Return on Equity	Inventory Turnover
Long-term debt-equity ratio	1.0								
Debt-equity ratio	.8	1.0							
Times interest earned	−.6	−.6	1.0						
Current ratio	−.4	−.6	.3	1.0					
Quick ratio	−.3	−.5	.3	.7	1.0				
Interval measure	−.1	−.2	.1	.2	.5	1.0			
Return on assets	−.3	−.4	.9	.2	.3	.1	1.0		
Return on equity	−.1	−.1	.6	.0	.1	.1	.8	1.0	
Inventory turnover	.1	.1	.2	−.4	.0	−.2	.2	.3	1.0

Source: G. Foster: *Financial Statement Analysis,* 1st ed., Prentice-Hall, Inc., Englewood Cliffs, N.J., 1978.

Figure 27-1 also shows the average earnings performance of other companies in the United States that do business in the tire and rubber industry. We can now start to ask sensible questions about Goodyear's record. For example, why were the earnings of tire and rubber companies so weak between 1978 and 1980 and

FIGURE 27-1
Earnings per share of Goodyear and a sample of other rubber companies 1972–1985, expressed as a percent of 1972 earnings per share. Note that the other rubber companies' earnings were negative in 1985.

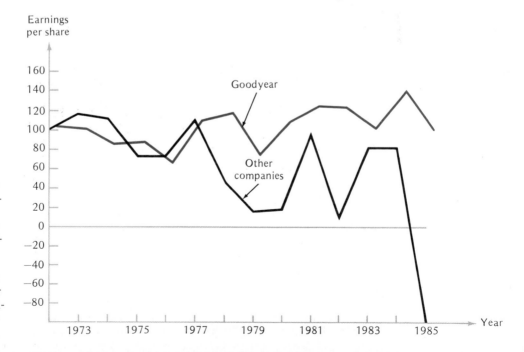

TABLE 27-6
Percentage of changes in net income due to economywide influences and industry influences (measured for 315 firms, 1964–1983)

	Economywide Influence	Industry Influence
Crude petroleum and natural gas	14%	21%
Paper and allied products	49	12
Drugs	14	26
Petroleum refining	37	23
Steel and blast furnaces	35	23
General industrial machinery	23	21
Radio and TV transmitting equipment	14	15
Electronic components	32	12
Trucking	21	27
Air transportation	12	13
Electric services	8	39
Natural gas distribution	13	8
Electric and other service combinations	6	45
Retail, grocery stores	9	17
State banks, Federal Reserve System	5	25
Average	17	26

Source: G. Foster, *Financial Statement Analysis,* 2d ed., Prentice-Hall, Inc., Englewood Cliffs, N.J., 1986.

then again in 1982? Was it because of the decline in auto production in those years? If so, we know one danger signal to look for in the future. What happened in 1985 and why did Goodyear buck the industry trend in that year? A study of the accounts for different business segments and geographical areas may offer some clues.

In the later years Goodyear's earnings have been better while its competitors' earnings have declined. Is this a sign that Goodyear has entered a period of more rapid growth? Not necessarily. Statisticians who have studied the time path of firms' reported earnings conclude that earnings behave much like stock prices— that is, they follow a random walk.[14] There is almost no relationship between a company's earnings growth in one period and that in the next. Therefore do not extrapolate growth mechanically. A firm with above-average earnings growth may sustain it, but it is equally likely to be followed by below-average growth.

Since earnings changes are unrelated from one year to the next, your best measure of past growth is the simple average of past annual percentage growth rates. There is little point in fitting a trend line to past earnings, and such a trend line tells you little about likely future earnings.

Of course there are many sources of information that may help you forecast earnings. For example, when a firm enjoys a high P/E ratio despite disappointing earnings, this suggests that investors should expect an earnings rebound. Or suppose a firm announces a significant technological jump ahead of its competitors; you don't need a Ph.D. to figure out the likely impact on earnings.

[14] See, for example, R. Ball and R. Watts, "Some Time Series Properties of Accounting Income," *Journal of Finance,* **27**: 663–682 (June 1972).

*The Meaning of Accounting Earnings

Economists often define earnings as cash flow plus the change in value of the company's assets. But we know from looking at the behavior of stock prices that changes in asset values are fundamentally unpredictable. So it looks as if the company's published earnings follow a much smoother path than economic earnings.

Accountants don't really try to track year-to-year economic income. They seem more interested in showing the long-run average profitability of the firm's assets.[15] However, they don't always achieve that objective either.

We described the biases in accounting profitability measures in Chapter 12. A few more words are needed here because accountants provide most of the input for financial ratios.

How Accounting Earnings Are Calculated. We emphasized in Chapter 6 that accounting earnings differ from cash flow. Accountants start with cash flow, then break it down into two categories—current and capital expenditures. Current expenditures are deducted from earnings right away.[16] Capital expenditures are capitalized and then depreciated over the following years.

A tricky problem for accountants is to decide which outflows are to be capitalized. When a company builds a new factory, there is an outflow of cash but shareholders also acquire an asset that is likely to bring higher cash flows in the future. Therefore, accountants are prepared to treat such expenditures as capital investments. But what about the cost of research and development, or staff training, or a new advertising campaign? These expenditures are also investments in the future but accountants are reluctant to recognize investments in intangible assets. Therefore, they deduct such expenditures from current earnings.[17]

If a high-tech company makes a large investment in research and development (R&D), financial statements are likely to understate true earnings. But investors recognize that some of the expenses are really an investment in the future. Therefore, the stock sells at a high price relative to published earnings. Subsequently, when the investment in R&D begins to pay off, published earnings are likely to rise rapidly. But investors are aware that the company is now running down its capital; so the stock price will not keep pace with earnings.[18]

A company's income statement shows the actual operating cash flows but it does not show the actual change in asset value. Instead, accountants set up a depreciation schedule ahead of time and, except in abnormal circumstances, they stick to it. Thus the company's income statement reflects partly what actually happened (the operating cash flow) and partly what was forecast to happen (the depreciation in asset value).

When accountants set up the depreciation schedule in advance, they do not make detailed forecasts of how the value of each asset is likely to vary over time.

---

[15] Fischer Black has made this point in an extreme and very interesting way in his article "The Magic in Earnings: Economic Earnings versus Accounting Earnings," *Financial Analysts Journal*, **36**: 3–8 (November–December 1980).

[16] This is obviously an oversimplification. Accountants also try to record income in the year in which it accrues rather than when the bills are paid.

[17] Accountants prefer assets you can kick. Since you can't see or touch intangible assets, how can you be *sure* they are there?

[18] When the stock price does not respond to the increased earnings, managers sometimes feel that investors are irrational or ungrateful. They forget that the *real* increase in earnings occurred several years earlier.

Instead they rely on a few standard rules of thumb such as straight-line depreciation. If an investment takes several years to reach full profitability, then in the early years straight-line depreciation will overstate the likely fall in the investment's value and in the later years it will understate it. For example, suppose that a paper manufacturer opens a new mill. Large new paper mills take a notoriously long time to reach maximum efficiency. Therefore, if the company depreciates its assets straight-line, the financial statements will initially understate true earnings and the stock will sell at a high price relative to published earnings.

Of course decisions on which items to capitalize and how to depreciate them are not the only potential sources of distortion in earnings. Our message, however, is a general one. If you wish to use a company's earnings as a guide to its value, you need to "normalize" those earnings for temporary distortions that stem from particular accounting techniques.

*How Inflation Affects Book Returns

We will steer clear of "inflation accounting" because the subject is so complex when one gets down to practical proposals. We will simply remind you how inflation bears on standard book earnings.

First, inflation increases the nominal value of work in process and finished inventory. Suppose you are a clothing manufacturer. In January you make up 1000 men's suits worth $300 apiece, but you do not sell the suits until June. During this time your competitors have raised their prices by 6 percent and you have quite literally followed suit. Thus the goods are finally sold for $300 \times 1.06 = \$318$. Part of your profit on this batch of suits can be attributed to inflation while the suits sat in inventory. You receive an inventory profit of $18 per suit.

Inventory profits are profits. You are better off with them than without. They are properly included in nominal income. However, they are not part of real income, except to the extent that the inventories appreciate faster than the general price level.

There is a second problem. As inflation progresses, the net book value of fixed assets becomes more and more out of date—that is, book value understates current value or replacement cost. So depreciation schedules that are based on book value may provide a misleading picture of the change in the current value of the assets.

Inflation has a third effect on book profits of firms that borrow. Lenders are paid back in inflated future dollars, so they demand a higher interest rate to compensate for the declining real value of their loan. The part of the interest rate which compensates for expected inflation is called the *inflation premium*.

The full interest payment, including the inflation premium, is deducted from the firm's net book income. But book income does not recognize the compensating gain that the stockholders make at the expense of lenders. Remember, lenders gain from the inflation premium but lose as inflation drives down the real value of their asset. Stockholders lose by paying the inflation premium but gain because inflation drives down the real value of their obligation. Book income recognizes stockholders' loss but not the offsetting gain.[19]

---

[19] For a provocative discussion of inflationary biases in book income see F. Modigliani and R. A. Cohn, "Inflation, Rational Valuation and the Market," *Financial Analysts Journal,* **35:** 24–44 (March–April 1979).

27-3 APPLICATIONS OF FINANCIAL ANALYSIS

We have discussed how to calculate and interpret summary measures of a company's financial position. We conclude this chapter with a brief glimpse at some of the ways that these measures can help the financial manager.

Suppose that you are a credit analyst or bank lending officer with the job of deciding whether a particular company is likely to repay its debts. What can you learn from the company's financial statements?

To answer this question William Beaver compared the financial ratios of 79 firms that subsequently failed with the ratios of 79 that remained solvent.[20] Beaver's sample of failed firms behaved much as you would expect. They had more debt than the surviving firms and they had a lower return on sales and assets. They had less cash but more receivables. As a result they had somewhat lower current ratios and dramatically lower cash ratios. Contrary to popular belief, the failed firms had less, rather than more, inventory.

Figure 27-2 provides some idea of the predictive power of these financial ratios. You can see that 5 years before failure the group of failed firms appeared to be consistently less healthy. As we move progressively closer to the date of collapse, the difference between the two groups becomes even more marked.

Instead of looking at a number of separate clues, it may be more useful to combine the different bits of information into a single measure of the likelihood of bankruptcy. We will describe in Chapter 30 how companies construct such a measure.

Using Financial Ratios to Estimate Market Risk

Chapter 9 described how the return that investors require from a company's stock depends on its market risk, or beta. If you have sufficient history of stock price data, you can estimate beta by looking at the extent to which the price was affected by fluctuations in the market.

Because such stock price data are not always available, financial economists have examined whether accounting data can be used to estimate beta. The pioneering study was by Beaver, Kettler, and Scholes.[21] In addition to calculating the usual financial ratios, Beaver, Kettler, and Scholes calculated an "accounting beta." In other words, they estimated the sensitivity of each company's earnings changes to changes in the aggregate earnings of all companies. An accounting beta of less than 1.0 means that on average the company's earnings changed by less than 1 percent for each 1 percent change in aggregate earnings. Conversely an accounting beta of more than 1.0 implies that the firm's earnings changed by more than 1 percent for each 1 percent change in aggregate earnings.

Table 27-7 summarizes the findings of this study. Not only the accounting beta but also the firm's leverage and payout ratio appear to provide useful clues to market risk.

Instead of looking at financial ratios one by one, Rosenberg and Marathe looked at a combination of ratios and obtained a single estimate of beta that was about

---

[20] See W. H. Beaver, "Financial Ratios and Predictors of Failure," *Empirical Research in Accounting: Selected Studies*. Supplement to *Journal of Accounting Research*, 1966, 77–111. Several later studies have come up with similar (but pictorially less eye-catching) findings. For a review of these studies see G. Foster, *Financial Statement Analysis*, 2d ed., Prentice-Hall, Inc., Englewood Cliffs, N.J., 1986.

[21] W. H. Beaver, P. Kettler, and M. Scholes, "The Association between Market-Determined and Accounting-Determined Risk Measures," *The Accounting Review*, **45**: 654–682 (October 1970).

FIGURE 27-2
Beaver's study showed that the financial ratios of firms which subsequently fail are different from those of firms which survive. Note that the horizontal axis measures the number of years *before* failure: thus moving from right to left brings the failed firms *closer* to failure. (*Source:* W. H. Beaver, "Financial Ratios and Predictors of Failure," *Empirical Research in Accounting: Selected Studies* Supplement to *Journal of Accounting Research*, 1966, pp. 77–111, fig. 1, p. 82.)

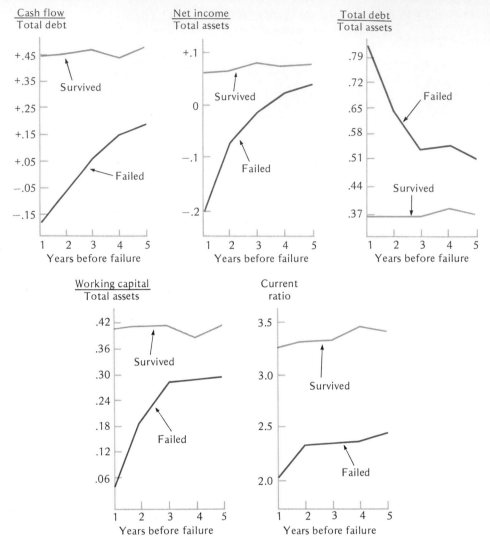

as accurate as you could get from stock price data.[22] They suggested that you can get even better estimates of risk by taking both accounting measures and stock price data into account.

Using Financial Ratios to Predict Bond Ratings

Moody's bond ratings are widely used as a yardstick of bond quality. Therefore, they indicate which investors are likely to buy your company's bonds and what interest rate they will require. Financial managers pay considerable attention to their company's bond ratings and would like to know in advance how a new issue of bonds would be rated and how a change in circumstances would affect the ratings on existing debt.

[22] See B. Rosenberg and V. Marathe, "The Prediction of Systematic and Residual Risk," *Proceedings of the Seminar on the Analysis of Security Prices,* Graduate School of Business, University of Chicago, November 1975.

TABLE 27-7

Correlations between stock market betas and
financial ratios

	1947–1956	1957–1965
Accounting beta	.44	.23
Leverage	.23	.22
Average payout ratio	−.49	−.29
Asset size	−.06	−.16
Asset growth	.27	.01
Liquidity	−.13	.05

Source: W. H. Beaver, P. Kettler, and M. Scholes, "The Association between Market-Determined and Accounting-
Determined Risk Measures," *The Accounting Review,* **45:**
654–682 (October 1970).

Kaplan and Urwitz found that issuers of the more highly rated bonds generally
had lower debt ratios, a higher ratio of earnings to interest, and a higher return
on assets.[23] The bonds were also more likely to be senior issues and the companies
tended to be larger with lower market and unique risk.

Kaplan and Urwitz also combined these variables into a single measure of bond
quality and looked at how well it could forecast Moody's ratings for a sample of
newly issued bonds. Table 27-8 shows that their forecast was spot on two-thirds
of the time and that it was never out by more than one category.

TABLE 27-8

Moody's bond ratings for a sample of new issues were similar
to the predicted ratings (for example, a total of 46 bonds were
predicted to have A ratings and of these, 33 actually received
an A rating)

Actual Ratings	PREDICTED RATINGS						
	Aaa	Aa	A	Baa	Ba	B	Total
Aaa	2						2
Aa	2	2	5				9
A		1	33	2			36
Baa			8	7			15
Ba				1			1
B					1		1
Total	4	3	46	10	1		64

Source: R. S. Kaplan and G. Urwitz, "Statistical Models of Bond Ratings:
A Methodological Inquiry," *Journal of Business,* **52:** 231–261 (April
1979).

[23] R. S. Kaplan and G. Urwitz, "Statistical Models of Bond Ratings: A Methodological Inquiry," *Journal
of Business,* **52:** 231–261 (April 1979).

27-4   SUMMARY

If you are analyzing a company's financial statements, there is a danger of being overwhelmed by the sheer volume of data. That is why managers use a few salient ratios to summarize the firm's leverage, liquidity, profitability, and market valuation. We have described some of the more popular financial ratios.

We offer the following general advice to users of these ratios.

1. Financial ratios seldom provide answers but they do help you ask the right questions.
2. There is no international standard for financial ratios. A little thought and common sense is worth far more than blind application of formulas.
3. Be selective in your choice of ratios. Different ratios often tell you similar things.
4. You need a benchmark for assessing a company's financial position. It is usual to compare financial ratios with the company's ratios in earlier years and with the ratios of other firms in the same business.

You can learn something about why a company's earnings change by comparing its earnings record with that of other firms. But be careful not to extrapolate past rates of earnings growth—earnings follow approximately a random walk.

Accounting earnings don't incorporate the year-by-year fluctuations in the value of the company's assets. Instead, accountants try to provide a picture of long-run sustainable earnings. Therefore, you can often get some idea of a company's value by multiplying its earnings by a standard price-earnings multiple. Sometimes the procedures used by accountants may temporarily depress earnings. For example, accountants generally deduct expenditure on intangible assets from current earnings. Also, if an investment takes a while to reach maximum profitability, straight-line depreciation will lead to an understatement of earnings in the early years. In these cases the earnings should be capitalized at a higher multiple.

Financial statement analysis helps you understand what makes the firm tick. We looked briefly at three particular applications. First, healthy firms have different financial ratios than firms that are heading for insolvency. Second, financial ratios provide valuable clues about a firm's market risk. Finally, we saw that a company's financial ratios can be used to predict the rating on a new issue of bonds.

FURTHER READING

There are some good general texts on financial statement analysis. See, for example:

G. Foster, *Financial Statement Analysis,* 2d ed., Prentice-Hall, Inc., Englewood Cliffs, N.J., 1986.

B. Lev, *Financial Statement Analysis: A New Approach,* Prentice-Hall, Inc., Englewood Cliffs, N.J., 1978.

Fischer Black's provocative paper argues that the object of accounting rules is to produce an earnings figure that moves as nearly as possible in line with company values:

F. Black, "The Magic in Earnings: Economic Earnings versus Accounting Earnings," *Financial Analysts Journal,* **36:** 3–8 (November–December 1980).

Three classic articles on the application of financial ratios to specific problems are:

W. H. Beaver, "Financial Ratios and Predictors of Failure," *Empirical Research in Accounting: Selected Studies.* Supplement to *Journal of Accounting Research,* 1966, 77–111.

W. H. Beaver, P. Kettler, and M. Scholes, "The Association between Market-Determined and Accounting-Determined Risk Measures," *The Accounting Review,* **45:** 654–682 (October 1970).

J. O. Horrigan, "The Determination of Long Term Credit Standing with Financial Ratios," *Empirical Research in Accounting: Selected Studies.* Supplement to *Journal of Accounting Research*, 1966, 44–62.

QUIZ

1. Table 27-9 gives abbreviated balance sheets and income statements for The May Department Store Company. Calculate the following financial ratios:
   (*a*) Debt ratio
   (*b*) Times interest earned
   (*c*) Current ratio
   (*d*) Quick ratio
   (*e*) Net profit margin
   (*f*) Inventory turnover
   (*g*) Return on net worth
   (*h*) Payout ratio

TABLE 27-9
Income statement and balance sheets for The May Department Store Company, January 31, 1987 (figures in millions)

*Income statement**		
Net sales	$10,376	
Cost of goods sold[†]	7,533	
Other expenses	2,048	
Earnings before interest and tax (EBIT)	795	
Interest	127	
Income before tax	668	
Tax	287	
Net income	381	
Dividends[‡]	138	

	Start of Year	End of Year
*Balance sheet**		
Assets		
Cash and marketable securities	$ 228	$ 469
Receivables	1,645	1,591
Inventories	1,455	1,432
Other current assets	43	33
Total current assets	3,371	3,525
Net property, plant and equipment	2,418	2,502
Other long-term assets	142	182
Total assets	$5,931	$6,209
Liabilities		
Payables	$ 790	$ 838
Other current liabilities	1,052	766
Total current liabilities	$1,842	$1,604
Long-term debt and capital leases	1,056	1,136
Other long-term liabilities	612	874
Shareholders' equity	2,421	2,595
Total liabilities	$5,931	$6,209

* Columns may not add because of rounding.
[†] Includes depreciation of 263.
[‡] Includes preferred dividends.

2. There are no universally accepted definitions of financial ratios, but five of the following ratios make no sense at all. Substitute the correct definitions.

(a) Debt-equity ratio = $\dfrac{\text{long-term debt} + \text{values of leases}}{\text{long-term debt} + \text{value of leases} + \text{equity}}$

(b) Return on equity = $\dfrac{\text{EBIT} - \text{tax}}{\text{average equity}}$

(c) Payout ratio = $\dfrac{\text{dividend}}{\text{stock price}}$

(d) Profit margin = $\dfrac{\text{EBIT} - \text{tax}}{\text{sales}}$

(e) Inventory turnover = $\dfrac{\text{sales}}{\text{average inventory}}$

(f) Current ratio = $\dfrac{\text{current liabilities}}{\text{current assets}}$

(g) Sales to net working capital = $\dfrac{\text{average sales}}{\text{net working capital}}$

(h) Interval measure = $\dfrac{\text{current assets} - \text{inventories}}{\text{average daily expenditure from operations}}$

(i) Average collection period = $\dfrac{\text{sales}}{\text{average receivables} \div 365}$

(j) Quick ratio = $\dfrac{\text{current assets} - \text{inventories}}{\text{current liabilities}}$

(k) Tobin's q = $\dfrac{\text{market value of assets}}{\text{replacement cost of assets}}$

3. True or false?
(a) A company's debt-equity ratio is always less than 1.
(b) The quick ratio is always less than the current ratio.
(c) The return on equity is always less than the return on assets.
(d) Successive earnings levels are unrelated to each other.
(e) Successive earnings changes are unrelated to each other.
(f) Earnings follow roughly a random walk. This means that if earnings turn out to be higher than expected, you should revise upward your forecast of future earnings by a similar proportion.
(g) Accounting earnings follow a less smooth path than economic earnings.
(h) If a project is slow to reach full profitability, straight-line depreciation is likely to produce an overstatement of profits in the early years.
(i) A substantial new advertising campaign by a cosmetics company will tend to depress earnings and cause the stock to sell at a low price-earnings multiple.

4. In each of the following cases, explain briefly which of the two companies is likely to be characterized by the higher ratio:
(a) Debt-equity ratio: a shipping company or a computer software company
(b) Payout ratio: United Foods Inc. or Computer Graphics Inc.

    (c) Ratio of sales to assets: an integrated pulp and paper manufacturer or a paper mill

    (d) Average collection period: a supermarket chain or a mail order company

    (e) Price-earnings multiple: Basic Sludge Company or Fledgling Electronics

    (f) Tobin's q: an iron foundry or a pharmaceutical company with strong patent protection

QUESTIONS AND PROBLEMS

1. Discuss alternative measures of financial leverage. Should the market value of equity be used or the book value? Is it better to use the market value of debt, the book value, or the book value discounted at the risk-free interest rate? How should you treat off-balance-sheet obligations such as pension liabilities? How would you treat preferred stock, deferred tax reserves, and minority interest?

2. As you can see, someone has spilt ink over some of the entries in the balance sheet and income statement of Transylvania Railroad (Table 27-10). Can you use the following information to work out the missing entries?

- Financial leverage   =   .4
- Times interest earned   =   8
- Current ratio   =   1.4
- Quick ratio   =   1.0

TABLE 27-10
Balance sheet and income statement of Transylvania Railroad

	MILLIONS OF DOLLARS	
	December 1988	December 1987
Balance sheet		
Fixed assets, net	■■■	25
Cash	■■■	20
Accounts receivable	■■■	34
Inventory	■■■	26
Total current assets	■■■	80
Total	■■■	105
Equity	■■■	30
Long-term debt	■■■	20
Notes payable	30	35
Accounts payable	25	20
Total current liabilities	■■■	55
Total	115	105
Income statement		
Sales	■■■	
Cost of goods sold	■■■	
Selling, general and administrative expenses	10	
Depreciation	20	
EBIT	■■■	
Interest	■■■	
Earnings before tax	■■■	
Tax	■■■	
Available for common	■■■	

- Cash ratio $\qquad$ = .2
- Return on total assets $\qquad$ = .18
- Return on equity $\qquad$ = .41
- Inventory turnover $\qquad$ = 5.0
- Receivables' collection period $\qquad$ = 71.2 days

3. Use financial ratio analysis to compare two companies chosen from the same industry.

*4. Read and discuss Fischer Black's paper "The Magic in Earnings."

5. Describe some of the ways that the choice of accounting technique can temporarily depress or inflate earnings.

6. At end 1985 Goodyear had unused lines of credit which would have allowed it to borrow a further $155 million. Suppose that it used this line of credit to raise short-term loans of $155 million and invested the proceeds in marketable securities. Would the company have appeared to be (*a*) more or less liquid, (*b*) more or less highly levered? Calculate the appropriate ratios.

7. Goodyear Tire and Rubber's income statement includes the income of its finance subsidiary, Goodyear Financial Corporation (GFC). However, the *balance sheet* of GFC is not consolidated. Here is an abbreviated version of GFC's balance sheet at the end of 1985:

	Millions of Dollars
Receivables	789
Other current assets	3
Total assets	792
Current liabilities	624
Loans from an affiliated company	15
Equity owned by Goodyear Tire and Rubber	153
Total liabilities	792

How would Goodyear Tire and Rubber's financial ratios change if you incorporated the assets and liabilities of GFC?

8. Recalculate Goodyear's financial ratios at the end of 1986. What problems arise in ensuring comparable figures with 1985? Discuss the effects of Goodyear's restructuring (referred to in Section 27-1).

9. Here are some data for five companies in the saucepan industry:

	COMPANY CODE				
	A	B	C	D	E
Net income (millions)	$ 10	.5	6.67	−1	6.67
Total book assets (millions)	$300	30	120	50	120
Shares outstanding (millions)	3	4	2	5	10
Share price	$100	5	50	8	10

You have been asked to calculate some measure of the industry price-earnings ratio. Discuss the possible ways that you might calculate such a measure. Does changing the method of calculation make a significant difference in the end result?

10. "When calculating 'times interest earned,' we average earnings over the past 5 years. This gives a better measure of the company's typical earnings."

    "For simplicity we just divide current earnings by interest payments."

    "We fit a trend line to earnings and then measure 'times interest earned' using the current trend value."

    "We also fit a trend line to earnings and then use that trend to forecast earnings. We then measure 'times interest earned' using forecasted earnings. After all, it is the future not the past that any credit analyst is concerned with."

    What assumptions is each of these speakers making? If you wished to measure the creditworthiness of a business, what would be the best way to compute "times interest earned" (perhaps there are alternatives that none of the speakers has considered)?

11. Look at the segment accounts of Goodyear for 1985. Calculate three profitability measures: sales to assets, profit margin, and return on assets for the different segments. Which appear to be the most profitable parts of the business? Do segments with a high sales-to-assets ratio tend to have a high or low profit margin? Why?

28

Approaches to Financial Planning

A camel looks like an animal designed by a committee. If the firm made all its financial decisions piecemeal, it would end up with a financial camel. Therefore, smart financial managers consider the overall effect of financing and investment decisions. This process is called *financial planning*, and the end result is a *financial plan*.

Financial planning is necessary because investment and financing decisions interact and should not be made independently. In other words, the whole may be more or less than the sum of the parts.

It is also necessary to help financial managers avoid surprises and think ahead about how they should react to those surprises that *cannot* be avoided. In Chapter 10 we stressed that financial managers are unwilling to treat capital investment proposals as "black boxes." They insist on understanding what makes projects work and what could go wrong with them. They attempt to trace out the possible impact of today's decisions on tomorrow's opportunities. The same approach is, or should be, taken when financing and investment decisions are considered in the aggregate. Without financial planning, the firm itself becomes a black box.

Finally, financial planning helps establish concrete goals to motivate managers and provide standards for measuring performance.

Financial planning is not easy to write about—it is the sort of topic that attracts empty generalities or ponderous detail. A full, formal treatment is beyond the scope of this book and probably beyond the capability of its authors. But there are a few specific helpful points we can make. We will first summarize what financial planning involves. Second, we will describe the contents of a typical completed financial plan. Finally, we will discuss the use of *financial models* in the planning process.

28-1 WHAT IS FINANCIAL PLANNING?

Financial planning is a *process* of:

1. Analyzing the financing and investment choices open to the firm
2. Projecting the future consequences of present decisions, in order to avoid surprises and understand the link between present and future decisions
3. Deciding which alternatives to undertake (these decisions are embodied in the final financial plan)
4. Measuring subsequent performance against the goals set in the financial plan

Of course, there are different kinds of planning. Short-term financial planning is discussed in the next chapter. In short-term planning the *planning horizon* is rarely longer than the next 12 months. The firm wants to make sure it has enough cash to pay its bills and that short-term borrowing and lending are arranged to the best advantage.

Here we are more concerned with long-term planning, where a typical horizon is 5 years, although some firms look out 10 years or more. For example, it can take at least 10 years for an electric utility to design, obtain approval for, build and test a major generating plant.

Financial Planning Focuses on the Big Picture

Financial planners try to look at the aggregate investment by each line of business and avoid getting bogged down in details. A large number of small investment proposals are aggregated and, in effect, treated as a single project.

For example, at the beginning of the planning process the corporate staff might ask each division to submit three alternative business plans covering the next 5 years:

1. An *aggressive growth* plan calling for heavy capital investment and new products, increased share of existing markets, or entry of new markets
2. A *normal growth* plan in which the division grows with its markets but not significantly at the expense of its competitors
3. A plan of *retrenchment* and specialization designed to minimize required capital outlays—this may amount to gradual liquidation of the division

The planners might add a fourth option:

4. *Divestiture*—the sale or liquidation of the division.

Each alternative has a stream of forecasted cash flows associated with it. Therefore the alternatives can be analyzed as four mutually exclusive capital projects.

Financial planners normally abstain from capital budgeting on a project-by-project basis. Planners address capital investment on a grander scale. Of course, some projects are large enough to have significant individual impact. When in 1978 Boeing committed $3 *billion* to two new planes (the 757 and 767 models), you can safely bet that these two capital projects were explicitly analyzed in the context of Boeing's long-range financial plan.

Financial Planning Is Not Just Forecasting

Forecasting concentrates on the most likely future outcome. Financial planners are not concerned solely with forecasting, for they need to worry about unlikely events as well as likely ones. If you think ahead about what could go wrong, then you are less likely to ignore the danger signals and you can react faster to trouble.

Also, financial planning does not attempt to *minimize* risk. Instead it is a process of deciding which risks to take and which are unnecessary or not worth taking.

Companies have developed a number of ways of looking at these "what if" questions. Some work through the consequences of the plan under the most likely set of circumstances and then vary the assumptions one at a time. For example, they might look at how badly the company would be hit if a policy of aggressive growth coincided with a recession. Other companies might look at the consequences of each business plan under a couple of plausible scenarios.[1] For example, one scenario might envisage high interest rates leading to a slowdown in world economic growth and lower commodity prices. The second scenario might involve a buoyant domestic economy, high inflation, and a weak currency.

---

[1] For a description of the use of different planning scenarios in the Royal Dutch/Shell group see P. Wack, "Scenarios: Uncharted Waters Ahead," *Harvard Business Review,* **63** (September–October 1985) and "Scenarios: Shooting the Rapids," *Harvard Business Review,* **63** (November–December 1985).

**Financial
Planning Is a
Communal
Activity**

Planning should never be the exclusive preserve of the planners. Unless management is widely involved in the process, it will lack faith in the output. Also financial plans should be tied in closely to the firm's business plans. A series of financial forecasts has little operational value unless management has thought about the production and marketing decisions which are needed to make those forecasts come about.

28-2 THE CONTENTS OF A COMPLETED FINANCIAL PLAN

A completed financial plan for a large company is a substantial document. A smaller corporation's plan would have the same elements but less detail and documentation. For the smallest, youngest businesses, the financial plan may be entirely in the financial manager's head. The basic elements of the plans will be similar, however, for firms of any size.

The plan will present pro forma (that is, forecasted) balance sheets, income statements, and statements describing sources and uses of cash. Because these statements embody the firm's financial goals, they may not be strictly unbiased forecasts. The earnings figure in the plan may be somewhere between an honest forecast and the earnings that management *hopes* to achieve.

The plan will also describe planned capital expenditure, usually broken down by category (for example, investment for replacement, for expansion, for new products, for mandated expenditures such as pollution control equipment) and by division or line of business. There will be a narrative description of why these amounts are needed for investment, and of the business strategies to be used to reach these financial goals. The descriptions might cover areas such as research and development efforts, steps to improve productivity, design and marketing of new products, pricing strategy, and so on.

These written descriptions record the end result of discussions and negotiations between operating managers, corporate staff, and top management. They ensure that everyone involved in implementing the plan understands what is to be done.[2]

**Planned
Financing**

Most plans contain a summary of planned financing together with narrative backup as necessary. This part of the plan should logically include a discussion of dividend policy, because the more the firm pays out, the more capital it will need to find from sources other than retained earnings.

The complexity and importance of financing plans varies tremendously from firm to firm. A firm with limited investment opportunities, ample operating cash flow, and a moderate dividend payout accumulates considerable "financial slack" in the form of liquid assets and unused borrowing power. Life is relatively easy for the managers of such firms, and their financing plans are routine. Whether that easy life is in the interests of their stockholders is another matter.

Other firms have to raise capital by selling securities. Naturally, they give careful attention to planning what kinds of securities are to be sold, and when. Such firms may also find their financing plans complicated by covenants on their existing debt. For example, electric utility bonds often prohibit the firm from issuing more bonds if interest coverage drops below a certain level. Typically, the minimum level is two times earnings.

---

[2] Managers come up with better strategies when they are forced to present them formally and expose them to criticism. Haven't you often found that you didn't *really* understand an issue until you were forced to explain it to someone else?

Utilities have enormous appetites for capital and relatively generous dividend payouts. In normal times they may issue a new series of bonds every year, almost like clockwork. But when earnings are depressed, as they were in the mid-1970s, alternative financing plans have to be developed. A common response was much heavier reliance on short-term loans from banks, coupled with more frequent stock issues than the utilities liked. But whatever the response, considerable midnight oil was burned by utility financial managers during this period.

Three Requirements for Effective Planning

The requirements for effective planning follow from the purposes of planning and the desired end result. Three points deserve emphasis.

Forecasting.   First is the ability to forecast accurately and consistently. Perfect accuracy is not obtainable—if it were, the need for planning would be much less. Still the firm must do the best it can.

Forecasting cannot be reduced to a mechanical exercise. Naive extrapolation or fitting trends to past data is of limited value. It is because the future is *not* likely to resemble the past that planning is needed.

To supplement their judgment, forecasters rely on a variety of data sources and forecasting methods. For example, forecasts of the economic and industry environment may involve use of econometric models which take account of interactions between economic variables. In other cases the forecaster may employ statistical techniques for analyzing and projecting time series. Forecasts of demand will partly reflect these projections of the economic environment, but they may also be based on formal models that marketing specialists have developed for predicting buyer behavior or on recent consumer surveys to which the firm has access.[3]

Because information and expertise may be inconveniently scattered throughout the firm, effective planning requires administrative procedures to ensure that this information is not passed by. Also, many planners reach outside for help. There is a thriving industry of firms, such as Data Resources, Inc. (DRI), and Chase Econometrics, that specialize in preparing macroeconomic and industry forecasts for use by corporations.

It is tempting to conduct planning in a vacuum and to ignore the fact that the firm's competitors are concurrently developing their own plans. Your ability to implement an aggressive growth plan and increase market share depends on what the competition is likely to do. In fact we can generalize by paraphrasing a recommendation that we made in Chapter 11. *When you are presented with a set of corporate forecasts, do not accept them at face value. Probe behind the forecasts and try to identify the economic model on which they are based.*

Inconsistency of forecasts is a potential problem because planners draw on information from many sources. Forecasted sales may be the sum of separate forecasts made by managers of several business units. Left to their own devices, these managers may make different assumptions about inflation, growth of the national economy, availability of raw materials, and so on. Achieving consistency is particularly hard for vertically integrated firms, where the raw material for one business unit is the output of another. For example, an oil company's refining division might plan to produce more gasoline than the marketing division plans

---

[3] For an interesting example of how forecasting is organized in one company, see R. N. Dino, R. E. Riley, and P. G. Yatrakis, "The Role of Forecasting in Corporate Strategy: The Xerox Experience," *Journal of Forecasting,* **1:** 335–348 (October–December 1982).

to sell. The oil company's planners would be expected to uncover this inconsistency and align the plans of the two divisions.

Corporations often find that working out a consistent aggregate forecast of sales, cash flow, income, and so on, is complex and time-consuming. However, many of the calculations can be automated by using a planning model. We will comment on such models in a moment.

Finding the Optimal Financial Plan. In the end the financial manager has to judge which plan is best. We would like to present a model or theory that tells the manager exactly how to make that judgment, but we cannot. There is no model or procedure that encompasses all the complexity and intangibles encountered in financial planning.

As a matter of fact there never will be one. This bold statement is based on Brealey and Myers's third law.[4]

- *Axiom:* The supply of unsolved problems is infinite.
- *Axiom:* The number of unsolved problems that humans can hold in their minds is at any time limited to 10.
- *The Law:* Therefore, in any field there will always be 10 problems which can be addressed but which have no formal solution.

You will note that the last chapter of this book discusses 10 unsolved problems in finance.

Financial planners have to face the unsolved issues, and cope as best they can by judgment. Take dividend policy, for example. At the end of Chapter 16 we were unable to say for sure whether a generous dividend policy was a good or bad thing. Nevertheless, financial planners have to *decide* on the dividend policy.

You sometimes hear managers stating corporate goals in terms of accounting numbers. They might say "Our objective is to achieve an annual sales growth of 20 percent," or "We want a 25 percent return on book equity and a profit margin of 10 percent."

On the surface such objectives don't make sense. Shareholders want to be richer, not to have the satisfaction of a 10 percent profit margin. Also a goal that is stated in terms of accounting ratios is nonoperational unless it is translated back into what that means for business decisions. For example, what does a 10 percent profit margin imply—higher prices, lower costs, a move into new, high-margin products, or increased vertical integration?

So why do managers define objectives in this way? In part such goals may be a mutual exhortation to try harder, like singing the company song before work. But we suspect that managers are often using a code to communicate real concerns. For example, the goal to increase sales rapidly may reflect managers' belief that increased market share is needed to achieve scale economies, or a target profit margin may be a way of saying that the firm has been pursuing sales growth at the expense of margins.

The danger is that everyone may forget the code and the accounting targets may be seen as goals in themselves.

Watching the Financial Plan Unfold. Long-term plans have an annoying habit of falling out of date almost as soon as they are made. They are then left to gather dust. Of course you can always restart the planning process from scratch but it may help if you can think ahead of time how to revise your forecasts in the light

---

[4] The second law is presented in Section 12-2.

of unexpected events. For example, suppose that profits in the first 6 months turn out to be 10 percent below forecast. Profits follow roughly a random walk, so they have no tendency to bounce back after a fall. Unless you have special information to the contrary, you should revise down your profit forecasts for later years by 10 percent.

We have mentioned that long-term plans are also used as a benchmark to judge subsequent performance. But performance appraisals have little value unless you also take into account the business background against which they were achieved. If you know how a downturn in the economy is likely to throw you off plan, then you have a standard to judge your performance during such a downturn.

Financial Planning as Managing a Portfolio of Options

Another problem that is often crucial in financial planning is the dependency of future investment opportunities on today's capital investment decisions. You often find firms investing to enter a market for "strategic" reasons, that is, not because the immediate investment has positive net present value, but because it establishes the firm in the market and creates *options* for possibly valuable follow-up investments.

In other words, there is a two-stage decision. At the second stage (the follow-up project) the financial manager faces a standard capital budgeting problem. But at the first stage projects may be valuable primarily for the options they bring with them. In principle the financial manager could value a first-stage project's "strategic value" using the option pricing theory introduced in Chapters 20 and 21.

Sometimes there are three or more stages. Think of the progress of a technological innovation from its inception in basic research, to product development, to pilot production and market testing, and finally to full-scale commercial production. The decision to produce at commercial scale is a standard capital budgeting problem. The decision to proceed with pilot production and test marketing is like purchasing an option to produce at commercial scale. The commitment of funds to development is like purchasing an option for pilot production and test marketing: The firm acquires an option to purchase an option. The investment in research at the very first stage is like acquiring an option to purchase an option to purchase an option.

Here we will stick our necks out by predicting that option pricing theory will eventually allow formal analysis of sequential investment decisions like the ones just discussed, and that financial planning eventually will be thought of not as a search for a single investment plan, but rather as the management of the portfolio of options held by the firm. This portfolio consists not of traded puts and calls, but of *real options* (options to purchase real assets on possibly favorable terms) or options to purchase other real options.[5] You can think of financial planning as, in part, a process of:

- Acquiring real options
- Maintaining these options—unlike financial options, real options based on technology, product design, or other competitive edges usually erode if put on the shelf and forgotten

---

[5] The concept of real options was introduced in S. C. Myers, "Determinants of Corporate Borrowing," *Journal of Financial Economics*, **5:** 147–175 (November 1977). The importance of real options to strategic decisions is emphasized in S. C. Myers, "Finance Theory and Financial Strategy," *Interfaces* 14:126–137 (January–February 1984).

- Exercising valuable real options at the right time
- Disposing of options that are too far "out of the money" and too expensive to maintain

28-3 FINANCIAL PLANNING MODELS

Most corporate financial models are simulation models designed to project the consequences of alternative financial strategies under specified assumptions about the future. The models range from general-purpose ones, not much more complicated than the illustration presented later in this section, to models containing literally hundreds of equations and interacting variables. Naturally the most complex models are used by the largest firms.

Most large firms have a financial model, or have access to one.[6] Sometimes they may use more than one, perhaps a detailed model integrating capital budgeting and operational planning, a simpler model focusing on the aggregate impacts of financing strategy, and a special model for evaluating mergers.

The reason for the popularity of such models is a simple and practical one. They support the financial planning process by making it easier and cheaper to construct pro forma financial statements. The models automate an important part of planning that used to be boring, time-consuming, and labor-intensive.

Executive Fruit's Financial Model

Table 28-1 shows current (year-end 1987) financial statements for Executive Fruit Company. Judging by these figures, the company is ordinary in almost all respects. Its earnings before interest and taxes were 10 percent of sales revenue. Net earnings were $90,000 after payment of taxes and 9 percent interest on $400,000 outstanding debt. The company paid out 60 percent of its earnings as dividends.

Executive Fruit's operating cash flow was not sufficient to pay the dividend and also to provide the cash needed for investment and to expand net working capital. Therefore $64,000 of common stock was issued. The firm ended the year with debt equal to 40 percent of total capitalization.

Now suppose that you are asked to prepare pro forma statements for Executive Fruit Company for 1988. You are told to assume business as usual *except* that (1) sales and operating costs are expected to be up 30 percent over 1987, and (2) common stock is not to be issued again. You interpret "business as usual" to mean that (3) interest rates will remain at 9 percent, (4) the firm will stick to its traditional 60 percent dividend payout, and (5) net working capital and fixed assets will increase by 30 percent to support the larger sales volume.

These assumptions lead to the pro forma statements shown in Table 28-2. Note that projected net income is up by 23 percent, to $111,000, which is heartening. But a glance at the "sources and uses of funds" statement shows that $404,000 has to be raised for additional working capital and for replacement and expansion of fixed capital[7] Executive Fruit's generous dividend payout and its decision against another stock issue mean that $255,600 has to be raised by additional borrowing.

---

[6] Some firms use general-purpose models developed by banks, management consultants, or commercial computer firms.

[7] Executive Fruit's existing fixed capital is assumed to depreciate by $104,000 in 1987. Thus it has to invest $104,000 simply to maintain the net book value of its fixed assets. Total investment is $104,000 plus the growth in net fixed assets required by the increased sales volume. Incidentally, we realize that requiring the net book value of fixed assets to grow in lockstep with sales volume is an arbitrary and probably unrealistic assumption. We adopt it only to keep things simple.

TABLE 28-1
1987 financial statements for Executive Fruit Company
(all figures in thousands of dollars)

INCOME STATEMENT

Revenue (REV)	2,160
Cost of goods sold (CGS)	1,944
Earnings before interest and taxes	216
Interest (INT)[a]	36
Earnings before taxes	180
Tax at 50% (TAX)	90
Net income (NET)	90

SOURCES AND USES OF FUNDS

Sources	
Net income (NET)	90
Depreciation (DEP)[b]	80
Operating cash flow	170
Borrowing (ΔD)	0
Stock issues (SI)	64
Total sources	234
Uses	
Increase in net working capital	
(ΔNWC)	40
Investment (INV)	140
Dividends (DIV)	54
Total uses	234

BALANCE SHEETS

	1987	1986	Change
Assets			
Net working capital (NWC)[c]	200	160	+40
Fixed assets (FA)	800	740	+60[d]
Total assets	1,000	900	+100
Liabilities			
Debt (D)	400	400	0
Book equity (E)	600	500	+100[e]
Total liabilities	1,000	900	+100

[a] Interest is 9 percent of the $400 in outstanding debt.
[b] Depreciation is a noncash expense. Therefore we add it back to net income to find operating cash flow.
[c] Net working capital is defined as current assets less current liabilities.
[d] The increase in the book value of fixed assets equals investment less depreciation. Change in FA = ΔFA = INV − DEP = 140 − 80 = 60.
[e] Book equity increases by retained earnings less dividends plus stock issues. Change in E = ΔE = NET − DIV + SI = 90 − 54 + 64 = 100.

The result is an increase in the book debt ratio to over 50 percent and a reduction in pretax interest coverage ratio to 4.8. (Earnings before interest and taxes divided by interest is 281/59 = 4.8.)

We have spared you the trouble of actually calculating the figures necessary for Table 28-2. The calculations do not take more than a few minutes for this

TABLE 28-2
1988 pro forma financial statements for Executive Fruit Company
(all figures in thousands of dollars)

INCOME STATEMENT		
Revenue (REV)	2,808	
Cost of goods sold (CGS)	2,527	(+30%)
Earnings before interest and taxes	281	
Interest (INT)	59	
Earnings before tax	222	
Tax (TAX)	111	
Net income (NET)	111	(+23%)

SOURCES AND USES OF FUNDS		
Sources		
Net income (NET)	111	
Depreciation (DEP)	104	
Operating cash flow	215	
Borrowing (ΔD)	255.6	
Stock issues (SI)	0	
Total sources	470.6	
Uses		
Increase in net working capital (ΔNWC)	60	(+30%)
Investment (INV)	344	
Dividends (DIV)	66.6	
Total uses	470.6	

BALANCE SHEETS			
	1988	1987	Change
Assets			
Net working capital (NWC)	260	200	+ 60
Fixed assets (FA)	1,040	800	+240
Total assets	1,300	1,000	+300
Liabilities			
Debt (D)	655.6	400	+255.6
Book equity (E)	644.4	600	+ 44.4
Total liabilities	1,300.0	1,000	+300.0

Assumptions:

CGS	Assumed to remain at 90 percent of REV.
INT	Nine percent of debt (D). This assumes all new debt is taken out early in 1988 so that a full year's interest must be paid.
TAX	Tax rate remains at 50 percent.
DEP	Remains at 10 percent of FA. This assumes all new investment is made early in 1988 so that a full year's depreciation is taken.
ΔD	Balancing item. Executive Fruit must borrow $255.6 to cover planned expenditures.
SI	Executive Fruit's management has decided not to issue stock in 1988, therefore SI = 0.
ΔNWC NWC	Net working capital expands in proportion to the increase in REV.
INV, FA	Required fixed assets FA are assumed to expand in proportion to the growth in sales. Investment must therefore cover depreciation plus the increase in FA.
DIV	Payout stays at 60 percent of NET.
E	The increase in equity equals retained earnings (NET − DIV) plus stock issues (SI). NET − DIV + SI = 111 − 66.6 + 0 = 44.4

simple example, *provided* you set up the calculations correctly and make no arithmetic mistakes. If that time requirement seems trivial, remember that in reality you probably would be asked for four similar sets of statements covering each year from 1989 to 1992. Probably you would be asked for alternative projections under different assumptions (for example, a 25 instead of 30 percent growth rate of revenue) or different financial strategies (for example, freezing dividends at their 1987 level of $54,000). This would require lots of work. Building a model and letting the computer toil in your place has obvious attractions.

Table 28-3 shows a 15-equation model for Executive Fruit. There is one equation for each variable needed to construct pro forma statements like Tables 28-1 and 28-2. Of the equations, six are accounting identities ensuring that the income statement adds up, the balance sheet balances, and sources of funds match uses. The functions of the equations are as follows: (1) and (8) set revenues and stock issues equal to values specified by the model user. Equations (2), (12), and (13) specify cost of goods sold, net working capital, and fixed assets as constant proportions of sales. The remaining equations relate interest to debt outstanding (3), taxes to income (4), depreciation to fixed assets (6), and dividends to net income (11).

The *input* for our model comprises nine items: a sales forecast (REV); a decision on the amount of stock to be issued (SI); and seven coefficients, a_1 through a_7, tying cost of goods sold to revenue, interest payments to borrowing, and so on. Take the coefficient a_5, for example. In developing Table 28-2 we assumed dividends to be 60 percent of net income. In the model this would be expressed as $a_5 = .6$.

TABLE 28-3
Financial model for Executive Fruit Company

INCOME STATEMENT EQUATIONS

(1)	REV = forecast by model user	
(2)	CGS = a_1REV	
(3)	INT = a_2D	(a_2 = interest rate)
(4)	TAX = a_3(REV − CGS − INT)	(a_3 = tax rate)
(5)	NET = REV − CGS − INT − TAX	(accounting identity)

SOURCES AND USES STATEMENT EQUATIONS

(6)	DEP = a_4FA	
(7)	ΔD = ΔNWC + INV + DIV − NET − DEP − SI	(accounting identity)
(8)	SI = value specified by model user	
(9)	ΔNWC = NWC − NWC(−1)	(accounting identity)
(10)	INV = DEP + FA − FA(−1)	(accounting identity)
(11)	DIV = a_5NET	(a_5 = dividend payout ratio)

BALANCE SHEET EQUATIONS

(12)	NWC = a_6REV	
(13)	FA = a_7REV	
(14)	D = ΔD + D(−1)	(accounting identity)
(15)	E = E(−1) + NET − DIV + SI	(accounting identity)

Note:
(−1) means a number taken from the previous year's balance sheet. These numbers are constants, not variables.

TABLE 28-4
Model forecast for Table 28-2

INCOME STATEMENT

---

(1)   REV = forecast = 2,808
(2)   CGS = .9 REV $(a_1 = .9)$
       = .9(2,808) = 2,527
(3)   INT = .09 D $(a_2 = .09)$
       = .09(655.6) = 59
(4)   TAX = .5(REV − CGS − INT) $(a_3 = .5)$
       = .5(2,808 − 2,527 − 59) = 111
(5)   NET = REV − CGS − INT − TAX
       = 2,808 − 2,527 − 59 − 111 = 111

SOURCES AND USES OF FUNDS STATEMENT

---

(6)   DEP = .1 FA $(a_4 = .1)$
       = .1(1,040) = 104
(7)   ΔD = ΔNWC + INV + DIV − NET − DEP − SI
       = 60 + 344 + 66.6 − 111 − 104 − 0 = 255.6
(8)   SI = specified as 0
(9)   ΔNWC = NWC − NWC(−1)
       = 260 − 200 = 60
(10) INV = DEP + FA − FA(−1)
       = 104 + 1,040 − 800 = 344
(11) DIV = .6 NET $(a_5 = .6)$
       = .6(111) = 66.6

BALANCE SHEET

---

(12) NWC = .093 REV $(a_6 = .093)$
       = .093(2,808) = 260
(13) FA = .37 REV $(a_7 = .37)$
       = .37(2,808) = 1,040
(14) D = ΔD + D(−1)
       = 255.6 + 400 = 655.6
(15) E = E(−1) + NET − DIV + SI
       = 600 + 111 − 66.6 − 0 = 644.4

Table 28-4 shows that our model works. In the table we insert the values for REV, SI, and a_1 through a_7 that correspond to the assumptions underlying Table 28-2. And we get the right answers, confirming that the model can be used to forecast Executive Fruit's financial results. All we would have to do is to give the computer the nine input items, tell it to solve the 15 simultaneous equations, and instruct it to print out the results in the format of Table 28-2.

Pitfalls in Model Design

The Executive Fruit model is too simple for practical application. You probably have already thought of several ways to improve it—by keeping track of the number of outstanding shares, for example, and printing out earnings and dividends per share. Or you might want to distinguish short-term lending and borrowing opportunities, now buried in net working capital.

But beware: There is always the temptation to make a model bigger and more detailed. You may end up with an exhaustive model that is too cumbersome for routine use.

Exhaustive detail gets in the way of the intended use of corporate planning models, namely, to project the financial consequences of a variety of strategies and assumptions. The fascination of detail, if you give in to it, distracts attention from crucial decisions like stock issues and dividend policy, and allocation of capital by business area. Sometimes decisions like these end up being "wired into" the model, just as the Executive Fruit model arbitrarily sets dividends equal to a constant proportion of net income.

There Is No Finance in Corporate Financial Models

Why do we say that there is no finance in corporate financial models? The first reason is that most such models incorporate an accountant's view of the world. They are designed to forecast accounting statements, and their equations naturally embody the accounting conventions employed by the firm. Consequently the models do not emphasize the tools of financial analysis: incremental cash flow, present value, market risk, and so on.[8]

Second, corporate financial models produce no signposts pointing toward optimal financial decisions. They do not even tell which alternatives are worth examining. All this is left up to their users.

Brealey and Myers's third law implies that no model can find the best of all financial strategies. However, it is possible to build linear programming models that help search for the best financial strategy subject to specified assumptions and constraints. These "intelligent" financial planning models should prove more flexible tools for sensitivity analysis and more effective in screening alternative financial strategies. Ideally they will suggest strategies that would never occur to the unaided financial manager.

The appendix to this chapter sketches a linear programming model based on the modern finance theory presented in this book.

28-4 SUMMARY

Most firms take financial planning seriously and devote considerable resources to it. What do they get for this effort?

The tangible product of the planning process is a financial plan describing the firm's financial strategy and projecting its future consequences by means of pro forma balance sheets, income statements, and statements of sources and uses of funds. The plan establishes financial goals and is a benchmark for evaluating subsequent performance. Usually it also describes why that strategy was chosen and how the plan's financial goals are to be achieved.

The plan is the end result. The process that produces the plan is valuable in its own right. First, planning forces the financial manager to consider the combined effects of all the firm's investment and financing decisions. This is important because these decisions interact and should not be made independently.

Second, planning, if it is done right, forces the financial manager to think about events that could upset the firm's progress and to devise strategies to be held in reserve for counterattack when unhappy surprises occur. Planning is more than forecasting, because forecasting deals with the most likely outcome. Planners also have to think about events that may occur even though they are unlikely.

To repeat, financial planning is a *process* of:

---

[8] Of course there is no reason that the manager can't use the output to calculate the present value of the firm (given some assumptions about growth beyond the planning period), and this is sometimes done.

1. Analyzing the interactions of the financing and investment choices open to the firm
2. Projecting the future consequences of present decisions, in order to avoid surprises and understand the links between present and future decisions
3. Deciding which alternatives to undertake (these decisions are embodied in the final financial plan)
4. Measuring subsequent performance against the goals set in the financial plan.

In this chapter we discussed "long-range" or "strategic" planning, in which the *planning horizon* is usually 5 years or more. This kind of planning deals with aggregate decisions; for example, the planner would worry about whether the broadax division should go for heavy capital investment and rapid growth, but not whether the division should choose machine tool A versus tool B. In fact, planners must be constantly on guard against the fascination of detail, because giving in to it means slighting crucial issues like investment strategy, debt policy, and the choice of a target dividend payout ratio.

There is no theory or model that leads straight to *the* optimal financial strategy. Consequently financial planning proceeds by trial and error. Many different strategies may be projected under a range of assumptions about the future before one strategy is finally chosen.

The dozens of separate projections that may be made during this trial and error process generate a heavy load of arithmetic and paperwork. Firms have responded by developing corporate planning models to forecast the financial consequences of specified strategies and assumptions about the future. These models are efficient and widely used. But remember that there is not much finance in them. Their primary purpose is to produce accounting statements. The models do not search for the best financial strategy, but only trace out the consequences of a strategy specified by the model user.

One of the most difficult aspects of deciding what strategies to examine closely is that the best strategy may not be an obvious one. In the appendix to this chapter we describe a linear programming model which is based on the concepts of finance rather than accounting, and which does help the financial manager search for the best financial plan.

APPENDIX LONGER

This appendix is a brief introduction to LONGER, a linear programming model devised by Myers and Pogue to support financial planners.[9] Other applications of linear programming to financial planning are described in "Further Reading" for this chapter.

LONGER differs from the typical corporate financial model described in this chapter in two important respects. First, it *optimizes:* It calculates the *best* financial plan, given specified assumptions and constraints. The typical planning model merely *projects* the consequences of a financial strategy chosen by the model user. Second, the model is based on finance theory rather than accounting. It assumes well-functioning capital markets. Consequently its objective is to maximize the firm's net present value. It relies on value additivity and the Modigliani-Miller theory that the chief advantage of debt is the tax shields created by debt interest payments.

LONGER will be introduced by a simple numerical example. Then extensions of

---

[9] S. C. Myers and G. A. Pogue: "A Programming Approach to Corporate Financial Management," *Journal of Finance,* **29:** 579–599 (May 1974).

the model are briefly described. The final part of this appendix shows how the shadow prices generated as part of LONGER's solution are interpreted. The shadow prices are an easy way to understand *adjusted present value* (APV), which measures the value of capital projects which have important financing side effects. APV and its practical implications were covered more fully in Chapter 19. This appendix should give a deeper appreciation of the APV method and the assumptions underlying it.

Example[10]

Consider a firm which has to decide how much to invest or borrow in the coming year. Let:

x = New investment, in millions of dollars. (We assume for simplicity that the firm has only one project.)
y = New borrowing, in millions of dollars.

Also, assume that:

1. Available investment opportunities can absorb $1 million at most. The investments generate a perpetual stream of after-tax cash flows. Let the expected average value of these flows be C. In this case $C = .09x$; thus the project offers a 9 percent internal rate of return.
2. Assume that the market will capitalize the returns at the rate $r = .10$. Thus, if all-equity financing is used, these assets generate a net present value of $-\$.10$ per dollar invested ($-x + .09x/.10 = -.1x$).
3. The firm's policy is to limit new debt to 40 percent of new investment.
4. The firm has $800,000 in cash available.
5. Any excess cash is paid out in dividends.
6. The additions to debt and equity are expected to be permanent.

For simplicity we begin with the Modigliani-Miller valuation formula for the firm.[11] If the firm does nothing (x and $y = 0$) then V will be given by

$$V = V_0 + T_c D$$

where V_0 = market value of firm's *existing* assets if they were all-equity-financed
T_c = marginal corporate income tax rate (.5 in this example)
D = amount of debt *already* outstanding, excluding any borrowing for new project

The amount $T_c D$ is the present value of the tax shields generated by the outstanding debt, assuming the debt is permanent.

For example,

$$V = V_0 + .5D - .1x + .5y$$

Now V_0 and D are fixed and therefore not relevant to the choice of x and y. Therefore we can just maximize the quantity $-.1x + .5y$, subject to constraints on the amount invested ($x \leq 1$), the amount of debt issued ($y \leq .4x$), and the balance of sources and uses of funds ($x \leq y + .8$).

This is the linear programming problem depicted in Figure 28-1. First look at the shaded area representing the set of feasible solutions. The feasible

---

[10] This example is based on one presented by Myers and Pogue, op. cit.

[11] See Section 18-1.

FIGURE 28-1
In this example, the firm can invest at most $1 million and borrow 40 percent of new investment. Funds for the new investment must come from existing cash ($.8 million) or new borrowing. The investment is not attractive in its own right (NPV $= -\$.1x$), but the firm is willing to invest in order to borrow because the tax shields created by borrowing outweigh the net loss in value attributable to the new investment.

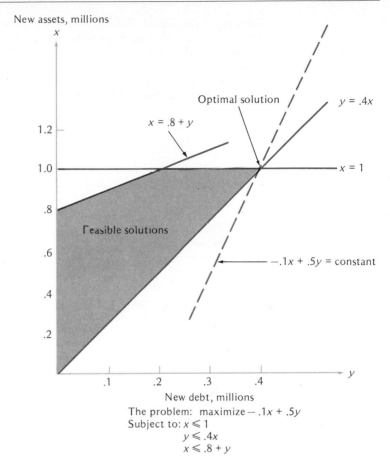

New assets, millions
x

The problem: maximize $-.1x + .5y$
Subject to: $x \leq 1$
$y \leq .4x$
$x \leq .8 + y$

region is below the line $x = 1$ because the firm's investment opportunity will absorb $1 million at most. It is below the line $x = .8 + y$ because the amount invested is limited to cash on hand ($.8 million) plus additional borrowing. It is above and to the left of the line $y = .4x$ because new debt is limited to 40 percent of new investment.

The firm does not want to invest (because NPV $= -\$.10$ per dollar invested) but it does want to borrow, and in order to borrow it has to invest. Thus, firm value is maximized when $x = 1$, $y = .4$. The firm invests and borrows as much as it can.

However, note that the constraint $x \leq .8 + y$ is not binding at the optimal solution. The firm borrows $200,000 more than it needs for investment. Thus it has $200,000 available for dividends.

Why does the optimal solution call for investing in a project with a negative net present value? The reason is that the project allows the firm to issue more debt, and the value of tax savings generated by the debt more than offsets the investment's inadequate return. (In fact, the optimal solution remains $x = 1.0$, $y = .4$ so long as the investment generates more than $-\$.20$ per dollar invested. If it generates less than that, $-\$.30$, for example, the solution becomes $x = y = 0$.) The debt capacity constraint thus makes financing and investment decisions interdependent.

Effects of Dividend Policy. The sources-uses constraint is not binding in the example, and therefore does not create an interaction of financing and investment decisions. However, what if it is binding? What if the firm has, say, only $500,000 cash on hand?

At first glance the effect is to change the sources-uses constraint to $x \le .5 + y$, which changes the optimal solution to $x = \frac{5}{6}, y = \frac{1}{3}$. However, if we consider dividend policy, then we should also allow new issues of equity. The constraint should really be

$$x + \text{DIV} \le .5 + y + \text{SI}$$

where DIV and SI are dividends paid and equity issued in millions. If dividend policy is irrelevant, then DIV and SI have no effect in the objective function, and the constraint itself is irrelevant. Thus, the optimal solution remains at $x = 1$, $y = .4$. The firm must make a $100,000 stock issue, but this is a mere detail once the investment and borrowing decisions are made.

However, in practice there would be transaction costs associated with the stock issue. These costs would have to be subtracted from the objective function, and the sources-uses constraint would become relevant and binding. The solution values for x and y will clearly be affected if the transaction cost is large enough.

Thus, the sources-uses constraint becomes important only if there are transaction costs to security issues or dividend policy matters for other reasons.

Extending the Model

The example we have just examined was limited to two variables by our goal of presenting it graphically on the two dimensions of the printed page. But the computer does not need a picture like Figure 28-1 to solve a linear program. We can extend LONGER to a practical level of detail by adding variables and constraints.

We have already referred to one extension. Suppose that the firm can pay dividends or issue common stock, but that cash available is cut to $.5 million. The linear program becomes

- Maximize: $-.1x + .5y + a\,\text{DIV} + b\,\text{SI}$

- Subject to: $x \le 1$
  $y \le .4x$
  $x + \text{DIV} \le .5 + y + \text{SI}$

If dividend policy is irrelevant, then both a and b are set at zero. But in practice b would have to be negative to reflect the transaction costs of a stock issue. And a might be positive, negative, or zero depending on your position on the dividend controversy (see Chapter 16).

Now suppose that there is a second investment opportunity to invest up to $2 million in a project offering $.12 of NPV per dollar invested. However, the performance of project 2 is less predictable than project 1's performance, and so the firm is willing to borrow only 20 percent of the amount invested in project 2. Our model now becomes

- Maximize: $-.1x_1 + .12x_2 + .5y + a\,\text{DIV} + b\,\text{SI}$

- Subject to: $x_1 \le 1$
  $x_2 \le 2$
  $y \le .4x_1 + .2x_2$
  $x_1 + x_2 + \text{DIV} \le .5 + y + \text{SI}$

Because present values add, we can include as many projects as we like without upsetting the linear form of the objective. Moreover, there is no need for included projects to have the same risk or time pattern of cash flows. There is nothing wrong with setting an office building alongside a wildcat oil well, so long as you can come up with a net present value for each.

If we introduce projects with irregular patterns of cash flow over time, we would naturally want to allow borrowing to vary period by period. Suppose that the firm has a 5-year planning horizon. Then we could replace the debt variable y with five new variables $y_1, y_2, \ldots, y_5$, where y_t is planned total borrowing for year t. This naturally suggests that dividends and stock issues should be allowed to vary over time also. Our objective function becomes

- Maximize: $-.1x_1 + .12x_2$
  $+ c_1y_1 + c_2y_2 + \ldots + c_5y_5$
  $+ a_1\text{DIV}_1 + a_2\text{DIV}_2 + \ldots + a_5\text{DIV}_5$
  $+ b_1\text{SI}_1 + b_2\text{SI}_2 + \ldots + b_5\text{SI}_5$

Also, we will now need twelve constraints: two limiting the amount that can be invested in each project, five limiting the amount that can be borrowed in each of the 5 years covered by the financial plan, and five constraints ensuring that planned uses of funds do not exceed planned sources in any year.

Still more constraints might be added. The financial manager might wish to try to avoid any planned cut in dividends, for example. This would call for five more constraints:

- $\text{DIV}_1 \geq$ dividends in period 0
- $\text{DIV}_2 \geq \text{DIV}_1$
- $\text{DIV}_3 \geq \text{DIV}_2$
- $\text{DIV}_4 \geq \text{DIV}_3$
- $\text{DIV}_5 \geq \text{DIV}_4$

Some firms might require that their financial plan generate a steady growth in reported (book) earnings. Suppose that the target growth rate is g. Then we would need five more constraints of the form $Z_t \geq (1 + g)Z_{t-1}$, where Z_t represents forecasted earnings in year t. The variable Z_t would be determined by the other decision variables in the programming model.

But we must immediately add a caveat: Any constraint on acceptable *book* earnings, as opposed to economic earnings, raises difficult issues. Should the firm be willing to sacrifice present value just to achieve regular growth in reported earnings? If capital markets are efficient, investors ought to be able to look through any fluctuations of short-run earnings to the true, underlying value of the firm. If so, any constraint on earnings is superfluous at best.

Constraints on the growth of book earnings might perhaps be useful for keeping track of how pursuit of present value affects reported earnings. It may be that the financial plan can be changed to generate a pretty earnings pattern. If there is real conflict between value and book earnings, comparing solutions with and without this constraint will at least awaken financial managers to the cost of that pretty pattern.[12]

There are several other items of optional equipment that most might wish to

---

[12] Eugene Lerner and Arnold Rappaport demonstrate the conflicts between pursuit of value and short-run earnings in "Limit DCF in Capital Budgeting," *Harvard Business Review*, **46:** 133–139 (September–October 1968).

add to LONGER, but we will stop at this point. You may wish to refer to Myers and Pogue's paper and the other suggested readings for the full story.

Comparison of LONGER with the Typical Corporate Planning Model

A full-scale linear programming model for financial planning would become formidably complex, but no more so than a typical simulation model.[13] The two models applied to the same firm would have approximately the same number of variables, and the number of constraints included in LONGER would about match the number of equations in the simulation model. But the input requirements for LONGER would be greater because an objective function must be specified. In return, LONGER allows the planner to screen all feasible financial strategies, to reject the inferior ones automatically, and to identify the best strategy consistent with the assumptions and constraints embodied in the model.

However, linear programming models do not automate the *decisions* required by the financial plan. No model can capture all the issues that the financial manager must face. Nor would access to an optimization model change the trial and error process of developing a financial plan; it only promises to make the process somewhat more efficient. The optimum plan generated by any run of LONGER does no more than reflect the assumptions and constraints specified by the model user, who will naturally explore a variety of assumptions and constraints before reaching a final decision.[14]

Shadow Prices, or Marginal Costs

The solution to any linear program includes a shadow price, or marginal cost, for each constraint. There are three constraints in the simple numerical example introduced at the start of this appendix, and therefore three shadow prices:

Constraint	Shadow Price	Explanation
Limit on investment ($x \leq 1$)	.1	Project NPV is $-.1x$. But investment supports .4x in debt worth $.50 per dollar borrowed. $-.1x + .4(.5x) = +.1x$
Limit on debt ($y \leq .4x$)	.5	$1 of additional debt generates tax shields worth $.50.
Limit on available cash ($x \leq .8 + y$)	0	Firm has surplus cash at optimal solution. Additional cash has NPV of zero.

A shadow price is defined as the change in the objective per unit change in the constraint.[15] In our example the objective is to increase net present value. Therefore the shadow price of .1 on the investment limit means that, if the firm were allowed to invest $1,000,001 instead of $1 million, net present value would increase by 10 cents. The shadow price of .5 on the debt limit means that if the firm were allowed to borrow $400,001 instead of $400,000, holding investment fixed at $1 million, value would increase by 50 cents.

[13] Note our warning on the temptation to excessive detail. See Section 28-3.

[14] Willard T. Carleton, Charles L. Dick, Jr., and David H. Downes give a comprehensive and insightful discussion of the differences in design and use of the two model types, and argue that optimization models are potentially more useful, in "Financial Policy Models: Theory and Practice," *Journal of Financial and Quantitative Analysis,* **8:** 691–709 (December 1973).

[15] Shadow prices are valid only for marginal shifts in the constraints. The range over which shifts qualify as marginal varies from problem to problem.

The limit on available cash is not binding at the optimal solution. The firm borrows $200,000 more than it needs, and so the shadow price on that constraint is zero. That is, extra cash would have a *net* present value of zero.

Consider a slightly more complex example. Cash on hand is reduced to $500,000. Equity issues and dividend payments are allowed, but transactions costs absorb 10 percent of the net proceeds of any issue. The linear programming problem changes to:

- Maximize: $-.1x + .5y + (0)\text{DIV} - .1\text{SI}$
- Subject to: $x \le 1$
  $y \le .4x$
  $x + \text{DIV} \le .5 + y + \text{SI}$

The solution is $x = 1$, $y = .4$, $\text{DIV} = 0$, and $\text{SI} = .1$. The firm invests and borrows as before, but has to issue $100,000 of equity to raise the necessary cash for investment.

The shadow prices for this problem are as follows:

Constraint	Shadow Price	Explanation
Limit on investment $(x \le 1)$	.04	(See below.)
Limit on debt $(y \le .4x)$	.6	$1 of additional debt generates tax shields worth $.50 *and* reduces equity issued by $1, saving $.10 in issue costs.
Limit on available cash $(x + \text{DIV} \le .5 + y + \text{SI})$	.1	Extra cash reduces equity issued and saves $.10 per $1.

The shadow price on project investment goes down by .06, from $.10 to $.04 per dollar invested. This occurs because additional investment can be only 40 percent debt-financed. The remainder must come from issuing new equity. Therefore, the value of the opportunity to invest an additional dollar decreases by .6 × .1 = .06.

The shadow prices on the investment limits are particularly interesting because they show the project's net marginal contribution to firm value, when all of the project's financing side effects are accounted for. In this example the project's marginal contribution is 4 cents per dollar invested. Remember that the project has negative NPV separately considered. But it has one favorable side effect (investment allows the firm to borrow) and one unfavorable side effect (investment requires equity issues and generates issue costs).

The shadow price for the project can be calculated by starting with its base-case NPV of $-.1$, adding the value of its marginal contribution to corporate borrowing, and subtracting the marginal cost of the equity issue needed to finance it:

$$
\begin{array}{c}
\text{Net contribution} \\
\text{to firm value}
\end{array} =
\begin{array}{c}
\text{base-case} \\
\text{NPV}
\end{array} +
\begin{array}{c}
\text{value of project's} \\
\text{marginal contribution} \\
\text{to borrowing power}
\end{array} -
\begin{array}{c}
\text{marginal cost} \\
\text{of equity issue} \\
\text{needed to finance} \\
\text{project}
\end{array}
$$

Investing $1 more effectively loosens the debt constraint by $.40 and tightens the cash constraint by $1. Therefore we can "price out" the project's financing side effects by noting the shadow prices on these two constraints. Extra borrowing power is worth 60 cents per dollar and cash used up costs 10 cents per dollar.

Therefore

$$\text{Net contribution to firm value} = -.1 + .40(.6) - (1.00)(.1) = .04$$

"Net contribution to firm value" is no more or less than *adjusted present value*, or APV. APV is calculated automatically as a by-product of LONGER. But, as you saw in Chapter 19, for simple problems you can calculate APV by hand. You need APV because it is the only generally reliable approach to capital budgeting when investment decisions have important financing side effects.

FURTHER READING

Corporate planning has an extensive literature of its own. Good books include:

R. N. Anthony, *Planning and Control Systems: A Framework for Analysis*, Division of Research, Graduate School of Business Administration, Harvard University, Boston, 1965.

A. C. Hax and N. S. Majluf, *Strategic Management: An Integrative Perspective*, Prentice-Hall, Inc., Englewood Cliffs, N.J., 1984.

P. Lorange and R. F. Vancil, *Strategic Planning Systems*, Prentice-Hall, Inc., Englewood Cliffs, N.J., 1977.

Our description of what planning is and is not was influenced by:

P. Drucker, "Long-Range Planning: Challenge to Management Science," *Management Science* **5**: 238–249 (April 1959).

The links between capital budgeting, strategy, and financial planning are discussed in:

S. C. Myers, "Finance Theory and Financial Strategy," *Interfaces*, **14**: 126–137 (January–February 1984).

Here are four references on corporate models:

W. T. Carleton, C. L. Dick, Jr., and D. H. Downes, "Financial Policy Models: Theory and Practice," *Journal of Financial and Quantitative Analysis*, **8**: 691–709 (December 1973).

W. T. Carleton and J. M. McInnes, "Theory, Models and Implementation in Financial Management," *Management Science*, **28**: 957—978 (September 1982).

D. Chambers, "Programming the Allocation of Funds Subject to Restrictions on Reported Results," *Operational Research Quarterly*, **18**: 407–432 (December 1967).

E. Lerner and A. Rappaport, "Limit DCF in Capital Budgeting," *Harvard Business Review*, **46**: 133–139 (September–October 1968).

LONGER is presented in:

S. C. Myers and G. A. Pogue, "A Programming Approach to Corporate Financial Management," *Journal of Finance*, **29**: 579–599 (May 1974).

QUIZ

1. True or false?

(a) Financial planning should attempt to minimize risk.

(b) The primary aim of financial planning is to obtain better forecasts of future cash flows and earnings.

(c) Financial planning is necessary because financing and investment decisions interact and should not be made independently.

(d) Firms' planning horizons rarely exceed 3 years.

(e) Individual capital investment projects are not considered in a financial plan unless they are very large.

(f) Financial planning requires accurate and consistent forecasting.

(g) Financial planning models should include as much detail as possible.

2. List the major elements of a completed financial plan.

3. "There is no finance in financial planning models." Explain.

QUESTIONS AND PROBLEMS

1. What are the dangers and disadvantages of using a financial model? Discuss.

2. Should a financial plan be considered an unbiased forecast of future cash flows, earnings, and other financial variables? Why or why not?

3. How would Executive Fruit's financial model change if dividends were cut to zero in 1988? Use the revised model to generate a new financial plan for 1988. Show how the financial statements given in Table 28-2 would change. Do you think the new plan is an improvement on the old one? Discuss.

4. The balancing item in the Executive Fruit model is borrowing. What is meant by *balancing item*? How would the model change if dividends were made the balancing item instead? In that case how would you suggest that planned borrowing be determined?

5. Construct a new model for Executive Fruit based on your answer to question 4. Does your model generate a feasible financial plan for 1988? (*Hint:* If it doesn't, you may have to allow the firm to issue stock.)

6. Executive Fruit's financial manager believes that revenues in 1988 could rise by as much as 50 percent or by as little as 10 percent. Recalculate the pro forma financial statements under these two assumptions. How does the rate of growth in revenues affect the firm's borrowing requirement?

7. (a) Use the Executive Fruit model (Table 28-3) to produce pro forma income statements, balance sheets, and sources and uses of funds statements for 1989 and 1990. Assume "business as usual" except that sales and costs expand by 30 percent per year, as do fixed assets and net working capital. The interest rate is forecasted to remain at 9 percent, and stock issues are ruled out. Executive Fruit also plans to stick to its 60 percent dividend payout ratio. (*Hint:* Interest expense depends on additional borrowing, which in turn depends on profit after interest and taxes. You may find it helpful to rearrange the equations so that you can calculate interest first.)

(b) What are the firm's debt ratio and interest coverage under this plan?

(c) Can the company continue to finance expansion by borrowing?

8. Discuss the relative merits of descriptive financial models, such as the Executive Fruit model, and optimizing models such as LONGER. Descriptive models are much more commonly used in practice. Why do you think this is so?

9. Table 28-5 shows the 1988 financial statements for the Executive Cheese Company. Annual depreciation is 10 percent of fixed assets at the beginning of this year, plus 10 percent of new investment. The company plans to invest a further $200 per year in fixed assets for the next 5 years, and forecasts that the ratio of revenues to total assets at the start of each year will remain at 1.75. Fixed costs are expected to remain at $53 and variable costs at 80 percent of revenue. The company's policy is to pay out two-thirds of net income as dividends and to maintain a book debt ratio of 20 percent.

(a) Construct a model like the one in Table 28-3 for Executive Cheese.

(b) Use your model to produce a set of financial statements for 1989.

10. Our model for Executive Fruit is an example of a "top down" planning model. Some firms use a "bottom up" financial planning model, which incorporates forecasts of revenues and costs for particular products, advertising plans, major

TABLE 28-5
Financial statements for Executive Cheese Company
(Figures in thousands of dollars)

INCOME STATEMENT FOR 1988

Revenue	$1,785
Fixed costs	53
Variable costs (80% of revenue)	1,428
Depreciation	80
Interest (at 8%)	24
Taxes (at 40%)	80
Net income	$ 120

SOURCES AND USES OF FUNDS FOR 1988

Sources	
Operating cash flow	$ 200
Borrowing	36
Stock issues	104
Total sources	$ 340
Uses	
Increase in net working capital	60
Investment	200
Dividends	80
Total uses	$ 340

BALANCE SHEET, YEAR-END

Assets	1988	1987
Net working capital	$ 400	$ 340
Fixed assets	800	680
Total assets	$1,200	$1,020
Liabilities		
Debt	$ 240	$ 204
Book equity	960	816
Total liabilities	$1,200	$1,020

investment projects, and so on. What are the advantages and disadvantages of the two model types? What sort of firms would you expect to use each type and what would they use them for?

11. Corporate financial plans are often used as a basis for judging subsequent performance. What do you think can be learned from such comparisons? What problems are likely to arise and how might you cope with these problems?

12. What problems are likely to be encountered in keeping the corporate financial plan up to date?

29 Short-Term Financial Planning

Most of this book is devoted to long-term financial decisions such as capital budgeting and the choice of capital structure. Such decisions are called *long-term* for two reasons. First, they usually involve long-lived assets or liabilities. Second, they are not easily reversed, and therefore may commit the firm to a particular course of action for several years.

Short-term financial decisions generally involve short-lived assets and liabilities, and usually they *are* easily reversed. Compare, for example, a 60-day bank loan for $50 million with a $50 million issue of 20-year bonds. The bank loan is clearly a short-term decision. The firm can repay it 2 months later and be right back where it started. A firm might conceivably issue a 20-year bond in January and retire it in March, but it would be extremely inconvenient and expensive to do so. In practice, such a bond issue is a long-term decision, not only because of the bond's 20-year maturity, but because the decision to issue it cannot be reversed on short notice.

A financial manager responsible for short-term financial decisions does not have to look far into the future. The decision to take the 60-day bank loan could properly be based on cash-flow forecasts for the next few months only. The bond issue decision will normally reflect forecasted cash requirements 5, 10, or more years into the future.

Managers concerned with short-term financial decisions can avoid many of the difficult conceptual issues encountered elsewhere in this book. In a sense, short-term decisions are easier than long-term decisions—but they are not less important. A firm can identify extremely valuable capital investment opportunities, find the precise optimal debt ratio, follow the perfect dividend policy, and yet founder because no one bothers to raise the cash to pay this year's bills. Hence the need for short-term planning.

In this chapter, we will review the major classes of short-term assets and liabilities, show how long-term financing decisions affect the firm's short-term financial planning problem, and describe how financial managers trace changes in cash and working capital. We will also describe how managers forecast month-by-month cash requirements or surpluses and how they develop short-term investment and financing strategies.

Part Nine of the book takes a more detailed look at working capital management. Chapter 30 examines the decision to extend credit to the firm's customers. Chapter 31 describes the decisions to hold cash (instead of investing cash to earn interest) and the relationship between firms and commercial banks. Chapter 32 describes the many channels firms can use to invest or raise funds for short periods.

TABLE 29-1

Current assets and liabilities for manufacturing corporations in the
United States, third quarter 1986 (figures in billions of dollars)

Current Assets[a]		Current Liabilities[a]	
Cash	62.5	Short-term loans	78.0
Marketable securities	62.9	Accounts payable	156.7
Accounts receivable	300.3	Accrued income taxes	29.1
Inventories	319.5	Current payments due	
		on long-term debt	28.7
Other current assets	63.1	Other current liabilities	222.7
Total	808.4	Total	515.2

[a] Net working capital (current assets − current liabilities) is $808.4 − $515.2
= $293.2 billion.
Source: U.S. Department of Commerce, *Quarterly Financial Report for Manufacturing, Mining and Trade Corporations,* Third Quarter 1986, p. 4.

29-1 THE COMPONENTS OF WORKING CAPITAL

Short-term or *current* assets and liabilities are collectively known as **working
capital.** Table 29-1 gives a breakdown of current assets and liabilities for all manufacturing corporations in the United States in 1986. Note that total current assets
were $808.4 billion and current liabilities $515.2 billion. **Net working capital**
(current assets less current liabilities) was $293.2 billion.

One important current asset is *accounts receivable.* When one company sells
goods to another company or a government agency, it does not usually expect to
be paid immediately. These unpaid bills, or *trade credit,* make up the bulk of accounts receivable. Companies also sell some goods on credit to the final consumer.
This *consumer credit* makes up the remainder of accounts receivable.[1] We will discuss the management of receivables in Chapter 30. You will learn how companies
decide which customers are good or bad credit risks and when it makes sense to
offer credit.

Another important current asset is *inventory.* Inventories may consist of raw
materials, work in process, or finished goods awaiting sale and shipment.

Firms *invest* in inventory. The cost of holding inventory includes not only storage cost and the risk of spoilage or obsolescence, but also the opportunity cost of
capital—that is, the rate of return offered by other, equivalent-risk investment
opportunities.[2] The benefits to holding inventory are often indirect. For example,
a large inventory of finished goods (large relative to expected sales) reduces the
chance of a "stockout" if demand is unexpectedly high. A producer holding a
small finished goods inventory is more likely to be caught short, unable to fill
orders promptly. Similarly, large raw materials inventories reduce the chance that

---

[1] Sales of all manufacturing corporations were $2295 billion in the year ending September 1986. Table
29-1 shows that accounts receivable were $300.3 billion, about 13 percent of the year's sales. This
amounts to .13 × 52 = 6.8 weeks. If this ratio of accounts receivable to annual sales is maintained,
accounts receivable will always reflect the last 6.8 weeks' sales.

[2] How risky are inventories? It is hard to generalize. Many firms just assume inventories have the same
risk as typical capital investments and therefore calculate the cost of holding inventories using the
firm's average opportunity cost of capital. You can think of many exceptions to this rule of thumb,
however. For example, some electronics components are made with gold connections. Should an
electronics firm apply its average cost of capital to its inventory of gold? (See Section 11-3.)

an unexpected shortage would force the firm to shut down production or use a more costly substitute material.

Bulk orders for raw materials, although they lead to large average inventories, may be worthwhile if the firm can obtain lower prices from suppliers. (That is, bulk orders may yield quantity discounts.) Firms are often willing to hold large inventories of finished goods, for similar reasons. A large inventory of finished goods allows longer, more economical production runs. In effect, the production manager gives the firm a quantity discount.

The task of inventory management is to assess these benefits and costs and to strike a sensible balance. In manufacturing companies the production manager is best placed to make this judgment. Since the financial manager is not usually directly involved in inventory management, we will not discuss the inventory problem in detail.

The remaining current assets are cash and marketable securities. The cash consists of currency, demand deposits (funds in checking accounts), and time deposits (funds in savings accounts). The principal marketable security is commercial paper (short-term, unsecured notes sold by other firms). Other securities include U.S. Treasury bills and state and local government securities.

In choosing between cash and marketable securities, the financial manager faces a task like that of the production manager. There are always advantages to holding large "inventories" of cash—they reduce the risk of running out of cash and having to raise more on short notice. On the other hand, there is a cost to holding idle cash balances rather than putting the money to work in marketable securities. In Chapter 31 we will tell you how the financial manager collects and pays out cash and decides on an optimal cash balance.

We have seen that a company's principal current asset consists of unpaid bills from other companies. One firm's credit must be another's debit. Therefore it is not surprising that a company's principal current liability consists of *accounts payable*—that is, outstanding payments to other companies.

To finance its investment in current assets, a company may rely on a variety of short-term loans. Commercial banks are by far the largest source of such loans, but an industrial firm may also borrow from other sources. Another way of borrowing is to sell commercial paper.

Many short-term loans are unsecured, but sometimes the company may offer its inventory or receivables as security. For example, a firm may decide to borrow short-term money secured by its accounts receivable. When its customers have paid their bills, it can use the cash to repay the loan. An alternative procedure is to *sell* the receivables to a financial institution and let it collect the money. In other words, some companies solve their financing problem by borrowing on the strength of their current assets; others solve it by selling their current assets. In Chapter 32 we will look at the varied and ingenious methods of financing current assets.

29-2 LINKS BETWEEN LONG-TERM AND SHORT-TERM FINANCING DECISIONS

All businesses require capital—that is, money invested in plant, machinery, inventories, accounts receivable, and all the other assets it takes to run a business efficiently. Typically, these assets are not purchased all at once but obtained gradually over time. Let us call the total cost of these assets the firm's *cumulative capital requirement*.

Most firms' cumulative capital requirement grows irregularly, like the wavy line in Figure 29-1. This line shows a clear upward trend, as the firm's business

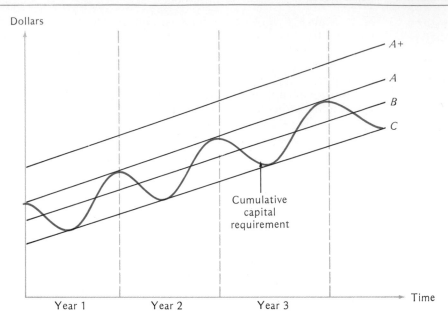

FIGURE 29-1

The firm's cumulative capital requirement (heavy line) is the cumulative investment in plant, equipment, inventory and all other assets needed for the business. In this case the requirement grows year by year, but there is seasonal fluctuation within each year. The requirement for short-term financing is the
difference between long-term financing (lines A^+, A, B, and C) and the cumulative capital requirement. If long-term financing follows line C, the firm *always*
needs short-term financing. At line B, the need is seasonal. At lines A and A^+,
the firm never needs short-term financing. There is always extra cash to invest.

grows. But there is also seasonal variation around the trend: In the figure the
capital-requirements line peaks late in each year. Finally, there would be unpredictable week-to-week and month-to-month fluctuations, but we have not attempted to show these in Figure 29-1.

  The cumulative capital requirement can be met from either long-term or short-
term financing. When long-term financing does not cover the cumulative capital
requirement, the firm must raise short-term capital to make up the difference.
When long-term financing *more* than covers the cumulative capital requirement,
the firm has surplus cash available for short-term investment. Thus the amount of
long-term financing raised, given the cumulative capital requirement, determines
whether the firm is a short-term borrower or lender.

  Lines A, B, and C in Figure 29-1 illustrate this. Each depicts a different long-
term financing strategy. Strategy A always implies a short-term cash surplus.
Strategy C implies a permanent need for short-term borrowing. Under B, which is
probably the most common strategy, the firm is a short-term lender during part
of the year and a borrower during the rest.

  What is the *best* level of long-term financing relative to the cumulative capital
requirement? It is hard to say. There is no convincing theoretical analysis of this
question. We can make several practical observations, however.

Matching Maturities

Most financial managers attempt to "match maturities" of assets and liabilities. That is, they finance long-lived assets like plant and machinery with long-term borrowing and equity.

Permanent Working-Capital Requirements

Most firms make a permanent investment in net working capital (current assets less current liabilities). They finance this investment from long-term sources.[3]

The Comforts of Surplus Cash

Many financial managers would feel more comfortable under strategy A than strategy C. Strategy A^+ (the highest line) would be still more relaxing. A firm with a surplus of long-term financing never has to worry about borrowing to pay next month's bills. But is the financial manager paid to be comfortable? Firms usually put surplus cash to work in Treasury bills or other marketable securities. This is at best a zero-NPV investment for a tax-paying firm.[4] Thus we think that firms with a *permanent* cash surplus ought to go on a diet, retiring long-term securities to reduce long-term financing to a level at or below the firm's cumulative capital requirement. That is, if the firm is on line A^+, it ought to move down to line A, or perhaps even lower.

29-3 TRACING CHANGES IN CASH AND WORKING CAPITAL

Table 29-2 compares 1986 and 1987 year-end balance sheets for Dynamic Mattress Company. Table 29-3 shows the firm's income statement for 1987. Note that Dynamic's cash balance increased by $1 million during 1987. What caused this increase? Did the extra cash come from Dynamic Mattress Company's additional long-term borrowing, from reinvested earnings, from cash released by reducing inventory, or from extra credit extended by Dynamic's suppliers? (Note the increase in accounts payable.)

The correct answer is "all the above," as well as many other activities and actions taken by the firm during the year. All we can say is that *sources* of cash exceeded *uses* by $1 million.

Financial analysts often summarize sources and uses of cash in a statement like the one shown in Table 29-4. The statement shows that Dynamic *generated* cash from the following sources:

1. It issued $7 million of long-term debt.
2. It reduced inventory, releasing $1 million.
3. It increased its accounts payable, in effect borrowing an additional $7 million from its suppliers.

---

[3] In a sense this statement is true by definition. If net working capital (current assets less current liabilities) is positive, it must be financed by long-term debt or equity. Our point is that firms *plan* it that way.

[4] But what is the NPV of an investment in Treasury bills? The answer depends on your position on the "debt and taxes" controversy discussed in Section 18-2. If there is a tax advantage to borrowing, as most people believe, there must be a corresponding tax *dis*advantage to lending, and investment in Treasury bills has a negative NPV. On the other hand, if Merton Miller is right, and there is no tax advantage to borrowing, then Treasury bills are a zero-NPV investment.

TABLE 29-2
Year-end balance sheets for 1986 and 1987 for Dynamic
Mattress Company (figures in millions of dollars)

	1986	1987
Current assets		
Cash	4	5
Marketable securities	0	5
Inventory	26	25
Accounts receivable	25	30
Total current assets	55	65
Fixed assets		
Gross investment	56	70
Less depreciation	−16	−20
Net fixed assets	40	50
Total assets	95	115
Current liabilities		
Bank loans	5	0
Accounts payable	20	27
Total current liabilities	25	27
Long-term debt	5	12
Net worth (equity and retained earnings)	65	76
Total liabilities and net worth	95	115

4. By far the largest source of cash was Dynamic's operations, which generated $16 million. See Table 29-3, and note: Income ($12 million) understates cash flow because depreciation is deducted in calculating income. Depreciation is *not* a cash outlay. Thus, it must be added back in order to obtain operating cash flow.

Dynamic *used* cash for the following purposes:

1. It paid a $1 million dividend. (*Note:* The $11 million increase in Dynamic's equity is due to retained earnings: $12 million of equity income, less the $1 million dividend.)

TABLE 29-3
Income statement for 1987 for Dynamic
Mattress Company (figures in millions
of dollars)

Sales	350
Operating costs	−321
	29
Depreciation	−4
	25
Interest	−1
Pretax income	24
Tax at 50 percent	−12
Net income	12

Note:
Dividend   = $1 million
Retained earnings = $11 million

TABLE 29-4
Sources and uses of cash for 1987 for Dynamic Mattress
Company (figures in millions of dollars)

Sources	
Issued long-term debt	7
Reduced inventories	1
Increased accounts payable	7
Cash from operations:	
Net income	12
Depreciation	4
Total sources	31
Uses	
Repaid short-term bank loan	5
Invested in fixed assets	14
Purchased marketable securities	5
Increased accounts receivable	5
Dividend	1
	30
Increase in cash balance	1

2. It repaid a $5 million short-term bank loan.[5]
3. It invested $14 million. This shows up as the increase in gross fixed assets in Table 29-2.
4. It purchased $5 million of marketable securities.
5. It allowed accounts receivable to expand by $5 million. In effect, it lent this additional amount to its customers.

Tracing Changes in Net Working Capital

Financial analysts often find it useful to collapse all current assets and liabilities into a single figure for net working capital. Dynamic's net working capital balances were (in millions):

	Current Assets	Less	Current Liabilities	Equals	Net Working Capital
Year-end 1986	$55	–	$25	=	$30
Year-end 1987	$65	–	$27	=	$38

Table 29-5 gives balance sheets which report only net working capital, not individual current asset or liability items.

"Sources and uses" statements can likewise be simplified by defining "sources" as actions or activities which contribute to net working capital, and "uses" as actions or activities which use up working capital. In this context working capital is usually referred to as *funds,* and a *"sources and uses of funds" statement* is presented.

---

[5] This is principal repayment, not interest. Sometimes interest payments are explicitly recognized as a use of funds. If so, operating cash flow would be defined *before* interest, that is, as net income plus interest plus depreciation.

TABLE 29-5

Condensed year-end balance sheets for 1986 and 1987 for
Dynamic Mattress Company (figures in millions of dollars)

	1986	1987
Net working capital	30	38
Fixed assets		
Gross investment	56	70
Less depreciation	−16	−20
Net fixed assets	40	50
Total assets	70	88
Long-term debt	5	12
Net worth	65	76
Long-term liabilities and net worth[a]	70	88

[a] When only *net* working capital appears on a firm's balance sheet, this
figure (the sum of long-term liabilities and net worth) is often referred
to as *total capitalization*.

In 1986, Dynamic contributed to net working capital by:

1. Issuing $7 million of long-term debt
2. Generating $16 million from operations

It used up net working capital by:

1. Investing $14 million
2. Paying a $1 million dividend

The year's changes in net working capital are thus summarized by Dynamic Mattress Company's "sources and uses of funds" statement, given in Table 29-6.

Profits and Cash Flow

Now look back to Table 29-4, which shows sources and uses of *cash*. We want to register two warnings about the entry called *cash from operations*. It may not actually represent real dollars—dollars you can buy beer with.

TABLE 29-6

Sources and uses of funds (net working capital) for 1987
for Dynamic Mattress Company (figures in millions
of dollars)

Sources	
Issued long-term debt	7
Cash from operations	
Net income	12
Depreciation	4
	23
Uses	
Invested in fixed assets	14
Dividend	1
	15
Increase in net working capital	8

First, depreciation may not be the only noncash expense deducted in calculating income. For example, most firms use different accounting procedures in their tax books than in their reports to shareholders. The point of special tax accounts is to minimize current taxable income. The effect is that the shareholder books overstate the firm's current cash tax liability,[6] and after-tax cash flow from operations is therefore understated.

Second, income statements record sales when made, not when the customer's payment is received. Think of what happens when Dynamic sells goods on credit. The company records a profit at the time of sale but there is no cash inflow until the bills are paid. Since there is no cash inflow, there is no change in the company's cash balance, although there is an increase in working capital in the form of an increase in accounts receivable. No net addition to cash would be shown in a "sources and uses" statement like Table 29-4. The increase in cash from operations would be offset by an increase in accounts receivable.

Later, when the bills are paid, there is an increase in the cash balance. However, there is no further profit at this point and no increase in working capital. The increase in the cash balance is exactly matched by a decrease in accounts receivable.

That brings up interesting characteristics of working capital. Imagine a company that conducts a very simple business. It buys raw materials for cash, processes them into finished goods, and then sells these goods on credit. The whole cycle of operations looks like this:

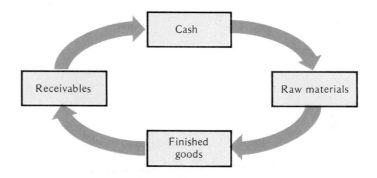

If you draw up a balance sheet at the beginning of the process, you see cash. If you delay a little, you find the cash replaced by inventories of raw materials and, still later, by inventories of finished goods. When the goods are sold, the inventories give way to accounts receivable and finally, when the customers pay their bills, the firm draws out its profit and replenishes the cash balance.

There is only one constant in this process—namely, working capital. The components of working capital are constantly changing. That is one reason why (net) working capital is a useful summary measure of current assets or liabilities.

---

[6] The difference between taxes reported and paid to the Internal Revenue Service shows up on the balance sheet as an increased deferred tax liability. The reason why a liability is recognized is that accelerated depreciation and other devices used to reduce current taxable income do not eliminate taxes, they only delay them. Of course this reduces the present value of the firm's tax liability, but still the ultimate liability has to be recognized. In the "sources and uses" statements an increase in deferred taxes would be treated as a source of funds. In the Dynamic Mattress example we ignore deferred taxes.

The strength of the working capital measure is that it is unaffected by seasonal or other temporary movements between different current assets or liabilities. But the strength is also its weakness, for the working capital figure hides a lot of interesting information. In our example cash was transformed into inventory, then into receivables, and back into cash again. But these assets have different degrees of risk and liquidity. You can't pay bills with inventory or with receivables—you must pay with cash.

29-4 CASH BUDGETING

The past is interesting only for what one can learn from it. The financial manager's problem is to forecast *future* sources and uses of cash. These forecasts serve two purposes. First, they alert the financial manager to future cash needs. Second, the cash-flow forecasts provide a standard, or budget, against which subsequent performance can be judged.

Preparing the Cash Budget: Inflow

There are at least as many ways to produce a quarterly cash budget as there are to skin a cat. Many large firms have developed elaborate "corporate models" which allow their computer to do much of the work. The procedures of smaller firms are less formal. But there are common issues that all firms must face when they forecast. We will illustrate these issues by continuing the example of Dynamic Mattress.

Most of Dynamic's cash inflow comes from the sale of mattresses. We therefore start with a sales forecast by quarter[7] for 1988:

	QUARTER			
	First	Second	Third	Fourth
Sales, millions of dollars	87.5	78.5	116	131

But sales become accounts receivable before they become cash. Cash flow comes from *collections* on accounts receivable.

Most firms keep track of the average time it takes customers to pay their bills. From this they can forecast what proportion of a quarter's sales is likely to be converted into cash in that quarter, and what proportion is likely to be carried over to the next quarter as accounts receivable. Suppose that 80 percent of sales are "cashed in" in the immediate quarter and 20 percent in the next. Table 29-7 shows forecasted collections under this assumption.

In the first quarter, for example, collections from current sales are 80 percent of $87.5, or $70 million. But the firm also collects 20 percent of the previous quarter's sales, or .2(75) = $15 million. Therefore total collections are $70 + $15 = $85 million.

Dynamic started the first quarter with $30 million of accounts receivable. The quarter's sales of $87.5 million were *added* to accounts receivable, but $85 million of collections were *subtracted*. Therefore, as Table 29-7 shows, Dynamic ended the

---

[7] Most firms would forecast by month instead of by quarter. Sometimes weekly or even daily forecasts are made. But presenting a monthly forecast would triple the number of entries in Table 29-7 and subsequent tables. We wanted to keep the examples as simple as possible.

TABLE 29-7
To forecast Dynamic Mattress's collections on accounts receivable you have to forecast sales and collection rates (figures in millions of dollars)

	First Quarter	Second Quarter	Third Quarter	Fourth Quarter
1. Receivables at start of period	30	32.5	30.7	38.2
2. Sales	87.5	78.5	116	131
3. Collections				
Sales in current period (80 percent)	70	62.8	92.8	104.8
Sales in last perod (20 percent)	15[a]	17.5	15.7	23.2
Total collections	85	80.3	108.5	128.0
4. Receivables at end of period	32.5	30.7	38.2	41.2
4 = 1 + 2 − 3				

[a] Sales in the fourth quarter of the previous year were $75 million.

quarter with accounts receivable of $30 + 87.5 − 85 = \$32.5$ million. The general formula is

$$\text{Ending accounts receivable} = \text{beginning accounts receivable}$$
$$+ \text{ sales} - \text{collections}$$

The top section of Table 29-8 shows forecasted sources of cash for Dynamic Mattress. Collection of receivables is the main source but it is not the only one. Perhaps the firm plans to dispose of some land, or expects a tax refund or payment of an insurance claim. All such items are included as "other" sources. It is also possible that you may raise additional capital by borrowing or selling stock, but we don't want to prejudge that question. Therefore, for the moment we just assume that Dynamic will not raise further long-term finance.

Preparing the Cash Budget: Outflow

So much for the incoming cash. Now for the outgoing cash. It is a universal fact that there seem to be many more uses for cash than there are sources. For simplicity, we have condensed the uses into four categories in Table 29-8.

1. *Payments on accounts payable.* You have to pay your bills for raw materials, parts, electricity, etc. The cash-flow forecast assumes all these bills are paid on time, although Dynamic could probably delay payment to some extent. Delayed payment is sometimes called *stretching your payables*. Stretching is one source of short-term financing, but for most firms it is an expensive source, because by stretching they lose discounts given to firms that pay promptly. This is discussed in more detail in Section 30-1.
2. *Labor, administrative, and other expenses.* This category includes all other regular business expenses.
3. *Capital expenditures.* Note that Dynamic Mattress plans a major capital outlay in the first quarter.
4. *Taxes, interest, and dividend payments.* This includes interest on presently outstanding long-term debt, but does not include interest on any additional borrowing to meet cash requirements in 1988. At this stage in the analysis, Dynamic does not know how much it will have to borrow, or whether it will have to borrow at all.

TABLE 29-8
Dynamic Mattress's cash budget for 1988 (figures in millions of dollars)

	First Quarter	Second Quarter	Third Quarter	Fourth Quarter
Sources of cash				
Collections on accounts receivable	85	80.3	108.5	128
Other	0	0	12.5	0
Total sources	85	80.3	121	128
Uses of cash				
Payments on accounts payable	65	60	55	50
Labor, administrative, and other expenses	30	30	30	30
Capital expenditures	32.5	1.3	5.5	8
Taxes, interest, and dividends	4	4	4.5	5
Total uses	131.5	95.3	95	93
Sources minus uses	− 46.5	− 15.0	+ 26	+ 35
Calculation of short-term financing requirement				
1. Cash at start of period	5	−41.5	− 56.5	− 30.5
2. Change in cash balance (sources less uses)	− 46.5	− 15.0	+ 26	+ 35
3. Cash at end of period[a] 1 + 2 = 3	− 41.5	− 56.5	− 30.5	+ 4.5
4. Minimum operating cash balance	5	5	5	5
5. Cumulative short-term financing required[b] 5 = 4 − 3	46.5	61.5	35.5	.5

[a] Of course firms cannot literally hold a negative amount of cash. This is the amount the firm will have to raise to pay its bills.

[b] A negative sign would indicate a cash *surplus*. But in this example the firm must raise cash for all quarters.

The forecasted net inflow of cash (sources minus uses) is shown in the box in Table 29-8. Note the large negative figure for the first quarter: a $46.5 million forecasted *outflow*. There is a smaller forecasted outflow in the second quarter, and then substantial cash inflows in the second half of the year.

The bottom part of Table 29-8 (below the box) calculates how much financing Dynamic will have to raise if its cash-flow forecasts are right. It starts the year with $5 million in cash. There is a $46.5 million cash outflow in the first quarter, and so Dynamic will have to obtain at least $46.5 − 5 = $41.5 million of additional financing. This would leave the firm with a forecasted cash balance of exactly zero at the start of the second quarter.

Most financial managers regard a planned cash balance of zero as driving too close to the edge of the cliff. They establish a *minimum operating cash balance* to absorb unexpected cash inflows and outflows. Also, banks usually require firms to maintain a minimum average cash balance as partial compensation for services the bank provides to the firm—this is described in more detail in Chapter 31. We will assume that Dynamic's minimum operating cash balance is $5 million. That means it will have to raise the full $46.5 million cash outflow in the first quarter, and $15 million more in the second quarter. Thus its cumulative financing requirement is $61.5 million in the second quarter. This is the peak, fortunately:

The cumulative requirement declines in the third quarter by $26 million to $35.5 million. In the final quarter Dynamic is almost out of the woods: Its cash balance is $4.5 million, just $.5 million shy of its minimum operating balance.

The next step is to develop a *short-term financing plan* that covers the forecasted requirements in the most economical way possible. We will move on to that topic after two general observations.

1. The large cash outflows in the first two quarters do not necessarily spell trouble for Dynamic Mattress. In part, they reflect the capital investment made in the first quarter: Dynamic is spending $32.5 million, but it should be acquiring an asset worth that much or more. In part, the cash outflows reflect low sales in the first half of the year; sales recover in the second half.[8] If this is a predictable seasonal pattern, the firm should have no trouble borrowing to tide it over the slow months.
2. Table 29-8 is only a best guess about future cash flows. It is a good idea to think about the *uncertainty* in your estimates. For example, you could undertake a sensitivity analysis, in which you inspect how Dynamic's cash requirements would be affected by a shortfall in sales or by a delay in collections. The trouble with such sensitivity analyses is that you are only changing one item at a time, whereas in practice a downturn in the economy might affect, say, sales levels *and* collection rates. An alternative but more complicated solution is to build a model of the cash budget, and then to simulate to determine the probability of cash requirements significantly above or below the forecasts shown in Table 29-8.[9] If cash requirements are difficult to predict, you may wish to hold additional cash or marketable securities to cover a possible unexpected cash outflow.

29-5 THE SHORT-TERM FINANCING PLAN

Dynamic's cash budget defines its problem: Its financial manager must find short-term financing to cover the firm's forecasted cash requirements. There are dozens of sources of short-term financing, but for simplicity we start by assuming that there are just two options.

Options for Short-Term Financing

1. *Unsecured Bank Borrowing:* Dynamic has an existing arrangement with its bank allowing it to borrow up to $41 million at an interest cost of 11.5 percent per year or 2.875 percent per quarter. The firm can borrow and repay whenever it wants so long as it does not exceed the credit limit. Dynamic does not have to pledge any specific assets as security for the loan. This kind of arrangement is called a **line of credit.**[10]

When a company borrows on an unsecured line of credit, it is generally obliged to maintain a **compensating balance** on deposit at the bank. In our example, Dynamic has to maintain a balance of 20 percent of the amount of the loan. In other words, if the firm wants to raise $100, it must actually borrow $125, because $25 (20 percent of $125) must be left on deposit in the bank.

---

[8] Maybe people buy more mattresses late in the year when the nights are longer.

[9] In other words, you could use Monte Carlo simulation. See Section 10-2.

[10] Lines of credit are discussed in more detail in Chapter 32.

2. *Stretching Payables:* Dynamic can also raise capital by putting off paying its bills. The financial manager believes that Dynamic can defer the following amounts in each quarter:

	QUARTER			
	1	2	3	4
Amount deferrable, millions of dollars	52	48	44	40

That is, $52 million can be saved in the first quarter by *not* paying bills in that quarter. (Table 29-8 assumes these bills *are* paid in the first quarter.) If deferred, these payments *must* be made in the second quarter. Similarly, $48 million of quarter 2's bills can be deferred to quarter 3 and so on.

Stretching payables is often costly, however, even if no ill will is incurred. The reason is that suppliers often offer discounts for prompt payment. Dynamic loses this discount if it pays late. In this example we assume the lost discount is 5 percent of the amount deferred. In other words, if a $100 payment is delayed, the firm must pay $105 in the next quarter.

The First Financing Plan

With these two options, the short-term financing strategy is obvious: Use the line of credit first, if necessary up to the $41 million credit limit. If cash requirements exceed the credit limit, stretch payables.

Table 29-9 shows the resulting financing plan. In the first quarter the plan calls for borrowing the full amount available under the line of credit ($41 million) and stretching $3.6 million of payables (see lines 1 and 2 in the table). In addition, the firm sells the $5 million of marketable securities it held at the end of 1987 (line 8). Thus, under this plan it raises $49.6 million in the first quarter (line 10).

Why raise $49.6 million when Table 29-8 shows a cash requirement of only $46.5 million? The major reason is that the $41 million borrowed under the line of credit requires a compensating balance of 20 percent of $41 million, or $8.2 million. Dynamic can cover part of this with its $5 million minimum balance, but $3.2 million still has to be raised (line 15).

In the second quarter, the plan calls for Dynamic to maintain line of credit borrowing at the upper limit and stretch $20 million in payables. This raises $16.4 million after the $3.6 million of payables stretched in the first quarter are paid.

Again, the amount of cash raised exceeds the amount required for operations ($16.4 versus $15 million). In this case, the difference is the interest cost of the first quarter's borrowing: $1.2 million for the line of credit and $.2 million for the stretched payables (lines 11 and 12.)[11]

In the third and fourth quarters the plan calls for Dynamic to pay off its debt. In turn, this releases cash tied up by the compensating balance requirement of the line of credit.

Evaluating the First Plan. Does the plan shown in Table 29-9 solve Dynamic's short-term financing problem? No: The plan is feasible, but Dynamic can probably

---

[11] The interest rate on the line of credit is 11.5 percent per year, or $11.5/4 = 2.875$ percent per quarter. Thus the interest due is $.02875(41) = 1.2$, or $1.2 million. The "interest" cost of the stretched payables is actually the 5 percent discount lost by delaying payment. Five percent of $3.6 million is $180,000, or about $.2 million.

TABLE 29-9
Dynamic Mattress's first financing plan (figures in millions of dollars)

	First Quarter	Second Quarter	Third Quarter	Fourth Quarter
New borrowing				
1. Line of credit	41	0	0	0
2. Stretching payables	3.6	20	0	0
3. Total	44.6	20	0	0
Repayments				
4. Line of credit	0	0	4.8	36.2
5. Stretched payables	0	3.6	20	0
6. Total	0	3.6	24.8	36.2
7. Net new borrowing	44.6	16.4	−24.8	−36.2
8. Plus securities sold	5[a]	0	0	0
9. Less securities bought	0	0	0	0
10. Total cash raised	49.6	16.4	−24.8	−36.2
Interest payments				
11. Line of credit	0	1.2	1.2	1.0
12. Stretching payables	0	.2	1.0	0
13. Less interest on marketable securities	− .1[a]	0	0	0
14. Net interest paid	− .1	1.4	2.2	1.0
15. Additional funds for compensating balance[b]	3.2	0	−1.0	−2.2
16. Cash required for operations[c]	46.5	15	−26	−35
17. Total cash required	49.6	16.4	−24.8	−36.2

[a] Dynamic held $5 million in marketable securities at the end of 1987. The yield is assumed to be 2.4 percent per quarter.
[b] Twenty percent of the amount borrowed on the line of credit in excess of $25 million. Dynamic's $5 million minimum operating cash balance serves as compensating balance for loans up to $25 million.
[c] From Table 29-8.

do better. The most glaring weakness of this first plan is its reliance on stretching payables, an extremely expensive financing device. Remember that it costs Dynamic 5 percent *per quarter* to delay paying bills—20 percent per year at simple interest. The first plan would merely stimulate the financial manager to search for cheaper sources of short-term borrowing. Perhaps the $41 million limit on the line of credit could be increased, for example.

The financial manager would ask several other questions as well. For example:

1. Does Dynamic need a larger reserve of cash or marketable securities to guard against, say, its customers stretching their payables (thus slowing down collections on accounts receivable)?
2. Does the plan yield satisfactory current and quick ratios?[12] Its bankers may be worried if these ratios deteriorate.[13]

[12] These ratios are discussed in Chapter 27.

[13] We have not worked out these ratios explicitly, but you can infer from Table 29-9 that they would be fine at the end of the year but relatively low in midyear, when Dynamic's borrowing is high.

3. Are there intangible costs of stretching payables? Will suppliers begin to doubt Dynamic's creditworthiness?

4. Does the plan for 1988 leave Dynamic in good financial shape for 1989? (Here the answer is yes, since Dynamic will have paid off all short-term borrowing by the end of the year.)

5. Should Dynamic try to arrange long-term financing for the major capital expenditure in the first quarter? This seems sensible, following the rule of thumb that long-term assets deserve long-term financing. It would also reduce the need for short-term borrowing dramatically. A counterargument is that Dynamic is financing the capital investment *only temporarily* by short-term borrowing. By year-end, the investment is paid for by cash from operations. Thus Dynamic's initial decision not to seek immediate long-term financing may reflect a preference for ultimately financing the investment with retained earnings.

6. Perhaps the firm's operating and investment plans can be adjusted to make the short-term financing problem easier. Is there any easy way of deferring the first quarter's large cash outflow? For example, suppose that the large capital investment in the first quarter is for new mattress-stuffing machines to be delivered and installed in the first half of the year. The new machines are not scheduled to be ready for full-scale use until August. Perhaps the machine manufacturer could be persuaded to accept 60 percent of the purchase price on delivery and 40 percent when the machines are installed and operating satisfactorily.

Short-term financing plans are developed by trial and error. You lay out one plan, think about it, then try again with different assumptions on financing and investment alternatives. You continue until you can think of no further improvements.

Trial and error is important because it helps you understand the real nature of the problem the firm faces. Here we can draw a useful analogy between the *process* of planning and Chapter 10, A Project Is Not a Black Box. In Chapter 10 we described sensitivity analysis and other tools used by firms to find out what makes capital investment projects tick and what can go wrong with them. Dynamic's financial manager faces the same kind of task: not just to choose a plan, but to understand what can go wrong with it, and what will be done if conditions change unexpectedly.[14]

We cannot trace through each trial and error in Dynamic Mattress's search for the best short-term financing plan. The reader may be buried in numbers already. Instead we will wrap up this chapter by looking at Dynamic's second try.

The Second Financing Plan

The second financing plan, shown in Table 29-10, reflects two significant new assumptions.

1. A commercial finance company[15] has offered to lend Dynamic up to 80 percent of its accounts receivable at an interest rate of 15 percent per year, or 3.75

---

[14] This point is even more important in *long-term* financial planning. See Chapter 28.

[15] Commercial finance companies are nonbank financial institutions that specialize in lending to businesses.

TABLE 29-10
Dynamic Mattress's second financing plan (figures in millions of dollars)

	First Quarter	Second Quarter	Third Quarter	Fourth Quarter
New borrowing				
1. Line of credit	41	0	0	0
2. Secured borrowing (receivables pledged)	6.1	16.4	0	0
3. Total	47.1	16.4	0	0
Repayments				
4. Line of credit	0	0	2.0	36.7
5. Secured borrowing	0	0	22.4	0
6. Total	0	0	24.4	36.7
7. Net new borrowing	47.1	16.4	−24.4	36.7
8. Plus securities sold	2.5[a]	0	0	0
9. Less securities bought	0	0	0	0
10. Total cash raised	49.6	16.4	−24.4	−36.7
Interest payments				
11. Line of credit	0	1.2	1.2	1.1
12. Secured borrowing	0	.2	.8	0
13. Less interest on marketable securities	− .1[a]	.1	− .1	− .1
14. Net interest paid	− .1	1.3	2.0	1.0
15. Additional funds for compensating balance[b]	3.2	0	− .4	−2.8
16. Cash required for operations[c]	46.5	15	−26	−35
17. Total cash required	49.6	16.4	−24.4	−36.7

[a] Dynamic held $5 million in marketable securities at the end of 1987.
[b] Twenty percent of the amount borrowed on the line of credit in excess of $25 million. Dynamic's $5 million minimum operating cash balance serves as compensating balance for loans up to $25 million.
[c] From Table 29-8.
Note: There are minor inconsistencies in this table because of rounding.

percent per quarter. In return, Dynamic is to pledge accounts receivable as security for the loan. This is clearly cheaper than stretching payables. It appears much more expensive than the bank line of credit—but remember that the line of credit requires a 20 percent compensating balance, whereas every dollar borrowed against receivables can be spent.

2. The financial manager is uncomfortable with the first plan, which includes no cushion of marketable securities. The second plan calls for a $2.5 million marketable securities portfolio held throughout the year.

A comparison of Tables 29-9 and Table 29-10 shows that the second plan is broadly similar to the first, except that borrowing against receivables replaces stretching payables, and the firm holds $2.5 million of marketable securities. The second plan is also cheaper than the first. This can be seen by comparing net interest paid (line 14) under the two plans.

	QUARTER				
	1	2	3	4	Total
First plan	−.1	1.4	2.2	1.0	4.5
Second plan	−.1	1.3	2.0	1.0	4.2

Over the year the second plan saves $\$4.5 - 4.2 = \$.3$ million, or about $\$300,000$ of interest.[16]

<table>
<tr><td>

A Note or Short-Term Financial Planning Models

</td><td>

Working out a consistent short-term plan requires burdensome calculations.[17] Fortunately much of the arithmetic can be delegated to a computer. Many large firms have built *short-term financial planning models* to do this. The financial manager specifies forecasted cash requirements or surpluses, interest rates, credit limits, etc., and the model grinds out a plan like those shown in Tables 29-9 and 29-10. The computer also produces balance sheets, income statements, and whatever special reports the financial manager may require.

</td></tr>
</table>

Smaller firms that do not want custom-built models can rent general-purpose models offered by banks, accounting firms, management consultants, or specialized computer software firms.

Most of these models are *simulation* programs.[18] They simply work out the consequences of the assumptions and policies specified by the financial manager. *Optimization* models for short-term financial planning are also available. These models are usually linear programming models. They search for the *best* plan from a range of alternative policies identified by the financial manager.

As a matter of fact, we used a linear programming model developed by Pogue and Bussard[19] to generate Dynamic Mattress's financial plans. Of course in that simple example we hardly needed a linear programming model to identify the best strategy: It was obvious that Dynamic should always use the line of credit first, turning to the second-best alternative (stretching payables or borrowing against receivables) only when the limit on the line of credit was reached. The Pogue-Bussard model nevertheless did the arithmetic quickly and easily.

Optimization helps when the firm faces complex problems with many interdependent alternatives and restrictions for which trial and error might never identify the *best* combination of alternatives.

Of course the best plan for one set of assumptions may prove disastrous if the assumptions are wrong. Thus the financial manager has to explore the implications

---

[16] These are pretax figures. We simplified this example by forgetting that each dollar of interest paid is a tax-deductible expense.

[17] If you doubt that, look again at Table 29-9 or 29-10. Notice that the cash requirements in each quarter depend on borrowing in the previous quarter, because borrowing creates an obligation to pay interest. Also, borrowing under a line of credit may require additional cash to meet compensating balance requirements; if so, that means still more borrowing and still higher interest charges in the next quarter. Moreover, the problem's complexity would have been tripled had we not simplified by forecasting per quarter rather than by month.

[18] Like the simulation models described in Section 10-2, except that the short-term planning models rarely include uncertainty explicitly. The models referred to here are built and used in the same way as the long-term financial planning models described in Section 28-3.

[19] G. A. Pogue and R. N. Bussard, "A Linear Programming Model for Short-Term Financial Planning under Uncertainty," *Sloan Management Review,* **13**: 69–99 (Spring 1972).

of alternative assumptions about future cash flows, interest rates and so on. Linear programming can help identify good strategies, but even with an optimization model the financial plan is still sought by trial and error.

29-6 SUMMARY

Short-term financial planning is concerned with the management of the firm's short-term, or *current,* assets and liabilities. The most important current assets are cash, marketable securities, inventory, and accounts receivable. The most important current liabilities are bank loans and accounts payable. The difference between current assets and current liabilities is called (*net*) *working capital.*

Current assets and liabilities are turned over much more rapidly than the other items on the balance sheet. Short-term financing and investment decisions are more quickly and easily reversed than long-term decisions. Consequently, the financial manager does not need to look so far into the future when making them.

The nature of the firm's short-term financial planning problem is determined by the amount of long-term capital it raises. A firm that issues large amounts of long-term debt or common stock, or which retains a large part of its earnings, may find that it has permanent excess cash. In such cases there is never any problem paying bills, and short-term financial planning consists of managing the firm's portfolio of marketable securities. We think that firms with permanent cash surpluses ought to return the excess cash to their stockholders.

Other firms raise relatively little long-term capital and end up as permanent short-term debtors. Most firms attempt to find a golden mean by financing all fixed assets and part of current assets with equity and long-term debt. Such firms may invest cash surpluses during part of the year and borrow during the rest of the year.

The starting point for short-term financial planning is an understanding of sources and uses of cash.[20] Firms forecast their net cash requirements by forecasting collections on accounts receivable, adding other cash inflows, and subtracting all forecasted cash outlays.

If the forecasted cash balance is insufficient to cover day-to-day operations and to provide a buffer against contingencies, you will need to find additional finance. It may make sense to raise long-term finance if the deficiency is permanent and large. Otherwise you may choose from a variety of sources of short-term finance. For example, you may be able to borrow from a bank on an unsecured line of credit, you may borrow offering receivables or inventory as security, or you may be able to finance the deficit by not paying your bills for a while. In addition to the explicit interest costs of short-term financing, there are often implicit costs. For example, the firm may be required to maintain a compensating balance at the bank, or it may lose its reputation as a prompt payer if it raises cash by delaying payment on its bills. The financial manager must choose the financing package that has lowest total cost (explicit and implicit costs combined) and yet leaves the firm with sufficient flexibility to cover contingencies.

The search for the best short-term financial plan inevitably proceeds by trial and error. The financial manager must explore the consequences of different as-

---

[20] We pointed out in Section 29-3 that sources and uses of *funds* are often analyzed rather than sources and uses of cash: Anything that contributes to working capital is called *source of funds;* anything that diminishes working capital is called a *use of funds.* "Sources and uses of funds" statements are relatively simple because many sources and uses of cash are buried in changes in working capital. However, in forecasting, the emphasis is on cash flow: You pay bills with cash, not working capital.

sumptions about cash requirements, interest rates, limits on financing from particular sources, and so on. Firms are increasingly using computerized financial models to help in this process. The models range from simple programs that merely help with the arithmetic to linear programming models that help find the best financial plan, given the financial manager's assumptions about cash requirements, interest rates, etc.

FURTHER READING

Here are three general textbooks on working capital management:

K. V. Smith, *Guide to Working Capital Management*, McGraw-Hill Book Company, New York, 1979.

D. R. Mehta, *Working Capital Management*, Prentice-Hall, Inc., Englewood Cliffs, N.J., 1974.

K. V. Smith, *Readings on the Management of Working Capital*, 2d. ed., West Publishing Company, New York, 1980.

Pogue and Bussard present a linear programming model for short-term financial planning:

G. A. Pogue and R. N. Bussard, "A Linear Programming Model for Short-Term Financial Planning under Uncertainty," *Sloan Management Review*, **13**: 69–99 (Spring 1972).

The following two references survey how firms use corporate models in financial planning:

P. H. Grinyer and J. Wooller, *Corporate Models Today—A New Tool for Financial Management*, 2d ed., Institute of Chartered Accountants, London, 1978.

J. W. Traenkle, E. B. Cox, and J. A. Bullard, *The Use of Financial Models in Business*, Financial Executive's Research Foundation, New York, 1975.

QUIZ

1. Listed below are six different transactions that Dynamic Mattress might make. Indicate how each transaction would affect each of the following:
(*a*) Cash
(*b*) Working capital
The transactions are:

1. Pay out $2 million cash dividend.
2. A customer pays a $2500 bill resulting from a previous sale.
3. Dynamic pays $5000 previously owed to one of its suppliers.
4. Borrow $1 million long-term and invest the proceeds in inventory.
5. Borrow $1 million short-term and invest the proceeds in inventory.
6. Sell $5 million of marketable securities for cash.

2. Here is a forecast of sales by National Bromide for the first 4 months of 1988 (figures in thousands of dollars):

	MONTH			
	1	2	3	4
Cash sales	15	24	18	14
Sales on credit	100	120	90	70

On the average 50 percent of credit sales are paid for in the current month, 30 percent in the next month, and the remainder in the month after that. What is the expected cash inflow from operations in months 3 and 4?

3. Fill in the blanks in the following statements:
    (a) A firm has a cash surplus when its _____ exceeds its _____ . The surplus is normally invested in _____ .
    (b) In developing the short-term financial plan, the financial manager starts with a _____ budget for the next year. This budget shows the _____ generated or absorbed by the firm's operations, and also the minimum _____ needed to support these operations. The financial manager may also wish to invest in _____ as a reserve for unexpected cash requirements.
    (c) Short-term financing plans are developed by _____ and _____ , often aided by computerized _____ .

4. State how each of the following events would affect the firm's balance sheet. State whether each change is a source or use of cash and whether it is a source or use of funds.
    (a) An automobile manufacturer increases production in response to a forecasted increase in demand. Unfortunately, the demand does not increase.
    (b) Competition forces the firm to give customers more time to pay for their purchases.
    (c) Inflation increases the value of raw material inventories by 20 percent.
    (d) The firm sells a parcel of land for $100,000. The land was purchased 5 years earlier for $200,000.
    (e) The firm repurchases its own common stock.
    (f) The firm doubles its quarterly dividend.
    (g) The firm issues $1 million of long-term debt and uses the proceeds to repay a short-term bank loan.

QUESTIONS AND PROBLEMS

1. Table 29-11 shows Dynamic Mattress's year-end 1985 balance sheet, and Table 29-12 shows its income statement for 1986. Work out statements of sources and uses of cash and sources and uses of funds for 1986.
2. Work out a short-term financing plan for Dynamic Mattress Company assuming the limit on the line of credit is raised from $41 to $50 million. Otherwise adhere to the assumptions used in developing Table 29-10.

TABLE 29-11
Year-end balance sheet for 1985 (figures in millions of dollars)

Current assets		Current liabilities	
Cash	4	Bank loans	4
Marketable securities	2	Accounts payable	15
Inventory	20	Total current liabilities	19
Accounts receivable	22		
Total current assets	48	Long-term debt	5
		Net worth (equity and	
Fixed assets		retained earnings)	60
Gross investment	50	Total liabilities	84
Less depreciation	−14	and net worth	
Net fixed assets	36		
Total assets	84		

TABLE 29-12
Income statement for 1986
(figures in millions of dollars)

Sales	300
Operating costs	−285
	15
Depreciation	−2
	13
Interest	−1
Pretax income	12
Tax at 50 percent	−6
Net income	6

Note:
  Dividend   = $1 million
  Retained earnings = $5 million

3. Look again at Dynamic Mattress's second plan in Table 29-10. Note that the line of credit is cheaper than borrowing against accounts receivable. Would you expect this to be true in practice? Why or why not?

4. Suppose that Dynamic's bank offers to forget about the compensating balance requirement if the firm pays interest at a rate of 3.375 percent per quarter. Should the firm accept this offer? Why or why not? (Except for this change, follow the assumptions underlying Table 29-10.) Would your answer change if Dynamic's cash requirements in quarters 1 and 2 were much smaller—say, only $20 million and $10 million, respectively?

5. In some countries the market for long-term corporate debt is limited, and firms turn to short-term bank loans to finance long-term investments in plant and machinery. When a short-term loan comes due, it is replaced by another one, so that the firm is always a short-term debtor. What are the disadvantages of such an arrangement? Does it have any advantages? (*Hint:* See Section 23-3, especially "Introducing Inflation.")

6. Suppose a firm has surplus cash, but is *not* paying taxes. Would you advise it to invest in Treasury bills or other safe, marketable securities? How about investment in the preferred or common stock of other companies? (*Hint:* Your answer will reflect your stand on the "debt and taxes" controversy. See Section 18-2.)

PART NINE

SHORT-TERM
FINANCIAL DECISIONS

30 Credit Management

Chapter 29 provided an overall idea of what is involved in short-term financial management. It is time to get down to detail.

When companies sell their products, they sometimes demand cash on or before delivery, but in most cases they allow some delay in payment. If you turn back to the balance sheet in Table 29-1, you can see that these accounts receivable constitute on the average about one-third of a firm's current assets. These receivables include both trade credit and consumer credit. The former is by far the larger and will, therefore, be the main focus of this chapter.

Credit management involves five main steps:

1. First, you must determine the terms on which you propose to sell your goods. How long are you going to give customers to pay their bills? Are you prepared to offer a cash discount for prompt payment?
2. Second, you must decide what evidence you need of indebtedness. Do you just ask the buyer to sign a receipt, or do you insist on some more formal IOU?
3. Third, you must consider which customers are likely to pay their bills. Do you judge this from the customers' past records or past financial statements? Or do you rely on a bank reference?
4. Fourth, you must decide how much credit you are prepared to extend to each customer. Do you play safe by turning down any doubtful prospects? Or do you accept the risk of a few bad debts as part of the cost of building up a large regular clientele?
5. Finally, after you have granted credit, you have the problem of collecting the money when it becomes due. How do you keep track of payments? What do you do about reluctant payers?

We will discuss each step in turn.

30-1 TERMS OF SALE

Not all business transactions involve credit. For example, if you are producing goods to the customer's specification or incurring substantial delivery costs, then it may be sensible to ask for cash before delivery (CBD). If you are supplying goods to a wide variety of irregular customers, you may require cash on delivery (COD).

If your product is expensive and custom-designed and built for each customer, a formal sales contract will be signed. Often such contracts provide for **progress payments** as work is carried out. For example, a large, extended consulting contract might call for 30 percent payment after completion of field research, 30 percent more on submission of a draft report, and the remaining 40 percent when the project is finally completed.

When we look at transactions that do involve credit, we encounter a wide variety of arrangements and considerable jargon. In fact each industry seems to have its own particular usage with regard to payment terms. These norms have a rough logic. The seller will naturally demand earlier payment if its customers are in a high-risk business, if their accounts are small, or if the goods are perishable or quickly resold.

In order to induce customers to pay before the final date, it is common to offer a cash discount for prompt settlement.[1] For example, a manufacturer may require payment within 30 days but offer a 5 percent discount to customers who pay within 10 days. These terms are referred to as *5/10, net 30*. If a firm sells goods on terms of *2/30, net 60*, customers receive a 2 percent discount for payment within 30 days and must pay in full within 60 days.

Cash discounts are often very large. For example, a customer who buys on terms of *5/10, net 30* may decide to forgo the cash discount and pay on the thirtieth day. This means that the customer obtains an extra 20 days' credit but pays about 5 percent more for the goods. This is equivalent to borrowing money at a rate of 155 percent per annum.[2] Of course any firm which delays payment beyond the due date gains a cheaper loan but damages its reputation for creditworthiness.

You can think of the terms of sale as fixing both the price for the cash buyer and the rate of interest charged for credit. For example, suppose that a firm reduces the cash discount from 5 to 4 percent. That would represent an *increase* in the price for the cash buyer of 1 percent but a *reduction* in the implicit rate of interest charged the credit buyer from just over 5 percent per 20 days to just over 4 percent per 20 days.

For many items that are bought on a recurrent basis, it is inconvenient to require separate payment for each delivery. A common solution is to pretend that all sales during the month in fact occur at the end of the month. Thus goods may be sold on terms of *8/10, EOM, net 60*. This allows the customer a cash discount of 8 percent if the bill is paid within 10 days of the end of month (EOM); otherwise the full payment is due within 60 days of the invoice date.[3] When purchases are subject to seasonal fluctuations, manufacturers often encourage customers to take early delivery by allowing them to delay payment until the usual order season. This practice is known as "season dating."

30-2   COMMERCIAL CREDIT INSTRUMENTS

The terms of sale define the amount of any credit but not the nature of the contract. Repetitive sales to domestic customers are almost always made on **open account** and involve only an implicit contract. There is simply a record in the seller's books and a receipt signed by the buyer.

---

[1] In addition, many companies allow an "anticipation rate"—that is, a discount calculated to give a normal rate of interest to those customers who miss the cash discount but pay before the final date. Some firms also add a service charge for late payment.

[2] The cash discount allows you to pay $95 rather than $100. If you do not take the discount, you get a 20-day loan, but you pay $5/95 = 5.26$ percent more for your goods. There are $365/20 = 18.25$ 20-day periods in a year. A dollar invested for 18.25 periods at 5.26 percent per period grows to $(1.0526)^{18.25} = \$2.55$, a 155 percent return on the original investment.

[3] Terms of 8/10, prox., net 60 would entitle the customer to a discount if the bill was paid within 10 days of the end of the following (or "proximo") month.

If an order is very large and there is no complicating cash discount, the customer may be asked to sign a **promissory note.** This is just a straightforward IOU, worded along the following lines:

New York
April 1, 1988

Sixty days after date I promise to pay to the order of the XYZ Company one thousand dollars ($1000.00) for value received.

Signature

Such an arrangement is not common, but it has two advantages. First, as long as it is payable to "order" or to "bearer," the holder may sell this note or use it as security for a loan. Second, the note eliminates the possibility of any subsequent disputes about the existence of the debt; the customer knows that he or she may be sued immediately for failure to pay on the due date.

If you want a clear commitment from the buyer, it is more useful to have it *before* you deliver the goods. In this case the simplest procedure is to arrange a **commercial draft.**[4] It works as follows. The seller draws a draft ordering payment by the customer and sends this draft to the customer's bank together with the shipping documents. If immediate payment is required, the draft is termed a **sight draft;** otherwise it is known as a **time draft.** Depending on whether it is a sight or a time draft, the customer either pays up or acknowledges the debt by adding the word *accepted* and his or her signature. The bank then hands the shipping documents to the customer and forwards the money or the **trade acceptance** to the seller.[5] The latter may hold the trade acceptance to maturity or may use it as security for a loan.

If the customer's credit is for any reason suspect, the seller may ask the customer to arrange for his or her bank to accept the time draft. In this case, the bank guarantees the customer's debt. These **bank acceptances** are often used in overseas trade; they have a higher standing and greater negotiability than trade acceptances.

The exporter who requires greater certainty of payment can ask the customer to arrange for an **irrevocable letter of credit.** In this case the customer's bank sends the exporter a letter stating that it has established a credit in his favor at a bank in the United States. The exporter then draws a draft on the customer's bank and presents it to the bank in the United States together with the letter of credit and the shipping documents. The bank in the United States arranges for this draft to be accepted or paid and forwards the documents to the customer's bank.

If you sell goods to a customer who proves unable to pay, you cannot get your goods back. You simply become a general creditor of the company, in common with other unfortunates. You can avoid this situation by making a *conditional sale,* so that title to the goods remains with the seller until full payment is made. The conditional sale is common practice in Europe. In the United States it is used only for goods that are bought on an installment basis. In this case, if the customer fails to make the agreed number of payments, then the equipment can be immediately repossessed by the seller.

---

[4] Commercial drafts are sometimes known by the more general term *bills of exchange.*

[5] You often see the terms of sale defined as SD-BL. This means that the bank will hand over the bill of lading in return for payment on a sight draft.

30-3 CREDIT ANALYSIS

Firms are not allowed to discriminate between customers by charging them different prices. Neither may they discriminate by offering the same prices but different credit terms.[6] You *can* offer different terms of sale to different *classes* of buyer. You can offer volume discounts, for example, or discounts to customers willing to accept long-term purchase contracts. But as a rule, if you have a customer of doubtful standing, you keep to your regular terms of sale for that customer class. You protect yourself by restricting the volume of goods that the customer may buy on credit.

There are a number of ways in which you can find out whether customers are likely to pay their debts. The most obvious indication is whether they have paid promptly in the past. Prompt payment is generally a good omen; but beware of the customer who establishes a high credit limit on the basis of a series of small payments and then disappears, leaving you with a large unpaid bill.

If you are dealing with a new customer, you will probably check with a credit agency. Dun and Bradstreet is by far the largest of these agencies: Its regular *Reference Book* provides credit ratings on nearly 3 million domestic and foreign firms. Figure 30-1 tells you how to interpret these ratings. In addition to its rating service, Dun and Bradstreet provides on request a full credit report on a potential customer.

Credit agencies usually report the experience that other firms have had with your customer. You can also get this information by contacting the firms directly or through a credit bureau. The Credit Interchange Service of the National Association of Credit Management provides a clearinghouse for such information.

Your bank can also make a credit check. It will contact the customer's bank and ask for information on the customer's average bank balance, access to bank credit, and general reputation.

In addition to checking with your customer's bank, it might make sense to check what everybody else in the financial community thinks about your customer's credit standing. Does that sound expensive? Not if your customer is a public company. You just look at the Moody's or Standard and Poor's rating for the customer's outstanding bonds.[7] You can also compare prices of these bonds to prices of other firms' bonds. (Of course the comparisons should be between bonds of similar maturity, coupon, etc.) Finally, you can look at how the customer's stock price has been behaving recently. A sharp fall in price doesn't mean that the company is in trouble, but it does suggest that prospects are less bright than formerly.

Financial Ratio Analysis

We have suggested a number of ways to check whether your customer is a good risk. You can ask your collection manager, a specialized credit agency, a credit bureau, a banker, or the financial community at large. But, if you don't like relying on the judgment of others, you can do your own homework. Ideally this would involve a detailed analysis of the company's business prospects and financing, but this is usually too expensive. Therefore credit analysts concentrate on the company's financial statements, using rough rules of thumb to judge whether the firm is a good credit risk. The rules of thumb are based on *financial ratios*. Chapter 27 described how these ratios are calculated and interpreted.

---

[6] Price discrimination, and by implication credit discrimination, is prohibited by the Robinson-Patman Act.

[7] See Section 23-4.

FIGURE 30-1
Key to Dun and Bradstreet ratings.

KEY TO RATINGS					
Estimated Financial Strength		Composite Credit Appraisal			
		Good	High	Fair	Limited
5A	$50,000,000 and over	1	2	3	4
4A	$10,000,000 to 49,999,999	1	2	3	4
3A	1,000,000 to 9,999,999	1	2	3	4
2A	750,000 to 999,999	1	2	3	4
1A	500,000 to 749,999	1	2	3	4
BA	300,000 to 499,999	1	2	3	4
BB	200,000 to 299,999	1	2	3	4
CB	125,000 to 199,999	1	2	3	4
CC	75,000 to 124,999	1	2	3	4
DC	50,000 to 74,000	1	2	3	4
DD	35,000 to 49,999	1	2	3	4
EE	20,000 to 34,999	1	2	3	4
FF	10,000 to 19,999	1	2	3	4
GG	5,000 to 9,999	1	2	3	4
HH	Up to 4,999	1	2	3	4

General Classification

Estimated Financial Strength		Composite Credit Appraisal		
		Good	Fair	Limited
1R	$125,000 and over	2	3	4
2R	$50,000 to $124,999	2	3	4

Explanation

When the designation "1R" or "2R" appears, followed by a 2, 3 or 4, it is an indication that the Estimated Financial Strength, while not definitely classified, is presumed to be in the range of the ($) figures in the corresponding bracket, and while the Composite Credit Appraisal cannot be judged precisely, it is believed to fall in the general category indicated.

"INV." shown in place of a rating indicates that the report was under investigation at the time of going to press. It has no other significance.

"FB" (Foreign Branch). Indicates that the headquarters of this company is located in a foreign country (including Canada). The written report contains the location of the headquarters.

Absence of Rating, expressed by two hyphens (--), is not to be construed as unfavorable but signifies circumstances difficult to classify within condensed rating symbols. It suggests the advisability of obtaining a report for additional information.

Employee Range Designations in Reports on Names
not Listed in the Reference Book

Certain businesses do not lend themselves to a Dun and Bradstreet rating and are not listed in the Reference Book. Information on these names, however, continues to be stored and updated in the D & B Business Information File. Reports are available on such businesses and instead of a rating they carry an Employee Range Designation (ER) which is indicative of size in terms of number of employees. No other significance should be attached.

Key to Employee Range Designations		
ER1	1000 or more	Employees
ER2	500-999	Employees
ER3	100-499	Employees
ER4	50- 99	Employees
ER5	20- 49	Employees
ER6	10- 19	Employees
ER7	5- 9	Employees
ER8	1- 4	Employees
ERN		Not Available

Numerical Credit Scoring

Analyzing credit risks is like police detective work. You have a lot of clues—some important, some minor, some fitting into a neat pattern, others contradictory. You must weigh these clues to come up with an overall judgment.

In a small village the local police officer can generally rely on experience and knowledge of the locality. Personal judgment is everything. In a large city the police force cannot operate like this. It needs a systematic way to gather and sort all the information that comes into police headquarters. Likewise, when the firm has a small, regular clientele, the credit manager can easily handle the investigation process informally. But when the company is dealing directly with consumers or with a large number of small trade accounts, some streamlining is essential. In these cases it may make sense to use a mechanical scoring system to prescreen credit applications.

One typical medium-sized bank required each loan applicant to answer a standard questionnaire, of which a condensed version is shown in Table 30-1.[8] It found that in total only 1.2 percent of these loans subsequently defaulted. Some categories of borrower, however, proved to be much worse credit risks than others. We have added the actual default rates for each category in the right-hand margin of Table 30-1. For example, you can see that 7.0 percent of the borrowers who had no telephone subsequently defaulted. Similarly, borrowers who lived in rented rooms, had no bank account, needed the loan to pay medical bills, and so on, were much worse credit risks than the average.

Given this experience, it might make sense for the bank to calculate an overall risk index for each applicant.[9] For example, it could construct a rough-and-ready index simply by adding up all the probabilities in Table 30-1. The wretch who gave the most unfavorable response to each question would have a risk index of

$$7.0 + 7.3 + 2.6 + \cdots + 2.6 = 51.8$$

As if he (or she) didn't have enough troubles!

Constructing Better Risk Indexes

Many lenders that use credit scoring systems employ ad hoc formulas. You should be able to do better than this.

Just adding up the separate probabilities, as in our bank example, isn't the answer, for it ignores the interactions between the different factors. It may be much more alarming when single applicants have a family of eight than when married ones do. On the other hand, you may not be so concerned when single applicants live in a rented room (unless, of course, they also have a family of eight).

Suppose that you take just two factors—time spent in last residence and time spent in last job. You then plot a scatter diagram like Figure 30-2. The x's represent customers that subsequently paid their debts; the o's represent customers that defaulted. Now try to draw a straight dividing line between the two groups. You can't wholly separate them but the line in our diagram keeps the two groups as far apart as possible. (Note that there are only three x's below the line and three o's above it.) This line tells us that, if we wish to *discriminate* between the good and bad risks, we should give only half as much weight to job stability as we give to home stability. The index of creditworthiness is

$$\text{Index of creditworthiness} = Z = 2 \text{ (months in last residence)}$$

$$+ 1 \text{ (months in last job)}$$

You minimize the degree of misclassification if you predict that applicants with Z scores over 60 will pay their bills and that those with Z scores below 60 will not pay.[10]

---

[8] See P. F. Smith, "Measuring Risk on Consumer Installment Credit," *Management Science,* **11:** 327–340 (November 1964).

[9] There are some measures you *cannot* use in calculating this risk index or in any other credit evaluation: the applicant's sex or race, for example.

[10] The quantity 60 is an arbitrary constant. We could just as well have used 6. In that case the Z score is

$$Z = .2 \text{ (months in last residence)} + .1 \text{ (months in last job)}$$

TABLE 30-1
A condensed version of a questionnaire used by a bank for personal loan applicants. We have added in parentheses the percentage of borrowers in each category who subsequently defaulted.

1. Do you have:	
1 or more telephones?	(.7)
No telephone?	(7.0)
2. Do you:	
Own your home?	(.7)
Rent a house?	(2.2)
Rent an apartment?	(3.3)
Rent a room?	(7.3)
3. Do you:	
Have 1 or more bank accounts?	(.8)
No bank account?	(2.6)
4. Is the purpose of the loan:	
To buy an automobile?	(.8)
To buy household goods?	(.6)
To pay medical expenses?	(2.5)
Other?	(1.3)
5. How long did you spend in your last residence:	
6 months or less?	(3.1)
7 to 60 months?	(1.4)
More than 60 months?	(.8)
6. How long did you spend in your last job?	
6 months?	(3.2)
7 to 60 months?	(1.5)
More than 60 months?	(.9)
7. What is your marital status:	
Single?	(1.6)
Married?	(1.0)
Divorced?	(2.9)
8. What is your postal zone?	(.1 to 11.4)
9. For how long do you require the loan:	
12 months or less?	(1.6)
More than 12 months?	(1.0)
10. What is your occupation?	(.4 to 3.5)
11. What is your monthly income:	
$200 or less?	(2.3)
$200 to $1000?	(1.1)
More than $1000?	(.7)
12. What is your age:	
25 or under?	(1.5)
26 to 30?	(1.8)
More than 30?	(1.0)
13. How many are there in your family:	
One?	(1.6)
Two to seven?	(1.1)
Eight or more?	(2.6)

Source: Reprinted by permission from P. F. Smith, "Measuring Risk on Consumer Installment Credit," *Management Science,* **11:** 327–340 (November 1964), Copyright 1964 The Institute of Management Science.

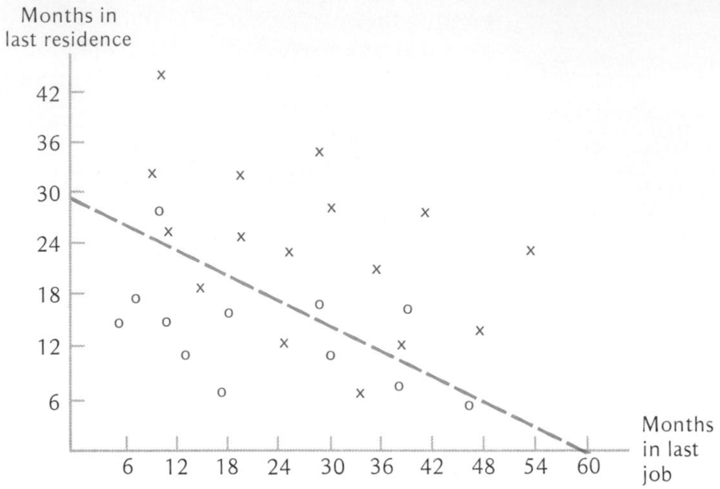

FIGURE 30-2
The x's represent a hypothetical group of
bank borrowers that subsequently repaid
their loans; the o's represent those that
defaulted. The sloping line discriminates
between the two groups on the basis of
time spent in last home and time spent in
last job. The line represents the equation
Z = 2 (months in last residence)
+ 1 (months in last job) = 60.
Borrowers who plot above the line have
"Z scores" greater than 60.

In practice we do not need to confine our attention to just two variables nor
do we need to estimate the equation by eye. Multiple discriminant analysis (MDA)
is a straightforward statistical technique for calculating how much weight to put
on each variable in order to separate the sheep from the goats.[11]

Edward Altman has used MDA to predict bad business risks. Altman's object
was to see how well financial ratios could be used to distinguish which firms would
go bankrupt during the period 1946–1965. MDA gave him the following index of
creditworthiness:[12]

$$Z = 3.3 \frac{\text{EBIT}}{\text{total assets}} + 1.0 \frac{\text{sales}}{\text{total assets}} + .6 \frac{\text{market value equity}}{\text{book value of debt}}$$

$$+ 1.4 \frac{\text{retained earings}}{\text{total assets}} + 1.2 \frac{\text{working capital}}{\text{total assets}}$$

This equation did a good job at distinguishing the bankrupt and nonbankrupt firms.
Of the former, 94 percent had Z scores of *less* than 2.7 the year before they went
bankrupt. In contrast 97 percent of the nonbankrupt firms had Z scores *above* this
level.[13]

Credit scoring systems should carry a health warning. When you construct a
risk index, it is tempting to experiment with many different combinations of variables until you find the equation that would have worked best in the past. Unfortunately, if you "mine" the data in this way, you are likely to find that the
system works less well in the future than it did previously. If you are misled by
these past successes into placing too much faith in your model, you may refuse

---

[11] MDA is not the only statistical technique that you can use for this purpose. Probit and logit are two
other potentially very useful techniques.

[12] EBIT is earnings before interest and taxes. E. I. Altman, "Financial Ratios, Discriminant Analysis
and the Prediction of Corporate Bankruptcy," *Journal of Finance,* **23:** 589–609 (September 1968).

[13] This equation was fitted with hindsight. The equation did slightly less well when used to *predict*
bankruptcies after 1965.

credit to a number of potentially good customers. The profits that you lose by turning away customers could more than offset the gains that you make from avoiding a few bad eggs. As a result you could be worse off than if you had pretended that you could not tell one customer from another and extended credit to all of them.

Does this mean that you should not use credit scoring systems? Not a bit. It simply implies that it is not sufficient to have a good credit scoring system; you also need to know how much to rely on it. That is the topic of the next section.

30-4 THE CREDIT DECISION

Let us suppose that you have taken the first three steps toward an effective credit operation. In other words, you have fixed your terms of sale; you have decided whether to sell on open account or to ask your customers to sign an IOU; and you have established a procedure for estimating the probability that each customer will pay up. Your next step is to work out which of those customers should be offered credit.

If there is no possibility of repeat orders, the decision is relatively simple. Figure 30-3 summarizes your choice. On the one hand, you can refuse credit. In this case you make neither a profit nor a loss. The alternative is to offer credit. Suppose that the probability that the customer will pay up is p. If the customer does pay, you receive additional revenues (REV) and you incur additional costs; your net gain is the present value of REV $-$ COST. Unfortunately, you can't be certain that the customer will pay; there is a probability $(1 - p)$ of default. Default means you receive nothing and incur the additional costs. The *expected* profit from the two courses of action is therefore as follows:

	Expected Profit
Refuse credit	0
Grant credit	p PV(REV $-$ COST) $- (1 - p)$ PV(COST)

You should grant credit if the expected profit from doing so is greater than the expected profit from refusing.

FIGURE 30-3
If you refuse credit, you make neither profit nor loss. If you offer credit, there is a probability p that the customer will pay and you will make REV $-$ COST; there is a probability $(1 - p)$ that the customer will default and you will lose COST.

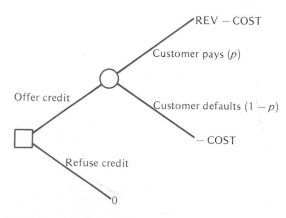

Consider for example the case of the Cast Iron Company. On each nondelinquent sale Cast Iron receives revenues with a present value of $1200 and incurs costs with a value of $1000. Therefore the company's expected profit if it offers credit is

$$p \text{ PV(REV} - \text{COST)} - (1 - p) \text{ PV(COST)} = p \times 200 - (1 - p) \times 1000$$

If the probability of collection is $\frac{5}{6}$, Cast Iron can expect to break even:

$$\text{Expected profit} = \frac{5}{6} \times 200 - \left(1 - \frac{5}{6}\right) \times 1000 = 0$$

Therefore Cast Iron's policy should be to grant credit whenever the chances of collection are better than 5 out of 6.

*When to Stop Looking for Clues

We told you earlier where to *start* looking for clues about a customer's creditworthiness, but we never said anything about when to *stop*. Now we can work out how your profits would be affected by more detailed credit analysis.

Suppose that Cast Iron Company's credit department undertakes a study to determine which customers are most likely to default. It appears that 95 percent of its customers have been prompt payers and 5 percent have been slow payers. On the other hand, customers with a record of slow payment are much more likely to default on the next order than those with a record of prompt payment. On the average 20 percent of the slow payers subsequently default but only 2 percent of the prompt payers do so.

In other words, consider a sample of 1000 customers, none of which has defaulted yet. Of these 950 have a record of prompt payment and 50 have a record of slow payment. On the basis of past experience Cast Iron should expect 19 of the prompt payers to default in the future and 10 of the slow payers to do so:

Category	Number of Customers	Probability of Default	Expected Number of Defaults
Prompt payers	950	.02	19
Slow payers	50	.20	10
All customers	1000	.029	29

Now the credit manager faces the following decision: Should the company refuse to give any more credit to customers that have been slow payers in the past?

If you are aware that a customer has been a slow payer, the answer is clearly "yes." Every sale to slow payers has only an 80 percent chance of payment ($p = .8$). Selling to a *slow* payer, therefore, gives an expected *loss* of $40:

$$\text{Expected profit} = p\text{PV(REV} - \text{COST)} - (1 - p)\text{PV(COST)}$$

$$= .8(200) - .2(1000) = -\$40$$

But suppose that it costs $10 to search through Cast Iron's records to determine whether a customer has been a prompt or slow payer. Is it worth doing so? The expected payoff to such a check is

$$\text{Expected payoff to credit check} = \text{probability of identifying a slow payer}$$

$$\times \text{ gain from not extending credit}$$

$$- \text{ cost of credit check}$$

$$= (.05 \times 40) - 10 = -\$8$$

In this case checking isn't worth it. You are paying $10 to avoid a $40 loss 5 percent of the time. But suppose that customer orders 10 units at once. Then checking is worthwhile because you are paying $10 to avoid a *$400* loss 5 percent of the time:

$$\text{Expected payoff to credit check} = (.05 \times 400) - 10 = \$10$$

The credit manager therefore decides to check customers' past payment records only on orders of more than five units. You can verify that a credit check on a five-unit order just pays for itself.

Our illustration is simplistic, but you have probably grasped the message. You don't want to subject each order to the same credit analysis. You want to concentrate your efforts on the large and doubtful orders.

*Credit Decisions with Repeat Orders

So far we have ignored the possibility of repeat orders. But one of the reasons for offering credit today is that you may get yourself a good, regular customer.

Figure 30-4 illustrates the problem.[14] Cast Iron has been asked to extend credit to a new customer. You can find little information on the firm and you believe that the probability of payment is no better than .8. If you grant credit, the expected profit on this order is

$$\text{Expected profit on initial order} = p_1 \times \text{PV(REV} - \text{COST)}$$

$$- (1 - p_1) \times \text{PV(COST)}$$

$$= (.8 \times 200) - (.2 \times 1000) = -\$40$$

You decide to refuse credit.

This is the correct decision if there is no chance of a repeat order. But look again at the example shown in the decision tree, Figure 30-4. If the customer does pay up, there will be a reorder next year. Because the customer has paid once, you can be 95 percent sure that he or she will pay again. For this reason any repeat order is very profitable:

$$\text{Next year's expected profit on repeat order} = p_2\text{PV(REV}_2 - \text{COST}_2)$$

$$- (1 - p_2)\text{PV(COST}_2)$$

$$= (.95 \times 200) - (.05 \times 1000)$$

$$= \$140$$

Now you can reexamine today's credit decision. If you grant credit today, you receive the expected profit on the initial order *plus* the possible opportunity to extend credit next year:

[14] Our example is adapted from H. Bierman, Jr. and W. H. Hausman, "The Credit Granting Decision," *Management Science,* **16:** B519–B532 (April 1970).

FIGURE 30-4
In this example there is
only a .8 probability that
your customer will pay in
period 1; but if payment is
made, there will be an-
other order in period 2.
The probability that the
customer will pay for the
second order is .95. The
possibility of this good
repeat order more than
compensates for the ex-
pected loss in period 1.

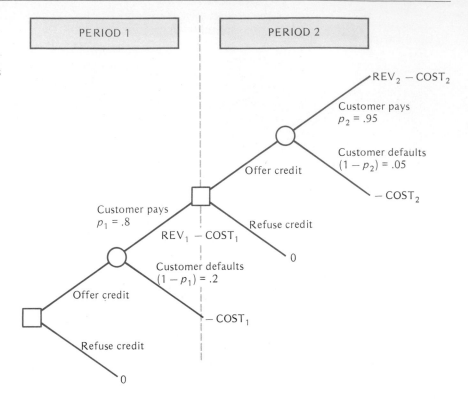

$$\text{Total expected profit} = \text{expected profit on initial order}$$
$$+ \text{ probability of payment and repeat order}$$
$$\times \text{ PV(next year's expected profit on repeat order)}$$
$$= -40 + .80 \times \text{PV}(140)$$

At any reasonable discount rate, you ought to extend credit. For example, if the discount rate is 20 percent,

$$\text{Total expected profit (present value)} = -40 + \frac{.8(140)}{1.2} = \$53.33$$

In this example you should grant credit even though you expect to make a loss on the order. The expected loss is more than outweighed by the possibility that you will secure a reliable and regular customer.

**Some General
Principles**

Sometimes the credit manager faces clear-cut choices. In these circumstances it may be possible to estimate fairly precisely the consequences of a more liberal or a more stringent credit policy. But real-life situations are generally far more complex than our simple examples. Customers are not all good or bad. Many of them pay consistently late; you get your money, but it costs more to collect and you lose a few months' interest. Then there is the question of risk. You may be able to measure the revenues and costs, but at what rate do you discount them?

Like almost all financial decisions, credit allocation involves a strong dose of judgment. Our examples are intended as reminders of the issues involved rather than as cookbook formulas. Here are the basic things to remember.

1. *Maximize Profit:* As credit manager your job is not to minimize the number of bad accounts; it is to maximize expected profit. You must, therefore, recognize that you are concerned with a trade-off. The best that can happen is that the customer pays promptly; the worst is default. In the one case the firm receives the full additional revenues from the sale less the additional costs; in the other it receives nothing and loses the costs. You must weigh the chances of these alternative outcomes. If the margin of profit is high, you are justified in a liberal credit policy; if it is low, you cannot afford many bad debts.

2. *Concentrate on the Dangerous Accounts:* You should not expend the same effort on analyzing all credit applications. If an application is small or clear-cut, your decision should be largely routine; if it is large or doubtful, you may do better to move straight to a detailed credit appraisal. Most credit managers don't make credit decisions on an order-by-order basis. Instead they set a credit limit for each customer. The sales representative is required to refer the order for approval only if the customer exceeds this limit.

3. *Look beyond the Immediate Order:* The credit decision is a dynamic problem. You cannot look only at the immediate future. Sometimes it may be worth accepting a relatively poor risk as long as there is a likelihood that the customer will grow into a regular and reliable buyer. New businesses must, therefore, be prepared to incur more bad debts than established businesses. This is part of the cost of building up a good customer list.

30-5 COLLECTION POLICY

It would be nice if all customers paid their bills by the due date. But they don't, and, since you may also occasionally "stretch" your payables, you can't altogether blame them.

The credit manager keeps a record of payment experiences with each customer. The manager knows that company A always takes the discount and that company Z is generally slow 90 days. In addition the manager monitors overdue payments by drawing up a schedule of the aging of receivables. This may look roughly like Table 30-2.

TABLE 30-2
An aging schedule of receivables (figures in dollars)

Customer's Name	Amount Not Yet Due	1 Month Overdue	2 Months Overdue	More Than 2 Months Overdue	Total Owed
A	10,000	—	—	—	10,000
.	.	;	.	.	.
.	.	.	.	.	.
.	.	.	.	.	.
Z	5,000	4,000	6,000	15,000	30,000
Total	200,000	40,000	15,000	43,000	265,000

When a customer is in arrears, the usual procedure is to send a statement of account and to follow this at intervals with increasingly insistent letters, telephone calls, or cables. If none of these has any effect, most companies turn the debt over to a collection agency or an attorney. The fee for such services is usually between 15 and 40 percent of the amount collected. An insolvent customer may seek relief by petitioning for bankruptcy. In the appendix to this chapter we describe what happens when an individual or firm files for bankruptcy.

There is always a potential conflict of interest between the collection department and the sales department. Sales representatives commonly complain that they no sooner win new customers than the collection department frightens them off with threatening letters. The collection manager, on the other hand, bemoans the fact that the sales force is concerned only with winning orders and does not care whether the goods are subsequently paid for.

Factoring and Credit Insurance

The large firm has some advantages in managing its accounts receivable. First, it may be possible for divisions to pool information on the creditworthiness of their customers. Second, there are potential economies of scale in record keeping, billing, etc., especially if the process can be computerized. Third, debt collection is a specialized business that calls for experience and judgment. The small firm may not be able to hire or train a specialized credit manager. However, it may be able to obtain some of these economies by farming part of the job out to a **factor.**

Factoring works as follows. The factor and the client agree on credit limits for each customer and on the average collection period. The client then notifies each customer that the factor has purchased the debt. Thereafter, for any sale the client sends a copy of the invoice to the factor, the customer makes payment directly to the factor, and the factor pays the client on the basis of the agreed average collection period regardless of whether the customer has paid. There are, of course, costs to such an operation, and the factor typically charges a fee of 1 to 2 percent of the value of the invoice.[15]

This factoring arrangement provides assistance with collection and insurance against bad debts. It is known as *maturity factoring.* In addition to these services, the factor is generally also willing to advance 70 to 80 percent of the value of the accounts at an interest cost of 2 or 3 percent above the prime rate. Factoring that provides collection, insurance, and finance is generally termed *old-line factoring.*[16]

If you don't want help with collection but do want protection against bad debts, you can obtain credit insurance. The credit insurance company obviously wants to be certain that you do not throw caution to the winds by extending boundless credit to the most speculative accounts. It therefore generally imposes a maximum amount that it will cover for accounts with a particular credit rating. Thus it may agree to insure up to a total of $100,000 of sales to customers with the highest Dun and Bradsteet rating, up to $50,000 to those with the next highest rating, and so on. You may claim not only if the customer actually becomes insolvent but also if an account is overdue. Such a delinquent account is then turned over to the insurance company which makes vigorous efforts to collect.

---

[15] Many factors are subsidiaries of commercial banks. Their typical client is a relatively small manufacturing company selling on a repetitive basis to a large number of industrial or retail customers. Factoring is particularly common in the clothing industry.

[16] Under an arrangement known as *with-recourse factoring,* the company is liable for any delinquent accounts. In this case the factor provides collection, but not insurance.

In 1962 the United States government encouraged a group of insurance companies to form a consortium known as the *Foreign Credit Insurance Association* (FCIA). The FCIA now accounts for the bulk of short-term and medium-term insurance of export credits. You will find that banks are much more willing to lend against receivables that are insured with the FCIA.

30-6 SUMMARY

Credit management involves five steps. The first task is to establish normal terms of sale. This means that you must decide the length of the payment period and the size of any cash discounts. In most industries these conditions are standardized.

Your second step is to decide the form of the contract with your customer. Most domestic sales are made on open account. In this case the only evidence that the customer owes you money is the entry in your ledger and a receipt signed by the customer. Particularly if the customer is foreign, you may require a more formal contract. We looked at three such devices—the promissory note, the trade acceptance, and the letter of credit.

The third task is to assess each customer's creditworthiness. There is a variety of sources of information—your own experience with the customer, the experience of other creditors, the assessment of a credit agency, a check with the customer's bank, the market value of the customer's securities, and an analysis of the customer's financial statements. Firms that handle a large volume of credit information often use a formal system for combining the various sources into an overall credit score. These numerical scoring systems help to separate the borderline cases from the obvious sheep or goats. We showed how you can use statistical techniques such as multiple discriminant analysis to give an efficient measure of default risk.

When you have made an assessment of the customer's credit standing, you can establish sensible credit limits. The job of the credit manager is not to minimize the number of bad debts; it is to maximize profits. This means that you should increase the customer's credit limit as long as the probability of payment times the expected profit is greater than the probability of default times the cost of the goods. Remember not to be too shortsighted in reckoning the expected profit. It is often worth accepting the marginal applicant if there is a chance the applicant may grow into a regular and reliable customer.

Finally, you must *collect*. This requires tact and judgment. You want to be firm with the truly delinquent customer, but you don't want to offend the good one by writing demanding letters just because a check has been delayed in the mail. You will find it easier to spot troublesome acounts if you keep a careful record of the aging of receivables.

These five steps are interrelated. For example, you can afford more liberal terms of sale if you are very careful about to whom you grant credit. You can accept higher-risk customers if you are very active in pursuing any late payers. A good credit policy is one that adds up to a sensible whole.

APPENDIX   BANKRUPTCY PROCEDURES

We are sure that nobody who reads this book is likely to go bankrupt. But you may still have occasion to deal with individuals or companies that are bankrupt. In this appendix we outline the procedures involved in bankruptcy.

**Personal
Bankruptcies**

Each year about 200,000 individuals file for bankruptcy. Their debts are usually small. William Zeckendorf listed personal liabilities of $79 million, but the typical figure is only about $20,000.

If a debtor defaults, the creditor may bring suit in a state court; state law offers a variety of remedies. If the debt is secured, the creditor may repossess the article and sell it. In most states the creditor may also seek a "garnishment" order, under which a deduction is made from the debtor's wages and assigned to the creditor.

Garnishment is a powerful inducement for debtors to seek some alternative solution to their difficulties. One simple and effective state-sanctioned technique is for a debtor to reach an informal agreement with the creditors. For example, the creditors may be willing to extend the payment period, or they may accept a partial payment to settle the debt.

A few states have provided for a formal payoff process that requires the debtor to send his or her wages to a trustee appointed by the local court. In other cases debts may be pooled and part of the debtor's income paid to an agent who prorates it among the creditors. Since debt pooling has been subject to considerable abuse, it is prohibited in many states.

Instead of seeking redress in the state courts, the debtor can rely on the federal bankruptcy system. The principal basis for this system is the Bankruptcy Reform Act of 1978, which extensively revised the earlier law embodied in the Bankruptcy Act of 1898 and the Chandler Act of 1938.

An individual may either file a petition for straight bankruptcy (under Chapter 7) or seek relief under Chapters 11 or 13 of the act. Since about 85 percent of individuals choose the first solution, we will look at it first.

If a debtor has committed certain "acts of bankruptcy," such as the written admission of bankruptcy or the concealment of property, the creditors can file to have him or her judged bankrupt. However, about 99 percent of straight bankruptcy petitions are voluntary. In such cases the debtor is automatically declared a bankrupt and any other proceedings against the debtor or his or her property are halted. The task of liquidating the debtor's assets then begins. Usually the bankruptcy judge calls a meeting of creditors to examine the bankrupt person and to elect a trustee who will sell off his or her assets and distribute the proceeds. On rare occasions the judge will appoint a receiver to protect the creditors' interests until the trustee can start work.

Since one of the goals of bankruptcy law is to give the debtor a fresh start, some of the debtor's property is protected.[17] For example, under California law the debtor's house is protected almost regardless of its magnificence, and in Alaska the debtor can keep, among other things, two reindeer or six dogs. Debtors can also choose to protect their assets under federal law which allows the debtor to keep, for example, $7500 equity in a home, $1200 in a motor vehicle, and $750 in books and tools used in the debtor's profession. Naturally the debtor will choose the federal list of exempt assets if it is more generous than the applicable state list.[18]

---

[17] The debtor is also protected from being pressured into reaffirming (agreeing to repay) debts *after* the debts have been discharged by bankruptcy. The Bankruptcy Reform Act of 1978 states that reaffirmations will be endorceable only if the bankruptcy court finds that it will not impose undue hardship and is either in the debtor's best interest or is a result of negotiations undertaken in good faith to settle a dispute about whether a particular debt should be discharged. Before the 1978 act, some creditors harassed bankrupt individuals into reaffirming debts, although the individuals were under no legal obligation to do so.

[18] However, the state can pass a law barring its residents from using the federal exemptions. Florida and Virginia have done so, for example.

Not every debt can be discharged by filing for bankruptcy. For example, you cannot escape liabilities for taxes or alimony. The debtor may be prohibited from discharging any debt if he or she has been through bankruptcy during the last 6 years, committed a crime, or been negligent in preserving adequate records. Also, valid claims against secured property, such as a mortgage on the debtor's house, cannot be escaped. Secured creditors appropriately receive up to the full value of the secured article; and if this is not sufficient to satisfy their claim, the remaining liability is treated as unsecured debt.[19]

Because the bankruptcy system is supposed to pay its way, a percentage of the value of the debtor's assets is paid to the U.S. Treasury and all court officers are paid directly from the "estate"—that is, from the debtor's assets. The trustee is paid a variable fee that depends in part on the size of the estate. Then come taxes. Finally, whatever remains is shared among the general creditors.

In only about 15 percent of straight personal bankruptcy cases are there any assets left after payment of administrative expenses. One survey of bankruptcies estimated that, taking personal and business straight bankruptcies together, creditors on average receive about 6 cents on every dollar. The return differs by class of creditor—secured creditors receive about 25 cents, priority creditors receive 14 cents, and unsecured creditors receive less than 3 cents. In these circumstances it is not surprising that after a personal bankruptcy petition is filed, creditors rarely go to great expense to attend meetings or to press their claims.

Instead of filing a petition for bankruptcy, an individual can opt for a Chapter 13 arrangement.[20] In this case the debtor meets his or her creditors to propose a plan for making repayment. This plan must be approved by a majority of the unsecured creditors and by each secured creditor. If it is also confirmed by the bankruptcy judge, money is collected from the debtor and paid to the creditors by a trustee appointed by the judge. If the repayment plan is successfully completed, the debts are discharged. Creditors' experience has been much more satisfactory in Chapter 13 cases; for example, between 1965 and 1978 they received on average about 93 cents on the dollar.

Business Bankruptcies

Business bankruptcies account for less than 10 percent of the total number of bankruptcies, but they involve about half of the claims by value. Like the individual debtor, the corporation may seek relief under state law. There are several state-sanctioned procedures. For example, the firm may negotiate an *extension*, that is, an agreement with its creditors to delay interest and principal payments. On the other hand, the firm may negotiate a *composition*, in which the firm makes cash payments to its creditors in exchange for being relieved of its debts.

If the business is worth more dead than alive, and therefore should be liquidated, an *assignment* may be arranged. The firm transfers its assets to a trustee, who sells them and distributes the proceeds to the creditors, thus discharging the firm's debts.[21]

These procedures resolve the firm's financial crisis by negotiation. The advantage of doing so is that the costs and delays of formal bankruptcy or reorganization

---

[19] The Bankruptcy Reform Act of 1978 gives the debtor the right to keep secured property if the debtor gives the fair market value of the property to the secured creditor. If this payment is not sufficient to satisfy the creditor's claim, the remainder is treated as an *unsecured* claim on the debtor's asset.

[20] Individuals can also use Chapter 11, described below.

[21] Distribution of the proceeds does not automatically discharge the debts. The creditors have to agree to settle the debts by accepting payments.

are avoided. However, the larger the firm, and the more complicated its capital structure, the less likely it is that a negotiated settlement can be reached. Most large, complicated bankruptcies and reorganizations are handled under federal law.

Under the federal system, the firm is subject to the same statutes as the individual. First, management must decide whether to petition for a straight bankruptcy (liquidation) or to seek to reorganize the firm's liabilities in order to maintain it as a going concern. The former solution—usually voluntary but sometimes involuntary—is adopted in more than 90 percent of the cases. Straight bankruptcy proceedings for businesses are essentially more elaborate versions of those used for individual debtors. Normally in business cases the bankruptcy judge will appoint a receiver, who will then continue to act as trustee. Frequently the receiver will need to seek restraining orders to prevent some creditors from trying to collect before the proceedings are finished or to recover property that a creditor has only recently repossessed.

As in personal bankruptcies, there is a pecking order of unsecured creditors. The U.S. Treasury, court officers, and trustee have first peck. Taxes have next priority, together with debts to some government agencies such as the Small Business Administration and the Pension Benefit Guarantee Corporation. Then wages payable (up to $2000 per employee) come ahead of the other creditors.

Since companies are more likely than individuals to possess valuable assets, creditors fare somewhat better than in personal cases; secured creditors receive about 31 percent of their claims, priority creditors 36 percent, and unsecured creditors 8 percent.

Instead of filing for straight bankruptcy, the company may attempt to rehabilitate the business. This is generally in the shareholders' interests—they have nothing to lose if things deteriorate further and everything to gain if the firm recovers.

Firms attempting reorganization seek refuge under Chapter 11 of the Bankruptcy Reform Act. (A firm may also be forced into Chapter 11 by petition of its creditors to the court.) Chapter 11 is designed to keep the firm alive and operating, and to protect the value of its assets,[22] while a plan of reorganization is worked out. During this period, other proceedings against the firm are halted and the company is operated by existing management as a "debtor in possession" or by a court-appointed trustee.

The responsibility for developing a plan may fall on the debtor firm. If no trustee is appointed, the firm has 120 days to present a plan to creditors. If it meets that deadline, it has 60 days more to get the plan approved. If these deadlines are *not* met, or if a trustee is appointed, anyone can submit a plan—the trustee, for example, or a committee of creditors.

The plan goes into effect if it is accepted by creditors and confirmed by the court. Acceptance requires approval by at least one-half of the creditors voting; also, the creditors voting "aye" must represent two-thirds of the value of creditors' aggregate claim against the firm. The plan must also be approved by two-thirds of the shareholders. Once a plan is accepted, the court normally approves it, provided that each *class* of creditors has approved it and that the creditors will be better off

---

[22] These two goals are sometimes in conflict. For example, in order to keep the firm alive it may be necessary to continue to use assets that had been offered as collateral, but this denies secured creditors access to their collateral. In order to resolve this problem, the Bankruptcy Reform Act makes it possible for firms operating under Chapter 11 to keep such assets as long as the creditors who have a claim on those assets are compensated for any decline in their value. Thus, the firm might make cash payments to the secured creditors to cover economic depreciation of the assets.

under the plan than if the firm's assets were liquidated and distributed. The court may, under certain conditions, confirm a plan even if one or more classes of creditors votes against it,[23] but the rules are in this case complicated, and we will not attempt to cover them here.

The reorganization plan is basically a statement of who gets what; each class of creditors gives up its claim in exchange for new securities. (Sometimes creditors receive cash as well.) The problem is to design a new capital structure for the firm that will (1) satisfy the creditors and (2) allow the firm to solve the *business* problems that got the firm into trouble in the first place. Sometimes satisfying these two requirements requires a plan of baroque complexity. When the Penn Central Corporation was finally reorganized in 1978 (7 years after the largest railroad bankruptcy ever), more than a dozen new securities were created and parceled out among 15 classes of creditors.

The Securities and Exchange Commission (SEC) plays a role in many reorganizations, particularly for large, public companies. The SEC's interest is to ensure that all relevant and material information is disclosed to the creditors before they vote on a proposed plan of reorganization. The SEC may take part in a hearing before court approval of a plan, for example.

| The Choice between Liquidation and Reorganization | Here is a simple view of the bankruptcy decision. Whenever a payment is due to creditors, management checks the value of the equity. If the value is positive, the firm pays the creditors (if necessary raising the cash by an issue of shares). If the equity is valueless, the firm defaults on its debt and petitions for bankruptcy. If the assets of the bankrupt firm can be put to better use elsewhere, the firm is liquidated and the proceeds are used to pay off the creditors. Otherwise, the creditors simply become the new owners and the firm continues to operate.[24] |

In practice, matters are rarely so simple. For example, we observe that firms often petition for bankruptcy even when the equity has a positive value. And firms are often reorganized even when the assets could be used more efficiently elsewhere. Here are some reasons.

1. Although the reorganized firm is legally a new entity, it is entitled to any tax-loss carry-forwards belonging to the old firm. If the firm is liquidated rather than reorganized, any tax-loss carry-forwards disappear. Thus there is an incentive to continue in operation.

2. If the firm's assets are sold off, it is easy to determine what is available to pay the creditors. However, when the company is reorganized, it needs to conserve cash as far as possible. Therefore, claimants are generally paid in a mixture of cash and securities. This makes it less easy to judge whether they receive their entitlement. For example, each bondholder may be offered $300 in cash and $700 in a new bond which pays no interest for the first 2 years and a low rate of interest thereafter. A bond of this kind in a company that is struggling to survive may not be worth much, but the bankruptcy court usually looks at the

---

[23] But at least one class of creditors must vote for the plan—otherwise, the court cannot approve it.

[24] If there are several classes of creditor, the junior creditors initially become the owners of the company and are responsible for paying off the senior debt. They now face exactly the same decision as the original owners. If their equity is valueless, they will also default and turn over ownership of the company to the next class of creditors.

face value of the new bonds and may therefore regard the bondholders as paid off in full.

Senior creditors who know they are likely to get a raw deal in a reorganization are likely to press for a liquidation. Shareholders and junior creditors prefer a reorganization. They hope that the court will not interpret the pecking order too strictly and that they will receive some crumbs.

3. Although shareholders and junior creditors are at the bottom of the pecking order, they have a secret weapon—they can play for time. Bankruptcies often take several years before a plan is presented to the court and agreed to by each class of creditor. (The bankruptcy proceedings of the Missouri Pacific Railroad took a total of 22 years.) When they use delaying tactics, the junior claimants are betting on a stroke of luck that will rescue their investment. On the other hand, the senior claimants know that time is working against them, so they may be prepared to accept a smaller payoff as part of the price for getting a plan accepted.

4. While a reorganization plan is being drawn up, the company is likely to need additional working capital. It is therefore allowed to buy goods on credit and borrow money. Postpetition creditors have priority over the old creditors and their debt may even be secured by assets that are already mortgaged to existing debtholders. This also gives the prepetition creditors an incentive to settle quickly, before their claim on assets is diluted by the new debt.

5. Sometimes profitable companies have filed for Chapter 11 bankruptcy to protect themselves against "burdensome" suits.[25] For example, Continental Airlines, which was bedeviled by a costly labor contract, filed for Chapter 11 in 1982 and immediately cut pay by up to 50 percent. In 1983 Manville Corp. was threatened by 16,000 damage suits alleging injury from asbestos. Manville filed for bankruptcy under Chapter 11, and the bankruptcy judge agreed to stay the damage suits. Needless to say, lawyers and legislators worry that these actions were contrary to the original intent of the bankruptcy acts.

FURTHER READING

Two of the standard texts on the practice and institutional background of credit management are:

T. N. Beckman and R. S. Foster: *Credits and Collections: Management and Theory,* 8th ed., McGraw-Hill Book Company, New York 1969.

R. H. Cole: *Consumer and Commercial Credit Management,* 4th ed., Richard D. Irwin, Inc., Homewood, Ill., 1972.

Much more analytical discussions of the credit granting decision are contained in:

H. Bierman, Jr., and W. H. Hausman: "The Credit Granting Decision," *Management Science,* **16:** B519–B532 (April 1970).

D. R. Mehta: *Working Capital Management,* Prentice-Hall, Inc., Englewood Cliffs, N.J., 1974.

Smith's and Altman's papers are both concerned with the problem of numerical credit scoring. Smith's interest, however, is with predicting default on personal loans, where Altman is interested in corporate failure.

P. F. Smith: "Measuring Risk on Consumer Installment Credit," *Management Science,* **11:** 327–340 (November 1964).

---

[25] See, for example, A. Cifelli, "Management by Bankruptcy," *Fortune,* October 1983, pp. 69–73.

E. I. Altman: "Financial Ratios, Discriminant Analysis and the Prediction of Corporate Bankruptcy," *Journal of Finance,* **23:** 589–609 (September 1968).

Altman's book provides a general survey of the bankruptcy decision. The other three studies listed below are principally concerned with an analysis of the conflicting interests of different security holders.

E. A. Altman: *Corporate Financial Distress: A Complete Guide to Predicting, Avoiding and Dealing with Bankruptcy,* John Wiley and Sons, New York, 1983.

J. I. Bulow and J. B. Shoven: "The Bankruptcy Decision," *Bell Journal of Economics and Management Science,* **9:** 437–457 (Autumn 1978).

M. White: "Bankruptcy and Reorganization: Economic and Public Policy Considerations," Summer Institute Paper No. 80–14, National Bureau of Economic Research, December 1980.

J. B. Warner: "Bankruptcy, Absolute Priority, and the Pricing of Risky Debt Claims," *Journal of Financial Economics,* **4:** 239–276 (May 1977).

QUIZ

1. Company X sells on a 1/30, net 60, basis. Customer Y buys goods with an invoice of $1000.
   (a) How much can Y deduct from the bill if he or she pays on day 30?
   (b) What is the effective annual rate of interest if Y pays on the due date rather than day 30?
   (c) Indicate if you would expect X to require shorter or longer payment if each of the following were true:
       (i) The goods are perishable.
       (ii) The goods are not rapidly resold.
       (iii) The goods are sold to high-risk firms.

2. The lag between purchase date and the date at which payment is due is known as the "terms lag." The lag between the due date and the date on which the buyer actually pays is termed the "due lag," and the lag between the purchase and actual payment dates is the "pay lag." Thus,

$$\text{Pay lag} = \text{terms lag} + \text{due lag}$$

State how you would expect the following events to affect each type of lag.
   (a) The company imposes a service charge on late payers.
   (b) A recession causes customers to be short of cash.
   (c) The company changes its terms from net 10 to net 20.

3. Complete the following passage by selecting the appropriate terms from the following list (some terms may be used more than once): *acceptance, open, commercial, trade, the United States, his or her own, note, draft, account, promissory, bank, the customer's, letter of credit, shipping documents.*

Most goods are sold on _____ _____ . In this case the only evidence of the debt is a record in the seller's books and a signed receipt. When the order is very large, the customer may be asked to sign a _____ _____ , which is just a simple IOU. An alternative is for the seller to arrange a _____ _____ ordering payment by the customer. In order to obtain the _____ _____ , the customer must acknowledge this order and sign the document. This signed acknowledgement is known as a _____ _____ . Sometimes the seller may also ask _____ _____ bank to sign the document. In this case it is known as a _____ _____ . The fourth form of contract is used principally in overseas trade. The customer's bank sends the exporter a _____ _____ _____ stating that it has established a credit in his or her favor at a bank in the United States. The exporter than draws a draft on _____ _____ bank and presents it to _____ _____ bank together with the _____ _____ _____ and _____ _____ . The bank then arranges for this draft to be accepted and forwards the _____ _____ to the customer's bank.

4. The Branding Iron Company sells its irons for $50 apiece wholesale. Production cost is $40 per iron. There is a 25 percent chance that wholesaler Q will go bankrupt within the next year. Q orders 1000 irons and asks for 6 months' credit. Should you accept the order? Assume a 10 percent per year discount rate, no chance of a repeat order, and that Q will pay either in full or not at all:

*5. Look back at Section 30-4. Cast Iron's costs have increased from $1000 to $1050. Assuming there is no possibility of repeat orders, answer the following:
   (a) When should Cast Iron grant or refuse credit?
   (b) If it costs $12 to determine whether a customer has been a prompt or slow payer in the past, when should Cast Iron undertake such a check?

*6. Look back at the discussion in Section 30-4 of credit decisions with repeat orders. If $p_1 = .8$, what is the minimum level of p_2 at which Cast Iron is justified in extending credit?

7. True or false?
   (a) Exporters who require greater certainty of payment arrange for the customers to sign a bill of lading in exchange for a sight draft.
   (b) Multiple discriminant analysis is often used to construct an index of creditworthiness. This index is generally called a "Z score."
   (c) It makes sense to monitor the credit manager's performance by looking at the proportion of bad debts.
   (d) If a customer refuses to pay despite repeated reminders, the company will usually turn the debt over to a factor or an attorney.
   (e) The Foreign Credit Insurance Association insures export credits.

8. (This question refers to the Appendix.) True or false?
   (a) Individuals may file for straight bankruptcy (under Chapter 7) or opt for a Chapter 13 arrangement. In the latter case, a repayment plan is drawn up and approved by the creditors.
   (b) When a company becomes bankrupt, it is usually in the interests of the equityholders to seek a liquidation rather than a reorganization.
   (c) A reorganization plan must be presented for approval by each class of creditor.
   (d) The Internal Revenue Service has first claim on the company's assets in the event of bankruptcy.
   (e) In a reorganization, creditors may be paid off with a mixture of cash and securities.
   (f) When a company is liquidated, one of the most valuable assets to be sold is often the tax-loss carry-forward.

QUESTIONS AND PROBLEMS

1. Here are some common terms of sale. Can you explain what they mean?
   (a) 2/30, net 60
   (b) net 10
   (c) 2/5, net 30, EOM
   (d) 2/10 prox, net 60

2. Some of the items in question 1 involve a cash discount. Calculate the rates of interest paid by customers who pay on the due date instead of taking the cash discount.

3. As treasurer of the Universal Bed Corporation, Aristotle Procrustes is worried about his bad-debt ratio, which is currently running at 6 percent. He believes that imposing a more stringent credit policy might reduce sales by 5 percent and reduce the bad-debt ratio to 4 percent. If the cost of goods sold is 80 percent of the selling price, should Mr. Procrustes adopt the more stringent policy?

4. Jim Khana, the credit manager of Velcro Saddles, is reappraising the company's credit policy. Velcro sells on terms of net 30. Cost of goods sold is 85 percent of sales and fixed costs are a further 5 percent of sales. Velcro classifies customers on a scale of 1 to 4. During the past 5 years, the collection experience was as follows:

Classification	Defaults as Percent of Sales	Average Collection Period in Days for Nondefaulting Accounts
1	.0	45
2	2.0	42
3	10.0	50
4	20.0	80

The average interest rate was 15 percent.

What conclusions (if any) can you draw about Velcro's credit policy? What other factors should be taken into account before changing this policy?

*5. Look again at question 4. Suppose (a) that it costs $95 to classify each new credit applicant and (b) that an almost equal proportion of new applicants falls into each of the four categories. In what circumstances should Mr. Khana not bother to undertake a credit check?

6. Until recently, Augean Cleaning Products sold its products on terms of net 60, with an average collection period of 75 days. In an attempt to induce customers to pay more promptly, it has changed its terms to 2/10, EOM, net 60. The initial effect of the changed terms is as follows:

Percent of Sales with Cash Discount	AVERAGE COLLECTION PERIODS, DAYS	
	Cash Discount	Net
60	30[a]	80

[a] Some customers deduct the cash discount even though they pay after the specified date.

Calculate the effect of the changed terms assuming that the change does not affect sales volume. Assume:
(a) The interest rate is 12 percent.
(b) There are no defaults.
(c) Cost of goods sold is 80 percent of sales.

7. Look back at question 6. Assume that the change in credit terms results in a 2 percent increase in sales. Recalculate the effect of the changed credit terms.

TABLE 30-3
Plumpton Variety Stores: Summary Financial Statements (figures in millions)

	1986	1985		1986	1985
Cash	$ 1.0	$ 1.2	Payables	$ 2.3	$ 2.5
Receivables	1.5	1.6	Short-term loans	3.9	1.9
Inventory	10.9	11.6	Long-term debt	1.8	2.6
Fixed assets	5.1	4.3	Equity	10.5	11.7
Total assets	$18.5	$18.7	Total liabilities	$18.5	$18.7

	1986	1985
Sales	$55.0	$59.0
Cost of goods sold	32.6	35.9
Selling, general and administrative expenses	20.8	20.2
Interest	.5	.3
Tax	.5	1.3
Net income	.6	1.3

8. Financial ratios were described in Chapter 27. If you were the credit manager, to which financial ratios would you pay most attention? Which do you think would be the least informative?

9. Discuss in which ways real-life decisions are more complex than the decision illustrated in Figure 30-4. How do you think these differences ought to affect the credit decision?

10. Discuss the problems with developing a numerical credit scoring system for evaluating personal loans.

11. If a company experiences a sudden decrease in sales, the aging schedule in Table 30-2 will suggest that an abnormally high proportion of payments is overdue. Show why this happens. Can you suggest an alternative form of presentation that would make it easier to recognize a change in customer payment patterns?

12. Why do firms grant "free" credit? Would it be more efficient if all sales were for cash and late payers were charged interest?

13. Sometimes a firm sells its receivables at a discount to a wholly owned "captive finance company." This captive finance company is financed partly by the parent, but it also issues substantial amounts of debt. What are the possible advantages to such an arrangement?

14. Explain why equity can sometimes have a positive value even when companies petition for bankruptcy.

15. Reliant Umbrellas has been approached by Plumpton Variety Stores of Nevada. Plumpton has expressed interest in an initial purchase of 5000 umbrellas at $10 each on Reliant's standard terms of 2/30, net 60. Plumpton estimates that if the umbrellas prove popular with customers, its purchases could be in the region of 30,000 umbrellas a year. After deducting variable costs, this would provide an addition of $47,000 to Reliant's profits.

Reliant has been anxious for some time to break into the lucrative Nevada market, but its credit manager has some doubts about Plumpton. In the past 5 years, Plumpton had embarked on an aggressive program of store openings.

In 1986, however, it went into reverse. The recession combined with aggressive price competition caused a cash shortage. Plumpton laid off employees, closed one store, and deferred store openings. The company's Dun and Bradstreet rating is only fair and a check with Plumpton's other suppliers reveals that, although Plumpton has traditionally taken cash discounts, it has recently been paying 30 days slow. A check through Reliant's bank indicates that Plumpton has unused credit lines of $350,000 but has entered into discussions with the banks for a renewal of a $1,500,000 term loan due at the end of the year.

Table 30-3 summarizes Plumpton's latest financial statements.

As credit manager of Reliant, what is your attitude to extending credit to Plumpton?

31 Cash Management

At the end of 1986 citizens and corporations in the United States held approximately $730 billion in cash. This included $183 billion of currency and $547 billion of demand deposits with commercial banks. Cash pays no interest. Why, then, do sensible people hold it? Why, for example, don't you take all your cash and invest it in interest-bearing securities? The answer of course is that cash gives you more *liquidity* than securities. You can use it to buy things. It is hard enough getting New York cab drivers to give you change for a $20 bill, but try asking them to split a Treasury bill.

In equilibrium all assets in the same risk class are priced to give the same expected marginal benefit. The benefit from holding Treasury bills is the interest that you receive; the benefit from holding cash is that it gives you a convenient store of liquidity. In equilibrium the marginal value of this liquidity is equal to the marginal value of the interest on an equivalent investment in Treasury bills. This is just another way to say that Treasury bills are investments with zero net present value—they are fair value relative to cash.

Does this mean that it does not matter how much cash you hold? Of course not. The marginal value of liquidity declines as you hold increasing amounts of cash. When you have only a small proportion of your assets in cash, a little extra can be extremely useful; when you have a substantial holding, any additional liquidity is not worth much. Therefore, as financial manager you want to hold cash balances up to the point where the marginal value of the liquidity is equal to the value of the interest forgone.

If that seems more easily said than done, you may be comforted to know that production managers must make a similar trade-off. Ask yourself why they carry inventories of raw materials. They are not obliged to do so; they could simply buy materials day by day, as needed. But then they would pay higher prices for ordering in small lots, and they would risk production delays if the materials were not delivered on time. That is why they order more than the firm's immediate needs.

But there is a cost to holding inventories. Interest is lost on the money that is tied up in inventories, storage must be paid for, and often there is spoilage and deterioration. Therefore production managers try to strike a sensible balance between the costs of holding too little inventory and those of holding too much.

That is all we are saying you need to do with cash. Cash is just another raw material that you require to carry on production. If you keep too small a proportion of your funds in the bank, you will need to make repeated small sales of securities every time you want to pay your bills. On the other hand, if you keep excessive cash in the bank, you are losing interest. The trick is to hit a sensible balance.

The trade-off between the benefits and costs of liquidity is one essential part of cash management. The other part is making sure that the collection and disbursement of cash is as efficient as possible. To understand this we will have to look closely at the relationships between firms and their banks. Most of the latter part of this chapter is devoted to the mechanics of cash collection and disbursement and the services offered by banks to assist firms in cash management.

31-1 INVENTORIES AND CASH BALANCES

Let us take a look at what economists have had to say about managing inventories and then see whether some of these ideas may help us to manage cash balances. Here is a simple inventory problem.

Everyman's Bookstore experiences a steady demand for *Principles of Corporate Finance* from customers who find that it makes a serviceable bookend. Suppose that the bookstore sells 100 copies of the book a year and that it orders Q books at a time from the publishers. Then it will need to place $100/Q$ orders per year:

$$\text{Number of orders per year} = \frac{\text{sales}}{Q} = \frac{100}{Q}$$

Just before each delivery, the bookstore has effectively no inventory of *Principles of Corporate Finance*. Just *after* each delivery it has an inventory of Q books. Therefore its *average* inventory is midway between 0 books and Q books:

$$\text{Average inventory} = \frac{Q}{2} \text{ books}$$

For example, if the store increases its regular order by one book, the average inventory increases by ½ book.

There are two costs to holding this inventory. First, there is the carrying cost. This includes the cost of the capital that is tied up in inventory, the cost of shelf space, and so on. Let us suppose that these costs work out to a dollar per book per year. The effect of adding one more book to each order is therefore to increase the average inventory by ½ book and the carrying cost by ½ × \$1.00 = \$.50. Thus the marginal carrying cost is a constant \$.50:

$$\text{Marginal carrying cost} = \frac{\text{carrying cost per book}}{2} = \$.50$$

The second type of cost is the order cost. Imagine that each order placed with the publisher involves a fixed clerical and handling expense of \$2. Table 31-1 illustrates what happens to order costs as you increase the size of each order. You

TABLE 31-1
How order cost varies with order size

Order Size, Number of Books	Number of Orders per Year	Total Order Costs, Dollars
1	100	200
2	50	100
3	33	66
4	25	50
10	10	20
100	1	2

FIGURE 31-1
Everyman's Bookstore minimizes inventory costs by placing 5 orders per year for 20 books per order. That is, it places orders at about 10-week intervals.

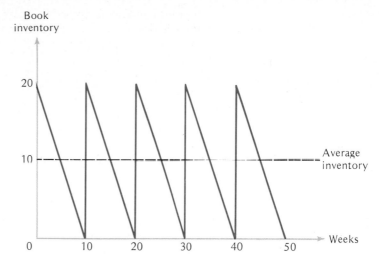

can see that the bookstore gets a large reduction in costs when it orders two books at a time rather than one, but thereafter the savings from increases in order size steadily diminish. In fact, the *marginal* reduction in order cost depends on the *square* of the order size:[1]

$$\text{Marginal reduction in order cost} = \frac{\text{sales} \times \text{cost per order}}{Q^2} = \frac{\$200}{Q^2}$$

Here, then, is the kernel of the inventory problem. As the bookstore increases its order size, the number of orders falls but the average inventory rises. Costs that are related to the number of orders decline; those that are related to inventory size increase. It is worth increasing order size as long as the decline in order cost outweighs the increase in carrying cost. The optimal order size is the point at which these two effects exactly offset each other. In our example this occurs when $Q = 20$:

$$\text{Marginal reduction in order cost} = \frac{\text{sales} \times \text{cost per order}}{Q^2} = \frac{\$200}{20^2} = \$.50$$

$$\text{Marginal carrying cost} = \frac{\text{carrying cost per book}}{2} = \$.50$$

The optimal order size is 20 books. Five times a year the bookstore should place an order for 20 books, and it should work off this inventory over the following 10 weeks. Its inventory of *Principles of Corporate Finance* will therefore follow the sawtoothed pattern in Figure 31-1.

---

[1] Let T = total order cost, S = sales per year, and C = cost per order. Then

$$T = \frac{SC}{Q}$$

Differentiate with respect to Q:

$$\frac{dT}{dQ} = -\frac{SC}{Q^2}$$

Thus, an *increase* of dQ reduces T by SC/Q^2.

The general formula for optimum order size is found by setting marginal reduction in order cost equal to the marginal carrying cost and solving for Q:

$$\text{Marginal reduction in order cost} = \text{marginal carrying cost}$$

$$\frac{\text{Sales} \times \text{cost per order}}{Q^2} = \frac{\text{carrying cost}}{2}$$

$$Q^2 = \frac{2 \times \text{sales} \times \text{cost per order}}{\text{carrying cost}}$$

$$Q = \sqrt{\frac{2 \times \text{sales} \times \text{cost per order}}{\text{carrying cost}}}$$

In our example,

$$Q = \sqrt{\frac{2 \times 100 \times 2}{1}} = \sqrt{400} = 20$$

The Extension to Cash Balances

William Baumol was the first to notice that this simple inventory model can tell us something about the management of cash balances.[2] Suppose that you keep a reservoir of cash that is steadily drawn down to pay bills. When it runs out you replenish the cash balance by selling Treasury bills. The main carrying cost of holding this cash is the interest that you are losing. The order cost is the fixed administrative expense of each sale of Treasury bills. In these circumstances your inventory of cash also follows a sawtoothed pattern like Figure 31-1.

In other words, your cash management problem is exactly analogous to the problem of optimum order size faced by Everyman's Bookstore. You just have to redefine variables. Instead of books per order, Q becomes the amount of Treasury bills sold each time the cash balance is replenished. Cost per order becomes cost per sale of Treasury bills. Carrying cost is just the interest rate. Total cash disbursements take the place of books sold. The optimum Q is

$$Q = \sqrt{\frac{2 \times \text{annual cash disbursements} \times \text{cost per sale of Treasury bills}}{\text{interest rate}}}$$

Suppose that the interest rate on Treasury bills is 8 percent, but every sale of bills costs you $20. Your firm pays out cash at a rate of $105,000 per month or $1,260,000 per year. Therefore the optimum Q is

$$Q = \sqrt{\frac{2 \times 1,260,000 \times 20}{.08}}$$

$$= \$25,100, \text{ or about } \$25,000$$

Thus your firm would sell approximately $25,000 of Treasury bills four times a month—about once a week. Its average cash balance will be $25,000/2, or $12,500.

---

[2] W. J. Baumol, The Transactions Demand for Cash: An Inventory Theoretic Approach," *Quarterly Journal of Economics*, **66**: 545–556 (November 1952).

In Baumol's model a higher interest rate implies a lower Q.[3] In general, when interest rates are high, you want to hold small average cash balances. On the other hand, if you use up cash at a high rate or if there are high costs to selling securities, you want to hold large average cash balances. Think about that for a moment. *You can hold too little cash.* Many financial managers point with pride to the tight control that they exercise over cash and to the extra interest that they have earned. These benefits are highly visible. The costs are less visible but they can be very large. When you allow for the time that the manager spends in monitoring her cash balance, it may make sense to forgo some of that extra interest.

The Miller-Orr Model

Baumol's model works well as long as the firm is steadily using up its cash inventory. But that is not what usually happens. In some weeks the firm may collect some large unpaid bills and therefore receive a net *inflow* of cash. In other weeks it may pay its suppliers and so incur a net *outflow* of cash.

Economists and management scientists have developed a variety of more elaborate and realistic models that allow for the possibility of both cash inflows and outflows. Let us look briefly at a model developed by Miller and Orr.[4] It represents a nice compromise between simplicity and realism.

Miller and Orr consider how the firm should manage its cash balance if it cannot predict day-to-day cash inflows and outflows. Their answer is shown in Figure 31-2. You can see that the cash balance meanders unpredictably until it reaches an upper limit. At this point the firm buys enough securities to return the cash balance to a more normal level. Once again the cash balance is allowed to meander until this time it hits a lower limit. When it does, the firm *sells* enough securities to restore the balance to its normal level. Thus the rule is to allow the cash holding to wander freely until it hits an upper or lower limit. When this happens, the firm buys or sells securities to regain the desired balance.

How far should the firm allow its cash balance to wander? Miller and Orr show that the answer depends on three factors. If the day-to-day variability in cash flows is large or if the fixed cost of buying and selling securities is high, then the firm should set the control limits far apart. Conversely, if the rate of interest is high, it should set the limits close together. The formula for the distance between barriers is[5]

$$\text{Spread between upper and lower cash balance limits} = 3\left(\frac{3}{4} \times \frac{\text{transaction cost} \times \text{variance of cash flows}}{\text{interest rate}}\right)^{1/3}$$

Have you noticed one odd feature about Figure 31-2? The firm does not return to a point halfway between the lower and upper limits. The firm always returns

---

[3] Note that the interest rate is in the denominator of the expression for optimal Q. Thus, increasing the interest rate reduces the optimal Q.

[4] M. H. Miller and D. Orr, "A Model of the Demand for Money by Firms," *Quarterly Journal of Economics*, **80:** 413–435 (August 1966).

[5] This formula assumes the expected daily change in the cash balance is zero. Thus it assumes that there are no systematic upward or downward trends in the cash balance. If the Miller-Orr model is applicable you need only know the variance of the daily cash flows, that is the variance of the daily *changes* in the cash balance.

FIGURE 31-2
In Miller and Orr's model the cash balance is allowed to meander until it hits an upper or lower limit. At this point the firm buys or sells securities to restore the balance to the return point, which is the lower limit plus one-third of the spread between the upper and lower limits.

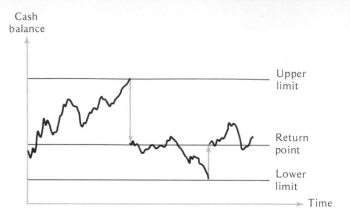

to a point one-third of the distance from the lower to the upper limit. In other words, the return point is

$$\text{Return point} = \text{lower limit} + \frac{\text{spread}}{3}$$

Always starting at this return point means the firm hits the lower limit more often than the upper limit. This does not minimize the number of transactions—that would require always starting exactly in the middle of the spread. However, always starting in the middle would mean a larger average cash balance and larger interest costs. The Miller-Orr return point minimizes the sum of transaction costs and interest costs.

Using the Miller-Orr Model

The Miller-Orr model is easy to use. The first step is to set the lower limit for the cash balance. This may be zero, some minimum safety margin above zero, or a balance necessary to keep the bank happy—more on bank requirements later in the chapter. The second step is to estimate the variance of cash flows. For example, you might record net cash inflows or outflows for each of the last 100 days and compute the variance of those 100 sample observations. More sophisticated measurement techniques could be applied if there were, say, seasonal fluctuations in the volatility of cash flows. The third step is to observe the interest rate and the transaction cost of each purchase or sale of securities. The final step is to compute the upper limit and the return point and to give this information to a clerk with instructions to follow the "control limit" strategy built into the Miller-Orr model. Table 31-2 gives a numerical example.

This model's practical usefulness is limited by the assumptions it rests on. For example, few managers would agree that cash inflows and outflows are entirely unpredictable, as Miller and Orr assume. The manager of a toy store knows that there will be substantial cash inflows around Christmastime. Financial managers know when dividends will be paid and when income taxes will be due. In Chapter 29 we described how firms forecast cash inflows and outflows and how they arrange short-term investment and financing decisions to supply cash when needed and put cash to work earning interest when it is not needed.

This kind of short-term financial plan is usually designed to produce a cash balance that is stable at some lower limit. But there are always fluctuations that

TABLE 31-2
Numerical example of the Miller-Orr model

A. Assumptions:
  1. Minimum cash balance = $10,000
  2. Variance of daily cash flows = 6,250,000 (equivalent to a standard deviation of $2,500 per day)
  3. Interest rate = .025 percent per day
  4. Transaction cost for each sale of purchase of securities = $20
B. Calculation of spread between upper and lower cash balance limits:

$$\text{Spread} = 3\left(\frac{\text{¾} \times \text{transaction cost} \times \text{variance of cash flows}}{\text{interest rate}}\right)^{1/3}$$

$$= 3\left(\frac{\text{¾} \times 20 \times 6{,}250{,}000}{.00025}\right)^{1/3}$$

$$= 21{,}634, \text{ or about } \$21{,}600$$

C. Calculate upper limit and return point:

  Upper limit = lower limit + 21,600 = $31,600

$$\text{Return point} = \text{lower limit} + \frac{\text{spread}}{3} = 10{,}000 + \frac{21{,}600}{3} = \$17{,}200$$

D. Decision rule:
  If cash balance rises to $31,600, invest $31,600 − 17,200 = $14,400 in marketable securities; if cash balance falls to $10,000, sell $7,200 of marketable securities and replenish cash.

---

financial managers cannot plan for, certainly not on a day-to-day basis. You can think of the Miller-Orr policies as responding to the cash inflows and outflows which cannot be predicted, or which are not *worth* predicting. Trying to predict *all* cash flows would chew up enormous amounts of management time.

The Miller-Orr model has been tested on daily cash-flow data for several firms. It performed as well as or better than the intuitive policies followed by these firms' cash managers. However, the model was not an unqualified success; in particular, simple rules of thumb seem to perform just as well.[6] The Miller-Orr model may improve our *understanding* of the problem of cash management, but it probably will not yield substantial savings compared with policies based on a manager's judgment, providing of course that the manager understands the trade-offs we have discussed.

Raising Cash by Borrowing

So far we have assumed that surplus cash is invested in securities such as Treasury bills and that cash is replenished when necessary by selling these securities. The alternative may be to replenish cash by borrowing—for example, by drawing on a bank line of credit.

Borrowing raises another problem. The interest rate that you pay to the bank is likely to be higher than the rate that you receive on securities. As financial manager, you therefore face a trade-off. To earn the maximum interest on your funds, you want to hold low cash balances, but this means that you are more

---

[6] For a review of tests of the Miller-Orr model, see D. Mullins and R. Homonoff, "Applications of Inventory Cash Management Models," in S. C. Myers, ed., *Modern Developments in Financial Management*, Frederick A. Praeger, Inc., New York, 1976.

likely to have to borrow to cover an unexpected cash outflow. For example, suppose you can either hold cash that pays no interest or you can invest in securities that pay interest at 10 percent. The cost of keeping cash balances is the interest forgone by not investing the money in securities.

$$\text{Cost of cash balances} = 10 \text{ percent}$$

If you need more cash at short notice, it may be difficult or costly to sell securities, but you can borrow from the bank at 12 percent. In this case, there is a simple rule for maximizing expected return. You should adjust the cash balances until the probability that you will need to borrow from the bank equals[7]

$$\frac{\text{Cost of cash balances}}{\text{Cost of borrowing}} = \frac{10}{12} = .83$$

When we look at the problem this way, the best cash balance depends on the cost of borrowing and the extent of uncertainty about future cash flow. If the cost of borrowing is high relative to the interest rate on securities, you should make sure that there is only a low probability that you will be obliged to borrow. If you are very uncertain about the future cash flow, you may need to keep a large cash balance in order to be confident that you will not have to borrow. If you are fairly sure about cash flow, you can keep a lower cash balance.

Cash Management in the Largest Corporations

For very large firms, the transaction costs of buying and selling securities become trivial compared with the opportunity cost of holding idle cash balances. Suppose that the interest rate is 8 percent per year, or roughly $8/365 = .022$ percent per day. Then the daily interest earned by $1 million is $.00022 \times 1,000,000 = \$220$. Even at a cost of $50 per transaction, which is generous, it pays to buy Treasury bills today and sell them tomorrow rather than to leave $1 million idle overnight.

A corporation with $1 billion of annual sales has an average daily cash flow of $1,000,000,000/365, about $2.7 million. Firms of this size end up buying or selling securities once a day, every day, unless by chance they have only a small positive cash balance at the end of the day.

Why do such firms hold any significant amounts of cash? There are basically two reasons. First, cash may be left in non-interest-bearing accounts to compensate banks for the services they provide. Second, large corporations may have literally hundreds of accounts with dozens of different banks. It is often better to leave idle

---

[7] See, for example, J. H. W. Gosling, "One-Period Optimal Cash Balances," unpublished paper presented to the European Finance Association, Scheviningen, Holland, 1981. Instead of keeping the money in cash you may be able to keep it in very liquid securities that are therefore easily sold, but pay only a low rate of interest. The model works in this case also. For example, suppose that the interest rate on these liquid balances is 4 percent. Then the cost of investing in liquid balances is the interest that you forgo by not investing in the less marketable securities:

Cost of liquid balances = $10 - 4 = 6$ percent

The cost of borrowing is the difference between the interest that you pay on the borrowing and the rate that you earn on liquid balances:

Cost of borrowing = $12 - 4 = 8$ percent

Our rule states that you should adjust the liquid balances until the probability that you will need to borrow equals

$$\frac{\text{Cost of liquid balances}}{\text{Cost of borrowing}} = \frac{6}{8} = .75$$

cash in some of these accounts than to monitor each account daily and make daily transfers between them.

One major reason for the proliferation of bank accounts is decentralized management. You cannot give a subsidiary operating autonomy without giving its managers the right to spend and receive cash.

Good cash management nevertheless implies some degree of centralization. You cannot maintain your desired inventory of cash if all the subsidiaries in the group are responsible for their own private pools of cash. And you certainly want to avoid situations in which one subsidiary is investing its spare cash at 7 percent while another is borrowing at 8 percent. It is not surprising, therefore, that even in highly decentralized companies there is generally central control over cash balances and bank relations.

31-2   CASH COLLECTION AND DISBURSEMENT SYSTEMS

We have talked loosely about a firm's cash balance; it is now time to be more precise about how cash enters and exits the corporation and how the available cash balance is computed. The first necessary step is understanding *float*.

Float

Suppose that the United Carbon Company has $1 million on demand deposit with its bank. It now pays one of its suppliers by writing and mailing a check for $200,000. The company's ledgers are immediately adjusted to show a cash balance of $800,000. But the company's bank won't learn anything about this check until it has been received by the supplier, deposited at the supplier's bank, and finally presented to United Carbon's bank for payment.[8] During this time United Carbon's bank continues to show in its ledger that the company has a balance of $1 million. The company obtains the benefit of an extra $200,000 in the bank while the check is clearing. This sum is often called *payment,* or *disbursement, float.*

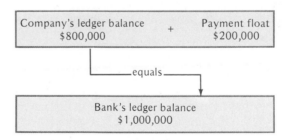

Float sounds like a marvelous invention, but unfortunately it can also work in reverse. Suppose that in addition to paying its supplier, United Carbon *receives* a check for $100,000 from a customer. It deposits the check, and both the company

---

[8] Checks deposited with a bank are cleared through the Federal Reserve clearing system, through a correspondent bank, or through a clearinghouse of local banks.

and the bank increase the ledger balance by $100,000:

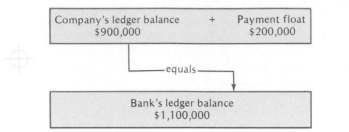

But this money isn't available to the company immediately. The bank doesn't actually have the money in hand until it has sent the check to, and received payment from, the customer's bank. Since the bank has to wait, it makes United Carbon wait too—usually 1 or 2 business days. In the meantime, the bank will show that United Carbon has an *available balance* of $1 million and *availability float* of $100,000:

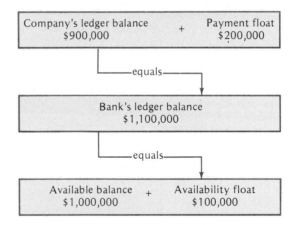

Notice that the company gains as a result of the payment float and loses as a result of the availability float. The difference is often termed the *net float*. In our example, the net float is $100,000. The company's available balance is therefore $100,000 greater than the balance shown in its ledger.

As financial manager your concern is with the available balance, not with the company's ledger balance. If you know that it is going to be a week or two before some of your checks are presented for payment, you may be able to get by on a smaller cash balance. This game is often called *playing the float*.

You can increase your available cash balance by increasing your net float. This means that you want to ensure that checks paid in by customers are cleared rapidly and those paid to suppliers are cleared slowly. Perhaps this may sound like rather small beer, but think what it can mean to a company like Ford. Ford's daily sales average over $140 million. Therefore if it can speed up the collection process by 1 day, it frees more than $140 million, which is available for investment or payment to Ford's stockholders.

Some financial managers have become overenthusiastic at managing the float. In 1985 E. F. Hutton pleaded guilty to 2000 separate counts of mail and wire fraud. Hutton admitted that it had created nearly $1 billion of float by shuffling funds between its branches, and through various accounts at different banks. These activities cost the company a $2 million fine and its agreement to repay the banks any losses they may have incurred.

Managing Float

Float is the child of delay. Actually there are several kinds of delay, and so people in the cash management business refer to several kinds of float. Figure 31-3 summarizes.

Of course the delays that help the payer hurt the recipient. Recipients try to speed up collections. Payers try to slow down disbursements.

Speeding Up Collections

One way to speed up collections is by a method known as **concentration banking.** In this case customers in a particular area make payment to a local branch office rather than to company headquarters. The local branch office then deposits the checks into a local bank account. Surplus funds are periodically transferred to a concentration account at one of the company's principal banks.

Concentration banking brings many small balances together in one large, central balance, which then can be invested in interest-paying assets through a single

FIGURE 31-3
Delays create float. Each heavy arrow represents a source of delay. Recipients try to reduce delay to get available cash sooner. Payers prefer delay so they can use their cash longer. *Note:* The delays causing availability float and presentation float are equal on average, but can differ from case to case.

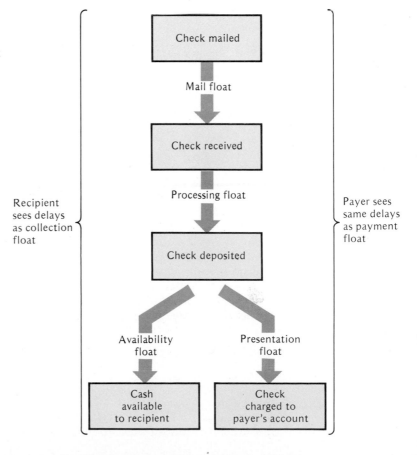

transaction. Concentration banking also reduces float in two ways. First, because the branch office is nearer to the customer, mailing time is reduced. Second, since the customer's check is likely to be drawn on a local bank, the time taken to clear the check is also reduced. Unfortunately, concentration banking also involves additional costs. First, the company is likely to incur additional administrative costs. Second, the company's local bank needs to be rewarded for its services. Third, there is the cost of transferring the funds to the concentration bank. The fastest but most expensive arrangement is wire transfer. A slower but cheaper method is a depository transfer check.[9]

Often concentration banking is combined with a **lock-box system.** In a lock-box system, you pay the local bank to take on the administrative chores. It works as follows: The company rents a locked post office box in each principal region. All customers within a region are instructed to send their payments to the post office box. The local bank, as agent for the company, empties the box at regular intervals and deposits the checks in the company's local account. Surplus funds are transferred periodically to one of the company's principal banks.

How many collection points do you need if you use a lock-box system or concentration banking? The answer depends on where your customers are and on the speed of the United States mail. For example, suppose that you are thinking of opening a lock box. The local bank shows you a map of mail delivery times. From that and knowledge of your customers' locations, you come up with the following data:

- Average number of daily payments to lock box   = 150
- Average size of payment   = $1200
- Rate of interest *per day*   = .02 percent
- Saving in mailing time   = 1.2 days
- Saving in processing time   = .8 days

On this basis, the lock box would increase your collected balance by:

150 items per day $\times$ $1200 per item $\times$ (1.2 + .8) days saved = $360,000

Invested at .02 percent per day, that gives a daily return of:

$$.0002 \times \$360,000 = \$72.00$$

The bank's charge for operating the lock-box system depends on the number of checks processed. Suppose that the bank charges $.20 per check. That works out at 150 $\times$ .20 = $30.00 per day. You are ahead by $72.00 − 30.00 = $42.00 per day, plus whatever your firm saves from not having to process the checks itself.

Our example assumes that the company has only two choices. It can do nothing or it can operate the lock box. But maybe there is some other lock-box location, or some mixture of locations, that would be still more effective. Of course, you can always find this out by working through all possible combinations, but it may be simpler to solve the problem by linear programming. Many banks offer linear programming models to solve the problem of locating lock boxes.[10]

---

[9] A depository transfer check is made out directly by the local bank to a particular company account at the concentration bank. It costs less than $1 compared with up to $20 for a wire transfer. See Bernell K. Stone and Ned C. Hill, "Alternative Cash Transfer Mechanisms and Methods: Evaluation Frameworks," *Journal of Bank Research,* **3:** 7–16 (Spring 1982).

[10] See, for example, A. Kraus, C. Janssen, and A. McAdams, "The Lock-Box Location Problem," *Journal of Bank Research,* **1:** 50–58 (Autumn 1970).

Controlling Disbursements

Speeding up collections is not the only way to increase the net float. You can also do so by slowing down disbursements. One tempting strategy is to increase mail time. For example, United Carbon could pay its New York suppliers with checks mailed from Nome, Alaska, and its Los Angeles suppliers with checks mailed from Vienna, Maine.

But on second thought you will realize that these kinds of post office tricks are unlikely to give more than a short-run payoff. Suppose you have promised to pay a New York supplier on February 29. Does it matter whether you mail the check from Alaska on the 26th or from New York on the 28th? Of course you could use a remote mailing address as an excuse to pay late, but that's a trick easily seen through. If you have to pay late, you may as well mail late.

There are effective ways of increasing presentation float, however. For example, suppose that United Carbon pays its suppliers with checks written on a New York City bank. From the time that the check has been deposited by the supplier, there will be an average lapse of little more than a day before it is presented to United Carbon's bank for payment. The alternative is for United Carbon to pay its suppliers with checks mailed to *arrive* on time, but written on a bank in Helena, Montana; Midland, Texas; or Wilmington, Delaware. In these cases, there will be an average lapse of nearly 4 days before each check is presented for payment. United Carbon, therefore, gains several days of additional float.[11]

Some firms even maintain disbursement accounts in different parts of the country. The computer looks up each supplier's zip code and automatically produces a check on the most distant bank.

The suppliers won't object to these machinations because the Federal Reserve guarantees a maximum clearing time of 2 days on all checks cleared through the Federal Reserve system. The Federal Reserve does object and has been trying to prevent remote disbursement.

A New York City bank receives several check deliveries each day from the Federal Reserve system as well as checks that come directly from other banks or through the local clearinghouse. Thus, if United Carbon uses a New York City bank for paying its suppliers, it will not know at the beginning of the day how many checks will be presented for payment. It must either keep a large cash balance to cover contingencies, or it must be prepared to borrow. However, instead of having a disbursement account with, say, Morgan Guaranty Trust in New York, United Carbon could open a *zero-balance* account with Morgan's affiliated bank in Wilmington, Delaware. Because it is not in a major banking center, this affiliated bank receives almost all check deliveries in the form of a single, early-morning delivery from the Federal Reserve. Therefore, it can let the cash manager at United Carbon know early in the day exactly how much money will be paid out that day. The cash manager then arranges for this sum to be transferred from the company's concentration account to the disbursement account. Thus by the end of the day (and at the start of the next day), United Carbon has a zero balance in the disbursement account.

United Carbon's Wilmington account has two advantages. First, by choosing a remote location, the company has gained several days of float. Second, because the bank can forecast early in the day how much money will be paid out, United Carbon does not need to keep extra cash in the account to cover contingencies.

---

[11] Remote disbursement accounts are described in I. Ross, "The Race Is to the Slow Payer," *Fortune*, 75–80, April 1983.

31-3 BANK RELATIONS

Banks have to be paid for the services they provide. They can be paid directly—a monthly fee based on services provided—or indirectly, by letting money sit in non-interest-bearing bank accounts.

Banks like demand deposits. After setting aside a portion of the deposit in a reserve account with the Federal Reserve Bank, they can relend these deposits and earn interest on them. Banks would, therefore, be prepared to pay interest to attract demand deposits, but the government prohibits them from doing so.

One thing that governments never learn is that it is very difficult to legislate prices. Although they stop banks from offering money in payment for demand deposits, they do not stop them from offering services to attract deposits. Therefore, if a firm keeps a sufficiently large balance with the bank, the bank will process the firm's checks without charge, it will operate a lock-box system—it will provide all kinds of advice and services. This system of **compensating balances** is a mechanism by which the banks pay for demand deposits.[12]

Thus firms can pay for bank services by maintaining interest-free demand deposits. These deposits generate "earnings credits" which are used to pay for bank services. The earnings credits are interest by another name.[13]

What Happens If Money Pays Interest?

Thus the prohibition on paying interest on demand deposits is breaking down. But even if explicit interest-bearing checking accounts become the norm, firms and individuals will still face a trade-off between liquidity and forgone interest, because checking accounts will normally offer lower interest rates than direct investment in securities. (Otherwise banks will lose money; and in the long run they cannot offer a money-losing service.) Thus, the less money kept in a checking account, the more interest earned. Yet low balances in checking accounts mean frequent sales or purchases of securities, and thus frequent transaction costs. This is the same problem we started the chapter with.

31-4 SUMMARY

Cash provides liquidity, but it doesn't pay interest. Securities pay interest, but you can't use them to buy things. As financial manager you want to hold cash up to the point where the marginal value of liquidity is equal to the interest that you could earn on securities.

Cash is just one of the raw materials that you need to do business. It is expensive keeping your capital tied up in large inventories of raw materials when it could be earning interest. Why do you hold inventories at all? Why not order materials as and when you need them? The answer is that it is also expensive to keep placing many small orders. You need, therefore, to strike a balance between holding too large an inventory of cash (and losing interest on the money) and making too

---

[12] For a discussion of the role of compensating balances, see D. W. Mullins, "Restriction on the Rate of Interest on Demand Deposits and a Theory of Compensating Balances," *Journal of Finance*, **31:** 233–251 (May 1976).

[13] Notice that this system of indirect rewards makes it much more difficult to determine how far you should be prepared to run down your cash balance before selling securities. If it is going to provide you with services, the bank will insist that you maintain a specified average level of balances over the month. Therefore you don't want to allow your cash inventory to run down to zero before replenishing it.

many small adjustments to your inventory (and incurring additional administrative costs). If interest rates are high, you want to hold relatively small inventories of cash. If your cash needs are variable and your administrative costs are high, you want to hold relatively large inventories.

If the securities are not easily sold, you have the alternative of borrowing to cover a cash deficiency. Again, you face a trade-off. Since banks charge a high interest rate on borrowing, you want to keep sufficiently large liquid funds that you don't need to keep borrowing. On the other hand, by having large liquid balances, you are also not earning the maximum return on your cash.

The cash shown in the company ledger is not the same as the available balance in your bank account. The difference is the net float. When you have written a large number of checks awaiting clearance, the available balance will be larger than the ledger balance. When you have just deposited a large number of checks which have not yet been collected by the bank, the available balance will be smaller. If you can predict how long it will take checks to clear, you may be able to *play the float* and get by on a smaller cash balance.

You can also *manage* the float by speeding up collections and slowing down payments. One way to speed collections is by *concentration banking.* Customers make payments to a regional office which then pays the checks into a local bank account. Surplus funds are transferred from the local account to a concentration bank. An alternative technique is *lock-box banking.* In this case customers send their payments to a local post office box. A local bank empties the box at regular intervals and clears the checks. Concentration banking and lock-box banking reduce mailing time and the time required to clear checks.

Banks provide many services. They handle checks, manage lock boxes, provide advice, obtain references, and so on. Firms either pay cash for these services, or they pay by maintaining sufficient cash balances with the bank.

In many cases you will want to keep somewhat larger balances than are needed to pay for the tangible services. One reason is that the bank may be a valuable source of ideas and business connections. Another reason is that you may use the bank as a source of short-term funds. Leaving idle cash at your bank may be implicit compensation for the willingness of the bank to stand ready to advance credit when needed. A large cash balance may, therefore, be good insurance against a rainy day.

FURTHER READING

Baumol and Miller and Orr were the pioneers in applying inventory models to cash management.

W. J. Baumol: "The Transactions Demand for Cash: An Inventory Theoretic Approach," *Quarterly Journal of Economics,* **66:** 545–556 (November 1952).

M. H. Miller and D. Orr: "A Model of the Demand for Money by Firms," *Quarterly Journal of Economics,* **80:** 413–435 (August 1966).

Models of the Miller-Orr type have been developed to cover a variety of more complicated situations. Two examples are:

W. H. Hausman and A. Sanchez-Bell: "The Stochastic Cash Balance Problem with Average Compensating Balance Requirements," *Management Science,* **21:** 849–857 (April 1975).

B. H. Stone: "The Use of Forecasts and Smoothing in Control Limit Models for Cash Management," *Financial Management,* **1:** 72–84 (Spring 1972).

Mullins and Homonoff review tests of inventory models for cash management.

> D. Mullins and R. Homonoff: "Applications of Inventory Cash Management Models," in S. C. Myers, ed., *Modern Developments in Financial Management,* Frederick A. Praeger, Inc., 1976.

Other useful readings include Mullins's discussion of reserve requirements, compensating balances, and the pricing of bank services; and analyses of the lock-box location problem by Kraus, Janssen, and McAdams, and by Corneujols, Fisher, and Nemhauser. The last two articles give an up-to-date view of banking systems.

> D. W. Mullins: "Restriction on the Rate of Interest on Demand Deposits and a Theory of Compensating Balances," *Journal of Finance,* **31**: 233–251 (May 1976).
>
> A. Kraus, C. Janssen, and A. McAdams: "The Lock-Box Location Problem," *Journal of Bank Research,* **1**: 50–58 (Autumn 1970).
>
> G. Corneujols, M. L. Fisher, and G. L. Nemhauser: "Location of Bank Accounts to Optimize Float: An Analytic Study of Exact and Approximate Algorithms," *Management Science,* **23**: 789–810 (April 1977).
>
> S. F. Maier and J. H. Van der Weide: "What Lock-Box and Disbursement Models Really Do," *Journal of Finance,* **37**: 361–371 (May 1983).
>
> B. K. Stone: "The Design of a Company's Banking System," *Journal of Finance,* **37**: 373–385 (May 1983).

The Journal of Cash Management, *published by the National Corporate Cash Management Association, is a good reference for recent developments. Two useful specialized texts are:*

> N. C. Hill, G. W. Emery, and W. L. Sartoris: *Essentials of Cash Management: A Study Guide,* National Corporate Cash Management Association, 1985.
>
> J. Van der Weide and S. F. Maier: *Managing Corporate Liquidity: An Introduction to Working Capital Management,* New York, John Wiley & Sons, Inc., 1985.

QUIZ

1. Everyman's Bookstore has experienced an increase in demand for *Principles of Corporate Finance.* It now expects to sell 200 books a year. Unfortunately inventory carrying costs have increased to $2 per book per year whereas order costs have remained steady at $2 per order.
   (*a*) What is the marginal carrying cost (for a unit increase in order size)?
   (*b*) At what point does the marginal carrying cost equal the marginal reduction in order cost?
   (*c*) How many orders should the store place per year?
   (*d*) What is its average inventory?
2. Now assume that Everyman's Bookstore uses up cash at a steady rate of $20,000 a year. The interest rate is 2 percent and each sale of securities costs $2.
   (*a*) What is the marginal carrying cost of the cash (for a $1 increase in order size)?
   (*b*) At what point does the marginal carrying cost equal the marginal reduction in order costs?
   (*c*) How many times a year should the store sell securities?
   (*d*) What is its average cash balance?
3. In the Miller and Orr cash balance model the firm should allow the cash balance to move within limits.
   (*a*) What three factors determine how far apart these limits are?
   (*b*) How far should the firm adjust its cash balance when it reaches the upper or lower limit?
   (*c*) Why does it not restore the cash balance to the halfway point?

4. Suppose that you can hold cash that pays no interest or invest in securities paying interest of 8 percent. The securities are not easily sold on short notice and, therefore, you must make up any cash deficiency by drawing on a bank line of credit which charges interest at 10 percent. Should you invest more or less in securities if
   (a) You are unusually uncertain about future cash flows?
   (b) The interest rate on bank loans rises to 11 percent?
   (c) The interest rates on securities and on bank loans both rise by the same proportion?
   (d) You revise downward your forecast of future cash needs?
5. A company has the following cash balances:

$$\text{Company's ledger balance} = \$600,000$$

$$\text{Bank's ledger balance} = \$625,000$$

$$\text{Available balance} = \$550,000$$

   (a) Calculate the payment float and availability float.
   (b) Why does the company gain from the payment float?
   (c) Suppose the company adopts a policy of writing checks on a remote bank. How is this likely to affect the three measures of cash balance?
6. Anne Teak, the financial manager of a furniture manufacturer, is considering operating a lock-box system. She forecasts that 300 payments a day will be made to lock boxes with an average payment size of $1500. The bank's charge for operating the lock boxes is *either* $.40 a check *or* compensating balances of $800,000.
   (a) If the interest rate is 9 percent, which method of payment is cheaper?
   (b) What reduction in the time to collect and process each check is needed to justify use of the lock-box system?
7. Explain why companies use zero-balance accounts to make disbursements.
8. Complete the following passage by choosing the appropriate term from the following list: *lock-box banking, wire transfer, payment float, concentration banking, availability float, net float, depository transfer check.*

   The firm's available balance is equal to its ledger balance plus the _____ and minus the _____ . The difference between the available balance and the ledger balance is often called the _____ . Firms can increase their cash resources by speeding up collections. One way to do this is to arrange for payments to be made to regional offices which pay the checks into local banks. This is known as _____ . Surplus funds are then transferred from the local bank to one of the company's main banks. Transfer may be by the quick but expensive _____ or by the slightly slower but cheaper _____ . Another technique is to arrange for a local bank to collect the checks directly from a post office box. This is known as _____ .

QUESTIONS AND PROBLEMS

1. How would you expect a firm's cash balance to respond to the following changes?
   (a) Interest rates increase.
   (b) The volatility of daily cash flow decreases.
   (c) The transaction cost of buying or selling marketable securities goes up.

2. A firm maintains a separate account for cash disbursements. Total disbursements are $100,000 per month spread evenly over the month. Administrative and transaction costs of transferring cash to the disbursement account are $10 per transfer. Marketable securities yield 1 percent per month. Determine the size and number of transfers that will minimize the cost of maintaining the special account.

3. Refer again to Table 31-2. Calculate the optimal strategy under the following alternative assumptions:
     Minimum cash balance = $20,000.
     Standard deviation of daily cash flows = $5000.
     Interest rate = .03 percent per day.
     Transaction cost of each purchase or sale of securities = $25.

4. Suppose that the rate of inflation accelerates from 5 to 10 percent per year. Would firms' cash balances go up or down relative to sales? Explain.

5. A parent company settles the collection account balances of its subsidiaries once a week. (That is, each week it transfers any balances in the accounts to a central account.) The cost of a wire transfer is $10. A depository transfer check costs $.80. Cash transferred by wire is available the same day, but the parent must wait 3 days for depository transfer checks to clear. Cash can be invested at 12 percent per year. How much money must be in a collection account before it pays to use a wire transfer?

6. The financial manager of JAC Cosmetics is considering opening a lock box in Pittsburgh. Checks cleared through the lock box will amount to $300,000 per month. The lock box will make cash available to the company 3 days earlier.
   (a) Suppose that the bank offers to run the lock box for a $20,000 compensating balance. Is the lock box worthwhile?
   (b) Suppose that the bank offers to run the lock box for a fee of $.10 per check cleared instead of a compensating balance. What must the average check size be for the fee alternative to be less costly? Assume an interest rate of 6 percent per year.
   (c) Why did you need to know the interest rate to answer (b) but not to answer (a)?

7. On January 25, Coot Company has $250,000 deposited with a local bank. On January 27, the company writes and mails checks of $20,000 and $60,000 to suppliers. At the end of the month, Coot's financial manager deposits a $45,000 check received from a customer in the morning mail and picks up the end-of-month account summary from the bank. The manager notes that only the $20,000 payment of the 27th has cleared the bank. What are the company's ledger balance and payment float? What is the company's net float?

8. Knob, Inc., is a nationwide distributor of furniture hardware. The company now uses a central billing system for credit sales of $180 million annually. First National, Knob's principal bank, offers to establish a new concentration banking system for a flat fee of $100,000 per year. The bank estimates that mailing and collection time can be reduced by 3 days. By how much will Knob's availability float be reduced under the new system? How much extra interest income will the new system generate if the extra funds are used to reduce borrowing under Knob's line of credit with First National? Assume the borrowing rate is 12 percent. Finally, should Knob accept First National's offer if collection costs under the old system are $40,000 per year?

9. A few years ago, Merrill Lynch increased its float by mailing checks drawn on west coast banks to customers in the east and checks drawn on east coast banks to customers in the west. A subsequent class action suit against Merrill Lynch

revealed that in 28 months from September 1976 Merrill Lynch disbursed $1.25 billion in 365,000 checks to New York State customers alone. The plaintiff's lawyer calculated that by using a remote bank Merrill Lynch had increased its average float by 1½ days.[14]

(a) How much did Merrill Lynch disburse per day to New York State customers?

(b) What was the total gain to Merrill Lynch over the 28 months, assuming an interest rate of 8 percent?

(c) What was the present value of the increase in float if the benefits were expected to be permanent?

(d) Suppose that the use of remote banks had involved Merrill Lynch in extra expenses. What was the maximum extra cost per check that Merrill Lynch would have been prepared to pay?

[14] See, for example, I. Ross, "The Race Is to the Slow Payer," op. cit.

32

Short-Term Lending and Borrowing

If a company has a temporary cash surplus, it can invest in short-term securities. If it has a temporary deficiency, it can replenish cash by selling securities or by borrowing on a short-term basis. In Chapter 31 you learned something about when to make such changes. But you need to know more than that. There is an elaborate menu of short-term securities; you should be familiar with the most popular entrées. Similarly there are many kinds of short-term debts and you should know their distinguishing characteristics. That is why we have included the present chapter on short-term lending and borrowing. You will encounter little in the way of new theory, but there is a good deal of interesting institutional material.

32-1 SHORT-TERM LENDING

The Money Market

The market for short-term investments is generally known as the **money market.** The money market has no physical marketplace. It consists of a loose agglomeration of banks and dealers linked together by telex, telephones, and computers. But a huge volume of securities is regularly traded on the money market, and competition is vigorous.

Most large corporations manage their own money-market investments, buying and selling through banks or dealers. Small companies sometimes find it more convenient to put their cash into a money-market fund. This is a mutual fund that invests only in short-term securities. In return for a fee, money-market funds provide professional management and a diversified portfolio of high-quality, short-term securities. We discussed money-market funds in Section 17-4.

In Chapter 24 we pointed out that there are two main markets for long-term dollar bonds. There is the domestic market in the United States and there is an international market for eurobonds. Similarly in this chapter we shall see that in addition to the domestic money market, there is also an international market for short-term eurodollar investments.

A eurodollar is not some strange bank note—it is simply a dollar deposit in a bank outside the United States. For example, suppose that an American oil company buys crude from an Arab sheik and pays for it with a $1 million check drawn on Morgan Guaranty Bank. The sheik then deposits the check with his account at Barclays Bank in London. As a result Barclays has an asset in the form of a $1 million credit in its account with Morgan Guaranty. It also has an offsetting liability in the form of a dollar deposit. The dollar deposit is placed outside the United States: It is, therefore, a eurodollar deposit.

We will describe in this chapter the principal domestic and eurodollar investments, but bear in mind that there is also a market for investments in other eurocurrencies. For example, if a United States corporation wishes to make a short-term investment in deutsche marks, it can do so either in the Frankfurt money market or in the international eurocurrency market.

If we lived in a world without regulation and taxes, the interest rate on a eurodollar loan would have to be the same as on an equivalent domestic dollar loan, the rate on a eurosterling loan would have to be the same as on a domestic sterling loan, and so on. However, the eurocurrency markets exist only because individual governments attempt to regulate domestic bank lending. For example, between 1963 and 1974 the United States government controlled the export of funds for corporate investment. Therefore companies that wished to expand abroad were forced to turn to the eurodollar market. This additional demand for eurodollar loans tended to push the eurodollar interest rate above the domestic rate. At the same time the government limited the rate of interest that banks in the United States could pay on domestic deposits; this also tended to keep the eurodollar rate of interest above the domestic rate. By early 1974 the restrictions on the export of funds had been removed and for large deposits the interest rate ceiling had also been abolished. In consequence, the differential between the interest rate on eurodollars and the rate on domestic deposits narrowed. But banks are not subject to Federal Reserve requirements on eurodollar deposits and are not obliged to insure these deposits with the Federal Deposit Insurance Corporation. On the other hand, depositors are exposed to the unlikely chance that a foreign government could prohibit banks from repaying eurodollar deposits. For these reasons eurodollar investments continue to offer slightly higher rates of interest than domestic dollar deposits.

The term *eurodollar* indicates that most of the business is conducted in Europe and principally in London. In addition there is a growing market for Asian dollar deposits. The United States government has become increasingly concerned that one consequence of regulation has been to drive banking business overseas to foreign banks and the overseas branches of American banks. In an attempt to attract some of this business back to the States, the government in 1981 allowed United States and foreign banks to establish so-called *International Banking Facilities* (IBFs). An IBF is the financial equivalent of a free-trade zone; it is physically situated in the United States, but as long as it conducts business only with non-American customers, it is not required to maintain reserves with the Federal Reserve and depositors are not subject to any United States tax.

Valuing Money-Market Investments

When we value long-term debt, it is important to take default risk into account. Almost anything may happen in 30 years; even today's most respectable company may get into trouble eventually. This is the basic reason why corporate bonds offer higher yields than Treasury bonds.

Short-term debt is not risk-free either. When Penn Central failed, it had $82 million of short-term commercial paper outstanding. After that shock, investors became much more discriminating in their purchases of commercial paper and the spread between interest rates on high- and low-quality paper widened dramatically.

Such examples of failure are exceptions that prove the rule; in general the danger of default is less for money-market securities issued by corporations than for corporate bonds. There are two reasons for this. First, the range of possible outcomes is less for short-term investments. Even though the distant future may be clouded, you can usually be confident that a particular company will survive for at least the next month. Second, only well-established companies can borrow in the money market. If you are going to lend money for only 1 day, you can't afford to spend too much time in evaluating the loan. Thus you will consider only blue-chip borrowers.

Despite the high quality of money-market investments, there are often substantial differences in yield between corporate and United States government securities. For example, in May 1987 the rate of interest on 3-month commercial paper was about 1.1 percentage points higher than on Treasury bills. Why is this? One answer is the risk of default on commercial paper. Another is that the investments have different degrees of liquidity or ''moneyness.'' Investors prefer Treasury bills because they are a little easier to turn into cash on short notice. Securities that can be converted quickly and cheaply into cash offer relatively low yields.

Calculating the Yield on Money-Market Investments

Many money-market investments are pure discount securities. This means that they don't pay interest: The return consists of the difference between the amount you pay and the amount you receive at maturity. Unfortunately, it is no good trying to persuade the Internal Revenue Service that this difference represents a capital gain. The IRS is wise to that one and will tax your return as ordinary income.

Two features make it difficult to work out the yield on money-market securities. One is the fact that they are often quoted on a discount basis; the other is that they are usually quoted on a 360-day year. For example, in May 1987 91-day Treasury bills were issued at a discount of 5.79 percent. This is a rather complicated way of saying that the price of a 91-day bill was $100 - 91/360 \times 5.79 = \$98.54$. For each $98.54 that you invested in May, the government agreed to pay $100 to you 91 days later. The yield over the 91 days was therefore $(100 - 98.54)/98.54 = 1.482$ percent, equivalent over a 365-day year to 5.94 percent simple interest and 6.08 percent if interest is compounded annually.[1] Notice that the yield is higher than the discount. When you read that Treasury bills are at a discount of 5.79 percent, it is very easy to slip into the mistake of thinking that they yield 5.79 percent.

U.S. Treasury Bills

Table 32-1 summarizes the characteristics of the principal money-market investments. The first item on our list is U.S. Treasury bills. These mature in 90,180, or 360 days.[2] Ninety-day and 180-day bills are issued every week and 360-day bills are generally issued every month. Sales are by auction. You can enter a competitive bid and take your chance of receiving an allotment at your bid price. Alternatively, if you want to be sure of getting your bills, you can enter a noncompetitive bid. Noncompetitive bids are filled at the *average* price of the successful competitive bids. You don't have to join in the auction in order to invest in Treasury bills. There is also an excellent secondary market in which billions of dollars of bills are bought and sold every day.

---

[1] Money-market dealers calculate yields on bills of 6 months or less on the basis of simple interest, using either a 360-day or a 365-day year. In other words, they multiply the 91-day yield by either 360/91 or 365/91. This is often confusing and not, in principle, the right way to do it. The compound rate is better:

$$(1.01482)^{365/91} - 1 = .0608, \text{ or } 6.08 \text{ percent}$$

[2] So-called 90-day bills actually mature 91 days after issue, 180-day bills mature 182 days after issue, and so on.

TABLE 32-1
Money-market investments

Investment	Borrower	Maturities When Issued	Marketability	Basis for Calculating Interest	Comments
Treasury bills	United States government	90, 180, and 360 days	Excellent secondary market	Discount	90- and 180-day bills auctioned weekly; 360-day bills auctioned monthly
Federal agency notes	FHLB, "Fannie Mae," "Sallie Mae," FHLMC, etc.	5 days to 1 year	Good secondary market	Usually discount	
Short-term tax-exempts	States, municipalities, local public housing agencies, urban renewal agencies	7 days to 1 year	Good secondary market	Usually interest-bearing; interest at maturity	Tax anticipation notes (TANs), bond anticipation notes (BANs), revenue anticipation notes (RANs), project notes (PNs), 7-day demand notes
Negotiable certificates of deposit (CDs)	Commercial banks	Usually 30 days to 3 months; also 6- and 12-month variable-rate CDs	Good secondary market	Usually interest-bearing, with interest at maturity on fixed-rate CDs	Receipt for time deposit at commercial bank
Eurodollar deposits	London branches of international banks	1 day to 1 year; also on 1-day call	No secondary market	Interest-bearing, with interest at maturity	
Negotiable London dollar certificates of deposit	London branches of international banks	Usually 30 days to 1 year; also variable-rate CDs up to 5 years	Somewhat less good market than for domestic CDs	Usually interest-bearing; on fixed-rate CDs interest annually or at maturity	Receipt for time deposit at overseas banks
Directly placed commercial paper	About 70 large sales finance companies and bank holding companies	Maximum 270 days	No secondary market; companies will usually consent to repurchase paper before maturity	Can be discounted or interest-bearing	Unsecured promissory notes placed directly with investor
Dealer commercial paper	Industrial firms and smaller finance companies	Maximum 270 days	No secondary market; buy-back arrangements can be negotiated with dealer	Can be discounted or interest-bearing	Unsecured promissory notes placed with dealer; also eurodollar dealer paper
Bankers' acceptances	Major commercial banks	1 to 6 months	Good secondary market	Discounted	Demands to pay that have been accepted by a bank
Repurchase agreements (RPs, repos, or buy-backs)	Dealers in U.S. government securities	Overnight to about 3 months; also continuing contracts (open repos)	No secondary market	Repurchase price set higher than selling price	Sales of government securities by dealer with simultaneous agreement to repurchase

Agency Securities

Agencies of the federal government such as the Federal Home Loan Bank or the Federal National Mortgage Association ("Fannie Mae"), borrow both short- and long-term. Corporations hold a significant part of the short-term obligations. They are actively traded and offer yields slightly above comparable Treasury securities. One reason for the slightly higher yield is that agency debt is not quite as marketable as Treasury issues. Another is that most agency debt is not backed by the "full faith and credit" of the United States government, but only by the issuing agency. It is possible that the government would allow one of its agencies to default on its debt, but most investors regard this risk as exceedingly remote.

Short-Term Tax-Exempts

States, municipalities, and local public housing and urban renewal agencies issue short-term notes.[3] These are slightly more risky than Treasury bills and not as easy to buy or sell. Nevertheless they have one particular attraction—the interest is not subject to federal income tax.

Yields on tax-exempts are substantially lower than pretax yields on comparable taxed securities. But if your company pays tax at the standard 34 percent corporate rate, the lower gross yield of the municipals may be more than offset by the savings in tax.

Bank Time Deposits and Certificates of Deposit

Banks offer lenders a variety of interest-bearing time deposits. One of the most popular is the regular savings account. You may invest almost any sum you choose in a savings account. The bank can insist that you give 30 days' notice before withdrawing funds, but in practice it is always prepared to pay out on demand. Savings accounts are, therefore, very liquid; and although they offer fairly low rates of interest, they are widely used by individuals and small companies.

Investment in a savings account is for an undefined period. In other words, you can withdraw funds as you need them. An alternative form of time deposit is the fixed-term deposit. In this case you lend the money for a fixed period. If you find that you need the money before maturity, the bank will usually allow you to withdraw, but you suffer a penalty in the form of a reduced rate of interest.

Fixed-term deposits are rather like short-term debt. The company "lends" the bank so many dollars; in return, the bank promises to repay the money with interest at the end of the agreed period. To attract large fixed-term deposits, banks regularly sell **certificates of deposit (CDs).** A CD is just the bank's promise to repay the loan. Most domestic CDs have a maturity of between 30 days and 6 months, but banks also issue longer-term CDs with a variable interest rate.

One attraction of CDs is that they are usually negotiable. Therefore, if you decide that you need the money before maturity, you don't have to ask the bank: You just sell your CD to another investor. When the loan matures, the new owner of the CD presents it to the bank and receives payment. CDs may be issued in amounts of $100,000, but a more normal minimum size is $1 million. There is an active market for these larger-denomination CDs issued by the principal commercial banks. Turning these CDs into cash is quick and relatively cheap.

Unlike domestic banking, eurocurrency banking is a wholesale rather than a retail business. The customers are corporations and governments—not individuals. They don't want checking accounts; they want to earn interest on their money.

---

[3] Issues by public housing agencies and urban renewal agencies are backed by the full faith and credit of the United States. They are usually known as *project notes* (PNs).

Therefore, all eurodollar bank deposits are either for a fixed term that may vary from 1 day to several years or they are for an undefined term but may be called at 1 day's notice. These fixed-term deposits are a more important source of funds for eurobanks than for domestic United States banks. However, the London branches of the major banks also issue eurodollar CDs, which are often for longer maturities than are available in the United States.

Commercial Paper

A bank is a kind of intermediary. It borrows short-term funds from one group of firms or individuals and relends the money to another group. It makes its profit by charging the borrower a higher rate of interest than it offers the lender.

Sometimes it is very convenient to have a bank in the middle. It saves lenders the trouble of looking for borrowers and assessing their creditworthiness, and it saves borrowers the trouble of looking for lenders. Depositors do not care whom the bank lends to: They need only satisfy themselves that the bank as a whole is safe.

There are also occasions on which it is *not* worth paying an intermediary to perform these functions. Large, safe, and well-known companies can bypass the banking system by issuing their own short-term unsecured notes. These notes are known as **commercial paper.**

Financial institutions, such as bank holding companies[4] and finance companies, also issue commercial paper, sometimes in very large quantities: $1 billion per month is not uncommon. Often such firms set up their own marketing department and sell their issues directly to investors. Other companies do so through dealers who receive a commission, or spread, of about $1000 for a $1 million trade.

Maturities of commercial paper may range from a few weeks to 270 days,[5] with the majority of issues maturing in 30 days. There is no regular secondary market for commercial paper, but the company or dealer that sells the paper is generally prepared to repurchase it from an investor before maturity.

Only nationally known companies can find a market for their commercial paper, and even then dealers are reluctant to handle a company's paper if there is any uncertainty about its financial position.[6] Companies generally back their issue of commercial paper by arranging a special backup line of credit with a bank. This guarantees that they can find the money to repay the paper. The risk of default is, therefore, small.

By cutting out the intermediary, major companies are able to borrow at rates that may be 1 to 1½ percent below the prime rate charged by banks. Even after allowing for a dealer's commission and the cost of any backup line of credit, this is still a substantial saving. Firms have generally been reluctant to imperil good relations with banks by reducing their borrowing too far. Nevertheless, there is no doubt that banks have felt the competition from commercial paper and have been prepared to reduce their rates to blue-chip customers. As a result, "prime rate"

---

[4] A bank holding company is a firm that owns a bank and also nonbanking subsidiaries. Thus a bank holding company might hold a bank (the major part of its business), and also a leasing company, a management consulting company, etc. Finance companies are firms that specialize in lending to businesses or individuals. In their lending they compete with banks. However, they raise funds not by attracting deposits, as banks do, but by issuing commercial paper and other, longer-term securities.

[5] Companies issuing securities are not required to file a registration statement with the SEC as long as the maturity does not exceed 270 days.

[6] Moody's and Standard and Poor's publish quality ratings for commercial paper. Investors rely on these ratings, along with other information, when they compare the quality of different firms' paper.

doesn't mean what it used to. It used to mean the rate banks charged their most creditworthy customers. Now the prime customers often pay less than the prime rate.

In recent years two new markets in commercial paper have developed. First, there is now a market for tax-exempt commercial paper issued by municipalities; second, there is a growing market for eurocommercial paper.[7]

Bankers' Acceptances

A banker's acceptance begins life as a written demand for the bank to pay a given sum at a future date. The bank then agrees to this demand by writing "accepted" on it. Once accepted, the draft becomes the bank's IOU and is a negotiable security. This security can then be bought or sold at a discount slightly greater than the discount on Treasury bills of the same maturity. A banker's acceptance may arise in one of two ways. We have already seen in Chapter 30 that an acceptance may be arranged when a company is buying goods on credit. Later in this chapter we shall see that acceptances are also occasionally used in connection with inventory financing.[8]

Acceptances by the large U.S. banks generally mature in 1 to 6 months and are known as *prime* acceptances. Money-market dealers make a good secondary market in prime acceptances.[9]

Repurchase Agreements

Repurchase agreements, RPs, repos, and buy-backs are all different names for the same thing—secured loans to a government security dealer. They work as follows. The investor buys part of the dealer's holding of Treasury securities and simultaneously arranges to sell them back again at a later date at a specified higher price.

Repos sometimes run for several months, but more frequently they are just overnight (24-hour) agreements. No other domestic money-market investment offers such liquidity. Corporations can treat overnight repos almost as if they were interest-bearing demand deposits.

Suppose that you decide to invest cash in repos for several days or weeks. You don't want to keep renegotiating agreements every day. One solution is to enter into a "continuing contract" with a security dealer. In this case there is no fixed maturity to the agreement; either side is free to withdraw at 1 day's notice. Alternatively, you may arrange with your bank to transfer any excess cash automatically into repos.[10]

For many years repos appeared to be not only very liquid instruments but also very safe. This reputation took a knock in 1982 when two money-market dealers went bankrupt. Each involved heavy use of repos or reverse repos (that is, buying securities with the promise to sell them back). One dealer, Drysdale Securities, had

---

[7] For a general discussion of the growth in commercial paper, see "Commercial Paper Market Since the Mid-Seventies," *Federal Reserve Bulletin*, **68:** 327–334 (June 1982).

[8] A banker's acceptance is used to finance specific transactions. The terms *working capital acceptance* and *finance bill* are used to describe drafts that are accepted by some banks to provide general funds. They are not often used.

[9] For further information see "Bankers' Acceptances," *Federal Reserve Bank of New York Quarterly Review,* **5:** 39–55 (Summer 1981) and "Recent Developments in the Bankers' Acceptance Market," *Federal Reserve Bulletin,* **72:** 1–12 (January 1986).

[10] See "Federal Funds and Repurchase Agreements," *Federal Reserve Bank of New York Quarterly Review,* **2:** 33–48 (Summer 1977).

been in existence for only 3 months and had a total capital of $20 million. However, it went bankrupt, owing Chase Bank $250 million. It's not easy to run up debts that fast, but Drysdale did it.

Ever since the Drysdale collapse lawyers have been trying to sort out the legal status of the repo. Is it, as the name implies, a promise to repurchase the bond at an agreed price, or is it, as some lawyers argue, a loan secured by a bond?

32-2 *FLOATING-RATE PREFERRED STOCK—AN ALTERNATIVE TO MONEY-MARKET INVESTMENTS

There is no law preventing firms from making short-term investments in long-term securities. If a firm has $1 million set aside for an income tax payment, it could buy a long-term bond on January 1 and sell it on April 15, when the taxes must be paid. However, the danger in this strategy is obvious: What happens if bond prices fall by 10 percent between January and April? There you are, with a $1 million liability to the Internal Revenue Service and bonds worth only $900,000. Of course bond prices could also go up, but why take the chance? Corporate treasurers entrusted with excess funds for short-term investment are naturally averse to the price volatility of long-term bonds.

You might think that common and preferred stock would be equally unattractive short-term investments for excess cash; that is not quite right, however, because these securities have an interesting tax advantage for corporations.

If the firm invests surplus cash in a short- or long-term debt, it must pay tax on the interest it receives. Thus, for $1 of interest, a firm in a 34 percent marginal tax bracket ends up with only $.66. However, firms pay tax on only 20 percent of dividends received from other corporations. Thus for $1 of dividends received, the firm gets to keep $1 - .20 \times .34 = \$.93$. The effective tax rate is only about 7 percent.

Suppose you consider putting that $1 million in some other corporation's preferred shares.[11] The 7 percent tax rate is very tempting. On the other hand, since preferred dividends are fixed, the prices of preferred shares change when long-term interest rates change. A $1 million investment in preferred shares could be worth only $900,000 on April 15, when taxes are due. Wouldn't it be nice if someone invented a preferred share that was insulated from fluctuating interest rates?

Well, there are such securities—the so-called *floating-rate preferreds*, which pay dividends that go up and down with the general level of interest rates.[12] The prices of these securities are less volatile than fixed-dividend preferreds, and they are a safer haven for the firms' excess cash.

Why would any firm want to *issue* floating-rate preferreds? Dividends must be paid out of *after-tax* income, whereas interest comes out of before-tax income. Thus, if a taxpaying firm wants to issue a floating-rate security, it would normally choose to issue floating-rate debt in order to generate interest tax shields.

However, there are plenty of firms that are not paying taxes. These firms cannot make use of the interest tax shield. Moreover, they have been able to issue floating-

---

[11] Preferred shares are usually better short-term investments for a corporation than common shares. The preferred shares' expected return is virtually all dividends; most common shares are expected to generate capital gains, too. The corporate tax on capital gains is usually 34 percent. Corporations therefore have a strong incentive to like dividends and dislike capital gains.

[12] Usually there are limits on the maximum and minimum dividends that can be paid. Thus if interest rates leap to 100 percent, the preferred dividend would hit a ceiling of, say, 15 percent. If interest rates fall to 1 percent, the preferred dividend would hit a floor at, say, 5 percent.

rate preferreds at yields *lower* than they would have to pay on a floating-rate debt issue. (The corporations buying the preferreds are happy with this lower yield because 80 percent of the dividends they receive escape tax.)

Floating-rate preferreds were invented in Canada in the mid-1970s, when several billion dollars' worth were issued before the Canadian tax authorities cooled off the market by limiting the dividend tax exclusion on some types of floating-rate issues. They were reinvented in the United States in May 1982, when Chemical New York Corporation, the holding company for the Chemical Bank, raised $200 million. The securities proved so popular that over $4 billion of floating-rate preferreds were issued by the following spring. Then the novelty wore off and the frequency of new issues slowed down. It was back to business as usual, with one important exception: There was one more item on the menu of investment opportunities open to corporate money managers.[13]

32-3 SHORT-TERM BORROWING

You now know where to invest your surplus cash. But suppose that you have the opposite problem and face a temporary cash deficit. Where can you find the short-term funds?

We have in part already answered that question. Remember that all those money-market investments that we discussed above must be *issued* by someone. So your firm may be able to raise short-term money by issuing commercial paper or discounting a banker's acceptance or (in the case of a bank) issuing CDs. But there are also other possible sources of cash that we have not yet discussed. In particular, you may take out a loan from a bank or finance company.

*Credit Rationing

Before we discuss the different types of bank loan, we should notice an interesting general point. The more that you borrow from the bank, the higher the rate of interest that you will be required to pay. However, there may come a stage at which the bank will refuse to lend you more, no matter how high an interest rate you are prepared to pay.

This takes us back to our discussion in Chapter 18 of the games that borrowers can play with lenders. Suppose that Henrietta Ketchup is a budding entrepreneur with two possible investment projects offering the following payoffs:

	Investment	Payoff	Probability of Payoff
Project 1	−12	+15	1.0
Project 2	−12	+24	.5
		0	.5

Project 1 is sure-fire and very profitable; project 2 is risky and a rotten project. Ms. Ketchup now approaches her bank and asks to borrow the present value of

---

[13] When investment bankers latch onto a good idea, they can't stop tinkering with it. In 1984 American Express invented *auction-rate preferred*. In this case the dividend is reset every 49 days by means of a Dutch auction which is open to all investors. An existing shareholder can enter the auction by stating the minimum dividend he is prepared to accept; if this turns out to be higher than the rate that is needed to sell the issue, the shareholder sells the stock on to the new investors at par. Alternatively, the shareholder can simply enter a noncompetitive bid, in which case he keeps his shares and receives whatever dividend is set by the other bidders. Since auction-rate preferred can be resold for par every 49 days, it proved popular with corporate treasurers as a temporary home for cash.

$10 (the remaining money she will find out of her own purse). The bank calculates that the payoff will be split as follows:

	Expected Payoff to Bank	Expected Payoff to Ms. Ketchup
Project 1	+10	+5
Project 2	$(.5 \times 10) + (.5 \times 0) = +5$	$.5 \times (24 - 10) = +7$

If Ms. Ketchup accepts project 1, the bank's debt is certain to be paid in full; if she accepts project 2, there is only a 50 percent chance of payment and the expected payoff to the bank is only $5. Unfortunately, Ms. Ketchup will prefer to take project 2, for if things go well she gets most of the profit and if they go badly, the bank bears most of the loss. Unless the bank can specify in the fine print which project must be undertaken, it will not lend to Ms. Ketchup the present value of $10. Suppose, however, that the bank agrees to lend the present value of *$5*. Then the payoffs would be

	Expected Payoff to Bank	Expected Payoff to Ms. Ketchup
Project 1	+5	+10
Project 2	$(.5 \times 5) + (.5 \times 0) = +2.5$	$.5 \times (24 - 5) = +9.5$

By rationing Ms. Ketchup to a smaller loan the bank has now made sure that she will not be tempted to speculate with its money.[14]

Unsecured Loans

We have so far referred to bank loans as if they were a standard product, but in practice they come in a variety of flavors. The simplest and most common solution is to arrange an unsecured loan from your bank. For example, many companies rely on unsecured bank loans to finance a temporary increase in inventories. Such loans are described as *self-liquidating*—in other words, the sale of the goods provides the cash to repay the loan. Another popular use of bank loans is for construction or "bridging" finance. In this case the loan serves as interim financing until a project is completed and long-term financing is arranged.[15]

Companies that frequently require short-term bank loans often ask their banks for a line of credit. This allows them to borrow at any time up to an established limit. A line of credit usually extends for a year and is then subject to review by the bank's loan committee. Banks are anxious that companies do not use a line of credit to cover their need for long-term finance. Thus, they often require the company to "clean up" its short-term bank loans for at least 1 month during the year.

---

[14] You might think that if the bank suspects Ms. Ketchup will undertake project 2, it should raise the interest rate on its loan. In this case Ms. Ketchup will not want to take on project 2 (they can't *both* be happy with a lousy project). But Ms. Ketchup also would not want to pay a high rate of interest if she is going to take on project 1 (she would do better to borrow less money at the risk-free rate). So, simply raising the interest rate is not the answer. If you find this surprising, imagine that you offered to lend someone a large sum at 100 percent. Would you be happier if he accepted or declined?

[15] For general information on trends in bank lending see "Changes in Loan Pricing and Business Lending at Commercial Banks," *Federal Reserve Bulletin,* **71:** 1–13 (January 1985).

The interest rate on a line of credit is usually tied either to the bank's prime rate of interest or to the CD rate—that is, the rate at which the bank can raise additional funds. In addition to the interest charge, banks often insist that in return for the line of credit the firm must maintain an interest-free demand deposit at the bank. For example, the firm might be asked to maintain a minimum average compensating balance equal to 10 percent of funds potentially available under the line of credit plus 10 percent of the amount actually borrowed. If as a result the firm maintains a higher cash balance than it otherwise would, the interest forgone on the additional deposit represents an extra cost to the loan.

Earlier in the chapter we noted that large companies sometimes bypass the banking system and issue their own short-term unsecured debt, i.e., commercial paper. Even after allowing for the issue expenses and the cost of backup lines of credit, commercial paper is generally substantially cheaper than a bank loan. Remember, however, that when times are hard and money is tight, the bank will give priority to its regular customers. Thus few firms bypass the banking system entirely, even in good times when commercial paper is cheap and easy to sell.

Loans Secured by Receivables

Banks often ask firms to provide security for loans. Since the bank is lending on a short-term basis, the security generally consists of liquid assets such as receivables, inventories, or securities. Sometimes the bank will accept a "floating lien" against receivables and inventory. This gives it a general claim against these assets, but it does not specify them in detail, and it sets few restrictions on what the company can do with the assets. More commonly, banks will require specific collateral.

If the bank is satisfied with the credit standing of your customers and the soundness of your product, it may be willing to lend you as much as 80 percent of accounts receivable. In return, you pledge your receivables as collateral for the loan. If you fail to repay your debt, the bank can collect the receivables and apply the proceeds to repaying the debt. If the proceeds are insufficient, you are liable for any deficiency. The loan is therefore said to be *with recourse.*

When you pledge receivables, you must keep the bank up to date on credit sales and collections. When you deliver goods to your customers, you send the bank a copy of the invoice, together with a form of assignment which gives the bank the right to the money your customers owe you. Then the firm can borrow up to the agreed proportion of this collateral.

Each day, as you make new sales, your collateral increases and you can borrow more money. Each day customers pay their bills. This money is placed in a special collateral account under the bank's control and is periodically used to reduce the size of the loan. Therefore, as the firm's business fluctuates, so does the amount of collateral and the size of the loan.

A few receivables loans are on a notification basis. In this case the bank informs your customer of the lending arrangement and asks for the money to be paid directly to the bank. Firms generally do not like their customers to know they are in debt, and therefore such loans are made more frequently without notification.

Receivables loans can be obtained not only from commercial banks but also from finance companies which specialize in lending to businesses.

Loans against receivables are flexible, and they provide a continuous source of funds. Also, banks are willing to lend the firm more with collateral than without it. However, it can be costly for borrower and lender alike to supervise and record changes in the collateral. Therefore the rate of interest on receivables financing is usually high, and there may be an additional service charge on the loan.

We discussed factoring in Chapter 30. Don't confuse factoring with lending against receivables. Factors *buy* your receivables and, if you wish, advance a portion of the money. They are, therefore, responsible for collecting the debt and suffer any losses if the customers don't pay. When you pledge your receivables as collateral for a loan, *you* remain responsible for collecting the debt and *you* suffer if a customer is delinquent.

If it moves, an investment banker will try to turn it into a security. In recent years receivables have sometimes been repackaged into securities. For instance, in 1986 First Boston Corporation set up a special-purpose subsidiary, which bought 367,000 vehicle loans from General Motors Acceptance Corporation (GMAC). It then bundled these loans into three packages, each with a different maturity, and resold the packages to investors in the form of notes with the huge total value of $4 billion. GMAC provided a limited guarantee on these notes, but if a large number of car buyers defaulted on their payments, the noteholders would suffer a loss.

Loans Secured by Inventory

Banks and finance companies also lend on the security of inventory, but they are choosy about the collateral they will accept. They want to make sure that they can identify and sell the inventory if you default. Automobiles and other standardized, nonperishable commodities are good collateral for a loan; work in process and ripe Camemberts are poor collateral.

The procedure for lending against inventories depends on where the goods are stored. If you place goods in a public warehouse, the warehouse company gives you a **warehouse receipt** and will then release the goods only on the instructions of the holder of the receipt. Because the holder of the receipt controls the inventory, the receipt can be used as collateral for a loan. Notice, however, that the warehouse receipt only identifies the goods and where they are stored. It doesn't guarantee the grade of the goods, nor does it guarantee your claim to the goods, nor does it provide insurance against fire, theft, and other hazards. Therefore the lender will also need to be satisfied on all these matters.

Lenders want to make sure that goods are not released without their permission. Therefore the law states that a warehouse receipt can be issued only by a bona fide warehouse company independent of the company that owns the goods. That is fine if you want to store your goods in a large public warehouse—but what do you do if you want to keep them on your own premises? The answer is that you establish a **field warehouse.** In other words, you arrange for a warehouse company to lease your warehouse or storage area. The warehouse company puts up signs stating that a field warehouse is being operated. It then remains responsible for storing your pledged goods and releases them only on the instructions of the holder of the warehouse receipt.

When you borrow from a bank, generally you sign an IOU and the bank hands you the money. Sometimes warehouse loans involve a somewhat more complicated arrangement. In exchange for your IOU the bank signs a banker's acceptance that matures on the same date. In other words, in exchange for your IOU the bank gives you not cash but *its* IOU. The advantage of this strange procedure is that the banker's acceptance is marketable whereas your promissory note is not. Therefore, you can sell your acceptance to the bank whenever you want the cash, and the bank can, if it chooses, resell the acceptance to another institution.

The important feature of warehouse loans is that goods are physically segregated and under the control of an independent warehouse company. Suppose, however, that you are an automobile dealer who needs to finance an inventory of new cars. You can't put the cars in a warehouse; you need to keep them in the showroom under your control. The common solution is to enter into a **floor planning** arrangement. Under this arrangement the finance company buys the cars from the manufacturer and you hold them in trust for the finance company. As evidence of this, you sign a *trust receipt* that identifies the cars involved. You are free to sell the cars, but when you do so, the proceeds are used to redeem the trust receipt. To make sure that the collateral is properly maintained, the finance company will make periodic inspections of the inventory.

The fact that liquid assets are easily saleable does not always make them good collateral. It also means the lender has to make sure that the borrower doesn't suddenly sell the assets and run off with the money. If you want to make your hair stand on end, read the story of the great salad oil swindle. Fifty-one banks and companies made loans of nearly $200 million to the Allied Crude Vegetable Oil Refining Corporation. Warehouse receipts issued by a field warehousing company were taken as security. Unfortunately, the cursory inspections by the employees of the field warehousing company failed to uncover the fact that, instead of containing salad oil, Allied's storage tanks were mainly filled with soap stock, seawater, and unidentifiable sludge. When the fraud was discovered, the president of Allied went to jail, the field warehousing company went into bankruptcy, and the 51 lenders were left out in the cold, looking for their $200 million. Lenders have been more careful since then.

32-4 TERM LOANS

The principal form of medium-term debt financing is the **term loan.** Most such loans are made by banks and have maturities of 1 to 8 years. Insurance companies often make longer-maturity term loans, and a number of term loans are split between banks and insurance companies.

Term loans are usually repaid in level amounts over the period of the loan, although often there may be a large final "balloon" payment or just a single "bullet" payment at maturity.

Banks can accommodate repayment patterns to the anticipated cash flows of the borrowing firm. For example, the first principal repayment might be delayed for a year pending completion of a new factory. Often term loans are renegotiated in midstream—that is, before maturity. Banks are usually willing to do this if the borrowing firm is an established customer, remains creditworthy, and has a sound business reason for making the change.

The rate of interest on the term loan is sometimes fixed for the life of the loan. But usually it is linked to the prime rate. Thus, if the rate is set at "1 percent over prime," the borrower may pay 5 percent in the first year when prime is 4 percent, $5\frac{1}{2}$ percent in the second year when prime is $4\frac{1}{2}$ percent, and so on. Occasionally these variable-rate loans include a "collar," which sets upper and lower limits on the interest that can be charged, or a "cap," which sets an upper limit only.

In addition to the interest cost the borrower is often obliged to maintain a minimum interest-free demand deposit with the bank. This compensating balance is commonly set at 10 to 20 percent of the amount of the loan, so that the true interest rate, calculated on the money the firm can actually use, may be significantly higher than the quoted interest rate.

Term loans are for the most part unsecured debt. The conditions of a term loan are like those of most unsecured bonds. They generally do not include the very restrictive negative conditions of private placement bonds, but they do stipulate minimum levels of net worth and working capital. Because many term loans are made to small companies, they often impose conditions on senior management. For example, the bank may require the company to insure the lives of senior managers, may place limits on management's remuneration, and may require personal guarantees for the loan.

A variant on the straight loan is the *revolving credit*. This is a legally assured line of credit with a maturity of up to 3 years. The borrower may be allowed to convert the credit at the end of the period into a straight term loan. Rather less common is the *evergreen credit*, which is a revolving credit without maturity that the *bank* may in any year convert into a straight loan. For both revolving credit and evergreen credit the company pays interest on any borrowings plus an "insurance premium" of about ½ percent on the unused amount, as well as maintaining a compensating balance with the bank.

Revolving credit agreements are relatively expensive compared to straight lines of credit or short-term bank loans. But in exchange for the extra cost, the firm receives a valuable option: It has guaranteed access to the bank's money at a fixed spread above the prime rate. This amounts to a put option, because the firm can sell its debt to the bank on fixed terms even if its own creditworthiness deteriorates.

Participation Loans

The large money center banks have more demand for loans than they can satisfy; for smaller banks it is the other way around. As a result there has been a rapid growth in shared lending. The most common form of shared lending is the participation loan. In this case the lead bank sells a portion of the loan to a second bank. This second bank usually just receives a "certificate of participation" which states that the lead bank will pay over a proportion of the cash flows from the loan. In many cases the borrower may not be aware that the sale has occurred.

Participation loans hit the headlines in 1982 when Penn Square National Bank went belly up. One reason for consternation was that Penn Square had sold more than $200 million of its loan portfolio to Chase Bank. To make matters worse, the borrowers had deposited money with Penn Square and the receiver claimed that the losses on these deposits should be deducted from the amount of the borrowers' debt. This reduced the cash flows to be paid over to Chase. Since the Penn Square collapse, banks and their lawyers have been more careful about the fine print in loan participations.

Eurodollar Lending

The major international banks also make unsecured eurodollar loans with short- or medium-term maturities. The interest rate on such loans is usually tied to the London interbank offered rate (LIBOR), which is the rate at which the banks lend eurodollars to one another. When the sums involved are very large, these eurodollar loans have traditionally been made by a syndicate of banks. These syndicated loans differ from the loan participations that we described earlier; with a syndicated loan each bank has a separate loan agreement with the borrower.[16]

During the 1980s there has been a trend away from syndicated eurodollar loans and toward more marketable types of debt. This process is generally known as "securitization."

---

[16] Occasionally banks would like to sell their share in a syndicated loan. They could do this by arranging for another bank to "participate" in their portion, but we have already seen the dangers of this approach. Therefore loan agreements sometimes make it possible for each bank to transfer its portion of the loan. Transferable syndicated loans are a response by the banks to the trend away from bank lending and toward marketable securities.

Securitization in the eurodollar market has taken two principal forms. Many firms, who would previously have borrowed by means of a syndicated bank loan, have chosen instead to issue floating-rate notes in the eurobond market (we described these notes in Section 24-2).

Other firms have preferred to borrow by means of **note issuance facilities** (NIFs).[17] NIFs have been one of the great growth products of the 1980s. A NIF is a line of credit that allows the borrower to issue a series of short-term euronotes, typically over a period of 5 to 7 years. These euronotes are marketed on behalf of the firm by one or more banks or investment banks. In order to make sure that the firm gets its money, a (possibly different) group of banks underwrites the issue by promising to take up any unsold notes. In exchange for this facility the firm usually pays an initial fee and an annual underwriting fee.[18]

Most of the euronotes issued under a note issuance facility have a 3- to 6-month maturity, but sometimes the firm will have a wide choice as to the maturity and currency of any debt that it issues. Many firms in the United States do not take up their option to issue euronotes but instead use the NIF either as an emergency source of funds or as a backup line of credit for their commercial paper programs in the United States.

32-5 SUMMARY

If you have more cash than you currently need, you can invest the surplus in the money market. The principal money market investments in the United States are:

- U.S. Treasury bills
- Short-term tax-exempts
- Certificates of deposit
- Commercial paper
- Bankers' acceptances
- Repurchase agreements

If none of these catches your fancy, you can make a short-term eurocurrency investment, such as a eurodollar time deposit or a London dollar certificate of deposit.

None of these securities is exactly the same. If you want to make effective use of your cash, you need to be aware of the differences in their liquidity, risk, and yield. Table 32-1 summarizes the main features of money-market instruments. Figure 32-1 shows money-market rates as reported in *The Wall Street Journal* for May 1, 1987.

Most corporations making short-term investments of excess cash buy one or more of the instruments described in Table 32-1. But there are many alternatives, including floating-rate preferreds. These securities are attractive for two reasons. First, corporations pay tax on only 20 percent of the dividends received. Second, the dividend moves up and down with changes in interest rates, so the preferred shares' prices are more or less stabilized.

For many companies surplus cash is not a worry; their problem is to finance a temporary cash deficiency. One of the main sources of short-term funds is the

---

[17] Other similar facilities are termed revolving underwriting facilities (RUFs) or note purchase facilities. Eurocommercial paper programs are sometimes referred to as nonunderwritten NIFs. The bank will agree to market the firm's short-term debt but will not promise to take up any unsold paper.

[18] See *Recent Innovations in International Banking,* Bank for International Settlements, Basel, April 1986.

MONEY RATES

The key annual interest rates below are a guide to general levels but don't always represent actual transactions.

PRIME RATE: 7¾%. The base rate on corporate loans at large U.S. money center commercial banks.

FEDERAL FUNDS: 8% high, 7¼% low, 7½% near closing bid, 8% offered. Reserves traded among commercial banks for overnight use in amounts of $1 million or more. Source: Prebon Money Brokers Inc., N.Y.

DISCOUNT RATE: 5½%. The charge on loans to depository institutions by the New York Federal Reserve Bank.

CALL MONEY: 7½% to 8¾%. The charge on loans to brokers on stock exchange collateral.

COMMERCIAL PAPER placed directly by General Motors Acceptance Corp.: 6⅝% 30 to 59 days; 6.55% 60 to 89 days; 6½% 90 to 119 days; 6.45% 120 to 149 days; 6.40% 150 to 179 days; 6.35% 180 to 270 days.

COMMERCIAL PAPER: High-grade unsecured notes sold through dealers by major corporations in multiples of $1,000: 6.65% 30 days; 6.70% 60 days; 6.775% 90 days.

CERTIFICATES OF DEPOSIT: 6.02% one month; 6.10% two months; 6.16% three months; 6.26% six months; 6.39% one year. Average negotiable rates paid by major New York banks on primary new issues of negotiable C.D.s, usually on amounts of $1 million and more. The minimum unit is $100,000. Typical rates in the secondary market: 6.50% one month; 6.65% three months; 6.95% six months.

BANKERS ACCEPTANCES: 6.60% 30 days; 6.66% 60 days; 6.71% 90 days; 6.74% 120 days; 6.76% 150 days; 6.76% 180 days. Negotiable, bank-backed business credit instruments typically financing an import order.

LONDON LATE EURODOLLARS: 6 15/16% to 6 13/16% one month; 7 1/16% to 6 15/16% two months; 7 3/16% to 7 1/16% three months; 7 3/16% to 7 1/16% four months; 7 5/16% to 7 3/16% five months; 7⅜% to 7¼% six months.

LONDON INTERBANK OFFERED RATES (LIBOR): 7⅛% three months; 7⅜% six months; 7 13/16% one year. The average of interbank offered rates for dollar deposits in the London market based on quotations at five major banks.

OTHER PRIME RATES: Canada 8.75%; Germany 6.25%; Japan 4.28%; Switzerland 5.25%; Britain 10%. These rate indications aren't directly comparable; lending practices vary widely by location. Source: Morgan Guaranty Trust Co.

TREASURY BILLS: Results of the Monday, April 27, 1987, auction of short-term U.S. government bills, sold at a discount from face value in units of $10,000 to $1 million: 5.79% 13 weeks; 6.14% 26 weeks.

FEDERAL HOME LOAN MORTGAGE CORP. (Freddie Mac): Posted yields on 30-year mortgage commitments for delivery within 30 days. 10.18%, standard conventional fixed-rate mortgages; 6.875%, 2% rate capped one-year adjustable rate mortgages.

FEDERAL NATIONAL MORTGAGE ASSOCIATION (Fannie Mae): Posted yields on 30 year mortgage commitments for delivery within 30 days (priced at par). 9.92%, standard conventional fixed rate-mortgages; 9.35%, 6/2 rate capped one-year adjustable rate mortgages.

MERRILL LYNCH READY ASSETS TRUST: 5.33%. Annualized average rate of return after expenses for the past 30 days; not a forecast of future returns.

FIGURE 32-1

Short-term interest rates of April 30, 1987. (*Source:* Reported by permission of *The Wall Street Journal.* © Dow Jones & Company, Inc., 1987. All rights reserved.)

unsecured bank loan. This is often taken out under a bank line of credit, which entitles the firm to borrow up to an agreed limit. The interest rate that banks charge on unsecured loans must be sufficient to cover not only the opportunity cost of capital for the loans but also the costs of running a loan department. As a result, large regular borrowers have found it cheaper to bypass the banking system and issue their own short-term unsecured debt. This debt is known as *commercial paper.*

Bank loans with maturities exceeding 1 year are called *term loans.* The firm agrees to pay interest based on the bank's prime rate and to repay principal in regular installments. Special patterns of principal payments over time can be negotiated to meet the firm's special needs, however. Often compensating balances are required.

Another form of medium-term bank finance is the revolving credit, which guarantees the firm access to a line of credit. Revolving credits can often be converted into regular term loans.

The international banks also make unsecured loans of eurodollars. The rate on these loans is usually tied to the London interbank offered rate (LIBOR). Sometimes a group of banks will arrange a line of credit that allows the borrower to issue euronotes up to some agreed limit. Such lines of credit are generally called *Note Issuance Facilities (NIFs)*.

If you ask to borrow more and more from a domestic bank in the United States, you will eventually be asked to provide security for the loan. Sometimes this security consists of a floating lien on receivables and inventories, but usually you will be asked to pledge specific assets. The bank or finance company will take precautions to make sure that the collateral is properly identified and within its control. For example, when you borrow against receivables the bank must be informed of all sales of goods and the resulting accounts receivable must be pledged to the bank. As customers pay their bills, the money is paid into a special collateral account under the bank's control. Similarly, when you borrow against stocks of raw materials, the bank will insist that the goods are held by an independent warehouse company. As long as the bank holds the warehouse receipt for these goods, they cannot be released without the bank's permission. Loans secured on finished goods are usually made under a floor planning arrangement. In this case you will be required to sign a trust receipt promising that you are merely holding the specified goods in trust for the lender, and the lender will make periodic inspections to see that you are keeping your promise.

You may also find that there comes a point at which the bank will not increase its lending no matter how high a rate of interest you are prepared to pay. Banks know that the more they lend, the more they are encouraging you to gamble with their money. Your aims and the bank's are more likely to coincide if your borrowing is kept to a responsible level.

FURTHER READING

For a detailed description of the money market and short-term lending opportunities, see:

> M. Stigum, *The Money Market: Myth, Reality and Practice,* 2d ed., Richard D. Irwin, Inc., Homewood, Ill., 1983.

Here are two practically oriented books on sources of short- and medium-term financing:

> D. A. Hayes, *Bank Lending Policies, Domestic and International,* Bureau of Business Research, University of Michigan, Ann Arbor, 1971.
>
> L. A. Moskowitz, *Modern Factoring and Commercial Finance,* Thomas Y. Crowell Co., New York, 1977.

QUIZ

1. Choose the investment that best fits the accompanying description.
   (a) Maturity often overnight: repurchase agreements or bankers' acceptances?
   (b) Maturity never exceeds 270 days: tax-exempts or commercial paper?
   (c) Maturity never less than 30 days: eurodollar deposits or U.S. certificates of deposit?
   (d) Often directly placed: finance company commercial paper or industrial commercial paper?
   (e) No secondary market: bankers' acceptances or finance company commercial paper?

    (*f*) Issued by the U.S. Treasury: tax-exempts or 360-day bills?

    (*g*) Quoted on a discount basis: certificates of deposit or Treasury bills?

    (*h*) Sold by auction: tax-exempts or Treasury bills?

2. On May 1, 1987, 6-month Treasury bills were issued at a discount of 6.14 percent. (See Figure 32-1.) What is the annual yield?

3. Complete the following passage by selecting the most appropriate terms from the following list: *floating lien, field warehouse, clean-up provision, commercial paper, floor planning, line of credit, prime rate, public warehouse, compensating balance, trust receipt, warehouse receipt, collateral, with recourse.*

> Companies with fluctuating capital needs often arrange a _____ with their bank. To make sure that this facility is not used to provide permanent funds, the bank usually incorporates a _____ . The interest on any borrowing is tied to the bank's _____ . In addition the bank generally requires that the company keep a _____ on deposit at the bank. Some large companies bypass the banking system and issue their own short-term unsecured debt. This is called _____ .
>
> Secured short-term loans are sometimes covered by a _____ on all receivables and inventory. Generally, however, the borrower pledges specific assets as _____ . If these assets are insufficient to repay the debt, the borrower is liable for the deficiency. Therefore such loans are said to be _____ . Warehouse loans are examples of secured short-term loans. The goods may be stored in a _____ or in a _____ that is established by the warehouse company on the borrower's premises. The warehouse company issues a _____ to the lender and releases the goods only on his or her instructions. Loans to automobile dealers are usually made on a different basis. The dealer holds the inventory on behalf of the lender and issues a _____ . This arrangement is known as _____ .

*4. Consider three securities:

    (*a*) A floating-rate bond

    (*b*) A preferred share paying a fixed dividend

    (*c*) A floating-rate preferred

    A financial manager responsible for short-term investment of excess cash would probably choose the floating-rate preferred over *either* of the other two securities. Why? Explain briefly.

5. Here are six questions about term loans:

    (*a*) What is the usual minimum maturity of a term loan?

    (*b*) Are compensating balances required?

    (*c*) Are term loans usually secured loans? That is, are they usually backed up by specific collateral?

    (*d*) How is the interest rate usually determined?

    (*e*) What is a balloon payment?

    (*f*) What is a revolving credit?

QUESTIONS AND PROBLEMS

1. Look up current interest rates offered by short-term investment alternatives. Suppose that your firm has $1 million excess cash to invest for the next 2 months. How would you invest this excess cash? How would your answer change if the excess cash is $5000, $20,000, $100,000 or $100 million?

2. At one point in 1987, 5-year Treasury notes sold at a 7.79 percent yield, while tax-exempts of comparable maturity offered 5.80 percent annually. Ignoring other factors, what was the marginal tax rate of investors just indifferent between the Treasury bills and tax-exempts? What other factors might affect an investor's choice between the two types of securities?

3. Interest rates on bank loans exceed rates on commercial paper. Why don't all firms issue commercial paper rather than borrowing from banks?

4. Do you think you could make money by setting up a firm which would (a) issue commercial paper and (b) relend money to businesses at a rate slightly higher than the commercial paper rate, but still less than the rate charged by banks?

5. Roy's Toys needs an extra $1 million in October to build up inventory for the Christmas season. First National has offered to lend at 9 percent subject to a 20 percent compensating balance. Hometown Trust will lend at 11 percent with no strings attached. Which bank is offering the better deal? Why? Would your answer change if Roy's Toys already had a $100,000 normal working balance at First National? (Assume in this case that the working balance can be used to cover part of the compensating balance.)

6. Axle Chemical Corporation's treasurer has forecast a $1 million cash deficit for the next quarter. However, there is only a 50 percent chance this deficit will actually occur. The treasurer estimates that there is a 20 percent probability the company will have no deficit at all, and a 30 percent probability that it will actually need $2 million in short-term financing. The company can either take out a 90-day unsecured loan at 1 percent per month or establish a line of credit, costing 1 percent per month on the amount borrowed plus a commitment fee of $20,000. Both alternatives also require a 20 percent compensating balance for outstanding loans. If excess cash can be reinvested at 9 percent, which source of financing gives the lower expected cost?

7. Suppose that you are a banker responsible for approving corporate loans. Nine firms are seeking secured loans. They offer the following assets as collateral:
   (a) Firm A, a heating oil distributor, offers a tanker load of fuel oil in transit from the Middle East.
   (b) Firm B, a wine wholesaler, offers 1000 cases of Beaujolais Nouveau, located in a field warehouse.
   (c) Firm C, a stationer, offers an account receivable for office supplies sold to the city of New York.
   (d) Firm D, a bookstore, offers its entire inventory of 15,000 used books.
   (e) Firm E, a wholesale grocer, offers a boxcar full of bananas.
   (f) Firm F, an appliance dealer, offers its inventory of electric typewriters.
   (g) Firm G offers 100 ounces of gold.
   (h) Firm H, a government securities dealer, offers its portfolio of Treasury bills.
   (i) Firm I, a boat builder, offers a half-completed luxury yacht. The yacht will take 4 months more to complete.
   Which of these assets are most likely to be good collateral? Which are likely to be poor collateral? Explain.

8. Any one of the assets mentioned in the preceding question *could* be acceptable collateral under certain circumstances if appropriate safeguards were taken. What circumstances? What safeguards? Explain.

*9. The first floating-rate preferreds were successfully issued at initial dividend yields *below* yields on Treasury bills. How was this possible? The preferreds were clearly riskier than the bills. What would you predict for the *long-run* relationship between yields on bills and floating-rate preferreds? (We say "long-run" to give time for all firms who will want to issue floating-rate preferreds to get around to doing so.)

*10 Most floating-rate preferreds have both a "floor" and a "ceiling" on their dividend rate. (See Section 32-2, footnote 12.) How do these limits affect the behavior of the *prices* of these securities as interest rates change? Why do you think the issuing companies included the limits in the first place?

11. Term loans usually require firms to pay a fluctuating interest rate. For example, the interest rate may be set at "1 percent above prime." The prime rate sometimes varies by several percentage points within a single year.

Suppose that your firm has decided to borrow $40 million for 5 years. It has three alternatives:

(*a*) Borrow from a bank at the prime rate, currently 10 percent. The proposed loan agreement requires no principal repayments until the loan matures in 5 years.

(*b*) Issue 26-week commercial paper, currently yielding 9 percent. Since funds are required for 5 years, the commercial paper will have to be "rolled over" semiannually. That is, financing the $40 million requirement for 5 years will require 10 successive commercial paper sales.

(*c*) Borrow from an insurance company at a fixed rate of 11 percent. As in the bank loan, no principal has to be repaid until the end of the 5-year period.

What factors would you consider in analyzing these alternatives? Under what circumstances would you choose *a*? Under what circumstances would you choose *b* or *c*? (*Hint:* Don't forget Chapter 23.)

12. The IRS prohibits companies from borrowing money to buy tax-exempts and also deducting the interest payments on the borrowing from taxable income. Should the IRS prohibit such activity? If it didn't, would you advise the company to borrow to buy tax-exempts?

PART TEN

MERGERS, INTERNATIONAL
FINANCE, AND PENSIONS

33 Mergers

The extent of merger activity in the United States is remarkable. For example, Table 33-1 lists just a few of the more important mergers in 1986. You can see that they involved big money. During periods of intense merger activity, financial managers spend significant amounts of time either searching for firms to acquire or worrying whether some other firm will acquire them.

When you buy another company, you are making an investment, and the basic principles of capital investment decisions apply. You should go ahead with the purchase if it makes a net contribution to shareholders' wealth. But mergers are often awkward transactions to evaluate. First, you have to be careful to define benefits and costs properly. Second, buying a company is more complicated than buying a new machine; in particular, special tax, legal, and accounting issues must often be addressed. Finally, you need a general understanding of why mergers occur and who typically gains or loses as a result of them.

We will start by reviewing the possible benefits and costs of a merger. We will also comment on the legal, tax, and accounting problems encountered in putting two firms together.

Many mergers are arranged amicably, but in other cases one firm will make a hostile takeover bid for the other. We will describe the principal techniques of modern merger warfare, and since the threat of hostile takeovers has stimulated corporate restructurings and leveraged buyouts, we will describe them too.

We would have liked to close by presenting a general theory explaining mergers, but unfortunately no satisfactory theory exists. In our opinion, no one has a complete economic explanation for the wide fluctuations in aggregate merger

TABLE 33-1
Some important mergers in 1986

Selling Company	Acquiring Company	Payment (Billions)
Beatrice*	Kohlberg Kravis Roberts	$6.3
RCA	General Electric	6.1
Sperry Rand	Burroughs	4.9
Safeway Stores*	Kohlberg Kravis Roberts	4.2
Allied Stores	Campeau	3.6
R. H. Macy*	Macy Acquiring	3.5
Midcon	Occidental Petroleum	3.0
Viacom International*	Viacom management and financial institutions	3.0
Texas Oil and Gas	USX	3.0

* Leveraged buyout (we explain leveraged buyouts in Section 33-7).

activity. On the other hand, a good deal is known about the profitability of mergers. We will summarize this evidence.

33-1 ESTIMATING THE ECONOMIC GAINS AND COSTS OF MERGERS[1]

Suppose that you are the financial manager of firm A and that you wish to analyze the possible purchase of firm B. The first thing to think about is whether there is an *economic gain* from the merger. There is an economic gain *only if the two firms are worth more together than apart.* For example, if you think that the combined firm would be worth PV_{AB}, and that the separate firms are worth PV_A and PV_B, then[2]

$$\text{Gain} = PV_{AB} - (PV_A + PV_B)$$

If this gain is positive, there is an economic justification for merger. But you also have to think about the *cost* of acquiring firm B. As we will show later, this can depend on the way the merger is financed. Let us begin, however, with the easy case in which payment is made in the form of cash. Then the cost of acquiring B is equal to the cash payment minus B's value as a separate entity. Thus

$$\text{Cost} = \text{cash} - PV_B$$

The net present value to A of a merger with B is measured by the difference between the gain and the cost. Therefore, you should go ahead with the merger if its net present value, defined as

$$NPV = \text{gain} - \text{cost} = PV_{AB} - (PV_A + PV_B) - (\text{cash} - PV_B)$$

is positive.

We like to write the merger criterion in this way because it focuses attention on two distinct questions. When you estimate the benefit, you concentrate on whether there are any gains to be had from the merger. When you estimate cost, you are concerned with the division of these gains between the two companies.

An example may help make this clear. Firm A has a value of $2 million, B a value of $200,000. Merging the two would allow cost savings with a present value of $120,000. This is the gain from the merger. Thus

$$PV_A = \$2,000,000$$
$$PV_B = \$200,000$$
$$\text{Gain} = +\$120,000$$
$$PV_{AB} = \$2,320,000$$

Suppose that B is bought for cash, say for $250,000. The cost of the merger is

$$\text{Cost} = \text{cash} - PV_B$$
$$= \$250,000 - \$200,000 = \$50,000$$

---

[1] This chapter's definitions and interpretations of the gains and costs of merger follow those set out in S. C. Myers, "A Framework for Evaluating Mergers," in *Modern Developments in Financial Management*, S. C. Myers (ed.), Frederick A. Praeger, Inc., New York, 1976.

[2] We use PV here to refer to the value of the whole firm—that is, its assets, not just its common equity.

Note that the stockholders of firm B—the people on the other side of the transaction—are ahead by $50,000. *Their* gain is *your* cost.[3] They have captured $50,000 of the $120,000 merger gain. Thus when we write down the NPV of the merger from A's viewpoint, we are really calculating that part of the gain that A's stockholders get to keep. The NPV of this merger therefore is

$$NPV = PV_{AB} - (PV_A + PV_B) - (cash - PV_B)$$

The net gain to A's stockholders equals the overall gain to the merger less that part of gain captured by B's stockholders:

$$\$70,000 = \$120,000 - \$50,000$$

Just as a check, let's confirm that A's stockholders really come out $70,000 ahead. They start with a firm worth $PV_A = \$2$ million. They pay out $250,000 cash to B's stockholders and end up with a firm worth $2,320,000. Thus their net gain is

$$NPV = \text{wealth with merger} - \text{wealth without merger}$$
$$= (PV_{AB} - cash) - PV_A$$
$$= (\$2,320,000 - \$250,000) - \$2,000,000$$
$$= + \$70,000$$

Suppose investors had not anticipated the merger between A and B. The announcement will cause the value of B's stock to rise from $200,000 to $250,000, a gain of 25 percent. If investors share management's assessment of the merger gains, the market value of A's stock will increase by $70,000, or 3½ percent.

It makes sense to keep an eye on what investors think are the gains from merging. If the stock price falls when investors learn of the bid, then the message is that the merger benefits are doubtful or that you are paying too much for them.

A Digression on the Right and Wrong Ways to Estimate the Benefits of Mergers

Some companies estimate the benefits of a merger by discounting detailed forecasts of the cash flows of the combined firm to give a figure for PV_{AB}. Then they deduct the current market values of the separate entities to give an estimate of the gain from the merger. There are two dangers in this procedure. First, current stock prices may already anticipate the gain. Second, and more important, you are likely to make large errors in your forecasts of the cash flows. Many mergers will, therefore, *appear* to offer gains just because you are overoptimistic in your forecasts of the target firm's cash flows. Concentrate instead on the *changes* in cash flow that would result from the merger. *Ask yourself why the two firms should be worth more together than apart.*

The same advice holds when you are contemplating the *sale* of part of your business. There is no point saying to yourself, "This is an unprofitable business and should be sold." Unless the buyer can run the business better than you can, the price you receive will reflect the poor prospects.

Sometimes you may come across managers who believe that there are simple

---

[3] In practice, arranging a merger may involve several million dollars in fees for investment bankers, lawyers, and accountants. For example, the leveraged buyout of Beatrice involved a huge $45 million in advisory fees and $46 million in legal and accounting fees. In that case there is a cash leakage: B's gain is *less* than A's cost.

rules for identifying good acquisitions. For example, they may say that they always seek to buy into growth industries or that they have a policy of acquiring companies that are selling below book value. But our comments in Chapter 11 about the characteristics of a good investment decision also hold true when you are buying a whole company. *You add value only if you can capitalize on a monopolistic advantage*—some competitive edge that other firms can't match.

One final piece of horse sense. Often two companies bid against one another to acquire the same target firm. In effect, the target firm puts itself up for auction. In these cases ask yourself whether the target is worth more to you than to the other bidder. If the answer is no, you should be cautious about getting into a bidding contest. Winning such a contest may be more expensive than losing it. (If you lose, you have simply wasted your time; if you win, then there is a better than even chance that you have paid too much.)

33-2 SENSIBLE MOTIVES FOR MERGER

Mergers are often categorized as *horizontal, vertical,* or *conglomerate.* A horizontal merger is one that takes place between two firms in the same line of business; most of the mergers around the turn of the century were of this type. During the 1920s vertical mergers were predominant. A vertical merger is one in which the buyer expands backward toward the source of raw materials or forward in the direction of the ultimate consumer. A conglomerate merger involves companies in unrelated lines of business. Conglomerate mergers have become common in recent years. For example, the Federal Trade Commission estimated that between 1965 and 1975, 80 percent of mergers were conglomerate.[4]

With these distinctions in mind, we will go on to consider motives for mergers—that is, reasons why two firms may be worth more together than apart. But first, a caveat. It would be nice if we could say that certain types of mergers are generally successful and other types fail. Unfortunately, we know of no such simple generalizations. Many mergers which seem to make economic sense fail because they are badly implemented. Sometimes mergers fail because the buyer misestimates the value of particular assets or liabilities. For example, perhaps the buyer does not notice that the inventory is not saleable or may overlook the warranties on a defective product. At other times mergers fail because managers cannot handle the complex task of integrating two firms with different accounting methods, remuneration policies, and production processes. And, perhaps most important of all, they fail because the buyer ignores the likely reactions of the people involved.

Economies of Scale

Just as most of us believe that we would be happier if only we were a little richer, so every manager seems to believe that his or her firm would be more competitive if only it were just a little bigger.[5]

These *economies of scale* are the natural goal of horizontal mergers. But such economies have been claimed in conglomerate mergers too. The architects of these

---

[4] Federal Trade Commission, *Statistical Report on Mergers and Acquisitions,* 1977, p. 106, table 19.

[5] Economies of scale are enjoyed when the average unit cost of production goes down as production increases. One way to achieve economies of scale is to spread fixed costs over a larger volume of production.

mergers have pointed to the economies that come from sharing central services such as office management and accounting, financial control, executive development, and top-level management.

There are innumerable examples of possible economies of scale. But merging isn't always the best way to achieve them. It is always easier to buy another business than it is to integrate it with yours afterward. Some companies that have got together for these reasons still operate as a collection of separate and sometimes competing operations with different production facilities, research efforts, and marketing forces. Even economies in central services may be elusive. The complicated structure of conglomerate companies may actually increase the administrative staff. And top-level managers of conglomerates find that their general skills are not easily applied to the specialized problems of individual subsidiaries.

Economies of Vertical Integration

Vertical mergers seek economies in vertical integration. Large industrial companies commonly like to gain as much control as possible over the production process by expanding back toward the output of the raw material and forward to the ultimate consumer. One way to achieve this is to merge with a supplier or a customer.

One reason for vertical integration is that it makes coordination and administration easier. We can illustrate by a somewhat extreme example. Think of an airline that does not own any planes. If it schedules a flight from Boston to San Francisco, it sells tickets and then rents a plane for that flight from a separate company. This strategy might work on a small scale, but it would be an administrative nightmare for a major carrier. There would be hundreds of flights and rental agreements daily. Moreover, the agreements could not be independently negotiated. For example, the airline might have to make sure that the plane from Boston shows up in San Francisco in time to be rented for a subsequent flight to Salt Lake City. In view of these difficulties, it is not surprising that all major airlines have integrated backward away from the consumer, by buying and flying airplanes rather than patronizing "rent-a-plane" companies.

Combining Complementary Resources

Many small firms are acquired by large ones which can provide missing ingredients necessary for the firm's success. The small firm may have a unique product but lack the engineering and sales organizations necessary to produce and market it on a large scale. The firm could develop engineering and sales talent from scratch, but it may be quicker and cheaper to merge with a firm that already has ample talent. The two firms have *complementary resources*—each has what the other needs—and so it can make sense for them to merge. The two firms are worth more together than apart because each acquires something it does not have and gets it cheaper than it would acting on its own. Also, the merger may open up opportunities that neither firm would pursue otherwise.

Of course two large firms may also merge because they have complementary resources. But we think that most gains of this nature occur when small firms are acquired by large ones.

Unused Tax Shields

Sometimes a firm may have potential tax shields but not have the profits to take advantage of them. For example, after the expropriation of its Cuban sugar plantations, Bangor Punta had substantial tax-loss carry-forwards which it could not use. It therefore combined with other firms that were generating taxable profits so that the tax-loss carry-forward could be used.[6]

Mergers as a Use for Surplus Funds

Here's another argument for mergers. Suppose that your firm is in a mature industry. It is generating a substantial amount of cash, but it has few profitable investment opportunities. Ideally such a firm should distribute the surplus cash to shareholders by increasing its dividend payment or by a stock repurchase. Unfortunately energetic managers are often reluctant to adopt a policy of shrinking their firm in this way.

If the firm is not willing to purchase its own shares, it can instead purchase someone else's. Thus firms with a surplus of cash and a shortage of good investment opportunities often turn to mergers *financed by cash* as a way of redeploying their capital.

In 1985 the 25 largest deals involved payment of about $50 billion in cash to the selling shareholders. That is more than half the total amount paid out in corporate dividends.[7]

Some firms have excess cash and do not pay it out to stockholders or redeploy it by acquisition. Such firms often find themselves targets for takeover by other firms who propose to redeploy the cash for them. During the oil price slump of the early 1980s many cash-rich oil companies found themselves threatened by takeover. This was not because their cash was a unique asset but because the acquirers hoped to prevent the cash from being frittered away searching for more oil.[8]

Eliminating Inefficiencies

Cash is not the only asset that can be wasted by poor management. There are always firms where there are opportunities to improve operations and increase earnings. Such firms are natural candidates for acquisition by other firms with better management.

If this motive is important, one would expect that firms that perform *poorly* would tend to be targets for acquisition. This seems to be the case. Palepu, for example, found that investors in firms that were subsequently acquired earned

---

[6] Mergers undertaken *just* to use tax-loss carry-forwards may be challenged by the Internal Revenue Service (IRS), and the use of the carry-forwards may be denied. Suppose that you own a profitable firm. You find another company on the ropes, with large cumulative losses. If you bought up that company and then liquidated its assets, the IRS would probably regard the tax-loss carry-forwards as liquidated also and not allow you to use them to reduce your taxable income. But the tax rules are funny: If the company on the rocks bought *you*, then gradually and discreetly closed down its old business and continued with yours, the IRS would probably accept the deal and let it use the tax-loss carry-forwards.

Since 1986 the amount of tax loss that the buyer can use in any one year is limited to the net worth of the company multiplied by the current tax-free bond yield.

[7] See J. B. Shoven, "New Developments in Corporate Finance and Tax Avoidance: Some Evidence," Working Paper No. 2091, National Bureau of Economic Research, December 1986.

[8] Michael Jensen has argued that the oil industry is not the only area in which mergers (or the threat of merger) have helped to unlock cash. He suggests that this has also been an important motive for mergers in the tobacco, forest products, food, broadcasting, and motion picture industries. See M. C. Jensen, "The Takeover Controversy: Analysis and Evidence," *Midland Corporate Finance Journal,* **4:** 6–32 (Summer 1986).

relatively low rates of return over several years before the merger.[9] Apparently many of these firms fell on bad times and were rescued by merger.

Of course a merger is not the only way to improve management. But it may be the only simple and practical way. Managers are naturally reluctant to fire or demote themselves, and stockholders of large public firms do not usually have much *direct* influence on how their firm is run or who runs it.[10]

Of course it is easy to criticize another firm's management and less easy to do better. Therefore many of the self-appointed scourges of poor management turn out to be less competent than those they replace. Here is how Warren Buffet, the chairman of Berkshire Hathaway, summarizes the matter:

> Many managers were apparently over-exposed in impressionable childhood years to the story in which the imprisoned, handsome prince is released from the toad's body by a kiss from the beautiful princess. Consequently, they are certain that the managerial kiss will do wonders for the profitability of the target company. Such optimism is essential. Absent that rosy view, why else should the shareholders of company A want to own an interest in B at a takeover cost that is two times the market price they'd pay if they made direct purchases on their own? In other words investors can always buy toads at the going price for toads. If investors instead bankroll princesses who wish to pay double for the right to kiss the toad, those kisses better pack some real dynamite. We've observed many kisses, but very few miracles. Nevertheless, many managerial princesses remain serenely confident about the future potency of their kisses, even after their corporate backyards are knee-deep in unresponsive toads.[11]

33-3   SOME DUBIOUS REASONS FOR MERGER

The benefits that we have described so far all make economic sense. Other arguments that are sometimes given for mergers are more dubious. Here are a few of the dubious ones.

Diversification

We have suggested that the managers of a cash-rich company may prefer to see it use that cash for acquisitions rather than distribute it as extra dividends. That is why we often see cash-rich firms in stagnant industries merging their way into fresh woods and pastures new.

What about diversification as an end in itself? It is obvious that diversification reduces risk. Isn't that a gain from merging?

The trouble with this argument is that diversification is easier and cheaper for the stockholder than for the corporation. No one has shown that investors pay a premium for diversified firms—in fact, discounts are common. For example, Kaiser

[9] K. Palepu, "Predicting Takeover Targets: A Methodological and Empirical Analysis," *Journal of Accounting and Economics,* **8:** 3–36 (March 1986).

[10] It is difficult to assemble a large enough block of stockholders to effectively challenge management and the incumbent board of directors at the firm's annual meeting. Stockholders can have enormous indirect influence, however. Their displeasure shows up in the firm's stock price. A low stock price may, for example, encourage a takeover bid by another firm.

[11] Berkshire Hathaway 1981 Annual Report, cited in G. Foster, "Comments on M&A Analysis and the Role of Investment Bankers," *Midland Corporate Finance Journal,* **1:** 36–38 (Winter 1983).

Industries was dissolved as a holding company in 1977 because its diversification apparently *subtracted* from its value. Kaiser Industries' main assets were shares of Kaiser Steel, Kaiser Aluminum, and Kaiser Cement. These were independent companies, and the stock of each was publicly traded. Thus you could value Kaiser Industries by looking at the stock prices of Kaiser Steel, Kaiser Aluminum, and Kaiser Cement. But Kaiser Industries' stock was selling at a price reflecting a significant *discount* from the value of its investment in these companies. The discount vanished when Kaiser Industries revealed its plan to sell its holdings and distribute the proceeds to its stockholders.

Why the discount existed in the first place is a puzzle. But the example at least shows that diversification does not increase value.[12]

There are exceptional cases in which personal diversification may be more expensive than corporate diversification. For example, perhaps you were lucky enough to invest in IBM in 1955. Since then the price of IBM stock has appreciated dramatically. If you just held on to your investment, you may now have a very undiversified portfolio. You know that is not a good idea. On the other hand, if you sell any of your IBM stock, you will be liable for a substantial capital gains tax. IBM would help you if it bought, say, a copper mining firm or other firms in areas unrelated to IBM's main business. Then by holding IBM stock you would hold a somewhat diversified portfolio.

If you are the president and majority owner of a closely held corporation, you are likely to have exactly the same problem. You may be wealthy, but you have all your eggs in one corporate basket. You could sell off a substantial part of your shares but this could result in a large liability for capital gains tax. It may be better to merge with a firm in another line of business, and hold on to the shares of that firm. By so doing you will have your eggs in two baskets rather than one.

The Bootstrap Game: Mergers and Earnings per Share[13]

During the 1960s some conglomerate companies made acquisitions which offered no evident economic gains. Nevertheless the conglomerates' aggressive strategy produced several years of rising earnings per share and stock prices. To see how this can happen, let us look at the acquisition of Muck and Slurry by the well-known conglomerate World Enterprises.

The position before the merger is set out in the first two columns of Table 33-2. Notice that because Muck and Slurry has relatively poor growth prospects, its stock sells at a lower price-earnings ratio than World Enterprises (line 3). The merger, we assume, produces no economic benefits, and so the firms should be worth exactly the same together as apart. The market value of World Enterprises after the merger should be equal to the sum of the separate values of the two firms (line 6).

Since World Enterprises stock is selling for double the price of Muck and Slurry stock (line 2), World Enterprises can acquire the 100,000 Muck and Slurry shares for 50,000 of its own shares. Thus World will have 150,000 shares outstanding after the merger.

Total earnings double as a result of the merger (line 5), but the number of shares increases by only 50 percent. Earnings *per share* rise from $2.00 to $2.67.

---

[12] The appendix to this chapter provides a simple proof that corporate diversification does not affect value in perfect markets as long as investors' diversification opportunities are unrestricted.

[13] The discussion of the bootstrap game follows S. C. Myers, "A Framework for Evaluating Mergers," op. cit.

TABLE 33-2
Impact of merger on market value and earnings per share of World Enterprises

	World Enterprises (Before Merger)	Muck and Slurry	World Enterprises (After Acquiring Muck and Slurry)
1. Earnings per share	$2.00	$2.00	$2.67
2. Price per share	$40.00	$20.00	$40.00
3. Price-earnings ratio	20	10	15
4. Number of shares	100,000	100,000	150,000
5. Total earnings	$200,000	$200,000	$400,000
6. Total market value	$4,000,000	$2,000,000	$6,000,000
7. Current earnings per dollar invested in stock (line 1 divided by line 2)	$.05	$.10	$.067

Note: When World Enterprises purchases Muck and Slurry, there are no gains. Therefore, total earnings and total market value should be unaffected by the merger. But earnings *per share* increase. World Enterprises only issues 50,000 of its shares (priced at $40) to acquire the 100,000 Muck and Slurry shares (priced at $20).

We call this a *bootstrap effect* because there is no real gain created by the merger and no increase in the two firms' combined value. Since stock price is unchanged, the price earnings ratio falls (line 3).

Figure 33-1 illustrates what is going on here. Before the merger $1 invested in World Enterprises bought 5 cents of current earnings and rapid growth prospects. On the other hand, $1 invested in Muck and Slurry bought 10 cents of current earnings but slower growth prospects. If the *total* market value is not altered by the merger, then $1 invested in the merged firm gives 6.7 cents of immediate

FIGURE 33-1
Effects of merger on earnings growth. By merging with Muck and Slurry, World Enterprises increases current earnings but accepts a slower rate of future growth. Its stockholders should be no better or worse off unless investors are fooled by the bootstrap effect. (*Source:* S. C. Myers, "A Framework for Evaluating Mergers," in S. C. Myers, ed., *Modern Developments in Financial Management*, Frederick A. Praeger, Inc., New York, 1976, fig. 1, p. 639.)

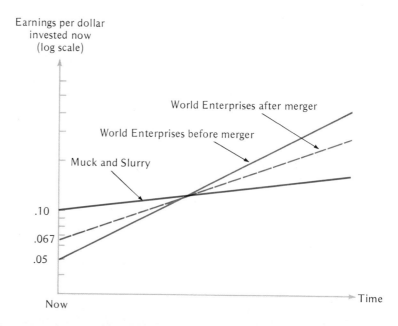

earnings but slower growth, and the Muck and Slurry shareholders get lower immediate earnings but faster growth. Neither side gains or loses provided everybody understands the deal.

The art of the financial manipulator is to ensure that the market does *not* understand the deal. Suppose that investors are fooled by the exuberance of the president of World Enterprises and by plans to introduce modern management techniques into the Earth Sciences Division (formerly known as Muck and Slurry). They could easily mistake the 33 percent postmerger increase in earnings per share for real growth. If they do, the price of World Enterprises stock rises and the shareholders of both companies receive something for nothing.

You should now see how to play the bootstrap, or "chain letter," game. Suppose that you manage a company enjoying a high price-earnings ratio. The reason why it is high is that investors anticipate rapid growth in future earnings. You achieve this growth not by capital investment, product improvement, or increased operating efficiency, but by purchasing slow-growing firms with low price-earnings ratios. The long-run result will be slower growth and a depressed price-earnings ratio, but in the short run earnings per share can increase dramatically. If this fools investors, you may be able to achieve the higher earnings per share without suffering a decline in your price-earnings ratio. But in order to *keep* fooling investors, you must continue to expand by merger *at the same compound rate*. Obviously you cannot do this forever; one day expansion must slow down or stop. Then earnings growth will cease, and your house of cards will fall.

This kind of game is not played so much now, after investors' bitter experience with it in the 1960s. But there is still a widespread belief that you should not acquire companies with higher price-earnings ratios than your own. Of course you know better than to believe that low-PE stocks are cheap and high-PE stocks are dear. If life were as simple as that, we should all be wealthy by now. Beware of false prophets who suggest that you can appraise mergers on the basis of their immediate impact on earnings per share.

Lower Financing Costs

You often hear it said that merged firms are able to borrow more cheaply than the separate units. In part this is true. We have already seen (in Chapter 15, Section 15-4) that there are significant economies of scale in making new issues. Therefore, if firms can make fewer, larger security issues by merging, there is a genuine saving.

But when people say that borrowing costs are lower for the merged firm, they usually mean something more than lower issue costs. They mean that when two firms merge, they can borrow at lower interest rates than they could separately. This of course is exactly what we should expect in a well-functioning bond market. While the two firms are separate, they do not guarantee each other's debt; if one fails, the bondholder cannot ask the other for money. But after the merger each enterprise effectively does guarantee the other's debt—if one part of the business fails, the bondholders can still take their money out of the other part. Because these mutual guarantees make the debt less risky, lenders demand a lower interest rate.

Does the lower interest rate mean a net gain to the merger? Not necessarily. Compare the following two situations:

1. *Separate issues:* Firm A and firm B each make a $50 million bond issue.
2. *Single issue:* Firms A and B merge and the new firm AB makes a single $100 million issue.

Of course AB would pay a lower interest rate, other things equal. But it does not make sense for A and B to merge just to get that lower rate. The firms' shareholders do gain from the lower rate but they lose by having to guarantee each other's debt. In other words, they get the lower interest rate only by giving bondholders better protection. There is no *net* gain.

In Chapters 20 (Section 20-2) and 23 (Section 23-4) we showed that

$$\text{Bond value} = \text{bond value (assuming no chance of default)} \\ - \text{value of shareholders' (put) option to default}$$

Merger increases bond value (or reduces the interest payments necessary to support a *given* bond value) only by reducing the value of stockholders' options to default. In other words, the value of the default option for AB's $100 million issue is less than the combined value of the two default options on A and B's separate $50 million issues.

Now suppose that A and B each borrow $50 million and *then* merge. If the merger is a surprise, it will be a happy one for the bondholders. The bonds they thought were guaranteed by one of the two firms end up guaranteed by both. The stockholders lose, other things equal, because they have given bondholders better protection but have received nothing for it.

There is one situation in which mergers can create value by making debt safer. In Chapter 18, Section 18-3 we described the choice of an optimal debt ratio as a trade-off of the value of tax shields on interest payments made by the firm against the present value of possible costs of financial distress due to borrowing too much. Merging decreases the probability of financial distress, other things being equal. If it allows increased borrowing, and increased value from the interest tax shields, there will be a net gain to the merger.[14]

*33-4 ESTIMATING THE COST OF A MERGER

To recapitulate: You should go ahead with a merger if the gain exceeds the cost. The gain is the difference between the value of the merged firm and the value of the separate entities.

$$\text{Gain} = PV_{AB} - (PV_A + PV_B)$$

We have looked at where these gains may come from and how to estimate them. It is now time to focus on the *costs*.

Estimating Cost When the Merger Is Financed by Cash

The cost of a merger is the premium that the buyer pays for the selling firm over its value as a separate entity. It is a straightforward problem to estimate cost as long as the merger is financed by cash. However, it is important to bear in mind that if investors *expect* A to acquire B, the market value of B may be a poor measure of its value as a separate entity. Thus it may help to rewrite our formula for cost as

[14] This merger rationale was first suggested by W. G. Lewellen, "A Pure Financial Rationale for the Conglomerate Merger," *Journal of Finance,* **26:** 521–537 (May 1971). If you want to see some of the controversy and discussion that this idea led to, look at R. C. Higgins and L. D. Schall, "Corporate Bankruptcy and Conglomerate Merger," *Journal of Finance,* **30:** 93–114 (March 1975), and D. Galai and R. W. Masulis, "The Option Pricing Model and the Risk Factor of Stock," *Journal of Financial Economics,* **3:** 53–81, esp. pp. 66–69 (January–March 1976).

$$\text{Cost} = (\text{cash} - \text{MV}_B) + (\text{MV}_B - \text{PV}_B)$$

$$= \text{premium paid over market value of B}$$
$$+ \text{difference between market value of B and its}$$
$$\text{value as a separate entity}$$

This is one of the few places in this book where we have drawn an important distinction between market value (MV) and the true, or "intrinsic," value (PV) of the firm as a separate entity. The problem here is not that the market value of B is wrong, but that it may not be the value of firm B as a separate entity. Potential investors in B's stock will see two possible outcomes and two possible values:

Outcome	Value of B's Stock
1. No merger	PV_B: Value per share of B as a separate firm
2. Merger occurs	PV_B *plus* some part of the benefits of the merger

If the second outcome is possible, the stock price we observe for B will overstate PV_B. This is exactly what *should* happen in a competitive capital market. Unfortunately it complicates the task of a financial manager evaluating a merger.

Here is an example. Suppose that just before the merger announcement we observe the following:

	Firm A	Firm B
Market price per share	$75	$15
Number of shares	100,000	60,000
Market value of firm	$7,500,000	$900,000

Firm A intends to pay $1.2 million cash for B. If B's market price reflects only its value as a separate entity, then

$$\text{Cost} = (\text{cash} - \text{MV}_B) + (\text{MV}_B - \text{PV}_B)$$

$$= \$300,000 + 0 = \$300,000$$

However, suppose that B's share price has already risen $2 because of rumors of a favorable merger offer. Then

$$\text{Cost} = (\text{cash} - \text{MV}_B) + (\text{MV}_B - \text{PV}_B)$$

$$= \$300,000 + \$120,000 = \$420,000$$

Notice that if the market made a mistake and the market value of B were *less* than its true value as a separate entity, the cost would be negative. In other words, B would be a *bargain* and the merger would be worthwhile from A's point of view, even if the two firms are worth no more together than apart.[15] Of course

---

[15] Of course, if the shares are bargain-priced, A doesn't need a merger to profit by its special knowledge. It can just buy up B's shares on the open market and hold them passively, waiting for other investors to wake up to B's true value.

A's stockholders' gain would be B's stockholders' loss, because B is being sold for less than its true value.

Firms have made acquisitions just because their managers believed they had spotted a company whose intrinsic value was not fully appreciated by the stock market. However, we know from the evidence on market efficiency that as often as not "cheap" stocks turn out to be expensive. It is not easy for outsiders, whether investors or managers, to find firms that are truly undervalued by the market.

If firm A is wise, it will not go ahead with a merger if the cost exceeds the gain. Conversely, firm B will not consent to a merger if it thinks the cost is negative, for a negative cost to A means a negative gain to B. This gives us a range of possible cash payments that would allow the merger to take place. Whether the payment is at the top or the bottom of this range depends on the relative bargaining power of the two participants. For example, if A makes an acquisition solely in order to use a tax-loss carry-forward, then it could equally well merge with B, C, or D; firm B has nothing special to offer, and its management is in no position to demand a large fraction of the gains. In this case, the cost of the merger to A is likely to be relatively low.

Estimating Cost When the Acquisition Is Financed by Stock

Estimating cost is more complicated when a merger is financed by an exchange of shares. Suppose that firm A offers 16,000 shares instead of $1.2 million in cash. Since A's share price before the announcement is $75 and B's market value is $900,000, the cost *appears* to be

$$\text{Apparent cost} = 16,000 \times \$75 - \$900,000 = \$300,000$$

However, the apparent cost may not equal the true cost. There are three reasons for this. First, B's value as a separate entity may not be $900,000. Second, A's value as a separate entity may not be $7.5 million. Third, because B's shareholders are partners in the merged firm, they will receive some part of the merger gains. In other words, the value of the shares paid over to B's shareholders depends on the value of the combined firms. If B's shareholders end up owning the fraction x of the combined firms, the true cost is

$$\text{Cost} = x\text{PV}_{AB} - \text{PV}_B$$

That is, $x\text{PV}_{AB}$ is the value of what B's stockholders get, and PV_B is the value of what they give up. Their net gain is their share of the merger benefits and also the cost of the merger from the viewpoint of A's stockholders.

In our example, B's shareholders will receive 16,000 shares. Thus their share of the merged firms will be

$$x = \frac{16,000}{100,000 + 16,000} = .138$$

Suppose that the market values just before the announcement of the merger accurately reflect the firm's separate values ($\text{MV}_A = \text{PV}_A$ and $\text{MV}_B = \text{PV}_B$). Assume that the merger produces gains with a present value of $400,000. Then

$$\text{PV}_{AB} = \text{PV}_A + \text{PV}_B + \text{gain} = \$7,500,000 + \$900,000 + \$400,000$$

$$= \$8,800,000$$

and

$$\text{True cost} = x\text{PV}_{AB} - \text{PV}_B = .138(\$8,800,000) - \$900,000$$
$$= \$314,000$$

The reason the true cost exceeds the apparent cost is that stock prices observed *before* the merger is announced do not reflect the merger gains or their division between A's stockholders and B's stockholders. Suppose that we calculate share prices and market values *after* the merger is negotiated and announced.

		Firm A	Firm B
1.	Proportions of ownership in merged firms	.862	.138
2.	Market value (line 1 × PV$_{AB}$, PV$_{AB}$ = \$8,800,000)	\$7,586,000	\$1,214,000
3.	Number of shares	100,000	60,000
4.	Price per share	\$75.86	\$20.23

With this information we can easily calculate the true cost, either as the difference between the value of firm A shares offered and the value of B as a separate entity,

$$\text{Cost} = 16,000(\$75.86) - \$900,000 = \$314,000$$

or as the gain in the market value of firm B following the merger announcement:

$$\text{Cost} = \text{MV}_B \text{ (after announcement)} - \text{MV}_B \text{ (before announcement)}$$
$$= 60,000(\$20.23) - \$900,000$$
$$= \$314,000$$

Unfortunately you cannot do these calculations until *after* the announcement of the merger. In negotiating the merger, you have to estimate its cost before it is announced. That is why you need the formula

$$\text{Cost} = x\text{PV}_{AB} - \text{PV}_B$$

We can now understand the key distinction between cash and stock as financing instruments. If cash is offered, the cost of the merger is unaffected by the merger gains. If stock is offered, cost depends on the gains, because they must be shared with B's owners.

Stock financing also mitigates the effect of overvaluation or undervaluation of either firm. Suppose, for example, that A overestimates B's value as a separate entity, perhaps because rumors of a merger have already driven up B's stock price. Thus A makes too generous an offer. Other things being equal, A's stockholders are better off if it is a stock offer rather than a cash offer. With a stock offer, the inevitable bad news about B's value will fall partly on the shoulders of B's stockholders.

33-5 THE MECHANICS OF A MERGER

Buying a company is a much more complicated affair than buying a piece of machinery. Thus we should look at some of the problems encountered in arranging mergers. In practice these problems are often *extremely* complex, and specialists must be consulted. We are not trying to replace those specialists; we simply want to alert you to the kinds of legal, tax, and accounting issues they deal with.

Mergers and Antitrust Law

One subject on which you may need early advice is the federal antitrust law. This is enshrined in three principal statutes. The first is the Sherman Act of 1890, which declared that "every contract, combination . . . or conspiracy, in restraint of trade" is illegal and that "every person who shall . . . attempt to monopolize . . . any part of . . . commerce" is acting illegally. The second is the Federal Trade Commission Act of 1914, which prohibits "unfair methods of competition" and (by amendment) "unfair or deceptive acts or practices." The third and most important statute is the Clayton Act of 1914. Section 7 of the Clayton Act[16] forbids the acquisition of assets or stock where "in any line of commerce" or "in any section of the country" the effect "*may be* substantially to lessen competition, or to *tend* to create a monopoly." Notice that under the Sherman Act a contract must not be in constraint of trade. The Clayton Act goes beyond that to prohibit *potential* restraints. As a result, prosecutions under the Sherman Act are now rare and Section 7 of the Clayton Act has become the principal weapon in the crusade against the ogre of monopoly.

Antitrust law can be enforced in one of two ways: by a civil suit by the Justice Department, or in a proceeding by the Federal Trade Commission (FTC). Both the Justice Department and the FTC have the right to seek injunctions delaying a merger, and in many cases this has been sufficient to ensure its failure.

In recent years relatively few mergers have been challenged on antitrust grounds but the threat is always there. For example, in 1977 the Texas department store group, Carter Hawley Hale, made a bid for Marshall Field. Marshall Field responded by buying Liberty House, another Texas department store group, thus leaving Carter Hawley Hale's bid exposed to the risk of antitrust proceedings. The risk was sufficient to cause Carter Hawley Hale to drop its bid.[17]

The Form of Acquisition

Let us suppose that you have been advised that the purchase of company B would not be challenged on antitrust grounds. The next thing you will want to consider is the best way to effect the acquisition.

One possibility is literally to *merge* the two companies, in which case one company automatically assumes *all* the assets and *all* the liabilities of the other. Such a merger must have the approval of at least 50 percent of the stockholders of each firm.[18]

An alternative is simply to buy the seller's stock in exchange for cash, shares, or other securities. In this case the buyer can, if he or she chooses, deal individually with the shareholders of the selling company. The seller's managers may not be involved at all, although their approval and cooperation are generally sought.

The third approach is to buy some or all of the seller's assets. In this case ownership of the assets needs to be transferred, and payment is made to the selling firm rather than directly to its stockholders.

---

[16] Together with the amending Celler-Kefauver Act of 1950.

[17] Subsequently a group of Marshall Field stockholders unsuccessfully sued the board of directors for a breach of duty.

[18] Corporate charters sometimes specify a higher percentage.

TABLE 33-3
Purchasing versus pooling in the merger of A Corporation and
B Corporation (figures in millions of dollars)

INITIAL BALANCE SHEETS							
A Corporation				B Corporation			
NWC	2.0	3.0	D	NWC	.1	0	D
FA	8.0	7.0	E	FA	.9	1.0	E
	10.0	10.0			1.0	1.0	

BALANCE SHEETS OF AB CORPORATION			
	AB Corporation		
Under pooling of interests:	NWC	2.1	3.0 D
	FA	8.9	8.0 E
		11.0	11.0
	AB Corporation		
Under purchase accounting,	NWC	2.1	3.0 D
assuming that A Corporation pays	FA	8.9	8.8 E
$1.8 million for B Corporation:	Goodwill	.8	
		11.8	11.8

Key:
NWC = Net working capital
FA   = Net book value of fixed assets
D   = Debt
E   = Book value of equity

A Note on Merger Accounting

Mergers sometimes raise complex accounting issues. One such issue is whether a merger should be treated as a *purchase of assets* or as a *pooling of interests.* In efficient capital markets, the choice between these two methods should make no difference whatsoever, but managers and accountants agonize over the choice anyway.

The essential differences between the two methods are illustrated in Table 33-3. The table shows what happens when A Corporation buys B Corporation, leading to a new AB Corporation. The two firms' initial (book) balance sheets are shown at the top of the table. The next balance sheet is AB Corporation's under pooling of interest. Note that this is nothing more than the two firms' separate balance sheets added together.

The final balance sheet shows what happens when purchase accounting is used. We assume that B Corporation has been purchased for $1.8 million, 180 percent of book value.

Why did A Corporation pay an $800,000 premium over book value? There are two possible reasons. First, the true values of B's *tangible* assets—its working capital, plant, and equipment—may be greater than $1 million. We will assume this is *not* the reason; that is, we assume the assets listed on its balance sheet are valued there correctly.[19] Second, A Corporation may be paying for *intangible* assets that

---

[19] If purchase accounting is used, and if B's assets are worth more than their previous book values, they would be reappraised and their current values entered on AB Corporation's balance sheet. Goodwill (see below) would be decreased by an amount equal to the write-up of tangible assets.

are not listed on B Corporation's balance sheet. The intangible asset may be a promising product or technology developed by B Corporation, for example. Or it may be no more than B Corporation's share of the economic gains from the merger.

Under the purchase method of accounting, A Corporation is viewed as buying an asset worth $1.8 million—as indeed it is. The problem is how to show that asset on the left-hand side of AB Corporation's balance sheet. B Corporation's tangible assets are worth only $1 million. This leaves $.8 million. The accountant takes care of this by creating a new asset category called *goodwill* and assigning $.8 million to it.

All this is somewhat arbitrary, but reasonable enough. Intangible assets do have value, and so there is no reason why such assets shouldn't be shown on the balance sheet when a firm buys them.

Nevertheless, most managers prefer to pool when they can. The reason is that goodwill has to be amortized over a period not exceeding 40 years, and the regular amortization charges have to be deducted from reported income. Thus AB Corporation's reported income will be reduced by at least $800,000/40 = $20,000 each year. Under pooling, goodwill never appears, and so reported income is at least $20,000 higher.

Now all this has absolutely no cash consequences. The amortization charges are *not* cash outflows and they are not tax-deductible expenses. Thus the choice between purchase and pooling should have no effect on the value of the merged firms.

Hong, Mandelker, and Kaplan tested this proposition by looking at a sample of 159 acquisitions made between 1954 and 1964, a period in which there were fewer restrictions on pooling than there are now.[20] They found no evidence that acquiring firms did better under pooling than under purchase accounting.

Some Tax Considerations

An acquisition may be either taxable or tax-free. In a taxable acquisition, the selling stockholders are treated, for tax purposes, as having *sold* their shares, and they must report any capital gains or losses on their income tax forms. In a tax-free acquisition, the selling shareholders are viewed as *exchanging* their old shares for essentially similar new ones; no capital gains or losses are recognized.

The tax status of the acquisition also affects the taxes paid by the firm afterward. After a tax-free acquisition, the firm is taxed as if the two firms had always been together. In a taxable acquisition, the assets of the selling firm are revalued, the resulting write-up or write-down is treated as a taxable gain or loss, and tax depreciation is recalculated based on the restated asset values.

A very simple example will illustrate these distinctions. In 1980 Captain B forms Seacorp, which purchases a fishing boat for $300,000. The boat is depreciated for tax purposes over 20 years on a straight-line basis (no salvage value). Thus annual depreciation is $300,000/20 = $15,000, and in 1990 the boat has a net book value of $150,000.

But in 1990, Captain B finds that, owing to inflation, careful maintenance, and

---

[20] H. Hong, G. Mandelker, and R. S. Kaplan: "Pooling vs. Purchase: The Effects of Accounting for Mergers on Stock Prices," *Accounting Review,* **53:** 31–47 (January 1978). The requirements for pooling were tightened in 1970 by the Accounting Principles Board of the American Institute of Certified Public Accountants. The requirements are set out in Opinion No. 16 and Opinion No. 17 of the board (New York, 1970). The opinions state, among other requirements for pooling, that the seller's stockholders must remain stockholders of the merged firm, and that the buyer must finance the merger by exchanging its common stock for at least 90 percent of the seller's shares.

TABLE 33-4
Possible tax consequences when Baycorp buys Seacorp for $330,000. Captain B's original investment in Seacorp was $300,000. Just before the merger Seacorp's assets were $50,000 of marketable securities and one boat with a book value of $150,000, but a market value of $280,000.

	Taxable Merger	Tax-Free Merger
Impact on Captain B	Captain B must recognize a $30,000 capital gain.	Capital gain can be deferred until Captain B sells the Baycorp shares.
Impact on Baycorp	Boat is revalued at $280,000. Baycorp must pay tax on the $130,000 write-up, but tax depreciation increases to $280,000/10 = $28,000 per year (assuming 10 years of remaining life).	Boat's value remains at $150,000, and tax depreciation continues at $15,000 per year.

good times in the fishing industry, the boat is really worth $280,000. In addition, Seacorp holds $50,000 of marketable securities.

Now suppose that Captain B sells the firm to Baycorp for $330,000. The possible tax consequences of the acquisition are shown in Table 33-4. In this case, Captain B is better off with a tax-free deal, because capital gains taxes can be deferred. Baycorp will probably go along; it covets the $13,000 per year extra depreciation tax shield that a taxable merger would generate, but these increased tax shields do not justify paying taxes on a $130,000 write-up.[21]

33-6 MERGER TACTICS

Many mergers are agreed upon by both parties, but in other cases the acquirer will go over the heads of the target firm's management and appeal directly to its stockholders. There are two ways of doing this. First it can seek the support of the target firm's stockholders at its next annual meeting. This is called a *proxy fight,* because the right to vote someone else's shares is called a *proxy.*

Proxy fights are expensive and difficult to win. The alternative is for the would-be acquirer to make a *tender offer* directly to the shareholders. The management of the target firm may advise its shareholders to accept the tender or it may attempt to fight the bid.

A tender offer may present shareholders with a difficult decision. Should they accept, should they wait to see if someone else produces a better offer, or should they sell their stock in the market? This dilemma presents an opportunity for the *arbitrageurs.* Arbitrageurs (or "arbs," as they are often called) speculate on the likely success of merger bids.[22] In other words, they take over from shareholders the risk that the deal will not go through. That is a useful social service. However,

---

[21] Before the 1986 Tax Reform Act, assets of the acquired company could be revalued *without* recognizing the write-up or write-down as taxable corporate income. This old rule would make a taxable merger much more attractive to Baycorp, which might pay Captain B a premium to accept a taxable deal.

[22] Strictly speaking, an arbitrageur refers to an investor who takes a fully hedged, that is, riskless, position. Arbitrageurs in merger battles often take very large risks indeed. Their activities are sometimes known as "risk arbitrage."

as Ivan Boesky demonstrated, arbs can make even more money if they learn about the offer *before* it is publicly announced. Because arbitrageurs may accumulate large amounts of stock, they can have an important effect on whether a deal goes through. So the bidding company may be tempted to take the arbitrageurs into its confidence. This is the point at which a legitimate and useful activity shades into an illegal and harmful one.

Tender battles resemble a complex game of poker in which the rules are set largely by the Williams Act of 1968 and by the courts. We will return to the subject of these rules shortly, but first let us look at two examples of takeover battles.

Case 1: The Fight for Cities Service[23]

The battle for Cities began in May 1982 when Boone Pickens, the chairman of Mesa Petroleum, began buying Cities shares as preparation for a takeover bid. Foreseeing the bid, Cities made an issue of equity that diluted Mesa's holding and followed this up with a retaliatory offer for Mesa.[24] Over the following month Mesa's bid was revised once and Cities' bid was revised twice before both companies agreed to drop their bids for one another. Cities repurchased the stock that had been bought by Mesa and in exchange Mesa agreed not to attempt a hostile takeover of Cities for 5 years.

The principal reason for the cessation of hostilities between Mesa and Cities was the announcement that Cities had found a more congenial partner in Gulf Oil. Also Gulf was prepared to pay substantially more than Mesa for Cities' stock. Unfortunately, this proposal fell afoul of the Federal Trade Commission (FTC), which issued a temporary restraining order. Shortly thereafter Gulf withdrew its offer.

In response, Cities charged Gulf with not attempting to resolve the FTC's objections and it filed a $3 billion lawsuit against Gulf. At the same time it began to look for another "white knight" who would take it over. The only interested suitor to emerge was Occidental Petroleum. Occidental's initial offer for Cities was revised twice and finally accepted. The battle for Cities Service had lasted 3 months and involved a total of nine bids from four separate companies.

Many of these bids consisted of a *two-tier offer*. For example, Occidental's final offer for Cities consisted of a tender offer of $55 a share for 45 percent of the stock and a package of fixed-income securities worth about $40 a share for the remaining stock. In effect, Occidental was saying, "Last one through the door does the washing up." The plan worked, for almost all Cities' stockholders rushed to take advantage of the cash offer.

In several instances the bidders employed both carrot and stick; for example, Occidental followed up its initial friendly offer for Cities with a hostile tender offer before finally reaching a friendly agreement.

The generous Gulf offer would have provided Cities' shareholders with a cumulative profit of almost 80 percent, but the collapse of that offer and the shortage of other suitors caused Cities' stock price to lose all its earlier gains. From then on Cities was in a relatively weak bargaining position and the Occidental offer resulted in a profit of only 12 percent for Cities' stockholders. The merger scarcely affected Occidental's stock price, which suggests that investors believed the merger to be a

---

[23] The Cities Service takeover is described in R. S. Ruback, "The Cities Service Takeover: a Case Study," *Journal of Finance*, **38**: 319–330 (May 1983).

[24] This practice of defending yourself against merger by making a counterbid for the predator's stock is sometimes known as the "pacman defense."

TABLE 33-5
Phillips's balance sheet was dramatically changed by its
leveraged repurchase (figures in billions)

	1985	1984		1985	1984
Current assets	$ 3.1	$ 4.6	Current liabilities	$ 3.1	$ 5.3
Fixed assets	10.3	11.2	Long-term debt	6.5	2.8
Other	.6	1.2	Other long-term liabilities	2.8	2.3
			Equity	1.6	6.6
Total assets	$14.0	$17.0	Total liabilities	$14.0	$17.0

zero-NPV investment. Gulf's stockholders fared the worst. Its high-priced offer led to a 14 percent fall in the price of Gulf stock. Even though this offer was subsequently withdrawn, the prospect of a costly lawsuit left Gulf's stock price depressed.

As with many real-life stories, there is an epilogue. One year after losing its battle for Cities, Gulf itself became a takeover target, when Mesa Petroleum proposed to buy Gulf stock in order to break the company up and sell it in pieces. At this point Chevron came to the rescue and acquired Gulf for $13.2 billion, more than double its value of 6 months earlier. Chevron's bid gave Mesa a profit of $760 million on the Gulf shares that it had bought. Asked for his views, Pickens commented, "Shucks, I guess we lost another one."[25]

Case 2: The Bid for Phillips Petroleum

Our second example also involves an oil company and the main protagonist is once again—you guessed it—Boone Pickens of Mesa Petroleum. In 1982 Mesa had been involved in a battle for General American Oil Co. (GAO) but had dropped its bid when GAO agreed to sell out to Phillips Petroleum.

Two years later Mesa bought 6 percent of Phillips stock at an average price of $38 a share and then bid for a further 15 percent at $60 a share.

Phillips responded in three ways. First, it agreed to buy back Mesa's holding, giving Mesa a profit on the deal of $89 million. Second, it raised its dividend by 25 percent, reduced capital spending, and announced a program to sell $2 billion of assets. Third, it agreed to repurchase about 50 percent of its stock and to issue instead $4.5 billion of debt.

Table 33-5 shows how this leveraged repurchase changed Phillips's balance sheet. The new debt ratio of about 80 percent not only signaled management's confidence that it could service the debt, but it also demonstrated that any surplus cash would be paid out to the security holders and not used for new corporate adventures.

Phillips's move to deter Mesa by buying out its holding at a premium is an example of greenmail. But giving in to greenmail can be dangerous, as Phillips soon discovered. Just 6 weeks later a group led by another corporate raider, Carl Icahn, acquired nearly 5 percent of Phillips stock and made an offer to buy the

[25] "Why Gulf Lost Its Fight for Life," *Business Week,* March 19, 1984, p. 76.

remainder. Phillips responded with a second greenmail payment: It bought out Icahn and his pals, giving them a profit of about $35 million.

Phillips also devised a *poison pill* that would make it a less appetizing morsel for future predators. This poison pill gave shareholders the right to exchange their stock for notes worth $62 a share if anyone bought 30 percent or more of Phillips's stock. (The purchaser who triggered this provision would not be entitled to any of the notes.)

Merger Regulation

Takeover battles such as these are undoubtedly exciting for the individuals involved, but many onlookers are concerned that the wheeling and dealing is not in the public interest. Hence the demand for some regulation of takeover tactics. The difficulty is that there is no agreement as to who needs protection from whom.

Should the Target Firm's Management Be Compelled to Act in the Interests of the Shareholders? The Cities Service and the Phillips cases provided plenty of examples of how managers can fight takeover bids for their companies. Frequently managers don't even wait for a takeover bid before taking defensive action. Instead they deter potential bidders by devising poison pills that make their companies unappetizing, or they persuade shareholders to agree to so-called shark repellant changes to the company charter. Table 33-6 summarizes the principal first and second levels of defense.

Why do managers contest takeover bids for their company? One reason is to

TABLE 33-6
A summary of takeover defenses

Type of Defense	Description
Preoffer defenses	
Shark repellant charter amendments:	
Staggered board	Board is classified into three equal groups. Only one group is elected each year. Therefore bidder cannot obtain control of the target immediately after obtaining majority.
Supermajority	High percentage of shares needed to approve a merger, usually 80%.
Fair price	Supermajority provisions waived if bidder pays all stockholders the same price. Prevents two-tier bids.
Other:	
Poison pills	Shareholders are issued rights to buy bonds or preferred stock. In the event of a merger these are convertible into stock of the acquiring firm or must be repurchased by the acquiring firm.
Dual class recapitalization	Distributes a new class of equity with superior voting rights. Allows target's managers to obtain a majority vote without owning a majority of shares.
Postoffer defenses	
Pacman defense	Make counterbid for stock of bidder.
Litigation	File suit against bidder for violating antitrust or securities laws.
Asset restructuring	Buy assets that bidder does not want or that will create antitrust problem. Sell the "crown jewels," i.e., assets that bidder wants.
Liability restructuring	Issue shares to a friendly third party or increase number of shareholders. Repurchase shares from existing shareholders at a premium.

Source: This table is loosely adapted from R. S. Ruback, "An Overview of Takeover Defenses," Working Paper No. 1836-86, Sloan School of Management, MIT, September 1986, tables 1 and 2.

extract a higher price from the bidder. (Contested takeovers produce a higher price for the shares in the acquired company.) Another possible reason is that managers believe their jobs may be at risk in the merged company. These managers are not trying to obtain a better price; they want to stop the bid altogether.[26]

If entrenched management is your worry, then you should campaign for legislation to limit the defensive tactics that managers can use. You might, for example, suggest that, once a bid has been announced, managers should be obliged to observe a "passivity principle" which would allow them to provide information and opinion but prohibit them from actively thwarting the bid. With this passivity principle shareholders would be free to make up their own minds on the merits of the bid. You might even want to go further and compel managers of target companies to search around for higher competing bids.[27]

Some companies reduce these conflicts of interest by offering their managers "golden parachutes"—that is, generous payoffs if they lose their jobs as the result of a takeover. Sometimes these payoffs can be very large; for example, Revlon offered its president $35 million. It may seem odd to reward managers for being taken over. However, if it overcomes their opposition to takeover bids, even $35 million may be a small price to pay.[28]

Any management that tries to develop improved weapons of defense must expect challenge in the courts. In the early 1980s the courts tended to give managers the benefit of the doubt and rely on their business judgment. But the courts' attitudes to takeover battles are changing. For example, they have ruled against some poison pills on the grounds that they discriminate against major shareholders. Also they have forced directors of the target company to "determine, seek and obtain maximum value for its shareholders."[29] As a result managers have become much less hasty about opposing bids or throwing themselves blindly into the arms of any white knight.

Do the Predators Employ Tactics that Are Unfair to the Target Shareholders?
For many other people a more important worry is the tactics employed by the predators. For example, in its battle to remain independent Phillips repurchased stock from Pickens and Icahn at hefty premiums. These premiums came out of the pockets of the remaining stockholders. Advocates of greenmail argue that managers like Pickens and Icahn are specialists in identifying desirable candidates for

---

[26] A failed bid is not in the interests of the target's shareholders. All their gains disappear when a bid is withdrawn. Shareholders *do* seem to be worried that managerial opposition may lead to withdrawal of the bid, for when the opposition is announced, the share price of the target company declines. See L. Y. Dann and H. DeAngelo, "Corporate Financial Policy and Corporate Control: A Study of Defensive Adjustments in Asset and Ownership Structure," unpublished paper, December 1986.

[27] For a discussion see R. J. Gilson, "Seeking Competitive Bids versus Pure Passivity in Tender Offer Defense," *Stanford Law Review,* **35:** 51–67 (November 1982); and F. H. Easterbrook and D. R. Fischel, "The Proper Role of a Target's Management in Responding to a Tender Offer," *Harvard Law Review,* **94:** 1161–1204 (April 1981).

[28] Of course excessively lavish parachutes may have the opposite effect and cause managers to throw themselves into the arms of almost any suitor.

[29] In *Edelman v. Fruehauf Corporation,* 1986. No. 86 CV 71332 DT, unpublished transcript at 22 (E.D. Mich. July 24, 1986). In 1985 a shiver ran through many boardrooms when the directors of Trans Union Corporation were held personally liable for being too hasty in accepting a takeover bid.

Changes in judicial attitudes to takeover defenses are reviewed in L. Herzel and R. W. Shepro, "Ups and Downs of U.S. Takeover Defense," *Securities Law Regulation Journal,* **15:** 116–135 (Summer 1987).

takeover and that the premium is their reward for this useful service.[30] But many do not go along with this rosy view. They believe that the success of greenmail does not depend on whether the firm is a desirable takeover candidate, and they are unhappy that a single shareholder can receive special treatment.[31]

Many states have been concerned that corporate raiders have developed coercive tactics, and they have therefore introduced legislation to protect companies against hostile bids. The courts have ruled most of these initiatives to be unconstitutional, but in 1987 the Supreme Court upheld a state law that allowed companies to deprive an investor of voting rights as soon as his or her share in the company exceeded a certain level.

Does Merger Regulation Inhibit Worthwhile Takeovers? Many people campaign to limit the activities of corporate raiders, yet there are others who believe that the dice are already loaded *against* the acquiring company. Suppose you are an expert in identifying firms with underutilized assets. You incur costs in uncovering such a firm but the Williams Act prohibits you from buying more than 5 percent of the stock without disclosing your hand.[32] If you make a tender offer, you must provide information about your plans for the company and give a waiting period of 20 business days during which other firms may come up with a better offer. These companies can free-ride on your good idea and rob you of the gains from it. In this case legislation that forces disclosure deters worthwhile mergers.[33]

Here's another example. You believe that a company is incompetently managed. You therefore propose to acquire a majority of the shares, replace the management, and realize a capital gain. The problem is that each of the shareholders will foresee that the share price will rise when the new management is in place and, therefore, won't sell to you below that price. But, if no one is willing to sell you shares at the low price, you won't get any of the benefits of your good idea. In this case each of the shareholders is trying to free-ride on your proposal and as a result is preventing worthwhile acquisitions.

33-7 CORPORATE RESTRUCTURING

Many recent takeover bids have sought to force mature, cash-rich companies to pay out that cash to shareholders instead of plowing the money back into the

---

[30] For some evidence that the shareholders of the target company gain from greenmail see C. G. Holderness and D. P. Sheehan, "Why Corporate Raiders Are Good News for Stockholders," *Midland Corporate Finance Journal*, **3:** 6–19 (Summer 1985). However, there is also some contrary evidence sugggesting that shareholders *lose* from greenmail. See L. Dann and H. DeAngelo, "Standstill Agreements, Privately Negotiated Stock Repurchases, and the Market for Corporate Control," *Journal of Financial Economics*, **11:** 275–300 (1983); M. Bradley and L. M. Wakeman, "The Wealth Effects of Targeted Share Repurchases," *Journal of Financial Economics*, **11:** 301–328 (1983); and W. H. Mikkelson and R. S. Ruback, "An Empirical Analysis of the Interfirm Investment Process," *Journal of Financial Economics*, **14:** 523–553 (December 1985).

[31] On one occasion the tables have been turned on the greenmailer. Unocal's response to a takeover attempt from Mesa Partners II was to tender at a premium for 29 percent of its own stock and to exclude Mesa from this offer. Discriminatory tender offers by either the bidder or the target company have since been banned by the SEC.

[32] Companies have 10 days within which to declare a 5 percent holding. During these 10 days they are free to make a "market sweep" and add considerably to their holding.

[33] The Williams Act also tries to ensure equal treatment among target shareholders by specifying that if the tender price is increased, the higher price must be paid to shareholders who have already tendered their stock.

business or using it to diversify into areas in which they have no expertise. The most effective response to such threats is to restructure the company so as to distribute more cash to the shareholders. For example, you may remember that as part of its defense against Mesa Petroleum's takeover attempt Phillips Petroleum repurchased about 50 percent of its stock and replaced it with debt. The high cost of servicing the mountain of debt ensured that in the future Phillips would not be in a position to undertake major new developments.

Although the leveraged repurchase has been one of the most popular ways to restructure to forestall or repell a takeover bid, it is not the only way. Here are some others.

Management Buyouts

Sometimes a company's management bands together to take over all or part of the business and turn it into a private company. Usually management shares the ownership with a small group of outside investors. When you concentrate a large equity investment in a few hands, you lose the benefits of risk-sharing. Thus the managers in such buyouts have all their eggs in one corporate basket. On the other hand, they are now working largely for themselves, which provides a wonderful incentive.

Table 33-1, which listed the largest mergers of 1986, included a number of management buyouts. For example, when Beatrice was bought out, the total payment was $6.3 billion. To make transactions of this size feasible, the common stock of the new firm is generally kept to 10 to 15 percent of capitalization and the rest is financed by the sale of debt and preferred stock.

These highly leveraged deals are known as *leveraged buyouts* (LBOs). LBO debt usually must be placed in the so-called *junk bond* market. So far, there have been relatively few defaults on junk bonds, but investors worry about their fate in a major recession. Two factors probably help to moderate the dangers. First, leveraged buyouts tend to involve mature companies with large cash flows and modest growth opportunities. Therefore the first order of the day for the new managers is to work off the debt burden. Second, the outside equity investors usually include the investment bank or LBO specialist that arranged the buyout and sold the bonds. Such a firm has an incentive to maintain its reputation by keeping a close eye on the firm's ability to service its debt.

Divestitures and Spin-offs

Firms not only acquire businesses; they also sell them. In recent years the number of divestitures has been about a third of the number of mergers. Many of them are a consequence of merger; others result from the threat of merger. For example, when Brunswick became the target of a takeover bid from Whittaker, it reacted by selling its Sherwood Medical Division to American Home Products and then distributing the cash to its shareholders. Since Whittaker's main object was to acquire Sherwood, it dropped its bid.[34]

Instead of selling a business to another firm, companies may spin off a subsidiary by distributing its stock to the shareholders of the parent company. Some spin-offs have tax or regulatory advantages. Others may widen investor choice by allowing them to invest directly in just one part of the business. However, probably the most frequent motive for spin-offs is that they improve efficiency. Companies

[34] See M. C. Jensen, "Takeovers: Folklore and Science," *Harvard Business Review,* **62:** 109–121 (November–December 1984); and L. Herzel and J. R. Schmidt, "Shareholders Can Benefit from Sale of 'Crown Jewels'," *Legal Times,* Oct. 24, 1983, p. 33.

sometimes refer to a business as being a "poor fit." By spinning it off, the management of the parent company can concentrate on its main activity. If each business must stand on its own feet, there is no risk that funds will be siphoned off from one in order to support unprofitable investments in the other. Moreover, if the two parts of the business are independent, it is easy to see the value of each and to reward managers accordingly.

Limited Partnerships and Other Structures	Sometimes corporate restructuring involves fundamental changes in the legal structure of the business. For example, some corporations have reorganized themselves as limited partnerships with a finite life. (Many limited partnerships are found in the oil industry, where producing oil wells have been spun off into partnerships.) In this case the shareholders are replaced by partners in the business and the firm's revenues and expenses are credited directly to the individual partners' accounts according to a predefined formula. Sometimes the partners' shares or "units" can be bought and sold in the same way as shares of common stock; these partnerships are generally known as *master limited partnerships*.

The management of a corporation has considerable discretion over whether to pay out income as dividends or reinvest it in the business. In a limited partnership there is no such discretion. Thus, if you are concerned that managers may be tempted to use the income from the business for imprudent investments, you will feel better if the business is reorganized as a limited partnership.

There can also be a tax advantage to a partnership. Shareholders in a corporation pay tax twice—once at the corporate level and once at the personal level. Income from an Internal Revenue Service–approved partnership is taxed only once—that is, when it appears on the partners' personal income tax forms.

33-8 MERGER WAVES AND PROFITABILITY

The vast literature on mergers contains a great deal of speculation but only a few general facts. The following three are the most important ones:

1. Mergers come in waves. The crests of the waves seem to coincide with buoyant stock prices.
2. Selling companies gain from mergers.
3. It is not clear whether acquiring companies gain from mergers but they certainly do not reap as large proportional gains as the selling companies.

Mergers Come in Waves	The first episode of intense merger activity occurred at the turn of the century and the second in the 1920s. There was a further boom from 1967 to 1969 and then again in the 1980s. Each episode coincided with a period of buoyant stock prices, though in each case there were substantial differences in the types of companies that merged and the way they went about it.

Nobody really knows why merger activity is so volatile. If mergers are prompted by economic motives, at least one of these motives must be "here today and gone tomorrow," and it must somehow be associated with high stock prices. But none of the economic motives that we review in this chapter has anything to do with the general level of the stock market. None burst on the scene in 1967, departed in 1970, and reappeared in 1981.

Some mergers may result from mistakes in valuation on the part of the stock market. In other words, the buyer may believe that investors have underestimated the value of the seller or may hope that they *will* overestimate the value of the combined firm. But we see (with hindsight) that mistakes are made in bear markets as well as bull markets. Why don't we see just as many firms hunting for bargain acquisitions when the stock market is low? It is possible that "suckers are born every minute," but it is difficult to believe that they can be harvested only in bull markets.

Companies are not the only active buyers and sellers in a bull market. Investors also trade much more heavily after a rise in share prices. Again, nobody has a good explanation of why this should be the case. Perhaps the answer has nothing to do with economics. Perhaps merger booms and stock market trading are behavioral phenomena—human beings, like some animals, are more active when the weather is sunny.

Do Mergers Generate Net Benefits?

There are undoubtedly good mergers and bad mergers but economists find it hard to agree as to whether mergers are *on balance* beneficial. To see what investors *think* are the consequences, we can look at what happens to the stock price when a merger is announced.

In most mergers there is a clear "buyer"—usually the larger firm—and a clear "seller." The selling stockholders almost always receive a premium over the premerger value of their shares. The average premium is about 20 percent in the case of agreed-upon mergers and 30 percent in the case of tender offers.[35] Sometimes premiums are much higher. When Du Pont acquired Conoco in 1981, it paid a premium of 81 percent, or $3 billion, for Conoco's stock.[36]

Figure 33-2 summarizes the results of a study by Asquith of about 200 mergers during the period 1962 to 1976. You can see that the sellers received a healthy gain.

Asquith's analysis of the stock market performance of the acquiring firms shows you how investors *expected* the mergers to work out. It would be difficult to argue with the view that on average investors thought that the acquirers would just about break even.[37]

Over the longer term Asquith's study shows a slight tailing off in the performance of the acquirers. Does that mean the mergers worked out slightly less well than investors expected? It's possible, but there may be so many other things happening to these firms that it is hard to be sure.

If buyers break even and sellers make substantial gains, shouldn't there be an overall gain? It looks that way but, once again, we can't be certain.[38] In most

[35] See M. C. Jensen and R. S. Ruback, "The Market for Corporate Control: The Scientific Evidence," *Journal of Financial Economics*, **11**: 5–50 (April 1983).

[36] Presumably Du Pont foresaw gains worth more than $3 billion, but it is not easy to spot where they were likely to come from. The two companies were in different industries, and Du Pont did not plan to change Conoco's management or to merge any part of its operations. The merger led to a fall of $800 million in the value of Du Pont stock. So presumably investors thought that the merger created more than $2 billion of additional value. For an interesting account of the Du Pont–Conoco merger, see R. S. Ruback, "The Conoco Takeover and Stockholder Returns," *Sloan Management Review*, **23**: 13–33 (Winter 1982).

[37] The small initial gain to the shareholders of acquiring firms is not statistically significant, although most researchers have observed a similar small positive return.

[38] Jensen and Ruback, *op. cit.*, after an extensive review of empirical work, conclude that "corporate takeovers generate positive gains" (p. 47). Richard Roll reviews the same evidence and argues that "takeover gains may have been overestimated if they exist at all." See "The Hubris Hypothesis of Corporate Takeovers," *Journal of Business*, **59**: 198 (April 1986).

FIGURE 33-2
Asquith's study confirms that selling firms receive substantial premiums. Stockholders of buying firms roughly break even. Note: The cumulative returns are adjusted to remove price fluctuations attributable to movements of the overall stock market. (*Source:* P. Asquith, "Merger Bids, Uncertainty, and Stockholder Returns," *Journal of Financial Economics,* **11:** 51–83 (April 1983), figures 1 and 2, pp. 62–63.)

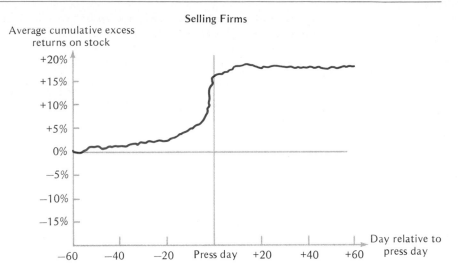

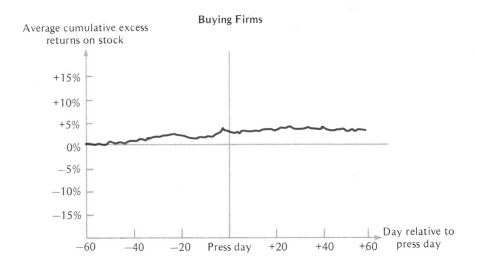

mergers the buyer is so much larger than the seller that even quite large gains or losses on acquisition would not show up very clearly in the buyer's share price. Therefore there may or may not be overall benefits to mergers. If there are, it is possible that the buyer gets some of those benefits. But it seems fairly clear that the buyer gets proportionately less than the seller out of a merger.

If you are concerned with public policy toward mergers, you do not want to consider solely their impact on the immediate protagonists. For example, many predators believe that the threat of takeover spurs the whole of corporate America to try harder. Others worry more about the costs of merger activity. Fighting off hostile mergers is expensive. For example, Phillips Petroleum spent an estimated $150 million defending itself. And that does not include the amount of time Phillips's management spent on the defense rather than running their business. Unfortunately, we don't know whether on balance the threat of merger makes more for active days or sleepless nights.

33-9 SUMMARY

A merger generates an economic gain if the two firms are worth more together than apart. Suppose that firms A and B merge to form a new entity, AB. Then the gain from the merger is

$$\text{Gain} = PV_{AB} - (PV_A + PV_B)$$

Gains from mergers may reflect economies of scale, economies of vertical integration, improved efficiency, fuller use of tax shields, the combination of complementary resources, or redeployment of surplus funds. We don't know how common these benefits are, but they do make economic sense. Sometimes mergers are undertaken to reduce the costs of borrowing, diversify risks, or play the bootstrap game. These motives are dubious.

You should go ahead with the merger if the gain exceeds the cost. Cost is the premium that the buyer pays for the selling firm over its value as a separate entity. It is easy to estimate when the merger is financed by cash. In that case,

$$\text{Cost} = \text{cash} - PV_B$$

When payment is in the form of shares, the cost depends on the value of the combined firm. For example, if B's shareholders end up owning the fraction x of the combined firm

$$\text{Cost} = xPV_{AB} - PV_B$$

The mechanics of buying a firm are much more complex than those of buying a machine. First, you have to make sure that the purchase is unlikely to fall afoul of the antitrust laws. Second, you have a choice of procedures: You can merge all the assets and liabilities of the seller into those of your own company; you can buy the stock of the seller rather than the company itself; or you can buy the individual assets of the seller. Third, you have to worry about the tax status of the merger. In a tax-free merger the tax position of the corporation and the stockholders is not changed. In a taxable merger the buyer can depreciate the full cost of the tangible assets acquired, but tax must be paid on any write-up of the assets' taxable value, and the stockholders in the selling corporation are taxed on any capital gains.

Mergers are often amicably negotiated between the management and directors of the two companies; but if the seller is reluctant, the would-be buyer can decide to make a tender offer or engage in a proxy fight. The cut and thrust of takeover battles can be fun to watch, but many believe that the battles are not in the public interest. Some are worried that the managers of the target company don't pay sufficient attention to the interests of their shareholders. Others are worried that some of the tactics used by the predator are unfair. And a third group think that the odds are weighted too heavily in favor of the shareholders of the target firm.

The threat of hostile takeover has stimulated corporate restructuring, which usually involves additional borrowing, selling or spinning off businesses, and buying back common stock. In a management buyout or leveraged buyout (LBO), all public shares are repurchased and the company "goes private." LBOs tend to involve mature businesses with ample cash flow and modest growth opportunities.

We conclude with three empirical facts about mergers. (1) Mergers occur in waves and are associated with buoyant stock prices. Nobody knows why. (2) Sellers gain from mergers—a typical premium is about 20 percent. Buyers on the average seem (roughly) to break even. (3) The typical merger appears to generate a net economic gain, but the size and significance of the gain are still controversial.

FURTHER READING

The approach to analyzing mergers presented in this chapter is based on:

> S. C. Myers, "A Framework for Evaluating Mergers," in S. C. Myers (ed.), *Modern Developments in Financial Management*, Frederick A. Praeger, Inc., New York, 1976.

The papers by Dodd and by Jensen and Ruback review the extensive empirical work on mergers. The same issue of the Journal of Financial Economics *also contains a collection of some of the more important empirical studies.*

> P. Dodd, "The Market for Corporate Control: A Review of the Evidence," *Midland Corporate Finance Journal*, **1:** 6–20 (Summer 1983).
>
> M. C. Jensen and R. S. Ruback, "The Market for Corporate Control: The Scientific Evidence," *Journal of Financial Economics*, **11:** 5–50 (April 1983).

There are two useful collections of articles on mergers and corporate restructuring. The first consists of a selection of papers previously published in The Chase Financial Quarterly *and* The Midland Corporate Finance Journal.

> J. M. Stern and D. H. Chew, Jr. (eds.), *The Revolution in Corporate Finance*, Basil Blackwell, Oxford, 1986.
>
> J. Coffee, L. Lowenstein, and S. R. Ackerman, *Knights, Raiders and Targets*, Oxford University Press, New York, forthcoming 1988.

QUIZ

1. Are the following hypothetical mergers horizontal, vertical, or conglomerate?
   (a) IBM acquires Control Data.
   (b) Control Data acquires Stop & Shop.
   (c) Stop & Shop acquires General Mills.
   (d) General Mills acquires IBM.
2. Velcro Saddles is contemplating the acquisition of Pogo Ski Sticks, Inc. The values of the two companies as separate entities are $20 million and $10 million, respectively. Velcro Saddles estimates that by combining the two companies, it will reduce marketing and administrative costs by $500,000 per year in perpetuity. Velcro Saddles can either pay $14 million cash for Pogo or offer Pogo a 50 percent holding in Velcro Saddles. If the opportunity cost of capital is 10 percent,
   (a) What is the gain from merger?
   (b) What is the cost of the cash offer?
   (c) What is the cost of the stock alternative?
   (d) What is the NPV of the acquisition under the cash offer?
   (e) What is its NPV under the stock offer?
3. Which of the following mergers are *not* likely to be classed as tax-free?

    (*a*) A merger undertaken solely for the purpose of taking advantage of tax-loss carry-forwards.

    (*b*) An acquisition of assets.

    (*c*) Payment is entirely in the form of voting stock.

    (*d*) Firm A acquires all of firm B's shares in a cash tender offer.

4. True or false?

    (*a*) Sellers almost always gain in mergers.

    (*b*) Buyers almost always gain in mergers.

    (*c*) Firms that do unusually well tend to be acquisition targets.

    (*d*) Merger activity in the United States varies dramatically from year to year.

    (*e*) On the average, mergers produce substantial economic gains.

    (*f*) Tender offers require the approval of the selling firm's management.

    (*g*) If a merger can be treated as a pooling of interest rather than a purchase, reported earnings are usually increased.

    (*h*) The cost of a merger is always independent of the economic gain produced by the merger.

    (*i*) The cost of a merger to the buyer equals the gain realized by the seller.

5. Which of the following motives for mergers make economic sense?

    (*a*) Merging to achieve economies of scale

    (*b*) Merging to reduce risk by diversification

    (*c*) Merging to redeploy cash generated by a firm with ample profits but limited growth opportunities

    (*d*) Merging to make fuller use of tax-loss carry-forwards

    (*e*) Merging just to increase earnings per share

6. Connect each term to its correct definition or description.

▪ LBO	▪ Payment to target firm's managers who leave after a takeover
▪ Master limited partnership	▪ Attempt to gain control of a firm by winning the votes of its stockholders
▪ Poison pill	▪ Offer to buy shares directly from stockholders
▪ Tender offer	▪ Target company buys out shareholders threatening takeover; repurchase price exceeds market price
▪ Greenmail	▪ Shareholders issued rights which must be repurchased by acquiring firm or which can be used to acquire shares of acquiring firm
▪ Golden parachute	▪ Company or business bought out by private investors, largely debt-financed
▪ Proxy fight	▪ Partnership "units" traded in the same way as common stock

QUESTIONS AND PROBLEMS

    1. Examine several recent mergers and suggest the principal motives for merging in each case.

    2. Examine a recent merger in which at least part of the payment made to the seller was in the form of stock. Use stock market prices to obtain an estimate of the gain from the merger and the cost of the merger.

    3. The Muck and Slurry merger has fallen through (see Section 33-3). But World Enterprises is determined to report earnings per share of $2.67. It therefore acquires the Wheelrim and Axle Company. You are given the following facts:

	World Enterprises	Wheelrim and Axle	Merged Firm
Earnings per share	$2.00	$2.50	$2.67
Price per share	$40.00	$25.00	?
Price-earnings ratio	20	10	?
Number of shares	100,000	200,000	?
Total earnings	$200,000	$500,000	?
Total market value	$4,000,000	$5,000,000	?

Once again there are no gains from merging. In exchange for Wheelrim and Axle shares, World Enterprises issues just cnough of its own shares to ensure its $2.67 earnings per share objective.

(a) Complete the above table for the merged firm.

(b) How many shares of World Enterprises are exchanged for each share of Wheelrim and Axle?

(c) What is the cost of the merger to World Enterprises?

(d) What is the change in the total market value of those World Enterprises shares that were outstanding before the merger?

4. Explain the distinction between a tax-free and a taxable merger. Are there circumstances in which you would expect buyer and seller to agree to a taxable merger?

5. Identify a few public companies that would not be suitable for an LBO. Then identify a few that would be suitable. Explain why the value of the companies in the second group might be increased by an LBO.

6. As treasurer of Leisure Products, Inc., you are investigating the possible acquisition of Plastitoys. You have the following basic data:

	Leisure Products	Plastitoys
Earnings per share	$5.00	$1.50
Dividend per share	$3.00	$.80
Number of shares	1,000,000	600,000
Stock price	$90.00	$20.00

You estimate that investors currently expect a steady growth of about 6 percent in Plastitoys' earnings and dividends. Under new management this growth rate would be increased to 8 percent per year, without any additional capital investment required.

(a) What is the gain from the acquisition?

(b) What is the cost of the acquisition if Leisure Products pays $25 in cash for each share of Plastitoys?

(c) What is the cost of the acquisition if Leisure Products offers one share of Leisure Products for every three shares of Plastitoys?

(d) How would the cost of the cash offer and the share offer alter if the expected growth rate of Plastitoys were not changed by the merger?

7. Look again at Table 33-3. Suppose that B Corporation's fixed assets are reexamined and found to be worth $1.2 million instead of $.9 million. How would this affect the AB Corporation's balance sheet under purchase accounting? How would the value of AB Corporation change? Would your answer depend on whether the merger is taxable?

8. Do you have any rational explanation for the great fluctuations in aggregate merger activity and the apparent relationship between merger activity and stock prices?

9. "Legislation is needed to ensure that shareholders of target companies are fairly treated."

   "Acquiring companies need some inducement to act. Legislation to protect the target shareholders is likely to remove this inducement."

   What do you think? For example, do you think that there should be a ban on two-tier bids, such as the Occidental bid for Cities Service?

10. What policy toward mergers would you wish to follow if you were head of the Federal Trade Commission?

APPENDIX   CONGLOMERATE MERGERS AND VALUE ADDITIVITY

A pure conglomerate merger is one that has no effect on the operations or profitability of either firm. If corporate diversification is in stockholders' interests, a conglomerate merger would give a clear demonstration of its benefits. But, if present values add up, the conglomerate merger would not make stockholders better or worse off.

In this appendix we examine more carefully our assertion that present values add. It turns out that values *do* add as long as capital markets are perfect and investors' diversification opportunities are unrestricted.

Call the merging firms A and B. Value additivity implies

$$PV_{AB} = PV_A + PV_B$$

where

PV_{AB} = the market value of the combined firms just after the merger

and

PV_A, PV_B = the separate market values of A and B just before the merger

For example, we might have

PV_A = $100 million ($200 per share times 500,000 shares outstanding)

and

PV_B = $200 million ($200 per share times 1,000,000 shares outstanding)

Suppose A and B are merged into a new firm AB, with one share in AB exchanged for each share of A or B. Thus there are 1,500,000 AB shares issued. *If* value additivity holds, then PV_{AB} must equal the sum of the separate values of A and B just before the merger, that is, $300 million. That would imply a price of $200 per share of AB stock.

But note that the AB shares represent a portfolio of the assets of A and B. Before the merger investors could have bought one share of A and two of B for $600. Afterward they can obtain a claim on *exactly* the same real assets by buying three shares of AB.

Suppose that the opening price of AB shares just after the merger is $200, so that $PV_{AB} = PV_A + PV_B$. Our problem is to determine if this is an equilibrium price, that is, whether we can rule out excess demand or supply at this price.

In order for there to be excess demand, there must be some investors who are willing to increase their holdings of A and B as a consequence of the merger. Who could they be? The only thing new created by the merger is diversification, but those investors who want to hold assets of A *and* B will have purchased A's and B's stock before the merger. The diversification is redundant and consequently won't attract new investment demand.

If there a possibility of excess supply? The answer is yes. For example, there will be some shareholders in A who did not invest in B. After the merger they cannot invest solely in A, but only in a fixed combination of A and B. Their AB shares will be less attractive to them than the pure A shares, so they will sell part or all their AB stock. In fact, the only AB shareholders who will *not* wish to sell are those who happened to hold A and B in exactly a 1:2 ratio in their premerger portfolios!

Since there is no possibility of excess demand, but a definite possibility of excess supply, we seem to have

$$PV_{AB} \leq PV_A + PV_B$$

That is, corporate diversification can't help, but it may hurt investors by restricting the types of portfolios they can hold. This is not the whole story, however, since investment demand for AB shares might be attracted from other sources if PV_{AB} drops below $PV_A + PV_B$. To illustrate, suppose there are two other firms, A* and B*, which are judged by investors to have the same risk characteristics as A and B, respectively. Then before the merger,

$$r_A = r_{A^*} \text{ and } r_B = r_{B^*}$$

where r is the rate of return expected by investors. We'll assume $r_A = r_{A^*} = .08$ and $r_B = r_{B^*} = .20$.

Consider a portfolio one-third invested in A* and two-thirds in B*. This portfolio offers an expected return of 16 percent.

$$r = x_A \cdot r_{A^*} + x_B \cdot r_{B^*}$$
$$= \tfrac{1}{3}(.08) + \tfrac{2}{3}(.20) = .16$$

A comparable portfolio of A and B before their merger also offered a 16 percent return.

As we have noted, a new firm AB is really a portfolio of firms A and B, with portfolio weights of $\tfrac{1}{3}$ and $\tfrac{2}{3}$. Thus it is equivalent in risk to the portfolio of A* and B*. Thus the price of AB shares must adjust so that it likewise offers a 16 percent return.

What if AB shares dropped below \$200, so that PV_{AB} is less than $PV_A + PV_B$? Since the assets and earnings of firms A and B are the same, the price drop means that the expected rate of return on AB shares has risen above the return offered by the A*B* portfolio. That is, if r_{AB} exceeds $\tfrac{1}{3}r_A + \tfrac{2}{3}r_B$, then r_{AB} must also exceed $\tfrac{1}{3}r_{A^*} + \tfrac{2}{3}r_{B^*}$. But this is untenable: Investors A* and B* could sell part of their holdings (in a 1:2 ratio), buy AB, and obtain a higher expected rate of return with no increase in risk.

On the other hand, if PV_{AB} rises above $PV_A + PV_B$, the AB shares will offer an expected return less than that offered by the A*B* portfolio. Investors will unload the AB shares, forcing their price down.

The only stable result is for AB shares to stick at \$200. Thus, value additivity will hold exactly in a perfect-market equilibrium if there are ample substitutes for the assets A and B. If A and B have unique risk characteristics, however, then PV_{AB} can fall below $PV_A + PV_B$. The reason is that the merger curtails investors' opportunity to custom-tailor their portfolios to their own needs and preferences.

This makes investors worse off, reducing the attractiveness of holding the shares of firm AB.

In general, the condition for value additivity is that investors' opportunity set—that is, the range of risk characteristics attainable by investors through their portfolio choices—is independent of the particular portfolio of real assets held by the firm. Diversification per se can never expand the opportunity set given perfect security markets. Corporate diversification may reduce the investors' opportunity set, but only if the real assets the corporations hold lack substitutes among traded securities or portfolios.

In a few cases the firm may be able to expand the opportunity set. It can do so if it finds an investment opportunity that is unique—a real asset with risk characteristics shared by few or no other financial assets. In this lucky event the firm should not diversify, however. It should set up the unique asset as a separate firm so as to expand investors' opportunity set to the maximum extent. If Gallo by chance discovered that a small piece of its vineyards produced wine comparable to Chateau Margaux, it would not throw that wine into the Hearty Burgundy vat.

34 International Financial Management

So far we have talked principally about doing business at home. But many companies have substantial overseas interests. Of course your objectives in international financial management are still the same. You want to buy assets that are worth *more* than they cost, and you want to pay for them by issuing liabilities that are worth *less* than the money raised. It is when you come to apply these criteria to your international business that you come up against some additional problems.

The unique feature of international financial management is that you need to deal with more than one currency. We will, therefore, look at how foreign exchange markets operate, why exchange rates change, and what you can do to protect yourself against exchange risks.

The financial manager must also remember that interest rates differ from country to country. For example, in spring 1987 the rate of interest was about 4 percent in Switzerland, 8 percent in the United States, and 270 percent in Brazil. We are going to discuss the reasons for these differences in interest rates, along with some of the implications for financing overseas operations. Should the parent company provide the money? Should it try to finance the operation locally? Or should it treat the world as its oyster and borrow wherever interest rates are lowest?

We will also discuss how international companies decide on capital investments. How do they choose the discount rate? And how does the financing method affect the choice of project? You'll find that the basic principles of capital budgeting are the same but there are a few pitfalls to look out for.

34-1   THE FOREIGN EXCHANGE MARKET

An American company that imports goods from Germany buys deutsche marks in order to pay for the purchase. An American company exporting to Germany receives deutsche marks, which it sells in exchange for dollars. Both firms make use of the foreign exchange market.[1]

Except in a few European centers, the foreign exchange market has no central marketplace. All business is conducted by telephone or telex. The principal dealers are the larger commercial banks and the central banks. Any corporation that wants to buy or sell currency usually does so through a commercial bank.

Turnover in the foreign exchange markets is huge. In each of the two major centers, Tokyo and London, nearly $200 billion of currency changes hands each day. Volume in New York is somewhat less.

---

[1] Alternatively, trade may take place in dollars. In this case the American importer pays for goods in dollars and the German exporter sells those dollars to buy deutsche marks. Similarly, the American exporter may demand payment in dollars; in this case the German importer must sell deutsche marks to buy those dollars.

Exchange rates in the United States are generally quoted in terms of the number of units of the foreign currency needed to buy one dollar. Therefore a rate of DM1.765/$ means that you can buy 1.765 deutsche marks for $1. Or, to put it another way, you need $1/1.765 = .5666$ dollars to buy one deutsche mark.[2]

Table 34-1 reproduces a table of exchange rates from *The Wall Street Journal*. Except where otherwise stated, the table gives the price of currency for immediate delivery. This is known as the **spot rate of exchange.** You can see that the spot rate for the deutsche mark is DM1.765/$.

The term *immediate delivery* is a relative one, for spot currency is usually purchased for 2-day delivery. For example, suppose that you need 100,000 DM to pay for imports from Germany. On Monday you telephone your bank in New York and agree to purchase 100,000 DM at DM1.765/$. The bank does not hand you a wad of banknotes over the counter. Instead it instructs its German correspondent bank to transfer DM 100,000 on Wednesday to the account of the German supplier. The bank debits your account by $100,000/1.765 = $56,666$ either on the Monday or, if you are a good customer, on the Wednesday.

In addition to the spot exchange market, there is a **forward market.** In the forward market you buy and sell currency for future delivery—usually in 1, 3, or 6 months' time, though in the major currencies banks are prepared to buy or sell for up to 10 years forward. If you know that you are going to pay out or receive foreign currency at some future date, you can insure yourself against loss by buying or selling forward. Thus, if you need 100,000 DM in 6 months, you can enter into a 6-month *forward contract.* The *forward rate* on this contract is the price you agree to pay in 6 months when the 100,000 deutsche marks are delivered.

If you look again at Table 34-1, you see that the 6-month forward rate for the deutsche mark is quoted at DM1.7300/$. If you buy deutsche marks for 6 months' delivery, you get fewer deutsche marks for your dollar than if you buy spot. In this case, the deutsche mark is said to trade at a forward *premium* relative to the dollar, because forward deutsche marks are more expensive than spot ones. Expressed as an annual rate, the forward premium is

$$2 \times \frac{1.765 - 1.730}{1.730} \times 100 = 4.05\%$$

You could also say that the dollar was selling at a 4 percent *forward discount*.

A forward purchase or sale is a made-to-measure transaction between you and the bank. It can be for any currency, any amount, and any delivery day. There is also an organized market for currency for future delivery known as the currency *futures* market. Futures contracts are highly standardized—they exist only for the main currencies, they are for specified amounts, and for a limited choice of delivery dates. The advantage of this standardization is that there is a liquid market in currency futures. Every day a huge number of contracts are bought and sold on the futures exchanges.[3]

When you buy a forward or a futures contract, you are committed to taking delivery of the currency. As an alternative, you can take out an *option* to buy or sell currency in the future at a price that is fixed today. Made-to-measure currency

---

[2] An exception is sterling which is usually quoted in terms of the number of dollars needed to buy one pound.

[3] See Chapter 25 for further discussion of the difference between forward and futures contracts and Table 25-1 for a list of currency futures. Chapter 25 also discusses swaps, which are (effectively) packages of forward contracts.

TABLE 34-1

An example of the foreign currency table in *The Wall Street Journal*

FOREIGN EXCHANGE

Monday, May 4, 1987

The New York foreign exchange selling rates below apply to trading among banks in amounts of $1 million and more, as quoted at 3 p.m. Eastern time by Bankers Trust Co. Retail transactions provide fewer units of foreign currency per dollar.

Country	U.S. $ equiv. Mon.	U.S. $ equiv. Fri.	Currency per U.S. $ Mon.	Currency per U.S. $ Fri.
Argentina (Austral)...	.6502	.6502	1.538	1.538
Australia (Dollar)	.6040	.7025	1.6556	1.4235
Austria (Schilling)	.08065	.07968	12.40	12.55
Belgium (Franc)				
Commercial rate	.02725	.02684	36.70	37.26
Financial rate.......	.02703	.02667	37.00	37.50
Brazil (Cruzado)......	.03625	.03658	27.59	27.34
Britain (Pound)	1.6843	1.6740	.5937	.5974
30-Day Forward....	1.6813	1.6708	.5948	.5985
90-Day Forward....	1.6772	1.6665	.5962	.6001
180-Day Forward....	1.6739	1.6615	.5974	.6019
Canada (Dollar)......	.7428	.7468	1.3463	1.3390
30-Day Forward....	.7422	.7462	1.3474	1.3401
90-Day Forward....	.7403	.7445	1.3508	1.3432
180-Day Forward....	.7370	.7418	1.3569	1.3480
Chile (Official rate)....	.0047	.004715	212.71	212.07
China (Yuan)........	.2687	.2687	3.722	3.722
Colombia (Peso)	.004264	.004305	234.50	232.28
Denmark (Krone)	.1504	.1493	6.6490	6.7000
Ecuador (Sucre)				
Official rate........	.005822	.006053	170.75	165.20
Floating rate.......	.0066	.006689	151.50	149.50
Finland (Markka)	.2316	.2295	4.3175	4.3575
France (Franc)	.1693	.1688	5.9075	5.9250
30-Day Forward....	.1691	.1686	5.9135	5.9310
90-Day Forward....	.1688	.1683	5.9245	5.9425
180-Day Forward....	.1685	.1680	5.9350	5.9515
Greece (Drachma)	.007634	.007582	131.00	131.90
Hong Kong (Dollar) ..	.1281	.1281	7.8060	7.8050
India (Rupee)........	.07899	.07893	12.66	12.67
Indonesia (Rupiah) ...	.000609	.0006086	1642.00	1643.00
Ireland (Punt)	1.5120	1.5010	.6614	.6662
Israel (Shekel)	.6293	.6254	1.589	1.599
Italy (Lira)	.0007918	.0007855	1263.00	1273.00
Japan (Yen).........	.007212	.007140	138.65	140.05
30-Day Forward....	.007234	.007162	138.23	139.63
90-Day Forward....	.007278	.007204	137.40	138.82
180-Day Forward....	.007348	.007267	136.10	137.60
Jordan (Dinar).......	2.9851	2.9851	.335	.335
Kuwait (Dinar)	3.6955	3.68	.2706	.2718
Lebanon (Pound)	.00860	.008889	116.25	112.50

Country	U.S. $ equiv. Mon.	U.S. $ equiv. Fri.	Currency per U.S. $ Mon.	Currency per U.S. $ Fri.
Malaysia (Ringgit)	.4056	.4045	2.4656	2.4720
Malta (Lira)	2.9197	2.8860	.3425	.3465
Mexico (Peso)				
Floating rate........	.0008425	.0008475	1187.00	1180.00
Netherland (Guilder) .	.5023	.4984	1.9910	2.0065
New Zealand (Dollar) .	.5740	.5760	1.7422	1.7361
Norway (Krone)	.1510	1497	6 6240	6.6800
Pakistan (Rupee).....	.0580	.0578	17.31	17.30
Peru (Inti)	.0657	.06570	15.22	15.22
Philippines (Peso)....	.0488	.04876	20.48	20.51
Portugal (Escudo)	.007273	.007225	137.50	138.40
Saudi Arabia (Riyal) .	.2666	.2666	3.751	3.751
Singapore (Dollar)....	.4726	.4713	2.1160	2.1220
South Africa (Rand)				
Commercial rate	.5020	.5020	1.9920	1.9920
Financial rate.......	.3313	.3225	3.0184	3.1008
South Korea (Won) ..	.0012	.001192	835.20	838.60
Spain (Peseta)	.008071	.007968	123.90	125.50
Sweden (Krona)	.1613	.1603	6.2000	6.2400
Switzerland (Franc) ..	.6916	.6878	1.4460	1.4540
30-Day Forward....	.6941	.6900	1.4408	1.4493
90-Day Forward....	.6978	.6938	1.4331	1.4414
180-Day Forward....	.7045	.6996	1.4195	1.4293
Taiwan (Dollar)......	.03049	.03040	32.80	32.90
Thailand (Baht)......	.0391	.03896	25.60	25.67
Turkey (Lira)	.0013	.001260	795.30	793.73
United Arab (Dirham) .	.2723	2.2723	3.673	3.673
Uruguay (New Peso)				
Financial	.0048	.004833	207.50	206.90
Venezuela (Bolivar)				
Official rate........	.1333	.1333	7.50	7.50
Floating rate.......	.0413	.04214	24.23	23.73
W. Germany (Mark) ..	.5666	.5634	1.7650	1.7750
30-Day Forward....	.5682	.5649	1.7598	1.7702
90-Day Forward....	.5715	.5681	1.7497	1.7601
180-Day Forward....	.5780	.5733	1.7300	1.7442
SDR	z	1.30526	z	0.766134
ECU	1.16776	z	....	....

Special Drawing Rights are based on exchange rates for the U.S., West German, British, French and Japanese currencies. Source: International Monetary Fund.

ECU is based on a basket of community currencies. Source: European Community Commission.

z-Not quoted.

options can be bought from the major banks, and standardized options are traded on the options exchanges.[4]

Finally, you can agree with the bank that you will buy foreign currency in the future at whatever is the prevailing spot rate *but subject to a maximum and minimum*

---

[4] A list of the traded currency options is given in Table 20-1. Some investment banks have also made one-off issues of currency warrants (i.e., long-term options to buy currency).

price. If the value of the foreign currency rises sharply, you buy at the agreed upper limit; if it falls sharply, you buy at the lower limit.[5]

34-2 SOME BASIC RELATIONSHIPS

You can't develop a consistent international financial policy until you understand the reasons for differences in exchange rates and interest rates. Therefore let us consider the following four problems:

- *Problem 1:* Why is the dollar rate of interest ($r_\$$) different from, say, the Swiss franc rate (r_{SFr})?
- *Problem 2:* Why is the forward rate of exchange ($f_{SFr/\$}$) different from the spot rate ($s_{SFr/\$}$)?
- *Problem 3:* What determines next year's expected spot rate of exchange between dollars and francs [$E(s_{SFr/\$})$]?
- *Problem 4:* What is the relationship between the inflation rate in the United States ($i_\$$) and the Swiss inflation rate (i_{SFr})?

Suppose that individuals were not worried about risk and that there were no barriers or costs to international trade. In that case the spot exchange rates, forward exchange rates, interest rates, and inflation rates would stand in the following simple relationship to one another:

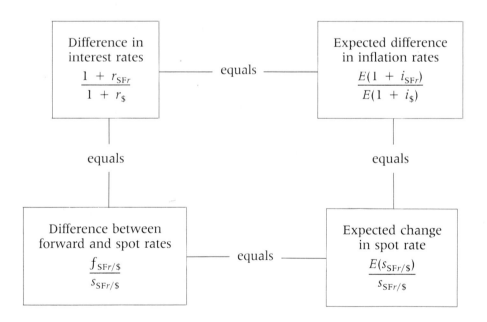

Why should this be so?

Interest Rates and Exchange Rates

You have $1 million to invest for 1 year. Is it better to make a dollar loan or a Swiss franc loan? Let's work out a numerical example.

- *Dollar loan:* The rate of interest on a 1-year dollar deposit is 7.875 percent. Therefore at the end of the year you get $1,000,000 \times 1.07875 = \$1,078,750$.
- *Swiss franc loan:* The current rate of exchange is SFr1.4460/$. For $1 million, you can buy $1,000,000 \times 1.446 = $ SFr1,446,000. The rate of interest on a 1-year Swiss franc deposit is 4 percent. Therefore at the end of the year, you get $1,446,000 \times 1.04 = $ SFr1,503,840. Of course you don't know what the exchange rate is going to be in 1 year's time. But that doesn't matter. You can fix today the price at which you will sell your francs. The 1-year forward rate is SFr1.392/$. Therefore, by selling forward, you can make sure that you will get $1,503,840/1.392 = \$1,080,345$ at the end of the year.

Thus, the two investments offer almost exactly the same rate of return. They have to—they are both risk-free. If the domestic interest rate were different from the "covered" foreign rate, you would have a money machine.

When you make the Swiss franc loan, you lose because you get a lower interest rate. But you gain because you sell francs forward at a higher price than you have to pay for them today.

The interest rate differential is

$$\frac{1 + r_{SFr}}{1 + r_{\$}}$$

And the differential between the forward and spot exchange rates is

$$\frac{f_{SFr/\$}}{s_{SFr/\$}}$$

Interest rate parity theory says that the interest rate differential must equal the differential between the forward and spot exchange rates.

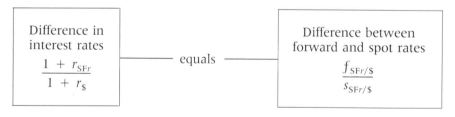

In our example,

$$\frac{1.04}{1.07875} = \frac{1.392}{1.446}$$

The Forward Premium and Changes in Spot Rates

Now let us think how the forward premium is related to changes in spot rates of exchange. If people didn't care about risk, the forward rate of exchange would depend solely on what people expect the spot rate to be. For example, if the 1-year forward rate on Swiss francs is SFr1.392/$, that can only be because traders expect the spot rate in 1 year's time to be SFr1.392/$. If they expected it to be higher than this, nobody would be willing to sell francs forward.

Therefore the *expectations theory* of exchange rates tells us that the percentage difference between the forward rate and today's spot rate is equal to the expected change in the spot rate:

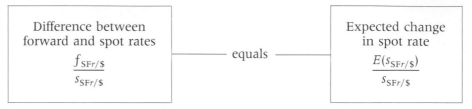

$$\frac{\text{Difference between forward and spot rates}}{\quad} \quad f_{\text{SFr}/\$} \atop s_{\text{SFr}/\$} \qquad \text{equals} \qquad \frac{\text{Expected change in spot rate}}{\quad} \quad \frac{E(s_{\text{SFr}/\$})}{s_{\text{SFr}/\$}}$$

In deriving the expectations theory we assumed that traders don't care about risk. If they do care, the forward rate can be either higher or lower than the expected spot rate. For example, suppose that you have contracted to receive SFr100,000 in 3 months. You can wait until you receive the money before you change it into dollars, but this leaves you open to the risk that the price of francs may fall over the next 3 months. Your alternative is to *sell* the francs forward. In this case, you are fixing today the price at which you will sell the francs. Since you avoid risk by selling francs forward, you may be willing to do so even if the forward price of francs is a little *lower* than the expected spot price.

Other companies may be in the opposite position. They may have contracted to pay out francs in 3 months. They can wait until the end of the 3 months and then buy francs, but this leaves them open to the risk that the price of francs may rise. It is safer for these companies to fix the price today by *buying* francs foward. These companies may, therefore, be willing to buy forward even if the forward price of francs is a little *higher* than the expected spot price.

Thus some companies find it safer to *sell* francs forward, while others find it safer to *buy* francs forward. If the first group predominates, the forward price of francs is likely to be less than the expected spot price. If the second group predominates, the forward price is likely to be greater than the expected spot price.

Changes in the Exchange Rate and Inflation Rates

Now we come to the third side of our quadrilateral—the relationship between changes in the spot exchange rate and inflation rates. Suppose that you notice that silver can be bought in New York for $8.50 a troy ounce and sold in Zurich for SFr13. You think you may be on to a good thing. You decide to buy silver for $8.50 and put it on the first plane to Zurich, where you sell it for SFr13. Then you exchange your SFr13 for $13/1.446 = \$8.99$. You have made a gross profit of $.99 an ounce. Of course you have to pay transportation and insurance costs out of this but there should still be something left over for you.

Money machines don't exist—not for long. As others notice the disparity between the price of silver in Zurich and the price in New York, the price will be forced down in Zurich and up in New York until the profit opportunity disappears. Arbitrage ensures that the dollar price of silver is about the same in the two countries.

Of course silver is a standard and easily transportable commodity, but to some degree you might expect that the same forces would be acting to equalize the domestic and foreign prices of other goods. Those goods that can be bought more cheaply abroad will be imported, and that will force down the price of the domestic product. Similarly, those goods that can be bought more cheaply in the United States will be exported, and that will force down the price of the foreign product.

This is often called the *law of one price*.[6] Just as the price of goods in Safeway must be roughly the same as the price of goods in A&P, so the price of goods in Switzerland when converted into dollars must be roughly the same as the price in the United States.

The law of one price implies that any differences in the rate of inflation will be offset by a change in the exchange rate. For example, if inflation is 5 percent in the United States and 1 percent in Switzerland, then in order to equalize the dollar price of goods in the two countries, the price of Swiss francs must rise by $(1.05)/(1.01) - 1$, or about 4 percent. Therefore the law of one price suggests that in order to estimate changes in the spot rate of exchange, you need to estimate differences in inflation rates:[7]

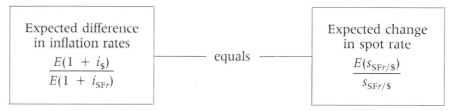

Expected difference in inflation rates

$$\frac{E(1 + i_{\$})}{E(1 + i_{SFr})}$$

equals

Expected change in spot rate

$$\frac{E(s_{SFr/\$})}{s_{SFr/\$}}$$

In our example,

$$\begin{array}{ccccc} \text{Current spot} & \times & \text{expected difference} & = & \text{expected spot} \\ \text{rate} & & \text{in inflation rates} & & \text{rate} \end{array}$$

$$1.446 \quad \times \quad \frac{1.01}{1.05} \quad = \quad 1.391$$

Interest Rates and Inflation Rates

Now for the fourth leg! Just as water always flows downhill, so capital always flows where returns are greatest. In equilibrium the expected *real* return on capital is the same in different countries.

But bonds don't promise a fixed *real* return: they promise a fixed *money* payment. Therefore we have to think about how the money rate of interest in each country is related to the real rate of interest. One answer to this has been provided by Irving Fisher, who argued that the money rate of interest will reflect the expected inflation.[8] In this case the United States and Switzerland will both offer the same expected *real* rate of interest, and the difference in money rates will be equal to the expected difference in inflation rates:

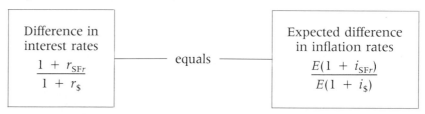

Difference in interest rates

$$\frac{1 + r_{SFr}}{1 + r_{\$}}$$

equals

Expected difference in inflation rates

$$\frac{E(1 + i_{SFr})}{E(1 + i_{\$})}$$

[6] Economists tend to use the phrase *law of one price* when they are talking about the price of a single good. The notion that the price level of goods in general must be the same in the two countries is often called the *purchasing power parity theory*.

[7] We are suggesting here that the *expected* difference in the inflation rate equals the *expected* change in the exchange rate. Notice, however, that the law of one price also implies that the *actual* difference in the inflation rate always equals the *actual* change in the exchange rate.

[8] We discussed the Fisher effect in Section 23-1 of Chapter 23.

Is Life Really That Simple?

We have described above four simple theories that link interest rates, forward rates, spot exchange rates, and inflation rates. Notice that the four theories are mutually consistent. This means that if any three are correct, the fourth must also be correct. Conversely, if any one is wrong, at least one other must be wrong.

Of course no economic theory is going to provide an exact description of reality, but we need to know how well these simple benchmarks can predict actual behavior.

1. *Interest rate parity theory:* Interest rate parity theory says that the Swiss franc rate of interest covered for exchange risk should be the same as the dollar rate. In the example that we gave you earlier we used the rates of interest on eurodollar and eurofranc deposits. The eurocurrency market is an international market that is very free of government regulation or tax. Since money can be moved easily between different eurocurrency deposits, interest rate parity almost always holds.[9] In fact dealers *set* the forward price of francs by looking at the difference between the interest rates on eurofrancs and eurodollars.

The relationship does not hold so exactly for the domestic money markets. In these cases taxes and government regulations sometimes prevent the citizens of one country from switching out of domestic bank deposits and covering their exchange risk in the forward market.

2. *The expectations theory of forward rates:* The expectations theory of forward rates does not imply that managers are perfect forecasters. Sometimes the *actual* future spot rate will jump above previous forward rates. Sometimes it will fall below. But if the theory is correct, we should find that *on the average* the forward rate is equal to the future spot rate. The theory passes this simple test with flying colors.[10] That is important news for the financial manager; it means that a company which always covers its foreign exchange commitments does not have to pay any extra for this insurance.

Although *on the average* the forward rate is equal to the future spot rate, it does seem to provide an exaggerated estimate of the likely change in the spot rate. Therefore, when the forward rate appears to predict a sharp rise in the spot rate, the actual rise generally turns out to be less. And when the forward rate appears to predict a sharp decline in the spot rate, the actual decline is also likely to be less. This result is *not* consistent with the expectations hypothesis. Instead it looks as if sometimes companies are prepared to give up a little return in order to buy forward currency and at other times they are prepared to give up return in order to sell forward currency.[11]

We should also warn you that the forward rate does not usually tell you very much about the future spot rate. This does not mean that the forward rate is a poor measure of managers' expectations; it just means that exchange rates are very

---

[9] See, for example, T. Agmon and S. Bronfield, "The International Mobility of Short-Term Covered Arbitrage Capital," *Journal of Business Finance and Accounting,* **2:** 269–278 (Summer 1975); and J. A. Frenkel and R. M. Levich, "Transactions Costs and Interest Arbitrage: Tranquil versus Turbulent Periods," *Journal of Political Economy,* **85:** 1209–1225 (November–December 1977).

[10] For some evidence on the average difference between the forward rate and subsequent spot rate see B. Cornell, "Spot Rates, Forward Rates, and Market Efficiency," *Journal of Financial Economics,* **5:** 55–65 (1977).

[11] For evidence that forward exchange rates contain risk premia that are sometimes positive and sometimes negative see, for example, E. F. Fama, "Forward and Spot Exchange Rates," *Journal of Monetary Economics,* **14:** 319–338 (1984).

tough to predict. Many banks and consultants produce forecasts of future exchange rates. But Richard Levich found that more often than not the forward rate provided a more accurate forecast than the currency advisory services.[12]

3. *The law of one price:* What about the third side of our quadrilateral—the law of one price? No one who has compared prices in foreign stores with prices at home really believes that the law of one price holds exactly. On the other hand, there is clearly some relationship between inflation and changes in exchange rates. For example, between 1980 and 1985, prices of goods in Turkey rose 5.1 times, compared with an average of 1.6 times in other countries. Thus

$$\frac{1 + i_{\text{average}}}{1 + i_{\text{Turkish lira}}} = \frac{1.6}{5.1} = .31$$

You could say that the purchasing power of the Turkish lira declined by $1 - .31 = 69$ percent more than the average. If exchange rates had not adjusted, Turkish exporters would have found it increasingly hard to sell their goods. But of course, exchange rates did adjust. In fact, on average, one unit of foreign currency bought 74 percent more Turkish lira than before. Thus a 69 percent relative decline in purchasing power was slightly more than offset by a 74 percent decline in the value of the Turkish currency.

Turkey is a somewhat extreme case,[13] but in Figure 34-1 we have plotted the relative change in purchasing power in 81 countries against the annual change in the exchange rate. You can see that, although the relationship is far from exact, large differences in inflation rates are generally accompanied by an offsetting change in the exchange rate.

Strictly speaking, the law of one price implies that the differential inflation rate is always identical to the change in the exchange rate. But we don't need to go as far as that. We should be content if the *expected* difference in the inflation rate equals the *expected* change in the spot rate. That's all we wrote on the third side of our quadrilateral. In order to test this, Richard Roll looked at exchange rates of 23 countries between 1957 and 1976.[14] He found that, on average, today's exchange rate provided the best estimate of the inflation-adjusted exchange rate. In other words, your estimate of the inflation differential is also your best estimate of the change in the exchange rate.

4. *Capital market equilibrium:* Finally we come to the relationship between interest rates in different countries. Do we have a single world capital market with the same *real* rate of interest in all countries? Can we even extend the notion and think of a single world market for risk capital, so that the real opportunity cost of capital for risky investments is the same in all countries? It is an attractive idea. Unfortunately, the evidence is scanty.

Since governments cannot directly control interest rates in the international eurocurrency markets, we might expect that in these markets, differences between

[12] See R. M. Levich, "How to Compare Chance with Forecasting Expertise," *Euromoney*, 61–78 (August 1981).

[13] There are *more* extreme cases. Between 1980 and 1985, inflation in Bolivia totaled 1,800,000 percent (or thereabouts).

[14] R. Roll, "Violations of the 'Law of One Price' and Their Implications for Differentially Denominated Assets," in M. Sarnat and G. Szego (eds.), *International Finance and Trade*, Ballinger Press, Cambridge, Mass., 1979.

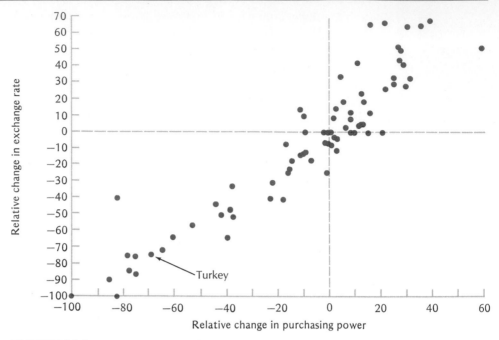

FIGURE 34-1

A decline in a currency's purchasing power and a decline in the exchange rate usually go hand in hand. In this diagram, each point represents the experience of a different country between 1980 and 1985. The vertical axis shows the change in the value of a foreign currency relative to the average. The horizontal axis shows the change in the currency's purchasing power relative to the average.

the expected real rates of interest would be small. Governments have more control over their domestic rates of interest, at least in the short run. Therefore, it's possible for a country to have a real rate of interest in the domestic market that is below the real rate in other countries. But it is not easy to maintain this position indefinitely. Individuals and companies are capable of great ingenuity in transferring their cash from countries with low real rates of interest to those with high real rates of interest.

We cannot show the relationship between interest rates and expected inflation, but in Figure 34-2 we have plotted the average interest rate in each of 15 countries against the inflation that subsequently occurred. You can see that in general, the countries with the highest interest rates also had the highest inflation rates. There were much smaller differences between the real rates of interest than between the nominal (or money) rates.

34-3 INSURING AGAINST CURRENCY RISKS

To hedge or not to hedge? Laker Airlines went bankrupt because it didn't. It had borrowed dollars aggressively, when much of its revenue was in sterling. When the dollar "took off" in the early 1980s, Laker could not meet debt service.

With examples like this in mind, most companies hedge or at least limit their foreign exchange exposures. Another British company, Thomas Cook, is a tour operator. When it sells a packaged vacation, it receives sterling but must pay

FIGURE 34-2
Countries with the highest interest rates generally have the highest subsequent inflation rates. In this diagram, each point represents the experience of a different country between 1980 and 1984. (*Source: Morgan Guaranty Bank, World Financial Markets.*)

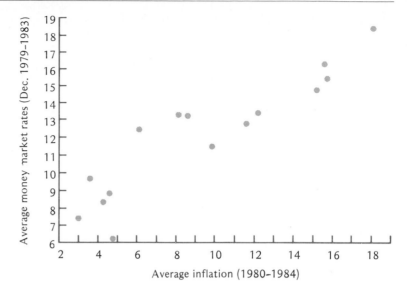

airlines in dollars and hotels in a different currency, for example, in Spanish pesetas. It has offset these liabilities by purchasing call options on dollars and buying pesetas forward.[15]

British Petroleum has used an interesting mixture of hedging and risk-taking:[16]

BP decided that the best way was to turn the foreign exchange operation into a profit centre. "The philosophy is that as far as possible the various [BP] businesses should identify and analyse what their exchange exposures are and seek to reduce those exposures. But the residual should be sold to BPFI [British Petroleum Finance International]," which treats the businesses as if they were third party customers. "And that gives them the cover, the protection of their risk, and puts the exposure onto our books, which we then manage on pure banking principles."

"Managing on pure banking principles" means a dozen traders, about $60 billion in transactions, and pretax profits on the order of $20 million in 1985. In other words, BP was big enough, and evidently skilled enough, to make money in international banking as well as oil.

But BP is hardly a typical case. We now look at a typical company in the United States, Outland Steel, and walk through its foreign exchange problems.

Example.   Outland Steel has a small but profitable export business. Contracts involve substantial delays in payment, but since the company has had a policy of always invoicing in dollars, it is fully protected against changes in exchange rates. More recently the export department has become unhappy with this practice and believes that it is causing the company to lose valuable orders to Japanese and German firms that are willing to quote in the customer's own currency.

---

[15] See "Dealing in Foreign Exchange Markets," Supplement to the July 1986 edition of *Corporate Finance* magazine, a monthly Euromoney Publication, pp. 30–31.

[16] Ibid., p. 34.

You sympathize with these arguments, but you are worried about how the firm should price long-term export contracts when payment is to be made in foreign currency. If the value of the currency declines before payment is made, the company may make a large loss. You want to take currency risk into account when you price these contracts, but you also want to give the sales force as much freedom of action as possible.

Notice that you can insure yourself against this currency risk by selling the foreign currency forward.[17] This means that you can separate the problem of negotiating individual contracts from that of managing the company's foreign exchange exposure. The sales force can allow for currency risk by pricing on the basis of the forward exchange rate. And you, as financial manager, can decide whether the company *ought* to insure.

What is the cost of insurance? You sometimes hear managers say that it is equal to the difference between the forward rate and *today's* spot rate. That is wrong. If Outland does not insure, it will receive the spot rate at the time that the customer pays for the steel. Therefore, the cost of insurance is the difference between the forward rate and the expected spot rate when payment is received.

Insure or speculate? We generally vote for insurance. First, it makes life simpler for the firm and allows it to concentrate on its main business.[18] Second, it does not cost much. (In fact, the cost is zero if the forward rate equals the expected spot rate as the expectations theory of forward rates implies.) Third, the foreign exchange market seems reasonably efficient, at least for the major currencies. Speculation should be a zero-NPV game unless financial managers have information superior to the pros who make the market.

Is there any other way that Outland can protect itself against exchange loss? Of course. It can borrow foreign currency against its receivables, sell the foreign currency spot, and invest the proceeds in the United States. Interest rate parity theory tells us that in free markets the difference between selling forward and selling spot should be exactly equal to the difference between the interest that you have to pay overseas and the interest that you can earn at home. But as we have seen, when capital markets are highly regulated, it may be cheaper to arrange foreign borrowing rather than forward cover.[19]

It is not always so simple to hedge exports against currency fluctuations. Suppose, for example, Outland has tendered for a large export order. It will not know for several weeks whether it has been successful in getting the order. If it sells the foreign currency forward and doesn't get the order, it stands to lose from a rise in the value of the foreign currency. If it doesn't sell the currency and *does* get the order, it stands to lose from a fall in the value of the foreign currency. When faced with this dilemma, many financial managers limit their downside risk by buying an option to sell the foreign currency at a specified price. That way they know the most they can lose is the cost of the option.[20]

---

[17] Of course, if you don't know the exact payment date, you cannot be sure of the appropriate delivery date for the forward contract. Banks are prepared to deal in forward contracts which allow the company some choice of when to deliver, but these are not common.

[18] It also relieves shareholders of worrying about the foreign exchange exposure they may have acquired by purchase of the firm's shares.

[19] Sometimes also governments attempt to prevent currency speculation by limiting the amount that companies can sell forward.

[20] It is even possible to buy options on options. In this case Outland could pay a small sum for an option now which would allow it to buy another option when it hears the results of its tender.

Our discussion of Outland's export business illustrates three practical implications of our simple theories about forward rates. First, you can use forward rates to tell you how to allow for exchange risk in contract pricing. Second, the expectations theory suggests that insurance against exchange risk is usually worth having. Third, interest rate parity theory is a reminder that you can insure either by selling forward or by borrowing foreign currency and selling spot.

Perhaps we should add a fourth implication. The cost of forward cover is not the difference between the forward rate and *today's* spot rate; it is the difference between the forward rate and the expected spot rate when the forward contract matures. There is a corollary to this. You don't make money simply by buying currencies that go up in value and selling those that go down. If investors anticipate the change in the exchange rate, then it will be reflected in the interest rate differential; therefore, what you gain on the currency you will lose in terms of interest income. You make money from currency speculation only if you can predict whether the exchange rate will change by more or less than the interest rate differential. In other words, you must be able to predict whether the exchange rate will change by more or less than the forward premium.

34-4 INTERNATIONAL INVESTMENT DECISIONS

Outland Steel's export business has risen to the point at which it is worth establishing a subsidiary in Holland to hold inventories of steel. Outland's decision to invest overseas should be based on the same criteria as the decision to invest in the United States—that is, the company must identify the incremental cash flows, discount them at a rate that reflects the opportunity cost of capital, and accept all projects with a positive NPV.

Here are two ways that Outland could calculate the net present value of its Dutch venture:

- *Method 1:* Outland could follow the practice of many multinational companies and do all its capital budgeting calculations in dollars. In this case it must first estimate the guilder cash flows from its Dutch operation and convert these into dollars at the projected exchange rate. These dollar cash flows can then be discounted at the dollar cost of capital to give the investment's net present value in dollars.
- *Method 2:* In order to avoid making forecasts of the exchange rate, Outland could simply calculate the project's net present value entirely in terms of guilders. Outland could then convert this figure into dollars at the current exchange rate.

Each method has three steps, but steps 2 and 3 are in different orders:

	Method 1	Method 2
Step 1	Estimate future cash flow in guilders	Estimate future cash flow in guilders
Step 2	Convert to dollars (at forecasted exchange rates)	Calculate present value (use guilder discount rate)
Step 3	Calculate present value (use dollar discount rate)	Convert to dollars (use spot rate)

Suppose it uses method 1. Where do the exchange rate forecasts come from? It would be foolish for Outland to accept a poor project just because management is particularly optimistic about the guilder—if Outland wishes to speculate in this way, it can simply buy guilders forward. Equally, it would be foolish for Outland to reject a good project just because it is pessimistic about the prospects for the guilder. The company would do much better to go ahead with the project and sell guilders forward. In that way, it would get the best of both worlds.

Thus, as long as a company can alter its exchange exposure, its international capital expenditure decisions should *not* depend on whether the manager feels that a currency is wrongly valued. Instead of using its own exchange rate forecasts, Outland should base its capital investment decision on the foreign exchange market's consensus forecasts. To measure this consensus forecast, Outland can make use of the simple relationships described earlier in the chapter. If investors are on their financial toes, the expected movement in the exchange rate is equal to the difference between the interest rates in the two countries.

If Outland uses either of our two methods, its investment decision is also going to be heavily influenced by its assumption about the Dutch inflation rate. Although Outland's financial manager may well have her own views about Dutch inflation, it would again be foolish to let these views influence the investment decision. After all there are more efficient ways to speculate on the inflation rate than by building (or not building) a steel distribution depot.[21] So the financial manager of Outland would do much better to assume that in efficient capital markets, the difference between the Dutch and American interest rates reflects the likely difference in the inflation rates.[22]

Does it matter which of our two methods Outland uses to appraise its investment? It does if Outland employs its own forecasts of the exchange rate and inflation rate. However, as long as Outland assumes our simple parity relationships between interest rates, exchange rates, and inflation, the two methods will give the same answer.

Example.   We will illustrate with a simple example. Suppose Outland's Dutch facility is expected to generate the following cash flows in guilders:

	YEAR				
	1	2	3	4	5
Cash flow in thousands of guilders	400	450	510	575	650

How much is this cash flow worth today if Outland wants a 16 percent *dollar* return from its Dutch investment?

Outland's financial manager looks in the newspaper and finds that the risk-free interest rate is 8 percent in the United States ($r_\$ = .08$) and 6 percent in Holland ($r_{\text{fl}} = .06$). She sees right away that if real interest rates are expected to be the same in the two countries, then the consensus forecast of the Dutch inflation

---

[21] For example, if the manager believes that investors have underestimated the Dutch inflation rate, she should issue long-term guilder bonds and invest in short-term guilder bills or notes.

[22] There is a general point here that is not confined to international investment. Whenever you face an investment that appears to have a positive NPV, decide what it is that you are betting on and then think whether there is a more direct way to place the bet. For example, if a copper mine looks profitable only because you are unusually optimistic about the price of copper, then maybe you would do better to buy copper futures rather than open a copper mine.

rate (i_{fl}) must be approximately two percentage points lower than the inflation rate in the United States ($i_\$$). For example, if the expected rate of inflation in the United States is 5 percent, then the real rate of interest and the expected Dutch inflation rate are calculated as follows:

	(1 + Nominal Interest Rate)	=	(1 + Real Interest Rate)	×	(1 + Expected Inflation Rate)
In dollars	1.08	=	1.029	×	1.05
In guilders	1.06	=	1.029	×	1.03

The financial manager therefore checks that the guilder cash flow forecasts are consistent with this inflation rate.

The current spot rate is 2.00 guilders to the dollar, but, since the expected inflation rate in Holland is lower than in the United States, the guilder is likely to appreciate against the dollar:

Expected spot rate = spot rate at × inflation rate
at end of year   start of year   differential

$$E(s_{fl/\$}) \qquad = s_{fl/\$} \qquad \times \frac{E(1 + i_{fl})}{E(1 + i_\$)}$$

For example,

$$\text{Expected spot rate at year 1} = 2.00 \times \frac{1.03}{1.05} = 1.96 \text{ guilders per dollar}$$

The financial manager can use these projected exchange rates to produce a forecast of the cash flows in *dollars:*

	YEAR				
	1	2	3	4	5
Cash flow (guilders)	400	450	510	575	650
Forecast spot rate	1.96	1.92	1.89	1.85	1.82
Cash flow (dollars)	204	234	270	311	357

Now she uses method 1 and discounts these *dollar* cash flows at the *dollar* cost of capital:

$$PV = \frac{204}{1.16} + \frac{234}{1.16^2} + \frac{270}{1.16^3} + \frac{311}{1.16^4} + \frac{357}{1.16^5} = \$863,000$$

Notice that she discounted at 16 percent, not the domestic interest rate of 8 percent. The cash flow is risky, so a risk-adjusted rate is appropriate.

Just as a check, the financial manager tries method 2. Since the guilder interest rate is lower than the dollar rate, the risk-adjusted discount rate must also be correspondingly lower:

	(1 + Risk-Adjusted Discount Rate)	=	(1 + Nominal Interest Rate)	×	(1 + Risk Premium)
In dollars	1.16	=	1.08	×	1.074
In guilders	1.139	=	1.06	×	1.074

To use method 2 the manager discounts the *guilder* cash flows by the *guilder* discount rate:

$$PV = \frac{400}{1.139} + \frac{450}{1.139^2} + \frac{510}{1.139^3} + \frac{575}{1.139^4} + \frac{650}{1.139^5}$$

$$= 1726, \text{ or } 1,726,000 \text{ guilders}$$

Now convert to dollars at the spot rate, 2.0fl/$:

$$NPV = \frac{1726}{2.0} = 863, \text{ or } \$863,000$$

34-5   THE COST OF CAPITAL FOR FOREIGN INVESTMENT

Now we need to think more carefully about the risk of overseas investment and the reward that investors require for taking this risk. Unfortunately, these are issues on which few economists can agree.[23]

Remember that the risk of an investment cannot be considered in isolation; it depends on the securities that the investor holds in his portfolio. For example, at one extreme, we can imagine a single world capital market in which investors from each country hold well-diversified international portfolios. In that case, Outland could measure the risk of its Dutch venture by the project's beta relative to the *world* market portfolio. Since Outland would face exactly the same risk on its Dutch project as a local Dutch steel company, it would need to earn exactly the same return.

At the other extreme, we can imagine a world in which capital markets are completely segmented so that American investors hold only American stocks and Dutch investors hold only Dutch stocks. In these circumstances, Outland and the Dutch company do not face the same risk. Outland could measure the project's risk by its beta relative to the *United States* market, whereas a Dutch company would want to measure it by its beta relative to the *Dutch* market. An investment in the Dutch steel industry would appear to be a relatively low-risk project to Outland's shareholders who hold only United States shares, whereas it might seem a relatively high-risk project to a Dutch company whose shareholders are already highly exposed to the fortunes of the Dutch market. In this case Outland would be satisfied with a lower return on the project than the Dutch company would demand.

---

[23] Why not? One fundamental reason is that economists have never been able to agree on what makes one country different from another. Is it just that they have different currencies? Or is it that their citizens have different tastes? Or is it that they are subject to different regulations and taxes? The answer affects the relationship between security prices in different countries. See, for example, F. L. A. Grauer, R. H. Litzenberger, and R. E. Stehle, "Sharing Rules and Equilibrium in an International Capital Market Under Uncertainty," *Journal of Financial Economics*, **3**: 233–256 (June 1976), B. H. Solnik, "An Equilibrium Model of the International Capital Market," *Journal of Economic Theory*, **8**: 500–524 (1974), and F. Black, "International Capital Market Equilibrium with Investment Barriers," *Journal of Financial Economics*, **1**: 337–352 (December 1974).

Here, in summary, are these two scenarios:

A Single World Capital Market	Completely Segmented Capital Markets
Individuals invest internationally	Individuals invest domestically
Risk measured relative to world market index	Risk measured relative to domestic index
No further gains from international diversification	Large gains from international diversification
Outland's Dutch subsidiary has same cost of capital as local Dutch company	Outland's Dutch subsidiary has lower cost of capital than local Dutch company

The truth seems to lie closest to the scenario in the right-hand column. Americans are free to hold foreign shares but they generally invest only a small part of their money overseas. This suggests that there are still unexploited opportunities for overseas investment to reduce risk through diversification. Therefore, investors may be willing to accept a somewhat *lower* return from international than they would from domestic investment.

Nobody knows quite why investors are so reluctant to buy foreign shares— maybe it is simply that there are extra costs in figuring out which shares to buy. Or perhaps investors are worried that a foreign government will expropriate their shares, restrict dividend payments, or catch them by a change in tax law.

Cooper and Kaplanis have tried to estimate the costs of foreign investment by asking how large the costs would need to be for the American holdings in foreign shares to make sense. They calculated that in the United States, investors behave *as if* the extra cost of investing in foreign shares is about 2 to 4 percent a year.[24]

Cooper and Kaplanis's estimates suggest a standard for American corporations that are investing abroad. If Americans are willing to pay an additional 2 to 4 percent for investing in overseas shares, they should be happy to see American corporations invest abroad even if they expect to earn 2 to 4 percent less than local companies.

We certainly don't pretend that we can put a precise figure on the cost of capital for foreign investment. But you can see that we disagree with the frequent practice of automatically marking *up* the domestic cost of capital when foreign investment is considered. We suspect that managers mark up the required return for foreign investment to cover the risk of expropriation, foreign exchange restrictions, or unfavorable tax changes. A fudge factor is added to the discount factor to cover these costs.

We think managers should leave the discount rate alone and reduce expected cash flows instead. For example, suppose that Outland is expected to earn 450,000 guilders in the first year *if no penalties are placed on the operations of foreign firms*. Suppose also that there is a 10 percent chance that Outland's operation may be expropriated without compensation.[25] The *expected* cash flow is not 450,000 guilders but $.9 \times 450 = 405,000$ guilders.

The end result may be the same when you add a fudge factor to the discount

---

[24] See I. A. Cooper and E. Kaplanis, "Cost to Crossborder Investment and International Equity Market Equilibrium," in J. Edwards, J. Franks, C. Mayer, and S. Schaefer (eds.), *Recent Developments in Corporate Finance,* Cambridge University Press, Cambridge, 1986.

[25] Our example is fanciful. Most measures of political risk place Holland as one of the most stable environments for investment.

rate. Nevertheless, adjusting cash flows brings management's assumptions about "political risks" out in the open for scrutiny and sensitivity analysis.

34-6 FINANCING FOREIGN OPERATIONS

Outland can pay for its Dutch venture in three ways. It can export capital from the United States, it can borrow Dutch guilders, or it can borrow wherever interest rates are lowest.

Notice that if the guilder is devalued, other things equal, the Dutch assets will be worth fewer dollars than before. In this case, Outland could protect itself against exchange risk by borrowing guilders. It would then have both a Dutch asset and an offsetting Dutch liability. If the guilder is devalued, the dollar value of the asset falls, but that is offset by the fact that Outland now needs fewer dollars to service its guilder debt.

Unfortunately, other things are rarely equal, for the devaluation may be accompanied by changes in the guilder value of Outland's assets. Remember that the law of one price states that any change in the guilder exchange rate will be exactly offset by a change in the relative price of Dutch goods. Of course you know better than to take that theory literally, but it may not be too bad an approximation in the case of readily exportable goods such as steel inventory. In other words, even if the guilder is devalued, Outland's steel inventory may largely hold its value in terms of dollars. Therefore, rather than finance the entire venture by guilder debt, it may be safer to finance it with a mixture of guilders and dollars.

Some overseas investments may have almost no exchange risk. For example, since oil prices are fixed in dollars, Exxon's investment in the British North Sea is largely immune to a devaluation of sterling. Exxon's least-risky strategy is therefore to finance its North Sea investment with dollars rather than pounds. Conversely, other firms may be exposed to exchange risk even though all their business is conducted in the United States. For example, since a devaluation of the yen is likely to reduce the dollar price of Japanese cars, a Ford dealer in Texas may be exposed to changes in the Japanese exchange rate and could protect herself against exchange risk by financing partly with yen.

One final example. Suppose that your company sites a plant in Taiwan to produce video recorders. The law of one price predicts that a high rate of inflation in Taiwan will be offset by a change in the exchange rate. So the *United States dollar* cash flows from the Taiwan plant are not affected by the level of inflation in Taiwan.

The problem occurs if the law of one price does *not* hold. For example, suppose that a relatively high rate of inflation in Taiwan coincides with a rise in the value of the Taiwan dollar. In this case there is a rise in the *real* value of the Taiwan dollar and, other things equal, a rise in the plant's cash flows when measured in United States dollars.

There are some other factors that you need to take into account. Because it is now more costly to manufacture in Taiwan, the plant will find it less easy to compete in export markets and profit margins are likely to be cut. This will tend to *reduce* cash flows when measured in United States dollars. You cannot determine how to hedge your exchange risk until you have decided whether on balance the firm gains or loses by a rise in the value of the Taiwan dollar.[26]

---

[26] Notice that it is the change in the *real* exchange rate that you would like to hedge against. In other words, the value of the Taiwan venture would be equally affected by a rise in the exchange rate and by a rise in the Taiwan inflation rate. Unfortunately, it is much easier to hedge against a change in the *nominal* exchange rate than against a change in the *real* rate.

Instead of worrying about reducing risk, why doesn't Outland follow our third alternative and borrow wherever interest rates are lowest? For example, instead of borrowing in Holland, where the interest rate is 6 percent, perhaps Outland should borrow in Switzerland, where the rate is about 5 percent. However, you must ask yourself *why* the Swiss rate is so low. Unless you know that the Swiss government is deliberately holding the rate down by restrictions on the export of capital, you should suspect that the real cost of capital is roughly the same in Switzerland as it is anywhere else. The nominal interest rate is low only because investors expect a low domestic rate of inflation and a strong currency. Therefore, the advantage of the low rate of interest is likely to be offset by the fact that when you come to repay the loan, each franc will cost you more dollars than it would currently.

We think that it makes sense for a firm to establish a "passive" or "normal" financing strategy. But sometimes you may come across an opportunity that truly does make it cheaper to depart from your normal strategy and finance in one particular country. For example, here is a deal worked out by Massey-Ferguson, the Canadian farm equipment manufacturer, as described in a paper by Donald Lessard and Alan Shapiro:[27]

> The key to Massey's strategy is to view the many foreign countries in which it has plants not only as markets, but also as potential sources of financing for exports to third countries. For example, in early 1978, Massey-Ferguson had the opportunity to ship 7200 tractors worth $53 million to Turkey, but was unwilling to assume the risk of currency inconvertibility. Turkey, at that time, already owed $2 billion to various foreign creditors and it was uncertain whether it would be able to come up with dollars to pay off its debts (especially since its reserves were at about zero).
>
> Massey solved this problem by manufacturing these tractors at its Brazilian subsidiary, "Massey-Ferguson do Brasil," and selling them to Brazil's Interbras, the trading company arm of Petrobas, the Brazilian national oil corporation. Interbras in turn arranged to sell the tractors to Turkey and pay Massey in cruzados. The cruzado financing for Interbras came from Cacex, the Banco de Brasil department that is in charge of foreign trade. Cacex underwrote all the political, commercial, and exchange risks as part of the Brazilian government's intense export promotion drive. Prior to choosing Brazil as a supply point, Massey made a point of shopping around to get the best export credit deal available.

Tax and the Financing Method

Outland's choice of initial financing may also depend on how it plans to use the profits of its Dutch subsidiary. In the early years the venture may well run a continuing deficit, but Outland hopes that it will generate a cash surplus eventually. You need to think about how you can best repatriate this surplus.

Broadly speaking, international affiliates make the following payments to the parent company:

- Dividends
- Interest payments and repayment of parent company loans
- Royalties for use of trade names and patents

[27] "Guidelines for Global Financing Choices," Working Paper, Sloan School of Management, MIT, October 1982, p. 17.

TABLE 34-2
How to calculate United States tax on dividends paid by Outland Steel's
Dutch subsidiary (figures in dollars)

	Dutch Corporate Tax = 42%	Dutch Corporate Tax = 30%
Profits before tax	100	100
Dutch company tax	42	30
Net profits	58	70
United States company tax	34	34
Less double-tax relief (maximum 34)	34	30
United States tax payable	0	4
Available for dividend	58	66

- Management fees for central services
- Payments for goods supplied by the parent

The form of payment is important because it affects the taxes paid. Companies are generally subject to local taxes on their local earnings. Therefore Outland's Dutch subsidiary will pay corporate tax in Holland on all profits that it earns there. In addition it is liable to United States corporate tax on any dividends that are remitted to the United States.[28]

Many countries (including Holland) have a double-taxation agreement with the United States. This means that the company can offset the payment of any local taxes against the United States tax liability on the foreign dividends. For example, suppose Outland Steel's subsidiary pays Dutch income tax of 42 percent on its profits plus a withholding tax of 5 percent on any dividends paid to the United States. The left-hand portion of Table 34-2 shows that Outland is, therefore, exempt from any additional tax on these dividends. The right-hand portion shows what would happen if the Dutch income tax rate is changed to 30 percent. In this case Outland could claim double tax relief only to the amount of taxes paid in Holland.

If the subsidiary is operating in a high-tax country with a double-tax agreement, dividend payments are not subject to additional taxes in the United States. On the other hand, in such cases you may do better to arrange a loan from the parent to the subsidiary. The parent company must pay United States tax on the interest, but the foreign subsidiary can deduct the interest before paying local tax. Another way to transfer income from high-tax areas to low-tax areas is to levy royalties or management fees on the subsidiary. Or it may be possible to change the transfer prices on sales of goods within the group. Needless to say, the tax and customs authorities are well aware of these incentives to minimize taxes and they will insist that all such intergroup payments be reasonable.

34-7 POLITICAL RISK

Think about what the political risk of a foreign investment really is. It is the threat that a foreign government will change the rules of the game—that is, break a

---

[28] If Outland's Dutch operation were a branch of the parent company rather than a subsidiary, the tax authorities in the United States would treat the income as part of the parent's income and tax it immediately rather than when it was remitted. That is usually a *disadvantage* when the foreign operation is showing profits but an *advantage* when it is making losses.

promise or understanding—*after* the investment is made. Some managers think of political risks as an act of God, like a hurricane or earthquake. But the most successful multinational companies structure their business to reduce political risks.

Foreign governments are not likely to expropriate a local business if it cannot operate without the support of its parent. For example, the foreign subsidiaries of American computer manufacturers or pharmaceutical companies would have relatively little value if they were cut off from the know-how of their parents. Such operations are much less likely to be expropriated than, say, a mining operation which can be operated as a stand-alone venture.

We are not recommending that you turn your silver mine into a pharmaceutical company, but you may be able to plan overseas manufacturing operations to improve your bargaining position with foreign governments. For example, Ford has integrated its overseas operations so that the manufacture of components, subassemblies, and complete automobiles is spread across plants in a number of countries. None of these plants would have much value on its own, and Ford can switch production between plants if the political climate in one country deteriorates.

Multinational corporations have also devised financing arrangements to help keep foreign governments honest. For example, suppose your firm is contemplating investing \$500 million to reopen the San Tomé silver mine in Costaguana, with modern machinery, smelting equipment, and shipping facilities.[29] The Costaguanan government agrees to invest in roads and other infrastructure and to take 20 percent of the silver produced by the mine in lieu of taxes. The agreement is to run for 25 years.

The project's NPV on these assumptions is quite attractive. But what happens if a new government comes to power 5 years from now and imposes a 50 percent tax on "any precious metals exported from the Republic of Costaguana"? Or changes the government's share of output from 20 to 50 percent? Or simply takes over the mine "with fair compensation to be determined in due course by the Minister of Natural Resources of the Republic of Costaguana"?

No contract can absolutely restrain a sovereign power. But you can arrange project financing to make these acts as painful as possible for the foreign government.[30] For example, you might set up the mine as a subsidiary corporation, which then borrows a large fraction of the required investment from a consortium of major international banks. If your firm guarantees the loan, make sure the guarantee stands only if the Costaguanan government honors its contract. The government will be reluctant to break the contract if that causes a default on the loans and undercuts the country's credit standing with the international banking system.

If possible, you should finance part of the project with a loan from the World Bank (or one of its affiliates). Include a *cross-default* clause, so that a default to any creditor automatically triggers default on the World Bank loan. Few governments have the guts to take on the World Bank.

Here is another variation on the same theme. Arrange to borrow, say, \$450 million through the Costaguanan Development Agency. In other words, the development agency borrows in international capital markets and relends to the San Tomé mine. Your firm agrees to stand behind the loan providing the government keeps *its* promises. If it does keep them, the loan is your liability. If not, the loan is *its* liability.

---

[29] The early history of the San Tomé mine is described in Joseph Conrad's *Nostromo*.

[30] We discussed project financing in Appendix B to Chapter 24.

These arrangements do work. In the late 1960s Kennecott Copper financed a major expansion of a copper mine in Chile using arrangements like those we have just described. In 1970 a new government came to power, headed by Salvador Allende, who vowed to take over all foreign holdings in Chile giving "ni un centavo" in exchange. Kennecott's mine was spared.

Political risk is not confined to the risk of expropriation. Multinational companies are always exposed to the criticism that they siphon funds out of countries in which they do business and, therefore, governments are tempted to limit their freedom to repatriate profits. This is most likely to happen when there is considerable uncertainty about the rate of exchange, which is usually when you would most like to get your money out.

Here again a little forethought can help. For example, there are often more onerous restrictions on the payment of dividends to the parent than on the payment of interest or principal on debt. So it may be better for the parent to put up part of the funds in the form of a loan. Royalty payments and management fees are less politically sensitive than dividends, particularly if they are levied equally on all foreign operations. A company can also, within limits, alter the price of goods that are bought or sold within the group, and it can require more or less prompt payment for such sales.

34-8 INTERACTIONS OF INVESTMENT AND FINANCING DECISIONS

You cannot entirely divorce the value of an international project from the way that it is financed. For example, the taxes paid on Outland Steel's Dutch venture depend on the form in which it remits profits to the United States. If it lends funds to the subsidiary rather than providing equity, the group will pay more tax in the United States and less in Holland.

Major international investments often have so many financing side effects that it's foolhardy to try to reduce the project analysis to one stream of cash flows and one adjusted discount rate. You need the adjusted present value (APV) rule, which we introduced in Chapter 19. Remember that APV is defined as (1) "base-case" project NPV plus (2) the sum of the present values of the project's financing side effects.

The base-case NPV of an international project is usually calculated assuming all-equity financing from the parent firm, and that all income is paid out as dividends at the first opportunity.

The next step is to value the financing side effects. If you finance the project in part by a loan from the parent rather than equity, you should calculate the value of any tax savings that result. And if the project also allows the firm *as a whole*[31] to borrow more on its own account, you should also calculate separately the value of any tax shields on this debt.

When you calculated your base-case net present value, you assumed that all funds were exported from the United States and all income was remitted as soon as possible. But you may do better to raise some of the money locally. Or you may already have surplus funds abroad that you are not allowed to repatriate or that you do not wish to repatriate for tax reasons. Instead of remitting all income by

---

[31] Don't confuse a foreign subsidiary's debt with its contribution to the firm's *overall* debt capacity. For example, we spoke of borrowing 80 to 90 percent of the $500 million cost of the San Tomé mine, but we did not assume the mine would support that debt. Instead we assumed the firm could use relatively more of its overall borrowing capacity in Costaguana and less in the United States. It could finance the project by committing its debt capacity instead of cash.

the normal channels, you may be able to remit some income more profitably in the form of royalties or management fees, or you may prefer to retain the funds overseas for further expansion. Such benefits should also be valued separately.[32]

There are many other financing side effects. The subsidized financing provided to Massey-Ferguson by Brazil is one example. So make a complete list, value each side effect separately, and add up all the values to get APV.

34-9 SUMMARY

The international financial manager has to cope with different currencies, interest rates, and inflation rates and must be familiar with a variety of different capital markets and tax systems. The most we can hope to do in these pages it to whet your appetite.

To produce order out of chaos, the international financial manager needs some model of the relationship between exchange rates, interest rates, and inflation rates. We described four very simple but useful theories.

Interest rate parity theory states that the interest differential between two countries must be equal to the difference between the forward and spot exchange rates. In the international markets, arbitrage ensures that parity almost always holds. There are two ways to hedge against exchange risk—one is to take out forward cover, the other is to borrow or lend abroad. Interest rate parity tells us that the cost of the two methods should be the same.

The expectations theory of exchange rates tells us that the forward rate equals the expected spot rate. If you believe the expectations theory, you will generally insure against exchange risks.

In its strict form the law of one price states that $1 must have the same purchasing power in every country. That doesn't square very well with the facts, for differences in inflation rates are not perfectly related to changes in exchange rates. This means that there may be some genuine exchange risks in doing business overseas. On the other hand, the difference in the inflation rates is just as likely to be above as below the change in the exchange rate.

Finally, we saw that in an integrated world capital market real rates of interest would have to be the same. In practice, government regulation and taxes can cause differences in real interest rates. But do not simply borrow where interest rates are lowest. Those countries are also likely to have the lowest inflation rates and the strongest currencies.

With these precepts in mind we looked at three common problems in international finance. First, we showed how you can use the forward markets or the loan markets to price and insure long-term export contracts.

Second, we considered the problem of international capital budgeting. We warned against making stupid investment decisions simply because you have a strong view about future exchange rates. And we showed that it makes no difference which currency you use for your calculations as long as you assume that prices, interest rates, and exchange rates are linked by the simple theories that we described above. The main difficulty is to select the right discount rate. If there is a free market for capital, the discount rate for your project is the return that your shareholders expect from investing in foreign securities. This rate is difficult to

[32]See, for example, D. R. Lessard, "Evaluating Foreign Projects—An Adjusted Present Value Approach," in D. Lessard (ed.), *International Financial Management: Theory and Application,* 2d ed., John Wiley and Sons, New York, 1986.

measure, but we argued against just adding a premium for the "extra risks" of overseas investment.

Finally, we looked at the problem of financing overseas subsidiaries. There are at least three issues that you should think about. Other things equal, you would like to protect yourself against exchange risk: you may be able to do this by borrowing part of the money in the local currency. Second, you need to think about tax: for example, you can reduce tax by borrowing in high-tax countries and lending in low-tax countries. Third, you should consider whether you can structure the financing to reduce the risk that governments will change the rules of the game.

The cash flow that the parent company receives from its overseas operations depends on the way that they are financed. Therefore an adjusted present value approach is needed to analyze international investment proposals.

FURTHER READING

There are a number of useful textbooks in international finance. Here is a small selection:

R. Z. Aliber: *Exchange Risk and Corporate International Finance,* Halsted Press, New York, 1978.

D. K. Eiteman and A. I. Stonehill: *Multinational Business Finance,* 3d ed., Addison-Wesley Publishing Company, Inc., Reading, Mass., 1982.

R. Rodriguez and E. Carter: *International Financial Management,* 3d ed., Prentice-Hall, Inc., Englewood Cliffs, New Jersey, 1984.

M. Levi: *International Finance: Financial Management and the International Economy,* McGraw-Hill, New York, 1983.

A. C. Shapiro: *Multinational Financial Management,* 2d ed., Allyn and Bacon, Inc., Boston, 1986.

Also, it's worth leafing through Euromoney *and* Euromoney Corporate Finance *for current events and developments in international finance.*

Here are some general discussions of the international investment decision and the exchange risk to which it may give rise:

A. C. Shapiro: "International Capital Budgeting," *Midland Corporate Finance Journal,* **1:** 26–45 (Spring 1983).

B. Cornell and A. C. Shapiro: "Managing Foreign Exchange Risks," *Midland Corporate Finance Journal,* **1:** 16–31 (Fall 1983).

E. Flood and D. Lessard: "On the Measurement of Operating Exposure to Exchange Rates: A Conceptual Approach," *Financial Management,* **15:** 25–36 (Spring 1986).

And here is a sample of the articles on some of the relationships between interest rates, exchange rates, and inflation rates:

Forward Rates and Spot Rates

B. Cornell: "Spot Rates, Forward Rates and Exchange Market Efficiency," *Journal of Financial Economics,* **5:** 55–65 (1977).

R. M. Levich: "Tests of Forecasting Models and Market Efficiency in the International Money Market," in J. A. Frenkel and H. G. Johnson (eds.), *The Economics of Exchange Rates; Selected Studies,* Addison-Wesley Publishing Company, Inc., Reading, Mass., 1978.

E. F. Fama: "Forward and Spot Exchange Rates," *Journal of Monetary Economics,* **14:** 319–338 (1984).

| Interest Rate Parity | T. Agmon and S. Bronfield: "The International Mobility of Short-Term Covered Arbitrage Capital," *Journal of Business Finance and Accounting,* **2:** 269–278 (Summer 1975).
J. A. Frenkel and R. M. Levich: "Covered Interest Arbitrage: Unexploited Profits?" *Journal of Political Economy,* **83:** 325–338 (April 1975). |

| Law of One Price | L. H. Officer: "The Purchasing Power Theory of Exchange Rates: A Review Article," *IMF Staff Papers,* March 1976.
R. Roll: "Violations of the 'Law of One Price' and Their Implications for Differentially Denominated Assets," in M. Sarnat and G. Szego (eds.), *International Finance and Trade,* Ballinger Press, Cambridge, Mass., 1979. |

| International Capital Market Equilibrium | F. Black: "International Capital Market Equilibrium and Investment Barriers," *Journal of Financial Economics,* **1:** 337–352 (December 1974).
F. L. A. Grauer, R. H. Litzenberger, and R. E. Stehle: "Sharing Rules and Equilibrium in an International Capital Market Under Uncertainty," *Journal of Financial Economics,* **3:** 233–256 (June 1976).
B. H. Solnik: "An Equilibrium Model of the International Capital Market," *Journal of Economic Theory,* **8:** 500–524 (1974).
R. M. Stultz: "A Model of International Asset Pricing," *Journal of Financial Economics,* **9:** 383–406 (December 1981). |

QUIZ

1. Look at Table 34-1.
   (a) How many Japanese yen do you get for your dollar?
   (b) What is the 6-month forward rate for the yen?
   (c) Is the dollar at a forward discount or premium on the yen?
   (d) Calculate the annual percentage discount or premium on the yen.
   (e) If the 6-month interest rate on eurodollars is 8 percent annually compounded, what do you think is the 6-month eurocurrency interest rate on the yen?
   (f) According to the expectations theory, what is the expected spot rate for the yen in 6 months' time?
   (g) According to the law of one price, what then is the expected difference in the rate of price inflation in the United States and Japan?

2. Define each of the following theories in a sentence or simple equation.
   (a) Interest rate parity theory
   (b) Expectations theory of forward rates
   (c) Law of one price
   (d) International capital market equilibrium (relationship of real and nominal interest rates in different countries)

3. The following table shows interest rates and exchange rates for the United States dollar and French franc. The spot exchange rate is 7.05 francs per dollar. Complete the missing entries:

	3 Months	6 Months	1 Year
Eurodollar interest rate (annually compounded)	11½%	12¼%	?
Eurofranc interest rate (annually compounded)	19½%	?	20%
Forward francs per dollar	?	?	7.5200
Forward discount on franc, percent per year	?	−6.3%	?

4. An importer in the United States is due to take delivery of silk scarves from Italy in 6 months. The price is fixed in lire. Which of the following transactions could eliminate the importer's exchange risk?
   (a) Sell 6-month call options on lire
   (b) Buy lire forward
   (c) Sell lire forward
   (d) Sell lire in the currency futures market
   (e) Borrow lire, buy dollars at the spot exchange rate
   (f) Sell lire at the spot exchange rate, lend dollars

5. You can see from Table 34-1 that spot and future deutsche marks cost $.5634/DM and $.5733/DM, respectively. Suppose a company has committed to pay 10 million DM to a German company in 180 days. What is the cost (in present value) of covering this liability by buying deutsche marks forward? The deutsche mark interest rate is 5.1 percent per year. Briefly explain.

6. A firm in the United States is due to receive payment of 1 million DM in 8 years' time. It would like to protect itself against a decline in the value of the deutsche mark but finds it difficult to get forward cover for such a long period. Is there any other way in which it can protect itself?

7. (a) Which of the following items do you need if you do all your capital budgeting calculations in your own currency?
      (i) Forecasts of future exchange rates
      (ii) Forecasts of the foreign inflation rate
      (iii) Forecasts of the domestic inflation rate
      (iv) Foreign interest rates
      (v) Domestic interest rates
   (b) Which of the above items do you need if you do all your capital budgeting calculations in the foreign currency?

8. Company A has two overseas subsidiaries in countries X and Y. The United States has a 50 percent rate of corporate tax, X has a 60 percent rate, and Y a 40 percent rate. Both X and Y have a double-tax agreement with the United States. Suppose that the company earns $100 pretax in both countries.
   (a) What taxes would be paid in the United States and overseas if it remitted all net income in the form of dividends?
   (b) What taxes would be paid if it remitted all net income in the form of interest?

QUESTIONS AND PROBLEMS

1. Look at the Foreign Exchange table in a recent issue of *The Wall Street Journal.*
   (a) How many United States dollars are worth one Canadian dollar today?
   (b) How many Canadian dollars are worth one United States dollar today?
   (c) Suppose that you arrange today to buy Canadian dollars in 180 days. How many Canadian dollars could you buy for each United States dollar?
   (d) If forward rates simply reflect market expectations, what is the likely spot exchange rate for the French franc in 90 days' time?
   (e) Look in the *Journal's* table of money rates. What is the 3-month interest rate on eurodollars?
   (f) Can you deduce the likely 3-month interest rate for eurocurrency French francs?
   (g) You can also buy currency for future delivery in the financial futures market. Look in the *Journal's* table of futures prices. What is the rate of

exchange for Canadian dollars to be delivered in approximately 6 months' time?

2. Table 34-1 shows the 180-day forward rate on the West German mark.
   (*a*) Is the dollar at a forward discount or a premium on the mark?
   (*b*) What is the annual *percentage* discount or premium?
   (*c*) If you have no other information about the two currencies, what is your best guess about the spot rate on the mark 6 months hence?
   (*d*) Suppose that you expect to receive 100,000 marks in 6 months. How many dollars is this likely to be worth?

3. Look at Table 34-1. If the 3-month interest rate on eurodollars is 7⅞ percent, what do you think is the 3-month eurocurrency interest rate on French francs? Explain what would happen if the rate was substantially above your figure.

4. Look in *The Wall Street Journal.* How many French francs can you buy for $1? How many deutsche marks can you buy? What rate do you think a German bank would quote for buying or selling French francs? Explain what would happen if it quoted a rate that was substantially above your figure.

5. What do our four basic relationships imply about the relationship between two countries' interest rates and the expected change in the exchange rate? Explain why you would or would not expect them to be related.

6. Ms. Rosetta Stone, the treasurer of International Reprints, Inc., has noticed that the interest rate in Switzerland is below the rates in most other countries. She is, therefore, suggesting that the company should make an issue of Swiss franc bonds. What considerations ought she first to take into account?

7. What considerations should an American company take into account when deciding how to finance its overseas subsidiaries?

8. An American firm is evaluating an investment in Switzerland. The project costs 20 million Swiss francs and it is expected to produce an income of 3 million francs a year in real terms for each of the next 10 years. The expected inflation rate in Switzerland is 1 percent a year and the firm estimates that an appropriate discount rate for the project would be about 8 percent above the risk-free rate of interest. Calculate the net present value of the project in dollars using each of the two methods described in this chapter. Exchange rates are given in Table 34-1. The interest rate was about 4 percent in Switzerland and 7⅞ percent in the United States.

9. "The decline in the value of the dollar has made chemical producers in the United States attractive purchases for European companies." Discuss.

10. Suppose you are the treasurer of Lufthansa. How is company value likely to be affected by exchange rate changes? What policies would you adopt to reduce exchange rate risk?

11. Suppose that you do use your own views about inflation and exchange rates when valuing an overseas investment proposal. Specifically, suppose that you believe that inflation will be 2 percent in Holland and 5 percent in the United States but that the exchange rate will remain unchanged. Recalculate the NPV of the Outland project using both of our methods. Each NPV implies a different financing strategy. What are they?

12. Companies may be affected by changes in the nominal exchange rate or in the real exchange rate. Explain how this can occur. Which risks are easiest to hedge against?

13. We suggested that a Ford dealer in the United States may be exposed to a devaluation in the yen if this leads to a cut in the price of Japanese cars. Suppose that the dealer estimates that a 1 percent decline in the value of the yen would result in a permanent decline of 5 percent in the dealer's profits.

How should she hedge against this risk and how should she calculate the size of the hedge position?

14. You have bid for a possible export order which would provide a cash inflow of 1 million DM in 6 months. The spot exchange rate is DM1.8/$ and the 6-month forward rate is DM1.7/$. There are two sources of uncertainty—(1) the deutsche mark could appreciate or depreciate, and (2) you may or may not receive the export order. Illustrate in each case the profits or losses that you would make if

(a) You sell 1 million DM forward

(b) You buy a 6-month put option on deutsche marks with an exercise price of DM1.7/$.

35

Pension Plans

At the end of 1986, current and past employees of Firestone Tire & Rubber had earned the right to pensions valued at \$542 million.[1] To help cover this liability, the company had put aside \$383 million in its pension fund, leaving an *unfunded liability* of \$159 million.[2]

This pension liability is a debt that one day the company will be obliged to honor. In fact it is Firestone's biggest debt, double the total amount of long-term loans shown on Firestone's balance sheet. The pension fund is also one of Firestone's biggest assets, amounting to a third of the book value of all its plant and equipment.

The company's pension plan is a major responsibility for you as financial manager. You can always call on the specialist advice of the actuary, pension consultant, and investment manager, but the buck (or lack of bucks) stops on your desk. Therefore you must understand the arguments behind the advice you receive, and grasp its implications for company policy. That is why we have included a chapter on pensions.

First, we consider briefly the pension benefits which companies offer. Second, we look at how the actuary calculates the cost of these benefits by drawing up a pension plan balance sheet. This balance sheet affects the amount of money that the company must put aside each year in its pension fund. Finally, we see how the financial manager helps to set the objectives of the pension fund and to monitor its performance.

We shall make frequent reference to the 1974 Employee Retirement Income Security Act (ERISA). This important and complex act lays down a set of standards for the pension plan and for the way in which the company should pay for it. No financial manager can now ignore the pension plan—ERISA has made sure of that.

35-1 TYPES OF PENSION PLAN

When they retire, most employees draw two pensions. One is the social security benefit that is provided by the government largely out of social security taxes. The other is the private company pension. For lower-paid workers the social security

---

[1] This figure is sometimes known as the accumulated-benefit obligation. It represents the value of vested and nonvested obligations but ignores the likely effects of future salary increases on pensions. We will discuss some of the different measures of the pension obligation below.

[2] We singled out Firestone because it had an unusually large unfunded liability. Most large companies in 1986 had pension plans that were in surplus; that is, the assets in the pension fund more than covered the accumulated liability.

benefit is likely to be larger than the company pension; for higher-paid workers it is the other way around.

Our focus in this chapter is on pension plans that are set up and paid for by the company. But those who are self-employed and proprietors of small unincorporated businesses can establish a so-called Keogh plan, which enjoys tax advantages similar to those of a company pension scheme. Also, anyone can set up his or her own personal pension plan known as an individual retirement account (IRA).

It is often said that there are at least as many types of company pension schemes in the United States as there are companies. That may be true, but we can notice some general categories.

Of employees covered by pensions, about one in four belong to a *defined-contribution* scheme. In this case the company promises to invest a specified sum each year on behalf of the employee. If the investments perform well, the employee receives a generous pension; if they perform badly, the employee loses out.

Most employees belong to *defined-benefit* plans. In this case the company promises the employee so many dollars a month on retirement or a specified proportion of his or her final salary. Thus with a defined-benefit scheme the company takes the risk of poor investment performance.

Some defined-benefit plans are negotiated directly between a company and a labor union. Typically these negotiated schemes provide for a flat annual benefit of, say, $300 for each year of service, but some schemes relate the benefit to both the length of service and the employee's wage classification.

The scale of benefits in union-negotiated plans is regularly *renegotiated* to take account of changes in wage levels. However, plans covering salaried or nonunion employees are not continuously revised in this way. Therefore, instead of promising a flat annual benefit, they almost always link the benefit directly to the employee's pay. This is done in one of two ways. *Career-average* formulas are based on the employee's average salary during the years of membership. For example, a company might pay a pension equal to 2 percent of the employee's salary in each year that he or she was a member of the plan.

Career-average plans offer relatively poor protection in periods of rapid inflation, so more and more companies have changed to *final-average* plans. These usually base the pension on the employee's average compensation in his or her final 5 years of service.

Pension plans rarely make promises to increase pensions after retirement, but many companies have given voluntary increases in times of high inflation. A few schemes have linked the pension to the Consumer Price Index.

An employee who leaves the company before the normal retirement age is usually entitled to some portion of the pension benefits that have been earned. This entitlement is known as *vesting*. The 1974 Employee Retirement Income Security Act (ERISA) laid down minimum standards for vesting. Companies must now offer one of the following:

1. 100 percent vesting after 10 years of service
2. 25 percent vesting after 5 years, increasing to 100 percent after 15 years
3. 50 percent vesting when age and service add up to 45, increasing to 100 percent 5 years later.

Notice the incentive for employees to stay on until they are fully vested. If it is expensive to train employees, it may pay the company to reward those who stay on and penalize those who quit.

TABLE 35-1
Pension plan balance sheet. Look first above the dashed line separating present from future: if the pension fund does not cover the present value of benefits employees have already earned, there is an unfunded liability. The firm must pay down this liability, although it can do so over an extended period. Actuaries also look below the dashed line; they require that the firm's planned future contributions cover the benefits employees will earn

Assets	Liabilities
Pension fund (current value) Unfunded liability*	PV (expected benefits for past service)
PV (contributions for future service)	PV (expected benefits from future service)
Total assets	PV (all expected benefits)

* Surplus if pension fund value is larger than PV (expected benefits from past service).

In addition to the basic pension check, pension plans usually provide a number of other benefits. For example, they include death benefits before and after retirement, and they offer special arrangements for employees who retire as a result of disability.

35-2   THE PENSION PLAN BALANCE SHEET

Table 35-1 shows the pension plan balance sheet. Note the dashed line separating present from future benefits and contributions. Above the line there is the current value of the pension fund, offset by the present value of the future pensions *already* earned by current and retired employees. If things work out *exactly* as the actuary plans, this asset and liability balance. But they never do: the pension fund investments may perform badly, for example, or the company may increase pension benefits. That would create an unfunded liability, which the firm must gradually pay off. On the other hand, if the pension fund assets perform exceptionally well, or if increased discount rates reduce PV (expected benefits for past service), there could be a surplus, which the firm can gradually recover through reduced future pension contributions.[3]

Below the dashed line there is the present value of the pensions that you expect current employees to earn by their future service. The actuary makes sure that this liability is offset by the present value of the regular contributions the firm plans to make to the pension fund on behalf of current employees.

So much for the bare bones of the pension plan balance sheet. Now we need to flesh them out.

Valuing the Liabilities

The actuary who values pension liabilities is asking how much the company needs to earmark if it is going to honor its promises to each member of the plan. The problem is that there are many things that could happen to the firm's employees. Some may leave the company and so receive only vested benefits. Some may die in harness, in which case their beneficiaries receive the preretirement death benefit.

[3] Sometimes large surpluses are captured in one fell swoop, by closing down an existing plan and starting a brand new one. More on this below.

Many will continue with the company until retirement and subsequently draw their pension to a ripe old age. And so on. The actuary needs to estimate how many employees are likely to fall into each category and what benefits they are likely to receive.[4] These benefits can then be discounted to arrive at the present value of expected benefits. This is the amount of money that the company needs to earmark—it is the total liability of the pension plan.

Employees have already earned part of these expected benefits by their service to date. They are expected to earn the remainder by their future service. The actuary divides the plan's liabilities into these two parts:

$$\begin{array}{ll} \text{PV (expected} & \text{PV (expected} \\ \text{benefits for} & + \text{ benefits for} & = \text{PV (expected benefits)} \\ \text{past service)} & \text{future service)} \end{array}$$

There are two common definitions separating what is due to the past from what is due to the future. Some actuaries like to think of the proportion of payments that have accrued as a result of past service. In that case, we have

Definition 1. *PV (expected benefits for past service) = PV (accrued benefits).*

Others say that all employees have so far earned is the pension that they would receive if they left the firm today. Thus we have

Definition 2. *PV (expected benefits for past service) = PV (vested accrued benefits).*

For employees who are fully vested, the two definitions are the same. For employees who are only partially vested, their past service earns them less if they leave the firm today than if they stay on. Therefore PV (vested accrued benefits) is *less than* PV (accrued benefits).

Valuing the Assets

Now let us look at the asset side of the balance sheet. The first asset is the **pension fund.** This results from past contributions by the company. These contributions are generally paid into a trust and invested in a diversified portfolio of securities.

If the assets of the fund do not cover the benefits that have accrued, the company has an *unfunded* liability. Thus for Firestone:

$$\text{Unfunded liability} = \text{PV (accrued benefits)} - \text{PV (pension fund assets)}$$

$$= 542 - 383 = \$159 \text{ million}$$

The second asset in the pension plan is the stream of contributions to cover future service. These are generally referred to as **normal costs.** Future normal costs should cover benefits resulting from future service.

Actuaries use several methods to estimate normal cost. If the plan offers a simple dollar payment based on years of service, the actuary generally bases the estimate on the *accrued-benefit cost method.* The basic idea behind this method is that the company should contribute each year the present value of any benefits that have accrued in that year.

---

[4] Often it is fairly easy to estimate the odds. For example, the actuary uses mortality tables to estimate the probability of death. It is far less easy to estimate whether an employee will leave the company or what his or her final salary will be.

The other methods of estimating normal cost are usually termed *projected-benefit cost methods* or *level cost methods*. Their object is to even out contributions so that each year the company provides an equal dollar amount per employee or an equal proportion of its wage bill.

Estimating the Deficit

If all goes well, the pension fund and the planned stream of contributions should be sufficient to cover the projected benefits. But things do not always go according to plan. Here are some of the things that can go wrong:

- There may be a decline in the value of securities in the pension fund.
- Fewer employees may quit before their benefits are vested.
- The union may negotiate increased pensions.

The first two are examples of what are called *experience losses*—that is, they are losses that result from the difference between expectations and experience. The third misfortune represents a new cost and gives rise to a *supplemental liability*.[5]

The company is not obliged to offset these shortfalls immediately. Under ERISA any experience losses (or losses resulting from a change in actuarial assumptions) must generally be made good over 15 years. Supplemental liabilities and unfunded past service costs must generally be made good over 30 years.

Another Look at the Pension Plan Balance Sheet

When you look at the pension plan balance sheet, remember that it is no better than the judgment of the plan's actuary. One of the actuary's most difficult decisions is the choice of discount rate. Perhaps as a result, they have tended to arbitrary choices. For example, actuaries have traditionally ignored wage inflation. They have counterbalanced this by choosing a relatively low discount rate.[6]

But you encounter some plans that assume a discount rate which is *less* than the projected rate of salary increase and others that assume a discount rate which can be 5 percent *higher* than the rate of salary increase. Increasing the discount rate reduces PV (benefits), reduces the annual contribution to the fund, and increases reported earnings. Many companies have found that a change in actuarial assumptions can do wonders to improve the earnings picture.

Actuarial discount rates are usually "sticky"—they don't increase right away even when market interest rates rise dramatically. But many pension plans have loosened their actuaries up by earmarking the portion of the fund that is needed to pay their fixed pensions, and then investing this money in a "dedicated" bond portfolio which generates future cash flows that exactly cover the fixed obligations.[7] In 1984 Bethlehem Steel dedicated 45 percent of its portfolio by investing $1.3 billion in bonds yielding 14.25 percent. As a result, the liabilities covered by

---

[5] When a plan is first established, a supplemental liability may arise if employees receive any credit for earlier service.

[6] It is sometimes said that as long as the actuary correctly estimates the difference between the discount rate and the growth in salaries, the absolute numbers don't matter. But if some of the benefits are not completely tied to the growth in salaries, the absolute numbers *do* matter.

[7] The investment manager tries to find the least expensive portfolio that perfectly hedges these pension obligations (see Chapter 25). This problem can be solved using a linear program. See S. D. Hodges and S. M. Schaefer, "A Model for Bond Portfolio Improvement," *Journal of Financial and Quantitative Analysis,* **12:** 243–260 (June 1977).

this bond portfolio were discounted at 14.25 percent rather than the 8 percent rate used for other liabilities.

ERISA, Fund Contributions, and Pension Insurance

You can imagine a system in which pension plans are not funded. The company does not put anything aside. It just waits until the pensions become due and then pays them out of current income.[8] That system is all very well as long as the company continues to grow and prosper; but if it runs into heavy weather, there may be no money to pay the pensioners. The law tries to prevent such problems in two ways. First, it requires the company to make minimum contributions to a pension fund; second, it provides a guarantee that the pensions will be paid.

Before 1974 companies were obliged to fund only normal costs (and the interest on supplemental liabilities). Some companies offered substantial increases in pension benefits but did not make any contributions to cover the supplemental liabilities. As a result the value of their pension funds fell far short of accrued liabilities. ERISA imposes more stringent funding rules. Companies are now obliged to cover normal costs and amortize any supplemental liabilities or other deficiency.

In 1964 Studebaker closed its plant at South Bend, Indiana, and terminated the pension plan. Employees at South Bend became entitled to all accrued benefits. But there was not enough money in the pension fund to cover these benefits, so most employees were left without a pension. To guard against such misfortunes ERISA set up a new agency, the Pension Benefit Guarantee Corporation (PBGC). If any plan is terminated and there is not enough money in the fund to pay pensions, the PBGC will make up most of the deficiency. But Congress did not want companies to be able to walk away from their pension promises. Therefore it also legislated that the PBGC could recover this money from the company itself. Its claim ranks alongside the tax collector's claim, *ahead of all unsecured creditors.*

Notice the importance of this change. Before ERISA, pension plans were essentially paper promises. A company could terminate a plan whenever it chose. If the fund was insufficient to cover benefits, the employees suffered. Since ERISA, the employee's pension is effectively guaranteed. On the other hand, any unfunded liabilities are now super-senior debt of the corporation. When the bank is deciding to lend your company money or when a bond analyst is rating your company's bonds, it should be looking not only at the debt shown on the balance sheet but also at the potentially very large debt to the PBGC.[9]

What ERISA gave with one hand, it partly took away with the other, for it limited the PBGC's claim on the company's assets to 30 percent of net worth. If the company's net worth was small, the PBGC could be left with a hefty bill to pay.[10]

---

[8] Although companies in the United States fund pension plans, they do not fund health benefits for retirees. The cost of these benefits may be almost as large as for pensions. For example, Firestone's income statement showed a deduction of $34 million for pension costs and $47 million for health benefits.

[9] For an account of how Moody's bond ratings reflect the company's pension liabilities, see "ERISA—A Bond Rater's View," *Moody's Bond Survey,* February 1978. Of course lenders are not the only ones affected by large unfunded pension liabilities. Feldstein and Morck have produced evidence that share prices also reflect such liabilities; see M. Feldstein and R. Morck, "Pension Funding Decisions, Interest Rate Assumptions and Share Prices," in Z. Bodie and J. Shoven (eds.), *Financial Aspects of the United States Pension System,* University of Chicago Press, Chicago, 1983.

[10] The PBGC has the right to terminate a plan if the PBGC's liability is likely to increase unreasonably. However, it has been reluctant to terminate while the company still has substantial net worth.

Plan Terminations

We have seen that the actuary calculates the present value of the pension liability by discounting the projected pension payments. A high interest rate reduces this present value; a low rate increases it. Of course the level of interest rates also affects the value of the bonds and stocks held in the pension fund, but to a lesser extent. Using the terminology of Chapter 25, we would say that pension fund assets have a lower duration than the liabilities. Thus when interest rates rise, pension plans move into surplus; when they fall, deficits are more common.

As interest rates rose during the first half of the 1980s, most pension plans moved into surplus. Many companies tried to lay their hands on this surplus and use it for their stockholders. They argued that if ERISA makes the shareholders responsible for any deficit, it is also fair that they should be able to repossess any surplus. At the moment the only way they can do this is by terminating the pension plan and starting a new one. Many companies have done this. For example, in 1986 Exxon withdrew more than $1 billion in surplus funds from its pension plan.[11]

You might think that if pension plans are in such a healthy state, the PBGC could shut up shop. But there have been some major defaults which threaten the agency's solvency. In 1985 plan terminations by Allis-Chalmers and Wheeling-Pittsburgh Steel cost the PBGC a total of $650 million. That was peanuts compared with the effect of LTV's bankruptcy, which is likely to end up costing the PBGC $1.5 billion.

Some companies in financial distress have even found that it paid them to terminate their pension plans voluntarily in order to escape their pension obligation. For example, in 1979 AlloyTek was a small company with large debts and a large unfunded pension liability—at least until it took advantage of a loophole in ERISA. By voluntarily terminating its pension plan, AlloyTek obliged the PBGC to take over the unfunded pension liability in exchange for 30 percent of the net worth of its nearly worthless equity.

How has the PBGC reacted to these hefty bills? First, it has secured a change in the law, so that it can refuse companies permission to terminate their plan unless they are bankrupt or incapable of continuing to service the plan.

Second, the law now entitles the PBGC to claim 30 percent of net worth *plus* three-quarters of whatever unfunded guaranteed benefits are not covered by the 30 percent claim.

Third, in 1986 the PBGC obtained an increase in the premium that it levies on firms from $2.60 per plan member to $8.50.

Finally, it has argued that with a flat insurance premium the "good guys" are paying for the mistakes of their less prudent fellows. Therefore, it has pressed Congress (so far, unsuccessfully) to allow it to levy a higher insurance premium on firms with underfunded plans.

Accounting for the Pension Plan

Until recently companies were obliged to show pension assets and liabilities only in the notes to the accounts. That was changed by Financial Accounting Standards Board Statement No. 87 (FASB 87) which brought the pension liability onto the balance sheet for the first time.

To find out whether there is a balance sheet liability the company must compare the value of the assets in the pension fund with the present value of accrued

---

[11] Contributions to the pension plan are tax-deductible and therefore withdrawals are taxable. In fact Congress sought to deter withdrawals by imposing a 10 percent surtax on them. However, in 1986 Exxon had substantial charges that it could use to offset this tax liability.

pensions.[12] If there's a surplus, nothing happens. If there's a deficit, it must be shown on the company's balance sheet as a liability.

If the pension fund's investment manager has a bad year, or if the value of accrued pensions increases, a pension liability may suddenly appear on the balance sheet (or an existing liability may get quite a bit bigger). This prospect worried many managers. To calm them down, FASB 87 included two mechanisms to smooth things out. First, when companies calculate the deficit, they can spread the effect of changes in the value of pension assets or liabilities over a number of years. Second, the Accounting Standards Board took the view that unfunded pension benefits produce a more contented and productive work force. Therefore, if improved benefits raise the deficit, the company is allowed to show an offsetting intangible asset that represents this prospective gain in worker productivity. This intangible asset is then amortized over several years, as the memory of the benefits increase fades, and employees begin to ask, "What have you done for us lately?" Isn't accounting wonderful?

FASB 87 also lays down procedures for calculating the pension expense deducted from each year's reported income. This has four components.

1. *Interest cost.* The company starts the year with a debtlike pension liability. Its cost is the interest rate times the accrued liability.[13]
2. *Service cost.* Employees earn additional benefits during the year.
3. *Amortization of deficit.* If the company has an accumulated pension deficit, it will also need to pay it off over time.
4. *Expected investment return.* Expenses 1, 2, and 3 are partly offset by the return that the company expects to earn on the pension assets.

The net expense is equal to:

$$
\begin{array}{l}
 (1)\ \text{Interest cost} \\
+\ (2)\ \text{Service cost} \\
+\ (3)\ \text{Amortization of plan deficit} \\
\underline{-\ (4)\ \text{Expected investment return}} \\
=\ \text{Net pension expense}
\end{array}
$$

This net annual expense may be higher or lower than the actual amount of cash that the company puts in the pension fund that year.

FASB 87 was an important step in pension accounting. It brought the pension debt onto the company's balance sheet and it substituted consistency for the ragbag of different approaches that companies previously used. It was also a controversial rule. Some critics believe that the opportunities for smoothing the impact of pension deficits result in a fudge. Corporate treasurers worry that the impact of the pension plan on the balance sheet and income statement could be severe. They argue that the debt ratios will deteriorate and lead to defaults on loan covenants. Or they suggest that the company's earnings may no longer reflect underlying business prospects.

35-3 MANAGING THE PENSION FUND

There are two methods of funding a pension plan. The employer can enter into a contract with an insurance company. The employer agrees to pay the pension

---

[12] In calculating the balance sheet liability, the company uses the *accumulated-benefit obligation.* This includes vested and unvested liabilities but ignores the effect of likely future salary increases.

[13] In this context, the accrued liability is called a *projected-benefit obligation,* which is the accumulated-benefit obligation (used to calculate the balance sheet liability) adjusted for future salary increases.

contributions over to the insurance company, which guarantees to provide a certain level of retirement benefits. The more common procedure (accounting for about 70 percent of contributions) is to pay the contributions into a trust fund.[14]

Some companies appoint their own investment manager to run the trust fund, but in the majority of cases management of the fund is given to one or more banks or investment management companies. The financial manager still retains responsibility for setting fund objectives and monitoring the performance of the investment manager. We will discuss these responsibilities in turn.

Risk and Pension Fund Policy

Some managers believe they can reduce the cost of a pension scheme by investing in securities with greater risk and greater expected return. But if the securities are properly priced, you cannot increase the *present value* of the pension fund by changing its composition.

Although the fund's composition cannot alter the size of the total pie, there are circumstances in which it can affect the size of the individual slices. For example, before ERISA pensions were not guaranteed. So, if the fund performed badly, employees could lose their pensions. On the other hand, if the fund performed better than expected, employees got no more than promised, and the company could reap the reward in the form of reduced contributions. Thus employees bore part of the risk of the pension fund investments but received none of the extra rewards that risk-bearing may bring.[15]

Since the establishment of the Pension Benefit Guarantee Corporation, the employee is largely protected against the consequences of a risky investment policy. However, the PBGC often has to pick up the tab when things go wrong. Companies that are close to the brink have an incentive to provide the minimum amount of funding and to invest the pension fund in relatively risky securities.[16] That incentive would disappear if the PBGC got its way and charged higher insurance premiums in such cases.

Tax and Pension Fund Policy

The PBGC guarantee tempts firms to underfund the pension plan and to invest in risky securities. But there is a second effect that works in the opposite direction and encourages firms to *overfund* the pension plan and invest in bonds.[17] To understand this argument we need to examine the plan's tax status.

The company's contribution to a pension fund is a tax-deductible expense just like the payment of wages. Also individuals are taxed when they receive a pension

[14] Some plans use a split-funded system, in which part of the contribution is placed with the insurance company and the remainder is put in the trust fund.

[15] The difference between the values of a safe and a risky pension equals the value of the company's option to default on promised benefits. By increasing the risk of the fund, management increased the value of this default option. As we explained in Chapter 20, the option to default is like a put option. The pension put was first discussed in W. Bagehot (pseud.), "Risk and Reward in Corporate Pension Funds," *Financial Analysts Journal,* **28:** 80–84 (January–February 1972). See also J. L. Treynor, W. Priest, and P. Regan, *The Financial Reality of Pension Funding Under ERISA,* Dow Jones–Irwin, Inc., Homewood, Ill., 1976.

[16] We do not wish to give the impression that anything goes. We have already seen that ERISA establishes a minimum level of funding; it also imposes a duty of prudence on the investment managers.

[17] Because the PBGC is at risk from underfunded plans, ERISA imposed minimum funding requirements. By contrast, the IRS is anxious that firms do not escape tax by overfunding their pension plans. Therefore the IRS imposes a maximum rate of funding. This is equal to normal cost plus the amount necessary to amortize supplemental liabilities and experience losses over 10 years.

TABLE 35-2
Two strategies for paying pension of P a year in perpetuity

	Current Cash Flows	Future Cash Flows
Strategy 1:		
Pay pensions when due	—	$-(1 - T_c)P$
Strategy 2:		
1. Borrow P/r	$+P/r$	$-(1 - T_c)r \times (P/r) = -(1 - T_c)P$
2. Place P/r in pension fund	$-(1 - T_c)P/r$	—
3. Invest fund in corporate bonds	—	$r \times (P/r) = +P$
4. Pay pensions from pension fund income	—	$-P$
Total cash flows, strategy 2:	$+T_cP/r$	$-(1 - T_c)P$
Cash-flow advantage of strategy 2 over strategy 1	$+T_cP/r$	—

just as they are taxed on wages. But pension plans do enjoy one important privilege: They are not taxed on investment income; therefore pension savings earn the pretax rate of return.[18]

Fisher Black and Irwin Tepper have argued that the tax privilege that pension funds enjoy has an important implication for investment policy.[19]

Imagine that a firm needs to pay pensions of P dollars a year in perpetuity, but does not set up a pension fund—it just makes each pension payment as it comes due. Since the pension payment is a tax-deductible expense, the net annual cost to the firm is $(1 - T_c)P$.

Table 35-2 outlines an alternative strategy. Rather than waiting until the pension becomes due, the firm can borrow P/r and put it in the pension fund. Since this pension fund contribution is tax-deductible, the firm receives an immediate tax savings of T_cP/r. If the pension fund invests in corporate bonds, it earns an annual income of $r \times (P/r) = P$, which is just sufficient to pay the future pensions. In addition, the firm has to pay interest on its borrowing, which after tax is equal to

$$(1 - T_c)r \times \frac{P}{r} = (1 - T_c)P$$

Both strategies involve future cash payments of $(1 - T_c)P$, but the second strategy provides an immediate cash benefit of T_cP/r. So it is best to borrow and give the proceeds to the pension fund to invest in bonds.

---

[18] Pension schemes are not the only way that companies can help individuals to earn pretax returns on their savings. ERISA also allowed companies to make tax-deductible contributions to an employee stock ownership plan (ESOP), which then uses the money to buy the company's stock on behalf of employees. This stock is held until the employee retires, when it is either distributed or rolled over into an individual retirement account (IRA). Employees are not taxed on their investment in an ESOP until it is distributed.

Instead of making a cash contribution, the company may issue new stock to the ESOP. For a discussion of the role of ESOPs see C. Rosen, "ESOPs: New Growth for Your Firm," *Financial Executive,* **9:** 10–20 (July 1983).

[19] See F. Black, "The Tax Consequences of Long-Run Pension Policy," *Financial Analysts Journal,* **36:** 1–28 (July–August 1980); and I. Tepper, "Taxation and Corporate Pension Policy," *Journal of Finance,* **36:** 1–14 (March 1981).

TABLE 35-3
Two strategies for paying pensions of $10 million per year in perpetuity
(figures in millions)

	Current Cash Flows	Future Cash Flows
Strategy 1:		
Pay pensions when due	—	$-(1 - .34)10 = -\$6.60$
Strategy 2:		
1. Borrow $10/.10 = \$100$	$+\$100$	$-(1 - .34)10 = -\$6.60$
2. Place $100 in pension fund	$-(1 - .34)100 = -66$	—
3. Invest fund in corporate bonds	—	$(+.10 \times 100) = +10$
4. Pay pensions from pension fund income	—	-10
Total cash flows, strategy 2:	$+\$34$	$-\$6.60$
Cash-flow advantage of strategy 2 over strategy 1	$+\$34$	—

It is tempting to think that this benefit comes from the decision to fund the pension scheme, but this is not so. Funding the pension scheme offers no advantage in itself. The benefit arises only because the firm is borrowing at the after-tax rate of interest and earning the pretax rate of interest on corporate bonds held in the pension fund.[20] Of course the more you put in the pension fund now, the more you can make from this tax arbitrage.

Example. We will put some numbers on this. Suppose that your company plans to set aside $10 million a year in perpetuity for the payment of pensions. Since this is a tax-deductible expense, the after-tax cash outlay is $(1 - .34)10 = \$6.6$ million per year. This is set out in the first line of Table 35-3.

The second section of Table 35-3 shows what happens if you follow Black and Tepper's advice. You arrange for your firm to borrow $100 million at 10 percent. The annual after-tax interest payment on this debt is $(1 - .34)10 = \$6.6$ million—exactly the same as the after-tax pension expense. The $100 million is placed in the pension fund and invested in bonds earning 10 percent. Thus each year the fund generates income of $.10 \times 100 = \$10$ million, which is just enough to pay the annual pensions. You have now substituted one fixed expense of $6.6 million a year (interest on the debt) for another (the cost of the pension). So all future cash flows are unchanged. But by contributing $100 million to the pension fund today, you also earn an immediate tax shield of $.34 \times 100 = \$34$ million. Thus Black and Tepper's strategy has made your shareholders $34 million better off.

Notice that your firm issues an additional $100 million of bonds, but through the pension fund it also *owns* an additional $100 million of bonds. So the firm's *aggregate* leverage is unchanged. But what if the pension fund invests in equities rather than bonds? In this case the aggregate leverage would increase. If your firm was at its optimal debt-equity ratio before the bond issue, it would no longer be so afterward.

---

[20] Suppose the earnings of the pension fund were taxed at the corporate rate T_c. Then under strategy 2 the firm would have to contribute $P/r(1 - T_c)$ to the pension fund. The after-tax cost would be $(1 - T_c)[P/r(1 - T_c)] = P/r$, which exactly offsets the amount borrowed. Thus strategy 2 would have no current cash-flow advantage over strategy 1. Try reworking Table 35-3 under this assumption.

Corporate pension funds hold more than $100 billion in stocks. So, if Black and Tepper are right, their idea is potentially worth $34 billion.[21] Some find it difficult to believe. Others agree that it works but believe that the gain comes from the issue of debt to fund the pension plan and that it doesn't matter whether the fund invests in debt or equity. A third group believes that it doesn't matter whether contributions are financed by borrowing as long as the pension fund invests in bonds.[22]

Setting Objectives

We have identified two considerations that could affect a firm's attitude toward funding and investment policy. Since the PBGC guarantees pensions, we would expect to find firms in financial distress underfunding the pension plan and investing in riskier assets. For profitable, taxpaying firms we are more likely to see borrowing in order to overfund and invest in bonds. And firms do in fact seem to behave in roughly this way.[23]

No manager likes to be caught by surprise, so investment companies and consultants have developed a range of tools that help the manager explore the consequences of any investment policy. For example, in Chapter 10 we saw how firms use Monte Carlo simulation to probe more deeply into their capital budgeting decisions.[24] In just the same way, financial managers sometimes use simulation to analyze their pension plans. It doesn't tell them the optimal investment or funding policy, but it does illustrate the possible consequences of any policy.

35-4 MEASURING FUND PERFORMANCE

You will pay an investment company a substantial fee for managing your pension fund. It makes sense to monitor how well it is doing its job. The need to measure pension fund performance has spawned an industry of consultants and analysts.

The first step in performance measurement is to calculate the fund's rate of return. Your concern is with *total* return. Therefore you must include in your calculations both dividends and capital appreciation. You are also interested only in market values. Therefore you must look at market prices and ignore the prices at which securities may be recorded in the fund's books.

One way to calculate the fund's rate of return is to list all cash flows in and out of the fund together with the final value of the fund; then you find the rate of discount that equates these benefits with the initial fund value:

---

[21] Approximately 1 in 10 pension plans are invested entirely in bonds. We don't of course know whether their managers are fans of Black and Tepper.

[22] Where you believe the gain comes from depends on your view on the debt and taxes controversy. See Section 18-2 of Chapter 18. If Miller's theory of debt and taxes is right, the pretax return on debt is higher than on (risk-free) equity and it is necessary to invest the pension fund in bonds in order to capture the tax advantage. If MM are right, the fund would earn the same pretax return whether it invested in debt or equity. However, the company would need to finance the pension fund contribution by an issue of debt in order to capture the interest tax shield.

[23] See Z. Bodie, J. O. Light, R. Morck, and R. A. Taggart, Jr., "Corporate Pension Policy: An Empirical Investigation," *Financial Analysts Journal,* **41:** 10–16 (September–October 1985).

[24] See Section 10-2 of Chapter 10. Irwin Tepper discusses pension plan simulation in "Risk vs. Return in Pension Fund Investment," *Harvard Business Review,* **55:** 100–107 (March–April 1977).

$$\begin{array}{c}\text{Initial}\\\text{fund}\\\text{value}\end{array} = \frac{\text{year 1 cash flow}}{1 + y} + \frac{\text{year 2 cash flow}}{(1 + y)^2} + \cdots + \frac{\text{year } N \text{ fund value}}{(1 + y)^N}$$

The quantity y in this formula is our old friend the internal rate of return.

Unfortunately the internal rate of return is inappropriate for measurement of performance, because it is affected by the timing of cash flows that may be beyond the manager's control. For example, suppose that you have two managers, each of whom follows a strategy of investing an entire fund in the market index. Each manager starts with $10 million. Over the first year the index falls by 50 percent, leaving each manager with an investment of $5 million. At that point company A puts $1 million more *into* its pension fund and company B takes $1 million *out* of its fund. Therefore A has $6 million invested in the market and B has $4 million. Over the second year the market recovers to its initial level giving A a fund worth $12 million and B a fund worth $8 million. To find the internal rate of return we set out the cash flows and final value and solve for the return y:

$$\text{Fund A:} \qquad 10 = \frac{-1}{1 + y} + \frac{12}{(1 + y)^2}, \quad y = +4.7\%$$

$$\text{Fund B:} \qquad 10 = \frac{+1}{1 + y} + \frac{8}{\cdot(1 + y)^2}, \quad y = -5.4\%$$

Notice that the manager of fund A was fortunate to receive a cash *inflow* at the bottom of the market and so has a positive rate of return. The manager of fund B was unfortunate to have a cash *outflow* at the bottom of the market and so has a negative rate of return. But you wouldn't want to conclude from this that the manager of A was more skilled at picking stocks than the manager of B.

The internal rate of return is sometimes called the **dollar-weighted rate of return**—it gives equal weight to each dollar invested. In performance measurement you need a measure of the return that gives equal weight to each unit of time. A familiar example of a **time-weighted rate of return** is the return on a share in a mutual fund. The value of *your* investment in a mutual fund is not directly affected by whether other people are putting money into the fund or taking it out.

When you measure the performance of a pension fund, you need to pretend that it is a mutual fund and then look at the performance of one share in the fund. In our example, that is easy. Whether you bought a share in fund A or fund B, the value of your investment would have halved in the first year and doubled in the second year. Therefore by the end of the 2 years you would have been back where you started. The time-weighted return is the same for both fund A and fund B.

To calculate the time-weighted rate of return you need to identify how much of the gain in the value of the fund was attributable to new cash. You can do that precisely only if you know the date of each cash flow *and* the market value of the fund at that date. Mutual funds value their portfolios every day, but some pension funds leave as much as a year between valuations. The Bank Administration Institute in cooperation with the University of Chicago sponsored a study of performance measurement which, among other things, devised two possible ways to estimate time-weighted rates of return in cases of infrequent fund valuations. It was an extremely careful study, and its recommendations have become a standard for performance measurers throughout the world.

Choosing the Performance Yardstick

Suppose that you now have an estimate of the time-weighted return on your pension fund. That in itself won't tell you whether the investment manager has done a good job. Maybe the average return was high because interest rates were high or because the stock market rose or because the manager held particularly volatile stocks. This may sound obvious, but it certainly was not so on Wall Street in 1967 and 1968. These were the heydays of the "high-growth" mutual funds. As the Dow Jones average rose 20 percent, many of these funds appreciated by more than 60 percent, and their youthful managers were widely acclaimed. Subsequently, when the Dow Jones declined by 10 percent, many of these funds depreciated by more than 40 percent and their managers were managers no more. The truth, of course, was that most of the managers of these funds were neither prodigies nor charlatans; they simply held high-beta portfolios which behaved accordingly.[25]

The object of performance measurement is to work out how far the fund's return was due to general market movements and how much was due to the skill of the manager.

Step 1. If a fund invests in Treasury bills, it can be sure of earning the risk-free rate of interest. If it invests in risky securities, the return may turn out to be higher or lower than the risk-free rate of interest. The premium that the fund receives for taking on risk is equal to the difference between the return on the fund and the risk-free rate of interest:[26]

$$\frac{\text{Fund risk}}{\text{premium}} = \frac{\text{average fund}}{\text{return}} - \frac{\text{average rate}}{\text{of interest}}$$

$$= r - r_f$$

Step 2. The fund may obtain a positive risk premium because markets in general have been buoyant or because the manager has been successful at picking stocks. It may obtain a negative risk premium because markets have been depressed or because the manager has picked the wrong stocks. You can break down the premium into two further components: the premium which *anyone* could have achieved and the additional premium that your manager achieved.

Suppose that the manager has invested in a portfolio with a beta (β) of .8. Anyone could have constructed a portfolio with a beta of .8 just by putting 80 percent of the portfolio in the market index and the remainder in Treasury bills. The risk premium on this benchmark portfolio would have been:

$$\frac{\text{Benchmark portfolio's}}{\text{risk premium}} = .8 \times \frac{\text{risk premium}}{\text{on market}}$$

$$= \beta(r_m - r_f)$$

The quantity $\beta(r_m - r_f)$ measures the risk premium on an unmanaged portfolio with the same market risk as your fund. This is the premium which anyone could have achieved. The difference between the risk premium on the actual fund and

---

[25] For an entertaining account of these years, read Adam Smith (pseud.), *The Money Game*, Random House, Inc., New York, 1967.

[26] Notice that in judging performance you are concerned with the *arithmetic* average of returns.

the risk premium on the benchmark portfolio must be due to the manager's success in picking stocks. This gain from picking stocks is often called alpha (α).[27]

$$\alpha = \text{gain from picking stocks}$$

$$= \frac{\text{fund risk}}{\text{premium}} - \frac{\text{benchmark portfolio's}}{\text{risk premium}}$$

$$= (r - r_f) - \beta(r_m - r_f)$$

Step 3. Unfortunately, a manager who tries to pick stocks cannot simultaneously hold the entire market. In other words, the manager's eggs must be put into a limited number of baskets. Some of the gains from picking stocks are needed just to compensate for the resulting unique risk.

In step 2 we measured the gains from picking stocks by comparing the reward on the actual fund with the reward on an unmanaged benchmark portfolio. The actual fund had the same market risk as the benchmark portfolio but it also had unique risk. Therefore it had more *total* risk.

You can imagine a second benchmark portfolio that is constructed to have the same *total* risk as the fund. If we call the total risk of the fund σ and the total risk of the market σ_m then this second benchmark portfolio would consist of the fraction σ/σ_m invested in the market index and the remainder invested in Treasury bills. The risk premium on the portfolio would be

$$\frac{\sigma}{\sigma_m}(r_m - r_f)$$

You can now measure the *net* gain from your manager's stock selection:

$$\textit{Net} \text{ gain from picking stocks} = \text{fund risk premium}$$

$$- \frac{\text{risk premium on benchmark}}{\text{portfolio with equal } \sigma}$$

$$= (r - r_f) - \frac{\sigma}{\sigma_m}(r_m - r_f)$$

The difference between the gain and the *net* gain from picking stocks is the extra return that is needed just to compensate for extra unique risk.[28]

Measuring Performance— An Example

Here is a free gift for you. You can use these techniques to measure the performance of your own common stock portfolio. Let us work through an example.

Table 35-4 sets out all the necessary data. It shows the risk-free interest rate and the yearly returns on your portfolio and the market index. At the bottom of

---

[27] Step 2 is equivalent to measuring the difference between the actual return and the return predicted by the capital asset pricing model. Thus the case for step 2 is strongest if we are sure that the capital asset pricing model is right and that we have measured the true market portfolio. Since we cannot be sure, we do not know that the benchmark portfolio is the *best possible* naive strategy. Nevertheless the benchmark is plausible and provides a useful way to adjust for market fluctuations.

[28] Our measures for gain from picking stocks and net gain from picking stocks were originally suggested by M. C. Jensen in "The Performance of Mutual Funds in the Period 1945–1964," *Journal of Finance,* **23:** 389–416 (May 1968), and in a slightly different form by W. F. Sharpe in "Mutual Fund Performance," *Journal of Business,* **39:** 119–138 (January 1966). Our description of these measures follows E. F. Fama, "Components of Investment Performance," *Journal of Finance,* **27:** 551–568 (June 1972).

TABLE 35-4
To measure the performance of your portfolio, you need the following data

	Your Portfolio	Standard & Poor's Composite Index
1979	+13	+18
1980	+28	+32
1981	+ 1	− 5
1982	+19	+21
1983	+17	+23
1984	+12	+ 6
1985	+30	+32
1986	+19	+18
Average return, %	$r = 17.4$	$r_m = 18.1$
Beta	$\beta = .70$	$\beta_m = 1.00$
Standard deviation, %	$\sigma = 8.6$	$\sigma_m = 11.7$

Note:
The average Treasury bill rate from 1978 to 1986 was 9.9%.

the table we have calculated three numbers: the average return, the market risk (β), and the total risk (σ).

Now we can start to analyze the average return on your portfolio.

Step 1. By investing in Treasury bills, you could have gotten an average return of $r_f = 9.9$ percent. Instead you took a riskier route and were rewarded with an average return of $r = 17.4$ percent, i.e. a premium of 7.5 percent:

$$r - r_f = 17.4 - 9.9 = 7.5\%$$

Step 2. Your portfolio had a beta of .70. Anyone could have constructed a portfolio with a beta of .70, just by putting 70 percent of his or her money in the market portfolio and the remainder in Treasury bills. The risk premium on this easy-to-pick portfolio would have been

$$\beta(r_m - r_f) = .70 \times (18.1 - 9.9) = 5.7\%$$

You got an average risk premium of 7.5 percent. Therefore your gain from picking stocks was

$$(r - r_f) - \beta(r_m - r_f) = 7.5 - 5.7 = 1.8\%$$

Step 3. If you tried to pick stocks, you must have been less than fully diversified. Therefore you took on some unique risk. Your total risk was $\sigma = 8.6$ percent. Anyone could have constructed a portfolio with a total risk of 8.6 percent just by putting $\sigma/\sigma_m = .74$, or 74 percent in the market portfolio and the remainder in Treasury bills. The risk premium on this second easy-to-pick portfolio would have been

$$\frac{\sigma}{\sigma_m}(r_m - r_f) = .74(18.1 - 9.9) = 6.0\%$$

The *net* gain from your efforts was, therefore,

$$(r - r_f) - \frac{\sigma}{\sigma_m}(r_m - r_f) = 7.5 - 6.0 = 1.5\%$$

If you can keep that up, you will beat most professional managers.

Some Cautions about Performance Measurement

We should issue three warnings about performance measurement. First, investment management is a highly competitive business, so that it is extremely rare to find managers that consistently outperform naive strategies by any dramatic amount. Occasionally you find portfolios that are clearly inferior to the unmanaged benchmark portfolio, so the principal value of performance measurement may well lie in spotlighting gross incompetence. Also, remember that there are many aspects of the manager's job that are not being measured, such as choosing an appropriate level of risk and undertaking various administrative functions.

Second, since you are looking for relatively minor differences in performance, it is all the more important to be careful in your comparisons.

Third, unusual performance in any one year will more often than not be due to chance rather than skill. To differentiate between skill and chance, you need to examine performance over many years. While you are waiting, don't attach undue significance to modest differences in performance.

The biggest problems in measuring performance arise when the fund has substantial holdings in real estate or overseas investments. In such cases, it does not make much sense to compare the fund with a package of United States common stocks and Treasury bills. Many performance measures, therefore, do not even try to adjust the fund return for the effect of market fluctuations. They simply report the return and leave the client to judge whether the risk was acceptable.

35-5 SUMMARY

By tradition, corporate finance texts ignore the company's pension plan. But the financial manager is spending more and more time worrying about it. On average the annual pension contribution amounted in 1985 to 16 percent of companies' pretax profits.[29] The obligation not covered by the pension fund is often substantially greater than the long-term debt shown in the balance sheet. That is why we have included this brief discussion of how the financial manager assesses the cost of the plan and oversees the management of the fund.

Most large companies have more than one pension plan. Some are regularly negotiated with the labor union; they typically offer employees a flat benefit based on years of service. Others are provided for nonunion or salaried employees; they generally offer a pension that is related to both years of service and final salary. Pension schemes also differ in the benefit they give to employees who quit *before* retirement age. But the 1974 pension law, ERISA, now lays down certain minimum standards for vesting.

The plan's actuary draws up a balance sheet of the plan. The liabilities consist of the value of all the benefits that the company expects to pay to current participants. They include those that have already accrued to them as a result of past service and those that are expected to accrue as a result of future service. To meet

[29] S. D. Bleiberg, *The 1986 BEA Pension Survey*, BEA Associates, Inc., New York, 1986.

these liabilities the pension plan has two principal assets. One is the value of the pension fund; the other is the present value of the planned contributions or "normal costs." If these assets fall short of the liabilities, there is a deficiency and the company must generally make additional contributions to eliminate this deficiency over 25 or 30 years.

Before the passage of ERISA, employees could be sure that they would get their pensions only if there were sufficient assets in the pension fund. Since ERISA the Pension Benefit Guarantee Corporation (PBGC) insures employees' pensions. But the PBGC can seek to recover from the company whatever is needed to pay the pensions. That makes the pension promise an important senior debt.

Company contributions may be paid to an insurance company which will, in exchange, contract to provide future benefits. More commonly the contributions are paid into a trust fund which is run by a bank or investment management company. The financial executive generally has the responsibility for coordination with the manager of the fund and thus has at least two things to worry about: deciding on the appropriate objectives for the fund, and monitoring the performance of the fund manager.

It is pointless to look for the optimal risk strategy for a pension fund. In an efficient market all securities are zero-NPV investments. Therefore you are unlikely to find a balance between bonds and stocks that makes everyone better off. But since the PBGC picks up the tab if things go wrong, there is an incentive for firms that are on the brink to underfund their pension plans and to invest them in risky assets. That helps the firm's shareholders, although only at the expense of the PBGC.

Because the income of the pension fund is not taxed, money held in the pension plan earns the pretax rate of return. That provides an incentive for the company to borrow, then fund the pension plan to the hilt and invest it in bonds.

Thus the risk-shifting effect tempts companies to underfund their pension plan and invest in risky stocks, while the tax effect tempts them to overfund and invest in safe bonds.

To measure the performance of the pension fund you first need to calculate its rate of return. It is useless to look at the internal rate of return, because that depends on when the company decides to put more money into the fund. You need to pretend that the fund is a mutual fund and that the new contributions are used to buy additional shares in the mutual fund. Then calculate the average return per share. In the pension business this is called the time-weighted rate of return.

Of course you need some benchmark against which to compare the fund's performance. The trick here is to compare the fund return with the return on a benchmark portfolio which has the same risk as the fund, but which anyone could have picked.

FURTHER READING

Munnell's book is a helpful general review of pensions and their role in the economy. Bodie and Shoven's book collects recent research studies on pensions.

   A. H. Munnell: *The Economics of Private Pensions,* Brookings Institution, Washington, D.C., 1982.

   Z. Bodie and J. Shoven (eds.): *Financial Aspects of the United States Pension System,* University of Chicago Press, Chicago, 1983.

Bagehot's article (which was written before ERISA) shows that the company's pension obligation resembles a risky debt. The value of this debt is reduced if the pension plan is unfunded or if the pension fund invests in risky securities. The studies of Sharpe and Treynor, Priest and Regan discuss how funding policy is affected by ERISA.

W. Bagehot (pseud.): "Risk and Reward in Corporate Pension Funds," *Financial Analysts Journal*, **28:** 80–84 (January–February 1972).

W. F. Sharpe: "Corporate Pension Funding Policy," *Journal of Financial Economics*, **3:** 183–193 (June 1976).

J. L. Treynor, W. Priest, and P. Regan: *The Financial Reality of Pension Funding Under ERISA*, Dow Jones–Irwin, Inc., Homewood, Ill., 1976.

The following articles discuss the implications of the pension fund's tax-free status for funding and investment policy:

F. Black: "The Tax Consequences of Long-Run Pension Policy" *Financial Analysts Journal*, 1–28 (July–August 1980).

J. Bulow: "Tax Aspects of Corporate Pension Funding Policy," National Bureau of Economic Research, Working Paper No. 724, July 1981.

A. F. Ehrbar: "How to Slash Your Company's Tax Bill," *Fortune*, 122–124 (Feb. 23, 1981).

I. Tepper: "Taxation and Corporate Pension Policy," *Journal of Finance*, **36:** 1–14 (March 1981).

The Bank Administration Institute provides a standard reference on the measurement of pension fund performance. The articles by Jensen, Sharpe, and Fama are concerned with the problem of adjusting for risk in performance measurement. Roll's article offers a contrary view and criticizes the modern theory of performance measurement.

Measuring the Investment Performance of Pension Funds, Bank Administration Institute, Park Ridge, Ill., 1968.

M. C. Jensen: "The Performance of Mutual Funds in the Period 1945–64," *Journal of Finance*, **23:** 389–416 (May 1968).

W. F. Sharpe: "Mutual Fund Performance," *Journal of Business*, **39:** 119–138 (January 1966).

E. F. Fama: "Components of Investment Performance," *Journal of Finance*, **27:** 551–568 (June 1972).

R. Roll: "Ambiguity When Performance is Measured by the Securities Market Line," *Journal of Finance*, **33:** 1051–1069 (September 1978).

QUIZ

1. True or false?
   (*a*) The time-weighted return is affected by the timing of cash flows into or out of the fund.
   (*b*) The dollar-weighted rate of return exceeds the internal rate of return in a rising market.
   (*c*) Vested benefits are those that are invested on behalf of the employee or pensioner.
   (*d*) If a pension plan defaults on promised benefits, the Pension Benefit Guarantee Corporation will make up the major part of any deficiency.
   (*e*) The PBGC's claim on the company's assets is limited to 50 percent of net worth.
   (*f*) Accountants now require that pension deficits be noted in footnotes to the company's financial statements.
   (*g*) Most pensions are linked to the employee's final salary.
   (*h*) Black and Tepper recommend that companies should increase their own borrowing and invest the money in the pension fund in bonds.

TABLE 35-5
See Quiz question 3

Assets	Liabilities
PV(pension fund)	PV(expected benefits for past service)
Deficit(surplus)	
PV(contributions)	PV(expected benefits for future service)
Total assets	PV(expected benefits)

    (*i*) Companies in financial difficulty are tempted to underfund their pension plans and invest pension funds in risky securities.

2. Explain the difference between a defined-benefit and defined-contribution pension plan.

3. Table 35-5 shows a pension plan balance sheet. Indicate where in the balance sheet you would enter the value of each of the following items:

    (*a*) 5000 shares of IBM, which are held in trust for members of the pension scheme

    (*b*) A pension of $10,000 a year which is currently being paid to Ms. Smith

    (*c*) A pension worth $20,000 a year which you expect to have to pay to Mr. Brown (age twenty-five) who has just joined the firm

    (*d*) An amount equal to 5 percent of Mr. Brown's salary, which the company plans to put aside each month in order to pay his pension

    (*e*) The total amount of $600 million that the company needs to earmark for pensions

    (*f*) Additional benefits worth $50 million that have just been negotiated by the union

4. Table 35-6 is the balance sheet for the pension plan of Mealy and Briars, Inc.

    (*a*) Explain the meaning of each of the terms in the table.

    (*b*) Calculate:

      (i) The unfunded vested accrued benefits

      (ii) The unfunded accrued benefits

    (*c*) Assuming that normal costs are not altered, show how the balance sheet would change if:

      (i) The value of securities in the pension fund falls by $50 million

      (ii) The union negotiates increased pensions worth $80 million

TABLE 35-6
See Quiz question 4 (figures in millions)

Assets		Liabilities	
Pension fund	$ 720	Vested accrued benefits	$ 540
Unamortized experience losses	90	Unvested accrued benefits	220
Unamortized supplemental liabilities	100	Expected future service costs	900
Losses from changes in actuarial			
assumptions	150		
Future normal costs	600		
Total assets	$1,660	Expected benefits	$1,660

5. If a pension fund is obliged to make a large cash disbursement near the bottom of the market, will the time-weighted rate of return be (a) the same as, (b) greater than, or (c) less than the internal rate of return?

6. The financial manager of Olde's Rope company has observed that the average return was 10 percent on common stocks, 5 percent on Treasury bills, and 11 percent on the firm's pension fund. The market return had an annual standard deviation of 20 percent and the fund return had an annual standard deviation of 16 percent and a beta of .6.
   (a) What was the risk premium on the pension fund?
   (b) What was the total gain from picking stocks?
   (c) After allowing for the unique risk, what was the net gain from picking stocks?

7. A pension fund starts the year with $50 million. By midyear it has appreciated to $60 million, at which point it pays out pensions of $20 million. In the second half of the year, the fund appreciates by a further 50 percent.
   (a) What is the annually compounded time-weighted rate of return?
   (b) Is the annually compounded dollar-weighted rate of return
        (i)   21.7 percent?
        (ii) 72.5 percent?
        (iii) 8 percent?
   (c) Suppose that the fund had a midyear cash inflow of $20 million rather than an outflow. Would this increase or reduce the time-weighted rate of return?
   (d) Would it increase or reduce the dollar-weighted rate of return?

QUESTIONS AND PROBLEMS

1. Explain the changes made by ERISA. How do they affect the employer, the employee, and the pension fund?

2. At year-end 1986, Ford's balance sheet was as follows (figures in millions):

Current assets	$18,458	Current liabilities	$15,626
Plant, equipment, and other assets	19,475	Debt and other liabilities	7,447
		Equity	14,860
Total assets	$37,933	Total liabilities	$37,933

   The company's pension plan for its United States employees had PV(benefits from past service) of $11,680 million. Pension assets were $12,500 million.
   (a) Would Ford's balance sheet change if the new pension accounting rules (FASB 87) were applied retroactively?
   (b) Draw up an augmented balance sheet for Ford that includes both its pension assets and its pension liabilities.
   (c) Show how the published and augmented balance sheets would change if Ford contributed an extra $1 billion in cash to the pension fund.
   (d) Show how the published and augmented balance sheets would change if the value of Ford's pension assets dropped by $2.5 billion.

3. Look at the annual report and accounts of any American company and calculate an augmented balance sheet that includes the assets and liabilities of the pension plan.

4. Show how an increase in the inflation rate is likely to affect the pension plan's surplus or deficit when most members of the plan:
   (a) Are still employed
   (b) Are retired

5. Find an American company with an underfunded pension and a pension deficit shown on the balance sheet in its annual report. Read the footnotes pertaining to its pension plan carefully. How much would the company have to contribute to the pension fund to wipe the pension deficit off its balance sheet?

6. The PBGC's ability to recover money from a company depends on the definition of "30 percent of net worth." What definition do you think would make most sense?

7. Suppose that a company must pay pensions of $30 million a year in perpetuity. The rate of interest is 8 percent and the corporate tax rate is 40 percent.
   (a) If the company does not fund the pension liability, what is the net annual cost to the company of these pensions?
   (b) If it does fund the pension liability, it eliminates this fixed future outflow. It can, therefore, increase its borrowing. How much more can the company afford to borrow if it funds the pension?
   (c) How much must the pension fund invest today in bonds to ensure that it can pay each year's pensions?
   (d) What is the net cost to the company of placing this money in the pension fund?
   (e) If the company borrows and funds the pension scheme in this way, what is the increase in stockholder wealth?

8. To illustrate Black and Tepper's strategy, we analyzed a company that has a fixed pension obligation in perpetuity. But their strategy does not assume perpetuities. Can you rework Table 35-2 for a company that must pay pensions of P in year t only?

9. In Section 35-3 we illustrated the Black and Tepper strategy with an example of a company paying pensions of $10 million a year. Assume that this company has assets of $200 million and no outstanding debt. Construct balance sheets for the company both before and after it follows the Black and Tepper strategy. Then construct the augmented balance sheets that include the assets and liabilities of the pension plan.

10. Does Black and Tepper's strategy increase the risk for (a) the bondholders, (b) the shareholders, or (c) the PBGC? Would the risk be any different if the company made an issue of new equity, which was then placed in the pension fund and invested in common stocks?

11. "Black and Tepper's strategy assumed that there is a tax shield to debt. If Miller's 'Debt and Taxes' article is right, the strategy no longer works." Is this true?

12. "Funded pension plans impose an excessive cost on the economy. We will be forced to change to a 'pay-as-you-go' system." What does the speaker mean? Is the statement right?

13. During the past decade, two pension funds had exactly the same cash inflows and outflows and provided the same internal rate of return. However, they provided different time-weighted rates of return. How is this possible?

14. You have been asked to evaluate the performance of your firm's pension fund over the last 5 years. You fit the following equation to 60 monthly returns:

$$r = \alpha + \beta(r_m - r_f)$$

where r = portfolio return
        r_m = market return
        r_f = risk-free interest rate

You estimate that α = .45 percent per month and β = .63. Other facts:

1. The average of the r's was .3 percent
2. The average of the r_m's was .14 percent
3. The average of the r_f's was .38 percent
4. The ratio of the standard deviation of the r's to the standard deviation of the r_m's was .90.

What can you infer from these statistics?

Can you say whether the fund management did a good job?

15. Here is a hard one. Should a pension fund's current investment policy be affected by the company's plans for future recruiting?

16. Why do we have company pension schemes? Would it be better to let individuals make their own savings arrangements for their old age?

PART ELEVEN

CONCLUSIONS

36 Conclusion: What We Do and Do Not Know about Finance

We have had our say and it is time to sign off. Let us finish by thinking about some of the things that we do and do not know about finance.

36-1 WHAT WE DO KNOW: THE FIVE MOST IMPORTANT IDEAS IN FINANCE

What would you say if you were asked to name the five most important ideas in finance? Here is our list.

1 Net Present Value

When you wish to know the value of a used car, you look at prices in the secondhand car market. Similarly, when you wish to know the value of a future cash flow, you look at prices quoted in the capital markets, where claims to future cash flows are traded (remember, those highly paid investment bankers are just secondhand cash-flow dealers). So when you wish to know the value of a future cash flow, you can look at the prices quoted in the capital market. If you can buy cash flows for your shareholders at a cheaper price than they would have to pay in the capital market, you have increased the value of their investment.

This is the simple idea behind *net present value* (NPV). When we calculate a project's NPV, we are asking whether the project is worth more than it costs. We are estimating its value by calculating what its cash flows would be worth if a claim on them were offered separately to investors and traded in the capital markets.

That is why we calculate NPV by discounting future cash flows at the opportunity cost of capital—that is, at the expected rate of return offered by securities having the same degree of risk as the project. In well-functioning capital markets, all equivalent-risk assets are priced to offer the same expected return. By discounting at the opportunity cost of capital, we calculate the price at which investors in the project could expect to earn that rate of return.

Like most good ideas, the net present value rule is "obvious when you think about it." But notice what an important idea it is. The NPV rule allows thousands of shareholders, who may have vastly different levels of wealth and attitudes toward risk, to participate in the same enterprise and to delegate its operation to a professional manager. They give the manager one simple instruction: "Maximize present value."

2 The Capital Asset Pricing Model

Some people say that modern finance is all about the capital asset pricing model. That's nonsense. If the capital asset pricing model had never been invented, our advice to financial managers would be essentially the same. The attraction of the model is that it gives us a manageable way of thinking about the required return on a risky investment.

Again, it is an attractively simple idea. There are two kinds of risk—those that you can diversify away and those that you can't. You can measure the *nondiversifiable*, or *market*, risk of an investment by the extent to which the value of the investment is affected by a change in the *aggregate* value of all the assets in the economy. This is called the *beta* of the investment. The only risks that people care about are the ones that they can't get rid of—the nondiversifiable ones. This is why the required return on an asset increases in line with its beta.

Many people are worried by some of the rather strong assumptions behind the capital asset pricing model, or they are concerned about the difficulties of estimating a project's beta. They are right to be worried about these things. In 10 or 20 years' time we will probably have much better theories than we do now. But we will be extremely surprised if those future theories do not still insist on the crucial distinction between diversifiable and nondiversifiable risk—and that, after all, is the main idea underlying the capital asset pricing model.

3   Efficient Capital Markets

The third fundamental idea is that security prices accurately reflect available information and respond rapidly to new information as soon as it becomes available. This *efficient-market theory* comes in three flavors, corresponding to different definitions of "available information." The weak form (or random-walk theory) says that prices reflect all the information in past prices. The semistrong form says that prices reflect all publicly available information, and the strong form holds that prices reflect all acquirable information.

Don't misunderstand the efficient-market idea. It doesn't say that there are no taxes or costs; it doesn't say that there aren't some clever people and some stupid ones. It merely implies that competition in capital markets is very tough—there are no money machines, and security prices reflect the true underlying values of assets.

4   Value Additivity and the Law of the Conservation of Value

The principle of *value additivity* states that the value of the whole is equal to the sum of the values of the parts. It is sometimes called the *law of the conservation of value*.

When we appraise a project that produces a succession of cash flows, we always assume that values are additive. In other words, we assume

$$PV(\text{project}) = PV(C_1) + PV(C_2) + \cdots + PV(C_t)$$

$$= \frac{C_1}{1 + r} + \frac{C_2}{(1 + r)^2} + \cdots + \frac{C_t}{(1 + r)^t} + \cdots$$

We similarly assume that the sum of the present values of projects A and B equals the present value of a composite project AB.[1] But value additivity also means that you can't increase value by putting two whole companies together unless you thereby increase the total cash flow. In other words, there are no benefits to mergers solely for diversification. And if the rule works for addition, it also works for subtraction. Therefore, financing decisions that simply subdivide the same cash flows in a different way just change the packaging: they don't increase overall firm

[1] That is, if

$$PV(A) = PV[C_1(A)] + PV[C_2(A)] + \ldots + PV[C_t(A)] + \ldots$$
$$PV(B) = PV[C_1(B)] + PV[C_2(B)] + \ldots + PV[C_t(B)] + \ldots$$

and if for each period t, $C_t(AB) = C_t(A) + C_t(B)$, then

$$PV(AB) = PV(A) + PV(B)$$

value. This is the basic idea behind Modigliani and Miller's famous article. Other things being equal, changes in capital structure do not affect value. As long as the *total* cash flow generated by the firm's assets and operations is unchanged by capital structure, total value is independent of capital structure. The value of the whole pie does not depend on how it is sliced.[2]

5 Option Theory

In everyday conversation we often use the word *option* as synonymous with *choice* or *alternative*; thus we speak of someone as *having a number of options*. In finance an option refers specifically to the opportunity to trade in the future on terms that are fixed today. Smart managers know that it is often worth paying today for the option to buy or sell an asset tomorrow.

If options are so important, the financial manager needs to know how to value them. Finance experts have known for some time the relevant variables—the exercise price and the exercise date of the option, the risk of the underlying asset, and the rate of interest. But it was Black and Scholes who first showed how these can be put together in a usable formula.

The Black-Scholes formula was developed for simple call options. It does not directly apply to the more complicated options often encountered in corporate finance. That is why one of the hottest areas of research is extending the basic principles of option valuation to cover the more complicated cases.

Are these five ideas exciting theories or plain common sense? Call them what you will, they are basic to the financial manager's job. If by reading this book you really understand these ideas and know how to apply them, you have learned a great deal.

36-2 WHAT WE DO NOT KNOW: 10 UNSOLVED PROBLEMS IN FINANCE

Since the unknown is never exhausted, the list of what we do not know about finance could go on forever. But, following Brealey and Myers's third law (see Section 28-2), we will list and briefly discuss 10 unsolved problems that seem ripe for productive research.

1 How Are Major Financial Decisions Made?

Arnold Sametz commented in 1964 that "we know very little about how the great nonroutine financial decisions are made."[3] That is no less true today. We know quite a bit about asset values, but we do not know very much about the decisions that give rise to these values. What is the process that causes one company to make a major investment and another to reject it? Why does one company decide to issue debt and another to issue equity? If we knew why companies make particular decisions, we would be better able to help improve those decisions.

Our ignorance is largest when it comes to major *strategic* decisions. In Section 12-1 we described strategic planning as "capital budgeting on a grand scale." Strategic planning attempts to identify the lines of businesses where the firm has the greatest long-run opportunities and to develop a plan for achieving success in those businesses. But it is hard to calculate the NPV of major strategic decisions. Think, for example, of a firm which makes a major commitment to the design and manufacture of computer memories. It is really embarking on a long-term effort

---

[2] If you *start* with the cash flow $C_t(AB)$ and split it into two pieces, $C_t(A)$ and $C_t(B)$, then total value is unchanged. That is, $PV[C_t(A)] + PV[C_t(B)] = PV[C_t(AB)]$. See footnote 1.

[3] A. W. Sametz, "Trends in the Volume and Composition of Equity Finance," *Journal of Finance,* **19:** 450–469 (September 1964). See p. 469.

which will require capital outlays over many years. It cannot identify all those future projects, much less evaluate their NPVs. Instead, it decides to go ahead because the computer memory business is growing rapidly, because firms already in that business are doing well, and because it has intangible assets—special technology, perhaps—which it thinks will give it a leg up on the competition.

Strategic planning is a "top-down" approach to capital budgeting: you choose the businesses you want to be in and make the capital outlays necessary for success. It's perfectly sensible and natural for firms to look at capital investments that way *in addition to* looking at them "bottom-up." The trouble is that we understand the bottom-up part of the capital budgeting process better than the top-down part.

Top-down and bottom-up should not be competing approaches to capital budgeting. They should be two aspects of a single integrated procedure. Not all firms integrate the two approaches successfully. No doubt some firms do so, but we don't really know how.

In Section 28-2 we suggested that option pricing theory might help unravel some of the mysteries of strategic planning. We will have to wait and see whether it does.

2 What Determines Project Risk and Present Value?

A good capital investment is one that has a positive NPV. We have talked at some length about how to calculate NPV, but we have given you very little guidance about how to find positive-NPV projects, except to say in Section 11-4 that projects have positive NPVs when the firm can earn economic rents. But why do some companies earn economic rents while others in the same industry do not? Are the rents merely windfall gains, or can they be anticipated and planned for? What is their source, and how long do they persist before competition destroys them? Very little is known about any of these important questions.

Here is a related question: Why are some real assets risky and others relatively safe? In Section 9-3 we suggested a few reasons for differences in project betas—differences in operating leverage, for example, or in the extent to which a project's cash flows respond to the performance of the national economy. These are useful clues, but we have as yet no general procedure for estimating project betas. Assessing project risk is therefore still largely a seat-of-the-pants matter.

3 Risk and Return—Have We Missed Something?

In 1848 John Stuart Mill wrote, "Happily there is nothing in the laws of value which remains for the present or any future writer to clear up; the theory is complete." Economists today are not so sure about that. For example, the capital asset pricing model is an enormous step toward understanding the effect of risk on the value of an asset, but there are many puzzles left, some statistical and some theoretical.

The statistical problems arise because the capital asset pricing model is hard to prove or disprove conclusively. It appears that average returns from low-beta stocks are too high (that is, higher than the capital asset pricing model predicts), and those from high-beta stocks are too low; but this could be a problem with the way the tests are conducted and not with the model itself.[4] In addition, some tests indicate that average return has been related to diversifiable risk as well as to beta.[5]

[4] See R. Roll, "A Critique of the Asset Pricing Theory's Tests; Part 1: On Past and Potential Testability of the Theory," *Journal of Financial Economics*, **4:** 129–176 (March 1977); and for a critique of the critique, D. Mayers and E. M. Rice, "Measuring Portfolio Performance and the Empirical Content of Asset Pricing Models," *Journal of Financial Economics*, **7:** 3–28 (March 1979).

[5] For example, see I. Friend, R. Westerfield, and M. Granito, "New Evidence on the Capital Asset Pricing Model," *Journal of Finance*, **33:** 903–916 (June 1978).

This is, of course, inconsistent with the capital asset pricing model, which states that diversifiable risk does not bother investors and therefore does not affect expected or average return. Of course, these statistical results could be spurious—an accidental result of inadequate testing procedures. But if they are true, they pose a puzzle: if investors are concerned with diversifiable risk, then corporations ought to be able to increase value just by diversifying. Yet there is evidence that investors do *not* pay extra for firms that diversify. It is hard to see why they would pay extra, because investors can usually diversify more cheaply and effectively than firms can. Maybe diversifiable risk only *appears* to matter because it happens to be correlated with some other variable x that, along with beta, truly determines the expected rates of return demanded by investors. That would resolve the puzzle; but we cannot yet identify variable x and prove that it matters.

Meanwhile, work is proceeding on the theoretical front to relax the simple assumptions underlying the capital asset pricing model. Here is an example: Suppose that you love fine wine. It may make sense for you to buy shares in a grand cru chateau, even if that soaks up a large fraction of your personal wealth and leaves you with a relatively undiversified portfolio. However, you are *hedged* against a rise in the price of fine wine: your hobby will cost you more in a bull market for wine, but your stake in the chateau will make you correspondingly richer. Thus you are holding a relatively undiversified portfolio for a good reason. We would not expect you to demand a premium for bearing that portfolio's undiversifiable risk.

In general, if two people have different tastes, it may make sense for them to hold different portfolios. You may hedge your consumption needs with an investment in wine making, whereas somebody else may do better to invest in Baskin and Robbins. The capital asset pricing model isn't rich enough to deal with such a world. It assumes that all investors have similar tastes: the "hedging motive" does not enter, and therefore they hold the same portfolio of risky assets.

Merton and Breeden have extended the capital asset pricing model to accommodate the hedging motive.[6] If enough investors are attempting to hedge against the same thing, their model implies a more complicated risk-return relationship. However, it is not yet clear who is hedging against what, and so the model remains difficult to test.

---

4 Are There Important Exceptions to the Efficient-Market Theory?

The efficient-market theory is strong, but no theory is perfect—there must be exceptions. What are the exceptions and how well does the evidence stand up?

We noted some apparent exceptions in Section 13-2. For example, we saw that the stocks of small companies appear to have yielded higher average returns than those of large companies with comparable betas. Thus, whatever your target portfolio beta, you can apparently generate superior average returns by investing in small companies.

Now this could mean one of several things:

1. The stock market is inefficient and consistently underprices stocks of small firms.
2. The difference between the stock market performance of small and large firms is just a coincidence. (The more researchers study stock performance, the more strange coincidences they are likely to find.)

---

[6] See R. Merton, "An Intertemporal Capital Asset Pricing Model," *Econometrica,* **41:** 867–887 (1973); and D. T. Breeden, "An Intertemporal Asset Pricing Model with Stochastic Consumption and Investment Opportunities," *Journal of Financial Economics* **7:** 265–296 (September 1979).

FIGURE 36-1
The relationship between firm
size and average daily abnormal returns for each month,
1963–1979. [*Source:* D. B.
Keim; "Size-Related Anomalies
and Stock Return Seasonality:
Further Empirical Evidence,"
Journal of Financial Economics,
12:21 (June 1983), figure 2.

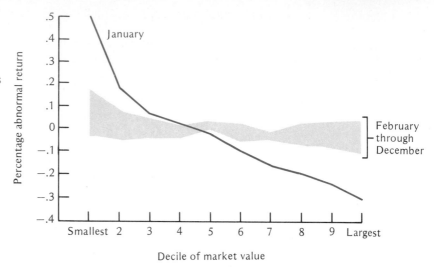

3. Firm size happens to be correlated with variable *x*, that mysterious second risk
variable that investors may rationally take into account in pricing shares.

In searching for an explanation of the small-firm phenomenon, researchers
have uncovered other puzzles. For example, look at Figure 36-1, which shows the
abnormal return on small- and large-company stocks for each month of the year.
You can see that almost all the extra return on small-company stocks occurred in
January. So the mystery deepens. Does the turn-of-the-year effect provide a clue
to the explanation of the small-company effect or is it just a false trail? Sorting
out what is really going on in these cases will take considerable work and thought.

If stocks were fairly priced, there would be no easy ways to make superior
profits. That is why most tests of market efficiency have analyzed whether there
are simple rules that produce superior investment performance. Unfortunately, the
converse does *not* hold: stock prices could deviate substantially from fair value and
yet it could be difficult to make superior profits.

For example, suppose that the price of IBM stock is always one half of its fair
value. As long as IBM is *consistently* underpriced, the percentage capital gain is the
same as it would be if the stock always sold at a fair price. Of course, if IBM stock
is underpriced, you get correspondingly more future dividends for your money,
but for low-yield stocks that does not make much difference to your total return.
So, while the bulk of the evidence shows that it is difficult to earn high returns,
we should be cautious about assuming that stocks are *necessarily* fairly priced.

**5 Is
Management
an Off–
Balance Sheet
Liability?**

Closed-end funds are firms whose only asset is a portfolio of common stocks. One
might think that if you knew the value of these common stocks, you would also
know the value of the firm. However, this is not the case. The stock of the closed-
end fund often sells for substantially less than the value of the fund's portfolio.[7]
All this might not matter much except that it could be just the tip of the iceberg.

[7] There are relatively few closed-end funds. Most mutual funds are *open-end*. This means that they
stand ready to buy or sell additional shares at a price equal to the fund's net asset value per share.
Therefore the share price of an open-end fund always equals net asset value.

For example, bank stocks appear to sell for less than the market value of the firms' net assets; so do real estate stocks. In the late 1970s and early 1980s the market value of many large oil companies was less than the market value of their oil reserves. Analysts joked that you could buy oil cheaper on Wall Street than in West Texas.

All these are special cases in which it was possible to compare the market value of the whole firm with the values of its separate assets. But perhaps if we could observe the value of other firms' separate parts, we might find that the value of the whole was often less than the sum of the values of the parts.

We don't understand why closed-end investment companies or any of the other firms sell at a discount on the market value of their assets. One explanation is that the value added by the firm's management is less than the cost of the management. That is why we suggest that management may be an off–balance sheet liability. For example, one rationalization of the discount of oil company shares from oil-in-the-ground value is that investors expected the profits from oil production to be frittered away in negative-NPV investments and bureaucratic excess. The present value of growth opportunites (PVGO) was negative!

Whenever firms calculate the net present value of a project, they implicitly assume that the value of the whole project is simply the sum of the values of each year's cash flow. We referred to this earlier as the law of the conservation of value. If we cannot rely on that law, the tip of the iceberg could turn out to be a very hot potato.

6 How Can We Explain the Success of New Securities and New Markets?

In the last 20 years companies and the securities exchanges have created an enormous number of new securities—options, futures, options on futures; zero coupon bonds, floating-rate bonds; bonds with collars, caps, and droplocks; dual currency bonds; bonds with currency options. . . . The list is endless. In some cases it is easy to explain the success of new markets or securities—perhaps they allow investors to insure themselves against new risks or they result from a change in tax or in regulation. Sometimes a market develops because of a change in the costs of issuing or trading different securities. But there are many successful innovations that cannot be explained so easily. Are we really better off by being able to trade options on stocks as well as the stocks themselves? Why are floating-rate bonds so much more common in the eurobond market than in the domestic U.S. market? Why do investment bankers continue to invent, and successfully sell, complex new securities that outstrip our ability to value them? The truth is we don't understand why some innovations in markets succeed and others never get off the ground.

7 How Can We Explain Capital Structure?

If firms are free to choose the level of borrowing that they think best, the total supply of debt in the economy will approximate the amount that investors demand. No manager can expect to increase (or reduce) the value of his or her firm just by changing the firm's capital structure. That is the idea behind Merton Miller's theory of capital structure (see Section 18-2). It is an appealing argument. But why, then, do firms have different capital structures? The Miller theory would reply that arbitrary but harmless differences in capital structure can persist indefinitely.

Does it really not matter how much your firm borrows? We have come across several reasons why it *may* matter. Perhaps managers are concerned with potential bankruptcy costs. Perhaps managers use capital structure to signal information to their shareholders.[8] Perhaps differences in capital structure reflect differences in the relative importance of growth opportunities. So far, none of these possibilities has been either proved relevant or definitely excluded.

The upshot of the matter is that we still don't have an accepted, coherent theory of capital structure. It is not for want of argument on the subject.

8 How Can We Resolve the Dividend Controversy?	We spent all of Chapter 16 on dividend policy without being able to resolve the dividend controversy. Many people believe dividends are good, others believe they are bad, and still others believe they are irrelevant. If pressed, we stand somewhere in the middle, but we can't be dogmatic about it.

We don't mean to disparage existing research; rather, we say that more is in order. Whether future research will change anybody's mind is another matter. In 1979 Joel Stern wrote an article for the editorial page of *The Wall Street Journal* arguing for low dividends and citing statistical tests in support of his position.[9] The article attracted several strongly worded responses, including one manager who wrote, ''While Mr. Stern is gamboling from pinnacle to pinnacle in the upper realms of the theoretical, those of us in financial management are down below slogging through the foothills of reality.''[10]

9 What Is the Value of Liquidity?	Unlike Treasury bills, cash pays no interest. On the other hand, cash provides more liquidity than Treasury bills. People who hold cash must believe that this additional liquidity offsets the loss of interest. In equilibrium, the marginal value of the additional liquidity must equal the interest rate on bills.

Now what can we say about corporate holdings of cash? It is wrong to ignore the liquidity gain and to say that the cost of holding cash is the lost interest. This would imply that cash always has a *negative* NPV. It is equally foolish to say that, because the marginal value of liquidity is equal to the loss of interest, it doesn't matter how much cash the firm holds. This would imply that cash always has a *zero* NPV.

We know that the marginal value of cash to a holder declines with the size of the cash holding, but we don't really understand how to value the liquidity service of cash. In our chapters on working-capital management we largely finesse the problem by presenting models that are really too simple,[11] or by speaking vaguely of the need to ensure an ''adequate'' liquidity reserve. We cannot successfully tackle the problem of working-capital management until we have a theory of liquidity.

The problem is that liquidity is a matter of degree. A Treasury bill is less liquid than cash, but it is still a highly liquid security because it can be sold and turned into cash easily and almost instantaneously.[12] Corporate bonds are less liquid than

---

[8] See S. Ross, ''The Determination of Financial Structure: The Incentive-Signaling Approach,'' *Bell Journal of Economics,* **8:** 23–40 (Spring 1977).

[9] Joel Stern, ''The Dividend Question,'' *Wall Street Journal,* July 16, 1973, p. 13.

[10] *Wall Street Journal,* August 20, 1979, p. 16. The letter was from A. J. Sandblute, senior vice-president of Minnesota Light and Power Company.

[11] For example, models based only on the transaction costs of switching between cash and interest-bearing assets. See Section 29-1.

[12] That is, you can realize the asset's true economic value in a quick sale. Liquidity means that you don't have to accept a discount from true value if you want to see the asset quickly.

Treasury bills; trucks are less liquid than corporate bonds; specialized machinery is less liquid than trucks; and so on. But even specialized machinery can be turned into cash if you are willing to accept some delay and cost of sale. The broad question is therefore not "How much cash should the firm hold?" but "How should it divide its total investment between relatively liquid and relatively illiquid assets?"—holding other things constant of course. That question is hard to answer. Obviously, every firm must be able to raise cash on short notice, but we have no good theory of how much cash is enough or how readily the firm should be able to raise it. To complicate matters further, we note that cash can be raised on short notice by borrowing, or selling other securities, as well as by selling assets. The financial manager with a $1 million unused line of credit may sleep just as soundly as one whose firm holds $1 million in marketable securities.

10 How Can We Explain Merger Waves?

In 1968, at the peak of the postwar merger movement, Joel Segall noted: "There is no single hypothesis which is both plausible and general and which shows promise of explaining the current merger movement. If so, it is correct to say that there is nothing known about mergers; there are no useful generalizations."[13] Of course there are many plausible reasons why two firms might wish to merge. If you single out a *particular* merger, it is usually possible to think up a reason why that merger could make sense. But that leaves us with a special hypothesis for each merger. What we need is a *general* hypothesis to explain merger waves. For example, everybody seemed to be merging in 1968 and nobody 5 years later. Why?

We can think of other instances of financial fashions. For example, from time to time there are hot new issue periods when there seems to be an insatiable supply of speculative new issues and an equally insatiable demand for them. In recent years economists have been developing new theories of speculative bubbles. Perhaps such theories will help to explain these mystifying financial fashions.

36-3 A FINAL WORD

That concludes our list of unsolved problems. We have given you the 10 uppermost in our minds. If there are others that you find more interesting and challenging, by all means construct your own list and start thinking about it.

It will take years for our 10 problems to be finally solved and replaced with a fresh list. In the meantime, we invite you to go on to further study of what we *already* know about finance. We also invite you to apply what you have learned from reading this book.

Now that the book is done, we sympathize with Huckleberry Finn. At the end of his book he says

So there ain't nothing more to write, and I am rotten glad of it, because if I'd a'knowed what a trouble it was to make a book I wouldn't a' tackled it, and I ain't a'going to no more.

---

[13] J. Segall, "Merging for Fun and Profit," *Industrial Management Review*, **9:** 17–30 (Winter 1968).

Appendix: Present Value Tables

APPENDIX TABLE 1

Discount factors: Present value of \$1 to be received after t years $= 1/(1 + r)^t$

Interest rate per year

Number of years	1%	2%	3%	4%	5%	6%	7%	8%	9%	10%	11%	12%	13%	14%	15%
1	.990	.980	.971	.962	.952	.943	.935	.926	.917	.909	.901	.893	.885	.877	.870
2	.980	.961	.943	.925	.907	.890	.873	.857	.842	.826	.812	.797	.783	.769	.756
3	.971	.942	.915	.889	.864	.840	.816	.794	.772	.751	.731	.712	.693	.675	.658
4	.961	.924	.888	.855	.823	.792	.763	.735	.708	.683	.659	.636	.613	.592	.572
5	.951	.906	.863	.822	.784	.747	.713	.681	.650	.621	.593	.567	.543	.519	.497
6	.942	.888	.837	.790	.746	.705	.666	.630	.596	.564	.535	.507	.480	.456	.432
7	.933	.871	.813	.760	.711	.665	.623	.583	.547	.513	.482	.452	.425	.400	.376
8	.923	.853	.789	.731	.677	.627	.582	.540	.502	.467	.434	.404	.376	.351	.327
9	.914	.837	.766	.703	.645	.592	.544	.500	.460	.424	.391	.361	.333	.308	.284
10	.905	.820	.744	.676	.614	.558	.508	.463	.422	.386	.352	.322	.295	.270	.247
11	.896	.804	.722	.650	.585	.527	.475	.429	.388	.350	.317	.287	.261	.237	.215
12	.887	.788	.701	.625	.557	.497	.444	.397	.356	.319	.286	.257	.231	.208	.187
13	.879	.773	.681	.601	.530	.469	.415	.368	.326	.290	.258	.229	.204	.182	.163
14	.870	.758	.661	.577	.505	.442	.388	.340	.299	.263	.232	.205	.181	.160	.141
15	.861	.743	.642	.555	.481	.417	.362	.315	.275	.239	.209	.183	.160	.140	.123
16	.853	.728	.623	.534	.458	.394	.339	.292	.252	.218	.188	.163	.141	.123	.107
17	.844	.714	.605	.513	.436	.371	.317	.270	.231	.198	.170	.146	.125	.108	.093
18	.836	.700	.587	.494	.416	.350	.296	.250	.212	.180	.153	.130	.111	.095	.081
19	.828	.686	.570	.475	.396	.331	.277	.232	.194	.164	.138	.116	.098	.083	.070
20	.820	.673	.554	.456	.377	.312	.258	.215	.178	.149	.124	.104	.087	.073	.061
25	.780	.610	.478	.375	.295	.233	.184	.146	.116	.092	.074	.059	.047	.038	.030
30	.742	.552	.412	.308	.231	.174	.131	.099	.075	.057	.044	.033	.026	.020	.015

Interest rate per year

Number of years	16%	17%	18%	19%	20%	21%	22%	23%	24%	25%	26%	27%	28%	29%	30%
1	.862	.855	.847	.840	.833	.826	.820	.813	.806	.800	.794	.787	.781	.775	.769
2	.743	.731	.718	.706	.694	.683	.672	.661	.650	.640	.630	.620	.610	.601	.592
3	.641	.624	.609	.593	.579	.564	.551	.537	.524	.512	.500	.488	.477	.466	.455
4	.552	.534	.516	.499	.482	.467	.451	.437	.423	.410	.397	.384	.373	.361	.350
5	.476	.456	.437	.419	.402	.386	.370	.355	.341	.328	.315	.303	.291	.280	.269
6	.410	.390	.370	.352	.335	.319	.303	.289	.275	.262	.250	.238	.227	.217	.207
7	.354	.333	.314	.296	.279	.263	.249	.235	.222	.210	.198	.188	.178	.168	.159
8	.305	.285	.266	.249	.233	.218	.204	.191	.179	.168	.157	.148	.139	.130	.123
9	.263	.243	.225	.209	.194	.180	.167	.155	.144	.134	.125	.116	.108	.101	.094
10	.227	.208	.191	.176	.162	.149	.137	.126	.116	.107	.099	.092	.085	.078	.073
11	.195	.178	.162	.148	.135	.123	.112	.103	.094	.086	.079	.072	.066	.061	.056
12	.168	.152	.137	.124	.112	.102	.092	.083	.076	.069	.062	.057	.052	.047	.043
13	.145	.130	.116	.104	.093	.084	.075	.068	.061	.055	.050	.045	.040	.037	.033
14	.125	.111	.099	.088	.078	.069	.062	.055	.049	.044	.039	.035	.032	.028	.025
15	.108	.095	.084	.074	.065	.057	.051	.045	.040	.035	.031	.028	.025	.022	.020
16	.093	.081	.071	.062	.054	.047	.042	.036	.032	.028	.025	.022	.019	.017	.015
17	.080	.069	.060	.052	.045	.039	.034	.030	.026	.023	.020	.017	.015	.013	.012
18	.069	.059	.051	.044	.038	.032	.028	.024	.021	.018	.015	.014	.012	.010	.009
19	.060	.051	.043	.037	.031	.027	.023	.020	.017	.014	.012	.011	.009	.008	.007
20	.051	.043	.037	.031	.026	.022	.019	.016	.014	.012	.010	.008	.007	.006	.005
25	.024	.020	.016	.013	.010	.009	.007	.006	.005	.004	.003	.003	.002	.002	.001
30	.012	.009	.007	.005	.004	.003	.003	.002	.002	.001	.001	.001	.001	.000	.000

E.g.: If the interest rate is 10 percent per year, the present value of $1 received at year 5 is $.621.

APPENDIX TABLE 2

Future value of $1 after t years $= (1 + r)^t$

Number of years		Interest rate per year													
	1%	2%	3%	4%	5%	6%	7%	8%	9%	10%	11%	12%	13%	14%	15%
1	1.010	1.020	1.030	1.040	1.050	1.060	1.070	1.080	1.090	1.100	1.110	1.120	1.130	1.140	1.150
2	1.020	1.040	1.061	1.082	1.102	1.124	1.145	1.166	1.188	1.210	1.232	1.254	1.277	1.300	1.323
3	1.030	1.061	1.093	1.125	1.158	1.191	1.225	1.260	1.295	1.331	1.368	1.405	1.443	1.482	1.521
4	1.041	1.082	1.126	1.170	1.216	1.262	1.311	1.360	1.412	1.464	1.518	1.574	1.630	1.689	1.749
5	1.051	1.104	1.159	1.217	1.276	1.338	1.403	1.469	1.539	1.611	1.685	1.762	1.842	1.925	2.011
6	1.062	1.126	1.194	1.265	1.340	1.419	1.501	1.587	1.677	1.772	1.870	1.974	2.082	2.195	2.313
7	1.072	1.149	1.230	1.316	1.407	1.504	1.606	1.714	1.828	1.949	2.076	2.211	2.353	2.502	2.660
8	1.083	1.172	1.267	1.369	1.477	1.594	1.718	1.851	1.993	2.144	2.305	2.476	2.658	2.853	3.059
9	1.094	1.195	1.305	1.423	1.551	1.689	1.838	1.999	2.172	2.358	2.558	2.773	3.004	3.252	3.518
10	1.105	1.219	1.344	1.480	1.629	1.791	1.967	2.159	2.367	2.594	2.839	3.106	3.395	3.707	4.046
11	1.116	1.243	1.384	1.539	1.710	1.898	2.105	2.332	2.580	2.853	3.152	3.479	3.836	4.226	4.652
12	1.127	1.268	1.426	1.601	1.796	2.012	2.252	2.518	2.813	3.138	3.498	3.896	4.335	4.818	5.350
13	1.138	1.294	1.469	1.665	1.886	2.133	2.410	2.720	3.066	3.452	3.883	4.363	4.898	5.492	6.153
14	1.149	1.319	1.513	1.732	1.980	2.261	2.579	2.937	3.342	3.797	4.310	4.887	5.535	6.261	7.076
15	1.161	1.346	1.558	1.801	2.079	2.397	2.759	3.172	3.642	4.177	4.785	5.474	6.254	7.138	8.137
16	1.173	1.373	1.605	1.873	2.183	2.540	2.952	3.426	3.970	4.595	5.311	6.130	7.067	8.137	9.358
17	1.184	1.400	1.653	1.948	2.292	2.693	3.159	3.700	4.328	5.054	5.895	6.866	7.986	9.276	10.76
18	1.196	1.428	1.702	2.026	2.407	2.854	3.380	3.996	4.717	5.560	6.544	7.690	9.024	10.58	12.38
19	1.208	1.457	1.754	2.107	2.527	3.026	3.617	4.316	5.142	6.116	7.263	8.613	10.20	12.06	14.23
20	1.220	1.486	1.806	2.191	2.653	3.207	3.870	4.661	5.604	6.727	8.062	9.646	11.52	13.74	16.37
25	1.282	1.641	2.094	2.666	3.386	4.292	5.427	6.848	8.623	10.83	13.59	17.00	21.23	26.46	32.92
30	1.348	1.811	2.427	3.243	4.322	5.743	7.612	10.06	13.27	17.45	22.89	29.96	39.12	50.95	66.21

Interest rate per year

Number of years	16%	17%	18%	19%	20%	21%	22%	23%	24%	25%	26%	27%	28%	29%	30%
1	1.160	1.170	1.180	1.190	1.200	1.210	1.220	1.230	1.240	1.250	1.260	1.270	1.280	1.290	1.300
2	1.346	1.369	1.392	1.416	1.440	1.464	1.488	1.513	1.538	1.563	1.588	1.613	1.638	1.664	1.690
3	1.561	1.602	1.643	1.685	1.728	1.772	1.816	1.861	1.907	1.953	2.000	2.048	2.097	2.147	2.197
4	1.811	1.874	1.939	2.005	2.074	2.144	2.215	2.289	2.364	2.441	2.520	2.601	2.684	2.769	2.856
5	2.100	2.192	2.288	2.386	2.488	2.594	2.703	2.815	2.932	3.052	3.176	3.304	3.436	3.572	3.713
6	2.436	2.565	2.700	2.840	2.986	3.138	3.297	3.463	3.635	3.815	4.002	4.196	4.398	4.608	4.827
7	2.826	3.001	3.185	3.379	3.583	3.797	4.023	4.259	4.508	4.768	5.042	5.329	5.629	5.945	6.275
8	3.278	3.511	3.759	4.021	4.300	4.595	4.908	5.239	5.590	5.960	6.353	6.768	7.206	7.669	8.157
9	3.803	4.108	4.435	4.785	5.160	5.560	5.987	6.444	6.931	7.451	8.005	8.595	9.223	9.893	10.60
10	4.411	4.807	5.234	5.695	6.192	6.728	7.305	7.926	8.594	9.313	10.09	10.92	11.81	12.76	13.79
11	5.117	5.624	6.176	6.777	7.430	8.140	8.912	9.749	10.66	11.64	12.71	13.86	15.11	16.46	17.92
12	5.936	6.580	7.288	8.064	8.916	9.850	10.87	11.99	13.21	14.55	16.01	17.61	19.34	21.24	23.30
13	6.886	7.699	8.599	9.596	10.70	11.92	13.26	14.75	16.39	18.19	20.18	22.36	24.76	27.39	30.29
14	7.988	9.007	10.15	11.42	12.84	14.42	16.18	18.14	20.32	22.74	25.42	28.40	31.69	35.34	39.37
15	9.266	10.54	11.97	13.59	15.41	17.45	19.74	22.31	25.20	28.42	32.03	36.06	40.56	45.59	51.19
16	10.75	12.33	14.13	16.17	18.49	21.11	24.09	27.45	31.24	35.53	40.36	45.80	51.92	58.81	66.54
17	12.47	14.43	16.67	19.24	22.19	25.55	29.38	33.76	38.74	44.41	50.85	58.17	66.46	75.86	86.50
18	14.46	16.88	19.67	22.90	26.62	30.91	35.85	41.52	48.04	55.51	64.07	73.87	85.07	97.86	112.5
19	16.78	19.75	23.21	27.25	31.95	37.40	43.74	51.07	59.57	69.39	80.73	93.81	108.9	126.2	146.2
20	19.46	23.11	27.39	32.43	38.34	45.26	53.36	62.82	73.86	86.74	101.7	119.1	139.4	162.9	190.0
25	40.87	50.66	62.67	77.39	95.40	117.4	144.2	176.9	216.5	264.7	323.0	393.6	478.9	581.8	705.6
30	85.85	111.1	143.4	184.7	237.4	304.5	389.8	497.9	634.8	807.8	1026	1301	1646	2078	2620

E.g.: If the interest rate is 10 percent per year, the investment of $1 today will be worth $1.611 at year 5.

APPENDIX TABLE 3

Annuity table: Present value of $1 *per year* for each of t years $= 1/r - 1/[r(1 + r)^t]$

Interest rate per year

Number of years	1%	2%	3%	4%	5%	6%	7%	8%	9%	10%	11%	12%	13%	14%	15%
1	.990	.980	.971	.962	.952	.943	.935	.926	.917	.909	.901	.893	.885	.877	.870
2	1.970	1.942	1.913	1.886	1.859	1.833	1.808	1.783	1.759	1.736	1.713	1.690	1.668	1.647	1.626
3	2.941	2.884	2.829	2.775	2.723	2.673	2.624	2.577	2.531	2.487	2.444	2.402	2.361	2.322	2.283
4	3.902	3.808	3.717	3.630	3.546	3.465	3.387	3.312	3.240	3.170	3.102	3.037	2.974	2.914	2.855
5	4.853	4.713	4.580	4.452	4.329	4.212	4.100	3.993	3.890	3.791	3.696	3.605	3.517	3.433	3.352
6	5.795	5.601	5.417	5.242	5.076	4.917	4.767	4.623	4.486	4.355	4.231	4.111	3.998	3.889	3.784
7	6.728	6.472	6.230	6.002	5.786	5.582	5.389	5.206	5.033	4.868	4.712	4.564	4.423	4.288	4.160
8	7.652	7.325	7.020	6.733	6.463	6.210	5.971	5.747	5.535	5.335	5.146	4.968	4.799	4.639	4.487
9	8.566	8.162	7.786	7.435	7.108	6.802	6.515	6.247	5.995	5.759	5.537	5.328	5.132	4.946	4.772
10	9.471	8.983	8.530	8.111	7.722	7.360	7.024	6.710	6.418	6.145	5.889	5.650	5.426	5.216	5.019
11	10.37	9.787	9.253	8.760	8.306	7.887	7.499	7.139	6.805	6.495	6.207	5.938	5.687	5.453	5.234
12	11.26	10.58	9.954	9.385	8.863	8.384	7.943	7.536	7.161	6.814	6.492	6.194	5.918	5.660	5.421
13	12.13	11.35	10.63	9.986	9.394	8.853	8.358	7.904	7.487	7.103	6.750	6.424	6.122	5.842	5.583
14	13.00	12.11	11.30	10.56	9.899	9.295	8.745	8.244	7.786	7.367	6.982	6.628	6.302	6.002	5.724
15	13.87	12.85	11.94	11.12	10.38	9.712	9.108	8.559	8.061	7.606	7.191	6.811	6.462	6.142	5.847
16	14.72	13.58	12.56	11.65	10.84	10.11	9.447	8.851	8.313	7.824	7.379	6.974	6.604	6.265	5.954
17	15.56	14.29	13.17	12.17	11.27	10.48	9.763	9.122	8.544	8.022	7.549	7.120	6.729	6.373	6.047
18	16.40	14.99	13.75	12.66	11.69	10.83	10.06	9.372	8.756	8.201	7.702	7.250	6.840	6.467	6.128
19	17.23	15.68	14.32	13.13	12.09	11.16	10.34	9.604	8.950	8.365	7.839	7.366	6.938	6.550	6.198
20	18.05	16.35	14.88	13.59	12.46	11.47	10.59	9.818	9.129	8.514	7.963	7.469	7.025	6.623	6.259
25	22.02	19.52	17.41	15.62	14.09	12.78	11.65	10.67	9.823	9.077	8.422	7.843	7.330	6.873	6.464
30	25.81	22.40	19.60	17.29	15.37	13.76	12.41	11.26	10.27	9.427	8.694	8.055	7.496	7.003	6.566

Interest rate per year

Number of years	16%	17%	18%	19%	20%	21%	22%	23%	24%	25%	26%	27%	28%	29%	30%
1	.862	.855	.847	.840	.833	.826	.820	.813	.806	.800	.794	.787	.781	.775	.769
2	1.605	1.585	1.566	1.547	1.528	1.509	1.492	1.474	1.457	1.440	1.424	1.407	1.392	1.376	1.361
3	2.246	2.210	2.174	2.140	2.106	2.074	2.042	2.011	1.981	1.952	1.923	1.896	1.868	1.842	1.816
4	2.798	2.743	2.690	2.639	2.589	2.540	2.494	2.448	2.404	2.362	2.320	2.280	2.241	2.203	2.166
5	3.274	3.199	3.127	3.058	2.991	2.926	2.864	2.803	2.745	2.689	2.635	2.583	2.532	2.483	2.436
6	3.685	3.589	3.498	3.410	3.326	3.245	3.167	3.092	3.020	2.951	2.885	2.821	2.759	2.700	2.643
7	4.039	3.922	3.812	3.706	3.605	3.508	3.416	3.327	3.242	3.161	3.083	3.009	2.937	2.868	2.802
8	4.344	4.207	4.078	3.954	3.837	3.726	3.619	3.518	3.421	3.329	3.241	3.156	3.076	2.999	2.925
9	4.607	4.451	4.303	4.163	4.031	3.905	3.786	3.673	3.566	3.463	3.366	3.273	3.184	3.100	3.019
10	4.833	4.659	4.494	4.339	4.192	4.054	3.923	3.799	3.682	3.571	3.465	3.364	3.269	3.178	3.092
11	5.029	4.836	4.656	4.486	4.327	4.177	4.035	3.902	3.776	3.656	3.543	3.437	3.335	3.239	3.147
12	5.197	4.988	4.793	4.611	4.439	4.278	4.127	3.985	3.851	3.725	3.605	3.493	3.387	3.286	3.190
13	5.342	5.118	4.910	4.715	4.533	4.362	4.203	4.053	3.912	3.780	3.656	3.538	3.427	3.322	3.223
14	5.468	5.229	5.008	4.802	4.611	4.432	4.265	4.108	3.962	3.824	3.695	3.573	3.459	3.351	3.249
15	5.575	5.324	5.092	4.876	4.675	4.489	4.315	4.153	4.001	3.859	3.726	3.601	3.483	3.373	3.268
16	5.668	5.405	5.162	4.938	4.730	4.536	4.357	4.189	4.033	3.887	3.751	3.623	3.503	3.390	3.283
17	5.749	5.475	5.222	4.990	4.775	4.576	4.391	4.219	4.059	3.910	3.771	3.640	3.518	3.403	3.295
18	5.818	5.534	5.273	5.033	4.812	4.608	4.419	4.243	4.080	3.928	3.785	3.654	3.529	3.413	3.304
19	5.877	5.584	5.316	5.070	4.843	4.635	4.442	4.263	4.097	3.942	3.799	3.664	3.539	3.421	3.311
20	5.929	5.628	5.353	5.101	4.870	4.657	4.460	4.279	4.110	3.954	3.803	3.673	3.546	3.427	3.316
25	6.097	5.766	5.467	5.195	4.948	4.721	4.514	4.323	4.147	3.985	3.834	3.694	3.564	3.442	3.329
30	6.177	5.829	5.517	5.235	4.979	4.746	4.534	4.339	4.160	3.995	3.842	3.701	3.569	3.447	3.332

E.g.: If the interest rate is 10 percent per year, the present value of $1 received in each of the next 5 years is $3.791.

APPENDIX TABLE 4

Values of e^{rt}: Future value of $1 invested at a *continuously compounded* rate r for t years

rt	.00	.01	.02	.03	.04	.05	.06	.07	.08	.09
.00	1.000	1.010	1.020	1.030	1.041	1.051	1.062	1.073	1.083	1.094
.10	1.105	1.116	1.127	1.139	1.150	1.162	1.174	1.185	1.197	1.209
.20	1.221	1.234	1.246	1.259	1.271	1.284	1.297	1.310	1.323	1.336
.30	1.350	1.363	1.377	1.391	1.405	1.419	1.433	1.448	1.462	1.477
.40	1.492	1.507	1.522	1.537	1.553	1.568	1.584	1.600	1.616	1.632
.50	1.649	1.665	1.682	1.699	1.716	1.733	1.751	1.768	1.786	1.804
.60	1.822	1.840	1.859	1.878	1.896	1.916	1.935	1.954	1.974	1.994
.70	2.014	2.034	2.054	2.075	2.096	2.117	2.138	2.160	2.181	2.203
.80	2.226	2.248	2.271	2.293	2.316	2.340	2.363	2.387	2.411	2.435
.90	2.460	2.484	2.509	2.535	2.560	2.586	2.612	2.638	2.664	2.691
1.00	2.718	2.746	2.773	2.801	2.829	2.858	2.886	2.915	2.945	2.974
1.10	3.004	3.034	3.065	3.096	3.127	3.158	3.190	3.222	3.254	3.287
1.20	3.320	3.353	3.387	3.421	3.456	3.490	3.525	3.561	3.597	3.633
1.30	3.669	3.706	3.743	3.781	3.819	3.857	3.896	3.935	3.975	4.015
1.40	4.055	4.096	4.137	4.179	4.221	4.263	4.306	4.349	4.393	4.437
1.50	4.482	4.527	4.572	4.618	4.665	4.711	4.759	4.807	4.855	4.904
1.60	4.953	5.003	5.053	5.104	5.155	5.207	5.259	5.312	5.366	5.419
1.70	5.474	5.529	5.585	5.641	5.697	5.755	5.812	5.871	5.930	5.989
1.80	6.050	6.110	6.172	6.234	6.297	6.360	6.424	6.488	6.553	6.619
1.90	6.686	6.753	6.821	6.890	6.959	7.029	7.099	7.171	7.243	7.316

rt	.00	.01	.02	.03	.04	.05	.06	.07	.08	.09
2.00	7.389	7.463	7.538	7.614	7.691	7.768	7.846	7.925	8.004	8.085
2.10	8.166	8.248	8.331	8.415	8.499	8.585	8.671	8.758	8.846	8.935
2.20	9.025	9.116	9.207	9.300	9.393	9.488	9.583	9.679	9.777	9.875
2.30	9.974	10.07	10.18	10.28	10.38	10.49	10.59	10.70	10.80	10.91
2.40	11.02	11.13	11.25	11.36	11.47	11.59	11.70	11.82	11.94	12.06
2.50	12.18	12.30	12.43	12.55	12.68	12.81	12.94	13.07	13.20	13.33
2.60	13.46	13.60	13.74	13.87	14.01	14.15	14.30	14.44	14.59	14.73
2.70	14.88	15.03	15.18	15.33	15.49	15.64	15.80	15.96	16.12	16.28
2.80	16.44	16.61	16.78	16.95	17.12	17.29	17.46	17.64	17.81	17.99
2.90	18.17	18.36	18.54	18.73	18.92	19.11	19.30	19.49	19.69	19.89
3.00	20.09	20.29	20.49	20.70	20.91	21.12	21.33	21.54	21.76	21.98
3.10	22.20	22.42	22.65	22.87	23.10	23.34	23.57	23.81	24.05	24.29
3.20	24.53	24.78	25.03	25.28	25.53	25.79	26.05	26.31	26.58	26.84
3.30	27.11	27.39	27.66	27.94	28.22	28.50	28.79	29.08	29.37	29.67
3.40	29.96	30.27	30.57	30.88	31.19	31.50	31.82	32.14	32.46	32.79
3.50	33.12	33.45	33.78	34.12	34.47	34.81	35.16	35.52	35.87	36.23
3.60	36.60	36.97	37.34	37.71	38.09	38.47	38.86	39.25	39.65	40.04
3.70	40.45	40.85	41.26	41.68	42.10	42.52	42.95	43.38	43.82	44.26
3.80	44.70	45.15	45.60	46.06	46.53	46.99	47.47	47.94	48.42	48.91
3.90	49.40	49.90	50.40	50.91	51.42	51.94	52.46	52.98	53.52	54.05

E.g.: If the continuously compounded interest rate is 10 percent per year, the investment of $1 today will be worth $1.105 at year 1 and $1.221 at year 2.

APPENDIX TABLE 5

Present value of $1 per year received in a continuous stream for each of t years (discounted at an *annually compounded* rate r) =

$$\{1/[\log(1 + r)]\} - \{1/[[\log(1 + r)][(1 + r)^t]]\}$$

Interest rate per year

Number of years	1%	2%	3%	4%	5%	6%	7%	8%	9%	10%	11%	12%	13%	14%	15%
1	.995	.990	.985	.981	.976	.971	.967	.962	.958	.954	.950	.945	.941	.937	.933
2	1.980	1.961	1.942	1.924	1.906	1.888	1.871	1.854	1.837	1.821	1.805	1.790	1.774	1.759	1.745
3	2.956	2.913	2.871	2.830	2.791	2.752	2.715	2.679	2.644	2.609	2.576	2.543	2.512	2.481	2.450
4	3.922	3.846	3.773	3.702	3.634	3.568	3.504	3.443	3.383	3.326	3.270	3.216	3.164	3.113	3.064
5	4.878	4.760	4.648	4.540	4.437	4.337	4.242	4.150	4.062	3.977	3.896	3.817	3.741	3.668	3.598
6	5.825	5.657	5.498	5.346	5.202	5.063	4.931	4.805	4.685	4.570	4.459	4.353	4.252	4.155	4.062
7	6.762	6.536	6.323	6.121	5.930	5.748	5.576	5.412	5.256	5.108	4.967	4.832	4.704	4.582	4.465
8	7.690	7.398	7.124	6.867	6.623	6.394	6.178	5.974	5.780	5.597	5.424	5.260	5.104	4.956	4.816
9	8.609	8.243	7.902	7.583	7.284	7.004	6.741	6.494	6.261	6.042	5.836	5.642	5.458	5.285	5.121
10	9.519	9.072	8.657	8.272	7.913	7.579	7.267	6.975	6.702	6.447	6.208	5.983	5.772	5.573	5.386
11	10.42	9.884	9.391	8.935	8.512	8.121	7.758	7.421	7.107	6.815	6.542	6.287	6.049	5.826	5.617
12	11.31	10.68	10.10	9.572	9.083	8.633	8.218	7.834	7.478	7.149	6.843	6.559	6.294	6.048	5.818
13	12.19	11.46	10.79	10.18	9.627	9.116	8.647	8.216	7.819	7.453	7.115	6.802	6.512	6.242	5.992
14	13.07	12.23	11.46	10.77	10.14	9.571	9.048	8.570	8.131	7.729	7.359	7.018	6.704	6.413	6.144
15	13.93	12.98	12.12	11.34	10.64	10.00	9.423	8.897	8.418	7.980	7.579	7.212	6.874	6.563	6.276
16	14.79	13.71	12.75	11.88	11.11	10.41	9.774	9.201	8.681	8.209	7.778	7.385	7.024	6.694	6.390
17	15.64	14.43	13.36	12.41	11.55	10.79	10.10	9.482	8.923	8.416	7.957	7.539	7.158	6.809	6.490
18	16.48	15.14	13.96	12.91	11.98	11.15	10.41	9.742	9.144	8.605	8.118	7.676	7.275	6.910	6.577
19	17.31	15.83	14.54	13.39	12.39	11.49	10.69	9.983	9.347	8.777	8.263	7.799	7.380	6.999	6.652
20	18.14	16.51	15.10	13.86	12.77	11.81	10.96	10.21	9.533	8.932	8.394	7.909	7.472	7.077	6.718
25	22.13	19.72	17.67	15.93	14.44	13.16	12.06	11.10	10.26	9.524	8.877	8.305	7.797	7.344	6.938
30	25.94	22.62	19.89	17.64	15.75	14.17	12.84	11.70	10.73	9.891	9.164	8.529	7.973	7.482	7.047

Interest rate per year

Number of years	16%	17%	18%	19%	20%	21%	22%	23%	24%	25%	26%	27%	28%	29%	30%
1	.929	.925	.922	.918	.914	.910	.907	.903	.900	.896	.893	.889	.886	.883	.880
2	1.730	1.716	1.703	1.689	1.676	1.663	1.650	1.638	1.625	1.613	1.601	1.590	1.578	1.567	1.556
3	2.421	2.392	2.365	2.337	2.311	2.285	2.259	2.235	2.211	2.187	2.164	2.141	2.119	2.098	2.077
4	3.016	2.970	2.925	2.882	2.840	2.799	2.759	2.720	2.682	2.646	2.610	2.576	2.542	2.509	2.477
5	3.530	3.464	3.401	3.340	3.281	3.223	3.168	3.115	3.063	3.013	2.964	2.917	2.872	2.828	2.785
6	3.972	3.886	3.804	3.724	3.648	3.574	3.504	3.436	3.370	3.307	3.246	3.187	3.130	3.075	3.022
7	4.354	4.247	4.145	4.048	3.954	3.865	3.779	3.696	3.617	3.542	3.469	3.399	3.331	3.266	3.204
8	4.682	4.555	4.434	4.319	4.209	4.104	4.004	3.909	3.817	3.730	3.646	3.566	3.489	3.415	3.344
9	4.966	4.819	4.680	4.547	4.422	4.302	4.189	4.081	3.978	3.880	3.786	3.697	3.612	3.530	3.452
10	5.210	5.044	4.887	4.739	4.599	4.466	4.340	4.221	4.108	4.000	3.898	3.801	3.708	3.619	3.535
11	5.421	5.237	5.063	4.900	4.747	4.602	4.465	4.335	4.213	4.096	3.986	3.882	3.783	3.689	3.599
12	5.603	5.401	5.213	5.036	4.870	4.713	4.566	4.428	4.297	4.173	4.057	3.946	3.841	3.742	3.648
13	5.759	5.542	5.339	5.150	4.972	4.806	4.650	4.504	4.365	4.235	4.112	3.997	3.887	3.784	3.686
14	5.894	5.662	5.446	5.245	5.058	4.882	4.718	4.564	4.420	4.284	4.157	4.036	3.923	3.816	3.715
15	6.010	5.765	5.537	5.326	5.129	4.945	4.774	4.614	4.464	4.324	4.192	4.068	3.951	3.841	3.737
16	6.111	5.853	5.614	5.393	5.188	4.998	4.820	4.655	4.500	4.355	4.220	4.092	3.973	3.860	3.754
17	6.197	5.928	5.679	5.450	5.238	5.041	4.858	4.687	4.529	4.381	4.242	4.112	3.990	3.875	3.767
18	6.272	5.992	5.735	5.498	5.279	5.076	4.889	4.714	4.552	4.401	4.259	4.127	4.003	3.887	3.778
19	6.336	6.047	5.781	5.538	5.313	5.106	4.914	4.736	4.571	4.417	4.273	4.139	4.014	3.896	3.785
20	6.391	6.094	5.821	5.571	5.342	5.130	4.935	4.754	4.586	4.430	4.284	4.149	4.022	3.903	3.791
25	6.573	6.244	5.945	5.674	5.427	5.201	4.994	4.803	4.627	4.464	4.314	4.173	4.042	3.920	3.806
30	6.659	6.312	6.000	5.718	5.462	5.229	5.016	4.821	4.641	4.476	4.323	4.181	4.048	3.925	3.810

E.g.: If the interest rate is 10 percent per year, a continuous cash flow of $1 a year for each of 5 years is worth $3.977. A continuous flow of $1 in year 5 only is worth $3.977 − $3.326 = $.651.

APPENDIX TABLE 6
Call option values, percent of share price

SHARE PRICE DIVIDED BY PV (EXERCISE PRICE)

	.40	.45	.50	.55	.60	.65	.70	.75	.80	.82	.84	.86	.88	.90	.92	.94	.96	.98	1.00
.05	.0	.0	.0	.0	.0	.0	.0	.0	.0	.0	.0	.0	.0	.0	.1	.3	.6	1.2	2.0
.10	.0	.0	.0	.0	.0	.0	.0	.0	.0	.1	.2	.3	.5	.8	1.2	1.7	2.3	3.1	4.0
.15	.0	.0	.0	.0	.0	.0	.1	.2	.5	.7	1.0	1.3	1.7	2.2	2.8	3.5	4.2	5.1	6.0
.20	.0	.0	.0	.0	.0	.1	.4	.8	1.5	1.9	2.3	2.8	3.4	4.0	4.7	5.4	6.2	7.1	8.0
.25	.0	.0	.0	.1	.2	.5	1.0	1.8	2.8	3.3	3.9	4.5	5.2	5.9	6.6	7.4	8.2	9.1	9.9
.30	.0	.1	.1	.3	.7	1.2	2.0	3.1	4.4	5.0	5.7	6.3	7.0	7.8	8.6	9.4	10.2	11.1	11.9
.35	.1	.2	.4	.8	1.4	2.3	3.3	4.6	6.2	6.8	7.5	8.2	9.0	9.8	10.6	11.4	12.2	13.0	13.9
.40	.2	.5	.9	1.6	2.4	3.5	4.8	6.3	8.0	8.7	9.4	10.2	11.0	11.7	12.5	13.4	14.2	15.0	15.9
.45	.5	1.0	1.7	2.6	3.7	5.0	6.5	8.1	9.9	10.6	11.4	12.2	12.9	13.7	14.5	15.3	16.2	17.0	17.8
.50	1.0	1.7	2.6	3.7	5.1	6.6	8.2	10.0	11.8	12.6	13.4	14.2	14.9	15.7	16.5	17.3	18.1	18.9	19.7
.55	1.7	2.6	3.8	5.1	6.6	8.3	10.0	11.9	13.8	14.6	15.4	16.1	16.9	17.7	18.5	19.3	20.1	20.9	21.7
.60	2.5	3.7	5.1	6.6	8.3	10.1	11.9	13.8	15.8	16.6	17.4	18.1	18.9	19.7	20.5	21.3	22.0	22.8	23.6
.65	3.6	4.9	6.5	8.2	10.0	11.9	13.8	15.8	17.8	18.6	19.3	20.1	20.9	21.7	22.5	23.2	24.0	24.7	25.5
.70	4.7	6.3	8.1	9.9	11.9	13.8	15.8	17.8	19.8	20.6	21.3	22.1	22.9	23.6	24.4	25.2	25.9	26.6	27.4
.75	6.1	7.9	9.8	11.7	13.7	15.8	17.8	19.8	21.8	22.5	23.3	24.1	24.8	25.6	26.3	27.1	27.8	28.5	29.2
.80	7.5	9.5	11.5	13.6	15.7	17.7	19.8	21.8	23.7	24.5	25.3	26.0	26.8	27.5	28.3	29.0	29.7	30.4	31.1
.85	9.1	11.2	13.3	15.5	17.6	19.7	21.8	23.8	25.7	26.5	27.2	28.0	28.7	29.4	30.2	30.9	31.6	32.2	32.9
.90	10.7	13.0	15.2	17.4	19.6	21.7	23.8	25.8	27.7	28.4	29.2	29.9	30.6	31.3	32.0	32.7	33.4	34.1	34.7
.95	12.5	14.8	17.1	19.4	21.6	23.7	25.7	27.7	29.6	30.4	31.1	31.8	32.5	33.2	33.9	34.6	35.2	35.9	36.5
1.00	14.3	16.7	19.1	21.4	23.6	25.7	27.7	29.7	31.6	32.3	33.0	33.7	34.4	35.1	35.7	36.4	37.0	37.7	38.3
1.05	16.1	18.6	21.0	23.3	25.6	27.7	29.7	31.6	33.5	34.2	34.9	35.6	36.2	36.9	37.6	38.2	38.8	39.4	40.0
1.10	18.0	20.6	23.0	25.3	27.5	29.6	31.6	33.5	35.4	36.1	36.7	37.4	38.1	38.7	39.3	40.0	40.6	41.2	41.8
1.15	20.0	22.5	25.0	27.3	29.5	31.6	33.6	35.4	37.2	37.9	38.6	39.2	39.9	40.5	41.1	41.7	42.3	42.9	43.5
1.20	21.9	24.5	27.0	29.3	31.5	33.6	35.5	37.3	39.1	39.7	40.4	41.0	41.7	42.3	42.9	43.5	44.0	44.6	45.1
1.25	23.9	26.5	29.0	31.3	33.5	35.5	37.4	39.2	40.9	41.5	42.2	42.8	43.4	44.0	44.6	45.2	45.7	46.3	46.8
1.30	25.9	28.5	31.0	33.3	35.4	37.4	39.3	41.0	42.7	43.3	43.9	44.5	45.1	45.7	46.3	46.8	47.4	47.9	48.4
1.35	27.9	30.5	33.0	35.2	37.3	39.3	41.1	42.8	44.4	45.1	45.7	46.3	46.8	47.4	47.9	48.5	49.0	49.5	50.0
1.40	29.9	32.5	34.9	37.1	39.2	41.1	42.9	44.6	46.2	46.8	47.4	47.9	48.5	49.0	49.6	50.1	50.6	51.1	51.6
1.45	31.9	34.5	36.9	39.1	41.1	43.0	44.7	46.4	47.9	48.5	49.0	49.6	50.1	50.7	51.2	51.7	52.2	52.7	53.2
1.50	33.8	36.4	38.8	40.9	42.9	44.8	46.5	48.1	49.6	50.1	50.7	51.2	51.8	52.3	52.8	53.3	53.7	54.2	54.7
1.55	35.8	38.4	40.7	42.8	44.8	46.6	48.2	49.8	51.2	51.8	52.3	52.8	53.3	53.8	54.3	54.8	55.3	55.7	56.2
1.60	37.8	40.3	42.6	44.6	46.5	48.3	49.9	51.4	52.8	53.4	53.9	54.4	54.9	55.4	55.9	56.3	56.8	57.2	57.6
1.65	39.7	42.2	44.4	46.4	48.3	50.0	51.6	53.1	54.4	54.9	55.4	55.9	56.4	56.9	57.3	57.8	58.2	58.6	59.1
1.70	41.6	44.0	46.2	48.2	50.0	51.7	53.2	54.7	56.0	56.5	57.0	57.5	57.9	58.4	58.8	59.2	59.7	60.1	60.5
1.75	43.5	45.9	48.0	50.0	51.7	53.4	54.8	56.2	57.5	58.0	58.5	58.9	59.4	59.8	60.2	60.7	61.1	61.5	61.8
2.00	52.5	54.6	56.5	58.2	59.7	61.1	62.4	63.6	64.6	65.0	65.4	65.8	66.2	66.6	66.9	67.3	67.6	67.9	68.3
2.25	60.7	62.5	64.1	65.6	66.8	68.0	69.1	70.0	70.9	71.3	71.6	71.9	72.2	72.5	72.8	73.1	73.4	73.7	73.9
2.50	67.9	69.4	70.8	72.0	73.1	74.0	74.9	75.7	76.4	76.7	77.0	77.2	77.5	77.7	78.0	78.2	78.4	78.7	78.9
2.75	74.2	75.4	76.6	77.5	78.4	79.2	79.9	80.5	81.1	81.4	81.6	81.8	82.0	82.2	82.4	82.6	82.7	82.9	83.1
3.00	79.5	80.5	81.4	82.2	82.9	83.5	84.1	84.6	85.1	85.3	85.4	85.6	85.8	85.9	86.1	86.2	86.4	86.5	86.6
3.50	87.6	88.3	88.8	89.3	89.7	90.1	90.5	90.8	91.1	91.2	91.3	91.4	91.5	91.6	91.6	91.7	91.8	91.9	92.0
4.00	92.9	93.3	93.6	93.9	94.2	94.4	94.6	94.8	94.9	95.0	95.0	95.1	95.2	95.2	95.3	95.3	95.4	95.4	95.4
4.50	96.2	96.4	96.6	96.7	96.9	97.0	97.1	97.2	97.3	97.3	97.3	97.4	97.4	97.4	97.5	97.5	97.5	97.5	97.6
5.00	98.1	98.2	98.3	98.3	98.4	98.5	98.5	98.6	98.6	98.6	98.6	98.7	98.7	98.7	98.7	98.7	98.7	98.7	98.8

STANDARD DEVIATION TIMES SQUARE ROOT OF TIME

Note: Based on Black-Scholes model. To obtain corresponding European put values, add present value of exercise price and subtract share price.

1.02	1.04	1.06	1.08	1.10	1.12	1.14	1.16	1.18	1.20	1.25	1.30	1.35	1.40	1.45	1.50	1.75	2.00	2.50	
3.1	4.5	6.0	7.5	9.1	10.7	12.3	13.8	15.3	16.7	20.0	23.1	25.9	28.6	31.0	33.3	42.9	50.0	60.0	.05
5.0	6.1	7.3	8.6	10.0	11.3	12.7	14.1	15.4	16.8	20.0	23.1	25.9	28.6	31.0	33.3	42.9	50.0	60.0	.10
7.0	8.0	9.1	10.2	11.4	12.6	13.8	15.0	16.2	17.4	20.4	23.3	26.0	28.6	31.1	33.3	42.9	50.0	60.0	.15
8.9	9.9	10.9	11.9	13.0	14.1	15.2	16.3	17.4	18.5	21.2	23.9	26.4	28.9	31.2	33.5	42.9	50.0	60.0	.20
10.9	11.8	12.8	13.7	14.7	15.7	16.7	17.7	18.7	19.8	22.3	24.7	27.1	29.4	31.7	33.8	42.9	50.0	60.0	.25
12.8	13.7	14.6	15.6	16.5	17.4	18.4	19.3	20.3	21.2	23.5	25.8	28.1	30.2	32.3	34.3	43.1	50.1	60.0	.30
14.8	15.6	16.5	17.4	18.3	19.2	20.1	21.0	21.9	22.7	24.9	27.1	29.2	31.2	33.2	35.1	43.5	50.2	60.0	.35
16.7	17.5	18.4	19.2	20.1	20.9	21.8	22.6	23.5	24.3	26.4	28.4	30.4	32.3	34.2	36.0	44.0	50.5	60.1	.40
18.6	19.4	20.3	21.1	21.9	22.7	23.5	24.3	25.1	25.9	27.9	29.8	31.7	33.5	35.3	37.0	44.6	50.8	60.2	.45
20.5	21.3	22.1	22.9	23.7	24.5	25.3	26.1	26.8	27.6	29.5	31.3	33.1	34.8	36.4	38.1	45.3	51.3	60.4	.50
22.4	23.2	24.0	24.8	25.5	26.3	27.0	27.8	28.5	29.2	31.0	32.8	34.5	36.1	37.7	39.2	46.1	51.9	60.7	.55
24.3	25.1	25.8	26.6	27.3	28.1	28.8	29.5	30.2	30.9	32.6	34.3	35.9	37.5	39.0	40.4	47.0	52.5	61.0	.60
26.2	27.0	27.7	28.4	29.1	29.8	30.5	31.2	31.9	32.6	34.2	35.8	37.4	38.9	40.3	41.7	48.0	53.3	61.4	.65
28.1	28.8	29.5	30.2	30.9	31.6	32.3	32.9	33.6	34.2	35.8	37.3	38.8	40.3	41.6	43.0	49.0	54.0	61.9	.70
29.9	30.6	31.3	32.0	32.7	33.3	34.0	34.6	35.3	35.9	37.4	38.9	40.3	41.7	43.0	44.3	50.0	54.9	62.4	.75
31.8	32.4	33.1	33.8	34.4	35.1	35.7	36.3	36.9	37.5	39.0	40.4	41.8	43.1	44.4	45.6	51.1	55.8	63.0	.80
33.6	34.2	34.9	35.5	36.2	36.8	37.4	38.0	38.6	39.2	40.6	41.9	43.3	44.5	45.8	46.9	52.2	56.7	63.6	.85
35.4	36.0	36.6	37.3	37.9	38.5	39.1	39.6	40.2	40.8	42.1	43.5	44.7	46.0	47.1	48.3	53.3	57.6	64.3	.90
37.2	37.8	38.4	39.0	39.6	40.1	40.7	41.3	41.8	42.4	43.7	45.0	46.2	47.4	48.5	49.6	54.5	58.6	65.0	.95
38.9	39.5	40.1	40.7	41.2	41.8	42.4	42.9	43.4	44.0	45.2	46.5	47.6	48.8	49.9	50.9	55.6	59.5	65.7	1.00
40.6	41.2	41.8	42.4	42.9	43.5	44.0	44.5	45.0	45.5	46.8	48.0	49.1	50.2	51.2	52.2	56.7	60.5	66.5	1.05
42.3	42.9	43.5	44.0	44.5	45.1	45.6	46.1	46.6	47.1	48.3	49.4	50.5	51.6	52.6	53.5	57.9	61.5	67.2	1.10
44.0	44.6	45.1	45.6	46.2	46.7	47.2	47.7	48.2	48.6	49.8	50.9	51.9	52.9	53.9	54.9	59.0	62.5	68.0	1.15
45.7	46.2	46.7	47.3	47.8	48.3	48.7	49.2	49.7	50.1	51.3	52.3	53.3	54.3	55.2	56.1	60.2	63.5	68.8	1.20
47.3	47.8	48.4	48.8	49.3	49.8	50.3	50.7	51.2	51.6	52.7	53.7	54.7	55.7	56.6	57.4	61.3	64.5	69.6	1.25
48.9	49.4	49.9	50.4	50.9	51.3	51.8	52.2	52.7	53.1	54.1	55.1	56.1	57.0	57.9	58.7	62.4	65.5	70.4	1.30
50.5	51.0	51.5	52.0	52.4	52.9	53.3	53.7	54.1	54.6	55.6	56.5	57.4	58.3	59.1	59.9	63.5	66.5	71.1	1.35
52.1	52.6	53.0	53.5	53.9	54.3	54.8	55.2	55.6	56.0	56.9	57.9	58.7	59.6	60.4	61.2	64.6	67.5	71.9	1.40
53.6	54.1	54.5	55.0	55.4	55.8	56.2	56.6	57.0	57.4	58.3	59.2	60.0	60.9	61.6	62.4	65.7	68.4	72.7	1.45
55.1	55.6	56.0	56.4	56.8	57.2	57.6	58.0	58.4	58.8	59.7	60.5	61.3	62.1	62.9	63.6	66.8	69.4	73.5	1.50
56.6	57.0	57.4	57.8	58.2	58.6	59.0	59.4	59.7	60.1	61.0	61.8	62.6	63.3	64.1	64.7	67.8	70.3	74.3	1.55
58.0	58.5	58.9	59.2	59.6	60.0	60.4	60.7	61.1	61.4	62.3	63.1	63.8	64.5	65.2	65.9	68.8	71.3	75.1	1.60
59.5	59.9	60.2	60.6	61.0	61.4	61.7	62.1	62.4	62.7	63.5	64.3	65.0	65.7	66.4	67.0	69.9	72.2	75.9	1.65
60.9	61.2	61.6	62.0	62.3	62.7	63.0	63.4	63.7	64.0	64.8	65.5	66.2	66.9	67.5	68.2	70.9	73.1	76.6	1.70
62.2	62.6	62.9	63.3	63.6	64.0	64.3	64.6	64.9	65.3	66.0	66.7	67.4	68.0	68.7	69.2	71.9	74.0	77.4	1.75
68.6	68.9	69.2	69.5	69.8	70.0	70.3	70.6	70.8	71.1	71.7	72.3	72.9	73.4	73.9	74.4	76.5	78.3	81.0	2.00
74.2	74.4	74.7	74.9	75.2	75.4	75.6	75.8	76.0	76.3	76.8	77.2	77.7	78.1	78.5	78.9	80.6	82.1	84.3	2.25
79.1	79.3	79.5	79.7	79.9	80.0	80.2	80.4	80.6	80.7	81.1	81.5	81.9	82.2	82.6	82.9	84.3	85.4	87.2	2.50
83.3	83.4	83.6	83.7	83.9	84.0	84.2	84.3	84.4	84.6	84.9	85.2	85.5	85.8	86.0	86.3	87.4	88.3	89.7	2.75
86.8	86.9	87.0	87.1	87.3	87.4	87.5	87.6	87.7	87.8	88.1	88.3	88.5	88.8	89.0	89.2	90.0	90.7	91.8	3.00
92.1	92.1	92.2	92.3	92.4	92.4	92.5	92.6	92.6	92.7	92.8	93.0	93.1	93.3	93.4	93.5	94.0	94.4	95.1	3.50
95.5	95.5	95.6	95.6	95.7	95.7	95.7	95.8	95.8	95.8	95.9	96.0	96.1	96.2	96.2	96.3	96.6	96.8	97.2	4.00
97.6	97.6	97.6	97.6	97.7	97.7	97.7	97.7	97.8	97.8	97.8	97.9	97.9	97.9	98.0	98.0	98.2	98.3	98.5	4.50
98.8	98.8	98.8	98.8	98.8	98.8	98.8	98.8	98.9	98.9	98.9	98.9	98.9	99.0	99.0	99.0	99.1	99.1	99.2	5.00

STANDARD DEVIATION TIMES SQUARE ROOT OF TIME

APPENDIX TABLE 7

Hedge ratios for call options, percent of share price

SHARE PRICE DIVIDED BY PV (EXERCISE PRICE)

	.40	.45	.50	.55	.60	.65	.70	.75	.80	.82	.84	.86	.88	.90	.92	.94	.96	.98	1.00
.05	.0	.0	.0	.0	.0	.0	.0	.0	.0	.0	.0	.1	.6	1.9	5.0	11.3	21.4	35.2	51.0
.10	.0	.0	.0	.0	.0	.0	.0	.2	1.5	2.7	4.5	7.2	11.0	15.8	21.7	28.5	36.0	44.0	52.0
.15	.0	.0	.0	.0	.0	.3	1.1	3.3	7.9	10.6	13.8	17.6	21.9	26.5	31.5	36.8	42.2	47.6	53.0
.20	.0	.0	.0	.2	.7	2.0	4.6	9.0	15.5	18.6	22.0	25.7	29.5	33.5	37.6	41.7	45.9	50.0	54.0
.25	.0	.1	.4	1.2	2.8	5.5	9.7	15.3	22.1	25.2	28.4	31.6	35.0	38.3	41.7	45.1	48.5	51.8	55.0
.30	.2	.6	1.5	3.3	6.0	9.9	14.9	20.9	27.6	30.4	33.3	36.2	39.1	42.0	44.9	47.8	50.6	53.3	56.0
.35	.7	1.8	3.6	6.3	9.9	14.6	19.9	25.9	32.2	34.8	37.3	39.9	42.5	45.0	47.5	49.9	52.3	54.7	56.9
.40	1.8	3.6	6.3	9.8	14.1	19.0	24.5	30.2	36.0	38.4	40.7	43.0	45.2	47.5	49.7	51.8	53.9	55.9	57.9
.45	3.5	6.1	9.4	13.5	18.1	23.2	28.5	33.9	39.3	41.4	43.5	45.6	47.6	49.6	51.6	53.5	55.3	57.1	58.9
.50	5.7	8.9	12.8	17.2	22.0	27.0	32.2	37.2	42.2	44.2	46.1	47.9	49.8	51.6	53.3	55.0	56.7	58.3	59.9
.55	8.2	12.0	16.2	20.8	25.7	30.6	35.4	40.2	44.8	46.6	48.3	50.0	51.7	53.3	54.9	56.5	58.0	59.4	60.8
.60	11.0	15.1	19.6	24.3	29.1	33.8	38.4	42.9	47.1	48.8	50.4	51.9	53.5	55.0	56.4	57.8	59.2	60.5	61.8
.65	13.9	18.3	22.9	27.6	32.2	36.8	41.1	45.3	49.3	50.8	52.3	53.7	55.1	56.5	57.8	59.1	60.3	61.6	62.7
.70	16.9	21.5	26.1	30.7	35.2	39.5	43.7	47.6	51.2	52.7	54.0	55.4	56.6	57.9	59.1	60.3	61.5	62.6	63.7
.75	19.9	24.5	29.1	33.6	38.0	42.1	46.0	49.7	53.1	54.4	55.7	56.9	58.1	59.3	60.4	61.5	62.6	63.6	64.6
.80	22.8	27.5	32.0	36.4	40.6	44.5	48.2	51.6	54.8	56.0	57.2	58.4	59.5	60.6	61.6	62.7	63.6	64.6	65.5
.85	25.7	30.3	34.8	39.0	43.0	46.7	50.2	53.4	56.5	57.6	58.7	59.8	60.8	61.8	62.8	63.8	64.7	65.6	66.5
.90	28.5	33.1	37.4	41.5	45.3	48.9	52.1	55.2	58.0	59.1	60.1	61.1	62.1	63.0	64.0	64.8	65.7	66.6	67.4
.95	31.2	35.7	40.0	43.9	47.5	50.9	54.0	56.8	59.5	60.5	61.5	62.4	63.3	64.2	65.1	65.9	66.7	67.5	68.3
1.00	33.9	38.3	42.3	46.1	49.6	52.8	55.7	58.4	60.9	61.9	62.8	63.7	64.5	65.3	66.2	66.9	67.7	68.4	69.1
1.05	36.4	40.7	44.6	48.2	51.5	54.6	57.4	59.9	62.3	63.2	64.0	64.9	65.7	66.4	67.2	67.9	68.7	69.3	70.0
1.10	38.9	43.0	46.8	50.3	53.4	56.3	58.9	61.4	63.6	64.4	65.2	66.0	66.8	67.5	68.2	68.9	69.6	70.3	70.9
1.15	41.2	45.2	48.9	52.2	55.2	57.9	60.4	62.7	64.8	65.6	66.4	67.1	67.9	68.6	69.2	69.9	70.5	71.1	71.7
1.20	43.5	47.4	50.9	54.1	56.9	59.5	61.9	64.1	66.1	66.8	67.5	68.2	68.9	69.6	70.2	70.8	71.4	72.0	72.6
1.25	45.7	49.4	52.8	55.8	58.6	61.0	63.3	65.4	67.2	67.9	68.6	69.3	69.9	70.6	71.2	71.8	72.3	72.9	73.4
1.30	47.8	51.4	54.6	57.5	60.1	62.5	64.6	66.6	68.4	69.1	69.7	70.3	70.9	71.5	72.1	72.7	73.2	73.7	74.2
1.35	49.9	53.3	56.4	59.2	61.7	63.9	65.9	67.8	69.5	70.1	70.7	71.3	71.9	72.5	73.0	73.5	74.0	74.5	75.0
1.40	51.8	55.2	58.1	60.8	63.1	65.3	67.2	69.0	70.6	71.2	71.8	72.3	72.9	73.4	73.9	74.4	74.9	75.4	75.8
1.45	53.7	56.9	59.8	62.3	64.5	66.6	68.4	70.1	71.6	72.2	72.7	73.3	73.8	74.3	74.8	75.2	75.7	76.1	76.6
1.50	55.5	58.6	61.3	63.7	65.9	67.8	69.6	71.2	72.6	73.2	73.7	74.2	74.7	75.2	75.6	76.1	76.5	76.9	77.3
1.55	57.3	60.3	62.8	65.1	67.2	69.0	70.7	72.2	73.6	74.1	74.6	75.1	75.6	76.0	76.5	76.9	77.3	77.7	78.1
1.60	59.0	61.8	64.3	66.5	68.5	70.2	71.8	73.2	74.6	75.0	75.5	76.0	76.4	76.9	77.3	77.7	78.1	78.4	78.8
1.65	60.6	63.3	65.7	67.8	69.7	71.4	72.9	74.2	75.5	76.0	76.4	76.8	77.3	77.7	78.1	78.5	78.8	79.2	79.5
1.70	62.2	64.8	67.1	69.1	70.9	72.5	73.9	75.2	76.4	76.8	77.3	77.7	78.1	78.5	78.8	79.2	79.6	79.9	80.2
1.75	63.7	66.2	68.4	70.3	72.0	73.5	74.9	76.1	77.3	77.7	78.1	78.5	78.9	79.2	79.6	79.9	80.3	80.6	80.9
2.00	70.6	72.6	74.3	75.8	77.2	78.4	79.4	80.4	81.3	81.6	81.9	82.2	82.5	82.8	83.1	83.4	83.6	83.9	84.1
2.25	76.4	77.9	79.3	80.5	81.5	82.5	83.3	84.1	84.8	85.0	85.3	85.5	85.7	86.0	86.2	86.4	86.6	86.8	87.0
2.50	81.2	82.4	83.5	84.4	85.2	85.9	86.6	87.2	87.7	87.9	88.1	88.3	88.5	88.6	88.8	89.0	89.1	89.3	89.4
2.75	85.1	86.1	86.9	87.6	88.3	88.8	89.3	89.8	90.2	90.4	90.5	90.7	90.8	90.9	91.1	91.2	91.3	91.4	91.5
3.00	88.4	89.1	89.8	90.3	90.8	91.3	91.6	92.0	92.3	92.4	92.5	92.6	92.7	92.9	93.0	93.0	93.1	93.2	93.3
3.50	93.2	93.6	94.0	94.3	94.6	94.8	95.0	95.2	95.4	95.5	95.5	95.6	95.7	95.7	95.8	95.8	95.9	95.9	96.0
4.00	96.2	96.4	96.6	96.8	96.9	97.1	97.2	97.3	97.4	97.4	97.5	97.5	97.5	97.6	97.6	97.6	97.7	97.7	97.7
4.50	98.0	98.1	98.2	98.3	98.4	98.4	98.5	98.6	98.6	98.6	98.6	98.7	98.7	98.7	98.7	98.7	98.7	98.8	98.8
5.00	99.0	99.0	99.1	99.1	99.2	99.2	99.2	99.3	99.3	99.3	99.3	99.3	99.3	99.3	99.3	99.4	99.4	99.4	99.4

STANDARD DEVIATION TIMES SQUARE ROOT OF TIME

Note: Based on Black-Scholes model. Subtract 1.0 to obtain corresponding hedge ratios for European puts.

SHARE PRICE DIVIDED BY PV (EXERCISE PRICE)

1.02	1.04	1.06	1.08	1.10	1.12	1.14	1.16	1.18	1.20	1.25	1.30	1.35	1.40	1.45	1.50	1.75	2.00	2.50	
66.3	79.1	88.3	94.1	97.3	98.9	99.6	99.9	100.	100.	100.	100.	100.	100.	100.	100.	100.	100.	100.	.05
59.8	67.1	73.7	79.4	84.2	88.2	91.3	93.8	95.6	96.9	98.9	99.6	99.9	100.	100.	100.	100.	100.	100.	.10
58.2	63.2	67.8	72.2	76.1	79.7	82.9	85.6	88.1	90.2	94.1	96.6	98.1	99.0	99.5	99.7	100.	100.	100.	.15
57.9	61.6	65.2	68.6	71.8	74.8	77.5	80.0	82.3	84.4	88.8	92.1	94.5	96.3	97.5	98.3	99.8	100.	100.	.20
58.1	61.1	64.0	66.7	69.4	71.8	74.2	76.4	78.4	80.4	84.6	88.0	90.7	92.9	94.6	96.0	99.1	99.8	100.	.25
58.6	61.1	63.5	65.8	68.0	70.1	72.1	74.0	75.9	77.6	81.4	84.7	87.5	89.8	91.8	93.3	97.8	99.3	99.9	.30
59.2	61.3	63.4	65.4	67.3	69.1	70.9	72.5	74.1	75.7	79.2	82.2	84.9	87.2	89.2	90.9	96.2	98.4	99.7	.35
59.9	61.7	63.5	65.3	66.9	68.6	70.1	71.6	73.0	74.4	77.6	80.4	82.9	85.1	87.1	88.8	94.5	97.3	99.4	.40
60.6	62.3	63.9	65.4	66.9	68.3	69.7	71.0	72.3	73.6	76.5	79.0	81.4	83.5	85.3	87.0	92.9	96.1	98.8	.45
61.4	62.9	64.3	65.7	67.0	68.3	69.6	70.8	71.9	73.1	75.7	78.1	80.2	82.2	84.0	85.6	91.5	94.9	98.1	.50
62.2	63.5	64.8	66.1	67.3	68.5	69.6	70.7	71.8	72.8	75.2	77.4	79.4	81.2	82.9	84.4	90.2	93.8	97.4	.55
63.0	64.3	65.4	66.6	67.7	68.8	69.8	70.8	71.8	72.7	74.9	77.0	78.8	80.5	82.1	83.5	89.1	92.7	96.6	.60
63.9	65.0	66.1	67.1	68.1	69.1	70.1	71.0	71.9	72.8	74.8	76.7	78.4	80.0	81.5	82.9	88.2	91.8	95.9	.65
64.7	65.8	66.8	67.7	68.7	69.6	70.4	71.3	72.1	72.9	74.8	76.6	78.2	79.7	81.1	82.4	87.5	91.0	95.1	.70
65.6	66.5	67.5	68.4	69.2	70.1	70.9	71.7	72.4	73.2	74.9	76.6	78.1	79.5	80.8	82.0	86.9	90.3	94.5	.75
66.4	67.3	68.2	69.0	69.8	70.6	71.4	72.1	72.8	73.5	75.1	76.7	78.1	79.4	80.6	81.8	86.4	89.7	93.9	.80
67.3	68.1	68.9	69.7	70.4	71.2	71.9	72.6	73.2	73.9	75.4	76.8	78.2	79.4	80.6	81.6	86.1	89.3	93.4	.85
68.2	68.9	69.7	70.4	71.1	71.8	72.4	73.1	73.7	74.3	75.7	77.1	78.3	79.5	80.6	81.6	85.8	88.9	92.9	.90
69.0	69.7	70.4	71.1	71.7	72.4	73.0	73.6	74.2	74.8	76.1	77.4	78.5	79.6	80.7	81.6	85.6	88.6	92.5	.95
69.8	70.5	71.2	71.8	72.4	73.0	73.6	74.2	74.7	75.2	76.5	77.7	78.8	79.9	80.8	81.7	85.5	88.4	92.2	1.00
70.7	71.3	71.9	72.5	73.1	73.7	74.2	74.7	75.3	75.8	77.0	78.1	79.1	80.1	81.0	81.9	85.5	88.2	91.9	1.05
71.5	72.1	72.7	73.2	73.8	74.3	74.8	75.3	75.8	76.3	77.4	78.5	79.5	80.4	81.3	82.1	85.5	88.1	91.7	1.10
72.3	72.9	73.4	74.0	74.5	75.0	75.5	75.9	76.4	76.8	77.9	78.9	79.8	80.7	81.5	82.3	85.6	88.1	91.5	1.15
73.1	73.7	74.2	74.7	75.2	75.6	76.1	76.5	77.0	77.4	78.4	79.4	80.2	81.1	81.8	82.6	85.7	88.1	91.4	1.20
73.9	74.4	74.9	75.4	75.8	76.3	76.7	77.1	77.6	78.0	78.9	79.8	80.7	81.4	82.2	82.9	85.8	88.1	91.3	1.25
74.7	75.2	75.6	76.1	76.5	76.9	77.4	77.8	78.2	78.5	79.4	80.3	81.1	81.8	82.5	83.2	86.0	88.2	91.2	1.30
75.5	75.9	76.4	76.8	77.2	77.6	78.0	78.4	78.7	79.1	80.0	80.8	81.5	82.2	82.9	83.5	86.2	88.3	91.2	1.35
76.2	76.7	77.1	77.5	77.9	78.3	78.6	79.0	79.3	79.7	80.5	81.3	82.0	82.6	83.3	83.9	86.4	88.4	91.2	1.40
77.0	77.4	77.8	78.2	78.5	78.9	79.3	79.6	79.9	80.3	81.0	81.8	82.4	83.1	83.7	84.2	86.7	88.6	91.3	1.45
77.7	78.1	78.5	78.9	79.2	79.5	79.9	80.2	80.5	80.8	81.6	82.2	82.9	83.5	84.1	84.6	86.9	88.7	91.3	1.50
78.5	78.8	79.2	79.5	79.9	80.2	80.5	80.8	81.1	81.4	82.1	82.7	83.4	83.9	84.5	85.0	87.2	88.9	91.4	1.55
79.2	79.5	79.9	80.2	80.5	80.8	81.1	81.4	81.7	82.0	82.6	83.2	83.8	84.4	84.9	85.4	87.5	89.1	91.5	1.60
79.9	80.2	80.5	80.8	81.1	81.4	81.7	82.0	82.3	82.5	83.2	83.7	84.3	84.8	85.3	85.8	87.8	89.3	91.6	1.65
80.6	80.9	81.2	81.5	81.8	82.0	82.3	82.6	82.8	83.1	83.7	84.2	84.8	85.3	85.7	86.2	88.1	89.6	91.8	1.70
81.2	81.5	81.8	82.1	82.4	82.6	82.9	83.1	83.4	83.6	84.2	84.7	85.2	85.7	86.2	86.6	88.4	89.8	91.9	1.75
84.4	84.6	84.8	85.0	85.3	85.5	85.7	85.9	86.1	86.2	86.7	87.1	87.5	87.9	88.2	88.5	90.0	91.1	92.8	2.00
87.2	87.3	87.5	87.7	87.8	88.0	88.2	88.3	88.5	88.6	89.0	89.3	89.6	89.9	90.1	90.4	91.5	92.4	93.7	2.25
89.6	89.7	89.9	90.0	90.1	90.2	90.4	90.5	90.6	90.7	91.0	91.2	91.5	91.7	91.9	92.1	93.0	93.7	94.7	2.50
91.7	91.8	91.9	92.0	92.1	92.2	92.3	92.3	92.4	92.5	92.7	92.9	93.1	93.3	93.4	93.6	94.3	94.8	95.6	2.75
93.4	93.5	93.6	93.6	93.7	93.8	93.9	93.9	94.0	94.1	94.2	94.4	94.5	94.7	94.8	94.9	95.4	95.8	96.4	3.00
96.0	96.1	96.1	96.2	96.2	96.3	96.3	96.3	96.4	96.4	96.5	96.6	96.7	96.8	96.8	96.9	97.2	97.4	97.8	3.50
97.8	97.8	97.8	97.8	97.9	97.9	97.9	97.9	97.9	98.0	98.0	98.1	98.1	98.1	98.2	98.2	98.4	98.5	98.7	4.00
98.8	98.8	98.8	98.8	98.8	98.9	98.9	98.9	98.9	98.9	98.9	99.0	99.0	99.0	99.0	99.0	99.1	99.2	99.3	4.50
99.4	99.4	99.4	99.4	99.4	99.4	99.4	99.4	99.4	99.4	99.5	99.5	99.5	99.5	99.5	99.5	99.5	99.6	99.6	5.00

STANDARD DEVIATION TIMES SQUARE ROOT OF TIME

Glossary

Accelerated depreciation Any depreciation method that produces larger deductions for depreciation in the early years of a project's life; e.g., *double-declining-balance depreciation, sum-of-the-years'-digits depreciation.**

Accounts payable (*payables, trade debt*) Money owed to suppliers.

Accounts receivable (*receivables, trade credit*) Money owed by customers.

Accrued-benefit cost method Method for estimating the *normal costs* of a pension plan. Its principle is that the company should contribute each year the present value of any benefits that have accrued (cf. *level cost method*).

Accrued interest Interest that has been earned but not yet paid.

Acid-test ratio *Quick ratio.*

Adjusted present value (*APV*) *Net present value* of an asset if financed solely by equity, plus the present value of any financing side effects.

Adverse selection A situation in which a pricing policy causes only the least desirable customers to do business, e.g., a rise in insurance prices that leads only the least-good risks to buy insurance.

Agency theory Theory concerning the relationship between a principal, e.g., a shareholder, and an agent of the principal, e.g., the company's manager.

Aging schedule Record of the length of time that *accounts receivable* have been outstanding.

AIBD Association of International Bond Dealers.

All-or-none underwriting The security issue is canceled if the *underwriter* is unable to resell the entire issue.

American option Option that can be exercised any time before the final exercise date (cf. *European option*).

Amortization (1) Repayment of a loan by installments; (2) allowance for depreciation.

* Italicized words are defined elsewhere in the glossary.

Annuity Investment that produces a level stream of cash flows for a limited number of periods.

Anticipation Arrangements whereby customers who pay before the final date may be entitled to deduct a normal rate of interest.

Appropriation request Formal request for funds for a capital investment project.

APV *Adjusted present value.*

Arbitrage Purchase of one security and simultaneous sale of another to give a risk-free profit. "Arbitrage" or "risk arbitrage" often used loosely to describe the taking of positions in related securities, e.g., at the time of a takeover bid.

ATS accounts Automatic transfer from savings to demand deposit accounts.

Auction-rate preferred A variant of *floating-rate preferred stock* where the dividend is reset every 49 days by auction.

Authorized share capital Maximum number of shares that a company can issue, as specified in the firm's articles of incorporation.

Availability float Checks deposited by a company that have not yet been cleared.

Aval Bank guarantee for debt purchased by *forfaiter.*

BA *Banker's acceptance.*

Balloon payment Large final payment (e.g., when a loan is repaid in installments).

Banker's acceptance (*BA*) Written demand that has been accepted by a bank to pay a given sum at a future date (cf. *trade acceptance*).

Basis point .01 percent.

Bear market Widespread decline in security prices (cf. *bull market*).

Bearer security Security for which primary evidence of ownership is possession of the certificate (cf. *registered security*).

Benefit-cost ratio *Profitability index.*

Best-efforts underwriting *Underwriters* do not commit themselves to selling a security issue but promise only to use best efforts.

Beta Measure of *market risk*.

Bill of exchange General term for a document demanding payment.

Bill of lading Document establishing ownership of goods in transit.

Blue-chip company Large and creditworthy company.

Blue-sky laws State laws covering the issue and trading of securities.

Boilerplate Standard terms and conditions, e.g., in a debt contract.

Bond Long-term debt.

BONUS (borrowers' options for notes and underwriting facilities) A borrowing facility that allows the firm to issue either euronotes or U.S. domestic debt. Also called *global note facility*.

Bracket A term signifying the extent of an *underwriter's* commitment in a new issue, e.g., major bracket, minor bracket.

Break-even analysis Analysis of the level of sales at which a project would just break even.

Bridging loan Short-term loan to provide temporary financing until more permanent financing is arranged.

Bull FRN *Reverse FRN*.

Bull-bear bonds *Bonds* whose principal repayment is linked to the price of another security. The bonds are issued in two tranches: In the first the repayment increases with the price of the other security; in the second the repayment decreases with the price of the other security.

Bulldog bond *Foreign bond* issue made in London.

Bullet payment Single final payment, e.g., of a loan (in contrast to payment in installments).

Bull market Widespread rise in security prices (cf. *bear market*).

Bunny bonds *Multiplier bonds*.

Buy-back *Repurchase agreement*.

Call option Option to buy an asset at a specified *exercise price* on or before a specified exercise date (cf. *put option*).

Call premium (1) Difference between the price at which a company can call its *bonds* and their *face value;* (2) price of an option.

Cap An upper limit on the interest rate on a *floating-rate note*.

Capital budget List of planned investment projects, usually prepared annually.

Capital lease *Financial lease*.

Capital market Financial market (particularly the market for long-term securities).

Capital rationing Shortage of funds that forces a company to choose between projects.

Capital structure Mix of different securities issued by a firm.

Capitalization Long-term debt, *preferred stock*, plus *net worth*.

CARs (Certificates of Automobile Receivables) *Pass-through* securities backed by automobile *receivables*.

CARDs (Certificates for Amortizing Revolving Debt) *Pass-through* securities backed by credit card *receivables*.

Career-average plan Pension plan offering a pension that depends on the employee's average compensation during his or her years of membership (cf. *final average plan*).

Cash and carry Purchase of a security and the simultaneous sale of a *future,* with the balance being financed with a loan or *repo*.

Cash budget Forecast of sources and uses of cash.

Cash-deficiency arrangement Arrangement whereby a project's shareholders agree to provide the operating company with sufficient *net working capital*.

CAT A U.S. Treasury *bond* reissued by Salomon Brothers as a series of *zero coupon bonds*.

CD *Certificate of deposit*.

CEDEL A centralized clearing system for *eurobonds*. Also *Euroclear*.

Certificate of Deposit (*CD*) A certificate providing evidence of a bank time deposit.

Closed-end mortgage Mortgage against which no additional debt may be issued. (cf. *open-end mortgage*)

Collar An upper and lower limit on the interest rate on a *floating-rate note*.

Collateral Assets that are given as security for a loan.

Collateral trust bonds *Bonds* secured by common stocks that are owned by the borrower.

Collection float Checks written by customers that have not been received, deposited, and added to the company's available balance. (cf. *payment float*)

Commercial draft (*bill of exchange*) Demand for payment.

Commercial paper Unsecured *notes* issued by companies and maturing within 9 months.

Compensating balance Non-interest-bearing demand deposits to compensate banks for bank loans or services.

Competitive bidding Means by which public utility *holding companies* are required to choose their *underwriter* (cf. *negotiated underwriting*).

Completion bonding   Insurance that a construction contract will be successfully completed.

Compound interest   Reinvestment of each interest payment on money invested, to earn more interest (cf. *simple interest*).

Concentration banking   System whereby customers make payments to a regional collection center. The collection center pays the funds into a regional bank account and surplus money is transferred to the company's principal bank.

Conditional sales   Sales in which ownership does not pass to the buyer until payment is completed.

Conglomerate merger   *Merger* between two companies in unrelated businesses (cf. *horizontal merger, vertical merger*).

Consol   Name of a perpetual *bond* issued by the British government. Sometimes used as a general term for *perpetuity*.

Contingent project   Project that cannot be undertaken unless another project is also undertaken.

Continuous compounding   Interest compounded continuously rather than at fixed intervals.

Controller   Officer responsible for budgeting, accounting, and auditing in a firm (cf. *treasurer*).

Conversion price   *Par value* of a *convertible security* divided by the number of shares into which it may be exchanged.

Conversion ratio   Number of shares for which a *convertible security* may be exchanged.

Convertible security   *Bond* or *preferred stock* that may be converted into another security at the holder's option.

Correlation coefficient   Measure of the closeness of the relationship between two variables.

Cost company arrangement   Arrangement whereby the shareholders of a project receive output free of charge but agree to pay all operating and financing charges of the project.

Cost of capital   *Opportunity cost of capital.*

Coupon   (1) Specifically, a coupon attached to the certificate of a *bearer bond* that must be surrendered to collect interest payment. (2) More generally, interest payment on debt.

Covariance   Measure of the comovement between two variables.

Covenant   Clause in a loan agreement.

Credit scoring   A procedure for assigning scores to companies on the basis of the risk of default.

Cross-default clause   Clause in a loan agreement stating that the company is in default if it fails to meet its obligation on any other debt issue.

Cum dividend   *With dividend.*

Cum rights   *With rights.*

Cumulative preferred stock   Stock which takes priority over common stock in regard to dividend payments. Dividends may not be paid on the common stock until all past *dividends* on the *preferred stock* have been paid.

Cumulative voting   A stockholder may cast all his or her votes for one candidate for the board of directors (cf. *majority voting*).

Current asset   Asset that will normally be turned into cash within a year.

Current liability   Liability that will normally be repaid within a year.

Current ratio   *Current assets* divided by *current liabilities*—a measure of liquidity.

DCF   *Discounted cash flow.*

Debenture   Unsecured *bond.*

Decision tree   Method of representing alternative sequential decisions and the possible outcomes from these decisions.

Dedicated portfolio   *Bond* portfolio that provides the cash flows to meet a series of fixed pension obligations at minimum cost.

Defeasance   Borrower sets aside cash or *bonds* sufficient to service the borrower's debt. Both the borrower's debt and the offsetting cash or bonds are removed from the balance sheet.

Delta   *Hedge ratio.*

Depository transfer check   Check made out directly by a local bank to a particular company.

Depreciation   (1) Reduction in the book or market value of an asset. (2) Portion of an investment that can be deducted from taxable income.

Dilution   Diminution in the proportion of income to which each share is entitled.

Direct lease   *Lease* in which the *lessor* purchases new equipment from the manufacturer and leases it to the *lessee* (cf. *sale and lease-back*).

Discount bond   Debt sold for less than its *principal* value. If a discount bond pays no interest, it is called a "pure" discount bond.

Discount factor   *Present value* of $1 received at stated future date.

Discount rate   Rate used to calculate the *present value* of future cash flows.

Discounted cash flow   Future cash flows multiplied by *discount factors* to obtain *present value.*

Disintermediation   Withdrawal of funds from a financial institution in order to invest them directly (cf. *intermediation*).

Dividend   Payment by a company to its stockholders.

Dividend yield   Annual *dividend* divided by share price.

Dollar-weighted rate of return   *Internal rate of return* (cf. *time-weighted rate of return*).

Double-declining-balance depreciation Method of *accelerated depreciation*.

Double tax agreement   Agreement between two countries that taxes paid abroad can be offset against domestic taxes levied on foreign *dividends*.

Drop lock   An arrangement whereby the interest rate on a *floating-rate note* or *preferred* becomes fixed if it falls to a specified level.

Dual currency bond   *Bond* with interest paid in one currency and *principal* paid in another.

Duration   The average time to an asset's *discounted cash flows*.

EBIT   Earnings before interest and taxes.

Economic income   Cash flow plus change in *present value*.

Economic rents   Profits in excess of the competitive level.

ECU   *European Currency Unit.*

Efficient market   Market in which security prices reflect information instantaneously.

Efficient portfolio   Portfolio that offers the lowest risk (*standard deviation*) for its *expected return* and the highest expected return for its level of risk.

Employee Stock Ownership Plan (*ESOP*)   Companies contribute to a trust fund that buys stock on behalf of employees.

EPS   Earnings per share.

Equipment trust certificate   Form of *secured debt* generally used to finance railroad equipment. The trustee retains ownership of the equipment until the debt is repaid.

Equity   (1) Common stock and *preferred stock*. Often used to refer to common stock only. (2) *Net worth*.

Equivalent annual cash flow   *Annuity* with the same *net present value* as the company's proposed investment.

ERISA   Employee Retirement Income Security Act.

ESOP   *Employee stock ownership plan.*

Eurobond   *Bond* that is marketed internationally.

Euroclear   A centralized clearing system for *eurobonds*. Also *CEDEL*.

Eurodollar deposit   Dollar deposit with a bank outside the United States.

European Currency Unit (*ECU*)   A basket of different European currencies.

European option   Option that can be exercised only on final exercise date (cf. *American option*).

Evergreen credit   *Revolving credit* without maturity.

Exchange of assets   Acquisition of another company by purchase of its assets in exchange for cash or shares.

Exchange of stock   Acquisition of another company by the purchase of its stock in exchange for cash or shares.

Ex dividend   Purchase of shares in which the buyer is not entitled to the *dividend* (cf. *with dividend, cum dividend*).

Ex rights   Purchase of shares in which the buyer is not entitled to the rights to buy shares in the company's *rights issue*   (cf. *with rights, cum rights, rights on*).

Exercise price (*striking price*)   Price at which a *call option* or *put option* may be exercised.

Expected return   Average of possible returns weighted by their probabilities.

Experience losses   In a pension plan, losses resulting from any difference between expectations and experience (e.g., a decline in the value of the pension fund's securities).

Extendable bond   Bond whose maturity can be extended at the option of the lender (or issuer).

External finance   Finance that is not generated by the firm: new borrowing or an issue of stock (cf. *internal finance*).

Extra dividend   *Dividend* that may or may not be repeated (cf. *regular dividend*).

Face value   *Par value.*

Factoring   Arrangement whereby a financial institution buys a company's *accounts receivable* and collects the debt.

FASB   Financial Accounting Standards Board.

FCIA   Foreign Credit Insurance Association.

FDIC   Federal Deposit Insurance Corporation.

Federal funds   Non-interest-bearing deposits by banks at the Federal Reserve. Excess reserves are lent by banks to each other.

Field warehouse   Warehouse rented by a warehouse company on another firm's premises (cf. *public warehouse*).

Final-average plan   Pension plan offering a pension that depends on the employee's average compensation in his or her final years of service (cf. *career-average plan*).

Financial assets   Claims on *real assets*.

Financial lease (*capital lease, full-payout lease*) Long-term, noncancelable *lease* (cf. *operating lease*).

Financial leverage (*gearing*)   Use of debt to increase the *expected return* on *equity*. Financial leverage is measured by the ratio of debt to debt plus equity (cf. *operating leverage*).

Fiscal agency agreement   An alternative to a bond *trust deed*. Unlike the trustee, the fiscal agent acts as an agent of the borrower.

Flip-flop note   *Note* which allows investors to switch backwards and forwards between two different types of debt.

Float   See *availability float, payment float*.

Floating lien   General *lien* against a company's assets or against a particular class of assets.

Floating-rate note (*FRN*)   *Note* whose interest payment varies with the short-term interest rate.

Floating-rate preferred   *Preferred stock* paying dividends which vary with short-term interest rates.

Floor planning   Arrangement used to finance inventory. A finance company buys the inventory, which is then held in trust by the user.

Foreign bond   A bond issued on the domestic *capital market* of another country.

Forex   Foreign exchange.

Forfaiting   Purchase of promises-to-pay (e.g., *bills of exchange* or *promissory notes*) issued by importers.

Forward cover   Purchase or sale of forward foreign currency in order to offset a known future cash flow.

Forward exchange rate   Exchange rate fixed today for exchanging currency at some future date (cf. *spot exchange rate*).

Forward interest rate   Interest rate fixed today on a loan to be made at some future date (cf. *spot interest rate*).

Forward rate agreement (*FRA*)   Agreement to borrow or lend at a specified future date at an interest rate that is fixed today.

FRA   *Forward rate agreement*.

Free cash flow   Cash not required for operations or reinvestment.

FRN   *Floating rate notes*.

Full-payout lease   *Financial lease*.

Full-service lease (*rental lease*)   *Lease* in which the *lessor* promises to maintain and insure the equipment (cf. *net lease*).

Funded debt   Debt maturing after more than 1 year (cf. *unfunded debt*).

Future   A contract to buy a commodity or security on a future date at a price that is fixed today. Unlike forward contracts futures are generally traded on organized exchanges and are *marked-to-market* daily.

Future service costs   Value of the pensions that are expected to accrue from employees' future service.

Garnishment   A procedure allowing debt to be paid off by deductions from the debtor's wages.

Gearing   *Financial leverage*.

General cash offer   Issue of securities offered to all investors (cf. *rights issue*).

Global Note Facility   BONUS.

Golden parachute   A large termination payment due to a company's management if they lose their jobs as a result of a merger.

Greenmail   A large block of stock is held by an unfriendly company, which forces the target company to repurchase the stock at a substantial premium to prevent a takeover.

Grey market   Purchases and sales of *eurobonds* that occur before the issue price is finally set.

Growth stocks   Stocks of companies that have an opportunity to invest money to earn more than the *opportunity cost of capital* (cf. *income stocks*).

Harmless warrant   *Warrant* that allows the user to purchase a *bond* only by surrendering an existing bond with similar terms.

Heaven-and-hell bonds   *Dual currency bonds* whose principal repayment is in a currency different from the interest payments. The size of the principal repayment is partially increased if the value of the currency falls, and vice versa.

Hedging   Buying one security and selling another in order to reduce risk. A perfect hedge produces a riskless portfolio.

Hedge ratio (*delta, option delta*)   The number of shares to buy for each option sold in order to create a safe position. More generally, the number of units of an asset that should be bought to hedge one unit of a liability.

Hell-or-high-water clause   Clause in a *lease* agreement that obliges the *lessee* to make payments regardless of what happens to the *lessor* or the equipment.

Holding company   Company whose sole function is to hold stock in other companies or subsidiaries.

Horizontal merger   *Merger* between two companies that manufacture similar products (cf. *vertical merger, conglomerate merger*).

Horizontal spread The simultaneous purchase and sale of two options that differ only in their exercise date (cf. *vertical spread*).

Hurdle rate Minimum acceptable rate of return on a project.

IBF *International Banking Facility.*

ICON *Indexed currency option note.*

IMM (International Monetary Market) The financial futures market within the Chicago Mercantile Exchange.

Immunization The construction of an asset and a liability that are subject to offsetting changes in value.

Income bonds *Bonds* on which interest is payable only if earned.

Income stocks Stocks with high *dividend yields* (cf. *growth stocks*).

Indenture Formal agreement, e.g., establishing the terms of a *bond* issue.

Indexed bonds *Bonds* whose payments are linked to an index, e.g., a consumer price index.

Individual Retirement Account (*IRA*) An *IRS*-approved pension plan for individuals.

Industrial revenue bond (*IRB*) Issued by local government agencies on behalf of corporations.

Intangible assets Nonmaterial assets such as technical expertise, trademarks, and patents (cf. *tangible assets*).

Integer programming Variant of *linear programming* where the solution values must be integers.

Interest cover *Times interest earned.*

Interest equalization tax Tax on foreign investment by residents of the United States (abolished 1974).

Interest-rate parity Theory that the differential between the *forward exchange rate* and the *spot exchange rate* is equal to the differential between the foreign and domestic interest rates.

Intermediation Investment through a financial institution (cf. *disintermediation*).

Internal finance Finance generated within a firm by retained earnings and *depreciation* (cf. *external finance*).

Internal rate of return (*dollar-weighted rate of return, IRR*) Discount rate at which investment has zero *net present value.*

International Banking Facility (IBF) A branch that an American bank establishes in the United States to do eurocurrency business.

Indexed currency option note A *eurobond* providing a principal repayment that is linked to the value of the bond's currency (e.g., a dollar bond whose principal repayment declines if the dollar appreciates against the yen).

Interval measure The number of days that a firm can finance operations without additional cash income.

In-the-money option An option that would be worth exercising if it expired immediately (cf. *out-of-the-money option*).

Investment banker *Underwriter.*

Investment-grade bonds *Bonds* rated Baa or above.

Investment tax credit Proportion of new capital investment that can be used to reduce a company's tax bill (abolished 1986).

IRA *Individual Retirement Account.*

IRB *Industrial revenue bond.*

IRR *Internal rate of return.*

IRS Internal Revenue Service.

Junior debt *Subordinated debt.*

Keogh plan An *IRS*-approved pension plan for the self-employed and owners of unincorporated businesses.

Lease Long-term rental agreement.

Legal capital Value at which a company's shares are recorded in its books.

Lessee User of a leased asset (cf. *lessor*).

Lessor Owner of a leased asset (cf. *lessee*).

Letter of credit Letter from a bank stating that it has established a credit in the company's favor.

Letter stock Privately placed common stock, so called because the *SEC* requires a letter from the purchaser that the stock is not intended for resale.

Level cost method (*projected-benefit cost method*) Method for estimating the *normal costs* of a pension plan. Its principle is that the company should contribute each year an equal amount per employee or an equal proportion of its wage bill (cf. *accrued-benefit cost method*).

Leverage See *financial leverage, operating leverage.*

Leveraged lease *Lease* in which the *lessor* finances part of the cost of the asset by an issue of debt secured by the asset and the lease payments.

Liabilities, total liabilities Total value of financial claims on a firm's assets. Equals (1) total assets *or* (2) total assets minus *net worth.*

LIBOR (London Interbank Offered Rate) The interest rate at which major international banks in London lend to each other. (LIBID is London Interbank Bid Rate; LIMEAN is mean of bid and offered rate).

Lien Lender's claims on specified assets.

Limited liability Limitation of a shareholder's losses to the amount invested.

Linear programming (*LP*) Technique for finding the maximum value of some equation subject to stated linear constraints.

Line of credit Agreement by a bank that a company may borrow at any time up to an established limit.

Liquid assets Assets that are easily and cheaply turned into cash—notably cash itself and short-term securities.

Liquidating dividend *Dividend* that represents a return of capital.

Liquidity premium (1) Additional return for investing in a security that cannot easily be turned into cash. (2) Difference between the *forward rate* and the expected *spot rate of interest.*

Load-to-load Arrangement whereby the customer pays for the last delivery when the next one is received.

Lock-box system Form of *concentration banking.* Customers send payments to a post office box. A local bank collects and processes the checks and transfers surplus funds to the company's principal bank.

LP *Linear programming.*

Maintenance margin Minimum margin that must be maintained on a *futures* contract.

Majority voting Voting system under which each director is voted upon separately (cf. *cumulative voting*).

Margin Cash or securities set aside by an investor as evidence that he or she can honor a commitment.

Marked-to-market An arrangement whereby the profits or losses on a *futures* contract are settled up each day.

Market capitalization rate *Expected return* on a security.

Market risk (*systematic risk*) Risk that cannot be diversified away.

Maturity factoring *Factoring* arrangement that provides collection and insurance of *accounts receivable.*

MDA *Multiple discriminant analysis.*

Merger Acquisition in which all assets and liabilities are absorbed by the buyer (cf. *exchange of assets, exchange of stock*). More generally, any combination of two companies.

Minimax bond *Floating-rate note* whose interest payments are subject to a narrow *collar.*

Mismatch bond *Floating-rate note* whose interest rate is reset at more frequent intervals than the rollover period (e.g., a note whose payments are set quarterly on the basis of the 1-year interest rate).

MMDA (money-market deposit account) In return for maintaining a minimum balance, the depositor receives both interest on the account and limited checking privileges.

Money center bank A major bank in the United States that undertakes a wide range of banking activities.

Money market Market for short-term safe investments.

Money-market fund *Mutual fund* which invests solely in short-term safe securities.

Monte Carlo simulation Method for calculating the probability distribution of possible outcomes, e.g., from a project.

Moral hazard The risk that the existence of a contract will change the behavior of one or both parties to the contract; e.g., an insured firm may take fewer fire precautions.

Mortgage bond *Bond* secured against plant and equipment.

Multiple discriminant analysis (*MDA*) Statistical technique for distinguishing between two groups on the basis of their observed characteristics.

Multiplier bonds *Bonds* that provide the option of taking the interest payment in the form of additional multiplier bonds. Also called *bunny bonds.*

Mutual fund Managed investment fund whose shares are sold to investors.

Mutually exclusive projects Two projects that cannot both be undertaken.

Naked option Option held on its own, i.e., not used to hedge a holding in the asset or other options.

NASD National Association of Security Dealers.

Negative pledge clause Clause under which the borrower agrees not to permit an exclusive *lien* on any of its assets.

Negotiated underwriting Method of choosing underwriters. Most firms may choose their *underwriter* by negotiation (cf. *competitive bidding*).

Net lease *Lease* in which the *lessee* promises to maintain and insure the equipment (cf. *full-service lease*).

Net present value A project's net contribution to wealth—*present value* minus initial investment.

Net working capital *Current assets* minus *current liabilities.*

Net worth Book value of a company's common stock, surplus, and retained earnings.

NIF   *Note issuance facility.*

Nominal interest rate   Interest rate expressed in money terms (cf. *real interest rate*).

Nonrefundable debt   Debt that may not be called in order to replace it with another issue at a lower interest cost.

Normal costs   Stream of contributions to a pension plan that is required to cover future employee service.

Normal distribution   Symmetric bell-shaped distribution that can be completely defined by its mean and *standard deviation*.

Note   Unsecured debt with a maturity of up to 10 years.

Note issuance facility (*NIF*)   In the eurocurrency market, a facility that guarantees the company the right to borrow from a group of banks up to some agreed maximum.

NOW account   "Negotiable order of withdrawal" account; a savings account that offers checking privileges.

NYSE   New York Stock Exchange.

Off-balance-sheet financing   Financing that is not shown as a liability in a company's balance sheet.

OID debt   *Original issue discount* debt.

Old-line factoring   *Factoring* arrangement that provides collection, insurance, and finance for *accounts receivable.*

Open account   Arrangement whereby sales are made with no formal debt contract. The buyer signs a receipt, and the seller records the sale in the sales ledger.

Open-end mortgage   Mortgage against which additional debt may be issued (cf. *closed-end mortgage*).

Operating lease   Short-term, cancelable *lease* (cf. *financial lease*).

Operating leverage   Fixed operating costs, so called because they accentuate variations in profits (cf. *financial leverage*).

Opportunity cost of capital (*hurdle rate, cost of capital*)   *Expected return* that is foregone by investing in a project rather than in comparable financial securities.

Option   See *call option, put option.*

Option delta   *Hedge ratio.*

Original issue discount debt (*OID debt*)   Debt that is initially offered at a price below *face value.*

Out-of-the-money option   An option that would not be worth exercising if it matured immediately (cf. *in-the-money option*).

Par value (*face value*)   Value of security shown on certificate.

Pass-through securities   *Notes* or *bonds* backed by a package of assets (e.g., mortgage pass-throughs, *CARs, CARDs*).

Payables   *Accounts payable.*

Payback period   Time taken for a project to recover its initial investment.

Payment float   Checks written by a company that have not yet cleared (cf. *availability float*).

Payout ratio   *Dividend* as a proportion of earnings per share.

PBGC   Pension Benefit Guarantee Corporation.

P/E ratio   Share price divided by earnings per share.

Perpetuity   Investment offering a level stream of cash flows in perpetuity (cf. *consol*).

PN   *Project note.*

Poison pill   An issue of securities that is convertible in the event of a merger into the shares of the acquiring firm or must be repurchased by acquiring firm.

Pooling of interest   Method of accounting for *mergers*. The consolidated balance sheet of the merged firm is obtained by combining the balance sheets of the separate firms.

Postaudit   Evaluation of an investment project after it has been undertaken.

Preemptive right   Common stockholder's right to anything of value distributed by the company.

Preferred stock   Stock that takes priority over common stock in regard to *dividends*. Dividends may not be paid on common stock unless the dividend is paid on all preferred stock (cf. *cumulative preferred stock*). The dividend rate on preferred is usually fixed at time of issue.

Present value   Discounted value of future cash flows.

Primary issue   Issue of new securities by a firm (cf. *secondary issue*).

Prime rate   Rate at which banks lend to their most favored customers.

Principal   Amount of debt that must be repaid.

Privileged subscription issue   *Rights issue.*

Production payment   Loan in the form of advance payment for future delivery of a product.

Profitability index (*benefit-cost ratio*)   Ratio of a project's *present value* to the initial investment.

Pro forma   Projected.

Project finance   Debt that is largely a claim against the cash flows from a particular project rather than against the firm as a whole.

Project note (*PN*)   *Note* issued by public housing agencies or urban renewal agencies.

Projected-benefit cost method   *Level cost method.*

Promissory note   Promise to pay.

Prospectus   Summary of the *registration* statement providing information on an issue of securities.

Proxy vote   Vote cast by one person on behalf of another.

Public warehouse (*terminal warehouse*)   Warehouse operated by an independent warehouse company on its own premises (cf. *field warehouse*).

Put option   Option to sell an asset at a specified *exercise price* on or before a specified exercise date (cf. *call option*).

q   The ratio of the market value of an asset to its replacement cost.

Quadratic programming   Variant of *linear programming* where the equations are quadratic rather than linear.

Quick ratio (*acid-test ratio*)   Measure of liquidity: (*current assets* − inventory) divided by *current liabilities.*

Real assets   *Tangible assets* and *intangible assets* used to carry on business (cf. *financial assets*).

Real interest rate   Interest rate expressed in terms of real goods, i.e., *nominal interest rate* adjusted for inflation.

Receivables   *Accounts receivable.*

Record date   Date set by directors when making dividend payment. *Dividends* are sent to stockholders who are registered on the record date.

Recourse   Term describing a type of loan. If a loan is with recourse, the lender has a general claim against the parent company if the *collateral* is insufficient to repay the debt.

Red herring   Preliminary *prospectus.*

Refunding   Replacement of existing debt with a new issue of debt.

Registered security   Security whose ownership is recorded by the company's *registrar* (cf. *bearer security*).

Registrar   Financial institution appointed to record issue and ownership of company securities.

Registration   The process of obtaining *SEC* approval for a public issue of securities.

Regression analysis   In statistics, a technique for finding the line of best fit.

Regular dividend   *Dividend* that the company expects to maintain in the future.

Regulation A issue   Security issues of under $400,000; partially exempt from *SEC registration* requirements.

Regulation Q   Limit on the rate of interest that banks may pay on (small) deposits.

Rental lease   *Full-service lease.*

Repo   *Repurchase agreement.*

Repurchase agreement (*RP, repo, buy-back*)   Purchase of Treasury securities from a securities dealer with an agreement that the dealer will repurchase them at a specified price.

Residual risk   *Unique risk.*

Retained earnings   Earnings not paid out as *dividends.*

Return on equity   Usually, equity earnings as a proportion of the book value of equity.

Return on investment (*ROI*)   Generally, book income as a proportion of net book value.

Reverse FRN (*bull FRN, yield-curve note*)   *Floating-rate note* whose payments rise as the general level of interest rates falls, and vice versa.

Revolving credit   Legally assured *line of credit* with a bank.

Revolving underwriting facility (*RUF*)   Issuance facility for short-term euronotes.

Rights issue (*privileged subscription issue*)   Issue of securities that is offered to current stockholders (cf. *general cash offer*).

Rights on   *With rights.*

Risk premium   Expected additional return for making a risky investment rather than a safe one.

ROI   *Return on investment.*

Roll-over CD   A package of successive *certificates of deposit.*

RP   *Repurchase agreement.*

R squared (R^2)   Square of the *correlation coefficient*—the proportion of the variability in one series that can be explained by the variability of one or more other series.

RUF   *Revolving underwriting facility.*

Sale and lease-back   Sale of an existing asset to a financial institution that then *leases* it back to the user (cf. *direct lease*).

Salvage value   Scrap value of plant and equipment.

Samurai bond   A yen *bond* issued in Tokyo by a non-Japanese borrower (cf. *bulldog bond, Yankee bond*).

SBIC   Small Business Investment Company.

Season datings   Extended credit for customers who order goods out of the peak season.

Seasoned issue   Issue of a security for which there is an existing market (cf. *unseasoned issue*).

SEC   Securities and Exchange Commission.

Secondary issue   Procedure for selling blocks of *seasoned issues* of stock. More generally, sale of already issued stock.

Secondary market   Market in which one can buy or sell *seasoned issues* of securities.

Secured debt   Debt which, in the event of default, has first claim on specified assets.

Securitization   Substituting tradeable securities for privately negotiated instruments.

Security market line   Line representing the relationship between *expected return* and *market risk*.

Self-liquidating loan   Loan to finance *current assets*. The sale of the current assets provides the cash to repay the loan.

Self-selection   Consequence of a contract that induces only one group (e.g., the low-risk individuals) to participate.

Semistrong-form efficient market   Market in which security prices reflect all publicly available information (cf. *weak-form efficient market* and *strong-form efficient market*).

Senior debt   Debt which, in the event of bankruptcy, must be repaid before *subordinated debt* receives any payment.

Sensitivity analysis   Analysis of the effect on project profitability of possible changes in sales, costs, and so on.

Serial bonds   Package of *bonds* that mature in successive years.

Series bond   *Bond* which may be issued in several series under the same *indenture*.

Shark repellants   Amendments to company charters intended to protect them against takeover.

Shelf registration   A procedure that allows firms to file one *registration* statement covering several issues of the same security.

Shogun bond   Dollar *bond* issued in Japan by a nonresident.

Short sale   Sale of a security that the investor does not own.

Sight draft   Demand for immediate payment (cf. *time draft*).

Signal   Action that demonstrates an individual's unobservable characteristics (because it would be unduly costly for someone without those characteristics to take the action).

Simple interest   Interest calculated only on the initial investment (cf. *compound interest*).

Simulation   *Monte Carlo simulation.*

Sinker   *Sinking fund.*

Sinking fund (*sinker*)   Fund that is established by a company to retire debt before maturity.

Skewed distribution   Probability distribution in which an unequal number of observations lie below and above the mean.

Special dividend (*extra dividend*)   *Dividend* that is unlikely to be repeated.

Specific risk   *Unique risk.*

Spot exchange rate   Exchange rate on currency for immediate delivery (cf. *forward exchange rate*).

Spot interest rate   Interest rate fixed today on a loan that is made today (cf. *forward interest rate*).

Spread (**underwriter's spread**)   Difference between the price at which an *underwriter* buys an issue from a firm and the price at which the underwriter sells it to the public.

Standard deviation   Square root of the *variance*—a measure of variability.

Standard error   In statistics, a measure of the possible error in an estimate.

Standby agreement   In a *rights issue*, agreement that the *underwriter* will purchase any stock that is not purchased by investors.

Step-up bond   *Bond* whose *coupon* is stepped up over time. (Also step-down bonds.)

Stock dividend   *Dividend* in the form of stock rather than cash.

Stock split   "Free" issue of shares to existing shareholders.

Straddle   The combination of a *put option* and a *call option* with the same exercise price.

Striking price   *Exercise price* of an *option*.

Stripped bond   A *bond* that can be subdivided into a series of *zero coupon bonds*.

Strong-form efficient market   Market in which security prices reflect instantaneously *all* information available to investors (cf. *weak-form efficient market* and *semistrong-form efficient market*).

Subordinated debt (*junior debt*)   Debt over which *senior debt* takes priority. In the event of bankruptcy, subordinated debtholders receive payment only after senior debt is paid off in full.

Sum-of-the-years'-digits depreciation   Method of *accelerated depreciation*.

Sunk costs   Costs which have been incurred and cannot be reversed.

Supermajority   A provision in a company's charter

requiring a majority of, say, 80 percent of shareholders to approve certain changes, such as a merger.

Super-NOW account Checking account with a specified minimum balance and on which interest is paid.

Supplemental liability Additional liability to a pension plan that results from an increase in promised benefits.

Sushi bond A eurobond issued by a Japanese corporation.

Swap An arrangement whereby two companies lend to each other on different terms, e.g., in different currencies, or one at a fixed rate and the other at a floating rate.

Swingline facility Bank borrowing facility to provide finance while the firm replaces U.S. *commercial paper* with eurocommerical paper.

Systematic risk *Market risk.*

Take-up fee Fee paid to *underwriters* of a *rights issue* on any stock that they are obliged to purchase.

Tangible assets Physical assets such as plant, machinery, and offices (cf. *intangible assets*).

Tax-anticipation bill Short-term bill issued by the U.S. Treasury that can be surrendered at *face value* in payment of taxes.

Tender offer General offer made directly to a firm's shareholders to buy their stock.

Tender panel Panel of underwriting banks established to bid for *notes* issued under a *note issuance facility.*

Terminal warehouse *Public warehouse.*

Term loans Medium-term, privately placed loans, usually made by banks.

Term structure of interest rates Relationship between interest rates on loans of different maturities (cf. *yield curve*).

Throughput arrangement Arrangement by which shareholders of a pipeline company agree to make sufficient use of pipeline to enable the pipeline company to service its debt.

TIGRS A U.S. Treasury *bond* reissued by Merrill Lynch as a series of *zero coupon bonds.*

Time draft Demand for payment at a stated future date (cf. *sight draft*).

Times interest earned (*interest cover*) Earnings before interest and tax, divided by interest payments.

Time-weighted rate of return Rate of return that gives equal weight to each time period; used in investment performance measurement (cf. *dollar-weighted rate of return*).

Tombstone Advertisement listing the *underwriters* to a security issue.

Trade acceptance Written demand that has been accepted by an industrial company to pay a given sum at a future date (cf. *banker's acceptance*).

Trade credit *Accounts receivable.*

Trade debt *Accounts payable.*

Transfer agent Individual or institution appointed by a company to look after the transfer of securities.

Treasurer Principal financial manager (cf. *controller*).

Treasury bill Short-term discount debt maturing in less than 1 year, issued regularly by the government.

Treasury stock Common stock that has been repurchased by the company and held in the company's treasury.

Trust deed Agreement between trustee and borrower setting out terms of *bond.*

Trust receipt Receipt for goods that are to be held in trust for the lender.

Underpricing Issue of securities below their market value.

Underwriter (*investment banker*) Firm which buys an issue of securities from a company and resells it to investors.

Unfunded debt Debt maturing within 1 year (cf. *funded debt*).

Unique risk (*residual risk, specific risk, unsystematic risk*) Risk that can be eliminated by diversification.

Unseasoned issue Issue of a security for which there is no existing market (cf. *seasoned issue*).

Unsystematic risk *Unique risk.*

Value additivity Rule that the value of the whole must equal the sum of the values of the parts.

Variance Mean squared deviation from the expected value—a measure of variability.

Variation margin The daily gains or losses on a *futures* contract that are credited to the investor's margin account.

Venture capital Capital to finance a new firm.

Vertical merger *Merger* between a supplier and its customer (cf. *horizontal merger, conglomerate merger*).

Vertical spread The simultaneous purchase and sale of two options that differ only in their exercise price (cf. *horizontal spread*).

Vesting Employee's entitlement to a part or all of a pension if he or she leaves before retirement.

Warehouse receipt Evidence that a firm owns goods stored in a warehouse.

Warrant Long-term *call option* issued by a company.

Weak-form efficient market   Market in which security prices instantaneously reflect the information in the past history of security prices. In such a market security prices follow a random walk (cf. *semistrong-form efficient market* and *strong-form efficient market*).

Weighted-average cost of capital   *Expected return* on a portfolio of all the firm's securities. Used as *hurdle rate* for capital investment.

White knight   A friendly potential acquirer sought out by a target company threatened by a less welcome suitor.

With dividend (*cum dividend*)   Term describing a purchase of shares by which the buyer is entitled to the forthcoming *dividend* (cf. *ex dividend*).

With rights (*cum rights, rights on*)   Purchase of shares in which the buyer is entitled to the rights to buy shares in the company's *rights issue* (cf. *ex rights*).

Withholding tax   Tax levied on *dividends* paid abroad.

Working capital   *Current assets* and *current liabilities*. The term is commonly used as synonymous with *net working capital*.

Writer   *Option* seller.

Yankee bond   A dollar *bond* issued in the United States by a non-U.S. borrower (cf. *bulldog bond, Samurai bond*).

Yield curve   *Term structure of interest rates.*

Yield-curve note   *Reverse FRN.*

Yield to maturity   *Internal rate of return* on a *bond.*

Zero coupon bond   *Discount bond* making no *coupon* payments.

Answers to Quizzes

Chapter 1

1. (a) Real
 (b) Executive airplanes
 (c) Brand names
 (d) Financial
 (e) Bonds
 (f) Investment
 (g) Capital budgeting
 (h) Financing

2. a, c, and d.

3. c, d, e, and g are real assets. Others are financial.

Chapter 2

1. (a) Negative

 (b) $PV = \dfrac{C_1}{1 + r}$

 (c) $NPV = C_0 + \dfrac{C_1}{1 + r}$

 (d) It is the return forgone by investing in the project rather than the capital market.
 (e) The return offered by default-free U.S. Treasury securities.

2. $DF_1 = .867$; discount rate $= .154$, or 15.4 percent.

3. (a) .909
 (b) .833
 (c) .769

4. (a) $Return = \dfrac{profit}{investment} = \dfrac{132 - 100}{100}$
 $= .32$, or 32 percent
 (b) Negative (if the rate of interest r equals 32 percent, $NPV = 0$).
 (c) $PV = \dfrac{132}{1.10} = 120$, or \$120,000
 (d) $NPV = -100 + 120 = 20$, or \$20,000

5. Net present value rule: Invest if NPV is positive. Rate-of-return rule: Invest if the rate of return exceeds the opportunity cost of capital. They give the same answer.

6. (a) $1 + r = 5/4$. Therefore $r = .25$, or 25 percent
 (b) $2.6 - 1.6 = \$1$ million
 (c) \$3 million
 (d) $Return = (3 - 1)/1 = 2.0$, or 200 percent

(e) Marginal return = rate of interest = 25 percent
 (f) $PV = 4 - 1.6 = \$2.4$ million
 (g) $NPV = -1.0 + 2.4 = \$1.4$ million
 (h) \$4 million (\$2.6 million cash + NPV)
 (i) \$1 million
 (j) \$3.75 million

7. They will vote for (a) only. The other tasks can be carried out just as efficiently by stockholders.

Chapter 3

1. \$1.00

2. $125/139 = .899$

3. $596 \times .285 = \$170$

4. $\dfrac{374}{(1.09)^9} = \$172$

5. $PV = \dfrac{432}{1.15} + \dfrac{137}{(1.15)^2} + \dfrac{797}{(1.15)^3}$
 $= 376 + 104 + 524 = 1004$

6. $100 \times (1.15)^8 = \$305.90$

7. $232 \times (1 + r)^2 = 312.18$ implies $r = .16$, or 16 percent

8. $NPV = -1548 + \dfrac{138}{.09} = -\$14.67$

9. Find g so that $NPV = 0$.
 $NPV = -2590 + \dfrac{220}{.12 - g} = 0$ implies $g = .035$,
 or 3.5 percent.

10. $PV = \dfrac{4}{.14 - .04} = \$40$

11. PV of \$502 at $t = 1, 2, \dots, 9$, at 13 percent $= 502 \times 5.132 = 2576$. Future value $= 2576 \times (1.13)^9 = \$7738$.

12. (a) Let $S_t = $ salary in year t

$PV = \displaystyle\sum_{t=1}^{30} \dfrac{S_t}{(1.08)^t} = \sum_{t=1}^{30} \dfrac{20,000\,(1.05)^{t-1}}{(1.08)^t}$

$= \displaystyle\sum_{t=1}^{30} \dfrac{20,000/1.05}{(1.08/1.05)^t} = \sum_{t=1}^{30} \dfrac{19,048}{(1.029)^t}$

$= 19,048 \left[\dfrac{1}{.029} - \dfrac{1}{.029\,(1.029)^{30}} \right] = 378,222$

(b) PV (salary) × .05 = 18,911.
Future value = 18,911 × $(1.08)^{30}$
= 190,295.

(c) Annual payment = initial value ÷ annuity factor; 20-year annuity factor at 8 percent = 9.818; annual payment = 190,295/9.818 = 19,382.

13.

Period	Discount Factor	Cash Flow	Present Value
0	1.0	−400,000	−400,000
1	.893	+100,000	+89,300
2	.797	+200,000	+159,400
3	.712	+300,000	+213,600
		Total = NPV	= $ 62,300

14. (a) PV = 1/.10 = $10

(b) PV = $\dfrac{1}{.10\,(1.10)^7} = \dfrac{10}{2}$ = $5 (approx.)

(c) PV = 10 − 5 = $5 (approx.)

(d) PV = $\dfrac{C}{r-g} = \dfrac{10,000}{.10-.05}$ = $200,000.

15. (a) From Appendix Table 1, $1/(1.05)^5$ = .784. You therefore need to set aside 10,000 × .784 = $7840.

(b) From Appendix Table 3, the present value of $1 a year for 6 years at 8 percent is $4.623. Therefore you need to set aside 12,000 × 4.623 = $55,476.

(c) From Appendix Table 2, 1.08^6 = 1.587. Therefore, at the end of 6 years you would have 1.587 × (60,476 − 55,476) = $7935.

(d) From Appendix Table 2, $1 grows to $1.762 by year 5 at an annually compounded rate of 12 percent. From Appendix Table 4, $1 grows to $1.762 by year 5 at a continuously compounded rate of about 11.4 percent.

Chapter 4

1. $PV_A = \dfrac{1060}{1.08}$ = 981.48

$PV_B = \dfrac{60}{1.08} + \dfrac{1060}{1.08^2}$ = 964.33

$PV_C = \sum_{t=1}^{3} \dfrac{60}{1.08^t} + \dfrac{1060}{1.08^4}$ = 933.76

$PV_D = \dfrac{100}{1.08} + \dfrac{1100}{1.08^2}$ = 1035.67

$PV_E = \sum_{t=1}^{3} \dfrac{100}{1.08^t} + \dfrac{1100}{1.08^4}$ = 1066.24

2. The increased return has larger impact on the longer-term bonds.

$PV_A = \dfrac{1060}{1.10}$ = 963.64

$PV_B = \dfrac{60}{1.10} + \dfrac{1060}{1.10^2}$ = 930.58

$PV_C = \sum_{t=1}^{3} \dfrac{60}{1.10^t} + \dfrac{1060}{1.10^4}$ = 873.21

$PV_D = \dfrac{100}{1.10} + \dfrac{1100}{1.10^2}$ = 1000

$PV_E = \sum_{t=1}^{3} \dfrac{100}{1.10^t} + \dfrac{1100}{1.10^4}$ = 1000

3. $P_0 = \dfrac{10+110}{1.10}$ = $109.09

4. $r = \dfrac{5}{40}$ = .125

5. $P_0 = \dfrac{10}{.08-.05}$ = $333.33

6. $\dfrac{15}{.08}$ + PVGO = 333.33; therefore PVGO = $145.83

7. (b) and (c); (a) ignores the cost of the investments needed to produce the earnings.

8. If present value of growth opportunities (PVGO) is zero.

Chapter 5

1. The opportunity cost of capital is the expected rate of return investors could earn at a given level of risk.

2. (a) A = 3 years, B = 2 years, C = 3 years
(b) B
(c) A, B, and C
(d) B and C (NPV_B = $3378; NPV_C = $2405)
(e) False
(f) True

3. $\dfrac{1000}{4000}$ = .25, or 25 percent

4. (a) True
(b) False

5. (a) $15,750; $4250; $0
(b) 100 percent

6. (a) (i) Both (IRR is greater than the cost of capital). (ii) The *incremental* cash flows on B are: −2000, +1100, +1210. The IRR on these incremental flows is 10 percent. Since this is greater than the cost of capital, the incremental investment in A is worthwhile.
(b) NPV of incremental investment = 690 − 657 = $33

7. (a) A = 2000/1600 = 1.25; B = 2400/2100 = 1.14
(b) (i) Both. (ii) The incremental flows on B are −500, +240, +288. The profitability index

on the incremental investment is 400/500 = .8. Therefore, accept A.

8. C (if both projects have NPV = 0 at the same discount rate, the project with the later cash flows must have the higher NPV if we use a lower discount rate).

9. No (you are effectively "borrowing" at a rate of interest higher than the opportunity cost of capital).

Chapter 6

1. a, b, d, g, h

2. Real cash flow = $100,000/1.1$ = $90,909$; real discount rate = $(1.15/1.1) - 1$ = $.0455$

$$PV = \frac{90,909}{1.0455} = 86,953,$$ four francs short because of rounding error.

3. (a) NPV_A = $100,000; NPV_B = $180,000
   (b) Equivalent cash flow of A = $100,000/1.736$ = $57,604; equivalent cash flow of B = $180,000/2.487$ = $72,376
   (c) Machine B

4. Replace at end of 5 years ($80,000 > 72,376$).

5. 1, 2, 4, and 6

6. Soft rationing means provisional capital constraints imposed by management as an aid to financial control. This doesn't rule out raising more money if necessary. Firms facing hard rationing can't raise money from capital markets.

Chapter 7

1. (a) About 12 percent
   (b) 8–9 percent
   (c) 0–1 percent
   (d) About 21 percent (less in recent years)
   (e) Less (diversification reduces risk)

2. Standard deviation of returns, correlated, less unique risk, market risk, capital asset pricing, security market line, zero, risk-free rate, one, market portfolio.

3. (a) False
   (b) True
   (c) False—its *risk premium* would be twice as high.
   (d) True
   (e) True
   (f) False
   (g) True—if "risk" means standard deviation.
   (h) False

4. A: 1.0; B: 2.0; C: 1.5; D: 0; E: -1.0

5. (a) 30 percent
   (b) zero
   (c) .75

(d) Less than 1.0 (the portfolio's risk is the same as the market, but some of this risk is unique risk).

6. 1.3 (Diversification does not affect market risk.)

7. (a) $\sigma^2 = 330$; $\sigma = 18.2$ percent
   (b) slightly lower.

8. (a) $r = r_f + \beta (r_m - r_f) = 4 + 1.73 (10 - 4)$ = 14.4 percent
   (b) Genentech: $r = 4 + 1.95 (10 - 4) = 15.7$ percent
   (c) General Mills: $r = 4 + .57 (10 - 4) = 7.4$ percent
   (d) Lower
   (e) Higher

9. b

10. $r_A = r_f + .5 (r_m - r_f) = 7$
   $r_B = r_f + 1.5 (r_m - r_f) = 15$
   $r_B - r_A = r_m - r_f = 8$ = market risk premium
   $r_A = r_f + .5 \times 8 = 7$ implies $r_f = 3$
   $r_m - 3 = 8$ implies $r_m = 11$ = expected return on market

Chapter 8

1. (a) Figure 8-15: Diversification reduces risk (e.g., a mixture of portfolios A and B would have less risk than the average of A and B).
   (b) Those along line AB in Figure 8-14.
   (c) See Figure 1, below.

2. (a) Portfolio A (higher expected return, same risk)
   (b) Cannot say (depends on investor's attitude toward risk)
   (c) Portfolio F (lower risk, same expected return)

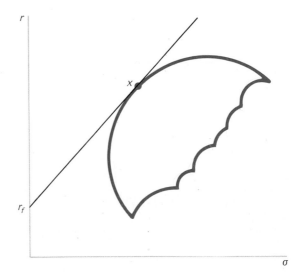

FIGURE 1
Chapter 8, Quiz question 1 (c).

3.

$x_1^2\sigma_1^2$	$x_1x_2\sigma_{12}$	$x_1x_3\sigma_{13}$
$x_1x_2\sigma_{12}$	$x_2^2\sigma_2^2$	$x_2x_3\sigma_{23}$
$x_1x_3\sigma_{13}$	$x_2x_3\sigma_{23}$	$x_3^2\sigma_3^2$

4. *a, b*
5. *d*
6. (a) See Figure 2, below.
  (b) A, D, G
  (c) F
  (d) 15 percent in C
  (e) Put 25/32 of your money in F and lend 7/32 at 12 percent:

  Expected return = 7/32 × 12 + 25/32 × 18 = 16.7 percent
  Standard deviation = 7/32 × 0 + 25/32 × 32 = 25 percent

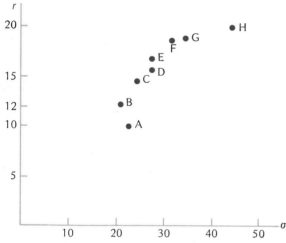

FIGURE 2
Chapter 8, Quiz question 6 (a).

If you could borrow without limit, you would achieve as high an expected return as you'd like, with correspondingly high risk of course.

Chapter 9
1. It will tend to overinvest in risky projects, and pass valuable safe projects by.
2. Suppose r_f = 7 percent.

$r = r_f + \beta(r_m - r_f) = 7 + 2.0\ (8) = 23$ percent

$\text{NPV} = -100{,}000 + \dfrac{150{,}000}{1.23} = +21{,}950$

3. BETA = market risk measure. Average risk would imply beta = 1.0

ALPHA = average price change on stock when market return was zero
R-SQR = ratio of market risk to total risk of stock—that is, proportion of variance of stock return attributable to market risk
RESID STD DEV-N = stock's unique risk, measured as a standard deviation
STD ERR OF BETA = measure of extent of possible error in beta estimate
ADJUSTED BETA = beta estimate adjusted for fact that high estimated betas tend to be overestimates of true betas, and low estimated betas tend to be underestimates
NUMBER OF OBSERV = number of monthly returns used to estimate beta and alpha

4. $\beta_{ASSETS} = 0 \times .40 + .5 \times .60 = .30$
  $r = 10 + .30\ (20 - 10) = 13$ percent
5. (a) $r_f + \beta(r_m - r_f) = 8 + 1.5 \times 10 = 23$ percent

  (b) $\beta_{ASSETS} = \beta_{DEBT}\left(\dfrac{\text{debt}}{\text{debt + equity}}\right)$
  $+ \beta_{EQUITY}\left(\dfrac{\text{equity}}{\text{debt + equity}}\right)$
  $= 0 \times \dfrac{4}{4 + 6} + 1.5 \times \dfrac{6}{4 + 6}$
  $= .9$

  (c) $r_f + \beta_{ASSETS}\ (r_m - r_f) = 8 + .9 \times 10$
  $= 17$ percent

  (d) $r = 17$ percent
  (e) $r_f + \beta(r_m - r_f) = 8 + 1.2 \times 10 = 20$ percent
6. Expected cash flow is an average of the cash flow from a dry hole and the cash flow from a producing well. The possibility of a dry hole should affect the discount rate only if the project's market risk is increased.
7. (a) A (higher fixed cost).
  (b) C (more cyclical revenues).
8. $CEQ_t / [(1 + r_f)^t]$; less than one; $r_f + \beta(r_m - r_f)$; decrease
9. (a) $PV = \dfrac{110}{1 + r_f + \beta(r_m - r_f)}$
  $+ \dfrac{121}{[1 + r_f + \beta(r_m - r_f)]^2}$
  $= \dfrac{110}{1.10} + \dfrac{121}{1.10^2} = \$200$

  (b) $\dfrac{CEQ_1}{1.05} = \dfrac{110}{1.10}\quad CEQ_1 = \$105$
  $\dfrac{CEQ_2}{1.05^2} = \dfrac{121}{1.10^2}\quad CEQ_2 = \$110.25$

  (c) $a_1 = \dfrac{105}{110} = .95$
  $a_2 = \dfrac{110.25}{121} = .91$

Chapter 10

1. (a) Detailed analysis of capital investment projects, to identify what cash flows depend on, what can go wrong, whether the project could be abandoned if performance is disappointing, and so on.
   (b) Analysis of how project profitability and NPV change if different assumptions are made about sales, cost, and other key variables.
   (c) Determines the level of future sales at which project profitability or NPV equal zero.
   (d) An extension of sensitivity analysis which explores all possible outcomes and weighs each by its probability.
   (e) A graphical technique for displaying possible future events and decisions taken in response to those events.
   (f) The additional present value created by the option to bail out of a project, and recover part of the initial investment, if the project performs poorly.
   (g) The additional present value created by the option to invest more and expand output, if a project performs well.

2. $-\$30$ million.

3. (a) NPV = old NPV
   $$- \begin{array}{c}\text{additional} \\ \text{investment}\end{array} + \begin{array}{c}\text{reduction in} \\ \text{net variable} \\ \text{costs}\end{array}$$
   $$+ \begin{array}{c}\text{increase in} \\ \text{depreciation tax} \\ \text{shield}\end{array}$$

$$= 34.3 - 150 + \sum_{t=1}^{10} \frac{(.5 \times 40)}{(1.10)^t}$$
$$+ \sum_{t=1}^{10} \frac{(.5 \times 15)}{(1.10)^t}$$
$$= \$53 \text{ million}$$

   (b) See Figure 3.
   (c) The left-hand chart in Figure 3 (below) shows that expected sales have to be at least 85,000 for the project to have a positive NPV. The right-hand graph shows that the firm can report an *accounting* profit if sales exceed 52,000.

4. (a) "Optimistic" and "pessimistic" rarely show the full probability distribution of outcomes.
   (b) Sensitivity analysis changes variables one at a time; in practice, all variables change, and the changes are often interrelated. Sensitivity analysis using scenarios can help in this regard.

5. (a) False
   (b) True
   (c) True
   (d) True
   (e) True
   (f) False
   (g) True
   (h) True

6. (a) Describe how project cash flow depends on the underlying variables.
   (b) Specify probability distributions for forecast errors for these cash flows.
   (c) Draw from the probability distributions to simulate the cash flows.

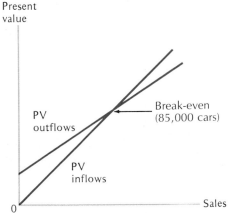

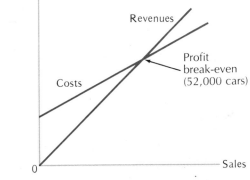

FIGURE 3
Chapter 10, Quiz question 3 (b).

7.

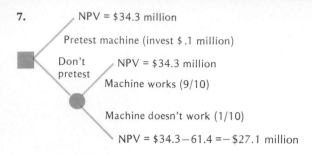

NPV = $34.3 million

Pretest machine (invest $.1 million)

Don't pretest

NPV = $34.3 million

Machine works (9/10)

Machine doesn't work (1/10)

NPV = $34.3−61.4 =−$27.1 million

NPV (pretest) = 34.3 − .1 = $34.2 million
NPV (don't pretest) = .9 × 34.3 + .1 × (−27.1)
= $28.2 million

8. See Table 1, below. The decision tree shows the probability of finding oil earlier. At 2000 feet, the expected payoff to further drilling is (.25 × 1) + (.75 × −3) = −$2 million. This is greater than the payoff to stopping. Therefore Big should drill to 3000 feet. At 1000 feet the expected payoff to drilling to 2000 feet is .8 × [(.25 × 1) + (.75 × −3)] + (.2 × 2) = −$1.2 million. This is greater than the payoff to stopping. Therefore Big should drill to 2000 feet. The expected payoff to drilling to 1000 feet is (.5 × 3) + (.5 × −1.2) = $.9 million. As long as the certainty equivalent value of this payoff is positive, Big should drill to 1000 feet.

Chapter 11

1. Your best estimate is $1000 per acre, the actual market value. Why do a discounted-cash-flow analysis to estimate market value when you can observe it directly?

2. (a) False
(b) True
(c) True
(d) False

3. $15

4. DC-8s should have been valued at market prices for used airplanes. The low *book* depreciation charge was irrelevant. Alitalia should have compared the total costs of operating 747s and DC-8s, in which the DC-8s' cost includes the opportunity cost of capital on, and depreciation of, their actual secondhand value. Note: If 747s and DC-8s were perfect substitutes in terms of range, passenger comfort, and so on, we would expect the DC-8s' secondhand value to adjust until their total operating costs per seat mile were the same as the 747s'.

5. It depends first on competition among capital equipment producers. If other producers can quickly match the new machine, its advantages are passed on to its buyers. But then the buyers will compete to pass on the machine's advantages to their customers. In the end, users will realize positive NPVs from buying the machine only if they are in a position to make better use of it than their competitors.

Chapter 12

1. (a) False
(b) False—top management usually makes the final decision on major projects.
(c) True
(d) True
(e) False
(f) True

2. Cash flow, economic, less, greater.

3.

	Year 1	Year 2	Year 3
Cash flow	0	78.55	78.55
PV at start of year	100.00	120.00	65.46
PV at end of year	120.00	65.46	0
Change in value during year	+ 20.00	− 54.54	− 65.46
Expected economic income	+ 20.00	+ 24.00	+ 13.09

TABLE 1
Chapter 10, Quiz question 8.

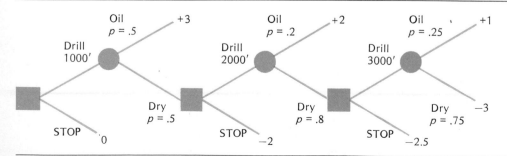

4. (*a*) False
   (*b*) False—firms have a considerable range of choice.
   (*c*) True
   (*d*) True

Chapter 13
1. *c*
2. Weak, semistrong, strong, fundamental, strong, technical, weak
3. *c* and *f*
4. (*a*) Decline to $200
   (*b*) Remain at 2 percent
   (*c*) Less
   (*d*) A slight abnormal fall (the split is likely to have led investors to expect an above-average rise in dividends)
5. (*a*) False
   (*b*) True
   (*c*) False
   (*d*) True
   (*e*) False
   (*f*) True (a small change in price *in the absence of new information* causes a large increase in demand)

Chapter 14
1. (*a*) 40,000/.50 = 80,000 shares
   (*b*) 78,000 shares
   (*c*) 2000 shares are held as Treasury stock
   (*d*) 20,000 shares
   (*e*)
Common stock	$ 45,000
Additional paid-in capital	25,000
Retained earnings	30,000
Common equity	100,000
Treasury stock	5,000
Net common equity	$ 95,000
2. (*a*) 80 votes
   (*b*) 10 × 80 = 800 votes
3. (*a*) Funded
   (*b*) Eurobond
   (*c*) Subordinated
   (*d*) Debentures
   (*e*) Sinking fund
   (*f*) Call
   (*g*) Prime rate
   (*h*) Floating rate
   (*i*) Lease
   (*j*) Convertible
   (*k*) Warrant; Exercise price
4.
Internally generated cash	79
Financial deficit	21
Net share issues	− 18
Debt issues	38
5. (*a*) False
   (*b*) True

(*c*) True
(*d*) True
(*e*) False
(*f*) True
(*g*) True

Chapter 15
1. (*a*) Issue of seasoned stock
   (*b*) Bond issue by utility holding company
   (*c*) Bond issue by industrial company
   (*d*) Bond issue by large industrial company
2. A (*d*); B (*f*); C (*c*); D (*a*); E (*b*); F(*e*)
3. (*a*) A large issue
   (*b*) A bond issue
   (*c*) A large competitive bond issue
   (*d*) A small private placement of bonds
4. (*a*) 50,000 shares
   (*b*) Primary: 500,000 shares
       Secondary: 400,000 shares
   (*c*) $15 or 19 percent, which is the same as the average underpricing observed by Ritter.

   (*d*)
	Millions
Underwriting cost	$ 4.5
Administrative cost	.82
Underpricing	13.5
Total	$18.82

5. (*a*) Net proceeds of public issue = 10,000,000 − 150,000 − 80,000 = $9,770,000
       Net proceeds of private placement = $9,970,000
   (*b*) PV of extra interest on private placement = $\sum_{t=1}^{10} \dfrac{.005 \times 10,000,000}{1.085^t}$ = $328,000, i.e., extra cost of higher interest on private placement more than outweighs saving in issue costs. N.b. We ignore taxes.
   (*c*) Private placement debt can be custom-tailored and the terms more easily renegotiated.
6. (*a*) Number of rights needed to purchase one share: 2
   (*b*) Number of new shares: 50,000
   (*c*) Amount of new investment: $500,000
   (*d*) Total value of company after issue: $4,500,000
   (*e*) Total number of shares after issue: 150,000
   (*f*) Rights-on price: $40
   (*g*) Ex-rights price: $30
   (*h*) Price of a right: $10

Chapter 16
1. (*a*) A, e; B, d; C, c; D, a; E, b
   (*b*) May 26 = ex-dividend date
   (*c*) (4 × .40)/50 = .032, or 3.2 percent

(d) $1.60/3.40 = .47$, or 47 percent
(e) $5, or 10 percent
2. (e) (they are taxed on 20 percent of dividends received)
3. (a) True
   (b) False (Managers prefer a smooth progression of dividends and move only partway to the dividend target.)
   (c) True
   (d) False (If earnings are expected to decline again, managers are less likely to increase dividends.)
4. (a) .35, or 35 percent
   (b) .77, or 77 percent
5. (a) Under MM's theory, the freeze should make no difference. Firms will have higher retained earnings and will either reduce the volume of new stock issues, repurchase more stock, or simply invest any extra cash in marketable securities. In any case, what investors lose in cash dividends is made up in capital gains.
   (b) If firms keep their investment decisions separate from their dividend and financing decisions, then the freeze will have no effect on real investment. If the freeze prevents in dividends, the firm can repurchase shares or "park" excess cash in marketable securities, possibly the shares of other firms.
      Some economists believe that firms do not separate investment from dividend and financing decisions, but look less critically at investments which can be financed from internal funds. In this case a dividend freeze could lead to increased real investment. (Of course if this investment is in negative-NPV projects, share prices will fall, but that would not disprove the MM argument. Prices would not fall because of forgone dividend increases, but because of the negative-NPV investments.)
6. A dividend increase signals management's optimism about future earnings (the company is putting its money where its mouth is).
7. Before the Tax Reform Act investors paid up to 50 percent tax on dividends versus a maximum 20 percent on capital gains. Since the act, individuals are taxed equally on dividends and realized capital gains. Because capital gains taxes can be deferred, individuals may still have a tax reason to prefer gains.
   Because effective tax rates on dividends and capital gains are now more alike, individual investors are less motivated to hold low-payout stocks. This would induce a *relative* fall in the price of low-payout stocks and a *relative* rise in their required pretax return.

Chapter 17

1. (a) $.10P$
   (b) Buy 10 percent of B's debt + 10 percent of B's equity
   (c) $.10(P - 100)$
   (d) Borrow an amount equal to 10 percent of B's debt and buy 10 percent of A's equity
2. Note the market value of Copperhead is far in excess of its book value:

	Market Value
Common stock (8 million shares at $2)	$16,000,000
Short-term loans	$2,000,000

Ms. Kraft owns .625 percent of the firm, which proposes to increase common stock to $17 million and cut short-term debt. Ms. Kraft can offset this by (a) borrowing $.00625 \times 1,000,000 = \$6250$, and (b) buying that much more Copperhead stock.

3. Expected return on assets is

$$r_A = .08 \times 30/80 + .16 \times 50/80 = .13$$

The new return on equity will be

$$r_E = .13 + 20/60 (.13 - .08) = .147$$

If stockholders pass on more of the firm risk to debtholders, expected return on equity will be *less* than 14.7 percent.

4. (a) (i) $\beta_A = \left(\dfrac{D}{D + E} \times \beta_D\right)$

$$+ \left(\dfrac{E}{D + E} \times \beta_E\right)$$

$1.0 = (.5 \times 0) + (.5 \times \beta_E)$
$\therefore \beta_E = 2.0$
   (ii) $\beta_D = 0$
   (iii) $\beta_A = 1.0$
   (b) (i) .10

   (ii) $r_A = \left(\dfrac{D}{D + E} \times r_D\right)$

$$+ \left(\dfrac{E}{D + E} \times r_E\right)$$

$.10 = (.5 \times .05) + (.5 \times r_E)$
$r_E = .15$
   (iii) $r_D = .05$
   (iv) $r_A = .10$
   (c) (i) 50 percent
   (ii) 6.7 (i.e., the P/E ratio falls to offset the increase in EPS).

5. (a)

Operating income, dollars	500	1000	1500	2000
Interest, dollars	250	250	250	250
Equity earnings, dollars	250	750	1250	1750
Earnings per share	.33	1.00	1.67	2.33
Return on shares, percent	3.3	10	16.7	23.3

(b) $\beta_A = \left(\dfrac{D}{D+E} \times \beta_D\right) + \left(\dfrac{E}{D+E} \times \beta_E\right)$

$.8 = (.25 \times 0) + (.75 \times \beta_E)$

$\beta_E = 1.07$

6. (a) True, so long as the market value of "old" debt does not change.

(b) False. MM's Proposition I says only that overall firm value ($V = D + E$) does not depend on capital structure.

(c) False. Borrowing increases equity risk even if debt is default-risk free.

(d) False. Limited liability affects the relative values of debt and equity, not their sum.

(e) True. Limited liability protects shareholders if the firm defaults.

(f) True—but the required rate of return on equity and the firm's assets are the same only if the firm holds risk-free assets. In this case r_A, r_D, and r_E all equal the risk-free rate of interest.

(g) False. The shareholders could make the same debt issue on their own account.

(h) True. To put it more precisely, it assumes that the expected rate of return to equity goes up, but stockholders' required rate of return goes up proportionately. Therefore, stock price is unchanged.

(i) False. The formula $r_E = r_A + D/E(r_A - r_D)$ does not require r_D = a constant.

(j) False. The clientele has to be willing to pay extra for the debt, which they will not do if plenty of corporate debt issues are already available.

7. See Figure 17-5.

Chapter 18

1. (a) PV tax shield

$= \dfrac{T_c\,(r_D D)}{1 + r_D} = \dfrac{.34(.08 \times 1000)}{1.08}$

$= \$25.19$

(b) PV tax shield

$= \displaystyle\sum_{t=1}^{5} \dfrac{T_c\,(r_D D)}{(1 + r_D)^t}$

$= \displaystyle\sum_{t=1}^{5} \dfrac{.34(.08 \times 1000)}{(1.08)^t} = \$108.60$

(c) PV tax shield $= T_c D = \$340$

2. (a) PV tax shield $= T_c D = \$16$

(b) $T_c \times 20 = \$8$

(c) New PV tax shield

$= \displaystyle\sum_{t=1}^{5} \dfrac{.40(.08 \times 60)}{(1.08)^t} = \$7.67$

Therefore, company value $= 168 - 24 + 7.67 = \$151.67$

3. (a)

	TAX PER DOLLAR OF GROSS INCOME	
	Equity	Debt
Corporate tax	.34	0
Personal income tax	$.38 \times .5 \times .66 = .13$	.38
Capital gains tax	$.28 \times .5 \times .66 = .09$	0
Total	$.56	$.38

(b) Total tax on equity $= \$.47$ per dollar of gross income. Tax on debt remains at $.38.

4. (a) Aggregate supply of debt falls. Only investors with tax rates below 24 percent will now prefer debt.

(b) Once new equilibrium is established, no single firm can gain an advantage by changing its capital structure.

5. A firm with no taxable income saves no taxes by borrowing and paying interest. The interest payments would simply add to its tax-loss carry-forwards. Such a firm would have little tax incentive to borrow.

6. (a) Stockholders win. Bond value falls, since the value of assets securing the bond has fallen.

(b) Bondholder wins if we assume the cash is left invested in Treasury bills. The bondholder is sure to get $26 plus interest. Stock value is zero, because there is no chance that firm value can rise above $50.

(c) The bondholders lose. The firm adds assets worth $10 and debt worth $10. This would increase Circular's debt ratio, leaving the old bondholders more exposed. The old bondholders' loss is the stockholders' gain.

(d) Both bondholders and stockholders win. They share the (net) increase in firm value. The bondholders' position is not eroded by the issue of a junior security. (We assume that the preferred does not lead to still more game playing, and that the new investment does not make the firm's *assets* safer or riskier.)

(*e*) Bondholders lose because they are at risk for longer. Stockholders win.

7. Specialized, intangible assets such as growth opportunities are most likely to lose value in financial distress. Safe, tangible assets with good second-hand markets are least likely to lose value. Costs of financial distress are thus likely to be less for, say, real estate firms or trucking companies than for advertising firms or high-tech growth companies.

8. More profitable firms have more taxable income to shield and are less likely to incur the costs of distress. Therefore the trade-off theory predicts high debt ratios. In practice the more profitable companies borrow least.

9. Firms have a pecking order of preference for new finance. Internal finance is preferred, followed by debt and then external equity. Each firm's observed debt ratio reflects its cumulative requirements for external finance. The more profitable companies borrow least because they have sufficient internal finance.

cent of project *value,* i.e., initial investment plus PV tax shield. To check this, we recalculate APV as follows:

$$\text{APV} = \text{base-case NPV} + \text{PV tax shield}$$
$$= 0 + \frac{.1 \times .2 \times .3 \,(1005.48)}{1.10}$$
$$= +5.48$$

5. $D = 75 \times .9 = \$67.5 \text{ million}$
$E = 42 \times 2.5 = \$105 \text{ million}$
$V = D + E = \$172.5 \text{ million}$
$r^* = (1 - T_c)r_D\,D/V + r_E\,E/V$
$\quad = (1 - .23).16(67.5/172.5)$
$\qquad + .25(105/172.5)$
$\quad = .20, \text{ or } 20 \text{ percent}$

6. No. The more debt you use, the higher rate of return equity investors will require. (Lenders may demand more also.) Thus there is a hidden cost of the "cheap" debt: It makes equity more expensive.

7. PV lease $= \displaystyle\sum_{t=0}^{5} \frac{(1 - .34)\,100{,}000}{[1 + (1 - .34).09]^t}$
$\qquad\quad = \$344{,}470$

Chapter 19

1. APV = base-case NPV ± PV financing side effects
(*a*) APV $= 0 - .15(500{,}000) = -75{,}000$
(*b*) APV $= 0 + 175{,}000 = +175{,}000$
(*c*) APV $= 0 + 76{,}000 = +76{,}000$
(*d*) APV $= 0 - .15(500{,}000) + 76{,}000 = +1{,}000$

2. PV tax shield $= (.10/.34)\,561{,}000 = \$165{,}000$
APV $= 170{,}000 + 165{,}000 = \$335{,}000$

3. (*a*) Base-case NPV $= -1000 + \dfrac{1200}{1.20} = 0$

(*b*) PV tax shield $= \dfrac{.1 \times .2 \times .3 \,(1000)}{1.10} = \$5.45$
APV $= 0 + 5.45 = \$5.45$

4. (*a*) $r^* = r(1 - T^*L) = .20(1 - .20 \times .30)$
$\quad = .188$

(*b*) $r^* = r - Lr_D T^* \left(\dfrac{1 + r}{1 + r_D}\right)$

$\quad = .20 - .30 \times .10 \times .20 \left(\dfrac{1.2}{1.1}\right)$

$\quad = .1935$

(*c*) NPV(@ $r^* = .188$) $= \dfrac{1200}{1.188} - 1000$

$\quad = +10.10$

NPV(@ $r^* = .1935$) $= \dfrac{1200}{1.1935} - 1000$

$\quad = +5.48$

Note: The Miles-Ezzell formula gives the correct NPV for a company that borrows 30 per-

Chapter 20

1. Call; exercise; put; exercise; European; call; assets; bondholders (lenders); assets; promised payment to bondholders.

2. (*a*) Call
(*b*) Put
(*c*) Call
(*d*) Call
(*e*) Put
(*f*) Call
(*g*) Call
(*h*) Put

3. Figure 20-11*a* represents a call seller; Figure 20-11*b* represents a call buyer.

4. (*a*) The exercise price of the put option (i.e., you'd sell stock for the exercise price).
(*b*) The value of the stock (i.e., you would throw away the put and keep the stock).

5. Buy a call and lend the present value of the exercise price.

6. The lower bound is the option's value if it expired immediately: either zero or the stock price less the exercise price, whichever is larger. The upper bound is the stock price.

7. (*a*) Zero
(*b*) Stock price less the present value of the exercise price.

8. The call price
(*a*) Increases
(*b*) Decreases
(*c*) Increases

(d) Increases
(e) Decreases
(f) Decreases

9. True. The beta and standard deviation of an option always exceeds its stock's. The risk of an option decreases as the stock price increases.

10. First, estimating expected cash flows from an option is difficult, although not impossible. Second, the risk of an option changes every time the stock price changes, so there is no single, well-defined risk-adjusted discount rate.

11. With an exercise price of 60,

$$\sigma \times \sqrt{t} = .06 \times \sqrt{3} = .10$$
$$P/EXe^{-rt} = 60/60e^{-.01 \times 3} = 1.03$$

(a) Call price = approximately .056 × 60
    = 3.4

Put price = call price + PV(EX)
          − stock price
          = 3.4 + 58.23 − 60
          = 1.6 (approximately)

(b) From Appendix Table 7 call option delta = .6. Thus replicating portfolio is .6 shares (cost = .6 × 60 = $36) and borrow balance (36 − 3.4 = $32.6).
Put option delta = .6 − 1 = −.4. Replicating portfolio is *sell* .4 shares (cash inflow = .4 × 60 = $24) and lend balance (24 + 1.6 = $25.6).

12. (a)

Payoffs	Stock Price = $100	Stock Price = $220
A. 1 call	$0	$60
B. 1 share	$100	$220
borrow PV(100)	−100	−100
	$0	$120

Value of 2 calls = share price − loan

$$\therefore \text{Value of 1 call} = \frac{140 − 90.9}{2} = \$24.55$$

(b) $p (57.1) + (1 − p)(−28.6) = 10$
$\therefore p = .45$

$$\text{Value of call} = \frac{(.45 \times 60) + (.55 \times 0)}{1.10}$$
$$= \$24.55$$

Wider range of stock prices does not increase loss to option holder if stock price falls, but it does increase gain if stock price rises.

Chapter 21

1. (a) Backwoods has an in-the-money call option on expansion.
   (b) Project provides call option on further projects.

(c) Standard equipment contains valuable abandonment (put) option.

2. (a) Using risk-neutral method
   $(p \times 20) + (1 − p)(−10) = 1$
   $p = .37$

   $$\text{Value of call} = \frac{(.37 \times 8) + (.63 \times 0)}{1.01}$$
   $$= 2.90$$

(b) $\text{Delta} = \dfrac{\text{spread of option prices}}{\text{spread of stock prices}} = \dfrac{8}{12} = .67$

(c)

	Current Cash Flow	Possible Future Cash Flows	
Buy call	−2.90	0	+8
equals			
Buy .67 shares	−26.67	+24	+32
Borrow 23.77	−23.77	−24	−24
	−2.90	0	+8

(d) Possible stock prices with call option prices in brackets:

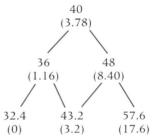

Option prices were calculated as follows:

Month 1: (i) $\dfrac{(.37 \times 17.6) + (.63 \times 3.2)}{1.01}$

= 8.40

(ii) $\dfrac{(.37 \times 3.2) + (.63 \times 0)}{1.01}$

= 1.16

Month 0: $\dfrac{(.37 \times 8.40) + (.63 \times 1.16)}{1.01}$

= 3.78

(e) $\text{Delta} = \dfrac{\text{spread of option prices}}{\text{spread of stock prices}}$

$= \dfrac{8.40 − 1.16}{48 − 36} = .60$

3. The period to expiration is subdivided into an indefinitely large number of subperiods (and when there is no incentive to early exercise).

4. (a) Yes (earn interest on exercise money)
   (b) No (dividend gain is less than loss of interest)
   (c) Yes (if the dividend becomes sufficiently larger than loss of interest to justify killing the option)

(d) Yes (if gain in deutsche mark interest more than offsets loss of dollar interest on exercise price)

5. (a) $(p \times 15) + (1 - p)(-10) = 10$
$p = .8$
Put value if exercised now $= EX - 60$
Value of put if not exercised now $=$
$$\frac{(1 - .8)(EX - 54)}{1.1}$$
∴ You are indifferent if $EX = 61.3$

(b) Higher interest rate reduces break-even exercise price (i.e., the benefit of the higher interest rate offsets the disadvantage of the lower exercise price).

6. (i) Keep gold stocks and buy put option with exercise "price" of £500,000.
(ii) Sell gold stocks, invest £472,000 in 6-month time deposit, and use balance of £128,000 to buy call option on gold stocks with exercise price of £500,000.

Chapter 22

1. (a) (i) 0
(ii) 0
(iii) 0
(iv) $10
(v) $20

(b)

Theoretical
value of warrant
(colored line)

Exercise price ($40)   Stock price

(c) Buy the warrant and exercise, then sell the stock.
Net gain $= -5 - 40 + 60 = +\$15$.

2. (a) No
(b) No
(c) $1/3 \times 30 = \$10$
(d) No
(e) Zero

(f) More
(g) (i) less; (ii) less; (iii) more; (iv) more; (v) more
(h) When the share price is no longer less than the warrant price plus the exercise price. This will occur when the dividends on the stock outweigh the interest on the exercise price.

3. (a) EPS $= \$2.00$
(b) Diluted EPS $= \$1.33$

4. (a) $1000/47 = 21.28$
(b) $1000/50 = \$20.00$
(c) $21.28 \times 41.50 = \$883.12$, or 88.31 percent
(d) $650/21.28 = \$30.55$
(e) No (not if the investor is free to convert immediately)
(f) $12.22, i.e., $(910 - 650)/21.28$
(g) $(47/41.50) - 1 = .13$, or 13 percent
(h) When the price reaches 102.75

Chapter 23

1. (a) Figure 4 shows that an increase in the demand for capital increases investment and saving. The rate of interest also rises.
(b) Figure 5 shows that an increase in the supply of capital also increases investment and saving. The rate of interest falls.

2. (a) $PV = \dfrac{50}{1 + r_1} + \dfrac{1050}{(1 + r_2)^2}$

(b) $PV = \dfrac{50}{1 + y} + \dfrac{1050}{(1 + y)^2}$

(c) Less (it is between the 1-year and 2-year spot rates).
(d) Yield to maturity; spot rate

3. (a) Fall
(b) Less than 100
(c) Less than the coupon
(d) Higher prices, other things equal

4. (a) 12 percent
(b) 70.88
(c) (i) Price rises from 71.33 to 73.51 if yield remains at 14 percent.
(ii) Price rises to 93.77 if yield falls to 10 percent.

5. (a) $(1 + r_2)^2 = (1 + r_1)(1 + f_2)$
$1.03^2 = 1.01 \times (1 + f_2)$
$f_2 = .05$, or 5 percent

(b) The expected one-year spot rate at time 1, $E(_1r_2)$, equals the forward rate f_2.
(c) Against (unless one believes that investors have generally expected interest rates to rise).
(d) The forward rate equals the expected spot rate *plus* a liquidity premium.
(e) Long-term bonds.
(f) Short-term bonds.

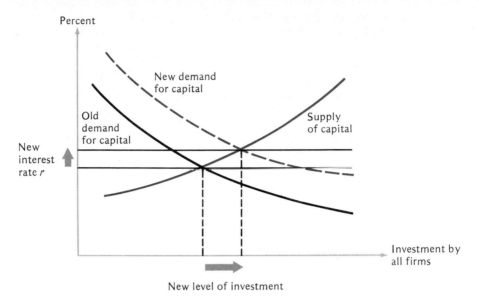

FIGURE 4
Chapter 23, Quiz question 1(*a*).

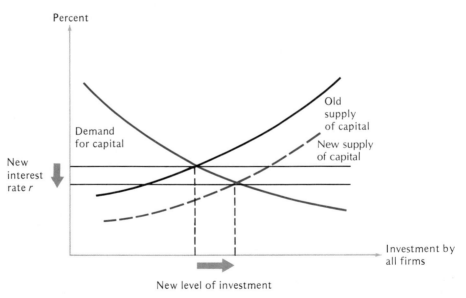

FIGURE 5
Chapter 23, Quiz question 1(*b*).

(g) The forward rate equals the expected spot rate plus a premium for the inflation risk.

6. (a) Aaa, Aa, A, and Baa
   (b) (i) Increase
      (ii) Increase
      (iii) Increase (Note: the value of the stockholders' call on the firm's assets increases with the interest rate.)
      (iv) Increase

7. (a) Value of guarantee = value of put (i.e., shareholders' option to put the company to the bondholders for the face value of the bond).
   (b) Put option; exercise price is face value of bond.

Chapter 24

1. (a) High-grade utility bonds
   (b) Short-dated notes
   (c) Industrial holding companies
   (d) Industrial bonds
   (e) Railroads
2. (a) Noncallable bonds (callable bonds neither rise nor fall as much in price).
   (b) They will disappear (each side should exercise its option at 100).
3. Sinking fund c (an optional sinking fund reduces bond value; a sinking fund that gives the firm the option to purchase in the market may decrease bond value).
4. (a) You would like an issue of junior debt.
   (b) You prefer it not to do so (unless it is also junior debt). The existing property may not be sufficient to pay off your debt.
5. (a) Salomon Bros; First Boston; Kidder Peabody; Merrill Lynch; Paine Webber; Prudential-Bache
   (b) Riggs National Bank
   (c) $990.99 - \dfrac{490,000}{75,000} = \$984.46$
   (d) Registered
   (e) No
   (f) 109.14
   (g) No
6. (a) Issue price + approximately 1 month's accrued interest $= 995.00 + \dfrac{112.5}{12} = \$1004.38$
   (b) May 1, 1986; $56.25 per bond
   (c) November 1, 2015; $75 million
   (d) November 2, 2002

Chapter 25

1. (a) True
   (b) True
   (c) False (depends on coupon)
   (d) False
   (e) False

(f) False
(g) True

2. Sell short $1.2 million of the market portfolio. In practice rather than "sell the market" you would sell futures on $1.2 million of the market index.

3.

	Year	C_t	PV(C_t)	Proportion of Total Value	Proportion × Time
Security A	1	40	37.04	.359	.359
	2	40	34.29	.333	.666
	3	40	31.75	.308	.924
		V =	103.08	1.0	
				Duration = 1.949 years	
Security B	1	20	18.52	.141	.141
	2	20	17.15	.131	.262
	3	120	95.26	.728	2.184
		V =	130.93	1.0	
				Duration = 2.587 years	
Security C	1	10	9.26	.088	.088
	2	10	8.57	.082	.164
	3	110	87.32	.830	2.490
		V =	105.15	1.0	
				Duration = 2.742 years	

Volatilities: A, 1.80; B, 2.40; C, 2.49.

4. Buy $\dfrac{100 \times 3}{1.949} = \$154$ of security A (i.e., $\dfrac{154}{103.08} = 1.49$ units)

   or $\dfrac{100 \times 3}{2.587} = \$116$ of security B (i.e., $\dfrac{116}{130.93} = .89$ units)

   or $\dfrac{100 \times 3}{2.742} = \$109$ of security C (i.e., $\dfrac{109}{105.15} = 1.04$ units)

   N.b. (i) To create a zero-value hedge, balance position with short-term borrowing (i.,e., duration of zero). For example, if you buy security A, you would need to borrow PV(A) − PV(liability) = 154 − $\dfrac{100}{1.08^3} = \$75$ to create zero-value hedge.

   (ii) To retain hedge, investments should be adjusted as time passes or interest rates change.

5. $\dfrac{\text{Value of future}}{1.049} = 95 - 4$

   ∴ Value of future = 95.46

6. $\dfrac{2408}{1.12} = 2550 + 100 - \text{PV (convenience yield)}$

   ∴ PV (convenience yield) = $500

7. (i) A promise to make a series of payments in one currency in exchange for receiving a series of payments in another currency.
   (ii) A promise to make a series of fixed-rate payments in exchange for receiving a series of

floating-rate payments (or vice versa). Also exchange of floating-rate payments linked to different reference rates (e.g., LIBOR and commercial paper rate).

Swaps may be used because a company believes it has an advantage in borrowing in a particular market or in order to change structure of existing liabilities.

Chapter 26

1. A, c; B, d or i; C, b or e; D, f; E, a; F, h; G, g
2. a, b, d, f, and h (though there may be other ways to reduce AMT).
3. (a) True
   (b) True
   (c) True
   (d) True
   (e) True
   (f) True
   (g) True
4. (a) $59,206, the present value of the lease cash flows from $t = 1$ to $t = 3$, discounted at $r(1 - T_c) = .10 (1 - .34) = .066$
   (b) $62,000 - 59,206 = 2794$
   (c) It should not invest. The lease's value of $+2794$ does not offset the machine's negative NPV. It would be happy to sign the same lease on a more attractive asset.

$$\text{Debt-equity ratio} = \frac{\substack{\text{long-term} \quad \text{value of} \\ \text{debt} \quad\quad + \text{ leases}}}{\text{equity}}$$

$$\text{Return on equity} = \frac{\text{earnings available for common}}{\text{average equity}}$$

$$\text{Payout ratio} = \frac{\text{dividend}}{\text{earnings per share}}$$

$$\text{Current ratio} = \frac{\text{current assets}}{\text{current liabilitied}}$$

$$\substack{\text{Average} \\ \text{collection} \\ \text{period}} = \frac{\text{average receivables}}{\text{sales} \div 365}$$

3. (a) False
   (b) True
   (c) False
   (d) False
   (e) True (as a general rule)
   (f) True
   (g) False
   (h) False
   (i) False—it will tend to increase the price-earnings multiple
4. (a) Shipping company
   (b) United Foods
   (c) Paper mill
   (d) Mail order company
   (e) Fledgling Electronics
   (f) Pharmaceutical company

Chapter 27

1. (a) $\dfrac{1136}{1136 + 2595} = .30$

   (b) $\dfrac{795 + 263}{127} = 8.33$

   (c) $\dfrac{3525}{1604} = 2.20$

   (d) $\dfrac{469 + 1591}{1604} = 1.28$

   (e) $\dfrac{795 - 287}{10,376} = .05$

   (f) $\dfrac{7533}{.5 (1455 + 1432)} = 5.22$

   (g) $\dfrac{381}{.5 (2421 + 2595)} = .15$

   (h) $\dfrac{138}{381} = .36$

2. The illogical ratios are a, b, c, f, and i. The correct definitions are:

Chapter 28

1. (a) False (it is a process of deciding which risks to take).
   (b) False (financial planning is concerned with possible surprises as well as expected outcomes).
   (c) True (financial planning considers both the investment and financing decisions).
   (d) False (a typical horizon for long-term planning is 5 years).
   (e) True (investments are usually broken down by category).
   (f) True (perfect accuracy is unlikely to be obtainable, but the firm needs to produce the best possible consistent forecasts).
   (g) False (excessive detail distracts attention from the crucial decisions).
2. Pro forma financial statements (balance sheets, income statements, and sources and uses of cash); description of planned capital expenditure, and a summary of planned financing.
3. Most financial models are designed to forecast accounting statements. They do not focus on the fac-

tors that directly determine firm value, such as incremental cash flow or risk.

Chapter 29

1. See Table 2, below.
2. Month 3: $18 + (.5 \times 90) + (.3 \times 120) +$
   $(.2 \times 100) = \$119,000$
   Month 4: $14 + (.5 \times 70) + (.3 \times 90) +$
   $(.2 \times 120) = \$100,000$
3. (a) Long-term financing, cumulative capital re-
       quirement, marketable securities
   (b) Cash, cash, cash balance, marketable securities
   (c) Trial, error, financial models
4. (a) Inventories go up (use).
   (b) Accounts receivable go up (use).
   (c) No change shown on the firm's books.
   (d) Decrease in assets (source).
   (e) Net worth declines (use).
   (f) Retained earnings fall (use).
   (g) Long-term debt increases (source), short-term
       debt falls (use).

TABLE 2
Chapter 29, Quiz question 1.

	Cash	Working Capital
1.	$2 million decline	$2 million decline
2.	$2,500 increase	Unchanged
3.	$5,000 decline	Unchanged
4.	Unchanged	$1 million increase
5.	Unchanged	Unchanged
6.	$5 million increase	Unchanged

Chapter 30

1. (a) 1 percent of $1000 = $10
   (b) 1 percent for 30 days = 12 percent per annum
       simple interest or 12.7 percent compound in-
       terest.
   (c) (i) Shorter
       (ii) Longer
      (iii) Shorter
2. (a) Due lag decreases, therefore pay lag decreases.
   (b) Due lag increases, therefore pay lag increases.
   (c) Terms lag increases, therefore pay lag in-
       creases.
3. Open account, promissory note, commercial draft,
   shipping documents, trade acceptance, the customer's, bankers' acceptance, letter of credit, the
   customer's, his or her own, letter of credit, shipping documents, shipping documents
4. Reject because PV of Q's order
   $= \dfrac{.75 \times 50}{1.10^{1/2}} - 40$
   $= -\$4.25$ per iron, or $-\$4250$ in total

5. (a) Expected profit $= p(1200 - 1050) - 1050$
       $(1 - p) = 0$
       $$p = .875$$
       Therefore, grant credit if probability of payment
       exceeds 87.5 percent.
   (b) Expected profit from selling to slow payer:
       $.8(150) - .2(1050) = -90$. Break-even point
       for credit check: $(.05 \times 90 \times \text{units}) - 12 =$
       0. Units $= 2.67$.
6. Total expected profit on initial order $= -40$
   $+ \dfrac{.8[(p_2 \times 200) - 1000 (1 - p_2)]}{1.2} = 0$
   $p_2 = .88$, or 88 percent
7. (a) False
   (b) True
   (c) False
   (d) False—should be collection agency or attorney.
   (e) True
8. (a) True
   (b) False
   (c) True
   (d) False
   (e) True
   (f) False. Tax loss carry-forwards are extinguished
       by liquidation.

Chapter 31

1. (a) Carrying cost per book/2 = $1
   (b) $(200 \times 2)/Q^2 = 1$
       $Q = \sqrt{400} = 20$ books
   (c) $200/20 = 10$ orders
   (d) $Q/2 = 10$ books.
2. (a) Carrying cost/2 = $.01
   (b) $(20,000 \times 2)/Q^2 = \$.01$
       $Q = \sqrt{4,000,000} = \$2000$
   (c) $20,000/2000 = 10$ orders
   (d) $Q/2 = \$1000$
3. (a) Interest rate, cost of each transaction, and var-
       iability of cash balance.
   (b) It should restore it to one-third of the distance
       between the lower and upper limits.
   (c) By holding a lower cash balance, the firm in-
       creases the transaction frequency but earns
       more interest.
4. (a) Less
   (b) Less
   (c) Invest the same amount
   (d) More
5. (a) Payment float = $25,000. Availability float =
       $75,000
   (b) It can earn interest on these funds.
   (c) Payment float increases. The bank's gross
       ledger balance and available balance increase
       by the same amount.

6. (a) The $.40 per check fee is cheaper at 300 × .40 = $120 per day. The cost of putting up $800,000 of compensating balances is .09 × 800,000 = $72,000 per year, or 72,000/365 = $197 per day.

(b) The lock-box system costs $120 per day, or $43,800 per year. You would need $487,000 additional cash to generate this much interest. Thus, the lock-box system must generate at least this much cash. The cash flow is 300 × 1500 = $450,000 per day. Thus the lock box must speed up average collection time by 487,000/450,000 = 1.08 days.

7. Because the bank can forecast early in the day how much money will be paid out, the company does not need to keep extra cash in the account to cover contingencies. Also, since zero-balance accounts are not held in a major banking center, the company gains several days of additional float.

8. Payment float; availability float; net float; concentration banking; wire transfer; depository transfer check; lock-box banking.

Chapter 32

1. (a) Repurchase agreements
(b) Commercial paper
(c) U.S. certificates of deposit
(d) Finance company commercial paper
(e) Finance company commercial paper
(f) Treasury bills
(g) Treasury bills
(h) Treasury bills

2. 6.4 percent simple interest or 6.5 percent compound interest

3. Line of credit; clean-up provision; prime rate; compensating balance; commercial paper; floating lien; collateral; with recourse; public warehouse; field warehouse; warehouse receipt; trust receipt; floor planning

4. Only 20 percent of the floating-rate preferred dividend is taxed versus 100 percent of bond interest. The fixed-dividend preferred also has this tax advantage but its price fluctuates more than the floating-rate preferred's.

5. (a) 1 year
(b) Often
(c) No
(d) Floating rate (e.g., linked to prime)
(e) A larger fraction of the loan is repaid at maturity.
(f) A legally assured line of credit that can be converted into a term loan

Chapter 33

1. (a) Horizontal
(b) Conglomerate
(c) Vertical
(d) Conglomerate

2. (a) $5 million (We assume that the $500,000 saving is an after-tax figure.)
(b) $4 million
(c) $7.5 million
(d) +$1 million
(e) −$2.5 million

3. a, b, d

4. (a) True
(b) False
(c) False
(d) True
(e) False (They may produce gains, but "substantial" is stretching it.)
(f) False
(g) True (assuming that the purchase price exceeds the value of the tangible assets acquired)
(h) False
(i) True

5. a and d; c can also make sense, although merging is not the only way to redeploy excess cash.

6. • LBO—buyout by private investors
• Master limited partnership—partnership "units" traded
• Poison pill—shareholders issued rights . . .
• Tender offer—offer to buy shares directly from stockholders
• Greenmail—target buys out shareholders threatening takeover
• Golden parachute—payment to target firm's managers
• Proxy fight—attempt to gain control by winning stockholders' votes

Chapter 34

1. (a) 138.65
(b) 136.10 yen = 1 dollar
(c) Discount
(d) $2 \times \dfrac{136.10 - 138.65}{138.65} = -.037$, or a discount of 3.7 percent
(e) $\dfrac{(1 + r_{yen})^{1/2}}{(1 + r_{\$})^{1/2}} = \dfrac{f_{yen/\$}}{s_{yen/\$}}$

$\dfrac{(1 + r_{yen})^{1/2}}{1.08^{1/2}} = \dfrac{136.1}{138.65}$

$r_{yen} = 4.1$ percent
(f) 136.10 yen = 1 dollar
(g) $\dfrac{E(1 + i_{yen})}{E(1 + i_{\$})} = \dfrac{f_{yen/\$}}{s_{yen/\$}} = .982$

That is, the 6-month inflation in Japan is expected to be 1.8 percent lower than in the United States.

2. (a) The interest rate differential equals the forward premium or discount, i.e.,

$$\frac{1 + r_x}{1 + r_\$} = \frac{f_{x/\$}}{s_{x/\$}}$$

(b) The expected change in the spot rate equals the forward premium or discount, i.e.,

$$\frac{f_{x/\$}}{s_{x/\$}} = \frac{E(s_{x/\$})}{s_{x/\$}}.$$

(c) Prices of goods in different countries are equal when measured in terms of the same currency. It follows that the expected change in the spot rate equals the expected inflation differential, i.e.,

$$\frac{E(1 + i_x)}{E(1 + i_\$)} = \frac{E(s_{x/\$})}{s_{x/\$}}$$

(d) Expected real interest rates in different countries are equal, i.e.,

$$\frac{1 + r_x}{1 + r_\$} = \frac{E(1 + i_x)}{E(1 + i_\$)}$$

3.

	3 Months	6 Months	1 Year
Eurodollar interest rate (percent)	11.5	12.25	12.5
Eurofranc interest rate (percent)	19.5	19.7	20
Forward francs per dollar	7.17	7.28	7.52
Forward discount on franc, percent per year	− 6.7	− 6.3	− 6.3

Note:
Spot dollars per franc = 1/7.0500 = .1418

4. (b)
5. Zero of course. You don't need to do any calculations.
6. It can borrow the present value of 1 million DM, sell the deutsche marks in the spot market, and invest the proceeds in a 2-year dollar loan.
7. (a) Foreign inflation rates to produce cash-flow forecasts
Future exchange rates to convert cash flows into domestic currency
Domestic interest rate to discount domestic currency cash flows
(b) Foreign inflation rates to produce cash-flow forecasts
Foreign interest rate to discount foreign currency cash flows

8. (a)

	Overseas	U.S.
X	60	0
Y	40	10*
	100	10

*$50 less double-tax relief of $40.

(b)

	Overseas*	U.S.
X	0	50
Y	0	50
	0	100

*Interest in most countries is deductible for corporate tax.

Chapter 35

1. (a) False
(b) False
(c) False
(d) True
(e) False
(f) False
(g) True, although "final salary" generally means an average over the last few years before retirement.
(h) True
(i) True
2. In a defined-benefit plan, the company promises specific benefits and then must set aside enough money to cover the promise. In a defined-contribution plan, the company promises to make a specific contribution. The employee's pension depends on the performance of the pension fund.
3. (a) Pension fund
(b) Expected benefits for past service
(c) Expected future service costs
(d) Future normal costs
(e) Expected benefits (i.e., total liabilities)
(f) Deficit
4. (a) Pension fund = investments held in trust for plan members
Future normal costs = contributions to cover future service
Unamortized experience losses = losses that result from difference between expectations and experience
Unamortized supplemental liabilities = liability from improved pension benefits
Losses from changes in actuarial assumptions = e.g., effect of change in assumed discount rate

Vested accrued benefits = benefits that would need to be paid if employees left firm immediately

Unvested accrued benefits = benefits that have accrued but will be paid only if employment continues

Expected future service costs = expected benefits to be paid for future service

(b) (i) $540 - 720 = -\$180$ million (i.e., vested benefits are fully funded)

(ii) $760 - 720 = \$40$ million

(c) (i) Pension fund = 670

Experience losses = 140

(ii) Supplemental liabilities = 180

Total assets = 1740

Total liabilities = 1740

Future service costs = 980

5. Greater
6. (a) $r - r_f = 6$ percent
   (b) $(r - r_f) - \beta(r_m - r_f) = 3$ percent
   (c) $(r - r_f) - (\sigma/\sigma_m)(r_m - r_f) = 2$ percent
7. (a) 80 percent
   (b) 72.5 percent
   (c) The time-weighted rate of return would not change.
   (d) The dollar-weighted rate of return would decrease.

Index

SOME USEFUL FORMULAS

(The section number indicates the principal reference in the text.)

Perpetuity (3-2)

The value of a perpetuity of $1 per year is:

$$PV = \frac{1}{r}$$

Annuity (3-2)

The value of annuity of $1 per period for t years (t-year annuity factor) is:

$$PV = \frac{1}{r} - \frac{1}{r(1 + r)^t}$$

A Growing Perpetuity (the "Gordon" model) (3-2)

If the initial cash flow is $1 at year 1 and if cash flows thereafter grow at a constant rate of g in perpetuity,

$$PV = \frac{1}{r - g}$$

Continuous Compounding (3-3)

If r is the continuously compounded rate of interest, the present value of $1 received in year t is:

$$PV = \frac{1}{e^{rt}}$$

Equivalent Annual Cost (6-3)

If an asset has a life of t years, the equivalent annual cost is:

$$\frac{PV(\text{costs})}{t\text{-year annuity factor}}$$

Measures of Risk (7-2 to 7-4)

Variance of returns $= \sigma^2$
$\qquad\qquad = $ expected value of $(\tilde{r} - r)^2$

Standard deviation of returns $= \sqrt{\text{variance}} = \sigma$

Covariance between returns of stocks 1 and 2
$= \sigma_{12} = $ expected value of $[(\tilde{r}_1 - r_1)(\tilde{r}_2 - r_2)]$

Correlation between returns of stocks 1 and 2 $=$

$$\rho_{12} = \frac{\sigma_{12}}{\sigma_1\sigma_2}$$

Beta of stock $i = \beta_i = \dfrac{\sigma_{im}}{\sigma_m^2}$

Variance of Portfolio Returns (8-1)

The variance of returns on a portfolio with proportion x_i invested in stock i is:

$$\sum_{i=1}^{N} \sum_{j=1}^{N} x_i x_j \sigma_{ij}$$

Capital Asset Pricing Model (8-2)

The expected risk premium on a risky investment is:

$$r - r_f = \beta(r_m - r_f)$$

Capital Asset Pricing Model (Certainty-Equivalent Form) (Chapter 9 Appendix)

The present value of a one-period risky investment is:

$$PV = \frac{C_1 - \lambda \text{Cov}(\tilde{C}_1, \tilde{r}_m)}{1 + r_f}$$

where

$$\lambda = \frac{r_m - r_f}{\sigma_m^2}$$

Value of Right and Ex-Rights Price (Chapter 15, Appendix A)

If N is the number of rights required to buy 1 share, the value of a right is:

$$\frac{\text{Rights-on price} - \text{issue price}}{N + 1}$$

$$= \frac{\text{ex-rights price} - \text{issue price}}{N}$$

The ex-rights price is:

$$\frac{1}{N + 1} (N \times \text{rights-on price} + \text{issue price})$$

Adjusted Cost of Capital (19-2 and 19-3)

If r is the cost of capital under all-equity financing, the adjusted cost of capital is:

MM formula:

$$r^* = r(1 - T_c L)$$